Professional Oracle 8i
Application Programming

Michael Awai

Matthew Bortniker

John Carnell

Sean Dillon

Drew Erwin

Jaeda Goodman

Bjarki Hólm

Ann Horton

Frank Hubeny

Thomas Kyte

Glenn E. Mitchell II

Kevin Mukhar

Gary Nicol

Daniel O'Connor

Guy Ruth-Hammond

Mario Zucca

Wrox Press Ltd. ®

Professional Oracle 8i
Application Programming

Published by Wrox Press Ltd,
Arden House, 1102 Warwick Road, Acocks Green,
Birmingham, B27 6BH, UK
Printed in Canada
ISBN 1-861004-84-2

Trademark Acknowledgements

Wrox has endeavored to provide trademark information about all the companies and products mentioned in this book by the appropriate use of capitals. However, Wrox cannot guarantee the accuracy of this information.

Credits

Authors
Michael Awai
Matthew Bortniker
John Carnell
The Churchill Team
Sean Dillon
Drew Erwin
Jaeda Goodman
Bjarki Hólm
Ann Horton
Frank Hubeny
Thomas Kyte
Glenn E. Mitchell II
Kevin Mukhar
Gary Nicol
Daniel O'Connor
Guy Ruth-Hammond
Mario Zucca

Contributing Authors
Sandeepan Banerjee
Frank Bell
Bambi Bellows
Kelly Cox
Shekhar Dhupelia
Michael Kay

Technical Architect
Tony Davis

Technical Editors
Fiver Löcker
Jim Molony
Mohammed Rfaquat
Robert Shaw

Managing Editor
Paul Cooper

Technical Reviewers
Duncan Ainsworth
Danny Ayers
Yogesh Bhandarkar
Graham Bowden
Luis Cabral
Robert Chang
Jitendra Chitkara
Daryl Collins
Michael Corning
Jeremy Crosbie
Dean Dameron
Robin Dewson
Sean Dillon
Drew Erwin
Mark Fehrenbacher
Dario Ferreira Gomes
Nikolay Fiykov
Frank Hubeny
Manzoor Hussain
Mike Kay
Aakash Kambuj
Doug Kanwischer
Victor Kolesov
Thomas Kyte
Todd Lauinger
Karen Little
Steven Livingston
Jim MacIntosh
Jennifer McGurk
Vinay Menon
Jon Millard
Brian Peasland
Sarma PRKV
John Roberts
Jordon Saardchit
Anunaya Shriwastava
Leslie Tierstein
Raj Vuchatu
Hiroko Wilensky

Author Agents
Tony Berry
Velimir Ilic

Project Administrators
Cilmara Lion
Chandima Nethisinghe

Indexers
Alessandro Ansa
Andrew Criddle

Production Coordinator
Tom Bartlett

Illustrations
Shabnam Hussain

Cover
Shelley Frazier

Proof Readers
Chris Smith
Keith Westmoreland
Agnes Wiggers

Production Manager
Simon Hardware

About the Authors

Michael Awai

Michael Awai lives near Charlotte, North Carolina, USA. He is currently a Consulting Partner with a successful privately owned consulting company. He works as a system architect, helping clients leverage the Internet, build extranet services and accomplish their application and business integration goals. He and his partner Karla are currently expecting their first baby and their first Irish wolfhound.

Matthew Bortniker

Matt has been in the computer field since 1982 and is an independent consultant for local businesses in the Washington DC area and for the US government. Currently his main tasks include upgrading client server applications to enterprise wide systems written entirely in Visual Basic and utilizing Oracle and Microsoft technologies. He is the author of *Professional VB6 MTS Programming*, ISBN 1861002440, and contributing author in *Professional Windows DNA*, ISBN 1861994451, (both Wrox Press). He can be reached at pc_geek37@hotmail.com.

John Carnell

John Carnell has had an obsession with computers since he was twelve years old, working on his Commodore 64. That obsession never waned and he is currently working as a Senior Systems Architect for Workscape, a leading provider of Human Resources and and Employee Benefits self-service solutions. John's favorite topic of discussion, much to his wife's chagrin, is component based N-tier architectures. John has extensive experience with Microsoft, Oracle and Java N-tier solutions. He lives in Waukesha, Wisconsin with his wife Janet and his two pups Ladybug and Ginger. John can be reached at john_carnell@yahoo.com.

For my mother Deborah: What I have achieved in my life is a summation of your hard work, dedication, and most importantly your sacrifices.
And to Janet: You are my inspiration. I love you both.

The Churchill Team

Chandrabhanu Ambatipudi, Ekta Rani Agarwal, John Ipe, and Makarand Kulkarni form the 'Oracle supreme & Java dream' team at Churchill Software Services India (CSSI). CSSI was established in 1996 in Bangalore India as an Oracle offshore development center, by an ex-Oracle UK management team. Since its inception the center has been serving the UK market with an exclusive focus on the Oracle platform, meshing cutting edge technologies with established Oracle technologies, and providing innovative road map solutions for the Internet age.

Sean Dillon

Sean got his start programming a Commodore Vic 20, back in 1980. Trying to program sprites and word games in the enormous 3.5Kb of user memory was truly a labor of love. He is now a Senior Oracle Technologist, working for Oracle Corporation based in Reston, Virginia. He has eight years of experience specializing in database architecture, tuning, web application development, and now XML-based technologies. Sean is one of the lead designers on Oracle's Web Education Initiative for children, Think.com. He is also an avid Quake player. Sean lives outside Washington, DC with his wife, Whitney, and two sons, Jordan and Cameron.

I would like to thank my wife for her never-ending support and encouragement.

Drew Erwin

Drew is a technical project leader and has been working with Oracle products for the last nine years. The last three of those have been dedicated to enterprise application development with the ever changing and improving Oracle toolset. Outside of work, Drew's interests include his family, Pam and Hannah, his Playstation, and traveling.

Jaeda Goodman

Jaeda Goodman is currently working as a Principal Software Engineer for Keane Ltd., the company who were responsible for the Sun Connect Framework. She has over four years experience working with Oracle and Java, encompassing everything from data warehousing to EJBs, servlets and JSPs – and also InfoBus, if anyone needs any advice or consultation about this now esoteric technology. Jaeda's non-technical interests include house restoration, American TV imports, and the ability to make an amazing blue punch, although of course the latter does not mix well with all of the former, especially InfoBus.

I'd like to dedicate this to everyone who went through the Synchromatic experience with me.

Bjarki Hólm

For more than three years Bjarki has been designing and developing commercial software tools at SALT Systems, Inc. His work includes the development of SALT Solutions, a website construction suite built with Java technology. His areas of (technical) interest include Enterprise Java, XML and e-commerce Oracle applications. In his working and waking hours, Bjarki is studying computer engineering at the University of Iceland, and with his Wrox authoring on top of this, he tends to get very little sleep. Bjarki can be reached at `holm@salt.is`.

Ann Horton

Ann Horton is the President of Horton Associates, Inc. and has over twelve years experience designing, developing, and managing Oracle projects. She has worked closely with Oracle Corporation for many years, is active in the Oracle User Group Community, and is a frequent presenter at ODTUG, IOUG-A, RMOUG, and ECO conferences. Ann has been extremely active in the Oracle Development Tools User Group (ODTUG) serving as a member of the Board of Directors, conference chairperson, and paper selection chair for numerous conferences, and ODTUG Volunteer of the Year for 2000. Ms. Horton has also worked as an Affiliate Professor for the Regis University evening MSCIS Program since 1992 teaching database classes to working students in the Denver area. In her spare time, Ann enjoys biking, hiking, bird watching, and scuba diving with her husband Dean.

Thanks to my husband Dean, my brother Tom, Jim, and Betty, and all my friends who have encouraged me to participate in this book project!

Frank Hubeny

Frank Hubeny is a certified Oracle 8i DBA and currently works for Experian doing data warehousing. He has recently worked for WExcel in Chicago where he designed and built databases for web applications and used the PL/SQL Toolkit extensively.

Thomas Kyte

Thomas Kyte is an Oracle professional who works for Oracle Corporation in the US. He specializes in database architecture, implementation, and tuning. In addition to his regular duties at Oracle, Tom writes an ongoing article for Oracle Magazine and can be found on the web answering questions via 'Ask Tom' on the Oracle Magazine website. Prior to working for Oracle, Tom worked with a contractor developing database applications and tools using many different commercial database products. Tom lives in Leesburg VA, USA with his wife Lori and two children, Alan and Megan.

Glenn E. Mitchell II

Glenn E. Mitchell II, who prefers 'Mitch', wears many different hats. He is president of .Com Consulting Group, a computer-consulting firm in Tallahassee, Florida. Mitch is also a faculty administrator at the University of South Florida in Tampa, Florida, where he directs the State Data Center on Aging, teaches graduate and undergraduate students, and earns lots of frequent flyer miles. He also holds a Ph.D. from the University of Iowa. Mitch writes and speaks at conferences extensively on object-oriented analysis and design, C++, Java, Visual Basic, and Microsoft SQL Server. When not a busy professional, Mitch is husband to Lillian and dad to Jessica. Lillian is a veterinarian, whose passion is small animal medicine. Jessica recently became a teen and spends her spare time alternately studying Latin and listening to pop music.

Mitch wants to dedicate his contribution to his wife, Lillian, who is also a busy professional and tolerates him spending countless hours in front of the computer.

Kevin Mukhar

Kevin Mukhar is a software engineer who lives and works in Colorado, USA. He spent 12 years in the US Air Force, where many of his jobs included using computers, but none of them involved writing software. Still, he managed to dabble in various languages as a hobby, and had enough practical experience to land a software engineering job when he left the Air Force. For the past two years he has been part of a team that developed a distributed system to manage and access large amounts of binary data from an Oracle database. His heroes are Steve McConnell and Philip Greenspun. Now that he has finished writing (part of) a book, he understands why many married writers thank their spouse; and so, he too, thanks his wife for tolerating him during the last few months.

Gary Nicol

Gary Nicol is a Senior Consultant within the eBusiness division of Mi Services Group, and has worked on a number of web-based projects involving integration of Oracle and Microsoft technologies. Having originally cut his teeth on a Sinclair ZX Spectrum, he took a twisted career path, via a degree in Electronic Engineering, followed by a brief incarnation as a semiconductor engineer, before realising that developing software was a much more fun way to spend his working day. In writing for this book, he has surprised not only himself, but probably a number of his high school teachers, who would never have believed he was capable of forming a coherent sentence (even when they could read his handwriting).

Daniel O'Connor

Daniel O'Connor is an independent software developer currently working on management applications using J2EE technologies, including EJB and JSP. He is a member of the board of directors for jBoss.org, an open-source application server featuring an EJB container. He is one of the authors of the *Professional Java Server Programming J2EE Edition*, Wrox Press, ISBN 186199463. He is also a principal of MVCSoft, Inc., which provides training and consulting on J2EE application development.

I would like to dedicate my efforts in this book to Christina Coughlin.

Mario Zucca

Some years ago Mario moved from the procedural world to the object-oriented one. Although it was a difficult step to take he's since fallen in love with Java and J2EE technologies and in particular with XML-related technologies such as XSL, XPath and SOAP.

I love freedom! I would like to dedicate this book to my daughter Federica. When she reads this book, many of the technologies will be prehistoric things, but I hope in an even freer world.

Table of Contents

Table of Contents

Table of Contents

Table of Contents

Table of Contents

Table of Contents

Table of Contents

Table of Contents

Table of Contents

Table of Contents

GRAMMINGORACLE8iAPPLICATIONPROGRAMMINGORACLE8iAPPL
ONPROGRAMMINGORACLE8iAPPLICATIONPROGRAMMINGORACLE8
ICATIONPROGRAMMINGORACLE8iAPPLICATIONPROGRAMMINGOR
iAPPLICATIONPROGRAMMINGORACLE8iAPPLICATIONPROGRAMM

Introduction

The life of the Oracle database programmer is in a state of flux. Oracle Corporation is advancing rapidly into the middle and presentation tiers of the enterprise application with an array of new products and technologies. Perhaps more significantly, with the launch of Oracle 8i, more and more enterprise features are being moved *into* the database, bringing with them a wealth of new programming possibilities.

There is no doubt that Oracle programmers will continue to be in high demand – Oracle database products still dominate the world market. But there is some work to be done to close the gap between the traditional database programming environment and today's world of the component-based enterprise-oriented application. That's why Oracle has moved heavily into supporting standards such as Java and XML. And that's the gap that this book fills.

What this Book is About

This is a book about developing applications that use the Oracle 8i database. Since the launch of Oracle 8i, developers have had the option of working not only with PL/SQL but also with Java and XML directly within the database. Oracle Corporation has vigorously supported the integration of these languages, and their associated development tools, into their core database products. These new languages may, or may not, be familiar to database programmers, but the chances are that even if you are experienced in PL/SQL, many of the new programming opportunities in the Oracle environment will be unfamiliar.

This book will show you how to build Java and XML-enabled applications that interact with Oracle 8i. You will be using a variety of tools, ranging from established ones such as Oracle Designer, to new tools such as Oracle Portal-to-Go. Mostly, however, you will be developing code by hand, learning about Java technologies, XML tools, building web applications, and solving enterprise development problems.

Who Should Use this Book

This book is primarily aimed at programmers with a database background. Oracle has adopted Java and XML in a big way. As a result, a host of new Oracle middle tier and web tier applications have appeared, based upon these and other new technologies. It is possible to continue following the PL/SQL stream, and to produce great applications, but sometime, someone is going to ask you to write your first Java stored procedure, an XML-enabled customer management system, or a wireless adapter for your existing PL/SQL web product.

This book will break down those barriers for you. You will see plenty of chapters with a mixture of the familiar and the unfamiliar. This will help you work out how these technologies can interact with, and enhance, each other.

How this Book is Structured

To help you use this book and structure your learning, we have divided it into the four sections outlined below. These are not rigid divisions, but they will help you navigate quickly to the area you need most.

- ❑ **Database**. Two introductory chapters on the Oracle 8i platform and Enterprise Application Design lead into chapters on database architecture and connectivity, and how to design your database using Oracle Designer 6i. We don't attempt to cover all the database issues that you will need to know in order to work effectively with PL/SQL and Oracle. Some database knowledge, and some SQL programming, are assumed. These chapters will serve as a quick reference point and a source of vital knowledge when you hit problems in your own designs and implementations.

- ❑ **PL/SQL and the Web**. In this section of the book, we focus on the web capabilities of Oracle's proprietary database language, PL/SQL. We will look at PL/SQL coding from the point of view of application design and from the point of view of making the best use of PL/SQL when it makes sense to use it in an enterprise application.

- ❑ **Java**. Although the Java section is divided approximately into individual Java technologies, there is significant cross-over and you will find that each chapter covers several Java tools, as well as focusing on how to integrate your Java with Oracle, PL/SQL and XML. We cover Java Stored Procedures, JDBC, SQLJ, EJB, BC4J, JavaMail, Servlets and JSPs. Each chapter in this section is database-oriented, and provides a starter database and full set-up instructions. Check out the Java Primer in Appendix B first, if you need to get yourself up to speed.

- ❑ **XML**. The idea behind XML is to provide a common communication and data representation language with which to bring together diverse platforms and enterprises. The chapters in this section will show you how to build applications based on an Oracle data tier and connect them to other tiers with XML. You will learn to use Oracle XML Developer's Kit, XML SQL utility, XSLT, ASP, SOAP, interMedia, and Portal-to-Go's SimpleResult XML, along with other techniques for building Java and PL/SQL-enabled applications. We provide an XML primer in Appendix C, for those who need to catch up with the basic XML notions.

This book has 25 chapters and 4 appendices. In the following sections we will give you a breakdown of the content of these chapters so that you can plan how to use this book to suit your needs best.

The Database

❑ Chapter 1, **Internet Programming with Oracle 8i**. This chapter presents the Oracle 8i platform, the new tools and technologies that have appeared or been updated in Oracle 8i and Oracle Internet Application Server (iAS). In particular we set the scene for Oracle and Java, and talk about the new features and programming opportunities that this combination has introduced.

❑ Chapter 2, **Enterprise Application Design**. Here we take a side step and remind ourselves of why we need to learn all these new languages and design patterns. Whether you are developing a company intranet, a simple web storefront, or a commercial N-tier application, you should be aware of the principles that are emerging in this field. In the chapter, we will look at the evolution of the N-tier approach, and at the challenges it presents to the programmer.

❑ Chapter 3, **Database Foundations**. Complementing Chapter 16, this is a chapter that will stand you in good stead in your applications programming. This chapter is aimed at those who are moving from middle tier to database tier programming and who need to brush up on what goes on inside the database and how it works.

❑ Chapter 4, **Scaling your Applications with Net8**. Communicating remotely to the Oracle 8i database introduces a new element: the fallibility and idiosyncrasies of networks. Net8 is the successor to Oracle's SQL*Net, and provides an integrated and homogenous networking solution for Oracle products. However good your application code, you will invariably spend time troubleshooting connectivity problems. This chapter will help you minimize that overhead and give you valuable insight into what is going on beneath the covers when you connect to Oracle.

❑ Chapter 5, **Enterprise Development with Designer 6i**. Any database application (which means any enterprise database solution) should consider using Oracle Designer and repository-based development to build a manageable and maintainable database infrastructure. This chapter will progress from designing the initial data model and translating it into a database design, to full generation of the database definition code. We'll build the foundations of a web application for an Education Center database, which we'll continue building in Chapter 10.

PL/SQL and the Web

❑ Chapter 6, **PL/SQL Development**. This is where the real programming starts. Whatever programs we use to access the database, our calls will be ultimately executed in PL/SQL. We concentrate on the fine art of effective, well-defined and re-usable PL/SQL packages. The chapter contains advice on how to program effectively in a group development environment and we build a test framework for reporting on the status of any P/SQL development effort. This will prepare us for developing with the PL/SQL web toolkit in the remaining chapters of this section of the book.

❑ Chapter 7, **PL/SQL Server Pages (PSP)**. New to Oracle 8.1.6 is the PSP system for serving up entire web applications directly from the database. Using PL/SQL as a scripting language, we can write our PSP pages, compile them and upload them to the database. The pages are then accessed via any web server running a PL/SQL Gateway, such as Apache/mod_plsql on Oracle iAS.

❑ Chapter 8, **The PL/SQL Web Toolkit**. This chapter covers everything you need to get coding with the PL/SQL Web Toolkit. We'll discuss how to exploit the reliability and scalability of the Oracle 8i database to deliver web content directly from stored PL/SQL procedures. We will develop a basic interactive web application for manipulating tabular information.

❏ Chapter 9, **A Stock Tracker using the PL/SQL Web Toolkit, XML and JavaScript**. Some of the elegance and power of the PL/SQL Web Toolkit will be explored in this case study. We'll build a stock tracking application with a web front end, focusing on good design and clarity in the implementation. As well as showcasing the toolkit features, we'll show how it can work alongside other technologies such as XML, JavaScript and Cascading Style Sheets, to generate finished web applications.

❏ Chapter 10**, Web PL/SQL Application Development using Designer 6i**. Whereas the previous chapter focused on hand coding of PL/SQL procedures, we look here at how Oracle Designer 6i can generate entire PL/SQL based web applications based on our design specifications. We will extend our Education Center example from Chapter 5 and show how the powerful Web PL/SQL Generator can enhance productivity and time-to-market for database-powered websites.

Java

❏ Chapter 11, **Oracle JVM and Java Stored Procedures**. Here we explain how PL/SQL and Java can work together. We look at the Oracle JVM, relating the use of Java to familiar database notions. The chapter progresses from getting your first Java stored procedure uploaded and callable from PL/SQL, to using Oracle Advanced Queuing and Java stored procedures with PL/SQL triggers.

❏ Chapter 12, **Oracle Access with JDBC**. Java Database Connectivity is the industry standard for accessing SQL databases from Java. Oracle supports JDBC with a number of Java database drivers and extended JDBC features for access to Oracle databases. In this chapter we explore the use of these drivers, with a sequence of clearly worked examples.

❏ Chapter 13, **Connection Pooling and Caching**. In this chapter, we build on Chapter 12, and move into the world of multiple concurrent JDBC access to the Oracle 8i database, from the middle-tier. We look at how we can reduce the burden on the database by pooling connection resources, instead of opening a new connection for each client. The chapter contains a complete example of a catalogue browser servlet, with middle-tier connection pooling using both JDBC 1.0 and the new JDBC 2.0 specification, and returning the results from the Oracle database.

❏ Chapter 14, **Database Connectivity with SQLJ**. Now that you have got to work on JDBC, you may have wondered whether there was any easier way of coding SQL into Java programs. SQLJ provides an interesting and productive way of writing more concise and maintainable database access code, using JDBC as the underlying connectivity technology. The chapter progresses through a number of clear examples, exploring the features of this ANSI standard, which is well supported, and has been enhanced, by Oracle.

❏ Chapter 15, **Enterprise JavaBeans and Oracle**. You will almost certainly have heard of EJBs, but you may not have heard of EJBs running inside an Oracle database. This chapter will introduce you to EJBs from the point of view of the J2EE specification, and then move on to show how we can get EJBs deployed in the Oracle 8i database. We will build a restaurant finder application with the searching and updating features coded into EJBs running in Oracle 8i.

❏ Chapter 16, **Inside the Database**. This chapter will cover vital ground for both experienced database programmers, and those keen to move on to more advanced Java programming. We will review the importance of knowing how the Oracle 8i database works. We will show how you can tune your client applications to make the best use of database features, and how to avoid inefficient and incorrect code. The chapter will give an example of tracing the SQL generated by JDBC code, and discussing what steps can be taken to make best use of Oracle features.

❑ Chapter 17, **Business Components for Java**. In this chapter we will build a restaurant booking application with a substantial web interface. We'll use Oracle's BC4J development environment, built into JDeveloper, to generate our application from scratch, modify it to our needs, and then deploy the business logic as an EJB to Oracle 8i. Then we will publish a JavaServer Pages front end to the Oracle HTTP Server, built into iAS.

❑ Chapter 18, **A Discussion Forum with PL/SQL and Java**. We extend here the work we did in Chapter 13 on connection pooling. We'll build a discussion forum with a JavaServer Pages interface. The forum will use PL/SQL stored procedures for database operations. We'll use Java code both inside and outside the database. We'll call PL/SQL procedures from Java using JDBC. And this is not all! Although completely self-contained, the case study will be further extended in Chapter 20.

❑ Chapter 19, **An Overview of Oracle interMedia Text**. Searching capability is a big issue in any enterprise application – the first thing many people do on reaching a website is to search for something. Searching is computationally intensive and therefore expensive. In this chapter we will study the elements of Oracle interMedia and the query language that is supported by this technology, as a way of collating information, creating indexes and optimizing searches.

❑ Chapter 20, **Building a Search Engine using Java and interMedia**. We build on the previous two chapters, adding a search facility to the Discussion Forum developed in Chapter 18. Using interMedia, we index all messages in the forum archives, and we can then use JDBC through our connection pooling infrastructure, to get back search results from a wide range of search queries. We display the results using Java Server Pages.

XML

❑ Chapter 21, **XML and Oracle**. We explore the Oracle XML Developer's Toolkit. We will examine the Oracle Java DOM and SAX parsers that can be used by client or database Java. We will use XSLT transformation, and explore Oracle's notion of combining XML and SQL data access into a scripted page using the XML SQL Utility (XSU). We'll run the XSQL servlet to process these pages. The Oracle Transviewer JavaBeans provide components for building XML-enabled Java applications, and we'll have a look at those too. All of these XML features are demonstrated using worked examples.

❑ Chapter 22, **A Case Study in Enterprise Application Development**. In this chapter we will put the material we reviewed in Chapter 2 into practice. We'll build an efficient and effective enterprise solution for an internal data centralization problem. We'll use XML as our representation language, XSL, JavaBeans, and a servlet on our web tier, and an EJB running in Oracle 8i.

❑ Chapter 23, **Application Integration using SOAP**. SOAP is a platform-neutral communications protocol based on XML. It is heavily supported by Apache and Microsoft and is rapidly developing into an important standard. This chapter will show how we can build connectivity between Oracle, Microsoft, Apache and other commercial products using SOAP, and we will work through a substantial case study. Though not directly supported by Oracle yet, this looks like being one to get familiar with now, because it has a big future.

❑ Chapter 24, **Wireless Applications with Oracle Portal-to-Go**. As we move into the mobile age, there is more and more demand for diverse information sources to be available via wireless devices. In this chapter we will look at setting up the Portal-to-Go client and server environment, and porting various network resources, such as HTML and LDAP, into a personalized wireless portal. We will examine the integrating protocol, SimpleResult XML, which maps resources to a common format before delivery to individual device types.

❑ Chapter 25, **ASP, XML and Oracle**. ASP is a Microsoft web page scripting language that is gaining a foothold on other platforms such as Solaris and Linux. We'll examine Microsoft's ActiveX Data Objects and how it works through Net8 to access Oracle 8i. We'll also look at how to use ASP with Oracle's XML SQL utility, to fetch and manipulate data in XML form.

Appendices

As well as an appendix covering installation issues, we have also provided two primers in the appendices for those who are unfamiliar with, or need to brush up on, Java and XML:

- ❑ Appendix A, **Installations Issues**. The appendix covers installing Oracle 8i and many of the tools used in the book.

- ❑ Appendix B, **Java Primer**. Here we will help get you up to speed on Java. Anyone who is starting out in Java will appreciate the handy reference material and tutorials. Intermediate programmers might appreciate not having to carry another Java book around!

- ❑ Appendix C, **XML Primer**. This appendix contains a refresher on XML for the reader who isn't familiar with basic XML concepts, or just needs to get back up to speed.

- ❑ Appendix D, **P2P, Support and Errata**. Find out about Wrox Press support and the forums at P2P (Programmer to Programmer™).

The Tools you Need for this Book

In this section we give you some advance warning of the software and tools you need to develop the applications in this book. You will need an Oracle 8i database. In order to obtain some reasonable performance from the database you will need a machine that exceeds certain minimum specifications (please see Appendix A for more details). The versions and editions of the database are covered in Chapter 1. You will need development kits, such as Sun Microsystems's JDK and Oracle's XDK. You will need a web server that can run servlets and JSPs. If you install Oracle iAS, then you will have an Apache installation that can be used for all the web applications, including those of the Portal-to-Go chapter. Alternatively, you will need to install Apache. In several chapters we use the Tomcat web server. This can be configured to run with Apache (either standalone or under iAS). To develop the BC4J application in Chapter 17 you will need Oracle JDeveloper.

All Oracle software products, including Oracle 8i, JDeveloper, Oracle iAS and Oracle Portal-to-Go, can be downloaded from the Oracle Technology Network (OTN or sometimes referred to as Technet) at the website http://technet.oracle.com.

> **Please note: This does not mean that Oracle products, or other downloadable software kits, are free! Before you download anything, please read the licensing agreement very carefully. Please ensure that you do not break the licensing agreement for any software that you download.**

Development Kits

- ❑ **JDK**. For Oracle 8.1.5, you will probably want to be working with JDK 1.1.6. For Oracle 8.1.6 and above, you will need to work with JDK 1.2.1. These kits can be obtained from http://java.sun.com.

- ❑ **XDK**. This product, along with several other XML packages used in the book can be downloaded from OTN at http://technet.oracle.com. Please see Appendix A for installation details.

- ❑ **PL/SQL Web Toolkit.** This is bundled with iAS, but can also be downloaded separately from OTN.

Web and Application Servers

- ❏ **Apache**. You can download the Apache web server from the **Apache Foundation** at http://www.apache.org.

- ❏ **Tomcat**. You can download the Tomcat web application server from the **Jakarta Project** at http://jakarta.apache.org.

- ❏ **JBoss**. This J2EE open source application server is available from **JBoss.org** at http://www.jboss.com. JBoss is used only in Chapter 23.

Tools

- ❏ **JDeveloper**. This Java, XML, BC4J and Oracle-enabled Integrated Development Environment is available for download at OTN. We used JDeveloper 3.1.1.2 for Chapter 17. You will also be able to use JDeveloper to explore most of the code from this book (all chapters with Java), by downloading appropriate material from the Wrox website.

- ❏ **Designer 6i**. This application can also be downloaded from OTN.

Conventions

We have used a number of different styles of text and layout in this book to help differentiate between the different kinds of information. Here are examples of the styles we use and an explanation of what they mean:

Code has several fonts. If it's a word that we're talking about in the text, for example when discussing a PL/SQL SELECT query, it's in this font. If it's a block of code that you can type as a program and run, then it's in a gray box:

```
public void close() throws EJBException, RemoteException
```

Sometimes you'll see code in a mixture of styles, like this:

```
<?xml version 1.0?>
<Invoice>
   <part>
      <name>Widget</name>
      <price>$10.00</price>
   </part>
</invoice>
```

In cases like this, the code with a white background is code we are already familiar with; the line highlighted in grey is a new addition to the code since we last looked at it.

Advice, hints, and background information comes in this type of font.

> **Important pieces of information come in boxes like this.**

Bullets appear indented, with each new bullet marked as follows:

- **Important Words** are in a bold type font
- Words that appear on the screen, in menus like File or Window, are in a similar font to that you would see on a Windows desktop
- Keys that you press on the keyboard like *Ctrl* and *Enter*, are in italics

Customer Support

We've tried to make this book as accurate and enjoyable as possible, but what really matters is what the book actually does for you. Please let us know your views, either by returning the reply card in the back of the book, or by contacting us via email at feedback@wrox.com.

Source Code and Updates

As you work through the examples in this book, you may decide that you prefer to type in all the code by hand. Many readers prefer this because it's a good way to get familiar with the coding techniques that are being used.

Whether you want to type the code in or not, we have made all the source code for this book available at our web site at the following address:

http://www.wrox.com/

If you're one of those readers who likes to type in the code, you can use our files to check the results you should be getting - they should be your first stop if you think you might have typed in an error. If you're one of those readers who doesn't like typing, then downloading the source code from our web site is a must!

Either way, it'll help you with updates and debugging.

Errata

We've made every effort to make sure that there are no errors in the text or the code. However, to err is human, and as such we recognize the need to keep you informed of any mistakes as they're spotted and corrected. Errata sheets are available for all our books at http://www.wrox.com. If you find an error that hasn't already been reported, please let us know.

Our web site acts as a focus for other information and support, including the code from all our books, sample chapters, previews of forthcoming titles, and articles and opinion on related topics.

1

Internet Programming with Oracle 8i

We stand at a crossroads in the evolution of the Oracle database platform. Over the last five years Oracle has transformed itself from being a database provider, to being a complete solution provider for almost every possible enterprise application development requirement.

It has achieved this by embracing open standards languages and technologies such as XML, and the J2EE framework, and by web-enhancing its proprietary PL/SQL standard. This book is for programmers who know their way around the core Oracle environment, but who need to catch up with the new features of this expanded platform.

Oracle's transformation has been the result of two things: the rise of the Internet as an application platform and the ever-growing demand to have front-to-backend data integration within the enterprise.

Organizations, in order to remain competitive, have to meet three basic criteria:

❑ An organization's data must be available any time and available quickly. With the rise of the Internet, organizations now compete in a global marketplace. This means that there can be no downtime. Data has to be available on a 24x7 basis. Having a stable, high performance database at the heart of your application is a must.

❑ An organization's data must be available from any place. Data has to be readily accessible to both employees and customers. Customers are no longer willing to tolerate organizations that do not "know" who they are.

❑ An organization's data must be available on any platform. While the PC is still the predominant tool for delivering data to the workforce and to customers, increasingly companies are having to consider how to deliver their application data to other devices such as cellular phones and Personal Digital Assistants (PDA).

Inherent in this challenge, is the ability to write powerful, flexible applications that can be adapted to incorporate the next "big" new technology that will enable them to maintain their competitive edge. If these companies – and their programming teams – cannot meet the criteria above their more nimble and adaptive competitors will overtake them. The global marketplace in which many companies now operate responds quickly and ruthlessly to inefficiency.

The irony is that while demands for such applications are increasing, funding and the time allocated to application development has often been shrinking. In order to support the development and delivery of such applications, developers require a comprehensive platform with a rich infrastructure and numerous architectural possibilities that also promotes a rapid development environment. Oracle provides such a platform, based on the 8i database, and a powerful collection of tools and supported technologies.

This chapter will provide a broad picture of the Oracle 8i database platform together with programming languages, tools, and Oracle technologies explored in this book. Specifically, we will cover:

- ❏ A background introduction to Oracle
- ❏ The Oracle 8i platform versions and editions
- ❏ Programming support in Oracle 8i
- ❏ Supported technologies and tools
- ❏ Oracle Internet Application Server

A Brief History of Oracle

Robert Minor and Lawrence Ellison (who is now Chairman and CEO) founded the Oracle Corporation in 1977. Two years later (1979), the Oracle Corporation presented the world with the first commercial Relational Database Management System (RDMS) that provided the first implementation of IBM's Structured Query Language (SQL).

> **IBM is credited with the development of Structured English Query Language (SEQUEL). It was not until later (exactly when is in question) that SEQUEL started being referred to as simply Structured Query Language (SQL).**

Although Oracle Corporation has made significant strides through the years, perhaps the most meaningful advance to modern computer professionals was the introduction of Oracle 7. It was here that stored procedures were introduced making client-server systems easier to work with. With the release of Oracle 7.3, extended datatypes such as spatial data and text were introduced.

Approaching more recent times, Oracle has evolved from a standard relational database to a combination between the object database model and the relational database model. Oracle 8 introduced a first attempt to incorporate object-oriented technology with current relational technology, thus creating a hybrid "object-relational" database in 1997. What this means is that object data can now be treated as relations, as well as treating relational data as objects.

Two years later, during the spring of 1999, Oracle released its most resent version – Oracle 8i, the 'i' standing for Internet. With it came a massive expansion in the choice of technology that developers had at their disposal for "internet" programming. Traditional languages and tools (PL/SQL, Forms...) have gained significant web-capability, Java is now a core programming language in the database, and the database can store and smoothly handle XML.

This chapter will provide a snapshot of the languages and tools that we will cover in significant detail throughout this book.

Versions and Editions of Oracle 8i

There are three releases of Oracle 8i.

- **Oracle 8i Release 1 (version 8.1.5)** This release introduced features such as an embedded Java VM in the database, summary table management via materialised views, function based indexes, invokers' rights procedures, among over 150 other new features and extensions to Oracle 8.

- **Oracle 8i Release 2 (version 8.1.6)** This release built on the capabilities of Oracle 8i Release 1 adding support for XML into the database, PL/SQL server pages, Single Sign On via the Oracle Internet Directory (LDAP), and advanced analytic extensions to SQL among many other features.

- **Oracle 8i Release 3 (version 8.1.7)** This release coincided with the final writing stages of this book. It has enhanced the capabilities of release 2 adding a JVM accelerator – the ability to translate Java byte code into C code to be compiled natively on your platform, resulting in large performance improvements; the database Oracle Servlet Engine (OSE), EJB 1.1 support, and support for HTTP/HTTPS calls to be made directly into the database – without a web server.

Please note:

- This book has been developed, and the code tested, on the Oracle 8.1.6 platform.

- This book focuses on cross-tier development with the new programming integration possibilities of Oracle 8i. The enhanced database programming features of Oracle 8i, such as Invokers' rights, materialized views etc.) will be explored not in this book, but in a future Wrox Press title: *Oracle Programming Masterclass*, due out early in 2001.

There are four distributions of Oracle 8i. Each distribution has it own unique niche within the corporate Information Technology (IT) environment. We will start with the smallest Oracle distribution, Oracle Lite, and work our way up to the largest, Oracle Enterprise Edition.

Oracle 8i Lite

Oracle 8i Lite is designed for mobile computing environments. It is used to develop applications that have to be disconnected and reside in a device as small as a Palm Pilot or other PDA device. Oracle 8i Lite consists of two different components:

- A stripped down version of the Oracle database. This version of the Oracle database is a lightweight object-relational database designed specially for mobile computers and devices. The database has minimal overhead, yet allows developers to write database application code using both PL/SQL and Java.

- A set of synchronization and replication tools called **iConnect**. iConnect empowers application developers to write applications that that can easily synchronize an Oracle 8i Lite database with any of the other Oracle 8i distributions. (Oracle 8i Personal Edition all the way up to Oracle 8i Enterprise Edition.)

Oracle 8i Lite was never meant to be a full-blown, fully functional DBMS. Instead Oracle has positioned this distribution to be the link between the mobile user and corporate Oracle databases.

Personal Oracle 8i

Personal Oracle 8i provides a single-user development license. This edition was designed with the student, consultant, and developer in mind. Personal Oracle 8i provides the same features as the standard Oracle 8i edition except that it only provides a single user license. One of Personal Oracle 8i's greatest strengths is the ability for developers to develop their applications on their own desktop or notebook computer. This minimizes development conflict between developers. We have all been in those situations before. Developer A just overwrote six hours of Developer B's work and it now appears as if Developer B is going to get physically violent with Developer A.

Using Personal Oracle 8i, developers can completely write and test their code locally and then easily deploy their work to any other Oracle environments.

Oracle 8i Standard Edition

Oracle 8i is the departmental/small-business version of the Oracle database. Applications written using Oracle 8i Standard Edition do not have the performance and fault tolerance needs found in their enterprise level brethren. Oracle 8i standard edition lacks the data partitioning and parallel server features of Oracle 8i. However, this Oracle distribution includes the most commonly used options and features that Oracle 8i has to offer. The Oracle 8i Standard Edition includes easy-to-use management tools for common database management tasks (like backing up and restoring an Oracle database), Oracle's Web Server and many of the web development tools need to develop robust Intranet applications.

Oracle 8i Enterprise Edition

This is the most feature-rich version of Oracle 8i. The Oracle 8i Enterprise Edition is designed for large scale, high-end data processing. Oracle 8i Enterprise Edition is perfect for data applications that require query-intensive data warehousing. Furthermore, Oracle 8i Enterprise Edition should be considered when business criteria demand large-scale Web applications as well as data-intense online transaction processing (OLTP).

Programming Support

This section will discuss the core programming languages and tools that are used in this book and their place within the Oracle 8i platform and architecture.

PL/SQL

PL/SQL is Oracle's proprietary database programming language, available in all the Oracle development tools. Based on the Ada programming language, it is easy to learn, well structured, and extensible. Because the execution modules are written in C and the procedures are stored in compiled form, it is a very fast language, optimized for database-oriented tasks.

PL/SQL has developed into a mature and powerful programming language. It encompasses many of the more advanced elements of a procedural programming language (control structures, user-defined data types, and so on) and, perhaps most importantly, it has a proven track record in Oracle database programming. Having said this, for a long time the language lacked much of the functionality found in more traditional languages like C or C++. PL/SQL had limited capabilities to interact with the underlying operating system on which the Oracle database runs. In addition, it offered no networking capabilities or ability to communicate with any kind of non-Oracle application residing on another machine. However, recent releases of the language have begun to address some of these issues:

❑ PL/SQL8 has many new language features and constructs, such as nested tables and variable-size arrays.

❑ PL/SQL is now fully object-oriented. It has progressed beyond support for the traditional database objects such as functions, triggers, procedures, and packages to encompass the ability to define object **types**.

❑ PL/SQL also has several new built-in functions, such as `utl_file`, that make it easier to manipulate files residing within the OS (see Chapter 6).

A full discussion of these new constructs and capabilities is out-of-scope for this book. Instead we will confine ourselves to an investigation of the ability of PL/SQL to deliver web content.

Oracle has supported web development with PL/SQL ever since the first release of its web server and the emergence of the PL/SQL Web toolkit. For the first time the same proven language used to obtain the content from the database language could be used to disseminate web content. With the second release of Oracle 8i, has been added the ability to develop PL/SQL Server Pages (PSP) (server-side web pages containing embedded PL/SQL).

Perhaps even more exciting is the recent capability to interface with languages such as Java and XML:

❑ Oracle 8i now allows developers to write stored procedures as Java stored within the database. However, Oracle has made sure that these new stored procedure types are seamlessly accessible from traditional PL/SQL code. The combination of PL/SQL and Java completely blows apart the limitations found in earlier versions of PL/SQL.

❑ PL/SQL can interface with XML through either the PLS XML utility – a set of stored procedures for generating XML documents from SQL statements, and manipulating XML documents in memory using the DOM (Document Object Model) API – or the XML SQL Utility (XSU), a set of Java classes for creating XML documents from SQL queries and loading these documents to and from the database.

As such it has become a powerful web content deliverer, used particular extensively in enterprise intranets and the business application arena. Designed for database programming, it suits the needs of the back-end server processes and at the same time can render the straightforward HTML pages typically used in an intranet application. Field-level validation can be accomplished by adding JavaScript into the PL/SQL-generated HTML, and the database operations and exception handling are native to PL/SQL. Oracle Designer can generate this code from a repository of business requirements, or it can be written by hand using any number of PL/SQL development tools.

The PL/SQL Web Toolkit

A set of packages containing procedures and functions that map to HTML commands, the PL/SQL Web Toolkit is the shortest link between database programs and Internet programs. PL/SQL web procedures are stored in the database, in compiled form, and retrieved via a URL that references a path belonging to the PL/SQL agent. These procedures can directly access database data through cursors and format this data for web display using the toolkit commands.

The PL/SQL Web Toolkit includes a few built-in utility functions that can display table data or date information relatively easily, but is mostly a rudimentary set of codes. There are functions dedicated to cookie processing, to images and image maps, and to text handling and pattern matching. Also included is the ability to retrieve data from other sites, to send e-mail, and to reference all services in the TCP/IP protocol, including FTP and news.

Writing code for the PL/SQL Web Toolkit can be as simple as entering some text in a text editor and pasting it into SQL*Plus to compile it. Most developers have a preferred development environment for PL/SQL, and Oracle offers a product called Procedure Builder to add a graphical front end to the development environment.

PL/SQL Server Pages

PL/SQL Server Pages (PSP) execute in the same way as Web Toolkit routines, but employ a different development approach. A PSP is developed in any HTML editor, and have embedded PL/SQL or SQL commands within special tags for Oracle to interpret. Once the HTML is ready, it is run through an Oracle utility that converts each HTML page into a PL/SQL procedure. This approach evolved from an older "unofficial" product called WebAlchemy, which would convert a static page of HTML into a single stored procedure that would produce exactly the same page of HTML. It was a first cut at turning a static page into a dynamic procedure.

PSPs are much easier for HTML developers to learn, and the pages can be designed using any HTML editing tool. Using this technique divides the labor quite neatly between graphical designer and PL/SQL programmer. PSPs are served by Oracle HTTP Server. This requires the setting up of a Data Access Descriptor (DAD) on Oracle HTTP Server to enable the PL/SQL gateway to redirect requests for pages to the database.

Traditional Oracle Development Tools

Traditionally, Oracle has always offered a number of different application development tools, including:

- ❑ Oracle Designer
- ❑ Oracle Forms and Oracle Reports
- ❑ Oracle Portal (previously WebDB)

Support for these tools has not diminished with the release of Oracle 8i. The Oracle development suite not only offers new and powerful functionality, along with numerous features for the development of web-based applications; in fact, all of Oracle's traditional development tools are now web-enabled to some extent. This allows Oracle developers a chance to leverage their existing skill sets and provides a smooth migration path for companies to move their "legacy" Oracle applications to the Web.

Although we do not cover the latter two in this book, they deserve a mention here.

Oracle Forms and Reports

Oracle Forms is a tool for developing interactive screens for transaction processing. It deploys the standard GUI styles and objects for accessing and manipulating data stored in a database. The latest version of Forms is Oracle Forms 6i. Oracle Reports 6i is a GUI tool for querying data from a database and presenting it in a structured fashion, employing a variety of fonts, colors, text, images, and multi-media objects. These tools are excellent for mission-critical data entry operations in an intranet environment. To quote the Oracle Technet site, "Forms 6i is not ready for prime-time Internet deployment".

Oracle Portal

Oracle Portal is the next generation of the WebDB product. It is a tool that enables access to enterprise information through portal pages. The Oracle Portal framework provides integrated and standardized access to web-enabled information contained within or without the corporate enterprise. Oracle Portal gathers this information and displays it through the use of portlets, which are areas of HTML or XML that that will present data in a uniform, repeatable, and secure manner. These portlets can be developed as in-house applications using Oracle's Portal Development Kit; they can be WebDB 2.2-like sites or components "exposed" as portlets; or they can be chosen from the ever-growing list of external Portlet Providers.

At the time of going to press the Oracle Portal Early Adopter (3.0.6.3.3) release had just become available. The full production version (3.0) is bundled with the 9i Internet Application Server.

Designer

Oracle Designer is an integrated database application development tool. Designer becomes useful when application requirements become complex, involving many tables and rich functionality for insert, update, and delete, in addition to display. It generates the Web PL/SQL described above based upon requirements entered into a repository. These requirements are stored in the database so future changes to the application theoretically only require changes to the requirements and re-generation. Entire applications, with complete query, data manipulation, and constraint validation features, can be developed in a shorter period of time than is required with manual coding.

The developer can specify what fields to use and the details of display and validation, but has limited capabilities regarding the page layout itself. This is an advantage in intranet applications, allowing the developer to concentrate on the business logic, but does not always result in attractive screens. With a certain amount of patience and willingness to work within the model, the developer can integrate custom graphics in headers and footers, create attractive frame sets, and format the data elements for custom display. For developers with a predisposition to generator-type tools, this product can be an extremely productive tool.

Oracle's commitment to repository-based development and code management is clear. While Designer is an obvious choice for Oracle veterans, it is by no means the only effective means of documenting the development process. The benefit of using a repository is that the business rules are stored in a central location and are easily retrieved and edited. Repository-generated code is then easily reproduced to reflect changes to the business rules. So much of the hastily produced code on the Web today is not documented, commented, or even understood by the next programmer. The sheer volume of both static and dynamic content is difficult to manage for many sites. With the average tenure of the web programmer as short as it is, many sites quickly find themselves in a desperation-maintenance mode. A code repository with source code control and business rule documentation alleviates this problem. One advantage of the repository is its use as a configuration management tool. Its versioning capabilities allow many developers to work in a coherent fashion on large projects without having to resort to third-party configuration management software. The tight integration of versioning control within the development environment reduces bureaucratic overhead and ensures adherence to best practice standards.

Although we do not cover the option in this book, Designer also supports generation to the Oracle Forms product, which then can be deployed via the Forms server.

Oracle 8i and Java

Java is an object-oriented, platform-independent tool for developing applications. Java as a development language and platform has radically altered the way developers design, develop, and deploy applications. Java applications can be developed and deployed in a number of different ways, including:

❑ **Stand-alone GUI Applications** – Java has built-in libraries, called Swing, for building GUI-based forms applications. Using Swing, developers can write sophisticated applications that reside on an end-user's desktop. While these applications are difficult to build, they are portable across multiple hardware and operating system platforms.

❑ **Applet running within a browser**. A Java application can be written as an applet that can be downloaded to an end-user's desktop. This applet can perform various tasks, but is severely limited in what actions it can take with an end-user's desktop.

❑ **A server-side application** serving up HTML and data to end-users. Developers can write server-side code (either as a Java Servlet or Java Server Pages) that takes user requests and returns data as HTML. The beauty of this solution is that end-users need nothing more than a web browser to use a server-side based application. Oracle has just achieved full support for Java Servlets and Java Server Pages in release 8.1.7.

Java was introduced in the Oracle database in the first release of Oracle 8i and is now an integral component of the Oracle Internet Platform. Oracle's commitment to Java is evident in the Java Virtual Machine built into Oracle 8i and in the tools it provides to support Java development (which we will review further a little later in this chapter).

Oracle supports Java because of the growing demand for integrated business solutions that use the Java component-based architecture for delivering robust and secure applications.

Java is inherently portable. You can take a Java program written and compiled on one platform and execute it on another. Oracle has always promoted portability issues and Java is a natural fit for this philosophy. Add to this the fact that the code you wrote that runs on the client could now be moved to a middle tier or even to the data tier – wherever it performs best – is an added bonus.

Another advantage of Java over other languages is its security features. Java has already proved itself as a sophisticated language that can nevertheless be downloaded from the Internet and executed securely in any client machine's browser. Security is surely a critical aspect of any code that runs in the same environment as valuable and sensitive data.

The reader is referred to Appendix B for a practical introduction to Java notions and terminology. In the following section, we refer below to Sun Microsystem's Java Developer Kits (JDK), which are covered in this appendix.

The Oracle Java Virtual Machine

A Java Virtual Machine (JVM) is an interpreter for Java programs. The idea behind a virtual machine, or virtual processor, is that it executes Java "bytecode" in the same way that a real processor executes native or "machine code". The virtual machine is a program compiled into native code, and runs in the computer's real processor. Java code then runs in the virtual processor. A problem that programmers generally face when trying to migrate applications to a different architecture, central processor, or operating system is that configuring the code to work with the new setup is something that has to be done again with each application. The idea behind the virtual machine is that these configurations issues are restricted to implementing the virtual machine correctly on the chosen platform. This then provides in principle the same virtual environment for compiled Java applications as a virtual machine on any other platform.

However, not all virtual machines are equal. In certain respects, the Java specification does place a burden on the developer to understand how the underlying operating system works in order ensure that the code runs as expected. For example, Java programs that utilize concurrency, or multi-threading features, may not execute the same on two different operating systems because, for reasons of efficiency and robustness, the virtual machines adopt the different threading models of the respective operating systems. The Java specification encourages developers to understand the code they are writing, and to take into account these issues.

Oracle has implemented a JVM to run alongside the Oracle 8i database. The Oracle JVM is the engine driving the Oracle 8i Java platform (previously known collectively as JServer). The platform consists of the following main structures:

❑ Java Stored Procedures

❑ Java Database Connectiviy (JDBC) interface for mediating database connections from both remote and local Java processes

❑ SQLJ translator for compiling SQLJ source files, and SQLJ Runtime classes for SQLJ

❑ Enterprise JavaBeans (EJB) container and an Inprise Visibroker ORB to manage access from and to deployed EJB and CORBA objects

❑ The JDK libraries, which are the standard compiled Java classes available for client stored procedures

❑ The Oracle Java Virtual Machine

❑ Oracle RDBMS libraries to interact with databases

❑ Operating system

The diagram below shows the conceptual arrangement of services:

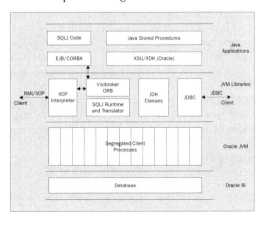

Advantages of the Oracle JVM

Why did Oracle write their own JVM rather than using an existing reference implementation? The demands placed upon a JVM in serving large numbers of client connections simultaneously are severe. The issues are scalability, reliability, and consistency. It is important to segregate client processes in order to prevent run-time errors in one connection adversely affecting another connection. Ideally, a new JVM process should be started for each client to deal with this. However, Sun's JVM release is large at several megabytes, and significant numbers of concurrent JVM processes would soon overwhelm even a powerful machine, using this strategy. Client connections to the Oracle JVM are allocated a new JVM process, and Oracle has solved the scalability problem by reducing the memory footprint for each process by a considerable factor.

The Oracle JVM is optimized for interaction with the Oracle database, and thus has a further advantage over other JVMs.

JDK Compatibility

Release 1 of Oracle 8i (8.1.5) is compliant with JDK 1.1.6, whereas 8.1.6 and 8.1.7 are JDK 1.2.1-compliant. From the development point of view, this means that provided that you use the appropriate JDK for testing and compilation, your Java code should load and run without modification on the Oracle JVM. However there are some significant differences to the way that the server deals with concurrency, which may lead to different observed behavior. There are some further remarks about multithreading in the JVM below.

It is important to realize that one cannot load newer versions of JDK library classes into an existing database and expect to obtain the functionality of new JDK releases. This is because the Oracle JVM must incorporate new system-level security requirements of the JDK before executing safely with new classes. You need to install an upgraded Oracle before you do that.

Java Stored Procedures

Once a Java class has been loaded into the Oracle 8i database, its static methods can be wrapped in a PL/SQL function or procedure and then called like any other PL/SQL procedure. Note that before a user has called any Java methods, no Java objects are accessible to that user. However static methods within a Java class belong to the class rather than to any specific instance of the class, and are therefore accessible as soon as the class has been loaded into memory. Static methods may then instantiate various new instances of other classes and call their methods, just like any Java program.

Differences between Oracle JVM and JDK

One powerful characteristic of Java is the multithreading features of the language. A Java programmer can easily write code that creates concurrently executing components within the same overall process. Although the Oracle JVM is compliant with the Java Language Specification, including support for multithreading, it does not adhere to the threading model that is available in most JVMs. The Oracle database already has a proven and reliable concurrency infrastructure: it can deal with a large number of concurrent connection and transaction processes. It has therefore adopted its own task scheduling systems as the preferred model for programmers to follow, rather than allowing them to develop multithreaded Java applications running within the same transaction context.

Like most application containers, Oracle JVM provides no support for graphical elements such as Java Swing components. The library classes are provided for compatibility, however they are not associated with any display context.

A notable difference to familiar Java environments is that source files and compiled bytecodes are stored in tables in the database rather than in familiar archive files or class directories. This can seem disconcerting at first. One major advantage of this approach is apparent: the database is able to exploit the same access control infrastructure for Java classes as it does for other data.

The J2EE Framework and Oracle

The Java 2 Platform Enterprise Edition builds on the standard Java platform. It provides a set of specifications, blueprints, and reference implementations for enterprise application development. In this section we review the components of the specification that play a significant part in this book, and outline the role these components play in Oracle 8i.

Java Database Connectivity (JDBC)

The JDBC standard is a programming interface that enables Java programs to access and modify data in just about any SQL database. For access to the Oracle platform, JDBC provides the tools for the Java programmer that Oracle Call Interface (OCI) provides to the C/C++ programmer: a means of calling basic RDBMS routines.

Database vendors provide JDBC drivers in the form of Java class libraries. Not all of the driver API, however, has be implemented in Java. Some types of driver link to native code libraries for enhanced performance.

Oracle 8i Release 2 (8.1.6) supports the latest release, the JDBC 2.0 specification, and provides a number of proprietary enhancements for optimising access to Oracle database features. Oracle 8.1.5 supports JDBC 1.0.

Oracle JDBC drivers are available for different application scenarios. A thin client, say an applet, requires a driver that is written purely in Java to maximize platform independence and portability. On the other hand, the middle tier of an enterprise application requires fast native code access to the backend database in order to maximize throughput and make optimal use of the underlying connectivity architecture. Oracle supports these different scenarios with a range of drivers, including a special driver for the use of Java code running in the database itself.

Although JDBC is widely used and is a very flexible interface to SQL, it has one significant disadvantage: the semantics of the SQL statements are generally lost within text strings in the program. The SQLJ specification provides a solution to this point.

SQLJ

Some of the drawbacks of JDBC are addressed in the SQLJ standard. Oracle, Sun Microsystems, IBM, and several other organizations maintain this ANSI standard for embedding SQL statements declaratively in Java programs. SQLJ implementations consist of a translator element, which converts SQLJ code into Java, and a run-time element, which is a set of library helper classes referred to in the generated code. The principal advantages of SQLJ are:

❑ Compile time "semantic" checking of referenced database objects: for example checking that a named table exists and has the attributes that the code expects.

❑ Support for the automatic construction of various helper classes such as iterators to aid in processing query results.

❑ More legible and maintainable code.

Oracle supports a number of custom extensions to the SQLJ ANSI standard, including support for a wider range of data types such as returning streams from a procedure call. The Oracle SQLJ Translator is available both as a stand-alone executable and as an Oracle JVM service. That is, one can upload and run SQLJ code directly into the database. Oracle also provides a presentation tier environment for SQLJ by allowing both SQLJ and Java to be used in Oracle JavaServer Pages.

Servlets and JavaServer Pages (JSP)

Servlets are small web components that help solve the problem of locating functionality within a complex web server application. That is, their small size and limited functionality enable them to be distributed optimally over the platform's architecture. Oracle 8i 8.1.7 provides a "container" for servlets (we will look at containers more closely in the next chapter), the Oracle Servlet Engine (OSE), for Servlet Specification 2.2. That is, servlets can execute within the secure transaction and scheduling environment of Oracle JVM.

JavaServer Pages (JSP) are scripted web pages containing Java code. The Java code dynamically controls the output of the page. In practice, JSPs are just an extension of the servlet specification, since a JSP is compiled to a Java class before execution in the web container. We will look more at Oracle's support for Servlets and JSPs in the section on Oracle HTTP Server later in this chapter.

Enterprise JavaBeans

A JavaBean is a reusable Java component, which often runs as a helper class in a web server, or as a modular component within an application. A Java class does not have to implement any specification to be a JavaBean, although there are some conventions by which the syntactic coding of the attribute methods in the class can be exploited. For example a JavaServer Page can call upon the services of a JavaBean to do some business or database processing, and can instantiate it directly with variables from the session context using a syntactic convention.

Although Enterprise JavaBeans (EJB) cannot be said to have evolved directly from JavaBeans, they share similar facets of portability and modularity. As mentioned, JavaBeans do not adhere to any particular specification, whereas EJB is essentially a specification rather than any particular implemented product. The principle behind EJBs is that they are program units that request certain services from the environment they run in, rather than trying to implement these services themselves. Typical services are management of execution privileges to specific functionality of the EJB, and management of any transactions with external resources. For example, if an external process attempts to locate an EJB and call one of its methods to update data in a database, the EJB's **container** authenticates the requestor of the service and verifies that this user is entitled to execute this process. When the call is completed by the EJB, the container instructs the database to commit the transaction. If an error occurs during processing, the container rolls back the transaction, and so on. This frees developers from tedious and difficult reimplementation of the same essential features in their business applications. Further more, an EJB can be packaged and deployed to any compliant container, without modification.

The EJB model is rapidly becoming a standard solution to some of the most complex problems facing enterprise application designers. Oracle introduced an EJB 1.0 specification-compliant container with the first release of Oracle 8i JVM. Developers can deploy "session" EJBs directly into the Oracle database.

Remote Method Invocation (RMI) with CORBA and IIOP

Remote Method Invocation is Sun Microsystems' specification for communication between JVMs running on different machines. Using the RMI infrastructure, a process on one machine can assign a Java object on another machine to one of its own variables. It can then execute methods on the remote object transparently – as if the remote object were in fact in the local address space. RMI is the high-level machinery that allows Java clients to connect remotely to Java processes, such as EJBs, in the Oracle JVM, and to access the functionality of the remote objects.

Sun and IBM have implemented the RMI-IIOP specification, which allows Java programs to interoperate through RMI with the Internet Inter-ORB Protocol (IIOP) as the underlying transport mechanism. IIOP is a version of the General Inter-ORB Protocol (GIOP) specifically designed for operation over TCP/IP. See http://java.sun.com/products/rmi-iiop/index.htm.

The Common Object Request Broker Architecture (CORBA) is a wider specification addressing inter-communication issues between object-oriented languages such as Java, C++, Smalltalk, and others (http://www.corba.org). The CORBA specification defines the Interface Definition Language (IDL), and designates how objects in separate process spaces can access each other's functionality through the IDL protocol. The inter-communication is achieved via a standardised Object Request Broker (ORB), a kind of server that acts as a intermediary between objects in a network. Oracle 8i fully integrates a third-party ORB, Inprise VisiBroker for Java 3.4 (which requires its own license), in the JVM and provides access to it via a Java IIOP interpreter running in the Oracle JVM.

The RMI-IIOP protocol provides Java clients with access to objects implementing the CORBA 2.0 specification, such as the ORB running in the Oracle JVM. In turn, the ORB acts as an intermediary for the clients with the EJB and CORBA objects deployed to the JVM.

JDeveloper

Based on Borland JBuilder technology, JDeveloper is an integrated development environment (IDE) for Java, XML and Oracle. It has been extended to support the Oracle-specific Java constructs available with the 8i server. For example, automated configuration and deployment of Java Stored Procedures and EJBs to 8i are supported; SQLJ development is well supported, with real-time semantic checking available during compilation; PL/SQL code can be edited and automatically deployed or executed in the database. Full support for web server deployment to Oracle Application Server is provided, but not yet for Oracle iAS. There are tools to connect to Oracle 8i database and interrogate database objects and deployed EJBs. An integrated web server Web-to-Go allows development testing of JSPs, servlets, XSQL servlet, and more. Finally, JDeveloper is used to develop Oracle's entity EJB-like technology BC4J.

A feature of this book is the provision of JDeveloper material for download at the Wrox web site. These folders can be imported into JDeveloper and provide ready-working solutions for the Java based applications in this book.

Business Components for Java (BC4J)

BC4J is a server-side framework for developing Java components and web applications from database structures. The BC4J development environment is built into JDeveloper. BC4J provides relational mapping tools for generating Java entity and view components from database tables. Business logic functionality is then coded into "application modules", which interact with the other generated components, and act as the exported interface to the tool-generated data objects and the database. The application module can then be packaged and deployed in various configurations. There is also support for generating JSP web applications to access the functionality of entire BC4J implementations.

Oracle XML Developer's Kit

Extensible Markup Language (XML) is on its way to becoming the standard for sharing data electronically due to its accessible and simple syntax, open standards, and industry support. XML is similar to Hyper Text Markup Language (HTML) in that they are both markup languages based on Standard Generalized Markup Language. However the similarity ends here. XML is a nonproprietary language that permits data to be shared. In other words, you can think of HTML as a method used to present data while XML is a method used to describe data content.

XML is crucial for business-to-business (B2B) data transfer, and is viewed by many as the answer to the dilemma of representing purchase orders and invoices online. While not viewed as a replacement for EDI (Electronic Data Interchange) because of the previous investment made by businesses in the infrastructure, XML is expected to open the marketplace for smaller businesses who would normally be reluctant to commit the capital required to enter the EDI network, as well as simplifying business-to-business transactions for all players. XML's other role is to support device independence in PDAs, cell phones, and other devices because of the ease with which XML's text-based format can be exchanged. Oracle directly supports XML in PL/SQL, Java, C, and C++ applications. Among other tools, transformers such as XSL transformer, can convert any XML document format into any other XML, HTML, WML (Wireless Markup Language), or custom document on demand, preserving the data but altering the markup tags used for presentation.

XML has applications in many development scenarios. XML is shaping up to be a significant player in any kind of business-to-business exchange. By specifying a format in which items are to be posted in terms of an XML schema or Document Type Definition (DTD), a site can permit buy and sell transactions with little or no human intervention. This use of the XML standard is still in its infancy, but is likely to represent one of the next waves in web technology.

The Oracle XML Developer's Kit (XDK) provides XML component libraries that can be used to enable XML support in applications. The components provided are:

❑ XML Parser for Java – Parses XML documents using DOM (Document Object Model) and SAX (Simple API for XML) so that Java applications can deal with them

❑ XML Class Generator – produces Java classes from a XML DTD that can be used to build XML documents that comply with this DTD

❑ XML Transviewer JavaBeans – Adds graphical or visual interfaces to XML documents for example the TreeViewer Bean will display an XML document as a graphical tree

❑ XSQL Servlet – processes SQL queries and produces an XML document

The Oracle Corporation has recognized the importance and value of XML. As a result, Oracle 8i is the first XML-enabled database on the market. Oracle provides XML parsers for major programming languages such as PL/SQL, C, C++, and Java. With XML parsers, businesses can easily incorporate XML into their applications without the need to rewrite them.

Oracle InterMedia

Oracle interMedia's role will continue to grow as the information we store becomes increasingly complex and user demands for intelligent retrieval continue to grow. InterMedia is important for any site that allows searches, which really is any site. B2C, B2B, and Content Management sites will make the most use of interMedia, as they need to provide the user with searches not only based on search terms, but on related words and item definitions. InterMedia is smart enough to recognize and index different document types based on what's important about each type, and does this in the background without user intervention. Using this option will speed up and improve the results of user searches.

When working with large video and audio files, storage quickly becomes an issue. Finding these files can be difficult if there are many of them, and giving users the additional capability of searching the video or audio content requires frame-by-frame indexing. Oracle's interMedia product offers this indexing, storage, and retrieval capability for any type of file, including audio, video, and image data.

InterMedia is actually a set of components that is fully integrated into Oracle 8i and is responsible for managing different types of text and multimedia services. The only component covered in depth in this book is the Text services – in Chapter 20 we demonstrate how interMedia in the database helps in the development of a search engine.

Text Services

InterMedia Text services provide powerful and fast text retrieval capabilities that evolved from Oracle's ConText text services. These text services makes it possible to query and analyze data from different text information sources including HTML, PDF, Word, Excel, online catalogs, and even online news feeds. Additionally, you can use text services to search XML documents that are stored in an Oracle 8i database, with full text search facilities rather than just record search.

Imaging, Audio, and Video Services

Aside from integrated management support of various multimedia files as previously discussed in this section, interMedia provides some cool features that make working with multimedia files easy. For example, multimedia objects can be dragged and dropped from within the Oracle 8i database to and from popular web applications and web authoring tools. Also, multimedia objects can be captured from within an Oracle 8i database or from external sources such as from digital cameras, scanners, and video cameras and streamed from the database to your application.

Oracle Spatial Cartridge

This cartridge help users locate information based on geocoded information stored in Oracle 8i. Information such as demographic regions, longitude and latitude, addresses, and other locations of interest can be represented through Geographic Locator Services. After data has been geocoded, distances between two or more locations can be calculated and displayed graphically through various applications such as seen with web sites that calculate driving distances and graphically display points of interest between various locations.

Oracle 8i and the Internet

Oracle 8i offers a number of different options for organizations looking at building web-based applications. While we have reviewed the development tools used for building applications in previous sections of this chapter, we have not yet looked at the platform that these applications run on.

Oracle offers a number of different platforms for running Internet-based applications. These platforms include:

❑ Oracle Internet Application Server (iAS)

❑ Oracle's Portal-to-Go technology

❑ Oracle Cache

Internet Application Server (iAS)

Oracle's latest application server, iAS, is the successor to, and marks quite a considerable departure from, Oracle Application Server (OAS). It provides an integrated application and web server platform for Oracle middle tier products and services. At the heart of the web platform is the Oracle HTTP Server built around Apache Web Server. The "cartridge" design of OAS has been replaced in principle by the Apache module system. Incoming HTTP requests are redirected by Apache to appropriate modules: requests for PSP pages are redirected by mod_plsql to the PL/SQL gateway and on to the database; mod_jserv redirects servlet requests to Apache JServ, mod_ose to the Oracle Servlet Engine within Oracle 8.1.7 and so on. Oracle iAS is available in three distributions:

Oracle iAS Standard Edition

Standard Oracle iAS lacks many of the features found in the enterprise edition including: support for Oracle Forms, caching services, and Oracle Enterprise Manager Console.

Oracle iAS Enterprise Edition

This product is a fully integrated enterprise application server and as such includes all the Oracle middle-tier services. In addition, Oracle iAS Enterprise Edition includes enhanced functionality for load-balancing and fail-over of the web server, and a much stronger suite of web server management tools. Oracle iAS features iCache, a read-only middle-tier caching service.

When required, the version of the Application server used in this book was iAS 1.0. At the time of going to press the second version of this server, known as 9iAS, had just been released.

9iAS Wireless Edition

This major enhancement edition bundles Oracle Portal-to-Go for delivering content to mobile devices.

Oracle HTTP Server

In adopting Apache as the heart of the presentation layer, Oracle are following an open standards approach to application integration that complements their support for Java and XML. For example, it is relatively easy to configure the Oracle HTTP Server to redirect requests for JSP pages or servlets to the Tomcat reference web container (http://jakarta.apache.org/tomcat/index.html). Oracle iAS is therefore an applications platform that opens up many different deployment and implementation opportunities to developers.

The Apache web server comes complete with a set of APIs that allow developers to easily extend its functionality. Requests are received by the web server and passed through to the relevant module for redirection to the appropriate web application

Oracle HTTP Server offers independent modules for application services. Among these are are Oracle Portal, Apache JServ, PL/SQL, Perl, Forms, Reports, Discoverer, and OpenSSL. Services can make use of Oracle iCache, which supports customizable caching of dynamic content. The administrator chooses how often and by what means the content is refreshed.

Oracle JSP

OracleJSP is a JSP 1.1-compliant implementation of the JavaServer Pages specification. It supports custom tag extensions (the ability to create user-defined tags implemented in Java). OracleJSP comes bundled with iAS but can also be installed on other web platforms. As well as providing its own set of custom tags (which anticipate but don't replicate many of the JSP 2.0 enhancements) it comes with ready-made Java data access components, which can be invoked in the session using the JSP JavaBean include directive.

Oracle 8i JVM

The release of the iAS 1.0 marked the first Oracle Application server to provide a Java Virtual Machine (8i JVM). The release of 9iAS is expected to provide a stable JVM that is a fully scalable environment and supports EJB 1.1, CORBA objects, and Java Stored Procedures. As a result, there will now be two possible targets for deployment, either into the database or onto the 9i Application Server.

Portal-to-Go

Portal-to-Go is a set of tools for delivering content to mobile devices such as WAP phones, Palm Computing Platform devices, and Windows CE devices. A difficulty arising from the proliferation of such devices is in configuring suitable content for each individual product type. Portal-to-Go solves this problem by defining an intermediate presentation layer Portal-to-Go XML. Content is mapped to this layer by customizable adaptors. The user of Portal-to-Go service can configure the resulting target format and deliver it via XSLT or Java transformers to a range of personal devices. The configuration is achieved using a web-based personalization tool. The Portal-to-Go server and client software sits on the middle tier and needs to be configured to run with a web server, either OAS or Apache on iAS. The Portal-to-Go server uses an Oracle 8i repository to configure and manage services, users.

Portal-to-Go can be downloaded as a stand-alone tool from http://technet.oracle.com and can be integrated into Apache in the Oracle HTTP Server.

Oracle iCache

Oracle iCache is a read-only window to an Oracle 8i database. It is quite simple to set up and can be easily monitored and customized using the database administration tool DBAStudio. It is installed on the middle tier and is specific to a single origin database instance. One can, however, have multiple cache instances across the same middle tier for access to multiple databases. As a simple example of how it works consider the following task: run SQL*Plus on the iAS node and connect to the database through a Transparent Network Substrate (TNS) connect string; then select some records from the employee table in the SCOTT schema. If you have iCache installed and configured to cache the employee table, then you will receive results from iCache. Otherwise you will receive them from the origin database. The connection request is transparently redirected in the TNS layer.

This facility is available to all applications in the iAS installation that use Net8 and TNS to connect to the database instance. The caching facility is ideal for intensive read-only applications and web services.

Summary

We have now reviewed many of the components of the Oracle 8i platform we will focus on in this book. We have not exhausted the tools one could use to develop against Oracle 8i – we've skipped over Oracle's flagship development environment Developer 2000 with Forms and Reports. We've neglected the C/C++ language by skipping Pro*C/C++ and OCI. We've not mentioned Oracle's tight integration with Visual Basic via Oracle Objects for OLE. These are not covered in this book.

We have looked at the technologies and tools supporting development on the Oracle platform:

❑ The different distributions of Oracle 8i

❑ The traditional Oracle Development Tools

❑ Oracle and Java

❑ Oracle and XML

❑ Oracle internet deployment platforms

These topics will of course be explored in far greater detail throughout this book. However, this book is meant to be more then just a text on how to write programs for Oracle. There are many ways in which these tools can be configured, and in which developed code can be deployed. In the next chapter we will look at application development from a wider perspective. We will review the design principles behind implementing and deploying enterprise applications.

We will address such questions as the following:

❑ What is an enterprise application design?

❑ How is it different from regular application development?

❑ What are the challenges we face in building enterprise level applications? Some of theses challenges include:

  ❑ Developing applications that are built on component-based architectures that emphasis designing and developing reusable business logic

  ❑ Building an integration strategy that will let you cleanly move data and processes throughout multiple systems within your organization

  ❑ Designing a hardware and software infrastructure that will meet the scalability and fault-tolerance needs of the enterprise-level Internet application

❑ Where and how do Oracle 8i technologies and tools fit into enterprise application design and development? Remember, Oracle offers a lot of options for application development. The challenge is trying to figure out what the appropriate tool is for the job at hand.

Many of these questions indicate there is more to developing enterprise-level applications (Internet or otherwise) than picking a technology and running with it. Oracle is not a silver-bullet cure that will solve all of your enterprise application needs. It is a means to an end, not the end in and of itself. Oracle is a very powerful set of tools that when combined with disciplined software engineering practices and a strong understanding of customer needs, can be used to build software systems that some may consider revolutionary.

2

Enterprise Application Design

Applications can no longer be developed in a vacuum. The application you are building may eventually have a life that goes beyond its original intent, has to integrate smoothly with external systems, and has to be modified in ways that fall far outside of its original scope. Applications are not stagnant, but evolutionary. The functionality within them must change and adapt over time to reflect the often-chaotic nature of the business process being supported. A good example of this phenomenon might be your company intranet. Many intranet applications started life as a small side-project with no funding, minimal work, and a small number of users. The intranet was an information "kiosk" that served the company's employees with static, unchanging web pages. However, as organizations realized the power of the intranet, the demand for new functionality, integration with existing company data sources, and number of users supported skyrocketed. Many organizations have constantly had to rewrite their intranet applications because the applications were designed for immediate functionality, not long-term flexibility and extensibility (not something that can be added onto the application after it has been written and deployed). It must be a fundamental part of the application design.

> Enterprise Application Design (EAD) is the process of designing applications that embrace change. EAD emphasizes building applications that integrate smoothly with internal and external processes, can be extended to reflect the constant state of change found within a business, and have high availability

In Chapter 1 we looked at the Oracle 8i platform and covered some of the development streams and programming choices that are now provided as an integrated enterprise solution within this platform. We shall be looking at these throughout this book. However, what you still need before launching into the book is some high-level analysis of what constitutes an effective enterprise application, what the pitfalls are in choosing strategies, and what challenges arise when developing such systems.

These notions are independent of your choice of design and its implementation. In reality, you have already decided, or are planning, to use Oracle 8i database as your data tier, and possibly Oracle Internet Application Server as your middle and/or web tiers. That's why you bought this book. There is little doubt that an Oracle 8i database will solve your data storage problems – provided you are aware of what your programs are doing to it. It is state-of-the-art. However, in the rest of this book, you will be able to test the criteria laid out in this chapter against Oracle's evolving support for enterprise-wide services.

This chapter tells you about how, and how not, to design a multi-tiered application. After reading this chapter you will have a basic understanding of why organizations need to design applications from an enterprise perspective. You will understand how client/server technology has evolved from a two-tier to an N-Tier implementation. We will cover:

- ❏ A breakdown of the transition of client/server technology from a two-tier to an N-Tier model
- ❏ Challenges and pitfalls that favor each possible scenario
- ❏ The challenges faced by the application developer in general
- ❏ The notion of a container and the services it offers
- ❏ The programming challenges related to each tier of the enterprise
- ❏ The solutions offered by the Oracle platform and its associated technologies

Chapter 22 in particular addresses many of the notions that we refer to in this chapter in the context of a real application.

The EAD Concept

The EAD concept did not just spring into existence overnight. Like all things in the business world, it was the result of competitive pressures. Companies that could integrate their heterogeneous information systems together and leverage these systems to better service their customers would outperform those organizations that could not. As stated in the previous section, most early IT systems focused on supporting organizations' operational activities. These systems were usually financial reporting systems that kept track of their accounts payable, accounts receivable, and general ledger or inventory systems that managed and controlled inventory levels. However, the twin forces of the Internet and competition in a global market have resulted in organizations looking at new ways to gain competitive advantage. These organizations want to leverage their information systems in the following ways:

- ❏ Reduce the transaction cost of doing business by tightly integrating their internal business processes with those of core vendors, suppliers, and customers
- ❏ Provide real-time, accurate access to data
- ❏ Break down the barriers that exist between departments within an organization
- ❏ Provide a consistent 360 degree view of their customers to their employees
- ❏ Develop new methods for customers to buy their products and services

IT applications that support these business needs can now be found in every part of the organization. Furthermore the individuals who use these systems are not necessarily internal employees. When we look at developing enterprise-level applications, our end-users can range from a customer looking at product information, through a vendor verifying the status of an order, to a customer service representative verifying whether or not a customer has any credit restrictions on their account.

The Evolution to N-Tier Computing

The basic idea behind a tiered (or "layered") architecture is to partition the application such that each layer represents a particular type of functionality and each layer provides that functionality to the layers that surround it. Communication will flow between the various tiers as the application goes about its work. This logical partitioning of the application usually (but not necessarily) also represents some form of physical partitioning in that the set of components composing a particular tier may exist in different processes (typically on different machines) from the components of another tier.

> **While the above statement is generally true, it is a mistake to use the reverse argument to say that a single machine represents a single type of functionality. An application architecture designed along physical boundaries in this manner is likely to be seriously flawed.**

At the heart of a well-designed, tiered architecture is an adherence to object-oriented programming concepts to produce components of specifically defined functionality, which present this functionality in the form of a well-defined interface. An interface is a contractual agreement between the different tiers. It defines the services (functionality) offered by each tier. An interface is a binding agreement that says the mechanism by which the services are invoked can never be changed. In the ideal situation, this can lead to plug'n'play interface implementations, where a component can be slotted into any tier of an application and, with little modification, can be accessed by other components thanks to its well-defined interface.

Having set the benchmark, let's examine the historical evolution towards the holy grail of distributed, n-tier, component-based computing.

Two-Tier Architecture

A two-tier architecture represents a very simple form of partitioning, with the application logic on one tier and the data access logic (and data) on a second tier:

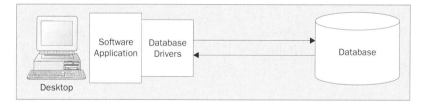

In practice this two-tier model emphasized separating computing power between a powerful back-end database server and a "fat" client residing on an individual's desktop, and hence is commonly referred to as client-server architecture. Traditionally, the individual's desktop would have a set of database-specific software drivers and a GUI application with the presentation and business logic for the application embedded within it. The application data was stored on a powerful database server (such as Oracle) that was accessible by the GUI application. Communication between the client and the server took place through the use of proprietary protocols like Oracle's SQL*Net or Microsoft's Open Database Connectivity standard (ODBC).

As organizations started developing and deploying two-tier client-server applications, some limitations became quickly apparent:

Scalability

Ultimately, two-tier client-server applications only scale up to a certain point.

People seem to have slightly different definitions of the word scalable. One definition states that if you get nearly linear performance gains from linear increases in hardware resources, then your application "scalable"

High transaction applications can quickly expose the scalability problems of two-tier architectures. When a large number of users hit a two-tier application, the network becomes saturated and database connections become exhausted because a database server can only handle a certain number of connections (based on the number of user licenses purchased and the size of the hardware). Once a critical threshold is hit on the database server, users may start being rejected when they want to use the application. Since you only have two tiers, your options are limited to upping the power of the hardware running on the user's desktop or of the database server (or increasing the network bandwidth available to the end user). However, when this sort of bottleneck occurs, your system ceases to be scalable according to the above definition.

Hidden Costs

Two-tier applications have high hidden costs. These costs come in three forms:

❑ Two-tier client-server applications have to be physically installed on each end-user's desktop. This means that every time an update or patch for the application is released every end-user's desktop has to be visited and upgraded. This is a costly process if the application is used by thousands of individuals located across multiple geographical areas.

❑ Most organizations do not have powerful desktop computers for each employee. Any organization can tell you that it is very rare for an employee to have to use only one application for their entire job. Multiple two-tier applications deployed to an employee's desktop quickly eat up resources.

❑ Multiple two-tier applications are deployed to each user's desktop, so it is extremely difficult to get any one group to take responsibility for their application. When something goes wrong, the different application support teams often point fingers over who is the cause of the problem. This leads to higher support costs, delays getting the problem solved and often results in end-users having their day-to-day work interrupted.

Flexibility Issues

Two-tier applications are often implemented with proprietary development tools (Oracle Forms, Visual Basic, Powerbuilder) that lock an organization's business rules into a specific technology. Two-tier applications that are built on a development tool, rather then a development platform (Enterprise Java Beans, CORBA, COM) face two challenges. First, most desktop application development tools do not integrate well. Sure, there are standards like COM that ease in sharing code but every development tool offers "special" features that cannot be "automatically" ported over to another tool. Taking advantage of a new or more scalable technology often requires an entire rewrite of the application. Secondly, because two-tier development tools are so proprietary, it is difficult if not impossible to reuse the business rules from one application to the next. The same set of business rules often has to be re-coded for each application deployed to the desktop. You have to find all of the applications that have the business rule embedded in them and apply the change. Multiple these by the hundreds, if not thousands, of user desktops that have these applications installed and you have a logistical nightmare for even the largest of IT departments. These high deployment and maintenance costs translate in longer release cycles and end-user needs not being met in a timely fashion.

Based upon the points above you can see there are two common problems that come out of two-tier client-server application development: physical partitioning of the application and logical partitioning of the business rules contained within the application. These two problems became the driving force from which three-tier client-server architectures arose.

Three-Tier Architecture

A three-tier architecture splits the logic (and as such, the code for an application) into three distinct tiers: a presentation tier, a business rules tier, and a data tier:

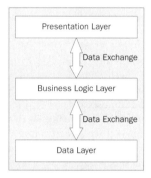

The presentation layer of the three-tier model contains all the code needed for the user interface. Included in this layer is the code that determines how data is presented (drop-down boxes, tables, etc.), user navigation, and data entry rules. The presentation tier in a three-tier model is considered a "thin" client that does not contain any business logic. Early three-tier applications were often written with a desktop development tool like Visual Basic, PowerBuilder, or Delphi. More recent three-tier application use a web-browser hosting HTML and JavaScript as the presentation layer.

The second layer – the business rules layer, contains all of the business logic for the business process being supported by the application. These business rules are often segmented into small software components that are accessed by the presentation layer. The business rules for the first three-tier applications were often written in a lower level language like C or a very vendor-specific development platform like Forte. Today, most three-tier applications are written around one of the three mainstream component architectures: Sun Microsystems' Enterprise Java Beans (EJB), Microsoft's Distributed Network Architecture (DNA), or the Object Manager Group's Common Object Request Broker Architecture (CORBA).

Business rules act on data keyed in by the end user and retrieved from a data store (like an Oracle or SQL Server database, or even a mainframe). However, the code in the business rules layer is never allowed to retrieve or manipulate data directly from a data store. Instead, the business rules layer must go through the data layer. The data layer in a three-tier application is responsible for retrieving data for the business layer and performing the common CRUD (Create, Replace, Update, and Delete) activities. Traditionally the data layer was a set of stored procedures that resided within the data store the application was accessing. Now many three-tier applications are implemented not as stored procedures, but rather as software components.

Advantages of Three-Tier

The first advantage is that a three-tier architecture offers greater flexibility then a two-tier architecture. Each layer in a three-tier architecture can only speak with the tier below it. For example the presentation tier never speaks directly to the data tier. The presentation tier only interacts with the business rules tier. Furthermore, if its interactions take place through well-defined interfaces, as it should, it becomes easier to replace or upgrade components in a particular tier without disrupting the entire application.

The tier using the services of another tier does not care how a service carries out its work. The invoking tier only cares that it has a method of invoking a service and that this method will never change. As long as each tier does not change the public interfaces that the tier above it interacts with, changes can be made without fear of "breaking" the application. Using well-defined interfaces at each of the different tiers abstracts away the details of the technical implementation.

The code in the presentation tier is completely decoupled from business and data code. The presentation client can be completely rewritten and deployed using another vendor's development tools with minimal impact on the other tiers. So, if an organization has written a three-tier application using Visual Basic as the thin client sitting on the user's desktop, they could easily port the application over to the web. The concept of interfaces applies to the business rules tier and data tiers as well. The business rules tier never manipulates data in a data store directly. It always goes through a set of well-defined interfaces that carry out database actions on its behalf. SQL statements can be optimized and tables normalized and denormalized without "breaking" the rest of the application.

Reuse of Code

Since, in a three-tier architecture, the tiers are more decoupled and communicate with each other through interfaces, it is possible to reuse business and data code. Business rules and database code in a three-tier application are no longer embedded within the client sitting on the user's desktop. They reside on a server and can be reused by any application that can communicate with that server. This translates into lower maintenance and support costs for the application. These lower costs are the second advantage of a three-tier architecture. IT staff no longer needs to visit each user's desktop when there are business rule or database changes to be made. They only have to update a single set of servers. However, many early three-tier applications still had a graphical client (written in Visual Basic, Delphi, etc.) residing on the end user's desktop. Any changes or updates to the graphical client still required updating each user's desktop. This problem has all but disappeared because most organizations now use the Web as the presentation tier for their applications. The presentation code for web applications is centralized on web-servers and now gains the deployment advantages that only the business rules and data tier had previously.

Minimizing the amount of code on the user's desktop means shorter and more frequent application release cycles. This translates into end users getting new functionality and bug fixes more frequently at a significantly lower overall cost.

The third advantage of three-tier architectures is that the processing load is spread across multiple machines. Conceptually the three tiers of a three-tier client-server implementation can reside on one machine. However, with many three-tier client-server applications the application is partitioned in the following manner:

❑ The end-user's desktop has a thin-client that contains only presentation logic. This means that the end-user does not have to have a powerful desktop computer and could have multiple applications running on their machine at the same time.

❑ The business tier is usually a single server that contains all of the business logic for the application. The server tends to be a high-end server that could easily process thousands of concurrent user requests.

❑ The data tier resides on a powerful server that handles all requests to retrieve and manipulate data.

The three-tier client-server architecture is a powerful model for building an application. However, many three-tier applications never lived up to the promises made with the architecture.

Problems with Three-Tier

As three-tier applications began to be deployed a number of limitations became apparent. Many of the issues that application developers ran into with three-tier development were exactly the same issues they dealt with when they were developing two-tier applications. These limitations included:

❑ The presentation tier of many early three-tier applications was still based on desktop development tools like Oracle Forms, Visual Basic, and Delphi. Changes in the client still meant physically deploying the update to a large number of desktops. This all changed when the web browser started becoming the tool of choice for developing the client used in many applications.

❑ Most three-tier architectures were built using a single-vendor's development tool(s). There were no widely accepted industry component-based standards that emphasized true cross-platform development and integration. This made it very difficult to integrate applications and reuse business logic written in one vendor's development tool with another's. This was a big problem for organizations try to reap the benefits of a three-tier architecture. Very few organizations build their applications with a single development tool. They buy their applications based on whether or not the application fulfills their need. They rarely make their choice based upon the development tool that was used to write the application.

❑ The data tier of a three-tier application was still very database-specific. Changing the back-end database for a large application still involved a great deal of effort. Much, if not all, of the data retrieval and manipulation code was written in stored procedure language specific to the database platform (such as Oracle's PL/SQL, or SQL Server's T-SQL).

Application developers also ran into problems that were unique to three-tier applications. These problems included:

❑ There was often too much attention paid to physically partitioning an application. Not enough attention was paid to logically partitioning the application. The right level of granularity was not achieved in the middle tier. This limited reuse. Three-tier applications had middle-tiers that were too specific and too tightly coupled to the application. This tight coupling resulted in very limited reuse of business rules outside of the application. Later in this chapter we will look at how middle-tier components can be broken down into different enterprise integration frameworks.

❑ Three-tier applications often required a great deal of "infrastructure" code. Infrastructure code is code that deals with such basic issues as transaction management, resource pooling, and network management. There were no standards for these services and three-tier developers often had to write their own implementations. This had two effects. One: it took time away from developers focusing on the primary task, which was developing an application that fulfilled a specific need. Two: it meant the development team became responsible for supporting this code. This added to overhead and dramatically increased the complexity of the application.

❑ Three-tier applications are still heavily centralized around a single application server and a single database server. If either of these two servers are a performance bottleneck, the only solution available is to upgrade to faster and more expensive hardware, while rarely leveraging your existing hardware investment.

The number of users demanding access to corporate data and services has exploded over the last five years. Organizations now have to develop systems that must support tens of thousands, if not hundreds of thousands of end users. These end users want access via a wide range of platforms including:

❑ Web browsers

❑ Cellular Phones

❑ Personal Digital Assistants (PDA)

❑ Desktop GUI clients

Three-tier applications – because of the limitations described above – could not meet the demands of all of these new users. However, the three-tier client-server architecture did not die and fade into obscurity. Instead the architecture evolved into a more powerful and ubiquitous model called N-Tier Architecture.

N-Tier Architecture

Creating an N-Tier architecture involves defining your components to a higher degree of granularity. The application's business logic may be split down into "data-centric" business logic and "presentation-centric" business logic. For the most demanding enterprise systems, it is common that each logical tier will not be confined to a single machine. With a well-designed N-Tier application you can move your logic between physical tiers as your application evolves and as you understand better its behavior, thus greatly enhancing scalability.

The holy grail of N-Tier architecture, and where it crosses the line to being an enterprise architecture, is to have each tier designed on a consumer/services model. A consumer/services model emphasizes exposing technology-independent services that a consumer (end user or an application) can access. These generic services provide a framework in which new applications can leverage existing business rules and existing applications can easily share data.

Ultimately we could build up an integration services "framework" is going to emphasize a "spoke and hub" model of integration. In this model, each system is a "spoke" that is integrated via a central "hub". This "hub" is a set of integration components that represent the different integration points between the systems. Applications are no longer allowed to talk directly to each other or to have independent integration points. Instead, all system integration must occur through software services that act as a mediator. The software services abstract integration details and more importantly provide an entry point for other services to integrate to the application. An integration services framework looks like this:

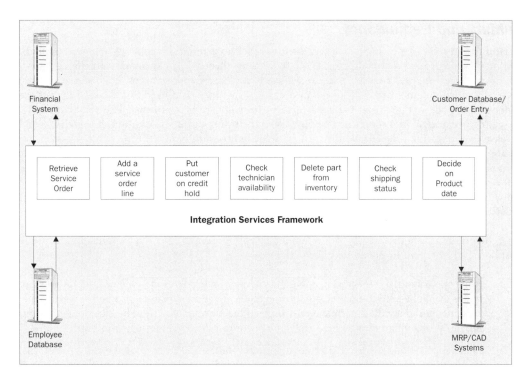

An integration services frameworks consists of centralized, coarse-grained services that encapsulate key business processes. These business processes are available for reuse in other applications throughout the enterprise via a set of public interfaces that never change.

The two keywords from the statement above are centralized and coarse. An integration services framework is centralized in the sense that all communication between applications must happen through the integration services. This means that an application is not allowed to communicate directly with another application. Instead, it has to go through a service that will perform the work for it. It has to be noted that the word centralized does not mean that all of the services have to be located on a single machine. Instead it means that all applications have to go a centralized logical layer. The second keyword "coarse" means that the service encapsulates an entire business process. It does not expose the consumer of the service to each of the individual steps needed to carry out the process. The consumer of the service does not care how the process is carried out. This is one of the main strengths of developing and using an integration services framework. Integration services abstract away both the business process and technical details of carrying out of task. As long as the public interfaces that consumers use to interact with the integration service does not change, the underlying business process and technical implementation of can be changed with minimal impact on other applications.

An N-Tier, services-based architecture provides a consistent interface in which to develop and integrate new applications. This is extremely important in the enterprise context. A successful application, or even a not so successful application, will often have a lifetime and use far outside of its original design. Let's have a look at some of the advantages an N-Tier architecture can bring.

Scalability and Redundancy

Scalability and redundancy in N-Tier architecture revolves around the concept of loose-coupled, share-nothing clusters processing user requests. Share-nothing clusters, also know as server farms, are groups of servers processing user requests that do not share any hardware resources. Each server (node) is a physically independent entity with its own processors, memory, and hard disks. User requests are load-balanced to a node in the cluster via hardware and/or software mechanisms. This load balancing allows for scaling because no one server is receiving all of the transactions. In addition, if there is a sudden increase in application usage scalability can be achieved by simply purchasing another server, installing the application code on the server, and configuring the cluster to accept this server. It is important to point out that the scaling achieved by a share-nothing cluster is not linear. Every additional server added to a cluster increases interprocess communication on the server and network traffic. Eventually, you will reach the point of diminishing returns where the overhead from the clustered servers will begin to detract from the performance of the application.

When determining whether or not to implement an application as an N-Tier application, two questions must be asked in regard to scalability. They are:

❏ Is the application, if it successful, going to experience a sudden spike in new users. A good example of this would be an e-commerce application that is mentioned in a major trade magazine and suddenly has to handle a permanent increase in the number of users. The lucky organization that has this problem has to be able to scale quickly or run the risk of losing customers.

❏ Is the application going to experience periodic spikes in user access? An example of this might be a web-based time-sheet entry system that is hardly used for most of the week. Every Friday at three o'clock the application has to suddenly handle thousands of employees trying to enter their time-sheet information.

Answering these questions is very important from an enterprise perspective. The gut reaction of most IT directors is to make a tactical decision (a.k.a. short-term) and purchase more or bigger hardware to handle these periodic spikes. However, this reaction is rarely cost-effective and often results in a proliferation of under-utilized servers. The more strategic solution (a.k.a. long-term) is to use share-nothing clusters to utilize existing server resources to handle these periodic spikes.

The share-nothing cluster model by its nature introduces a great deal of redundancy and fail-over within the application. Share-nothing clusters eliminate many of the single-points of failure within an application.

> **A single point of failure within an application can be defined as the loss of a single resource – hardware or software – that can completely cripple the application and make it unavailable to end-users.**

Each node in the cluster is completely independent of the other servers. If a node goes down, the other servers pick up the load. Usually, depending on the load-balancing mechanism chosen, the work on the down server will be lost and the end user will receive some kind of error message. The challenge when designing an N-Tier architecture with redundancy is to have enough server power to be able to serve the additional load if one of the nodes in the cluster goes down. A common mistake made when designing an enterprise level N-Tier application is to purchase only enough server power to adequately handle the current user load. However, the moment one of the servers in the cluster goes down, a domino effect takes place. Each server becomes overloaded and in turn fails. This vicious cycle continues until the application becomes unusable. Designing for server redundancy can be summed up as follows: always have enough server capacity to handle a node failing in the cluster. Never buy just enough hardware.

Integration

Organizations have to build relationships with their customers, be solution providers, and gain a competitive advantage by leveraging the data locked within their information systems. Those organizations that do not learn these (albeit often painful) lessons will find themselves being beaten in the market by more agile competitors.

Although information has grown to be a key business asset, much of this information exists as data in old and outdated information systems. In order to maximize the usefulness of this information, applications need to be able to integrate with the existing information system – not necessarily an easy task as current technologies have often advanced far ahead of some of these legacy systems. The ability to combine old and new technologies is key to the success of developing for today's enterprise.

Enterprise Application Integration is a huge field of study. There are many vocal proponents in it and to go into any great depth would be outside the scope of this book. However, we can review some of the basic principles of EAI:

- ❑ **EAI focuses on business processes, not just technology**. Enterprise Application Integration is not about writing reusable applications or using cool software. It is about integrating and supporting business processes. Everything else is just implementation detail.

- ❑ **EAI happens at an enterprise level not an application level**. Enterprise Application Integration is not solved with one or two applications talking to each other. There has to be conscious commitment from an organization to build a cross-functional team of business and IT personnel who are responsible for identifying key business processes and how to integrate them.

- ❑ **EAI is about process-orientated software development**. Enterprise Application Integration is not captured in a technology. Technologies like N-Tier architectures, component-based software development and Message-Orientated-Middleware (MOM) are all just tools for implementing EAI solutions. EAI is a formalized approach for understanding business processes, identifying and using technologies to integrate these processes, and creating the organization and methodologies in your software development team to focus on the larger picture of enterprise development.

- ❑ **EAI is a continuous process**. Enterprise Application Integration focuses on building an infrastructure that will let applications share business processes, data, and code. This is not a one-time project that can be implemented by an organization and forgotten about.

Adaptability

In order to maintain a competitive edge, the adoption of new technologies has become a key factor in a company's ability to best exploit its information assets. More importantly, adapting these new technologies to work in tandem with the existing legacy systems has become one of the foremost requirements of the enterprise.

The high-paced, fast-changing information-driven economy means that responding quickly to new directions and information is critical in establishing and maintaining a competitive edge. The functionality within business systems must change and adapt over time to reflect the often-chaotic nature of the business process being supported. An N-Tier architecture that supports plug'n'play interface deployment has the best chance of being able to adapt in such a demanding environment.

Remember, EAD is the process of designing applications that embrace change. It emphasizes building applications that integrate smoothly with internal and external processes, and can be extended to reflect the constant state of change found within a business.

Before we start painting too rosy a picture of N-Tier development, we should consider some of the downsides. Successful N-Tier (and three-tier), distributed applications require a huge amount of expertise to get right, and now and for the unforeseeable future, expertise is in very short supply. Most developers still find that their most successful projects are two-tier projects.

Problems with N-Tier

N-Tier architectures are not a hammer that can be used to "pound away " at IT solutions. N-Tier applications need a serious level of time, money, and patience from an organization. Some examples of projects and organizations that should not undertake N-Tier application development include:

- ❏ **Small organizations** – Building N-Tier architectures requires resources and talent. Many small organizations have a small IT budget. Developing N-Tier applications can significantly add to the time it takes to deploy an application. Small companies will often not have the time needed to properly develop and deploy N-Tier applications.

- ❏ **Small projects** – Many times applications are very narrowly focused and might have a one or two time use. Examples of these projects include departmental applications, some corporate intranets, and application prototypes. N-Tier applications increase upfront development costs because of their strong emphasis on modeling and application partitioning. If the application does not have any longevity then this extra time (a.k.a. money) is wasted. This said determining whether or not an application has longevity can be like looking in a crystal ball. A careful analysis of the business problem the application is solving is needed.

- ❏ **Organizations that lack commitment** – Companies, especially large companies, will often say that the have a commitment to enterprise application design. However, when it comes time to fund N-Tier projects these companies are the first to say "forget design, we have to deploy this now". If this attitude cannot be overcome do not try and write an N-Tier application. You will be hamstrung and will not be able to complete the project. The fact that you pursued the N-Tier path will often lead to you or your team getting the blame for the failure of the project. The words "you spent too much time in design and not enough time writing code" are words that have burned the ears of many application developers.

- ❏ **Organizations that lack the people skills** – N-Tier architectures are unique in that they emphasize partitioning an application into different tiers. Each tier is often implemented using a different technology. N-Tier architectures need developers who are familiar with implementing each of the tiers. This means that you cannot take a mainframe programmer with little or no experience in middle-tier development and ask them to build a scalable application. If a company cannot hire the talent, build their own talent in-house or locate consultants who can assist in developing these applications, they should not pursue an N-Tier strategy.

As you can tell all of the reasons for not using an N-Tier design revolve around size (of the company and the organization) and the availability of resources (time, money, and programming resources). Most N-Tier projects do not fail because of technology. They fail because of poor planning or lack of resource and organizational commitments.

Oracle and EAD

One of the great challenges is to maintain programming productivity in the face of the increasing complexity of modern enterprise application design and development.

Some of the recent developments in the Oracle platform – adoption of the Java language, support for XML, an ever-increasing cast of supporting tools and technologies – have been in direct response to the many challenges (adaptability, integration...) that have been mapped out in the preceding discussion.

However, with Oracle the problem is in danger of becoming "too many choices"! Achieving high productivity can be complicated by the sheer variety of technologies and standards that have been developed over the years, requiring highly developed skill sets, the acquisition of which is a problem in itself. Moreover, the rapid pace of change in standards poses significant challenges in ensuring efficient meshing of technologies

None of these problem domains are especially new to the enterprise developer, but solving these problems in a comprehensive and economic manner is still crucial.

The key to creating usable, flexible, and maintainable applications is to apply technologies that are appropriate to the *context* of the problem being solved. Over the following sections, we will look at a couple of development scenarios that are discussed in more detail in various sections of this book.

PL/SQL Development

Do not over-engineer a solution. It is perfectly possible to build logically tiered applications, with well-defined interfaces using traditional PL/SQL programming, as we hope to demonstrate in the "PL/SQL and the Web" section of this book:

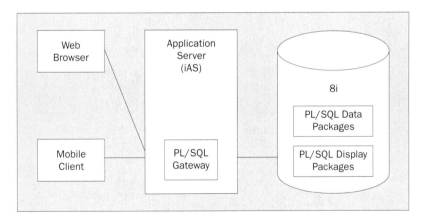

On the face of it the above solution is 3-tier, but in terms of physical partitioning of the code, it is basically "1-tier". All of the code is stored and executes in the Oracle database, with all the stability and security that brings. As an application grows more complex and attracts a wider user base there is obviously a limit to the scalability of this solution. However, Oracle is a powerful database and, these applications, if correctly designed, can certainly service the needs many enterprises.

Remember, that whatever language you use for your application logic, what actually interacts with the Oracle database tier is going to be PL/SQL. Consider using PL/SQL for any part of your application when:

- ❑ **Skills**. Your development staff is already well versed in the language.

- ❑ **Intranet**. You need fast, powerful internal or intranet applications. Although the PL/SQL Web Toolkit is sufficiently well-supported to enable development of fully fledged e-commerce sites, it is inherently well-suited to internal business systems which can centralize their intranet content to a single tier.

- ❑ **Local processing**. Any heavy processing can make effective use of PL/SQL procedures, even when the presentation layer is written in another language. If you pay big license fees for a state-of-the-art database, and you are able to exploit the native processing power of PL/SQL in your application, then it is sensible to make use of that facility.

Some of the benefits are:

- ❑ **Intuitiveness**. PL/SQL is easy to learn and write, and is reasonably intuitive to database programmers. Most experienced Oracle developers already know PL/SQL.

- ❑ **Network overhead**. PL/SQL is native to the database, requiring no establishment of connections or external data processing. This is a particular weakness of the JVM interoperation model based on RMI. In standard RMI, arguments are passed between machines by transferring the entire data structure: since the machines use different address spaces, they cannot refer to a structure by its address.

- ❑ **Compilation**. Code is stored in compiled form, eliminating the need for compilation or interpretation at runtime. Note that in Oracle 8.1.7, the JAccelerator is available for server-side compilation of Java bytecode to machine code, so this issue of compilation efficiency is no longer so clear.

Java Development

The biggest difference between Java and PL/SQL is that PL/SQL requires more resources on the database server as it grows, while Java demands can usually be distributed between application and database servers.

With the emergence of Oracles new Internet Application Server (iAS), with its adoption of the Apache Web server with JServ web container, Oracle middle-tier options now include programming web applications with Java Server Pages and Servlets:

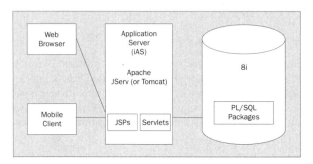

Direct adoption of new technologies is insufficient unless they are utilized to their full potential and appropriately integrated with other relevant technologies. Thus the ability to develop and then deploy applications as effectively and as quickly as possible is also important. In Chapter 18 of this book we show how to utilize and meld two technologies and skill sets: PL/SQL database programming and Java web programming, to develop an effective discussion forum that are becoming vital pieces in the drive to create a sense of community on a Web site.

We also have Oracle's adoption of the advanced and complex EJB framework, that allows Oracle developers to deploy beans on the middle or database tier:

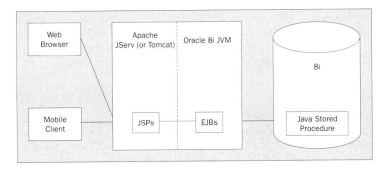

The development of frameworks such as EJB, and its adoption by Oracle, is in direct response to the difficulties faced by programmers in a distributed n-tier environment.

In a distributed environment method calls are no longer deterministic, as they are in local processing. There are associated problems with network failure etc.

Other factors must also be considered:

❑   Many orders of magnitude increase in the overhead of method calls

❑   The potential for communication to dominate computation

❑   Implicit concurrency in the system

❑   The need to repeatedly locate remote components as they migrate between servers over time

❑   The levels of unpredictability make it difficult or impossible to guarantee the consistency of all the data in the system at any one time

EJBs work in containers that provide numerous services – things the programmer will not have to code themself – that can ease the burden of this type of development. We take an in-depth look at the use of EJBs in Oracle applications in Chapter 15. It should be noted that, with the only recent emergence of iAS technology, the database JVM currently provides the most stable platform for deployment of EJBs (we certainly found this to be true in the case of iAS 1.0 at least).

Containers and the Middle Tier

A container is an execution environment for a component. The component lives in the container and the container provides services for the component. Similarly, a container often lives in an application server, which provides an execution environment for it and other containers.

We look closely at one particular container type, the **EJB container** proposed in Sun Microsystems' J2EE specification, as an example of the issues that can be dealt with by this component-based and declarative approach to implementation of business logic.

Technically, a component interacts only with its container and the resources the container provides. As the interface between the container and an application server isn't well defined, a single vendor will almost always provide both and the distinction is often meaningless. If an API between a container and an application server is ever standardized, at that time the distinction will become more important.

The primary reason that you would write an Enterprise JavaBeans component for example is to take advantage of the services that the container (the execution environment) provides. Understanding what these services comprise will help you understand why you should make the decision to use EJB components in your design in a certain situation, and what role they should play. Here are some of the services you can expect from an EJB container.

Services

The EJB container exists to provide the bean programmer with services. For the most part, the bean programmer just needs to follow the rules to automatically take advantage of these services. They can simply tell the container the details of what should be provided. This "telling the container" is known as **declarative semantics**, and is one of EJB's best features. Declarative information is specified in an XML file known as the deployment descriptor. For many features, even this declarative information is not necessary, and the container will provide the feature without any work on the bean programmer's part at all.

Transaction Management

It's true that the JDBC API provides functionality to manage a transaction, and this could conceivably be done from a servlet or JSP. However, transaction management can be complex, particularly if multiple data-access components and/or multiple data sources are involved. Complex transactions with EJBs can be managed without any coding.

Declarative Security

In a real-world application, access to data and business logic functionality must be secure. It is possible for the developer to provide security using servlets or JSP pages, but this can be a complex and error-prone task. This is especially true if multiple servlets or JSP pages use classes with common business logic; a custom security framework would need to be provided by the application. Access to EJB components can be regulated without any coding.

Error Handling

The EJB specification clearly defines how errors affect transactions, client results, server logging, and component recovery.

Business Logic

Developing software that represents complex business logic requires a large investment in an enterprise's resources. Realizing this, software developers have for decades been pursuing the goal of software reuse. Component reuse has been one of the most successful strategies. EJBs are server-side components that can be used simultaneously by many different clients: web server presentation logic represented by servlets and JSPs as well as a multitude of others (such as Swing GUI clients, Visual Basic programs, Excel spreadsheets, and Palm Pilots, to name a few). If the business logic embodied in your application requires a large development investment, this is an ideal way to enable maximum returns.

Scalability

The Enterprise JavaBeans specification requires the application developer to follow certain rules in coding their business logic components. These rules are designed to enable the application server to manage large numbers of simultaneous clients making significant demands on business logic components and data access components. They are also designed to enable the application server to work in a cluster (across multiple machines) and to recover from the failure of any clustered node. Although web servers can be made to scale as well, web containers are not designed specifically to scale components, like EJB containers are with business logic and data access code. For instance, Chapter 22 discusses how many users can share instances of a pooled service session bean, conserving system resources. The equivalent service component on the web tier, a JavaBean, will not be pooled without custom programming.

Portability

Although the application developer can provide some of the same services as an Enterprise JavaBeans container, each of those services must be developed and integrated separately. If a changing business environment imposes new requirements on an application, those new requirements must be met with custom code (or at least purchased technology that must be integrated by hand). Since Enterprise JavaBeans are written to an industry-standard API, they can often be run unmodified in a new application server that provides increased functionality.

The important point to understand about all these services is that they are implemented by the container developer, not by the business-logic programmer. This is possible, even though the container developer knows nothing about the business logic, because the business logic components – the Enterprise JavaBeans – follow the contract defined in the specification.

When to Use Java

Consider Java when your requirements include:

❑ **Scalability**. The ability to deploy interoperating Java components within a cluster of machines versus heavy database procedure loading. Note that reference Java virtual machines probably do not have the scalability and performance of commercial products, including Oracle JVM – particularly when load-balancing and interprocess security is critical. On the other hand, if you insist on a PL/SQL solution, Oracle almost certainly has the tools to deploy it: iCache nodes in the middle tier can reduce backend loading; Oracle Parallel Server (OPS) spreads data services between multiple processors.

❑ **User interface design.** Most Oracle consoles and graphic based tools are written in Java!

❑ **Independent reusable components**. This is the inspiration behind Java, but it is harder to realize in practice than in theory. Oracle JVM still has to catch up with the latest JDK releases and EJB releases, and making sure that your respective runtime environments are compatible is an issue here. (It is fair to say that many of the compatibility issues are GUI related and therefore of little relevance within Oracle JVM.)

Some of the benefits of using Java:

❑ **Skills**. Expert programmers are becoming available by the thousand, and this supply seems likely to increase.

❑ **Security**. Sophisticated compiler-enforced error handling and security features encourage the development of predictable and manageable code.

❑ **Integration**. Java has standardized library classes, development kits, and development tools, that should work anywhere.

❑ **Memory management**. Java is a high-level language, and all memory management is handled by the runtime. In older languages, one had to specifically allocate and deallocate memory to dynamic program elements – a source of subtle and dangerous bugs.

Possible drawbacks of Java:

❑ **Speed**. Java is still quite slow compared to other languages, even with faster servers and precompilation and caching techniques.

❑ **Learning**. The learning curve for Java is steep. Programmers accustomed to object-oriented techniques tend to pick it up faster, but it is a huge leap for someone coming from an PL/SQL or other procedural background.

How, you might ask, does one tell if a language is future-proof? Looking at installed base, industry support, and openness should give us a reasonable indicator as to a language's staying power. Clearly, there is significant industry support for Java. But what about PL/SQL? Aren't proprietary languages outdated? That's probably true, but the installed base, the comfort level among so many in the Oracle field, and the stated corporate commitment to the language will most likely keep it around at least another ten years or so.

The Supporting Cast of Oracle Software

Don't forget that, Oracle now provides a staggering range of technologies and tools that are available to you whatever core language you choose for your applications.

Whether or not you ultimately program the application in Java you can use Designer to design your database and as a repository for all database objects required by the application (see Chapter 5). With Oracle interMedia support in the database, it is a relatively simple programming task to come up with some Java classes for a search engine (see Chapter 20). And so on.

Of course, a considerable advance in the Oracle development platform is its burgeoning support for XML, which is at the heart of many enterprise application integration projects (see Chapters 21 and 22).

XML

Will HTML ultimately be replaced by XML? This is a general misconception: XML is not intended to be a replacement for HTML. HTML is a presentation markup language, whereas XML is a data definition markup language. XML is a serious competitor for EDI (Electronic Data Interchange), though, since XML applications don't require the heavy infrastructure investment EDI demands, making it more interesting to smaller businesses. If your application will ever exchange data with any other organization, or if you will ever consider deploying to a mobile device, you would be wise to begin evaluating XML's role in your enterprise. Broadly, this definition should include everyone who is currently writing web code, but the reality is that the majority of your content will be written for and delivered to a browser via HTML for many years to come.

Communication Issues

N-Tier architectures have finally broken many of the vendor dependencies found in the earlier two- and three-tier application models. This has happened for two reasons. First there is a "standard" set of protocols that break many of the vendor dependencies found in early development efforts. Software vendors like Oracle, IBM, Sun, and Microsoft have realized, sometimes begrudgingly, that the future of computing is not desktop-centric applications that tie an end user to a particular operating system or hardware platform. Rather the future revolves around giving users access to applications and services that reside on a global network of computers (the Internet). End users want this access to be independent of any one vendor's technology. In response to this demand software vendors are adopting common protocols for networking computers and requesting, presenting, and exchanging data. These protocols are not owned by any vendor. They include:

❑   **TCP/IP** – TCP/IP stands for Transport Control Protocol/Internet Protocol. It is the *lingua franca* for networking different types of systems to communicate with one another. TCP/IP can run across a multitude of physical networks (Ethernet, SNA, Token Ring, Banyan) and is the protocol used by the Internet.

❑   **HTTP** – HTTP stands for HyperText Transport Protocol. It is a request/response protocol used by web browsers and web servers to request and retrieve web pages. It is also used heavily by other types of applications to request and receive data.

❑   **HTML** – HTML stands for HyperText Markup Language. HTML is a standard used by web browsers to present web pages returned from a web server. HTML is the standard that has allowed the development of the universal desktop client. Developers can now write truly portable applications that can be deployed across multiple hardware and software platforms with minimal effort.

Summary

Enterprise application design is a very broad subject. This chapter has attempted to give a conceptual framework in which to understand and pursue EAD. In summary the topics covered included:

❑   A definition of the term Enterprise Application Design

❑   The business needs for EAD

❑   The evolution of client-server technology from a two-tier model to an N-Tier model

❑   The Internet and how it has driven the use of EAD principles

❑   When to use and not use an N-Tier implementation

N-Tier design, like so many other design methodologies before it, is not a silver-bullet solution. It will not solve all of an organization's problems, nor will it mystically transform a development staff's productivity overnight. The design and implementation of N-Tier applications is a slow, iterative and incremental process that should not be rushed into. In order to consider an application for an N-Tier implementation, the following requirements and constraints need to be considered:

❑   The application has a high volume of transactions and needs to be scalable.

❑   The application is mission-critical. The loss of the application could seriously hamper the organization's ability to do business.

❑   The application encapsulates business rules and processes that have a high degree of reuse.

❑   The organization has made the commitment of time, resources, and patience to properly implement the architecture.

We examined Java and PL/SQL in the light of various criteria that will guide you towards good solutions in N-Tier development. The notion of application and component container is rapidly becoming a standard one in N-Tier design, and we looked at one specification in particular, the EJB container.

In closing, the design and implementation of integrated enterprise applications will be the key to many companies moving successfully from a "brick and mortar" business model to the Internet based "click and mortar" model. When looking at Enterprise application design remember these basics:

❑   Applications must be designed from a cross-functional (a.k.a. interdepartmental) perspective.

❑   Applications often have a life outside of their original purpose.

❑   Applications must be envisioned as services based. The application can be composed of three different frameworks (application development, business domain, integration services). Each one of these frameworks has component pieces that offer different levels of granularity and reuse.

❑   The benefits of EAD do not appear overnight. Reuse, consistency, and abstraction are all things that are developed incrementally and iteratively over time.

❑   N-Tier applications must be developed with a clear business need and a definable return on investment (ROI). The ROI for N-Tier application must be communicated back to all the projects stakeholders. It's important to define not just the ROI on the work, but in what time frame each of the shareholders will start seeing a return.

In the next chapter we begin along the road to deploying effective applications with the Oracle 8i platform. We start by looking at the database itself. It is possible to use JDBC, RMI-IIOP, SQLJ, etc. to access and modify data, or programs, in Oracle 8i without really knowing what a database is or how it works. We don't want you to develop your programs that way. It is crucial to have some knowledge of the internal structure of the database so that you can take the material of this chapter forward to reliable, scalable, and efficient applications. In Chapter 22 we will look at many of the specific issues in this chapter in relation to a real application.

ORACLE8iAPPLICATIONPROGRAMMING

3

Database Foundations

Why do we need to learn how a database works? To a novice database programmer, this may sound like a reasonable question. After all, Oracle 8i provides numerous tools that appear to make database administration easy. However, an experienced Oracle database programmer will notice that I said "appear to make..." in the previous statement.

It's true: using Oracle tools, a DBA can keep an Oracle database system working under normal circumstances. It's like driving a car. All you have to do is turn the key and give it some gas. Voila, you're cruising down the highway and the best part is, you don't need to know a thing about how the internals of the car operate. But what would you do if one day you turned the key and nothing happened? If you took time to learn the basics of how a car operates, there would be a reasonable chance you may be able to figure out what is wrong and take appropriate action on your own to quickly get things running again.

As a programmer, you will need to know how the systems, components and structures of the database work, and you will often have to deal with technical material that includes these terms. This chapter provides a reference and a tutorial over the internal workings of an Oracle 8i database, which can be used in conjunction with the rest of this book.

After completing this chapter, you should understand the following concepts:

- ❑ What is the difference between a hierarchical, network, and a relational database?
- ❑ Types of relationships in a RDBMS
- ❑ Components of an Oracle 8i database
- ❑ What are Oracle objects?
- ❑ How does Oracle use memory locations?
- ❑ What are redo logs and how do they work?
- ❑ What are the five required background processes and what types of optional processes are available to Oracle users?
- ❑ The difference between an Oracle database and an Oracle Instance

Database History

Database management systems (DBMS) go back to the late 1950's. At the time, the predominant database management system was based on models using hierarchal relationships. This was well suited to the early mainframe computers with their limited storage and memory requirements. Hierarchical databases were based on tree structures that could be easily and quickly traversed. One such hierarchical structure is shown in the next diagram:

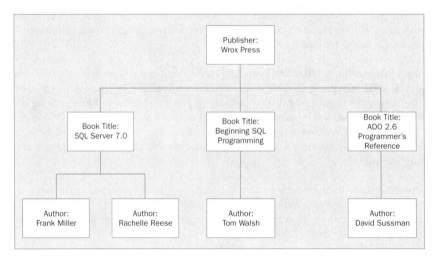

The way the hierarchical model works is through the organization of data elements that are placed in tabular rows. In other words, each row represents an entity. Looking back at the diagram for the hierarchical tree, notice the first row at the top of the hierarchy represents Wrox Press, Inc. This top row (Publisher) represents a relationship with the next row down which is shown as Book Titles. These Book Titles imply a relationship with the next row down where we see the Authors for the titles in the previous row. In other words, the relationships we just looked at represent that the authors write books (book titles) that are published by Wrox Press, Inc.

It is important to realize that the hierarchical model is really a logical abstraction based on a linear tree. In actuality, data tends to be scattered across numerous locations and these relationships are only formed as a logical proximity is required.

The hierarchical model presents numerous shortcomings largely due to the restrictive nature of its tree-like branching structure used in making relationships. In 1964, a General Electric employee by the name of Charles Bachman proposed an alternative to the hierarchal model by providing a new model for database management called the network model. The network model provided a way to handle non-hierarchical relationships and was based on linking data records together with a system of intersecting circular chains. Look at the following diagram:

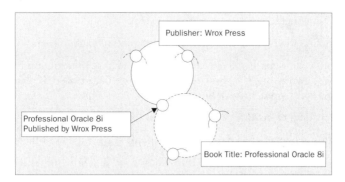

Notice that one intersecting circular chain is solid indicating the Publisher Wrox Press Inc., while the other circular chain indicating the book title Professional Oracle 8i is shown using dashes. The smaller circles located on the solid circular chain represent other publishers. The smaller circles located on the dashed circular chain represent other titles of books. When a small circle intersects both chains, then the Publisher originating from the solid chain published the book title originating from the circle with dashed lines. In this example, we can see that the book title Professional Oracle 8i intersects with the publisher Wrox Press indicating that Wrox Press published the book titled Professional Oracle 8i.

It was the year 1970 when Dr. Edgar F. Codd first promoted his relational database theory in a number of papers, *A Relational Model of Data for Large Shared Data Banks* that first appeared in the publication, *Association of Computer Machinery*; and *System R4 Relational* that appeared in an independent IBM research journal. What's interesting is as much as 10 years after Dr. Codd's relational theory was first introduced few relational databases were yet to be implemented. As a matter of fact, as late as 1980, most database systems in existence still were based on either a hierarchical or network database management systems.

Today, most of the hierarchical and network database management systems are mere memories and the relational model is now accepted as the standard model. What makes the relational database management system (RDBMS) so popular is its ability to organize and store data in easily joined tables and views and normalization to eliminate duplications in data.

Logical Structures

Although relationships are at the heart of an RDBMS, there is more to it than simply relating tables. A typical RDBMS contains several logical structures. For example, every relational database will have a database schema. A database schema is like a roadmap that includes all the logical structures that are a part of a database system. A schema does not physically organize objects within a database. Objects represented in schemas are logically organized. Some of the other major elements and components within a schema include:

- ❏ Tables (with Rows and Columns) as previously described.

- ❏ Numbered Sequences.

- ❏ Datatypes define the type of values that are assigned to each column in a table.

- ❏ Views enable data to be displayed in such a manner that information from several tables and rows can be shown at once. Views are nothing more than stored SQL statements that are designed to display predefined table information.

- ❏ Indexes allow data to be accessed quicker.

- ❏ Synonym, this is like an alias or an alternate name for a database object.

- ❏ Snapshot is a read-only representation of data stored in a table or tables.

Components of an Oracle 8i Database

The Oracle 8i database management system is a rather complex structure that is made up of numerous files, processes, and memory structures each interacting to form a complete and robust database environment.

Before we look at the different items making up an Oracle database management system, let's start with an analogy. Pretend you are standing outside a public library. Take a look at the library building from the outside. Now think about what is inside. Inside you will find lots of books arranged on shelves. There is a card catalog that keeps a listing of all the books in the library as well as a decimal convention that makes it easy to locate any book in the library. Also, there are librarians and building maintenance personnel who maintain the library. All of these objects and people work together to make a library functional. As we continue our tour of Oracle's components, we will return frequently to our library analogy. We will see example of how things such as the librarians and building personnel are similar to Oracle background processes and how the card catalog is similar to Oracle indexes.

Data Dictionary

Every Oracle database contains data that describes the structure of objects stored within the database. This describing data is referred to as metadata. More specifically, metadata contains information about database objects such as tables, views, indexes, user privileges, roles, and constraints. This metadata is stored in a special read-only table referred to as the data dictionary. You can query the data dictionary using standard SQL statements, however you should never attempt to manually override the dictionary (it is read-only) by forcing changes to it.

We have looked at most of the types of objects found in an Oracle database (such as tables, datafiles, memory structures, etc.). It stands true that each database object contains its own set of system tables and views in the data dictionary, which can be accessed by issuing the following SQL statement:

```
SQL>SELECT * FROM DICT;
```

The data dictionary can be broken into four sections:

❑   Internal RDBMS Tables

❑   Data Dictionary Tables

❑   Data Dictionary Views

❑   Dynamic Performance Views

Internal RDBMS Tables

The internal RDBMS Tables are easy to identify because they contain an X$ or XX$ sign toward the beginning of the table name such as with XX$KSMSS. Although it may be easy to identify internal RDBMS tables by their designated prefixes, they are very difficult to make sense of. In actuality, these tables are not meant to provide meaningful information to a DBA or user, although Oracle has no problem letting you look at them.

First, you will find that these tables are cryptically named as previously indicated and secondly these system tables are undocumented. The reason for this is they are designed to provide Oracle with essential system information and internal statistics, thus they are not meant for DBAs and other users to poke around in. Nevertheless, these tables do exist and the curious DBA can query them.

Data Dictionary Tables

The data dictionary tables are very much like a map to the library. Using data dictionary tables, you can learn just about everything about the database itself without ever looking at what is being stored in the database (like books in the library). The data dictionary is responsible for storing metadata about Oracle's tables, indexes, constraints, and database constructs. Data dictionary tables can be identified by table names ending with a "$" sign such as with the tables TAB$ and SEG$.

As with the internal RDBMS Tables, data dictionary tables can be queried however, most of the information contained in the data dictionary tables can be presented in the form of user friendly views as described in the next sections: Data Dictionary Views and Dynamic Performance Views

Data Dictionary Views

Data dictionary views provide ways to query meaningful information for DBAs as well as regular database users. Recall that views are nothing more than predefined stored SQL statements that are designed to display predefined table information. You can categorize data dictionary views into three types of views: DBA, USER, ALL, which are accessible to different levels of users based on their privileges. If a user is defined in the database as being a DBA, he or she will have the DBA privilege. All users can access both the USER and ALL views.

DBA Views

DBA views as the name suggests, are designed for providing DBAs with pertinent information. Data dictionary views intended for DBAs are identified with DBA_ as the first three characters followed with an underscore and then the name of the view. As a matter of fact, the only users that can access DBA views are users with system privileges that equate to Select Any Table. A DBA with appropriate privileges can query DBA_Tablespaces to retrieve comprehensive information about all the tablespaces within the data dictionary tables.

User Views

User views provide methods for a user to query the data dictionary for information about objects a user owns. These views are designated with a prefix of user_ as in the view user_ tables, that being a view which shows all the tables the user has created.

All Views

Data dictionary views designated with a prefix of "all_" are designed to provide data dictionary views containing information about all objects which a user has permission to access. For example, a DBA may be able to view the entire listing for all_ tables while a user querying all_ tables may only see tablespace objects that are permitted for that particular user.

Dynamic Performance Views

Up to this point, all the views we have looked at are referred to as static views. Simply, static views provide us with information dealing with the overall structure of an Oracle database such as we see when we query dba_tables. Dynamic performance views, on the other hand, are views designed to provide real-time performance information such as current memory utilization and current I/O statistics. Dynamic views are identified with the prefix "v$". For example, data dictionary tables containing metadata about SGA memory structures (covered later in this chapter) can be found in dynamic table views v$sga and v$sgastat.

Oracle Instance

A lot of times you see the terms Oracle database and Oracle Instance used interchangeably. This is poor form and only indicates a lack of understanding of how Oracle operates. An Oracle database is made up of all the items that are stored on disk. An Oracle Instance is made up entirely of memory (such as the SGA and PGA, which will be discussed at length later in this chapter) as well as background processes (such as SMON, PMON, etc) that operate at the server. In other words, an Oracle instance is logical while an Oracle database is physical. To make these distinctions clearer, you must realize that a user does not access an Oracle database directly but only through an Oracle instance.

Let me give you an analogy for an Oracle database and an Oracle instance. Think about interacting with a Web site such as at www.wrox.com. The web site may consist of HTML files which reside on disk (like the database files reside on disk), and the server processes which keep the web site active (like the processes associated with an instance). Now suppose Wrox web server goes down. You cannot access the web site, and may say that it is down, but in fact all the files behind the scene are still intact on disk. You simply cannot access these files directly and need the processes behind the scenes to get to the data. In the same way, you cannot simply read data off the disk, you need to access the data through an instance.

A database may be mounted and opened by many instances concurrently (parallel server) while an instance may open and mount at most one database at a time. A single database might have many instances configured for it (for example, an instance for batch loading, an instance for OLTP operations, an instance for DSS operations).

Now that you understand the difference between an Oracle database and an Oracle instance, you can impress the most experienced DBA and Oracle developer by speaking the proper lingo. Let's move on to see how an Oracle instance is created.

Data Files and Tablespaces

Beyond the logical constructs associated with the database are the physical constructs which the database uses to store the data. The most obvious case differentiation between logical and physical constructs occur with data files and tablespaces. In a nutshell, data files are files located on disk used to store information. There are two types of information that are stored within data files: system data and user data. System data is the information that the database is required to have in order to operate correctly while the user data is your application data.

But data is not stored directly into data files on the disk. Each logical construct that stores data, whether it be a table or even an index, must reside in a container. Oracle calls this container a tablespace. A tablespace may be physically stored in one or more data files, but it is one continuous logical construct. Think back to our library analogy. The library building as viewed from the outside is one large physical structure residing on a piece of land (disk); but it may consist of several wings built at different times as the library expanded. Similarly, data files can be added to tablespaces as they hold more and more data, but it is still logically the same structure serving the same function.

However, tablespaces are more than just providing a container for data files, they provide a method for organizing. More specifically, tablespaces are designed to help organize data by allowing a DBA to group similar types of data into one area. For example, a DBA can allocate one tablespace specifically for data objects while allocating another tablespace specifically for index objects. Going back to the library analogy again, the library will have separate sections for books on history, classical literature, and autobiographies. It will have certain space set aside for the card catalog which tells people where to find the books they're looking for. Similarly, tablespaces are divided in terms of what data "goes together" and there are separate tablespaces set aside for indexes (which closely approximate the job of the card catalog).

Tablespaces offer the DBA a lot of control. A DBA can create, drop, size, and resize a tablespace as needed. For example, if a data file begins to grow it may be necessary to make more room on disk. A DBA can easily expand the table space by enlarging the data file(s) comprising the tablespace. Additionally, a DBA can create a tablespace anywhere on disk, even on another machine. Furthermore, you can define tablespaces to be temporary or permanent and you can take them offline and bring them back online as necessary. It should be noted that although a DBA can drop a tablespace, a DBA cannot remove a data file from a tablespace. This, again, is a separation of the logical from the physical. A DBA can manipulate the logical structure – make it larger or smaller as need be – but once there is data in a data file, that data file cannot be removed from the physical structure which comprises the tablespace. It would be like removing a floor from a library once it's filled up with books.

Blocks

A **data block** or simply a **block**, is the smallest logical unit of storage that Oracle 8i can read or write to in an Oracle database at a given moment in time. Perhaps in simpler terms, a data block is the smallest database storage unit available to Oracle 8i. Typically an Oracle 8i database block size is set using a multiple of 2k bytes, which is associated with an operating system's pagesize. Some operating systems deal with a 512 byte block, in which case, the DBA is free to use a block size which is a multiple of 512 bytes. Notice that I said a data block size is set. This means a DBA should determine Oracle's block size at the time an Oracle 8i database is created. It is important to understand that once a block size has been set, it cannot be changed without recreating the database.

Segments

You just learned that the storage container of an Oracle database is called a tablespace. Now that we have a place to hold things, we need to put something into these tablespaces. Oracle provides five types of objects referred to as **segments** that can be placed into an Oracle tablespace: table, index, cluster, rollback, and temporary segments. In simpler terms, you can think of segments as the object components in an Oracle database. Tables, clusters, and indexes are referred to as user-created objects, while rollback, and temporary segments are referred to as system segments.

It is important to understand that a segment can only belong to one tablespace.

Let's take a look at each of these five types of segments:

Table Segments

We talked about tables at the beginning of this chapter under relational databases. In summary, a table is composed of one or more named columns where each column has been assigned a datatype. In an Oracle database, tables are the database segments that hold data.

Index Segments

Index segments are objects designed to increase the speed of data accessed in a table. Going back to our library analogy, think about how a card catalog works. Suppose we want to find where the book, "Professional Oracle 8i" is located in the library. We can wander around the library and hope to stumble upon this book or we can go to the card catalog to find its location. The card catalog is an index of all the books available in the library including their locations. We can jump to a listing of library books starting with the letter "O" to quickly find our book. Once our book has been located with the card catalog, we can look up the book's unique decimal number that provides a path to the physical location of the book we want. Back to index segments, an index contains the value for one or more columns in a table. Furthermore, a ROWID is used to identify values located in any corresponding columns. What this means is that Oracle can access data directly from a table by first looking up the ROWID in an index.

Indexes are not always the most efficient way for retrieving data. This particularly holds true for smaller tables that require less than 100 data blocks.

Oracle 8i provides many types of index, of which the most commonly used are: B*-Tree, reverse key, bitmapped, and function-based.

B*Tree Index

The B*Tree (B for balance) Index is the most common type of index in an Oracle database and Oracle uses this index by default. In other words when an index is created using the standard CREATE INDEX, a B*Tree index will be created by default. To help explain how a B*Tree index works, let's take a look at the following diagram:

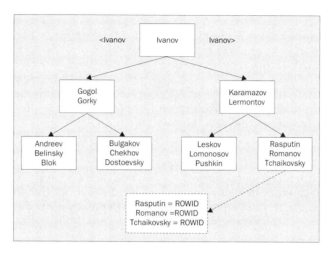

It is claimed that B*Tree acquired its name because it follows the structure of an inverted tree. The structures at the top of the tree are referred to as branch blocks while each level down is referred to as its depth.

In B*Tree indexes, there are usually one or more levels containing branch blocks. Each block reflects information about other blocks at the next level down. Again, take a look at the diagram; the upper-most branch block is labeled with the last name Ivanov while the next level down, the blocks are broken down between names that fall alphabetically "less" than Ivanov to the left while names that are alphabetically "greater" than Ivanov are on the right.

What is happening in this diagram is for each row entry in a table, the B*Tree index has recorded an entry for it. When a query is submitted, Oracle works its way down from the top of the index until it finds a match. Once a match between the index and the information being requested from the query has been found, Oracle will be directed to the actual data through the ROWID that is specified with corresponding leaf node. This is similar to the way the card catalog at the library is used. Once the book title from the card catalog is found, you can use its decimal number to locate the physical location for the book title you are searching for.

Aside from making data easy to locate, indexes can also be used to enforce column uniqueness. When you create a primary key constraint on a table, Oracle will automatically create an index. (In fact Oracle will either create an index on the columns or it will "take over" an existing index on those columns. It does not always create an index (if one is already in place). It would be interesting to note that the index in place does not have to be a unique index – we can and will use non-unique indexes to enforce primary keys and under some circumstances even the automatically generated index will be non-unique (deferrable constraints)). The reason an index is automatically created is to guarantee that all key values for rows in a table remain unique. Although primary key uniqueness can be ensured, it is important to realize that foreign key constraints are not automatically indexed but should be considered by the DBA and manually created. By creating indexes to foreign key columns, performance can be greatly enhanced particularly when joining tables together (using foreign key columns).

Reverse Key Indexes

We just learned that B*Tree indexing is the most common method used for indexing in an Oracle database. However, as with all great features, they also have their negatives. The major problem that occurs with B*Tree indexes is that over time the leaf structures begin to take on numerous entries toward the right side of the tree thus creating a lopsided and unbalanced structure. What this means is this unbalanced growth causes an increase to the depth of the B*Tree index. The greater the depth, the more I/O is required. The final outcome is a decrease in performance. There are two solutions to fixing this problem. The method I prefer is to periodically rebuild them and, in Oracle8i, we can perform an **online** rebuild. However, some prefer to solve their index problems by using a reverse key index. As you may have guessed, this index reverses the order of values. Actually the reverse key index reverses the bytes that are stored in the index. For example, suppose the value in a row is "12345". Instead of having the values "12345" stored as a key value in a B*Tree index, the reverse key index will store its key value as "54321". The result of reversing the order of index values causes them to be more evenly distributed across the leaf nodes, thus reducing unnecessary I/O.

Bitmapped Indexes

You learned that B*Tree indexes store complete ROWIDs in each leaf block. B*Tree indexes can take up large amounts of storage space. In contrast, a bitmapped index only needs a fraction of storage space because it can represent ROWIDS as on and off bits. Furthermore, bitmapped indexes include Null values which is a luxury other indexes do not offer.

Pets_Owned		Bitmaps Equivalent			
Owner_ID	Pets	Pets = Dog	1	0	0	0
1	Dog	Pets = Cat	0	1	0	0
2	Cat	Pets = Horse	0	0	1	0
3	Horse	Pets = Elephant	0	0	0	1
4	Elephant	Owner_ID	1	2	3	4

The way a bitmap works is like this – if a row in a table contains a number of columns with limited values, ideally booleans, a bit is either turned on or off accordingly. This may sound confusing so let's take a look at an example:

The above diagram shows a database table called Pets_Owned and a chart indicating a bitmapped equivalent for column Pets in the Pets_Owned table. Notice that a bitmapped index for the column Pets with the data Dog may be represented as 1000, while a bitmapped index for elephant may be indicated as 0001. Let's look at this a little closer. We just said the bitmap for Dog is 1000. If we look at the corresponding column called Owner_ID, we can see that for Owner_ID: 1 shows a bit setting of 1 for dog, 0 for cat, 0 for horse, and 0 for elephant. Now looking at Owner_ID number 4, we can see a bit setting of 0 for dog, 0 for cat, 0 for horse, and 1 for elephant, thus giving us a bitmap of 0001. Suppose we had a fifth person who owned a horse and an elephant. Then the bitmap would be represented as 0011. In order for Oracle to decipher these bitmap equivalents, a special mapping function will convert the bits into the ROWID that we are accustomed to.

Bitmapped indexes are best suited to situations where columns don't exhibit numerous different values relative to the number of rows existing in a table, such as shown in our example. Other real life examples are columns like gender (which can be either Male or Female), Marital_Status (which can be either Married or Divorced or Unmarried or Widow), Employed (where the value will be either Yes or No). The fewer the number of possible values the better. The reason for this is that as the number of different values increases in a column, the more space will be required to store the index. Furthermore, bitmapped indexes tend to be best suited for data warehousing applications where data is mainly queried as opposed to being subject to frequent insert and update procedures. So if we are not careful when implementing bitmapped indexes, we can create a counter-productive situation.

Function-Based Indexes

New to Oracle 8i are function-based indexes that allow you to base an index on the result from a SQL function as opposed to basing the result solely on a column or columns value. In a way, this is creating an index based on virtual fields, or fields that don't exist as such in the table.This is a very powerful feature particularly because Oracle 8i allows you create your own functions. By creating your own functions and then creating indexes based on your custom functions, you can enhance query performance as well as executing other functions on tables, such as updates, and deletes, because instead of having to execute a function on every row in a table, you can select directly from an index.

Cluster Segments

You just learned how indexes can be used to increase the speed of data accessed in a table. Cluster segments can be an alternative for using indexes. By using cluster segments, data retrieval performance in addition to cutting down on disk I/O can be achieved. When Oracle needs to access data, it can only read one data block at a time. So it makes sense that if we can store related data into one area, we can increase system performance as well as decrease excess I/O. This is what cluster segments do.

Cluster segments make use of a column or columns in a table called a cluster key that is used to determine how cluster data is going to be stored. There are two types of cluster segments: Table Clusters and Hash Clusters. Although both use a cluster key, they each physically store row information in a different manner.

One important thing to keep in mind is that table cluster segments can inhibit the performance of insert and update procedures. Performance issues are particularly noticeable when using hash clusters. Nevertheless, ensuring that you don't use a value for a clustered column that is likely to exhibit a lot of changes can prevent these performance issues.

Table Clusters

Table Clusters, sometimes referred to as Index Clusters, physically organize row data based on the cluster key value. More specifically, table clusters store both the cluster key value that is based on a column or columns to join the tables, as well as storing the values of the columns in the clustered tables. Table clusters are, in effect, clustered together. In a way, they are already pre-joined on the cluster key. Table clusters, therefore, are most effective for select queries that need to access tables based on joins. For example, think of a computerized version of a library card catalog. Suppose we have a table cluster for two tables, Subjects and Book_Titles. The table cluster can store all the book titles in close proximity (or even within the same data block) as the data specifying the various subjects one can select. So when someone executes a typical select statement for the retrieval of all the books about a particular subject, Oracle can quickly access the data with only one or two disk I/O operations as opposed to retrieving data that is not clustered, which may involve several I/O operations as data is retrieved from several locations. Be aware, however, that querying only one of the clustered tables, or querying the tables not using the cluster key, will have worse performance than were the tables not clustered at all.

Hash Clusters

Hash Clusters operate differently from table clusters in that they use a mathematical function to calculate a key value for the row's cluster key value. This mathematical function is referred to as a hash function. What this means is that Oracle will physically store all rows in the same data block that yields the same hash result.

As far as hash clusters go, what is good for organizing data is also good for retrieving it. The same process of using a hash calculation to locate rows that have been physically stored in the same location is used for every data retrieval request. In other words, a hash value must first be calculated. However, the calculated value points directly to the requested row data. What is actually happening here is that row data can be accessed directly without the need to first consult a cluster index. In simple terms, the hash cluster points directly to the row locations in a table. By eliminating the middleman being the cluster index, a hash cluster can perform faster data retrieval than table clusters and at the same time eliminates excess disk I/O.

So why aren't hash clusters used more extensively than indexes? Aside from space considerations (hash clusters take up substantially more space than indexes), hash clusters require exact matches. In the case where equalities are to be used, hash clusters can dramatically improve query performance. B*-Tree indexes tend to perform better for queries that search for ranges of rows as opposed to using exact match searches.

Rollback Segments

When a database transaction either fails or is aborted, it is mandatory to restore the database object back to its original state in order to guarantee data integrity. In other words, in the event of a failed or aborted transaction, data in the database is rolled back (restored) to its original state as if the transaction never occurred. This rolling back of data is accomplished through a database object called a rollback segment. The rollback segment actually stores an image of the original data before a transaction can modify any data. More specifically, when a transaction is initiated, the original data in a data block is first written to a rollback segment. This "old" information that is stored in a rollback segment can be called upon to restore the data blocks back to their original state in the event that a transaction fails or aborts.

Temporary Segments

As you read through this chapter, you will discover that Oracle does a lot of work in memory. Many user requests will require information to be sorted. Most of the time, Oracle can process data procedures such as data summarizing, sorting, and grouping in memory. However there may be times when memory available for these procedures may not be sufficient. In this case Oracle will create a temporary workspace within a temporary tablespace. This temporary workspace is referred to as a temporary segment. As soon as the information is sorted, the temporary segment is deleted. Needless to say, numerous temporary segments are not desirable as it increases disk I/O.

Extents

Over time, segments within a data or index tablespace will grow to the point where it requires space beyond its current allocation. As a result the segment(s) must be extended. An extent is a unit of storage that stores database information in a contiguous set of data blocks. Once Oracle has claimed an extent, it cannot be changed, however the definition for the size of the next extent to be claimed can be modified at any time.

Going back to our library analogy, think about the binders that keep magazines together. For example, a binder for Oracle Magazine may hold issues 1-6 before reaching their maximum storage. A second binder is used to store issues 7-12, thus extending the original storage for Oracle Magazines.

Oracle 8i Object/Relational Database

With the release of Oracle 8 in 1997, the Oracle Corporation extended its RDBMS into the object-oriented world. As a result, a new hybrid for object-relational databases was born. Oracle's new Object-Relational Database Management System keeps all the relational characteristics we previously covered; yet at the same time, we can now surpass the two-dimensional related database table and represent real life items through objects. More specifically, Oracle 8i objects can be created as reusable components that are capable of representing real life business functions and procedures.

You may be asking yourself, "Do I have to use Oracle 8i extensions for object support?" The answer is, absolutely not! You can still utilize all of Oracles RDBMS capabilities without working with objects. To prove this point, I challenge you to take any legacy Oracle 7 application and run it within Oracle 8i without any modifications whatsoever – the odds are very good that it will work!

Now that I told you that you don't need to use any of Oracle 8i object technology, let me give you some good reasons why Oracle objects should be used.

First, Oracle 8i allows you to mix object technology with its relational technology through the use of object types and collections. This allows for Oracle developers who are new to object technology as well as the seasoned database developer to slowly migrate from using Oracle's relational features over to its object features. For the die-hard object programmer, you can take Oracle 8i to its farthest by designing your database using the latest object oriented technology.

If you create objects you probably will find that you can use them over and over in your database. Reuse of code is one of the main advantages with object-oriented programming. Using Oracle's object technology also leads to an adherence of standards that is defined specifically for your system. In other words, if you create a data object for a particular data type in a database, then you can be sure the same object type will keep the same internal format throughout the entire database. For example, if we were to create an object type for user names, we don't have to worry about different formats for user names anywhere else within the database, as they will all maintain the same characteristics that were originally defined when the object was created.

Oracle 8i provides several built-in capabilities for supporting object-oriented development including support for user defined data types as well as other data types representing relations and collections. Although Oracle 8i is a hybrid of an object oriented database, it is important to understand that Oracle 8i is not a true object-oriented database because (currently) it lacks certain aspects of object orientation, including inheritance, polymorphism and encapsulation. In fact, it is better to say that Oracle 8i is an object-based product rather than an object-oriented product. Nevertheless, you will find that Oracle objects come in handy in many areas within an Oracle 8i database and you can be sure as new releases of Oracle come out, so will enhancements for its object capabilities. Lets take a look at the basic building blocks for Oracle objects starting with Object Types.

Object Types

Object types are the basic building blocks for object modeling within an Oracle 8i database. You can think of an object type as being similar to an object class found in object-oriented languages such as C++ and Java. What this boils down to is an object type is like a template for the creation of individual instances of an object.

Oracle 8i object types allow you to extend Oracle's predefined data type definitions into customized user-defined data types. These user-defined data types, also called UDFs, are referred to as object types. Furthermore, you can also use other existing user-defined object types to create new object types. However, as with most things, there are a few exceptions. You cannot use Oracle's pre-defined datatypes for Long, Long Raw, RowID, and %Type for defining object types. Other than these few exceptions, you have full rein to create what you want.

Let's take a look at a simple object type. All we need to do is name our object type and associate it with one or more attributes:

```
CREATE TYPE pet_owner AS OBJECT (
ID             NUMBER(7)
First_Name  VARCHAR2(10)
);
```

Looking at the sample statement, we have named our object `pet_owner` while giving it two attributes called `ID` and `First_Name`. Remember, attributes are nothing more than characteristics of the object you are trying to describe. The key point to remember is attributes must be unique just as names of columns in tables must be unique. However, it is OK to use the same attribute names in other object types. Oracle 8i object types can also contain methods that are simply procedures or functions that can model the actions of the object. Typically methods are written using PL/SQL although methods can be written externally using other languages such as C, C++, Java, and Visual Basic.

Object types can be used to further bring together the gap between the relational aspects for Oracle 8i and 8i's objects through the use of Object Columns within a relational table, Object Views, and Object Tables. Let's briefly take a look to see what can be done with Oracle objects.

Object Columns

You can create tables that contain both standard relational columns that use standard relational datatypes one or more columns containing object types (as opposed to standard relational datatypes). These columns that are defined by an object type as its datatype are referred to as object columns.

Object Views

Previously we talked about relational views that enable data to be displayed in such a manner that information from several tables and rows can be displayed. It would seem logical with the introduction of object tables in Oracle 8 there should be a way to create views that support Oracle's object tables. Sure enough, views fully support all of Oracle 8's object extensions. What this means is you can not only create views for typical relational tables, you can create views for relational tables that contain object types as well as creating views of entire object tables.

Object Table

Instead of using relational tables consisting of one or more object columns, an object table can be used entirely in place of a relational table. What this means is a table can be created consisting entirely of object types as opposed to using traditional relational columns and their datatypes. Although Object tables are unlike traditional relational tables, object tables can make use of primary keys for unique identifiers as well as using indexes. Perhaps more importantly, object tables can be related to other object tables through the use of a special datatype called REF (object reference). REF works similar to the way a foreign key in a standard relational table works in order for two objects to relate. Also, the columns within an object table correspond to the object type's attributes. Furthermore, an object table can have methods associated with it that provide a means of data manipulation. These methods are stored within the table's definition.

Object Identifier

Whenever an Oracle 8i row object is created a unique and immutable Object Identifier (OID) is system generated. You learned that ROWIDs were used by indexes in order to quickly locate data within a table. Object identifiers are an object's equivalent to ROWID. Simply an OID is used to describe the location of a row object. Oracle guarantees that an OID is universally unique across all Oracle databases. Oracle even touts that OIDs are universally unique.

 An analogy for an OID is the globally unique identifiers (GUIDs) that Microsoft generates for its COM classes and interfaces. OIDs are guaranteed to be unique and immutable just as GUIDs are. GUIDs are generated using complex algorithms that utilize the systems clock and the network card's MAC address. Oracle is a little more esoteric in telling how OIDs are generated, but rumour has it that they are somehow based on a unique identification number that accompanies Oracle's installation CD-ROM SYS_GUID() and generates and returns a globally unique identifier (RAW value) made up of 16 bytes. On most platforms, the generated identifier consists of a host identifier and a process or thread identifier of the process or thread invoking the function, and a non-repeating value (sequence of bytes) for that process or thread:

```
SELECT SYS_GUID() FROM DUAL;

SYS_GUID()
--------------------------------
01BfC3CAC58D11D49AAB00B0D06725AB
```

Collections

Anything that we can group together is called a collection. Oracle 8i has three object types that can be used for collections. These are nested tables, index-by table types (that can only be declared through PL/SQL) and varrays.

There are two major distinguishing features between nested tables and varrays. Nested tables use an unordered method of grouping while varrays group data together in an orderly fashion. Furthermore, nested tables have an unlimited number of rows available while varrays have a finite limitation to the amount of rows they can have.

Nested Tables

Nested Tables are tables that can be stored within tables. With a nested table, you can take a collection of rows from one table and place them into a single column in another table. In a way, what you are doing is storing a one-to-many relationship within one table. This is roughly equivalent to a hierarchical table structure. For example, suppose you want to record data reflecting information from the tables Pet_Owners and Pets_Owned. Instead of creating two relational tables using a join, we can create one table for Pet_Owners and imbed a complete table for Pets_Owned into one of the columns in the Pet_Owners table. Now we can directly access Pets_Owned from the Pet_Owners table. This is cool stuff! By nesting these two tables, we make it easier for users to access data because we don't need to traverse numerous tables with a join. However, like hash clusters, this is efficient only when the design is such that this is the only way that this data is supposed to be retrieved; otherwise, performance may be degraded.

Varrays

The variable array, more commonly referred to as varray, provides you with a way to store repeating attributes into a table. In other words, a varray is a set of objects that have the same datatype. The varray is of defined size and is ordered, as opposed to the nested tables which are not ordered. This can come in handy by saving space and possibly eliminate the need for some tables, where there are a set number of possibilities of a repeating datatype. For example, if `Pet_Owners` need to be contacted by phone, there might be a home number, an office number, a fax number and a cell phone. The varray could be used to store the phone numbers in that order and eliminate the need for two other tables: an `owner_phone_numbers` table and a `phone_number_types` lookup table.

Oracle Memory Structures

As I previously hinted, the Oracle database is extremely memory oriented. It differs from many other database systems in that Oracle tries to keep as much information cached in memory as possible. Keeping information in memory greatly enhances the system's overall performance because information in cached memory is quicker to access as opposed to requiring large amounts of disk I/O that is time consuming. Of course, the memory must be allocated properly. Too little memory allocated will force Oracle to go to disk with great frequency, whereas too much memory allocated may affect performance of other processes on the machine. If extraordinary amounts of memory are allocated, there may not be sufficient physical memory on the machine and there will be a performance hit due to extensive paging.

System Global Area

Each Oracle database instance (see later in the chapter) requires its own dedicated memory area called the System Global Area or SGA. Although the SGA requires its own dedicated memory area, it is shared among currently connected users.

The SGA is comprised of the following three major structures: **Shared Pool**, **DB Buffer Cache**, and the **Redo Log Buffer**. Let's look at each in detail.

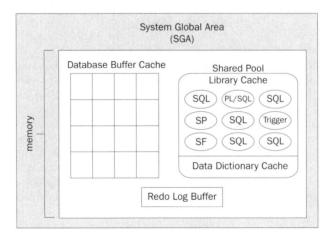

Shared Pool

The shared pool can be divided into two major sections, the library cache and the dictionary cache. The library cache is designed to increase SQL efficiency by allowing SQL and PL/SQL statements to be shared among users. In other words, the library cache stores all parsed SQL statements. Because SQL statements residing in memory are already parsed, they are ready for quick execution. Lets see how this works:

When referring to SQL statements, I also mean PL/SQL blocks, Stored Procedures, Stored Functions, and Triggers making use of Oracle's Shared Pool.

When an SQL statement is submitted, two things need to happen. First, Oracle will check to see if an identical SQL statement has already been placed into the library cache. If Oracle does not find an identical SQL statement, the statement must first be parsed and then it will be placed into the library cache. Parsing requires several tasks to be completed which means overhead for the system. First, a parsed call creates in memory a private SQL area where the SQL statement will temporarily reside while the SQL statement is validated. Second, it needs to be checked for correct syntax. Next, the data dictionary (we will talk more about the data dictionary shortly) is checked in order to verify important criteria such as whether the tables or views actually exist, and whether the user executing the SQL statement actually has user rights to the tables or views involved, and whether they even have rights to execute a statement in the first place. As soon as all pertinent requirements are verified, Oracle's query optimizer will create a plan of execution. You can think of this plan of execution as an internal list of procedures that will be followed in order to access the requested data from the SQL statement. As soon as the SQL is successfully parsed, the SQL statement is placed into the library cache.

> **A query optimizer is a set of routines designed to find the most efficient path for accessing data requested from an SQL statement.**

Now, suppose a user sends a SQL statement that is identical to the statement recently stored in the library cache. This time, when Oracle checks the library cache, it will find a parsed tree for an identical SQL statement and its path for execution, it will check the privileges to make sure it can be run, and, if so, it will execute the statement.

As you can see, the library cache can be very efficient because repeated SQL statements do not need to be reparsed. However, there is one very important snag to be aware of. In order to take advantage of a cached item, it must be 100% identical to the SQL statement already residing in the library cache. In other words, there cannot be the slightest difference between statements including differences in punctuation. For example, look at the following two SQL statements:

```
Select  * From book_titles where publisher = "Wrox" and title = "Oracle 8i"

Select  * from book_titles where publisher = "Wrox"  and title="Oracle 8i"
```

As you should recognize, both of these statements have the same syntax and both will yield the same results. However, both statements are not identical. Notice the keywords "From" in both statements. The first statement uses a capital letter "F" while the second statement uses a lower case "f". As far as syntax is concerned, both are correct. Unfortunately, using these two statements will only take up memory in the library cache because as far as Oracle is concerned, these two statements are not identical. The trick is to create identical SQL and PL/SQL code that is likely to be used often in day-to-day business.

The second part of the shared pool is the data dictionary cache. Previously I mentioned that during the parsing of an SQL statement, the data dictionary was consulted to verify whether pertinent information such as tables, views, and user permissions were correct and valid. The data dictionary is part of the shared pool and is responsible for maintaining metadata information about the database itself.

The purpose of the data dictionary cache is to cut down on expensive I/O by the Oracle system. The data dictionary works similar to the library cache in that it keeps recent information in memory. Oracle will first check the data dictionary cache when it needs information about the database. If Oracle cannot find the information it needs in the data dictionary's cache, then Oracle has no choice but to use expensive I/O resources by going to disk in order to retrieve the necessary dictionary information. I will talk more about the data dictionary later in this chapter.

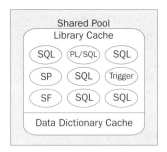

DB Buffer Cache

The DB buffer cache is used to place data blocks that have recently been accessed from data files into memory. Recall that a data block is the smallest logical unit of storage that Oracle 8i can read or write to an Oracle database at a given time.

What's important to understand is that before any user process can access a block of data, the data must first reside in the DB Buffer Cache. This means that if data being accessed does not reside in the DB Buffer Cache, the data must first be retrieved from the data file on disk and then placed into the DB Buffer Cache. To take this further, all data manipulations are changed to these data blocks located in memory. In other words, data is not directly changed to the data file located on disk. As you may surmise, data already residing in cache can be accessed almost instanteously as opposed to potentially long delays resulting from disk I/O. Let's take a look and see how the DB Buffer Cache works.

I just mentioned a data block must first be stored in cache memory before it can be accessed. It does not take much to realize that if numerous data blocks are accessed the DB Buffer Cache will start to fill up. Oracle has a rather elegant way of taking care of this problem. Oracle makes use of an algorithm called LRU that stands for **Least Recently Used**. This algorithm uses a process called "aging" to move data blocks around in order to make room for new data blocks. More specifically, LRU keeps track of each data block and how often it is accessed. You can think of the LRU as keeping a list of active and inactive data blocks. Newly accessed data is kept at the top of LRU's list while data that has been sitting around without being accessed or data that has not been recently accessed is moved towards the bottom of the list. When more space is needed in the DB Buffer Cache, the LRU will begin to move the inactive or least recently used data blocks out of cache.

When a data block has been modified, it is said to be dirty. A dirty data block is a term used to describe a block of memory where data has been modified since the original data was retrieved from a data file.

In addition to keeping track of dirty data blocks, the LRU keeps track of clean data blocks (data blocks that have not been modified) as well as keeping track of data blocks that are currently being used (pinned data blocks.)

For example, suppose a SQL statement is issued to retrieve the names of leading book publishers. Naturally Wrox Press would be retrieved from a data file and placed into a memory block located in the database buffer cache. Currently, this data is exactly the same as it resided in the data file located on disk. Now suppose a user decides that the entry should be changed from Wrox Press to Wrox Press, Inc. The user issues an update command and now the data block in memory has been altered to reflect these changes. Keep in mind that the data file located on the disk is not directly updated. Furthermore, when a data block is modified, these changes are also written to the redo logs (discussed later) in order for the new data to be written back to the data file. Because the data block containing Wrox Press Inc. is different from the original data in the data file located on disk, the data block containing Wrox Press Inc. is said to be dirty.

Oracle 8 introduced some new enhancements to the DB Buffer Cache. You now have the ability to index data to be cached into specific areas of the buffer pool. In previous versions, there was only one cache. Now with Oracle 8i there are three cache areas referred to as pools:

❏ **Default Pool**: This is still considered the standard DB buffer cache and unless otherwise specified, all objects will be placed in this area.

❏ **Keep Pool**: This pool can be used to place objects that you know will be used frequently. These objects will not be "aged out", as the LRU ignores the keep pool.

❏ **Recycle Pool**: The recycle pool allows you to place objects that you are not likely to use again. These objects will be "aged out" first, as the LRU moves the objects in the recycle pool to the beginning of the items to be flushed out of the buffer.

Being able to determine where data objects will be placed in cache, the DBA has the ability to help eliminate excess I/O that occurs when the LRU is needed to free up space. If the DBA or developer doesn't explicitly state which buffer an object should go in, it will go into the Default Pool. As far as the Default Pool is concerned, the LRU will continue to track and move data as deemed necessary.

You may be wondering why Oracle does not write changes immediately to disk. The reason is instead of continuously writing changes to disk, the Oracle system tries to avoid the high cost of continuous disk I/O. Instead, Oracle defers writing to disk by using large multi-block increments when it is more efficient – such as time when other processes are idle and disk I/O is down. It bears repeating that it is very important to allocate the correct amount of memory to Oracle for it to process its I/O efficiently.

Redo Log Buffer

> In a nutshell, the redo log buffer temporarily holds redo log entries until they can be written to disk. Because modified data blocks reside in memory (DB Buffer Cache), they are not immediately written to disk. As a result, it is important that Oracle provide a safety feature in the event of some unforeseen accident such as a power outage. Thanks to the redo log buffer in conjunction with the redo logs, a database can be restored up to the point of failure.

How Redo Logs Work

Every Oracle database requires at least two redo log files although it is highly recommended to have three or more redo logs for performance. For the sake of fault tolerance, it is recommended to have an additional redo log group on a separate disk. Each redo log in the second group is a perfect copy of the associated redo log in the first group. We will come back to fault tolerance shortly. For now, lets keep things simple by looking at an example that uses two redo logs:

Suppose you have a database that uses the minimum requirement of two redo logs. For simplicity, let's call the first redo log, redo_log1 and the other redo_log2. When data in the DB Buffer Cache is modified, changes are sent to the Redo Log Buffer. From the Redo Log Buffer, Oracle will record these changes by making an entry into one of the redo logs. In this example let suppose redo_log1 is the active log. Redo logs follow a circular pattern. When redo_log1 becomes filled, Oracle makes a transition referred to as a log switch to the next Redo log available. In this case redo_log2 now becomes the active log. As soon as redo_log2 is filled, Oracle's log switch would proceed to the next redo log. If we had a third redo log, Oracle would continue with a switch made to redo_log3. However, because there are no additional redo logs, Oracle will switch back to redo_log1. What happens to the data previously recorded? It is written over with new and current data!

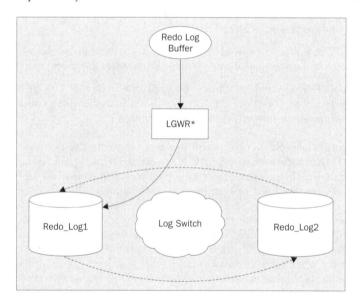

Redo logs work in a circular pattern. The LGWR is a required background process (see below) specifically for writing to the redo logs.

We have just learned that redo logs write over themselves with new current data. This method for not keeping old redo logs as just described is Oracle's standard out of the box default and is referred to as being in NOARCHIVELOG mode. So what exactly does this mean to a database user and the administrator? It means that you are only protected for instance failures that cause the memory areas to be lost such as the sudden powering down of an Oracle Database server. In other words, when running your Oracle database in NOARCHIVELOG mode, you cannot go back to a point of time and restore through your redo logs because once redo information has been written over, the backup data (redo log data) is gone. This is a very important concept to keep in mind. I have heard many horror stories where a DBA believed that a complete database could be recovered only to later learn that this is not true.

Understanding redo logs is such an important concept, I think this is worth repeating: – When using Oracle's default NOARCHIVELOG mode, your database is only protected for instance failures such as power loss. NOARCHIVELOG mode will not provide the information necessary to restore an Oracle database. It will only provide the minimum information needed to bring the database back to the point in time when failure occurred.

However, a savvy database administrator will be aware of certain additional configurations that can be administered to provide full fault tolerance in order to recover an Oracle database. Let me tell you about the mechanisms which allow for a full recovery:

An Oracle database can be set to run in ARCHIVELOG mode. What this means is a copy of every redo log is recorded and kept in another location. Typically, these redo logs are written to another storage device such as another hard drive or tape device. Now if a serious failure such as a disk crash occurs, a DBA can restore the entire database up to the point of failure.

You may be wondering why Oracle does not use ARCHIVELOG mode as its default. As with any extended feature, you must pay a price. First, with ARCHIVELOG mode, you are increasing more I/O demands in order to save all the transaction logs. The second problem (that can be solved in a well configured system!) is that Oracle may temporarily come to a halt in the event of a redo log not yet having a chance to be backed up. For example, if redo_log2 is full and needs to switch back to redo_log1 but redo_log1 is still making copies of its logs to another location, then Oracle will halt transaction activities until everything from redo_log1 is saved.

Of course the savvy DBA will recognize if this problem occurs and will know that adding one or more redo logs will eliminate the chances of the system from temporarily halting.

There is one more thing that can be done to increase fault tolerance concerning redo logs and that is mirroring the redo logs. By default, Oracle's redo logs present a single point of failure. If you lose your redo logs perhaps through a hardware or a power failure, you have no way of restoring your system back to the point of failure. However, Oracle provides a mirroring feature that allows redo logs to be simultaneously copied to another location, preferably to another disk drive.

Program Global Area

The Program Global Area (PGA) is also a designated memory structure, however unlike the SGA that is shared by all server and client processes, the PGA is allocated to a single process. There are several purposes of the PGA, including:

❏ Providing a place in memory for Oracle processes to perform sorting procedures before returning data to the user

❏ Containing data and control information for a single process

❏ Holding a stack space to hold a session's variables, arrays and process information

However, when the database is configured to use a multi-threaded server configuration (MTS), nearly all of the PGA's functions are performed by the SGA instead.

We briefly cover the setting up of MTS in Appendix A. For now, understand that correctly allocating memory to the PGA can be a very important aspect for tuning because if the PGA cannot handle its processing in memory, reduced system performance results due to extra disk I/O in order to create extra work areas.

Background Processes

So far we have covered Oracle files and memory structures that are found in a typical Oracle database instance. However, we have yet to talk about how Oracle actually performs certain operations such as moving information from the DB Buffer Cache to disk. These operations or tasks are performed in the background and are referred to as Oracle processes. Before we continue our discussion about processes, lets try and clear up a confusing issue, namely what is the difference in terminology between processes and threads.

If you come from a Unix environment, you should be aware that Unix uses processes to perform various background tasks often called to daemons. In other words, Unix uses an architecture that is based on processes. When Oracle 8 was introduced to the Windows NT platform it used only one operating system process per database instance. What this boils down to is that with Windows NT, each Oracle process equates to one thread that executes within one Windows NT process. Perhaps in simpler terms, Windows NT actually consolidates all of the Oracle processes such as SMON, PMON, etc., into one single executable that is composed of multiple concurrent threads.

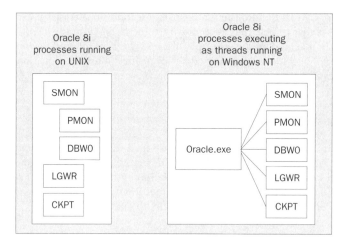

Oracle.exe is the Windows NT executable for running Oracle Processes

OK, now that you understand the difference between NT threads and Oracle processes, let's continue our discussion regarding Oracle's background processes. For the purpose of this book, I will continue using the term process to generically reflect either processes or threads when describing the way Oracle executes tasks that occur in the background.

In order for an Oracle database to operate (see Oracle Instance), there are five processes that must be running: System Monitor, Process Monitor, Database Writer, Redo Log Writer and the Checkpoint process.

System Monitor (SMON)

SMON, which stands for System Monitor, is a very important Oracle process. SMON begins its functions at database startup time when it determines whether a recovery needs to be performed, and, if so, performs it. After the database is up, it is responsible for cleaning up temporary segments which are no longer being used, and coalesces free space. It also tries to perform recovery if there are data file errors.

Process Monitor (PMON)

PMON, which stands for Process Monitor, oversees Oracle's database connections. PMON keeps track of Oracle's database connections, by making sure that each connection is operating correctly. For example, if a user terminates their session with the database abnormally, such as powering their workstation down without properly closing the database session, it is possible for a severed connection to remain open. Furthermore, with a severed connection or other abnormal condition, it is possible to place and keep certain data locked such that other users will not be able to access the same rows. Oracle's solution to these problems is with PMON. PMON will release any locks and resources as well as rollback any uncommitted changes to the database due to a users abnormal termination of their Oracle database session. If you have experienced these problems with other databases you are probably aware that it is often necessary to reboot the database server in order to properly release severed connections and to restore locked rows. It doesn't take much to recognize that PMON is a wonderful feature of Oracle's database system and that many other databases don't offer a close equivalent.

Database Writer (DBWn)

Previously you learned that the DB Buffer Cache maintains database manipulations in memory and does not immediately write these changes directly to the database. You also learned that data modifications in memory, called "dirty data" blocks are eventually written to the database. Writing these data modifications from the DB Buffer Cache to the database (datafiles) is DBW0's (database writer) job. However, DBW0 does not immediately write data modifications to disk. As a matter of fact, DBW0 tends to sit idle more than it actually writes data to disk. The purpose of DBW0 is to reduce large disk I/O by staying idle and then intermittently writing several blocks at one time. So how does Oracle ensure manipulated data is not accidentally lost in the event of a power loss or other unforeseen event causing loss to Oracles memory structures? Oracle records the changes to its redo logs.

If you have worked with pre-Oracle 8 databases, you may notice that its name has changed from DBWR to DBW0. Oracle 8 and Oracle 8i now can provide up to 10 database writers (0-9) as opposed to only one in pre-Oracle 8 versions. Having multiple writers can come in handy when DBW0 alone has difficulty in keeping up with the system demands on platforms that do not exhibit asynchronous I/O. However, you will gain very little by using multiple writers using a Windows NT platform because NT fully supports asynchronous I/O.

Redo Log Writer (LGWR)

The Redo Log Writer (LGWR) tends to be the most active writing process in an Oracle database yet LGWR rarely causes any performance problems. Like DBW0, the LGWR is responsible for writing information to disk once a transaction has been committed. In this case, the LGWR moves database changes from the Redo Log Buffer and records them in the physical redo logs that reside in the datafile on disk. LGWR writes log sequence information to the header block within each datafile in an Oracle database system. The first data block in a datafile is referred to as a header. This block of data is responsible for keeping track of important information such as a logical timestamp that is generated each time changes are written to a datafile. If you guessed that this timestamp is critical for data recovery, you are correct. In order to restore the datafiles back to the time of failure, Oracle will need to access these timestamps from the header blocks in each datafile in order to determine which redo logs contain the latest information.

You may be wondering what happens when something goes wrong before LGWR has had a chance to write its information to the redo logs. Oracle has built in a safeguard to ensure data integrity is maintained. Simply, Oracle treats all database changes (transactions) that have not yet been written to the redo logs as non-committed. In other words, if something were to go wrong before data is written to the redo logs, these items that are still in memory will be rolled back. What this means is just because data has successfully been recorded in the data files by DBW0 they are not committed until they have been successfully written to the redo logs. In other words, the final commit is not issued by successfully writing to the data files, but through the successful completion of the redo logs.

> *Interesting trivia: When an Oracle database is first created, the log sequence number begins with the number "1". Every time a redo log switch occurs, a log sequence number is generated that is incremented by one integer from the previous log sequence. In time, this log sequence number can grow to be very large. Think about how many log sequence numbers may be generated over a day, a month, or a year!*

Checkpoint (CKPT)

The scenario just described works very well, however as we have seen before, there are always exceptions to the rule. In very active Oracle database systems, the numerous signaling for DBW0 and updating header blocks can slow down the efficiency for LGWR to carry out its main function which is to move database changes to the redo logs. The solution lies in the background process called CHECKPOINT (CKPT). The purpose of CKPT is fairly straightforward; it is designed to conduct checkpoints in place of LGWR, thus allowing LGWR to concentrate solely on moving data to the redo logs.

Optional Processes

In addition to the five required processes necessary for an Oracle database instance to operate, there are several optional processes that can be used to enhance Oracle's database. Let's look at the major optional processes.

Redo Log Archiver (ARCH)

Earlier in this chapter we talked about running in noarchive mode vs archive mode. We said that running in Oracle's default noarchive mode only allows the restoring of transactions up to the moment of failure. However, by configuring Oracle's database to run in archive mode you keep a copy of all transactions that have occurred. The ARCH process is only required when running in archive mode and the purpose of ARCH is to copy all the old redo logs to a designated location (preferably on another disk) and are typically referred to as the archived redo logs.

We have covered several items relating to redo logs and archiving. Let's retrace our steps a little and look at the overall picture to see how each interacts with the other.

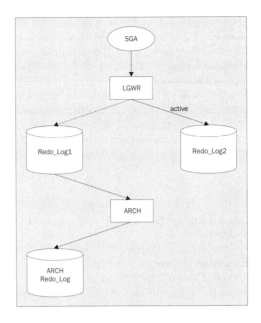

1. New data and modifications are placed into the DB Buffer Cache. At the same time, data modifications are written to the redo log buffer.

2. From the redo log buffer, information is recorded to the redo logs.

3. As soon as the active redo log becomes full, a log switch occurs where the LGWR moves to the next redo log. This is where the ARCH process kick in – The ARCH's job is to copy all the items in the old redo logs to a designated location. At the same time LGWR must make sure the new active redo log has completed saving its information to the database otherwise the system will halt until the logs have been copied.

Recoverer (RECO)

The Recoverer (RECO) process is used when implementing Oracle's two-phase commit protocol. Simply, RECO is designed to recover in-doubt transactions that can occur when using distributed databases. Let's look at the basic theory for Oracle's two-phase commit protocol and how RECO processes affect it:

An Oracle 8i system can utilize more than one database and treat them all as a single database. These separate databases are logically linked together and communicate through a network. This means that a database in Washington, DC, one in Chicago, and another database in England, can be logically linked together through the Internet to form one large database system.

In a distributed database system, the main concern is maintaining data integrity. Suppose a user in Washington, DC, creates a transaction that involves updating all three databases. The goal of the two-phase commit is to make sure the transaction either completes in its entirety or fails in its entirety by restoring (roll back) the distributed database back to its original state before the update request. When a transaction is made, every database that is involved with the transaction will signal the initiating database (referred to as the **global coordinator**) that they are ready to commit. If all databases check in with an "OK to commit", the global coordinator will send a message back to each database for the commit to occur. Again, all databases must report back to the global coordinator and indicate that a commit successfully occurred. During any of these stages, if a transaction fails at any database, the entire transaction must be rolled back to bring the database back to its original state before the transaction was attempted.

As you can see, Oracle's two-phase commit protocol is very important to keeping the integrity of data in a distributed database system. However, the two-phase commit protocol only works if all network communications are open. Unfortunately, networks do go down and the more databases are linked together in a network environment the more potential points of failure. This is where the Recoverer (RECO) processes come in. In the event communication is lost (such as with a downed server) between a node or nodes during a two-phase commit operation, RECO will try to re-establish communication until it is either successful or until it times out. In the event, RECO fails to re-establish communications with a node or nodes, the transaction will be flagged as in-doubt. It is important to distinguish between a transaction failing to commit due to errors as opposed to a transaction not committing or failing due to lost communication. An in-doubt transaction can still be completed at a later time through the manual intervention of the DBA.

Starting an Instance

When starting an Oracle database instance, three things must complete in a specified order before users can begin working with the database:

1. **Starting an Oracle database instance**: is initiated by opening the database initialization file (INIT.ORA) that contains a list of Oracle's parameter settings. Based on these parameters settings, Oracle will first initialize the SGA by allocating appropriate memory structures. After the SGA has been initialized, Oracle will initialize the background processes.

2. **Mounting the Oracle database**: is initiated by accessing the control files. One of the parameters found in the INIT.ORA file is a parameter called Control_Files=location. This parameter instructs the Oracle database instance where to find the control files (for init.ora and control files, see below). As soon as this stage of Oracle's database instance is achieved, the database instance is said to be in the mount state. In mount state, the DBA is now able to perform some types of database administration such as renaming, moving, and updating datafiles. However, no one else but the DBA is able to access the Oracle instance and the DBA is limited only to certain administrative tasks.

3. **Opening the Oracle database**: One last step is necessary before the Oracle instance is ready for user access. The redo log files and datafiles must first be initiated based on the information provided by the control files. Once these are in place, the database instance is fully operational and anyone with proper access privileges can access it.

Oracle's Database Initialization File

When starting an Oracle database instance, Oracle's initialization file (INIT.ORA) is first read. The INIT.ORA file is a text file that contains all the parameters necessary for an Oracle database instance to start. More specifically, the parameters in the INIT.ORA files contain information such as how much memory to allocate to the System Global Area (SGA) and how large each component of the SGA (such as the Shared Pool, Redo Log Buffer, etc.) will be, which background processes to start as well as providing several other parameters including many that are undocumented.

You can easily look at and edit the INIT.ORA file by opening it in a standard text editor. Alternatively you can edit the initialisation parameters through DBAStudio: select the Intstance node in the top level tree, and you should see an Initialization parameters... button. (You must have SYSDBA privileges to change parameters.) You may be surprised to see that a typical INIT.ORA file allows over 200 different parameters to be set, and, as previously mentioned, many are undocumented. The odds of having to use more than a handful, however, are slim. If you are curious about many of these parameters, the Oracle website provides an excellent of them including a listing of their defaults.

Control Files

Control files are small binary files that are maintained externally from an Oracle database. The purpose of control files is to mount and open an Oracle database. Thus it is necessary to have at least one control file in an Oracle database. In fact, it is highly recommended that there be at least three control files mounted on separate physical devices. Without an Oracle control file, a database cannot be started. An analogy for a control file would be the front door of a library building. If the librarian has a key to open the door, he (she) can open the door for you so you can go in. If he has lost the key, the library will remain closed and no one can get in.

Control files provide physical database structure information such as what datafiles and redo log files belong to the database, the types of character sets a database uses as well as other physical database structure information including the name of the database, its creation date and time and even records of database backups that have been performed and whether the database itself was closed properly the last time it was shut down.

Control files are in binary form, thus they cannot be viewed or manually edited. This shortcoming can be overcome using the command alter database backup control file to trace.

Now that you know how to protect yourself in the event a control file becomes damaged, what about the poor DBA who does not have another control file. This poor DBA still has a chance to keep his/her job, as there are ways to rebuild them (just as the librarian can call a locksmith.) But don't let this bit of optimism fool you. Rebuilding control files does not guarantee things will work properly. Furthermore rebuilding control files typically will be difficult at best and they will take a fair amount of time to recreate. This means downtime, something your users will not be happy about.

Recap

We have covered a lot of material here and you have seen that many parts of the Oracle database system are controlled by physical files, as well as memory structures. Let's take a quick review of the major parts making up an Oracle database system:

- ❑　INIT.ORA: The INIT.ORA is at the heart of an Oracle database instance as it is the first file read. INIT.ORA is the file that contains all the parameters necessary for an Oracle database instance to start. It includes information such as how much memory to allocate to the System Global Area (SGA) and how large each component of the SGA (such as the Shared Pool, Redo Log Buffer, etc.) will be. Also it determines which background processes to start as well as providing many other parameters including several that are undocumented.

The other physical files in an Oracle database include:

- ❑　**Data files:** Data files are files located on disk that are used to store information. We learned that there are two types of information stored within data files, system data and user data. System data is the information that the database is required to have in order to operate correctly while the user data is your application data.

- ❑　**Control files:** These are small binary files that are maintained externally from an Oracle database with the sole purpose of allowing mounting and opening an Oracle database.

- ❑　**Redo log files:** We also learned that every Oracle database requires at least two redo log files. Redo logs are physical files where current redo (translog) information is recorded.

We also have seen how an Oracle instance is composed of various memory structures:

- ❑ **DB Buffer Cache**: The DB Buffer Cache is a part of the SGA and is responsible for placing data blocks that have been recently accessed from datafiles into memory.

- ❑ **Library Cache:** The library cache is a part of the shared pool (that resides in the SGA) and is used to reduce disk I/O by placing recently parsed SLQ statements into memory so they can be reused (shared) by other users.

- ❑ **Data Dictionary Cache:** The data dictionary cache is also a part of the shared pool (that resides in the SGA) and is used to reduce expensive disk I/O by storing recent information about the database in memory.

- ❑ **Redo Log Buffer:** Also a memory structure that is a part of the SGA and temporarily holds redo data until it is written to the redo log files located on disk.

And we have seen Oracle's required five background processes:

- ❑ **SMON:** SMON for system monitor whose job is to monitor the overall well-being of the database. If a problem exists, SMON will try and take the database system down in an orderly manner.

- ❑ **PMON:** PMON stands for Process Monitor. It is an invaluable process that will release any locks and resources as well as rollback any uncommitted changes to the database due to a user's abnormal termination of their Oracle database session.

- ❑ **DBWn:** (DBW0 to – possibly – DBW9) for database writer is responsible for writing data modifications from the DB Buffer Cache to the database (datafiles) on disk.

- ❑ **LGWR:** LGWR is responsible for moving database changes from the Redo Log Buffer and records them in to the physical redo logs that reside in the datafile on disk.

- ❑ **CKPT:** CKPT conducts checkpoints in place of LGWR, thus allowing LGWR to concentrate solely on moving data to the redo logs.

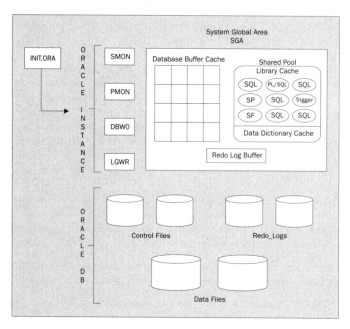

Summary

We have covered a lot of material in this chapter that will serve as a solid foundation for the rest of this book. Now that you have taken a look under the hood of Oracle 8i, you will be able to apply your skills as well as develop new skills for managing and developing Oracle 8i database systems.

We started this chapter with a little database history and took a look at two legacy database systems, the hierarchical and the network database. Next we reviewed concepts for relational databases.

Next we learned about the components in an Oracle 8i database. We looked at data files, tablespaces, blocks, and segments. We also took an in-depth look at the types of indexes such as B*Tree, Reverse Key, Bitmapped, and Function Based. We then moved on to look at segments and learned about the different types including clusters, rollback, and temporary segments.

The next section introduced Oracle 8i objects where you learned about the basic building blocks called object types. Next you took a look at other objects including object columns, views, tables, and collections.

The second half of this chapter consisted of Oracle 8i's memory structures, background processes and physical files.

Under memory structures you learned about the SGA and its various parts such as DB Buffer Cache, Redo Log Buffer and the parts of the shared pool including the Library Cache and the Data Dictionary Cache.

Next you took a look at the four required background processes, designated as SMON, PMON, DBW0, and LGWR. You also took a tour of a few of the major optional processes that can run with Oracle 8i.

Finally, you learned about many of the physical files such as Oracle's initialization file `init.ora`. You also learned about control files and the data dictionary files. You learned the difference between the Oracle 8i database and an Oracle 8i instance.

Having looked at the main database structures and systems, we turn to connectivity issues. If you can't get in, you can't do anything. Chances are you've not been able to get a connection to a Oracle database sometime. Your JDBC connections might hang or throw unusual exceptions. Your EJBs may not be contactable, or throw security exceptions when you try to access them. Mostly there'll be nothing wrong with the database, but networks are fallible and you need to know about them to make your code robust and to troubleshoot your setup.

ORACLE8iAPPLICATIONPROGRAMMING

4

Scaling Your Application with Net8

In this chapter we will take brief look at Net8 – the networking solution for Oracle8 – from the developer's perspective. The idea behind Net8 as far as the developer is concerned is that they can concentrate on building business functionality into their applications while letting Net8 automatically handle important services such as location transparency and data conversion. Thus, in a sense, Net8 encourages developers to write distributed business solutions and in this complex environment it is important to have a good understanding of what Net8 is and what it does.

Net8 combines transparent client/server application connectivity with a rich set of network services. The resulting Net8 client applications can operate in a heterogeneous network environment, unaware of multiple network protocols, multiple operating systems, or different hardware architectures. Oracle databases and applications can reside on different computers and still communicate client-to-server or server-to-server as peer applications. In other environments, like Microsoft SQL Server, the enterprise developer has to shoulder more work to create applications that are interoperable across differing operating systems and hardware architectures.

Net8 is the successor to Oracle7's SQL*Net. It is more than just an iterative release of SQL*Net, hence the name change. Net8 supports application programming interfaces, Java-enabled Internet browsers, and network services such as naming and security. While Net8 offers a richer set of services and superior performance, it is fully compatible with SQL*Net Version 2, allowing both to interoperate and easing the migration path.

What Net8 Does

Net8 brokers communication sessions between client applications and remote databases. It provides three basic services that should interest enterprise application developers:

❑ **Connection Services** – Net8 establishes sessions that open and close connections between client applications and remote database servers over a network protocol.

❑ **Data Transfer Services** – Once a session is established, Net8 acts as a data conduit, packaging and sending data requests and data responses between client applications and remote databases.

❑ **Exception Handling Services** – Network disconnects and other errors can occur in a distributed application. Net8 allows clients and servers to raise and respond to interrupts.

Why Use Net8?

Net8 provides important benefits to a distributed computing environment. Some of the benefits are particularly attractive to DBAs and network engineers. Net8 also offers features important to enterprise application developers, including:

❑ **Location Transparency** – Net8 provides all of the services required for an Oracle client to connect to an Oracle database, maintain that connection, process transactions on the database, and receive results from the database. This is done without regard for the location of the server or the client.

❑ **Network Transparency** – Net8 provides support for a broad range of network protocols, including TCP/IP, SPX/IPX, IBM LU6.2, Novell, Named Pipes, and DECnet. This enables Net8 to transparently connect any combination of PCs, UNIX servers, and legacy mainframes together.

❑ **Data Conversion** – Data conversion is invisible to the user and the application with Net8. Net8 automatically converts national-language character sets, such as those used in European and Asian languages. It also converts computer character sets, such as ASCII and EBCDIC. Net8 even allows machines with different word sizes, bit and byte orderings, and native number formats to interoperate transparently.

❑ **Large Scale Scalability** – Net8 offers improved scalability through two new features:

  ❑ **Connection Pooling**
  ❑ **Connection Multiplexing**

Idle sessions are a common feature of interactive enterprise applications. When hundreds or thousands of clients connect with a server, many sessions may be idle at any moment. Connection pooling allows more sessions to a server over the available physical connections by recycling open connections from idle sessions to newly active sessions. Connection multiplexing is another new scalability feature offered in Net8. The **Oracle Connection Manager** (**CMAN**) can multiplex traffic between a large number of clients and an Oracle8 server along a single transport connection.

- ❑ **Extensibility** – Net8 includes an application interface (API) called **Net8 OPEN**, which enables developers to:

    - ❑ Develop database and non-database applications that make use of an existing Net8 network.

    - ❑ Deploy an application developed on one machine to another without needing to port network API calls.

  Net8 OPEN provides applications with all of the benefits of Net8, including protocol independence, full security, cross-protocol interoperability, and comprehensive network management.

- ❑ **Easy Deployment** – JDBC-based applications can benefit from downloadable data access when they implement the **Oracle Thin Driver**. The Oracle Thin Driver, with its small footprint, allows users to run a downloadable client/server application from within a web browser. Applets using the Oracle Thin Driver, when serviced through the Oracle Connection Manager, can be routed to all of the available Oracle data services on a network, effectively overcoming the single node access limitations common to Java applets.

- ❑ **Security** – Three complementary products are optionally available to enhance security:

    - ❑ **Oracle Security Server** – an X.509 certificate-based server that provides support for e-commerce.

    - ❑ **Oracle Advanced Networking Option** – supports data encryption, checksums, and biometric user authentication.

    - ❑ **Oracle Enterprise Manager** – allows administrators to maintain uniform identities for users throughout an enterprise via unique identities and roles.

Typical Scenarios

Because of the breadth of its network services, Net8 eases the development of highly scalable enterprise applications. Net8 services are compatible with traditional two-tier client/server applications and the distributed multi-tier architectures that characterize enterprise application development.

Two-Tier Client/Server

The classic configuration for Net8 involves a client application that accesses an Oracle database through Net8. This requires the deployment of Net8 on both the server and the client. When the client needs the services of an Oracle database, Net8 establishes a connection to the database and routes the requests from the client to the server.

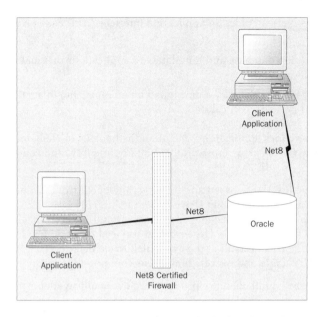

Net8 services support a broad range of clients. These include Oracle applications and application developer solutions. Developers can write Net8-compatible applications using C, C++, COBOL, Fortran, or Java. Oracle JDBC drivers support the JDBC 2.0 standard and the JDBC 2.0 optional package, which includes features like connection pooling and distributed transactions. They also provide Oracle-defined extensions to Oracle datatypes.

Oracle offers three different JDBC drivers:

- ❏   JDBC/OCI driver.
- ❏   Oracle Thin JDBC driver.
- ❏   JDBC Server driver.

The JDBC Server driver is a client-side Java driver, intended to complement Oracle8i, which allows Java programs to run inside the database. We will not consider it further in the discussion of Net8.

The JDBC/OCI Driver

The JDBC/OCI driver is well-suited for building client-server Java applications in an Intranet situation and for developing middle-tier servers. It is a JDBC Type II driver.

In the first situation, the client/server Java Intranet application, the Java application is installed on a client machine, which could be a personal computer or a workstation. Extranets are also practical, when a Net8 Certified firewall is included in the network.

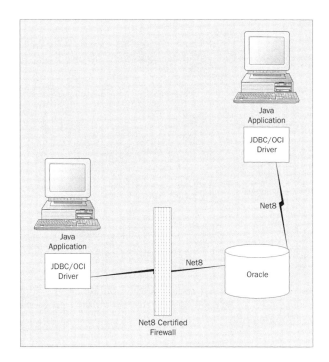

In the second circumstance, the middle-tier Java server, a browser-based client communicates with a Java-based server. The middle-tier executes the Java application logic and returns the result. The Java/OCI driver and Net8 handle the communication between the middle-tier Java server and the Oracle database server.

A two-tier client/server application makes calls to the JDBC/OCI driver, just like any other JDBC application. No additional programming effort is required to leverage the services of Net8. The JDBC/OCI driver translates the JDBC calls directly into Net8 network protocol.

The Thin JDBC Driver

The Oracle Thin JDBC driver is targeted at Java applet developers. JDBC drivers designed for applets intended to run in a Web browser cannot require any client-side installation. The Oracle Thin JDBC driver is a JDBC Type IV driver. It is 100% Java.

The Oracle Thin JDBC driver has a smaller footprint than the JDBC/OCI driver. The Oracle Thin JDBC driver is downloaded with the applet. The user simply selects a Uniform Resource Locator (URL) containing a Java applet tag from an HTML page. The driver provides its own lightweight implementation of the TCP/IP version of Net8. *The Oracle Thin JDBC driver, therefore, only works with TCP/IP networks. Applications running on non-TCP/IP networks instead need to use the JDBC/OCI driver.*

While the Thin JDBC driver does not offer full Net8 functionality, it allows users to run a downloadable client/server application from within a browser.

The initial HTTP request to download the applet (and associated JDBC Thin driver) is stateless. Once the JDBC Thin driver establishes the database connection, the communication between the browser and the database is a stateful two-tier configuration.

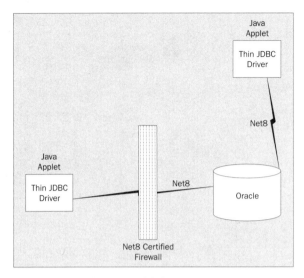

In this configuration, the Thin JDBC driver establishes a separate connection for each browser to the database. Net8 offers two solutions for achieving greater scalability in this configuration: connection multiplexing and connection pooling.

The Net8 Connection Manager can multiplex connections between many different browser clients to a single physical database connection. This reduces the number of physical connections that the database server must maintain.

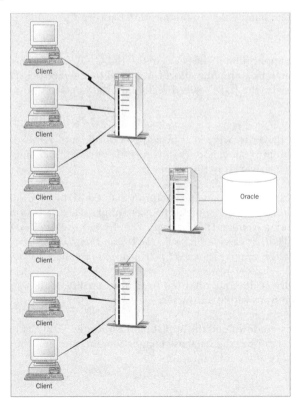

The Oracle8 database server can also transparently leverage connection pooling. The Multi-Threaded Server dispatcher creates a pool of connections and can automatically reallocate connections from inactive browser clients to active clients. When an idle client resumes activity, Net8 re-establishes the database connection.

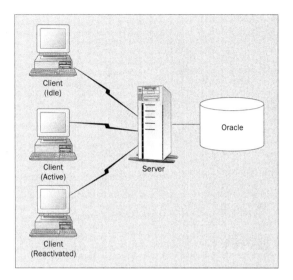

The important feature is that the enterprise application developer does not need to write any application code to take advantage of connection multiplexing or connection pooling.

Multi-Tier Client/Server

The following figure indicates how the JDBC/OCI driver can be used in a three-tier configuration. The three-tier client/server application can be safely deployed on Extranets with a SQL*Net/Net8 certified firewall.

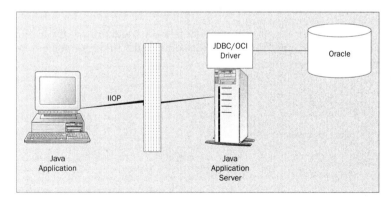

The figure above shows an **IIOP** client talking to a Java application across a firewall. IIOP (Internet Inter-Orb Protocol) is a standard transport protocol used by CORBA for distributed computing. Transport protocols pass data across a network from one computer to another. The client in the example above could even use HTTP. IIOP was chosen to illustrate the flexibility of Net8. The key feature in the diagram above is the Java application server, which uses the JDBC/OCI driver to communicate with the Oracle8 database via Net8.

An alternative multi-tier scenario is a Web browser connected to a Web application server via HTTP. A Java application running on the application server then fulfills the requests from the browser application, using the JDBC/OCI driver and Net8 to invoke database services.

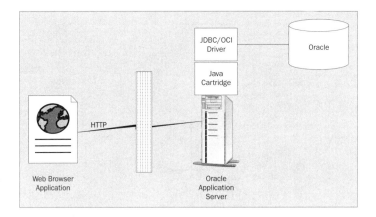

Oracle Connectivity

Net8 is designed to work on top of an existing network protocol. It is independent of particular network hardware and software. As long as Net8 is using the same protocol on both sides of the connection (for example TCP/IP, IPX/SPX, LU6.2, etc.), Net8 is unconcerned with how the underlying network protocol transmits the data. Net8 itself is unaware that a network exists.

Net8 is a software layer that is required to communicate between Oracle clients and servers. The **Transparent Network Substrate** (**TNS**) is an underlying layer of Net8 that handles all of the generic connectivity functions, such as opening and closing a session or sending and receiving requests or responses. TNS then passes control to an **Oracle Protocol Adapter** to make the protocol-specific call (for example TCP/IP)

The following figure shows the basic connectivity architecture and process for Net8 when a client, such as SQL*Plus, initiates a connection. Any information returned by a database query flows in the reverse direction.

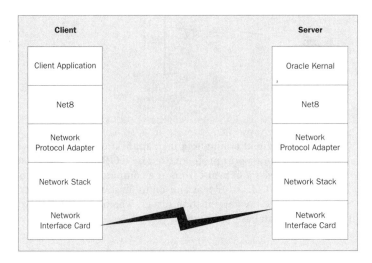

When Oracle is installed, both Net8 and one or more supported network protocol adapters must be installed on the server. Net8 requires an existing network protocol stack to make the machine-level connection between two machines. The network protocol is responsible only for getting the data from the client machine to the server machine. Once the data passes across the network, it is passed to the Oracle Protocol Adapter. An Oracle Protocol Adapter maps function calls of specific network protocols (such as TCP/IP) into equivalent function calls of the Transparent Network Substrate.

Connecting to a Server

The Network Service Name

When an end user connects to a database service from across the network, a "connect string" identifies the service through a **Network Service Name**. The following example uses the SQL*Plus utility but the generic syntax applies from all application environments:

```
SQL> CONNECT username/password@network_service_name
```

The username and password are standard authorization information to be passed along. The interesting item here is the network service name. This provides the link to the information needed to locate the service on the network. Net8 resolves a network service name into the **Network Route** to the service and a service name (typically, the **Global Database Name**) that used to identify the database service at the remote end.

Network Route

The network route is defined by the location of the entry point to the service (for example network address) along with the protocol to be used and such protocol-specific items as may be necessary to establish a network connection.

The entry point to a service in Net8 terms is a listener process. As we'll see later, this process waits for incoming connection requests, and if all is satisfactory, grants the connection so operations can continue between client and server.

Global Database Name

The global database name is the means of uniquely identifying a database across the entire network. Each node in the network must be uniquely identified. Although a database **System Identifier** (**SID**) has to be unique on any particular node (for example there can only be one ORCL on node mysys.myco.com), there is nothing to stop the same name being used on a different system (for example ORCL on node yoursys.myco.com).

The Connection Process

Clients initiate a connect request by passing information such as a username and password along with a network service name for the database service that they wish to connect. Net8 uses the service names to identify the specific connect descriptor needed by a client. Depending upon your specific network configuration, connect descriptors may be stored in one of the following:

- ❑ Local names configuration file (called tnsnames.ora).
- ❑ Oracle Names server.
- ❑ A native naming service, such as NIS or DCE CDS (via an Oracle Native Naming Adapter).

Net8 uses a **Network Listener** to coordinate sessions. The network listener is a process that runs on the server. It receives connection requests from client applications. The network listener is configured to "listen" on a specific address in the listener configuration file (listener.ora).

The network listener responds to client connect requests in one of three ways:

❑ Bequeath the session to a new dedicated server process.

❑ Redirect to an existing server process (such as a dispatcher or pre-spawned server process).

❑ Refuse the session.

Bequeathed Sessions to Dedicated Server Processes

A bequeathed connection is one the network listener passes directly to the Oracle database server. The network listener may create (that is, 'spawn') dedicated server processes *when the listener and server exist on the same node.* Most Oracle dedicated server processes are bequeathed. When a client disconnects, the dedicated server process associated with the client closes.

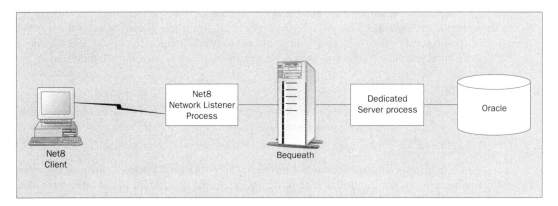

The sequence of events that occur when the listener `bequeaths' control of a session is as follows:

1. The network listener is started and listens on an address specified in a listener configuration file (listener.ora).

2. A client connects to the listener with the network address from the tnsnames.ora file or from the Oracle Names server.

3. The listener receives the session request and determines if the client's request can be serviced. If not, the listener refuses the session and then continues listening for incoming sessions.

4. The listener spawns a new dedicated server process to serve the incoming session and bequeaths the session to that server process. Once the session is established, data flows directly between the client and dedicated server process.

5. The listener continues listening for incoming sessions.

Redirected Sessions to Existing Server Processes

Net8 can redirect the request to an existing server process. In the case of a redirect, the network listener sends the address of an existing server process back to the client. The client will then resend its connection request to the server address provided.

Existing server processes include:

- ❑ **Pre-spawned server processes**.

- ❑ **Dispatcher processes**.

Pre-spawned server processes are aptly named. They are dedicated server processes that the network listener starts at startup and they last for the life of the listener. Pre-spawned processes can be passed to clients requesting dedicated processes.

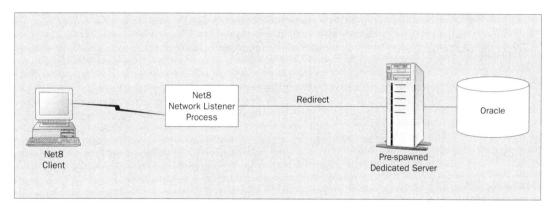

The process for redirecting control of a session to a pre-spawned process is slightly more complicated than bequeathing control to a dedicated server process.

1. The listener is started and listens on an address specified in a listener configuration file (listener.ora).

2. The listener then spawns a pool of dedicated server processes until it reaches the specified pool size.

3. Each pre-spawned server process performs a wildcard listen and provides the network listener with the address it is listening on. The listener initially marks all pre-spawned servers as idle.

4. A client connects to the network listener with the network address from the tnsnames.ora file or from the Oracle Names server.

5. The network listener receives the session request and determines if the client's request can be serviced. If not, the network listener refuses the session and then continues listening for incoming sessions.

6. The network listener issues a redirect message to the client containing the network address of one of the pre-spawned processes. The listener marks the pre-spawned process as active.

7. The client dissolves the session to the network listener and establishes a session to the pre-spawned process using the address provided in the redirect message.

8. The network listener spawns another server process to replace the active pre-spawned process (provided a value called PRESPAWN_MAX in the listener configuration file is greater than the number of active *and* idle pre-spawned server processes).

9. The network listener continues listening for incoming sessions.

A multi-threaded server can service many client connections with a relatively small number of server processes. This reduces memory and server resource requirements when there are a large number of concurrent clients. The technique is especially well suited for applications that support a large number of concurrent connections *and* do not transmit a high volume of data. E-commerce Web applications are an example.

A dispatcher handles and directs multiple incoming session requests to a multi-threaded server. Incoming sessions are always routed to the dispatcher unless the session specifically requests a dedicated server (by specifying SERVER=DEDICATED in the connect string for the requesting client) or the multi-threaded server connections are exhausted.

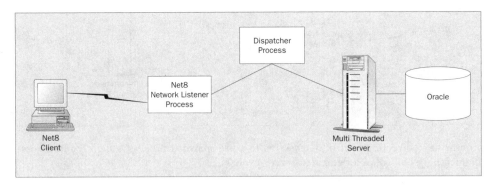

When a multi-threaded server Oracle instance and the network listener start up, the following events occur:

1. The network listener begins listening on the addresses specified in the listener.ora file.

2. A database instance starts. Dispatchers start according to the configuration parameters in the init.ora file. Each dispatcher then performs a listen on the address assigned to it.

3. Each dispatcher informs the network listener if its wildcard address is registered.

The multi-threaded server and the network listener are now ready to accept connections. The steps for handling sessions with a dispatcher continue as follows:

1. The client connects to the network listener with the network address from the tnsnames.ora file or from the Oracle Names server.

2. The network listener receives the session request and determines if the client's request can be serviced. If not, the network listener refuses the session and then continues listening for incoming sessions.

3. The network listener issues a redirect message to the client containing the network address of the least-used dispatcher for the shared server (unless SERVER=DEDICATED is requested by the client).

4. The client dissolves the session to the network listener and establishes a session to the dispatcher using the network address provided in the redirect message.

5. The dispatcher updates the network listener with the new load value because of the presence of the new session. This allows the listener to balance the incoming session requests between dispatchers.

6. The listener resumes listening for incoming sessions.

Refused Sessions

The network listener will refuse a session if it does not know about the server being requested *or* if the server is unavailable. The network listener refuses the session by sending a refuse response packet back to the client.

Disconnecting from a Server

Requests to disconnect from the server can be initiated in the following ways:

- **User-Initiated Disconnect** – A client can request a disconnection from the server when a client-server transaction completes. A server can disconnect from a server-to-server connection when all server-server data transfers have been completed.

- **Additional Connection Request** – When a client application is connected to a server and requires access to another user account on the same (or other) server, most Oracle tools will first disconnect the application from the server to which it is currently connected and then initiate a connection request to the new user account.

- **Abnormal Connection Termination** – Other components will occasionally disconnect or abort communications without giving notice to Net8. Net8 will recognize the failure during its next data operation and clean up client and server operations, disconnecting the current session.

- **Dead Connection Detection** – Dead connection detection allows Net8 to identify connections that have suffered abnormal termination of a client. This feature automatically forces a database rollback of uncommitted transactions and locks held by the user of a broken connection.

Data Operations

Net8 supports four client/server data operations:

- Send data synchronously
- Receive data synchronously
- Send data asynchronously
- Receive data asynchronously

Basic send and receive requests are synchronous with Net8. Once a client initiates a request, it waits for the server to respond. Once the server responds, the client can then issue an additional request.

Net8 also includes the capability to send and receive data requests asynchronously. Asynchronous data operations were added to support the Oracle multi-threaded server, which requires asynchronous calls to service incoming requests from multiple clients on a small number of server processes.

Migrating to Net8

Net8 is backwards compatible with SQL*Net version 2. Net8 clients can transparently connect to an Oracle7 database. Existing SQL*Net version 2 clients can also connect to an Oracle8 database.

Upgrading to Net8 is not required, but migrating to Net8 offers important advantages.

- ❑ Net8 simplifies the process of setting up your network components. You can use the Oracle Net8 Assistant to create or modify your existing local naming files, profile, and Oracle Names configuration file.

- ❑ Net8 offers extended network functionality. Many of the features previously available with SQL*Net version 2 were replaced with enhanced functionality.

- ❑ Net8 includes an application program interface (API) called Net8 OPEN. Application developers can use Net8 to develop applications (database and non-database) that make use of the Net8 network services. One important advantage that Net8 OPEN offers application developers is a single common interface to all industry standard network protocols.

Net8 Tuning

Developers can apply some basic techniques to improve the performance of enterprise applications running under Net8. These fall under techniques to reduce the number of round-trip messages between the clients and the database server and techniques to reduce the amount of data exchanged between clients and the server.

- ❑ Setting your application's ARRAY_SIZE parameter to reduce the number of fetches.

- ❑ Using stored procedures. Especially when combined with server cursors, stored procedures can reduce both network round-trips and the amount of information crossing the network.

Net8 performance is also related to Oracle network features outside the control of the typical developer. Enterprise developers should, however, become familiar with Net8 tuning basics in order to work collaboratively with network administrators and DBAs to isolate performance bottlenecks. Keep the following issues in mind:

- ❑ **Performance Tuning of MTS** – Scalability under Net8 can be improved by performance tuning the configuration of any multi-threaded server instances. Tuning MTS is largely a function of configuring the optimal number of dispatchers and adding/reducing the number of server processes.

- ❑ **Performance Tuning of Dedicated Processes** – Dedicated server processes require an operating system process for each user connection. As a consequence, it is easy to run out of system memory. If you intend to service a large number of clients with dedicated processes, configure the server with a large amount of RAM.

❑ **Connection Pooling and Multiplexing** – Net8 includes connection pooling and connection multiplexing capabilities. Scalability can be greatly improved by employing connection pooling or multiplexing.

If your enterprise application must process a high volume of connection requests (for example a popular e-commerce Web site), load balancing the network listeners can increase scalability. Multiple network listeners can process sessions for a single database server.

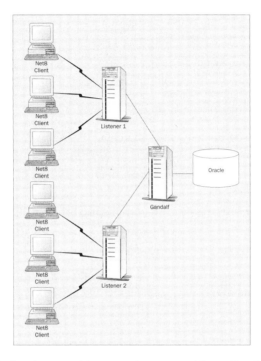

Load balancing can be further increased in an environment with an Oracle parallel server environment or with symmetric replication. Multiple network listeners can each be configured so that they redirect sessions to the least busy dispatchers among all of the available masters.

Net8 Troubleshooting

Developers should understand the basics of Net8 troubleshooting. Problems can and do sometimes occur when client applications run under Net8. Developers, network administrators, and DBA's will not always agree initially about the source of the problem. Finger pointing back and forth is a common occurrence.

The Net8 Administrator's Guide jumps right to log file analysis for troubleshooting. Log file analysis is not a task recommended for the squeamish. Fortunately, it is a task better suited to network administrators and DBAs. There are other considerations to try first.

The most common problem that will plague developers is a failure to connect. This is especially frustrating when it appears that the client and the server are perfectly configured.

There are some common causes for connection difficulties to consider:

❏ A problem with a Net8 configuration parameter (for example, an incorrect entry in the tnsnames.ora file).

❏ A non-functioning or malfunctioning network protocol (for example, an incorrect IP address, a DNS configuration error).

❏ A failure in the physical network (for example, bad cable, malfunctioning NIC, unplugged connection).

❏ A failure in the logical network (for example, a router).

Troubleshooting is largely a process of logical deduction and elimination. Oracle provides tools that can help diagnose Net8 operations. Operating system tools and network analysis tools are also helpful in determining whether a problem lies in the installation and configuration of Net8, the network protocol layer, or the physical network itself.

Diagnosing the Network

Most operating systems include diagnostic tools for verifying proper operation of the network. The Windows, Windows NT, and Unix operating systems, for example, include a simple utility called ping to determine whether TCP/IP packets are being properly transmitted and received between two nodes on a network.

The ping utility can be use in a TCP/IP network to test the HOSTS file and the DNS. It will return the time for a packet to make a roundtrip or it will fail with an error.

Oracle 8 includes a similar utility called tnsping to verify Oracle database connections. You can invoke the Oracle utility in the following way:

```
tnsping service_name count
```

The tnsping utility does not try to connect to the network listener. The tnsping utility does, however, try to reach the listener. The count parameter determines the number of attempts tnsping makes. The count parameter is optional and defaults to 1.

The Net8 Easy Configuration utility provides an additional mechanism for testing whether a workstation can reach a network listener process.

1. *Start the Net8 Easy Configuration utility.*

2. *Select "Test" and enter an existing service name.*

3. *A "Connection Test" window appears. Enter a username and password and click the "Test" button.*

4. *The test result will be displayed.*

Diagnosing the Server

There is a simple question to ask when diagnosing server connectivity. Can *any* workstation or server access the server? Yes. Then move your attention to the client. Other simple questions include:

❏ Is the database running? No. Start the database and test the connection again.

❏ Is the listener running? No. Start the listener and test the connection again.

❏ If you are using Oracle Names, is the Oracle Names server running? No. Start the Oracle Names server and test the connection again.

Performing a loopback test is one of the easiest ways to determine whether Net8 is installed, properly configured, and running on a particular server. A loopback test tries to connect locally to a server using SQL*Plus. You start by using SQL*Plus to establish a local connection to the database. This will verify the database is up and running:

```
sqlplus scott/tiger
```

The loopback test then tries a loopback connection by specifying a Net8 connect string. Assuming you are still logged into SQL*Plus, just enter:

```
connect scott/tiger@host
```

For this to work, the tnsnames.ora file must exist and must contain an entry for the database running on this host. (A correctly configured Oracle Names server with an entry for the database running on this host is another possibility.) If the tnsnames.ora file requires TCP/IP name resolution, appropriate entries must exist in an accessible DNS or in the local HOSTS file.

If the loopback test is successful, you should move your attention to the client. If the test is unsuccessful, the usual suspects include a faulty Net8 configuration or an errant network protocol stack on the server.

Diagnosing the Client

Diagnosing the client will usually begin with verifying network connectivity. For TCP/IP networks, this will involve the ping utility. Can the workstation reach the server? If the workstation cannot reach the server, check the following:

❑   Does the tnsnames.ora file use logical service names resolved by a DNS server? Yes. Verify the DNS server is properly resolving the logical name by using the logical name in the ping instead of the server's IP address.

❑   If the service name is not resolved by a DNS, is the logical name entered in HOSTS file on the client computer? No. Enter the logical name in HOSTS file.

If the logical name still cannot be resolved, try using the server's IP address in the tnsnames.ora file. This will narrow the problem to logical name resolution on the client computer.

Once network connectivity is verified, your attention should shift to Net8 client operation. Some common problems to consider include the following:

❑   Is Net8 installed on the client?

❑   Is the correct protocol adapter installed on the client?

❑   Is the tnsnames.ora file installed on the client? Installed in the correct directory? In the alternative, is the Oracle Names server properly configured? Does it contain an entry for the database server?

❑   Is the sqlnet.ora file installed on the client? Installed in the correct directory?

Some Common ORA Errors and What To Do

There are some common ORA messages when Net8 goes wrong. Here is a short list, (based on a more complete list in *Oracle Net8 Administrator's Guide*, Release 8.0):

ORA Error	Message	What To Do
ORA-12154	TNS:could not resolve service name	Check that service name exists in the `tnsnames.ora` file.
ORA-12162	TNS:service name is incorrectly specified	Check the syntax of the `tnsnames.ora` file. *Mismatched parentheses are the usual suspect.*
ORA-12163	TNS:Connect descriptor is too long	Shorten the connection description.
ORA-12197	TNS:keyword-value resolution error	Check the syntax of the `tnsnames.ora` file. *Mismatched parentheses are the usual suspect.*
ORA-12198	TNS:could not find path to destination	Check the `tnsnav.ora` file for errors.
ORA-12203	TNS:Unable to connect to destination	Run `LSNRCTL` and check whether a listener is running for the specified SID. If this doesn't identify the problem, check for physical and logical network problems.
ORA-12208	TNS:could not find the TNSNAV.ORA file	Check that the `tnsnav.ora` file is in the correct directory.
ORA-12210	TNS:error in finding Navigator data	Check the `tnsnav.ora` file for errors.
ORA-12224	TNS:no listener	Check the `listener.ora` file for errors. Make sure the supplied destination address matches one of the addresses used by the listener.
ORA-12500	TNS:listener failed to start a dedicated server process	Check the process count in the operating system. Check the `listener.ora` file for errors.
ORA-12504	TNS:listener was not given the SID in CONNECT_DATA	Check `CONNECT_DATA` in the `tnsnames.ora` file.
ORA-12505	TNS:Listener could not resolve SID given in connect descriptor	Check the `listener.ora` file for errors. Run `LSNRCTL` and check whether a listener is running for the specified SID. *The usual suspect here is a mistyped SID in the CONNECT_DATA section or a mistyped machine name.*
ORA-12510	TNS:database lacks resources to handle the request for this SID	Increase the number of available dispatchers.

Table continued on following page

ORA Error	Message	What To Do
ORA-12511	TNS:service handler found but it is not accepting connections	Either try again or increase the number of available dispatchers.
ORA-12533	TNS:illegal ADDRESS parameters	Check the ADDRESS section of the tnsnames.ora file.
ORA-12545	TNS:name lookup failure	Verify that the ADDRESS in the tnsnames.ora file and the listener.ora file is correct. Run LSNRCTL and verify that the listener has been started.

Summary

Net8 provides an enterprise-wide data solution that application developers can leverage easily. Enterprise application developers do not need to write code to move data across different network protocols, translate character sets or word sizes or byte orderings, manage multiple clients, or apply security. Net8 handles these details transparently for the enterprise application developer.

Net8 is designed to support data services for thousands of concurrent users. Employing features like connection pooling and connection multiplexing do not require any changes to client applications.

Enterprise application developers will find that Oracle Net8 is an ideal complement to the deployment of large OLTP solutions, such as e-commerce Web sites.

Before moving on to hand-coding our applications, we will take a look at one way of quickly building robust and powerful database applications using one of Oracle's well-established tools.

5

Enterprise Development with Designer 6i

The Oracle Designer product focuses on the challenges of enterprise application development by a team of developers. Oracle Designer provides a set of repository-based tools for modeling, designing, and generating databases and application systems. The latest version, Designer 6i, is a major new release with many new features including:

- ❑ The new **Oracle Repository**, which provides a datastore for the numerous source files, binary files, documents, and structured data involved with Oracle 8i enterprise application development using Java, PL/SQL, Oracle Forms 6i, Oracle Reports 6i, JDeveloper 3.2, or any other development tool. Repository management tools provide fine-grained versioning of objects, object check-in and check-out, release management, and object dependency analysis.

- ❑ Enhanced support for Oracle 8i database features including index-organized tables, function-based indexes, Java in the database, advanced queuing, new Oracle object types, and materialized views.

- ❑ Numerous new features in the **Web PL/SQL generator** including multi-row forms, separate LOV components, and a security API.

- ❑ New features in the **Forms generator** for navigator style forms, list of values components, split blocks, side-by-side blocks, and a relative tab stop layout editor.

Professional Oracle developers should consider applying Designer and the Oracle Repository to their large Oracle application development projects in one or more of the following areas:

❏ **Database Design and Development** – Getting the Oracle 8i database design "right" is the key to the success of any database project. Designer provides tools for diagramming conceptual and physical data models, generating DDL scripts, reverse engineering existing databases into the Repository, and reconciling Repository definitions with physical schemas. Later in this chapter we will present a hands-on example of using Designer 6i to design and build a database.

❏ **Web PL/SQL Application Design and Generation** – Designer offers a quick approach to designing and generating full-function Web PL/SQL applications based upon the Oracle Web Developer Toolkit. These applications can be run against any web server with a PL/SQL gateway (for example iAS, OAS, Oracle Portal, or WebDB). Web PL/SQL applications are generated based on module and database design specifications recorded in the Oracle Repository, and may include custom code to provide enhanced functionality. We will discuss using the PL/SQL Web toolkit with Designer to create a web application in Chapter 10.

❏ **Developer Application Design and Generation** – Designer is a powerful development tool for model-based development of Developer Forms and Reports applications to be deployed as either web applications or client-server applications.

❏ **Software Configuration Management** – Managing all the data and files involved with enterprise development is a major challenge for any software development project. The Oracle Repository provides all the capabilities of configuration management or source code control systems such as PVCS or ClearCase plus the extensive capabilities of Oracle Designer. Developer 6i and JDeveloper 3.2 include the capability to use the Oracle Repository for source code control.

❏ **Software and Database Change Impact Analysis** – Use the Repository's new Dependency Analysis capabilities to assess the impact of a software or database change, and to manage the implementation of that change.

Designer 6i Software Architecture

Designer 6i has a client-server software architecture. The Designer client software and the Repository client software run on a Windows-based client. The Repository must be loaded on an Oracle 8.1.6+ database. In most development organizations, the Designer Repository is installed on a shared database server, but it is possible to install both the client tools and the Repository on a single NT 4.0 or Windows 2000 computer.

The Repository consists of numerous PL/SQL packages plus the meta data (the structured objects and unstructured files).

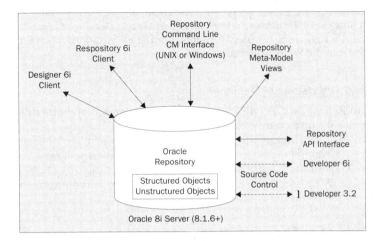

The Oracle Repository includes a command line interface for performing configuration management transactions from either a UNIX or Windows command line. The Oracle Repository has an open, documented meta-model – that is, a model of the meta data stored in the Repository. A set of meta-model views are provided for reporting data stored in the Repository, and an Application Programming Interface (API) is provided for developing custom programs to load, update, and query data in the Repository.

The new Oracle Repository is bundled with Designer 6i, but exists as a separate product that can be used with or without Designer.

Designer has been traditionally offered as a separate product but is now included in Oracle's **Internet Development Suite**. Designer 6i may be installed alone, or with one or more of the other development tools in the suite:

❑   Developer 6i – Oracle Reports and Oracle Forms

❑   JDeveloper

❑   Discoverer

❑   Oracle Portal

The Designer 6i client includes Developer 6i Forms and Reports runtime modules. If you plan to use Designer to generate Forms or Reports modules, then you will need to install the full Developer software with the Forms Builder and Reports Builder components on your workstation. Both Developer 6i and JDeveloper 3.2 are 'repository-enabled' with the capability to use the Oracle Repository for source code control.

Designer 6i was first released in June 2000. At the time of writing Designer 6i Release 2 is imminent. It is expected to include support for Windows 2000, support for Oracle's Universal Installer (greatly simplifying the installation process), integration with Developer 6i Release 2, and numerous patches. The latest version of Designer 6i is downloadable from http://technet.oracle.com together with the documentation.

You should plan your Designer installation thoroughly to ensure success. The Designer 6i installation must be coordinated with the installation and configuration of other Oracle software components on both the client-side and server-side. The Designer 6i Software CD includes a very thorough Oracle *Designer 6i Installation Guide* and also a Release Notes file. More information on installation issues can be downloaded from the Wrox web site.

Migrating from Previous Versions of Designer

Before migrating to Release 6i, clean up your existing repository and optimize it. Designer 1.3.2, 2.1, or 2.1.2 repositories must be upgraded first to Designer 2.1.2 or 6.0. Then the 2.1.2 or 6.0 repository can be migrated to Designer 6i. This migration must be performed from a **live** Designer 2.1.2 or 6.0 repository to a **live** Designer 6i repository. The Designer 6i migration process will write data into the existing 2.1.2 or 6.0 repository. Be sure to make a backup of your repository before attempting to migrate. Conditions may be encountered which would necessitate re-running the migration.

The New Oracle Repository

With the release of Designer 6i, the Designer repository was completely re-structured and greatly expanded in capability. The new Oracle Repository provides a datastore and tools for managing both:

❑ Traditional Designer structured meta-data definitions

❑ Any operating system file – for example source files, binary files, document files

All structured meta data defined in Designer 6i is automatically stored in the Oracle Repository. Any flat file (such as source files, binary files, document files) may also be uploaded into the Oracle Repository for management. The Oracle Repository provides the capability to manage all structured and unstructured meta data involved with enterprise application development using Java, PL/SQL, Oracle Forms or Reports, or any other development tool.

Repository Objects

A repository object is an individual item of meta data. Each repository object is a specific instance of a particular **element type**. The Oracle Repository provides a basic set of element types, and Oracle Designer provides a larger set of pre-defined element types. A few of the these are:

❑ Business processes

❑ Business functions

❑ Entities

❑ Domains

❑ Table definitions

❑ View definitions

❑ Sequence definitions

❑ Module definitions

❑ Diagrams

Each repository element type has a standard set of **properties**. For example, each Table Definition has properties of Name, Alias, and Description.

Certain element types are dependent upon a "parent" element type and only exist within the context of that parent. For example, a column definition or an index may only exist within the context of a table. The independent element types are called **primary access controlled (PAC) elements** and the dependent element types are called **secondary access controlled (SAC) elements**.

An Oracle Repository **object** consists of a single PAC element, plus any SAC elements defined for it, plus any references defined to other objects. For example, a table object would consist of:

❑   The table's properties

❑   All dependent column definitions

❑   Any allowable values defined for the columns

❑   Any constraint definitions

❑   Any index definitions

❑   Any usage references to other objects.

> **When you copy or delete a PAC element, all its dependent SAC elements are copied or deleted as well.**

A **reference** or association may be defined between two repository objects. For example, an entity definition may have a "usage association" with a table definition. Designer provides a standard set of **association types** for defining references between repository objects.

Designer also provides a standard set of **text types** for defining various kinds of free-format text for an element type or an association type. For example, a Description or Notes text property may be associated with a given element type.

User Extensibility

The Oracle Repository provides the capability for the repository owner to extend the standard data element types, association types, and text types. The available extensions include:

❑   **User-defined properties** for a particular element type – in addition to the standard properties for that type. Once defined, repository users can define values for those user-defined properties.

❑   **User-defined association types** between repository elements.

❑   **User-defined text types** for an element type or association type.

Containers

A **container** is a logical subdivision of the repository – similar to a directory in a file system. A container is a means of organizing repository objects. Objects are defined within a container. Each object is owned by the container in which it is defined. An object may be moved to another container causing the object's ownership to be transferred to the new container.

There are two types of containers in the Oracle Repository:

❑ **Application Systems**

❑ **Folders**

The Repository also supports the concept of sub-containers. An application system may contain folders or sub-application systems. A folder may contain an application systems, or sub-folders.

Previous releases of Designer only supported Application Systems. Folders have been added to manage operating system files, and to support other new and planned features of the Oracle Repository.

Both Application Systems and Folders can hold instances of any type of repository object. However, you should be aware of two constraints on the use of containers in Designer 6i:

❑ The Designer Systems Modeling Tools can only access objects owned by an application system. Therefore you will have to define and use an Application System to contain your Designer meta data, rather than using a Folder.

❑ Operating systems directories can only be mapped to Root Level Folders – not to subfolders. Therefore, you will want to define a root level folder for each operating system directory that will be used to routinely to download and upload files.

Container Access Rights

A container is owned by the repository user who creates the container. The owner of the container controls access to the container and its objects. The owner may grant access to other users to use, create, or modify objects in that container. The owner of a container may also transfer ownership of a container to another user. There is more information on access rights in a later section of this chapter.

File Objects

The new Oracle Repository provides the ability to create and store files and file systems within the Repository. Any file type may be stored in the Repository including source files, binary files, and documents. You can use these new features to:

❑ Place files or folders under version control. Use the Repository as a source control system.

❑ Store files used or generated by Designer in the Repository. For example, you can store your generated modules, generated DDL files, cascading style sheets, or Forms object libraries in the Repository.

You can **create** a file directly in a container in the repository using the Repository Object Navigator. If the file name has an extension with a Windows program association, then you can open and **edit** that file directly from the Repository.

You can **upload** individual operating system files or an entire directory structure and its contents into a selected Repository folder. Subdirectories are automatically stored as subfolders under the selected folder.

Files created in the Repository or previously uploaded to the repository can be **downloaded** to any operating system directory accessible from your workstation.

Uploaded files can also be edited directly in the Repository. Note that once a file is uploaded into the Repository, the Repository access rights take over for that file. A file that was read-only in the operating system could become editable in the Repository.

The Repository also provides the ability to **map** an operating system directory to a Repository folder. The mapped directory then becomes the default location for uploading into that folder or downloading from that folder.

Changes made to either the operating system files or the files stored in the Repository will not automatically be reflected in the other location. The Repository provides the capability to **synchronize** the files contained in a mapped folder with the files in its operating system directory.

Files are stored in the Repository in either **uncompressed** or **compressed** format. By default, all files are stored uncompressed. In the Repository Object Navigator, use the Utilities | Edit File Registry menu option to specify how a particular type of file, or even a file with a specific name, is to be stored.

Version Control

The version control features of the Repository allow you to record changes made to an object during its life-cycle. Version numbers and version labels are provided for easy identification.

Version control applies to a repository object at the PAC element level. You cannot version individual SAC elements of a Repository object. The object and all its dependent elements must be versioned together.

Version control is implemented via a **check-in** and **check-out** mechanism. Each time an object is checked in, a new version is created for that object. The record of changes to a particular object is known as the version history of the object. Notes describing the version change may be logged at the time an object is checked in or out.

Version control for an object is initiated when that object is checked-in for the first time. **If an object has not been checked in, it is not under version control**. Containers may also be placed under version control. If a container is under version control, then it must be checked out before any of its objects can be checked out.

> Each organization should decide on its approach to object version control. Some development organizations may choose to place an object under version control only when the object is stable and ready for review. Other organizations may prefer to check-in and check-out all objects on a daily basis.

Object versions are organized into a **version tree structure with branches**. Each branch has a user-defined label. When checking in an object version, the user may decide whether to include the new object version in its originating version branch, or to create a new branch.

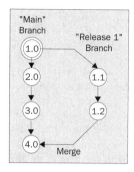

An automatic **compare** feature is available to compare two versions of an object and to report differences in those objects. A rule-based **merge** feature is available to assist in merging branched objects. The Repository currently supports comparing and merging the following kinds of objects:

❏ Structured objects – Designer objects

❏ Oracle Forms Files

❏ Text files

> **Each organization should decide upon its branching strategy. In general, organizations should try to control and limit the number of branches.**

Configurations

To support release management, you can define a configuration of specific object versions. For example, all the components in Release 1.1. This might include Order version 1.1, Order Line version 1.0.1, and Org 2.0. Together they form a configuration that you can version control and track as a unit. When you create a configuration, you are its owner.

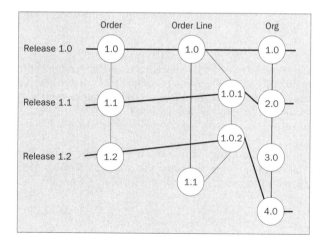

Dependency Analysis

Dependency analysis identifies the relationships between objects in a workarea, and answers the questions:

- ❑ Tell me everything that uses an object
- ❑ Tell me everything that is used by an object
- ❑ If I release a new version of a module, what other components must I compile or run?

The new Oracle Repository includes the capability to analyze the dependencies between structured and unstructured objects held in the repository. For structured objects, dependency usage data is retrieved directly from the Repository. Unstructured files are first parsed, and dependency information extracted. Parsers for a variety of file types come with the Oracle Repository, and instructions are provided for creating additional parsers.

Analysis and compilation of the dependencies is performed externally from the Repository, and then loaded into the Repository as Dependency Data. The Dependency Manager is a tool for examining dependency information in the Repository. Dependency data is current only at the point of time it is analyzed, and will need to be purged and re-compiled periodically.

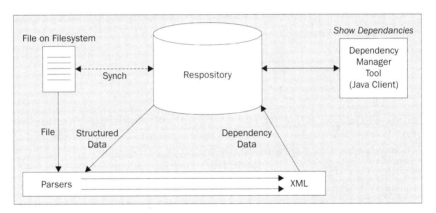

Workareas

An organization's Repository may contain many versions of many objects. An individual user may not want to see all objects within the Repository.

A **workarea** is a view of repository objects. It provides a working context for a user or a project team. A workarea contains only one version of any single object. A workarea's **rules** define:

- ❑ Which objects and/or containers are included in the workarea
- ❑ Which objects and/or containers are excluded from the workarea
- ❑ Which version of each object is included in that workarea – for example, the most current version on the "Patch 1" branch

Workareas may be defined to meet an organization's requirements. For example, a workarea might be created for:

❏   A specific project or project phase

❏   A specific software release

❏   A specific department within an organization

The workarea concept is tightly coupled with version control. Objects created in a workarea are only visible from that workarea until they are checked in and placed under version control. Deleting a workarea does not delete the version controled objects included in that workarea, but will delete any new objects or objects which have been checked-out and not yet checked back in.

The user who creates a workarea is the owner of that workarea, and controls the access privileges on that workarea. A workarea is always created as a **private workarea**. When access rights are granted to other users, the workarea becomes a **shared workarea**.

When the Designer Repository is installed, a default **Global System Workarea** is created. By default, the PUBLIC user role is granted full access privileges on this workarea. Any new user account should be able to access and use the Global System Workarea.

> **If versioning is not turned on for the Repository, then the Global System Workarea is the sole workarea in the repository. No additional workareas can be created in a non-versioned repository.**

Overview of Designer 6i Tools

When you first invoke Designer 6i from the Start Menu, you will be asked to log into the Repository, and to choose a Default Workarea. Note that your Oracle Repository must have been installed before you can use Designer 6i. From you main **Designer** window, you can access all the components of Designer including the tools for modeling data, designing and generating database elements, and repository maintenance.

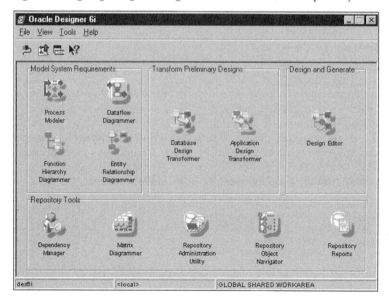

Four Designer tools are specifically focused on Modeling Systems Requirements:

❑ The **Process Modeler** is a tool to assist with the analysis and re-engineering of an organization's business processes. A Business Process Re-engineering effort may be closely related to an IT development effort since it is often desirable to revise an inefficient business process before automating it. The Process Modeler captures business processes, process steps, organization units, and associated flow and timing. Business processes captured in the Process Modeler may map to business functions in the Function Hierarchy.

❑ The **Dataflow Diagrammer** can be used to diagram how information flows between a system's functions. Designer supports Gane and Sarson style dataflow diagrams (DFDs) with functions, datastores, dataflows, and externals. A single dataflow diagram can be decomposed to increasingly detailed levels. Dataflow diagrams can on occasion be quite useful, but are not used as often as the other modeling tools.

❑ **The Function Hierarchy Diagrammer** is a tool for documenting the functions of a business or system as a hierarchical chart. Function hierarchy diagrams (FHDs) can be useful for defining the scope of a system and for documenting the individual modules to be built and their data usages.

❑ **The Entity Relationship Diagrammer** can be used to create and present entity relationship diagrams (ERDs) for an application's conceptual data model. In Designer, an ERD is a view of one or more entities and relationships defined with the Oracle Repository. The use of ERDs will be presented in the case study.

Under **Transform Preliminary Designs**, two components are available for transforming the system models into preliminary designs:

❑ The **Database Design Transformer** transforms a selected set of entities and relationships into a preliminary database design. We will use this tool to transform your ERD.

❑ The **Application Design Transformer** transforms a selected set of functions defined in a Function Hierarchy Diagram (FHD) into preliminary module designs.

Under **Design and Generate**, all of Designer's capabilities are grouped into a single component:

❑ The **Design Editor** is an integrated environment for the many design and generation capabilities of Designer. This environment includes facilities for database design and DDL generation for Oracle and non-Oracle databases; module design for Forms, Reports, and Web PL/SQL applications; and reverse engineering of databases and modules into Designer. We will use the Design Editor extensively throughout the case study to create the database and the web application.

Under **Repository Tools**, five components are shown for managing and using data in the Oracle Repository:

❑ The **Dependency Manager** provides access to Designer's components and utilities for creating and maintaining dependency analysis information in the Repository.

❑ The **Matrix Diagrammer** is a tool for cross-referencing elements in the Repository. It is widely used for logging a function's usage of entities, or a module's usage of tables. Any Repository object type may be cross-referenced to any other object type.

❑ The **Repository Administration Utility** (RAU) is a tool for installing, upgrading, and maintaining the Oracle Repository; maintaining user privileges to the Repository; and registering physical database schemas in the Repository (new with Release 6i). The Repository's administrator is the primary user of this tool. Note that this tool is also available from the separate Oracle Repository 6i item on the Start Menu. Initial installation of the Repository must be run from the separate Oracle Repository 6i menu item.

❑ The **Repository Object Navigator** (RON) is a tool for creating and maintaining workareas and for viewing and editing object definitions within a Workarea. This tool is heavily used by developers and DBA's. Note that this tool is also available from the Start Menu via the separate Oracle Repository 6i item.

❑ The **Repository Reports** component provides pre-canned reports on structured data stored in the Oracle Repository. These reports are particularly useful for reporting function definitions, entity definitions, table definitions, and module definitions.

Setting up the Oracle Repository

The Oracle Repository physically consists of a set of database objects and packages installed in an Oracle 8i database. The **Repository Owner** account owns all the repository objects. The Repository Owner cannot be the SYSTEM or SYS user account. See the Designer 6i Installation Guide and the Designer 6i Release Notes for detailed instructions on setting up the Repository Owner account, installing the Oracle Repository, and migrating an existing Designer repository from a previous version of Designer to Designer 6i.

The **Repository Administration Utility** (RAU) enables the Repository Owner to install the repository and administer the repository environment:

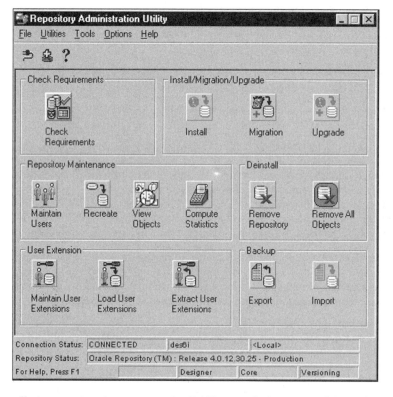

During the installation or migration process, the RAU can only be accessed from the Oracle Repository Client via the Start Menu. Once the Repository has been installed, the Repository Owner can access the RAU from either the Oracle Repository Client or from the Designer 6i client's main window.

Enabling Version Control

The Designer installation process installs the Oracle Repository with the Repository Versioning feature turned off. With a non-versioned repository:

- ❏ A single workarea called the System Global Workarea is available. No other workareas can be created.

- ❏ Multiple Application Systems and folders may be created within the Global System Workarea.

- ❏ You cannot create an Application Version in the same way as you could in previous releases. Versioning must be enabled in order to create an Application Version.

You can enable versioning at any time. **Once Versioning is turned on, it can not be turned off. It is a permanent feature of that repository.** Within a Versioned Repository, applications systems, folders, and objects will remain un-versioned until they are checked in for the first time. This feature allows you to keep un-versioned objects in a versioned repository. Please note that un-versioned objects are only available from the Workarea where they were created.

To turn versioning on for your Repository, select Options | Enable Version Support from the RAU menu. Once Versioning is enabled, the RAU menu option Enable Version Support will be grayed out.

Maintaining Users

The Oracle userid used to install the Repository becomes the Repository Owner and automatically has a full set of Repository privileges and access to all the functions of Designer. After installing the Designer Repository, the Repository Owner account should generally be used only for repository administration and configuration management tasks.

You should set up separate Repository user accounts for each of the other Designer users. These other users are sometimes referred to as **subordinate users**. Most repository administration tasks will be performed by the Repository Owner user account. However, subordinate users may be granted certain administration privileges – such as maintaining users.

Creating User Accounts

Use the following steps to create a new Designer user account:

1. Use SQL*Plus to create an Oracle database account for each Designer user:

```
CREATE USER scott IDENTIFIED BY tiger;
GRANT resource, connect TO scott;
```

2. Log onto the Repository Administration Utility (RAU) as the Repository Owner and invoke the Maintain Users icon to bring up a **User Maintenance** window. (The Repository privilege of "Allow Management of Users" is required to run this facility.)

3. Expand the Users node to see the existing users, and then click the Add icon to bring up a **Repository User Properties** window. Select the Oracle User Name from the list of current database user accounts, and fill in the Full User Name and Description fields with appropriate documentation text:

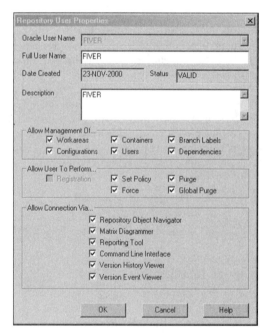

4. Assign the user object management privileges:

❏ **Workareas** – privilege to create, edit, refresh, and delete workareas.

❏ **Configurations** – privilege to create, edit, delete, and purge configurations.

❏ **Containers** – privilege to create, edit, delete, and purge containers (a.k.a. Application Systems and Folders).

❑ **Users** – privilege to use the RAU User Maintenance facility to create, edit, and set these user privileges for other users.

❑ **Branch Labels** – for a versioned repository, privilege to create, edit, and delete branch labels for repository object versions.

❑ **Dependencies** – privilege to use all the features available in the Dependency Manager. Without this privilege, a user can only use the Dependency Manager in read only mode.

5. Assign the user repository management privileges:

❑ **Registration** – not used in this release.

❑ **Set Policy** – privilege to enable or disable repository policies.

❑ **Force** – privilege to **force delete** or purge repository object versions. Note that force delete is a convenient privilege for the development leader to have! To use this privilege, the user must also have delete privileges on the container involved.

❑ **Purge** – privilege to purge repository object versions, even if they are checked in. To use this privilege, the user must also have delete privileges on the container involved.

❑ **Global Purge** – privilege to purge any or all versions of an object not owned by a container, for example objects in a wastebasket.

> **Most users will not need Object Management privileges or Repository Management privileges. Consider limiting the assignment of these privileges to your administrators or technical leads.**

6. Assign the user privileges to connect to one or more of the repository tools. If a check box is not selected, the user cannot connect to the repository using that tool and therefore, cannot use the tool. Click OK to finish creating the new Repository User and close the window.

7. When you install the Repository, you will be given a choice of using either public synonyms or private synonyms for the Repository objects. If the Repository is using **private synonyms**, you will also need to click the Reconcile button after you Add or Delete a new user(s). Reconcile creates and organizes the private synonyms for all users. A new user cannot use the Repository until you reconcile his private synonyms.

Editing User Repository Privileges

You can edit a User's Repository Privileges at any time. Select the user's name from the User Maintenance Screen and click the Properties icon to bring up the Repository User Properties window (or use the right mouse button's Menu | Properties) to bring up the window). Revise the user's repository privileges as desired, and commit those changes.

Object Access Rights

Before a user can access objects in the Repository, that user's account must also be granted access privileges on specific Workareas and Containers. The Owner of each Workarea or Container will need to use the RON to grant specific access rights to the user for the objects that the user should be able to view or edit. Viewing and granting Access Rights is presented in the introduction of the RON later in this chapter.

Designer 6i includes a new PUBLIC role, which is displayed on the **User Maintenance** window. A Repository User will automatically receive any access privileges assigned to PUBLIC for Workareas, Application Systems, and Folders.

Note that access rights are not assigned to individual objects, but are instead derived based upon a user's access privileges to the current Workarea and the Container which owns the Object.

> **If a subordinate user creates a Workarea or Container, the Repository Owner will not have privileges on that Workarea or Container unless the Owner grants them to their userid or to PUBLIC. Therefore, the Repository Owner may want to restrict the users given Workarea and Container creation rights.**

Reconciling the Grants for All Repository Users

A full reconcile organizes the roles, grants, and synonyms for all repository users. It also resolves the ownership of workareas and containers. If the owner of a workarea or container is not defined (for example the user's Oracle account was deleted), the repository owner becomes the owner. You must use Full Reconcile after you publish a user-defined object type to make it available to repository users.

To perform a full reconcile, select the Repository Maintenance: Recreate icon from the **RAU** window. This will bring up a Select **Recreate Option** window. Select the Full Reconcile radio button, and click Start. See the Repository Help Text for more information about this process.

Administering the Oracle Repository

Like any large Oracle database, the Oracle Repository will require on-going administration of its storage usage and performance. On a routine basis the repository administrator should use the capabilities of the RAU to:

❑   Backup the Repository Objects

❑   Compute Index Statistics

In previous versions of the Repository, the RAU provided an option to PIN the repository PL/SQL packages in the Oracle database server's System Global Area (SGA). With Designer 6i, this capability is no longer available from the RAU. However, your DBA may want to consider pinning some of the more frequently used repository packages.

Introducing the Repository Object Navigator (RON)

The Repository Object Navigator (RON) is a tool for creating, maintaining, and viewing repository objects. The RON can be used to:

❑   Administer workareas, containers, and configurations and to set repository-wide policies.

❑   Maintain repository objects, and to perform file upload, download, and synchronization between the repository and a file system.

❑   Perform version control of objects including checking in or out, viewing version history, and comparing and merging object versions.

The RON may be invoked from:

❏ The Designer main window

❏ From the Start Menu: select Oracle Repository 6i | Repository Object Navigator

❏ From within various Designer tools – for example, from within the Entity-Relationship Diagrammer or the Design Editor

The RON's **Navigator** window presents a hierarchical list of the objects in the repository. The actual contents of the display depend on the level of the tree structure selected when the window was opened. For example, a **Navigator** window may be opened for a specific workarea or a specific application system. In the screenshot below, the RON was invoked for the Global Shared Workarea. Notice that the top level node in the Navigator represents the workarea – GLOBAL SHARED WORKAREA. Underneath that node, nodes are displayed for the two types of containers: Application Systems and Folders.

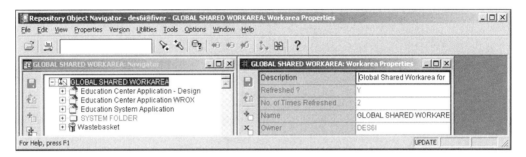

The Wastebasket node refers to the workarea's wastebasket and contains objects deleted, but not yet completely removed from the repository. Wastebaskets are discussed further in the next section of this chapter.

The right-hand **Properties** window displays the properties of the object currently highlighted in the **Navigator** window. The Property sheet for the object GLOBAL SHARED WORKAREA is displayed.

To view all the objects in the workarea, select the menu option View | Hide Group Tabs. Now all objects in the RON will be visible.

The group tab view partitions the objects displayed in the Navigator by Category. The objects in a category are only visible if that tab is selected. For example, to view or create entity definitions, you would have to select either the Enterprise Model or E/R Model tab.

Within a RON session, you can open any number of **Navigator** windows. A **Navigator** window can be opened at one of the following hierarchy levels:

❏ The entire repository

❏ Private workareas

❏ Shared workareas

❏ A single workarea

❏ All configurations

❏ A single configuration

❏ All containers

❏ A single container

To open another window in the RON, select File | Open and pick the hierarchy level from the **Open Navigator** window. If the folder or object is versioned, you can pick a specific version using either the buttons on the toolbar or a drop-down list that will appear above the Help button.

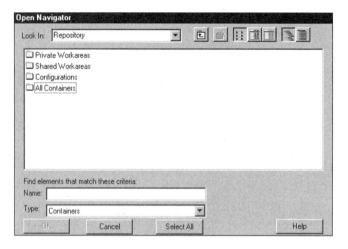

The All Containers view is particularly useful. It shows all the containers in the repository to which you have access. It also shows the Lost+Found node with those objects that have no owning container anywhere in the repository.

About Wastebaskets

There is a separate wastebasket for each workarea in the repository. In addition, there is a global wastebasket, which includes the contents of all the workarea wastebaskets and also any objects or object versions that are not visible in any workarea.

If you delete a PAC element (for example, a table definition), the object is not immediately removed from the repository but is placed in a wastebasket. From a wastebasket you can either remove the object completely, or restore it. If you delete a SAC element (for example, a column in a table definition), it is immediately removed from the repository and cannot be restored. To restore one or more PAC elements from the wastebasket:

1. Within the wastebasket node of the RON, select the element(s) to be restored

2. From the RON's menu, select Edit | Restore from Wastebasket

3. Then re-query the Navigator's display using the Menu Edit | Requery All or the requery button on the tool palette

To permanently remove all of the objects in the wastebasket from the repository, select Edit | Empty Wastebasket from the RON's menu.

> **Be sure to periodically check and empty the Repository Wastebasket!**

Selecting a Repository Workarea

All work within Designer is performed within the context of a Workarea. A Workarea is a logical view of the objects in the Oracle Repository. The Repository installation process automatically creates a default workarea called GLOBAL SHARED WORKAREA. We recommend that you use this workarea for your hands-on exercises in this book. By default, full access privileges on the GLOBAL SHARED WORKAREA are granted to the Repository role PUBLIC, so all new users are automatically granted full access privileges to this default workarea.

If your Repository has versioning enabled and your system administrator does not want you to use the GLOBAL SHARED WORKAREA, then another workarea must be defined and privileges must be granted to your Designer account to use this workarea. See the Designer Help Text for more information about creating and using workareas.

Also, if you do create a new workarea for the hands-on exercises in this book, be sure to include the SYSTEM FOLDER into your new Workarea. You will need it for Chapter 10 where you will be designing and generating a Web PL/SQL application with Designer. The System Folder is a special folder containing a number of predefined language types, such as Java or Oracle Forms. You can use these when defining application modules, for example. The system folder also contains a predefined preference set for use with the Forms Generator to optimize the look-and-feel of generated applications.

Create an Application System Container

If your workarea has no containers, you will need to create a new container before you can create objects in the Repository or use the Designer tools. For a new development project, you should create a new Application System to contain your Designer structured objects and a new root Folder to contain your operating system files. For the hands-on exercises in this book, you will need to create a new Application System called 'Education Center Application'.

In order to create a container, your repository account must have the following two privileges (See the section *Setting up the Oracle Repository: Maintaining Users* above for more information):

❑ The Containers repository privilege – allows you to manage containers. If you are logged in as the Repository Owner, you should have the Containers privilege.

❑ The Insert privilege on the selected Workarea. By default, full use privileges are granted to PUBLIC for the SHARED GLOBAL WORKAREA.

To create a new container:

1. Open the workarea in the RON and select the Workarea node on the Navigator.

2. Click the Create as Child icon (or Edit I Create Child from the menu).

3. Select the type of container to be created – either an Application System or a Folder.

4. Then type in a name for the new container on the Navigator node.

> **Be aware that you cannot move a container from one workarea to another without first checking in the container and all of its objects.**

Viewing and Granting Access on Containers and Workareas

Access rights for a single Workarea or Container must be granted to individual users or to the role PUBLIC. Access rights granted to PUBLIC are automatically inherited by all Repository users. The access rights that can be granted on a workarea or container are:

- ❑ administrate – Grant, revoke, or delete access rights on a repository object
- ❑ compile – Refresh a workarea
- ❑ delete – Delete an object (or perform force delete or purge if they have the necessary repository privileges)
- ❑ insert – Create an object
- ❑ select – Query an object
- ❑ update – Modify an object
- ❑ update spec – Redefine a workarea
- ❑ version – Check out/check in an object

Access rights are controlled by the owner of the workarea or container. The owner may grant administrate rights to another user.

To view the access privileges on a container or a workarea,

- ❑ Select File | Access Rights | View Access Rights from the RON's menu. This will bring up the View Access Rights window.
- ❑ Drill down into the list of objects and select a specific container or workarea.

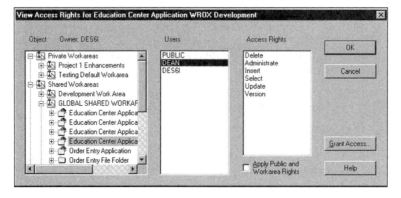

The View Access Rights window will show the owner of the selected container or workarea, the users who have access to this container or workarea, and the access rights granted to each user (or to PUBLIC).

To grant additional access rights for your container or workarea, select the Grant Access button on this window to bring up the Grant Access Rights window for the selected object.

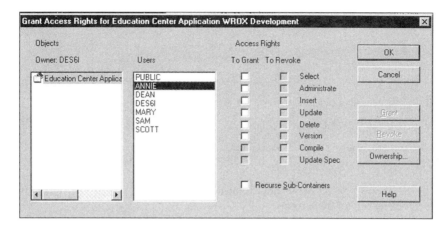

To grant a user access, select the user's name, select the access rights to be granted, and then click the Grant button.

> Remember that a user's access rights on a container are constrained by their access rights on the workarea in which that container is visible. A user may have access rights for a container, but if they do not have access rights to a workarea in which that container is visible, the user will not use able to use their access rights on the container.

The Case Study

Oracle's Designer 6i provides a powerful, comprehensive set of capabilities to support database design, development, and maintenance. Most enterprise application development projects currently use or should be using an automated design and development tool to:

❑   Manage the details of the database design process

❑   Generate diagrams of their conceptual data model and database design

❑   Automate the creation of Data Definition Language (DDL) scripts

❑   Manage changes to the database design and the physical database

Enterprise application development organizations using Oracle 8i should consider using Designer 6i to manage their database design and development. Designer 6i provides an extensive set of features to support the design, development, implementation, and evolution of Oracle 8i database objects across multiple physical schemas. The new file management, configuration management, and impact analysis features of the Oracle Repository provide additional capabilities for database management support.

This chapter presents an overview of Designer's capabilities for database design and development, and then provides a hands-on case study using Designer to design and build the Oracle 8i database for an Education Center Application. In Chapter 10 Designer will be used to design and generate a Web PL/SQL Application based upon this database.

Getting Started

To follow this case study, you should have:

❑ Access to a working copy of Designer 6i with an Oracle Repository

❑ An Oracle user account and a Designer 6i user account

❑ Full privileges on the Designer default workarea named GLOBAL SHARED WORKAREA

❑ Full privileges a new Designer Application System container called 'Education Center Application' included in the GLOBAL SHARED WORKAREA

Please see the beginning of this chapter for an introduction to Designer and the Oracle Repository, and information about setting up these items.

Overview

When first introduced to the database design capabilities of Designer, some developers are put off by the 'complexity' of Designer. To many new developers, database design and development involves **just** defining a few relational tables and creating SQL DDL scripts to create those tables. Why are all the features of Designer even required? Why do I need both entity-relationship diagrams and server model diagrams? If you are only building simple databases, perhaps you don't need Designer. Perhaps all you need is a diagramming tool like Visio.

Over the years, Oracle Corporation has developed and continually extended the database design and development capabilities in Designer to support large, enterprise application development shops with demanding database design and management requirements. In these organizations, database design often involves:

❑ Identifying, documenting, and refining new database requirements from multiple users in multiple organizations

❑ Determining how those database requirements relate to existing enterprise databases

❑ Designing numerous relational tables, integrity constraints, indexes, sequences, views, and object types to meet the new requirements

❑ Designing modifications and extensions to a variety of existing database objects

❑ Defining reference tables for code validation or lookup

❑ Designing and building server-side PL/SQL and Java database triggers, functions, and procedures for enforcing business rules and performing application functions

❑ Defining data access control procedures, database roles, and user privileges

❑ Designing and implementing auditing and journaling capabilities

❑ Defining database instances, tablespaces, and storage allocations for the multiple implementations of database objects required for the project's development, test, production, and maintenance phases

❑ Defining public and private synonyms for database objects

❑ Tracking, impacting, and controlling changes to any and all of the database objects as the project progresses to completion and into production and maintenance

❏   Managing operating system files containing DDL (data definition language), server-side code, data initialization scripts, and test data

❏   Documenting and communicating all aspects of the database design among the database designers, developers, testers, database administrators, information security officers, and other team members who need to be aware of the many details of the database design

The extensive capabilities of Designer 6i are a solution for enterprise development projects with complex database design, development, and management requirements. Not all projects or organizations will require all the database design and development capabilities of Designer, but a lot of organizations do. Designer is easily the most powerful automated tool in existence for supporting the design, development, and maintenance of large enterprise databases.

In the limited page count of this chapter, it is impossible to do justice to (or even mention) all the extensive database design capabilities of Designer. A high-level, summary view of those capabilities would have to mention the Entity Relationship Diagrammer, the Database Design Transformer, the integrated Design Editor environment, and the DDL generators.

This chapter follows a top-down approach to database design and development.

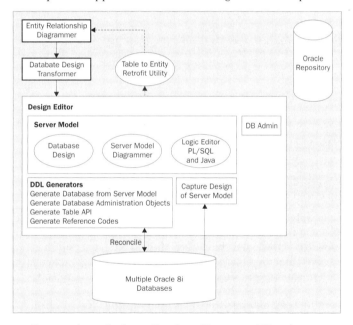

In this chapter, you will see and use the basic Database Design and Development components of Designer:

❏   The **Entity Relationship Diagrammer** – for developing a conceptual model of your data requirements

❏   The **Database Design Transformer** – to transform your Entity Relationship model into a preliminary database design

❏   The **Design Editor** – for refining your database design and generating DDL for your database objects.

The concepts presented in this chapter are fundamental to anyone new to Designer who wants to get started using Designer for database design and web application development.

Database Design and Development Process Using Designer

Fundamentally, database design is a top-down process:

❑   Develop an Entity Relationship Model

❑   Transform the Entity Relationship Model into a Preliminary Set of Tables

❑   Refine the Database Design and design other physical objects

❑   Generate the DDL and build the Database

However, practitioners will be quick to point out that database design is iterative and incremental. Requirements are discovered throughout the development cycle, and changes are being made at all phases of development. No matter how systematic an organization's development process, it is normal to build the database for an application, and then the next day or next week to re-build it.

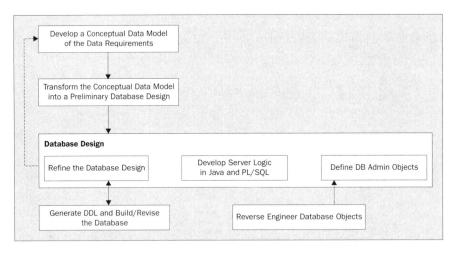

No automated tool can 'solve' all the challenges of evolving database designs and changing requirements, but you will find that Designer has numerous features to help with those changes. For example, since version 2.1 of Designer, the Server Model DDL generator has provided the capability to automatically check what database objects already exist in your target schema, and only generate the DDL scripts necessary to amend your existing database with the new objects.

If your organization is not keen on entity relationship modeling, you will likely discover that Designer's database design features are extremely useful for organizations only using the Design Editor, the DDL generators, and the Design Capture Features of Designer.

Develop a Conceptual Data Model of Requirements

If possible, a database development project should begin with a definition of the business requirements for the database and the development of a Conceptual Data Model of those data requirements. A Conceptual Data Model is a formal, detailed definition of a business's data requirements. There are a numerous techniques for developing a conceptual data model of a business's requirements including:

❑   Entity Relationship Modeling

❑   Object Modeling using the Unified Modeling Language (UML)

Oracle Designer and its predecessor products have traditionally supported entity relationship modeling using Richard Barker's diagramming conventions. In the mid-1990's, the Oracle Designer product development team began developing an object-oriented data modeling facility and demonstrated it to the Oracle user group community. With the advent of Oracle 8 and its object-oriented capabilities, Oracle's object modeling facility was offered as a package called Object Data Diagrammer (ODD). ODD was subsequently loosely bundled with Designer versions 2.1 and 6.0.

Like many object modeling tools, ODD did not fully support the eventual UML standard. As Oracle rushed to evolve its JDeveloper product into a competitive integrated development environment for Java enterprise components, it was not immediately clear if or how ODD could be integrated into JDeveloper. In late 1999, Oracle announced that a UML modeling capability would be included with JDeveloper, and efforts to develop a more complete UML modeling facility in Designer 6i were apparently dropped. When Designer 6i was released for production in June 2000, ODD was no longer included as part of the Designer package. Thus entity relationship modeling is the only conceptual modeling technique available in Designer 6i.

Case Study Data Requirements

The following high-level requirements have been identified for the Education Center database:

"The Education Center offers courses to students in the local community, and would like to provide a web site where currently enrolled students can browse the schedule of classes, and register on-line for a class. The initial database for this application prototype should include the following data:

❑ Course data – descriptive information about each course offered at the Education Center. For example, a course on "Introduction to Oracle" which runs for 3 days.

❑ Course Session data – each course session offered. For example, course sessions for the course "Introduction to Oracle" might be offered starting on June 9, July 15, and August 25.

❑ Student data – information about each student.

❑ Instructor data – information about each instructor.

❑ Registration data – a record of each student registered for a particular Course Session."

After several discussions with the management and users of the Education Center, our expert business analyst has developed the following entity relationship diagram (ERD) of the data requirements of the Education Center data:

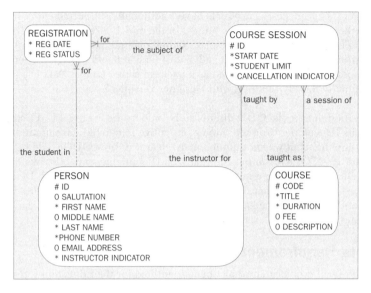

In this ERD, you will recognize the REGISTRATION, COURSE SESSION, and COURSE entities from the business requirements listed above. Our business analyst chose to model the requirements for Student and Instructor information with a single PERSON entity. This will allow an instructor to also be a student. An attribute, **Instructor Indicator**, was included in the PERSON entity to tag a Person who is an Instructor.

Oracle's Entity-Relationship Diagramming Conventions

Designer uses Oracle Corporation's ERD diagramming conventions which may vary slightly from the data modeling conventions you may have used with other CASE tools. Here is a brief summary of those conventions:

❑ An **entity** is a "thing of significance" about which information needs to be kept. A "soft box" is used to represent an entity. An entity name should always be singular.

❑ **Attributes** are significant details about an entity. They are shown in their entity's box. An attribute must describe the entity. Each attribute will be tagged with one of the following symbols:

\# an attribute in the entity's unique identifier and also mandatory

* a mandatory attribute

o an optional attribute

> **Unlike some modeling approaches, "foreign key columns" are not considered attributes, and are not shown in the related entity's box. For example, Course Code is not an attribute of COURSE SESSION.**

❑ A **relationship** is a significant association between two entities.
A "crow's foot" ⤙ signifies **one or more** (a.k.a. "many").
A plain line signifies **one and only one**.

❑ A relationship is **bi-directional** and can always be read in two directions:

❑ Each Course may be *taught as* one or more Course Sessions.

❑ Each Course Session must be *a session of* one and only one Course.

A solid line is used to represent **must be**, and a dashed line is used to represent **may be**. Note that the end of the relationship line next to COURSE SESSION is solid and the end of the relationship line next to COURSE is dashed.

❑ A **unique identifier** (UID) serves to distinctly identify a specific instance of an entity from all other instances of that entity. A unique identifier may be comprised of:

❑ An attribute

❑ A combination of attributes

❑ A combination of relationships

❑ A combination of attributes and relationships.

All attributes and relationships included in a UID must be mandatory. An attribute included in a UID is tagged with a "#" symbol. A relationship included in a UID is marked with a "UID bar" ⋝⊢.

It is Oracle's standard practice to always layout an ERD so that "Crows fly south and east" – the many end of the "crow's foot" should always point to either the left or the top. This results in placing the high volume entities in the top, left-hand corner of a diagram – the corner of importance. The low-volume, reference entities will end up in the bottom right corner.

Although not required for this case study, Oracle's ERD conventions supports additional data modeling constructs including recursive relationships, super-types and subtypes, and arcs. For more information on Oracle's entity relationship diagramming conventions, see:

❑ The Designer tool's Help Text topic "Entity Relationship Diagram elements and notation"

❑ *CASE*METHOD Entity Relationship Modeling*, by Richard Barker, ISBN: 0-201416-96-4

Develop the Education Center Entity-Relationship Model

To create the Education Center Entity Relationship Model in Designer, you will follow these steps:

❑ Log on to Designer

❑ Create a new Entity Relationship Diagram (ERD)

❑ Create the entities

❑ Create the relationships

❑ Add the attributes

❑ Define domains

❑ Link attributes to domains

❑ Define a unique identifier for each entity

❑ Print the ERD

❑ Print Entity and Attribute Definition Reports

❑ Review and quality check the ERD

Log on to Designer

The Designer 6i client installation process automatically loads a program group and icons into your workstation's Start Menu for the Designer 6i client.

You can log into Designer from the Start Menu. This brings up a screen to log you into the Oracle Server where the Oracle Repository resides. Access privileges on repository objects are assigned by Oracle database user account. If your Oracle Repository has versioning enabled, then multiple workareas can exist within your Repository. Each time you log into Designer you will be presented with the workarea window. This window shows all workareas that your Oracle user account has access rights to. Select the GLOBAL SHARED WORKAREA for the Education Center case study. (Or the workarea your repository manager told you to use.) Click OK.

After successfully logging into Designer and selecting a Default Workarea, the **Designer** window is displayed:

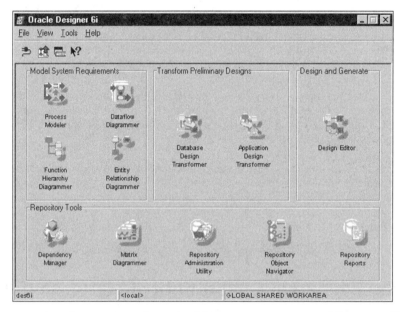

The **Designer** window shows an icon for each of the major components of Designer. These icons are grouped into four major categories:

❑ **Model System Requirements** – components for diagramming and modeling systems requirements.

❑ **Transform Preliminary Designs** – components for transforming a data model into a preliminary database design and for transforming system functions into preliminary module designs.

❑ **Design and Generate** – The Design Editor is an integrated environment for the many design and generation capabilities of Designer. This environment includes facilities for database design and DDL generation for Oracle and non-Oracle databases; module design for Forms, Reports, and Web PL/SQL applications; and reverse engineering of databases and modules into Designer.

❑ **Repository Tools** – components for managing and using data in the Oracle Repository. These repository tools will be used throughout a project's life cycle. Only the system administrator or configuration manager will use the Repository Administration Utility (RAU).

The status bar on the bottom of the **Designer** window reflects current connection information.

Create an Entity-Relationship Diagram

An Entity-Relationship Diagram is a view of a subset of the entities in the repository. In an Enterprise wide application, there are likely to be hundreds of entities defined in a Repository. Separate diagrams are created to reflect the entities that are relevant to a particular user group. A single entity can appear on multiple diagrams. The diagrams can also overlap. To use the Entity Relationship Diagrammer to create a new entity-relationship diagram:

1. From the **Designer** window, click the Entity Relationship Diagrammer icon. The Entity Relationship Diagrammer will come up with a blank, diagram window. The window's title bar will display your default Workarea name – such as GLOBAL SHARED WORKAREA. From the Entity Relationship Diagrammer's Menu, select File | New. This brings up a **Choose Container** window: choose the Education Center Application container that your system administrator set up for you.)

2. Click the list box icon to bring up a list of the containers you have accessed recently. If you are a new user of Designer, this list may be empty. If the list box does not contain the Education Center Application, then select the extended list icon ▤ to bring up the **Select Object** window:

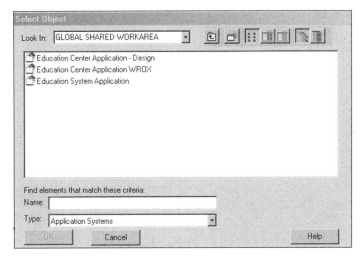

In this Select Object window, the Look In and Type contexts are extremely important when selecting an object. Whenever the objects you expect do not appear in the Select Object window, check these two fields to verify your context.

3. Select the Education Center Application and exit the **Choose Container** dialog. Now you will see a new, blank ERD canvas with a window title of ERD1 (Education Center Application). Now save this new diagram with a name of ERD – Education Center.

Now you are ready to create Entities in your new diagram.

Create the Entities

You will create four entities for the Education Center prototype:

❏ **PERSON**. Short name: 'PER'. Description: 'An instructor or a student of importance to the Education Center. Occasionally, an instructor may also be a student.'

❏ **COURSE**. Short name: 'COU'. Description: 'A specific course offered by the Education Center. For example, a course on "Introduction to Oracle". '

❏ **COURSE_SESSION**. Short name: 'CS'. Description: 'An offering of a specific course. For example, an offering of the course "Introduction to Oracle" beginning on a certain date.'

❏ **REGISTRATION**. Short name: 'REG'. Description: 'A single Person registered for a specific Course Session.'

First create a **PERSON** entity on our new Entity Relationship Diagram:

1. Click on the Entity Icon 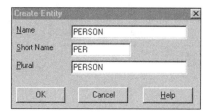 on the Entity Relationship Diagrammer's Toolbar, then click on the diagram's canvas to place a new Entity on that diagram. This will bring up the **Create Entity Dialog** box. Fill in the box as shown:

The entity's Short Name and the Plural properties will be automatically derived if you leave those fields blank. Both of those values will be important later:

❏ The entity's Short Name property will be used as the prefix for unique identifier names, constraint names, and module components based on the corresponding table. The default is the first letter of each word in the name of the entity, which in most cases is not what you want. Therefore it pays to think these names through prior to creating the entities.

❏ The Database Transformer will use the entity's Plural property as the default Table Name. If you prefer singular table names, then you will want to change all your Plural properties to singular! Designer will occasionally create a very awkward plural entity by automatically adding an 'S' to your entity name.

> **For this case study, please be sure to set the Short Name to the specified value and to make the Plural property singular to match the screenshots and instructions for this case study.**

2. Click the OK button to complete the creation of this entity. The PERSON entity will now appear on the diagram.

3. Next you will add a description to the PERSON entity. Double click on the PERSON entity box, and the **Edit Entity** window will appear. Click on the Text tab of this **Edit Entity** window to bring up a text box for the Description of this PERSON entity.

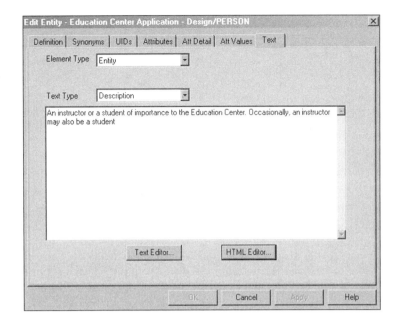

4. Enter the entity description supplied above in the requirements section as shown. The drop-down list on Text Type can be used to enter other text properties Click the OK button to save this description and exit this window. Repeat these same steps to create the other three Entities. Be sure to:

❑ Type the Entity Name and Short Name exactly as presented above.

❑ Make the Entity Plural Names **singular** – these will translate to table names. Later sections of this case study assume that you followed these conventions. Now Save your ERD Diagram.

Here are some tips for handling situations that you may encounter when creating entities:

❑ An entity name must be unique within your application. If you try to create a new entity, but an entity already exists with the same name or short name, you will receive an error window describing a Uniqueness violation and you will not be able to create the new entity.

❑ If you receive this error message, you should first check the open diagram and determine if this entity already appears on the diagram, but is just not visible in your current window's view. Try zooming out to view your entire diagram.

❑ If the existing entity is not shown on your diagram, then it must exist in the Repository so you will need to **include** this entity onto your diagram if it represents the same business concept. From the Entity Relationship Diagrammer's menu, select Edit | Include | Entity. This will bring up an **Include Entity** window that lists entities defined in the Repository which could be included on your diagram.

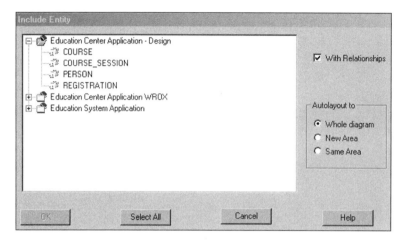

Select any entities not on your diagram. Select the **With Relationships** check box in the top right corner of this window to also include any relationships associated with the selected entities. Click the **OK** button to include the selected entities and associated relationships on your diagram.

There are three ways to remove an entity from an entity relationship diagram:

❑ Select and cut the entity – This will remove the entity from the diagram, but leave it in the Repository.

❑ Select the entity and from the menu select **Edit | Delete from Repository** – This will remove the entity from the diagram and also from the repository. The *Delete* key performs the same function.

Create the Relationships

The next step is to create the relationships between the entities. You will first create the relationship between COURSE and COURSE SESSION. Refer to the section above for Oracle's entity relationship diagramming conventions.

When you are finished, your relationship should look like this:

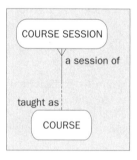

To add this relationship to your diagram:

1. Click on the M:1 Relationship icon ➤·· to select a mandatory to optional (M:1) relationship. Click inside the COURSE SESSION entity to anchor the Many end of the relationship. Then click inside the COURSE entity to anchor the One end of the relationship.

2. A **Create Relationship** box will appear for entry of the relationship names. 'From' is the first entity clicked on, regardless of the cardinality. Make sure that the first entity box that you click on agrees in cardinality with the iconic button you selected.

3. Enter the relationship names (From Name: "a session of" and To Name: "taught as") and then click OK. Now examine the relationship line on the diagram and validate that it appears as you expected.

4. Now repeat these same steps to enter the other relationships, following the entity diagram above:

Editing Relationship Lines

Diagramming relationships can be tricky, and initially you may make mistakes. Here are some tips for correcting some of the situations that you may get into:

❑ To delete a relationship completely from the Repository, you select it, and then use the delete key or Edit | Delete from the menu. Cutting a repository does not delete it. It only removes it from your diagram.

❑ Edit a relationship's definition by double-clicking on the relationship to bring up the **Edit Relationship** window. In this window, you can edit the names on the relationship and change the optionality or degree on either end:

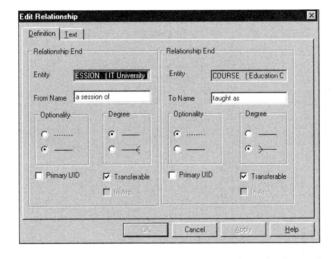

Use the Autolayout Tool to adjust the layout of one or more selected relationships:

1. Select the line or lines to be straightened either by:

❑ Manually clicking on one relationship, and *CTRL*-clicking on any additional relationships, OR

❑ Select one relationship line by clicking, and then on the Menu select Edit | Select Same Type to select all the rest of the relationship lines.

2. Click the Autolayout icon or select Layout | Autolayout from the menu.

The Autolayout Tool can be used to autolayout all the entities and relationships on your diagram, or it can be used to just autolayout a few selected relationships. **As a rule never run autolayout on your entire diagram – it will totally scramble your diagram!**

Get into the habit of Saving your ERD diagram regularly – after any significant changes. The Entity Relationship Diagrammer is known for crashing on crowded, complex diagrams. When it does crash, you will loose all layout work since the last save. If the Entity Relationship Diagrammer does crash, and you have not saved your work recently, any entities or relationships that you created will still be available in the Repository, but your diagram will not display them. To bring your diagram up to date with the Repository:

❑ From the menubar, select Edit | Requery | All. This will make all the elements displayed in the diagram consistent with the definitions stored in the Repository.

❑ If a relationship or entity still does not appear on the diagram but is defined in the Repository, you will need to **Include** it on your diagram (see the Include instructions in the *Create the Entities* section above).

In a multi-user repository, a diagram element may get out of date with what is stored in the Repository. For example, another user might update an entity, but not update your diagram. If Designer detects that an element on your diagram is out-of-date, a **red dot** may be displayed by that element in your diagram. To bring the elements on your diagram up to date with the definitions in the Repository, select Edit | Requery | All.

Add the Attributes

The next step is to add attributes to your entities. The systems analyst has determined that the following attributes are required for the COURSE entity:

Attribute Name	Seq	OPT ?	Data Type (Max Length, Num of Decimals)	Comments
CODE	10	no	VARCHAR2(8)	A code uniquely identifying a course
TITLE	20	no	VARCHAR2(50)	The title of a course
DURATION	30	no	NUMBER(30)	Number of days in a typical course session
FEE	40	no	NUMBER(8,2)	Standard fee for the course
DESCRIPTION	50	yes	VARCHAR2(1000)	A description of the course

To add these attributes to the COURSE entity:

1. Double-click on the COURSE entity in your ERD to bring up the **Edit Entity** window that you used previously. Select the Attributes tab of the **Edit Entity** window. This tab shows a list of all the attributes defined for this entity. Enter the attributes as shown in the table above. Type "CODE" in the Name column.

❑ **Seq** (sequence) column – This number will be used to sequence attributes within an entity on the Entity Relationship Diagram. To facilitate adding attributes or re-ordering attributes later, sequence your attributes by 10's or leave gaps between the Seq numbers.

❑ **Opt** (optional) box – shows a check mark for an optional attribute. To make this CODE attribute mandatory clear the checkbox.

❏ **Format** property – defines the column format.

❏ **MaxLen** property – This is the maximum length for this attribute. Leave the Dec (decimal point) property blank. A VARCHAR2 attribute has no decimal points.

❏ **COMMENT** – Enter comments for your attributes, and they will be copied to the resulting column definition.

2. Repeat step 1 to add the remaining attributes for the COURSE entity. Validate that the attribute names required are displayed on the COURSE entity in the diagram. Repeat the same steps to enter the attributes required for the PERSON, COURSE SESSION, and REGISTRATION entities.

PERSON Entity

Attribute Name	Seq	Opt ?	Data Type (Max Length, Dec)	Comments
ID	10	no	NUMBER(6)	A identifier assigned to uniquely identify a person
SALUTATION	20	yes	VARCHAR2(6)	A salutation for a person: Mr., Ms., Mrs., Dr.
FIRST NAME	30	no	VARCHAR2(60)	A person's first name
MIDDLE NAME	40	yes	VARCHAR2(40)	A person's middle name or middle initial
LAST NAME	50	no	VARCHAR2(60)	A person's last name
PHONE NUMBER	60	no	VARCHAR2(20)	Phone number where the person can be contacted
EMAIL ADDRESS	70	yes	VARCHAR2(50)	The person's e-mail address
INSTRUCTOR INDICATOR	80	no	VARCHAR2(1)	A flag indicating this PERSON is a certified Instructor for the Education Center. 'Y' means Yes. 'N' means No

COURSE_SESSION Entity

Attribute Name	Seq	Opt ?	Data Type (Max Length, Dec)	Comments
ID	10	no	NUMBER(6)	A identifier assigned to uniquely identify a Course Session
START DATE	20	no	DATE	The date a course session starts
STUDENT LIMIT	30	no	NUMBER(2)	The maximum number of students who can enroll in this class session
CANCELLATION INDICATOR	40	no	VARCHAR2(1)	A flag indicating this COURSE SESSION has been cancelled. 'Y' means Yes. 'N' means No.

REGISTRATION Entity

Attribute Name	Seq	Opt ?	Data Type (Max Length, Dec)	Comments
REG DATE	10	no	DATE	Date and time the registration was created
REG STATUS	20	no	VARCHAR2 (1)	Status of the registration: A – Active, D – Dropped, W – Wait-Listed

Create Domains

A domain is a set of format properties and allowable values. Often several attributes and columns will share the same domain. A domain allows those format properties and allowable values to be defined once, and then to be assigned to each attribute and column. If a change or addition needs to be made to a domain, that change can be made to the domain and then be automatically propagated to the attributes and columns which use that domain.

Use a domain to:

❑ Ensure that the properties and values are consistently defined across attributes and columns

❑ Define allowable values for an attribute

From the Entity Relationship Diagrammer, create a REG STATUS domain:

1. From the menu, select Edit I Domains. This brings up the **Domains** window listing all the domains currently defined in this Application System. Type REG STATUS for the Name property in the **Name** column. This will be the REG STATUS domain. Click on the Detail tab. Enter the data format properties for attributes and columns assigned to this domain as shown below.

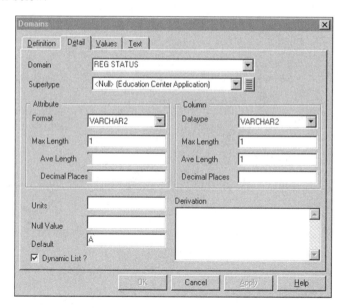

2. Click on the Values Tab. Add the domain values shown below. Note that domain values are case sensitive. If both the upper and lower case values are valid, then both values must be included in the values list. Click the Apply button to save these domain values and leave the **Domains** window open.

REG STATUS Domain Values

Sequence	Value	Abbreviation	Meaning
5	A	A	Active
10	D	D	Dropped
15	W	W	Wait-Listed

3. Now create a YESNO domain. On the Definition tab, enter:

    a. Name: YESNO

    b. Comment: A domain for Indicator Columns.

4. Click the Detail tab and set the format properties as shown below:

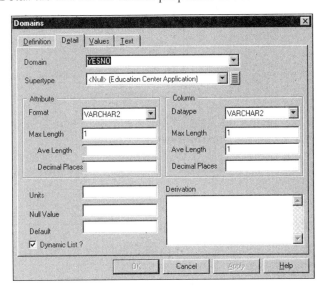

5. Click the Values tab and add the two YESNO domain values:

Sequence	Value	Abbreviation	Meaning
10	Y	Y	Yes
20	N	N	No

Assign a Domain to an Attribute

A domain may be attached to one or more attributes or columns. When a domain is assigned to an attribute or column, all of the domain's properties and allowed values are automatically assigned to that attribute.

Now attach the REG STATUS domain to the REG STATUS attribute of the REGISTRATION entity:

1. Double-click on the REGISTRATION entity in the diagram. The **Edit Entity** dialog box will appear. Select the Att Detail tab. In the Name field, select the REG STATUS attribute. Be sure to select the correct attribute, or the domain's characteristics will be assigned to the wrong attribute!

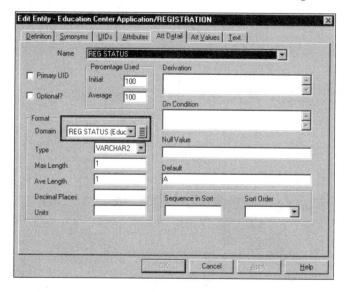

2. In the Domain field select the REG STATUS domain. Validate again that you are assigning the correct domain to the correct attribute.

3. Repeat steps 1 and 2 to attach the YESNO domain to the following attributes:

Entity	Attribute
PERSON	INSTRUCTOR INDICATOR
COURSE SESSION	CANCELLATION INDICATOR

Propagate Domain Properties to Attributes and Columns

When a domain is assigned to an attribute or to a column, that attribute or column's properties are automatically re-set to the properties of the domain. If a domain's properties are later revised, the properties of the associated attributes and columns are not automatically revised to match the new properties of the domain.

To explicitly update attributes with revised domain values:

- ❑ From the Entity Relationship Diagrammer's menu, select Utilities | Update Attributes in Domains. This brings up the **Update All Attributes within Domains** window.
- ❑ Select specific domains to update or use the Select All button to select all domains within the workarea. Then click the OK button to update the attribute definitions.

Use the Design Editor to explicitly update columns with revised domain values:

- ❑ On the Design Editor's navigator, select the domain to be propagated.
- ❑ From the menu, select Utilities | Update Columns/Attributes in a Domain. To proceed with the update, click the OK button on the dialog window.

Define a Unique Identifier for each Entity

A unique identifier (UID) allows each instance of an entity to be distinctly identified from all other instances of that entity. A unique identifier may be an attribute, a combination of attributes, a combination of relationships, or a combination of attributes and relationships. Only mandatory attributes or relationships should be included in a UID.

> **Be sure all entities have a unique identifier defined before you finish the data modeling step.**

The unique identifier for an entity will be mapped to the primary key of the resultant table. Per Oracle's ERD conventions, "foreign key columns" are *not* shown on an ERD, but are instead represented entirely by a relationship line. In the resultant table, foreign key columns will be included in the table at the many end of the relationship. If a Unique Identifier includes a relationship, then the resultant primary key will include the foreign key columns.

The systems analyst has defined the following unique identifiers for the Education Center's entities:

Entity	UID Name	Primary	Components
COURSE	COU_PK	yes	Attribute: code
PERSON	PER_PK	yes	Attribute: ID
REGISTRATION	REG_PK	yes	Relationship: for PERSON
			Relationship: for COURSE SESSION
COURSE_SESSION	CS_PK	yes	Attribute: ID

To create the unique identifier for the COURSE entity:

1. In the Entity Relationship Diagrammer, double-click on the COURSE entity. The **Edit Entity** dialog box will appear. Select the UID tab to display the Unique Identifier window. The first section will list the UIDs defined for this entity. (A UID will automatically be created for an entity if the **"Primary" attribute property** is checked in the Attributes tab section of the Edit Entity dialog box. The default naming convention is the Short Name of the Entity. If the name of an entity changes after it is created initially, validate that the short name is still sensible. If it must change as well, also change any existing unique identifiers.)

2. To add a UID for this entity enter a UID Name in the first empty row. For the COURSE entity, enter a name of "COU_PK". Check the Primary? Property to specify that this is the **primary unique identifier** for COURSE. The primary UID will be transformed into a primary key of the table. Occasionally, an entity may have both a primary UID and also a secondary UID. A secondary UID will be transformed into a unique key for the table.

3. Next select the Unique Identifier Contents from the lists of Candidate Attributes and Candidate Relationships in the middle of the window. In the Candidate Attributes section, highlight any attributes to be included in this UID. For the COURSE entity, highlight the attribute CODE. Click the Down Arrow to include the highlighted attributes into the UID. In the Candidate Relationships section, highlight any relationships to be included in this UID. For the COURSE entity, no relationships will be highlighted. Relationships will be included in the UID for the REGISTRATION entity. Click the Down Arrow to include the highlighted relationships into the UID.

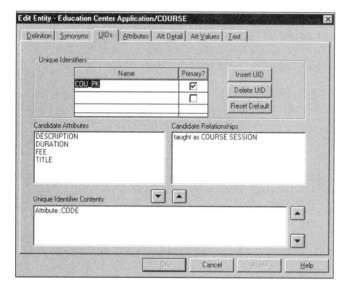

4. Remove any unwanted attributes or relationships from the UID by highlighting them in the Unique Identifier Contents field, and clicking on the Up Arrow. Adjust the desired order of the UID components using the Up arrow and Down arrow on the right side of the Unique Identifier Contents box. Click the OK button to create the UID as defined. Validate that the UID is displayed correctly on the diagram:

❑ A # sign indicates that an attribute is contained in the primary UID.

❑ A "UID bar" indicates that the relationship is part of the primary UID.

5. Repeat the steps above to add Unique Identifiers for the other Entities in the Education Center as per the table above. Relationships will be included in the UID for the REGISTRATION entity only. Click the Down Arrow to include the highlighted relationships into the UID.

Print Entity and Attribute Reports

Repository Reports can be printed to review the details of the data model, and to perform quality assurance on the data model before proceeding to the Transformation stage. To print reports showing the details of your ERD:

1. From the **Designer** window, click the Repository Reports icon. This brings up the Repository Reports tool. Its window title shows your default workarea – the GLOBAL SHARED WORKAREA.

2. Expand the Entity/Relationship Modeling node. Select the Entities and their Attributes Report. This brings up a Report Parameters Palette on the right side of the **Repository Reports** window. In the Parameters Palette, select:

- ❑ Destination Type: 'Printer'.

- ❑ Destination Name: your printer's name (may be detected automatically).

- ❑ Container Name: Education Center Application.

- ❑ Entity Name field: % to select all entities (default).

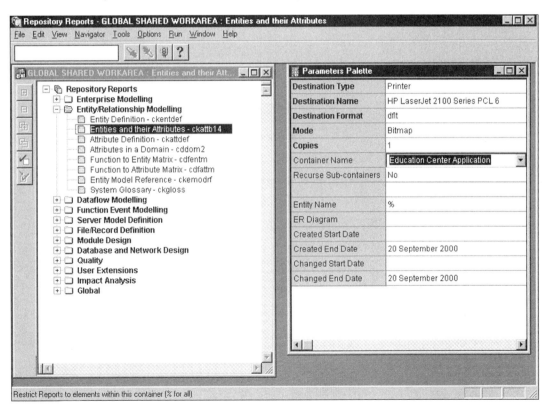

3. Now click on the Run Report icon on the toolbar to run this Report and send it to your printer.

Review the ERD's Quality

You should always review and check the quality of your entity relationship data model before you transform it to a preliminary database design. Here are some basic quality checks that you should routinely perform:

❏ **ERD Scope Checks**

Does your ERD contain all the entities and attributes required for your application?

Are there any entities or attributes that will not be used at all by your application?

❏ **Entity Definition Checks**

Does each entity have a definition?

Review the entity Short Name and Plural.

❏ **Relationships**

Do the relationship patterns look normal?

The first two relationships below are quite common.

The third relationship is usually a modeler's error, but not always.

The Rare relationship occurs quite rarely in business requirements.

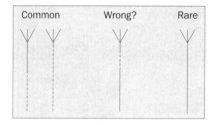

Are the relationships "readable" in both directions?

Do the relationship names fit within the convention of: **may be** 'name' and **must be** 'name'?

❏ **Attributes**

Does each attribute 'describe' or 'belong to' its entity?

Are all 'foreign key' attributes deleted? Here are two examples where the foreign key attributes appear and are redundant with the relationships. Each will result in duplicate columns in the tables!

Right:

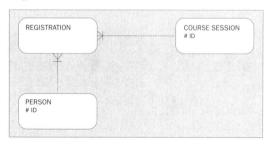

Wrong:

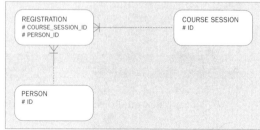

Right:

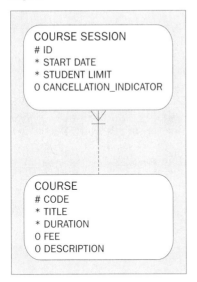

Wrong:

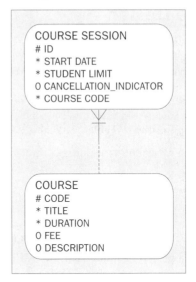

Are the attribute names descriptive?

Does the same attribute appear in more than one entity? If so make sure the descriptions clearly delineate the differences.

Is the entity name excluded from the attribute name?

Are the attributes decomposed? Avoid embedded or compound attributes.

Are all "repeating groups" removed from each entity and placed in a separate entity?

❏   **Unique Identifiers**

Does each entity have a unique identifier defined?

Are the components of the UID mandatory? It is unfortunately possible to create a unique ID in Designer that does not have mandatory attributes!

Do the UID names reflect the entity Short Name?

Would an artificial key be a more appropriate UID?

Revise your ERD to correct any quality errors that you discover in this quality review.

Transform the Conceptual Data Model into a Preliminary Database Design

Once your ERD is complete, you are ready to transform your data model into a preliminary database design using Designer's **Database Design Transformer**. This database design will consist of preliminary table definitions within Designer. Designer refers to a database design as a **Server Model**.

The Database Design Transformer will perform the following transformations on a selected set of entities:

❑ **Map Entities to Tables**. The table name will be taken from the entity's 'Plural Name' property.

❑ **Map Attributes to Columns** - with any domain associations.

❑ **Map Relationships** to:

    ❑ Foreign key columns at the many end

    ❑ Foreign key constraints

    ❑ Indexes on the foreign key columns

❑ **Map primary Unique Identifiers** to Primary Keys.

❑ **Map secondary unique identifiers** to unique keys.

During this process, the Transformer will also create implementation usage to link the source entities to the resultant tables.

> If you did not resolve a many-to-many relationship in your Data Model, the Database Design Transformer will automatically create an additional intersection table to resolve that relationship for you. Designer will arbitrarily name the intersection table. Resolving all your many-to-many relationship prior to Transformation is the recommended approach.

To run the Database Design Transformation, you will follow these steps:

❑ Select the Run Set for transformation.

❑ Select the Settings for transformation.

❑ Run the Database Design Transformer.

Select the Run Set for Transformation

The database transformation **run set** is the set of entities to be transformed by this "run" (single execution) of the Transformer. To begin the transformation process and define the run set:

1. From the **Designer** window, click the Database Design Transformer icon. This brings up an **Application System** window. Select Education Center Application and click OK. Wait while the Database Design Transformer initializes.

When invoked from the **Designer** window, the Database Design Transformer selects all the entities in the Application for the default run set. If you have a large application with many entities, this initialization process will take a lot of time. If you only want to include a small number of those entities in your Run Set, you can save time by invoking the Database Design Transformer from the Repository Object Navigator. First select the entities that you want to transform on the navigator's window, and then invoke the Database Design Transformer from the menu by selecting Utilities | Designer | Database Design Transformer.

2. When initialization is complete, the **Database Designer Transformer** window will appear with the Mode tab active. The Database Design Transformer comes up ready to run in Default Mode. In default mode, the Run Set consists of all the entities in this Application System which have not previously been mapped to tables. In the lower right hand corner of this screen, you will see that the four entities of the Education Center Application have been included in this default run set. None of these entities have been mapped to tables before.

3. Click on the Show Run Set button to view a cryptic list of all these entities, and their attributes, relationships, and unique identifiers, which have been selected by default to be included in this run set.

4. On the **Database Design Transformer** window, click on the option to Customize the Database Design Transformer. At the top of the window, three additional tabs will appear. This option allows you to select the entities to include in a run set rather than using the default run set selected by the Transformer. It also allows you to customize the behavior of the Transformer.

5. Click on the Table Mappings tab to view a list of the entities in your application:

	Database Design Transformer GLOBAL SHARED WORKAREA (Education Center Application)			
	Mode Table Mappings Other Mappings Run Options			

In Set	Entity	Map Type	Arc	Table
☑	PERSON	Mapped	■	PERSON
☑	COURSE SESSION	Mapped	☐	COURSE_SESSION
☑	COURSE	Mapped	☐	COURSE
☑	REGISTRATION	Mapped	☐	REGISTRATION

Run   Commit   Show Run Set   Settings   Cancel   Help

The In Set column displays those entities which have been selected for inclusion in the Run Set. You would click the checkbox to remove or add an entity.

6. Click on the Run Options tab to bring up the Run Options for the Transformer.

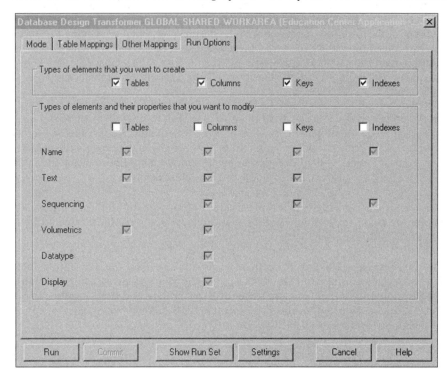

Note that only the top section, **Types of elements that you want to create**, has check marks in it. By default, the Transformer will not re-map entities which have already been mapped. This is the mode that you want to use for our case study. For later projects, you may need to select the modify options to propagate changes made to an entity relationship model in a database design.

7. Click on the Mode tab to return to the main **Database Design Transformer** window.

Select the Settings for Transformation

Designer provides numerous options for mapping the entities in a Run Set into database design elements. The **Transformation Settings** define which options will be used.

To select the transformation settings for your ERD:

1. From the main **Database Design Transformer** window (or from any of its tabs), click on the Settings button. This brings up a tabbed group of **Settings** windows:

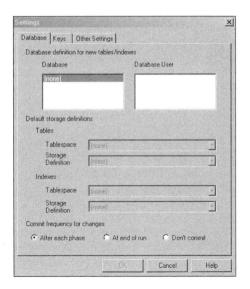

The first **Settings** window tab, the Database tab, provides options for defining **Implementations** for each new table and index definition created by the transformation process.

Implementations are defined in the Database Administration tab of the Design Editor, and are used to create more complete DDL definitions for a physical database. An Implementation is defined within the context of a Designer Database Definition and a User Definition. Tablespace definitions and storage definitions may be assigned to a Table Implementation or an Index Definition.

2. Accept the default null values for these settings. You do not need to create Implementations for the Education Center database design. You will create DDL without these implementations for your initial database.

3. Click on the Keys tab to bring up Settings for primary keys and foreign keys.

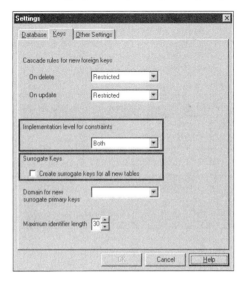

4. Accept the default Restricted for the first two settings. These settings define the referential integrity rules to be applied to the new foreign key definitions if a row in a related table is deleted or updated.

5. Set the Implementation level for constraints to Both. This setting will direct Designer to generate DDL and code to validate the constraint both on the server and in any Web PL/SQL modules or Forms modules generated using these tables.

> **If you are using Designer for application design and generation, your foreign key constraint validation must be set to Both or Client. Designer cannot use server-only foreign key constraints in its module designs.**

6. Make sure the option to create surrogate keys for all new tables is de-selected. In the Education Center ERD, you defined unique identifiers for all your entities, and you want those UIDs to be used as the primary keys of your tables. Note that some database administrators insist that surrogate, artificial keys be created for all tables, in which case you would select this option.

7. Click on the Other Settings tab. This brings up additional transformation settings. Verify that the first box is selected. You do want the transformer to generate prefixes for Foreign key columns. This will prefix any foreign key columns with the Table Alias of the primary key column. For example, a foreign key to the ID column of the PERSON table will be named: PER_ID. The Table Alias is derived from the Entity Short Name.

8. Verify that the other options are **not** selected, and click OK to accept these changes. If no changes had been made, the OK button would not be active, and you would just Cancel the dialog.

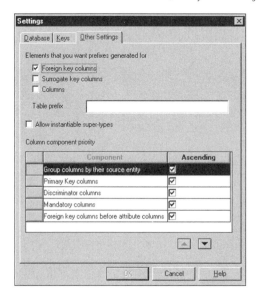

In the next step, the Run button will automatically save any altered Database Transformer Settings, and then runs the Transformer. To only save the revised settings and not run the transformer, click the Commit button.

Execute the Database Design Transformer

Now that you have selected the Run Set and the Settings for the Database Design Transformer, you are ready to run the Transformer and create definitions in the Repository for tables, columns, primary keys, foreign keys, and indexes.

To start the transformer:

1. Click the Run button on the **Database Design Transformer** window. The actions of the transformer will be displayed in the **Database Design Transformer Output** window as the transformation progresses.

2. When the transformer has completed, it will display a message Waiting for Close to be pressed. Use the vertical scroll bar to review the output messages. Click the Close button to return to the Database Transformer main window.

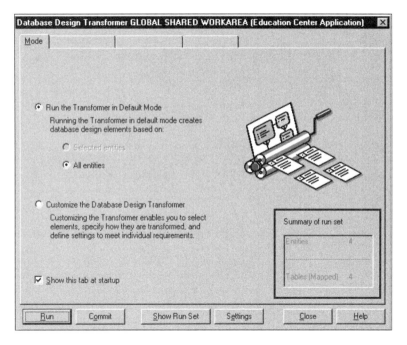

3. The Summary of run set box has been updated to reflect that the Education Center prototype's four entities have been mapped to four tables. Click the Table Mappings tab to view the table mappings created by the Database Design Transformer. Click the Other Mappings tab to view mapping details. The window initially comes up with a display of the attribute to column mapping for the COURSE entity.

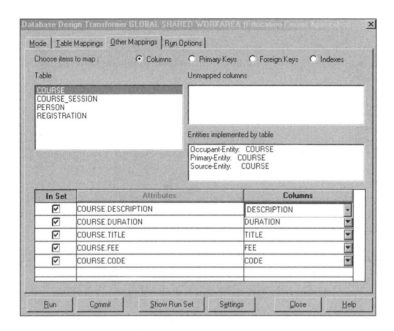

To view additional mappings for the COURSE entity, click the other radio buttons at the top of this window: **Primary Keys, Foreign Keys,** and **Indexes.**

4. Click on the table **COURSE_SESSION,** and view the mappings for that entity. Notice that two foreign key columns were created for the COURSE_SESSION table from the relationships: COU_CODE and PER_ID. Click on the **Foreign Key** radio button to see the foreign key constraints defined from those relationships.

5. Next view the mappings for the PERSON and REGISTRATION entities. After viewing these mappings, click the **Close** button to dismiss the Database Design Transformer.

While reviewing the mappings of the Database Design Transformer, you may discover that you have made an error in either your Entity Relationship Model, your Run Set, or your Transformer Settings, and that you would like to correct that mistake, and re-run the Database Design Transformer. The cleanest and safest approach to rerunning the Database Design Transformer is to first delete the table definitions completely using the Design Editor. See the later section *'Deleting a Preliminary Database Design'* for instructions on using the Design Editor to delete table definitions.

Refine the Database Design

Now that you have a preliminary database design, you are ready to refine it and complete it in preparation for generating your DDL. You will use the Design Editor to view and refine your database design. In this section, you will:

❑ Get an Introduction to the Design Editor

❑ Create a Server Model Diagram of the preliminary database design

❑ Review the preliminary database design

❑ If necessary, delete the preliminary table definitions and repeat the database transformation process

❑ Review and revise each table's column order

❑ Define database sequences for ID columns

❑ Add change history columns

❑ Review column properties

❑ Review and refine database constraints and indexes

❑ Print a revised server model diagram

❑ Print Table Definition Reports

Introducing the Design Editor

The **Design Editor** is the primary Designer component for design and generation tasks. It provides an integrated environment for:

❑ Database design

❑ Module design for Forms, Reports, and Web PL/SQL applications

❑ Developing server logic in PL/SQL and Java

❑ Defining Database administration objects

❑ DDL generation

❑ Reverse engineering database objects into Designer

To invoke the Design Editor:

1. From the **Designer** window, click the Design Editor icon. This brings up the Design Editor and a **Welcome to the Design Editor** window. Select the Server Model radio button. De-select the Use a Guide option. You will not use the guide dialog this time. Click the OK button. This brings up the **Design Editor** window.

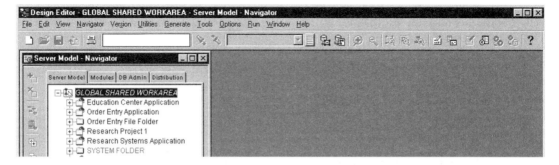

Note the workarea name in the window's title bar. The Design Editor operates within the context of a single workarea. On the left side you will see the Design Editor's Navigator and on the right side a workspace for creating and manipulating diagrams. Property palettes, property dialog windows, and wizards may be also displayed on the right side.

Design Editor Navigator

The Designer Editor Navigator has four tabs, that is, four different views of design elements. The Server Model tab displays the database objects and server-side PL/SQL and Java modules in the Repository. To view the newly created table definitions:

1. Verify that the Server Model tab is selected. The Design Editor Navigator displays a hierarchical view of the design objects of the current Workarea. Application Systems and Folders are at the top level of this hierarchy. A list of the Applications and Folders in your current Workarea is shown in the Navigator. Expand the Education Center Application node and display the categories of server model objects. Expand the Relational Table Definitions node to display the tables defined for the Education Center Application.

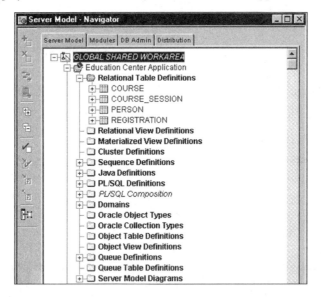

> **Please note that these "tables" exist as definitions only in the Repository at this point. They will not exist physically in an Oracle database until you generate the DDL to create them and then run that DDL via SQL*Plus to actually create them in the database.**

2. Expand the COURSE table's node to view the table's columns and key constraints.

Property Palette and Property Dialog Box

Each Designer element type has a standard set of properties. The Design Editor provides two different detailed views of any object:

❑ A **Property Palette** lists all the properties for the currently selected object. Using a property palette to define and edit design objects requires that a user have more knowledge of how the properties are used and how they interrelate.

❑ A **Property Dialog Box** displays the commonly used set of properties for the selected object and may also show the properties of any dependent or secondary objects. A Property Dialog box is easier to use, since its Wizard-like interface guides you through the properties.

Double-clicking an object in the Design Editor, clicking on the toolbar's Properties icon, or using the right mouse button and selecting Properties will bring up either a property palette or a property dialog box – depending upon the current setting of the Design Editor. On the toolbar, the Dialog/Palette button displays the current properties mode and also functions as a toggle switch between the two modes. Another way to view or to change between the two displays is to select Options from the menubar and look at its submenu items:

❑   Use Property Dialogs

❑   Use Property Palette

A dot indicates the current properties mode. The *F4* key will always bring up a property palette window within the Design Editor. You can use a combination of the property displays and a server model diagram to review and enhance your preliminary database design.

Create a Server Model Diagram

A server model diagram is a graphical representation of the table definitions in the Designer repository. A server model is the "design level" equivalent of an entity-relationship diagram. An entity-relationship diagram generally contains the business data requirements, and the server model contains implementation-specific and physical characteristics of the database. The server model generally matches the physical database. A server model may contain artificial keys, additional database foreign key constraints, denormalized tables, views, and other 'non-business' requirements.

To create a server diagram model of the Education Center's database design:

1.   From the Design Editor's menu, select File | New | Server Model Diagram. A blank diagram window will appear in the right-hand side of your Design Editor's window.

An alternative method for creating a new Server Model Diagram is to select a table from the Navigator, and drag it to the blank workspace to the right of the navigator. A new Server Model Diagram will appear and the selected table will be displayed on that diagram.

2.   Select the COURSE table definition from the Design Editor Navigator and drag it to the diagram. A COURSE table box will appear on the diagram. Select the other three table definitions and drag them to the diagram canvas.

You can also include tables, foreign key constraints, or views in a Server Model Diagram by selecting the menu option Edit | Include and selecting the objects to be included from the **Include Tables/Views/Foreign Keys** window.

3.   Use your mouse to adjust the layout of your diagram. The Server Model Diagrammer is similar to the Entity Relationship Diagram. Here are some tips for refining your diagram's layout:

❑   Page boundaries will appear as dashed lines on the diagram canvas. To change the orientation of the diagram from portrait to landscape, select File | Print Setup from the menu.

❑   From the menu, select Layout | Minimize Number of Pages to have the diagrammer automatically minimize the number of pages used by the diagram.

4.   Review your Server Model Diagram, and note that the optional relationships in your ERD were mapped to optional foreign key columns and optional foreign key constraints represented by dashed lines. You can view all keys and indexes by clicking on the icons below the table name in the box on the Server Model Diagram. Save the Server Model diagram as EDUCATION CENTER SERVER MODEL.

Review the Preliminary Database Design

The Database Design Transformer automatically created your table definitions for you. It is a good idea to check the definitions that were generated, and verify that the preliminary database design is what you wanted: Compare your Server Model diagram to your ERD, and identify any discrepancies. Identify new columns in your tables that do not map to attributes in your ERD:

❏   Do you know where they came from, and why they were generated?

❏   Do the names of the new foreign key columns have a **table prefix** (the related table's alias)?

❏   Check the optionality of the new foreign key columns. Are they optional where you expected them to be, and mandatory where you expected them to be?

❏   Check the primary key columns for each of your tables. Are they what you expected them to be? Or did the Database Design Transformer create surrogate keys when you did not want them?

Deleting a Preliminary Database Design

While reviewing your Preliminary Database Design, you may discover that you made an error in either your Entity Relationship Model or in running the Database Design Transformer, and that you would like to correct that mistake and re-run the Database Design Transformer.

It is possible to use the Database Design Transformer to modify an existing preliminary database design; however, re-running the Database Design Transformer will not completely replace any existing table definitions. Therefore, especially since you have not made any changes to the server Model since the Transformer created it, the best approach is to completely delete the preliminary table definitions, and then to re-run the Database Design Transformer. (Deleting table definitions later in the database development life-cycle or after modules have been defined against table definitions is **not recommended**, and will result in the loss of substantial design work.)

To delete the table definitions created in a preliminary database design:

1.   In the Design Editor Navigator, select the tables to be deleted. From the left-hand toolbar, click the Delete icon. This will bring up a **Delete from Repository** window:

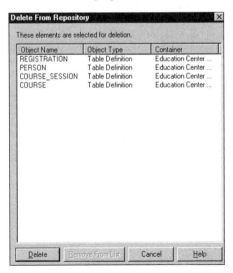

2. Review the list, and if it contains the tables that you want to delete, click the Delete button. Designer will try to delete the tables in the order in which they are listed in the Delete from Repository window. If you have foreign key constraints between these objects, the delete process may attempt to delete an table that has a foreign key constraint defined on it. In this case you will get an Internal API error window reporting that the table cannot be deleted due to an existing Foreign Key.

3. After reviewing the error messages, click OK, and the deletion process will continue deleting all the tables that it can. When the deletion process is complete, a Delete from Repository window will appear listing elements not deleted during this first pass. Click the Delete button to re-run the delete process and delete the remaining tables.

4. Check the Design Editor Navigator to verify that the table definitions were indeed deleted. You may need to re-query the Navigator using Edit | Requery All. Once the table definitions are deleted, you are clear to re-run the Database Design Transformer.

Designer includes a **Force Delete utility** that will delete an element regardless of its usage by other repository elements. For example, it will delete a table even if it has foreign key references and module usages. The Force Delete utility requires the Repository User Privilege "Allow user to perform force". Due to its potential impact on repository elements, many organizations limit the Force Delete privilege to their repository managers or project technical leads. To invoke the Force Delete utility, select the object(s) to be force deleted and then select the menu option Utilities | Force Delete.

Revise Each Table's Column Order

When you compared your Server Model diagram to your ERD, you discovered that the columns appeared in somewhat random order, and not in the same order as in the ERD. It is customary to show the primary key of a column first in a table. The remaining columns may be ordered "logically" or with the mandatory columns first and the optional columns second, and the columns arranged alphabetically within each group.

Revise the column order of your tables to place the primary key columns first, and the remaining columns in the 'logical order' of your ERD:

1. Select a table on the Design Editor Navigator. Verify that the Properties toggle button is set for the Dialog Box. Click the Properties icon from the toolbar to bring up the **Edit Table** Properties Dialog. On the Columns tab re-sequence the primary key columns to appear first, and the remaining columns to the logical order they are listed in the ERD.

2. Examine the table boxes on the Server Model Diagram, and verify that the columns are now in the same order as the corresponding attributes were on the ERD.

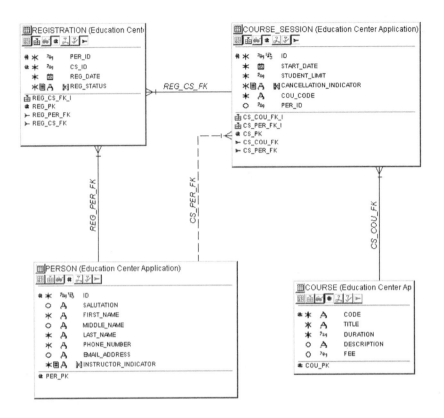

Define Database Sequences

A database sequence is an Oracle 8i database object that generates a list of numbers in sequence. A sequence can be used to automatically generate unique values that can be used to populate primary keys for tables. See your Oracle 8i reference for more information about defining and using sequences. In the Education Center database, you will use Oracle database sequences to populate the ID columns of the COURSE_SESSION and PERSON tables.

Create Sequence Definitions

To define these two database sequences:

1. In the Design Editor Navigator, select the node Sequence Definitions. Click the Create icon to bring up the Create Sequence dialog. Enter a sequence name of PER_ID_SEQ and a Purpose: Sequence for the PER_ID column.

2. Click the Finish button to create the Sequence Definition. If a Default Database Implementation window is displayed, select Do not assign database objects to databases and click the Finish button.

> Designer's use of a database, database users, and implementations is beyond the scope of this case study. However, it would be of great interest to DBAs and application developers, who might need to deploy the same application (and its tables) in several environments and optimize it for those environments.

3. Repeat steps 1 through 2 to create a second sequence:

Name: CS_ID_SEQ

Purpose: Sequence for the COURSE_SESSION.ID column.

4. Verify that the two new sequences now appear in the Design Editor's Navigator. If necessary, requery the navigator's view.

Associate Sequences with Columns

Each sequence must be assigned to the column that it will populate. It is possible to assign a single sequence to multiple columns. To assign these sequences:

1. In the Design Editor navigator, expand the COURSE_SESSION table's node until the ID column's definition is visible. Select the ID column in the navigator, and hit the *F4* key to bring up the Column Property Palette for ID. Scroll down to the property **Sequence**, and select the **CS_ID_SEQ** from the pop-up list.

2. Set the **Server Derived** property to Yes. Setting this property to Yes means that Designer will generate code in the Table API to automatically populate the column with the next value of the sequence when a row is inserted. (This is discussed in Chapter 10: *Web PL/SQL Application Development Using Designer 6i.*).

3. Repeat steps 1 through 2 to assign the PER_ID_SEQ to the ID column of the PERSON table.

Add Change History Columns

It is general practice to add change history columns to each table to record:

❑ The username and date/time that the record was created

❑ The username and date/time that the record was last modified.

Designer can generate code to automatically populate change history columns. Details on this code, and how it is generated, are included in the chapter on Web PL/SQL Application Development later in this book.

In this section, you will add four change history columns to each of your tables:

1. To add the change history columns after the other columns in the COURSE table, select the COURSE table in the Design Editor Navigator. Bring up the COURSE Property Dialog box. Select the last column on the **Columns** tab of this Properties Dialog.

2. Click the **Add** button to add the column CREATED_BY. Type in the following column definition information:

Column name	Datatype	Length	Mandatory
CREATED_BY	VARCHAR2	30	yes

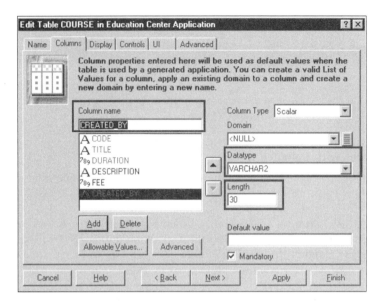

3. Click the Advanced button to bring up the **Advanced** window. Scroll down to the Derivation properties. Enter the following Derivation Properties:

AutoGen Type	Server Defaulted?	Server Derived?
Created By	No	Yes

4. Commit the new column and its properties. Repeat the above steps to add the following additional change history columns to the COURSE table:

Column Name	Datatype	Length	Mandatory?	AutoGen Type	Server Defaulted?	Server Derived
DATE_ CREATED	DATE		yes	Date Created	No	Yes
MODIFIED_ BY	VARCHAR2	30	no	Modified By	No	Yes
DATE_ MODIFIED	DATE		no	Date Modified	No	Yes

5. Repeat steps 1 through 4 to add all four change history columns to the other three tables.

> If your application requires the complete tracking of change history, consider using the Designer features to generate and populate Journal tables. For more information on Journal tables see the Designer Help Text.

Review and Refine Database Constraints and Indexes

The Database Design Transformer created primary keys and unique keys based upon the UIDs in the entity relationship model. It created foreign keys, foreign key columns, and indexes for the foreign keys based upon the relationships in the entity relationship model. It is a good idea to review the database constraints and indexes that were created, and to validate that the definitions are what you want. You may want to:

❑   Change the constraint names or index names assigned by the Database Design Transformer

❑   Re-order the columns in a primary key, unique key, or index

❑   Delete redundant indexes

❑   Add additional indexes for queries that are expected on the database

❑   Add any data value constraints (such as upper case) to your table and column definitions

To review the database constraints and indexes defined for the Education Center:

1.   In the Design Editor Navigator, expand the COURSE table definition. Select the primary key constraint COU_PK and click *F4* to view its properties. In the Navigator, expand the COURSE_SESSION table definition, and review the primary key constraint, foreign key constraints, and indexes defined for this table. Notice that an index was created for each foreign key constraint.

2.   In the Navigator, expand the REGISTRATION table definition, and review the component of the primary key and the components of the two indexes created for the foreign keys. The primary key REG_PK will automatically have an index on: PER_ID, CS_ID. Therefore, the index REG_PER_FK_I is redundant with the primary key.

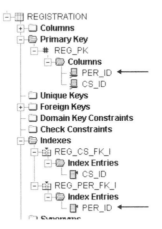

3.   Delete the index REG_PER_FK_I, by selecting it on the Navigator and clicking the Delete icon.

Print the Revised Server Model Diagram

Now that you have refined your database design, print a final version of your Server Model Diagram. Open the Education Center Server Model Diagram and Edit | Requery All to bring it up to date. Review and adjust the layout of your diagram as necessary, save it, and then print it.

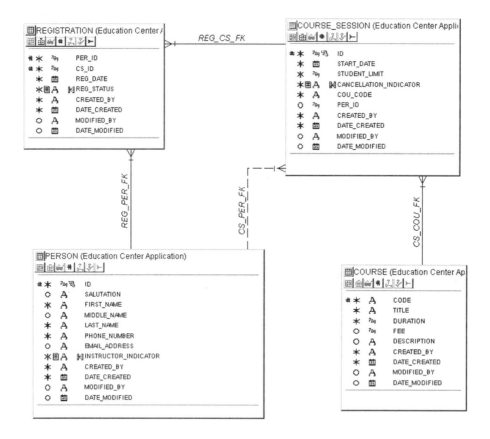

Generate DDL and Create a Physical Database

Once your database design is complete, you are ready to generate data definition language (DDL) SQL files, and then to run those scripts to create your physical database objects.
You will use the following steps to generate and run the required DDL:

- ❑   Invoke the Server Model Generator and select generation options

- ❑   Select the Objects to Generate

- ❑   Execute the Server Model Generator and its Results

- ❑   Execute the generated DDL

- ❑   Review the physical database

Invoke the Server Model Generator and Select Options

To invoke the Server Model Generator:

1. On the **Server Model** tab of the Design Editor Navigator, select all four of the Education Center Application's tables

2. From the Design Editor's menu, select **Generate | Generate Database from Server Model**. The **Generate Server Model Definitions** window will appear.

3. For the Target for Generation, select the **Database** option. This option will:

❑ Read the existing database schema and determine differences between the current Repository definitions and any existing database objects

❑ Create the DDL files

❑ Create a reconciliation report of differences

❑ Provide an option to view the created DDL files

❑ Provide an option to execute SQL*Plus to run the DDL scripts to create the physical database objects

4. Enter the username, password, and connect string of the database schema where the physical database objects are to be created. Note that this schema does not have to be the same as your current Designer userid. Specify a file name prefix for the DDL files to be created– for example, proto. Specify a directory where the DDL files should be stored – for example, E:\EdCenter\SQL. (You will need to create this directory).

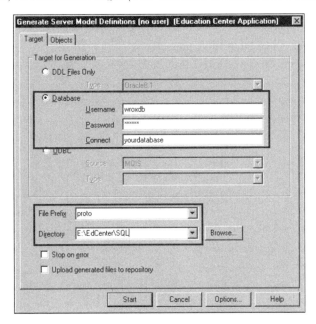

5. Click the Options button to bring up the **Options** window. By default, all of the Options are selected. For the Education Center prototype, only the options shown below are required. De-select the other options. The **Generate Valid Value Constraints** option will create a table named CG_REF_CODES and populate it with the domain values for dynamic list domains.

6. Click the OK button to establish the revised options and close the Options window.

Select Objects to Generate

To select the objects for which DDL will be generated:

1. Click the Objects tab to bring up the list of objects for which DDL will be generated:

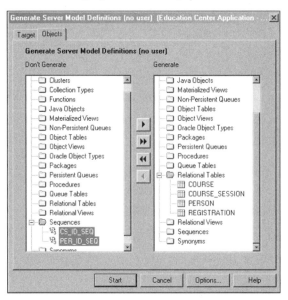

The four tables should appear in the list of objects to generate on the right-hand side of this window. Use the right arrow to also move the sequences to the right-hand list of objects to be generated.

> The two sequences are referenced by columns in the COURSE_SESSION and PERSON tables. The Server Model Generator will detect that these sequence objects are used by these tables, and will automatically include them in the objects to be generated – even if you do not explicitly include them in list of objects to be generated.

2. Verify that all objects to be generated and no unwanted objects appear on the right-hand side.

Execute the Server Model Generator and Review its Results

1. Click the Start button to begin the process of generating the DDL files. A generation Message window will appear at the bottom of the window. If any errors are encountered, they will be displayed in this window in red.

2. When the DDL has been successfully generated, the **DDL Generation Complete** window will be displayed. Use the buttons on the **DDL Generation Complete** window to review the Server Model Generator's results.

Click the View DDL button to view the DDL files. Six files are shown:

a. proto.tab – CREATE TABLE statements for the four tables and for the CG_REF_CODES table which will contain the Domain values for the YESNO and REGISTRATION STATUS domains.

b. proto.ind – CREATE statements for the indexes.

c. proto.con – ALTER TABLE ADD CONSTRAINT statements for the primary key, foreign key, and check constraints.

d. proto.sqs – CREATE SEQUENCE statements for the two sequences.

e. proto.avt – INSERT statements to load the domain values into the CG_REF_CODES table for the YESNO and REG STATUS domains.

f. proto.sql – a script file that executes the five DDL files.

These files will be saved to the target Directory specified on the first Server Model Generator Dialog window.

3. Click the View Report button to view the reconciliation report. This report shows a list of objects and then whether they are in the repository or in the existing database. Since this is the first time that you have generated DDL for this schema, all of your database objects will show *** * NOT IN DATABASE * *** in the far right-hand column of this report. This reconciliation report is saved in a seventh file, proto.lis, in the target file directory.

Execute the Generated DDL

If you are satisfied with the generated DDL files, you are now ready to run the DDL scripts to build the database objects in the database:

1. Click the Execute DDL button to run all the DDL files. When the Message window ends with:

```
Processing Complete:  0 error(s), 0 warning(s)
```

2. Close the message window. If any errors are displayed (for example missing FK and Index components), you should research them by looking at the DDL files in the target directory. Executing the proto.sql script will create another file, proto.1st, in the target Directory. This file should also contain a listing of any errors encountered.

Review the Physical Database

1. Invoke SQL*Plus from the Start menu specifying the username, password, and connect string of the schema where the Education Center tables were created. Describe each of the new physical tables:

```
DESCRIBE COURSE
DESCRIBE PERSON
DESCRIBE COURSE_SESSION
DESCRIBE REGISTRATION
DESCRIBE CG_REF_CODES
```

2. Review the table constraints created:

```
SELECT table_name,constraint_name, constraint_type
FROM user_constraints
ORDER BY 1,2;

SELECT table_name, constraint_name, position, column_name
FROM user_cons_columns
ORDER BY 1,2,3;
```

3. Review the domain values created in the CG_REF_CODES table:

```
SELECT rv_domain, rv_low_value, rv_meaning FROM cg_ref_codes
ORDER BY rv_domain, rv_low_value;
```

You have now successfully generated the required DDL to create the Education Center database and you have executed that DDL to create a physical Oracle 8i database for the Education Center database.

Summary

This chapter has presented the fundamentals steps of Database Design and Development using Designer:

- ❏ Develop a conceptual model
- ❏ Transform it into a preliminary set of tables
- ❏ Refine the database design, and design other physical objects
- ❏ Generate the DDL and build the database

Hopefully you found these basic steps fairly 'simple', and you had a successful experience using the Designer toolset. Using the steps presented in this chapter, you should be able to use Designer to design and develop other Oracle 8i databases for your upcoming development projects.

Designer doesn't just support the design and creation of databases, but will allow the generation of PL/SQL-based web applications. Chapter 10 will extend the database you created in this chapter with a web application that allows the user to query the database, insert, update, and delete records.

As mentioned in the Overview section of this chapter, database design and development for large, enterprise databases can be quite complex and many faceted. You will very likely need many of the additional features of Designer not covered in this chapter. Just because a feature was not presented in this chapter, do not assume Designer does not provide it!

Additional features Designer provides for the design and development of Oracle 8i databases include the ability to define:

- ❏ Databases, roles, users, and other Oracle 8i "Database Administration" objects
- ❏ Implementations for tables that include tablespace and storage parameters
- ❏ Database trigger logic
- ❏ PL/SQL packages, procedures, and functions
- ❏ Java server-side code
- ❏ Materialized views.

If you need an additional feature, check the Designer Help Text and see what capabilities Designer provides. You will be pleased to discover numerous developer-friendly Wizards for defining other database objects.

If you still have questions after checking the Designer Help Text, consider joining the Designer listserver sponsored by the Oracle Development Tools Users Group (http://www.odtug.com). On the ODTUG listserver, you will find lots of experienced Designer users more than willing to answer your questions on the use of Designer.

And remember, even if your organization is not keen on entity relationship modeling, you should still consider using Designer's Design Editor, the DDL generators, and the Design Capture Features of Designer. You don't have to use the Entity Relationship Diagrammer!

6

PL/SQL Development

There are many people in the world who think PL/SQL is beyond its prime, and that Java will take its place as the core programming language in the Oracle database. On the other hand, according to Perl advocates, Java will never perform fast enough to support the enterprise. Regardless of the various opinions and proficiencies people might have, the fact is that SQL is *the* API of the relational database and PL/SQL is the *lingua franca* of the Oracle database. It will be around for a long time to come and is more than capable of delivering enterprise-class applications. PL/SQL is in the database. It uses the database as its execution environment, and with that it inherits the scalability, reliability, and performance for which the Oracle database is renowned.

The remaining chapters in this section are concerned with "PL/SQL and the Web": delivering output from the database directly to a Web server using the PL/SQL Web toolkit as a foundation. This chapter, however, will concentrate on the fundamental art of programming efficient PL/SQL **packages**, with advice as to how to do this productively in a group development environment.

> *This knowledge will stand you in good stead for the coming chapters since the PL/SQL Web Toolkit is, in fact, a set of pre-defined packages in the database.*

The chapter will be structured as follows:

- ❑ First, a description of a minimal, but effective, development environment
- ❑ Second, a quick refresher of some of the main PL/SQL constructs, for the relative newcomer to the language
- ❑ Finally, an example will be developed using a set of PL/SQL packages, five in all, that could be the start of an application that monitors the PL/SQL development process itself. Specifically, they will construct a set of batch-run html reports on the user_source view, provided by the database when you compile PL/SQL code (it provides the line-by-line text of the compiled source code). The reports will format this text adding comments derived from automated testing of the PL/SQL codes.

In the example application design is paramount. A well-designed package will yield a clearly defined API. This, in turn, means that a package constructed for a specific but often-required purpose (display formatting, for example) can be reused in numerous applications. The example may not do everything you might like but in some ways that is the point: hopefully the reader will be able to continue the application or initiate a new one after reading this primer and will be able to design the new application effectively.

Minimal Development Environment

The following sections describe an environment for productive group PL/SQL development. If one works alone, one might get by with even simpler tools and habits than are suggested here, but they are good habits to adopt nevertheless.

This section assumes that the reader is developing on a Windows platform, regardless of which operating system hosts the 8i database. If you are using a non-Windows platform, it should be easy to gather the materials required to set up a similar development environment.

Occasionally, I will mention specific tools that I, personally, have found useful in my development work. I reference these tools primarily to highlight their existence, and encourage the reader to seek out other tools that may be more suited to their individual requirements and taste.

Reference Material

Reference material is a key part of your toolset – do not neglect it. Books such as this and numerous others published in the field are often excellent sources of practical information. Also, one should certainly not neglect the Oracle online documentation (even if you, like many, find them difficult to read!). A few of the most important online documents for PL/SQL development are as follows:

- ❑ **Oracle 8i SQL Reference** for SQL syntax

- ❑ **Oracle 8i Supplied Packages** for information on some of the PL/SQL package available to the developer

- ❑ **Oracle 8i PL/SQL User's Guide** for a comprehensive description of the PL/SQL language and

- ❑ **Oracle 8i Designing and Tuning for Performance** for information on how to make SQL efficient

You will find them at the Oradoc site, (http://oradoc.photo.net) or as PDF files from http://technet.oracle.com.

Occasionally, I will highlight terms using the same format that I used to highlight the titles of these online books. This usually indicates that additional information is available in one or more of these documents

Programming Editor

You might argue that all you really need to start programming is a text editor such as Notepad. However, for serious development I would recommend the use of a proper programming editor. There are many inexpensive shareware editors available that can be used to build PL/SQL. The editor does not have to be complicated, but it is convenient if it can do the following:

❏ It should allow the user to run external programs, such as SQL*Plus or a version control program such as RCS, from within the editor. This makes it convenient to perform simple tasks, such as compiling the code or checking the file in and out of a version control system, from within the editor.

❏ It should not silently overwrite read-only files, thereby voiding the locking feature of version control software. This requirement eliminates the more primitive text editors.

❏ It should allow the user to define keywords and choose the colors in which to represent them. This makes it convenient to see which part of the code represents keywords.

❏ It should be able to associate line numbers with text or allow the user to go quickly to a specific line. This would allow the user to find errors that are usually identified by line numbers.

Ultraedit (http://www.ultraedit.com) is an example of an editor that passes all these tests and is inexpensive (around the $30 mark at the time of this book going to press), but there are others available. An example of a free PL/SQL editor is TOAD (Tool for Oracle Application Developers), which is available from http://www.toadsoft.com (although, personally, I find TOAD to be inferior to Ultraedit).

Version Control Software

Developers on Windows systems often don't appreciate the value of version control software. It doesn't come with the Windows operating system as it does on Unix (with sccs) and therefore the developer is not likely to be familiar with it. Many of the people I have introduced to version control, kicking and screaming, eventually find it indispensable, especially in a group environment. Changes are preserved without having to concoct new filenames, entire projects can be recovered at once, version information can be automatically placed into the source code itself, and an accounting of who changed what is always available.

A simple version control system, that is quite adequate for PL/SQL, is RCS. One can, for a small price, get RCS and a GUI interface to it from Component Software (http://www.componentsoftware.com). Many other version control solutions exist (such as WinCVS). The reader is encouraged to explore these other options. The only relevant feature to look for is whether the software has keyword substitution so that it may automatically update the source file with version information.

SQL Performance Tools

You may have heard the expression: "*Fast, fat computers breed slow, lazy programmers*" (Robert Hummel), and it's certainly true that, to some extent, today's fast machines can "mask" inefficient code. However, if you write inefficient SQL code in PL/SQL (or Java or Perl, or any other language that allows you to embed SQL) the mask will ultimately slip, and you may find yourself needing to totally re-write the SQL or reworking the logic of the language calling it.

The simple reason for this is that the primary activity of a database-driven application is to manipulate and deliver data. Therefore, it makes sense that the programmer take every possible step to ensure that this activity is efficient – which usually means to make SQL run as rapidly as possible.

> *If you're keen on analogies, then writing poor SQL is analogous to posting a letter to your next door neighbor by first sending it to Siberia and then having it returned to their mailbox from there. It might get there eventually but the more efficient option is to deliver it by hand.*

The tool that is principally used to measure SQL performance is **SQL Trace**. The output is often formatted with `tkprof`. For ad hoc tuning, one can also use the autotrace feature in SQL*Plus or Enterprise Manager. The goal is to verify that each SQL statement runs acceptably fast.

We will encounter these tools again in Chapter 16 ("Inside the Database"), when we investigate the performance of the SQL code generated in the database by an Enterprise Java Bean. However, a simple example might be beneficial here.

Consider the following anonymous PL/SQL block that sets the value of a variable, `mydate`, to the current date, `sysdate`:

```
SQL> alter session set sql_trace = true;

Session altered.

SQL> set serveroutput on
SQL> declare
  2      mydate date;
  3  begin
  4      mydate := sysdate;
  5  end;
  6  /

PL/SQL procedure successfully completed.

SQL> alter session set sql_trace = false;

Session altered.
```

Notice how we assign a value to our `mydate` variable, using `:=`. We enable tracing with the initial `alter session` statement. Note that there does not appear to be any SQL statement in the code. However, the reference to `sysdate` hides a SQL statement, as the `tkprof` report will later show.

We can find where the trace file is located by looking for the value of the parameter `user_dump_dest`. We can do this from SQL*Plus by issuing the following command (you will need the appropriate privileges to do this):

```
SQL> show parameter user_dump_dest

NAME                                 TYPE     VALUE
------------------------------------ -------- --------------------------------
user_dump_dest                       string   E:\Oracle\admin\da\udump
```

In that directory, locate the most recent file. Assuming the most recent file is `ora00345.trc`, we then run `tkprof.exe` on that file to generate the output file `out.lst`:

```
tkprof ora00345.trc out.lst.
```

Following are listed the relevant features of the out.1st file:

```
declare
    mydate date;
begin
    mydate := sysdate;
end;
```

call	count	cpu	elapsed	disk	query	current	rows
Parse	1	0.01	0.02	0	0	0	0
Execute	1	0.00	0.00	0	0	0	1
Fetch	0	0.00	0.00	0	0	0	0
total	2	0.01	0.02	0	0	0	1

```
Misses in library cache during parse: 1
Optimizer goal: CHOOSE
Parsing user id: 61
*************************************************************************

SELECT SYSDATE
FROM
 SYS.DUAL
```

call	count	cpu	elapsed	disk	query	current	rows
Parse	0	0.00	0.00	0	0	0	0
Execute	1	0.01	0.01	0	0	0	0
Fetch	1	0.00	0.00	0	1	4	1
total	2	0.01	0.01	0	1	4	1

```
Misses in library cache during parse: 0
Optimizer goal: CHOOSE
Parsing user id: 61      (recursive depth: 1)
```

Note that the reference to sysdate involved running a SQL statement:

```
SELECT SYSDATEFROM SYS.DUAL
```

The most important columns are count, which shows how often the SQL command was run and the disk, query and current columns that show how many blocks of data were involved in completing the query. One can improve SQL performance by reducing the number of times a statement is executed in the database (say by caching results) or by reducing the amount of blocks it takes to finish a single run (say by using an index).

Debugging

A minimal, productive PL/SQL environment requires no special debugging tools. The major reason for this is that PL/SQL is not a general-purpose language. It exists for two reasons:

❏   To provide a namespace for SQL

❏   To add procedural elements to SQL's declarative language

Although PL/SQL keeps getting more powerful, it is the SQL that is the most likely to require debugging or tuning. However, it is useful to have an ad hoc way to trace through code, storing variables, or the values returned by a SQL query, for display later. There are many ways to do this – I can think of the following at the moment:

❏   Write the values to a temporary table using SQL that can be queried later.

❏   Write the values to a file using the utl_file supplied package.

❏   Write the values to a web page using the PL/SQL Web Toolkit so that the browser can see the results.

❏   Use dbms_output to display the values in SQL*Plus.

Following is a trivial example of using dbms_output (since SQL*Plus will likely be the first display the reader uses in learning PL/SQL, this will probably be the easiest way to begin ad hoc debugging):

```
SQL> set serveroutput on
SQL> declare
  2      v number := 1;
  3  begin
  4      dbms_output.put_line(to_char(v));
  5  end;
  6  /
1

PL/SQL procedure successfully completed.
```

The first line enables display of the buffer to which dbms_output writes. An anonymous PL/SQL block defines a number variable, v, the value of which dbms_output then displays.

Profiling

Profiling should not be confused with performance tuning of SQL queries. Rather it involves measuring the non-SQL code steps that are involved in PL/SQL.

Like debugging, profiling is not required, but occasionally you will want to know whether a certain PL/SQL construct is faster than another. One can then build a benchmark using the supplied procedure dbms_utility.get_time.

For example, let's expand on our SQL Trace example and try to find out how long it takes to set a variable, mydate, to the current date, sysdate (since we are using SQL*Plus to do this, we will also display the values using dbms_output described in the section above):

```
SQL> set serveroutput on
SQL> declare
  2      mydate     date;
  3      starttime number;
  4      endtime    number;
  5  begin
  6      starttime := dbms_utility.get_time;
  7      mydate := sysdate;
  8      endtime := dbms_utility.get_time;
  9      dbms_output.put_line(to_char(starttime));
 10      dbms_output.put_line(to_char(endtime));
 11      dbms_output.put_line(to_char(endtime-starttime));
 12  end;
 13  /
8726303
8726303
0

PL/SQL procedure successfully completed.
```

As the result shows, it goes so fast that we are not really able to measure it. At this point, we might be either happy with the result, or try to put the block into a loop until we get some measurable elapsed time.

As we saw when this was measured with SQL Trace, the assignment really involves the SQL statement, select sysdate from dual. It is that SQL statement that would likely yield the most benefit from tuning, rather than trying to reduce the cost of doing the assignment in PL/SQL.

Benchmarking PL/SQL with the above technique is a useful way to determine if a PL/SQL construct should be used over another technique. It does not, however, require a full profiler to get this information.

Testing

Testing is usually performed manually, with a human tester validating the results. This is time consuming and error prone. On top of this it is often unclear how to go about automating this process: setting up an automated test framework is difficult and the time required has to be balanced against the benefits this testing has for code quality. The net result is that testing is often overlooked.

> *Proponents of Extreme Programming (http://www.xprogramming.com/) **require** automated testing and this has elevated people's awareness of this process. Steven Feuerstein has provided a PL/SQL test framework that follows the principles set out by Extreme Programming (http://oracle.oreilly.com/utplsql/).*

In this chapter, I hope to show how to construct the rudiments of a simple test framework that not only performs a quality task for development, but also helps document the PL/SQL code itself. When the automated tests also serve as documentation, their value increases – which means that they are likely to get built.

Programming Style

Before actually writing any PL/SQL code, you need to consider a suitable coding style. It is not necessary to imitate the style that is found in the online manuals or programming guides. There is no need to even follow the style that I will be presenting in the later example. The only requirement is to **be consistent**, so that the code may be easily read and understood.

Code formatters are available with special purpose PL/SQL editors, but their use is not necessary to achieve the desired clarity. One such formatter, PL/FORMATTER, is available from RevealNet (http://www.revealnet.com) as a standalone product.

Following are a couple of style issues that come up often, and are therefore worth mentioning:

❑ People get used to certain styles. One is the use of capitalization of Oracle keywords that is used in the Oracle documentation. Personally, I see no need to continue the tradition of capitalizing Oracle keywords. Modern editors are able to color code these keywords and so the need for capitalization is outmoded.

❑ Many developers, myself included, like to align parameters and arguments vertically. It is important to do this alignment using only spaces, not tabs. When "tabbed" code is viewed in a browser the vertical alignment can be destroyed, rendering the code difficult to read. The tab character should not be used to quickly format text within a line unless that tab represents the initial indentation of the line. In the packages provided, I use no tabs at all, only spaces. If the reader is not interested in vertical alignment, this issue of using tabs is probably irrelevant.

Writing PL/SQL

PL/SQL is Oracle's propriety language that allows one to provide SQL code with namespaces and procedural functionality.

SQL itself is not procedural, but declarative, code. When you ask the database to `select text from user_source`, you do not specify how this is done, just what should be done. Sometimes this is all that one needs. Other times, for more complicated queries, one just can't figure out a way to get the desired output without using standard programming features such as flow-of-control structures and variables. PL/SQL provides the developer with that additional functionality.

Often it is also convenient to group SQL statements together under a single transaction and reference this transaction with a name. Sometimes one just wants to name a single SQL statement itself so that it can be reused. SQL does not provide this namespace functionality. However by including SQL statements within PL/SQL subprograms and packages as cursors a namespace is made possible. This namespace can be used to pin SQL code into memory for added performance, enhance security by granting execute on code within the namespace to only certain users and in general help organize the basic SQL statements that are used by an application.

So the reason to write PL/SQL is to augment SQL code with procedural logic and to provide a namespace for SQL. Recent advances in the language allow it to call C shared libraries and Java classes as well as to communicate with a web server.

Building a PL/SQL Test Framework

The full power of the PL/SQL language cannot be demonstrated and explained with one example and about 20 pages. However, I've tried to make the most efficient use of this space. Instead of trying to explain every nuance directly, this example provides the rudiments – that is, nothing too advanced and certainly nothing obsolete – of a useful test framework. In the process the reader will be exposed to at least some of the possibilities that are available with the language.

The example is not trivial. Every PL/SQL project needs to see documented PL/SQL code that represents the current state of development and this example shows one way of doing this. Hopefully it will provide a foundation, which the serious developer can then modify and improve, making it fit into their own specific development environment.

Packages

We will start and end with the major namespace creation device PL/SQL offers: packages. Since packages contain the other namespace devices, named procedures and functions, we are really not leaving anything out. Earlier, one saw examples of anonymous PL/SQL blocks that were used to show how SQL Trace and debugging could be implemented. Anonymous blocks are useful for test purposes and examples, but all PL/SQL code written today that wants to be considered professional needs to be packaged.

A **package** is a way to group the following together under a common name:

- ❑ **Types** (datatypes), and **subtypes**. A subtype would obey the same rules as its parent datatype but be constrained to a specific set of values.

- ❑ **Constants** and **variables** to store internal data in a PL/SQL program and which have a name a datatype and a value.

- ❑ **Subprograms**, such as procedures and functions, both modules of code that can be precompiled and stored in the database, the difference being that a function always returns a value.

- ❑ **Cursors**, a storage mechanism that allows us to loop through the rows selected from the database. It is our "pointer" to the current row selected in the database

This namespace creation is one of the major benefits that PL/SQL provides to SQL. It provides a way to quickly assign execute permissions to all of these pieces as a whole. A package consist of two "sections". Code definitions (for example, implementation of a procedure) are contained ("hidden") within the **body** and anything that can be referenced outside of the package is declared ("exposed") through the **specification**.

I like to divide packages into functional groups. I will consider four distinct functional groups in this chapter:

- ❑ Data packages, responsible for retrieving, storing and constructing datatypes for structuring data

- ❑ Display packages, responsible for formatting the data

- ❑ Exception packages to handle errors

- ❑ Test packages, to provide automated tests for other packages

Packages are often built as two separate files, a **specification** file and a **body** file, although it is possible to combine both the specification and body into one file. There are two reasons to use files. First, when errors occur the associated line numbers are easier to find if the specification is separated from the body, since the line count begins at the top of the body or specification source code. And second, all of the specification files can be compiled in advance of the body files. This allows all the public interfaces to be made known even before one can actually run them. Then when code in the body of package A references code in another package B, the specification of B will exist allowing the body of A to successfully compile.

Data Packages

The goal of the data package, which we will call src, will be to retrieve rows from the user_source view that provides the text of compiled PL/SQL programs. However, to ease the reader into using packages, we will build the src package in steps. Other packages will be presented in their final form right from the start.

Implementing Version Control

The first step will show how version control can be added to a package. This will make a package that is very simple because it is mostly empty, but gives the first-time user of packages something to compile and use quickly. It also provides a template for the implementation of version control in other packages. In the following section we will build the full src package.

The specification file for implementing version control in the src package is as follows:

```
create or replace package src
is
    function ver return varchar2;
end;
/
show errors
```

The following points are of interest:

❑   It was created in a file called src.sql and placed in a subdirectory called src. This makes it easy to find and separate from other packages.

❑   The package at this stage contains only one subprogram, a **function** called ver, which returns data as a varchar2.

❑   The last three lines of the file are useful for compiling the file in SQL*Plus. The line containing / compiles the package. The call to show errors is just a query on the user_errors view in the database, which displays any errors that might have occurred. The last line containing no text is there just to avoid a nuisance message stating the number of characters in the last line. If the last line has no characters, the message does not display.

Corresponding to the specification file, src.sql, for the src package there is a body file, srcb.sql, which adds the definitions for code declared in the specification. Both files refer to the same package, src, and so some convention should be agreed upon to distinguish the file containing the specification from the file containing the body. Here, we use the letter b in the filename to signify that the file contains the body of the package.

For this example, the body file, srcb.sql, would look as follows:

```
create or replace package body src
is

    /* The constant defined below is provided automatically by the
       RCS keyword substitution. We do not have to keep it up-to-date.
    */

    cversion constant varchar2(25) := '$Revision: 1.0 $';

    /* Here we create the ver function. It takes no parameters because
       it is just returning RCS version information from the package body.
       It returns a varchar2 datatype that is a string that gives the
       version information.
    */

    function ver return varchar2
    is
    begin
        return cversion;
    end;
end;
/
show errors
```

Now this code needs to be entered into the database. The specification is compiled first and then the body. There are many ways to get this done, especially if one has a programming editor that will allow you to compile the code directly from the editor. It is worth exploring your chosen editor to see exactly how this is done. In Ultraedit this involves using the Tool Configuration feature. Unless your editor is very primitive, this feature should be available somewhere.

A general solution that should work in most environments is to open a command window or DOS prompt and navigate to the directory containing the specification and body files. Next, start up SQL*Plus from this directory using the login to the schema that will own the package. At the SQL*Plus prompt type @src to compile the specification file as follows (if you have not navigated to the file directory, then you'll need to enter the full path after @):

```
SQL> @src

Package created.

No errors.
```

Note that since we used the default .sql extension for the file, we do not have to add this extension. Upon compilation we get two messages. The first tells the user that the src package was successfully created. A message would have displayed if this were not the case. The second is the result of running the SQL*Plus command show errors and it says that no errors occurred. If no errors are displayed, type @srcb in the SQL*Plus command line to compile the body.

If any errors did occur when compiling these simple files, it is likely to be due to typing errors. Messages will be displayed with line numbers referring to the errors. Simply, turn line numbering on in your editor, go to the line where the error was noted and look for a mistyped word.

After compiling both the spec and the body, we can confirm the current version of the package SQL*Plus, as follows:

```
SQL> select src.ver as "SRC Version" from dual;

SRC Version
-----------------------------------
$Revision: 1.0 $
```

All we're doing here is requesting that the function `ver` in the package `src` be run for every row in the `dual` table.

> *The `dual` table in the database is available to all users. It contains one column, called `dummy` (datatype: `varchar2`) and one row, with a value of x. It provides a useful way to test functions etc. without having to build sample tables.*

Also, at this point, we can see the information available in the `user_source` view for our new package:

```
SQL> select text from user_source where name = 'SRC' and type = 'PACKAGE';

TEXT
---------------------------------------------------------------------------
package src
is
    function ver return varchar2;
end;
```

Note that we are getting back almost the entire specification file except for the `create or replace` SQL command and the SQL*Plus commands that compiled (`/`) the package and displayed errors (`show errors`).

The goal of this project will be to display this query as an HTML page with added information that is derived from some automated tests. Let's start building the full packages for our example.

The SRC Package Specification

We now need to build the full `src` package so that, among other things, it will retrieve rows from the `user_source` view for our report. We will need to provide a procedure that other packages may use to get these rows, and also to define a datatype to make this communication more convenient.

Here is the source code for the specification file, `src.sql` (if you are somewhat overwhelmed by the syntax, don't worry – we walk through the code directly afterwards):

```
create or replace package src
is

    subtype   adequate is varchar2(25);

    ctype_default constant adequate := 'PACKAGE';
    spec          constant adequate := 'PACKAGE';
    body          constant adequate := 'PACKAGE BODY';
```

```
      type src_row is record (
         text user_source.text%type,
         line user_source.line%type
      );

      type src_table is table of src_row
         index by binary_integer;

      procedure pkg_code (pname in  varchar2,
                          ptype in  varchar2 default ctype_default,
                          pinfo out src_table);

      function ver return varchar2;
   end;
   /
   show errors
```

This is the same package that was created previously. It now has additional functionality. Let's walk through the code. The create or replace syntax does just what it says: if the package does not exist it is created. Since src already exists it will replace it with this new version:

```
   create or replace package src
   is
```

Next, we define a subtype, adequate, which allows us to take the varchar2 datatype and constrain it to 25 characters in length, which is actually more than adequate to store the literals PACKAGE and PACKAGE BODY. Why do this? Well, it cuts down on the number of times that we have to type the numeric literal "25" from three to one. Our exposure to literals is reduced. As the package grows we might expect there to be more literals of this size, thus increasing the benefit of the subtype:

```
      subtype adequate is varchar2(25);
```

Next we define three constants, of subtype adequate, and assign literal values to them. The syntax constant means that this code will not be permitted to change dynamically. WE will have to recompile the package to change these values:

```
      ctype_default constant adequate := 'PACKAGE';
      spec          constant adequate := 'PACKAGE';
      body          constant adequate := 'PACKAGE BODY';
```

Next we define a src_row datatype that is not a subtype of a more primitive datatype, but a record data structure, which is composite of two primitive datatypes (each having its own value). However, note that we define each component by referencing the datatype used for a field of the user_source view. The text component has the same datatype as the text field of the user_source view. We do this to avoid exposing the code to any more literals than are necessary. You may not really expect the datatype for the text field in user_source to change, but it very well could in a new version of the database:

```
      type src_row is record (
         text user_source.text%type,
         line user_source.line%type
      );
```

Since we need more than one row, we define a `src_table` datatype as an `index-by` table containing rows of `src_row` type. Although it is called a `table`, it can also be thought of as an array:

```
type src_table is table of src_row
    index by binary_integer;
```

Note that all of the above types, since we are defining them in the specification file are **public**. That is, they are available to any schema which has been granted the execute privilege on this package. The same goes for our first procedure, pkg_code, below: by placing it in the specification, we are exposing it to use by schemas with the privilege to execute this package. Specifically note that the procedure has three parameters:

- ❑ pname is data being sent in to the procedure and has a `varchar2` datatype
- ❑ ptype is similar to pname except that it has a default value defined as the constant `ctype_default`, defined at the start of the package
- ❑ pinfo is a parameter returned from the procedure. Its datatype is the `index-by` table that was defined above

```
procedure pkg_code (pname in  varchar2,
                    ptype in  varchar2 default ctype_default,
                    pinfo out src_table);
```

One point of extra note is how the three constants we defined earlier (ctype, spec and body) provide assistance to schemas owners that have execute privilege on this package in using the pkg_code procedure. For example, with these constants, a call to the procedure could be:

```
exec src.pkg_code('SRC',src.body,pinfo)
```

where `src.body` is a reference to the literal "PACKAGE BODY". It saves the caller of the procedure the risk of getting this literal wrong. The caller can always use the string "PACKAGE BODY", but using the constant lessens the impact of future changes and mistyping.

> *If you are picking up the notion that I am wary of any literals in my code, much like someone constantly washing their hands is worried about germs, then you are definitely getting the point of this defensive architecture.*

Besides the constants, a user with permission to execute the package can also use the newly defined datatypes src_row and src_table. This is true even if the user does not use these datatypes in the third parameter of the pkg_code procedure.

Finally, we get back to the original function that was part of the first pass at creating this package:

```
    function ver return varchar2;
end;
/
show errors
```

The SRC Package Body

Now let's move on to the body of the package, `srcb.sql`, which has to retrieve this information.

> Please take careful note that this file relies on a separate package, **ex.sql**, for exception handling (explained a little later). If you wish to compile this code immediately you must either skip forward and compile the specification for the **ex** package first, or remove the exception handling section denoted in the following code until after we have discussed and created the **ex** package in the next section.

Here is the code for `srcb.sql`:

```
create or replace package body src
is

    /* We can use the subtype "adequate" here because the specification
       has already been compiled and so it is available to us.
    */

    cversion constant adequate := '$Revision: 1.1 $';

    /* Here is where the pkg_code is defined.  Note that the declaration
       is repeated exactly as it appears in the specification.
    */

    procedure pkg_code (pname in  varchar2,
                        ptype in  varchar2 default ctype_default,
                        pinfo out src_table)
    is

        cursor cur_src(ppkg  in varchar2,
                       ptype in varchar2)
        is
        select text,
               line
          from user_source
         where name = upper(ppkg)
           and type = upper(ptype);
    begin

        dbms_application_info.set_action('src.pkg_code');

        for v in cur_src(pname,ptype) loop
           pinfo(pinfo.count).text := v.text;
           pinfo(pinfo.count).line := v.line;
        end loop;

        dbms_application_info.set_action(null);

    /*  Exception handling section. If there are any errors then log
        the error.  After the logging occurs the error is raised again.
    */
```

```
    exception
        when others then
            ex.err;
            raise;

    end;

    function ver return varchar2
    is
    begin
        return cversion;
    end;
end;
/
show errors
```

This completes the code on the src package. The pkg_code procedure now has a complete **block structure** with a **declarative** part between the is and begin keywords, an **executable** part between the begin and exception keywords and an **exception-handling** part between the exception and end keywords.

We'll now discuss the code that may be new to you. We define a cursor, cur_src, to hold the rows we slect from the user_source view.

This particular cursor is an example of an **explicit** cursor (it has a name). It has parameters as well and note how the parameters are used to filter the results. One other thing to note about the cursor is that it is defined within the procedure pkg_code. If WE build another procedure in this package, it will not be able to reference this cursor because it is out of scope. This is a handy way to hide functionality within the package body itself:

```
cursor cur_src(ppkg  in varchar2,
               ptype in varchar2)
is
select text,
       line
  from user_source
 where name = upper(ppkg)
   and type = upper(ptype);
```

An important, and often missed, piece of functionality is the ability of PL/SQL to inform the database of what it is doing at any period of time. It does this through the dbms_application_info supplied package. Here we are setting the field action in the v$session view to have the value of src.pkg_code. As a result, whoever is maintaining the database will have a bit more information about what is running:

```
dbms_application_info.set_action('src.pkg_code');
```

Next, we open, fetch, and load values into an index-by table and close the cursor. Note that we have not defined the variable v anywhere. This is done by the loop construction:

```
for v in cur_src(pname,ptype) loop
   pinfo(pinfo.count).text := v.text;
   pinfo(pinfo.count).line := v.line;
end loop;
```

Note how `pinfo` is indexed by the number of elements in the "table". Also note how each component of the composite datatype is referenced by name and separated by a "." from the name of the variable. After this `loop` is finished the `pinfo` parameter is completely loaded and ready to be received by whoever requested it.

When the procedure ends, we set the action field to `null`:

```
dbms_application_info.set_action(null);
```

Those of you who are paying close attention will have noticed that we skipped over a certain section of code in the above explanation:

```
exception
   when others then
       ex.err;
       raise;
end;
```

This section of code is our exception handling, which provides the ability to catch errors and process them. Usually there isn't much one can do about errors except to log that they occur and then raise them again. You'll notice that we're not doing much work here – we are relying on a separate package to do this for us (we call the `err` procedure in the package called `ex`). Note that the exception is reraised so that it will be sent to the calling subprogram.

The architectural decision was basically this: should we include exception handling within the `src` package or create another package to deal with all exceptions? If we place exception-processing code in the `src` package there might be some code that is redundant, since exception handling is required by other packages. This is especially true of any logging feature. This is basically the reason that leads me to choose to create another package for exceptions. Let's now take a look at that package.

The ex Exception Package

The exception package, which I am calling `ex`, depends on a table that is used to store errors received. This table can be defined in many ways, and if you wish to develop this application further, you will no doubt have other information to store about an error. However, a simple error table would look something like the following:

```
create table err_table (
   username varchar2(30),
   when     date              default sysdate,
   stack    varchar2(4000),
   error    varchar2(4000),
   info     varchar2(4000)
);
```

The ex Specification

The following code defines the specification file for the ex package, `ex.sql`:

```
create or replace package ex
is
    procedure err (pinfo in varchar2 default null);

    procedure no_code (pcount in number,
                       pname  in varchar2);

    function ver return varchar2;
end;
/
show errors
```

This `err` procedure logs error information. Generally, we cannot anticipate what errors will occur. What this procedure does is record the error and then raises it again. It is used in all error handling sections of the code. The `pinfo` parameter allows for additional text that we might want to add to the error, such as which subprogram the error occurred in.

```
    procedure err (pinfo in varchar2 default null);
```

The following is an example of a check to see if an error should be raised. Sometimes the developer would like to raise errors that Oracle would not raise. It is used in the display package that will be built later to signal if data has been returned. Since we always expect some data, not having any is a user-defined error. Rather than specifying the details of how this error is handled in the calling subprogram, we send in the conditions that allow us to test if the error should be raised, and then proceed to raise it if necessary:

```
    procedure no_code (pcount in number,
                       pname  in varchar2);
```

The ex Body

The ex package body, `exb.sql`, shows how these subprograms are implemented:

```
create or replace package body ex
is
    cversion constant varchar2(25) := '$Revision: 1.0 $';

    cno_code  constant number := -20001;
    cno_codes constant varchar2(500) :=
        'No package source data was returned for ';

    procedure err (pinfo in varchar2 default null)
    is
        pragma autonomous_transaction;
        vsqlerrm varchar2(4000) := substr(sqlerrm,1,4000);
    begin
        dbms_application_info.set_action('ex.err');
```

```
    insert
      into err_table
           (username,
            stack,
            error,
            info)
    values (user,
            substr(dbms_utility.format_error_stack,1,4000),
            vsqlerrm,
            substr(pinfo,1,4000));
    commit;

    dbms_application_info.set_action(null);
  end;

  procedure no_code (pcount in number,
                     pname  in varchar2)
  is
  begin
    if pcount < 1 then
       raise_application_error(cno_code,cno_codes || pname);
    end if;
  end;

  function ver return varchar2
  is
  begin
    return cversion;
  end;
end;
/
show errors
```

As usual, let's examine this code in more detail. The following lines of code define an error number and an error message when no data has been returned. The permitted error numbers start with -20001 and end with -20999:

```
cno_code  constant number := -20001;
cno_codes constant varchar2(500) :=
   'No package source data was returned for ';
```

The err procedure has the interesting pragma autonomous_transaction. This is a directive that tells the database that the commit performed within this procedure will occur independently of any transaction that called this procedure:

```
procedure err (pinfo in varchar2 default null)
is
   pragma autonomous_transaction;
```

The value entered into the error field is checked to be not larger than the largest value we have permitted for this table, 4000 bytes:

```
vsqlerrm varchar2(4000) := substr(sqlerrm,1,4000);
```

However, if this ever should get larger than 4000 bytes, we will be prepared. As we load the error information into our err_table, we make a call to dbms_utility.format_error_stack, an important Oracle supplied package to provide information about the state of the program:

```
insert
  into err_table
        (username,
        stack,
        error,
        info)
  values (user,
        substr(dbms_utility.format_error_stack,1,4000),
        vsqlerrm,
        substr(pinfo,1,4000));
  commit;
```

The no_code procedure is an example of a check whether an exception should be raised:

```
procedure no_code (pcount in number,
                   pname  in varchar2)
is
begin
   if pcount < 1 then
      raise_application_error(cno_code,cno_codes || pname);
   end if;
end;
```

The test is just to see whether the value of pcount is less than 1. If it is then an exception is raised using our cno_code and cno_codes constants. In general, we would expect to have one of these procedures for every user-defined error that was recognized in the design of the application. By placing all such code in this package we have isolated exception raising and handling to one package.

Should an error be generated, the user would see the assigned error number and error message. To see what this error would look like, just execute the procedure in SQL*Plus with a value that will generate an error. Since 0 is less than 1, we should get an error if the following is executed:

```
SQL> exec ex.no_code(0,'test')
BEGIN ex.no_code(0,'test'); END;

*
ERROR at line 1:
ORA-20001: No package source data was returned for test
ORA-06512: at "WROX.EX", line 59
ORA-06512: at line 1
```

That completes our discussion of the ex package. If you did not include the exception section in the src code before, go back and add it in now.

The Test Framework

Although you can probably download a test framework that will allow you to automatically test PL/SQL code, it is useful to build one to fit a project's needs. The use of a test framework is two-fold:

❑ It provides a way to automatically validate PL/SQL functionality

❑ It provides information that will be used by the display package to document the package code

The test package framework stores the results in the following database table. Results of tests may be viewed by querying this table:

```
create table test_results (
    ran          date,
    pkg          varchar2(30),
    subprogram   varchar2(30),
    success      number,
    failure      number
);
```

The tpk Package Specification

The test package specification, tpk.sql, is a bare minimum to illustrate what a framework can provide. It is a good foundation for a fully-fledged test framework:

```
create or replace package tpk
is

    type test_result is
        record (
            ran          test_results.ran%type,
            pkg          test_results.pkg%type,
            subprogram   test_results.subprogram%type,
            success      test_results.success%type,
            failure      test_results.failure%type
        );
    type test_result_table is
        table of test_result
        index by binary_integer;

    procedure starttest (pname in varchar2);
    procedure subprogram (pname in varchar2);
    procedure endtest;
    procedure test(presult   in boolean,
                   pexpected in boolean);

    procedure gettest (ppkg  in  varchar2,
                       pinfo out test_result_table);
end;
/
show errors
```

The test_result datatype is created to store results from the test_results table. An index-by table accompanies it, which is an array of test_results:

```
type test_result is
   record (
       ran            test_results.ran%type,
       pkg            test_results.pkg%type,
       subprogram     test_results.subprogram%type,
       success        test_results.success%type,
       failure        test_results.failure%type
   );
type test_result_table is
   table of test_result
   index by binary_integer;
```

Note how we do not have to specify the exact type in any of the columns, we just use the %type modifier to return whatever those values happen to be at the moment. It solves problems arising from mistyping these values and protects us against changes to the test_results table that we forgot to make in this code:

We now define the four procedures that constitute the test framework. The starttest procedure initializes variables for a test to begin. The subprogram procedure names a subprogram being tested. The endtest wraps up any summary information required by the test framework. The test procedure performs a specific test that will be recorded:

```
procedure starttest (pname in varchar2);
procedure subprogram (pname in varchar2);
procedure endtest;
procedure test(presult   in boolean,
               pexpected in boolean);
```

Finally, the gettest procedure provides a means to retrieve test results from the test_results table without actually querying the table directly:

```
procedure gettest (ppkg  in  varchar2,
                   pinfo out test_result_table);
end;
```

The ppkg parameter is the name of the package that is being tested. The pinfo parameter is an array type test_results, as defined previously.

The tpk Package Body

The package body, tpkb.sql, implements the framework.

```
create or replace package body tpk
is

    /* The following variables are global to this
       package. They will persist in the user's session until
       the session is closed
    */
```

```
gtests      test_result_table;
gpkg        test_results.pkg%type;
gran        date;
gsubprogram test_results.subprogram%type;

/* The starttest procedure initializes the global variables. */

procedure starttest(pname in varchar2)
is
   vtests test_result_table;
begin
   gtests      := vtests;
   gpkg        := pname;
   gran        := sysdate;
   gsubprogram := null;
end;

/* The subprogram procedure provides a name for the
   packaged subprogram being tested.
*/

procedure subprogram (pname in varchar2)
is
begin
   gsubprogram := pname;
end;

/* The endtest procedure cleans up and stores new results
   into the test_results table.
*/

procedure endtest
is
begin
   if gtests.count > 0 then

/* As the reader will notice, no history is kept of
   the test results.  The reader is welcome to record
   this history if desired.
*/

      delete
        from test_results
       where pkg = gpkg;

/* Note the for loop that goes through all the
   stored tests and inserts them into the test_results table.
*/

      for i in gtests.first .. gtests.last loop
         insert
           into test_results
                (ran,
                 pkg,
                 subprogram,
                 success,
```

```
                              failure)
              values (gtests(i).ran,
                     gtests(i).pkg,
                     gtests(i).subprogram,
                     gtests(i).success,
                     gtests(i).failure);
        end loop;
    end if;
    commit;
end;

/* This procedure adds a new test to the array of test results. */

procedure test(presult   in boolean,
               pexpected in boolean)
is
    vsuccess number := 0;
    vfailure number := 0;
    i number;
begin
    if presult = pexpected then
        vsuccess := 1;
    else
        vfailure := 1;
    end if;
    i := gtests.count;
    if i = 0 then
        gtests(i).ran          := gran;
        gtests(i).pkg          := gpkg;
        gtests(i).subprogram   := gsubprogram;
        gtests(i).success      := vsuccess;
        gtests(i).failure      := vfailure;
        gtests(i).ran          := sysdate;
    else
        if gtests(i-1).pkg = gpkg and
           gtests(i-1).subprogram = gsubprogram then
           gtests(i-1).success := gtests(i-1).success + vsuccess;
           gtests(i-1).failure := gtests(i-1).failure + vfailure;
        else
           gtests(i).ran          := gran;
           gtests(i).pkg          := gpkg;
           gtests(i).subprogram := gsubprogram;
           gtests(i).success      := vsuccess;
           gtests(i).failure      := vfailure;
           gtests(i).ran          := sysdate;
        end if;
    end if;
end;

/* This procedure retrieves information about a concluded test. */

procedure gettest (ppkg  in  varchar2,
                   pinfo out test_result_table)
is
```

```
    /* A cursor is explicitly named for the query to be used
       to retrieve the test information.
    */
    cursor getinfo (ppkg in varchar2)
    is
    select ran,
           subprogram,
           success,
           failure
      from test_results
     where pkg = lower(ppkg);
    v binary_integer;
begin
    dbms_application_info.set_module('tpk','gettest');

    /* The cursor is opened, fetched and closed.  In the meantime
       its values are loaded into an index-by table to be passed
       back to the calling procedure.
    */

    for i in getinfo(ppkg) loop
        v := pinfo.count;
        pinfo(v).ran        := i.ran;
        pinfo(v).pkg        := ppkg;
        pinfo(v).subprogram := i.subprogram;
        pinfo(v).success    := i.success;
        pinfo(v).failure    := i.failure;
    end loop;

    dbms_application_info.set_module(null,null);
    end;
end;
/
show errors
```

Not many of the concepts and structures in the above code are new to you any more, so we're not going to walk through the code in such detail. One point of new interest is regarding the use of global variables:

```
gtests       test_result_table;
gpkg         test_results.pkg%type;
gran         date;
gsubprogram  test_results.subprogram%type;
```

They will persist in the user's session until the session is closed. They are denoted as variables and not constants, because they do not have the constant keyword. The benefit of globals is their persistence – they maintain their state between different calls to subprograms in this package. This persistence is also their liability – one cannot assume they are null when first using them. They may have been set by a previous subprogram.

The src_test Package

To use the framework, one constructs another test package for each package in the application. For the src package I have called the specification file src_test.sql and the test body file src_testb.sql. I store these files in the same directory, src, that contains the src package files and then load them into the database through SQL*Plus. Placing the production packages with the test packages is just one way to organize these files. The reader may come up with a better approach:

```
create or replace package src_test
is
    procedure test;
end;
/
show errors
```

The src_test body contains the individual tests for the src package:

```
create or replace package body src_test
is
    procedure test
    is
        vdata src.src_table;
        vver  varchar2(100);
    begin

    /* The test of the src package begins. */

        tpk.starttest('src');

    /* The first subprogram to be tested is the pkg_code
       procedure in the src package.
    */

        tpk.subprogram('pkg_code');

    /* This is the first test. We are testing to see if
       any data is returned from the pkg_code procedure
       in the second parameter, as well as if the first
       line of code is numbered 1.
    */
        begin
            src.pkg_code('src',src.spec,vdata);
            tpk.test(vdata.count>0,true);
            tpk.test(vdata(0).line=1,true);

        /* If the exception is raised then something went
           wrong. Whatever it is, it is logged against the
           package as an error.
        */

        exception
            when others then
                tpk.test(true,false);
        end;
```

```
    /* Now we begin testing the ver function by calling the tpk.subprogram
       procedure.
    */

       tpk.subprogram('ver');
       begin
           vver := src.ver;
           tpk.test(length(vver)>0,true);
       exception
           when others then
               tpk.test(true,false);
       end;

   /* The test of the package is over. */

       tpk.endtest;
   end;
end;
/
show errors
```

Notice how each test is enclosed in its own `begin...end` block. If an exception occurs it is captured, a test error is recorded and the test continues.

After compiling this package and executing `src_test.test` in SQL*Plus, the results are stored in the `test_results` table for use by the display package. There will be a success and a failure for the `pkg_code` procedure and a success for the `ver` function. The following shows how this would look through SQL*Plus:

```
SQL> exec src_test.test

PL/SQL procedure successfully completed.

SQL> select * from test_results;

RAN         PKG    SUBPROGRAM   SUCCESS     FAILURE
---------   -----  ----------   ----------  ----------
22-NOV-00   src    pkg_code              1           1
22-NOV-00   src    ver                   1           0
```

Display Packages

The display package, `disp`, will provide one type of display for the `user_source` information, by writing an HTML file using the PL/SQL supplied package `utl_file`. If the reader has the PL/SQL Web Toolkit, a more dynamic display could be constructed, but this technique illustrates a way to generate batch HTML reports that should complement the dynamic reports returned with the web toolkit.

The PL/SQL Web toolkit is described and used throughout the following two chapters.

Not all reports need to be constructed on demand. Some can be run once and then saved for future reference as web pages. Indeed some reports are too resource-intensive to be run anew at every request. This is one way to generate this sort of report.

Since the package uses the `utl_file` supplied package, be aware of the following issues that often cause problems when using `utl_file` for the first time:

❑   The `utl_file` package writes to files on the server not to the developer's local machine. The server is only permitted to write to those files that can be found in directories specified under the `utl_file_dir` parameter specified in the `init.ora` file. The reader should ensure that this parameter is set to the correct output path.

❑   Directories or locations are not specified with a trailing slash or backslash. A directory in Windows would look like `C:\wrox\web` and not like `C:\wrox\web\`. An obscure error will be generated if the trailing end character is added to the path where the file is stored.

The disp Display Package Specification

The specification, `disp.sql`, is as follows:

```
create or replace package disp
is

    /* The only procedure in this package provides a means of printing
       the user_source information.
    */

    procedure print (pname in varchar2,
                     ptype in varchar2 default src.ctype_default);

    function ver return varchar2;
end;
/
show errors
```

The `ptype` parameter has the same default as the `ptype` default in the `src` package. This package will make use of the default value defined in `src` rather than redefining it again here. Although we can compile this package within the same schema as we compiled the `src` package, it is not necessary to do so. However, it would provide a further level of isolation between the data and the display.

The disp Display Package Body

Here is the `dispb.sql` package body:

```
create or replace package body disp
is
    cversion        constant varchar2(25) := '$Revision: 1.0 $';

    /* This is a set of literals that could be configured for
       different environments.
    */

    cwebdirectory constant varchar2(30) := 'e:\wrox\web';
    cwebextension constant varchar2(6)  := '.html';
    cbodysuffix   constant varchar2(30) := 'b';

    /* This is a set of literals for reuse. */
```

```
cwrite          constant varchar2(1)   := 'w';
chash           constant varchar2(1)   := '#';
cstarttag       constant varchar2(1)   := chr(60);
cendtag         constant varchar2(1)   := chr(62);
cstartendtag    constant varchar2(2)   := chr(60) || '/';

/* This is a set of global variables.  The first literal
   provides a file reference to the file being created.
   The last three provide communication between separate
   calls to the same function.  If a tag has been opened
   they are set to true.  This determines whether the
   function generating the html, body or pre tag should
   output an opening or closing tag.
*/

gfile           utl_file.file_type;
ginpre          boolean := false;
ginbody         boolean := false;
ginhtml         boolean := false;

/* The following are private general subprograms not dependent
   on utl_file.
*/

/* This function builds the opening html tag. */

function starttag (ptag in varchar2) return varchar2
is
begin
   return chr(10) || cstarttag || ptag || cendtag;
end;

/* This function builds the closing html tag. */

function endtag (ptag in varchar2) return varchar2
is
begin
   return cstartendtag || ptag || cendtag;
end;

/* This functions builds a tagged piece of data. */

function tag(ptext in varchar2,
             ptag  in varchar2) return varchar2
is
begin
   return starttag(ptag) || ptext || endtag(ptag);
end;

/* The following are private specific tag subprograms
   not dependent on utl_file.
*/
```

199

```
/* The next two functions illustrate how a subprogram may
   be overloaded by changing the number of parameters
   that are required.  In the first case the <a> tag
   has a name attribute rather than an href attribute.
*/

function a (pname in varchar2) return varchar2
is
begin
   return cstarttag || 'a name="' || pname || '"' ||
          cendtag || endtag('a');
end;

function a (phref in varchar2,
            ptext in varchar2) return varchar2
is
begin
   return cstarttag ||'a href="' || phref || '"' ||
          cendtag || ptext || endtag('a');
end;

/* The next three functions build the body, html and pre
   tags and record if the tag has been opened or not.
   This information is recorded in a global variable and
   is used to either open or close the tag depending on
   how the global variables are set.
*/

function body return varchar2
is
begin
   if ginbody then
      ginbody := false;
      return chr(10) || endtag('body');
   else
      ginbody := true;
      return starttag('body');
   end if;
end;

function html return varchar2
is
begin
   if ginhtml then
      ginhtml := false;
      return chr(10) || endtag('html');
   else
      ginhtml := true;
      return starttag('html');
   end if;
end;

function pre return varchar2
is
begin
   if ginpre then
```

```
            ginpre := false;
            return chr(10) || endtag('pre');
        else
            ginpre := true;
            return starttag('pre');
        end if;
    end;

    /* This css function provides a link to a style sheet. */

    function css(pfile in varchar2) return varchar2
    is
    begin
        return chr(10) || cstarttag ||
               'link rel="stylesheet" type="text/css" href="' ||
               pfile || '"' || cendtag;
    end;

    /* The following procedures are dependent on utl_file package. */

    /* This is a general print procedure. */

procedure prt(ptext in varchar2)
 is
 begin
     utl_file.putf(gfile,ptext);
 end;

 procedure closing
 is
 begin
     prt(body || html);
 end;

 procedure heading(pname in varchar2)
 is
     vtitle varchar2(100) := 'Package ' || pname || ' Listing';
 begin
     prt(html || tag(vtitle,'title') ||
         css('primer.css') || body ||
         tag(vtitle,'h1'));
 end;

 /* Only the following procedure is available outside the package. */

 procedure print (pname in varchar2,
                  ptype in varchar2 default src.ctype_default)
 is
     vinfo       src.src_table;
     vprog       varchar2(30);
     vtype       varchar2(30);
     vurl        varchar2(4000);
     vtest       tpk.test_result_table;
     vcounttest binary_integer := 0;
```

```
/* Note how this function is defined within the print procedure.
   It almost appears as if the print procedure is acting like
   a package in that it can contain procedures of its own.
   Alternatively, one can view the package as a kind of procedure.
*/
   function make_url (ptype in varchar2,
                      pname in varchar2,
                      pprog in varchar2) return varchar2
   is
   begin
      if ptype = src.spec then
         return pname || cbodysuffix || cwebextension || chash || pprog;
      else
         return pname || cwebextension || chash || pprog;
      end if;
   end;
   function make_filename (ptype in varchar2,
                           pname in varchar2) return varchar2
   is
   begin
      if ptype = src.spec then
         return lower(pname) || cwebextension;
      else
         return lower(pname) || cbodysuffix || cwebextension;
      end if;
   end;
   function divtest (ptext in varchar2) return varchar2
   is
   begin
      return cstarttag || 'div class="testresult"' || cendtag ||
             ptext || endtag('div');
   end;
begin
   dbms_application_info.set_module('disp.print '||pname,null);

   /* Here data is obtained from user_source and test results. */

   src.pkg_code(pname,ptype,vinfo);

/* Here is where a possible error is tested.  If no data was
   returned this would generate an error and the block would
   exit.  Otherwise processing would continue.
*/
   ex.no_code(vinfo.count,pname);
   tpk.gettest(pname,vtest);

/* If we get to this point, there are no exceptions and so we
      will build the report.
*/
   gfile := utl_file.fopen(cwebdirectory,
                           make_filename(ptype,pname),
                           cwrite);

/* This next part may seem difficult, but it simply builds the
   content of the html page.
*/
   heading(pname);
```

```
        if vtest.count > 0 then
            for r in vtest.first .. vtest.last loop
                vcounttest := vcounttest + vtest(r).success + vtest(r).failure;
            end loop;
        end if;
        prt(divtest('Total Tests: ' || to_char(vcounttest)));
        prt(pre);
        for i in vinfo.first .. vinfo.last loop
            if instr(vinfo(i).text,'procedure ') > 0 or
                instr(vinfo(i).text,'function ') > 0  then
                if vtest.count > 0 then
                    for j in vtest.first .. vtest.last loop
                        -- if any tests match then record results.
                        if instr(vinfo(i).text,lower(vtest(j).subprogram))>0 then
                            prt(pre);
                            prt(a(vtest(j).subprogram) ||
                                a(make_url(ptype,pname,vtest(j).subprogram),
                                    tag(vtest(j).subprogram,'h2'))));
                            prt(divtest('Success: ' || to_char(vtest(j).success)));
                            prt(divtest('Failure: ' || to_char(vtest(j).failure)));
                            prt(pre);
                        end if;
                    end loop;
                end if;
            end if;
            prt(vinfo(i).text);
        end loop;
        prt(pre);
        closing;
        utl_file.fclose(gfile);

        dbms_application_info.set_module(null,null);

        /* And if there are errors they are logged by the ex package. */

    exception
        when others then
            ex.err;
            raise;
    end;

    function ver return varchar2
    is
    begin
        return cversion;
    end;
end;
/
show errors
```

Although the disp body appears to be extremely long, only the length of the print procedure is indicative of what would be required to build a report. The other private procedures at the top of the package are primarily used to format HTML. While this print procedure displays the content from user_source and ignores the line number, another version of the print function, that the reader might be interested in writing, could use this additional line information.

The only feature the `print` procedure illustrates is to insert a link from the body to the spec and back based upon the name of the subprogram that has been tested. Subprograms that have not been tested do not get this treatment. Also the number of tests performed is also recorded. This is how linking test information with the documentation of the PL/SQL code is effected. With more sophisticated tests, more information can be supplied to the HTML report.

Other features could be included such as creating a contents list at the top of the package, color-coding certain keywords, linking calls to package code or providing comments on parameters and subprograms.

Formatting the Display

For the sake of creating a nice display the following cascading style sheet, `test.css`, has been included. The reader may conveniently and often drastically change the look of the report by modifying this file and reloading the report file:

An overview of Cascading Style Sheet syntax is available at the W3C site (http://www.w3.org/Style/CSS/)

```
body, h1, h2, div {
    font-family: arial,sans-serif;
    font-size: 10pt;
    margin-left: 15%;
    margin-right: 10%;
}
pre {
    font-family: courier;
}
h1 {
    text-align: center;
    font-size: 1.7em;
}
h2 {
    text-align: left;
    font-size: 1.3em;
    margin-left: 0%;
}
div.testresult {
    text-align: left;
    font-size: 8pt;
    color: green;
    margin-left: 0%;
}
```

Generating the Report

To generate the reports one would execute `disp.print('src')` and `disp.print('src','package body')`. This would build the two files in the location specified by the `utl_file_dir` parameter. They may now be loaded into Netscape or IE for viewing.

The following is a portion of what the browser would show. Note that entries Total Tests, Success and Failure, come from the `test_results` table. The procedure titles are linked to the specification file.

```
Package src Listing - Microsoft Internet Explorer        _ □ ×

File   Edit   View   Favorites   Tools   Help

← Back  ·  →  ·  ⊗  ▣  ⌂   ◯ Search  ▣ Favorites   »   Address   Links »
```

Package src Listing

Total Tests: 3

```
package src
is

   subtype   adequate is varchar2(25);

   ctype_default constant adequate := 'PACKAGE';
   spec          constant adequate := 'PACKAGE';
   body          constant adequate := 'PACKAGE BODY';

   type src_row is record (
      text user_source.text%type,
      line user_source.line%type
   );

   type src_table is table of src_row
      index by binary_integer;
```

pkg_code

Success: 1
Failure: 1

```
  ⌚ Local intranet
```

Summary

This chapter provides the beginning of an application that monitors the PL/SQL development process. Five packages were created, a display package called disp, a data package called src, an exception package called ex, a test framework called tpk and a test package called src_test.

Many other features could be added to this initial application structure by mimicking and expanding the code in the above packages. Some of the other pieces that might be of interest are table and column comments, tablespace properties or lists of triggers. The data package may also be combined with the PLS/SQL Web Toolkit by changing only the display package or adding an additional display package to dynamically generate reports.

7

PL/SQL Server Pages

Introduction

Until relatively recently, there was really only one option when it came to serving dynamic data directly from the database using PL/SQL and that was to use the PL/SQL cartridge and associated PL/SQL Web Toolkit provided with the Oracle Application Server. Then along came WebDB, a tool that not only allowed developers to create entire websites inside the database, but then acted as a listener to serve these sites out to users. The latest version of WebDB has now been renamed as Portal. The next variation in the use of PL/SQL for the dynamic provision of content to web pages is PL/SQL Server Pages (PSPs). Support for PL/SQL Server Pages was first introduced in Oracle 8i Release 2 and is therefore only available where Oracle 8.1.6 and above has been installed.

In short, a PL/SQL Server Page, PSP, is a server side web page that contains PL/SQL within predefined tags.

This chapter will look at the use, anatomy, and creation of PSPs, and we will examine a sample architecture that they could be deployed into.

If you intend to try the examples, there are a few prerequisites:

❑   You must have Oracle 8i Release 2 (8.1.6) installed.

❑   You must have a PL/SQL Gateway installed and configured. For iAS, the instruction can be found in the `apache/modplsql/cfg/help` folder of your iAS install. This will take you through the installation of the PL/SQL Web Toolkit and how to grant access to and from the Internet.

It should be noted that the setup and installation of these does require some knowledge of the products, so you should refer to the relevant documentation or sections in this book if you run into any problems.

When to Use PSPs

There are no hard or fast rules as to when to use PSPs as opposed to say WebDB, JavaServer Pages or Java servlets, etc. But the following points may help to decide if PSPs are a suitable technology for your project:

❑ PSPs are deployed directly into and served from the database, and so enjoy the security, scalability and reliability inherent in the Oracle 8i database

❑ PSPs are only available in version 8.1.6 and above of the database

❑ PSPs easily allow the combination of cutting edge web page design from a third party with proven data manipulation techniques

❑ PSPs are only for server side scripting and so all load balancing must be performed by the database server

Often the overruling consideration for the project technology will be the skills of the development team and the project timelines. So if your project has aggressive timescales and the overall skill set for the development team will be the core Oracle Database languages of PL/SQL and SQL, and you have a heavy dependence on another company to produce the HTML look and feel for your company, then PSPs will provide a good, sound platform for your application.

PSP Architecture

The sample application that we will use in this chapter will be based around the traditional 3-tier internet application architecture. The following diagram illustrates this architecture with each tier residing on a separate machine. It is, however, feasible to have each tier residing on the same machine and still be able to create, deploy and run the sample application. The sample application was created on a single machine, a P2 300MHz with 128MB RAM and a 6GB Disk, which was running all 3 tiers.

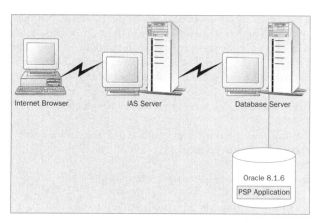

In this scenario, the Internet Browser connects through to the PSP Application using the iAS (Oracle Internet Application Server) mod_plsql, the module for Apache that enables the translation of PL/SQL into HTML, and a predefined Data Access Descriptor (DAD). The DAD is used by iAS to identify which database to connect and when connected, which application module to run.

Having said all this, the final deployment architecture has only 2 stipulations:

❑ The version of the database must support PSPs, so it must be 8.1.6 or above.

❑ There must be a PL/SQL gateway available to serve the PL/SQL Server Pages. This can be obtained from either Oracle Internet Application Server, iAS as shown in the above diagram, WebDB or Oracle Application Server, OAS. For further information as to how to set this up please refer to the documentation provided with each product.

The Anatomy of a PSP

The anatomy of a PSP is made up of 4 main elements

❑ **Directives** – these provide information for the current page

❑ **Declaratives** – these are where all variables are declared for use within the current page.

❑ **Scriptlets** – here any valid PL/SQL code can be included, including variable declarations

❑ **Expressions** – formats the expression for inclusion in the displayed page

We will explore these elements using PSP that created the following customer detail form from our sample application, a simple on-line catalog. For more details about the sample application please refer to the What Now? Section towards the end of this chapter.

As we look at each of the elements and attributes, it is worth remembering that they are case sensitive and if you are going to type in the code for this screen, rather than using the source code file, please ensure that these key words are entered correctly and saved as `cuts_dets.psp`. The entire source code for this is given later. The following section will look at the anatomy using code snippets from this file. It will help to prevent frustrating errors; believe me, I know.

PSP Directives

A PSP directive is a statement that gives the PSP compiler information about the page it is about to load into the database. The general syntax is:

```
<%@ directive attribute="value" [ attribute="value" ... ] %>
```

One of the first things to notice is that there is a % inside the <. This differentiates the special PSP tags from normal HTML tags and lets the compiler know that there is something of interest to it inside the tags.

There are currently 4 directives available. These are:

❏   page – information specific for the page

❏   procedure – the name for the procedure

❏   parameter – name, type and default value for parameters

❏   include – files to be included

The Page Directive

There are 3 attributes associated with the page directive:

❏   the language

❏   the contentType

❏   the errorPage to be used

The general syntax of the page directive is:

```
<%@ page [language="PL/SQL"] [contentType="content type"] [errorPage="error page"]
%>
```

The only language allowed within a PSP is PL/SQL so this attribute, if provided, must be set to PL/SQL.

The contentType attribute defines the content type of a PSP page. The internet browser uses this to determine the action to be taken when interpreting the page contents. As text/HTML is the default contentType if the page is HTML it is not necessary to set this attribute

The last attribute is the errorPage attribute. I will come back to error pages later.

In our sample page, the page directive is:

```
<%@ page language="PL/SQL" errorPage="error.psp"%>
```

The procedure Directive

There is only one attribute associated with the `procedure` directive:

❏ The target `procedure` name

It is not necessary to provide this directive, but if it is to be used, as a rule, it must only be used once in any single PSP and the name assigned should be different from the names used in any of the other PSPs as this will be the name assigned to the database stored procedure. If it is not supplied the PSP loading program uses the name of the PSP file. We will look at the PSP loading program later.

In our example we have used this directive and assigned the name `cust_dets` to be the name of the generated procedure:

```
<%@ plsql procedure="cust_dets" %>
```

The parameter Directive

There are 3 attributes associated with the `parameter` directive:

❏ The parameter `name`
❏ The `type`, which can be any supported PL/SQL type
❏ The `default` value

If there are any input parameters that will be used by the PSP they should be defined using these attributes. The only mandatory attribute is the `parameter` attribute. If there is no `type` provided this defaults to `varchar2` and if there is no `default` value, this will default to `NULL`.

In our example we will use the `cust_id` in our query to retrieve the relevant customer details, so we have to declare this as follows:

```
<%@ plsql parameter="cust_id" type="number" %>
```

These parameters must then appear in the URL that calls this page as shown below:

```
localhost/psp/psp_test.cust_dets?cust_id=2
```

If we want to add another parameter we must add another directive line. So in our example if we wanted to add a `new_customer` flag that defaulted to `Y` we have to add another line and so the resulting parameters directives would be:

```
<%@ plsql parameter="cust_id" type="number" %>
<%@ plsql parameter="new_customer" type="varchar2" default="Y"%>
```

The resulting URL for this page would become:

```
localhost/psp/psp_test.cust_dets?cust_id=354&new_customer=
```

The include Directive

There is only one attribute associated with the `include` directive:

❏   the `file` name, this can be a file of any browser compatible material, HTML, XML, JavaScript

This directive may occur anywhere within a PSP as the file will be inserted in place of it.

In our example, we do not have a file to include, but say it was necessary to include an advertising banner that, due to its changing nature was held in a different file called `banner.ads`, the format for this directive would be:

```
<%@ include file="advertising/pages/banner.ads" %>
```

Note that this insertion occurs only once, when the PSP is compiled, and not every time the page is executed, so it is not dynamic. Another good use of `include` files is to make a consistent interface, with all decoration elements (backgrounds, styles, navigation bars) inside an `include` file that all pages in the application utilize. If you have to change something, you will change only one file (but you will have to recompile all the pages that use it).

PSP Declarations

The declaration element is used to define anything that will be used by the PL/SQL within the PSP like variables, constants and cursors. They are optional as these can also be defined within the PL/SQL scriptlets. But for ease of maintenance it is preferable to define all variables within one block at the start of the page. The general syntax is:

```
<%! PL/SQL declaration %>
```

In our example the declarative element is:

```
<%!
    firstname   varchar2(30);
    lastname    varchar2(30);
    housename   varchar2(30);
    address1    varchar2(30);
    address2    varchar2(30);
    town        varchar2(30);
    region      varchar2(30);
    zip         varchar2(10);
    country_id number(2);
%>
```

These variables are used to hold data that will be used to populate the fields of the form.

PSP Scriptlets

Any PL/SQL or SQL code can be embedded inside the Scriptlet element, including variable declarations, statements and exception handlers. The general syntax is:

```
<% PL/SQL script %>
```

In our example there are several scriptlets, but we will take a look at the code, both HTML and PL/SQL, used to create the Country pick list:

```
<tr>
 <td width="153" align="right">
  <font face="Arial">
   Country
  </font>
 </td>
 <td width="2"></td>
 <td width="220">
  <!--beginning of pick list--!>
  <select size="1" name="country_id" >
  <% if country_id is null then %>
  <% for c1 in (select id, country from countries) loop %>
     <option value="<%= c1.id %>"><%= c1.country %> </option>
    <% end loop; %>
   <% else %>
    <% for c1 in (select id, country from countries) loop %>
     <% if country_id = c1.id then %>
      <option selected value="<%= c1.id %>"><%= c1.country %> </option>
     <% else %>
      <option value="<%= c1.id %>"><%= c1.country %> </option>
     <% end if; %>
    <% end loop; %>
   <% end if; %>
  </select>
 </td>
 <td width="278">
  <font size="1" color="#FF0000" face="Arial">
   <b>
    At the moment we can only deliver to these countries
   </b>
  </font>
 </td>
</tr>
```

A walk through this code shows that a new row is created in the HTML table to hold the Country data. The row is divided into 3 cells, one for the Country label, one for the spacer, and one to hold the pick list. The pick list is generated from the data held within the countries table. Then finally the row is closed.

Let's take a closer look at the creation of the pick list, as this is where our Scriptlet element is used:

```
<% if country_id is null then %>
```

The first step is to test to see if the `country_id` defined in the Declarative section has been assigned a value. If not then the pick list is simply populated using a cursor `for-loop` and the first value will default as the selected item in the pick list:

```
<% for c1 in (select id, country from countries) loop %>
  <option value="<%= c1.id %>"><%= c1.country %> </option>
<% end loop; %>
```

Notice that the syntax within the script follows that required for standard PL/SQL. This also includes ensuring that if a semi-colon is required to finish a line then it is provided.

The other option for the pick list is where the form has retrieved data and will use this to ensure that the correct country is selected in the pick list.

```
<% else %>
 <% for c1 in (select id, country from countries) loop %>
  <% if country_id = c1.id then %>
   <option selected value="<%= c1.id %>"><%= c1.country %> </option>
  <% else %>
   <option value="<%= c1.id %>"><%= c1.country %> </option>
  <% end if; %>
 <% end loop; %>
<% end if; %>
```

The final element of a PSP page, the PSP **expression** is also illustrated in this example but I will look at that further in the next section.

It is worth noting that both Scriptlet and Declarative elements can be used to hold comments. In our example I have used the Scriptlet element for my comments:

```
<%
 /***************************************************/
 /* The cust_dets.psp is used to allow a customer   */
 /* to either register with the site or amend data  */
 /* stored for them.                                 */
 /*                                                  */
 /* If the cust_id parameter contains a value then  */
 /* it will be assumed that this is a customer       */
 /* returning to amend their details and the form   */
 /* will be populated. Otherwise a blank form will  */
 /* be displayed                                     */
 /***************************************************/
%>
```

PSP Expressions

The Expression element allows something that will return a value to be embedded into the PSP. The general syntax is:

```
<%= a PL/SQL expression %>
```

As shown below, in our example we will assign the value for the pick list item to be the selected id and the text to be displayed will be the country name:

```
<% for c1 in (select id, country from countries) loop %>
 <option value="<%= c1.id %>"><%= c1.country %> </option>
<% end loop; %>
```

Source for cust_dets.psp

Putting these elements together along with the HTML results in the following PSP source file. It is not necessary to type this code in as the source code and database definition files are available from the Wrox web site as detailed in the What Next? section at the end of this chapter.

```
<%@ page language="PL/SQL" errorPage="error.psp"%>
<%@ plsql procedure="cust_dets" %>
<%@ plsql parameter="cust_id" type="number" %>

    /**************************************************/
    /* The cust_dets psp is used to allow a customer  */
    /* to either register with the site or amend data */
    /* stored for them.                               */
    /*                                                */
    /* If the cust_id parameter contains a value then */
    /* it will be assumed that this is a customer     */
    /* returning to amend their details and the form  */
    /* will be populated. Otherwise a blank form will */
    /* be displayed                                   */
    /**************************************************/

 /* set up the variable to be used in the query */
    <%!firstname   varchar2(30);
    lastname    varchar2(30);
    housename   varchar2(30);
    address1    varchar2(30);
    address2    varchar2(30);
    town        varchar2(30);
    region      varchar2(30);
    zip         varchar2(10);
    country_id number(2);
%>
 /* populate the variables */
  <% if cust_id is not null then
    select firstname,
           lastname,
           housename,
           address1,
           address2,
           town,
           region,
           zip,
           country_id
    into   firstname,
           lastname,
           housename,
```

```
          address1,
          address2,
          town,
          region,
          zip,
          country_id
   from   cust
   where  id = cust_id;
  end if;
%>
<HTML>

<head>
 <title>The Big Shop</title>
</head>

<body>

<font face="Comic Sans MS" color="#000080" size="7">The Big Shop</font>

<% if cust_id is null then %>
  <p>
   <font face="Arial" size="4">
    <b>Please enter your details.</b>
   </font>
  </p>
<% else %>
  <p>
   <font face="Arial" size="4">
    <b>Please amend your details.</b>
   </font>
  </p>
<% end if; %>

/* Build the form and populate with the contents of the variables */ %>

<form method="POST" action="commit_cust">
 <input type="hidden" name="cust_id" value="<%= cust_id %>" >
  <table border="0" width="679">
   <tr>
    <td width="153"></td>
    <td width="2"></td>
    <td width="220"></td>
    <td width="278"></td>
   </tr>
   <tr>
    <td width="153" align="right">
     <font face="Arial">
      First Name
     </font>
    </td>
    <td width="2"></td>
    <td width="220">
     <input type="text" name="firstname" size="30" value="<%= firstname %>">
    </td>
    <td width="278"></td>
```

```
      </tr>
      <tr>
       <td width="153" align="right">
        <font face="Arial">
         Last Name
        </font>
       </td>
       <td width="2"></td>
       <td width="220">
        <input type="text" name="lastname" size="30" value="<%= lastname %>">
       </td>
       <td width="278"></td>
      </tr>
      <tr>
       <td width="153" align="right">
        <font face="Arial">
         House Name/Number
        </font>
       </td>
       <td width="2"></td>
       <td width="220">
        <input type="text" name="housename" size="30" value="<%= housename %>">
       </td>
       <td width="278"></td>
      </tr>
      <tr>
       <td width="153" align="right">
        <font face="Arial">
         Street
        </font>
       </td>
       <td width="2"></td>
       <td width="220">
        <input type="text" name="address1" size="30" value="<%= address1 %>">
       </td>
       <td width="278"></td>
      </tr>
      <tr>
       <td width="153" align="right"></td>
       <td width="2"></td>
       <td width="220">
        <input type="text" name="address2" size="30" value="<%= address2 %>">
       </td>
       <td width="278"></td>
      </tr>
      <tr>
       <td width="153" align="right">
        <font face="Arial">
         Town/City
        </font>
       </td>
       <td width="2"></td>
       <td width="220">
        <input type="text" name="town" size="30" value="<%= town %>">
       </td>
       <td width="278"></td>
```

```
      </tr>
      <tr>
       <td width="153" align="right">
        <font face="Arial">
         Region
        </font>
       </td>
       <td width="2"></td>
       <td width="220">
        <input type="text" name="region" size="30" value="<%= region %>">
       </td>
       <td width="278"></td>
      </tr>
      <tr>
       <td width="153" align="right">
        <font face="Arial">
         ZIP / Postcode
        </font>
       </td>
       <td width="2"></td>
       <td width="220">
        <input type="text" name="zip" size="30" value="<%= zip %>">
       </td>
       <td width="278"></td>
      </tr>
      <tr>
       <td width="153" align="right">
        <font face="Arial">
         Country
        </font>
       </td>
       <td width="2"></td>
       <td width="220">
        <select size="1" name="country_id" >
         <% if country_id is null then %>
          <% for c1 in (select id, country from countries) loop %>
           <option value="<%= c1.id %>"><%= c1.country %> </option>
          <% end loop; %>
         <% else %>
          <% for c1 in (select id, country from countries) loop %>
           <% if country_id = c1.id then %>
            <option selected value="<%= c1.id %>"><%= c1.country %> </option>
           <% else %>
            <option value="<%= c1.id %>"><%= c1.country %> </option>
           <% end if; %>
          <% end loop; %>
         <% end if; %>
        </select>
       </td>
       <td width="278">
        <font size="1" color="#FF0000" face="Arial">
         <b>
         At the moment we can only deliver to these countries
         </b>
        </font>
       </td>
```

```
      </tr>
    </table>
    <p> </p>
    <table border="0" width="50%">
      <tr>
        <td width="22%"><input type="submit" value="Save"></td>
        <td width="78%"><input type="reset" value="Reset"></td>
      </tr>
    </table>
  </form>

  <% if cust_id is not null then %>
    <p>
      <font face="Arial">
        <a href="psp_test.welcome?cust_id=<%= cust_id %>"><b>Home</b></a>
      </font>
    </p>
  <% else %>
    <p>
      <font face="Arial">
        <a href="psp_test.home"><b>Home</b></a>
      </font>
    </p>
  <% end if; %>

</body>

</HTML>
```

Handling Errors in a PSP

There are two ways to handle errors, one is to use a dedicated error page, the other is to use standard PL/SQL exception handling. As exception handling is not particular to PSPs we will not cover this, rather we will look at how to use an error page.

In our example, we defined the error page using the `errorPage` attribute of the `page` directive:

```
<%@ page language="PL/SQL" errorPage="error.psp"%>
```

So, for example, if there is a `no_data_found` error in our customer details screen, the error page would be displayed:

This is a pretty crude interpretation of the error and if you intend to show these errors to users they should give a more user friendly explanation of what has happened.

The code used to produce this error page, error.psp is:

```
<%@ page language="PL/SQL" %>
<%@ plsql procedure="error" %>
<HTML>
<head>
 <title>The Big Shop</title>
</head>
<body>
<p>
 <font face="Comic Sans MS" color="#000080" size="7">
  The Big Shop
 </font>
</p>
<b>
 <font face="Arial">
  Awooga Awooga there has been an error
 </font>
</b>
<p>
 <font face="Arial">
  <%= SQLERRM %>
 </font>
</p>
</body>
</HTML>
```

Note that SQLERRM is an Oracle core function that returns the error message when an error occurs.

This page should be implemented as a PSP and as such, can have the same anatomy as any PSP with the one important exception, it cannot have any parameter attribute of the page directive set.

Loading a PSP into the Database

As PSPs are stored in the database they need to be loaded in such a way that they can be easily retrieved at run time. This is achieved by the loadpsp utility, a standard utility provided by Oracle with Oracle 8.1.6 and above. It reads in the PSP and translates it into a stored procedure using the attributes provided in the directives. The general syntax is:

```
loadpsp -user username/password@database file.psp
```

In our example, assuming the file name is cust_dets.psp, files must have the .psp extension. The command would be:

```
loadpsp -replace -user username/password@database error.psp cust_dets.psp
```

Note that I have used the -replace keyword, this is because I have already loaded the cust_dets psp. It is the same as when you create a procedure. After the first time you must either drop it or use the create or replace commands before the procedure name.

You will notice that the error page is included in the command. If it does not appear in the same loadpsp command before the main PSP page, the load will fail, this is the same with any files that you intend to include.

The result of this command is:

```
"error.psp" : procedure "error" created
"cust_dets.psp" : procedure "cust_dets" created
```

If we have a look at the resulting procedure created for the error page we can see that the loadpsp utility uses the PL/SQL Web Toolkit to web-enable the page.

```
PROCEDURE error  AS
 BEGIN NULL;
htp.prn('
');
htp.prn('

<HTML>

<head>
<title>The Big Shop</title>
</head>

<body>

<p><font face="Comic Sans MS" color="#000080" size="7">The Big Shop</font></p>
<b><font face="Arial">There has been an error</font></b>
<p><font face="Arial">');
htp.prn( SQLERRM );
htp.prn('</font></p>

</body>

</HTML>
');
  END;
```

The -replace flag is optional, but if you plan to load the file many times it must be provided from the second time on.

What Now?

If you want to develop this application further then the source code required can be obtained from the Wrox website.

If you do decide to use this sample application as the basis for any part of a real application it should be understood that the whole purpose of the application is to support this introduction to PSPs and as such there have been no considerations made for security, user interface or performance.

A full description of the application and how to set it up are included with the source files from the Wrox website.

Summary

A PL/SQL Server Page, PSP, is a server side stored procedure that contains PL/SQL within predefined tags. These tags can be grouped into 4 main elements:

- **Directives** – these provide information for the current page. We set the page language to be PL/SQL.

- **Declaratives** – these are where all variables are declared for use within the current page.

- **Scriptlets** – here any valid PL/SQL code can be included, including variable declarations.

- **Expressions** – formats the expression for inclusion in the displayed page

Each of these elements have their own attributes that are used by the `loadpsp` utility to translate the PSP file into a database stored procedure that can provide dynamic data content directly from the database to the internet browser.

For further information please see the documentation included with your Oracle 8i Release 2 and above software.

The PL/SQL Web Toolkit

Hopefully Chapter 6 served as both a refresher in the art of programming good PL/SQL packages and an introduction to new ideas for effective PL/SQL programming in a group production environment. With that knowledge under you belt, we can move on to discuss the PL/SQL Web Toolkit, which is a suite of predefined PL/SQL packages in the database that allow developers to deploy enterprise applications to the Web.

The Web toolkit has been in existence since the first version of Oracle Web Application Server, as a way to dynamically build simple web pages based on data stored in the database. The intent of the PL/SQL Web Toolkit hasn't actually changed much since then and, indeed many custom, enterprise-wide applications have this toolkit as their foundation.

The chapter will be structured as follows:

- ❑   Evolution of the Toolkit and when you might consider using it
- ❑   Setting up to use the Toolkit
- ❑   How Toolkit-based applications work
- ❑   An overview of the various components of the Toolkit
- ❑   A sample application using the `htp` package

The toolkit encompasses far more functionality than we can demonstrate in this short section, but it will give you a solid understanding of what the toolkit can do and how it does it, and this is knowledge that will be augmented by the case study in the following chapter that utilizes the toolkit to build a personal stock tracker.

A Brief History of the Toolkit

Back in the "old" days, an "enterprise computing system" might have comprised several computers linked on an intranet, with a web server dishing out static HTML pages. Webmasters around the world were learning how to create HTML pages, and figuring out the best way of storing and organizing those pages on the filesystem-based architecture of the web server. The problem back in "those days" was that all of the valuable information was being maintained in a database. We had the information we wanted to publish; we had an audience interested in the information we wanted to publish. We simply had no way to take the data in our database and deploy it to our audience.

In 1994, Oracle put a small team of developers together to build a product for accessing the database through a web browser. Out of this came the PL/SQL Agent. This was one part of Oracle Web Server, and it allowed web browsers to call a PL/SQL procedure, inside the database, and return the results of that procedure to the web browser. From this beginning, we now have enterprises around the world publishing data, conducting business, and coming up with the 'next-best-thing' based on the technology originally created by this small team at Oracle.

Since then, the Oracle Web Server has grown up and matured, and the PL/SQL Agent has done the same. In addition, various other technologies have been included in Oracle's Internet offering. Oracle Internet Application Server is the name of Oracle Web Server as it exists today, and the PL/SQL Agent is now known as mod_plsql. If you read through Chapter 1 of this book, then you will know that, along with mod_plsql, there are numerous other extensions to iAS, including mod_perl, mod_ose, and support for XML, Java Servlets, and JSPs and EJBs. So the question arises: with all these new technologies around, why use the PL/SQL Web Toolkit?

When to Use the Toolkit

There are a number of reasons to use PL/SQL for web-based application development, instead of the various other options at your disposal. I am a big fan of using the right tool for the job. You wouldn't go out and rent a bulldozer to dig a hole in your yard for a fence post. Along the same lines, there is no need to 'over engineer' a technology solution; or as a famous man once said: "Don't use technology for technology's sake".

One of the most compelling reasons for using the toolkit was mentioned in Chapter 6. PL/SQL Web Toolkit pages are written as stored procedures and so are deployed directly into and served from the database and so enjoy the security, scalability, and reliability inherent with the Oracle database. Others include:

❑ As noted above, PL/SQL Web Toolkit pages have been available since early versions of the Oracle Web Server. Essentially, they have been proven to work.

❑ PL/SQL Web Toolkit utilizes PL/SQL and SQL, which are native data manipulation languages and so are quicker for these tasks.

Often the overruling consideration for the project technology may be the skills of the development team and the project timelines. So if your project has aggressive timescales and the overall skill-set for the development team will be the core Oracle Database languages of PL/SQL and SQL then PL/SQL Web Toolkit-based pages will provide a good, sound platform for your application.

There have been numerous applications, web sites, and tools built on the foundation of PL/SQL in the Oracle database. Oracle Portal, formerly known as Oracle WebDB, has its roots in the PL/SQL Web Toolkit – as it is largely written in PL/SQL internally.

Now that we've established what the toolkit is, and how it came to be, let's look at the architecture in which it is employed.

The Toolkit Architecture

There are a variety of architectures to choose from when it comes to developing and deploying any web-based application, and the PL/SQL Web Toolkit is no different. In order to build and deploy an application using the toolkit, there are a variety of components you will need to understand and configure. The architecture, as we are going to discuss it, is primarily an Oracle environment, but this isn't necessarily a requirement. You will need the Oracle database server in order to run the toolkit on the database tier but beyond that, whether you use Oracle or some third party solution is up to you.

The following diagram illustrates where the toolkit fits, in relation to the rest of the architecture:

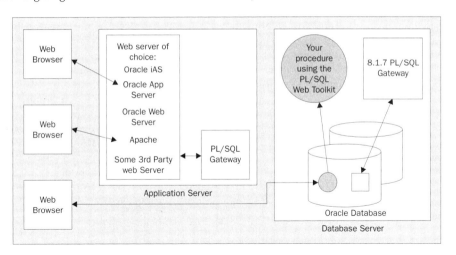

Here we see the classic 3-tier architecture, with the application server and the database server on separate machines. In your environment, however, you could easily deploy these on the same server. Many considerations will affect the choice of architecture for your production environment: budget, including scalability requirements, existing hardware and software environments, user requirements, and so on.

Let's start at the front end with the web browsers that are accessing the application. The PL/SQL Web Toolkit was originally designed for generating HTML pages for a web browser but, today, browsers are only one of many types of devices capable of using your PL/SQL Web Toolkit applications. Cellular telephones, personal data assistants (PDAs), digital picture frames, and a variety of other devices are being outfitted with the capability to browse the Web and use these network-centric applications. Although our examples are going to be targeting Internet Explorer and Netscape, keep it in the back of your mind that you may be writing applications for a wireless handheld device or a cell phone before long.

In the middle is the Application Server tier. Most of the application server solutions listed in the diagram come packaged with a **PL/SQL Gateway** in some form or fashion (Oracle iAS, OAS, Oracle Web Server). In Oracle iAS, for example, this gateway is mod_plsql. Since Oracle application servers are tightly integrated with the database, configuring the PL/SQL Gateway to talk to your database is a pretty simple affair. Later in the chapter, we will configure the Database Access Descriptor (DAD) in Oracle iAS to talk to the database via Net8 (Net8 is Oracle's network communication software, which acts as the data transport layer for Oracle software on one machine talking to Oracle software on another machine – see Chapter 4).

On the back end in our diagram is the database server. Although the PL/SQL Web Toolkit is typically installed as a part of the web server or PL/SQL Gateway product, it resides inside the database in the form of compiled PL/SQL packages. The application we are going to write will also live inside the database, as will most products that are built on top of the PL/SQL Web Toolkit.

> *We do not actually explore this in the book, but it's worth mentioning that Oracle is also considered a "gateway" into many legacy applications.*

Custom PL/SQL Gateways have been written for many non-Oracle web servers that will allow you to use the PL/SQL Web Toolkit. The problem you may encounter here is that most of these products are unsupported and may or may not have continued development/bug fixes/enhancements being built. Also, typically, many of the authors of these third party PL/SQL Gateway solutions don't port their solutions to the wide variety of operating systems that Oracle does. Having said this, many of these custom-written gateways come with pretty installation procedures and configuration walkthroughs, in order to get you up and running with little to no pain. We discuss a few third party options a little later in the chapter.

Different Oracle products offered different ways of installing the toolkit, and different recommendations were made with regard to how best to use it. Up until OAS 4.0 it was recommended that you perform a separate installation of the toolkit for each user in the database that planned on using it. Later versions of OAS recommended one installation of the toolkit in one schema only, with public synonyms and public execution access to the packages that made up the toolkit. The supported installation method for iAS 1.0.1 is to install the toolkit with a utility account in the database. The installation procedures in iAS include the creation of the public synonyms and appropriate grants to allow other users in the database to use the toolkit.

Setting up the Environment

You're all ready to dive right in and start building applications, right? Well, first things, first. We need to properly configure the products in our architecture for database connections, mod_plsql settings, etc. In this section, we'll walk through the major steps in getting your environment configured to run applications built on the PL/SQL Web Toolkit.

Bear in mind that covering installation and configuration issues for all flavors of web server products that support this architecture would take an entire book. The following sections aren't meant in any way to replace the installation/administration documentation for your particular product. Indeed you should consult this documentation as a matter of course, whether or not you read the sections here. The purpose is simply to highlight the important components you will need to have configured in order to get off the ground and running.

Configuring iAS

Once iAS is installed, you need to configure your application server for your database and your environment. There are a few files in your iAS installation you should be concerned with:

```
UNIX:   <IAS_HOME>/Apache/Apache/conf/httpds.conf


NT/2000:  <IAS_HOME>\Apache\Apache\conf\httpd.conf
```

This is the Apache HTTP Server configuration file. It is responsible for configuring how the actual web listener works. You can define such settings as the document root (where your `.html` static files are kept), the port(s) on which your server listens, which modules your installation supports (such as mod_plsql), virtual directory mappings, and so on.

Mapping Virtual directories in iAS is relatively painless. Simply edit the `httpd` or `httpds.conf` file, and add the following line at the bottom:

```
Alias /images/ "C:\Oracle\iAS\Apache\images\"
```

In effect, this makes a folder on the operating system of the web server machine. This new folder is then accessible via requests made to the web server.

> *You may need to stop and restart your web server product in order to make that change to the configuration public.*

In addition to the `httpd.conf` and the `httpds.conf` files, there are configuration files available with iAS that serve entirely different purposes. For example, the following configuration files are additional files used by iAS:

```
UNIX:   <IAS_ROOT>/Apache/modplsql/cfg/plsql.conf


NT/2000:  <IAS_ROOT>\Apache\modplsql\cfg\plsql.conf
```

The `plsql.conf` file is an extension to the original `httpd(s).conf` file. When mod_plsql is loaded, this file is loaded as an extension to the Apache directives specified in the `httpd(s).conf`:

```
UNIX:   <IAS_ROOT>/Apache/modplsql/cfg/wdbsvr.conf


NT/2000:  <IAS_ROOT>\Apache\modplsql\cfg\wdbsvr.conf
```

This is the mod_plsql configuration file that specifies the DAD settings. There is no need to modify this file directly. Oracle iAS has a mod_plsql configuration page that will allow you to create, edit, and remove DADs from your iAS configuration.

Configuring a Simple Database Access Descriptor (DAD)

The DAD is a collection of settings that allow iAS to talk to the database. You will need to configure a DAD in order to connect through the PL/SQL Gateway to your database. Follow these steps:

1. Go to http://<hostname>, where <hostname> is the name of your computer.

2. With a default iAS installation, you'll be presented with a list of pages you can view. Toward the bottom of the list you will find mod_plsql. Click on mod_plsql.

3. This will bring you to the Gateway Configuration Menu.

4. From this menu, click on Gateway Database Access Descriptors. This will take you to the DAD administration screen.

5. Click on Add Default (blank configuration) on the DAD administration screen. From here we can create a new DAD.

There are a handful of options you have when configuring your DAD. Here we will only create the simplest DAD possible to get us up and running. Enter the following information:

❑ Database Access Descriptor Name: scott_dad

❑ Oracle User Name: SCOTT

❑ Oracle Password: TIGER

❑ Oracle Connect String: **<your connect string>**

You will also need to specify the Oracle Connect String. When you installed iAS, you would have had the option of specifying a database alias to the database you are using. You can use this alias as your connect string, or you can create another alias by using the tools provided with iAS. The Net8 Assistant (or the Net8 Configuration Assistant) will do the job equally well. One word of warning, however: if you are running both your database and iAS on the same machine, make sure that you specify the correct Net8 environment. The best way to test this is to view the Net8 configuration files manually:

```
UNIX:   <IAS_HOME>/network/admin/tnsnames.ora


NT/2000:   <IAS_HOME>\network\admin\tnsnames.ora
```

My particular tnsnames.ora file looks like this (my connect string is SDILLON.US.ORACLE.COM) :

```
SDILLON.US.ORACLE.COM =
  (DESCRIPTION =
    (ADDRESS_LIST =
      (ADDRESS = (PROTOCOL = TCP)(HOST = SDILLON)(PORT = 1521))
    )
    (CONNECT_DATA =
      (SID = ORCL)
    )
  )
```

> **NOTE:** Editing the Net8 configuration files manually is strongly discouraged by Oracle. Unless you are well versed in the ways of SQL*Net and Net8, stick to using the tools for making updates to this environment. One missed parenthesis or quotation mark can spell disaster.

Once you have configured your DAD, you're ready to move on to installing the PL/SQL Web Toolkit packages.

You Don't Have iAS, You Say?

The PL/SQL Web Toolkit is fairly web server agnostic. Just because you don't have iAS, it does not mean you can't build enterprise class web-based applications with PL/SQL! For most of the web server solutions out there today, there is a corresponding PL/SQL Gateway solution. Oracle Application Server (OAS) 4.0 was built on a flexible architecture, which allowed you to use Netscape, Microsoft, or Apache web server solutions with the extended services of OAS behind them. This means that you could continue to use Netscape, Microsoft IIS, or Apache as your web listener, and then install OAS as an "add-on service" behind the HTTPD listener.

There are some third-party solutions built for providing access to the PL/SQL Web Toolkit from many other web servers. One example is DBPrism, a servlet-based PL/SQL Gateway, which extends the PL/SQL functionality and adds various other services, as well. Additionally, DBPrism also supports a variety of other technologies (see http://www.plenix.com/dbprism/xml/wwwIndex.html).

Installing the Toolkit

The toolkit is basically a set of packages in a common schema. Execute privileges on these packages are then granted to the database users who will be hosting PL/SQL based web applications. (Typically, I grant execute to PUBLIC. This is the way to make the toolkit available to any database user. You should evaluate whether or not that is necessary in your environment.)

If the database you are using is your own, you are probably aware of whether the toolkit has been installed or not. If you have been given access to a database and you are unaware of whether or not the toolkit has been installed, run the following query:

```
system@SDILLON.US.ORACLE.COM> select owner, object_name, object_type
  2      from dba_objects
  3    where object_name like 'HT%'
  4    /

OWNER                             OBJECT_NAME                       OBJECT_TYPE
--------------------------------  --------------------------------  ----------------
OWAUTIL                           HTF                               PACKAGE
OWAUTIL                           HTF                               PACKAGE BODY
OWAUTIL                           HTP                               PACKAGE
OWAUTIL                           HTP                               PACKAGE BODY
PUBLIC                            HTF                               SYNONYM
PUBLIC                            HTP                               SYNONYM
```

You are looking for two packages in particular. If the HTF and HTP packages are visible, you will know (1) that the PL/SQL Web Toolkit exists in the database, and (2) whether public synonyms have been created for access to these packages.

231

> **NOTE:** I ran this query as the **SYSTEM** database user, which is a privileged account. If you do not have DBA privilege, you would query the **ALL_OBJECTS** view instead of the **DBA_OBJECTS** view. The results of this can be inconclusive, however. The toolkit may be installed, but if your non-privileged account does not have access to the packages, you will not see the records. In cases where you do not have a privileged account to check the database, I recommend asking to your database administrator if the packages exist.

If the packages are not installed, you will need to run the installation scripts necessary to compile the packages into the database. The files you need to install the toolkit are distributed with iAS (or Oracle Application Server, or Oracle Web Server, etc.).

On UNIX operating systems, you will find the files here:

```
<IAS_HOME>/Apache/modplsql/owa
```

For Windows NT and/or Windows 2000, the installation scripts will be found here:

```
<IAS_HOME>\Apache\modplsql\owa
```

The "driving script" used to install the toolkit is `owaload.sql`. This script is responsible for installing all the necessary packages. The latest iAS documentation recommends installing the toolkit as the SYS user. The purpose of this is to ensure only one user in the database owns the toolkit, and is meant to prevent multiple users from installing the toolkit themselves.

```
sys@SDILLON.US.ORACLE.COM> connect sys/change_on_install;
Connected.

sys@SDILLON.US.ORACLE.COM> @@owaload owaload.log
<serveroutput removed for brevity>
```

The script goes through the following steps:

1. Installs a package called SYS.WPIUTL. This package is for internal use only.

2. Drops all the packages in the toolkit (if they are present).

3. Creates each of the toolkit packages.

4. Grants all privileges on the packages to PUBLIC.

5. Drops public synonyms that reference these packages.

6. Creates public synonyms for each of the toolkit packages.

There are a variety of packages installed, all of which contribute to the final product of the PL/SQL Web Toolkit. In our examples later in the chapter, you will learn how to use a small subset of the functionality included in this toolkit. For more information about the packages and their abilities, I recommend you review the documentation included with iAS regarding the Web Toolkit API. This will give you details about what packages are available, what each of the packages does, and how to use each one of them.

Debugging Your Configuration

At this point, it would be wise to ensure your installation is working properly. There is an easy way to test your installation of the toolkit itself, without involving a web browser, web server, or PL/SQL Gateway. What we are going to do is short circuit the need for the HTTP protocol altogether. We can write some simple code that uses the toolkit, and use a utility in the OWA_UTIL package to view the data that is in the response buffer. Typically, this response buffer is returned to the end-user's browser via the PL/SQL Gateway. When the PL/SQL Gateway invokes the toolkit, it initializes the CGI environment of the toolkit. It's not important to understand the details of the CGI environment at this stage, but in order to test your configuration you must initialize the CGI environment and pass some name/value pair:

```
scott@SDILLON.US.ORACLE.COM> begin
2    l_name owa.vc_arr;
3    l_val owa.vc_arr;
4 begin
5    l_name(1) := 'SOME_NAME';
6    l_val(1) := 'SOME_VALUE';
7    owa.init_cgi_env(1, l_name, l_val);
8 end;
9 /

PL/SQL procedure successfully completed.
```

Next, launch SQL*Plus and enter the following code, as any user (provided you granted execute privilege to PUBLIC during the installation of the toolkit):

```
scott@SDILLON.US.ORACLE.COM> set serveroutput on
scott@SDILLON.US.ORACLE.COM> begin
2    htp.p('Testing...  1, 2, 3, ... Testing');
3    owa_util.showpage;
4  end;
5  /
Content-type: text/html
Content-length: 33
Testing...  1, 2, 3, ... Testing

PL/SQL procedure successfully completed.
```

As you can see, my installation is configured properly. htp is a package in the PL/SQL Web Toolkit, and p is a procedure that prints to the response buffer. owa_util.showpage is a PL/SQL procedure that acts much the same as dbms_output.put_line, but it dumps the response buffer to the standard output (in this case, SQL*Plus).

There are a few different errors that you may encounter when there is something wrong with the installation.

CGI Environment Not Initialized

```
begin
*
ERROR at line 1:
ORA-06502: PL/SQL: numeric or value error
ORA-06512: at "SYS.OWA_UTIL", line 318
ORA-06512: at "SYS.HTP", line 859
ORA-06512: at "SYS.HTP", line 974
ORA-06512: at "SYS.HTP", line 992
ORA-06512: at line 2
```

Failure to initialize your CGI environment will result in this error stack. When you try to execute the HTP package, it attempts to access the CGI environment, which was supposed to be set up by the PL/SQL Gateway. If it is not initialized, an exception is thrown. In order to fix this, simply run the script above, which calls the OWA.INIT_CGI_ENV() procedure with a name-value pair.

Improper privileges

```
ERROR at line 1:
ORA-06550: line 2, column 3:
PLS-00201: identifier 'SYS.HTP' must be declared
ORA-06550: line 2, column 3:
PL/SQL: Statement ignored
```

This happens when execute permission has not been granted to either PUBLIC or the database user you are logged in as. An easy way to resolve this is to grant execute privileges on the toolkit packages to PUBLIC, or to the user who owns the application code. In the "Installing the Toolkit" section above, you will find instructions for running the installation scripts. One of the scripts grants the appropriate privileges to PUBLIC for the toolkit.

Can't Resolve Package/Procedure Name

```
ERROR at line 1:
ORA-06550: line 2, column 3:
PLS-00201: identifier 'HTP.P' must be declared
ORA-06550: line 2, column 3:
PL/SQL: Statement ignored
```

There are a couple of potential solutions to this problem. You can either create a private synonym for this user that maps to the packages in the toolkit owner's schema, or, again, you can create public synonyms for the packages in the toolkit (see "Installing the Toolkit").

These are the most common errors you will encounter when debugging your toolkit installation. If you encounter additional problems, I would encourage you to re-read your toolkit installation documentation.

OK, your environment is configured; the toolkit is installed, and now we are ready to start building applications.

Building Applications Using the Toolkit

We are going to create a quick, simple sample page with the PL/SQL Web Toolkit to ensure that everything is working and to introduce a few core concepts.

In order to build applications using the PL/SQL Toolkit, you first need to understand the tool and have a cursory knowledge of the functionality it provides. To set aside three or four weeks trying to understand every nuance and parameter involved in the packages of the toolkit would most likely be overkill. On the other hand, sitting down to re-write your company's general ledger using the toolkit without understanding how to create pages, forms, and reports would be a project headed for disaster.

Your First Dynamic Page

We're going to start off slow, developing a few simple dynamic pages with PL/SQL. We can then move on to investigate some additional features, ultimately developing a simple application, which should give some idea of how you might approach designing and building applications of your own.

In SQL*Plus, run the following script:

```
sdillon@SDILLON.US.ORACLE.COM> create or replace procedure helloworld
  2  as
  3  begin
  4     -- call the HTP procedures necessary to produce an HTML page
  5     htp.htmlopen;
  6     htp.bodyopen;
  7     htp.header('1','Hello,World!');
  8     htp.bodyclose;
  9     htp.htmlclose;
 10  end;
 11  /
Procedure created.
```

Then, in a web browser, point to the following URL:

http://<your hostname>/pls/scott_dad/helloworld

The hostname is the name of the web server hosting your PL/SQL gateway. You should receive a very simple web page with the infamous words "Hello, World!" at the top, in large, bold letters. If you received an error message, check that your web server is up and running, have a look through the debugging section above, consult you documentation, and so on until the issue is resolved. We're now going to have a look at what the above URL actually means, and what happens when you submit such a request.

Nomenclature of a Request

Our request for a web page takes the form of a URL. This request is submitted to the Web server where it is handled by the PL/SQL Gateway. Let's have a closer look at the exact format of this URL:

protocol://hostname[:port]/prefix/dad/[[!][schema.][package.]procedure[?querystring]

For example, my URL is as follows:

http://slaphappy.us.oracle.com/pls/scott_dad/helloworld

Let's break this down further because there are a few features that don't actualy appear in our simple request:

❑ **Protocol**. In our case, HTTP, which simply specifies that we are making a web request for an HTML document. We can also use HTTPS for Secure Sockets Layer (SSL) requests. These are the only valid entries for the purposes of the PL/SQL Web Toolkit.

❑ **Hostname**. As stated above, this is the name of the server handling our request . My particular server is named SLAPHAPPY and it lives in the US.ORACLE.COM domain.

❑ **Prefix**. Your web or application server uses this prefix to map your request to the PL/SQL gateway. Using the standard installation of iAS, the default mapping to mod_plsql is `pls` (this is configurable via the iAS configuration options). If you are using the WebDB product, this prefix is most likely to be `webdb`

❑ **dad**. This is the name of your Database Access Descriptor (DAD). In our case: `scott_dad`.

❑ **"!"**. The optional exclamation character indicates that the parameter passing mechanism is "flexible", rather than hard coded. We'll talk more about this later.

❑ **Package**. As discussed in Chapter 6, we often create packages to logically sort our procedures and functions. If your procedure is part of a package, specify the package name here.

❑ **Procedure**. The procedure name is the actual code that will execute in the database. Often, this procedure is responsible for generating an HTML page, which will be delivered to the user's browser via the PL/SQL Gateway. In our example, this is the `helloworld` procedure.

❑ **?querystring**. The query string, which is attached to the end of the URL request, indicates all the parameters that are passed to the target procedure. Unless flexible parameter passing has been enabled (via the '!' symbol), the procedure you are calling must map exactly to the query string indicated.

Lifecycle of a Request

Once the request has been submitted, the web server will accept the request and determine how to handle it. The request prefix is the key to determining how to handle a particular request. If the prefix is a virtual directory that has been mapped in the web server's configuration, then the web server knows to serve up a static file. For example, consider the following URL:

http://slaphappy.us.oracle.com/downloads/index.html

The web server will look up `downloads` to determine how it should handle this request. In my case, I have a virtual directory mapped to `downloads` that points to a folder on my server. In that folder is a file named `index.html`. So for that request, the web server reads the `index.html` file and returns it to the browser. If the request is as follows:

http://slaphappy.us.oracle.com/cgi-bin/dostuff?user=sdillon

The web server then knows to use `cgi-bin` to handle the request. According to the web server's configuration settings, `cgi-bin` is configured to execute some external functionality such as a C procedure, Perl script, etc. The web server will then call on the `dostuff` procedure, and pass it a parameter named `user`, with a value of `sdillon`.

For iAS we use the `pls` prefix and mod_plsql uses its own configuration files to determine what the settings are for the DAD. In the "*Configuring iAS*" section we discussed a few such configuration files that define how mod_plsql handles these requests. In the `WDBSVR.APP` file, there will be entries for each of your DADs, including `scott_dad`:

```
[DAD_mydad]
connect_string   =   SDILLON.US.ORACLE.COM
username   = SCOTT
password   = TIGER
;document_table   =
```

```
;document_path    =
;document_proc    =
;upload_as_long_raw    =
;upload_as_blob    =
name_prefix    =
;always_describe    =
;after_proc    =
;before_proc    =
reuse    =  Yes
;connmax    =
;pathalias    =
;pathaliasproc    =
enablesso    =  No
;sncookiename    =
stateful    =  No
;custom_auth    =
```

mod_plsql is responsible for reading the URL request and translating it into a database call. In order to look at this process in more detail we're going to define a slightly more interesting helloworld procedure that accepts parameters:

```
/*
 *  A parameterized HELLOWORLD
 */

create or replace procedure helloworld(
   p_greeting   in   varchar2 default 'Hello',
   p_addressee  in   varchar2 default 'World' )
is
begin
   -- call the HTP procedures necessary to produce an HTML page
   htp.htmlopen;
   htp.bodyopen;
   -- concatentate the input parameters to this procedure in order
   -- to allow for a dynamic header tag.
   htp.header(1,p_greeting||', '||p_addressee||'!');
   htp.bodyclose;
   htp.htmlclose;
end;
/
show errors
```

Once the new helloworld procedure is created, we can call it using the following URL request:

http://slaphappy.us.oracle.com/pls/mydad/helloworld?p_greeting=Hello&p_addressee=Readers

You should see the words Hello, Readers! in your browser. So how does this happen? Well, once we make this request, the PL/SQL Gateway is then responsible for converting this URL request into a PL/SQL block that will execute our procedure and pass in the correct parameters. Based on the above request, the block created would be:

```
begin
   helloworld(p_greeting=>'Hello',
             p_addressee=>'Readers');
end;
/
```

This PL/SQL block is then executed in the database as the user specified in the DAD. The results of the request are then sent back to the user via the web server and PL/SQL Gateway.

The following diagram gives an overview of the entire lifecycle:

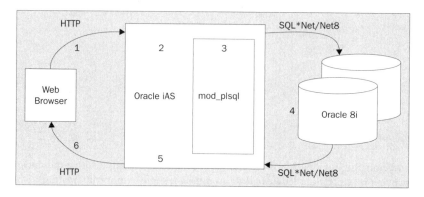

1. The browser sends a URL request to iAS via HTTP. The browser then waits for a response from the web server.

2. iAS parses the request and determines how to handle the request. Upon determining mod_plsql should handle the request, it is passed to mod_plsql for processing.

3. mod_plsql translates the URL request into a PL/SQL block. A connection is established to the database, and the PL/SQL block is passed to the database for execution.

4. Oracle 8i processes the PL/SQL block. The response buffer in the PL/SQL Toolkit is populated with data from the PL/SQL block (dependent on the block, of course)

5. The contents of the response buffer are sent back to mod_plsql and given back to iAS.

6. iAS ships the results to the web browser.

The diagram shown is specific to Oracle iAS using mod_plsql. For other types of web servers, the architecture is pretty much the same. The request is interpreted in the web server, it is handed of to some form of PL/SQL Gateway, and the PL/SQL Gateway then connects to the database to process the procedure. The results are then shipped back to the browser via the PL/SQL Gateway and web server.

The Toolkit API

Our helloworld procedure served as our 'get-your-feet-wet' routine. We didn't go into any details at all regarding the toolkit packages, how to call them, what happens when you call them, etc. Let's now have a quick overview of the packages that are available with the PL/SQL Web Toolkit.

HTF & HTP

The htp and htf packages contain procedures and functions (respectively) that generate HTML tags and place those tags in the response buffer. The designers of the toolkit knew that when calling the htp procedures, you would need to have additional tags generated within these procedure calls. That's where the htf functions come into play. For instance, in the following code procedure:

```
create or replace procedure show_image(p_url        in varchar2,
                                        p_align      in varchar2 DEFAULT 'LEFT',
                                        p_alt        in varchar2 DEFAULT 'Image',
                                        p_attributes in varchar2 DEFAULT
'BORDER="0"')
is
begin
  htp.htmlopen;
  htp.bodyopen;
  htp.print('Here is an image:  <img src="'|| p_url ||'" align="'|| p_align ||
            '" alt="'|| p_alt ||'" '||p_attributes||'>');
  htp.bodyclose;
  htp.htmlclose;
end;
/
```

The line that draws the image tag can be changed to use the `htf` function for creating an image tag, as follows:

```
create or replace procedure show_image(p_url        in varchar2,
                                        p_align      in varchar2 DEFAULT 'LEFT',
                                        p_alt        in varchar2 DEFAULT 'Image',
                                        p_attributes in varchar2 DEFAULT
'BORDER="0"')
is
begin
  htp.bodyopen;
  htp.print('Here is an image: '||
    htf.img(p_url, p_align, p_alt, null, p_attributes));
  htp.bodyclose;
  htp.htmlclose;
end;
/
```

This helps to cut down on string concatenation, and can produce cleaner code. These two packages are by far the most commonly used packages in the toolkit.

OWA_CACHE

This package provides cache functions for storing PL/SQL generated content. Using OWA_CACHE, we can specify content in our PL/SQL web applications as "cacheable items". This means that after the content has been requested once, it will be cached in your middle tier and subsequent requests will retrieve it from there, rather than requesting it from the database. If the this content results from a frequently accessed database query, caching on the middle tier can considerably enhance the performance of your PL/SQL web applications

OWA_COOKIE

The cookie package is a wrapper enabling the use of web browser based Cookies in your generated web pages. Cookies are one way to have the browser maintain some locally managed cache of information. That cookie, or cached data, is resubmitted to the web server on each subsequent page request.

OWA_CUSTOM

This package is used as a callback mechanism when the application is interested in using it's own custom authentication. For example, when using the PL/SQL Gateway, developers can decide how they want to implement their own security. The developer can override the standard OWA_CUSTOM package body, and use their own authentication in the AUTHORIZE function.

OWA_IMAGE

This package is provided as a utility to assist in dealing with image map coordinates. When a user clicks on an image, routines in OWA_IMAGE can retrieve the coordinates of where this event took place. Use this package when you have an image map that has destination links that invoke mod_plsql.

OWA_OPT_LOCK

Contains subprograms that enable you to impose database optimistic locking strategies, so as to prevent lost updates. Lost updates can occur if a user selects and then attempts to update a row whose values have been changed in the meantime by another user. This is a very helpful package, considering the (normally) stateless environment of the Internet.

OWA

This contains procedures that are used directly from mod_plsql. There are no procedures or functions publicly available in the specification of this package. In the installation files, it states that the procedures within OWA should not be called by an end user.

OWA_PATTERN

This package contains routines that allow you to use regular expressions to perform string matching and string manipulation. String matching and manipulation are more and more important on the Internet, because most of the data you deal with on your sites is textual in nature.

OWA_SEC

This package contains routines that are used by mod_plsql for authenticating requests to the PL/SQL Gateway. Developers can use OWA_SEC to access the web client's authentication information to perform custom authentication in their PL/SQL web applications.

OWA_TEXT

This package contains procedures and functions for manipulating large amounts of text. The utilities in OWA_TEXT mainly provide the ability to break up large streams of text into an array of individual lines. This is especially useful when used in conjunction with OWA_PATTERN.

OWA_UTIL

This package is a helper package to assist in a few different areas. First, there are utilities to allow you to retrieve the values of the CGI environment variables. This can be useful in any number of ways. You can track statistics based on the distribution of client machine types, browsers, and so on. You can also use the IP address of the connecting client (as indicated in the CGI environment) as a key into some security algorithm.

There are also routines to allow OWA_UTIL users to produce pages with dynamically generated SQL code, and also to perform functions such as casting text data retrieved from the web into DATE datatypes in our PL/SQL routines.

WPG_DOCLOAD

This package is used to implement file upload and file download to/from the database via a web browser on the front end. These files can be loaded into the database itself, and/or stored on the operating system in a `BFILE`.

Building the Sample Application

It's finally time to build a sample application to exercise the toolkit. The approach I've taken to building web-based applications is to start small, and start simple. Don't try to jump straight in and design a 250-table front-office/back-office solution. We're going to build an example based around the `htp` and `htf` packages and the classic (!) `EMP` – `DEPT` tables in the `SCOTT/TIGER` demo database that will generate web-based reports.

The Department Report

In this first stage we're going to create an application that will allow us to see all the departments that live in the `DEPT` table. This shouldn't be too difficult. Start with the following specification:

```
set define off
create or replace package dept_tool
as

    -- procedure DEPARTMENTS is used for listing departments on a web page.
    -- It accepts one parameter, p_currentdept

    procedure departments(p_currentdept in varchar2 default NULL);

end dept_tool;
/
show errors
```

...and then define the body for this package as follows:

```
set define off
create or replace package body dept_tool
as

    /*
     * ITE:  This function takes three parameters.  First, the boolean
     *       parameter which will be evaluated.  If p_condition is true,
     *       p_true is returned.  If p_condition is false, p_false is
     *       returned.  This is just a shortcut function for performing an
     *       if/then/else throughout the package.
     */

    function ite(
      p_condition in boolean,
      p_true      in varchar2,
      p_false     in varchar2)
      return varchar2
    is
```

```
begin
  if p_condition then
    return p_true;
  end if;
  return p_false;
end ite;

/*
 * DEPT_ERROR:  In the case of an error, this procedure will simply create
 *              a web page which either displays a message to the user, or
 *              if no message was passed, displays a message indicating an
 *              error was encountered.
 */

procedure dept_error(
  p_msg in varchar2 default NULL)
is
begin
  htp.htmlopen;
  htp.bodyopen;
  htp.p(ite(p_msg is null,'The department tool encountered an error.',p_msg));
  htp.br;
  htp.p('Click '||htf.anchor('dept_tool.departments',
                              'here')||' to return to the departments report');
  htp.bodyclose;
  htp.htmlclose;
end dept_error;

/*
 * DEPARTMENTS:  This procedure is for listing all those departments in the
 *               DEPT table.
 */

procedure departments(
  p_currentdept in varchar2 default NULL)
is
  l_empcnt number := 0;
  l_dname  varchar2(30);
begin
  htp.htmlopen;
  htp.bodyopen(cattributes=>'BGCOLOR="WHITE"');
  htp.header(2,'Departments');
  htp.tableopen(cattributes => 'CELLSPACING="3" CELLPADDING="3"');

  /* This is an implicit cursor, which will loop through each record returned
   * from the query "select * from dept" and create an HTML table row for each
   * department.  Additionally, each department will be an anchor to this
   * procedure passing along the selected department as the current department.
   */

  for d in (select * from dept) loop
    htp.tablerowopen;
    htp.tabledata(
      htf.anchor('dept_tool.departments?p_currentdept='||d.deptno,
                 initcap(d.dname)), cattributes=>'BGCOLOR="'||
                 ite(d.deptno=p_currentdept, 'YELLOW', 'WHITE')||'"');
    htp.tabledata(initcap(d.loc), cattributes=>'BGCOLOR="'||
                  ite(d.deptno=p_currentdept,'YELLOW','WHITE')||'"');
    htp.tablerowclose;
    if d.deptno=p_currentdept then
      l_dname := d.dname;
```

```
      end if;
    end loop;
    htp.tableclose;
    htp.bodyclose;
    htp.htmlclose;
  end departments;
end dept_tool;
/
show error
```

With this package, you can now open your browser to
http://hostname:port/pls/dadname/dept_tool.departments and you will get a list of your departments
that looks a lot like the following:

If you click on each department, it should be highlighted in yellow, but nothing much else appears to
happen at this point. However, observe the URL as you click on each department and you will see that the
value assigned to the p_currentdept parameter corresponds to the appropriate value of the deptno
field in the dept table. For example, when you click on the Accounting department, it should read:

http://oas/pls/scott_dad/dept_tool.departments?p_currentdept=10

Let's move on and build in the functionality that will allow us to view a list of employees for each department.

Changing the Department

We are going to list all of the employees in a particular department along with some of their details. A
couple of changes need to be made in the package body for dept_tool. Replace the last few lines of
code in the existing package:

```
    htp.htmlclose;
  end departments;
end dept_tool;
/
show error
```

...with the following:

```
        -- separate the department listing and the employee listing by a horizontal
        -- rule

        htp.hr(cattributes=>'HEIGHT="1" WIDTH="300" ALIGN="LEFT"');

        htp.header(2,'Employees');
        htp.tableopen(cattributes => 'CELLSPACING="3" CELLPADDING="3"');
        htp.tabledata('<b>Name</b>');
        htp.tabledata('<b>Manager</b>');
        htp.tabledata('<b>Job</b>');

        /* This is an implicit cursor, which will loop through each record returned
         * from the employee query below and create an HTML table row for each
         * employee.
         */

        for e in (select e.empno, e.ename, e.mgr, e.job, e2.ename mgrname
                    from emp e,emp e2
                  where e.mgr = e2.empno
                    and e.deptno = to_number(p_currentdept)) loop
          -- increment the number of employees for each record returned.  We will
          -- show this count after we close the loop.
          l_empcnt := l_empcnt + 1;
          htp.tablerowopen;
          htp.tabledata(initcap(e.ename));
          htp.tabledata(initcap(e.mgrname));
          htp.tabledata(initcap(e.job));
          htp.tablerowclose;
        end loop;
        htp.tableclose;

        -- if there is a department selected, show the number of employees
        -- in the dept.

        if p_currentdept is not null then
          htp.p(l_empcnt||' employees in the '||initcap(l_dname)||' department.');
        end if;

        htp.bodyclose;
        htp.htmlclose;
    end departments;

end dept_tool;
/
show error
```

Now when you click on a particular department, you should be presented with the department information as before, and also all of the employees that are assigned to that particular department:

As you can see we are now given the manager and job for each employee. At the bottom of the employee list, we also roll up the number of employees in the department and display that information to the user.

Showing the User's Detail Record

What's the next logical step in our sample application? Well, it wouldn't be right if we couldn't view a detail screen for each employee, and edit his or her details through the web browser. The next step is to modify the `dept_tool` package so that we can accomplish that.

This will involve changes to both the specification and body. Here is the full `dept_tool` specification, `depttool.sql`:

```
set define off
create or replace package dept_tool
as

  -- procedure DEPARTMENTS is used for listing departments on a web page.
  procedure departments(
    p_currentdept in varchar2 default NULL);

  -- procedure EDIT_EMP allows the end-user to edit an employees details
  -- via the web.

  procedure edit_emp(
    p_empno  in varchar2);
```

```
-- procedure UPDATE_EMP is necessary to allow the changes made in
-- EDIT_EMP to be submitted.

procedure update_emp(
  p_empno  in varchar2,
  p_ename  in varchar2,
  p_job    in varchar2,
  p_mgr    in varchar2,
  p_sal    in varchar2,
  p_comm   in varchar2,
  p_deptno in varchar2);

end dept_tool;
/
show error
```

Here is the complete, corresponding body file, `depttoolb.sql`:

```
set define off

create or replace package body dept_tool
as

  /*
   * ITE:   This function takes three parameters.  First, the boolean
   *        parameter which will be evaluated.  If p_condition is true,
   *        p_true is returned.  If p_condition is false, p_false is
   *        returned.  This is just a shortcut function for performing an
   *        if/then/else throughout the package.
   */

  function ite(
    p_condition in boolean,
    p_true      in varchar2,
    p_false     in varchar2)
    return varchar2
  is
  begin
    if p_condition then
      return p_true;
    end if;
    return p_false;
  end ite;

  /*
   * DEPT_ERROR:  In the case of an error, this procedure will simply create
   *              a web page which either displays a message to the user, or
   *              if no message was passed, displays a message indicating an
   *              error was encountered.
   */

  procedure dept_error(
    p_msg in varchar2 default NULL)
  is
  begin
```

```
      htp.htmlopen;
      htp.bodyopen;
      htp.p(ite(p_msg is null,'The department tool encountered an error.',p_msg));
      htp.br;
      htp.p('Click '||htf.anchor('dept_tool.departments',
                                 'here')||' to return to the departments report');
      htp.bodyclose;
      htp.htmlclose;
  end dept_error;

  procedure departments(
    p_currentdept in varchar2 default NULL)
  is
    l_empcnt number := 0;
    l_dname  varchar2(30);
  begin
    htp.htmlopen;
    htp.bodyopen(cattributes=>'BGCOLOR="WHITE"');

    htp.header(2,'Departments');

    htp.tableopen(cattributes => 'CELLSPACING="3" CELLPADDING="3"');

    /* This is an implicit cursor, which will loop through each record returned
     * from the query "select * from dept" and create an HTML table row for
     * each department. Additionally, each department will be an anchor to
     * this procedure passing along the selected department as the current
     * department
     */

    for d in (select * from dept) loop
      htp.tablerowopen;
      htp.tabledata(htf.anchor('dept_tool.departments?p_currentdept='||d.deptno,
                               initcap(d.dname)), cattributes=>'BGCOLOR="'||
                               ite(d.deptno=p_currentdept,'YELLOW','WHITE')||'"');
      htp.tabledata(initcap(d.loc), cattributes=>'BGCOLOR="'||
                               ite(d.deptno=p_currentdept,'YELLOW','WHITE')||'"');
      htp.tablerowclose;
      if d.deptno=p_currentdept then
        l_dname := d.dname;
      end if;
    end loop;
    htp.tableclose;

  /* separate the department listing and the employee listing by a
   * horizontal rule
   */

  htp.hr(cattributes=>'HEIGHT="1" WIDTH="300" ALIGN="LEFT"');

  htp.header(2,'Employees');

  htp.tableopen(cattributes => 'CELLSPACING="3" CELLPADDING="3"');
  htp.tabledata('<b>Name</b>');
```

```
      htp.tabledata('<b>Manager</b>');
      htp.tabledata('<b>Job</b>');

      /* This is an implicit cursor which will loop through each record returned
       * from the employee query below and create an HTML table row for each
       * employee.
       */

      for e in (select e.empno, e.ename, e.mgr, e.job, e2.ename mgrname
                  from emp e, emp e2
                where e.mgr = e2.empno
                  and e.deptno = to_number(p_currentdept)) loop
        l_empcnt := l_empcnt + 1;
        htp.tablerowopen;

        /* Now notice this has changed.  Instead of simply listing the
         * employee's ENAME, we add in an anchor to a procedure called edit_emp.
         * See below for details regarding this procedure.
         */

        htp.tabledata(htf.anchor('dept_tool.edit_emp?p_empno='||e.empno,
                                 initcap(e.ename)));
        htp.tabledata(initcap(e.mgrname));
        htp.tabledata(initcap(e.job));
        htp.tablerowclose;
      end loop;
      htp.tableclose;

      /* if there is a department selected, show the number of employees in
       * the dept.
       */

      if p_currentdept is not null then
        htp.p(l_empcnt||' employees in the '||initcap(l_dname)||' department.');
      end if;

      htp.bodyclose;
      htp.htmlclose;
    end departments;

    /*
     * EDIT_EMP:  This procedure is for allowing the end-user to see and edit
     *            all the details about an employee's record.
     */

    procedure edit_emp(
      p_empno  in varchar2)
    is
      l_emp emp%rowtype;
    begin
      begin
        select *
          into l_emp
          from emp
        where empno = p_empno;
      exception
```

```
    when NO_DATA_FOUND then

-- if the employee passed in doesn't exist, display an error

    dept_error('We encountered an error when trying to edit employee #
            '||p_empno);
    return;
end;

htp.htmlopen;
htp.bodyopen(cattributes=>'BGCOLOR="WHITE"');

htp.header(1,'Edit Employee '||initcap(l_emp.ename));

-- Open the form tag, which will identify the procedure to be run when
-- we submit this update. In this case, it is the UPDATE_EMP procedure,
-- which you will see further along in this package.

htp.formopen('dept_tool.update_emp');

-- This makes a hidden variable in the HTML itself. This value is not
-- displayed on the web browser, but is still passed along to the
-- UPDATE_EMP call.

htp.formhidden('p_empno',p_empno);

-- Show the employee's name
htp.tableopen(cattributes=>'CELLPADDING="3"');
htp.tablerowopen;
htp.tabledata('Name: ','RIGHT');
htp.tabledata(htf.formtext('p_ename',13,10,initcap(l_emp.ename)));
htp.tablerowclose;

-- Show the employee's title, and let the end-user edit this value freely
htp.tablerowopen;
htp.tabledata('Job: ','RIGHT');
htp.tabledata(htf.formtext('p_job',13,10,initcap(l_emp.job)));
htp.tablerowclose;

-- Select a list of all the employees EXCEPT the employee being edited,
-- and allow the end-user to select a manager for this user
htp.tablerowopen;
htp.tabledata('Mgr: ','RIGHT');
htp.p('<td>'||htf.formselectopen('p_mgr'));
htp.formselectoption('%',ite(l_emp.mgr is null,'SELECTED',''));
for e in (select empno,ename from emp) loop
  htp.formselectoption(initcap(e.ename),ite(e.empno=l_emp.mgr,'SELECTED',''),
                                'VALUE="'||e.empno||'"');
end loop;
htp.p('</td>');
htp.formselectclose;
htp.tablerowclose;
```

```
      -- Select a list of all the departments and allow the end-user to select
      -- a new department for this user.
      htp.tablerowopen;
      htp.tabledata('Department: ','RIGHT');
      htp.p('<td>'||htf.formselectopen('p_deptno'));
      htp.formselectoption('%',ite(l_emp.deptno is null,'SELECTED',''));
      for d in (select deptno,dname from dept) loop

   /* The ITE function call is necessary to determine whether the current
    * department being drawn from the loop is the employee's department. If
    * it is, we will pass 'SELECTED' as the second parameter to the
    * HTP.formselectoption procedure request.  (The second parameter is
    * CSELECTED).
    */

 htp.formselectoption(initcap(d.dname),
                      ite(d.deptno=l_emp.deptno,'SELECTED',''),
                      'VALUE="'||d.deptno||'"');
      end loop;
      htp.p('</td>');
      htp.formselectclose;
      htp.tablerowclose;

      -- Allow the user to select an arbitrary salary.  I wish I could edit my
      -- own employee record!
      htp.tablerowopen;
      htp.tabledata('Salary: ','RIGHT');
      htp.tabledata(htf.formtext('p_sal',13,10,initcap(l_emp.sal)));
      htp.tablerowclose;

      -- Allow the user to select an arbitrary salary.  I wish I could edit my
      -- own employee record!
      htp.tablerowopen;
      htp.tabledata('Commission: ','RIGHT');
      htp.tabledata(htf.formtext('p_comm',13,10,initcap(l_emp.comm)));
      htp.tablerowclose;

      -- Draw the save button, which is used to submit the form.
      htp.tablerowopen;
      htp.tabledata(htf.formsubmit(null,'Save'),'RIGHT',cattributes=>'COLSPAN="2"');
      htp.tablerowclose;
      htp.tableclose;
      htp.formclose;

      -- This is simply a quick link back to the departments report.
      htp.p('Click '||htf.anchor('dept_tool.departments?p_currentdept=
                  '||l_emp.deptno, 'here')||' to return to the departments report');
      htp.bodyclose;
      htp.htmlclose;
    end edit_emp;

    /*
     * This procedure updates the employee record.
     */
    procedure update_emp(
      p_empno  in varchar2,
      p_ename  in varchar2,
      p_job    in varchar2,
      p_mgr    in varchar2,
      p_sal    in varchar2,
      p_comm   in varchar2,
```

```
      p_deptno in varchar2)
   is
   begin
     update emp
        set ename  = p_ename,
            job    = p_job,
            mgr    = p_mgr,
            sal    = p_sal,
            comm   = p_comm,
            deptno = p_deptno
      where empno = p_empno;
     edit_emp(p_empno);
   exception
     when OTHERS then

   -- instead of writing a stack of data value validation code,
   -- we'll simply disallow the update. You would most likely want
   -- to check the values explicitly.
        dept_error('There was an error when updating employee '||p_ename);
   end update_emp;

end dept_tool;
/
show error
```

Now when the list of employees pops up, the employee's names should be hyperlinked:

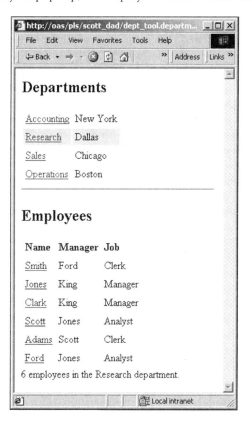

Click on one of the employee's names and you should be presented with their details, which you will be able to edit and update in the table:

This application isn't terribly complex, but it does provide a representative example of functionality in order to get you somewhat familiarized with the process of application development using the PL/SQL Web Toolkit. As I mentioned earlier, the PL/SQL Web Toolkit is a highly scalable, secure, robust platform for developing web-based solutions for a variety of customers' requirements.

The Departments Procedure, Explained

Now that we can see dynamic web pages being generated from the PL/SQL Web Toolkit, let's take the `departments` procedure and break it down.

The procedure starts by declaring the procedure name and specifying the input parameter, `p_currentdept`, which will be the selected department on the page. You will notice that `p_currentdept` has a default value of `NULL`, which means passing this parameter is optional.

```
procedure departments(
    p_currentdept in varchar2 default NULL)
is
```

In the declaration, we have a variable for the count of employees in the department, and a variable to store the department name for use later in the page:

```
l_empcnt number := 0;
l_dname  varchar2(30);
begin
```

As we learned earlier in the chapter, `htp` procedures generate HTML tags and place those tags in the response buffer. The next few statements are responsible for creating the beginnings of the HTML page. From the next three lines:

```
htp.htmlopen;
htp.bodyopen(cattributes=>'BGCOLOR="WHITE"');
htp.header(2,'Departments');
```

...the following HTML is generated into the response buffer:

```
<HTML>
<BODY BGCOLOR="WHITE">
<H2>Departments</H2>
```

The next task is to create an HTML table listing all the departments. Each department will also be an HTML anchor linking back to the department report, passing it's own Department ID (deptno) as the p_currentdept parameter:

```
htp.tableopen(cattributes => 'CELLSPACING="3" CELLPADDING="3"');
for d in (select * from dept) loop
  htp.tablerowopen;
  htp.tabledata(htf.anchor('dept_tool.departments?p_currentdept='||d.deptno,
                          initcap(d.dname)), cattributes => 'BGCOLOR="' ||
                          ite(d.deptno=p_currentdept,'YELLOW','WHITE')||
                              '"');
  htp.tabledata(initcap(d.loc), cattributes => 'BGCOLOR="' ||
                   ite(d.deptno=p_currentdept,'YELLOW','WHITE')||'"');
  htp.tablerowclose;
  if d.deptno=p_currentdept then
    l_dname := d.dname;
  end if;
end loop;
htp.tableclose;
```

htp.tableopen generates the HTML necessary to open the HTML table. The implicit cursor parses through each row of the DEPT table. Inside the loop, we open a new HTML table row and two HTML table data cells for each department. In the first cell, we are going to list the name of the department, which will also be a link to select the current department. The second cell will list the location of the department. The ITE function call is used to determine the background color of the cells. If we are painting the current department in the HTML table, the background color will be yellow. Otherwise, it will be white. We then close the HTML table row. Again if we are painting the current department, we assign the local variable (l_dname) to the name of the department in the query. Finally, we close the HTML table. The HTML code generated from this block of code would look something like this:

```
<TABLE CELLSPACING="3" CELLPADDING="3">
<TR>
<TD BGCOLOR="YELLOW"><A
HREF="dept_tool.departments?p_currentdept=10">Accounting</A></TD>
<TD BGCOLOR="YELLOW">New York</TD>
</TR>
<TR>
<TD BGCOLOR="WHITE"><A
HREF="dept_tool.departments?p_currentdept=20">Research</A></TD>
</TR>
```

```
<TD BGCOLOR="WHITE">Dallas</TD>
<TR>
<TD BGCOLOR="WHITE"><A
HREF="dept_tool.departments?p_currentdept=30">Sales</A></TD>
<TD BGCOLOR="WHITE">Chicago</TD>
</TR>
<TR>
<TD BGCOLOR="WHITE"><A
HREF="dept_tool.departments?p_currentdept=40">Operations</A></TD>
<TD BGCOLOR="WHITE">Boston</TD>
</TR>
</TABLE>
```

The next block of code does basically the same thing, but here we are showing the employees in the current department:

```
htp.hr(cattributes=>'HEIGHT="1" WIDTH="300" ALIGN="LEFT"');
htp.header(2,'Employees');

htp.tableopen(cattributes => 'CELLSPACING="3" CELLPADDING="3"');
htp.tablerowopen;
htp.tabledata('<b>Name</b>');
htp.tabledata('<b>Manager</b>');
htp.tabledata('<b>Job</b>');
htp.tablerowclose;
for e in (select e.empno, e.ename, e.mgr, e.job, e2.ename mgrname
            from emp e,emp e2
          where e.mgr = e2.empno
            and e.deptno = to_number(p_currentdept)) loop

    l_empcnt := l_empcnt + 1;
    htp.tablerowopen;
    htp.tabledata(htf.anchor('dept_tool.edit_emp?p_empno='||e.empno,
                            initcap(e.ename)));
    htp.tabledata(initcap(e.mgrname));
    htp.tabledata(initcap(e.job));
    htp.tablerowclose;
end loop;
htp.tableclose;
```

And the employee HTML table looks something like this:

```
<TABLE CELLSPACING="3" CELLPADDING="3">
<TR>
<TD><B>Name</B></TD>
<TD><B>Manager</B></TD>
<TD><B>Job</B></TD>
</TR>
<TR>
<TD><A HREF="dept_tool.edit_emp?p_empno=CLARK">Clark</A></TD>
<TD>King</TD>
<TD>Manager</TD>
</TR>
<TR>
<TD><A HREF="dept_tool.edit_emp?p_empno=KING">King</A></TD>
<TD></TD>
<TD>President</TD>
</TR>
</TABLE>
```

The footer of the code shows the count of the employees in the current department, and closes the HTML page:

```
    -- if there is a department selected, show the number of employees in
    -- the dept.
    if p_currentdept is not null then
      htp.p(l_empcnt||' employees in the '||initcap(l_dname)||' department.');
    end if;

    htp.bodyclose;
    htp.htmlclose;
  end departments;
```

...which generates:

```
2 employees in the Accounting department.
</BODY>
</HTML>
```

In review, we have walked through the `dept_tool.departments` procedure and shown how writing PL/SQL generates dynamic HTML pages. Using cursors and simple HTP/HTF procedures and functions, we have created a functional departmental user management application.

Summary

In this chapter, we have covered everything you need to know in order to get started writing your own web-based PL/SQL applications using the PL/SQL Web Toolkit. We began with getting familiar with the environment in which you use the PL/SQL Web Toolkit and it's associated technologies.

We attained a high level understanding of the "Lifecycle of a Request", and the "Nomenclature of a Request". This helps us to understand what happens behind the browser when we click on a link to a dynamic page build on the PL/SQL Web Toolkit. We wrapped up with some examples that should help to get you started with the toolkit.

In the end, the most important thing you need to learn is that PL/SQL is a great choice for building enterprise applications for the web. By living inside the Oracle 8i database, the PL/SQL Web Toolkit and subsequently your applications benefit from the scalability, reliability, and performance of the database platform. You should view PL/SQL not as a library that allows you to write HTML data to a buffer, which in turn gets redirected to some user's browser... but instead, as your set of keys into Oracle and all the features and benefits that it provides.

ORACLE8iAPPLICATIONPROGRAMMING

A Stock Tracker using the PL/SQL Web Toolkit and JavaScript

Now that the fundamentals of the toolkit have been discussed, we are going to look at a somewhat more detailed example that has the toolkit at its heart.

As we discussed in Chapter 8, the PL/SQL Web Toolkit allows a developer to send database output directly to a web server using stored procedures compiled from within the database. This is an architectural breakthrough – it is the database opening its door to the web server. Most other architectures assume that the code controlling the application's display resides outside the database. That external code has to negotiate a connection with the database, communicate with the database through stored procedure calls, or bare SQL, and format information for the web server.

Placing data validation near the data in a constraint, table definition or trigger has the advantage that a user who attempts to violate business rules by manipulating the data outside of the application will be forced to modify triggers, constraints or tables to do this, rather than performing simple inserts, updates or deletes.

On top of this, the language used to disseminate web content is the same proven language used to obtain the content from the database. Think about it – there is no watering-down of either the front-end display language or the back-end data language because data type translations between the two languages don't quite match. They match. They originate from the same release of the same language. Which means that you can use the full power of PL/SQL stored procedures not only to gather data but also to publish it.

The case study that is provided in this chapter will not explore the toolkit packages to anything like their full extent. Instead it will, without the aid of any wizard-based development, examine just what can be done with the "simple" ability to communicate with a web server from within the database. Talking to a web server involves other technologies as well. In this case study, JavaScript and Cascading Style Sheets will be used to complement the work that the toolkit will perform.

Overview of the Case Study

This case study builds a personal stock tracker using the PL/SQL Web Toolkit as its cornerstone. I should say immediately, to avoid disappointment, that in its current state, this stock tracker is not what some might term "the complete article". It does not, for example, use "real-time" data. The current value of stocks is stored in a `current_value` table, and the user must update this table themselves.

It may seem odd to start off by saying what an example **doesn't** do but my primary objective was to highlight a good **design**. Whatever flashy feature I might have incorporated, there would be people who were unsatisfied and would feel that another feature should have been incorporated instead. What I've tried to do here is provide a well-designed foundation that is useful in a broader sense.

> *Whatever its merits and disadvantages, bear in mind the fundamental point that this is a web application, not a client-server application. That means that a dissatisfied reader has a very powerful recourse – they can simply open up a programmer's editor and "fix" the application to his or her heart's content. Try to do that with your latest client-server software.*

Besides, I think you'll find that, when you start to study the structure and design, as I hope you will, it does actually do quite a bit:

❑ It uses XML as an internal communication medium, proving that the developer is not limited to HTML when using the toolkit

❑ It shows how to integrate use of the toolkit with JavaScript on the client, to maintain state

❑ It uses Cascading Style Sheets for display formatting

Indeed, it does so much that you may wonder if the toolkit gets lost in the process. Just recall that the source of the information is transmitted directly to the Web Server, from code running within the database, not outside of it. This is not a trivial point.

Most importantly, I have tried to use a flexible "tiered" design that keeps display and data logic separate and that can be easily adapted and expanded to suit personal tastes. If you like what I've provided as a foundation and want to use the application seriously, then, for example, stock information might be made available automatically by using the Oracle supplied package `utl_http` to get the information from a web site and PL/SQL to parse and store it in the database.

Essentially, our application will allow a user to enter and update stock buying-and-selling transactions through a Web page and track and report on the financial position of each of their stock accounts. We will walk through our stock tracker application as follows:

❑ First, we'll take a high level overview of the application architecture, and how it works Screen shots will be provided of the available web pages supporting the application.

❑ Second, we will construct the database tables, add constraints and build triggers. This is the core of the application. Initial test data for the application is provided via a SQL script, `data.sql`

❑ We will implement the application using two PL/SQL packages:

  ❑ A back-end package, `backend`, to insert and update records in the database tables, in order to support a web front-end package

  ❑ A frontend package, created using the PL/SQL Web Toolkit. The `frontend` package is separate from the `backend` package in order to isolate the data from the display.

❑ Assisting the `frontend` package on the client side will be two JavaScript libraries, `stocks.js` and `htm.js` and a style sheet, `stocks.css`, to format the display.

The client files, that is, the JavaScript files and the style sheet, are very important. They will ultimately display the HTML and help preserve state in the client browser between transitions of the web page. Unlike Java, with its Servlet technology, there is no concept of maintaining state within a PL/SQL application. The fact that the PL/SQL toolkit doesn't itself completely do this work is irrelevant. What is important is that it integrates well with technology that does.

Clearly, knowledge of HTML, style sheets and JavaScript would be useful for a full understanding of this case study. However, I hope that I've given sufficient information for all readers to get the application up and running and to learn from it.

The application was built using an Oracle 8i database to house the PL/SQL packages, the PL/SQL gateway to deliver database content to JavaScript libraries, sent to the browser (IE 5.5 or Netscape 4.7) from an Apache Web Server. No wizards from WebDB or any other such product were used (I doubt that it is possible to reproduce this application's functionality through these wizards). The only development tool required was a shareware programmer's editor used to construct the files.

Application Architecture

The following diagram shows the components of the application. On the data tier are the tables, triggers and data as well as the `backend` package. Also on this tier is the `frontend` package and the PL/SQL Toolkit. The reader will note the line dividing the data tier into two parts. This is meant to symbolize the separation between the data and the display components on this tier. There are numerous middle tier options, as described in the previous chapter. Here we are using iAS and its built in Apache web server. The middle tier provides access to the files and the stored PL/SQL `frontend` package required by the application. The client tier is where the JavaScript and style sheet are actually run although as files they are physically located on the middle tier.

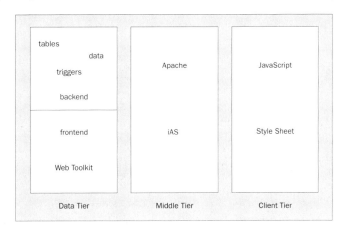

Maintaining State on the Client

As we discussed earlier, we cannot preserve state within a PL/SQL application but it is not too difficult to difficult to preserve state with or without PL/SQL (or with or without Java). Two techniques that are routinely used to preserve state in web pages are cookies and frames. Since cookies are well known and more restrictive, this example will use frames. When using frames to preserve state, one frame, usually the parent, persists throughout the application's existence in the browser. It is in this frame that state information is stored.

When discussing state it is helpful to keep in mind what benefit state preservation would provide. When one sees it this way, state preservation has a client-side and a database-side because it is in these two tiers that state information is useful.

On the client, preserving state allows the user to experience less disruption from slow network traffic to and from the other tiers in the application. The principal goal is to avoid delivering the same data to the client more than once. On the client side, state is closely related to cache. On the database side, state implies that the client is identified and storage is available for preserving messages from clients. This data is analyzed later to improve client relationships.

In our application, the browser is divided into frames as the following diagram illustrates. The parent frame contains the code that builds the child frames. It also contains all the JavaScript code that builds the child frame contents. Communication between the server and the client is done through the message frame (which is hidden as well as being a child frame). Some readers will recognize frames as a technique to format the display of browser content. That is not the purpose of frames here. Only the display frame is actually visible in the browser – formatting of its content is done through a style sheet.

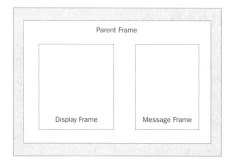

The User Interfaces

It's useful to take a high-level overview of what the application does, then we can look under the hood and see how it works. The application displays only two Web pages, a data entry page ("Update Position") and a report page ("Trade Report").

The initial trade report calls a PL/SQL procedure, `frontend.stocks`, to build the initial frameset of the application. This procedure calls the `backend` package to get the data that is loaded into the parent frame. It uses JavaScript and style sheets on the browser to build the content of the display page. The display frame contains the Trade Report shown alongside using the data supplied by the `data.sql` script (see later):

Trade Report

Summary

Account	Start Date	Gains	Trade Cost	Net Gains	Investment	Cash	Capital
acc011	Oct 02, 2000	0.00	29.97	−29.97	18543.75	8876.82	27420.57
acc033	Oct 02, 2000	0.00	19.98	−19.98	4050.00	7950.00	12000.00

Portfolio: acc011

Stock	Average Purchase Price	Current Price	Shares	Investment	Current Portfolio
CA	25	32.3125	500	12500.00	16156.25
LU	33	24.5625	100	3300.00	2456.25
MOT	27.4375	24.6875	100	2743.75	2468.75
				18543.75	21081.25

Portfolio: acc033

Stock	Average Purchase Price	Current Price	Shares	Investment	Current Portfolio
ADSK	23	22	100	2300.00	2200.00
CA	25	32.3125	70	1750.00	2261.88
				4050.00	25543.13

Now, suppose we want to purchase some ORCL stock, set the current price of LU stock and sell CA stock, all from the acc011 account. Clicking on the acc011 link in the Summary table will take us to the data entry page:

Update Position: acc011

Stock	Purchase Price	Shares	Selling Price	Quantity	Current Price
CA	25.0000	500	30	200	
LU	33.0000	100			26
MOT	27.4375	100			
orcl	30	100			

Report Submit

In the above screenshot you can see that we wish to:

❑ Purchase 100 shares of ORCL at $30 per share

❑ Sell 200 shares of CA at the current market value of $30 per share, making a tidy profit on the purchase price of $25 per share

❑ See that the current price of LU to $26 per share.

If we click the Report button, the report page will be displayed with this updated position calculated.

What happens is that JavaScript formats the content of the HTML form into an XML message, which is sent back to the frontend package with a target for the response in the hidden message frame. A PL/SQL procedure calls the backend package, which records the message and updates the position in the database returning the new state of the account to the frontend package. It in turns sends this information back to the message frame and reloads the JavaScript values in the parent frame. Finally, JavaScript reloads the display frame with updated information from the parent frame.

The process can be illustrated as follows:

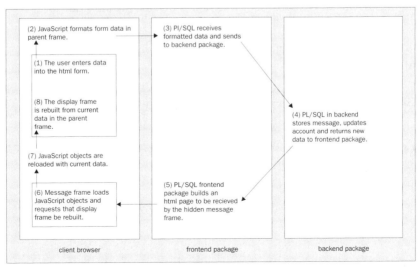

When we click Submit, the database state is updated, the client state is updated and the new report is displayed from information in the client preserved state. Note that the LU current price now is listed as $26, our CA holding has reduced from 500 to 300 shares, and ORCL has an entry. Updates are also evident in the Summary table. The assumption is that each trade costs $9.99 and from this the net gains are calculated:

Trade Report

Summary

Account	Start Date	Gains	Trade Cost	Net Gains	Investment	Cash	Capital
acc011	Oct 02, 2000	1000.00	49.95	950.05	16543.75	11826.87	27420.57
acc033	Oct 02, 2000	0.00	19.98	−19.98	4050.00	7930.02	12000.00

Portfolio: acc011

Stock	Purchase Price	Current Price	Shares	Investment	Current Portfolio
CA	25	32.3125	300	7500.00	9693.75
LU	33	26	100	3300.00	2600.00
MOT	27.4375	24.6875	100	2743.75	2468.75
ORCL	30	30	100	3000.00	3000.00
				16543.75	17762.50

Portfolio: acc033

Stock	Purchase Price	Current Price	Shares	Investment	Current Portfolio
ADSK	23	22	100	2300.00	2200.00
CA	25	32.3125	70	1750.00	2261.88
				4050.00	22224.38

Data Model

Five tables store the data for the application (the scripts to build the physical model are available in the file stock.sql.):

❑ The accounts table describes companies through which the user is permitted to buy and sell stocks

❑ The funds table stores information about the source of initial capital (there is currently no business rule that specifics a minimum funding level to trade)

❑ The trades table stores details about each market trade

❑ The current_value table stores the most recent closing price for the stock (which, at the moment, the reader must look up from a Web site and enter manually)

❑ Finally, the track_user table stores information about user activity

Although this allows for application code to reside on a physically separate tier, it brings up the question of where data validation should occur: in the database or in a middle tier code library.

Placing this validation within the GUI application and not in the database opens a backdoor to data integrity problems.

The term "business rules" is often used today. An interesting exercise might be to identify the business rules for this simple application. Personally, I view the table definitions, constraints and triggers that are presented in this section as the primary business rules of the application. Since the back-end package could contain some of the trigger code, it would also be considered part of the business rule logic.

Accounts Table

The accounts table describes the organization (broker) that makes the trade for the user. This table can be loaded with data using a SQL script we discuss a little later.

> *You may argue that a GUI should be provided as a front-end to this table and this is possibly true. However, I don't expect that many people can name an example of a GUI application on top of a database that could do everything that the reader could imagine doing using straight SQL on the base tables. All applications are deliberately selective. They provide an interface to only the most important features of a database application.*

Here is the DDL that creates the accounts table:

```
create table accounts
(
    id            number        constraint accounts_nn1 not null,
    account_name  varchar2(50)  constraint accounts_nn2 not null,
    company       varchar2(100) constraint accounts_nn3 not null,
    created       date          default sysdate
                                constraint accounts_nn4 not null,
    account_type  varchar2(10)  default 'IRA'
                                constraint accounts_nn5 not null,
    constraint accounts_pk primary key (id)
);
```

So, what "business rules" are rolled in to this definition of the accounts table? Well, quite a few in actual fact:

❑   The name of the account is permitted to be only 50 characters long

❑   An account name must always exist, it cannot be null

❑   If no date is provided for the start of an account, it will be defined to start the day the account was identified

If the business rules change, the table would change to reflect this. Once one gets used to viewing constraints as business rules, the construction of constraints takes on a new level of interest. For example, let's create a new business rule stating that the account types are limited to three values (two of which refer to US retirement plans:

```
alter table accounts
    add constraint accounts_ck1
    check(account_type in ('IRA','ROTH','OTHER'));
```

With the following sequence and trigger we implement two further rules:

❑ The broker will be identified by a unique number

❑ The company names will be represented using capital letters

We implement the latter by forcing the name to be in upper case before inserting into the `company` field. You might not think much of this business rule but, without actually modifying or disabling this trigger, I would like to see someone enter a name in lower-case into this table! Here is the code:

```
create sequence accounts_seq;
create or replace trigger accounts_bef
before insert or update on accounts
for each row
begin
    if inserting then
        select accounts_seq.nextval into :new.id from dual;
    end if;
    if :new.company is not null then
        :new.company := upper(:new.company);
    end if;
end;
/
```

Funds Table

Once an account is identified, then funds can be entered into it. Recording these initial funds is the job of the `funds` table. As with the `accounts` table, there is no GUI interface to load data into the table. It is done with straight SQL.

One business rule that may not be obvious is "Each fund is determined by the broker holding the funds and the name of an account where the funds are deposited." This is implemented by a primary key constraint on the `account` and `fund_name` fields, as well as a foreign key constraint identifying the broker with a record in the `accounts` table.

```
create table funds
(
    account       number         constraint funds_nn1 not null,
    fund_name     varchar2(100)  constraint funds_nn2 not null,
    received      date           constraint funds_nn3 not null,
    amount        number         constraint funds_nn4 not null,
    constraint funds_pk primary key (account, fund_name)
);

alter table funds
    add constraint funds_fk1
    foreign key (account) references accounts (id);
```

Trades

The third table, trades, is where market trades or transactions are stored. Each record records a buy and perhaps also a sell of the stock. This is where the GUI part of the application tries to shine. Inserts and updates to most of this table are provided by the web portion of the application, as we saw earlier.

As one looks for business rules one will perhaps note that there is no constraint on the number datatype that represents money in columns such as buy_price. However, there is a check constraint that forces buy_price to be positive. Some might look at the number data type and think that because this is a money field it should be of type number(9,2). However, if the business rule says, "All prices are positive values which represent the exact value of the stock", then it is not acceptable to restrict the number data type to only two decimal digits.

```
create table trades
(
    id              number        constraint trades_nn1 not null,
    account         number        constraint trades_nn2 not null,
    stock           varchar2(10)  constraint trades_nn3 not null,
    bought          date          default sysdate
                                  constraint trades_nn4 not null,
    buy_price       number        constraint trades_nn5 not null,
    shares          number        constraint trades_nn6 not null,
    trade_cost      number        default 0
                                  constraint trades_nn7 not null,
    sold            date,
    sell_price      number,
    constraint trades_pk primary key (id)
);
```

Similarly to the accounts table, we implement a trigger and a sequence that ensure that it will be identified by a unique numeric value, and that the stock symbol will be capitalized:

```
create sequence trades_seq;

create or replace trigger trades_bef
before insert or update on trades
for each row
begin
  if inserting then
    select trades_seq.nextval into :new.id from dual;
  end if;
  if :new.stock is not null then
      :new.stock := upper(:new.stock);
    end if;
end;
/
```

By now the reader should be able to determine the business rules from the following constraints. However, just to make sure, here's a test: where are the following two business rules implemented?

❑   Stocks are sold after they are bought. (Answer: sold is null or sold >= bought)

❑   When a stock is purchased at least one share must be bought." (Answer: shares > 0)

```
alter table trades
   add constraint trades_ck1
   check (buy_price > 0);
alter table trades
   add constraint trades_ck2
   check (shares > 0);
alter table trades
   add constraint trades_ck3
   check (sold is null or sold >= bought);
alter table trades
   add constraint trades_ck4
   check (sell_price is null or sell_price > 0);
alter table trades
   add constraint trades_ck5
   check (trade_cost >= 0);
alter table trades
   add constraint trades_fk1
   foreign key (account) references accounts (id);
```

Current Value Table

The current_value table is used to store the current price of the stocks. It doesn't hang on to any of the other tables, but is used as a source of information about the stocks. The application does provide a way to insert or update data in this table through the web page.

One use of this table is to record the closing price of the stocks for the data, or perhaps the current price. It could even be used to enter the desired selling price for the stock. The user must enter this data into the web page manually. A possible extension to this application would allow the user to automatically update this table with current stock prices through a call to some on-line quote service to which the reader subscribes:

```
create table current_value (
   stock   varchar2(10),
   price   number        constraint current_value_nn1 not null,
   constraint current_value_pk primary key (stock)
);

alter table current_value
   add constraint current_value_ch1
   check (price > 0);
```

Track User Table

The track_user table records the change in state of the user when entering information into forms or doing other recordable activities in the browser. The user is identified through a sequence, track_user_seq, that labels the user's session when it begins. PL/SQL helps to load the track_user table with messages from a client machine and gets the value of the sequence to pass to the client. Although, a "real" application could make the data collection more voluminous, including anything that JavaScript could conceivably track, the principle is the same: to preserve state for the database means to assign an identification number to the client and to record information about what the client has done or the messages received. There isn't much else to it.

Tables such as `track_user` are examples of database objects that will grow rapidly. These tables should be frequently pruned, perhaps every hour, and the pruned data placed in a larger database warehouse where the analysis of user activity can take place. This keeps the database that communicates with the client small. For the particular application at hand, however, this is additional work is unnecessary.

```
create sequence track_user_seq;

create table track_user (
    userid     number          constraint track_user_nn1 not null,
    entered    date            default sysdate
                               constraint track_user_nn2 not null,
    submitted varchar2(4000)
);
```

Loading Initial Data

The following `data.sql` file is available from the Wrox web site for initial loading. This data will be used to illustrate the examples below.

```
declare
    v_id number; -- used to receive the id of an account.
begin

    -- Insert some funds into one account.
    insert into accounts (account_name, company)
    values ('acc033','My Broker1') returning id into v_id;
    insert into funds (account,fund_name,received,amount)
    values (v_id,'My Fund 1',to_date('09292000','MMDDYYYY'),12000);
    insert into trades (account,stock,bought,trade_cost,buy_price,shares)
    values (v_id,'CA',to_date('10022000','MMDDYYYY'),9.99,25,70);
    insert into trades (account,stock,bought,trade_cost,buy_price,shares)
    values (v_id,'ADSK',to_date('10042000','MMDDYYYY'),9.99,23,100);

    -- Insert some funds into another account.
    insert into accounts (account_name, company)
    values ('acc011','My Broker2')
    returning id into v_id;
    insert into funds (account,fund_name,received,amount)
    values (v_id,'My Fund 2',to_date('09292000','MMDDYYYY'),12803.22);
    insert into funds (account,fund_name,received,amount)
    values (v_id,'My Fund 3',to_date('09292000','MMDDYYYY'),14617.35);
    insert into trades (account,stock,bought,trade_cost,buy_price,shares)
    values (v_id,'CA',to_date('10022000','MMDDYYYY'),9.99,25,500);
    insert into trades (account,stock,bought,trade_cost,buy_price,shares)
    values (v_id,'LU',to_date('10062000','MMDDYYYY'),9.99,33,100);
    insert into trades (account,stock,bought,trade_cost,buy_price,shares)
    values (v_id,'MOT',to_date('10062000','MMDDYYYY'),9.99,27 + (7/16),100);

    -- Insert some guestimates of current prices.
    insert into current_value values ('ADSK',22+(0/16));
    insert into current_value values ('CA',32+(5/16));
    insert into current_value values ('LU',24+(9/16));
    insert into current_value values ('MOT',24+(11/16));
end;
/
commit;
```

267

After the database has been constructed from the data model, one could say, with tongue-in-cheek, that the application is finished. The user could use SQL and SQL*Plus to manipulate data and provide reports. However, as the application becomes complicated, it is usually desirable if not necessary to provide some type of GUI interface between the database and the user to insure higher input accuracy and convenience, if mere mortals are going to use the system. So although often necessary, one can view the GUI interface as the frosting on the cake. The cake probably cannot be sold without the frosting, but without the cake the frosting is just a gooey mess.

The PL/SQL Packages

The first thing to note about this architecture is that it contains not one, but two PL/SQL packages. This represents an effort to isolate the data from the display. There are two reasons to do this:

❑ The display can be maintained independently of the code used to manipulate the data. For example, if one wants to use SVG rather than HTML, it would involve only changing the display side, not the package that touches the data.

❑ If the display package were in a different schema from that housing the backend package, the user could be prohibited from directly connecting to the schema that owns the data. This would prohibit the user from directly writing SQL to achieve a result, thus increasing security by forcing the user to use the application. However, this places an additional burden upon the application to provide a more complete interface for the user so that direct SQL is not necessary.

Backend Data Package

The backend package is responsible for manipulating, retrieving and defining datatypes and communicating the information that resides in the database. It is the application's gatekeeper over the data.

The backend package could be further divided into an exception package and a data package, as we did for the test framework in Chapter 8. However, for this application, there is no exception package. The readers should now be well able to implement this themselves.

The backend Specification

The specification file for the back end package, backend.sql, follows. It is broken down into bite-size chunks, with explanations of each section of code.

```
create or replace package backend
is
```

The first thing we do is to declare a tag subtype that restricts the varchar2 data type to 12 characters. This is used as the datatype for a set of partial XML tag names that follow:

```
subtype tag is varchar2(12);
csell           constant tag    := '_sell';
cquantity       constant tag    := '_quantity';
cstock          constant tag    := '_stock';
cbuy            constant tag    := '_buy';
cbuystock       constant tag    := '_buystock';
cbuyshare       constant tag    := '_buyshare';
```

By defining the subtype we save ourselves having to write `varchar2(12)` five times. We can define the XML tags here rather than using a Document Type Definition (see Chapter 21) simply because the application is simple. XML is used for internal communication – we know what the tags are, so we can handle all processing without reference to other, more general XML tools.

Another constant, `ctrade_cost`, is also defined. Since we generally have to pay our broker a certain sum for each trade, we (arbitrarily) assign a cost of $9.99 per trade:

```
ctrade_cost    constant number := 9.99;
```

The following types define data structures that are used to communicate the information retrieved by this `backend` package, so that the `frontend` package can reference the information. We could have allowed the front-end package to directly access the data using SQL. Instead, the data is accessed through three `index-by` tables, effectively "hiding" the database data from the front-end display.

Admittedly, in this simple application, hiding the back-end is unimportant. However, in a larger application, this is desirable for security and maintainability.

The first set of datatypes provides a way to communicate a set of market trades. The second set provide a way to display summary information about each of the accounts in which trades occur:

```
type trade_row is record (
    id                trades.id%type,
    account .         trades.account%type,
    stock             trades.stock%type,
    buy_price         trades.buy_price%type,
    shares            trades.shares%type,
    trade_cost        trades.trade_cost%type,
    current_price current_value.price%type
);
type trade_table is table of trade_row
    index by binary_integer;

type summary_row is record (
    accountid    number,
    accountno    accounts.account_name%type,
    tradecost    number,
    earn         number,
    leverage     number,
    capital      number,
    startdate    date);
type summary_table is table of summary_row
    index by binary_integer;
```

The following procedures and functions are declarations that expose this code to those who have execute permission on this package. We will discuss these in more detail when we describe the package body:

```
procedure process (pdata in varchar2 default null,
                   psummary out summary_table);

procedure get_summary (psum out summary_table);
procedure get_trades (ptrades out trade_table);
procedure insert_state (pid      in number,
                        pmessage in varchar2);
function new_user return number;
end;
/
show errors
```

The backend Package Body

The following backend body has a few features worth noting:

- ❑ The procedure process receives XML data from the web page through the pdata parameter. This XML markup is parsed using the procedure parse within the procedure process. Were this a larger application, the XML processing could be carried out in a separate package.

- ❑ There are no implicitly defined cursors.

- ❑ The application uses the Oracle supplied package dbms_application_info to allow monitoring of application activity through the v$session view (used by DBAs to monitor the current state of the database). If you are not familiar with dbms_application_info, it can be found in the Supplied Packages online documentation.

Let's build the code for the body, backendb.sql, in a step-by-step fashion:

```
create or replace package body backend
is
```

The package body introduces a cursor that holds the data resulting from the execution of a SQL command (that can be used through the package body, but not outside of it). The cursor returns information that will be loaded into an index-by table whose datatype, trade_data, was defined in the specification:

```
cursor current_trades
is
select a.id,
       a.account,
       a.stock,
       a.buy_price,
       a.shares,
       a.trade_cost,
       b.price
  from trades a,
       current_value b
 where a.sold is null
   and a.stock = b.stock (+)
 order by a.stock;
```

The get_trades procedure returns the results of the current_trades cursor into the ptrades parameter. One can think of this as a "firewall" between the display package and the data. The display package, frontend, must call get_trades in order to retrieve information from the trades and current_value tables in the database. It is not permitted to directly access those tables itself:

```
procedure get_trades (ptrades out trade_table)
is
    i binary_integer;
begin
    dbms_application_info.set_action('backend.trades');

    for c in current_trades loop
        ptrades(ptrades.count) := c;
    end loop;

    dbms_application_info.set_action(null);
end;
```

The insert_state procedure inserts change-of-state information from the browser into a table. In a larger application such a table is likely to be more complicated, but the basic idea is the same: record user activity in the browser. The pid value is the identification number that is assigned to the browser's session so that continuity may be preserved. The pmessage value is information that is returned from the JavaScript code in the browser that keeps track of what the user is doing. The procedure uses an autonomous transaction pragma to commit this information independently of any other transaction that is performed on the part of the user:

```
procedure insert_state (pid       in number,
                        pmessage in varchar2)
is
   pragma autonomous_transaction;
begin
   insert
     into track_user
          (userid,
           submitted)
   values (pid,
           pmessage);
   commit;
end;
```

The procedure process receives information through the pdata parameter and returns a new state through the psummary parameter. This is called when the user at the browser requests to update the position of a portfolio. The update is recorded here and then a new state is returned to the user:

```
procedure process (pdata    in  varchar2 default null,
                   psummary out summary_table)
is
   vtag        varchar2(100);
   vvalue      varchar2(100);
   vdata       varchar2(32767) := substr(pdata,1,32767);
   vsell       number;
   vsellshares number;
   vstock      number;
   vprice      varchar2(100);
   vshares     varchar2(100);
   vaccount    varchar2(100) := '1';
```

I would like to draw the reader's attention to one limitation in the code. Note how the pdata input parameter is assigned to the vdata local variable and potentially truncated in the process. For this application, I am not likely to get data larger than 32K bytes, but in other applications, one cannot be so sure. The largest value that a varchar2 can be assigned in PL/SQL is 32K and so I have used that rather than defining a new datatype, say an index-by table, of varchar2 values, to hold a larger amount of input data.

Inside the process procedure is another procedure called parse. This procedure helps extract XML tags and values from the input data, which is all XML. Why use XML? Well, everyone is formatting with it today and it is easy to parse, as the procedure shows. I am not using more general tools to process XML because it is just too easy to do-it-oneself and the general tools add their own processing load that I will not need. Even if this application became larger, I would still use the technique provided here until a standard DTD were identified and communication with external businesses were desired. I often describe this as XML 101. It is the simplest XML that could conceivably go by that name and it serves the very useful purpose of communication between the browser and the database.

```
procedure parse(pstring in out varchar2,
                ptag        out     varchar2,
                pvalue   out     varchar2)
is
    vstart  number := instr(pstring,'>')+1;
    vlast   number := instr(pstring,'>',1,2);
    vsecond number := instr(pstring,'<',1,2);
begin
    ptag    := substr(pstring,2,vstart-3);
    pvalue  := substr(pstring,vstart,vsecond-vstart);
    pstring := substr(pstring,vlast+1);
end;
```

An additional procedure is also placed within the process procedure to simplify inserting data into the current_value table.

```
procedure curr_val (pstock in varchar2,
                    pprice in number)
is
begin
    insert
        into current_value
            (stock,
             price)
        values (pstock,
                pprice);
exception
    when others then
    update current_value
        set price = pprice
        where stock = pstock;
end;
```

Although I consider the next loop to be "simple", I would certainly be infuriated if someone passed it off to me with that description. What it does is to go through each tagged value, find what the tag is and what the value is and then, depending upon the name of the tag, it does something to the value.

If you recall at the beginning of this chapter, the screen shots showed the user requesting an update of the position of the portfolio. To achieve that update the following XML was returned to this parse procedure. The first tag tells us the id of the account that was updated. The second row tells us that I sold the stock I bought in the third trade. The fourth row says that I am claiming that LU is worth $26 per share. The last row is a set of three items that describe what I purchased:

```
<account>2</account>
<3_sell>30</3_sell>
<LU_stock>26</LU_stock>
<_buystock>orcl</_buystock><_buy>30</_buy><_buyshare>100</_buyshare>
```

If the reader is curious how I got this, I just looked in the track_user table after performing the update that generated the screen shots. The text of the message is saved there as part of recording the state of the session.

```
begin
    dbms_application_info.set_action('backend.parse');

    parse(vdata,vtag,vaccount);
    loop

        exit when vdata is null;
        parse(vdata,vtag,vvalue);

        vsell        := instr(vtag,csell);
        vstock       := instr(vtag,cstock);
        if vsell > 0 then
            vid := to_number(substr(vtag,1,vsell-1));
            parse(vdata,vtag,vsellshares);
            open cur_shares(vid);
            fetch cur_shares into vcur_shares;
            close cur_shares;
            vremaining := vcur_shares.shares - to_number(vsellshares);
            if vremaining > 0 then
                vsold := to_number(vsellshares);
            else
                vsold := vcur_shares.shares;
            end if;
            update trades
                set sold         = sysdate,
                    shares       = vsold,
                    trade_cost = trade_cost + ctrade_cost,
                    sell_price = to_number(vvalue)
              where id           = vid;

            if vremaining > 0 then
                insert
                  into trades
                        (stock,
                         account,
                         buy_price,
                         bought,
                         shares,
                         trade_cost)
                values (vcur_shares.stock,
                         vaccount,
                         vcur_shares.buy_price,
                         vcur_shares.bought,
                         vremaining,
                         0);
            end if;

        elsif vstock > 0 then
            curr_val(upper(substr(vtag,1,vstock-1)),to_number(vvalue));
        elsif instr(vtag,cbuystock) > 0 then
            parse(vdata,vtag,vprice);
            parse(vdata,vtag,vshares);
            insert
              into trades
                    (stock,
                     account,
```

```
                        buy_price,
                        shares,
                        trade_cost)
               values (vvalue,
                        to_number(vaccount),
                        to_number(vprice),
                        to_number(vshares),
                        ctrade_cost);
               curr_val(upper(vvalue),to_number(vprice));
          end if;
      end loop;
      commit;

      dbms_application_info.set_action(null);
   end;
```

The summary of each account is returned through the get_summary procedure. Like the get_trades procedure, it acts as a firewall to the database. A couple of cursors are defined as private to this procedure, since they are not used outside of it, to return the information to populate the psum output parameter.

The cur_trade_cost cursor is traversed and the information available from it is loaded. For each row the cur_capital cursor is run to get summary information about the total capital available to the account originally. One thing to be wary about here is that the cur_capital cursor is called within a loop. If there are more than a few iterations of this loop, the cost of retrieving this data could get high. In this case, there are only a handful of iterations and the cost is insignificant.

```
procedure get_summary (psum out summary_table)
   is
      cursor cur_trade_cost
      is
      select b.account_name,
             a.account,
             sum(a.trade_cost) tradecost,
             sum(nvl(a.shares*(a.sell_price-a.buy_price),0)) earn,
             min(a.bought) startdate,
             sum(a.shares*a.buy_price*decode(a.sold,null,1,0)) leverage
        from trades a,
             accounts b
       where a.account = b.id
       group by b.account_name, a.account
       order by b.account_name;

      cursor cur_capital (paccount in varchar2)
      is
      select sum(a.amount)
        from funds a,
             accounts b
       where b.account_name = paccount
         and a.account = b.id;

      i binary_integer;
   begin
      dbms_application_info.set_action('backend.get_summary');
      for c in cur_trade_cost loop
          i                     := psum.count;
          psum(i).accountid  := c.account;
          psum(i).accountno  := c.account_name;
          psum(i).tradecost  := c.tradecost;
```

```
            psum(i).earn        := c.earn;
            psum(i).leverage    := c.leverage;
            psum(i).startdate   := c.startdate;
            open cur_capital(c.account_name);
            fetch cur_capital into psum(i).capital;
            close cur_capital;
        end loop;

        dbms_application_info.set_action(null);
    end;
```

In order to maintain state for the database, the session has to be identified. We will do that through the new_user procedure that returns a value from the track_user_seq sequence.

```
    function new_user return number
    is
        cursor c is
        select track_user_seq.nextval
           from dual;
        vnum number;
    begin
        open c;
        fetch c into vnum;
        close c;
        return vnum;
    end;
end;
/
show errors
```

Frontend Display Package

This is the package that illustrates the use of the PL/SQL Web Toolkit. The most interesting thing about this package is what it does not contain.

❑ It does not contain direct SQL against database tables. Only those packaged procedures defined in the backend package are called to change the database state. This allows the separation between data and display for maintenance. It also potentially isolates the owner of the data from the schema requesting the data if the back-end and front-end packages are separated into different schemas.

❑ It does not contain any JavaScript, except for calls, hidden within the PL/SQL code. This is to avoid a maintenance nightmare and to facilitate development. JavaScript is difficult enough to debug. Placing it within a PL/SQL string that does not validate it in any meaningful way only adds to this difficulty. Admittedly, it initially appears easy to include simple JavaScript in PL/SQL (or any other language that builds HTML pages). After all the reader does not have to build a JavaScript object and link to this file. And building that JavaScript object may not be familiar to the developer who specializes in some other language. But separating JavaScript from PL/SQL allows independent development of the JavaScript to occur as well as independent testing that does not require that the PL/SQL application be running at all for the test to take place. Those who know JavaScript work on JavaScript. Those who know PL/SQL work on PL/SQL.

The reader who is familiar with the PL/SQL Web Toolkit will note that I am not using many procedures from the `htp` or `htf` packages that belong to the toolkit in the `frontend` package. The reason for this is that I am using JavaScript in the browser to generate the HTML and so I do not need these packages to build the HTML on the server. This allows me to preserve state in the browser by letting a language available on the browser generate the HTML. However, all of the data that is communicated for formatting goes through the `frontend` package. And it uses the open door that allows to the web server to accomplish this.

To put it another way, any language that can send text to a web server through a print procedure and an ability to set a mime-type, can generate HTML, or generally, XML. Only the toolkit, so far, is able to open the door for that communication from within the database to the web server. I'm concentrating on that door.

The specification file that follows shows that the package `frontend` contains only three procedures. They will be described in more detail when the package body is presented.

```
create or replace package frontend is
    procedure stocks;
    procedure initialpage;
    procedure blank;
    procedure process(pid   in number,
                      pdata in varchar2 default null);
end;
```

The `frontend` package builds the initial frameset, loads the data into JavaScript and calls JavaScript to build the initial display frame content. This might be a little different from the approach taken by most users of the PL/SQL Web Toolkit, who often use large quantities of code from the `htp` or `htf` packages to build the content on their web pages. You won't find that here, because the JavaScript on the client handles that task.

Which approach is better? Use JavaScript on the client or let the database generate the web content through the PL/SQL toolkit? For the current application either approach would be adequate. However, for more complicated applications some data should be stored on the client so that the server does not have to reconstruct this data for every call. Indeed, limiting the number of calls that have to be made back to the server improves the user's flow experience. It makes the user more likely to return to the site.

The package body follows.

```
create or replace package body frontend
is
```

The following constants are configuration parameters for the application. Change them here and recompile and they will be available with their new values. They also avoid having to look through code for these values should the reader want to change them later. Note that the value for `site` will likely have to be changed to suit your own environment. I set it to my wife's name:

```
subtype adequate is varchar2(100);
cmoney_format constant adequate := '9999999D99';
cprice_format constant adequate := '9999999D9999';
site    constant adequate := 'http://xiaoyan.at.home/';
```

The script procedure is written because it is used often. I suppose I could use a PL/SQL procedure from the `htp` package, but this does the job of linking a JavaScript library file using less coding. In general, I use the `htp` package when it most economically gets me the HTML that I want. When it doesn't, I build a procedure that I can reuse that does. That is why this procedure exists. Note that the only `htp` procedures that are really necessary are the procedures that allow you to communicate with the web server. The one I am using here is the `p` procedure to do that:

```
procedure script (psource in varchar2)
is
begin
    htp.p ('<script src="' || psource || '"></script>');
end;
```

The message frame needs to be loaded with something. The next procedure loads an empty page into it.

```
procedure blank
is
begin
    htp.htmlopen;
    htp.htmlclose;
end;
```

The `display` frame is initially displayed by this procedure when the application begins. It does only two things:

❑   It lets JavaScript in the top parent frame know about the existence of the display frame object which has just been constructed

❑   It requests that JavaScript display the data that has been provided to it when the top frame was constructed:

```
procedure initialpage
is
begin
    dbms_application_info.set_module('frontend.initialpage',null);

    htp.script('parent.htm.document(this.document)');
    htp.script('parent.stocks.report()');

    dbms_application_info.set_module(null,null);
end;
```

This procedure is the workhorse of this package. It gets the current state of the accounts and sends this information to JavaScript objects in the top frame. It can be called initially when the top frame is constructed or later from the `message` frame. For those who think I am not using any `htp` procedures, note the use of the `htp.script` procedure to send data to JavaScript.

There are two loops that take data stored using the `backend` package's data types and loads them into JavaScript arrays of objects. Just ignore the syntax for a moment to see the transitions that have occurred so far. The `backend` package retrieved the data from a cursor, that is, from SQL. It converted this data into new data types of its own construction in order to hide direct access to the tables. The `frontend` package received data using the `backend` package's data types, not directly from SQL and, in turn, converted them into the data types used by JavaScript. JavaScript is the language that we will use on the browser to store state and rebuild the HTML.

```
procedure updateInfo(pwhere in varchar2 default null)
    is
        vsummary backend.summary_table;
        vtrades  backend.trade_table;
    begin
        backend.get_summary(vsummary);
        if vsummary.count > 0 then
            htp.script(pwhere || 'stocks.s.length=0');
            for i in vsummary.first .. vsummary.last loop
            htp.script(pwhere || 'stocks.s['||pwhere||
                'stocks.s.length]=new '||pwhere||'sRec("'||
                to_char(vsummary(i).accountid)||'","'||
                vsummary(i).accountno||'","'||
                ltrim(to_char(vsummary(i).tradeCost,cmoney_format)) ||
                '","'||
                ltrim(to_char(vsummary(i).earn,cmoney_format))||
                '","'||
                ltrim(to_char(vsummary(i).leverage,cmoney_format))||
                '","'||
                ltrim(to_char(vsummary(i).capital,cmoney_format))||
                '","'||
                to_char(vsummary(i).startdate,'Mon DD, YYYY')||'")');
            end loop;
        end if;
        backend.get_trades(vtrades);
        if vtrades.count > 0 then
            htp.script(pwhere || 'stocks.d.length=0');
            for i in vtrades.first .. vtrades.last loop
            htp.script(pwhere || 'stocks.d['||pwhere||
                'stocks.d.length]=new '||pwhere||'dRec('||
                to_char(vtrades(i).id)||',"'||
                vtrades(i).account||'","'||
                vtrades(i).stock||'","'||
                ltrim(to_char(vtrades(i).buy_price,cprice_format))||
                '","'||
                to_char(vtrades(i).shares)||'","'||
                ltrim(to_char(vtrades(i).trade_cost,cmoney_format))||
                '","'||
                ltrim(to_char(vtrades(i).current_price,cprice_format))||
                '")');
            end loop;
        end if;
    end;
```

The stocks procedure is the first call made. For example, in my browser, I would reference the first page by http://xiaoyan.at.home:8001/WebDB/wrox.frontend.stocks. This procedure loads the JavaScript libraries into the parent frame by loading files containing these libraries. These files create JavaScript utility objects. It then loads data through the updateInfo procedure into the newly loaded JavaScript objects and then builds the two child frames of the application, a frame named display to show the GUI interface and a hidden frame named message to send messages back and forth to the server. A call to backend.new_user gets an identification number that is associated with this construction of the parent frame. This identification number is used to track activity performed by the user and thereby record state.

```
procedure stocks
   is
   begin
      dbms_application_info.set_module('frontend.stocks',null);

      htp.htmlopen;
      script(site || 'js/htm.js');
      script(site || 'js/stocks.js');
      htp.script('stocks.s.length=0');
      htp.script('stocks.d.length=0');
      htp.script('stocks.sellLabel="'||backend.csell||'"');
      htp.script('stocks.quantityLabel="'||backend.cquantity||'"');
      htp.script('stocks.stockLabel="'||backend.cstock||'"');
      htp.script('stocks.buyStockLabel="'||backend.cbuystock||'"');
      htp.script('stocks.buyLabel="'||backend.cbuy||'"');
      htp.script('stocks.buyShareLabel="'||backend.cbuyshare||'"');
      htp.script('stocks.id='||to_char(backend.new_user));
      updateInfo;
      htp.framesetopen('100%,*','100%,*',cattributes=>'border="0"');
      htp.frame('frontend.initialpage','display');
      htp.frame('frontend.blank','message');
      htp.framesetclose;
      htp.htmlclose;

      dbms_application_info.set_module(null,null);
   end;
```

The process procedure receives changes that the user at the browser wishes to make. These changes are sent to the backend package for processing and recording of state. The new state of the database is loaded into the JavaScript objects with the updateInfo procedure and it requests that the trade report page be written to the display frame.

When the process procedure is called from JavaScript, the call requests that the HTML be sent to the hidden message frame. The message frame is hidden and so this information is not directly displayed to the user. When requested JavaScript displays the updated information to the display frame that the user can see.

```
procedure process(pid    in number,
                  pdata in varchar2 default null)
   is
      vsummary backend.summary_table;
   begin
      dbms_application_info.set_module('frontend.process',null);

      backend.insert_state(pid,pdata); -- Handles server state.
      backend.process(pdata,vsummary); -- Processes request.

      htp.htmlopen;
      updateInfo('parent.');
      htp.script('parent.stocks.report()');
      htp.htmlclose;

      dbms_application_info.set_module(null,null);
   end;
end;
/
show errors
```

Support Files

The JavaScript and style sheet files do the real work of displaying HTML in the browser. They are isolated from the PL/SQL code because their development, testing, versioning and document management can be done more easily on the file system with a wider variety of tools to choose from.

It is possible to place all of these files into PL/SQL code. However, just because something is possible doesn't mean that it should be done. The liability of storing these languages within another language is that strings are usually used to write the JavaScript code or styles. These strings introduce errors that are not easy to debug since as strings in PL/SQL they are not evaluated until they are live in the browser. Separating out the JavaScript and styles allows for the possibility that these files can be independently built from PL/SQL as well as independently tested.

As discussed at the start of this chapter, the browser is divided into frames, the parent frame containing the code that builds the child frames (`message` and `display`) as well as the JavaScript code to build the frame contents. The `display` frame is the only one genrally visible to the user, but occasionally , during development, it is interesting to view what appears in the `message` frame. Errors are generally sent to that frame from the database. To make this frame appear, the line in the `frontend.stocks` procedure that opens the frameset could be set as follows:

```
htp.framesetopen('100%,*','50%,*',cattributes=>'border="0"');
```

To make this example generate an error, there thereby show something interesting in the `message` frame, I modified the name of the procedure that loaded the initial `message` frame to `rblank` that does not exist in the `frontend` package.

```
htp.frame('frontend.rblank','message');
```

The browser would then see two frames, one with the original content and the `message` frame displaying an error:

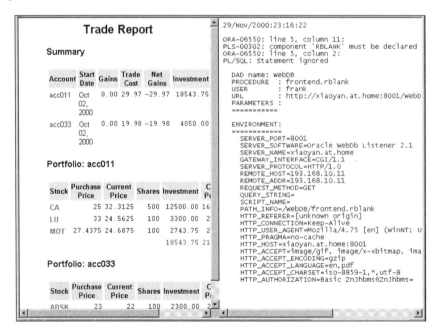

JavaScript: htm.js

The sole purpose of the `htm.js` library is to format HTML to write to the display frame. Some might argue that it is very simple to do this using the JavaScript `writeln` method. They are correct that it is simple to do, but it involves the use of more strings than are necessary to get the job done. More strings means more inconsistencies and errors and hence more debugging. Therefore this formatting is provided in a separate JavaScript utility object.

This support file contains a utility object called `htm` that provides a convenient way to write just the HTML that is required by the application. No attempt is made to generalize this library to write all HTML.

```
var htm = new Object()
```

One configuration parameter is needed to store the name of the cascading style sheet file.

```
htm.stylesheet = http://xiaoyan.at.home/css/stocks.css
```

Since the `display` frame is not yet built it cannot be specified here, but a variable is available so that when the `display` frame is created it can identify itself to the `htm` object.

```
htm.doc = ""
```

Some variables are used to indicate if a tag has been opened or not. This allows the same call to open the tag if the flag is `false` or close it if the flag is `true`.

```
htm.htmlFlag = false
htm.bodyFlag = false
htm.tdFlag   = false
htm.trFlag   = false
htm.formFlag = false
htm.tdsFlag  = false
```

One method, `document`, is available which allows the `display` frame to identify itself once it has been created.

```
htm.document = function(d) { this.doc = d; }
```

Two other methods provide a general way to construct tags. The class attribute of the tag is important for using style sheets.

```
htm.tag = function(tag,t,c,a) {
this.doc.writeln("<"+tag+
                 (c==undefined?"":" class='"+c+"'")+
                 (a==undefined?"":" "+a)+">"+
                 (t==undefined?"":t)+"</"+tag+">")
}
htm.singleTag = function(tag,flag,attributes) {
    if (flag) {
       this.doc.writeln("</"+tag+">")
       return false
    } else {
       this.doc.writeln("<"+tag+
                        (attributes==undefined?"":" "+attributes)+">")
       return true
    }
}
```

The other methods call the general methods to construct specific tags.

```
htm.html  = function() {
    if (!this.htmlFlag) {this.doc.open()} // open a new document
    this.htmlFlag = this.singleTag("html",this.htmlFlag)
    if (!this.htmlFlag) {this.doc.close()} // close a written document
}
htm.body  = function() {
    this.bodyFlag = this.singleTag("body",this.bodyFlag)
}
htm.div   = function(text,c,attr) {
    this.tag("div",text,c,attr)
}
htm.form  = function(attr) {
    this.formFlag = this.singleTag("form",this.formFlag,attr)
}
htm.h1    = function(text,c,attr) {
    this.tag("h1",text,c,attr)
}
htm.h2    = function(text,c,attr) {
    this.tag("h2",text,c,attr)
}
htm.span  = function(text,c,attr) {
    this.tag("span",text,c,attr)
}
htm.style = function() {
    this.singleTag("link",false,
            "rel='stylesheet' type='text/css' href='"+this.stylesheet+"'")
}
htm.table = function() {
    this.tableFlag = this.singleTag("table",this.tableFlag)
}
htm.td    = function(text,c,attr) {
    this.tag("td",text,c,attr)
}
htm.tds   = function(c,attr) {
    this.tdsFlag = this.singleTag("td",this.tdsFlag,attr)
}
htm.th    = function(text,c,attr) {
    this.tag("th",text,c,attr)
}
htm.tr    = function() {
    this.trFlag = this.singleTag("tr",this.trFlag)
}
htm.a     = function(text,c,attr) {
    this.tag("a",text,c,attr)
}
```

Javascript: stocks.js

The JavaScript file, stocks.js, does many things:

❏ It stores data that is returned from the server so that this data does not have to be re-sent often. This eases the load on the server and provides the user with a smoother experience.

❏ It displays the entire frame that the user sees. When building the display frame through PL/SQL, only a call to JavaScript was invoked after the data was loaded.

❏ Data collected from a form is tagged in JavaScript on the browser so that it may be sent to the database for storage.

There are some who will argue that the PL/SQL Web Toolkit should build the `display` frame. The toolkit is able to do this, directly from the database. However, by choosing a language that is in the browser, and by caching information obtained from the server in data structures maintained by this language, persistence can be created at the client level.

Constructors for the data structures that will store the PL/SQL `trade_row` and `summary_row` data are first created.

```
function sRec(id,account,tradeCost,earn,leverage,capital,startDate) {
    this.id        = id
    this.account   = account
    this.tradeCost = tradeCost
    this.earn      = earn
    this.leverage  = leverage
    this.capital   = capital
    this.startDate = startDate
}
function dRec(id,account,stock,buy_price,shares,tradeCost,price) {
    this.id        = id
    this.account   = account
    this.stock     = stock
    this.buy_price = buy_price
    this.shares    = shares
    this.tradeCost = tradeCost
    this.price     = price
}
```

The utility object `stocks` is constructed to store arrays of data as well as to construct the content for the `display` frame.

```
var stocks = new Object
// This next data value should probably be changed.
stocks.plsqlGateway = "http://xiaoyan.at.home:8001/WebDB/"
// State preservation information.
stocks.id = 0;  // Used on the server to keep track of this user.
// Data storage.  The goal is to bring this data to the client
// only once and then to display in multiple ways.
stocks.account = ""
stocks.s = new Array()
stocks.d = new Array()
stocks.blanks = 3 // Number of blank rows for new purchases.
// These are used for xml building and are received from PL/SQL.
stocks.sellLabel = ""
stocks.stockLabel = ""
stocks.buyStockLabel = ""
stocks.buyLabel = ""
stocks.buyShare = ""
stocks.quantityLabel = ""
```

A convenience method to format a number is provided.

```
stocks.format = function(n) {
   var n1 = Math.round(n*100)/100
   var s  = n1.toString()
   var w  = s.indexOf('.')
   if (w==-1) {
      s = s+".00"
   } else {
     if (w==(s.length-2)) {
        s = s+"0"
     }
   }
   return s
}
```

The `stocks.process` JavaScript code generates XML in the browser from the HTML form in order to allow an arbitrary number of fields to be displayed on the **Update Position** page. This allows any number of fields to be displayed and the developer does not have to worry about exceeding some limit. It also means that only one field is returned to the PL/SQL program to receive the data that the user entered in that arbitrary number of fields in the html form. This is the reason XML is used and it is probably one of the earliest uses of XML in web pages.

The `backend` package now has to parse and store this XML. It is easy to store the XML and that is being in the `track_user` table. One stores the XML to record information about the user session. But parsing it requires some code. That code could be from a general-purpose parser, but if the developer knows what XML to expect and the kinds of tags are limited, it is straightforward to do the parsing oneself. That is what is done in the `backend` package `process` procedure:

```
stocks.process = function (f) {
   var r = "<account>"+this.account+"</account>";
   // Loop through all the elements in the form f.
   for (var i = 0; i < f.elements.length; i++) {
      // Find those that are not empty.
      if (f.elements[i].value != "") {
         // Tag these field elements.

         r = r + "<" + f.elements[i].name + ">" +
             (isNaN(f.elements[i].value)?
             f.elements[i].value:
             eval(f.elements[i].value)) +
             "</" + f.elements[i].name + ">"
      }
   }
   if (r=="") {
      alert("No changes were made.")
   } else {
      message.location = this.plsqlGateway+
         "frank.frontend.process?pid="+
         this.id+"&pdata="+r;
   }
}
```

The `report` method displays the report page. Note how it uses the `htm.js` library to display the HTML:

```
stocks.report = function () {
    var current = 0
    var currentvalue = 0
    var earn, tradeCost, leverage, capital
    var buy_price, price, shares
    htm.html()
    htm.style()
    htm.body()
    htm.h1('Trade Report')
    htm.h2('Summary')
    htm.table()
    htm.tr()
    htm.th("Account")
    htm.th("Start Date")
    htm.th("Gains")
    htm.th("Trade Cost")
    htm.th("Net Gains")
    htm.th("Investment")
    htm.th("Cash")
    htm.th("Capital")
    htm.tr()
    for (var i in this.s) {
        earn = parseFloat(this.s[i].earn)
        tradeCost = parseFloat(this.s[i].tradeCost)
        leverage  = parseFloat(this.s[i].leverage)
        capital   = parseFloat(this.s[i].capital)
        htm.tr()
        htm.td("<a href='JavaScript:parent.stocks.form("+this.s[i].id+")'>"+
                this.s[i].account+"</a>")
        htm.td(this.s[i].startDate)
        htm.td(this.format(earn),"number")
        htm.td(tradeCost,"number")
        htm.td(this.format(earn-tradeCost),"number")
        htm.td(this.format(leverage),"number")
        htm.td(this.format(capital+earn-tradeCost-leverage),"number")
        htm.td(this.format(capital),"number")
        htm.tr()
    }
    htm.table()

    for (i=0;i<this.s.length;i++) {
        htm.h2("Portfolio: "+this.s[i].account)
        htm.table()
        // Report Header
        htm.tr()
        htm.th("Stock")
        htm.th("Average Purchase Price")
        htm.th("Current Price")
        htm.th("Shares")
        htm.th("Investment")
        htm.th("Current Portfolio")
        htm.tr()
        // Report Data
        for (var j=0;j<this.d.length;j++) {
```

```
            if (this.d[j].account==this.s[i].id) {
                buy_price = parseFloat(this.d[j].buy_price)
                price     = isNaN(price)?buy_price:price
                shares    = parseFloat(this.d[j].shares)
                htm.tr()
                htm.td(this.d[j].stock,"stock")
                htm.td(buy_price,"number")
                if (this.format(buy_price<=price)) {
                    htm.td(price,"number")
                } else {
                    htm.td(price,"alert")
                }
                htm.td(shares,"number")
                htm.td(this.format(buy_price*shares),"number")
                currentvalue = price*shares
                htm.td(this.format(currentvalue),"number")
                htm.tr()
                current = current + currentvalue
            }
        }
        // Conclusion
        htm.tr()
        htm.td()
        htm.td()
        htm.td()
        htm.td()
        htm.td(this.format(this.s[i].leverage),"total")
        htm.td(this.format(current),"total")
        htm.tr()
        htm.table()
    }
    // Navigation Buttons
    htm.body();
    htm.html();
}
```

The update page is constructed by the `form` method:

```
stocks.form = function(account) {
    this.account = account.toString()
    var Aname
    for (var f=0;f<this.s.length;f++){
        if (this.s[f].id==account) {
            Aname = this.s[f].account
        }
    }
    htm.html();
    htm.style()
    htm.body()
    htm.h1("Update Position: "+Aname)
    htm.form("name='stocks'")
    htm.table()
    // Heading
    htm.tr()
    htm.th("Stock")
    htm.th("Purchase Price")
```

```
            htm.th("Shares")
            htm.th("Quantity")
            htm.th("Selling Price")
            htm.th("Current Price")
            htm.tr()
            for (var i=0;i<this.d.length;i++) {
                if (this.d[i].account==this.account) {
                    htm.tr()
                    htm.td(this.d[i].stock,"stock")
                    htm.td(this.d[i].buy_price,"number")
                    htm.td(this.d[i].shares,"number")
                    htm.td("<input type='text' name='"+
                        this.d[i].id+this.sellLabel+"' size=5>")
                    htm.td("<input type='text' name='"+
                        this.d[i].id+this.quantityLabel+"' size=5>")
                    htm.td("<input type='text' name='"+
                        this.d[i].stock+this.stockLabel+"' size=5>")
                    htm.tr()
                }
            }
            for (var j=1;j<this.blanks;j++) {
                htm.tr()
                htm.td("<input type='text' name='"+this.buyStockLabel+"' size=5>")
                htm.td("<input type='text' name='"+this.buyLabel+"' size=5>")
                htm.td("<input type='text' name='"+this.buyShareLabel+"' size=5>")
                htm.tr()
            }
            htm.table()
            htm.form()
            // Navigation Buttons
            htm.table()
            htm.tr()
            htm.td("<a href='JavaScript:parent.stocks.report()'>Report</a>",
                    "button")
            htm.td("<a "+
        "href='JavaScript:parent.stocks.process(this.document.stocks)'>Submit</a>",
                    "button")
            htm.tr()
            htm.table()
            htm.body();
            htm.html();
        }
```

Style Sheet: stocks.css

Simple changes to a style sheet can result in drastic changes globally in the application. Just try removing the style sheet and see what difference it makes! The style sheet allows individual preferences to be readily expressed.

The reader might ask what style sheets have to do with the PL/SQL toolkit. The answer is that using style sheets, especially external style sheets, means that less PL/SQL code needs to be written. Since the style sheet may be more easily tested with a plain HTML page from the file system using different browsers than by running the full application, PL/SQL should only reference a style sheet, not incorporate the style information into the PL/SQL code.

```css
body, div, h1, h2, div, td, th, span {
    font-family:arial;
    font-size:10pt;
    font-color:black;
}
body {
    margin-left:15%;
    margin-right:10%;
}
h1 {
    font-size:17pt;
    text-align:center;
}
h2 {
    font-size:14pt;
}
th {
    background-color:yellow;
}
td {
    vertical-align:top;
}
.alert {
    background-color:#66ff33;
    text-align:right;
    font-family:courier;
}
.button {
    background-color:#66ccff;
    font-weight:bold;
    font-family:arial;
    border:4pt;
    padding:4pt;
}
.number {
    text-align:right;
    font-family:courier;
}
.stock {
    text-align:left;
    font-weight:bold;
    color:#339999;
}
.total {
    text-align:right;
    font-family:courier;
    color:red;
}
```

Summary

This case study demonstrates a useful, even if simple, product that could be built with this Toolkit. Many parts are involved: a data model, a set of two PL/SQL packages that attempt to interface the database to the user and JavaScript and style sheet support files. I hope that it will prove to be the foundation for further improvements and developments.

Here are a few suggestions along those lines:

❏   The UML design phase has been ignored, although at least a detailed Use Case Diagram with documentation is worth building for a more complicated application.

❏   No exception handling occurs in the PL/SQL code. To some extent this was done out of laziness on my part. However, when I thought of inserting it, I felt it would distract attention from the major features of the application. In general, an entire package should be devoted to exceptions and how they are handled and recognized.

❏   No exception handling was done in the JavaScript either. Certainly, adding a check that an expected numeric value is indeed numeric and positive would be valuable. Note that this data validation would be done only as a convenience to the user to avoid receiving an error from the database. The primary place this data validation occurs is in the database.

❏   No automated tests were conducted for these files. This is a serious fault and I would recommend that the reader rectify the situation. Note that it is possible to build PL/SQL test packages to check that both the `backend` and `frontend` packages work correctly. It is also possible to build JavaScript testing tools that would exercise the JavaScript when it is loaded in a browser. And a simple HTML page linked to the style sheet would test whether the styles did what one expected when loaded into each browser that the application claimed to support.

Of all the technologies that involve databases and web servers, the ones that allow databases to communicate directly with the web server, without going through an external language in the middle-tier, are the most exciting. A door to the database, that only a few years ago did not exist, is now available.

10

Web PL/SQL Application Development Using Designer 6i

This chapter presents the use of Designer's Web PL/SQL Generator to quickly build production-quality web applications. The Web PL/SQL Generator generates PL/SQL packages that dynamically create HTML pages using Oracle's Web PL/SQL Toolkit presented in Chapter 8. Complete, robust Oracle 8i database applications can be generated from design specifications without writing any code. The Web PL/SQL Generator is one of several generators included in the Designer toolset.

This chapter includes hands-on exercises to design, generate, and execute several Web PL/SQL modules for the Education Center database built in Chapter 5. These modules provide a representative sample of the page layouts easily generated using Designer. These exercises cover several of the new features of the Designer 6i Web PL/SQL Generator including multi-row insert forms and list of values (LOV) components.

To follow this case study, the readers should have:

- ❑ Access to a working copy of Designer 6i with an Oracle Repository.

- ❑ An understanding of Oracle's PL/SQL Web Toolkit and Web PL/SQL applications

- ❑ Access to a web server with a PL/SQL gateway – for example, iAS, OAS, Oracle Portal, or WebDB.

Getting Started

Ideally, the reader should have successfully completed the Chapter 5 database design case study using Designer 6i. However, if you're keen to jump straight into application development with Designer, then a Designer 6i export (.dmp file) of the Education Center Application database design is available from the Wrox web site. If you did not create the database design from Chapter 5 in your Repository, you can use this export to load that data so that you can proceed with the hands-on exercises in this chapter. Instructions for loading this data into your Designer Repository are included with the .dmp file on the Wrox web site.

Overview

Designer 6i provides the capability to design and generate full-function Web PL/SQL applications that enable users to query, input, update, and delete information in an Oracle 8i database across an Intranet or across the World Wide Web. Designer generates applications based upon the Oracle PL/SQL Web Toolkit.

Any HTML browser may access the generated Web PL/SQL applications – for example, Netscape 3+ or Internet Explorer 5+. The browser sees HTML pages with optional Javascript for client-side validation. The browser submits HTTP requests to the HTTP listener on the Application Server with a PL/SQL gateway. The Application Server processes the HTTP request based upon the specified URL. Requests for static pages are performed on the Application Server, and application requests are routed to the PL/SQL module packages in the Oracle Database.

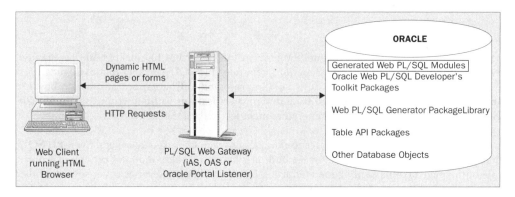

The Web PL/SQL Generator creates a set of module PL/SQL packages that dynamically create application-specific HTML pages. The Web PL/SQL Module processes the requests, retrieves the requested data from the database, and returns dynamically generated HTML pages with the data.

Each generated module PL/SQL package contains application-specific logic, and uses the standard functionality provided by Designer's Web Server Generator Library for HTML document syntax and layout, text/message handling, SQL statement construction, navigation links, environment information, button/control creation, domain validation, URL manipulation, and security.

The Designer Web Server Generator Library packages (the WSGLx packages) use the Oracle Web PL/SQL Toolkit for standard web PL/SQL application logic. The generated module packages may also include application-specific calls to the Web Toolkit. See Chapter 8 for a detailed discussion of the Web Toolkit

The generated Web PL/SQL modules use Designer-generated Table API procedures rather than performing direct data manipulation on the Oracle tables. Designer generates a Table Application Programming Interface (API) package for each table, which includes query, insert, update, delete, and lock procedures for that table. Custom business logic may also be defined and include in the Table API packages.

Designer's **Design Editor** provides an integrated environment for the design and development of database objects and modules. Designer generates Web PL/SQL applications from Module Designs and Database Designs recorded in the Oracle Repository. Generator Preferences can be defined to control the characteristics and behavior of the generated application modules.

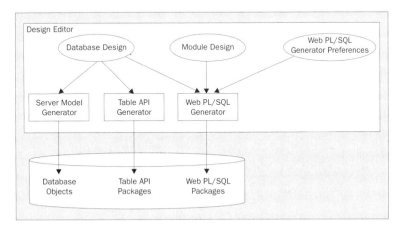

The Designer components used for web PL/SQL application development include:

- ❏ The **Design Editor**'s navigator, property dialogs, and diagramming tools are used to create Module Designs and Database Designs.

- ❏ The **Server Model Generator** creates the DDL for the database objects and for custom PL/SQL packages for the application.

- ❏ The **Table API Generator** creates the Table API Packages based upon the Database Design and associated column display and validation specifications.

- ❏ The **Web PL/SQL Generator** produces the Web PL/SQL Modules based upon the Module Designs, Database Design, and Generator Preferences.

Chapter 5 introduced the Design Editor, and covered the Server Model Generator. This chapter will focus on the Module Design capabilities of the Design Editor, the Table API Generator, and the Web PL/SQL Generator.

Designer's Web PL/SQL Application Development Process

The diagram below shows the major steps in the design and development of a Web PL/SQL application using Designer.

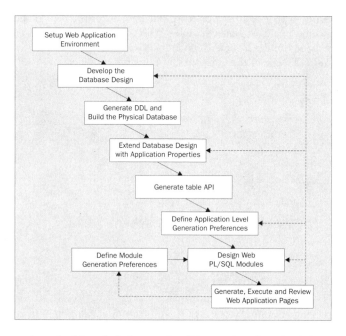

Each of these steps is described briefly below and will be explored in depth later in this chapter:

- **Setup the Web Application Environment** – You must setup up an Application Schema(s) to contain the physical database, the Table API, and your web PL/SQL modules. You must install Designer's Web PL/SQL Library and the Web PL/SQL Toolkit. In your web server's configuration, define a Database Access Descriptor (DAD) for your application schema and virtual directories for your static web pages.

- **Develop the Database Design** – The Database Design must be defined in the Oracle Repository in the form of Table Definitions with columns, constraints, default values, any associated value lists, and any associated database sequences. Other server-side database objects, including database triggers, PL/SQL, and Java logic, may also be defined in the Designer Repository and used to support the Web PL/SQL applications. This Database Design may be derived from an Entity Relationship Model and/or by reverse engineering a physical database.

- **Generate DDL and Build the Physical Database** – From the Database Design, generate DDL for the physical database objects, and build the physical database in your application schema.

- **Extend the Database Design** – To support web application development, the Database Design must be extended with additional database 'application' properties, including column display formats, prompts, validation criteria, and error messages. These properties will be incorporated into the generated Table API and in the Module Design and generated Web PL/SQL modules.

- **Generate and Build the Table API** – Based upon the extended Database Design, generate and install the Table API packages in your application schema. If the database design changes, the Table API must be re-generated. Custom business logic may also be defined and included in the generated Table API packages.

- ❑ **Design Web PL/SQL Modules** – Create a Module Design for each Web PL/SQL module. For each module, define:

  - ❑ the database tables used by the module
  - ❑ operations allowed on those tables and columns – insert, update, select, and/or delete
  - ❑ the data fields to be displayed on each page
  - ❑ data validation criteria and lists of values
  - ❑ page layout and static text to be displayed
  - ❑ custom logic

- ❑ **Define Module Generation Preferences** – Define generation preferences for module layout, style, and other generated characteristics. Preferences may be defined at various levels – for example, at the Application Level for all modules, or at the module level for a specific module.

- ❑ **Generate, Execute, and Review the Web Application Pages** – Once the Module Definition is complete, run the Web PL/SQL Generator to create and install the Web PL/SQL module packages into the application schema. Execute and evaluate the newly generated module or modules via your Web Browser.

Application design and generation using Designer is usually an iterative process. The generator is run, and then the resulting module is executed and evaluated. Based upon the evaluation, revisions are made to the Module Design, Database Design, or Generator Preferences. The affected components are then re-generated and re-installed in the application schema. The Web pages are then re-executed and re-evaluated. If needed, another iteration of design and generation may be performed.

Ideally, the Web PL/SQL Generator will produce a complete application that meets all user requirements and expectations. In other words, the application will be "100% generated". If the module needs to be modified, the Module Design, or Database Design, or Preferences would be updated, and the module re-generated.

Designer provides several ways to include custom Javascript and PL/SQL code into a Web PL/SQL Module Design or Table API. This custom code will automatically be included in the generated PL/SQL packages. It is best to put as many customizations into Designer through the Module Designs or the Server Designs as possible. This guarantees those customizations will be generated every time the module is re-generated.

Some organizations may still have the need to customize a generated Web PL/SQL application with custom "wrapper" code, additions to the generated code, or modifications to the generated code. These customizations are referred to as **post-generation mods**, and will be lost if a module is re-generated from Designer and will have to be manually re-applied to the new version of the package. Designer does not support reverse engineering or design capture of post-generation modifications to Web PL/SQL modules or to a Table API – although it does support

Each organization should consciously define their strategy for post-generation mods. In some cases, post-generation mods may make excellent business sense. In other cases, they may not be wise.

> **Try to minimize post-generation mods to your Web PL/SQL Modules and Table APIs. Always document each post-generation mod thoroughly. Use the Repository's configuration management capabilities to check-in each version of a package and track changes.**

The remainder of this chapter will discuss each of these steps in detail, and present hands-on exercises to design and generate a prototype Web PL/SQL Application.

Setup the Web Application Environment

You must setup your physical web application environment before you will be able to install, execute, and test the Web PL/SQL applications that Designer generates. The required components of this environment include:

❏ An Application Schema – a database userID to contain the physical database and the various PL/SQL packages you will create for this application.

❏ The Oracle Web PL/SQL Toolkit – a set of packages that come with your PL/SQL gateway. These packages include HTF, HTP, OWA, OWA_UTIL.

❏ A Web server configured for your Web Application's use – you will need a Database Access Descriptior (DAD) defined for your application schema and a virtual directory definition mapped to a physical directory for your static web pages.

❏ Designer's Webserver Generator Library – a set of PL/SQL packages with names like WSGLx.

If you do not have your web server installed, you may want to stop and get it installed.

> **If you do not have a working web server, you can still enjoy these hands-on exercises through the generation steps. However, you will not be able to actually execute your modules in the browser until you get your web server working.**

Create an Application Schema

For your web application environment, create a single physical database userID to contain your physical database and various PL/SQL packages. In this chapter, this Oracle database account will be referred to as the wroxweb user. Note that this user account does not have to be the same user account that you use to access the Designer Repository. Also, this user account does not even have to reside on the same Oracle database as your Designer Repository.

To create this user account: logon to SQL*Plus as system/manager or some other DBA privileged account and create this user account:

```
SQL> CREATE USER wroxweb IDENTIFIED BY wroxweb;
SQL> GRANT resource, connect TO wrox;
```

Throughout the remainder of this chapter, the term **application schema** or wroxweb/wroxweb@yourdatabase will be used to reference this account.

> **Creating a single application schema is the easiest way to set up your physical Web Application Environment. It is possible to configure your web application using multiple schemas but this approach is more confusing. Note that the Designer 6i Help Text does present an approach using three schemas – a Table Owner Schema, an Application Schema, and a Toolkit Schema. To minimize reader confusion, this chapter presents the user of a single application schema.**

Obtain Access to the PL/SQL Web Toolkit

Your application schema will require EXECUTE privileges on the Web Toolkit packages. Some of the required Web Toolkit packages are: HTF, HTP, OWA, OWA_UTIL.

The Oracle PL/SQL Web Toolkit may have been automatically installed on your Oracle 8*i* database when your webserver and its PL/SQL gateway were installed. The location of the Web Toolkit will vary depending on the Webserver that you are using. For example:

❑ With OAS and WebDB, the Web Toolkit is routinely installed in a schema called OAS_PUBLIC.

❑ With iAS and Oracle Portal, the Web Toolkit is installed in the SYS schema. This installation script also creates public synonyms and grants all privileges on each of these packages to public.

> **With iAS and Oracle Portal, the Web Toolkit installation scripts are hard-coded for installation in the SYS schema, and will require modification to install into another schema. Your DBA should examine this default installation and modify it to meet your organization's access and security needs.**

First determine if your application schema already has access to the Web Toolkit packages and can EXECUTE one of the toolkit procedures:

1. Logon to SQL*Plus as the application schema:

```
wroxweb/wroxweb@yourdatabase
```

2. Try describing each package:

```
SQL>DESCRIBE HTF
SQL>DESCRIBE HTP
SQL>DESCRIBE OWA
SQL>DESCRIBE OWA_UTIL
```

If your Application Schema can see these packages, you will get a long list of the procedures contained in each package. This is what you want to see!

3. Validate that the application schema has EXECUTE privileges on the HTP package using the following:

```
SQL>EXECUTE htp.htmlopen;
```

You should see the message:

```
PL/SQL procedure successfully completed.
```

If you can DESCRIBE the Toolkit packages and EXECUTE a toolkit procedure from your Application Schema, then your Application Schema probably has the required access to the PL/SQL Web Toolkit, and you should proceed to the next section.

If you cannot see the Web Toolkit packages, then they may not be installed correctly. Try the following to diagnose the situation further:

1. Logon to SQL*Plus as system/manager or with another DBA privileged account.

2. Run the following query to determine if and where the Toolkit Packages are installed:

```
SELECT owner, object_name, object_type, status
FROM all_objects
WHERE object_name in ('HTF','HTP','OWA','OWA_UTIL')
AND object_type like 'PACKAGE%'
ORDER BY owner;
```

The result should look like the following:

```
OWNER                    OBJECT_NAME      OBJECT_TYPE       STATUS
-----------------------------------------------------------------------
DES6I                    HTF              PACKAGE           VALID
DES6I                    HTF              PACKAGE BODY      VALID
DES6I                    HTP              PACKAGE           VALID
DES6I                    HTP              PACKAGE BODY      VALID
DES6I                    OWA              PACKAGE           VALID
DES6I                    OWA              PACKAGE BODY      VALID
DES6I                    OWA_UTIL         PACKAGE           VALID
etc...
```

If you find the Web Toolkit packages, then the Web Toolkit may be installed but not shared with your Application Schema. Check with your DBA or your web server administrator to obtain access rights on the Web Toolkit. Check your web server installation documentation for instructions for installing and sharing the Web Toolkit packages.

If you do not find the Web Toolkit packages in your Oracle 8i database, then you or your DBA will need to install the Web Toolkit. Check your webserver installation documentation for instructions on how to install the Toolkit.

To install the Web Toolkit for iAS:

1. Logon to the computer where iAS is installed. Locate the script owaload.sql in:

    C:\<iAS_ORACLE_HOME>\Apache\modsql\owa\owaload.sql

    where <iAS_ORACLE_HOME> is your home directory for the iAS software.

2. Logon to SQL*Plus as: SYS. **This script must be run as** SYS. Run the script:

    SQL>@x:\<iAS_ORACLE_HOME>\Apache\modsql\owa\owaload.sql

If this script runs successfully, repeat the steps above to verify that your Application Schema can DESCRIBE the Toolkit packages, and can EXECUTE one of the Toolkit procedures.

Configure Your Webserver

Next you should configure your web server for your Application Schema. You will need to define:

❑ A Database Access Descriptor (DAD) for your application schema: you will run your generated Web applications using this DAD

❑ A directory mapping for your static web pages

Setting and Testing Your DAD

See your web server documentation on how to set up a DAD. Once your DAD is set up, you will run your Web PL/SQL applications from Internet Explorer or Netscape using the following URL:

<web agent's URL>/packagename.procedurename

For example:

http://ias.wrox.com/pls/wroxweb/dad_test.hello

Once you have created a DAD for your application schema, test it using the following procedure:

1. Logon to SQL*Plus as your Application Schema: Create this dad_test package and its HELLO procedure:

```
CREATE OR REPLACE PACKAGE dad_test IS
   PROCEDURE hello;
END dad_test;
/


SQL> Package created.


CREATE OR REPLACE PACKAGE BODY dad_test IS
   PROCEDURE hello IS
      BEGIN
       htp.print('Hello world! Your DAD is Working!);
      END hello;
   END dad_test;
/


SQL> Package body created.
```

2. Now invoke your browser and go to the URL:

http://<your DAD's URL>/data_test.hello

3. You should see the following message displayed in your browser:

Hello World! Your DAD is Working!

If this test does not work, then you may have your URL wrong. Or your DAD is not configured correctly. Or the Web Toolkit is not completely installed. You should diagnose and fix this problem before proceeding to configure Designer's Webserver Generator Library.

Setting up Directory Mappings

You should also setup directory mappings in your DAD for your static web pages. In Web PL/SQL applications, static pages may include images, static HTML pages, or stylesheets.

For example, to set up two virtual directories for the `wroxweb` DAD:

Go into your web server's Listener administration screens. Drill down into the subsection on Directory Mappings. Add the following virtual directory mappings:

Physical Directory	Virtual Directory
E:\your_physical_directory\images\	/images/
E:\ your_physical_directory\docs\	/docs/

Be sure to add a trailing slash to each file-system and virtual directory name. Make sure the physical directories exist as well. Once these directory mappings are set up, you can store your images and documents in the specified physical directories, and then reference those static files using the virtual directory paths in your Web PL/SQL modules.

The Designer Web PL/SQL generator uses several GIF images in its generated web pages. For example, on a multi-row Insert page, it uses the file: `cg_tick.gif`. The generated pages will look for these images in the physical directory on your web server that you may map to the virtual directory: `/images/`. After creating your directory mappings, you should copy the Designer image files from the directory `C:\orant\cgenw61\cvwimg` to the physical directory on your server mapped `/images/`.

Install the Designer Webserver Generator Library

After you get your web server configured correctly, you should install the Designer Webserver Generator Library (WSGL) packages into your application schema. Designer 6i includes a script to load the WSGL packages:

```
<orahome>\CGENW61\cvwetc\wsgl.sql
```

To support a multi-schema configuration setup, this script also includes commands to create PUBLIC SYNONYMS for these packages. However, for this chapter, you do not need to create these PUBLIC SYNONYMS.

To install the Webserver Generator Library:

1. From the Start Menu, select Designer 6I | Install Web PL/SQL Generator. This will start SQL*PLUS and invoke the `wsgl` script.

2. This script will prompt you to enter your connect string for toolkit user: Supply the connect string for your Application Schema, which is:

```
wroxweb/wroxweb@yourdatabase
```

You want to install the Webserver Generator Library into your application schema.

The script will connect to your application schema and load the Webserver Generator Library packages. It automatically spools its messages into the file: `wsgl.log`. You should see the following messages indicating a successful execution of this script:

```
This user does not have CREATE PUBLIC SYNONYM system privileges.
There were no errors
```

After this script completes, logon to SQL*Plus as the application schema user. Check that all the packages were successfully installed:

```
SELECT object_type, status, count(*)
FROM user_objects
GROUP BY object_type, status;
```

You should see:

OBJECT_TYPE	COUNT(*)	
INDEX	8	
PACKAGE	9	(including DAD_TEST)
PACKAGE BODY	8	(including DAD_TEST)
SEQUENCE	2	
TABLE	5	

This script installs the following packages:

```
CG$ERRORS
WSGFL
WSGJSL
WSGL
WSGLM  (package spec only)
WSGMC_OUTPUT1
WSGMC_OUTPUT2
WSGOC
```

> There are additional Designer Web PL/SQL libraries, which must be installed if you are running Oracle ConText search options on your Query Form, or if you are generating non-English web PL/SQL applications. Check the Designer Help for more information about installing these packages.

Develop the Database Design in Designer

Before you can begin the design and development of Web PL/SQL applications with Designer, you must have developed your Database Design in the Oracle Repository in the form of Table Definitions with columns, constraints, default values, any associated values lists, and any associated database sequences. Other server-side database objects, including database triggers, PL/SQL and Java logic, may also be defined in the Designer Repository and be used to support the Web PL/SQL applications.

A Database Design may be captured in Designer and the Oracle Repository using one or more of these methods:

❑ Transform an Entity Relationship Model into a Database Design as presented in Chapter 5

❑ Directly enter Table Definitions and other Database Objects into Designer using the Design Editor

❑ Use the Design Editor's Design Capture utility to capture an existing Database Schema in Designer. (Generate I Capture Design of I Server Model).

❑ Import of a Designer repository export file (.dmp file) from another repository.

If you have completed the case study in Chapter 5, then you will already have this database design captured in your repository. If you are familiar with the use of Designer and did not complete the Chapter 9 case study, then you can load the Education Center Database Design into your Repository using the Designer repository export .dmp file on the Wrox web site.

The Server Model for the Education Center database is:

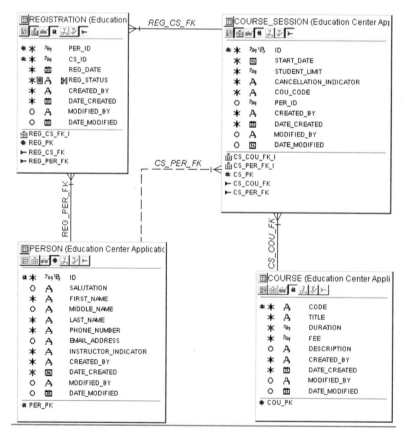

You will use the PERSON, COURSE_SESSION, and COURSE tables as the basis for your Web PL/SQL applications.

> The Web PL/SQL Generator requires that Table API packages be built for each table used in your web application. Currently a Table API can only be built for a Designer Table Definition. If you need to base your Web PL/SQL Applications on a view, you can create Table API packages for a view by first defining a 'fake' table definition in Designer for your view, generating the Table API, and then deleting the 'fake' table definition.

Generate DDL and Build the Physical Database

In Chapter 5, you generated Data Definition Language (DDL) for this database, and created the physical database for this application. However, you may not have created this database in the application schema you are using in your Web Application Environment.

If you have not generated and run your DDL in your application schema yet, then please do so now. Follow the steps outlined in *Generate DDL and Create a Physical Database* in Chapter 5. When you have successfully completed building your database, verify that all of your physical objects have been created. Log on to SQL*Plus as the application schema.

Enter the following query:

```
SQL> SELECT object_type, count(*) FROM user_objects GROUP BY object_type;
```

The result should be:

```
OBJECT_TYPE          COUNT(*)
------------------   ----------
INDEX                       8
PACKAGE                     9
PACKAGE BODY                8
SEQUENCE                    2
TABLE                       5
```

Insert Instructor Data into the PERSON Table

Later in this chapter, you will need to have data in the PERSON table for Instructor data. This chapter does not include the development of a module to load Instructor data. Until you have a chance to build a module to maintain the PERSON table, you should use SQL*Plus to insert a few Instructor records into this table:

1. Invoke SQL*Plus, and log into the Application Schema where the Education Center tables are.

> If you invoke SQL*Plus from within Designer, you will automatically be logged in with your repository user account. Type SHOW USER to see which user you are logged in as.

2. View the PERSON table:

```
DESC PERSON
```

3. Then insert some records into the PERSON table (this script can be downloaded from Wrox):

```
INSERT INTO person VALUES
(per_id_seq.nextval,'MR.','BOB',null,'DAVIS',
'615-555-1212','Y',null,'MANUAL',sysdate,null,null);
INSERT INTO person VALUES
(per_id_seq.nextval,'MS.','MARY','JANE','SMITH',
'401-889-7887','Y',null,'MANUAL',sysdate,null,null);
INSERT INTO person VALUES
(per_id_seq.nextval,'MRS.','KATHY','LEE','JONES',
'915-567-4112','Y',null,'MANUAL',sysdate,null,null);
```

Commit your changes and exit SQL*Plus.

Extend the Database Design with Application Properties

In Chapter 5, you designed your database, generated your DDL, and built your physical database. At that time, you did not pay much attention to the "application properties" for each column and constraint definition. These "application properties" include column display formats, prompts, validation criteria, and error messages. Now you will begin your application design by defining the relevant **application database properties** for your application. These properties will be used in the code generated for the Table API packages or the module packages.

For a Web PL/SQL application, the primary **table-related application database properties** are:

- ❑ **Table alias** – the short name for the table. This table short name will be used throughout the generated Table API and module PL/SQL code.

- ❑ **Display title** – a default title to be used for module components generated for this table.

- ❑ **Journal** – have Designer create a journal table, and generate code to automatically maintain that journal table.

The primary **column application database properties** are:

- ❑ **Domain** – a domain of valid values for this column. If this property is set, it may be used to lookup valid values in the CG_REF_CODES table.

- ❑ **Upper case ?** – Only store upper case values in the database. The Table API will generate code to translate a column's values to upper case before storage and also during data query and entry. Note that setting this property prior to DDL generation will cause a database constraint to be generated to enforce this constraint.

- ❑ **Sequence** – a database sequence to be used to automatically create values for this column.

❑ **Default values.**

❑ **Display ?** – whether this column will be displayed or not.

❑ **Display type** – how this column will be displayed. For example, as a text box, a pop-up list, or a radio button.

❑ **Display sequence** – the order this column will appear on a page relative to other columns in this table.

❑ **Display height and length** – default height and length for this item. For example, for a text box.

❑ **Format mask** – a mask for formatting the display of this data value.

❑ **Prompt** – the default label to be shown for this colum.

❑ **Order by sequence** – the position this column will appear in an ORDER BY clause for the entire table.

❑ **Auto-generation types** – if values will be automatically generated for this column, what method will be used to assign these values. For example, Created By userID, Date Created, Modified By userID, Date Modified, Sequence in Parent.

❑ **Server derived** – whether this value will be derived from server-side logic. This property should be set to 'Yes' for auto-generated columns.

❑ **Server defaulted** – whether this value is defaulted by server-side logic.

You may also want to define error message text for primary key, unique key, and foreign key constraints. Default error messages will be created if no explicit error message text is defined. For example, if you attempt to enter a new COURSE record with a course code which duplicates an existing COURSE record, you will receive the following default error message:

```
Error! Primary key COU_PK on table COURSE violated
```

You might want to define a more user friendly message: 'A record already exists for that Course code.'

Now extend your Education Center Database Design with application properties. Some of these application properties may have been set by earlier database design tasks:

1. Select the COURSE table definition in the **Server Model** tab of the Design Editor's Navigator, and click the properties icon to bring up the **Properties** dialog for that table.

2. On the **Name** tab, note that the Display Title "Course" will have been propagated to your Module Design. At this point, accept that title.

3. Click the **Columns** tab, and review the **Default** value for each column. The DURATION column should have a Default value of 3. Select each change history column (date_created, created_by, modified_by, date_modified) and review its Advanced Properties:

❑ **AutoGen Type** – should match the column name.

❑ **Server Defaulted?** – should be No

❑ **Server Derived?** – should be Yes

4. Click the Display Tab. The list on the right shows all the columns that will be displayed on one or more of your web pages for this table. Note that this is the "default" display order for these columns, and it can be over-ridden during Module Design. None of the change history columns should be displayed. Select the four change history columns, and use the left arrow to move them to the right-hand window. Review the order in which the columns will be displayed on your page, and if necessary, use the Up or Down icons to be in the following order:

CODE
TITLE
DURATION
FEE
DESCRIPTION

Click Apply to save these changes.

5. Click the Controls tab, and view the display properties for each Displayed column. Note these default display properties can be over-ridden during Module Design.

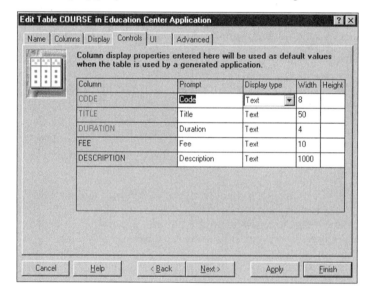

6. Validate that each column has a meaningful prompt. These values will be used both on your generated web pages and by the Table API. Review each column's Display type. For these 5 columns, "Text" is appropriate. Revise the Display properties of the Description column to show: Width: 40, Height: 5 (This will display a scrollable region for the Description). Click Apply to save these changes.

7. Click the UI Tab, and review the User Interface Properties. Verify that CODE and TITLE are set to Uppercase, and specify a display format for FEE ($99G999D9). Click Finish to save these changes, and close this dialog.

8. Review and refine the application database properties for the other tables repeating the steps above:

Table PERSON

Controls tab	Prompt	Display Type
SALUTATION	Salutation	Pop List
INSTRUCTOR INDICATOR	'Instructor?'	Pop List
UI tab	**Uppercase**	
	SALUTATION	
	FIRST_NAME	
	MIDDLE_NAME	
	LAST_NAME	
	INSTRUCTOR_INDICATOR	

Table COURSE_SESSION

Columns tab	Default Value	
STUDENT_LIMIT	15	
CANCELLATION_INDICATOR	N	
Controls tab	**Prompt**	**Display Type**
CANCELLATION_INDICATOR	'Canceled?'	Pop List

Table REGISTRATION

Columns tab	Default Value
REG_DATE	SYSDATE
REG_STATUS	A
Controls tab	**Display Type**
REG_STATUS	Radio Group Across

For this prototype application, you will use the default error messages created by Designer. If you were building a production application, you would want to assign an error message to each primary key, unique key, and foreign key constraint definition in your application. Just select that constraint (that is COU_PK in the Primary Key folder of the COURSE table) in the Navigator, and click the Properties button on the toolbar to bring up the property dialog window for this Primary Key. Select the Validation Tab, and then enter an Error message for the constraint.

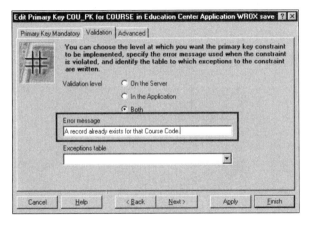

Generate the Table API

After reviewing and defining the Extended Database Design, you are ready to create the Table API in your application schema. The Table API consists of a package for each table, and an optional set of database triggers. Each package includes query, insert, update, delete, and lock procedures for that table. These procedures incorporate routine data integrity checks, set values on the server-side, and can optionally incorporate custom server-side logic.

The implementation of the Table API database triggers is optional. If implemented, these triggers force **any** access to this table to go through the API rather than manipulating the table directly. Thus the logic in the Table API cannot be by-passed using SQL*Plus directly or by using other third-party tools.

The Web PL/SQL Generator creates Web PL/SQL modules that call the API procedures rather than executing SQL data manipulation commands directly upon each table. Thus, the Table API must be generated before a Web PL/SQL application can be executed.

> **If the database design changes, the Table API must be re-generated to reflect any changes to the physical or application database design.**

To generate the Table API for the Education Center Application:

1. In the Designer Editor Navigator, select the four Education Center tables. From the menu select Generate | Table API. The Generate Table API window will appear.

2. Specify your application schema as the Target for Generation. Specify a file prefix and a directory for the API DDL files. Verify that the option to Generate Table API Triggers is not selected. For the Education Center application, you will only use the API packages.

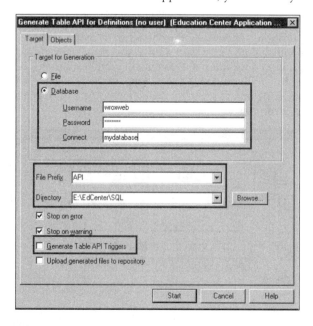

3. Select the **Objects** tab to view the **Generate List**. Verify that all the Education Center tables are included in the list. Click the **Start** button to bring up a **Message Window**. Watch the messages as the API Server Generator generates the API packages and then executes the script to load those packages into the application schema.

4. When the API Server Generator is complete, you should see the following messages displayed:

```
Finished. ...
DDL execution complete
Processing Complete:  0 error(s), 0 warning(s)
```

5. From the message window, click the **List Action** button. This lists each file, which can then be viewed:

```
API.sql
Reg.pks
Reg.pkb
Per.pks
Per.pkb
Cs.pks
Cs.pkb
Cou.pks
Cou.pkb
```

A .pks and .pkb file were created for each table. The SQL file contains commands to execute these files and build the packages. A file named CDSTAPI.LOG is created in your <oracle_home>\bin directory that contains the results of executing the SQL file.

6. Invoke SQL*Plus for your target database, and validate that the packages were created, and that they compiled correctly:

```
SELECT object_name, object_type, status
FROM user_objects
WHERE object_name like 'CG$%' AND object_type LIKE 'PACK%';
```

You should see the following new packages:

```
CG$COURSE
CG$COURSE_SESSION
CG$PERSON
CG$REGISTRATION
```

Your Table API is now ready to use. Web PL/SQL developers should become familiar with the packages and code generated for the Table API. Designer provides the capability to define custom Table API/Trigger logic for a table, and then to have that logic incorporated into the generated Table API packages.

Introduction to Web PL/SQL Module Design

Now that you have built your physical Education Center Database and generated the Table API for that database, you are ready to design and generate Web PL/SQL modules. This section presents an overview of Web PL/SQL Module Designs. Each Module Design will define the module components and table usages for that module. A **Module Component** is a "block" of data associated with a single base table and one or more lookup tables. One or more list of values components may also be associated with a Web PL/SQL module design.

Let's explore the format of a generated Web PL/SQL module and possible layout options.

Format of Generated Web PL/SQL Modules

For each Module Design, the Web PL/SQL Generator creates a set of PL/SQL packages that dynamically build a series of linked web pages:

❑ **Startup Page** – the initial page for a module with introductory text and hyperlinks to other pages and to the About Page

❑ **About Page** – displays version information for the module (optional)

❑ **Query Form** – supports querying by field values (optional)

❑ **Record List** – displays a set of queried records in an HTML table, or in an ordered or bulleted list

❑ **View Form** – displays full details of a single record and supports updating that record

❑ **Insert Form** – allows entry of a new record.

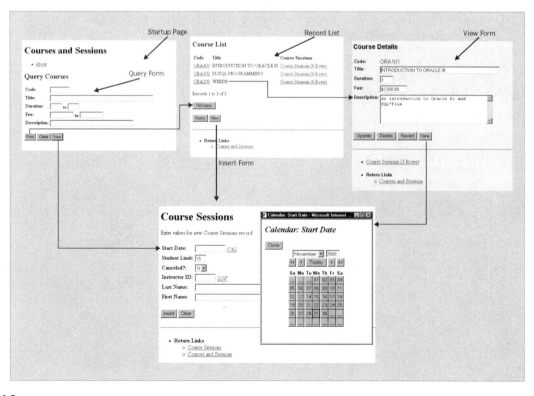

For a single module, there may be multiple query forms, record lists, view forms, and insert forms – one set per component.

The Module Design and the Generator Preferences define the contents and format of these web pages. These pages may be displayed separately, or within frames on a single page. Custom text, HTML script, JavaScript, and calls to PL/SQL procedures may be embedded in the pages. Action items (displayed as buttons, hyperlinks, or image links) may be defined to control navigation or execute a specific piece of user-defined application logic. Custom stylesheets and framesets may be used to customize the layout and look of these pages.

Designer incorporates JavaScript in the generated Web PL/SQL applications to provide:

- ❏   Validation during data entry

- ❏   Client-side handling of check constraints and derivation expressions

- ❏   Client-side conversion to uppercase for database columns defined as uppercase

- ❏   List of values windows to help a user select lookup column values

- ❏   JavaScript message boxes with warning messages and confirmation messages

- ❏   User-defined JavaScript logic

Module Component Layout Styles

The Layout Style property assigned to a Module Component drives the overall appearance, content, and sequence of pages generated for that module component. Three layout styles are available for Web PL/SQL module components:

- ❏   **List** – The Query Form, Record List, View Form, and Insert Form all appear on separate pages. This style is useful for presenting module components with a large number of columns, or if your users are running web browsers that do not support HTML frames.

- ❏   **List/Form** – The Query Form, Record List, View Form, and Insert Form can all appear within HTML frames on the same page. This style is effective only if your users have browsers that support HTML frames and the content of each form is small enough to be displayed within a frame.

- ❏   **Form** – No Record List is created. The View Form is used to navigate through the detailed records one record at a time.

The default layout generated for each of these styles may be modified (or refined) using preferences.

Define Application-Level Generator Preferences

Generator Preferences are parameters that control the appearance and behavior of generated applications. Designer comes with a set of default Web PL/SQL Generation Preference settings. These preferences can be changed for each application. Preferences are an important tool to assist in reaching 100% generation.

Generator Preferences can be set at the application system level, in which case they are inherited by all modules in that container, or they can be set on a module-by-module basis. Certain preferences can also be set on individual table definitions or module components.

In this section, you will define a **Preference Set** of preferences to be applied to the Education Center Application. This preference set will combine primarily 'factory' preference values with a few custom values. After you create this Preference Set, you will associate it with the Education Center Application. If you later define other application Systems, you will be able to associate this preference set or a revised version of this set to your new application systems.

Define an Application-Level Preference Set

To create an application-level preference set for the Education Center Application:

1. In the Modules tab of the Design Editor's Navigator, expand the Preference Sets node and select the PL/SQL Web Generator node.

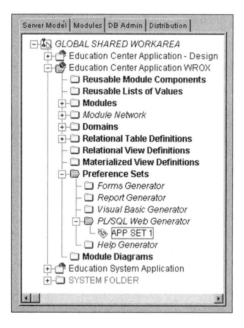

2. Click the Create icon on the left-hand toolbar to create a new Preference Set. The Preference Set Properties window will appear on the right-hand side. Enter a Name field value of APP SET 1 and click Save.

3. Select the new APP SET 1 preference set node on the Navigator, and click the Generator Preferences icon on the horizontal tool bar to bring up the Generator Preferences Palette for the APP SET 1.

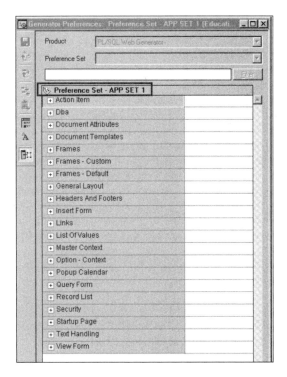

The preferences that can be set for a repository element are divided into preference categories. These categories are shown on the palette and can be expanded to show the preferences they contain.

4. Expand the General Layout node, and set the preference:

❑ Default format for date fields: **MM/DD/RRRR**

The modified preference setting changes to blue font. The color of the preference name indicates the level at which it is set:

❑ Red: The preference is mandatory, and displays its default value

❑ Black: The preference is optional, and displays its default value

❑ Blue: The preference value has been modified at this level.

5. Set the following preference values:

❑ QUERY FORM: Display Default Caption: No

❑ RECORD LIST: Add Table Border: No

❑ RECORD LIST: Always Display Count Information: Yes

❑ **STARTUP PAGE**: Title Format: leave this blank

❑ TEXT HANDLING: Substitute HTML Reserved Characters: No

❑ VIEW FORM: Display Context Header: No Heading

❑ STARTUP PAGE: About Hyperlink Required: Yes

6. Click the Save button on the Property Palette's vertical toolbar to save these changes.

The Generator Preferences Palette provides two tool icons to change a preference setting back to what it was before:

❏ **Revert** – Reverts an unsaved preference setting change to the previously saved version.

❏ **Inherit** (this is not recursive) – Changes a preference back to the preference setting inherited from the higher preference level.

> **Preference settings are often referred to by their short names – for example, ZONITC or ZONIBR. The Show Name icon will switch the Preference Palette to show short names rather than full names. Use the Filter block in the Preference Palette's header to find the preference line for a given short name.**

Assign the Preference Set to the Application

Once a preference set is created, it must be explicitly assigned to the application to apply that set of preferences across the application. To assign the APP SET 1 to the Education Center Application:

❏ Select the Education Center Application node on the Design Editor's Navigator, and click the Generator Preferences icon on the horizontal tool bar to bring up the Generator Preferences window at the application level. Verify that the Preferences Palette is labeled Application System – Education Center Application. All preference palettes look the same and it is very easy to accidentally define preferences at the wrong level.

❏ Select the Product: PL/SQL Web Generator. Note that the Preference Set property contains No Preference Set Used. Select APP SET 1 for this property. Click the Save icon to implement this assignment.

Now all Web PL/SQL modules within this application will inherit the preferences in this application-level preference set.

> **If you revise the Application-Level Preference set, those revisions will automatically be inherited by the modules within the application. However, preferences are only applied at generation time, so you will need to re-generate all your modules in order to implement those revisions.**

Using Cascading Stylesheets (Optional Exercise)

The Designer Web PL/SQL Generator uses a set of standard, built-n styles to format the dynamic web pages that it creates. These may initially meet your requirements, but at some point you will likely discover that you need to control the font and style of your web pages. For example, the default fonts may be too large for a List/Form style module with multiple frames. Designer provides several preferences for customizing the styles used on a web page using standard, HTML styles and stylesheets. For more information, see the Designer Help Text on About Templates and Style Sheets. For more information about HTML styles and cascading style sheets, see the following web sites:

http://www.w3.org/MarkUp/
http://www.htmlhelp.com/reference/

> **Stylesheets are not a solution to all HTML layout challenges. At this point in time, not all browsers support stylesheets or cascading stylesheets fully. Support for stylesheets only starts with Netscape 5 and Internet Explorer 4. If a browser does not support a given style, then the page will be displayed using the browser's default settings.**

In the exercise below, you will create and use a cascading stylesheet to define font sizes so that your List/Form module fits better on a single page. You will create a Designer document template with a reference to your cascading stylesheet:

1. First create a document template file with a reference to the cascading stylesheet (CSS) you will create. Use your favorite text editor to create a text file named edctr_ref.txt containing the following text:

```
<LINK REL=stylesheet  TYPE="text/css" HREF="/docs/edctr_css.css" >
<META http-equiv="charset" content="iso-8859-1">
```

Note that your CSS will be stored in the virtual directory /docs/. For this example to work, you must have defined a Directory Mapping in your web server to a virtual directory named /docs/. Store this document template file in a physical directory of your choice which is accessible to your Designer 6i client. This file and directory will **only** be accessed when the module is being generated by the Web PL/SQL generator. It will not be used during the Web PL/SQL module's execution.

2. Use your favorite text or CSS editor to create the referenced cascading stylesheet named edctr_css.css with the following lines of text. This will establish variables for each font/style you will want to use on your pages. The variables will become tags in your HTML text:

```
H1 {font: bold 16pt Arial}
H2 {font: bold 14pt Arial}
H3 {font: bold 12pt Arial}
H4 {font: bold 10pt Arial}
H5 {font: bold  8pt Arial}
H6 {font: 10pt Arial}
P  {font: 10pt Arial}
B  {font: bold 10pt Arial}
EM  {font: 10pt Arial}
SMALL {font: 8pt Arial}
BODY {background-color: EFFFEF }
```

3. Store this cascading stylesheet file in the physical directory on your web server which is mapped to the virtual directory named /docs/ in your web server's Listener for your application's DAD. Now set your **Generator Preferences** to use your document template file:

```
C:\<your_physical_directory>\docs\edctr_ref.txt
```

❑ Select the Preference Set **APP SET 1** on the Navigator, and click the **Generator Preferences** icon to open the **Property Palette** for the **APP SET 1** preference sheet. Verify that the **Property Palette** is labeled: Preference Set: APP SET 1.

❑ Expand the Document Templates node and set all the Document Template Filename preferences to the full path name of your Document Template file:

Preference Set - APP SET 1	
– Document Templates	
About Page Template Filename	e:\your_physical_directory\docs\edctr_ref.txt
Insert Form Template Filename	e:\your_physical_directory\docs\edctr_ref.txt
List Of Values Template Filename	e:\your_physical_directory\docs\edctr_ref.txt
Module Content Template Filename	e:\your_physical_directory\docs\edctr_ref.txt
Query Form Template Filename	e:\your_physical_directory\docs\edctr_ref.txt
Record List Template Filename	e:\your_physical_directory\docs\edctr_ref.txt
Text Frame Template Filename	e:\your_physical_directory\docs\edctr_ref.txt
View Form Template Filename	e:\your_physical_directory\docs\edctr_ref.txt

4. Click Save to commit these preference settings. Now all of your modules will automatically be generated using the Cascading Stylesheet that you defined.

This section has only briefly introduced Web PL/SQL Generator Preferences. As you become more familiar with the Web PL/SQL Generator, you will want to experiment with various preference settings to better understand what options are available for your applications.

Design and Generate Web PL/SQL Modules

In this section, you will design and generate the following Web PL/SQL Modules:

❑ A COURSE module – a single table module with a List layout style and a Multi-row Insert Form

❑ A FRCOURSE module – a second COURSE Module with a List/Form layout style with frames

❑ A MDCOURSE module – a master-detail module for Course and Course Sessions with a lookup table usage and a list of values (LOV) component

❑ A MAIN module – An Application Launch Page

In these exercises, you will use various Module Design Wizard Dialogs in the Design Editor to create each Module Design.

> **Many organizations use Designer's Function Modeling capabilities to define business function hierarchies, and then transform those functions into preliminary module designs. This is another viable approach to application design. This approach is not presented due to the limited scope of this chapter.**

COURSE Module

In this section, you will design, generate, and run your first Web PL/SQL module. You will use the List layout style for this first COURSE module. For the Insert Form page, you will design a multi-row Insert Block for a Course record. You will use the Design Editor's Wizards to design your Module, Module Component, and Base Table Usage definitions.

Create the Module Definition

Your first step is to develop a Module Definition for the COURSE module:

1. Select the Modules tab and highlight the modules folder in the Design Editor's Navigator. Highlight and expand the Education Center Application, and then highlight the Modules node. Then click the Create icon to bring up the Create Module dialog. Enter a name, purpose, and select the language Web PL/SQL:

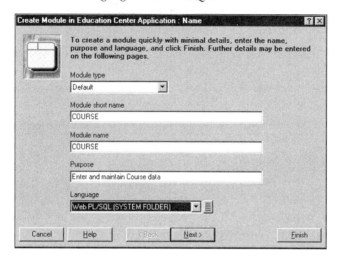

If your Language pop-up list is empty, then the SYSTEM FOLDER is not included in your WorkArea. Talk with your Repository Administrator about including that folder in your WorkArea. You cannot proceed until this is fixed. Briefly, open your WorkArea in the Repository Object Navigator. From the menu, select Edit | Include in Workarea. Then click the Browse button and select the SYSTEM FOLDER.Click Next, and then enter the following fields for this Module:

❑   Hyperlink text – Course Information. This text will appear on any page that displays a link to the COURSE Module.

❑   Startup Page title – Course Information. This title will appear on the Startup Page of the Module.

2. Click Next to move through the following windows:

❑   Files window: Set the Implementation Name to: COURSE

❑   User Text window – Do not define any user text at this time

❑   Module Network window – If this module called another module, you would define the module called here and any parameters passed to that module

❑   Advanced window – Leave Default Values.

3. Select the second option on the Goodbye window to invoke the next wizard:

❑ Create the module then invoke a wizard to create a Module Component.

4. Then click Finish.

Create a Module Component and Table Usages

A Module Component is a "block" of data associated with a single base table and one or more lookup tables. A Module will usually contain one or more module components – the exception being a menu module.

The Create Module Component wizard will automatically appear after the Create Module wizard finishes:

1. Name the module component COURSE_MC. The _MC suffix will differentiate this module component from the COURSE module. Leave the Title field empty.

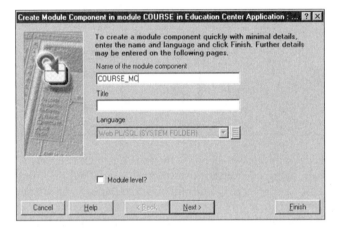

2. Click Next, and select the COURSE table as your Base Table Usage. This module will not have any Lookup table usages. Click Next twice, and then define the operations that can be performed on this base table:

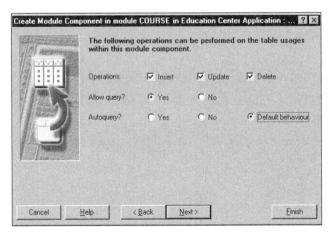

3. Click Next, and select the columns to be used for this module component. Use the All icon to first select **all** the columns. Then use the de-select icon to de-select the **change history columns**. These columns will be maintained by the Table API, and should not be included in the module. The Selected items appear in the display order you defined for the COURSE table definition in your extended database design. Verify that this is the order they should appear on your web page. You could change their order here if you wanted to:

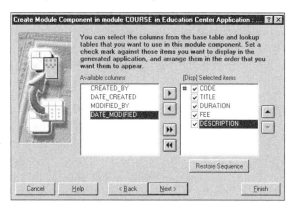

4. Click Next twice, and define the operations to be performed on the columns. These settings determine which columns will appear on which web page generated for the module:

❑ **Query** – Yes means that the column will appear on the Query Page of the module. Always means that it will appear and must always be used to constrain a query.

❑ **Insert** – Check means that the column will appear on the Insert Page.

❑ **Update** – Check means that the column will appear on the Update Page.

Include all the fields on the Query Page with a YES. Include all the fields on the Insert Page with a check, and include all but the CODE field on the Update Page.

5. Click Next, and review the list of mandatory columns. The module component inherits the properties from the extended table definition. The initial mandatory list reflects the mandatory columns in the table. If you want to make a column mandatory for this module, you could add it here.

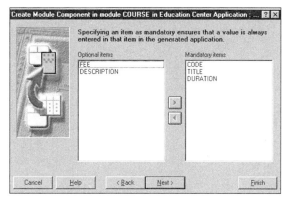

6. Click Next and select the Display: Layout Style of List for this module. Click Next and then select the second option: this will invoke the Display Wizard next. Click Finish.

Module Component Display Wizard

The Module Component Display wizard will appear next:

1. On the Display tab, verify that a layout style of List is selected.

2. On the Context tab, select the columns to be displayed in the Record List page. The layout style of this module is List, so select all of the available items to be Context Items (a Context Item is an item that should appear on the Record List page).

3. Click Finish and the COURSE module will be visible in the Navigator with COURSE_MC as a component.

Use a Module Diagram to Refine the Module Design

Now create a Module Diagram for your new COURSE module and use it to refine your Module Design:

1. Select the COURSE module from the Navigator, and drag it to the workspace to the right of the Navigator. A Module Diagram window will appear. In this Data View, the column names are listed alphabetically:

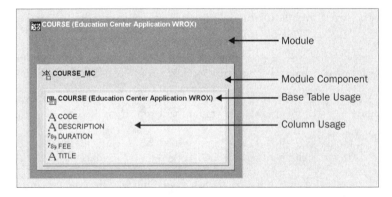

> It is not necessary to save a Module Diagram because the diagram can be easily re-created by selecting the Module from the Navigator and dragging it to the diagram workspace. In fact having diagrams saved in a versioned repository means you have to check out the module and diagram – so it is easier not to save diagrams.

2. Click on the COURSE_MC Module Component to bring up the Edit Module Component COURSE_MC window. Browse these tabs and view the information that you just defined with the Wizards. Click the User Text tab of this window. In any User Text field, you can define text to be displayed. The formats are:

- ❑ Plain text
- ❑ HTML tagged text
- ❑ Oracle toolkit `htf.xxx` functions
- ❑ JavaScript

Note that if you specify HTML tags, then you must have set the preference: Text Handling: Substitute HTML Reserved Characters: No. If this preference is not set, the HTML tag <H2> will appear on your page when you execute your module!

3. Select the Text Location 'Top of Record List', and type the User Text <H2>Course List</H2>. Then click the Apply button.

4. Repeat step 3 to define the following User Text values for this module component:

- ❑ Top of View Form: <H2>Course Details</H2>
- ❑ Top of Query Form: <H2>Query Courses</H2>
- ❑ Top of Insert Form: <H2>Define New Courses</H2>

Then click Finish to close this dialog.

Define Module Component Preferences for Multi-Row Insert Form

Next you will assign Generator Preferences to the module component COURSE_MC to create a multi-row Insert Form:

1. Select the COURSE_MC module component box on the Module Diagram, and click the Generator Preferences icon on the horizontal tool bar to bring up the Generator Preferences palette for the Module Component COURSE_MC. Verify that this Preference Sheet is set at the Module Component level for COURSE_MC, and not the module level.

2. In the Generator Preferences Palette, expand the Insert Form node, and set the following two preferences to create a multi-row Insert Form:

- ❑ Insert Form: Number of Blank Rows: 3
- ❑ Insert Form: Number of items per Line: 3

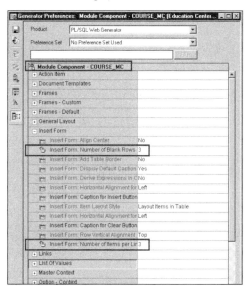

3. Click the Save icon on the Generator Preferences Palette to save these new settings, and then close the Generator Preferences window.

Generate and Execute the First Course Module

Now you are ready to generate and run the first Course Module. This step requires that the table APIs have been generated and installed in the application schema.

1. From the Design Editor's Navigator, select the module to be generated: COURSE. From the menu, select Generate | Generate Module or click the Generate icon from the horizontal toolbar. This will bring up the Generate Web PL/SQL window.
Click the Options button to bring up the Web PL/SQL Generator Options window.

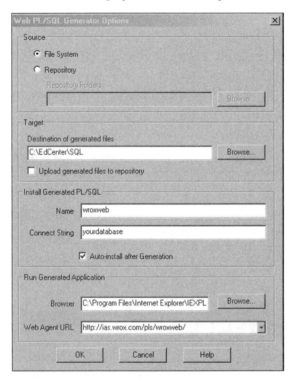

❏ Enter a Target destination directory for the generated files.

❏ Enter the username and connect string for your application schema where the Web PL/SQL modules will be installed.

❏ Select the physical location of your browser. After generating the module, you will be able to run the module using this browser.

❏ Specify the Web Agent URL for your WebDB or iAS PL/SQL gateway.

2. Click the OK button to save these settings and close this options window. Note that these setting will be used the next time you invoke the Web PL/SQL generator.

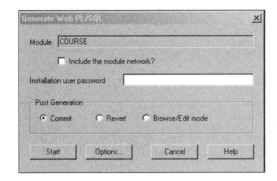

3. In the Generate Web PL/SQL window, enter the password for the application schema that you supplied on the Generator Options window.

   Verify that the Commit option is selected for Post Generation. This option will update the repository objects when generation is complete. As part of the generation process, the Web PL/SQL Generator will detect inconsistencies in your Module Design, and automatically correct those inconsistencies if this option is set.

   Click Start to begin generation of the Web PL/SQL module. A Message window will appear and display messages as the generation process progresses.

4. Once the Web PL/SQL modules have been generated, the Web PL/SQL generator will invoke SQL*Plus and install the generated modules in the Application Schema.

   At the completion of the generation process, you should see the following messages in the Message Window:

   Compilation Report
   There were no errors
   Generation Complete

   These messages indicate that the generated PL/SQL packages compiled successfully.

5. Use the vertical scroll bars on the Message window to browse Message window:

   ❑ Critical Errors are displayed in red

   ❑ Warnings are displayed in blue

   ❑ Adjustments made automatically to the module design are displayed in green.

   ❑ If generation errors are incurred, use the flag icons in the Message window's toolbar to review each error, and the source of the error in the module design

   ❑ If a critical error is encountered, the generation will stop and the module's PL/SQL files will not be generated

   ❑ The messages displayed in this window are also logged in the files

   `c:\<ORAHOME>\bin\oratst.txt`

   `c:\<ORAHOME>\bin\cvwsgin.log`

6. Click the List Actions icon from the Message window to bring up the Build Action window.

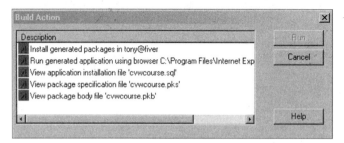

7. Select the View package specification and View package body file actions to view the PL/SQL packages which were generated for this module. Three packages were created for this COURSE module: COURSE$, COURSE$COURSE_MC, and COURSEJSCOURSE_MC. Notice that the COURSE$ package contains a procedure named STARTUP. A generated Web PL/SQL module is always invoked by <module implementation name>$.startup. For example:

> http://ias.wrox.com/pls/wroxweb/course$.startup

8. In the Generate Options window, you checked the option to Auto-Install after Generation. So the Action Install generated packages has already been performed and the packages were loaded into your application schema.

9. Select the action Run generated application to run your new COURSE module from your browser. If your web server has database authentication set to On invocation, you will be prompted to log on as the application schema user. Note the URL which is invoked.

10. The combined **Startup/Query Form** for your COURSE module will appear.

   ❑ Click the New button to bring up the multi-row **Insert Form**, and add the three COURSE records listed on the record list screen below to the COURSE table. Try adding a lower case Course code and watch it change to upper case. The Insert 'tick' mark appears when you add some data. If you aren't getting your GIF images, then check the installation instruction above regading virtual directories. Click the Insert button to commit your new records.

   ❑ Use the Return Link or the Back button on your browser to return to the Startup/Query Form page.

   ❑ On the **Query Form**, you can either click the Find button to query all the Course records, or you can specify query criteria – for example A% in the Course code field – and then click Find.

   ❑ Your query will bring up the **Record List**. Double-click on one of the Course Codes to bring up the View Form for that Course.

   ❑ On the **View Form**, to update the selected course record, change one of the fields and click the Update Button. To delete the selected course record, just click the Delete button. Use the browser's back button to return to the Record List page. You may have to re-query this page to see your updates.

Startup/Query Form

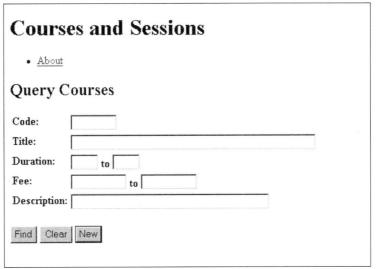

Insert Form

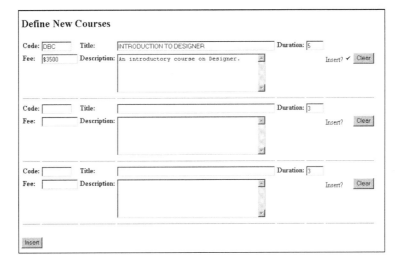

Record List

View Form

> **Course Details**
>
> Code: ORA101
> Title: INTRODUCTION TO ORACLE 8I
> Duration: 3
> Fee: $2,500.00
> Description: An introduction to Oracle 8i and SQL
>   Plus
>
> [Update] [Delete] [Revert] [New]

FRCOURSE Module

It is quite common to include a generated web application within an organization's standard frameset, or perhaps within an organization's portal. Some web application developers like to use frames within their database applications. Others have found that their users tend to get confused by multiple frames, and the refresh constraints of framesets.

In this section you will create a copy of the COURSE module, and change its layout style to use List/Form Frames. Then you will be able to explore the capabilities and constraints of using frames within a Web PL/SQL application, and be able to give your users a choice of styles.

Copy COURSE Module

First you will use the Copy-and-Paste method to create a new FRCOURSE Module from the COURSE module that you just developed:

1. Select the COURSE Module on the Design Editor's Navigator. Then select Edit | Copy from the menu. Nothing will appear to happen. Then select Edit | Paste. A Copy Dialog box will appear.

   ❑ Select the **Deep Copy** option to copy the module's dependent objects

   ❑ De-select the **Auto checkout** option – you are not using versioning

   ❑ De-select **Copy Dependencies** – you have not run any dependency analyses on this object

   ❑ De-select **Don't show this dialog again** – you do want to see this dialog again

2. Click **OK** and a progress bar will be displayed while the copy is made

3. Once the copy is complete, select the new COURSE_1 module on the Navigator and hit *F4* to bring up the module's property sheet. Set the following properties for this module to FRCOURSE: Short Name, Name, and Implementation Name. Save and close the Properties window.

Revise the Module Definition

Next revise the Titles associated with this FRCOURSE module:

1. Close any open diagram windows. Remember that you don't need to save a Module Diagram because it can be easily re-created whenever you need it. On the menu, select Options | Use Property Dialogs if it is not already selected.

2. Select the FRCOURSE module from the Design Editor's Navigator, and drag it over to the diagram workspace. Double click the FRCOURSE module box, and bring up the Edit Module FRCOURSE dialog.

3. On the Titles tab window, revise the module titles Hyperlink text and Startup Page text as follows: Course Information in Frames. Click Finish to close the Edit Module dialog.

Revise the Module Component

To revise the Module Component for the FRCOURSE module:

1. On the Module Diagram, double-click the COURSE_MC icon and bring up the Edit Module Component COURSE_MC dialog. Make the following changes:

    ❑ Name tab – change the Name of the module component to FRCOURSE_MC

    ❑ Operations tab – Autoquery? Yes. This will automatically query the record list when the module starts up.

    ❑ Display tab – change the Layout style to List/Form.

Revise the Base Table Usage

Next, you should revise the COURSE table usage to reduce the number of Context columns to be displayed on the Record List:

1. On the Module Diagram, double-click the COURSE table usage box (the inside yellow one) and bring up the Edit Base Table Usage COU dialog. On the Operations tab, set the following columns to Query = NO:

    ❑ DURATION

    ❑ FEE

    ❑ DESCRIPTION

2. On the Context tab, move the above columns from the right-hand Context items list to the left-hand Available items list. Click Finish to save these changes and close the dialog.

Revise the Module's Generator Preferences

Next you will change a few module-level preferences to adjust the module's layout to a List/Form style:

1. Select the FRCOURSE module on either the Module Diagram or on the Navigator, and click the Generator Preferences icon to bring up the Generator Preferences: Module – FRCOURSE Property Palette. Set the following preference at the Module – FRCOURSE level:

❑ Frames: Place Query Form on Separate Page: NO. This will place the Query Form on the same page with the Record List.

❑ Startup Page: About Page Hyperlink Required: NO. This will cause the About Hyperlink not to be displayed.

2. Save these changes.

Revise the Module Component Preferences

The multi-row Insert Form was nice for the full-page Insert Form, but it is not really appropriate for an Insert Form within a frameset. To revise the Module Component preferences to change this page:

1. Select the Module Component FRCOURSE_MC on either the Module Diagram or on the Navigator, and click the Generator Preferences icon to bring up the Generator Preferences: Module Component: FRCOURSE_MC window. Verify that the Preferences Palette is for the FRCOURSE_MC module component.

In the Generator Preferences Palette, expand the Insert Form node. Use the Inherit icon to re-set the following two preferences to inherit their settings from the next higher level – in this case from the factory settings. First select the preference setting, and then click the Inherit icon:

❑ Insert Form: Number of Blank Rows Displayed

2. To minimize the space used by the query form, set the following preference:

❑ Insert Form: Number of items per Line

❑ Query Form: Number of Items Per Line: 2

Generate and Execute the FRCOURSE Module

Now generate the FRCOURSE Module:

1. From the Design Editor's Navigator, select the module to be generated: FRCOURSE. From the menu, select Generate | Generate Module or click the Generate icon from the horizontal toolbar. This will bring up the Generate Web PL/SQL window.

2. Click the Options button, and verify that the generator settings are still correct. In the Generate Web PL/SQL window, enter the password for the Application Schema that you supplied on the Generator Options window. Click Start to begin Generation of the Web PL/SQL module. When generation is complete review the results as you did for the COURSE module.

3. Click the List Actions icon from the Message window to bring up the Build Action window.

❑ Select the view actions to examine the PL/SQL packages built for this module.

❑ Select the action 'Run generated application' to run your new FRCOURSE module from your browser. Review how the pages fit into the frames. If necessary, select and pull your top frame down to view the entire Query page.

❑ Enter query criteria in the top frame and click Find. Notice how the Course List changes.

❑ Click the New button, and see what happens.

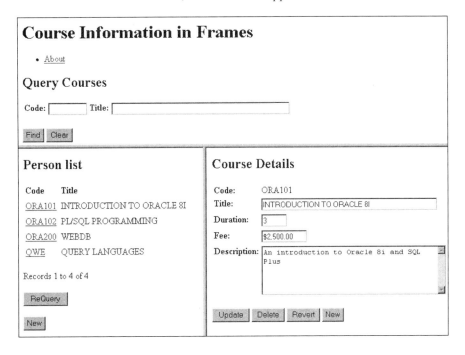

MDCOURSE Module

Next you will build a master-detail module for Courses and their dependent Course Sessions. This module will include:

❑ Two module components

❑ A lookup table usage on the PERSON table

❑ A list of values (LOV) component on the PERSON table with a restrictive WHERE clause.

The MDCOURSE module will build upon the design of the COURSE module you built earlier.

Copy COURSE Module

The first step is to create a new MDCOURSE Module from the COURSE module that you developed earlier:

1. Copy the COURSE Module like you did for the FRCOURSE Module in the section above.

2. Once the copy is complete, select the new Module – COURSE_1 and hit *F4* to bring up the module's property sheet. Set the following properties for this module:

- ❑ Short Name: MDCOURSE
- ❑ Name: MDCOURSE
- ❑ Implementation Name: MDCOURSE
- ❑ Top Title: 'Courses and Sessions' (This is the module title 'Startup Page Text'.)
- ❑ Short Title: 'Course and Sessions' (This is the module title 'Hyperlink Text'.)

3. Then click the Save icon to commit these name and title changes and close the properties window.

Add the CS Module Component

Now add a second Module Component to the MDCOURSE module:

1. Close any previous module diagrams, and drag the **MDCOURSE** module over to the diagram workspace to create a new Module Diagram.

2. Select the **Create Specific Component** icon on the diagram's vertical toolbar, and then click inside the module box below the current **COURSE_MC** module component. A Create Module Component window will appear. Enter the following properties:

- ❑ Name of the module component: CS_MC
- ❑ Title: Course Sessions (This title will appear in the hyperlink drill-down in your module.)

3. Click **Next**, and define the table usages for this module component:

- ❑ Base Table Usage – COURSE_SESSION. This table should be available from the popup list.
- ❑ Lookup Usage – check the PERSON table.

Note that **COURSE** should not be selected as a Lookup usage as it is the 'master'.

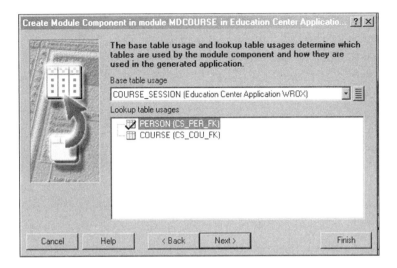

4. Click **Next** twice, and define the **Operations** for this module component: Do not select Delete. A Course Session can be canceled but not deleted from the table.

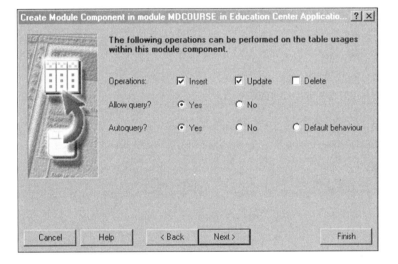

5. Click **Next**, and define the columns in the base table and the lookup table to be displayed in the CS module component. The lookup table columns are shown with a prefix of **L_PER_xxxx**. Use the **Add** button to select each column individually, and then use the **Up** and **Down** buttons to place the columns in display order. Select the following columns and arrange them in this order:

❑ ID: **checked**

❑ COU_CODE: **unchecked**

❑ START_DATE: **checked**

❑ STUDENT_LIMIT: **checked**

❑ CANCELLATION_INDICATOR: **checked**

❑ PER_ID: **unchecked**

❑ L_PER_ID: **checked**

❑ L_PER_LAST_NAME: **checked**

❑ L_PER_FIRST_NAME: **checked**

❑ L_PER_MIDDLE_NAME: **unchecked**

❑ L_PER_INSTRUCTOR_INDICATOR: **unchecked**

Do not select the change history columns – they will be maintained by the Table API. Click Next twice, and define the Operations to be performed on each column as per the following table:

Item	Query	Insert	Update
ID	No	–	–
COU_CODE	No	√	√
START_DATE	Yes	√	√
STUDENT_LIMIT	No	√	√
CANCELLATION_INDICATOR	No	√	√
PER_ID	No	–	√
L_PER_ID	No	–	√
L_PER_LAST_NAME	Yes	√	√
L_PER_FIRST_NAME	No	√	√
L_PER_MIDDLE_NAME	No	–	–
L_PER_INSTRUCTOR_INDICATOR	No	–	–

6. Click Next twice and then select the COURSE_MC master component to create **a key based link** to the master. This key based link will be used to link the Master Pages for COURSE to the Child pages for COURSE_SESSION.

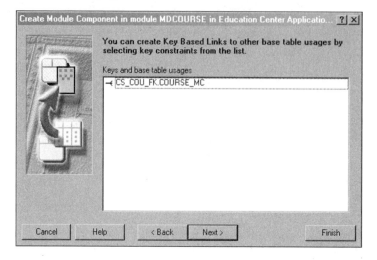

7. Click Next and select a Layout style of List. Click Next. Select the option to invoke the Display Wizard (the second option), and click Finish.

Refine the Module Component's Display

The Display Wizard will automatically appear after the Create Module Component wizard ends. Now refine the CS module component's display properties:

1. On the Display tab, validate that the Layout style is List.
On the Displayed Items tab, you should see the following:

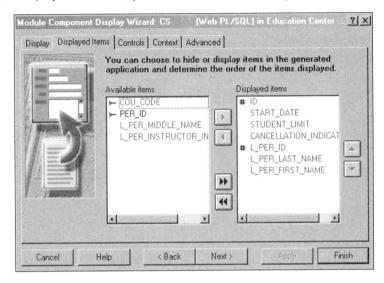

2. On the Controls tab, change the Labels for two columns:

❑ ID: Session ID

❑ L_PER_ID: 'Instructor ID'

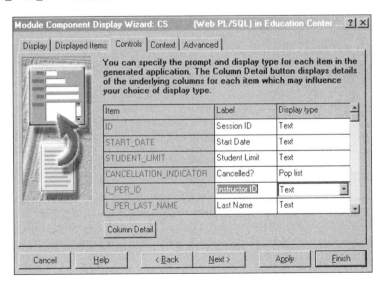

3. Click Next, and select the Context items to appear on the Record List as shown below. These items will appear in the order that they are listed.

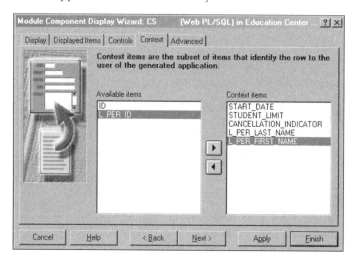

4. Click Finish, and look at your revised MDCOURSE Module Diagram and note the new Module Component, the Key Based Link, and the Lookup Table usage:

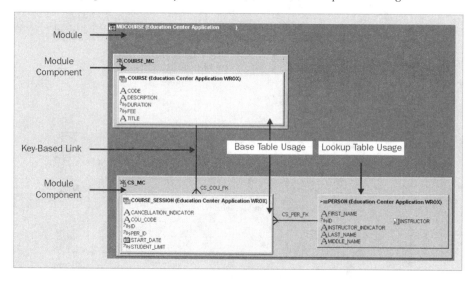

Create LOV Component

Next you will create a List of Values (LOV) component to look up instructors in the PERSON table to assign to a COURSE SESSION. LOV Components are a new feature of Designer 6i. With this version, you have to define an LOV component when you want an LOV to be built. However, you can define a single LOV component and then use it for multiple fields or even multiple modules. To create an LOV Component in the MDCOURSE module:

1. In the Design Editor Navigator, select the List of Values node under the MDCOURSE. Click the Create icon to bring up the Create List of Values wizard. Enter a Name: INSTRUCTOR and Title: Instructors. Click Next, and select the PERSON table as the base table usage. This LOV will be based upon the PERSON table. Click Next twice, and select the columns to be included in the LOV component as shown below:

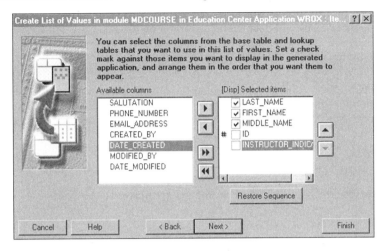

2. Click Next twice, and set the following properties:

- ❏ Used For: Data Entry (This LOV is not needed for query.)

- ❏ In the middle window, under the CS_MC module component, select L_PER.L_PER_ID. This will associate this LOV with the L_PER.L_PER_ID in the module component. Note that this is the ID in the PERSON lookup table.

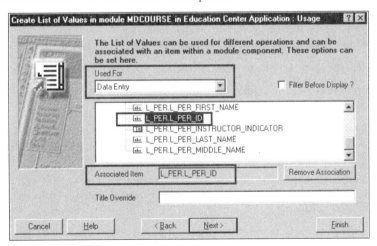

3. Click Next and add an Additional Restriction to only show PERSON records for instructors:Instructor_indicator='Y'.
Click Next twice, and select the first option :Create the list of values with the information provided, and then click Finish.

View the new LOV component on the bottom of the MDCOURSE module diagram. The association to the ID column PERSON lookup table usage will also be shown.

Revise the Module's Generator Preferences

Designer will display a hypertext link on the master module component view form that will take the user to the detailed records for a given master record. There are two additional preferences that can be set to display a hypertext link and detailed record count on the Record List page.

To set those two preferences for the MDCOURSE module:

1. Select the MDCOURSE module on either the Module Diagram or on the Navigator, and click the Generator Preferences icon to bring up the Generator Preferences: Module – MDCOURSE Property Palette. Verify that this property palette window does indeed say 'MDCOURSE'.

2. Set the following preferences at the Module – MDCOURSE level:

❑   RECORD LIST – Add Detail Hyperlinks to Record List: YES

❑   LINKS – Display Number of Rows in Hyperlink to Detail: YES

3. Save these changes.

Generate and Execute the MDCOURSE Module

Now the module design for MDCOURSE is complete, and you are ready to generate it:

1. Select the module and click the Generate icon. Enter the password for the application schema and click Start to generate it. When the generation process completes, review the Message window and close it.

2. When generation is complete, review the results as you did for the COURSE module.

3. Click the List Actions icon from the Message window to bring up the Build Action window.

❑   Select the View actions to examine the PL/SQL packages built for this module.

❑   Select the Action Run generated application to run your new MDCOURSE module from your browser.

❑   On your first page, you will find your old friend the COURSE Query Page. Remember that this is a master-detail module, and the master is essentially the COURSE module.

❑   Click Find, and examine your master record list form. Note the new Course Sessions column with hyperlinks and counts to the Detailed Records. The two preferences that we just set added these columns. Until you add some detailed records, all your hyperlinks will show 0 Rows.

❑   Select one of the Course Sessions hyperlinks, and you will go to the Course Session record list page for this course. It will be empty at first. Click the New button to bring up the Insert page.

❑   On the Course Session Insert page, notice the calendar window that was automatically created for the Start Date field. Also try the Instructor LOV component that you created.

❑   Add a few Course Sessions, and then return to your Master COURSE Record List, and view the revised record count. You may have to requery before the counts will show up correctly.

Course Query Page

Courses and Sessions

- About

Query Courses

Code:
Title:
Duration: to
Fee: to
Description:

Find Clear New

Master List Form

Note the hyperlinks and counts to the Detailed Records:

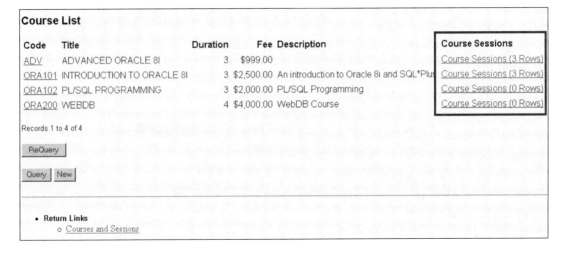

Course List

Code	Title	Duration	Fee	Description	Course Sessions
ADV	ADVANCED ORACLE 8I	3	$999.00		Course Sessions (3 Rows)
ORA101	INTRODUCTION TO ORACLE 8I	3	$2,500.00	An introduction to Oracle 8i and SQL*Plus	Course Sessions (3 Rows)
ORA102	PL/SQL PROGRAMMING	3	$2,000.00	PL/SQL Programming	Course Sessions (0 Rows)
ORA200	WEBDB	4	$4,000.00	WebDB Course	Course Sessions (0 Rows)

Records 1 to 4 of 4

ReQuery

Query New

- **Return Links**
  - Courses and Sessions

Course Session Record List Page

Initially this page will be empty. Click the New button to add some detailed records.

Course Sessions

No Records returned

ReQuery

Query New

- **Return Links**
  - Courses and Sessions

337

Insert Form

A Calendar lookup was automatically created on Start Date field:

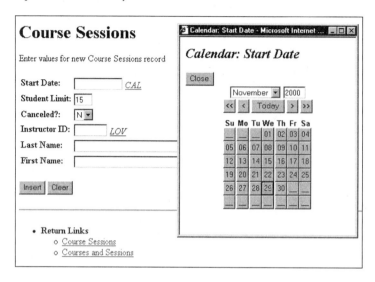

Insert Form

With the LOV Component on PERSON:

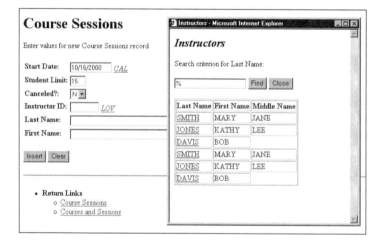

Master View Form

Note hyperlinks and counts to the Detailed Records:

Course Details

Code:	ORA101
Title:	INTRODUCTION TO ORACLE 8I
Duration:	3
Fee:	$2,500.00
Description:	An introduction to Oracle 8i and SQL*Plus

[Update] [Delete] [Revert] [New]

- Course Sessions (3 Rows)

- **Return Links**
  - o Courses and Sessions

MAIN Module

It is always helpful to have a single, application web page with hyperlinks to your application's modules. Some developers prefer to build this launch page or menu page by hand so that they can easily jazz it up. Designer also offers a way to quickly generate a launch page to other modules. In this section, you will create a MAIN module to serve as a Launch Page for the three modules you have just created.

Create the Main Module

First create a Module Definition for this module:

1. Select the Modules node in the Navigator, and click the Create icon to bring up a Create Module dialog. Enter the information shown below:

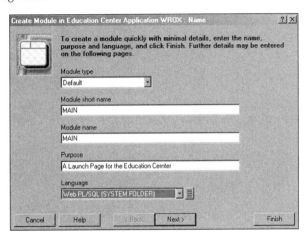

Create Module in Education Center Application WROX : Name

To create a module quickly with minimal details, enter the name, purpose and language, and click Finish. Further details may be entered on the following pages.

Module type
Default

Module short name
MAIN

Module name
MAIN

Purpose
A Launch Page for the Education Center

Language
Web PL/SQL (SYSTEM FOLDER)

[Cancel] [Help] [< Back] [Next >] [Finish]

2. Click Next to bring up the Titles page, and enter the following title for both the Hyperlink text and the Startup Page: Education Center Main Page. Click Next twice and enter the following User Text for the Top of the First Page:

```
<H3>Please select a detailed page from the list below:</H3>
```

Click the Next button to create hyperlinks from this Launch Page to your three Modules as shown in the figure below:

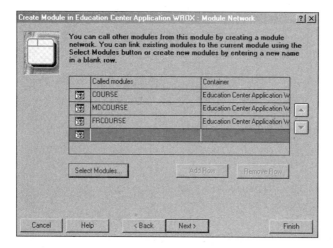

3. Use the Select Modules button to select each of your modules. Use the up and down arrows on the right to order those modules. Click Finish to complete this module definition. Close any open Module Diagrams and drag the MAIN module from the Navigator to the diagram workspace to view a Module Diagram for this module.

This diagram shows a Module box for the MAIN module, and then links to the Modules that it calls. The MAIN module box contains no module components because it does not need to access the database.

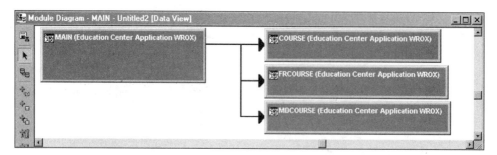

Generate and Execute the MAIN Module

Now generate and execute the MAIN module as you did above. The result should look like the following figure:

Education Center Main Page

Please select a detailed page from the list below:

- Course Information
- Course Information in Frames
- Course and Sessions

Try out each of the links to invoke the modules you generated.

Summary

In this chapter, you walked through the entire process of Web PL/SQL Application Design and Development. You designed and generated the following modules without writing a line of code:

- ❑ A MAIN module: An Application Launch Page

- ❑ A COURSE module: a single table module with a List layout style and a Multi-row Insert Form

- ❑ A FRCOURSE module: a second COURSE Module with a List/Form layout style with frames

- ❑ A MDCOURSE module: a master-detail module for Course and Course Sessions with a lookup table usage and a list of values (LOV) component

This chapter has covered a lot of material in a few pages. The features of the Web PL/SQL Generator are quite extensive. In these few pages, it was not possible to address many important topics or to present the extensive features of Designer's Web PL/SQL Generator. The only real way to learn about any tool is to build applications with it. Look at the generated PL/SQL code for the Module Packages and the Table API code. As you study the code, you will come to appreciate the robust and powerful nature of the code that the Web PL/SQL generator creates automatically. Browse and study the Designer Help Text pages. You will find a wealth of information in the Help text. Network with and learn from other Oracle Developers through the listservers and conferences of the Oracle Development Tools Users Group: http://www.odtug.com; and Oracle's Technology Network; a free membership group on Oracle's Internet web site, http://technet.oracle.com.

11

Oracle JVM and Java Stored Procedures

The Oracle Java Virtual Machine (JVM) is the engine driving the Oracle 8i Java platform. One of the core services provided by the JVM is in making static methods of Java classes available to PL/SQL as stored Java procedures. Over the next four chapters, we will be looking at various other services provided by the JVM. In this chapter, we start with Java Stored Procedures. We will find out to invoke Java from PL/SQL, from which point our Java code will run as any normal Java.

In my opinion, there are two basic approaches to covering the Oracle Java infrastructure:

- ❏   Focus on the technology and its relationship to the Oracle database platform,
- ❏   Concentrate on the application of the technology

The first approach would provide a thorough explanation of the components of the current Oracle Java infrastructure, the relationships between these components, and how these components are engineered to interoperate with core Oracle services. Such information is invaluable, but is covered in detail in the Oracle manual *Oracle 8i Java Developer's Guide* – a component of the Oracle 8i documentation library provided on the Oracle Technology network. I would argue that there is little value in re-phrasing the contents of this document.

Here, we take the second approach, focusing more on application than theory and, thus, the chapter will be structured as follows:

- ❏   Fundamental features of the Oracle JVM
- ❏   Introduction to stored procedures and preparing the development environment
- ❏   Practical examples

The opening sections will cover the core competencies needed for developing any kind of Java application for Oracle 8i, and on stored procedures in particular, the goal being to provide a quick path to getting your first Java stored procedure developed, deployed, and running in the database. The heart of the chapter then provides a series of carefully constructed examples and discussions aimed at consolidating this knowledge and preparing you for exploring the possibilities on your own. Hopefully, it will demonstrate that the Java infrastructure in Oracle 8i provides a significant improvement in the toolset available to application developers.

By adopting this approach, I hope that the chapter will be of significant interest to a diverse readership, from the experienced PL/SQL developer with little or no Java experience to the experienced Java developer who wants a fast track through the Oracle 8i Java features. Indeed, it should have value for any developers and architects looking to understand how to position the Oracle 8i Java features amidst the set of available tools and services for software development.

Java-enabling Infrastructure

With the release version 8.1.5 of their 8i database, with its integrated JVM (then known as JServer), Oracle began to blur the traditional distinction between the sort of functionality that was provided by the database and that traditionally provided by the "middle tier".

For the first time, Oracle leveraged the Java technology foundation to enhance the capabilities of its database platform. Specifically, it provided the ability to create stored procedures, functions, triggers, and object type methods in the Java language, and seamlessly integrate them with their PL/SQL counterparts.

> *These Java-based enhancements to the Oracle database platform are the focus of this chapter. For simplicity, I will refer to these enhancements collectively as "Java stored procedures".*

It also provided support for the EJB/CORBA component-based programming models (the specifics of developing CORBA and EJB-based services are not covered in this chapter).

With subsequent releases these services have been enhanced, such that today an Oracle "instance" can no longer be assumed to mean a database instance. Today, an Oracle instance can be a database instance, an application server instance (an EJB/CORBA platform), a web application server instance (Servlet and JavaServer Pages platform) or any combination of the three.

> **With Oracle 8.1.5, the JVM was named JServer. This name is sometimes still used but, with the release of 8.1.6, it officially changed to 8i JVM. The code in this chapter was tested on the 8i JVM.**

Before introducing Java stored procedures, let us look in more detail at the 8i JVM.

The Oracle 8i Java Virtual Machine

As noted above, the 8i JVM provides the run-time infrastructure on which Java stored procedures and other application components written in Java (EJBs, CORBA servers, JavaServer Pages, and Servlets) run in Oracle 8i. The Oracle 8i JVM runs within the Oracle server, using the Oracle server's architecture and core services. To put this another way: in the same way that Sun provides JVMs that run on different operating systems, and Microsoft provides a JVM that runs on Windows, Oracle has provided a JVM that is tightly integrated with Oracle's database server infrastructure. This means that it purportedly provides optimized data access and scalability and can exploit the built-in memory management, thread management, and other infrastructure services provided by the Oracle server architecture.

The thread-management feature is critically important because it means that, from a threading perspective, the Oracle 8i JVM behaves differently from other JVMs. Multi-threaded Java code executing in the Oracle 8i JVM, be it a Stored Procedure, EJB, or CORBA object, is executed on a single operating system thread. Therefore, instead of writing multi-threaded Java code to realize throughput benefits as you could on a traditional JVM, Oracle recommends writing single-threaded applications and relying on the JVM multi-user features to provide scalability.

For a more comprehensive treatment of the threading advantages and disadvantages of the 8i JVM and JServer, refer to the Oracle document *Oracle 8i Java Developer's Guide.* Other Oracle resources, including the white paper *Oracle JServer Scalability and Performance* are available at http://www.oracle.com/java.

Java Namespace Implementation

The closely-knit relationship between the JVM and RDBMS infrastructure means that the Oracle 8i JVM also works differently from traditional JVMs in some other respects. The most striking of these differences from a development and deployment perspective is that the JVM implements Java namespace functionality using database schema objects rather than the operating system's filesystem. This means that if you want to use the Oracle 8i Java compiler, you have to load your source code into a database schema. Similarly, if you want to run an already-compiled .class file or access classes and resources stored in an archive, you must load the .class or archive file into a database schema.

You should also be aware of a couple of features of Oracle's naming implementation. The first is that only one package.class name can exist within a database schema. For example, let's say a class called GregorianCal in Java package com.wrox.calendar has been compiled with the JDK compiler, version 1.2, into GregorianCal.class, and we want to load this class into the SCOTT schema. We might navigate to the {project-dir}/classes/com/wrox/calendar directory and invoke the command line utility loadjava as follows:

```
loadjava -thin scott/tiger@host:port:SID GregorianCal.class
```

Let us say that we want to try a different implementation of the same class using a new project. When we execute loadjava scott/tiger@host:port:SID GregorianCal.class from <project2> \classes\com\wrox\calendar, the original class will be overwritten in the SCOTT schema.

The second notable characteristic is that you can load the source definition of a Java class into a schema or you can load the .class bytecodes into the schema, but you cannot load both into the same schema. In other words, if you load the GregorianCal source like this:

```
loadjava -thin scott/tiger@host:port:SID GregorianCal.java
```

and then load the GregorianCal.class file into the same schema, the source will be overwritten by the bytecodes.

Compilers: BCOMP and the Oracle 8i JVM Accelerator (NCOMP)

The Oracle 8i JVM comes with two compilers:

❑   BCOMP (bytecode compiler)

❑   NCOMP (native compiler, now officially called the Oracle 8i JVM Accelerator)

BCOMP compiles Java source code into Java bytecodes. These bytecodes can then be interpreted by the JVM just like in a traditional Java run-time environment. BCOMP creates the same bytecodes that Sun's JDK compiler would produce. In Oracle 8i Release 2 and 3 (version 8.1.6 and 8.1.7), BCOMP is JDK 1.2 compliant. In the original release of Oracle 8i (8.1.5), BCOMP is JDK 1.1.x compliant.

There are two ways to invoke the Java compiler (BCOMP). One is using `loadjava`; the other is using the `CREATE JAVA` statement. Executing BCOMP places an enormous strain on the Oracle 8i JVM because it requires a tremendous amount of memory to run.

BCOMP is not the only compilation option, nor is it the best choice in my opinion. The best choice is to use the Sun JDK compiler (`javac`) and load the compiled `.class` files into the database.

NCOMP is a Java bytecode-to-C translator. Translating Java bytecodes to C allows the use of native compilers to compile the final executable code, resulting in substantial performance gains. Pre 8.1.7, only the JDK classes in the Oracle 8i JVM (all versions) are processed by NCOMP and compiled into native binaries for the respective platforms. Thus, whenever you invoke JDK classes from Java Stored Procedures, you are running native code rather than JIT-interpreted bytecodes. In other words, use of the JDK classes in the Oracle 8i JVM is heavily optimized, while use of your own classes is interpreted and slower. Oracle 8.1.7 is the first version of Oracle 8i to make NCOMP generally available – in Oracle 8.1.7, you can now natively compile your own Java code.

The Resolver

The resolver is the component of the Oracle 8i JVM responsible for finding Java classes at installation and execution time. More will be said about it when we discuss loading classes into the database.

JDBC and SQLJ

Java programs can access data via JDBC or SQLJ (a set of directives that simplify the coding of data-access functions). These APIs are covered in Chapters 12 and 14, respectively. Briefly, Oracle 8i ships with 3 JDBC drivers:

❑   **The thin driver**. This is a pure Java Type IV driver that is wellsuited for use from applets and other clients sitting across network boundaries.

❑   **The OCI8 driver**. This is a Type II driver that utilizes native code and the Oracle Call Interface for database connectivity.

❑   **The server-side driver**.

The server-side driver is an internal driver that has a very efficient channel into the database infrastructure. You can use any of these drivers in Stored Procedures, but most often you will use the server-side driver to access the local database, as it provides the most functionality and best performance. On the other hand, accessing data in another database instance requires the OCI8 or thin driver.

While simplicity is an advantage of SQLJ over JDBC, SQLJ doesn't support dynamic SQL so there are instances in which it cannot be used.

Java Stored Procedures

With 8i, Oracle has added the ability to develop Stored Procedures using Java. Java Stored Procedures can be called just like PL/SQL Stored Procedures. You can:

❑ Use them as functions in SQL (as in `SELECT myJavaFunction() FROM dual;`)

❑ Call them from any form of external client using JDBC, ODBC, ADO, OCI APIs

❑ Use them in triggers

❑ Call them from other Stored Procedures (PL/SQL or Java)

❑ Run them with the `CALL` statement

From within Java Stored Procedures you may:

❑ Execute data manipulation language (DML) commands (for example, `UPDATE`, `INSERT`, `DELETE` SQL statements) and data definition language (DDL) commands (for example, `CREATE TABLE`, `ALTER TABLE`, `DROP PROCEDURE`) against the database using Oracle's JDBC drivers (especially Oracle's internal, optimized driver).

❑ Execute static DML, DDL, and DCL statements against the database using two APIs: JDBC and SQLJ. SQLJ consists of a set of directives that greatly simplify the coding of static SQL statements.

❑ Call PL/SQL and Java Stored Procedures and functions (again through JDBC and SQLJ).

❑ Invoke other Java classes to capitalize on the rich functionality provided by the JDK third party Java classes, and other reusable software components. For example, in this chapter we'll look at how Java Stored Procedures can leverage XML and Oracle Advanced Queuing Java APIs.

> You should be aware that the Oracle JVM places one restriction on the use of JDK classes: you cannot display GUI objects using classes in the `java.awt` and `javax.swing` packages. This makes sense since code executing as server-side application components (as Java Stored Procedures, CORBA server objects, and EJBs would be) can have no graphical context. Therefore, you can use the graphics-oriented classes from Stored Procedures just as long as you don't try to display any GUI features (an `oracle.aurora.awt.UnsupportedOperation` exception will be thrown if you do).

Thus, Java Stored Procedures can function as an alternative to PL/SQL Stored Procedures or as an augmentation, enabling you to use the best data-tier technology for the job, given factors like resource availability, corporate standards, performance requirements, and so on. Additionally, you can take advantage of a standard language, a rich development environment, and internal and external marketplaces of reusable code.

Considering this flexibility, interesting possibilities come to mind. For example, in 3-tiered solutions, business tier to data tier communications have in the past originated in the business tier. With Java Stored Procedures, however, events can originate in the data tier. For example, a database trigger can execute a Java Stored Procedure that invokes an EJB method that then updates a Microsoft SQLServer database.

In addition to new possibilities in the application architecture realm, you have a new deployment configuration option in Oracle 8i: business and data tier services can be physically located not only on the same box, but also in the same address space.

Later, we'll discuss the criteria that influence the decision of when to use Java Stored Procedures, when to use PL/SQL, and how to use them together. But first, we need to discuss how to set the development environment and server.

Preparing the Development Environment

To start developing applications for the Oracle JVM, you need to set up your Java development environment, and ensure that the Oracle 8i Java features have been properly installed.

First of all, be aware that different versions of Oracle 8i support different versions of the JDK. Oracle 8i version 8.1.5 supports JDK 1.1.8, Oracle 8.1.6 and 8.1.7 (9i) support the Java 2 SDK version 1.2.2. If you are running Oracle 8.1.6 or Oracle 8.1.7, simply compile your code with JDK 1.2.2. However, if you are running Oracle 8.1.5, you will probably want to compile your code with JDK 1.1.8. While you *can* use JDK 1.2.2 to develop applications for JServer 8.1.5, your code will generate exceptions if it attempts to use Java 2 features that are not supported.

As with any Java application, you can compile your Java code for the JVM using `javac` from the command line, or with integrated development environment tools, or a combination of the two.

If you're just getting started with Java, I recommend you carry out the following tasks.

Identify and Install the Appropriate JDK

If you are deploying to Oracle version 8.1.5, you are developing for the Java platform version 1.1.8. If you are deploying to Oracle version 8.1.6 or 8.1.7, you are developing for the Java platform version 1.2.2. If a new version comes out, find in the Oracle Java documentation (available at http://technet.oracle.com) what Java platform version is supported – that is the platform that you are developing for.

Install on your development machine the correct version of the Java software development kit. For example, if you identified your target platform as Java 1.2.2, download the Java 2 SDK version 1.2.2 from Sun Microsystems (http://java.sun.com). The JDK setup will prompt you for an installation directory. For example, on my Windows 2000 development machine, my installation directory is `C:\jdk1.2.2`. In the rest of this chapter, I'll refer to this directory as `<JAVA_HOME>`. Wherever you see `<JAVA_HOME>` substitute the path to the directory where you installed the JDK.

Use Your JDK Documentation

Look for a directory called `<JAVA_HOME>/docs`. The documentation may be available on the CD from which you installed the JDK, or you can download the JDK documentation from Sun Microsystems or view it on the Web at http://java.sun.com. If you download the documentation, you should extract it to the `<JAVA_HOME>` directory such that it is available in `<JAVA_HOME>/docs`.

In the JDK documentation, there is a section called "SDK Tool Documentation" (in JDK 1.2), or "Tool Documentation" (in JDK 1.1.x). This documentation can be very useful for beginning Java developers because it explains the directory structure of the JDK, how to use the tools, and how classpaths work.

In the examples in this chapter, I provide the required steps to compile the code from the command line using the JDK tools directly. I also demonstrate the equivalent procedure if you are using Oracle JDeveloper. However, as you create your own applications or modify the examples to try new things, you may find the documentation mentioned above a valuable reference.

Install Your IDE

If you decide to use an IDE like Oracle JDeveloper, Borland JBuilder, WebGain VisualCafe, you can realize great productivity gains. However, bear in mind that these tools can mask the underlying characteristics of the JDK. For this reason, consider using an IDE's editor, but compiling the code with `javac` from the command line until you get familiar with the JDK tools. Once comfortable with how the JDK works, you can work the IDE's features into your build process.

Check Your Path Environment Variable

You need to be sure that the directories in the table below are in your PATH shell or environment variable. At this point, the JDK installation and Oracle Universal Installer should have made the required path modifications. However, in the event that you have trouble running `loadjava`, `javac`, etc., here are the paths for your reference:

Directory	Description
`<ORACLE_HOME>\bin`	Substitute the location of your Oracle 8i directory for `<ORACLE_HOME>`. This directory contains SQL*Plus, and other Oracle utilities.
`<JAVA_HOME>\bin`	Substitute the location of your JDK. For example `\jdk1.2.2\bin`. This directory contains the Java compiler (`javac`) and other utilities.

In addition to the APIs that comprise the JDK, the examples in this chapter use several other Java packages. These are listed in the table below:

Description/Source	Packages used	Directory/filename

Oracle JDBC drivers and native Oracle JDBC types
 	
(Installed with Oracle 8i)
	`oracle.jdbc.driver`
	
	`oracle.sql`
		Java 1.2 and up:
		`<ORACLE_HOME>/jdbc/lib/classes12.zip`
		or `classes12.tar`
		
		Java 1.1.x:
		`<ORACLE_HOME>/jdbc`
		`/lib/classes111.zip`

Oracle Advanced Queueing
 	
(Installed with Oracle 8i)
	`oracle.AQ`	Java 1.2 and up:
		`<ORACLE_HOME>/rdbms/jlib/aqapi.jar`
		
		Java 1.1.x:
		`<ORACLE_HOME>/rdbms`
		`/jlib/aqapi11.jar`

Oracle XSU
 	
(Available from http://technet.oracle.com)
	`oracle.xml.sql.query`
	
	`oracle.xml.sql.dml`
		Java 1.2 and up:
		`<xsu_dir>/lib/ xsu12.jar`
		`<XSU_DIR>/lib/xmlparserv2.jar`
		
		Java 1.1.x:
		`<XSU_DIR>/lib/ xsu111.jar`
		`<XSU_DIR>/lib/xmlparserv2.jar`

Naturally, to compile the examples that use these additional APIs, you will need to set your classpath correctly. For readers who are just getting started with Java, it is vital that you understand how the `javac` and `java` programs use the CLASSPATH environment/shell variable and command line parameter to reconcile API dependencies. Comfortable Java developers can skip the next two sub-sections.

Classpath Notes – Using Javac from the Command Line

When you compile a Java application that uses APIs that are not part of the JDK, you must tell the Java compiler how to find the Java classes that comprise those APIs. This is called "setting the classpath". You do this explicitly by using the `-cp` parameter, or implicitly by omitting the `-cp` parameter. Here are the rules for `javac`:

❑ `javac` always includes the JDK, so you never have to include the path to the JDK classes in the classpath.

❑ If the `-cp` parameter is omitted, `javac` checks for an environment or shell variable called CLASSPATH in `autoexec.bat` and uses its contents to reconcile dependencies.

❑ If the `-cp` parameter is provided, `javac` ignores the CLASSPATH setting and uses whatever string follows `-cp`. This is the preferred way. By always compiling your code using `-cp` and saving the compile command line in a shell script (Unix/Linux) or `.bat` file (Windows 95/98/NT/2000), so that you always have a record of classpath dependencies. Over time, you might have multiple versions of application code on your file system. Eventually, you may find that relying on the integrity of the CLASSPATH variable leads to bugs, confusion and other threats to engineering good software.

The examples in this chapter always use the `-cp` parameter, when required, for compiling the sample code.

Developing Stored Procedures in Java

There are several steps required to develop and deploy a Java Stored Procedure. These steps are summarized in the table below, and then I have covered them in more detail in the first example.

	Step	Tools
1	Code and compile the Java class	Coding: Your preferred IDE (Borland JBuilder, Oracle JDeveloper, WebGain VisualCafé).
		Compiling: Sun JDK 1.2.2 (or 1.1.x for Oracle 8.1.5) compiler (javac)
2	Load the compiled class into the database	`loadjava` command-line utility
3	Optionally specify a resolver spec.	`loadjava -resolver` option
4	Optionally request resolution at load time (otherwise resolution will happen the first time the class is run)	`loadjava -resolve` option
5	Publish the class to the SQL layer by defining a call spec	Any tool that can send data definition language commands to Oracle (for example, SQL*Plus), using the CREATE PROCEDURE | FUNCTION... AS LANGUAGE JAVA statement

A Date-Formatting Function

The first example will be a simple one. Its basic purpose will be to:

❏ Demonstrate how to develop, deploy, and publish an Oracle function written in Java.

❏ Begin to show that the ability to wrap JDK functionality in Stored Procedures can provide an enriched programming toolset.

We will not do any data access from inside of the class (we'll start to examine that in the next example).

In its simplest form, a Java Stored Procedure or function is a `public static` Java class method. Methods that will be used as the entry point for calls to Stored Procedures have to be defined as `public static`. Once inside the static method, the class can create custom and JDK library objects, just as in any Java application.

The method's parameters act like Stored Procedure parameters and the method's return value, if it has one, works just like an Oracle function's return value (we'll discuss Java-to-SQL type issues later).

Coding and Compiling the Java Class

This first example class is called `TimestampFormatter`. It has one method, `format()`, which simply takes an SQL date parameter and formats it using the JDK `SimpleDateFormat` class. This is a simplistic example of leveraging the functionality provided by the JDK in an Oracle Stored Procedure.

```
package com.wrox.examples;

import java.sql.*;
import java.text.SimpleDateFormat;

public class TimestampFormatter {
  // This method formats a date according to
  // US locale. You may want to replace the
  // pattern string with your own, based on
  // your locale.
  public static java.lang.String
        format(java.sql.Timestamp datetime) {

    String pat =
        "MM/dd/yyyy 'at' hh:mm:ss a zzzz";
    String outStr = null;
    SimpleDateFormat formatter =
        new SimpleDateFormat(pat);

    if(datetime != null)
    {
      outStr = formatter.format(datetime);
      System.out.println(outStr);
      return outStr;
    }
    else
      return "";
  }
}
```

Editing and Compiling the Code from the Command Line

Create a text file called `TimestampFormatter.java` in a directory of your choice (we've used `com\wrox\examples`) and edit the file with a text or code editor of your choice, typing in the code as listed (You can also download the code from http://www.wrox.com).

From a command or shell prompt, navigate to your chosen directory and compile the Java source with javac thus:

```
javac TimestampFormatter.java
```

The JDK compiler will create a file called `TimestampFormatter.class` in the same directory. In the next step towards making the `format()` method a Stored Procedure, we'll load this class into Oracle.

> **If you have trouble running javac, make sure that the `<JAVA_HOME>/bin` directory is in your path (where `<JAVA_HOME>` is the directory in which you installed the JDK). All the dependent classes are in the `java.sql` and `java.text` packages, which are contained in the JDK. Therefore, you don't need to specify a classpath when compiling `TimestampFormatter`.**

Editing and Compiling the Code in Oracle JDeveloper

Create a new JDeveloper workspace and project in a directory of your choosing. Using the File | New menu item, add a new Java class to the project as shown below.

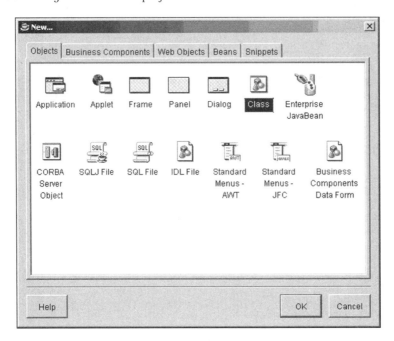

Next, enter the details for our date formatting class:

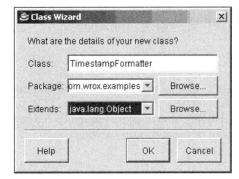

The `TimestampFormatter.java` file will appear in the Navigator pane. The file will already contain a shell of a Java class. Edit it with the JDeveloper editor, typing in the `import` statements and the `format()` method.

Before compiling, make sure that you're targeting the right Java platform version. Click the **Project |
Properties...** menu item. The project properties dialog box will appear as shown below (obviously the directory detail will be specific to your set up). In the drop-down list labeled **Target JDK version** select version 1.1.8 if you are targeting Oracle 8.1.5, or version 1.2.2 if you are targeting Oracle 8.1.6 or higher.

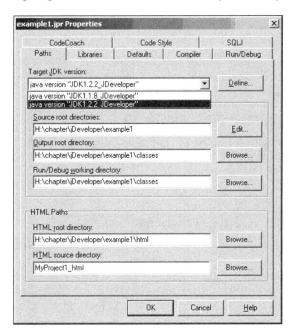

To compile the code in JDeveloper, click the menu item **Project | Make** `TimestampFormatter.java`.
JDeveloper will manage the compilation and direct the compiler to place the resulting
`TimestampFormatter.class` file in the `<ProjectOutput>\class\com\wrox\examples`
directory. `ProjectOutput` is your specified output directory. If you refer to the screen print, you'll see that I based my output directory on my project directory.

Examining the Code

Before we deploy, publish and execute this code, let us take a look at what it is doing. First of all, we import the JDBC API classes and the `java.sql` package:

```
import java.sql.*;
import java.text.SimpleDateFormat;
```

Specifically, we do this in order to use the `Timestamp` class used in the `format()` method's only parameter. The JDBC Timestamp class is compatible with the SQL DATE type (SQL type-to-JDBC class compatibility will be discussed in more detail later). As you'll see later on, `java.sql.Timestamp` is not the only Java class that could be used to accept an SQL DATE.

The second import allows us to use the `java.text.SimpleDateFormat` class. The `java.text` package is again a part of the core JDK, and contains classes that encapsulate functionality related to manipulating and formatting text.

`TimestampFormatter.format()` returns a `java.lang.String` which, as we'll soon see, is compatible with the Oracle VARCHAR2 data type. Inside the `TimestampFormatter.format()` method, we create two `String` objects: `pat`, which contains the text that will specify how we want the date formatted, and `outStr`, which will hold the formatted text to be returned.

```
public static java.lang.String
        format(java.sql.Timestamp datetime) {

    String pat =
           "MM/dd/yyyy 'at' hh:mm:ss a zzzz";
    String outStr = null;
```

Next we create a `java.text.SimpleDateFormat` object, passing the format pattern into the constructor.

```
    SimpleDateFormat formatter =
           new SimpleDateFormat(pat);
```

After that a call to the `SimpleDateFormat.format()` method takes the raw JDBC date and formats it into a text string as specified by the pattern String. The `TimestampFormatter.format()` method then returns that formatted String.

```
    if(datetime != null)
    {
      outStr = formatter.format(datetime);
      System.out.println(outStr);
      return outStr;
    }
    else
      return "";
  }
}
```

You might be wondering what benefit there is to this method, given that Oracle has the TO_CHAR function. The `SimpleDateFormat` Java class has certain rich, locale-specific formatting capabilities that TO_CHAR doesn't. Therefore by leveraging this Java class you can easily do locale-sensitive date formatting inside of a Stored Procedure that may have been more difficult to do before. This is an over-simplified example, but it serves to hint at how the functionality of Oracle Stored Procedures can be expanded and enriched by the features available through Java APIs (both JDK and external).

Simple Debugging with System.out() and System.err()

In the code we have a simple debugging statement `System.out.println(outStr)` that is used to display the value of `outStr`. To redirect the output of `System.out` and `System.err` calls to the SQL*Plus buffer, run the following commands from the SQL*Plus prompt:

```
SQL> SET SERVEROUTPUT ON SIZE 4000
SQL> CALL dbms_java.set_output(4000);
```

Simple debugging statements sent to `System.out` and `System.err` will then be written to the console when testing with SQL*Plus. More powerful debugging techniques are discussed later.

Deploying to the Database

In the Sun JVM and its derivatives, when a class is executed, the Java run-time environment resolves class dependencies by searching the classpath (either using the list of directories specified with the `-cp` parameter, or the `CLASSPATH` environment variable if no classpath parameter is supplied).

Recall that all Java classes that are to run in the Oracle 8i JVM must be loaded into the database (though not necessarily in the same schema). Dependency resolution works differently with the Oracle 8i JVM since you are working with database schemas, not directories. Instead of specifying a classpath at run-time, you specify a resolver spec at installation time (that is, when you load the class into Oracle). A resolver spec is a list of database schemas to search for dependent classes. If you do not provide a resolver spec, Oracle provides a default resolver which consists of classes in the `SYS` schema, the install destination schema, and any public synonyms.

Deploying from the Command Line

When you install the Java features of Oracle 8i, the JDK classes are automatically deployed to the database. However, once you compile your own applications with `javac`, you must load the classes into a database schema using the `loadjava` command line utility. Some examples of using `loadjava` are shown below:

❑   To display all the loadjava options:

```
loadjava -help
```

❑   To load the `TimestampFormatter` class into the `SCOTT` schema using the thin JDBC driver, using the default resolver spec, and deferring dependency resolution until the first time the class is run:

```
loadjava -user scott/tiger@host:port:SID -thin TimestampFormatter.class
```

Note that specifying the `-thin` or `-oci8` option does not have anything to do with the driver used internally in the `TimestampFormatter` class. It just specifies which driver `loadjava` should use to communicate to the database. If you have Oracle networking client software installed on your development machine, you can use either the thin or OCi8 driver. If you do not, then you will have to use the thin driver. Your choice of which driver you use with `loadjava` does not affect the functionality of your software – the end result is the same.

Also note that if you defer resolver activities until run-time, your class will appear to run *extremely* slowly the first time it is executed as it waits for the resolver to complete this lengthy task. By no means should you defer dependency resolution until run-time when deploying to production.

❑ To load the `TimestampFormatter` class into the `SCOTT` schema using the OCI8 driver, accepting the default resolver spec, but forcing resolver activity at install time:

```
loadjava -user scott/tiger@orcl -oci8 -resolve TimestampFormatter.class
```

❑ To load the `TimestampFormatter` class into the `SCOTT` schema using the thin driver, manually specifying the schemas the resolver should search (`SCOTT` and `sys` in this case), and forcing immediate dependency resolution:

```
loadjava -user scott/tiger@host:port:SID -thin -resolve \
    -resolver "((* SCOTT)(* SYS))" TimestampFormatter.class
```

Resolver Syntax

The resolver spec is a list of pattern/schema pairs, where the pattern specifies *which classes should be searched for in which schema*. For example, in the code above, (* `SCOTT`) tells the JVM to search the `SCOTT` schema for all the classes. You can narrow the search by changing the pattern, and this has practical uses.

For example, suppose we have two separate applications – an e-commerce system, and a Customer Relations Management (crm) system – which keep their Java classes in their respective schemas, `COMMERCE` and `CRM`. Suppose further that we are introducing a reporting application (schema: `REPORTING`) that uses the e-commerce `Orders` class and the crm `Customer` class. In our `ReportManager` class we have imports thus:

```
    import com.myCompany.Ecommerce.Order;
    import com.myCompany.CRM.Customer;

    public class ReportManager  {
    ...
```

We can speed up and add clarity to our install scripts by clearly specifying the source of the various dependencies, thus:

```
    loadjava -user reporting/reportingpwd@myServer:1521:o8i -thin -resolve \
        -resolver '(("com/myCompany/Ecommerce/*" commerce) \
                   ("com/myCompany/CRM/*" crm)(* sys))' ReportManager.class
```

When you don't specify a resolver spec, you tell Oracle to use the default resolver spec. Oracle responds by searching the current user's schema (the user specified in the `-user` parameter to `loadjava`) and the `sys` schema for all dependencies. That will work fine for the examples in this chapter, but when working with a development team, deploying to shared development, test, and production servers, and building applications from many different Java APIs, explicitly (and properly) specifying the resolver spec will help reduce your exposure to obscure bugs.

Checking Installation Status

To check the status of a class that you've loaded, you can query the `USER_OBJECTS` view from SQL*Plus or other query tool. For example, if you omitted the `-resolve` option when you loaded the Java class the query shown below will display a status of `INVALID` for the class. A status of invalid indicates that the class has not been resolved. As mentioned before, the first time the class is run, Oracle will automatically attempt to resolve it:

```
SELECT object_name, status
FROM user_objects
WHERE OBJECT_TYPE = 'JAVA CLASS';


OBJECT_NAME                         STATUS
----------------------------------- -------
/3ec063f_TimestampFormatter         INVALID
```

If you *did* specify the -resolve option and Oracle was able to resolve the class dependencies, your query output should look like this (it will also show this if you attempted to run the class and Oracle resolved it at run-time):

```
OBJECT_NAME                         STATUS
----------------------------------- -------
/3ec063f_TimestampFormatter         VALID
```

Notice the rather strange OBJECT_NAME that Oracle generated for the class. Due to the limits on the length of SQL identifiers, Oracle generates an internal hexadecimal name for package qualified class names that exceed 30 characters. To see the full class name, you can use the DBMS_JAVA.longname() method:

```
SELECT DBMS_JAVA.longname(object_name), status
FROM user_objects
WHERE OBJECT_TYPE = 'JAVA CLASS';


OBJECT_NAME                         STATUS
----------------------------------- -------
com/wrox/examples/TimestampFormatter INVALID
```

With suitable permission, you can similarly query the ALL_OBJECTS view to see all the Java classes throughout the database, including the JDK and Oracle JDBC driver classes.

Other Java object types are: JAVASOURCE and JAVARESOURCE. Note that there is no object type for archives. This is because when you pass an archive to loadjava, it extracts and loads the contents of the archive, not the archive itself.

Other loadjava Options for Class Loading/Resolving

These additional options can be used to change the behavior of loadjava when loading and resolving classes. The option -encoding is not discussed here because it applies to loading Java source code into the database.

- ❑ -f, -force forces loadjava to reload a class, even if it detects that the bytecodes in the database and .class file are identical.

- ❑ -d, -definer gives the methods of the class definer's rights.

- ❑ -g, -grants <grants> grant execute permission on all loaded classes and resources, to the users and roles listed in the comma separated list <grants>.

- ❑ -noverify skips verification of bytecodes.

- ❑ -order resolves classes in the bottom-up order.

❏ -schema <schema> if this option is not specified, the classes are loaded into the schema of the user specified with -user. Otherwise you can use this option to load classes into a different schema.

❏ -o, -oci8 tells loadjava to use the OCI8 JDBC driver to connect to the database. This is *currently* the default connection method used by loadjava, so you don't have to specify it. You might want to explicitly use this option for any installation scripts you want to keep since the default connection method could theoretically change.

❏ -resolve tells loadjava to resolve class dependencies.

❏ -resolver tells loadjava which schemas to search for which classes when attempting to resolve dependencies. When you do not specify a custom resolver spec, it searches the destination schema (*not* necessarily the -user schema) and the JDK schema for all classes. The resolver spec has quite a flexible syntax.

❏ -thin tells loadjava to use the JDBC thin driver to connect to the database. This enables you to install classes from a remote machine with no OCI8 client software.

❏ -user specifies the user who is installing the Java classes, their password, and an appropriate connect string depending on whether they've specified -oci8 or -thin.

❏ -v, -verbose turns on more extensive logging from loadjava. This information can be very useful, especially when you're just getting started with Java in Oracle 8i . For example, if you attempt to reload a class that hasn't changed, you get no output from loadjava. But add -verbose, and you'll see:

```
initialization complete
identical: com/wrox/examples/TimestampFormatter is unchanged from previously
loaded file
```

If you load and resolve with a custom resolver spec, loadjava gives you no feedback if successful. To see all the steps in action use -v and you'll get:

```
initialization complete
loading   : com/wrox/examples/TimestampFormatter
creating : com/wrox/examples/TimestampFormatter
resolver :  resolver ((* scott)(* sys))
resolving: com/wrox/examples/TimestampFormatter
```

Un-installing Java Classes with dropjava

To remove Java classes from a schema, you should use the dropjava utility, which has similar options to loadjava. Note that the Java classes, source or JAR files that you want to unload must not only be passed on the command-line, they must physically exist in the directory. In other words, it is best to call dropjava to remove the Java objects from the database *before* deleting the corresponding files.

Publish a Java Class Using a Call Spec

Once a Java class has been installed (loaded and resolved), it can be called from other Java classes in the database. However, to be called from the SQL layer, its methods must be published as Stored Procedures or functions. Before we discuss what a call spec is, consider the following:

❏ A fully qualified Java method name can be longer than the Oracle Stored Procedure maximum name length of 30 characters. We need to reference the method from PL/SQL using another name.

❑ If the Java class is part of a package, that method name contains the "." character, such as in com.wrox.examples.TimestampFormatter.format(). This character is not permitted in Oracle Stored Procedure names. We will therefore define wrapper PL/SQL functions.

❑ There is not a one-to-one relationship between Java and SQL data types, and these types are represented differently.

Thus, for the Oracle SQL engine to be able to locate and execute a Java method, pass it parameters, receive output parameters and a return value, a translation layer is needed. Specifically, this layer must define a SQL-friendly name by which to call the Java method and it must translate between the SQL and Java data types. A **call spec** is simply a specialized CREATE FUNCTION or CREATE PROCEDURE statement that defines that SQL-friendly name and data-type mappings.

In the case of TimestampFormatter, we want to publish a call spec for the format() method so that we can use it as an Oracle function (just like we use TO_CHAR()). Let's say we want the SQL-friendly name for the function to be ts_format(). Executing the following SQL DDL statement from within SQL*Plus will create the desired call spec:

```
CREATE OR REPLACE FUNCTION
ts_format(in_datetime IN DATE) RETURN VARCHAR2
AS LANGUAGE JAVA
NAME 'com.wrox.examples.TimestampFormatter.format
(java.sql.Timestamp) return java.lang.String';
/
```

Note the following:

❑ The function name and method name don't have to be the same

❑ The method name must be qualified by the full package name. Just using TimestampFormatter.format, for example, does not work. The call spec will be created, but at run-time it will fail, thus:

```
select ts_format(sysdate) from dual;
                   *
ERROR at line 1:
ORA-29540: class TimestampFormatter does not exist
```

❑ The Java type names must also be fully qualified.

Once this call spec is created, the Java class method can be used similarly to a PL/SQL function. For example, the following query will return a formatted date:

```
SELECT ts_format(sysdate) FROM dual;
```

For me, in the eastern US, the query returns something like:

```
08/10/2000 at 04:19:00 PM Eastern Daylight Time
```

Publishing a Call Spec into an Oracle Package

Java Stored Procedures and functions can be published as members of a PL/SQL package. To do this, you put the procedure's specification in the package header and the procedure's implementation in the package body just like for PL/SQL Stored Procedures. For example, here are the package header and body for a package called `CalendarPackage` in which we might place `ts_format`:

```
CREATE PACKAGE CalendarPackage AS
    public_var INT := 5;

    FUNCTION ts_format(in_datetime IN DATE) RETURN VARCHAR2;

END;
/
```

The package body is:

```
CREATE PACKAGE BODY CalendarPackage IS

    private_var INT := 10;

    FUNCTION ts_format(in_datetime IN DATE) RETURN VARCHAR2
    AS LANGUAGE JAVA
    NAME 'com.wrox.examples.TimestampFormatter.format(java.sql.Timestamp)
      return java.lang.String';

END;
/
```

Just like with PL/SQL, if you wanted the function or procedure to be local to the package (that is not accessible from outside elements) you would omit the procedure specification from the package header.

However, Oracle packages can contain more than procedures. They can also have variable declarations and type definitions that can be specified in the package header (in which case they are global) or body (in which case they are only accessible by package members). Currently, only `public` package variables can be accessed from Java Stored Procedures using `packageName.publicVar` as shown below. Private package variables cannot be accessed from Java Stored Procedures.

```
Connection cn = new OracleDriver().defaultConnection();
CallableStatement st =
      cn.prepareCall("{call ? := CalendarPackage.publicVar}");
```

You'll find out more about `CallableStatement` objects when we discuss using OUT and IN OUT parameters, a little later.

First-time Activation

The first time a Java class method is invoked (after being recompiled and reloaded or after a database restart), it incurs considerable overhead as it is loaded into memory. From that point on, the Oracle 8i JVM caches the class in memory. All users that access the class use the cached class resulting in much faster access but more memory usage.

Deploying and Publishing with Oracle JDeveloper

With JDeveloper, you can deploy and optionally publish Java classes right from the IDE using Deployment Profiles. To create a deployment profile to deploy and publish TimestampFormatter, select the Project I Deploy I New Deployment Profile... menu item as shown below:

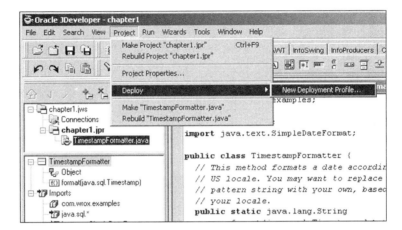

This brings up the Deployment Profile Wizard. The first step is to select "Classes and Java Stored Procedures to Oracle8i" as the deployment type:

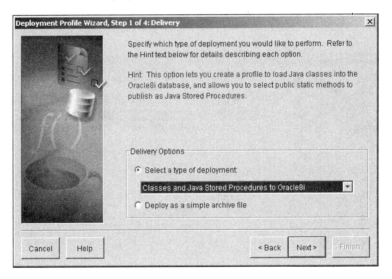

Step 2 involves selecting the Java classes to deploy. Make sure that `TimestampFormatter.java` is checked:

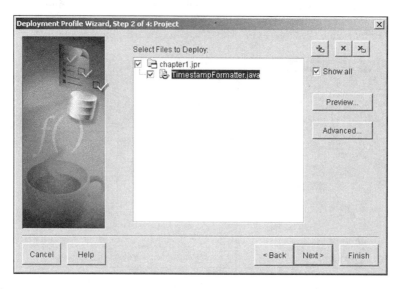

In step 3, the wizard will automatically figure out and list those methods that can be used as Stored Procedures (that is, which are `public static`). To select the `format()` method for publication as an Oracle function, check the checkbox under the Publish column for the format method row as shown below. Also, if you want to put the function in a package you can specify the package name.

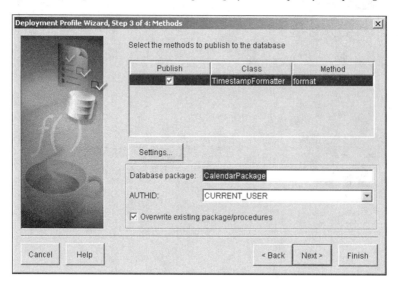

Before clicking Next, click the Settings button to specify more information about how you want the `format()` method represented as an Oracle function. This brings up the settings dialog box where you can set the Oracle function name, and define the type mappings. For example, we need to change the Publish As field to `ts_format` and ensure that the PL/SQL type for the lone argument is DATE.

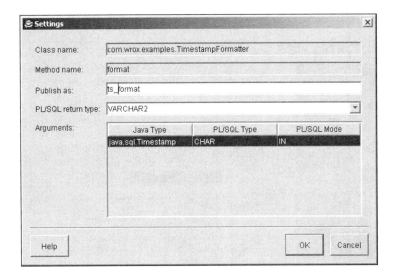

The next step is to define the database and schema to deploy to. If you already have an appropriate JDeveloper connection defined, select it and click Next. If you don't, click the New button to create a new JDeveloper connection. In the screenshots below, a connection using the thin driver to connect to scott/tiger at a HOST:PORT:SID of "localhost:1521:dev1" is created. Once the connection is created, it is auto-selected back in the Deployment Profile Wizard.

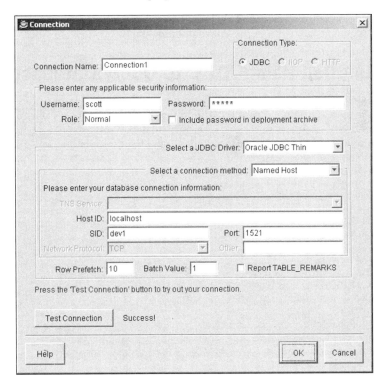

Next, specify the connection details:

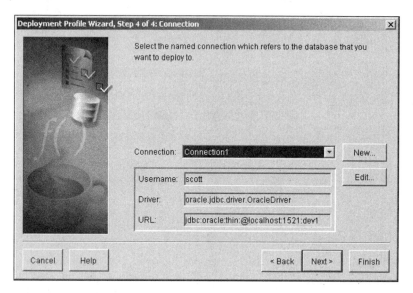

The final wizard page prompts you for where you want to save the profile. Once you click finish, JDeveloper displays a message box allowing you to choose to deploy immediately. Back at the project navigator pane in JDeveloper, the deployment profile shows up in the Deployment folder. You can redeploy it by selecting it from the Project | Deploy menu. When you execute the deployment profile, JDeveloper displays all its activities in the JDeveloper log pane.

A Simple Function Using JDBC to Query Database

This example reviews sales performance for a fictitious company and demonstrates another Oracle function written in Java. This time it uses JDBC to query the database for a value to return. Note this example uses the DEMO schema. The script to create the database objects in the DEMO schema is installed by the Oracle Universal Installer's server installation (not client installation) as <ORACLE_HOME>\rdbms\admin\demo.sql.

```java
package com.wrox.examples;

import java.sql.*;
import oracle.jdbc.driver.*;

public class SalesPerformance {

  public static java.lang.Double
      getAvgSalesPerf() throws Exception {

    // Note that demo.sales is a VIEW in the DEMO
    // schema. You should ensure that the Oracle example DEMO
    // has been set up: run the <ORACLE_HOME>\rdbms\admin\Demo.sql
    // script as user SYSTEM.
    String query = "SELECT AVG(total_sales) " +
            "FROM " +
            "(SELECT salesperson_id, " +
```

```
                       "SUM(amount) AS total_sales " +
                       "FROM demo.sales " +
                       "GROUP BY salesperson_id)";

        Connection cn = null;
        PreparedStatement ps = null;
        ResultSet rs = null;

        try {
          cn= new OracleDriver().defaultConnection();
          ps = cn.prepareStatement(query);
          rs = ps.executeQuery();

          if(rs.next())
            return new
                java.lang.Double(rs.getDouble(1));
          else
            throw(new Exception("Unexpected exception: SELECT returned no rows"));
        }
        finally {
          if(rs != null) rs.close();
          if(ps != null) ps.close();
        }
      }
    }
  }
```

The `SalesPerformance` class has a single method, `getAvgSalesPerf()`, that doesn't take any parameters. It performs a simple calculation, returning the result as a `Double`. It can be tested with the query `SELECT getAvgSalesPerf() FROM dual;`. It barely does anything but provide first steps in using JDBC to communicate with the local Oracle 8i database from a Java Stored Procedure.

Once the example builds the query string, it gets a JDBC connection to Oracle via the internal server-side JDBC driver. This driver is only available to Java applications running in the Oracle 8i JVM. Notice that the connection doesn't have to be created, we just called the `defaultConnection()` method. This is always the case with the server-side JDBC driver.

Next we create a `PreparedStatement`, a Java wrapper around any kind of SQL statement, in this case an SQL query. Then we execute the query and get the results in a resultset. The resultset has one column containing a `float` which we return to the calling application.

> Notice that we used a **finally** clause to ensure that the **ResultSet**, and **PreparedStatement** objects **close()** methods are called even if an exception occurs. The Oracle 8i JDBC Developer's Guide points out that **ResultSet** and **Statement** objects should be closed explicitly, and warns that not doing so can lead to severe memory and cursor leaks.

Editing and Compiling the Code

Create a text file called `SalesPerformance.java` in directory `com\wrox\examples`. Edit the file with a text or code editor of your choice, typing in the code as listed.

From a command or shell prompt, compile the Java source with `javac` as shown below. Note that if you're using JDK 1.1.x, use `classes111.zip` or `classes111.tar` instead:

```
javac -classpath "<ORACLE_HOME\jdbclib\classes12.zip" SalesPerformance.java
```

> As mentioned earlier, you have to specify a classpath whenever you use Java APIs external to the JDK. This is true in the case of **SalesPerformance**, where we're using the Oracle server-side JDBC driver. In order for javac to locate the **OracleDriver** class, it needs to be told to search in the Oracle JDBC driver archive.

Deploying SalesPerformance from the Command Line

Once the class is compiled, you can load and resolve it as shown below, making the appropriate substitutions to connect to your Oracle server:

```
loadjava -user "scott/tiger@host:port:sid" -thin -resolve -verbose \
    SalesPerformance.class
```

`loadjava` should respond with:

```
initialization complete
loading   : com/wrox/examples/SalesPerformance
creating  : com/wrox/examples/SalesPerformance
resolver  :
resolving : com/wrox/examples/SalesPerformance
```

Publishing SalesPerformance.getAvgSalesPerf()

Here's a call spec that maps the SQL function `getAvgSalesPerf()` to Java class method `com.wrox.examples.SalesPerformance.getAvgSalesPerf()`.

```
CREATE OR REPLACE FUNCTION getAvgSalesPerf
RETURN number
AS language java
name 'com.wrox.examples.SalesPerformance.getAvgSalesPerf()
    return java.lang.Double';
/
```

Java to Oracle Type Mappings

So far we've used Stored Procedure call specs to map the `java.lang.String` data type to the `VARCHAR2` Oracle data type, the `java.sql.TimeStamp` JDBC data type to the `DATE` Oracle type, and `java.lang.Double` to the Oracle `NUMBER` type. The following table shows the full spectrum of Java/JDBC to Oracle type compatibilities:

Oracle Types	Compatible non-JDBC JDK Types and Classes	Compatible JDBC 2.0 Classes	Compatible Oracle Native Classes
All types	--	--	oracle.sql. CustomDatum oracle.sql. Datum
BLOB	--	java.sql.Blob oracle.jdbc2.Blob	oracle.sql. BLOB
BFILE	--	--	oracle.sql. BFILE
CHAR VARCHAR2 LONG NCHAR NVARCHAR2	byte,double,float int, short java.lang.Byte java.lang.Double java.lang.Float java.lang.Integer java.lang.Long java.lang.Short java.lang.String	java.sql.Date java.sql.Time java.sql.Timestamp	oracle.sql. CHAR
CLOB NCLOB	--	java.sql.Clob oracle.jdbc2.Clob	oracle.sql. CLOB
DATE	java.lang.String	java.sql.Date java.sql.Time java.sql.Timestamp	oracle.sql. DATE
NUMBER	byte, double, float, int, short java.lang.Byte java.lang.Double java.lang.Float java.lang.Integer java.lang.Long java.lang.Short java.math.BigDecimal	--	oracle.sql. NUMBER
OBJECT	--	java.sql.Struct oracle.jdbc2.Struct	oracle. sqljData oracle.sql. STRUCT
REF	--	java.sql.Ref oracle.jdbc2.Ref	oracle.sql. REF
ROWID	java.lang.String	--	oracle.sql. CHAR oracle.sql. ROWID
TABLE	--	java.sql.Array oracle.jdbc2.Array	oracle.sql. ARRAY
VARRAY	--	java.sql.Array oracle.jdbc2.Array	oracle.sql. ARRAY

Note that the classes in the `oracle.jdbc2` package are JDBC 2.0 classes designed for use in JDK 1.1.x versions (for example, with Oracle 8.1.5). When using JDK 1.2, these classes are found in the `java.sql` package.

Use of the type mappings in columns two and three ensures the most portable code, and in many instances, the most functionality. However, when data is copied from a native Oracle type to a JDK/JDBC type you incur translation overhead. This occurs in the following instances:

❑ When you pass parameter data into and out of a Stored Procedure or function

❑ When you return values to SQL or PL/SQL clients

❑ When you access data through a standard JDBC `ResultSet` object

❑ When you access data through a `Statement` object

The Oracle native classes are very thin wrappers around the native Oracle SQL types. These classes are stored in the `oracle.sql` package. Use of these classes affects your portability. In addition, since these classes are meant to be used as wrappers, their functionality is severely limited to keep their footprint small. Leverage them in situations where you have to iterate through a large amount of `ResultSet` rows, which then, for example, need to be inserted into another Oracle table.

Boolean Issues

When publishing a call spec for a Java Stored Procedure or function with boolean parameters or a boolean return value, you currently can't use the PL/SQL `BOOLEAN` type. For example, the following call spec is currently invalid:

```
CREATE PROCEDURE setLimitExceeded(boolval IN BOOLEAN)
AS LANGUAGE JAVA
NAME
'com.wrox.examples.CreditManager.setLimitExceeded(Boolean);
```

The workaround is simple: publish the call spec using `NUMBER` instead of `BOOLEAN`:

```
CREATE PROCEDURE setLimitExceeded(boolval IN NUMBER)
AS LANGUAGE JAVA
NAME
'com.wrox.examples.CreditManager.setLimitExceeded(Boolean);
```

Any non-zero value passed in `boolval` will be interpreted as true, while zero will be false.

Using OUT and IN OUT Parameters

Here we expand on the sales performance example to demonstrate the use of OUT and IN OUT parameters.

Java method parameters that you want to publish as OUT or IN OUT arguments have to be array types. You refer to the data using the 0-index array member. In this example, the first parameter will be published as IN OUT, and the others as OUT. The IN OUT parameter `cm_total_sales` (cumulative total sales) allows us to pass in a running total and have the total sales number added to it. This running total could have practical use in a scenario where we made different calls to get different region totals and we wanted to maintain a running total.

```
package com.wrox.examples;

import java.sql.*;
import oracle.jdbc.driver.*;

public class BasicStats {

  public static void getSalesStats(
      Double[] cm_total_sales,
      Double[] total_sales,
      Double[] avg_sales,
      Integer[] above_avg_cnt)
      throws Exception {
    Double totalSales;
    Double avgSales;
    Integer aboveAvg;
    Connection cn = null;
    PreparedStatement ps = null;
    ResultSet rs = null;

    String query =
        "SELECT AVG(total_sales), " +
        "SUM(total_sales) " +
        "FROM " +
        " (SELECT salesperson_id," +
        "  SUM(amount) AS total_sales" +
        "  FROM demo.sales" +
        "  GROUP BY salesperson_id)";

    // This query counts how many sales persons
    // performed at or above the average sales
    // numbers
    String aboveQry =
        "SELECT COUNT(*) FROM " +
        " (select salesperson_id , " +
        "  SUM(amount) AS total_sales " +
        "  FROM demo.sales " +
        "  GROUP BY salesperson_id) " +
        "WHERE total_sales >= ? ";

    try {
      // Get the default Connection. Could also
      // use an OracleConnection object.
      cn =
          new OracleDriver().defaultConnection();

      // Prepare and execute the query to get the
      // average and total sales numbers. Throw
      // an exception if we have any trouble
      ps = cn.prepareStatement(query);
      rs = ps.executeQuery();
      if(!rs.next())
        throw(new Exception("Unexpected " +
            "exception: AVG/TOTAL query " +
            "returned no rows"));
```

```
        // Get the average and total numbers, then
        // close the objects
        avgSales = new Double(rs.getDouble(1));
        totalSales = new Double(rs.getDouble(2));
        rs.close();
        ps.close();

        // Prep and execute query,substituting in
        // the average sales number
        ps = cn.prepareStatement(aboveQry);
        ps.setDouble(1, avgSales.doubleValue());
        rs = ps.executeQuery();
        if(!rs.next())
          throw(new Exception("Unexpected " +
              "exception: Above-average query " +
              "returned no rows"));

        // Get the below-average number, then
        // close the objects
        aboveAvg = new Integer(rs.getInt(1));
        rs.close();
        ps.close();

        // Set the IN OUT parameters
        if(cm_total_sales[0] == null)
          cm_total_sales[0] =
              new Double(totalSales.doubleValue());
        else
          cm_total_sales[0] = new
            Double(cm_total_sales[0].doubleValue()
                  + totalSales.doubleValue());
        total_sales[0] = totalSales;
        avg_sales[0] = avgSales;
        above_avg_cnt[0] = aboveAvg;
      }
      finally {
        if(rs != null) rs.close();
        if(ps != null) ps.close();
      }
    }
  }
```

The getSalesStats() method does a bit more work than previous examples. First off, we have two query strings: query and aboveQry. The former calculates the average and total sales for all sales persons. The latter, shown again below, gets a count of how many salespersons sold more than the average:

```
String aboveQry =
        "SELECT COUNT(*) FROM " +
        " (select salesperson_id , " +
        "  SUM(amount) AS total_sales " +
        "  FROM demo.sales " +
        "  GROUP BY salesperson_id) " +
        "WHERE total_sales >= ? ";
```

The character ? in the query is a placeholder for a value. The idea is to substitute in the SUM(total_sales) value retrieved by executing the first query, prior to executing the second. Once aboveQry is prepared and assigned to the variable ps with ps = cn.prepareStatement(aboveQry), the PreparedStatement object recognizes the placeholder as a positional parameter. Therefore, we can set the value by calling one of the PreparedStatement set methods; in this case, the setDouble(int parameterIndex, double x) method.

Once it executes the second query, the code does some straightforward assignments to set the OUT and IN OUT parameters.

Compiling the BasicStats class is similar to the previous example; we have not introduced any new Java package dependencies:

```
javac -classpath  <ORACLE_HOME>/jdbc/lib/classes12.zip BasicStats.java
```

Once again we load the class:

```
loadjava -user scott/tiger@host:port:sid -thin -resolve -verbose BasicStats.class
```

And here's a call spec to publish the getSalesStats() method as a PL/SQL stored procedure named getSalesStats:

```
CREATE OR REPLACE PROCEDURE
  getSalesStats(cm_total_sales IN OUT NUMBER,
  total_sales OUT NUMBER, avg_sales OUT NUMBER,
  above_avg_cnt OUT NUMBER)
AS LANGUAGE JAVA
NAME
  'com.wrox.examples.BasicStats.getSalesStats(
  java.lang.Double[], java.lang.Double[],
  java.lang.Double[], java.lang.Integer[])';
/
```

Testing this Stored Procedure in SQL*Plus on my system yields the results shown below. I initialized the cm_total_sales bind variable to simulate a running total.

```
SQL> VAR cm_total_sales NUMBER
SQL> VAR total_sales NUMBER
SQL> VAR avg_sales NUMBER
SQL> VAR above_avg_cnt NUMBER

SQL> BEGIN
  2   :cm_total_sales := 15692.35;
  3   END;
  4   /

PL/SQL procedure successfully completed.

SQL> CALL getSalesStats(:cm_total_sales, :total_sales, :avg_sales, :above_avg_cnt);

Call completed.

SQL> SELECT :cm_total_sales, :total_sales, :avg_sales, :above_avg_cnt  FROM dual;

:CM_TOTAL_SALES :TOTAL_SALES :AVG_SALES :ABOVE_AVG_CNT
--------------- ------------ ---------- --------------
      252929.1    237236.75 26359.6389              5
```

Deploying getAvgSalesPerf() with JDeveloper

There isn't much difference between deploying `SalesPerformance.getAvgSalesPerf()` and earlier examples. The main thing to note is that the arguments' directions need to be set to IN OUT for `cm_total_sales`, and OUT for the remainder as shown below.

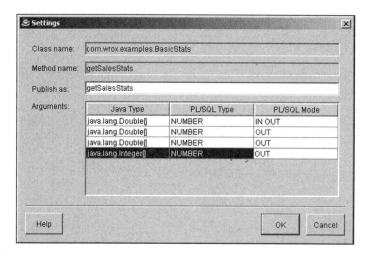

Calling Stored Procedures from Java Stored Procedures

In this example, we'll call the `getSalesStats` and `getAvgSalesPerf` Stored Procedures from a new Java Stored Procedure to demonstrate how to call Stored Procedures via JDBC passing IN, IN OUT, and OUT parameters, and retrieving a return value. The class will be called `SalesDriver` since it is used to test, or "drive" the other procedures.

```java
package com.wrox.examples;

import java.sql.*;
import oracle.jdbc.driver.*;

public class SalesDriver {

    public static String test() throws Exception {

        // Different ways to call Stored Procedures
        // from JDBC.
        String sp1 =
            "{? = call ts_format(SYSDATE)}";
        String sp2 =
            "BEGIN ? := getAvgSalesPerf; END;";
        String sp3 =
            "{call getSalesStats(?, ?, ?, ?)}";

        Double cmTotal = null;
        Double total = null;
        Double average = null;
        Integer aboveCount = null;
```

```
      Connection cn = null;
      CallableStatement cs1 = null, cs2 = null,
                        cs3 = null;

   try {
      cn = new OracleDriver().defaultConnection();

      cs1 = cn.prepareCall(sp1);
      cs2 = cn.prepareCall(sp2);
      cs3 = cn.prepareCall(sp3);

      cs1.registerOutParameter(1,
                          java.sql.Types.CHAR);
      cs2.registerOutParameter(1, Types.DOUBLE);
      cs3.setDouble(1, 1.0);
      cs3.registerOutParameter(1, Types.DOUBLE);
      cs3.registerOutParameter(2, Types.DOUBLE);
      cs3.registerOutParameter(3, Types.DOUBLE);
      cs3.registerOutParameter(4, Types.INTEGER);

      cs1.execute();
      cs2.execute();
      cs3.execute();

      return "SalesDriver.test run date: " +
            cs1.getString(1) + "\n" +
            "Total sales from getAvgSalesPerf: " +
            cs2.getDouble(1) + "\n" +
            "Sales stats: " + cs3.getDouble(1) +
            ", " + cs3.getDouble(2) + ", " +
            cs3.getDouble(3) + ", " +
            cs3.getInt(4);
   }
   finally {
      if(cs1 != null) cs1.close();
      if(cs2 != null) cs2.close();
      if(cs3 != null) cs3.close();
   }
  }
}
```

Using `loadjava` should be familiar territory, and our package dependencies have not changed from the previous example, so here is the call spec only:

```
CREATE OR REPLACE FUNCTION
sdTest RETURN VARCHAR2
AS LANGUAGE JAVA
NAME 'com.wrox.examples.SalesDriver.test()
   return java.lang.String';
/
```

Calling this example with SELECT sdTest FROM dual should yield:

```
SalesDriver.test run date: 08/15/2000 at 03:09:06 PM Eastern Daylight Time
Total sales from getAvgSalesPerf: 26359.6388888889
Sales stats: 237237.75, 237236.75, 26359.6388888889, 5
```

In the example, we use three `CallableStatement` objects. The first demonstrates how to pass an `IN` parameter and retrieve a return value from a stored function using SQL92 call syntax. This syntax requires the keyword "call" be in lower case; use `CALL` and you will get an error.

The second object `cs2`, shows how to retrieve a return value using Oracle Stored Procedure syntax.

The third `CallableStatement` demonstrates how to pass and retrieve `IN` and `IN OUT` parameters to/from Stored Procedures. The call to `cs3.setDouble(1, 1.0)` passes the value 1.0 into the `IN OUT` parameter. This value is replaced by the called procedure and is accessed with `cs3.getDouble(1)`.

DML and Transactions

So far we've looked at Java Stored Procedures that queried Oracle database objects. This example:

❏   Shows how to execute `INSERT`, `UPDATE` and `DELETE`

❏   Discusses transactions in Java Stored Procedures

❏   Discusses related issues

The example consists of a Java class called Order. Order is responsible for managing order persistence. For this simple demo, it has only two methods: `AddItem()` and `RemoveItem()`. `AddItem()` adds an item to an existing order; `RemoveItem()` removes an item from an existing order. In `AddItem()` a row must be added to the item table and the total column in the corresponding `sales_order.order` row must be updated. `RemoveItem()` is similar, except that the first DML operation is a delete.

Here's the source listing for the two methods:

```
package com.wrox.examples;

import java.sql.*;
import oracle.jdbc.driver.*;

public class Order {

  public static void AddItem(int order_id, int product_id,
          int quantity) throws Exception {

    String dmlAddItem = null;
    String dmlUpdateTotal = null;
    String qryPriceAndItem =
            "SELECT list_price, next_item_no " +
            "FROM demo.price, " +
            "(SELECT MAX(item_id) + 1 " +
            "   AS next_item_no " +
            "   FROM demo.item    " +
            "   WHERE order_id = " + order_id + ") " +
            "WHERE product_id = " + product_id +
            "   AND end_date IS NULL";

    String csUpdateTotal =
            "DECLARE " +
            "new_total NUMBER; " +
            "BEGIN " +
```

```
                    "SELECT SUM(total) INTO new_total " +
                    "FROM demo.item " +
                    "WHERE order_id = " + order_id + "; " +
                    "UPDATE demo.sales_order " +
                    "SET total = new_total " +
                    "WHERE order_id = " + order_id + "; " +
                    "END; ";

    Connection cn = null;
    PreparedStatement ps = null;
    CallableStatement cs = null;
    ResultSet rs = null;

    double price = 0;
    double itemTotal = 0;
    int nextItemID = 0;

    try {
      cn = new OracleDriver().defaultConnection();
      ps = cn.prepareStatement(qryPriceAndItem);
      rs = ps.executeQuery();
      if(!rs.next()) throw(new Exception("Unexpected " +
                  "exception: SELECT returned no rows"));

      price = rs.getDouble(1);
      nextItemID = rs.getInt(2);
      itemTotal = (price * (double)quantity);
      rs.close();
      ps.close();

      dmlAddItem = "INSERT INTO demo.item VALUES(" +
                  order_id + ", " + nextItemID + ", " +
                  product_id + ", " + price +
                  ", " + quantity + ", " + itemTotal + ")";
      ps = cn.prepareStatement(dmlAddItem);
      ps.execute();
      ps.close();

      cs = cn.prepareCall(csUpdateTotal);
      cs.execute();

      cn.commit();
    }

    finally {
      if(rs != null) rs.close();
      if(ps != null) ps.close();
    }
  }

  public static void RemoveItem(int order_id, int item_id)
                    throws Exception {

    String dmlRemoveItem = null;
    String dmlUpdateTotal = null;
```

```
        String csUpdateTotal =
                    "DECLARE " +
                    "new_total NUMBER; " +
                    "BEGIN " +
                    "SELECT SUM(total) INTO new_total " +
                    "FROM demo.item " +
                    "WHERE order_id = " + order_id + "; " +
                    "UPDATE demo.sales_order " +
                    "SET total = new_total " +
                    "WHERE order_id = " + order_id + "; " +
                    "END; ";

        Connection cn = null;
        PreparedStatement ps = null;
        CallableStatement cs = null;
        ResultSet rs = null;

        try {
          cn = new OracleDriver().defaultConnection();

          dmlRemoveItem = "DELETE FROM demo.item " +
                      "WHERE order_id = " + order_id +
                      "AND item_id = " + item_id;
          ps = cn.prepareStatement(dmlRemoveItem);
          ps.execute();
          ps.close();

          cs = cn.prepareCall(csUpdateTotal);
          cs.execute();
          cn.commit();
        }

        finally {
          if(rs != null) rs.close();
          if(ps != null) ps.close();
        }
      }
    }
}
```

Compiling and deploying this class is similar to previous examples. Call specs are shown below:

```
CREATE OR REPLACE PROCEDURE
  orderAddItem(order_id IN NUMBER,
  product_id IN NUMBER,
  quantity IN NUMBER)
AS LANGUAGE JAVA
NAME
  'com.wrox.examples.Order.AddItem(int, int, int)';
/
```

```
CREATE OR REPLACE PROCEDURE
  orderRemoveItem(order_id IN NUMBER,
  item_id IN NUMBER)
AS LANGUAGE JAVA
NAME
  'com.wrox.examples.Order.RemoveItem(int, int)';
/
```

To test these methods you can execute the following statements in SQL*Plus, then query the ITEM and SALES_ORDER tables to ensure that the item was indeed added/deleted and the total computed properly.

```
SQL> call orderAddItem(501, 100860, 7);
SQL> call orderRemoveItem(501, 1);
```

If you run into permission problems executing the procedures as user SCOTT, this is because when the DEMO schema is created, ready-only permission is granted to PUBLIC. Therefore SCOTT doesn't have permission to INSERT into the ITEM table or UPDATE the sales_order table. Issuing the following GRANT operations while connected as user DEMO should enable running the tests successfully:

```
GRANT UPDATE ON sales_order TO SCOTT;
GRANT INSERT ON item TO SCOTT;
GRANT DELETE ON item TO SCOTT;
```

This class makes extensive use of dynamic SQL. In the AddItem method, the query string stored in qryPriceAndItem is built dynamically using the order_id and product_id arguments. Similarly a dynamic PL/SQL block is built and stored in csUpdateTotal.

Restrictions on DML-Enabled Java Stored Procedures

If you perform DML (Data Manipulation Language) actions inside of a Java Stored Procedure, Oracle places these restrictions on how the procedure or function can be used:

❑ It cannot be called from a SELECT statement or parallelized DML statement.

❑ It cannot be called from an INSERT, UPDATE, or DELETE statement if the statement modifies the same tables as the Stored Procedure

❑ It cannot be called from a SELECT, INSERT, UPDATE, or DELETE statement if it performs any transaction management (for example, calling commit() or rollback()). By extension, it cannot execute any DDL (Data Definition Language) statements since these are automatically committed by Oracle.

❑ It cannot be called from a SELECT, INSERT, UPDATE, or DELETE statement if it performs system or session control functions.

Attempts to violate these restrictions are met with a run-time error.

Transactions and Sessions in Java Stored Procedures

The Connection you receive when you call the defaultConnection() method of the Oracle internal JDBC driver from within a Java Stored Procedure inherits the session and transaction context from the client. For example, when you run a Java Stored Procedure or function from SQL*Plus, the Connection your Stored Procedure gets inherits your SQL*Plus session. Let's say for some reason you execute the following DML statement:

```
UPDATE sales_order SET ship_date = sysdate WHERE order_id = 305;
```

Subsequently you call a Java Stored Procedure. If that Stored Procedure calls the Connection instance's commit() or rollback() method, your UPDATE will be committed or rolled-back as well. If the Stored Procedure has an exception prior to committing or rolling-back, or simply fails to decide, your UPDATE will be left in limbo until a commit or rollback is performed.

If a Servlet calls a Java Stored Procedure, the same is true – the Stored Procedure inherits the session and transaction state established by the Servlet's Connection object that managed the Stored Procedure call. The Stored Procedure does *not* inherit the client connection's auto-commit setting: it will always execute with auto-commit off. Therefore, if the Servlet's Connection has auto-commit enabled, the database changes performed in the Stored Procedure will be committed as a unit when the statement completes.

The table below summarizes this transaction behavior:

Client auto-commit setting	Stored procedure behavior (i.e. commits/rolls back/neither)	Outcome
true	None	All actions that took place in the Stored Procedure will be committed as a whole when the call to the Stored Procedure returns.
true	Rollback	All uncommitted actions that took place in the Stored Procedure up to the rollback statement will be undone.
		Previous actions initiated in the client are not affected as they were already subject to auto-commit.
true	Commit	Actions in the Stored Procedure up to the commit point are committed.
		No effect on the client.
false	None	Actions in the Stored Procedure are committed if the client explicitly commits or when the connection is closed.
false	Rollback	All uncommitted actions initiated using the client's Connection object since the last commit/rollback point will be rolled back. This potentially includes calls to other Stored Procedures.
false	Commit	All uncommitted actions initiated using the client's Connection object since the last commit or rollback will be committed.

Triggers and Advanced Queuing with Java Stored Procedures

The ability to implement Stored Procedures in Java and call them from a trigger enables us to easily tie together triggers and Oracle Advanced Queuing (AQ) functions.

Consider the following example where an order that exceeds the customer's credit limit gets posted to a queue. The order is still placed in the example. In a more realistic scenario, the order might only get placed if the customer had a certain rank; otherwise it might get placed in a hold state. A possible subscriber to the queue could be a CRM application that would alert the account manager and send an acknowledgement to the customer that the credit issue is being worked on. Note that the example does not take into consideration existing balances; it treats the credit limit as a per-order limit for simplicity.

Setting up the Queue

Firstly we need to set up the Oracle Advanced Queuing environment. We define an Oracle TYPE that encapsulates the credit increase request by executing the DDL statement below from SQL*Plus:

```
CREATE TYPE CustCreditBreach AS OBJECT (
customer_id NUMBER(6),
credit_limit NUMBER(9,2),
credit_gap NUMBER(9,2));
/
```

Next, we need to create a Java class to represent this type in our Java code. We can create this easily using the jpub utility (JPublisher) at the command prompt. jpub is a utility that is installed with the Oracle 8i server and client installations which is used to generate Java or SQLJ source code that is compatible with Oracle object and collection types and packages. In this case, we're using it to quickly generate a Java class that encapsulates the CustCreditBreach Oracle object type.

```
jpub -user=scott/tiger -url=jdbc:oracle:thin:@host:port:SID \
   -sql=SCOTT.CustCreditBreach -case=mixed -usertypes=oracle -methods=none
      -package=com.wrox.example\
```

As used above, jpub will connect to the database specified by the JDBC connection string (specified with −url) as the user specified with -user. Once connected, it locates the Oracle object type CustCreditBreach (specified with −sql) in the SCOTT schema (to access a type defined in a different schema, prefix the type with the schema name, e.g. DEMO.CustCreditBreach). It then creates a directory called com\wrox\examples, and places two generated Java source files in it: CustCreditBreach.java and CustCreditBreachRef.java.

> The **jpub utility uses either the thin or OCI8 JDBC driver to communicate with Oracle, as specified by the JDBC connection string passed as the −url parameter. It also uses the Java class oracle.jpub.java.Main, which is installed by Oracle Univeral Installer as part of SQLJ. jpub relies on the CLASSPATH environment variable to locate these two libraries. Therefore for jpub to run successfully, your CLASSPATH must include <ORACLE_HOME>\jdbc\lib\classes12.zip (or classes111.zip for 8.1.5) and <ORACLE_HOME>\sqlj\lib\translator.zip.**

Thirdly, we'll create a queue table in the SCOTT schema. Note that our payload will be the CustCreditBreach type. That is to say, the queue messages will have the same structure as the CustCreditBreach Oracle object, consisting of three NUMBER variables: customer_id, credit_limit, and credit_gap. To execute the dbms_aqadm.create_queue_table Stored Procedure, the user you connect with must have been granted permission to manage queues. Normally, this is a DBA function. To grant this permission to SCOTT, the SYSTEM or other DBA account must issue the following GRANT:

```
GRANT EXECUTE ON sys.dbms_aqadm to SCOTT;
```

If SCOTT (or whatever user you're connecting as) cannot be granted this privilege, the SYSTEM or other DBA account can still execute the following to create the schema objects required in the SCOTT schema.

```
execute dbms_aqadm.create_queue_table (Queue_table =>
'SCOTT.MultiConsumerMsgs_qtab', Multiple_consumers => TRUE, Queue_payload_type =>
'SCOTT.CustCreditBreach');
```

379

Executing the statement above results in the creation of three database objects in the SCOTT schema:

❑ a view called AQ$MULTICONSUMERMSGS_QTAB

and two tables:

❑ AQ$_MULTICONSUMERMSGS_QTAB_I

❑ MULTICONSUMERMSGS_QTAB

It also writes rows to the:

❑ SYSTEM.AQ$_QUEUES

❑ SYSTEM.AQ$_QUEUE_TABLES tables.

Now, to create and start the queue:

```
EXECUTE dbms_aqadm.create_queue (Queue_name => 'SCOTT.CustCreditBreachQ',
    Queue_table => 'SCOTT.MultiConsumerMsgs_qtab');
```

```
EXECUTE dbms_aqadm.start_queue(queue_name => 'SCOTT.CustCreditBreachQ');
```

One more thing: we need to define at least one subscriber to the queue, otherwise we'll get a "no recipients for message" exception when we try to post to the queue. Paste the following into SQL*Plus:

```
DECLARE
    subscriber sys.aq$_agent;
BEGIN
    subscriber := sys.aq$_agent ('GREEN', null, 0);
    DBMS_AQADM.ADD_SUBSCRIBER(
      queue_name => 'SCOTT.CustCreditBreachQ',
      subscriber => subscriber);
  END;
/
```

Coding the Stored Procedure

The code for the Java Stored Procedure that will post to this queue appears below:

```
package com.wrox.examples;

import java.sql.*;
import oracle.jdbc.driver.*;
import oracle.AQ.*;
import java.math.*;

import com.wrox.examples.CustCreditBreach;

public class CreditManager {

  public static void checkLimit(Integer customerId,
                    Double creditNeeded)
```

```
                      throws Exception
{
   String qry = "SELECT credit_limit FROM demo.customer " +
                "WHERE customer_id = " +
                customerId.toString();

   Connection cn = null;
   PreparedStatement ps = null;
   ResultSet rs = null;

   oracle.AQ.AQSession aqs = null;
   oracle.AQ.AQQueue ccbq = null;
   oracle.AQ.AQMessage ccbm = null;

   CustCreditBreach ccb = null;
   double creditLimit = 0;
   double difference = 0;

   try {
      cn = new OracleDriver().defaultConnection();
      ps = cn.prepareStatement(qry);
      rs = ps.executeQuery();

      if(!rs.next())
         throw(new Exception("Unable to retrieve credit " +
                             "limit for customer "));

      creditLimit = rs.getDouble(1);
      difference = creditNeeded.doubleValue() - creditLimit;

      if(difference > 0)
      {
         // Initialize the message
         ccb = new CustCreditBreach();
         ccb.setCustomerId(
            BigDecimal.valueOf((long)customerId.intValue()));
         ccb.setCreditLimit(new BigDecimal(creditLimit));
         ccb.setCreditGap(new BigDecimal(difference));

         // Get a reference to the Queue
         oracle.AQ.AQDriverManager.registerDriver(
                       new oracle.AQ.AQOracleDriver());
         aqs = AQDriverManager.createAQSession(cn);
         ccbq = aqs.getQueue("scott", "CustCreditBreachQ");

         // Put the message on the queue
         ccbm = ccbq.createMessage();
         ccbm.getMessageProperty().setExpiration(1);
         ccbm.getObjectPayload().setPayloadData(ccb);

         ccbq.enqueue(new AQEnqueueOption(), ccbm);
         cn.commit();

         System.out.println(
                     "Successfully created AQ session");
      }
```

```
        System.out.println("Done");
     }

     finally {
        if(rs != null) rs.close();
        if(ps != null) ps.close();
  }
   }
 }
```

First of all, we have two new imports: `oracle.AQ.*` and `com.wrox.examples.CustCreditBreach`.
The first provides access to the Oracle Advanced Queueing Java package, from which we use the
`AQSession`, `AQQueue`, and `AQMessage` classes. The second imports one of the classes we created
earlier with `jpub`. This is the class that will encapsulate the queue's payload.

There is one method in the `CreditManager` class: `checkLimit`. This method takes two parameters:
`customerId`, which identifiers the customer and `creditNeeded` which specifies how much credit the
customer requires (that is the purchase amount, as we're assuming all purchases are made on credit in
this business-to-business scenario).

Inside `checkLimit()`, we first create a dynamic query that get's the customer's credit limit from the
`DEMO.customer` table. Then, in the try clause, standard JDBC functionality is used to execute the
query and retrieve the credit limit as a `Double`. At that point, the difference between the credit limit
and the amount of credit requested is calculated and stored in the variable `difference`.

If the credit limit would be exceeded (the difference is greater than 0), we need to write a
`CustomerCreditBreach` message to the queue. First of all, a `CustCreditBreach` object is created to
encapsulate the message, then we use the accessor methods that `jpub` generated to set the customer ID,
credit limit, and credit gap fields:

```
ccb = new CustCreditBreach();
ccb.setCustomerId(
        BigDecimal.valueOf((long)customerId.intValue()));
        ccb.setCreditLimit(new BigDecimal(creditLimit));
        ccb.setCreditGap(new BigDecimal(difference));
```

Next, we establish a connection to the queue. There are three steps to this. First, we register the
Advanced Queueing driver:

```
oracle.AQ.AQDriverManager.registerDriver(new oracle.AQ.AQOracleDriver());
```

Then we create an AQ session using the existing JDBC connection:

```
AQDriverManager.createAQSession(cn);
```

Finally, we connect to the `CustCreditBreachQ` queue:

```
ccbq = aqs.getQueue("scott", "CustCreditBreachQ");
```

Now that we have a connection to the queue, we can post a message. The next four statements enable
this. The first creates an `AQMessage` object with the `createMessage()` method of our `AQQueue` object.
The second specifies when the message should expire. The third sets the payload by passing in the
`CustCreditBreach` object. The fourth places the message on the queue.

```
ccbm = ccbq.createMessage();
ccbm.getMessageProperty().setExpiration(1);
ccbm.getObjectPayload().setPayloadData(ccb);
ccbq.enqueue(new AQEnqueueOption(), ccbm);
```

Once the `commit()` method of our JDBC connection is called, the message is queued.

Compiling Using the JDK from the Command Line

To compile successfully, we need to include the Oracle Advanced Queueing Java package in the classpath. If you are using the JDK 1.2 and up, use the package
`<ORACLE_HOME>\RDBMS\jlib\aqapi.jar`. JDK 1.1.x users should use
`<ORACLE_HOME>\RDBMS\jlib\aqapi11.jar`. The following is for JDK 1.2:

```
javac -classpath \
    "<ORACLE_HOME>\jdbc\lib\classes12.zip;<ORACLE_HOME>\RDBMS\jlib\aqapi.jar" \
        -sourcepath "./" CreditManager.java
```

If you executed all the commands without changes, this should result in a new file called `CreditManager.class` in the same directory as `CreditManager.java`, and another called `CustCreditBreach.class` in `com\wrox\examples`.

Loading the Classes and Publishing the Call Spec

This time around, our loading requirements are a little more complex. The Advanced Queuing `oracle.AQ` and JPublisher `oracle.jpub` packages should already be loaded into Oracle. The query shown below should list the contents of the `oracle.AQ` package. If you have any problems the JAR file is `<ORACLE_HOME>/rdbms/jlib/aqapi.jar`. If jpub is not installed for some reason, chances are SQLJ isn't either. The packages for SQLJ and jpub are in `<ORACLE_HOME>\sqlj\lib`.

```
SELECT dbms_java.longname(object_name)
FROM all_objects
WHERE object_type = 'JAVA CLASS'
AND dbms_java.longname(object_name) like '%AQ/%';
```

The classes `CreditManager` and `CustCreditBreach` must be loaded with `loadjava`:

```
loadjava -user scott/tiger@host:port:sid -thin -resolve -verbose \
    com/wrox/examples/CustCreditBreach.class CreditManager.class
```

The call spec is:

```
CREATE OR REPLACE PROCEDURE cmCheckLimit(customerId IN NUMBER,
    creditNeeded IN NUMBER)
AS LANGUAGE JAVA
NAME
'com.wrox.examples.CreditManager.checkLimit(java.lang.Integer, java.lang.Double)';
/
```

Defining the Trigger

Before creating the trigger, we need to connect to SQL*Plus as SCOTT and grant execute permissions on SCOTT.cmCheckLimit to DEMO as follows:

```
GRANT EXECUTE ON cmCheckLimit TO DEMO;
```

The trigger calls cmCheckLimit whenever there is an attempt to update or insert an order. If the order exceeds the credit limit, cmCheckLimit will post a CustCreditBreach message to the queue. To create the trigger connect as DEMO/DEMO and issue the following:

```
CREATE OR REPLACE TRIGGER checkOrder
BEFORE INSERT OR UPDATE OF total ON demo.sales_order
FOR EACH ROW
BEGIN
SCOTT.cmCheckLimit(:new.customer_id, :new.total);
END;
/
```

Testing the Solution

To test the solution, we'll connect to SCOTT and insert some rows into the DEMO.sales_order table. However, to be able to create an AQSession etc., SCOTT needs EXECUTE permission on the SYS.DBMS_AQIN package. On my test Oracle server, the SYSTEM account did not have the right to GRANT this privilege. You may run into the same problem, so I've provided the full SQL*Plus script to rectify this and (finally) give SCOTT execute privileges on DBMS_AQIN:

```
CONNECT SYS/CHANGE_ON_INSTALL
GRANT EXECUTE ON SYS.DBMS_AQIN TO SYSTEM WITH GRANT OPTION;
CONNECT SYSTEM/MANAGER
GRANT EXECUTE ON SYS.DBMS_AQIN TO SCOTT;
```

Also, SCOTT needs INSERT privileges on the DEMO.sales_order table:

```
CONNECT DEMO/DEMO
GRANT INSERT ON sales_order TO SCOTT;
```

To test the trigger/Java Stored Procedure combo, let's insert some rows. Customer 227, "The Tour", has a per-order credit limit of 5000. Executing the two inserts below should create one order that breaches the credit limit, and one that doesn't:

```
insert into DEMO.sales_order (select max(order_id) + 1, sysdate, \
    227, NULL, 495000 FROM DEMO.sales_order);
```

```
insert into DEMO.sales_order (select max(order_id) + 1, sysdate, \
    227, NULL, 4000 FROM DEMO.sales_order);
```

Once you've inserted a couple of rows that do and don't exceed the customer's credit limit, you can query the SCOTT.AQ$MULTICONSUMERMSGS_QTAB view to see the messages that have been queued:

```
SELECT queue, expiration, user_data FROM AQ$MULTICONSUMERMSGS_QTAB;
```

Results in my database were:

```
QUEUE                   EXPIRATION    USER_DATA(CUSTOMER_ID, CREDIT_LIMIT, CREDIT_GAP)
-----------------------------------------------------------------------------
CUSTCREDITBREACHQ    1               CUSTCREDITBREACH(227, 5000, 495000)
CUSTCREDITBREACHQ    1               CUSTCREDITBREACH(227, 5000, 5000)
```

Returning Query Results as XML

Returning query results in XML format means that virtually any client software on any platform can read and manipulate the results information without having to deal with the limitations and intricacies of data access APIs like JDBC, ODBC, ADO, etc.

This simple example demonstrates how to use an OracleXMLQuery object (in package oracle.xml.sql.query) to format query results to be returned by a Java Stored Procedure. The OracleXMLQuery class is a part of the Oracle XML SQL Utility (XSU) product, currently available for download from Oracle Technology Network. Pay close attention to the version information; you want the correct download depending on whether you're running Oracle 8.1.5 or 8.1.6.

> **Instructions on how to load the XSU classes into the database are provided with the download, and it's highly recommended that you read them. Below is a summary of the steps required.**

Installing XSU

The directory into which you extracted the contents of the XSU archive will be referred to as <XSU_DIR>. These instructions are for XSU version 1.2.0.

The first step is to make sure your ORACLE_HOME environment variable is set properly. The next step, which is to edit, then execute <XSU_DIR>\env.bat (or env.sh), requires that ORACLE_HOME is properly set.

Edit env.bat or env.sh, changing the value that is assigned to environment variable PD. For example, for Windows platforms, change:

```
set PD=C:\downloads\OracleXSU%JDBCVER%
```

To the command below, substituting the XSU install directory for <XSU_DIR>:

```
set PD=<XSU_DIR>
```

Also in env.bat or env.sh, set the JAVA_HOME and JDKVER environment variables to the directory in which you installed the JDK and the appropriate version. For example, on a Windows machine with the JDK version 1.2.2 installed in C:\jdk1.2.2, change:

```
set JDKVER=1.2
set JAVA_HOME=C:\JDK${JDKVER}
```

to:

```
set JDKVER=1.2.2
set JAVA_HOME=C:\jdk1.2.2
```

> Note that as of this writing, there is a bug in the Windows **env.bat** script where
> **${JDKVER}** is used instead of **%JDKVER%**.

Next, if you want to load XSU into any schema **other than** the SCOTT schema, edit
<XSU_DIR>/oraclexmlsqlload.bat (or oraclexmlsqlload.csh), and change the
USER_PASSWORD environment variable appropriately. The example assumes that you installed the
packages into a schema called XSU.

Finally, on the command line run <XSU_DIR>\env.bat or env.sh, then navigate to the
<XSU_DIR>/lib directory and run oraclexmlsqlload.bat or oraclexmlsqlload.sh.

This script will initiate the extensive procedure of loading and resolving the XSU and Oracle XML
Parser Java packages.

Coding the Customer Class

Here's the class definition:

```java
package com.wrox.examples;

import java.sql.*;
import oracle.jdbc.driver.*;
import oracle.xml.sql.query.OracleXMLQuery;

public class Customer {

  public static String getCustomers()
            throws Exception
  {

    String qry = "SELECT customer_id, name, address, " +
            "city, state, zip_code, area_code, " +
            "phone_number, salesperson_id, " +
            "credit_limit FROM demo.customer";

    String xmlOutput = null;
    Connection cn = null;

    try {
      cn = new OracleDriver().defaultConnection();

      OracleXMLQuery oxq = new OracleXMLQuery(cn, qry);

      oxq.setRowsetTag("Customers");
      oxq.setRowTag("Customer");
      oxq.setMaxRows(5);
      return oxq.getXMLString();
    }

    finally {
  }
 }
}
```

The Customer class starts with the usual JDBC imports followed by an import of the OracleXMLQuery class which is part of the XSU package. Customer has one method: getCustomers(), which retrieves a simple customer list and returns it as an XML string.

The XSU processing begins with the creation of an OracleXMLQuery object. The JDBC connection and query string that we want to execute are passed to the constructor, thus:

```
OracleXMLQuery oxq = new OracleXMLQuery(cn, qry);
```

This prepares the oxq object to execute our SELECT on our database connection. Next, we manipulate the format of the XML document that it will generate using three methods: setRowsetTag specifies the XML tag that is to enclose the entire document; setRowTag specifies the enclosing tag for each row returned by the query; setMaxRows places a limit on the amount of rows returned. Finally, the query is executed with getXMLString(), which returns the results in an XML string formatted as specified.

Compiling and Deploying the Customer Class

To compile, we need to include the Oracle JDBC drivers and XSU package in the classpath as follows:

```
javac -classpath "<ORACLE_HOME>/jdbc/lib/classes12.zip;<XSU_DIR>/lib/xsu12.jar" \
    Customer.java
```

I used a resolver spec, since I loaded the Oracle XML SQL Utility into a schema XSU to keep it separate:

```
loadjava -thin -user scott/tiger@host:port:sid -resolve \
    -resolver "((* xsu)(* scott)(* sys))" -verbose Customer.class


CREATE OR REPLACE FUNCTION getCustomers RETURN VARCHAR2
AS LANGUAGE JAVA
NAME
'com.wrox.examples.Customer.getCustomers() return java.lang.String';
/
```

A subset of the results of a simple test using SELECT getCustomers() FROM dual; is shown below:

```
<?xml version = '1.0'?>
<Customers>
    <Customer num="1">
        <CUSTOMER_ID>100</CUSTOMER_ID>
        <NAME>JOCKSPORTS</NAME>
        <ADDRESS>345 VIEWRIDGE</ADDRESS>
        <CITY>BELMONT</CITY>
        <STATE>CA</STATE>
        <ZIP_CODE>96711</ZIP_CODE>
        <AREA_CODE>415</AREA_CODE>
        <PHONE_NUMBER>5986609</PHONE_NUMBER>
        <SALESPERSON_ID>7844</SALESPERSON_ID>
        <CREDIT_LIMIT>5000</CREDIT_LIMIT>
    </Customer>
    <Customer num="2">
        <CUSTOMER_ID>101</CUSTOMER_ID>
        <NAME>TKB SPORT SHOP</NAME>
```

```
        <ADDRESS>490 BOLI RD.</ADDRESS>
        <CITY>REDWOOD CITY</CITY>
        <STATE>CA</STATE>
        <ZIP_CODE>94061</ZIP_CODE>
        <AREA_CODE>415</AREA_CODE>
        <PHONE_NUMBER>3681223</PHONE_NUMBER>
        <SALESPERSON_ID>7521</SALESPERSON_ID>
        <CREDIT_LIMIT>10000</CREDIT_LIMIT>
    </Customer>
</Customers>
```

DML Operations in XML

Stored procedures are frequently used to manage INSERTs and UPDATEs. Typically, the stored procedure is passed a set of parameters, each of which corresponds to a table column. As the table columns change, the Stored Procedure parameters change, and the procedure must be recompiled. Using XML to describe the table data to be inserted or updated in tandem with the OracleXMLSave class's DML capability provides a more flexible solution:

```
package com.wrox.examples;

import java.sql.*;
import oracle.jdbc.driver.*;
import oracle.xml.sql.dml.OracleXMLSave;

public class Department {

  public static void insertDepartment(String deptDataXML)
                   throws Exception
  {
    String tableName = "demo.department";
    Connection cn = null;
    OracleXMLSave savemgr = null;

    try {
      cn = new OracleDriver().defaultConnection();
      savemgr = new OracleXMLSave(cn, tableName);
      savemgr.setRowTag("DEPARTMENT");
      savemgr.insertXML(deptDataXML);
    }

    finally {
    }
  }
}
```

To compile, we need both the XSU and XML Parser packages in the classpath:

```
javac -classpath "<ORACLE_HOME>/jdbc/lib/classes12.zip; \
   <XSU_DIR>/lib/xsu12.jar;<XSU_DIR>/lib/xmlparserv2.jar" Department.java
```

Deployment again requires a resolver spec if the XSU packages were installed into a schema other than SCOTT (in this case schema XSU):

```
loadjava -thin -user scott/tiger@host:port:sid -resolve \
    -resolver "((* xsu)(* scott)(* sys))" -verbose Department.class


CREATE PROCEDURE insertDepartment(deptDataXML VARCHAR2)
AS LANGUAGE JAVA
NAME
'com.wrox.examples.Department.insertDepartment(java.lang.String)';
/
```

The method Department.insertDepartment in this example accepts an XML document corresponding (as far as Oracle XML SQL Utility is concerned) to the DEMO.department table, and inserts the data using the Oracle XMLSave.insertXML() method. The client, likely some business-tier object, would construct this document by transforming the business-tier XML representation of the department using XSLT.

Sometimes, though, there are different INSERT scenarios in a solution. For example, in our contrived scenario, a new department might be added to the database with a location_id, and also without a location_id (for example, if the department has been established but not situated). You can pass any subset of the columns to OracleXMLSave, and as long as you don't violate any constraints it will insert only the columns you specified. In that way, it is left up to the business tier to decide which combinations of inserted columns meet or violate the business rules, but the data-tier retains the responsibility of maintaining data integrity. Here are some example calls to show the Stored Procedure in action:

If testing the procedure as SCOTT, user SCOTT needs INSERT privileges on DEMO.department:

```
GRANT INSERT ON department TO SCOTT;
```

A call with all three columns:

```
CALL insertDepartment(
  '<?xml version="1.0"?>
  <DEPARTMENT>
    <DEPARTMENT_ID>51</DEPARTMENT_ID>
    <NAME>IT</NAME>
    <LOCATION_ID>124</LOCATION_ID>
  </DEPARTMENT>');
```

A call with two columns:

```
CALL insertDepartment(
  '<?xml version="1.0"?>
  <DEPARTMENT>
    <DEPARTMENT_ID>54</DEPARTMENT_ID>
    <NAME>IT</NAME>
  </DEPARTMENT>');
```

A call without a primary key will fail:

```
CALL insertDepartment(
  '<?xml version="1.0"?>
   <DEPARTMENT>
     <NAME>IT</NAME>
   </DEPARTMENT>');
```

The following exception will be thrown:

```
ERROR at line 1:
ORA-29532: Java call terminated by uncaught Java exception:
oracle.xml.sql.OracleXMLSQLException:
Exception 'oracle.jdbc.driver.OracleSQLException:ORA-01400:
cannot insert NULL into ("DEMO"."DEPARTMENT"."DEPARTMENT_ID")'
encountered during processing ROW element 1
All prior XML row changes were rolled back. in the XML
document.
```

System Architecture Considerations

Based on the features and relative performance of the Oracle 8i implementation of Java Stored Procedures, we can derive some guidelines regarding their use.

Performance

To start with, for heavily iterative data access operations, PL/SQL Stored Procedures can be expected to perform considerably better than their Java counterparts. However, systems typically have both heavy duty and light to medium duty SQL operations to support. The performance burden of implementing relatively light duty data access is minimal. Part of the reason for this is that the data access layer (JDBC and SQLJ) has been optimized via native compilation with NCOMP. The other half is, of course, the availability of the server-side embedded JDBC driver.

In addition, SQL operations may improve in performance dramatically when they are moved from a remote application server to the Oracle 8i Java Virtual Machine. If these operations were originally implemented in Java, the complexity of migrating the functionality to Stored Procedures is greatly reduced.

In addition to the obvious issues like number of user sessions to be supported and the number of Java classes being accessed, the memory footprint required to run Java in the server depends on the server configuration (Dedicated versus Multi-Threaded Server), and what kinds of Java components are being run. EJBs and CORBA components place considerably higher memory demands than Java Stored Procedures, for example. The store of memory dedicated to Java components is called Java Pool Memory. To see the current Java Pool utilization you can use:

```
select * from v$sgastat where pool = 'java pool';
```

Features

Theoretically, Stored Procedures implemented in Java have a vast, rich set of reusable classes to draw on to accomplish tasks. Realistically, though, Stored Procedures are primarily concerned with getting data into and out of database structures. When it comes to features for managing data, transaction support, and performance tweaking, PL/SQL is the choice platform.

Looking forward, more and more application component interfaces are going to employ XML. As it is, PL/SQL is arguably far less elegant and more unwieldy than Java. Java can be leveraged for faster implementations, especially as more APIs (like those supporting XML) are introduced into the mix. Excellent IDEs are available for Java, excellent modeling and documentation interfaces exist for Java, and the Java package construct means that Java source and binaries are far easier to manage and track. Anyone who's had to manage hundreds of PL/SQL procedures in a dozen-odd packages will know what I'm getting at.

Summary

All things considered, implementing the data-tier in Stored Procedures in Oracle 8i is probably best served by a hybrid of PL/SQL and Java. Either implementation can call on the other to perform its best work, there's no reason to reject one or the other. For example, if a data-intensive data-tier operation also requires several calls to functionality in a JDK, Oracle XML, or other Java API, embed the Java calls in a Java Stored Procedure and call them from the PL/SQL implementation.

The examples in this chapter use Oracle-supplied utilities like the Oracle XML SQL Utility and Oracle Advanced Queuing API. These utilities also have PL/SQL APIs. Choosing the PL/SQL APIs may provide better performance today at the expense of greater maintainability and portability in the future. Third-party utilities (third-party tools for XML/SQL manipulation, for example), on the other hand, do not typically ship with PL/SQL APIs. With the Oracle JVM that large, competitive marketplace is now available to Oracle developers for use on all tiers.

ORACLE8iAPPLICATIONPROGRAMMING

12

Oracle Access with JDBC

Java is designed to be platform independent. A pure Java program written for a Windows machine will run without recompilation on a Solaris Sparc, an Apple Macintosh, or any platform with the appropriate Java virtual machine.

JDBC extends this to databases. If you write a Java program with JDBC, given the appropriate database driver, that program will run against any database without having to recompile the Java code. Without JDBC, your Java code would need to run platform specific native database code, thus violating the Java motto, *Write Once, Run Anywhere.*

JDBC allows you to write Java code, and leave the platform (database) specific code to the driver. In the event you change databases, you simply change the driver used by your Java code and you are immediately ready to run against the new database.

This chapter will present a tour of using JDBC code to access and use the data in an Oracle database. Some information in this chapter will apply to both the original JDBC specification, which will be referred to as JDBC 1.0, and the current specification, JDBC 2.0. Other information in this chapter is JDBC 2.0 specific. Finally, Oracle has implemented some JDBC 2.0 features using Oracle extensions to the JDBC 1.0 specification. The text will indicate when a feature is an Oracle extension to JDBC 1.0, or a feature that is specific to JDBC 2.0. If neither is indicated, then the information applies to both JDBC versions.

The JDBC API specification can be found at
http://java.sun.com/j2se/1.3/docs/guide/jdbc/index.html.

The following topics are covered in this chapter:

❑ Registering a driver

❑ Connecting to a database and sending SQL statements to a database

❑ Retrieving and modifying data using a result set

❑ Reading and writing BLOBs, CLOBs, and BFILES

❑ Using a `DataSource` object to get a database connection

Driver Types

As mentioned in the introduction, your Java JDBC code is portable because the database specific code is contained in a Java class known as the driver. The two most common kinds of driver for connecting to an Oracle database are the thin driver and the OCI driver.

The thin driver is known as a Type IV driver; it is a pure Java driver that connects to a database using the database's native protocol. While you can use the thin driver in any environment, the Type IV driver is intended for use in Java applets and other client-side programs. A Java client can be run on any platform. For that reason, the JDBC driver downloaded with an applet or used by a Java client may not have access to platform native code and must be pure Java.

The OCI8 driver is known as a Type II driver. It uses platform native code (contained in `ocijdbc8.dll` for Windows) to call the database. Because it uses a native API, it can connect to and access a database faster than the thin driver. For the same reason, the Type II driver cannot be used where the program does not have access to the native API. This usually applies to applets and other client programs which may be deployed on any arbitrary platform.

Sun's Java web site maintains a database of JDBC drivers. They list 122 drivers for various databases in their driver database; 25 of them are Type II drivers, 67 of them are Type IV drivers. For more information on JDBC drivers, check http://java.sun.com/products/jdbc/drivers or the Oracle8i JDBC Developer's Guide and Reference, which can be found with your Oracle installation or at http://technet.oracle.com.

Installing JDBC

In the following sections you will learn how to get a driver for your development environment, where to put the driver in your system, and how to configure your system.

Where to Get Drivers

If your development computer includes an Oracle distribution, or has network access to an Oracle distribution, you may already have access to the JDBC drivers. The Oracle JDBC 1.0 drivers are in a Java archive file named `classes111.zip`. The JDBC 2.0 drivers are in a file named `classes12.zip`. They are normally located in the `<ORACLE_HOME>\jdbc\lib` directory.

The basic JDBC driver files support NLS characters in the Oracle character set. Support for other character sets is provided in another Java archive. The NLS files are named similarly to the JDBC driver files: `nls_charset11.zip` for JDBC 1.0 and `nls_charset12.zip` for JDBC 2.0. These files are to be found in the same location as `classes111.zip` and `classes12.zip`.

If the driver files are already loaded on your system, you can go to the next section. If you do not have local or network access to the drivers, but you do have access to an Oracle distribution, you can install the driver files from the CD. Perform a custom installation and select the JDBC driver files from the list of available components.

If you don't have a distribution CD, you can download the appropriate driver files from Oracle at http://technet.oracle.com/software/.

> At the time this chapter was written, when you download the driver files, they have a slightly different name than those given in this section. For instance, `classes12.zip` is downloaded as `classes12_01.zip`. As part of the download, rename the file to `classes12.zip`. Once the file is downloaded, do NOT unzip this file. The same applies to the NLS file: rename `nls_charset12_01.zip` to `nls_charset12.zip` when you download it. If you do not rename it at download time, you can easily rename it later.

If you have Oracle installed on your computer, download the files to `<ORACLE_HOME>\jdbc\lib`. If you do not have an Oracle directory, you can create one for the JDBC files. Alternately, if you have JDK 1.1, you could download the files to `<JAVA_HOME>\lib`. If you have Java 2, see the next section.

Installing the Oracle JDBC Classes

After you've put the class file archive (say `classes12.zip`) into a directory as explained in the previous section, half the installation is complete. The other half of installation is to change the classpath environment variable to include the directory where the class file archive is located.

Putting `<ORACLE_HOME>` for the location of your Oracle home directory, and assuming that you are using a Java 2 compiler with the JDBC 2.0 driver, add `<ORACLE_HOME>\jdbc\lib\classes12.zip` to the `CLASSPATH` environment variable. For a Unix installation, add `<ORACLE_HOME>/jdbc/lib/classes12.zip` to the `classpath variable`. If you need full NLS character set support using the `nls_charset12.zip` archive, add that file to the classpath in the same manner.

> For archives (`.jar` or `.zip` files) the entire path and file name must be part of the classpath setting.

If you are using JDK 1.2, you can avoid having to change the classpath by copying the driver files to the Java development extension directory at `<JAVA_HOME>\jre\lib\ext\`. The classpath environment variable does not need to include classes in the extension directory. The Java virtual machine automatically uses class files in the extension directory. When you deliver your Java application, the target computer will likely not have a JDK installed and it will run Java programs using the Java Runtime Environment (JRE); for this situation, the `classes12.zip` file should be placed in the `<JAVA_HOME>\lib\ext` directory.

For example, assume that you have JDK 1.2 installed in your development environment into `C:\java\jdk1.2`. Then for development, copy the driver files to `C:\java\jdk1.2\jre\lib\ext\`. On my home computer, the JRE is installed at `C:\Program Files\JavaSoft\JRE`, so if your application were to be installed onto my computer, you would ensure that the driver files were copied to `C:\Program Files\JavaSoft\JRE\1.2\lib\ext\`.

On a Unix development system, you may have the JDK 1.2 installed at `/usr/java1.2`. The driver files would be installed in `/usr/java1.2/jre/lib/ext`. For a delivery system, if the JRE is installed at `/usr/jre` for example, you would copy the driver files to `/usr/jre/lib/ext`.

If you cannot put the driver files into the extension directory, you can, of course, change the classpath just as is done for Java 1.1 environments.

The other change you may need to make to your environment is to change the `PATH` environment variable in Windows (`LD_LIBRARY_PATH` for Unix). If you are using an OCI8 (Type II) driver, then the native code shared library must be accessible to Java. The shared library is called `ocijdbc8.dll` for Windows and `libocijdbc8.so` for Unix. It will be located in `<ORACLE_HOME>/lib`. Add this directory to your `PATH` or `LD_LIBRARY_PATH` environment variable.

The shared library file can be downloaded from Oracle from the same location as the JDBC archive `classesnnn.zip`.

Finally, if you are using the thin (Type IV) driver, a TNS (Transparent Network Substrate) listener must be configured and running on the database server host machine.

The database administrator for the database will be able to tell you on which machine the database resides and configure the listener for you. If you need to do this yourself, information on configuring a listener can be found in the Net8 Administrator's Guide, supplied with your Oracle installation or at http://technet.oracle.com.

Java Requirements

To use the JDBC drivers, you will need one required Java package and one optional Java package: The required package is the java.sql package. This package comes standard with the JDK 1.1 onwards. If you are using the JDBC 2.0 driver from Oracle, you may also want to get the Java extension package `javax.sql`.

The optional package `javax.sql` contains additional classes needed for some JDBC 2.0 features. The two significant features of the package are the interfaces `DataSource` and `RowSet`. The `DataSource` object provides a distributed method for obtaining database connections. A database client can access a datasource via a naming service over a network and obtain a connection object from the `DataSource`. The `RowSet` object is a `ResultSet`, because it implements the `ResultSet` interface; however, it can also be used as a JavaBean component. At the time this chapter was written, Oracle's JDBC driver did not provide an implementation for `RowSet`, so it will not be discussed in this chapter. Datasources are discussed in the Advanced Topics section at the end of the chapter.

The package `javax.sql` comes with the Java 2 SDK Enterprise Edition. You can get it by downloading the Java 2 SDK Enterprise Edition, or you can download the package separately from the Java web site at http://java.sun.com/products/jdbc/download.html. The downloaded Java archive should be put into the JRE extension directory as explained above.

Checking Your Installation

When you have the driver files in place and the classpath and path set, create the following simple Java file TestJdbc.java in a new directory jdbc\driverTest:

```
package jdbc.driverTest;

import java.sql.*;

public class TestJdbc {
  public TestJdbc() {
    try {
      DriverManager.registerDriver(new oracle.jdbc.driver.OracleDriver());
    } catch (Exception e) {}
  }
}
```

Save and compile the file. If the drivers are installed correctly, and your environment is properly configured, the program will compile with no errors. If your installation is incorrect, you will see something like the following:

```
C:\java\projects>c:\java\jdk1.1\bin\javac jdbc\driverTest\TestJdbc.java
TestJdbc.java:5: Class oracle.jdbc.driver.OracleDriver not found in type
declaration.
        DriverManager.registerDriver(new oracle.jdbc.driver.OracleDriver());
                                                                  ^
1 error
```

There are two possible causes for the error message above. Check and correct as necessary:

❑ The driver file does not exist on your development system. Check for the existence of the file named classes111.zip or classes12.zip. If the file does not exist on the system, reinstall it as described above.

❑ The driver file exists on your system, but the classpath does not point to it. Either adjust the classpath to include the driver file (remember to include the path **and** file name); or, if you are using Java 2, move the driver files to the JRE extension directory. (Also recall you should normally include the path '.' in your classpath; this points to the current working directory.)

> The example classes in this chapter are declared to be part of a package with a name that starts with **jdbc**. For example, the **TestJdbc** class above is declared to be in the package **jdbc.driverTest**. This means that the source file should be saved as **jdbc\driverTest\TestJdbc.java**.

JDBC Basics

All Java database programs (programs that access and use a database), whether they consist of one class or dozens of classes, perform their work in three fundamental steps. Those steps are

- ❑ Loading a driver and making a connection to the database
- ❑ Executing an SQL statement against tables
- ❑ Accessing and using the results of the SQL statement

Database Connections

Accessing a database involves loading a driver class, and then using the driver to connect to the database. In JDBC 2.0, another method of obtaining a connection was introduced. This method, part of the JDBC extension javax.sql, involves getting a reference to a DataSource object, and getting the connection from the DataSource object. The DataSource object will be discussed this later in this chapter.

Loading a Driver

The first step to making a connection to the database is to load the driver. There are several ways to load the driver:

- ❑ You can load the driver within your code using Class.forName(String).
- ❑ You can have the DriverManager automatically load drivers specified using a System property.
- ❑ You can directly register the driver using the DriverManager method registerDriver(Driver).

Using Class.forName

The first method uses the method forName(String) from java.lang.Class. Calling forName(String) instructs the Java virtual machine to find, load, and link the class file identified by the String parameter. The linking of the class causes any static initialization blocks to be executed. Inside this initialization block, the driver class calls the DriverManager.RegisterDriver(Driver) method.

> *A static initialization block is a block of Java statements beginning with the static keyword, for example:*
> ```
> public class MyDriverClass {
>    static{
>        DriverManager.registerDriver(new MyDriverClass());
>    }
> }
> ```
> *The static block (or each static block if there are several within the class) is called only once the first time the class is referenced. It is used to perform one-time initialization for the class. Note that inside the static block, one can only reference static variables or call static methods.*

The class name used for the Oracle driver in both JDBC 1.0 and JDBC 2.0 is oracle.jdbc.driver.OracleDriver. Here's an example of using the forName(String) method. Start by creating and compiling a prototyping class to hold variables needed by the driver:

```
public class DriverData {
  public static String url = "jdbc:oracle:thin:@dbserver:1521:proead";
  public static String user = "scott";
  public static String passw = "tiger";
}
```

We will use this class as a simplified method of sharing connection information between the applications in this chapter. In the class above, set the values of the variables url, user, and passw with strings appropriate for your system. The url part will be discussed in detail later in this chapter. For now, the three parameters dbserver, 1521, and proead, need to be replaced with values for your system as follows:

❑   dbserver is the hostname of the database server.

❑   1521 is the port number where the database listens for connections; 1521 is the Oracle default. Consult your DBA to determine if your system uses 1521 or a different port.

❑   proead is the Local Service Name (or SID prior to 8.1.6) for the required database instance.

Here is the class that actually loads the driver and then attempts to connect to the database to determine if the driver was correctly loaded:

```
package jdbc.driverLoader;

import java.sql.*;
import DriverData;

/** Load a jdbc driver using Class.forName() */
public class ForNameLoader {
  public static void main(String[] args) {
    try {
      Class.forName("oracle.jdbc.driver.OracleDriver");
      //check the driver by trying to get a connection
      Connection conn = DriverManager.getConnection(DriverData.url,
                        DriverData.user, DriverData.passw);
      if (conn != null) {
        System.out.println("Driver loaded: Connection made to db.");
      } else {
        System.out.println("No Connection to db. Driver problem.");
      }
    } catch (Exception e) {
        e.printStackTrace();
    }
  }
}
```

The class above is in the package jdbc.driverLoader so you need to save it in the directory jdbc\driverLoader as ForNameLoader.java. The DriverData class is not in any package, so it can be placed in any directory that is in the classpath. Compile both files and then run the ForNameLoader class.

Using a System Property

When the DriverManager is first referenced, it looks for a java.lang.System property with the name jdbc.drivers. If it finds this property, it attempts to load each driver listed in the property. To use this technique, you can create a property file with a line similar to the following:

```
jdbc.drivers=jdbc.oracle.driver.OracleDriver:com.dataSolutions.driver.Driver:com.x
teligent.DBDriver
```

Each driver is listed by full package specification and class name. Note in the example above that several drivers are specified in the same `jdbc.drivers` property (although only the Oracle driver is real; the other two names are fictitious and are used only to illustrate how to specify multiple drivers). A colon separates each driver. If you already have a properties file for your program, add the line to that file. For the next example, create a property file named `Larch.properties` that contains the single line:

```
jdbc.drivers=jdbc.oracle.driver.OracleDriver
```

Next, inside your application, you would load the properties and set the `System` property. Assume for this example that your application main class is called `Larch`, and you are going to set additional system properties in the constructor. The properties file is called `Larch.properties`, and the properties file is accessible to the `Larch` class:

```java
package jdbc.propertyLoader;

import java.sql.*;
import java.io.*;
import java.util.*;
import DriverData;

/**
 * A class that demonstrates loading the driver using a System property.
 * To load the driver using a property file, start the program and provide
 * the name of the property file as a command line parameter like this:
 *    java jdbc.propertyLoader.Larch Larch.properties
 * To use just the filename, the directory where the properties file is
 * located must be the current directory. If you run from another
 * directory, use the full path and filename for the file
 *
 * To load the driver using the JVM option -D, start the program like this:
 *    java -Djdbc.drivers=oracle.jdbc.driver.OracleDriver
 *         jdbc.propertyLoader.Larch
 */
public class Larch {
  public static void main(String[] args) {
    try {
      if (args.length > 0) {
        //the command line argument is the name of the property file
        //System.getProperties() gets the System Properties object,
        // the load(InputStream) method loads properties from the file
        System.getProperties().load(new FileInputStream(args[0]));
        System.out.println("Loaded driver " +
                    System.getProperty("jdbc.drivers") +
                    " from Larch.properties");
      } else {
        //if no command line argument, then assume the System property set
        //on command line using -D option
        System.out.println("Loaded driver " +
                    System.getProperty("jdbc.drivers") +
                    " from -D option");
      }
```

```
        Connection conn = DriverManager.getConnection(
          DriverData.url,DriverData.user,DriverData.passw);
        if (conn != null) {
          System.out.println("Driver loaded: Connection made to db.");
        } else {
          System.out.println("NO Connection to db. Driver problem.");
        }

      } catch (Exception e) {
        e.printStackTrace();
      }
    }
  }
```

Alternatively, as mentioned in a comment in the code above, you can specify a system property on the command line with the -D option:

```
java -Djava.drivers=jdbc.oracle.drivers.OracleDriver Larch
```

Specifying the property on the command line causes the virtual machine to set the property at startup, without your code needing to open and set properties from a property file. The first time you call a DriverManager method, getConnection() for instance, the DriverManager will look for the system property. If it finds the property, it will attempt to load and link each driver.

Using registerDriver(Driver)

Oracle recommends using the following method for loading the driver:

```
DriverManager.registerDriver(new oracle.jdbc.driver.OracleDriver());
```

> **Almost every JDBC method can throw an SQLException. For the sake of brevity, the code snippet above and every other code snippet in this chapter does not show the try-catch block for this exception. However, try-catch blocks are included in the source code listings for Java classes, and you will need to include the blocks in your code.**

This technique is illustrated in the TestJdbc class earlier in the chapter. There are at least two reasons for using this technique. First, there is a bug in the JDK 1.1.x virtual machine (http://java.sun.com/products/jdbc/faq.html#13) that sometimes prevents the static initialization block from executing when the class is loaded when using Class.forName(String). If you are using JDK 1.1, you may want to use registerDriver(Driver) or one of the techniques from this section other than Class.forName(String) to load the driver.

The other reason again has to do with the Class.forName(String) method. The Microsoft Java Virtual Machine does not correctly initialize a class when loading it with Class.forName(String). So if you are using a Microsoft Virtual Machine (for instance, any applet running in Internet Explorer), use the registerDriver(Driver) technique or the System property technique for loading the driver.

The Right Way

Given the methods above, which is the right way? If you are using JDK 1.1 or want to ensure that your code works in all environments, you should use the `registerDriver(Driver)` method. On the other hand, using `registerDriver(Driver)` makes the class less portable. If you use `registerDriver(Driver)` in your code, then if someone ever needs to use a different driver, that other user would need access to your source code so that they could edit and recompile the class to use the new driver. If you are concerned about portability, you should avoid using `registerDriver(Driver)`.

If your project is using Enterprise JavaBeans, or has decided to use the JDBC 2.0 optional package, then you should disregard the methods above and use a `DataSource` object to get the connection. With this method, there is no need for your code to load the driver; loading the driver is handled by the datasource. `DataSource` objects will be discussed later in this chapter.

Getting a Connection

Once the driver is registered, you use the `getConnection()` method of `DriverManager` to actually make the connection. There are several versions of the `getConnection()` method:

- ❏ `public static synchronized Connection getConnection(String url) throws SQLException`

- ❏ `public static synchronized Connection getConnection(String url, String user, String password) throws SQLException`

- ❏ `public static synchronized Connection getConnection(String url, Properties info) throws SQLException`

All three method calls use a `url` parameter. The URL generally takes the form:

```
protocol:subprotocol:subname
```

- ❏ `protocol`
  Always `jdbc`

- ❏ `subprotocol`
  Substring used by the `DriverManager` to select the correct driver from the registered drivers

- ❏ `subname`
  Varies by driver. The subname usually consists of additional information for the driver or database server. With oracle, the subname is of the form `<drivertype>:@<database>`. This chapter uses only the Type II and Type IV drivers, so drivertype is either `thin` or `oci8`. The `<database>` parameter must be a string in one of the following forms:

  a. a Net8 keyword-value pair

  b. a string of the form `<host_name>:<port_number>:<SID>` (thin driver only)

  c. a TNSNAMES entry (OCI driver only)

Here are some example URLs for the Oracle driver. This URL uses the JDBC thin driver to connect to a database on the same machine (`localhost`); the connection listener is listening to port 1521, and the Oracle SID is `orcl`:

```
jdbc:oracle:thin:@localhost:1521:orcl
```

This URL uses the OCI8 driver to connect to a database:

```
jdbc:oracle:oci8:@
```

If you are using the getConnection(String) method, the URL must be of the form:

```
jdbc:oracle:<type>:<username>/<password>@<host>
```

You can also specify connection parameters in a properties file and pass the Properties object to the connect method. The Oracle driver looks for any of the following properties in the Properties object:

Property Name	Property Value Type	Property Description
user	String	The user name for logging into the database.
password	String	The password for logging into the database.
database or server	String	The connect string for the database as described in the bullet for subname above.
defaultRowPrefetch or prefetch	int	The default number of rows to prefetch from the server. The default value is 10.
remarksReporting or remarks	boolean	true if getTables() and getColumns() should report TABLE_REMARKS; equivalent to using setRemarksReporting(). The default value is false.
defaultBatchValue or batchvalue	int	The default batch value that triggers an execution request. The default value is 10. See the section on Oracle update batching below.

After getting a Connection object, you can use the Connection object to send SQL statements to the database. You send SQL statements to the database using an instance of a statement object.

Commit and Rollback

When you open a connection to an Oracle database, that connection starts in a state that is known as autocommit enabled. That means that every statement that is sent to the database is executed by the database and then, if appropriate, immediately committed. In this situation, each statement sent to the database is a discrete transaction.

Transactions can also consist of multiple statements. You can send any number of statements to the database where each one is executed, but nothing is committed. When you are ready, you can explicitly commit or rollback all the statements with a method call of the Connection class. To accomplish this, you set the autocommit mode to false (this disables autocommit). The method used to commit the changes to the database is commit(). Here is a code snippet illustrating this:

```
//disable autocommit
connection.setAutoCommit(false);
//execute one or more SQL statements, then commit all changes
connection.commit();
```

Closing the *connection* with the `close()` method will also cause any changes to be committed. Closing the *statement* will not commit the changes. Changes that have not been committed can be rolled back with the `rollback()` method:

```
//statements have been sent to the database but there was some problem,
//so rollback the changes
connection.rollback();
```

Closing a Connection

If your explicitly obtained a connection to the database, then your code should explicitly close the database connection. This frees the database resources so other code or programs can use them. The connection is closed with the `close()` method:

```
connection.close();
```

If you got a connection from a connection pool, you may or may not need to call the `close()` method. Consult the documentation for the connection pool to determine whether or not to call `close()`.

Statements

Once you have a connection to the database, you can interact with the database. The `java.sql.Statement` object, or one of its subclasses, the `java.sql.PreparedStatement` or the `java.sql.CallableStatement`, handles this interaction.

There are six methods for creating statements, two methods for each of the three kinds of statements. Those methods are:

❑   `createStatement()` and `createStatement(int, int)` for `Statement`

❑   `prepareStatement(String)` and `prepareStatement(int, int, String)` for `PreparedStatement`

❑   `prepareCall(String)` and `prepareCall(int, int, String)`.

You will notice that of the six methods, three methods take int parameters and three do not. The int parameters are used by the `Statement` objects to control the kind of resultset obtained when the database is queried.

> *In several places, this section on statements mentions a Java interface named `ResultSet`. It's difficult to talk about statements without also talking about resultsets; but it's just as difficult to discuss a resultset without knowing about statements. In code, you will create a statement object first and use it to get a resultset. So this chapter has a section about statements first, followed by a section on resultsets.*

What is meant by "the kind of resultset?" A `ResultSet` is a Java object that allows you to view the rows returned by a query. A resultset is the return value of certain statement methods. When JDBC was first released, resultsets provided a one-way (first row to last row) read-only view of the rows. Three methods that take int parameters were added with JDBC 2.0 and allow you to create a statement that can return a resultset that is scrollable (you can move forwards and backwards) and that can be used to update the underlying table. Since the use of the `Statement` is the same regardless of which kind of `ResultSet` is created, discussion of the use of the methods that use the int parameters will be postponed until the `ResultSet` section.

java.sql.Statement

Statement objects are used to send SQL statements to the database. However, since java.sql.Statement is an interface, you cannot directly instantiate an instance:

```
Statement statement = new Statement();          //this won't compile
```

You get a Statement object using a method of the Connection class:

```
String url = "jdbc:oracle:oci8:scott/tiger@localhost";
Connection connection = DriverManager.getConnection(url);
Statement statement = connection.createStatement();
```

In the code above, the createStatement() method is used to get an instance of a Statement object. Using the Statement object, various SQL statements can be executed against the database. Statement can be used to execute almost any kind of legal SQL statement: SELECT, INSERT, UPDATE, CREATE, DELETE. As a minimum, the JDBC specification requires that a driver support at least ANSI SQL92 Entry Level.

> *As mentioned above, java.sql.Statement (and java.sql.Connection in the previous section) is an interface. So how can the paragraph above refer to a Statement object? Even though a Statement can't be instantiated, the Connection object must return a reference to some concrete object. That object must implement the Statement interface. Although you don't know the actual name of the object, you do know that the object will provide all the methods defined in the Statement interface. Thus, with the object, you can safely call any method defined by the Statement interface. In this chapter, I use the phrase "Statement object" in place of "an object which implements the Statement interface." (If you are really interested, you can determine the name of the concrete statement class provided by Oracle. Use an archive program, such as the jar program that comes with the JDK, to view the contents of classes111.zip or classes12.zip file.)*

Once you have a statement object, you use it to pass a String containing the SQL to the database. The executeQuery() method is used when the SQL statement is a SELECT statement. The rows that are returned from the query can be examined using the ResultSet object. Here is a code snippet which shows how to query the emp table from Oracle sample database schema SCOTT:

```
String sql = "select * from emp";
ResultSet rs = statement.executeQuery(sql);
```

The ResultSet object will be discussed later in this chapter. If the SQL statement is any other type of SQL (INSERT, DELETE, CREATE, etc.), then the method to use is the executeUpdate(String) or execute(String) method. Here is a code snippet showing an insert into the dept table in the Oracle sample database schema SCOTT:

```
String sql = "insert into emp values (50, 'ETHICS', 'Seattle')"
int rowCount = statement.executeUpdate(sql);
//or use boolean result = statement.execute(sql);
```

The method executeUpdate(String) returns an int which indicates how many rows were affected by the SQL statement. For SQL statements that do not affect rows (such as a CREATE TABLE statement), executeUpdate(String) returns a 0.

While the execute(String) method could be used in place of either executeQuery(String) or executeUpdate(String), it is meant to be used in special situations. The method execute(String) is used when the SQL statement may return multiple resultsets, multiple row counts, or a combination of either. Using the initial return value, and the Statement methods getMoreResults(), getResultSet(), and getUpdateCount(), you can extract the multiple results and row counts.

Here is code which shows how to use a statement to create a table and insert some rows of data into that table. This code creates a statement and then uses it to execute various SQL statements. It uses executeUpdate() to create two tables and insert data into those tables. The table created in this code will be used in other examples later in this chapter. Then it uses the executeQuery() method to query the data that was inserted:

```java
package jdbc.SimpleStatement;

import java.sql.*;

/**
 * A class to demonstrate the use of a non-scrollable,
 * non-updateable Statement. This code will compile under either
 * JDBC 1.0 or JDBC 2.0
 *
 * This class creates the hospital database tables used in later examples
 * of the JDBC chapter.
 */
public class SimpleStatement {
  Connection connection;
  Statement statement;
  ResultSet resultSet;

  //constructor
  SimpleStatement() throws ClassNotFoundException, SQLException {
    Class.forName("oracle.jdbc.driver.OracleDriver");
    //change the parameters in the next line, or use the DriverData
    //class as shown in previous examples
    connection = DriverManager.getConnection("jdbc:oracle:oci8:@",
      "scott", "tiger");
    statement = connection.createStatement();
  }

  /** Use the executeUpdate method to create two tables */
  void createTable() throws SQLException {
    String sql = "create table patients (" +
      "patient_id number(9) not null primary key," +
      "surname varchar(50)," +
      "given_name varchar(50)" +
      ")";
    int rows = statement.executeUpdate(sql);
    //return value from a 'create table' should be zero
    System.out.println("create table statement return value is " + rows);
    System.out.println("Table patients created");

    sql = "create table hospital_stays (" +
      "patient_id references patients(patient_id)," +
      "admit_date date," +
      "discharge_date date" +
```

```
      ")";
    rows = statement.executeUpdate(sql);
    System.out.println("create table statement return value is " + rows);
    System.out.println("Table hospital_stays created");
  }

  /** Use the executeUpdate method to insert data */
  void insertData() throws SQLException {
    String sql = "insert into patients (patient_id, surname, given_name) " +
      "values (10000, 'Smith', 'Joe')";
    int rows = statement.executeUpdate(sql);
    //return value from inserting a row should be 1
    System.out.println("Inserted " + rows + " row");

    //How does one insert a String with an embedded apostrophe (')?
    //Use two apostrophes like this:
    sql = "insert into patients (patient_id, surname, given_name) " +
      "values (10001, 'O''Grady', 'Bridget')";
    rows = statement.executeUpdate(sql);
    System.out.println("Inserted " + rows + " row");

    sql = "insert into hospital_stays (patient_id, admit_date, discharge_date) " +
      "values (10000, '10-Aug-2000', '13-Aug-2000')";
    rows = statement.executeUpdate(sql);
    System.out.println("Inserted " + rows + " row");

    sql = "insert into hospital_stays (patient_id, admit_date) " +
      "values (10001, '11-Sep-2000')";
    rows = statement.executeUpdate(sql);
    System.out.println("Inserted " + rows + " row");
  }

  /** Use the executeQuery method to query the table */
  void checkData() throws SQLException {
    String sql = "select p.patient_id, p.given_name, p.surname, " +
      "h.admit_date, h.discharge_date " +
      "from patients p, hospital_stays h " +
      "where h.patient_id = p.patient_id";
    resultSet = statement.executeQuery(sql);
    //resultSet.next() advances to the next row in the ResultSet and
    //return true. When there are no more rows, it returns false
    while (resultSet.next()) {
      System.out.print(resultSet.getInt(1) + " ");
      System.out.print(resultSet.getString(2) + " ");
      System.out.print(resultSet.getString(3) + " ");
      System.out.print(resultSet.getDate(4) + " ");
      System.out.println(resultSet.getDate(5) + " ");
    }
  }

  void disableCommit() throws SQLException {
    connection.setAutoCommit(false);
  }
  void commit() throws SQLException { connection.commit(); }
  void rollback() throws SQLException { connection.rollback(); }
  void close() throws SQLException {
```

```
      if (resultSet != null) { resultSet.close(); }
      if (statement != null) { statement.close(); }
      if (connection != null) { connection.close(); }
    }

  public static void main(String[] args) {
    SimpleStatement ss = null;
    try {
      ss = new SimpleStatement();
      ss.disableCommit();
      ss.createTable();
      ss.insertData();
      ss.checkData();
      ss.commit();
    } catch (Exception e) {
      e.printStackTrace();
      //if there was any exception, try to rollback the changes
      try { ss.rollback(); } catch (Exception e2) { e2.printStackTrace(); }
    } finally {
      try { ss.close(); } catch (Exception e2) { e2.printStackTrace(); }
    }
  }
}
```

java.sql.PreparedStatement

The PreparedStatement interface is a subinterface of the Statement. It is used to optimize database calls. Every time you use an instance of Statement to execute some SQL, the SQL string is sent to the database where it is compiled to a form usable by the database, and then executed. Even if you send the same string of SQL, the SQL is sent to the database and compiled again. This obviously can have an impact on performance. If you had an SQL statement where the only thing that changed was the IN parameters, you could gain execution time by being able to use a precompiled version of the SQL statement. PreparedStatement does this for you.

Suppose you were programming a hospital database that kept patient information. You know that one often-executed query will be a query to look for a patient with a specific surname. The two hospital tables used in this and other examples were created with a Java class in the previous section. You can also create the tables using the following SQL:

```
CREATE TABLE patients (
  patient_id NUMBER(9) NOT NULL PRIMARY KEY,
  surname VARCHAR2(50),
  given_name VARCHAR2(50)
)

CREATE TABLE hospital_stays (
  patient_id REFERENCES patients(patient_id),
  admit_date DATE,
  discharge_date DATE
)
```

The SQL for selecting patients with the surname "Smith" might look like this:

```
SELECT surname, given_name, patient_id
FROM patients
WHERE surname = 'Smith';
```

If you used a `Statement` object, then every time this query was performed you would have code that was something like this:

```
String surname = "Smith";
String sql = "SELECT surname, given_name, patient_id FROM patients "
    + "WHERE surname = '" + surname + "'";
Statement s = connection.createStatement();
ResultSet rs = s.executeQuery(sql);
```

Each time the code above is executed a new string is sent to the database, it is compiled, and the result returned.

Using a `PreparedStatement`, the SQL string is created with place holders for the bind variables which can change each time the SQL is executed. The code looks like this:

```
String sql = "select surname, given_name, patient_id from patients " +
    "where surname = ?";
PreparedStatement ps = connection.prepareStatement(sql);
ps.setString(1, surname);
ResultSet rs = ps.executeQuery();
```

Each bind variable parameter, or `IN` parameter, in the SQL statement is represented by a question mark. The SQL string is passed to the `PreparedStatement` when it is created. The JDBC driver passes this string to the database where it is compiled, but not executed. Before executing the SQL, you must tell the `PreparedStatement` the value to use for each bind variable.

The `PreparedStatement` class has methods for inserting every kind of Java object into the SQL. Like the `setString(int, String)` call in the code above, each call begins with `set` and uses the object type as the rest of the method name. Here are a few of the `setXXX()` methods:

- `setDate(int, java.sql.Date)`
- `setFloat(int, float)`
- `setLong(int, long)`.
- `setBlob(int Blob)` (this is a JDBC 2.0 method)
- `setObject(int, Object)`

Consult the JDBC API Javadoc for the complete list of `setXXX()` methods for `PreparedStatement` objects.

> The Oracle API Javadoc can be found in the Oracle **jdbc** subdirectory; it can also be
> downloaded from the same location as the drivers at Oracle's web site
> **http://technet.oracle.com.**

Each setXXX() method takes two parameters: the first indicates which bind parameter is to be set; the second gives the value for the bind parameter. The bind parameters are numbered as they appear in the SQL statement: the first bind parameter is 1, the second is 2, etc. Note that for some of the setXXX() methods the second parameter is a Java primitive, for some methods it is a Java object reference.

> *If your code is using many PreparedStatements, you may want to use SQLJ for these statements. SQLJ code performs the same function as a PreparedStatement, but more concisely. In addition, with SQLJ the SQL syntax can be checked at compile time, while the PreparedStatement SQL syntax is not checked until run time. See Chapter 14 for more information.*

Since java.sql.PreparedStatement extends java.sql.Statement, the same execute methods as in Statement are available to the PreparedStatement. The method executeQuery() is used when the prepared statement is a SELECT statement; executeUpdate() is used when some other kind of statement is used; execute() is used when the return value of the SQL is unknown or if it returns multiple values or resultsets. Note that unlike the Statement methods, these methods do not take a String parameter.

> Since **PreparedStatement** extends **Statement**, you can call the method **executeQuery(String)** on subinterface. However, if you mix this method call with calls to **executeQuery()**, the Oracle driver will most likely throw an exception at run time. When using **PreparedStatement**, do not call **executeQuery(String)**, **execute(String)** or **executeUpdate(String)**.

Another point to note about PreparedStatements is that as objects, they retain state. This means that if you set a particular parameter, that variable remains set for subsequent calls, until you change the parameter. So if you have a PreparedStatement with several parameters, you don't necessarily need to set each variable for every call.

Looking at the code for the Statement object, you may wonder why one would use a PreparedStatement. After all, it takes only two lines of code to use a Statement while the PreparedStatement requires an extra line of code for each parameter. While the PreparedStatement code may be a bit more involved (imagine that there are several parameters to be set), it is potentially better optimized. When using a PreparedStatement, the SQL statement can be sent to the database before the query is executed; the database can precompile the SQL and optimize the database call, thus providing faster execution time for the SQL statement. The PreparedStatement SQL is compiled only once, when the PreparedStatement is created; each time the PreparedStatement is reused, the bind variables are sent to the database where the statement is executed. Since the SQL does not need to be compiled every time you use it, the execution performance is improved.

java.sql.CallableStatement

The CallableStatement is a subinterface of PreparedStatement, and thus a subinterface of Statement. Callable statements are used to call database stored procedures. Stored procedures or functions are similar to methods in Java code. A Java method is a set of code that is executed by calling a method name. A stored procedure or function consists of a set of PL/SQL statements that is stored in the database and that can be executed by calling a name. The difference between the functions and procedures is that a function returns a value, a procedure does not.

Both procedures and functions can take parameters. Like the `PreparedStatement`, these parameters are represented as question marks in the SQL string in the Java code. In a `PreparedStatement`, the parameters are all `IN` parameters; in other words, they are write-only parameters. With CallableStatement you can have `IN` parameters, `OUT` parameters, and `IN OUT` parameters. The `OUT` or `IN OUT` parameters are used to get the return value from the stored function. Even though a procedure does not have a return value, it can have parameters in its parameter list that are `OUT` or `IN OUT` parameters. Take the `hospital_stays` table created in a previous section. A common action will be to update a patient's record with the discharge date. First, a stored procedure is created for that feature.

```
CREATE OR REPLACE PROCEDURE set_discharge (
    id IN NUMBER,
    discharged IN DATE
    admitted IN DATE
)
AS
BEGIN
    UPDATE hospital_stays
    SET discharge_date = discharged
    WHERE patient_id = id
    AND admit_date = admitted;
END;
/
```

The procedure above uses the table `hospital_stays`. The procedure uses three `IN` parameters for the caller to pass the `patient_id`, the `admit_date`, and the `discharge_date`.

Likewise, there is a function to read the discharge date. Here's the SQL for that procedure:

```
CREATE OR REPLACE FUNCTION get_discharge (
    id IN NUMBER,
    admitted IN DATE)
RETURN DATE IS adate DATE;
BEGIN
    SELECT discharge_date INTO ADATE
    FROM hospital_stays
    WHERE patient_id = id AND admit_date = admitted;
RETURN (adate);
end;
/
```

Although Oracle SQL*Plus was used to create the procedures, they could just as easily have been sent to the database with a `Statement` object using the `executeUpdate(String)` method. Java classes showing how to do this are included with the downloadable code for this chapter.

Calling Stored Procedures and Functions with a CallableStatement

Now these procedures can be called from Java code. Here's a Java class showing how to call the procedures:

```
package jdbc.CallableStatement;

import java.sql.*;
import java.util.*;
import DriverData;
```

411

```java
public class ManageDischarge {
  private Connection connection;
  private CallableStatement callStmt;

  /** Constructor. Makes database connection */
  public ManageDischarge() throws ClassNotFoundException, SQLException {
    Class.forName("oracle.jdbc.driver.OracleDriver");
    connection = DriverManager.getConnection(DriverData.url,
      DriverData.user, DriverData.passw);
  }

  /** Calls the set_discharge procedure in the hospital database. Uses a
      callable statement to call a procedure.
      All input parameters should be non-null */
  public void setDate (int patientId,
                       java.sql.Date admitDate,
                       java.sql.Date dischargeDate) throws SQLException
  {
    callStmt = connection.prepareCall("{ call SET_DISCHARGE(?, ?, ?) }");
    callStmt.setInt(1, patientId);
    callStmt.setDate(2, admitDate);
    callStmt.setDate(3, dischargeDate);
    callStmt.executeUpdate();
  }

  /** Calls the get_discharge procedure in the hospital database. Uses a
      callable statement to call a function that returns a value.
      All input parameters should be non-null */
  public java.sql.Date getDate(int patientId,
                       java.sql.Date admitDate) throws SQLException
  {
    callStmt = connection.prepareCall("{ ? = call GET_DISCHARGE(?, ?) }");
    callStmt.setInt(2, patientId);
    callStmt.setDate(3, admitDate);
    callStmt.registerOutParameter(1, java.sql.Types.DATE);
    callStmt.executeUpdate();
    return callStmt.getDate(1);
  }

  public static void main(String[] args) {
    try {
      int patientId = 10001;
      GregorianCalendar cal = new GregorianCalendar();
      cal.set(2000, 8, 11);
      java.sql.Date admitDate = new java.sql.Date(cal.getTime().getTime());
      cal.set(2000, 8, 15);
      java.sql.Date dischargeDate =
          new java.sql.Date(cal.getTime().getTime());

      ManageDischarge md = new ManageDischarge();
      md.setDate(patientId, admitDate, dischargeDate);
      System.out.println("Discharge date for patient " + patientId +
        " was updated");
```

```
            dischargeDate = null;
            System.out.println("dischargeDate is set to " + dischargeDate);
            dischargeDate = md.getDate(patientId, admitDate);
            System.out.println("dischargeDate from database is " +
                                dischargeDate);
        } catch (Exception e) {
            e.printStackTrace();
        }
    }
}
```

In the `main(String[])` method, an instance of the class `ManageDischarge` is created. That instance is used to call the method `setDate(int, Date, Date)` to set the discharge date. Note that for this code to work properly, a patient record with the identifier 10001 and an `admit_date` of 11 Sep 2000 must already have been inserted into the `patients` and `hospital_stays` tables. The `SimpleStatement` class presented in the `java.sql.Statement` section can do this for you. If you did not run that code, you can insert the data from that class into the tables. After setting the discharge date, the code calls the method `getDate(int, Date)` to check that the discharge date was updated correctly.

Just as with a `PreparedStatement`, you use `setXXX()` methods to set the IN parameters in the `CallableStatement`. Also, the above code calls the stored function `GET_DISCHARGE` which has an OUT parameter. The OUT parameters in the `CallableStatement` are set with a call to the `registerOutParameter(int, int)` method. This method is discussed further below.

The last point to note about the above code is that it uses the Java core class `java.sql.Date` rather than `java.util.Date`. A `java.util.Date` object contains date and time information whereas the type SQL date only has date information. For this reason Java provides the `java.sql.Date` class. Also, like `java.util.Date`, months in `java.sql.Date` are zero based, which is why the code above used the number 8 to represent September.

There are three general forms for the string used when creating the `CallableStatement` object. Each form encloses the procedure or function call inside curly braces. As shown in the code above, if the procedure takes one or more parameters, you would use the form:

```
    { call procedure_name(? [, ?, . . . ] ) }
```

where the square brackets are not part of the syntax; the brackets show which syntax is optional. Each parameter that is sent to the procedure is represented by a question mark. When you are calling a function that returns a value, use:

```
    { ? = call function_name[(? , . . . )] }
```

Finally, if the stored procedure takes no parameters and returns no values, then the form is simply:

```
    { call procedure_name }
```

The IN parameters represented by the question marks are set using the methods from `Prepared Statement` that were discussed earlier. If the parameter is a `String`, use `setString(int, String)`; if it is an `int`, use `setInt(int, int)`; for a `float`, use `setFloat(int, float)` and so on.

In addition to IN variables, stored procedures and functions can have OUT and IN OUT parameters. These parameters return values from the procedure or function. The IN OUT parameter has a dual role: it sends a parameter to the database and returns a value from the procedure or function.

Getting the value from an OUT or IN OUT parameter takes two methods calls. One to set up the return value before the CallableStatement is executed; the other to retrieve the value after it is executed.

The method to register an OUT parameter is:

```
registerOutParameter(int position, int jdbcType);
```

The first parameter is the position of the OUT bind parameter in the statement. Each parameter, whether it is IN, OUT, or IN OUT, is numbered from left to right in the string, beginning with the value 1. The second parameter in registerOutParameter(int, int) is a value from the class java.sql.Types. This class contains a static int variable for every JDBC type. You generally use the variable rather than the actual value. So, for instance, in the ManageDischarge class above, an SQL DATE is returned from the get_discharge function, so the registerOutParameter call is made with the variable java.sql.Types.DATE:

```
callStmt.registerOutParameter(1, java.sql.Types.DATE);
```

To get the value of the parameter after executing the CallableStatement, you would use a get method similar to the set method: getString(int), getFloat(int), getBoolean(int), etc. Again, the first parameter indicates the position in the SQL string of the parameter. Parameters are numbered left to right, starting with 1.

Using an IN OUT parameter is a combination of the methods for IN and OUT parameters. You will call both setXXX(int) and registerOutParameter(int, int) for the IN OUT parameter prior to the execute, and then getXXX() to get the return value. For example, suppose that the third parameter passed to SET_DISCHARGE above was an IN OUT parameter. The code in the ManageDischarge class to set and get the value would be written like this:

```
callStmt = connection.prepareCall("{ call SET_DISCHARGE(?, ?, ?) }");
callStmt.setInt(1, patientId);
callStmt.setDate(2, admitDate);
//pretend that param three is INOUT, set the value for IN
callStmt.setDate(3, dischargeDate);
//and also register it for OUT
callStmt.registerOutParameter(3, java.sql.Types.DATE);
callStmt.executeUpdate();
//now get the OUT parameter
java.sql.Date date = callStmt.getDate(3)
```

It should be obvious that if you register an OUT parameter as a particular JDBC type, you must use the correct getXXX() method to get the value. Likewise, if you have an IN OUT parameter, the particular setXXX(), registerOutParameter(), and getXXX() methods must set, register, or get the same JDBC type. If you register a float, get a float; if you register a byte, get a byte; etc.

> As with the PreparedStatement, do not call the executeQuery(String), executeUpdate(String), or execute(String) methods of the CallableStatement.

Getting a ResultSet from a CallableStatement

The examples for `PreparedStatement` and `CallableStatement` have shown how to use `OUT` parameters to get the basic JDBC types such as `int`, `float`, `String`, etc. Stored functions can return other kinds of objects that you can retrieve from an `OUT` parameter. One common JDBC question is whether a `ResultSet` can be retrieved using a `CallableStatement`. The answer is yes, and to do this, there must be a stored function in the database that returns a **cursor**. A cursor is a database feature that is analogous to a `ResultSet`. Start by defining a type to represent a cursor:

```
CREATE OR REPLACE PACKAGE types AS
  TYPE cursorType IS REF cursor;
END;
/
```

Here is the PL/SQL for a function that will return the patient name, `admit_date`, and `discharge_date` for a given `patient_id`:

```
CREATE OR REPLACE FUNCTION list_patient (id IN NUMBER)
RETURN types.cursorType IS patient_cursor types.cursorType;
BEGIN
  OPEN patient_cursor FOR
  SELECT p.given_name, p.surname,
         h.admit_date, h.discharge_date
         FROM patients p, hospital_stays h
         WHERE p.patient_id = id AND
         p.patient_id = h.patient_id;
  RETURN patient_cursor;
END;
/
```

And here is a very short Java program that gets a `ResultSet` as the return value from calling the stored function. The code works the same as the other code in this section which calls a stored function and procedure with one exception. The code uses an Oracle specific JDBC type, `OracleTypes.CURSOR` when registering the `OUT` parameter.

```
package jdbc.CallableStatement;

import java.sql.*;
import oracle.jdbc.driver.*;
import DriverData;

public class CallListPatients {
  public static void main(String[] args) throws Exception {
    int patient_id = 10001;

    //register the driver and connect
    Class.forName("oracle.jdbc.driver.OracleDriver");
    Connection connection = DriverManager.getConnection(DriverData.url,
      DriverData.user, DriverData.passw);

    //create and prepare the CallableStatement
    String sql = "{ ? = call LIST_PATIENT(?) }";
    CallableStatement callStmt = connection.prepareCall(sql);
    //Use OracleTypes.CURSOR as the OUT parameter type
```

```
callStmt.registerOutParameter(1, OracleTypes.CURSOR);
callStmt.setInt(2, patient_id);

//Execute the function and get the return object from the call
callStmt.executeUpdate();
ResultSet rset = (ResultSet) callStmt.getObject(1);

while(rset.next()) {
    System.out.print(rset.getString(1) + " ");
    System.out.print(rset.getString(2) + " ");
    System.out.print(rset.getDate(3) + " ");
    System.out.println(rset.getDate(4));
    }
  }
}
```

Batch Updates

In JDBC 1.0, you have the ability to use the concept of a transaction. Rather than automatically committing each statement as it is executed, you can execute a series of statements and then commit or rollback all the statements. However, each statement is still sent to the database and executed before the next is sent.

With JDBC 2.0, a `Statement` object can hold a set of SQL statements that are sent to the database together and then executed. To use this facility, the SQL commands must not be queries, but SQL statements that return an update count. This method can be used with any of the three statement classes. The Oracle JDBC driver supports two different techniques for executing SQL as a batch. The Oracle driver has supported an Oracle specific batch update process that is available with JDBC 1.0. Starting with Oracle 8.1.6, the Oracle driver supports the JDBC 2.0 standard for batch updates. Neither technique is better than the other. The Oracle specific version is a little easier to use since the driver determines when to send the batch. However, using the JDBC standard version your code is more platform independent.

JDBC Batch Updates

Before batch processing begins, auto-commit must be disabled. If this is not done, then each SQL command will be committed as it is executed.

```
connection.setAutoCommit(false);
```

Next, the SQL commands that are part of the batch update are added to the Statement object. This is done with the `addBatch(String)` method. As mentioned previously, none of the SQL statements must be queries that return a `ResultSet`. If any of the SQL commands is a `SELECT` statement, an exception will be thrown.

```
Statement statement = connection.createStatement();
statement.addBatch("insert into patient values " +
    "('John Smith', 12345,'3-Aug-2000', NULL)");
```

When you are ready to send the SQL statements to the database, you call the `executeBatch()` method. This method returns an `int` array. Each entry in the array is the row update count that corresponds to each SQL statement.

```
int[] results =  statement.executeBatch();
```

Here's a program that demonstrates the above. Start by entering and compiling this base class. The base class is used because the functionality it provides will be used again when Oracle batch updating is demonstrated. The base class provides a method to read a data file. Each line in the file becomes a `String` stored in a `Vector`. The other method in the base class, `sqlEncode()` is used to prepare Strings for inserts. It goes through each string and ensures that any single tick marks (') are converted to two tick marks (") so that single tick marks are stored properly. Save this file in the directory `jdbc\BatchUpdates` as `Batch.java`.

```java
package jdbc.BatchUpdates;

import java.util.*;
import java.io.*;

public class Batch {
  public Vector readData(String filename) throws IOException
  {
    BufferedReader bin = new BufferedReader(new FileReader(filename));
    Vector v = new Vector();
    String s = bin.readLine();
    do {
      v.addElement(s);
      s = bin.readLine();
    } while (s != null);
    return v;
  }

  /** Insert an extra single quote into strings with a single quote.
      So, input O'Grady return O''Grady */
  protected String sqlEncode(String s) {
    if (s.indexOf("'") == -1) return s;

    StringBuffer sb = new StringBuffer();
    int start = 0;
    int index = 0;
    while ((index = s.indexOf("'", start)) != -1) {
      sb.append(s.substring(start, index)).append("''");
      start = index+1;
    }
    return sb.toString();
  }
}
```

Next you will create a data file that contains the data for an `INSERT` statement. Each line in the data file is a row of data where each field is delimited by a plus (+) sign. This data will be inserted into the `patients` and `hospital_stays` tables which were created earlier. The elements in the line consist of the `patient_id`, `given_name`, `surname`, `admit_date`, and `discharge_date`. Save this file as `JDBCBatch.data` in a directory named `jdbc\Data`:

```
10012+Kevin+Charles+23-Sep-2000+25-Sep-2000
10013+Laura+Lister+24-Sep-2000+26-Sep-2000
10014+Michael+Moorstone+26-Sep-2000+28-Sep-2000
10015+Nancy+Nelson+23-Sep-2000+25-Sep-2000
10016+Oscar+D'Estanger+28-Sep-2000+30-Sep-2000
10017+Pauline+Perrin+29-Sep-2000+1-Oct-2000
```

```
10018+Roger+Van Briggle+24-Sep-2000+26-Sep-2000
10019+Susan+Howard+25-Sep-2000+27-Sep-2000
10020+Timothy+Himmelman+26-Sep-2000+28-Sep-2000
10021+Barbara+Dominguez+28-Sep-2000+30-Sep-2000
10022+Catherine+Taylor+29-Sep-2000+1-Oct-2000
10026+Elizabeth+Tyson+28-Sep-2000+30-Sep-2000
10027+Kimberly+Bergquist+29-Sep-2000+1-Oct-2000
```

Finally, here is the derived class that provides the JDBC batch updating:

```
package jdbc.BatchUpdates;

import java.sql.*;
import java.util.*;
import java.io.*;
import DriverData;

/** A class to demonstrate batch updates. This class requires JDBC 2.0
    to work properly */
public class JDBCBatch extends Batch {
  Connection connection;
  Statement pStmtPatient;
  Statement pStmtStays;

  //constructor
  JDBCBatch() throws SQLException, ClassNotFoundException {
    Class.forName("oracle.jdbc.driver.OracleDriver");
    connection = DriverManager.getConnection(DriverData.url,
                    DriverData.user, DriverData.passw);
  }
```

The constructor above is used to get the database connection. Note that it uses the `DriverData` class that was presented early in the chapter. The method that follows is the `insert(Vector)` method. The `Vector` contains the data that was read from the data file. The `insert(Vector)` method first disables autocommit. Then it creates two `Statement` objects, one for the `patients` table and one for the `hospital_stays` table. Then it takes each line from the vector, splits it into its tokens, and then uses the tokens to update the two tables. After all the data has been added to the batch, the `executeBatch()` method is called for both statements and the update counts are totaled. Finally, the changes are committed.

```
//insert the data from the vector into the tables
//each element of the vector must be a new row in the patients table
public void insert(Vector data)
  throws SQLException, NumberFormatException
{
  //set batching parameters
  connection.setAutoCommit(false);

  //create prepared statements
  pStmtPatient = connection.createStatement();
  pStmtStays = connection.createStatement();

  //parse and add the data to the batch
  for (int i = 0; i < data.size(); i++) {
```

```
      StringTokenizer stData =
        new StringTokenizer((String) data.elementAt(i), "+");
      int id = new Integer(stData.nextToken()).intValue();
      String firstName = sqlEncode(stData.nextToken());
      String lastName = sqlEncode(stData.nextToken());

      String sql = "insert into patients " +
        "(patient_id, given_name, surname) " +
        "values (" + id + ", '" + firstName + "', '" +
        lastName + "')";
      pStmtPatient.addBatch(sql);
```

In the next section, the admit and discharge data are extracted from the data, and inserted into the hospital_stays table. Note that because Oracle will automatically convert a properly formatted string into a DATE field, we do not have to convert the String to a DATE in the Java code.

```
      String admitted = stData.nextToken();
      String discharged = stData.nextToken();
      sql = "insert into hospital_stays " +
        "(patient_id, admit_date, discharge_date) " +
        "values (" + id + ", '" + admitted + "', '" +
        discharged + "')";
      pStmtStays.addBatch(sql);
    }

    int total = 0;
    int[] rows = pStmtPatient.executeBatch();
    for (int i = 0; i < rows.length; i++) { total += rows[i]; }

    rows = pStmtStays.executeBatch();
    for (int i = 0; i < rows.length; i++) { total += rows[i]; }

    System.out.println(total + " rows updated");

    //auto commit is disabled, so need to explicitly commit data
    //NOTE: if this method throws any exception, the data does not
    //get committed
    connection.commit();
  }
```

The last method is the main() method. This create an instance of the class, calls readData() to read the data file, then calls the insert method:

```
  public static void main(String[] args) {
    try {
      JDBCBatch ob = new JDBCBatch();
      Vector data = ob.readData("JDBCBatch.data");
      ob.insert(data);
    } catch (Exception e) {
      try { connection.rollback(); } catch (Exception ignored) {}
      e.printStackTrace();
    }
  }
}
```

Batch updates can be performed with Statement, PreparedStatement, or CallableStatement objects. The class above used two Statement objects. To use batch updates with a CallableStatement, only stored procedures, not functions, can be called; also, the stored procedure must not have OUT or IN OUT parameters and must return a row update count. Since the above class used SQL where only the bind variables changed, it could have been written using a PreparedStatement. Here's how the above code would look with a PreparedStatement:

```java
public void insert(Vector data)
   throws SQLException, NumberFormatException
{
   //set batching parameters
   connection.setAutoCommit(false);

   //create prepared statements
   String sql = "insert into patients " +
       "(patient_id, given_name, surname) " +
       "values (?, ?, ?)";
   pStmtPatient = connection.prepareStatement(sql);
   sql = "insert into hospital_stays " +
     "(patient_id, admit_date, discharge_date) " +
     "values (?, ?, ?)";
   pStmtStays = connection.prepareStatement(sql);

   //parse and add the data to the batch
   for (int i = 0; i < data.size(); i++) {
     StringTokenizer stData =
       new StringTokenizer((String) data.elementAt(i), "+");
     int id = new Integer(stData.nextToken()).intValue();
     String firstName = sqlEncode(stData.nextToken());
     String lastName = sqlEncode(stData.nextToken());

     pStmtPatient.setInt(1, id);
     pStmtPatient.setString(2, firstName);
     pStmtPatient.setString(3, lastName);
     pStmtPatient.addBatch();

     String admitted = stData.nextToken();
     String discharged = stData.nextToken();
     pStmtStays.setInt(1, id);
     pStmtStays.setString(2, admitted);
     pStmtStays.setString(3, discharged);
     pStmtStays.addBatch();
   }

   int total = 0;
   int[] rows = pStmtPatient.executeBatch();
   for (int i = 0; i < rows.length; i++) { total += rows[i]; }

   rows = pStmtStays.executeBatch();
   for (int i = 0; i < rows.length; i++) { total += rows[i]; }

   System.out.println(total + " rows updated");

   //auto commit is disabled, so need to explicitly commit data
   //NOTE: if this method throws any exception, the data does not
   //get committed
   connection.commit();
}
```

One other method call may be useful when doing batch updating. After inserting statements into the batch, you may decide that you do not want to execute them after all. If you need to clear the list of SQL statements from the statement object, use:

```
statement.clearBatch();
```

Note that calling `clearBatch()` only clears the list of SQL statements that have not been sent to the database. If you also need to undo statements that were sent and executed but not committed, you still must call the `rollback()` method of the `Connection` class.

Oracle Update Batching

Oracle specific JDBC update batching is very similar to the batch updates specified by JDBC 2.0. One difference is that Oracle update batching works only with a prepared statement, an `OraclePreparedStatement` to be specific. The other difference is that SQL statements are sent automatically as a batch rather than requiring a specific method call to send the batch as in JDBC batch updating.

> **You cannot mix the Oracle specific batch process with the JDBC 2.0 batch process in the same application. If you try to use both methods in a single application, the Oracle JDBC driver will throw exceptions.**

In the next few paragraphs, the general algorithm will be illustrated. Following that, complete source code for a class that uses the algorithm will be presented. Start by disabling autocommit. Then set the number of statements that are to be sent in a batch. Note that you have to use a reference of type `OracleConnection` to call `setDefaultExecuteBatch(int)`. In the snippet below, the number of statements that complete a batch is set to 10, although any positive number can be used.

```
OracleConnection connection =
    (OracleConnection) DriverManager.getConnection(url);
connection.setAutoCommit(false);
connection.setDefaultExecuteBatch(10);
```

Now get an `OraclePreparedStatement` object and set the parameters for the prepared statement.

```
OraclePreparedStatement statement =
    (OraclePreparedStatement) connection.prepareStatement(
        "insert into patient values (?, ?, ?, ?)");
statement.setString(1, "John Smith");
```

After all the parameters for the prepared statement have been set, call the `executeUpdate()` method. Calling this method tells the driver that the SQL statement is ready to be sent to the database:

```
int result = statement.executeUpdate();
```

However, since the execute batch value was set to 10, the driver does not actually send or execute the SQL statement; it queues the SQL statement until 10 statements have been set. The return value of the call above will be 0 at this point. Now assume that the code has looped 9 times to set the parameters and call `executeUpdate()`. The next snippet of code will be the tenth call to `executeUpdate()`:

```
result = statement.executeUpdate();
```

On this tenth call, the entire batch of queued SQL statements is sent to the database where it is executed. The return value is the number of rows that were changed. For the general SQL statement, this value will not necessarily be the same as the default execute batch value. In the above example, each SQL statement inserted a single row, so assuming that all the rows are successfully inserted, the result should be 10; however, if each SQL statement updated more than one row, the return value will be more than 10.

After all the statements have been executed, you must still commit the changes with a call to the commit() method.

Here is a Java class demonstrating Oracle JDBC batch updating. Note that in many ways it is the same as the JdbcBatch class presented in the previous section. The main differences are that the code below uses an OracleConnection and OraclePreparedStatements. The data to be used with this class is shown after the Java source code.

```java
package jdbc.BatchUpdates;

import java.sql.*;
import oracle.jdbc.driver.*;
import java.util.*;
import java.io.*;
import DriverData;

/** A class to demonstrate batch updates. This class works with
    either JDBC 1.0 or JDBC 2.0 */
public class OracleBatch extends Batch {
  OracleConnection connection;
  OraclePreparedStatement pStmtPatient;
  OraclePreparedStatement pStmtStays;

  //constructor
  OracleBatch() throws SQLException, ClassNotFoundException {
    Class.forName("oracle.jdbc.driver.OracleDriver");
    connection = (OracleConnection) DriverManager.getConnection(
      DriverData.url, DriverData.user, DriverData.passw);
  }

  //insert the data from the vector into the tables
  //each element of the vector must be a new row in the patients table
  public void insert(Vector data) throws SQLException, NumberFormatException
  {
    //set batching parameters
    connection.setAutoCommit(false);
    connection.setDefaultExecuteBatch(6);

    //create prepared statements
    pStmtPatient = (OraclePreparedStatement) connection.prepareStatement(
      "insert into patients " +
      "(patient_id, given_name, surname) values (?, ?, ?)");
    pStmtStays = (OraclePreparedStatement) connection.prepareStatement(
      "insert into patient " +
      "(patient_id, admit_date, discharge_date) values (?, ?, ?)");
```

```
    //parse and submit the data
    int rows;
    for (int i = 0; i < data.size(); i++) {
      StringTokenizer stData =
        new StringTokenizer((String) data.elementAt(i), "+");
      int id = new Integer(stData.nextToken()).intValue();

      pStmtPatient.setInt(1, id);
      pStmtPatient.setString(2, sqlEncode(stData.nextToken()));
      pStmtPatient.setString(3, sqlEncode(stData.nextToken()));
      rows = pStmtPatient.executeUpdate();

      if (rows > 0) {
        System.out.println(rows + " rows were updated");
      }

      pStmtStays.setInt(1, id);
      pStmtStays.setString(2, stData.nextToken());
      pStmtStays.setString(3, stData.nextToken());
      rows = pStmtStays.executeUpdate();

      if (rows > 0) {
        System.out.println(rows + " rows were updated");
      }
    }
    //submit any remaining data
    System.out.println("Sending unsubmitted updates");
    rows = pStmtPatient.sendBatch();
    System.out.println(rows + " rows were updated");
    rows = pStmtStays.sendBatch();
    System.out.println(rows + " rows were updated");

    //auto commit is disabled, so need to explicitly commit data
    //NOTE: if this method throws any exception, the data does not
    //get committed
    connection.commit();
  }

  public static void main(String[] args) {
    try {
      OracleBatch ob = new OracleBatch();
      Vector data = ob.readData("OracleBatch.data");
      ob.insert(data);
    } catch (Exception e) {
      try { connection.rollback(); } catch (Exception ignored) {}
      e.printStackTrace();
    }
  }
}
```

The data file for the class above is saved in the jdbc\Data directory as OracleBatch.data:

```
10002+Mary+Smith+2-Jul-2000+3-Jul-2000
10003+John+Adams+12-Aug-2000+13-Aug-2000
10004+Dianne+Barns+12-Aug-2000+15-Aug-2000
10005+George+Custer+13-Aug-2000+23-Aug-2000
10006+Dan+Davis+14-Aug-2000+24-Aug-2000
10007+Ethel+Esther+15-Aug-2000+16-Aug-2000
10008+Frank+Frankland+4-Sep-2000+6-Sep-2000
10009+Gina+Gratowski+5-Sep-2000+7-Sep-2000
```

```
10010+Harold+Haster+6-Sep-2000+22-Sep-2000
10011+John+Jameson+13-Sep-2000+18-Sep-2000
10023+George+Smith+2-Sep-2000+15-Sep-2000
10024+George+Grand+22-Sep-2000+30-Sep-2000
10025+Harold+Genovese+03-Sep-2000+12-Sep-2000
```

There are a few other methods that can be used with Oracle update batching. When you call the `setDefaultExecuteBatch(int)` method of the `Connection` class, that sets the execute batch value for all statement objects created from the connection. To change that value for a particular instance of `OraclePreparedStatement`, call:

```
statement.setExecuteBatch(int);
```

To send the current set of SQL statements without waiting for a number of statements to reach the execute batch value, call:

```
statement.sendBatch();
```

There are three other situations that will cause the driver to send the current set of queued SQL statements:

❑ The statement is closed

❑ The connection is closed

❑ The transaction is committed

Resultsets

Resultsets were mentioned extensively in the previous section as the return value from a statement that executed a query against a database. In JDBC 1.0, resultsets were useful, although somewhat limited. With a JDBC 1.0 resultset, you started at the first returned row, and stepped through the results row by row with no ability to go to a specific row, either forwards or backwards. JDBC 2.0 introduces the scrollable resultset. With a scrollable resultset, you can move forwards or backwards within the resultset, or jump to a specific row. The other big change in JDBC 2.0 is that you can now use the resultset directly to update the data in the database.

As mentioned at the beginning of this section on statements, there were originally three methods for creating statements: `createStatement()`, `prepareStatement(String)`, and `prepareCall(String)`. JDBC 2.0 still supports those method calls. If you use one of those methods, and then call `executeQuery()`, the resultset that is returned is a non-scrollable, non-updateable resultset. To get a scrollable, updateable resultset, you have to prepare the statement to return a scrollable resultset. Three additional method calls were added to the API to do this:

❑ `connection.createStatement(int resultSetType, int resultSetConcurrency);`

❑ `connection.prepareStatement(String sql, int resultSetType, int resultSetConcurrency);`

❑ `connection.prepareCall(String sql, int resultSetType, int resultSetConcurrency);`

The first additional parameter sets the type of the resultset that is returned from a query. The type refers to whether the resultset will be scrollable or non-scrollable. The parameter must be one of three fields that are part of the JDBC 2.0 `ResultSet` interface:

❏ `ResultSet.TYPE_FORWARD_ONLY` indicates that the resultset is non-scrollable.

❏ `ResultSet.TYPE_SCROLL_SENSITIVE` indicates that the resultset is scrollable and is sensitive to changes committed by other transactions or other statements within the same transaction.

❏ `ResultSet.TYPE_SCROLL_INSENSITIVE` indicates that the resultset is scrollable but is insensitive to changes committed by other transactions or other statements within the same transaction.

The second parameter sets the **concurrency** of the resultset returned from a query. Concurrency refers to whether a resultset can be used to update the underlying table or whether it is a read-only resultset. Again the parameter must be a field from the resultset interface:

❏ `ResultSet.CONCUR_READ_ONLY`

❏ `ResultSet.CONCUR_UPDATABLE`

> **Note that both of the new parameters are of type int. This means that if you enter TYPE_SCROLL_SENSITIVE where you meant to enter CONCUR_READ_ONLY, and vice versa, the compiler will compile the code successfully. Only at run time will you possibly discover a problem when the resultset does not behave as you expected.**

Resultset objects returned by a call to `executeQuery()` or `execute()` will be able to scroll and can be updated as indicated by the parameters used to create the statement. Since the ability to scroll is independent of the ability to update, this leads to six different possible kinds of resultsets from a statement object:

❏ `connection.createStatement(ResultSet.TYPE_FORWARD_ONLY, ResultSet.CONCUR_READ_ONLY)` – same as a JDBC 1.0 `ResultSet`, a query returns a `ResultSet` that can't go backwards and can't be used to update the underlying data

❏ `connection.createStatement(ResultSet.TYPE_SCROLL_SENSITIVE, ResultSet.CONCUR_READ_ONLY)` – a query returns a resultset that can be scrolled to any particular row but can't be used to update the underlying data

❏ `connection.createStatement(ResultSet.TYPE_SCROLL_INSENSITIVE, ResultSet.CONCUR_READ_ONLY)` – a query returns a resultset that can be scrolled to any particular row but can't be used to update the underlying data

❏ `connection.createStatement(ResultSet.TYPE_FORWARD_ONLY, ResultSet.CONCUR_UPDATABLE)` – a query returns a resultset that can't go backwards; it can be used to update or delete rows, but can't be used to insert a new row

❏ `connection.createStatement(ResultSet.TYPE_SCROLL_SENSITIVE, ResultSet.CONCUR_ UPDATABLE)` – a query returns a resultset that can be scrolled to any particular row and can be used to update, delete, or insert rows

❏ `connection.createStatement(ResultSet.TYPE_SCROLL_INSENSITIVE, ResultSet.CONCUR_ UPDATABLE)` – a query returns a resultset that can be scrolled to any particular row and can be used to update, delete, or insert rows

The prepareStatement(String, int, int) and prepareCall(String, int, int) methods work in the same manner as the createStatement(int, int) method. The only difference being that the prepareStatement() and prepareCall() methods have the SQL String as the first parameter in the method call.

Getting And Moving Through Resultsets

A resultset is returned by executing a query using the executeQuery() or execute() method of a statement object. A resultset returned from a query has the cursor positioned before the first row. Once you have a ResultSet reference, you call the method next() to step through the rows. The first call to next() advances to the first row in the resultset and returns true. If there is a row following the current row, next() advances to that row and returns true; if there is no following row, next() returns false. Since next() returns a boolean, you can use it directly in a while loop. The checkData() method from the SimpleStatement class earlier in the chapter executes a query that returns a resultset, then uses next() in a while loop to traverse the rows of data:

```
void checkData() throws SQLException {
    String sql = "SELECT p.patient_id, p.given_name, p.surname, " +
        "h.admit_date, h.discharge_date " +
        "FROM patients p, hospital_stays h " +
        "WHERE h.patient_id = p.patient_id";
    resultSet = statement.executeQuery(sql);
    //resultSet.next() advances to the next row in the ResultSet and
    //return true. When there are no more rows, it returns false
    while (resultSet.next()) {
        System.out.print(resultSet.getInt(1) + " ");
        System.out.print(resultSet.getString(2) + " ");
        System.out.print(resultSet.getString(3) + " ");
        System.out.print(resultSet.getDate(4) + " ");
        System.out.println(resultSet.getDate(5) + " ");
    }
}
```

The assumption up to this point is that there are actually rows in the resultset. However, sometimes the resultset may be returned without a row to act upon. In this case, the resultset will return false on the first call to next().

A frequently asked question with resultsets is how to determine the number of rows returned from a query before actually traversing the rows and reading the data. With a non-scrollable resultset, there is no easy way. The common techniques for determining the number of rows returned both involve executing two queries against the database.

The first way is the brute force approach: get the result, then count the rows. With this technique, if you need to do something with the rows, you will need to execute the query a second time:

```
String sql = "SELECT * FROM emp";
int rowCount = 0;
ResultSet rs = statement.executeQuery(sql);
while (rs.next()) {
    ++rowCount;
}
rs = statement.executeQuery(sql);
while (rs.next()) {
    //access the data...
}
```

The other technique is slightly more elegant. You let the database count for you. Then when you need the data, you execute the select statement that returns the rows, rather than the count.

```
String sql = "SELECT count(*) FROM emp";
ResultSet rs = statement.executeUpdate(sql);
rs.next();
//the count is the first and only column, get the first column with
int rowCount = rs.getInt(1);
```

Neither of the above techniques is very satisfactory. One problem is that the underlying data could change between the first and second query. Also, you have to be careful to use the same query both times. Unfortunately, if you only have a non-scrollable resultset, you don't have much choice. With a scrollable resultset, though, you have many more options for moving through a resultset.

Scrollable Resultsets

The JDBC 2.0 `ResultSet` interface provides an entire set of new methods to enable random access to a resultset's rows. In addition to the `next()` method, the `ResultSet` implements methods for moving to any row in a `ResultSet`. These additional methods only work if the `ResultSet` is scrollable; if the `ResultSet` is non-scrollable, the methods will throw an `SQLException` when called. Here are the methods:

❑   `boolean first()` – moves to the first row in the resultset. Returns `true`, unless there are no rows in the resultset.

❑   `boolean last()` – moves to the last rows in the resultset. Returns `true`, unless there are no rows in the resultset.

❑   `boolean previous()` – moves to the previous row in the resultset. Similar to `next()`, returns `true` if the resultset is positioned at a valid row; returns `false` when `previous()` causes the resultset to be positioned before the first row.

❑   `boolean absolute(int row)` – moves to the row given by the parameter. If the parameter is positive, moves to the given row from the beginning; if negative, moves to the given row from the end (that is, `absolute(-1)` is the last row). If `absolute(int)` moves beyond the first or last row, the cursor is left before the first row or after the last row. Returns `true` when the row is valid. Throws an exception if the parameter is 0.

❑   `boolean relative(int offset)` – moves forwards or backwards from the current row by an amount given by the offset parameter. If `relative(int)` moves beyond the first or last row, the cursor is left before the first row or after the last row. Returns `true` when the row is valid. Do not call when the resultset is positioned before the first or after the last row.

❑   `void beforeFirst()` – moves to a position before the first row in the resultset.

❑   `boolean isFirst()` – returns `true` if the resultset is positioned at the first row.

❑   `boolean isBeforeFirst()` – returns `true` if the resultset is positioned before the first row in the resultset.

❑   `void afterLast()` – moves to a position after the last row in the resultset.

❑   `boolean isLast()` – returns `true` if the resultset is positioned at the last row.

❑   `boolean isAfterLast()` – returns `true` if the resultset is positioned after the last row.

❑   `int getRow()` – returns the row number of the current row.

> The Oracle database does not support a scrollable cursor, so the scrollable resultset is supported directly by the driver. It does this by caching the rows in memory. For this reason, the driver may consume all the memory if there are a large number of rows in a scrollable resultset and a scrollable resultset should not be used when the query returns a large number of rows. The exact value of "large" will depend on your environment (memory, number of columns in a row, number of rows, etc.)

Recall the problem from the previous section of determining the numbers of rows in a resultset before accessing the data in each row. Using these new methods, the problem becomes much easier to solve:

```
String sql = "SELECT * FROM emp";
ResultSet rs = statement.executeQuery(sql);
rs.last();
int rowCount = rs.getRow();
```

'Easier' is a relative term. The code snippet above is easier in the sense that it needs only a single database query to get the rows and to know how many rows are returned. If you executed a query that returned a million rows, it might be easier to execute select count(*) from emp *first and then get the rows with a second query.*

Retrieving Data from a Resultset

Whether a resultset is a forward only or a scrollable resultset, you still need a way to access the data from the resultset. The resultset interface defines numerous methods for getting the data from each column in the resultset.

For each primitive Java type, there are two corresponding getXXX() methods. For example, suppose that you have an Oracle table with a column that holds a number. This hypothetical table is defined such that the column value is a whole number from 0 to 1,000,000. In Java, you would use a variable of type int to ensure that the largest possible value in the table could be assigned to the variable. To get that value from a resultset, you would use one of two forms of the getInteger() method.

- ❑ getInteger(String)
- ❑ getInteger(int)

When you know the name of the column, you can use the getInteger(String) method. The String parameter is the name of the column in the resultset that you want to retrieve. When using getInteger(int) the int parameter is the number of the column in the resultset that you want to retrieve. Columns in a resultset are numbered starting with 1. The order of the columns is either the same order as in the query when each column is explicitly named, or the order specified in the table definition when using SELECT * in the query.

> The first column in a resultset is number 1 (as compared to Java arrays, vectors, etc., where the first element is number 0).

Earlier in this resultset section of the chapter, the checkData() method from the SimpleStatement class was shown. That method performed a query that retrieved the rows from the patients and hospital_stays tables using the SQL here:

```
String sql = "SELECT p.patient_id, p.given_name, p.surname, " +
    "h.admit_date, h.discharge_date " +
    "FROM patients p, hospital_stays h " +
    "WHERE h.patient_id = p.patient_id";
```

In this example, the columns in the resultset are the columns as named in the SELECT statement. The first column is the patient_id which is an int, the second is the String given_name, etc. The checkData() method retrieved and printed the columns with this code:

```
System.out.print(resultSet.getInt(1) + " ");
System.out.print(resultSet.getString(2) + " ");
System.out.print(resultSet.getString(3) + " ");
System.out.print(resultSet.getDate(4) + " ");
System.out.println(resultSet.getDate(5) + " ");
```

Since this code "knows" the column names, it could also have been written like this:

```
System.out.print(resultSet.getInt("patient_id") + " ");
System.out.print(resultSet.getString("given_name") + " ");
System.out.print(resultSet.getString("surname") + " ");
System.out.print(resultSet.getDate("admit_date") + " ");
System.out.println(resultSet.getDate("discharge_date") + " ");
```

When using the String parameter, you use the name of the column in the resultset, not the name in the table. The code sample above used the column names as defined by the table. If, however, the SQL had been:

```
String sql = "SELECT p.given_name as First_Name, " +
    "p.surname AS Last_Name, FROM patients p";
```

Then the String parameters would have to be First_Name and Last_Name:

```
System.out.print(resultSet.getString("First_Name") + " ");
System.out.print(resultSet.getString("Last_Name") + " ");
```

The JDBC 1.0 specification includes accessor methods for all the primitive Java types along with some additional accessors such as getTime() and getObject(). The JDBC 2.0 specification added support for additional SQL types including BLOBs (Binary Large Object), CLOBs (Character Large Object), and BFILEs (Binary File). You can consult the Oracle Java API Javadoc for the complete list of methods and descriptions of what those methods do. (If it was installed, you can find the Javadoc in the Oracle jdbc directory)

Updatable Resultsets

The second big change in JDBC 2.0 is the ability to update the data in a resultset, and have those changes be reflected in the underlying database. In JDBC 1.0 the only way to change the data in a table was to execute some SQL using a statement. With JDBC 2.0, you can update the data directly through the resultset.

> Unlike some JDBC 2.0 features that Oracle supports in classes111.zip, updateable resultsets are supported only in Oracle's JDBC 2.0 implementation, classes12.zip.

To be able to do this, you have to indicate whether the resultset is updatable or not when you create the Statement object. The parameters passed to the connection when creating the statement were discussed above in the "Statement Concurrency and Type" section. To review, when creating a statement, you can pass a parameter that indicates whether the statement is updatable or not. That parameter can have one of two values:

- ❑ ResultSet.CONCUR_READ_ONLY
- ❑ ResultSet.CONCUR_UPDATABLE

A statement created with ResultSet.CONCUR_READ_ONLY cannot be updated. If, however, a statement is created with ResultSet.CONCUR_UPDATABLE, you can update the data in the table using the resultset.

Updating Data in a Resultset

To update the data in a resultset, there are updateXXX() methods corresponding to each Java primitive type. There are also update methods for some SQL types that correspond to Java objects, such as Date. After you've changed the data in the resultset, the changes are propagated to the underlying table by calling the updateRow() method.

The updateRow() method causes the change to be applied to the table, but may or may not cause the change to be committed. If autocommit is enabled, then calling updateRow() will cause the change to be committed immediately. When autocommit is disabled, changes are committed only when commit() is called, or when the connection is closed. If autocommit is disabled, then the change can be rolled back by a call to connection.rollback().

To cancel an update before updateRow() or commit() is called, your code calls:

```
    rs.cancelRowUpdates();
```

The method cancelRowUpdates() discards all changes that were made to the current row. Previous changes which were "committed" using the updateRow() method are not affected by the cancel. Another way to discard changes to the current row is to call a method that moves to another row, such as next(), previous(), lastRow(), etc. Moving to another row in the resultset has the effect of canceling changes made to the current row. Canceling changes will not undo any changes that were previously committed; if autocommit is disabled, the rollback() method can be called to discard any changes which were made but not committed.

The code that follows demonstrates the techniques for scrolling and updating a table. The DBTable class below is used to connect to the database and query a table in the database. You will need to use Java 2 and JDBC 2.0 for the next class and the other classes in this example. The query() method of this class makes a connection to the database and queries for all the columns in a given table. The connection parameters and table name for the query are passed in the constructor.

```
package jdbc.ResultSet2;

import java.sql.*;

/** class that queries a table and produces a scrollable and updatable
result set */
public class DBTable {
  String url, username, password, tablename;
```

```
      Connection connection;
      Statement statement;
      ResultSet rset;

      /** constructor */
      public DBTable(String url, String username, String password, String tablename) {
        this.url = url;
        this.username = username;
        this.password = password;
        this.tablename = tablename;
      }

      /** makes connection to database and queries all columns for a specific table */
      public void query() throws SQLException {
        Connection connection = DriverManager.getConnection(url, username,
                                                  password);
        statement = connection.createStatement(ResultSet.TYPE_SCROLL_SENSITIVE,
                                      ResultSet.CONCUR_UPDATABLE);
        //NOTE: for the result set to be updatable, you must explicitly specify
        //each column OR you must use tablename.* syntax
        String sql = "select " + tablename + ".* from " + tablename;
        rset = statement.executeQuery(sql);
      }

      /** create the view for the result set */
      public TableView getTableView() throws SQLException {
        return new TableView(rset);
      }
    }
```

The DBTable class above creates a TableView object in its getTableView() method. The
TableView class shown below provides the functionality for scrolling and updating the ResultSet.
The TableView constructor gets the first row of data from the resultset and displays it using the
JPanel functionality it inherits from its parent class:

```
    package jdbc.ResultSet2;

    import java.awt.*;
    import javax.swing.*;
    import java.sql.*;

    /** A class which can be used to view any result set */
    public class TableView extends JPanel {
      ResultSet rset;
      ResultSetMetaData rsmd;
      JTextField[] fields;
      int cols;

      /** constructor, initializes to first row of data in result set.
          Result set must be scrollable and updatable */
      public TableView(ResultSet rset) throws SQLException {
        this.rset = rset;
        rsmd = rset.getMetaData();

        setLayout(new GridLayout(0,2));
        if (rset.next()) {
          adjustView();
        }
      }
```

The adjustView() method below determines the number of columns that need to be displayed, and then extracts the data for a row and displays the data. To do this it uses an object obtained from the resultset with the getMetaData() call in the constructor. The getMetaData() method returns a ResultSetMetaData object which holds information about the resultset. This object is used to get the column names for the display. (The ResultSetMetaData object is discussed at the end of the ResultSet section.) Note also, that since each value must be converted to a String for the display, the code uses the getString() method and lets the ResultSet handle the conversion of the column value to a String.

```
/** adds a name and value for each column to the JPanel (this class).
Uses ResultSetMetaData to dynamically get the column count, column name,
and column value for a row */
void adjustView() throws SQLException {
  removeAll();
  cols = rsmd.getColumnCount();
  fields = new JTextField[cols+1];
  for (int i = 1; i <= cols; i++) {
    String name = rsmd.getColumnName(i);
    JPanel namePanel = new JPanel(new FlowLayout(FlowLayout.RIGHT));
    namePanel.add(new JLabel(name));
    add(namePanel);

    String value = rset.getString(i);
    JPanel valuePanel = new JPanel(new FlowLayout(FlowLayout.LEFT));
    JTextField text = new JTextField(value,20);
    text.setEditable(false);
    fields[i] = text;
    valuePanel.add(text);
    add(valuePanel);
  }
  validate();
  setVisible(true);
}
```

The next set of methods are used to scroll through the TableView. The methods are public so that they can be called by the user interface; the TableView class accepts the call and then delegates to the ResultSet:

```
/** scrolls to next row in result set */
public void next() throws SQLException { rset.next(); adjustView(); }
/** scrolls to previous row in result set */
public void previous() throws SQLException {
  rset.previous();
  adjustView();
}
/** scrolls to first row in result set */
public void first() throws SQLException { rset.first(); adjustView(); }
/** scrolls to last row in result set */
public void last() throws SQLException { rset.last(); adjustView(); }
/** returns true if the result set is not on the last row */
public boolean hasNext() throws SQLException {
  if (rset.isLast()) return false; else return true;
}
/** returns true if the result set is not on the first row */
public boolean hasPrevious() throws SQLException {
  if (rset.isFirst()) return false; else return true;
}
```

This next method changes the text fields in the `JPanel` so that they can be edited. The test fields are initialized to be non-editable (see the `adjustView()` method above). This method is provided for the user interface to call when the user wants to edit a record.

```java
/** Enables the text fields for editing */
public void enableEdit() {
  for (int i = 1; i < fields.length; i++) {
    fields[i].setEditable(true);
  }
}
```

The final method does the updating of the resultset. Using the `ResultSetMetaData`, the method finds every column in the resultset that is a VARCHAR2 or NUMERIC. It then finds the corresponding text field in the `JPanel` and uses the value in the text field to update the row. The method only updates VARCHAR2 or NUMERIC types for simplicity and brevity. In a real application, you would want to handle all the SQL types.

```java
/** Updates the database table based on the text fields. Updates every
column that is VARCHAR or NUMERIC. Other types are not handled. To avoid
trying to determine if a value has actually been edited, updates every
column even if the value did not change */
public void update() throws SQLException, NumberFormatException {
  for (int i = 1; i <= cols; i++) {
    int type = rsmd.getColumnType(i);
    switch (type) {
      case java.sql.Types.VARCHAR:
        rset.updateString(i, fields[i].getText());
        break;
      case java.sql.Types.NUMERIC:
        //handle blank values
        String textValue = fields[i].getText();
        if (textValue == null || textValue.equals("")) textValue = "0";

        //if the type is NUMERIC, determine whether it is int/long or
        //double/float. Use long or double for all values
        int scale = rsmd.getScale(i);
        if (scale == 0) {
            long value = Long.parseLong(textValue);
            rset.updateLong(i, value);
        } else {
          double value = Double.parseDouble(textValue);
          rset.updateDouble(i, value);
        }
        break;
    }
  }
  //updateRow commits the changes
  rset.updateRow();
}
```

For reasons of space and relevance, the user interface code is not shown. However, it is provided as part of the downloadable code for this chapter.

Inserting a Row Through a Resultset

Rows are inserted into a resultset and the underlying table by moving to a special row in the resultset and updating the contents of each column in this row. The special staging row is known as the insert row, and you move to it using the method:

```
rs.moveToInsertRow();
```

Changes are made to this row with the updateXXX() methods, and then applied using the insertRow() method. Even though the row is inserted into the database, the row is **not** added to the resultset. New rows will only be visible in the resultset if a new query is executed and the new rows are selected as part of the query.

The rules for committing changes with insertRow() are the same as for updateRow() shown before: when auto-commit is enabled, changes are automatically committed by calling insertRow(); when auto-commit is disabled, changes can be committed or rolled back; moving to a different row cancels the current change (unlike updating, though, there is no cancelRowInsert() method). Here's an illustration of inserting a row through a resultset into the patients table:

```
//assume stmt creates a scrollable, updatable ResultSet
//for Oracle must include table name with * for "select *" syntax
rs = stmt.executeQuery("SELECT patients.* FROM patients");
rs.moveToInsertRow()
rs.updateInt(1, 92375);   //patient_id
rs.updateString(2, "Chapman"); //surname
rs.updateDate(3, new Date()); //given name
rs.insertRow();
```

There is one important difference between updating row data and inserting a row. When updating a resultset, it does not matter if only some of the columns from the table were retrieved by the query; update acts on individual columns. When inserting a row, it does make a difference. Inserting a row acts upon an entire row; so you must be able to insert data into all columns that are required to be NOT NULL. If the resultset does not retrieve all NOT NULL columns, you will not be able to update the resultset or the table. If you try to insert a row under these circumstances, an SQLException will be thrown.

> When updating an Oracle table through a resultset, you must select all the columns using the **table_name.*** syntax (using just "**SELECT** *" will throw an **SQLException**) or by specifically naming the columns to be selected.

The resultset keeps track of which row was the current row, before the method moveToInsertRow() was called. You can return the resultset to that row by calling

```
rs.moveToCurrentRow();
```

You can also use any of the other movement methods. When that method is a relative move, like next() or previous(), that move is made relative to the current row, not the insert row.

Deleting a Row Through a Resultset

Deleting a row is performed by moving to a row and calling the `deleteRow()` method. For example, to delete the last row in a resultset, use the code below to move to the last row and delete it:

```
rs.last();
rs.deleteRow();
```

Note that the `deleteRow()` method deletes the row from the resultset and the underlying table. If autocommit is enabled, the delete is also immediately committed. A delete can only be undone if autocommit is disabled, and `rollback()` is called before the delete is committed.

MetaData

So far, this chapter has discussed getting the data from a table with a resultset. The JDBC specification also provides two ways to get information about the database and tables. This data about the data is known as **metadata**. One metadata object was used in the `TableView` class presented previously in the chapter. The `TableView` class used a `ResultSetMetaData` object to get information about the data in the `ResultSet`. Here are the method calls that were used in the `TableView` class:

```
rsmd = rset.getMetaData();
String name = rsmd.getColumnName(i);
int type = rsmd.getColumnType(i);
```

The first method, `getMetaData()` returns the `ResultSetMetaData` object. The `TableView` class used the `getColumnName(int)` method to get the name used by the `ResultSet` for each column. The `getColumnType(int)` method returns one of the variables from the `java.sql.Types` class to identify the type of data held by a particular column. The `int` parameter in these methods and all the `ResultSetMetaData` methods that take an int parameter is the column number of the column in the resultset for which you want the information. You can find the complete list of the `ResultSetMetaData` methods in the Oracle JDBC API Javadoc.

Database MetaData

The second metadata object is obtained from a `Connection` object and it provides information about the entire database. This object is a `DatabaseMetaData` object. Here is the method call to get an instance of `DatabaseMetaData`:

```
DatabaseMetaData dbmd = connection.getMetaData();
```

Among the many methods of the `DatabaseMetaData` class are methods to get information about the driver, the features supported by the database, the maximum and minimum values for various database features, table names in the database, the table structure of tables in the database, and the primary and foreign keys in the database.

A `DatabaseMetaData` object can be obtained by calling `getMetaData()` on the `Connection` object you are using to interact with the database, and it can then be used to retrieve comprehensive information about the database as a whole. Information about the database itself can be obtained, such as what the maximum length of an SQL statement is, and whether full outer joins are supported. This type of information might be useful if you are writing an application to run on multiple databases, where you want the code to take different courses of action depending on the actual database being used. It is also possible to retrieve the contents of the database: the tables, packages, procedures, and so on. For example:

```
getProcedureColumns(String catalog, String schemaPattern, String
procedureNamePattern, String columnName pattern)
```

retrieves a `ResultSet` containing stored procedure parameters and result columns for procedures matching the patterns which are passed in as parameters. The `ResultSet` which is returned contains the procedure name, parameter names, parameter types (`IN`, `OUT`, etc.), data types, and so on. The JDBC API documentation (http://java.sun.com/j2se/1.3/docs/api/index.html) gives full details about these.

This area of functionality is useful for writing programs to access many different procedures by reusing the same Java code. You do not have to know which procedures the Java code is going to call as you are writing it; you can instead dynamically find out what procedures are in the database and then create `CallableStatement` objects to access them, setting their parameters according to what `DatabaseMetaData` has told you they need to be.

Another use of `DatabaseMetaData` might be to generate Java programs based on your database procedures, in the same way as Oracle Designer provides the facility to generate packages based on the tables. You could write a program which, given a package or procedure name, creates a Java class to call that package or procedure, thus saving developers the tedium of generating many almost identical classes.

Advanced Topics

This section of the chapter will show how to access BLOB, CLOB, and BFILE data from an Oracle database. The last part of the chapter will briefly discuss using a `DataSource` to get a database connection.

BLOBs

Binary Large Objects (BLOBs) are, as the name suggests, a large amount of binary data stored in a database table. You can store any kind of data in a BLOB column, such as raw binary data, an MP3 file, an image file: anything that is a sequence of bytes. The only limitation is that the size of a BLOB is limited to 4 gigabytes in Oracle 8i.

Accessing BLOB data is performed using many of the same JDBC methods that have been presented previously in this chapter. One important difference is that when you query a table that contains BLOB data, the actual binary data is not sent to the client software. Rather the JDBC code receives a "reference" or locator to the actual data in the database. The locator allows your code to use the BLOB without actually accessing the bytes that make up the BLOB. When you need to read or write the bytes, you will use an input or output stream.

Writing a BLOB from One Table to Another

As mentioned previously, when you query a table that contains a BLOB column, you get a "reference" or locator to the BLOB field. This locator allows you to use the BLOB field without actually accessing the bytes of the BLOB. Later in this section you will see a Java class that opens input and output streams to read and write binary data. However, if you want to transfer BLOB data directly from one table to another, you can use the locator without needing to open an input or output stream. Here is a very short code snippet illustrating this technique.

```
//assume sql is a query which returns a Blob in column 1
ResultSet rs = statement.executeQuery(sql);
rs.next();
```

For JDBC 1.0 use:

```
oracle.jdbc2.Blob blob = ((OracleResultSet) rs).getBlob(1);
//for JDBC 2.0 use
java.sql.Blob blob = rs.getBlob(1);

//assume sql is now an insert statement with one bind variable
PreparedStatement ps = connection.prepareStatement(sql);
//use the blob locator that was retrieved above
//for JDBC 1.0 use
((oracle.jdbc.driver.OraclePreparedStatement)ps).setBlob(1, blob);
```

For JDBC 2.0 use:

```
ps.setBlob(1, blob);
ps.executeUpdate();
```

Reading and Writing Binary Data

If you need to access the binary data in a BLOB field, you must use input and output streams. This section presents an application that shows how to read and write binary data. The sample code uses JDBC 2.0 to read and write the BLOB. The SQL to create the BLOB table used in the example code is:

```
CREATE TABLE media (
  name VARCHAR2(200),
  data BLOB
);
```

Here is the code that will read binary data from a file and write it to the media table presented above.

```
package jdbc.lob;

import javax.swing.*;
import java.io.*;
import java.sql.*;
import DriverData;

public class WriteBlobToDb {
  Connection conn;
  Statement stmt;
```

```java
  ResultSet rs;
  int bufferSize;

  public WriteBlobToDb() throws SQLException, ClassNotFoundException
  {
    //Load driver and make connection
    Class.forName("oracle.jdbc.driver.OracleDriver");
    conn = DriverManager.getConnection(DriverData.url,
      DriverData.user,DriverData.passw);
    stmt = conn.createStatement();
  }

  public void sendToDb() {
    String pathname, name;
    int amount = 0;
    OutputStream out = null;
    BufferedInputStream in = null;

    //Use a JFileChooser to let the user select the file to be
    //read and written to the media table
    JFileChooser chooser = new JFileChooser();
    int returnVal = chooser.showOpenDialog(null);
    if(returnVal == JFileChooser.APPROVE_OPTION) {
      pathname = chooser.getSelectedFile().getAbsolutePath();
      name = chooser.getSelectedFile().getName();
      chooser = null;
    } else {
      System.out.println("No file selected for write to db");
      System.out.println("Program terminating");
      return;
    }

    try {
      //Since BLOB is written with stream, disable autocommit
      conn.setAutoCommit(false);
      //insert a row into the BLOB table, use the empty_blob()
      //construct for the BLOB field. empty_blob() creates the
      //BLOB locator
      stmt.executeUpdate("insert into media values ('" + name +
        "', empty_blob())");
      //Retrieve the row that was just inserted
      //NOTE: Must use 'select for update syntax' to write BLOB
      rs = stmt.executeQuery(
        "select data from media where name = '" +
        name + "' for update");
      if (rs.next()) {

        //Get the BLOB locator
        Blob blob = rs.getBlob(1);
        //Get the output stream which will be used to send
        //data to the table. Use Oracle extension because
        //JDBC 2.0 does not support writing data to BLOB
        out = ((oracle.sql.BLOB)blob).getBinaryOutputStream();

        //Let driver compute buffer size for writing to BLOB
        bufferSize = ((oracle.sql.BLOB)blob).getBufferSize();
```

```
        //Create a buffered stream to read from the file
        in = new BufferedInputStream(
          new FileInputStream(pathname), bufferSize);

        //Create a byte buffer and start reading from the file
        byte[] b = new byte[bufferSize];
        int count = in.read(b, 0, bufferSize);

        //write the bytes using the OutputStream
        //loop until all bytes are written to the table
        while (count != -1) {
          out.write(b, 0, count);
          amount += count;
          System.out.println("Processed " + amount + " bytes.");
          count = in.read(b, 0, bufferSize);
        }
        System.out.println("Processed " + amount + " bytes. Finished.");

        //Close the Input and Output Streams
        out.close();
        out = null;
        in.close();
        in = null;
        //And finally, commit the changes
        conn.commit();
      }
    } catch (Exception e) {
      e.printStackTrace();
      try { conn.rollback(); } catch (Exception ignored) {}
    } finally {
      //if an exception occurred, the streams may not have been closed
      //so close them here if needed
      if (out != null) try { out.close(); } catch (Exception ignored) {}
      if (in != null) try { in.close(); } catch (Exception ignored) {}
    }
  }

  public static void main(String[] args) {
    try {
      WriteBlobToDb w = new WriteBlobToDb();
      w.sendToDb();
    } catch (Exception e) {
      e.printStackTrace();
    } finally {
      System.exit(0);
    }
  }
}
```

All the steps needed to write binary data to a table are commented in the above code, so only a few points about the above code will be mentioned. First two important points need to be emphasized:

❑   The binary data is written to the table using an output stream. The autocommit mode **must** be disabled for this to work correctly.

❑   The code uses a select statement to get the BLOB locator. The select statement **must** use the FOR UPDATE clause if the locator will be used to write binary data to the table.

The code uses two Oracle specific methods to write the data to the database. First, because JDBC 2.0 does not support writing binary data to a table, an Oracle method is used to get the output stream which is used to write the data. Second, an Oracle method is used to calculate the optimal buffer size for writing the binary data to the table.

The code uses a very minimal user interface. When you run the code, a file chooser dialog is displayed; use the dialog to select a file from your filesystem that will be written to the table. After choosing a file, the dialog is closed. The code reads the data from the file and writes it to the media table. If you do not choose a file, the program exits. The status of the write operation is reported by printing to System.out.

Reading binary data from a table and writing it out to an output stream is almost as easy as changing the OutputStream and InputStream in the code above. Here is the code that reads binary data from the BLOB column in the media table, and writes the data to a file. The class is named ReadBlobFromDb and the method that does the work is named readFromDb(). Other than the readFromDb() method and the class name, this class is identical to the class above, so only the readFromDb() method is shown. As usual, the complete source code can be downloaded from Wrox.

```java
public void readFromDb() {
    String pathname, name;
    int amount = 0;
    BufferedOutputStream out = null;
    InputStream in = null;

    //Use a JFileChooser to let the user select the file to be
    //read and written to the media table
    JFileChooser chooser = new JFileChooser();
    int returnVal = chooser.showOpenDialog(null);
    if(returnVal == JFileChooser.APPROVE_OPTION) {
      pathname = chooser.getSelectedFile().getAbsolutePath();
      name = chooser.getSelectedFile().getName();
      chooser = null;
    } else {
      System.out.println("No file selected for writing data from db");
      System.out.println("Program terminating");
      return;
    }

    try {
      //Retrieve the row that has the selected name
      rs = stmt.executeQuery(
        "select data from media where name = '" + name + "'");
      if (rs.next()) {

        //Get the BLOB locator
        Blob blob = rs.getBlob(1);
        //Get the input stream which will be used to read
        //data from the table. GetBinaryStream() is standard JDBC 2.0
        in = blob.getBinaryStream();

        //let the driver determine the buffer size
        bufferSize = ((oracle.sql.BLOB)blob).getBufferSize();

        //Create a buffered stream to write to the file
        out = new BufferedOutputStream(
          new FileOutputStream(pathname), (int)bufferSize);
```

```
                    //Create a byte buffer and start reading from the file
                    byte[] b = new byte[(int)bufferSize];
                    int count = in.read(b, 0, (int)bufferSize);

                    //write the bytes using the OutputStream
                    //loop until all bytes are written to the table
                    while (count != -1) {
                      out.write(b, 0, count);
                      amount += count;
                      System.out.println("Processed " + amount + " bytes.");
                      count = in.read(b, 0, (int)bufferSize);
                    }
                    System.out.println("Processed " + amount + " bytes. Finished.");

                    //Close the Input and Output Streams
                    out.close();
                    out = null;
                    in.close();
                    in = null;
                  } else {
                    //file not found in table
                    System.out.println("The name " + name + " was not " +
                      "found in the media table");
                  }
                } catch (Exception e) {
                  e.printStackTrace();
                } finally {
                  //if an exception occurred, the streams may not have been closed
                  //so close them here if needed
                  if (out != null) try { out.close(); } catch (Exception ignored) {}
                  if (in != null) try { in.close(); } catch (Exception ignored) {}
                }
              }
```

With the readFromDb() method, the JFileChooser is used to identify the directory where the binary data will be written. You must enter a file name into the dialog that matches the name field stored in the media table, although the directory can be any directory. You should choose a directory different than that where the original file is stored so that you can see that the binary data is actually written to a file.

CLOBs

Character large objects (CLOBs) are similar to BLOBs, except they are used when saving large blocks of text (with a 4Gb limit) to a database. Another difference is that to materialize the data from the table, you have your choice of using an InputStream (as you did with a BLOB) or a Reader.

Like BLOBs, when querying one table for CLOB data and inserting that data into another table in the same database, you can treat the CLOB locator just as though it was the actual CLOB data. The CLOB data can be inserted into another table using the setClob() method of a PreparedStatement. The code used would be identical to that shown in the "Writing a BLOB from One Table to Another" section above (except for replacing getBlob() or setBlob() with getClob() or setClob()).

Reading and Writing Character Data

In this section, the `WriteBlobToDb.java` and `ReadBlobFromDb.java` code from the previous section will be modified to read and write CLOB data using streams.

The CLOB example uses a different database table. Here's the table definition:

```
CREATE TABLE reports (
  name VARCHAR2(200),
  data CLOB
);
```

The code to read and write CLOB data to the table is almost identical to the code that reads and writes BLOB data. Rather than repeating two complete classes, here is the section of the `writeToDb()` and `readFromDb()` methods that needs to be changed. The only other change is to change the class name. The complete source code can be downloaded from Wrox as `WriteClobToDb.java` and `ReadClobFromDb.java`. First, code changes to the `writeToDb()` method:

```
//Since CLOB is written with stream, disable autocommit
conn.setAutoCommit(false);
//insert a row into the CLOB table, use the empty_clob()
//construct for the CLOB field. empty_clob() creates the
//CLOB locator
stmt.executeUpdate("insert into reports values ('" + name +
    "', empty_clob())");
//Retrieve results for the row that was just inserted
rs = stmt.executeQuery(
    "select data from reports where name = '" +
    name + "' for update");
if (rs.next()) {

    //Get the CLOB locator
    Clob clob = rs.getClob(1);
    //Get the output stream which will be used to send
    //data to the table. Use Oracle extension because
    //JDBC 2.0 does not support writing data to CLOB
    out = ((oracle.sql.CLOB)clob).getAsciiOutputStream();

    //Let driver compute buffer size for writing to CLOB
    bufferSize = ((oracle.sql.CLOB)clob).getBufferSize();
```

You'll notice that besides the name change for the class, only five lines of code are actually changed in the source code. Four of the five changes involved replacing `Blob` with `Clob`; the fifth modification was to change the `getBinaryOutputStream()` call to `getAsciiOutputStream()`. A similarly small change is needed for the `readFromDb()` method of the `ReadClobFromDb.java` source code:

```
//Retrieve the row that has the selected name
rs = stmt.executeQuery(
    "select data from reports where name = '" + name + "'");
if (rs.next()) {

    //Get the CLOB locator
    Clob clob = rs.getClob(1);
    //Get the input stream which will be used to read
    //data from the table.
    in = clob.getAsciiStream();

    //let the driver determine the buffer size
    bufferSize = ((oracle.sql.CLOB)clob).getBufferSize();
```

Reading and Writing Character Data Using Readers and Writers

CLOB data can also be read and written using character streams instead of the byte streams used above. To use a `Writer` in the `WriteClobToDb.java` source, only a few lines of code need to be changed. The three lines are shown below. For the interests of space, only a small amount of the other code from the `WriteClobToDb.java` source is shown.

First, the `OutputStream` variable is changed to a `Writer` and the `BufferedInputStream` is changed to a `BufferedReader`:

```
int amount = 0;
Writer out = null;
BufferedReader in = null;
```

Next, the code calls `getCharacterOutputStream()` rather the `getAsciiOutputStream()`:

```
out = ((oracle.sql.CLOB)clob).getCharacterOutputStream();
```

The member variable in is created as a `BufferedReader`:

```
in = new BufferedReader(new FileReader(pathname), bufferSize);
```

Last, a `char` buffer is used instead of a `byte` buffer:

```
//Create a char buffer and start reading from the file
char[] b = new char[bufferSize]; int count = in.read(b, 0, bufferSize);
```

Likewise, only a few lines of code need to be changed to use a `Reader` with the `ReadClobFromDb.java` source code. Again, only the lines that need to be changed are shown below:

First, the `InputStream` is changed to a `Reader` and the `BufferedOutputStream` is changed to a `BufferedWriter`:

```
int amount = 0;
BufferedOutputStream out = null;
InputStream in = null;
```

Next, the code gets a character stream from the CLOB locator:

```
in = clob.getCharacterStream();
```

The member variable out is created as a `BufferedWriter`:

```
out = new BufferedWriter(new FileWriter(pathname), (int)bufferSize);
```

Last, a `char` buffer is used instead of a `byte` buffer:

```
//Create a char buffer and start reading from the file
char[] b = new char[(int)bufferSize];
```

443

BFILEs

The previous section looked at reading and writing BLOBs and CLOBs in a database. BLOBs and CLOBs are also referred to as internal large objects. That is, the data for the BLOB or CLOB is stored in the database in a table. While these types can be used to hold very large amounts of data, they still have a limitation. With Oracle 8i, BLOBs and CLOBs are limited to 4 gigabytes of data.

BFILEs provide a way to include more than 4 gigabytes of data with a table. The name BFILE stands for external binary file. The data itself is stored outside the database system, on a hard drive, CD-ROM, or other media separate from the database files. Like BLOBs and CLOBs, you get a locator from the database table, and use that locator to manipulate the BFILE field.

Getting a BFILE Locator

If you are accessing a table with a BFILE column, you can access the BFILE locator just like you access a BLOB locator, or like any other JDBC type, by using a getXXX() method of the resultset. Use the getBFILE() or getObject() methods to get a BFILE locator from a resultset. Note that the ResultSet reference must be of type oracle.jdbc.driver.OracleResultSet, or must be cast to that type to use the getBFILE() method. This is because BFILEs are an Oracle specific feature and are not part of JDBC 2.0.

```
//use an OracleResultSet with getBFILE()
oracle.sql.BFILE bfile = ((OracleResultSet)rs).getBFILE(1);
//getObject returns an Object, so cast it to oracle.sql.BFILE
bfile = (oracle.sql.BFILE) rs.getObject(1);
```

Using the Bfile Locator to Insert a BFILE

After obtaining a BFILE locator in your JDBC code, you can use the locator to insert the BFILE into another table. You are not actually moving the BFILE data, you are simply using the locator as a value to be inserted into the other table. You can use a PreparedStatement or a CallableStatement to write BFILE data from one table to another using the setObject() method:

```
//assume the BFILE is the first column in the ResultSet
bfile = (oracle.sql.BFILE) rs.getObject(1);
//assume the BFILE column is the first column in the table bfile_table
PreparedStatement ps =
    conn.prepareStatement("INSERT INTO bfile_table VALUES (?)");
ps.setObject(1, bfile);
ps.executeUpdate();
```

An alternative to using setObject() is to use setOracleObject() or setBFILE(). To do this you need to use the OraclePreparedStatement or OracleCallableStatement.

```
bfile = (oracle.sql.BFILE) rs.getObject(1);
OraclePreparedStatement ps = (OraclePreparedStatement)
    conn.prepareStatement("INSERT INTO bfile_table VALUES (?)");
ps.setOracleObject(1, bfile);
// or ps.setBFILE(1, bfile);
ps.executeUpdate();
```

Reading BFILE Data

Reading BFILE data is similar to reading BLOB or CLOB data. Using the BFILE locator, you can open the file represented by the locator, get an input stream from the BFILE, and use that input stream to read the data. After the code has finished reading the data, the BFILE is closed. The code below is analogous to the code in the `readFromDb()` method in the source `ReadBlobFromDb.java`.

```
ps.executeQuery("SELECT bfile_loc FROM bfile_table");
rs.next();
oracle.sql.BFILE bfile = ((OracleResultSet)rs).getBFILE(1);
if (bfile.fileExists()) {
  bfile.openFile();
  InputStream in = bfile.getBinaryStream();
  byte[] byte_array = new byte[bufferSize];
  int count = in.read(byte_array, 0, bufferSize);
  while (count != -1) {
    //do something with data
  }
  in.closeFile();
} else {
  //file doesn't exist
}
```

Inserting BFILE Data

Before you can insert BFILE data into a table, you need a table. As a minimum the table must have a column to hold the BFILE and a column for the directory alias for the directory where the external file is located. Using either a JDBC program or SQL*Plus, execute the following two statements:

```
CREATE TABLE bfile_table (
  name VARCHAR2(200),
  data BFILE
);

CREATE DIRECTORY bfile_dir AS 'C:\import\bfiles';
```

You can name the table and the directory alias to whatever you wish. In addition, the BFILE directory can be any directory on your computer that is readable by the database, even a removable disk or network resource. Now copy a file into the C:\import\bfiles directory (or whichever directory you used in the CREATE DIRECTORY statement above. The following code can be used to create a BFILE entry in the table for the file:

```
Statement stmt = conn.createStatement();
//change some_file_name in the next line to the name of the file
//that was copied into the bfile directory
String name = "some_file_name";
//change c:\import\bfiles to the directory you used
String sql = "insert into bfile_table values ('" + name +
  "', bfilename(bfile_dir, '" + name + "'))";
stmt.executeUpdate(sql);
```

Alternately, you can insert a NULL value into the table, and update the entry later with a BFILE locator and a PreparedStatement:

```
Statement stmt = conn.createStatement();
stmt.executeUpdate("insert into bfile_table values ('file_name', null)");
//assume table bfile_table2 has a BFILE column named bfile_loc
stmt.executeQuery("select bfile_loc from bfile_table2");
rs.next()
BFILE bfile = (oracle.sql.BFILE) rs.getObject("bfile_loc");
//assume bfile_table2 has a column named name
String name = rs.getString("name");
//insert the BFILE locator into bfile_table
PreparedStatement ps =
    conn.prepareStatement("insert into bfile_table values (?, ?)");
ps.setString(1, name);
ps.setObject(2, bfile);
ps.executeUpdate();
```

Datasources

Datasource objects were introduced with JDBC 2.0. An object implementing javax.sql.DataSource is like a server for database connections. The datasource is set up with the parameters needed to connect to a particular database. Clients can get a reference to the datasource object, and then ask the datasource for a Connection. Thus, clients do not need to worry about connection URLs, database passwords, listener ports, etc. To get the datasource reference, all the client needs is information for contacting a Java Naming and Directory Interface (JNDI), and the name by which the JNDI knows the datasource.

The JNDI is a way for clients to access services in a distributed environment. JNDI is a Java interface to existing directory services such as Lightweight Directory Access Protocol (LDAP) servers or Domain Name Server (DNS) servers. Services bind (register) themselves with JNDI using a name. Clients use the name to ask the JNDI for the service.

In the Java class that follows, a DataSource object is created and registered with JNDI. The code will use a JNDI FileSystem Naming Server. To compile and run this code, you will need additional Java libraries: jndi.jar, fscontext.jar, and providerutil.jar. If you do not already have these libraries, then you can download them from the JNDI area at http://java.sun.com. The .zip files that contain the libraries used for the examples in this section are:

❏   jndi1_2_1.zip, the JNDI 1.2.1 class libraries and sample code

❏   fscontext1_2beta3.zip, the File system service provider, 1.2 beta 3 release

Newer releases may be available when you go to the Java web site, so download the current versions of the JNDI and FSContext libraries. After downloading the .zip archives, extract the library files jndi.jar, fscontext.jar, and providerutil.jar from the jndi.zip and fscontext.zip files. Copy the .jar files to a directory that is part of the classpath, or add the path to these files to the classpath environment variable.

When the libraries have been installed, you will be able to compile and run the `DataSourceServer` class. In the source that follows, two major tasks are performed. In the constructor, the class creates a `Context` object. The `Context` object is the object that maintains the set of bindings between a name and a `DataSource`. In this sample code, the `Context` saves the binding information to a file named `.bindings` in a directory in the filesystem, `C:\temp\oracle`. This directory must be created before the program is run. The other important task occurs in the `createDataSource()` method. In that method, the `DataSource` object is created and then bound to the name `jdbc/wrox` using the `Context` method `rebind()`. The rebind method takes a `String` parameter that will be the name used by clients to access the `DataSource` and a reference to the `DataSource`. Notice that all the database specific connection parameters are set in the `DataSource` object; no client will ever need to know or use these parameters.

```java
package jdbc.DataSource;

import java.sql.*;
import javax.sql.*;
import oracle.jdbc.pool.OracleDataSource;
import javax.naming.*;
import java.util.*;
import DriverData;

public class DataSourceBinder {
  public DataSourceBinder() {
    Context context = null;

    try {
      //create and store parameters which are used to create the context
      Hashtable env = new Hashtable();
      env.put(Context.INITIAL_CONTEXT_FACTORY,
        "com.sun.jndi.fscontext.RefFSContextFactory");
      env.put(Context.PROVIDER_URL, "file:/C:/temp/oracle");
      //create the context
      context = new InitialContext(env);
      //call method to create and bind the data source
      createDataSource(context, "jdbc/wrox");
    } catch (Exception e) {
      e.printStackTrace();
    }
  }

  //create and bind the data source
  static void createDataSource(Context ctx, String bindName)
    throws SQLException, NamingException
  {
    //Create an OracleDataSource object
    OracleDataSource dataSource = new OracleDataSource();

    //set the connection parameters
    dataSource.setUser(DriverData.user);
    dataSource.setPassword(DriverData.passw);
    dataSource.setDriverType("thin");
    dataSource.setNetworkProtocol("tcp");
    dataSource.setServerName("localhost");
    dataSource.setPortNumber(1521);
    dataSource.setDatabaseName("orcl");
```

```
        //bind it, rebind is used to that the DataSource replaces any
        //service that was previously bound with the same name
        ctx.rebind(bindName, dataSource);
    }

    public static void main(String[] args)
        throws SQLException, NamingException
    {
        //start the server
        new DataSourceBinder();
    }
}
```

When the `rebind()` method is called in the code above, the `Context` object saves the binding to a file in the `C:\temp\oracle` directory. Client objects, as will be seen in the next class, create a `Context` object, and then call the `lookup()` method to get a reference to a `DataSource`. The `DataSourceServer` class must be run prior to the `DataSourceClient` class. If the database connection parameters do not change, the `DataSourceServer` class only needs to be run once. After it is run, you can run the `DataSourceClient` code as often as desired. If the database connection parameters change, the `DataSourceServer` class must be run again.

Here is the client code that will get the `DataSource` from the JNDI and use it to connect to and query the database. Notice that unlike all the other JDBC programs in this chapter, the client does not need any information about how to connect to the database. All it needs is knowledge of how to contact the JNDI and the name by which the `DataSource` was bound to JNDI. Also, multiple clients can use the same `DataSource` to get a connection.

The constructor of this class is almost identical to the constructor of the server. A `Context` object is created and then passed to the `getDataSource()` method. In the `getDataSource()` method, the `lookup(String)` method of the `Context` is called. If the `String` parameter matches a name that is bound with a service by the `Context`, the `Context` returns a reference to the service, a `DataSource` in this case. Once a `DataSource` reference is obtained, it is used to get a `Connection`. Finally, the `query()` method uses JDBC to query the `patients` table and display the rows returned by the query:

```
package jdbc.DataSource;

import java.sql.*;
import javax.sql.*;
import javax.naming.*;
import java.util.*;
import DriverData;

public class DataSourceClient {
    Connection conn;

    public DataSourceClient() {
        Context context;

        try {
            //create and store parameters which are used to create the context
            Hashtable env = new Hashtable();
            env.put(Context.INITIAL_CONTEXT_FACTORY,
                "com.sun.jndi.fscontext.RefFSContextFactory");
```

```
          env.put(Context.PROVIDER_URL, "file:/C:/temp/oracle");
          //create the context
          context = new InitialContext(env);
          //call method to get DataSource and Connection
          getDataSource(context, "jdbc/wrox");
          //call query method
          query();
      } catch (Exception e) {
          e.printStackTrace();
      }
  }

  //get the DataSource and use it to get a connection
  void getDataSource(Context context, String bindName)
      throws SQLException, NamingException
  {
      //Don't need url or username/password in client,
      //all that is needed is the bind name for lookup
      DataSource source = (DataSource) context.lookup(bindName);
      conn = source.getConnection();
  }

  //use the connection to query the patients table
  void query() throws SQLException {
      Statement statement = conn.createStatement();
      String sql = "select * from patients";
      ResultSet rset = statement.executeQuery(sql);

      while (rset.next()) {
          System.out.println("Patient: " + rset.getInt("PATIENT_ID") +
              " " + rset.getString("GIVEN_NAME") +
              " " + rset.getString("SURNAME"));
      }

      rset.close();
      statement.close();
      conn.close();
      conn = null;
  }

  public static void main(String[] args) {
      //create and execute the client
      new DataSourceClient();
  }
}
```

In the future, using datasources will become the standard technique for database connections. The big advantage of using the datasource is that all the database specific connection code and parameters are abstracted out of the JDBC code. This provides a more flexible architecture when compared against the DriverManager. Using a DataSource, the database administrator can change the connection parameters for the database server and the only code that might need to be recompiled is the class that creates the DataSource.

Summary

This chapter was a brief introduction to accessing an Oracle database using Java and JDBC. Here's what you have learned:

❏ JDBC is used to dynamically create SQL statements that can be sent to a database. JDBC can also be used to call stored procedures and functions.

❏ Every database program opens a connection to a database, uses `Statement` objects to execute SQL statements, and uses a `ResultSet` to view the rows from a table.

❏ Database connections in JDBC are created with the help of a `DriverManager`. After registering a driver with the `DriverManager`, the `getConnection()` method returns a `Connection` object.

❏ You can also get a `Connection` with a `DataSource` object, which provides a more flexible technique for obtaining a `Connection`. `DataSource` objects are the preferred method for obtaining a database connection.

❏ SQL can be sent to a database using `Statement`, `PreparedStatement`, or `CallableStatement`. `Statement` objects are used for dynamic SQL. `PreparedStatement` is used when a particulare SQL string is often used and only the bind variables change. `CallableStatement` is used for calling stored procedures and functions.

❏ A `ResultSet` is a Java class that is used to iterate through the rows returned by a query. JDBC 1.0 `ResultSet` is traversed from beginning to end; JDBC 2.0 `ResultSet` can be accessed randomly.

❏ JDBC 1.0 `ResultSet` cannot be used to update the data in a table. JDBC 2.0 `ResultSet` can be used to update table data. JDBC 2.0 `ResultSet` can also be used to insert a row, or delete a row.

❏ BLOB and CLOB data in a table can be inserted into a table and read from a table using Java input and output streams.

❏ An external file can be "stored" in an Oracle database table as a BFILE type. The BFILE type is a locator that can be used to access the external file.

13

Connection Pooling and Caching

Just as in real life, the concept of sharing and recycling limited resources is very important in computer science. Apart from the obvious economic profit, this usually ensures better performance and prevents bottlenecks.

When dealing with networked resources, sharing becomes essential. In most database applications, the actual connection requires substantial amounts of time to create and destroy. In case of high-throughput, such as with web services, this time delay can dramatically reduce the capabilities of the network application. However, by sharing and reusing these valuable connection resources, this expensive overhead can be greatly minimized, increasing performance.

Although some of the distribution of network resources is often configured with the database system, the real work of reducing overhead lies with the client application. In this chapter we will study powerful methods of sharing database resources, by pooling and caching connection objects at the middle tier. This is opposed to, for example, Net8 connection pooling, which deals with pooling physical connections at the database level. In this context, we will study the implementation of a connection pool model for any type of JDBC compliant network application, focusing on web-based services.

In this chapter we will:

- ❑ Explain the concept of connection pooling

- ❑ Discuss the advantages of connection pooling

- ❑ Implement a basic connection pool

- ❑ Extend our connection pool to include JDBC 2.0 extensions.

Pooling

An object pool is a set of limited resources that can be reserved for use by clients and then returned for reuse when the object is no longer needed. In this chapter we will discuss one such type of object pool in detail, namely a pool of database connection objects, a **connection pool**.

Each time a resource connects with a database, it creates a physical database connection. In JDBC this translates to creating a specific `Connection` object. A database connection incurs overhead – it requires resources to create the connection, maintain it, and then release it when it is no longer required. By using a connection pool for reserving and returning pooled connection objects, this overhead of separately creating and destroying can be largely avoided, except, of course, for the initial connections in the pool.

The cost of dynamically creating database connections can be particularly high for web-based applications. Web users connect and disconnect frequently, and their user interaction is typically short, due to the surfing nature of the Internet. In addition, online usage volumes can be large and difficult to predict, which requires the database connection procedure to be fast and efficient. With connection pooling, the connection overhead can be spread across several user requests, thus conserving resources and improving response times.

Put short, a connection pool is a cache of database connections, allowing:

❑ reuse of connections

❑ increased performance

Connection Pool Advantages

We have already mentioned some of the advantages of connection pooling, such as lower response times for database applications. To support our case, we did a series of tests where we compared accessing a database by using pooled connections on one hand, and a new connection per access on the other.

What we measured was the time it took to get a connection and create an executable statement for a particular database schema. We repeated these tests for both connection schemes, for up to 100 executed statements in a row. From the results of these measures, we then plotted a graph of statements executed vs. time, as can be seen from the following diagram:

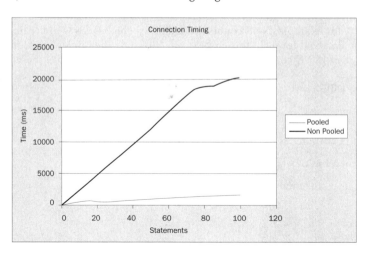

The graph shows the statements vs. time relationship for both the pooled and non-pooled connection schemes. It becomes apparent by comparing the two that the time it took to execute the statements with non-pooled connections was much longer than the time it took using pooled connections – in fact, it took approximately 10 times more time with the first scheme. With the exception of the initial rise in time for the pooled connection scheme (which reflects the time it took to create the initial connections), both the schemes show a fairly linear relationship between statements executed and the time it took to execute them. Therefore, we may condclude that the general use of pooled connections has obvious advantages over using non-pooled connections, in terms of time and database resources.

> *These measures were conducted for Oracle 8.1.5, running on Solaris 7. We had a pooling scheme of 5 initial and 150 maximum connections, using the pool implementation we introduce in the following section.*

Different Types of Connection Pooling

As we have already mentioned, the connection pooling we discuss in this chapter takes place at the middle tier, in the database application. This is opposed to connection pooling at the actual database level, which can be done with, for example, Net8.

Net8 Connection Pooling

Net8 connection pooling is a feature that allows you to maximize the number of physical network connections to a server. When a connection has been idle for a specified length of time, Net8 connection pooling makes these connections available for swapping out in favor of incoming connection requests. This essentially "recycles" server resources that would otherwise be unavailable for use. Using connection pooling, the server maintains a logical connection with the idle session, so that it may re-establish the physical connection upon request. The largest benefit of Net8 connection pooling is the recycling and distribution of physical connections.

Connection Object Pooling

Connection object pooling, which we will implement in this chapter, is different from the type of database connection pooling used with Net8. With connection object pooling, we pool and cache connection **objects**, which each stand for a physical database connection. Unlike database-tier connection pooling, this type of pooling does not swap connections when they are idle; it is up to the client to return connections to the pool. The largest benefit of object connection pooling is the reduced need of resources to establish and maintain the database connections.

Both the mentioned pooling methods can be used within the same application. Net8 connection pooling is a configuration issue for the DBA, while the application developer configures the connection object pooling.

Overview

Now that we have discussed the general nature of connection pools, we will move to the actual implementation of a pooling model. In the next section, we will create a connection pool, using the JDBC 1.0 core API. Although JDBC 2.0, with its built-in pooling support, would spare us some of the work in this implementation, there are several reasons for starting the discussion on explicitly using JDBC 1.0. Firstly, some applications still have to use JDK 1.1.x, for some reasons, and must therefore suffice with JDBC 1.0 API. Secondly, the JDBC 1.0 implementation serves as a good introduction to the pooling concepts. When we implement a pool with JDBC 2.0 later in this chapter, we will find that the details of the pooling process are often hidden. Thus, by studying the JDBC 1.0 implementation, we get knowledge of the logic behind connection pooling, regardless of whether we use this rather obsolete technique or move directly to JDBC 2.0. In the JDBC 2.0 section, we provide an overview of the updates necessary to update the pooling classes from JDBC 1.0 to JDBC 2.0.

Standard Connection Pool

Pooling connections can be accomplished with any type of database, using any type of connection mechanism. In this section, we will show you how to implement a connection pool using the JDBC 1.0 core API. Later on, when we introduce the JDBC 2.0 optional packages, we will extend our basic implementation to include those techniques.

Our implementation follows a fairly standard pooling pattern. Using no specific features other than those defined in the core API, this model should be able to fit all kinds of networking applications.

Specifically, with our connection pool model, a client

- ❑ gets a reference to a pool manager object, which contains multiple connection pools
- ❑ gets a connection from a specified pool from the pool manager
- ❑ uses the connection
- ❑ returns the connection to the pool

Actually, instead of returning an actual Connection object to the client, we will implement a Connection wrapper class, that allows the client to call close() on the connection in order to return it to the pool. The procedure of getting the Connection wrapper is further emphasized in the following figure:

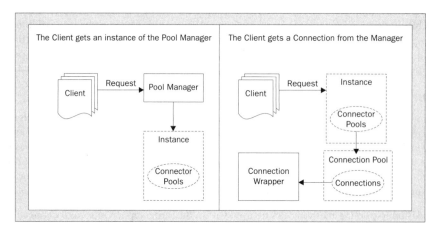

On the left side of the figure, the client gets an instance (actually, **the** instance, as we explain later) of the pool manager class. Then, as we show on the right side, the client requests a new Connection wrapper from a certain connection pool of the pool manager. The pool manager object obtains the connection pool instance specified, and requests a Connection from the pool. A wrapper class containing the actual Connection instance is then created and returned to the client.

Our connection pool model consists of a single instance of a DBPoolManager class, managing one or more DBConnectionPool objects. Each DBConnectionPool stands for pool of connections to a single database account and contains a number of DBConnection objects. The DBConnection class is actually a wrapper around an actual Connection instance and serves the purpose of ensuring that that the Connection will never be actually closed by the user, just returned to the connection pool. The following class diagram gives overview of these classes, in addition to the Logger class, which we will use to keep a log of pooling activity.

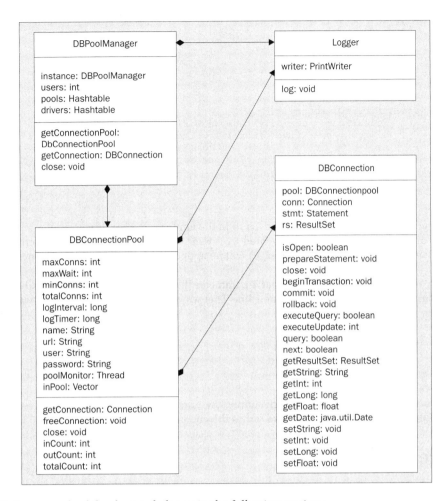

We will discuss each of the depicted classes in the following sections.

Logger

To be able to track down errors and monitor the status of the connection pool, we must have a proper logging mechanism. In this section we will show how to implement a `Logger` class for that purpose.

The `Logger` class contains a single instance of the `PrintWriter` class used for writing messages to the log file. The `Logger` constructor takes as a parameter the log file name, which is used to construct a `PrintWriter` instance:

```
import java.io.*;
import java.util.Date;

public class Logger {

    private PrintWriter writer;
    public Logger( String logName ) throws IOException {
```

```
        File dir;
        FileWriter filewriter;

        dir = new File(".","logs");
        if ( !dir.exists() ) {
            dir.mkdir();
        }
        if ( dir.isDirectory() ) {
            filewriter = new FileWriter(new File("logs",logName));
            writer = new PrintWriter(filewriter, true);
        } else {
            throw new IOException("The log directory is a file!");
        }
    }
}
```

The constructor creates a directory named `logs` in the application root directory. If a log file with the given file name does not exist, the instantiated `FileWriter` object will automatically create a new file with that name. Otherwise, new log messages will be appended at the end of the existing file.

The `log()` method of the `Logger` takes as a parameter the message to log. The method automatically adds the current date in the front of the new line That way, it will be easier later on to track down messages by their logging date.

```
    public void log(String msg) {
        writer.println(new Date() + ": " + msg);
    }
```

This is basically all there is to it. Although simple, the `Logger` class serves its purpose and will be used by most of the classes implemented in the rest of the chapter.

DBConnection

In order to be able to actually return a connection back to the pool instead of closing it when the client calls the `close()` method of a `connection` object, we implement a wrapper for the `Connection` class. The wrapper class contains all the JDBC objects necessary for database access: the `Connection`, `Statement`, and `ResultSet`. Methods of the `Connection` class are implemented for `DBConnection`, where they are usually just relayed to the actual `Connection`. In addition, wrapper methods are included to get datatypes from the `ResultSet` and manipulate the `Statement`. The `ResultSet` can also be obtained separately, for further manipulation, although, to preserve control, neither the `Statement` nor `Connection` objects can be referenced directly.

Instance Variables

The `DBConnection` class has a few instance variables that are used for the database access:

```
    package pooling;

    import java.sql.*;
    import java.util.*;
    import java.io.*;
    import Logger;
```

```
public class DBConnection {

    private DBConnectionPool pool;
    private Connection conn = null;
    private Statement stmt = null;
    private ResultSet rs = null;
```

As has been mentioned, the DBConnection keeps instances of the Connection, ResultSet, and Statement classes. The latter two are obtained from the Connection as will be later explained. The class also has an instance of the DBConnectionPool that is used for initially getting the pooled Connection object.

Constructor

The DBConnection is constructed with an instance of the DBConnectionPool it associates with:

```
public DBConnection( DBConnectionPool pool ) throws SQLException {
    this.pool = pool;
}
```

The DBConnectionPool instance will be used when the DBConnection is first opened in order to get a physical Connection object from the pool.

Connecting

Before clients begin using the DBConnection, it must get a Connection instance from the DBConnectionPool. Each of the database methods that we will implement call the open() method before commencing. That way, we ensure that the Connection instance used is always open and ready.

```
private synchronized void open() throws SQLException {
    connect();
    stmt = conn.createStatement();
}
```

The open() method calls connect() to initialize the database Connection and create a Statement instance. The Connection instance is obtained by a call to the getConnection() method of the DBConnectionPool class, which we will discuss in more detail in the next section.

```
private synchronized void connect() throws SQLException {
    if ( isOpen() ) {
        rsClose();
        stmtClose();
    } else {
        conn = pool.getConnection();
    }
}
```

If there is already an open Connection, connect() ensures that the any previous Statement and ResultSet objects are closed.

Closing the Connection

The purpose of implementing a Connection wrapper in the first place was to ensure that clients calling close() on the connection class would not actually close the physical database connection, but rather return it to the underlying connection pool. This is exactly what the close() method of the DBConnection does:

```
public synchronized void close() throws SQLException {
        if ( isOpen() ) {
            rsClose();
            stmtClose();
            conn.setAutoCommit(true);
            pool.freeConnection(conn);
            conn = null;
        }
    }
```

Naturally, close() does nothing if the Connection has never been opened in the first place. Otherwise, it calls rsClose() and stmtClose() to close the ResultSet and Statement objects, respectively. It then sets the auto commit state of the Connection (in case it had been altered from its original state) and then calls the freeConnection() method of the DBConnectionPool instance to send the Connection object back to the pool.

This is the code for the rsClose() and stmtClose() methods:

```
private synchronized void stmtClose() throws SQLException {
        if ( stmt != null) {
            stmt.close();
            stmt = null;
        }
    }

    private synchronized void rsClose() throws SQLException {
        if ( rs != null) {
            rs.close();
            rs = null;
        }
    }
```

Database Methods

Most of the other methods we implement are simply relayed to the Connection, ResultSet, and Statement instances. These include methods for setting statement parameters (relayed to the Statement instance) and obtaining results (relayed to the ResultSet).

Connection Methods

The DBConnection class contains a few methods relayed to the Connection instance. These methods can be used to create a PreparedStatement instance or to begin a continuous transaction, which can then be either committed or rolled back with the appropriate methods.

```java
public synchronized void prepareStatement(String sql) throws SQLException {
       connect();
       stmt = conn.prepareStatement(sql);
   }

public synchronized void prepareStatement(String sql) throws SQLException {
    connect();
    stmt = conn.prepareStatement(sql);
}
public void beginTransaction() throws SQLException {
       open();
       conn.setAutoCommit(false);
   }

public void beginTransaction() throws SQLException {
       open();
       conn.setAutoCommit(false);
   }
public void commit() throws SQLException {
       open();
       conn.commit();
       conn.setAutoCommit(true);
   }

   public void rollback() throws SQLException {
       open();
       conn.rollback();
       conn.setAutoCommit(true);
   }
```

ResultSet Methods

The following methods, used for obtaining data from an executed query, are relayed to the `ResultSet` instance:

```java
public String getString(String field) throws SQLException {
       try {
           String s = rs.getString(field);
           if (s != null) {
               return s;
           } else {
               return "";
           }
       } catch (NullPointerException e) {
           throw new SQLException( "Please call getResultSet() only after "
                       +    "calling query()/executeQuery().");
       }
   }
   public int getInt(String field) throws SQLException {
       try {
           return rs.getInt(field);
       } catch (NullPointerException e) {
           throw new SQLException( "Please call getResultSet() only after "
                           +    "calling query()/executeQuery().");
```

```
            }
        }
        public long getLong(String field) throws SQLException {
            try {
                return rs.getLong(field);
            } catch (NullPointerException e) {
                throw new SQLException( "Please call getResultSet() only after "
                                    +   "calling query()/executeQuery().");
            }
        }
        public float getFloat(String field) throws SQLException {
            try {
                return rs.getFloat(field);
            } catch (NullPointerException e) {
                throw new SQLException( "Please call getResultSet() only after "
                                    +    "calling query()/executeQuery().");
            }
        }
        public java.util.Date getDate(String field) throws SQLException {
            try {
                return rs.getDate(field);
            } catch (NullPointerException e) {
                throw new SQLException( "Please call getResultSet() only after "
                                    +    "calling query()/executeQuery().");
            }
        }
    }
```

Note that, as these methods do not cover all of the possible get() methods of the ResultSet, we provide a method for explicitly obtaining the active ResultSet instance, for further manipulation:

```
        public ResultSet getResultSet() throws SQLException {
            try {
                return rs;
            } catch (NullPointerException e) {
                throw new SQLException( "Please call getResultSet() only after "
                                    +    "calling query()/executeQuery().");
            }
        }
```

Finally, the next() method returns true if the ResultSet has more results:

```
    public synchronized boolean next() throws SQLException {
        try {
                return rs.next();
        } catch (NullPointerException e) {
                throw new SQLException("Please call next() only after calling
query().");
        }
    }
```

Statement Methods

We finally define the methods that are relayed to the `Statement` instance of the `DBConnection`. We use these methods for executing statements (queries, updates, inserts, etc.) and setting parameters when we execute a `PreparedStatement`, with the previously mentioned `prepareStatement()` method.

```java
public synchronized boolean executeQuery() throws SQLException {
    try {
        rs = ((PreparedStatement)stmt).executeQuery();
        return true;
    } catch (NullPointerException e) {
        throw new SQLException("Please call executeQuery() only after calling
prepareStatement() and appropriate set methods.");
    }
}

public void finalize() throws Throwable {
    close();
}

public boolean isOpen() {
    return conn != null;
}

public void setString(int parameterIndex, String x) throws SQLException {
    try {
        ((PreparedStatement)stmt).setString(parameterIndex, x);
    } catch (NullPointerException npe) {
        throw new SQLException( "Please call set() only after calling "
                        + "prepareStatement().");
    } catch (ClassCastException cce) {
        throw new SQLException( "You have already created a Statement. "
                        + "Close it and use prepareStatement().");
    }
}
public void setInt(int parameterIndex, int x) throws SQLException {
    try {
        ((PreparedStatement)stmt).setInt(parameterIndex, x);
    } catch (NullPointerException npe) {
        throw new SQLException( "Please call set() only after calling "
                        + "prepareStatement().");
    } catch (ClassCastException cce) {
        throw new SQLException( "You have already created a Statement. "
                        + "Close it and use prepareStatement().");
    }
}
public void setLong(int parameterIndex, long x) throws SQLException {
    try {
        ((PreparedStatement)stmt).setLong(parameterIndex, x);
    } catch (NullPointerException npe) {
        throw new SQLException( "Please call set() only after calling "
                        + "prepareStatement().");
    } catch (ClassCastException cce) {
        throw new SQLException( "You have already created a Statement. "
                        + "Close it and use prepareStatement().");
    }
}
```

```
    }
    public void setFloat(int parameterIndex, float x) throws SQLException {
        try {
            ((PreparedStatement)stmt).setFloat(parameterIndex, x);
        } catch (NullPointerException npe) {
            throw new SQLException( "Please call set() only after calling "
                        +   "prepareStatement().");
        } catch (ClassCastException cce) {
            throw new SQLException( "You have already created a Statement. "
                        +   "Close it and use prepareStatement().");
        }
    }
    public void setDate(int parameterIndex, java.sql.Date x) throws SQLException {
        try {
            ((PreparedStatement)stmt).setDate(parameterIndex, x);
        } catch (NullPointerException npe) {
            throw new SQLException( "Please call set() only after calling "
                        +   "prepareStatement().");
        } catch (ClassCastException cce) {
            throw new SQLException( "You have already created a Statement. "
                        +   "Close it and use prepareStatement().");
        }
    }
}
```

Now that we have discussed the DBConnection class, we will next cover the DBConnectionPool, which contains the pooled Connection objects we use for the DBConnection.

DBConnectionPool

The DBConnectionPool class represents a pool of connections to one database account. It provides methods for:

❑ getting connections from the pool

❑ creating new connections

❑ returning connections to the pool

❑ monitoring pool activity

The DBConnectionPool class is instantiated with information on the database account it is built on. This includes the database URL and possibly username and password. In addition, the DBConnectionPool takes a number of other settings, which will be described in the next section.

Instance Variables

The DBConnectionPool has many instance variables. Most of them are used to store information on the underlying database account and pool settings. For example, the pool stores the maximum number of Connection objects in the pool, the total number of active connections, the database username and password, and more.

```
package pooling;

import java.sql.*;
import java.util.*;
import java.io.*;
import Logger;

public class DBConnectionPool {

    private final int SLEEP_INTERVAL = 2000;
    private int maxConns;
    private int maxWait;
    private int minConns;
    private int totalConns = 0;
    private int next = -1;
    private int inConns = -1;
    private Logger log;
    private long logInterval;
    private long logTimer;
    private String name;
    private String url;
    private String user;
    private String password;
```

In addition, two other instance variables are of special interest:

```
    private Connection[] inPool;
    private Thread poolMonitor;
```

The first of these is the `inPool` array, which stores `Connection` objects that are lying in the pool. When a client requests a `Connection` from the pool, one of the instances in the `inPool` is returned. Also, when a `Connection` instance is returned back to the pool, it is added to the `inPool`. We will discuss the `inPool` in more detail later. Secondly, the `DBPoolManager` creates a thread for monitoring the pool activity. The thread, which runs the `DBConnectionPool monitor()` method, is started when the pool is first initialized. It then updates the `inPool` with fresh `Connection` objects when necessary, and logs the pool state after every `logInterval` seconds.

Maintaining the Pool of Connections

As we have already mentioned, we use an array to store the `Connection` objects for the pool. At the time of construction, we create an array that can hold the maximum number of connections allowed (`maxConns`). Then, we use the two variables `inConns` and `next` to maintain the pool status by storing information of the array index at which the last connection is kept and the index from which we will take the next connection, respectively. Both variables are initialized with the value of –1, which at any time means that the pool is empty.

The pool can only change its state in one of the following ways:

❑ When a `Connection` is returned to the pool, with the `freeConnection()` method, we add it behind the last connection present in the array and increase the `inConns` variable, if the maximum number has not been reached.

❑ When we get a Connection from the pool, with the getPooledConnection() method, we return the Connection from index next of the array. If next is set to -1 and inConns is not -1 (in which case the pool would be empty), we set next to the value of inConns (effectively wrapping around the array, starting at the end) and return the Connection at that index, creating a gap in the array. When we have returned the Connection, we take the last Connection from the array (at index inConns) and move it to the gap, that is, if we are not currently at the end. Finally, we decrease the values of both next and inConns.

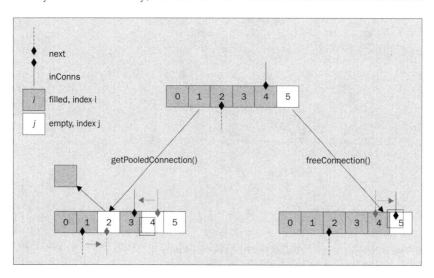

Both of these methods are further clarified in the figure shown above, which shows how the pool array is affected by either the getPooledConnection() or the freeConnection() method. In the first example, we return a Connection from index 2 of the array, and move the Connection at index 4 to this gap. Both inConns and next are decreased. In the latter example, we add a Connection after the last existing Connection in the array, and increase inConns.

Note that we implement the pool by using an array and pointer variables, instead of, for example, using a Vector class with its addElement() and removeElement() methods, to spare array extensions/contractions, and thus minimize garbage collection.

Constructor

As we will explain in the next section, we use the DBPoolManager class to store all the DBConnectionPool objects for a single application. Although the DBPoolManager may store more than one DBConnectionPool instance, it will store only a single instance of each specific pool we define for the application. Therefore, as we only want the DBConnectionPool class instantiated from the DBPoolManager, we omit the visibility modifiers for the class constructor. Thereby, it becomes visible only for classes of the same package.

```
DBConnectionPool( String name, String url, String user,
    String password, int maxConns, int minConns, int maxWait,
    long logInterval ) throws SQLException {

    this.name = name;
    this.url = url;
    this.user = user;
```

```
            this.password = password;
            this.maxConns = maxConns;
            this.minConns = minConns;
            this.maxWait = maxWait;
            this.logInterval = 1000 * logInterval;
            inPool = new Connection[maxConns];
            logTimer = System.currentTimeMillis();

            // Initialize logging
            if ( logInterval > 0 ) {
                try {
                    this.log = new Logger("DBConnectionPool_" + name);
                } catch ( IOException e ) {
                    throw new SQLException( "Unable initialize logging for "
                                    +   "DBConnectionPool " + name  + ": "
                                    +   e.getMessage() );
                }
            }

            // Create the monitor Thread.
            poolMonitor = new Thread (
                new Runnable() {
                    public void run() {
                        monitor();
                    }
                }
            );
            poolMonitor.start();
        }
```

Specifying a `logInterval` of equal to or below zero omits logging, as can be seen from the constructor.

Monitoring the Connection Pool

At the end of the constructor, the `poolMonitor` thread is initialized. The somewhat peculiar initialization of the `Thread` class allows us to implement an instance of the `Thread` without creating a special class file, which, of course, could just as easily be done.

When the `poolMonitor` has been created, it calls `start()` to run the `monitor()` method. This method serves the purposes of:

❑   creating initial `Connection` objects and adding them to the pool

❑   supplying the connection pool with the minimum number of free `Connection` objects

❑   logging pool state and activity at regular intervals, which can, for example, be used to ensure that clients return their connections back to the pool

Note that we only want a single thread to monitor our connection pool, as there is only a single active instance of the class for each pool type, as we will see in the `DBPoolManager` section later. Otherwise, we would have put the `monitor()` code in the actual `run()` method of the monitor thread, to allow for multithreading.

```
    private void monitor() {
        Connection conn;
        while ( true ) {

            // Each time the Thread wakes up, it checks whether
            // the total number of connections is lower than
            // the specified minimum. If so, it creates
            // necessary new connections and adds them to the pool.
            while ( totalConns < minConns ) {
                try {
                    conn = getNewConnection();
                    freeConnection(conn);
                } catch(SQLException e) {
                    log.log("SQL Exception in the monitor function:\n"
                        +   e.getMessage());
                }
            }
        }
    private void monitor() {
            while ( true ) {

                Connection conn;

                // Each time the Thread wakes up, it checks whether
                // the total number of inConns is lower than
                // the specified minimum. If so, it creates the
                // necessary new inConns and adds them to the pool.
                while ( totalConns < minConns ) {
                    try {
                        conn = getNewConnection();
                        freeConnection(conn);
                    } catch(SQLException e) {
                        log.log("SQL Exception in the monitor function:\n"
                            +   e.getMessage());
                    }
                }

                // This is only done every logInterval seconds.
                if ( (logInterval != 0) &&
                    ((System.currentTimeMillis() - logTimer) > logInterval) ) {
                    log();
                    logTimer = System.currentTimeMillis();
                }
    // This is only done every logInterval seconds.
                if ( (logInterval != 0) &&
                    ((System.currentTimeMillis() - logTimer) > logInterval) ) {
                    log();
                    logTimer = System.currentTimeMillis();
                }

                // Rest the Thread on a regular basis.
    try {
                    Thread.sleep(SLEEP_INTERVAL);
                } catch (InterruptedException e) {
                    log.log("Interrupted in the monitor function");
                }
            }
        }
```

The monitor() method examines whether the number of active Connection instances created are below the specified minimum. If so, it creates the necessary number of new Connection objects and adds them to the inPool array. Additionally, for every logInterval milliseconds, the method calls the log() method to log the current pool state. This can become useful when we suspect clients of not returning their connections back to the pool. In such a case, we may want to log the number of connections inside and outside the pool, and for that purpose we define the additional methods totalCount(), inCount(), and outCount(), which give us the total number of created connections, number of connections in the pool, and number of connections with clients, respectively.

```java
    public int totalCount() {
        return totalConns;
    }

    public int inCount() {
        return (inConns+1);
    }

    public int outCount() {
        return totalConns - inCount();
    }

    private void log() {
        log.log("IN + OUT = TOTAL: " + inCount()
            +   "+" + outCount() + "=" + totalCount() );
    }

    private void log(String msg) {
        log.log(msg);
    }
private void log() {
    log.log("IN + OUT = TOTAL: " + inCount() +
        +   "+" + outCount() + "=" + totalCount() );
}

public int totalCount() {
    return totalConns;
}

public int inCount() {
    return (inConns+1);
}

public int outCount() {
    return totalConns - inCount();
}
```

Getting a Connection From the Pool

The public getConnection() is used for checking a Connection out of the pool:

```java
public synchronized Connection getConnection() throws SQLException {
        Connection connection = null;
        if ( inConns == -1 && totalConns < maxConns ) {
            connection = getNewConnection();
        } else {
            connection = getPooledConnection();
        }
        return connection;
    }
```

469

This method checks on the state of the `inPool` and calls either one of the private methods, `getNewConnection()` or `getPooledConnection()`. If there are no connections currently in the pool **and** the total number of connections that have been created is lower than the specified maximum connection count, the method calls `getNewConnection()`. The `getNewConnection()` method creates a new `Connection` object and increments the number of current active connections:

```
private Connection getNewConnection() throws SQLException {
    Connection conn = DriverManager.getConnection(url,user,password);
    totalConns++;
    return conn;
}
```

On the other hand, if the pool is not empty or one cannot make more connections, we call the `getPooledConnection()` method. Obviously, in the latter case, the object calling the `getConnection()` method will have to wait for its connection. A possible solution to this problem is to increase the maximum number of connections allowed and make sure that clients always close their connections as soon as possible.

The `getPooledConnection()` method returns a `Connection` instance from the `inPool`. If there are connections in the pool, the next `Connection` instance to be returned (at array index `next`) is taken from the pool. If we have reached beyond the first element of the array, we set `next` to the value of `inConns` and take the `Connection` at the end. If the chosen `Connection` is valid, it is returned. Otherwise, the total number of active connections is decremented and we try again. We will wait for a connection from the pool for a maximum of the specified `maxWait` milliseconds. If that time has elapsed, we throw an exception. This is most likely to happen when users forget to return connections back to the pool.

```
private synchronized Connection getPooledConnection() throws SQLException {
    long timer = System.currentTimeMillis();
    Connection conn;
    while ( (maxWait == 0) ||
            ((System.currentTimeMillis() - timer) < maxWait) ) {
        if ( inConns > -1 ) {
            if ( next == -1 ) {
                next = inConns;
            }
            conn = inPool[next];
            inPool[next] = null;

            // Swap the last Connection in this
            // gap, if it is not at the end.
            if ( next != inConns ) {
                inPool[next] = inPool[inConns];
                inPool[inConns] = null;
            }
            next--;
            inConns--;
            if ( isValid(conn) ) {
                return conn;
            } else {
                totalConns--;
            }
        } else {
            notify();
        }
    }
    throw new SQLException( "Did not get a Connection "
                        +   "from the Pool in time");
}
```

There is one more method left to discuss in this context, isValid(). This method takes a Connection object as its parameter and returns true if it is valid. When checking for validity, we first make sure that the Connection instance is open and not null. If that proves correct, and no exceptions are thrown, we assume the Connection is valid, and return true.

```
private boolean isValid( Connection conn ) {
    try {
        return (conn != null && !conn.isClosed());
    } catch ( SQLException x ) {
        return false;
    }
}
```

Returning Connections to the Pool

When the close() method of the DBConnection class is invoked, the DBConnection in turn returns its Connection instance back to the connection pool. The DBConnectionPool freeConnection() method returns the Connection back to the pool:

```
public synchronized void freeConnection(Connection conn) throws SQLException {
    if ( isValid(conn) && inConns < maxConns - 1 ) {
        inConns++;
        inPool[inConns] = conn;
        notifyAll();
    } else {
        totalConns--;
    }
}
```

First of all, freeConnection() calls isValid() to check whether the Connection instance is actually valid. If not, it is not added to the pool, and the total number of active connections is decremented. If, however, the connection is valid, it is added to the back of the inPool array and all threads possibly waiting for a free connections are alerted, via notifyAll().

Cleaning Up Resources

The close() method of the DBConnectionPool serves the purpose of cleaning up resources and closing the connections. This method is either invoked by the DBPoolManager before server shutdown, as we will discuss later, or when the object is valid for garbage collection, through finalize(). Either way, this method takes every Connection instance in the inPool and calls close() on it.

```
public void finalize() throws SQLException {
    close();
    log.log("DBConnectionPool finalized");
}

public synchronized void close() throws SQLException {

    Connection conn;
    while (inConns > 0) {
        try {
            conn = inPool[inConns];
            inPool[inConns] = null;
            inConns--;
```

```
                    conn.close();
            } catch ( SQLException e ) {
                log.log(e.getMessage());
            }
        }
    }
}
```

Note that if an exception occurs in this process, it doesn't halt the shutdown, instead the error message is logged and the method loops through the rest of the `inPool`.

Managing the Connection Pools

By now, we have discussed in detail the `DBConnection` and `DBConnectionPool` classes. A single `DBConnectionPool` maintains a set of pooled connections, which are wrapped up in the `DBConnection` class before sent to the requesting client.

The `DBPoolManager` class, which we will discuss next, allows us to use multiple connection pools. The pool manager provides the user interface for getting pooled connections and connection pool instances. An instance of the `DBPoolManager` will:

❑   create `DBConnectionPool` objects from a property file

❑   register JDBC drivers

❑   provide methods for getting connections from a specified connection pool

In our implementation of the `DBPoolManager`, we would like to keep a single instance of the class so that clients will always access the same `DBConnectionPool` objects. A simple approach to this situation is to use static members and methods for the desired functionality. For these elements, no instance is required. The class can be made final with a private constructor in order to prevent any instance of the class from being created.

A better approach is to use the Singleton pattern by creating a static wrapper around a reference to a single instance of the class. A Singleton is a design pattern that constrains a class to a single unique instance which clients can reference by calling a static method, in our implementation this is called `getInstance()`. This method is shown later on in the chapter. Further discussion on the Singleton pattern can be found in various design books, such as *Design Patterns* by Erich Gamma, Richard Helm, Ralph Johnson, and John Vlisseides, ISBN: 0-201633-61-2.

Property Files

When the `DBPoolManager` instance is initialized, it must have access to information on each of the connection pools it should manage. In our implementation, it does so by reading a property file, which stores the necessary attributes of each connection pool. A property file is a text file with a list of key-value pairs, which all have the same standard format:

```
property1=value1
property2=value2
property3=value3
```

In Java, property files are usually given the extension .properties and placed somewhere in the classpath. These files can then be read by any object and conveniently manipulated by constructing an object of the Properties class with the file input stream. The following code shows how to create a Properties object from a properties file, in this case pools.properties:

```
import java.io.*;


char c = File.separatorChar;
InputStream is = getClass().getResourceAsStream(c + "pools.properties");
Properties props = new Properties ();
try {
    props.load(is);
} catch (Exception e) {
    System.err.println("Unable to read database properties file.");
}
```

The first line of code reads the actual properties file. The getClass() method is a method of Object and is inherited by all objects. It returns a new object of the Class class, which is associated with the same object as called the method. The getResourceAsStream() method of the getClass class is used to open an InputStream to the properties file. The InputStream is then fed to the load() method of the Properties class, which converts the properties file content to a Properties hash table.

The Properties class, being an extension of the Hashtable class, provides methods similar to those of the Hashtable for getting property names and values:

```
String key;
for ( Enumeration e = props.propertyNames(); e.hasMoreElements(); ) {
    key = (String) e.nextValue();
    System.out.println(key + "=" + props.get(key));
}
```

In our connection pool implementation, we create a properties file that holds necessary information on each of the pools to be constructed. When the DBPoolManager is first initialized, the database properties file is read and a Properties file created, as has already been explained. Each of the pool properties starts with the name of the pool, separated from the property name by a period:

poolname.driver	The database driver.
poolname.url	The database URL.
poolname.user	The username for the database account.
poolname.password	The password for the database account.
poolname.maxConns	The maximum number of connections that can be created.
poolname.minConns	The minimum number of connections at any time.
poolname.maxWait	The maximum waiting period for a connection, before an exception is thrown.

All properties, except for the database URL, are optional, though recommended. If no username and password are supplied, they will have to be included in the database URL.

In addition, there is one more property for each pool defined in the properties file, namely, the pool name. The pool name appears ahead of all other properties, and has the format:

```
name # = poolname
```

The following sample shows what our properties file might look like. Here `musicpool` is the pool name we use in our example and the file is saved as `pools.properties`:

```
name0=oracle
oracle.driver=oracle.jdbc.driver.OracleDriver
oracle.url=jdbc:oracle:thin:@127.0.0.1:1521:DB
oracle.user=test
oracle.password=test
oracle.maxConns=150
oracle.minConns=5
oracle.maxWait=500

name1=mssql
mssql.driver=com.ashna.jturbo.driver.Driver
mssql.url=jdbc:JTurbo://127.0.0.1:1433/msdb/sql70=true
mssql.user=demo
mssql.password=demo
name1=mssql
mssql.driver=com.ashna.jturbo.driver.Driver
mssql.url=jdbc:JTurbo://127.0.0.1:1433/msdb/sql70=true
mssql.user=demo
mssql.password=demo

name2=musicpool
musicpool.driver= oracle.jdbc.driver.OracleDriver
musicpool.url= jdbc:oracle:thin:@127.0.0.1:1521:Database
musicpool.user=scott
musicpool.password=tiger
musicpool.maxConns=150
musicpool.minConns=1
musicpool.maxWait=500
```

DBPoolManager

The `DBPoolManager` class defines a set of `DBConnectionPool` objects from a given set of data in a property file. For the purpose of storing the `DBConnecionPool` instances, the pool manager contains the `Hashtable` pools. When the `Hashtable` has been populated, individual `DBConnectionPool` objects can be accessed by their pool name.

Instance Variables

The `DBPoolManager` class maintains a few instance and class variables. As we have already mentioned, it contains a `static` instance of itself, which is kept in the `instance` variable. The `users` variable is also `static` and keeps a count of the number of clients that are currently holding an instance of the `DBPoolManager`. In addition, the class instance keeps the two `Hashtable` objects for containing `DBConnectionPool` objects and their respective drivers. Finally, an instance of the `Logger` class is kept for keeping a log file for the pools:

```
    package pooling;

    import java.io.*;
    import java.util.*;
    import java.sql.*;
    import Logger;

    public class DBPoolManager {

        private static DBPoolManager instance;
        private static int users;
        private Hashtable pools;
        private Hashtable drivers;
        private Logger log;
```

Getting an Instance

As we have described, the DBPoolManager constructor is kept private so that the class cannot be freely instantiated. Clients get a reference to the DBPoolManager instance by a call to the getInstance() method, which creates the instance if it has not already been done, and returns it:

```
    private DBPoolManager() throws SQLException {
        init();
    }

        public static synchronized DBPoolManager getInstance()
            throws SQLException {
            if( instance == null ){
                instance = new DBPoolManager();
            }
            users++;
            return instance;
        }
```

The private constructor calls the init() method, described below. Note that a call to getInstance() increments the users count by one, enabling the class to keep track of the number of users. The opposite of this, releasing the DBPoolManager instance and decrementing the number of users, is done with the close() method, which we will discuss later.

Initializing the Connection Pools

The init() method serves the purpose of reading the database properties file, registering database drivers, and adding constructed DBConnectionPool objects to the pools hash table:

```
    private synchronized void init() throws SQLException {

        char c = File.separatorChar;

        DBConnectionPool pool;
        Enumeration propertyNames;

        int maxConns;
        int logInterval;
        int minConns;
```

```
        int maxWait;
        //int p = 0;
        int p = 2;

        Properties props;
        InputStream is;

        String driver;
        String poolname = "";
        String prop;
        String password;
        String url;
        String user;

        users = 0;
        pools = new Hashtable();
        drivers = new Hashtable();

        // Initialize the pool manager Logger class.
        try {
            log = new Logger("poolmanager.log");
        } catch (IOException e) {
            throw new SQLException(e.getMessage());
        }
        log.log("\n--------------------------------\n"
            +   "--- INITIALIZING CONNECTION POOLS\n"
            +   "--------------------------------\n");
```

Here we will read the properties file:

```
        is = getClass().getResourceAsStream(c + "properties" + c
                                    +   "pools.properties");
        props = new Properties ();
        try {
            props.load(is);
        } catch (Exception e){
            e.printStackTrace();
            log.log("Unable to read database properties file.");
        }
```

Then we load the connection pool properties:

```
        propertyNames = props.propertyNames();
        while( propertyNames.hasMoreElements() ){
            prop = (String) propertyNames.nextElement();
            if( prop.equals("name" + p) ){

                // Parse the new pool name.
                poolname = props.getProperty(prop);

                // Read numeric valued properties.
                maxConns        =   intValue(props.getProperty(
                                    poolname + ".maxConns"));
                logInterval     =   intValue(props.getProperty(
```

```
                                            poolname + ".logInterval"));
                minConns        =   intValue(props.getProperty(
                                            poolname + ".minConns"));
                maxWait         =   intValue(props.getProperty(
                                            poolname + ".maxWait"));

                // Read character valued properties.
                password = props.getProperty(poolname + ".password");
                url      = props.getProperty(poolname + ".url");
                user     = props.getProperty(poolname + ".user");
                driver   = props.getProperty(poolname + ".driver");

                // Register the JDBC driver.
                registerDriver(driver);
```

Now we create the connection pool object and add it to the hash table of pools:

```
                pool = new DBConnectionPool(poolname,url,user,password,
                                    maxConns,minConns,maxWait,
                                    logInterval );
                pools.put(poolname,pool);
                p++;
                log.log("Initialized DBConnectionPool " + poolname);
            }
        }
    }
```

The method starts by initializing all the global instance variables the DBPoolManager defines. It then proceeds to reading the database properties file and loads the file content in a Properties object. Next, it scrolls through all the pool properties and creates a set of DBConnectionPool objects, registering each pool's JDBC driver as it is encountered.

> *Please note that the registration of drivers is usually unnecessary, as database drivers are supposed to register themselves, as is discussed in chapter 12. However, this is unfortunately not always the case, as some drivers lack this autoregistration property, and also because of a bug in the JDK 1.x machine (Sun's reference version) that prevents drivers from registering automatically. You should always consult your database driver manual and check your Java version before deciding whether to explicitly register the drivers or not.*

The registerDriver() method that is called in init() when a new driver is encountered, serves the purpose of the registering the specified JDBC driver with the DriverManager. All registered drivers are kept for unregistering them when the DBPoolManager instance is released.

```
    private void registerDriver( String name ){
        try {
            Driver driver = (Driver) Class.forName(name).newInstance();
            DriverManager.registerDriver(driver);
            drivers.put(name,driver);
            log.log("Registered JDBC driver " + name);
```

```
        } catch ( Exception e ){
            log.log("Unable to register JDBC driver " + name + "."
                +   "Check the driver name suppled.");
        }
    }
    public DBConnectionPool getConnectionPool( String poolname ){
        return (DBConnectionPool) pools.get(poolname);
    }
```

Note the use of the `intValue()` method in the properties loading. The `intValue()` method takes a `String` and tries to convert it to an `int`:

```
private static int intValue( String str ){
    int i;
    try {
        i = Integer.parseInt(str);
    } catch ( NumberFormatException e ){
        i = 0;
    }
    return i;
}
```

If an exception is thrown in the parsing, the method simply returns the value of zero, which is the default behavior for some of the numeric properties.

Getting Connections

Clients requesting a database connection from one of the connection pools must interact directly with the `DBPoolManager` for that purpose. The `getConnection()` method of the `DBPoolManager` takes a pool name as the only parameter and returns a free `DBConnection` instance from the pool specified:

```
public DBConnection getConnection( String poolname ){
    DBConnection conn = null;
    DBConnectionPool pool = (DBConnectionPool) pools.get(poolname);
    if( pool != null ){
        try {
            conn = new DBConnection(pool);
        } catch ( SQLException e ){
            log.log("Unable to get a connection "
                +   "from the " + poolname + " pool.");
        }
    }
    return conn;
}
```

The `getConnection()` method gets the `DBConnectionPool` instance corresponding to the given pool name from the connection pools hash table. If there is no matching object found, the method returns `null`. Clients should be aware of this, and always check their `DBConnection` instance against `null`, in order to avoid nasty null pointer exceptions later on. On the other hand, if there was a matching `DBConnectionPool` to the given pool name, the method instantiates a `DBConnection` wrapper with the pool object obtained. If there is an error at this stage, a value of `null` will again be returned.

Closing the Pool Manager

When a client gets an instance of the DBPoolManager with the getInstance() method, the DBPoolManager increments the number of clients with an instance, thus keeping track of usage. Ideally, clients should also release their instance before server shutdown, by calling the close() method of the DBPoolManager.

```
public void close(){

        // Do nothing until the last client
        // has released its instance.
        if( --users != 0 ){
            return;
        }

        // Close down all DBConnectionPool objects.
        for( Enumeration e = pools.elements(); e.hasMoreElements(); ){
            try {
                ( (DBConnectionPool) e.nextElement() ).close();
            } catch ( SQLException s ){}
        }

        // Unregister all database drivers.
        for( Enumeration e = drivers.elements(); e.hasMoreElements(); ){
            try {
                DriverManager.deregisterDriver( (Driver) e.nextElement() );
            } catch ( SQLException s ){}
        }
    }
}
```

This method actually does nothing unless all clients have released their instances. As soon as that happens, all the DBConnectionPool objects are closed with their corresponding close() method, and all registered JDBC drivers are unregistered with the DriverManager. Note that in case of an SQLException in the unregistering process nothing can actually be done; the error is caught but not really handled.

Client Example

The DBConnection, DBConnectionPool, and DBPoolManager classes we have implemented can be used with any type of JDBC compliant drivers, in any Java application. In this section we will give an example of a client using these classes for accessing an Oracle database.

What we will look at is a servlet using the DBPoolManager to get a pooled DBConnection from the DBConnectionPool. It will use the DBConnectionPool to select information from a database of CD albums, based on a request for a specific artist. The servlet will display the CD information in an HTML format, with which you are probably familiar.

Prepare the Database

Before we implement the actual servlet, we will have to create the database table that stores the CD information and add some initial data entries.

Create Table

In this example, all the CDs are stored in the `cd_table` table. This table contains information on each CD's name, price, publication date, and artist:

```
CREATE TABLE CD_TABLE (
     CD                   NUMBER          NOT NULL,
     CD_NAME              VARCHAR2(500)   NOT NULL,
     ARTIST               VARCHAR2(500)   NOT NULL,
     PUBLISH_DATE         NUMBER          NOT NULL,
     PRICE                VARCHAR2(100)   NOT NULL,
     PRIMARY KEY (CD)
);
```

Create Sequence

The `CD_TABLE` table has the `CD` ID as its primary key. This value is generated with the `CD_SEQ` sequence:

```
CREATE SEQUENCE CD_SEQ;
```

Add Entries

Before we implement the servlet, we add some initial entries to the `CD_TABLE`, just so that we get some results when we run the servlet with a specified query:

```
INSERT INTO CD_TABLE (CD,CD_NAME,ARTIST,PUBLISH_DATE,PRICE)
VALUES (CD_SEQ.NEXTVAL, 'New Connection','The Connection',1995,'$16.99');

INSERT INTO CD_TABLE (CD,CD_NAME,ARTIST,PUBLISH_DATE,PRICE)
VALUES (CD_SEQ.NEXTVAL,'Best Of','OraCool',1999,'$12.99');

INSERT INTO CD_TABLE (CD,CD_NAME,ARTIST,PUBLISH_DATE,PRICE)
VALUES (CD_SEQ.NEXTVAL,'Bean Me Up!','The Java Beans',2000,'$19.99');

INSERT INTO CD_TABLE (CD,CD_NAME,ARTIST,PUBLISH_DATE,PRICE)
VALUES (CD_SEQ.NEXTVAL,'T.N.S.','OraCool',1995,'$7.99');

INSERT INTO CD_TABLE (CD,CD_NAME,ARTIST,PUBLISH_DATE,PRICE)
VALUES (CD_SEQ.NEXTVAL,'OK Computer','The Java Beans',1997,'$16.99');

INSERT INTO CD_TABLE (CD,CD_NAME,ARTIST,PUBLISH_DATE,PRICE)
VALUES (CD_SEQ.NEXTVAL,'Cool by the Pool','OraCool',1997,'$7.99');
```

Create the Servlet

Next, we will implement the actual servlet. This servlet stores a static instance of the `DBPoolManager`, which is obtained through the `init()` method.

```
package pooling.servlet;

import pooling.*;
import java.io.*;
import javax.servlet.*;
import javax.servlet.http.*;
import java.sql.*;
```

```
public class CDServlet extends HttpServlet {

    private DBPoolManager manager;
    public void init() throws SQLException {
        manager = DBPoolManager.getInstance();
    }
```

The actual work of the servlet takes place within its doGet() method. The servlet requests an artist's name through the getParameter() method. If there was an artist specified, then that means we should display CD information exclusively on the specified artist, otherwise, we just display all the CDs in the database.

```
protected void doGet(  HttpServletRequest request,
                        HttpServletResponse response)
                        throws ServletException, IOException {

    DBConnection conn;
    ServletOutputStream out;
    String artist;
    String query;

    out = response.getOutputStream();

    // Request a specified artist.
    artist = request.getParameter("artist");
    artist = (artist == null) ? "" : artist.trim();

    // Create the HTML page header.
    out.println("<html>");
    out.println("<head>");
    out.println("<title>" + artist + " CDs</title>");
    out.println("</head>");
    out.println("<body>");

    // Display the page header
    out.print  ("<h1>" + artist + " CDs</h1><br>");
```

Next, the method requests a DBConnection from the DBPoolManager instance, giving the pool name "musicpool", which we assume has been specified in the database properties file. If the getConnection() method returns null at this stage, we print a message indicating so and return. We assume that there is a connection pool named musicpool.

```
    conn = manager.getConnection("musicpool");

    // Checking the DBConnection against null.
    if ( conn == null ) {
        out.println("Unable to get a valid connection.");
        out.println("</body>");
        out.println("</html>");
        return;
    }
```

When we have created all necessary database objects and displayed the HTML page header, we proceed to query the database. As we have said, we query for a specific artist if we have previously requested an artist name. Otherwise, all the CDs in the database are displayed.

481

```
                          // Start the table
                          out.print  ("<table width=\"400\" border=\"0\" ");
                          out.print  ("cellpadding=\"3\" cellspacing=\"1\" ");
                          out.println("bgcolor=\"#000000\">");

                          // Print the table header, with gray background.
                          out.println("<tr bgcolor=\"#F4F4F4\">");
                          if ( artist.equals("") ) {
                              out.println("<td><b>Artist</b></td>");
                          }
                          out.println("<td><b>CD name</b></td>");
                          out.println("<td><b>Year</b></td>");
                          out.println("<td><b>Price</b></td>");
                          out.println("</tr>");

                          // Loop through all the ResultSet, displaying
                          // the CD information.
                          do {
                              out.println("<tr bgcolor=\"#FFFFFF\">");
                              if ( artist.equals("") ) {
                                  out.print("<td>");
                                  out.println(conn.getString("artist") +"</td>");
                              }
                              out.print("<td>");
                              out.println(conn.getString("cd_name") +"</td>");
                              out.print  ("<td>" + conn.getString("publish_date"));
                              out.println("</td>");
                              out.println("<td>" + conn.getString("price") +"</td>");
                              out.println("</tr>");

                          } while ( conn.next() );

                          out.println("</table>");
                      }
              } catch ( SQLException e ) {
                  out.println(e.getMessage() + "<br>");
              }
              finally {
                try {
                  // Close the connection.
                  conn.close();
                } catch (Exception e) {
                }
              }

          out.println("</body>");
          out.println("</html>");
      }
```

Note the simplicity of using the DBConnection to wrap the ResultSet and Statement objects. Instead of having to create and manage three database objects, using the wrapper class allows the user to have a single object do all the database work.

Finally, the `destroy()` method of the servlet is used to notify the `DBPoolManager` that this particular client is shutting down and no longer using the pool:

```
public void destroy() {
        manager.close();
        super.destroy();
    }
}
```

When this servlet is invoked, it should produce results similar to these shown in the following figure:

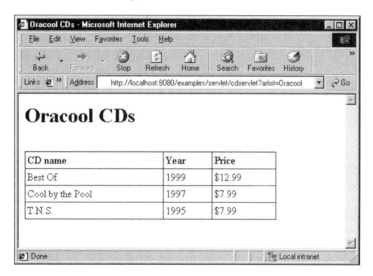

Deploying the Servlet

Once you have prepared the database and created the servlet, you must, in order to get things going, deploy the servlet to your preferred application server. In this section, we will give instructions on how to deploy our CD servlet on a particular type of server, namely the Tomcat application server.

To deploy a servlet to Tomcat, there are a few steps you must take:

- ❑   compile the servlet in its right place

- ❑   modify `web.xml` to include the servlet

- ❑   mount the servlet in `tomcat.conf`

- ❑   restart the server

Modify web.xml

The `web.xml` configuration file can be found under `TOMCAT_HOME/webapps/examples/WEB-INF`. The following should be add to the file, beneath the `<web-app>` entry :

```
<servlet>
  <servlet-name>
        cdservlet
  </servlet-name>
```

```
    <servlet-class>
          pooling.servlet.CDServlet
    </servlet-class>
    <!-- Load this servlet at server startup time -->
    <load-on-startup>
          -2147483646
    </load-on-startup>
</servlet>

<servlet-mapping>
   <servlet-name>cdservlet</servlet-name>
   <url-pattern>/cdservlet /*</url-pattern>
</servlet-mapping>
```

This way, you have mapped your CDServlet to the cdservlet URL extension.

Compiling

Before you compile your servlet, you should add it to your servlet package, or create one if it does not exist. Add the following line above the imports clause in the servlet code and the Java files:

```
package pooling.servlet;
```

The Java files are put into a folder called pooling or your own package and this is then placed in TOMCAT_HOME/webapps/examples/WEB-INF/Classes. This folder should contain all the Java files, and two other folders - properties and servlet, which contain the property file and the CDServlet the Java file. Compile all the files, from within Classes folder using:

```
classes> javac pooling/*.java
```

This compiles all the files in the pooling directory. To compile the servlet, use:

```
classes> javac pooling/servlet/*.java
```

Modify tomcat.conf

Next, you must mount the servlet in the tomcat.conf configuration file. You do so by adding the following clause below the line that says "ApJServMount default /root":

```
ApJServMount /cdservlet / cdservlet
<Location /WEB-INF/ >
    AllowOverride None
    Deny from all
</Location>
```

Restart the Server

Finally, you must restart the Tomcat server to be able to access the new servlet. Go to <TOMCAT_HOME>/bin and execute either the tomcat.bat (in Windows) or tomcat.sh (on UNIX) script with the following commands:

```
tomcat.bat/tomcat.sh stop
tomcat.bat/tomcat.sh start
```

Now your servlet should be accessible by visiting http://mysite/examples/servlet/ CDServlet, where *mysite* is the path of your deployment site; in our deployment this was the localhost. To find information about a CD from the database, use the normal CGI arguments such as ?name=OraCool at the end of the URL.

JDBC 2.0 Connection Pooling

The release of the JDBC 2.0 core API and the JDBC 2.0 Standard Extension API added significant functionality to database connectivity. New concepts and new solutions greatly simplified the process of connection pooling, which for the first time became officially supported by standard classes.

Since most of the features of the JDBC 2.0 API have already been introduced in previous chapters, we will now examine only those parts specifically related to connection pooling. These classes are all part of the Standard Extension packages, occasionally abbreviated to SE from now on.

First, before going into any details, let's get some perspective on how the Standard Extension API fits into the JDBC 2.0 API. The JDBC 2.0 API includes two packages:

❑ The java.sql package, which is the JDBC 2.0 core API. This includes the original JDBC API, referred to as the JDBC 1.0 API, plus the new core API that has been added. This package is included in the download of the Java 2 Platform SDK, Standard Edition.

❑ The javax.sql package, which is the JDBC 2.0 Standard Extension API. This package is entirely new and is available as a separate download or as part of the Java 2 Platform SDK, Enterprise Edition.

New Features

With the JDBC 2.0 SE came a number of new features and improvements to the core API. Two of the new features of the JDBC 2.0 Standard Extension package are of particular concern to us, namely the concept of **data sources** and support for **connection pooling**, which we will discuss in the next two sections.

The SE classes we will be working with in this section are described in the following table:

DataSource	A DataSource object is a factory for Connection objects.
OracleDataSource	Oracle's version of the DataSource class.
ConnectionPoolDataSource	A ConnectionPoolDataSource object is a factory for PooledConnection objects.
PooledConnection	A PooledConnection object is a connection object that provides hooks for connection pool management.

DataSource

With the JDBC 2.0 came the new concept of **data sources**. A data source is a standard, general-use object for specifying databases or other resources to use. A data source can optionally be bound to JNDI (Java Naming and Directory Interface) entities in order to access a database by a logical name, for convenience and portability.

> Using JNDI functionality requires the file **jndi.zip** to be in the classpath. This file is
> included in the Oracle file hierarchy, but is not included in the **classes12.zip** or
> **classes111.zip** files. You must add it to the classpath.

The data source facility provides a complete replacement for the previous JDBC DriverManager
facility, that is, registering a driver with the Class.forName() technique. The following example
emphasizes the difference in getting a Connection with the two procedures:

```
// JDBC 1.0 core API
Class.forName("oracle.jdbc.driver.OracleDriver");
String url = jdbc:oracle:thin:@127.0.0.1:1521:DB;
String user = test;
String password = test;
Connection conn = DriverManager.getConnection(url,user,password);

// JDBC 2.0 with JNDI
Context ctx = new InitialContext();
DataSource source = (DataSource) ctx.lookup("jdbc/testDB");
Connection conn = ds.getConnection();
```

In the first example, we use the DriverManager.getConnection() method to get a database
Connection object. This method of including the driver name, database port, and host name is
immobile, as any small change in, for example, the server setup would call for major changes in the
code. In the latter example, we use the Context.lookup() method to find a database schema that has
been associated, a logical name (in this case, "testDB"). This way, we could change the underlying
database specs without ever having to modify our code; we would still get our Connection objects
from the DataSource, it does not matter what the underlying database specs are.

Connection Pooling

Whereas connection pooling was largely neglected in the JDBC 1.0 core API, the JDBC 2.0 SE packages
include the foundations for a connection pool.

As we saw in the last section, a DataSource instance can be used to obtain Connection objects. In
addition to the standard DataSource interface, the SE packages additionally define a
ConnectionPoolDataSource, which returns pooled connections instead of the standard connections.
To be more precise:

- ❏ the DataSource returns Connection objects
- ❏ the ConnectionPoolDataSource returns PooledConnection objects

In creating a connection pool using a data source, you must actually implement a DataSource interface
to use the ConnectionPoolDataSource. The ConnectionPoolDataSource getConnection()
method returns a PooledConnection instance, which can be used to obtain a Connection, which the
DataSource returns from its getConnection() method. The following example should clarify
this further:

```
// Create a OracleConnectionPoolDataSource instance
OracleConnectionPoolDataSource ocpds =  new
    OracleConnectionPoolDataSource();
// Set connection parameters
ocpds.setURL(...);

...

// Create a pooled connection
PooledConnection pc  = ocpds.getPooledConnection();

// Get a logical connection
Connection conn = pc.getConnection();
```

The difference in using this method, rather than the one shown earlier lies in the **action listener**. A Connection object produced by calling PooledConnection.getConnection() is somewhat different from a usual Connection object. Although a new Connection instance is produced each time that the getConnection() method is called, this does not imply that a new physical database connection is created. A Connection object produced by the PooledConnection is actually just a temporary handle that an application can use to access an underlying physical database connection being pooled. When the application calls close() on the Connection handle, the DataSource that produced it is alerted that a connection is being closed, and instead of actually closing the Connection, it *returns it back to the pool.*

> **If you are wondering how the Connection class can be a wrapper for a physical connection, you must remember that the Connection is actually an *interface*, which can be implemented and extended to suit different specifications.**

This is the apparent magic behind how the DataSource interface producing the PooledConnection registers itself as an event listener for the object through the addConnectionEventListener() method. This way, the DataSource is informed about what happens to the Connection wrapper, such as when it is closed, so that the actual PooledConnection that produced the Connection can be returned to the connection pool, instead of being closed.

The biggest benefit of the data source connection pool model is that an application can use connection pooling without the client ever knowing it. That way, the designer could possibly switch back and forth between connection schemes, without ever disturbing the underlying application. Actually, this will also be the case with our updated connection pool classes from the first section, as we will see in the rest of the chapter.

Oracle JDBC 2.0 Extensions

In this section, we will introduce Oracle specific extensions and additions to the JDBC 2.0 API. Although the Oracle JDBC framework contains a large number of classes, we will discuss only those beneficial to the connection pool model, leaving the rest up to you to study.

The following set of classes will be discussed in this section:

OracleConnectionEventListener	An object that registers itself to receive events generated by a PooledConnection.
OracleConnectionCache	An interface that needs to be extended in order to implement Oracles own version of connection caching.
OracleConnectionCacheImpl	An Oracle supplied implementation of the OracleConnectionCache interface.
OracleConnection	Implements the Connection interface.
OracleResultSet	Implements the ResultSet interface.
OracleStatement	Implements the Statement interface.

The first three classes in the previous table are in the oracle.jdbc.pool package, while the last three are in the oracle.jdbc.driver package.

The most notable feature supplied with the Oracle extensions is **connection caching**, a technique similar to traditional connection pooling. In the next two sections, we will discuss this concept in more detail.

Connection Caching

Basically, connection caching is a means of keeping and using caches of physical database connections. Each connection cache is represented by an instance of a **connection cache class** and a group of pooled connections. For a single connection cache instance, the associated pooled connections must all represent physical connections to the same database account. The connection cache class creates pooled connection instances as needed, which is whenever a connection is requested and the connection cache does not have any free instances.

The connection pool, in setting up a connection cache, will create an instance of a connection cache class and set its data source connection properties as appropriate. An example of a connection cache class is OracleConnectionCacheImpl. This class extends the OracleDataSource class and so includes the setter methods to set connection properties.

Getting Connections from the Cache

Whenever a JDBC application wants a connection to a database in a connection-caching scenario, it will call the getConnection() method of the connection cache instance associated with the database. The getConnection() method checks if there are any free pooled connection instances in the cache. If not, one is created. This behavior is similar to the getConnection() method of DBConnectionPool we discussed in the first section of this chapter. A logical Connection instance can be retrieved from a previously existing or newly created pooled connection instance, and this logical connection instance will be supplied to the application.

Returning Connections to the Cache

When a pooled connection is created for the cache, the connection cache instance creates a connection event listener and associates it with the chosen pooled connection instance. The association with the pooled connection instance is accomplished by calling the standard addConnectionEventListener() method specified by the PooledConnection interface, as we discussed in the section on connection pooling with the JDBC SE.

488

Then, when a JDBC application calls the close() method of a logical connection instance, an event is triggered and communicated to the event listener associated with the PooledConnection instance that produced the logical connection. This event will trigger a connection-closed event and inform the pooled connection instance that its physical connection can be reused. This means that the pooled connection can be put back into the cache.

The exact point at which a connection event listener is created and registered with a pooled connection instance is implementation-specific. For example, this could happen when the pooled connection instance is first created or each time the logical connection associated with it is closed. The same logic applies to our previous discussion of the ConnectionPoolDataSource.

Oracle Connection Cache Implementation

Oracle offers a sample implementation of connection caching and connection event listeners, providing the OracleConnectionCacheImpl class. This class implements the OracleConnectionCache interface and uses instances of the OracleConnectionEventListener class for listener functionality. Of course, you can always implement the OracleConnectionCache interface for your own connection cache class.

If you choose to use the OracleConnectionCacheImpl class in your own connection pooling implementation, these are the steps you must take in order to get things going:

❑   instantiate OracleConnectionCacheImpl and set its properties

❑   set a maximum number of pooled connections

❑   select a scheme for creating new pooled connections

Instantiation

A connection pool that uses the OracleConnectionCacheImpl can set its connection properties in one of two ways:

❑   it can use the OracleConnectionCacheImpl constructor that takes an existing connection pool data source as input

❑   or it can use the default OracleConnectionCacheImpl constructor and then set the properties individually, using setter methods

The following code shows both methods of construction:

```
// Using an existing data source object.
ConnectionPoolDataSource cpds;
...
OracleConnectionCacheImpl ocacheimpl = new OracleConnectionCacheImpl(cpds);

// Using a default constructor and setting properties.
OracleConnectionCacheImpl ocacheimpl = new OracleConnectionCacheImpl();

ocacheimpl.setDriverType("oci8");
ocacheimpl.setServerName("127.0.0.1");
ocacheimpl.setNetworkProtocol("tcp");
ocacheimpl.setDatabaseName("DB");
ocacheimpl.setPortNumber(1521);
ocacheimpl.setUser("test");
ocacheimpl.setPassword("test");
```

Pooled Connections Settings

In any connection caching implementation, the developer must decide:

❑ whether there should be a maximum number of pooled connections in the cache

❑ and if so how to handle situations where no pooled connections are available and the maximum number has been reached.

The `OracleConnectionCacheImpl` class includes a maximum cache size that can be set using the `setMaxLimit()` method (taking an `int` as input). Following is an example, presuming `ocacheimpl` is an `OracleConnectionCacheImpl` instance:

```
ocacheimpl.setMaxLimit(10);
```

This limits the cache to a maximum size of 10 pooled connection instances. The default value is 1.

The `OracleConnectionCacheImpl` class supports three so-called cache schemes, for situations where the application has requested a connection, all existing pooled connections are in use, and the maximum number of pooled connections in the cache has been reached. (We actually discussed this same situation in our discussion of the `getConnection()` method of the `DBConnectionPool` class.) The first scheme is known as the **dynamic cache scheme**, the second is known as the **fixed-with-no-wait scheme**, and the third one as the **fixed-with-wait scheme**.

Using the default dynamic scheme, new pooled connections will be created above and beyond the maximum limit, but each one is automatically closed and freed as soon the logical connection instance that it provided is no longer in use.

In the fixed-with-no-wait scheme, the maximum limit cannot be exceeded. Requests for connections when the maximum has already been reached will return `null`.

In the fixed-with-wait scheme, the maximum limit cannot be exceeded, but instead of returning `null`, as in the previous scheme, the cache class will wait for a connection to be returned to the cache.

You can set the cache scheme by invoking the `setCacheScheme()` method of the `OracleConnectionCacheImpl` instance, using one of the following class static constants as input:

```
public static final int DYNAMIC_SCHEME
public static final int FIXED_RETURN_NULL_SCHEME
public static final int FIXED_WAIT_SCHEME
```

For example, presuming `ocimpl` is an `OracleConnectionCacheImpl` instance:

```
ocimpl.setCacheScheme(OracleConnectionCacheImpl.FIXED_RETURN_NULL_SCHEME);
```

Additional OracleConnectionCacheImpl Methods

In addition to the key methods already discussed, the following `OracleConnectionCacheImpl` methods might be useful:

❑ `getActiveSize()`

Returns the number of currently active pooled connections in the cache (pooled connection instances with an associated logical connection instance being used by the JDBC application).

❑ `getCacheSize()`

Returns the total number of pooled connections in the cache, both active and inactive.

Altering the Standard Pool

By now, we have discussed the most notable features of the JDBC 2.0 Standard Extension and Oracle extension packages relevant to connection pooling. It is time for us to show how all these features fit together in an actual connection pool implementation. In doing so, instead of writing a new set of classes, we will instead update our previous connection pool implementation from the first section to work with JDBC 2.0.

In updating the standard connection pool implementation to the JDBC 2.0 extensions, the following features have to be included to resemble the JDBC 2.0 suggested model:

- ❑ database access using data sources and JNDI

- ❑ connection caching

- ❑ a wrapper class for physical connections

When we examine the first item in the list above, we notice that our old connection pool implementation does in fact fulfill the role of JNDI when it comes to identifying a database. That is, using the DBPoolManager class, we have already implemented access to a database schema by giving a logical name instead of supplying database account details (giving the pool name, remember), where the actual directory object creation takes place in the DBPoolManager with a supplied database properties file. Therefore, the first part of the update is in fact unnecessary. However, you may of course implement a solution by creating DBConnectionPool objects, registering them with a JNDI directory instance, and locating them with a Context.lookup() method, as shown in chapter 12.

The second part, using Oracle connection caching, will fit very nicely into our standard implementation. What we have to do is to have the DBConnectionPool class contain an instance of the OracleConnectionCacheImpl class (or any other implementation, if appropriate), which replace the inPool array we had used for representing the actual connection pool. This we will discuss in more detail later.

As for the implementation of a connection wrapper class, we already have our DBConnection class, which will easily fit in our new implementation without much alteration. We will, however, update some of the classes used to their Oracle specific counterparts defined in the oracle.jdbc.driver package, as will be shown below.

Summary of Updates from JDBC 1.0

The following list of items gives a summary of the updates needed to adapt our JDBC 1.0 connection pool to the JDBC 2.0 standard.

- ❑ **DBConnection**

  Import the oracle.jdbc.pool, oracle.jdbc.driver, and oracle.sql packages.

  Replace the Statement, PreparedStatement, Connection, and ResultSet classes with OracleStatement, OraclePreparedStatement, OracleConnection, and OracleResultSet. This *may* require typecasting at the appropriate places, that is casting Statement to OracleStatement, ResultSet to OracleResultSet, and so on.

  Instead of calling the freeConnection() method of the DBConnectionPool, we simply call Connection.close() when we free the Connection instance in the close() method.

❑ **DBConnectionPool**

Import the `oracle.jdbc.pool` and `oracle.sql` packages.

Store an instance of the `OracleConnectionCacheImpl` class. Remove most of the instance variables used to store the database settings.

Update the constructor.

Update `getConnection()` to use the `OracleConnectionCacheImpl` instance to get `Connection` objects.

Remove `getPooleConnection()`.

Remove `getNewConnection()`.

Remove `isValid()`.

Modify the `totalCount()`, `outCount()`, and `inCount()` methods.

Modify the `close()` method, so that it calls close on the `OracleConnectionCacheImpl` instance.

Modify the `monitor()` method, which no longer serves the purpose of supplying the pool with fresh connections.

❑ **DBPoolManager**

Replace the `maxWait` property with the `cacheScheme` property.

Modify the `init()` method to construct the `DBConnectinPool` instances with `cacheScheme` and to skip the driver registration.

Remove the `registerDriver()` method.

Remove the `deregisterDriver()` method.

Modify the `close()` method, so that it doesn't deregister drivers.

DBConnection Updates

We have already mentioned some of the new classes of the `oracle.jdbc.driver` package. Since we are developing for Oracle, we would prefer to use some of these Oracle counterparts of the standard `java.sql` database classes in the updated `DBConnection` class. These include:

❑ `OracleConnection`, instead of `Connection`

❑ `OracleResultSet`, instead of `ResultSet`

❑ `OracleStatement`, instead of `Statement`

❑ `OraclePreparedStatement`, instead of `PreparedStatement`

All of these new classes implement their standard counterparts in a manner better adapted to the Oracle environment. Although using these classes will probably not result in greatly increased performance on the short run, the long-term effects can be considerable, especially when considering applications with frequent transactions, such as web services.

Note that by changing to the Oracle counterparts of the JDBC classes, we may need to typecast return values and parameters, as we show below.

The new class header of the DBConnection is the following; this is in the package pooling2:

```
package pooling2;

import oracle.sql.*;
import oracle.jdbc.pool.*;
import oracle.jdbc.driver.*;
import java.sql.*;
import java.util.*;
import java.io.*;

public class DBConnection {
```

The actual DBConnection code is more or less intact, except for the fact that we have replaced all mention of Connection, ResultSet, PreparedStatement, and Statement. The following examples should clarify this further:

```
private synchronized void connect() throws SQLException {
    if ( isOpen() ) {
        rsClose();
        stmtClose();
    } else {
        conn = (OracleConnection)ocp.getConnection();
        conn.setAutoCommit(true);
    }
}

public synchronized void prepareStatement( String sql ) throws SQLException {
    connect();
    stmt = (OraclePreparedStatement)conn.prepareStatement(sql);
}

public int getInt(String field) throws SQLException {
    try {
        return rs.getInt(field);
    } catch (NullPointerException e) {
        throw new SQLException( "Please call getResultSet() only after "
                        +    "calling query()/executeQuery().");
    }
}

public void setInt(int parameterIndex, int x) throws SQLException {
    try {
        ((OraclePreparedStatement)stmt).setInt(parameterIndex, x);
    } catch (NullPointerException npe) {
        throw new SQLException( "Please call set() only after calling "
                        +    "prepareStatement().");
    } catch (ClassCastException cce) {
        throw new SQLException( "You have already created a statement. "
                        +    "Close it and use prepareStatement().");
    }
}
```

493

DBConnectionPool Updates

As we have mentioned, in order to update our original DBConnectionPool class to use the JDBC 2.0 extensions, we will have to provide it with an implementation of the OracleConnectionCache interface. In this example, we use the supplied OracleConnectionCacheImpl class, but of course, any other valid implementation could have been used for this purpose.

Instance Variables

Since the actual pooling logic is now included in the connection cache class, which is initialized in the constructor, there is no need to keep all the pool settings of the standard implementation as instance variables. Instead, in the new implementation, there are now only four instance variables, the OracleConnectionCacheImpl instance, the logInterval, the Logger instance, the monitor Thread, and the sleep interval constant:

```
package pooling2;

import oracle.sql.*;
import oracle.jdbc.pool.*;
import java.sql.*;
import java.util.*;
import java.io.*;

public class DBConnectionPool {

    private final int SLEEP_INTERVAL = 2000;
    private OracleConnectionCacheImpl oci;
    private Logger log;
    private long logTimer;
    private long logInterval;
    private Thread poolMonitor;
```

Constructor

The new constructor resembles the original standard implementation constructor, except that the maximum wait for connection property has been replaced by the cache scheme type. This is done because the OracleConnectionCacheImpl does not contain methods for explicitly setting this property, whereas some other implementations might. If using any other implementation, check for this property, as it can often be necessary to alter the length of this period for different types of applications.

```
public DBConnectionPool( String name, String url, String user,
    String password, int maxConns, int minConns, int cacheScheme,
    long logInterval ) throws SQLException {
```

We then create the OracleConnectionCacheImpl instance with the default constructor, and explicitly set the pool properties with the corresponding set() methods:

```
oci = new OracleConnectionCacheImpl();
oci.setURL( url );
oci.setUser( user );
oci.setPassword( password );
oci.setMaxLimit( maxConns );
oci.setMinLimit( minConns );
```

```
        // Set the cache scheme.
        if ( cacheScheme == 1 ) {
            oci.setCacheScheme(OracleConnectionCacheImpl.
            FIXED_RETURN_NULL_SCHEME);
        } else if ( cacheScheme == 2 ) {
            oci.setCacheScheme(OracleConnectionCacheImpl.FIXED_WAIT_SCHEME);
        }
```

As we have mentioned, a dynamic cache scheme is the default behavior, so a cacheScheme value of zero which corresponds to omitting the cacheScheme property from the database properties file; remember intValue() will result in a dynamic scheme.

The rest of the constructor, setting the log file and starting the monitor thread, is unchanged from the standard implementation.

```
        // Initialize logging
        if ( logInterval > 0 ) {
            try {
                this.log = new Logger("DBConnectionPool_" + name);
            } catch ( IOException e ) {
                throw new SQLException( "Unable initialize logging for "
                            +   "DBConnectionPool " + name  + ": "
                            +   e.getMessage() );
            }
        }
        this.logInterval = logInterval;
        logTimer = System.currentTimeMillis();

        // Create the monitor Thread.
        poolMonitor = new Thread (
            new Runnable() {
                public void run() {
                    monitor();
                }
            }
        );
        poolMonitor.start();
    }
```

Getting a Connection from the Pool

Just as in the standard implementation of the DBConnection class, we call the getConnection() method to get a physical database Connection instance from the pool. The only difference from the previous method is that, instead of determining the pool state and using either the getPooledConnection() or the getNewConnection() method based on that assumption, we simple request a Connection straight from the connection cache, which now encapsulates the pooling logic:

```
    public synchronized Connection getConnection() throws SQLException {

        Connection conn = oci.getConnection();
        if ( conn == null ) {
            throw new SQLException( "Maximum number of connections "
                            +   "in pool succeeded.");
        }
        return conn;
    }
```

This is where the connection cache scheme we specified for the pool will begin to make a difference. As we have mentioned, there are three types of connection cache schemes, the dynamic scheme, the fixed-with-wait-scheme, and the fixed-with-no-wait-scheme scheme. The first one will dynamically create necessary Connection objects when needed, as the other two will stop at the specified maximum number of connections. The difference between the latter two is just that the fixed-wait scheme will wait for a connection to get back to the pool, and the fixed-with-no-wait-scheme scheme will not wait, returning null if it encounters an empty pool. Each one of the three caching schemes will fit different applications and circumstances and none of them is actually better than the others, they just behave differently.

Pool Status

In the JDBC 1.0 implementation, we had the totalCount(), inCount(), and outCount() methods, that gave us the status of the connection pool. These methods have to be updated for the JDBC 2.0 version, as we no longer get the pool size from our own instance variables. Instead, we use the getActiveSize() and getCacheSize() methods of the OracleConnectionCacheImpl class for the same purpose:

```
public int totalCount() {
    return oci.getCacheSize();
}

public int inCount() {
    return (totalCount() - outCount());
}

public int outCount() {
    return oci.getActiveSize();
}
```

The Monitor Thread

We have to do little modifications on the monitor() method for the JDBC 2.0 implementation. The new monitor() method only serves the purpose of logging the pool state; keeping the connection minimum is now up to the connection cache:

```
private void monitor() {
    while ( true ) {

        // This is only done every logInterval seconds.
        if ( (logInterval != 0)
        && ((System.currentTimeMillis() - logTimer) > logInterval) ) {
            log();
            logTimer = System.currentTimeMillis();
        }

        // Rest the Thread on a regular basis.
        try {
            Thread.sleep(SLEEP_INTERVAL);
        } catch (InterruptedException e) {
            log("Interrupted in the monitor function");
        }
    }
}
```

Closing the Pool

In the close method of the JDBC 1.0 DBConnectionPool, we had to go through each of the Connection objects in the pool and call close() on them, deregister drivers, and such. In the JDBC 2.0 implementation, we only have to call close() on the OracleConnectionCacheImpl instance, which takes care of closing all the pooled connections:

```
public synchronized void close() throws SQLException {
    oci.close();
}
```

DBPoolManager Updates

As for the final class in our connection pool implementation, the DBPoolManager, the only updates that have to be done there are replacing the maxWait property with the cacheScheme property, in both the database properties file and the construction of the DBConnectionPool. As it should be unnecessary to register drivers with JDBC 2.0, we will throw away the registerDriver() and deregisterDriver() methods in the init() and close() methods, respectively. The JDBC 2.0 version of the class constructor is the following:

```
private synchronized void init() throws SQLException {

    char c = File.separatorChar;

    DBConnectionPool pool;
    Enumeration propertyNames;

    int maxConns;
    int logInterval;
    int minConns;
    int cacheScheme;
    int p = 0;

    Properties props;
    InputStream is;

    String driver;
    String poolname = "";
    String prop;
    String password;
    String url;
    String user;

    users = 0;
    pools = new Hashtable();
    drivers = new Hashtable();

    // Initialize the pool manager Logger class.
    try {
        log = new Logger("poolmanager.log");
    } catch (IOException e){
        throw new SQLException(e.getMessage());
    }
    log.log("\n----------------------------------\n"
        +   "--- INITIALIZING CONNECTION POOLS\n"
        +   "----------------------------------\n");
```

```
        // Read the properties file.
        is = getClass().getResourceAsStream(c + "properties" + c
                                      +  "pools.properties");
    props = new Properties ();
    try {
        props.load(is);
    } catch (Exception e){
        e.printStackTrace();
        log.log("Unable to read database properties file.");
    }

    // Load the connection pool properties.
    propertyNames = props.propertyNames();
    while( propertyNames.hasMoreElements() ){
        prop = (String) propertyNames.nextElement();
        if( prop.equals("name" + p) ){

            // Parse the new pool name.
            poolname = props.getProperty(prop);

            // Read numeric valued properties.
            maxConns      =    intValue(props.getProperty(
                               poolname + ".maxConns"));
            logInterval   =    intValue(props.getProperty(
                               poolname + ".logInterval"));
            minConns      =    intValue(props.getProperty(
                               poolname + ".minConns"));
            cacheScheme   =    intValue(props.getProperty(
                               poolname + ".cacheScheme"));

            // Read character valued properties.
            password = props.getProperty(poolname + ".password");
            url      = props.getProperty(poolname + ".url");
            user     = props.getProperty(poolname + ".user");
            driver   = props.getProperty(poolname + ".driver");

            // Create the connection pool object
            // and add it to the hash table of pools.
            pool = new DBConnectionPool(poolname,url,user,password,
                                    maxConns,minConns,cacheScheme,
                                    logInterval );
            pools.put(poolname,pool);
            p++;
            log.log("Initialized DBConnectionPool " + poolname);
        }
    }
}
```

Closing the Pool Manager

When we call close() on the updated DBPoolManager, we wait for all clients to release their instances, and then close each of the connection pools:

```
public void close(){

    // Do nothing until the last client
    // has released its instance.
    if( --users != 0 ){
        return;
    }

    // Close down all DBConnectionPool objects.
    for( Enumeration e = pools.elements(); e.hasMoreElements(); ){
        try {
            ( (DBConnectionPool) e.nextElement() ).close();
        } catch ( SQLException s ){}
    }
}
```

When all the necessary updates have been finished, our connection pool implementation should now be JDBC 2.0 compliant. Now, the good part in all of this is that although we have now altered all of the classes comprising our connection pool implementation, it should still be transparent to the client. The client will still request a DBConnection object from the DBPoolManager using the getConnection() method, and all of the methods of the DBConnection are left intact, at least from the user's perspective. On the other hand, if we had been using the Connection, ResultSet and Statement classes instead of a Connection wrapper in the first place, we would have had to rewrite most of the client code to reflect our update.

Summary

In this chapter, we have studied the concept of connection pooling and its implementation using JDBC. To be more precise, we have:

- ❏ discussed the advantages of pooling resources

- ❏ implemented a connection pool using the JDBC 1.0 core API

- ❏ discussed how the JDBC 2.0 Standard Extension packages support connection pooling

- ❏ introduced Oracle extension packages and connection caching

- ❏ updated our connection pool implementation to use the JDBC 2.0 extensions

14

Database Connectivity with SQLJ

Oracle 8i introduced a feature that allowed developers to embed SQL statements directly in Java code, thus easing development of database applications. This means that instead of using the JDBC API to open connections, create statements, call methods to execute SQL, and parse through a result set, you can write just a few lines of embedded SQL and achieve the same result.

This feature is known as SQLJ. With SQLJ, you embed SQL statements directly in Java code and use a special preprocessor to translate those statements to pure Java source code. Finally, you compile and run your code with access to the SQLJ library classes.

Make no mistake; SQLJ does not eliminate the need to write JDBC code. SQLJ is a pre-compiler environment and works in those situations where the SQL statements are static, that is, where the SQL statements are known at compile time and do not change dynamically during the execution of the program. In these situations, you can let the computer create the JDBC code from a few lines of SQL embedded in your Java code.

> **A SQLJ program is a Java program that contains static embedded SQL code.**

In many programming situations, however, we do not know what SQL will be executed until runtime (for example, SQL in which the column names in a WHERE clause are dynamically built) – on these occasions, you'll still need to use JDBC.

Embedded SQL is a feature that is not unique to Oracle. SQLJ is an industry standard that was developed by numerous companies, including Oracle. The standard for SQLJ is ANSI SQL/OLB X3.135.10-1998. You can find information on SQLJ at the website: http://www.sqlj.org.

In this chapter you will learn how to:

- ❑   Embed SQL executable statements in Java code

- ❑   Compile a Java application using the SQLJ translator preprocessor and Java compiler

- ❑   Create `Iterator` classes and use them to receive multiple rows from a database table query

- ❑   Use SQLJ `Connection` classes and `Execution` classes to create multiple connections to a database

- ❑   Load and run SQLJ classes in the Oracle JVM

SQLJ Code

Within your Java code, you can have SQLJ executable statements or SQLJ declarations. Each kind of SQLJ code does what its name implies: executable statements are compiled into Java JDBC code that sends SQL statements to the database to do something or produce a result; SQLJ declarations are used to create new Java types or classes.

> The classes which support embedded SQL are located in the Java archives
> `translator.zip` (for development) or `runtime.zip` (for deployment). See
> Appendix A for the location of these archives and how to install them. Information on
> the classes in these archives can be found at the Javadoc for Oracle SQLJ, usually
> located at: `<ORACLE_HOME>\sqlj\doc\runtime\javadoc`

Executable Statements

Executable statements are any legal SQL statements that you want the code to execute and that are supported by your database driver. Legal SQLJ statements can be:

- ❑   Data Definition Language (DDL) statements: `CREATE`, `ALTER`, etc.

- ❑   Data Manipulation Language (DML) statements: `SELECT`, `INSERT`, `UPDATE`, etc.

- ❑   PL/SQL declarations, blocks, and comments

The SQLJ standard specifies that SQLJ statements must support the SQL92 standard, but allows a vendor to support additional features. If you are planning to use the SQLJ code in multiple environments, you may want to avoid using any Oracle SQLJ extensions. See the translator section later in this chapter for more information on how to identify Oracle specific extensions.

Here is the syntax for an SQLJ statement where the angle brackets < > mark optional syntax:

```
#sql <[<connection_context>,<execution_context>]> <iterator = >
    { SQL statements };
```

At its simplest, a SQLJ executable statement consists of the token `#sql` followed by SQL statements placed between curly braces and terminated by a semicolon.

In addition, there are optional components to the SQLJ statement. These optional components are the connection context, the execution context, and the iterator. The optional clauses are discussed later in this chapter:

❑ The #sql token can be followed by an optional connection context reference, or an optional execution context instance, or both

❑ If the SQL statement will return results, a reference to an iterator can receive the results of the SQL expression

The SQLJ code can appear any place inside a class where executable statements are allowed. Everything between the braces is treated as a SQL statement and must conform to the SQL standard.

Sample SQLJ expressions:

```
#sql { INSERT INTO employee (lastname, firstname,
                            salary_grade)
                 VALUES ('Smith', 'John', 45) };
#sql { SET :sales_tax = 0.1 };
#sql { SET :OUT sales_tax = 0.1 };
```

The variable sales_tax above is preceded by a colon and, in one case, a mode specifier (OUT); the colon identifies the variable as a host expression.

Host expressions and mode specifiers are explained in the next section.

In the next line of SQL, a stored procedure is called:

```
#sql { CALL PROCESS_ORDERS() };
```

The next statement uses an iterator to receive the results of the select statement. (Iterators are discussed in more detail later in this chapter):

```
#sql iter = { SELECT lastname, firstname
                FROM employee };
```

You can embed PL/SQL statements as well:

```
#sql { BEGIN if salary_grade < 47 then
                salary_grade := salary_grade + 1;
            end if;
       END; };
```

Host Expressions

A host expression is simply a Java expression or variable that can be used inside SQLJ code. Host expressions are used to retrieve or send data values. Since they are Java expressions or variables, they follow the same scope rules as any other Java expression or variable. The syntax rules for host expressions are:

❑   A colon must precede the host expression.

❑   A mode specifier that is one of IN, OUT, or IN/OUT can optionally precede the host
    expression. In this case, the colon appears before IN, OUT, or IN/OUT and a space character
    between the mode specifier and the host expression. Host expressions with a mode of IN are
    used to send values to the database. The OUT mode is used to receive values from the
    database. IN OUT host expressions can do both.

❑   With two exceptions, host expressions in SQLJ statements have a default mode of IN. The two
    exceptions are the SELECT INTO and SET statements where the default access mode is OUT.

❑   If the mode is OUT or IN OUT, the host expression must be a legal l-value (that is, it must be
    legal to have the expression on the left side of an assignment statement).

❑   Any host expression that is not a simple Java variable is a complex expression. Complex
    expressions should be enclosed in parentheses, with the colon preceding the opening
    parenthesis if there is no mode specifier.

Two complex expressions are used in the code snippet below:

```
#sql { UPDATE emp
          SET department = .
              :IN(getDeptName()),
              salary = :(oldSalary * 1.05)
          WHERE emp='SMITH' };
```

In the first case, the return value of the method call getDeptName() is used as a host expression. In the
second case, a variable oldSalary is multiplied by 1.05, and the result is used as a host expression.

The simplest form of a host expression is a local variable. The local variable must be of the correct type
to hold the particular data that will be stored. The full listing of the correspondence between Java types
and Oracle datatypes can be found in Oracle's SQLJ documentation. Here is a partial extract from
Oracle's SQLJ documentation showing some supported data types:

Java Type/Standard JDBC Types	Oracle Datatype
int	NUMBER
Integer	NUMBER
long	NUMBER
float	NUMBER
Float	NUMBER
double	NUMBER
java.lang.String	CHAR
java.lang.String	VARCHAR2

In the list above, you may have noticed the Java objects Integer and Float. In fact, all the Java
primitive wrapper types can be used as host expression types: Byte, Short, Integer, Long, Double,
Float, and Boolean. They are supported for those cases where a column in a table can be NULL.
When NULL is returned from the database, it is converted to a Java null. If your code tries to store a
Java null into a Java primitive, then an SQLException will be thrown.

Below is the source for a Java class, which demonstrates the use of host expressions. It accesses the SCOTT.emp table from the starter database that can be created as part of an Oracle installation. In the Java class below, one row from the table is retrieved. The fields from that row are assigned to host variables, which are then printed for display. As explained above, because the emp table defines empno to be NOT NULL, the Java primitive int can be used; but the salary field could be NULL, so the code uses the Java Double for that field. Save this source file as sqlj\simple\SQLJHost.sqlj:

```
package sqlj.simple;

import oracle.sqlj.runtime.Oracle;

public class SQLJHost {
  public static void main(String[] args) {
    //initialize host expressions
    int employeeNumber = 0;
    Double salary = null;
    String name = "";
    String job = "";

    try {
      //the url string "jdbc:oracle:oci8:@proead" tells
      //the driver how to connect to database with local
      //TNS service name proead (set up with Net8 assistant).
      //the next two parameters are the username and password
      //the parameter 'true' enables auto-commit
      Oracle.connect("jdbc:oracle:oci8:@proead", "scott", "tiger", true);

      //this SQL statement selects a row from the emp table and stores the
      //results in the host expressions
      #sql { select empno, ename, job, sal
               into :employeeNumber, :name, :job, :salary
             from emp
             where empno=7566 };
    } catch (Exception e) {
      e.printStackTrace();
    } finally {
      try {
        Oracle.close();
      } catch (Exception ignored){}
    }

    System.out.println("Employee       : " + name);
    System.out.println("Employee Number: " + employeeNumber);
    System.out.println("Job            : " + job);
    System.out.println("Salary         : " + salary);
  }
}
```

To compile and run the code above, you will need to have SQLJ 8.1.6 or installed. See Appendix A for more information on how to do this. If you are using SQLJ 8.1.5, add import sqlj.runtime.ref.DefaultContext to the beginning of the source file; in place of Oracle.close(), use DefaultContext().getDefaultContext().close():

```
    } finally {
      try {
        DefaultContext.getDefaultContext().close();
      } catch (Exception ignored){}
    }
```

When SQLJ is installed as directed in Appendix A, the code can be compiled from the command line using the command below; more detailed explanation of how the translator works and the command line options are provided later in the chapter.

```
sqlj -v -passes sqlj\simple\SQLJHost.sqlj
```

This command will run the SQLJ translator and the Java compiler. The −v option tells the translator to report each step as the step is performed. More information on the translator is provided later in this chapter. If the code does not compile, check the code and the SQLJ installation. When the code is compiled, you can run the code from the command line using:

```
java sqlj.simple.SQLJHost
```

And this is the output you should see:

```
Employee        : JONES
Employee Number: 7566
Job             : MANAGER
Salary          : 2975.0
```

The SQLJ translator creates a `.java` source file from the `.sqlj` file. It will be located in the same directory as `SQLJHost.sqlj`, and it will be named `SQLJHost.java`. You can load this source file into an editor and compare it to the `.sqlj` source file. For example, the SQL statement

```
#sql { select empno, ename, job, sal
         into :employeeNumber, :name, :job, :salary
       from emp
       where empno=7566 };
```

becomes 24 lines of JDBC code. Clearly, using SQLJ can make database programming easier than using JDBC.

The Default Connection

The last thing to cover before actually writing an SQLJ class is the connection. As with all other database programs, before you can talk to the database, you must create a connection to the database.

For the first half of this chapter, we'll use a single connection, known as the default connection context. After making the connection, all the SQLJ statements in the class file will use that single connection to talk to the database. This connection is used to send SQL statements to the database for execution and to receive the results of the SQL. You'll see how to create and use multiple connection contexts later in this chapter.

There are two basic ways to get a database connection:

- ❑   `oracle.sqlj.runtime.Oracle.connect()`
- ❑   `oracle.sqlj.runtime.Oracle.getConnection()`

The `oracle.sqlj.runtime.Oracle` class is in the Oracle `translator.zip` and `runtime.zip` Java archives.

Oracle.connect()

There are 12 overloaded varieties of the connect() method. That is, there are 12 methods named connect(). Each method provides a different means to supply four required parameters. The four required parameters are:

- ❑ The connection URL
- ❑ The connection user name
- ❑ The connection password
- ❑ The auto-commit setting

> **Unlike the JDBC driver, the SQLJ driver defaults to auto-commit disabled.**

The Oracle.connect() method is a public static method, which returns a reference of type DefaultContext. Full information on the different forms of the connect() method can be found in the SQLJ Javadoc, which is usually located at <Oracle Home>\sqlj\doc\runtime\javadoc. When using this method for obtaining a connection, you only need to call the connect() method.

This chapter will use one of two forms of connect(). One form explicitly passes the four parameters listed above:

```
Oracle.connect("jdbc:oracle:oci8:@proead","scott", "tiger", true);
```

The previous line of code was used in the sample program SQLJHost.sqlj listed above. The first parameter is the driver URL and it tells the JDBC driver how to connect to the database. The URL used above tells the driver to connect to the database using the Oracle OCI library. This is also known as a Type II driver; this driver uses platform native code to connect to the database. In this case, we are using the alias proead, which has been set up on our client machine using the Net8 Assistant to point to the Oracle 8i database (with the same service name) on a remote machine with host address dbserver. It is possible to omit the service name proead from the driver URL, if a default database is specified in the local TNS naming service.

The other driver you may be using is known as a thin driver or a Type IV driver. This driver is a pure Java driver. The URL for the thin driver looks like jdbc:oracle:thin:@host:port:service. To use this URL: replace host with the server name or IP address of the machine running the database, replace port with the Net8 Listener port (the standard default value is 1521) and replace service with the database service name (called the Service Identifier or SID in Oracle 8.1.5 and earlier). A TNS listener must be running on host. Since this driver is pure Java, it does not require any native Oracle code to run, and it does not refer to a local naming service to resolve the URL. If in doubt, contact your database administrator for suitable values for the parameters for your driver URL. More information on drivers and driver URLs can be found at http://java.sun.com/products/jdbc/drivers or the Oracle8i JDBC Developer's Guide and Reference, http://technet.oracle.com.

The other form used in this chapter is:

```
Oracle.connect(getClass(), "connect.properties");
```

The getClass() method is a method of all Java classes, because it is a method of the Object class. It returns a Class object that represents the class. The connect call uses this Class object to determine where to look for the property file named by the second parameter. This property file contains the driver URL, the username, and the password. The format of the property file is shown later in this chapter.

Calling Oracle.connect() creates a default connection that can be used by all the SQLJ statements in your class file. The connection is used when sending SQL to the database or returning a result from the database. You do not even need to keep a reference to the DefaultContext instance which is returned by the connect() method (although you can if you really want to), because the oracle.sqlj.runtime.Oracle class keeps a reference to the connection. What happens if you call this method a second time in your code? The class recognizes that a DefaultContext has already been created, and simply returns a null from the method without replacing the original connection.

Oracle.getConnection()

For every connect() method, there is a corresponding getConnection() method with the same parameter list. This is because connect() calls getConnection() to do part of its connection work. If you use any of the getConnection() methods directly, though, you need to do a bit more work. Here's how the getConnection() method would be used in the SQLJHost class above:

```
//the url string "jdbc:oracle:oci8:" tells the driver how to connect
//the next two parameters are the username and password
//the parameter 'true' enables auto-commit
DriverManager.registerDriver(new OracleDriver());
DefaultContext dc = Oracle.getConnection("jdbc:oracle:oci8:@proead",
    "scott", "tiger", true);
DefaultContext.setDefaultContext(dc);
```

After registering the driver and making the connection, you need to either set the default context as shown, or use the connection context explicitly in each SQL statement. Using the connection context explicitly will be covered later in the section on connection contexts.

The code above is essentially what connect() does for you when you call Oracle.connect(). You can use connect() when all you need is the default connection. When you need multiple connections, as shown later in the section on connection contexts, you'll need to use getConnection() to get additional connection contexts.

Closing the Connection

When you explicitly open a connection to a database, you should close that connection as soon as possible. The number of available connections is a limited system resource. By closing the connection you ensure that there will be a connection available for the next user. With SQLJ 8.1.6 and later, the connection is closed using the following code:

```
oracle.sqlj.runtime.Oracle.close()
```

Both the code above and the code that follows can throw an SQLException, so you will need to add exception handling as appropriate. If you are using Oracle 8.1.5, import sqlj.runtime.ref.DefaultContext and close the connection using this code:

```
DefaultContext.getDefaultContext().close();
```

A Simple SQLJ Application

Enough material has been introduced so that we can now start to build an application using SQLJ. Let's start by defining a problem domain, and designing the tables needed to hold the data. Then we'll write the code to start solving the problem.

We want to create an application that will help a small business manage its activities. The business we will focus on is one that sells some type of product in an on-line store.

> **Although the data is fictitious and the code will not be used by a real business, the problems being addressed are based on a real business.**

The business owner has provided the following description of some activities to be tracked and managed using an Oracle database and Java SQLJ code. The system should provide solutions in the following areas:

❏ **Customer relationships**: keep a list of customers and contact information for these customers

❏ **Business inventory**: be able to get a report on the current inventory available

❏ **Product orders**: to allow customers to order products electronically

In the course of the chapter, we'll develop code for each of the three areas. For now, we'll look at customer relationships. We will develop a simple application that will let the businees record and track customer personal information.

Now let's build some tables to help us manage this information. Here's the SQL to do this:

```
CREATE TABLE customer (
    email VARCHAR2(100) NOT NULL primary key,
    password VARCHAR2(20) NOT NULL,
    surname VARCHAR2(40) NOT NULL,
    given_name VARCHAR2(40)
);

CREATE SEQUENCE order_id_sequence;

CREATE TABLE product (
    product_id VARCHAR2(20) primary key,
    name VARCHAR2(100),
    description VARCHAR2(400),
    price NUMBER(6,2) not null,
    count_in_stock NUMBER(9),
    on_order CHAR(1) DEFAULT 'n' CHECK (on_order IN ('y', 'n'))
);

CREATE TABLE orders (
    order_id INTEGER PRIMARY KEY,
    customer_id VARCHAR2(100) REFERENCES customer(email),
    product_id VARCHAR2(20) REFERENCES product(product_id),
    quantity NUMBER(4),
    state VARCHAR2 (10) default 'NEW'
      check (state IN ('NEW', 'PAID', 'SHIPPED'))
);
```

You can enter these tables into your database using many different techniques. Typing the above into SQL*Plus would be one method. You could also create these tables using an SQLJ program. Here is the code to create the `customer` table using a Java class with SQLJ. Save this source file as `sqlj\tables\CreateCustomer.sqlj`:

```
package sqlj.tables;

import oracle.sqlj.runtime.Oracle;

public class CreateCustomer {
  public static void main(String[] args) {

    try {
      Oracle.connect("jdbc:oracle:oci8:@proead", "scott", "tiger", true);

      #sql { CREATE TABLE customer (
              email VARCHAR2(100) NOT NULL primary key,
              password VARCHAR2(20) NOT NULL,
              surname VARCHAR2(40) NOT NULL,
              given_name VARCHAR2(40))
            };
    } catch (Exception e) {
      e.printStackTrace();
    }
  }
}
```

The program can be translated and compiled from the command line using the following command:

```
sqlj -v -passes sqlj\tables\CreateCustomer.sqlj
```

If the code does not compile, check the code and the SQLJ installation. When the code is compiled, run the code from the command line using:

```
java sqlj.tables.CreateCustomer
```

We will now create a Java application that will allow a user to add, edit, or remove an entry from the customer table in the database.

The point of the application is to demonstrate some simple SQLJ statements. This application will provide a means to add a customer to the customer table, delete a customer from the table, and query the table for an entry. The application performs only rudimentary validation of the fields, and has limited exception handling.

The Customer Class

First we'll create a class to represent a customer. The customer class will have fields to hold the various pieces of data that go into a customer record in the CUSTOMER table. We'll also provide three methods, one to add the customer, one to remove the customer record, and one to query for a customer record. Here's the source code, `Customer.sqlj` (note that this file is named with the extension `.sqlj`).

For information on how to install and configure your system to use SQLJ, see Appendix A For help on how to use Java, see the Java Primer Appendix, or one of the many Java programming books published by Wrox Press. Save this source file as `sqlj\crms\Customer.sqlj`:

```
package sqlj.crms;

import java.sql.SQLException;
import sqlj.runtime.ref.DefaultContext;
import oracle.sqlj.runtime.Oracle;

/**
 * Represents a customer of a business. Provides methods to add or remove
 * a customer from the business database. Also provides
 * a method to query for a customer record.
 */
public class Customer {
  private String email;
  private String password;
  private String surname;
  private String given_name;
```

The class Customer defines four instance variables. These variables are used to hold the information for a customer. If a customer is being created, then these fields will be filled and then sent to the database. If the table is being queried, the query will set the values of these variables. The constructor is shown below. It requires that the e-mail and password always be non-null. Whether the code is adding, removing, or querying, these fields will always be required:

```
  /**
   * Constructor for a customer object, the email and password
   * must be non-null and non-empty. If either is null or empty, an
   * IllegalArgumentException is thrown.
   * Attempts to connect to the database; If a connection cannot
   * be made, an SQLException is thrown.
   */
  public Customer (String email, String password,
                   String surname, String given_name)
    throws SQLException, IllegalArgumentException
  {
    if (email == null || password == null ||
        email.equals("") || password.equals(""))
    {
      throw new IllegalArgumentException();
    }

    this.email = email.toLowerCase();
    this.password = password;
    this.surname = surname;
    this.given_name = given_name;

    makeConnection();
  }
```

The makeConnection() method below uses a different version of the connect() method than was used in previous code. This version needs an instance of a Class object and the name of a properties file. The Class instance is obtained using the getClass() method call and is used to determine where to look for the properties file. The contents of the properties file will be detailed at the end of the source listing of this class. The properties file does not enable the auto-commit setting, so by default, auto-commit is disabled.

```
/**
 * Make a connection to the database. Connection parameters are obtained
 * from the properties file connect.properties
 */
private void makeConnection()
  throws SQLException
{
  Oracle.connect(getClass(), "connect.properties");
}
```

The add() method shown below adds a record to the database. It checks to ensure that the surname field is non-null and non-empty. Since the e-mail and password were checked in the constructor, the method "knows" that those fields are non-null and non-empty. It allows the given_name field to be null. Since auto-commit is disabled, the code must explicitly call commit(). The method catches any SQLException thrown and attempts to rollback the change. Note that rollback will also throw an SQLException; if it does then this exception is ignored. If the original SQLException is for the Oracle error ORA-00001, then the e-mail is already being used and the exception is thrown from the method. If it is any other exception, the method prints the stack trace and exits.

```
/**
 * Adds a customer record to the database.  The email address must be
 * unique, that is, not used by any other customer. If the email address
 * is already in the database an SQLException is thrown. The surname
 * must not be null or empty; an IllegalArgumentException is thrown
 * if it is.
 */
public void add()
  throws SQLException, IllegalArgumentException
{
  if (surname == null || surname.equals(""))
  {
    throw new IllegalArgumentException();
  }

  try {
    #sql { insert into customer ( email, password,
                                  surname, given_name )
                     values ( :email, :(encrypt(password)),
                              :surname, :given_name )
         };
    #sql { commit };
  } catch (SQLException e) {
    try { #sql { rollback }; } catch (SQLException ignored) {}
    //ORA-00001 is 'unique constraint violated',
    //ie, email was not unique
    if (e.getMessage().indexOf("ORA-00001") != -1)
    {
      throw e;
    }
    e.printStackTrace();
  } finally {
    closeConnection();
  }
}
```

The `remove()` method is shown below. This method uses an SQL delete statement to attempt to delete a row from the table. Notice that the SQL uses a complex host expression, a method call to `encrypt(String)`. Because the method call is a complex host expression, the entire method call is wrapped in parentheses, and the colon is placed in front of the opening parenthesis. If the SQL does not cause an exception, the delete is committed; if an `SQLException` is thrown, the code attempts to perform a rollback.

```
/**
 * Removes a customer record from the database. Both the email
 * and password must match a row in the database for the customer
 * record to be removed.
 */
public void remove()
{
  try {
    #sql { delete from customer
                where email = :email
                    and password = :(encrypt(password)) };
    #sql { commit };      } catch (SQLException e) {
    try { #sql { rollback }; } catch (SQLException ignored) {}
    e.printStackTrace();
  } finally {
    closeConnection();
  }
}
```

The query method attempts to get a row from the table. The query method uses a `SELECT INTO` statement to select a single row into host expressions. A query that returned multiple rows cannot be performed without an iterator class; since that has not been covered yet, and because only a single row was needed, the `SELECT INTO` syntax was used. Since this method only performs a query, there is no need to commit or rollback. The method uses a complex host expression just like the `remove()` method above.

```
/**
 * Queries for a specific customer in the database. Both the email and
 * the password must match, otherwise no entry is returned.
 */
public boolean query()
{
  surname = null;

  try {
    #sql { select email, surname, given_name
            into :email, :surname, :given_name
            from customer
          where email = :email
              and password = :(encrypt(password))
        };

  } catch (SQLException e) {
    e.printStackTrace();
  } finally {
    closeConnection();
  }
  if (surname != null)
  {
    return true;
```

```
    } else {
        return false;
    }
}
```

The encrypt() method below is part of the class. Its primary purpose is to demonstrate using a method call within an SQLJ statement in the remove() and query() methods. It simply takes a String object and converts each character in the String to be the character eight positions ahead:

```
/**
 * Takes the input String and encrypts it
 */
private String encrypt(String inString)
{
    //in a production environment, we would use real encryption
    StringBuffer outString = new StringBuffer(inString);
    int length = outString.length();
    for (int i = 0; i < length; i++)
    {
        outString.setCharAt(i, (char)(outString.charAt(i) + 8));
    }
    return outString.toString();
}
```

In each of the methods above is a call to a method to close the connection. This method is shown below. It obtains a handle to the default connection context and calls the close() method:

```
private void closeConnection() {
    try {
        Oracle.close();
    } catch (Exception ignored) {}
}

public String getSurname() { return surname; }
public String getGivenName() { return given_name; }
}
```

For this code to be able to connect to the database, you'll need to provide the correct properties file, named connect.properties. Oracle provides a sample connect.properties file in the SQLJ installation. It's located at <ORACLE_HOME>\sqlj\demo. Place a copy in the same directory as the class file, or create a file called connect.properties in that directory. Edit the properties file so that the correct driver URL, user, and password is in the file. Here's a configuration that uses the OCI8 driver:

```
sqlj.url=jdbc:oracle:oci8:@proead
# User name and password here
sqlj.user=scott
sqlj.password=tiger
```

If you are using a JDBC thin driver over a network, you'll need to use this line instead:

```
sqlj.url=jdbc:oracle:thin:@hostaddress:port:SID
```

You'll need to replace `hostaddress`, `port`, and `SID`, with appropriate values for your configuration. For Oracle 8.1.6 and higher, the value `SID` will be the service name of the database. In 8.1.5 it was called the service identifier or SID.

The User Interface Class

Now we'll provide some very simple user interface code. This code will create a window with four textfields, one for each parameter in the `Customer` class. It will have three buttons, one to add a customer, one to remove a customer, and one to query for a customer. Save the following file as `sqlj\crms\CustomerManager.java`:

```java
package sqlj.crms;

import java.awt.*;
import java.awt.event.*;
import java.sql.SQLException;

public class CustomerManager extends Frame
    implements ActionListener
{
```

Instance variables are defined for the buttons and the textfields:

```java
    protected Button add_button = new Button("Add");
    protected Button remove_button = new Button("Remove");
    protected Button query_button = new Button("Query");

    protected TextField email = new TextField(40);
    protected TextField password = new TextField(40);
    protected TextField surname = new TextField(40);
    protected TextField given_name = new TextField(40);
    protected TextArea userMsg = new TextArea(3,40);
```

The constructor starts by setting up the application to exit when the window is closed:

```java
    public CustomerManager()
    {
      //create an anonymous inner class that allows the window
      //to be closed, close connection when window closes
      addWindowListener(new WindowAdapter()
        {
          public void windowClosing(WindowEvent ev)
          {
            System.exit(0);
          }
        }
                      );

      setSize(400, 300);
      setTitle(getClass().getName());

      createButtons();
```

The next section of code calls methods to position the buttons and text fields in the window:

```
        setLayout(new GridBagLayout());
        GridBagConstraints constraints = new GridBagConstraints();
        constraints.weightx = 100;
        constraints.weighty = 100;

        add(new Label("email address:"), constraints, 0, 0, 1, 1);
        add(email, constraints, 1, 0, 2, 1);
        add(new Label("password"), constraints, 0, 1, 1, 1);
        add(password, constraints, 1, 1, 2, 1);
        add(new Label("given_name"), constraints, 0, 2, 1, 1);
        add(given_name, constraints, 1, 2, 2, 1);
        add(new Label("surname"), constraints, 0, 3, 1, 1);
        add(surname, constraints, 1, 3, 2, 1);
        add(add_button, constraints, 0, 4, 1, 1);
        add(remove_button, constraints, 1, 4, 1, 1);
        add(query_button, constraints, 2, 4, 1, 1);
        add(userMsg, constraints, 0, 5, 4, 4);
    }

    /** Method to add a component to the frame */
    public void add (Component comp, GridBagConstraints constraints,
                     int x, int y, int w, int h)
    {
      constraints.gridx = x;
      constraints.gridy = y;
      constraints.gridwidth = w;
      constraints.gridheight = h;
      add(comp, constraints);
    }

    /** This method calls methods to configure the buttons */
    private void createButtons() {
      add_button.addActionListener(this);
      add_button.setActionCommand("add");

      remove_button.addActionListener(this);
      remove_button.setActionCommand("remove");

      query_button.addActionListener(this);
      query_button.setActionCommand("query");


    }
```

Next comes the heart of the user interface. Just above in the code, a reference to this class was added as an Action Listener to each button, like this:

```
        query_button.addActionListener(this);
```

When the button is clicked, the button code calls the `actionPerformed()` method of each `ActionListener` that was added to the button. In the `actionPerformed()` method, a `Customer` object is created. Then, depending on which button was clicked, the appropriate method of the `Customer` class is called:

```java
public void actionPerformed(ActionEvent ev) {
  String command = ev.getActionCommand();

  Customer c = null;

  userMsg.setText("");

  try {
    c = new Customer(email.getText(), password.getText(),
                     surname.getText(), given_name.getText());
  } catch (IllegalArgumentException e) {
    userMsg.setText("Both the email field and the ,\n" +
                    "password field must have\n" +
                    "an entry. Please try again\n");
    return;
  } catch (SQLException e) {
    userMsg.setText("The database is not responding\n" +
                    "Please try again later\n");
    return;
  }

  if (command.equals("add")) {
    try {
      c.add();
      userMsg.setText("Customer successfully added.");
    } catch (IllegalArgumentException e) {
      userMsg.setText("All three of the fields email,\n" +
                      "password, surname must\n" +
                      "have an entry. Please try again\n");
    } catch (SQLException e) {
      userMsg.setText("That email is already in use. \n" +
                      "Apparently you're already a customer \n" +
                      "or you mistyped your email address");
    }

  } else if (command.equals("remove")) {
    c.remove();
    userMsg.setText("Customer successfully removed.");

  } else if (command.equals("query")) {
    if (c.query()) {
      surname.setText(c.getSurname());
      given_name.setText(c.getGivenName());
      userMsg.setText("Customer found");
    } else {
      userMsg.setText("Customer was not found\n" +
                      "Check the email and password\n");
    }
  }
}
```

The `main()` method for the application is shown below. This method creates an instance of the `CustomerManager` class and calls the `show()` method to display the frame with buttons and text fields:

```
public static void main(String[] args)
{
  try {
    Frame f = new CustomerManager();
    f.show();
  } catch (Exception e) {
    e.printStackTrace();
  }
}
}
```

The program can be translated and compiled from the command line using the following command:

```
sqlj -v -passes sqlj\crms\Customer.sqlj sqlj\crms\CustomerManager.java
```

If the code does not compile, check the code and the SQLJ installation. When the code is compiled, run the code from the command line using:

```
java sqlj.crms.CustomerManager
```

You should get a window like the one below:

Using the SQLJ Translator

We've already used the SQLJ translator several times in this chapter. With the beginning of the application in the previous section, it's time to look at the translator in a little more detail. The Oracle SQLJ translator is a Java class that processes the Java code and the SQL statements in the code, and creates standard Java source files that are then compiled with the Java compiler.

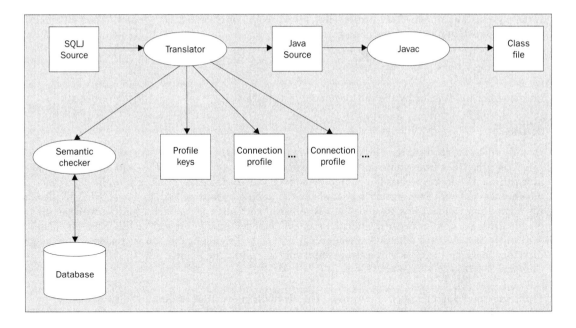

Basic Translator Operations

At its simplest, here's the command to compile your SQLJ code from the command line (you have already compiled this file in the above section):

```
sqlj sqlj\crms\Customer.sqlj
```

The `sqlj` command calls Oracle's SQLJ translator. The SQLJ translator works like a preprocessor, taking your `.sqlj` file, replacing the `#sql` statements with JDBC and SQL code, and writing the new code to a Java source file. Then the SQLJ translator calls the Java compiler to compile the source code into class files.

> **Note for Oracle 8.1.5:** Oracle's SQLJ documentation reports that on a Windows platform, the translator sometimes doesn't complete properly. To deal with this, there is a command line option that instructs the translator to compile the code in two passes. The option is '-passes.' While compiling in two passes may take a little more time, I recommend you always use the -passes option. So the command above for translating the code changes to `sqlj -passes Customer.sqlj`. This problem has been resolved in Oracle 8.1.6.

If you have not yet done so, compile both the above classes. You can compile them both in the same command as follows:

```
sqlj -passes sqlj\crms\Customer.sqlj sqlj\crms\CustomerManager.java
```

If the compilation attempt finds errors, look at your code, or classpath, as needed. When all compilation errors are fixed, you can run the code by typing

```
java sqlj.crms.CustomerManager
```

on the command line, or by the run command in your IDE.

Profiles

In addition to the Java source files that correspond to the SQLJ source file, the SQLJ translator also produces other files from your source file. These other files are called Profiles and there will always be at least two. The first is a class file named by adding _SJProfileKeys.class to the class name from which it was created. The second is a serialized file named by adding _SJProfilen.ser to the class file name from which it was created; the n is replaced with a sequential digit, starting with the digit 0. A profile file is created for every connection context class declared in the source file. Since the class previously uses only the default connection context, only a single profile file is created. If you check the directory to which the class files were written, you will find a file named Customer_SJProfile0.ser.

Profiles are used for a number of purposes. They contain information about the SQLJ statements in the class file. During the translation process, the profiles are created, then they are customized, which allows your code to use database specific features without putting those database specific features directly in the source code. This allows your source code to be portable between SQLJ implementations.

Normally you will not need to worry about profiles. They are created automatically for you. They are customized automatically. All you need do is include them in the distribution of your application or applet.

Catching SQL Errors

The earlier you catch errors in the code, the better your code will be. It's better for you to catch the error than have the software fail after it's been released.

The SQLJ translator provides a method to check the correctness of your SQLJ statements against the actual database schema. This is known as semantic checking. You do that by providing the -user (-u for short) option to the translator.

Edit the Customer.sqlj code presented earlier. Find the add() method, and change one of the column names in the INSERT statement so that it is incorrect. Here's the change we should make:

```
#sql { insert into customer ( email, passwrd,
                              surname, given_name )
                    values ( :email, :password,
                             :surname, :given_name
                           )
     };
```

Notice that I changed the column name password to passwrd.

Now run the translator as originally shown above. When the SQLJ translator is run against this code, what warning does the translator report? Nothing!

Without a connection to the database, the translator can only check the syntax of the SQL statements, but it cannot check the use, or semantics, of the table names or column names.

What happens when the code above is run? The code throws a SQLException. Here's the first line of the long stack trace:

```
java.sql.SQLException: ORA-00904: invalid column name
```

Now compile the code by telling the translator how to connect to the database:

```
sqlj -passes -user=scott/tiger sqlj\crms\Customer.sqlj
```

The compiler is able to check the complete SQL statement for syntax and semantics. Here's the complete error message for mistyping a column name:

```
Customer.sqlj:46.6-50.4: Warning: Database issued an error: PLS-00390: undefined
column 'PASSWRD' in INSERT statement
insert into customer ( email, passwrd,
                              ^^^^^^^
        surname, given_name )
                        values (  ...  ,   ...  ,
        ...  ,  ...  )
    ;
```

When the -user option does not specify a driver, the default driver is the OCI8 driver. If you want or need to use a different driver, such as the OCI7 driver, just add it to the -user option:

```
-user=scott/tiger@jdbc:oracle:oci7@
```

If you're using a thin driver, you only need to specify the host, port, and sid:

```
-user=scott/tiger@hostaddress:port:sid
```

You can also specify each part of the connection separately for online semantics checking by using the following options on the command line or in a property file:

- ❑   -user
- ❑   -password
- ❑   -url
- ❑   -default-url-prefix
- ❑   -driver

Other Basic Operations

There are other options you can use with the SQLJ translator.

- ❑   -props=filename
  This option tells the translator to get additional options from the named property file. Some options are command line only, such as props and classpath. When used in the property file, the option is preceeded by sqlj rather than a hyphen. For example: sqlj.user=user, sqlj.d=pathspec.

- ❑   -classpath=pathspec
  This option passes the indicated classpath to the Java compiler and Virtual Machine.

521

❑   `-d=pathspec`
This option tells the translator where to put compiled files. It works the same as the Java `-d` option.

❑   `-warn=option,option,option`
This option provides a list of possible warning levels. The possible options are shown below.

❑   `-linemap=true/false`
When `true`, this option tells the translator to map line numbers for debugging to the SQLJ source file, rather than the java source file. The default is `false`.

`precision` (default)	Provides a warning when there is a loss of precision when storing database values in host expressions.
`noprecision`	No warning for loss of precision.
`nulls` (default)	Warns for a possible loss of precision between database and host expressions.
`nonulls`	No warning.
`portable`	Warns if your SQL statements are not portable to ANSI92.
`noportable` (default)	No warning for non-portable SQL.
`strict` (default)	Warns if the number of columns in an iterator do not match the number of columns in the select statement. See the section on iterators.
`nostrict`	No warning unless the number of columns in the select statement is less than the number of columns in the iterators.
`verbose`	More information about the translation process.
`noverbose` (default)	Less information about the translation process.
`all`	All warnings turned on.
`none` (default)	No warnings.

Advanced Translator Operations

When you invoke the Oracle SQLJ translator, it actually runs inside a Java Virtual Machine. If you need to pass options to the virtual machine, you would use the `-J` option. This is a command line option only. So, for example, if you wanted to pass a system property to the virtual machine that runs the translator, you would use this syntax:

```
sqlj -J-Dproperty_name=property_value
```

Sometimes you may need to pass some options to the Java compiler that is compiling the translated SQLJ source files. When passing options to the compiler, you use the `-C` option on the command line, or the `compile` property within a property file. For example, if you wanted to pass a specific classpath to the compiler, you would use this syntax inside a property file:

```
compile.classpath=pathspec
```

When customizing profile files, you can pass options to the customizer through the translator using either -P (for generic customizer options) or -P-C (for vendor specific options). The default customizer for Oracle sqlj is the class `oracle.sqlj.runtime.OraCustomizer`. Some of the general profile customization options are:

- ❑ `-backup`
  Instructs the customizer to make a backup of the profile before customizing it

- ❑ `-context=classname<,classname,...>`
  Only customize profiles for the given connection context classname

- ❑ `-customizer=classname`
  Identifies a customizer class to use instead of the default class

There is one last flag that may be helpful when translating your files, the -ser2class flag. There are some browsers that are unable to process the .ser profile file created during translation. For whatever reason, you can have the translator create class files from the serialized profile files. You do that by specifying the -ser2class options when calling the SQLJ translator.

Declarations

SQLJ declarations allow you to create specialized Java 'types' to simplify certain common programming patterns with SQLJ. Declarations are used when you want to create the following:

- ❑ An **iterator**, which allows us to receive and process multiple rows returned by a query

- ❑ A **connection context**, which allows us to make multiple connections to a database schema or connections to different schemas

Declarations are only legal in certain places in the Java code:

- ❑ Top level scope in its own source file. For example:

```
//source file Product_Iterator.sqlj
#sql iterator Product_Iterator (String product_id);
```

- ❑ Top level scope – within another source file, but outside any class declaration. For example:

```
//source file ProductQuery.sqlj
#sql iterator Product_Iterator (String product_id);

public class ProductQuery {
}
```

- ❑ Class scope – inside a class, but not inside any method. For example:

```
//source file ProductQuery.sqlj
public class ProductQuery {
  #sql iterator Product_Iterator (String product_id);
}
```

❏ Nested class scope – inside a nested class, but again, not inside any method. For example:

```
//source file ProductQuery.sqlj
public class ProductQuery {
  //inner class
  class PQInner {
    #sql iterator Product_Iterator (String product_id);
  }
}
```

Let's examine iterators in more detail.

SQLJ Iterators

An SQLJ iterator is a strongly typed version of the cursor construct with which we retrieve the multiple rows returned by a query; it is analogous to a resultset. An iterator declaration causes the SQLJ translator to create a new type, or class, that is, an iterator class. You then create an iterator reference in your Java code to receive the results of a query.

Each different iterator has a common base class, but because the iterators themselves are different classes, one cannot assign one iterator reference to a variable of a different iterator type. Just like Integer and Float are two classes with the same parent class, but it's not possible to assign an object of one type to a variable of the other type.

In addition, iterators, especially named iterators, are specific to only certain queries or tables. If you had an iterator with all integer values, you wouldn't use it for a query that returned all strings. The compiler will produce a warning or signify an error if you try to assign a query result to an iterator that isn't correct for the query.

Declaring an Iterator

The iterator declaration statement has the following form:

```
#sql <modifiers> iterator iterator_classname
      <implements interface_name>
      <with (name=value<,name=value>)>
      (type declarations);
```

❏ #sql
   Each declaration must start with this token. As with SQLJ statements, it signals the translator that this line is embedded SQL.

❏ <modifiers>
   Modifiers are one or more optional Java class modifiers: public, private, final, static or no modifier. The modifier is applied to the class that is created from the iterator declaration. That is, the iterator class can be public, private, final, or static. Here are the different scopes and the modifiers allowed in that scope:

   ❏ (package access), public, or final.

   ❏ When the iterator is declared in another class' source file the modifier can be blank (package access), or final.

❑   When the iterator is defined inside a class the modifier can be blank (package access), `public`, `private`, `final`, or `static`.

❑   An iterator defined in class scope is known as an inner class. Oracle recommends that these inner class iterators be declared as `private static` iterators. Declaring an inner class as `public` or package access is allowed, but it defeats the purpose of an inner class.

❑   Although `final` is an allowed modifier, its use is superfluous at this time. The SQLJ standard does not allow subclassing an iterator, and Oracle does not support iterator subclassing. When the iterator declaration is in its own source file the modifier can be blank

❑   `iterator`
This token tells the translator that this is an iterator declaration.

❑   `iterator_classname`
This is any legal Java class name. Since the declaration creates a Java class, the class must be named.

❑   `implements` clause
Since this declaration causes a class to be created, you can optionally specify that the class implements one or more Java interfaces in addition to the default `sqlj.runtime.NamedIterator` interface. This clause must come before any `with` clause. More detail on using this option appears at the end of this section.

❑   `with` clause
Causes the iterator class to be created with a public static final member with a name and value as specified in the `with` clause.

❑   Type declarations
One or more Java types and optional Java variables enclosed in parentheses. The Java types you would use are those that correspond to the column being retrieved from a table. Because an iterator declaration creates a new type, just like any Java class, you can even use an iterator in the type list. There are two ways you can specify the type declarations. One kind of declaration is called a named iterator. In this declaration you must name both the data type and the column name using a host expression. The second type is a positional iterator. For this iterator, only the data type is specified; the order of the data types must match the table's column types. The next section will give examples of these two types of iterators.

Iterator Examples

Previously in the chapter, a table named `product` was defined, which contained the following fields:

❑   `product_id VARCHAR2(20),`

❑   `name VARCHAR2(100),`

❑   `description VARCHAR2(400),`

❑   `price NUMBER(6,2),`

❑   `count_in_stock NUMBER(9)` (notice we did not specify NOT NULL for this field)

❑   `on_order CHAR(1)`

Creating an Iterator

To create a private named iterator to receive query results for these fields the declaration would be:

```
#sqlj private iterator Product_Iterator (String product_id,
                                         String name,
                                         String description,
                                         float price,
                                         Integer count_in_stock,
                                         String on_order );
```

A positional iterator with Java package scope would be created like this:

```
#sqlj iterator Product_Iterator (String, String, String,
                                 float, Integer, String);
```

The iterator uses strings for columns, which are defined as VARCHAR2. Since price was defined as NOT NULL, a variable of type `float` can be used for this column. However, because `count_in_stock` could be NULL, an Integer object is used to represent the field. Remember that if a table column can be NULL, a Java object (such as String, Byte, Short, Integer, Long, Float, or Double) must be used in the SQLJ iterator declaration to hold the value. Compare that to the price field in the iterator where a primitive type, a `float`, was used; the corresponding column in the table is declared NOT NULL.

Notice that in the example, each named field in the iterator matched a column name in the table. If you use a SELECT * syntax for the query, the iterator fields **must** match the column names exactly. Also, the SELECT statement must return at least as many columns as fields named in the iterator. If the SELECT statement returns more columns, then the unmatched columns are ignored; if it returns less matching columns than iterator fields an SQLException is thrown.

However, if you name the columns in the SELECT statement (SELECT column, column...), you can name the iterator fields differently. To do this, you use an alias to map the database column names in the select statement to the field names in the iterator. For example:

```
#sqlj private iterator Product_Iterator (String id,
                                         String shortName,
                                         String backordered );

. . . . .

Product_Iterator prod iter;
#sql prod_iter = { SELECT name as shortName,
                          product_id as id,
                          on_order as backordered
                   FROM product };
```

In the code snippet above, notice also that the fields in the iterator do not need to be in the same order as the column names in the SELECT statement, nor as the columns in the table. All that is needed is that the names match and the SELECT statement returns as many matching columns as named in the iterator declaration.

On the other hand, for a positional iterator, the column names are omitted. To create a public positional iterator the declaration would be:

```
#sqlj public iterator Product_Iterator (String, String, String,
                                        float, Integer, String );
```

For this iterator, the columns selected from the table are stored in the iterator in the same order as they appear in the select statement. Because of this, the columns named in the SELECT statement must have a data type that can be stored in the field in the iterator. For example, given the positional iterator declaration above, the following SQL statement would be incorrect:

```
Product_Iterator prod_iter;
#sql prod_iter = { SELECT count_in_stock, name, product_id,
                          price, description, on_order
               FROM product };
```

The above statement is incorrect for at least the following two reasons:

❑   It selects a NUMBER field (count_in_stock) from the database and tries to store it in a field of type String

❑   It selects a VARCHAR2 field (description) and tries to store it in a field of type Integer

Multiple Row Selection Using Iterators

In this section, an iterator will be used to retrieve data from a table. The Java SQLJ code will query the product table that was defined previously in this chapter. Here is some data that can be loaded into the table using SQL* Loader or Oracle SQL*Plus. It is available as a download on the website http://www.wrox.com:

The product table:

product_id	name	description	price	count	on_order
Rose-1	Candy Kiss Roses	Blooming Rose Favor	3.25	100	n
Rose-2	Candy Kiss Roses	Rose Bud Favor	2.25	5	n
Rose-3	Candy Kiss Roses	3 Boxed Rose Buds	7.95	43	n
Rose-4	Candy Kiss Roses	6 Boxed Rose Buds	15.95	23	n
Candle-1	Candles	Dove votive candles	1.65	0	n
Candle-2	Candles	Love votive candles	1.65	32	n
Candle-3	Candles	Rose votive candles	1.65	0	y
Candle-4	Candles	Baby hands candles	1.65	20	n
Wrapper-1	Candy Wrappers	Wedding bells 15	2.95	NULL	y
Wrapper-2	Candy Wrappers	Doves sheet of 15	2.95	25	n
Wrapper-3	Candy Wrappers	Doves and Rings 15	2.95	13	y
Wrapper-4	Candy Wrappers	Teddy Bear 15	2.95	45	n

As mentioned above in the introduction to iterators, the iterator declaration results in a Java class being created. The SQLJ translator actually writes the Java class code for you, code that is the same as if you had manually designed and created a Java class.

After translating the SQLJ code, you can look at the iterator source code. The source code for the iterator will be in the .java file that corresponds to the .sqlj file.

When you use a named iterator, the class that is created also has accessors that provide you a simple way to get the results of the query you've performed. Each name that was used in the iterator declaration becomes the name of an accessor function in the new class.

For example, the code snippet below shows a declaration of a named iterator:

```
#sql iterator Product_Iterator (String product_id,
                                String name,
                                String description,
                                float price,
                                Integer count_in_stock,
                                String on_order );
```

When that declaration is translated, the translator creates Java code. If you examine the Java code, you will find that the code creates a class called `Product_Iterator` that has methods with the following signatures:

```
public String product_id() throws java.sql.SQLException
public String name() throws java.sql.SQLException
public String description() throws java.sql.SQLException
public float price()throws java.sql.SQLException
public Integer count_in_stock()throws java.sql.SQLException
public String on_order()throws java.sql.SQLException
```

Here is a class that uses the iterator declaration above to query and display the rows from the product table. The class has a `makeConnection()` method to make the connection to the database. The `doLowInventoryQuery()` method performs the query of the product table. The iterator that results from the query is returned by the `doLowInventoryQuery()` method. Save this file as `sqlj\declarations\ProductQuery.sqlj`:

```
package sqlj.declarations;

import java.sql.SQLException;
import sqlj.runtime.ref.DefaultContext;
import oracle.sqlj.runtime.Oracle;

//Declare the named iterator here. Use default (package) access
#sql iterator Product_Iterator (String product_id,
                                String name,
                                String description,
                                float price,
                                Integer count_in_stock,
                                String on_order );

/**
 * A class to demonstrate the usage of an iterator
 * to receive multiple query results
 */
public class ProductQuery
{

    /**
     * Query for information about the products in the product table
     */
    public Product_Iterator doLowInventoryQuery()
       throws SQLException
    {
```

```
      Product_Iterator pi = null;
        //perform the query and assign the result to a Product_Iterator reference
      #sql pi = { SELECT * FROM product
                              WHERE count_in_stock < 10
                                OR count_in_stock IS NULL
                    };

      return pi;
    }

    private void makeConnect()
      throws SQLException
    {
      Oracle.connect(getClass(), "connect.properties");
    }

    public static void main(String[] args) {
      //declare an instance of this class and a Product_Iterator reference
      ProductQuery p = new ProductQuery();
      Product_Iterator pi = null;

      try {
        //make the connection and call the query method
        p.makeConnect();
        pi = p.doLowInventoryQuery();

        //now print the results
        if (pi.next()) {
          System.out.println("Here are the products" +
                "that need to be ordered:");
          do {
            //each field named in the iterator declaration becomes the
            //name of a method used to get the value from the iterator
            System.out.println("Product id:   " + pi.product_id());
            System.out.println("Product name: " + pi.name());
            System.out.println("Description:  " + pi.description());
            System.out.println("Inventory:    " + pi.count_in_stock());
          } while(pi.next());
        } else {
          System.out.println("Query returned no results");
        }
      } catch (Exception e) {
        e.printStackTrace();
      } finally {
        try { pi.close(); } catch (Exception ignored) {}
        try { Oracle.close();
        } catch (Exception ignored) {}
      }
    }
  }
```

One of the first things in the code above is the iterator declaration. This is a named iterator that does not have any access modifier. Thus, it has the default package access; only classes in the same package can use the iterator. If the iterator had been declared public, it would have to be in its own source file; but because it has package access, we can put it in the same source file as the ProductQuery class.

In the method `doLowInventoryQuery()`, the query is performed and the iterator is returned to the caller. When the results are first returned, the iterator is positioned prior to the first returned row. If you called one of the accessors at this point, an `SQLException` would be thrown. So, the first action to perform after a query is to call the method `next()`. This will position the iterator at the first returned row and return a value of `true`; each subsequent call to `next()` will position the iterator at the next row and return `true`. When there are no more rows, `next()` will return `false`.

To get the actual column values, we call the accessor methods of the iterator. Each accessor has a signature based on the type and name used in the iterator declaration.

Finally, the iterator and the connection are closed when they are no longer needed.

> Oracle's Javadoc documentation for the iterator states that the iterator is automatically closed when it is garbage collected. It's not safe to rely on garbage collection, though, so you should always explicitly close the iterator as soon as it is no longer needed. The code above also explicitly closed the connection. In Oracle 8.1.5, the only way to close the connection is by calling `DefaultContext.getDefaultContext().close()`. In Oracle 8.1.6, you should call the static method `oracle.sqlj.runtime.Oracle.close()` to close the connection.

To use a positional iterator in the code above, copy the `ProductQuery.sqlj` source file to a new directory named `declarations2` and name the file `ProductQuery2.sqlj`; then make this change to the iterator declaration:

```
package sqlj.declarations2;

import java.sql.SQLException;
import sqlj.runtime.ref.DefaultContext;
import oracle.sqlj.runtime.Oracle;

//Declare the iterator here. Use default (package) access
#sql iterator Product_Iterator (String, String, String,
                                float, Integer, String );

/**
 * A class to demonstrate the usage of an iterator
 * to receive multiple query results
 */
public class ProductQuery2
{
```

While you can use the SELECT * syntax with both named and positional iterators, it is safer, especially with the positional iterator, to name the columns:

```
/**
 * Query for information about the products in the product table
 */
public Product_Iterator doLowInventoryQuery()
  throws SQLException
{
  Product_Iterator pi = null;
```

```
    #sql pi = { SELECT name, product_id, description,
                        price, count_in_stock, on_order
                  FROM product
                 WHERE count_in_stock < 10
                    OR count_in_stock IS NULL
            };

    return pi;
}

private void makeConnect()
  throws SQLException
{
  Oracle.connect(getClass(), "connect.properties");
}
```

The biggest change is made to the code that accesses the results:

```
public static void main(String[] args) {
  ProductQuery2 p = new ProductQuery2();
  Product_Iterator pi = null;

  try {
    p.makeConnect();
    pi = p.doLowInventoryQuery();

    //declare some local variables to hold the results
    String id = null;
    String name = null;
    String description = null;
    Integer inventory = null;
    String backordered = null;
    float price = 0.0f;

    //print some of the results
    while (true) {
      #sql { FETCH :pi INTO :id, :name, :description,
                           :price, :inventory, :backordered };

      if (pi.endFetch()) break; //Must test AFTER fetch,
                                //but before results
                                //are processed.
      System.out.println("Product id:   " + id);
      System.out.println("Product name: " + name);
      System.out.println("Description:  " + description);
      System.out.println("Inventory:    " + inventory);
    }
  } catch (Exception e) {
    e.printStackTrace();
  } finally {
    try { pi.close(); } catch (Exception ignored) {}
    try { Oracle.close();
    } catch (Exception ignored) {}
  }
}
}
```

As shown above, when using the positional iterator, a different technique for retrieving the results must be employed. You must use an SQL FETCH INTO statement to store the results into host expressions. After the FETCH statement but before using the host expressions, you must call the endFetch() method of the iterator. When the iterator is positioned after the last row, endFetch() returns true. This signals that there is no more data, and that the previous FETCH was not on a row.

Using the Implements Clause

The implements clause allows you to modify the behavior of the iterator class that is created using the named iterator syntax. As mentioned, a named iterator provides accessors to all the fields named in the iterator declaration. There may be situations where you want to provide an instance of the class to some code, but you do not want to allow access to all the fields declared in the iterator. For instance, perhaps you are publishing your iterator as part of an application programming interface (API) for customers of your application. Internally, you can use the same iterator code as your customers, but for customers you provide limited access to table columns by exposing the iterator using an interface.

You can accomplish this by writing your own interface class. Save this file as sqlj\declarations3\ProductIterSimple.java:

```java
package sqlj.declarations3;

import java.sql.SQLException;

public interface ProductIterSimple {
    public String name() throws SQLException;
    public String description() throws SQLException;
    public boolean next() throws SQLException;
    public void close() throws SQLException;
}
```

> Along with the field accessors provided for the user, the interface should expose the methods **next()** and **close()**. You could get by without providing a **next()** method by positioning the iterator for the user. However, you should always provide the **close()** method.

Then implementing the interface in the iterator declaration:

```
#sql iterator Product_Iterator
    implements ProductIterSimple
        (String product_id,
         String name,
         String description,
         float price,
         Integer count_in_stock,
         String on_order);
```

The ProductQuery class is rewritten so that it only performs the actual query and then returns a reference to the iterator. This file is saved as sqlj\declarations3\ProductQuery3.sqlj:

```
package sqlj.declarations3;

import java.sql.SQLException;
import sqlj.runtime.ref.DefaultContext;
import oracle.sqlj.runtime.Oracle;

/**
 * A class to demonstrate the usage of an iterator
 * to receive multiple query results. This class performs
 * the query but returns the iterator reference as type
 * ProductIterSimple, which is an interface which
 * exposes only two accessors.
 */
public class ProductQuery3
{

  //iterator as inner class, access is private
#sql private iterator Product_Iterator
  implements ProductIterSimple
    (String product_id,
     String name,
     String description,
     float price,
     Integer count_in_stock,
     String on_order );

  /**
   * Query for information about the products in the product table
   */
  public ProductIterSimple doLowInventoryQuery()
    throws SQLException
  {
    Product_Iterator pi;
    #sql pi = { SELECT * FROM product
                        WHERE count_in_stock < 10
                            OR count_in_stock IS NULL
              };
    return pi;
  }

  private void makeConnect()
    throws SQLException
  {
    Oracle.connect(getClass(), "connect.properties");
  }

  public static void main(String[] args) {
    //declare an instance of this class and a Product_Iterator
    ProductQuery3 p = new ProductQuery3();
    ProductIterSimple pi = null;

    try {
      //Make the connection and call the query method
      p.makeConnect();
      pi = p.doLowInventoryQuery();
```

```
        //print out the results
        if (pi.next()) {
          System.out.println("Here are the products that" +
                      " need to be ordered:");
          do {
            //each field named in the iterator declaration becomes
            //the name of a method used to get the value from the iterator
            //because pi is type ProductIterSimple, calls to product_id()
            //and count_in_stock() are not legal
            //System.out.println("Product id:    " + pi.product_id());
            System.out.println("Product name: " + pi.name());
            System.out.println("Description:   " + pi.description());
            //System.out.println("Inventory:     " + pi.count_in_stock());
          } while(pi.next(  ));
        } else {
          System.out.println("Query returned no results");
        }
      } catch (Exception e) {
        e.printStackTrace();
      } finally {
        //close the iterator and the connection
        try { pi.close(); } catch (Exception ignored) {}
        try { Oracle.close();
        } catch (Exception ignored) {}
      }
    }
  }
}
```

The new `ProductQuery3` class represents a class you would write and publish as part of your API.
When users want to perform a query, they create an instance of this class, and call the
`doLowInventoryQuery()` method. As before, the SQLJ statement returns an object of type
`Product_Iterator`, and the reference is assigned to a local variable. The return type of the method,
though, is `ProductIterSimple`; since `Product_Iterator` implements `ProductIterSimple`, the
reference is automatically cast to that type when it is returned.

The `Product_Iterator` class that is created still contains all the accessor methods. However, the methods
will only be accessible if the user has a reference variable of type `Product_Iterator`. If the reference
variable is of type `ProductIterSimple`, only the methods exposed in the interface can be used.

*If you want to see that all the methods are in the class file, type `javap Product_Iterator` from
the command line after the program below is compiled. The `javap` program is a Java disassembler tool
that comes with many distributions of the Java development kit. If you are using an IDE, temporarily
rename the source files, and then open the class file in the IDE to see the methods in the class file.
Renaming the source files shows that the IDE actually loads the class file and not the source file.*

The `main()` method represents the code an API user would write. The code creates a `ProductQuery3`
instance and calls the `doLowInventoryQuery()` method. To compile this code, compile the interface
first, and then the `ProductQuery3.sqlj` file, or compile them at the same time using:

```
sqlj -v -passes sqlj\declarations3\ProductIterSimple.java \
   sqlj\declarations3\ProductQuery3.sqlj
```

Because the compiler knows only that the `pi` reference in the `main()` method is of type `ProductIterSimple`, the compiler allows the code to call only the four defined methods in `ProductIterSimple`. The compiler will not allow the following two lines of code to be uncommented as shown:

```
System.out.println("Product id:    " + pi.product_id());
System.out.println("Product name: " + pi.name());
System.out.println("Description:   " + pi.description());
System.out.println("Inventory:    " + pi.count_in_stock());
```

If you try to compile the change above, the compiler responds with:

```
ProductReporter.sqlj:18: Method product_id() not found in interface
ProductIterSimple.
        System.out.println("Product id :    " + pi.product_id());
                                                      ^
ProductReporter.sqlj:21: Method count_in_stock() not found in interface
ProductIterSimple.
        System.out.println("Inventory    :    " + pi.count_in_stock());
                                                         ^
2 errors
```

Connection Contexts

Near the beginning of the chapter, the technique for making a connection to the database was presented. After making the connection and setting the default context, all the SQLJ statements can use the default context without any additional effort on your part. Up to this point in the chapter, that is all that has been needed.

However, there may be cases when your code needs more than one connection, or you may want to create and use a specific connection context in addition to the default connection context. For these cases, you can create your own connection context classes, and use instances of these classes in your SQL statements. Oracle identifies the following motivations for using multiple connection context instances:

❑   If you are connecting to different kinds of databases from the same application (such as Oracle8 and Sybase)

❑   You are connecting to a single database and a single schema, but you need separate concurrent transactions

❑   You are connecting to a single database but are using multiple types of schemas from the same application (in other words, you are using different sets of SQL objects such as tables, views, and stored procedures)

Since you probably don't have two different databases available to connect to, we'll look at connecting to the same database.

To create a connection context class, you use an SQLJ declaration:

```
#sql <modifiers> context class_name
    <implements interface_name>
    <with (name=value<,name=value>)>;
```

- ❏ `#sql`
  This token tells the translator that a SQLJ statement follows.

- ❏ `<modifiers>`
  Modifiers are one or more optional Java class modifiers: `public`, `private`, `static`, `final`, or no modifier. Here are the different scopes and the modifiers allowed in that scope:

  - ❏ Top level scope, context in its own source file: no modifier (package access), public, final.

  - ❏ Top level scope, context in another class's source file: no modifier, final.

  - ❏ Class scope or nested class scope – no modifier, `public`, `private`, `final`, `static`.

- ❏ `context`
  This token tells the translator that a connection context class is being defined.

- ❏ `class_name`
  This is any legal Java class name. The declaration causes the translator to create the code for a Java class. This will be the name of the class.

- ❏ `implements` clause
  The name of any other Java interfaces that you want the connection context class to implement. This clause is used to limit the methods available to users of the connection context class, rather than to add functionality. This feature works the same as it does for the iterator declaration; for more details, see the end of the previous section.

- ❏ `with` clause
  Creates the class with one or more public static final variables with a name and value as indicated by the expression (name=value, etc.).

One reason for multiple connection context instances is in connecting to different database schemas. Notice, however, that the context declaration does not inherently use any particular schema. There is nothing in the declaration that identifies the schema being used. The schema used by a particular connection context instance is determined when the connection to the database is made.

Connecting to the Same Schema

As mentioned earlier, the Java classes up to this point have used a single default connection context. You can, however, create multiple instances of the `DefaultConnection` class, and use each instance separately for an SQLJ statement. You would do this where all the SQL statements were against a single schema.

Let's start by developing a class that allows users to place orders. This class will be used to insert rows into the orders table. Each request from a customer will be performed against the same schema. Since we expect multiple customers to place orders concurrently, we will need to make sure the code is multi-thread safe. Oracle's documentation states that in a multi-threaded application, each thread must have its own execution context. One way to do this is to create a connection context for each thread.

> *In production, this would be implemented in a server application using Java servlets, Enterprise JavaBeans, or within the Oracle database. Here we present a simple Java application which simulates concurrent client requests for service.*

First, a class that represents an order will be created. The `Order` object creates an instance of the class `DefaultConnection` every time it is asked to insert its member data into the database. It does that by calling the `Oracle.connect()` method. The reference to the connection context instance is included in the SQLJ statement. Here's the syntax for including a connection context with SQL:

```
#sql [connection_context] { SQL statements };
```

Replace `connection_context` with the variable; the square brackets are mandatory. This connection context is used rather than the default connection (which is never created in this code) when connecting to the database. Here's the source for `Order.sqlj` (saved as `sqlj\orders\Order.sqlj`):

```
package sqlj.orders;

import java.sql.SQLException;
import sqlj.runtime.ref.DefaultContext;
import oracle.sqlj.runtime.Oracle;

/**
 * Represents an order for a product by a customer
 */
public class Order
{
  private static final String newOrder = "NEW";

  /**
   * Store the order in the database
   */
  public void create(String customerId, String productId, int quantity)
    throws SQLException
  {
    DefaultContext context = null;

    context = Oracle.getConnection("jdbc:oracle:oci8:@proead","scott","tiger");

    if (context == null) return;

    System.out.println(customerId + " placing order for " +
                       quantity + " " + productId);

    try {
```

Here's one place where the connection context is used. The variable context is set above, and then used in the SQLJ statement in the line below:

```
#sql [context] { INSERT INTO orders
                 VALUES (order_id_sequence.nextVal, :customerId,
                         :productId, :quantity, :newOrder)
               };
```

Then the variable context is used in the commit statement:

```
#sql [context] { commit };
    } finally {
      context.close();
    }
  }
}
```

This next class is the test driver. It creates a single `Client` instance. Then it starts some threads that run in the `Client` instance. Each thread will create an order. When all the clients are complete, the test driver terminates. This file is saved as `sqlj\orders\OrderTest.java`:

```java
package sqlj.orders;

public class OrderTest {
  public static void main(String[] args)
  {
    if (args.length == 0) {
      System.out.println("Usage: java OrderServer n\n" +
          "where n is a non-negative integer");
      System.exit(0);
    }

    int c = new Integer(args[0]).intValue();

    //this code will simulate client requests
    //create a client object and start threads that will each
    //place an order
    Client client = new Client();
    Thread[] t = new Thread[c];

    for (int i = 0; i < c; i++) {
      //Note that each Thread object uses the same client object
      t[i] = new Thread(client);
      t[i].start();
    }

    //wait for all the clients to finish before terminating
    for (int i = 0; i < c; i++) {
      try {
    t[i].join();
      } catch (InterruptedException e) {
      }
    }
  }
}
```

And finally here's the code for the simulated clients. Each thread that enters the `run()` method randomly creates a value for customer_id, the product_id, and the quantity. It then calls the `Order.create()` method.

For this code to work, the product data presented earlier in the chapter should be entered into the database, if it was not done previously. In addition, the following data must be entered into the customer table:

email	password	surname	given_name
Alice@wrox.com	Alice	Adams	Alice
Bob@wrox.com	Bob	Baker	Bob
Cynthia@wrox.com	Cynthia	Carter	Cynthia

The following code is saved as sqlj\orders\Client.java:

```
package sqlj.orders;
/**
 * A class that simulates a client placing an order
 */
public class Client implements Runnable
{   /**
     * An array holding the valid product_id values, these must already
     * exist in the product table
     */
    private static String[] products = {
        "Rose-1", "Rose-2", "Rose-3", "Rose-4",
        "Candle-1", "Candle-2", "Candle-3", "Candle-4",
        "Wrapper-1", "Wrapper-2", "Wrapper-3", "Wrapper-4"
    };

    /**
     * The valid users, these must be already in the customer table
     */
    private static String users[] = {
        "Alice@wrox.com", "Bob@wrox.com", "Cynthia@wrox.com"
    };

    private static java.util.Random r = new java.util.Random();

    private int getRandom(int high) {
        return (r.nextInt() & Integer.MAX_VALUE) % high;
    }

    public String getUser() {
        return users[getRandom(users.length)];
    }

    public String getProduct() {
        return products[getRandom(products.length)];
    }

    public void run()
    {
        String user = getUser();
        String product = getProduct();
        int quantity = getRandom(10) + 1;
        try {
            Order order = new Order();
            order.create(user, product, quantity);
        } catch (Exception e) { e.printStackTrace(); }
    }
}
```

Compile the code with this command:

```
sqlj -v sqlj\orders\Order.sqlj sqlj\orders\OrderTest.java \
    sqlj\orders\Client.java
```

Then and run it using:

```
java sqlj.orders.OrderTest 10
```

After the program finishes, you can check the table using SQL*Plus to verify that the orders were inserted as reported by the program.

Connecting to Different Schemas

When you are connecting to different schemas, Oracle recommends that you use different connection context classes for each schema. This is because you may be using a different driver URL, different username, different password, or different auto-commit setting, (in any combination) for each connection. In this situation, your code must declare the connection context. The declaration causes the translator to create a new class; you create instances of this class in your code when you want a different connection context.

To see how this works, Order.sqlj will be modified by adding a method that allows a user to query the orders. A default connection context will be used to query the orders table, and a different connection context class will be used to query the customer table. First, use SQL*Plus, SQL Worksheet, or DBA Studio to create a new user, and give that user access to the SCOTT schema:

```
create user keith identified by texas;
grant create session to keith;
grant all privilege on customer to keith;
```

The code will use this new user to simulate connecting to a different schema. Here is the modified Order class. Put this code under sqlj\orders2\Order.sqlj

```
package sqlj.orders2;

import java.sql.SQLException;
import sqlj.runtime.ExecutionContext;
import sqlj.runtime.ConnectionContext;
import sqlj.runtime.ref.DefaultContext;
import oracle.sqlj.runtime.Oracle;

#sql context CustomerContext;

#sql iterator OrderIterator (long id, String customerId, Integer quantity);

/**
 * Represents an order for a product by a customer
 */
class Order
{

  private static final String newOrder = "NEW";

  public Order() throws SQLException {
    //the default connection context
    Oracle.connect("jdbc:oracle:oci8:@proead","scott","tiger");
  }
```

```
    /**
     * Query for orders where quantity is greater than input parameter
     */
    public void query(int quantity)
      throws SQLException
    {
      OrderIterator iter = null;
      CustomerContext context = null;
      try {
        //use the default connection context to query orders
        #sql iter = { SELECT order_id as id, customer_id as customerId,
                             quantity
                        FROM orders
                       WHERE quantity > :quantity
                    };

        DefaultContext d_ctx =
          Oracle.getConnection("jdbc:oracle:oci8:@", "keith", "texas");
        context = new CustomerContext(d_ctx);

        if (iter.next()) {
          String firstName;
          String lastName;

          System.out.println("Here are the customers who placed orders " +
                             "for more than " + quantity + " items");

          do {
            #sql [context] { SELECT surname, given_name
                               INTO :lastName, :firstName
                               FROM scott.customer
                              WHERE email = :(iter.customerId())
                           };

            System.out.println("Name: " + lastName.trim() + ", " +
                              firstName.trim() + "  Quantity: " +
                              iter.quantity());
          } while (iter.next());
        }
      } catch (SQLException e) {
        e.printStackTrace();
      } finally {
        if (context != null) { context.close(); }
        if (iter != null) { iter.close(); }
        Oracle.close();
      }
    }

    //create method
  }
```

(The create() method is as before.)

The first declaration is for a context name CustomerContext. The translator will turn this declaration into a Java class. This context class will be used when the customer table is queried. The second declaration is for an iterator.

A default connection context is created in the constructor. Because no context class reference is included with the SELECT statement that queries the orders table, that query uses the default context. After that query is executed, a CustomerContext instance is created by using Oracle.getConnection() to make another database connection. This second connection uses a different username and password than the default connection. The connection returned by getConnection() is then passed to the CustomerContext constructor. All context classes have 12 overloaded constructors with the same parameter list as Oracle.connect() or Oracle.getConnection().

After getting a CustomerContext, that connection context is used for the query of the customer table. Even though this second connection context actually connected to the SCOTT schema, the point is that it could be used to connect to any other schema in the data, and access any tables that the owner of that schema can access.

Execution Contexts

Although it has not been explicitly mentioned, all the examples so far have been using the default execution context in which to execute the SQL statements. Each connection context, whether it's been the default connection context or an explicitly created connection context instance, has an execution context associated with it. You don't need to do anything to get the execution context instance; it comes automatically with the connection.

Like connection contexts, an execution context is a class from which you can create instances. You can use those instances in any SQLJ statements. Unlike a connection context, you do not need to declare an execution context before creating and using it. You create an instance of the class just like any other Java class:

```
ExecutionContext context = new ExecutionContext();
```

The ExecutionContext class contains a number of methods that you can use to control, or get information about, the execution environment. Here is a list of some of the more frequently used methods:

- ❑ getWarnings()
  Returns the warnings from the most recent operation using a java.sql.SQLWarning object.

- ❑ getUpdateCount()
  Returns an int specifying the number of rows updated by the last SQL operation that completed using this execution context instance.

- ❑ getQueryTimeout()
  Returns an int specifying the timeout limit, in seconds, for any SQL operation that uses this execution context instance.

- ❑ setQueryTimeout(int)
  Takes an int as input to modify the query timeout limit.

- ❑ cancel()
  Cancels an operation being executed with this execution context instance.

- ❑ execute()
  Performs a generic execute on the currently registered statement.

- ❑ executeQuery()
  Performs an execute query on the currently registered statement.

❑ `executeUpdate()`
    Performs an execute update on the currently registered statement.

❑ `registerStatement(ConnectionContext, Object, int)`
    Registers the statement.

❑ `releaseStatement()`
    Releases the currently registered statement.

(You will find the full listing in the Javadoc documentation in `<ORACLE_HOME>\sqlj\doc\runtime`). You can explicitly create an execution context instance and use it rather than the default execution context in an SQL statement. This is useful in the following circumstances:

In multithreaded code, you can use the same connection context instance, and create a separate execution context for each thread. This allows different threads to execute SQL statements concurrently.

You are using the same connection context instance for several SQL statements, but you want to use different execution control operations with each statement.

You are using the same connection context for several SQL statements, but you want to retain the status information from each SQL statement separately (only the status information for the last SQL operation is retained in the execution context instance).

Your code can use any combination of connection contexts and execution contexts. You can have multiple connection contexts and a single execution context, or a single connection context and multiple execution contexts, or any combination in between. You provide a reference to the execution context in the same manner as you specify a connection context for an SQL statement:

```
#sql [execution_context] { SQL Statement };
```

❑ `execution_context` is replaced by a variable that references an instance of `sqlj.runtime.ExecutionContext`.

❑ If neither connection context or execution context is specified, then the translator uses a default connection and execution context.

❑ If a connection context is specified, the connection context reference must appear before the execution context reference in the brackets.

❑ The square brackets are a required part of the syntax.

As mentioned above, one purpose for using different execution contexts is to provide multithreaded code. Let's modify `Order.sqlj` one more time. This time we will use the same connection context for all the queries. The difference is that we'll update both the product and order tables in concurrent threads using a separate execution context for each query. Save the following code as `sqlj\orders3\Order.sqlj`

```
package sqlj.orders3;

import java.sql.SQLException;
import sqlj.runtime.ExecutionContext;
import sqlj.runtime.ConnectionContext;
import sqlj.runtime.ref.DefaultContext;
```

```
import oracle.sqlj.runtime.Oracle;

#sql context CustomerContext;

#sql iterator OrderIterator (long id, String customerId, Integer quantity);
#sql iterator ProductIterator (String product_id);

/**
 * Represents an order for a product by a customer
 */
class Order {
```

The constructor for this class and the query() method are the same as before and for brevity, they are not shown here. The first change is to the create() method, which no longer takes quantity as an order parameter. This method now returns the order_id when an order is successfully created. At that point, the client needs to call the updateQuantity() method with the order_id, product_id, and quantity desired.

```
/**
 * Store the order in the database
 */
public long create(String customerId, String productId)
{
  DefaultContext context = null;

  try {
    context = Oracle.getConnection("jdbc:oracle:oci8:@proead","scott","tiger");

    if (context == null) return -1;

    System.out.println(customerId + " placing order for " +
                        productId);

    //remove quantity from order creation, client must make request
    //to checkout method to update inventory
    Long order_id;
    #sql [context] { SELECT order_id_sequence.nextVal
                       INTO :order_id
                       FROM dual
                   };

    if (order_id == null) return -1;

    #sql [context] { INSERT INTO orders
                       (order_id, customer_id, product_id, state)
                     VALUES (:(order_id.longValue()), :customerId,
                             :productId, :newOrder)
                   };

    #sql [context] { commit };
    return order_id.longValue();
  } catch (SQLException e) {
    e.printStackTrace();
    return -1;
  } finally {
    try {
      context.close();
    } catch (SQLException e2) {
    }
  }
}
```

The updateQuantity() method uses several different execution contexts to perform its work. First it checks that the order_id and product_id parameters match an order in the system. Then it checks the product table to ensure there is inventory available for the order. If there is sufficient inventory, it proceeds to update the product table with the inventory reduction and the order table with the product quantity. It does this by creating an instance of the inner classes OrderUpdater and ProductUpdater, and starting a thread for each object:

```
/**
 * Update the orders table and the product table with the inventory change.
 * Set the quantity of the order to quantity, reduce the count_in_stock
 * of the product by quantity
 */
public void updateQuantity(long orderId,
                           String product_id,
                           int quantity)
{
    //create an instance of execution context for the initial query
    ExecutionContext eCtx = new ExecutionContext();
    ProductIterator iter;
    try {
        //use the default connection
        #sql [eCtx] iter = { SELECT product_id
                             FROM orders
                             WHERE order_id = :orderId
                               AND product_id = :product_id
                           };
    } catch (SQLException e) {
    }

    //check for a result
    if (eCtx.getUpdateCount() == 0) {
        System.out.println("Order " + orderId + " with product " + product_id +
                           " not found");
        return;
    }

    Integer inventory = new Integer(0);
    //fetch the count_in_stock from the product table,
    //use same execution context
    try {
        #sql [eCtx] { SELECT count_in_stock INTO :inventory
                      FROM product
                      WHERE product_id = :product_id
                    };
    } catch (SQLException e) {
        e.printStackTrace();
        System.out.println("Server error...try again later");
        return;
    }

    if (inventory == null || inventory.intValue() < quantity) {
        System.out.println("Cannot place order at this time, " +
                           "not enough inventory");
        return;
    }
```

```
ExecutionContext updateOrderCtx = new ExecutionContext();
Thread t1 = new Thread(new OrderUpdater(updateOrderCtx,
                    orderId, product_id, quantity));

ExecutionContext updateProductCtx = new ExecutionContext();
Thread t2 = new Thread(new ProductUpdater(updateProductCtx,
                product_id, (inventory.intValue() - quantity)));

t1.start();
t2.start();

try {
    t1.join();
    t2.join();
} catch (InterruptedException e) { e.printStackTrace(); }

try {
    //check to ensure the operation can be committed
    if (updateOrderCtx.getUpdateCount() == 0 ||
        updateProductCtx.getUpdateCount() == 0)
    {
        #sql { ROLLBACK };
        System.out.println("Error placing order. Operation aborted");
    } else {
        #sql { COMMIT };
        System.out.println("Order placed for " + quantity +
            " " + product_id);
    }
} catch (SQLException e) {
    e.printStackTrace();
}
}
```

There are two private inner classes that handle the table updating, `OrderUpdater()` and `ProductUpdater()`. The `updateQuantity()` method creates two threads, one thread for each method. After the threads complete, the code in the `updateQuantity()` method above checks the status of both inserts by calling the `ExecutionContext.getUpdateCount()` method. If both table updates were successful, then the whole transaction is committed.

> In your application, you might be tempted to commit statements separately for each thread or **ExecutionContext** instance. That would be a mistake. Committing each **ExecutionContext** individually will quickly lead to what appears to be a deadlock in your code. If you are using multiple **ExecutionContexts** with a single **ConnectionContext** to support multithreading, you should commit after all the **ExecutionContexts** associated with a **ConnectionContext** are complete.

```
/**
 * Private inner class that updates the order table with the
 * quantity of the product to be ordered
 */
private class OrderUpdater implements Runnable {
```

```java
    private ExecutionContext updateOrderCtx;
    private int quantity;
    private long order_id;
    private String product_id;
    private OrderUpdater(ExecutionContext ctx, long order_id,
                        String product_id, int quantity)
    {
      updateOrderCtx = ctx;
      this.order_id = order_id;
      this.product_id = product_id;
      this.quantity = quantity;
    }
    public void run() {
      try {
        #sql [updateOrderCtx] { UPDATE orders
                                    SET quantity = :quantity
                                WHERE order_id = :order_id
                                AND product_id = :product_id
                              };
      } catch (SQLException e) {
        e.printStackTrace();
      }
    }
  }


  /**
   * Private inner class that updates the product table with a new
   * count_int_stock value for inventory that is ordered
   */
  private class ProductUpdater implements Runnable {
    private ExecutionContext updateProductCtx;
    private int newCountInStock;
    private String product_id;
    private ProductUpdater(ExecutionContext ctx, String product_id,
                           int newCountInStock)
    {
      updateProductCtx = ctx;
      this.product_id = product_id;
      this.newCountInStock = newCountInStock;
    }
    public void run() {
      try {
        #sql [updateProductCtx] { UPDATE product
                                      SET count_in_stock = :newCountInStock
                                  WHERE product_id = :product_id
                                };
      } catch (SQLException e) {
        e.printStackTrace();
      }
    }
  }
}
```

Here are the changes to the `Client.java` source file. This new file is saved as `sqlj\orders3\Client.java`

```
package sqlj.orders3;
/**
 * A class that simulates a client placing an order
 */
public class Client implements Runnable
{
```

The other methods and variable are the same, but are not shown for brevity. Only the method `run()` needs to be changed:

```
public void run()
{
  String user = getUser();
  String product = getProduct();
  int quantity = getRandom(10) + 1;
  try {
    Order order = new Order();
    long order_id = order.create(user, product);
    if (order_id == -1) {
      System.out.println("Error creating order");
    } else {
      order.updateQuantity(order_id, product, quantity);
    }
  } catch (Exception e) { e.printStackTrace(); }
}
}
```

These source files can be compiled using:

```
sqlj -v -passes sqlj\orders3\Order.sqlj sqlj\orders3\Client.java \
     sqlj\orders3\OrderTest.java
```

Then run it using:

```
java sqlj.orders3.OrderTest
```

SQLJ in the Server

Oracle has, for some time, allowed you to store procedural program statements in the database. These stored procedures or functions could be called from other stored procedures, by an explicit call from a sufficiently privileged database user, or by an external program. See the Chapter 11 for further material in this area.

You can have this same kind of functionality with Java and SQLJ. You can write a Java program with embedded SQL statements, compile the program, and load the resulting class files into the database for later use. Alternatively, you can load the source files directly into the database, where the database will translate and compile the source files using an embedded SQLJ translator. With few exceptions, all the techniques presented in this chapter are applicable to writing an SQLJ program for the server.

The server side SQLJ code can run as a stored procedure, a stored function, a trigger, an Enterprise JavaBean, or a CORBA server. While a discussion of which of these you should use is beyond the scope of this chapter, we can discuss general techniques for deploying server-side SQLJ.

Server vs Client SQLJ

SQLJ Runtime Classes

When you create an external SQLJ program, you must distribute runtime.zip with your application. The archive runtime.zip contains the Oracle SQLJ classes needed for your application to run properly. For example, it contains the oracle.sqlj.runtime.Oracle class needed to open a database connection. When you create an application for Oracle server-side processing, the runtime classes are already present in the server, so you do not need to provide them with your application.

The Database Connection

Unlike Java code that executes outside the database, there is no need for server-side Java code to create an explicit connection. The connection automatically exists by virtue of the fact that a user has made a connection to the database to execute the Java code. The SQLJ statements use this pre-existing connection.

Just as there is no need to open a connection, there is no need to close the connection. If you try to close the connection, the server will quietly ignore the request. Likewise, if you make a call to:

```
DefaultContext.setDefaultContext(null);
```

in an attempt to set the default context to null, the request is essentially ignored. You cannot, nor is there a need to, close the database connection from within your Java program.

Auto-commit

Because there is no need to create a connection to the database, there is also no way to set the auto-commit value for the connection. For server-side Java classes, the auto-commit setting is turned off. All of your database transactions must explicitly be committed or rolled-back.

The Default Output Device

System.out.println is a handy tool for the Java programmer. However, without some explicit direction from the programmer, in a server-side SQLJ program, all System.out.println calls will write their output to the current trace file, not to the screen.

There are two things you can do if you want to display output on the user's screen.

First, you can explicitly redirect System.out.println. Before any use of System.out.println in your Java code, call the following two procedures:

```
//call the procedures with the size of the desired buffer,
//set output buffer to 5000 bytes
#sql { CALL DBMS_JAVA.SET_OUTPUT(5000) };
#sql { CALL DBMS_OUTPUT.ENABLE(5000) };
```

The other alternative is to use a stored procedure for output:

```
//enable the buffer first
#sql { CALL DBMS_OUTPUT.ENABLE(5000) };
#sql { DBMS_OUTPUT.PUT_LINE(:("Query returned " + x + "results")); }
```

Note that the String parameter is a complex host expression, so it has a leading ':' and the String is wrapped in parentheses. The PUT_LINE() function can take arguments of type VARCHAR2, NUMBER, or DATE.

SQLJ Server Example

Recall the ProductQuery.sqlj class from earlier in the chapter. Suppose you wanted to supply the functionality of this class as a stored procedure in the server. To do this, you could rewrite the doLowInventoryQuery() method as a static method. Here are the changes:

ProductQuery.sqlj

```
package sqlj.declarationsServer;

import java.sql.SQLException;

//Declare the iterator here. Use default (package) access
#sql iterator Product_Iterator (String product_id,
                                String name,
                                String description,
                                float price,
                                Integer count_in_stock,
                                String on_order );

/**
 * A class to demonstrate the usage of server-side SQLJ
 */
public class ProductQuery
{

    /**
     * Query for information about the products in the product table
     */
    public static void doLowInventoryQuery()
      throws SQLException
    {
      Product_Iterator pi = null;

      try {
        #sql pi = { SELECT * FROM product
                            WHERE count_in_stock < 10
                              OR count_in_stock IS NULL
                  };


        //now let's print out some of the results
        if (pi.next()) {
          #sql { CALL DBMS_JAVA.SET_OUTPUT(500) };
          #sql { CALL DBMS_OUTPUT.ENABLE(500) };
          System.out.println("Here are the products that" +
```

```
               "need to be ordered:");
          do {
            System.out.println("Product id:    " + pi.product_id());
            System.out.println("Product name: " + pi.name());
            System.out.println("Description:   " + pi.description());
            System.out.println("Inventory:     " + pi.count_in_stock());
          } while(pi.next());
        } else {
          System.out.println("Query returned no results");
        }
      } finally {
        if (pi != null) {
          pi.close();
        }
      }
    }
  }
```

Notice that there's no need to create a connection in the code above. As mentioned previously, the connection is implicit and the programmer does not need to perform any connection management.

However, you still must explicitly close the iterator. If you do not call the close method of the iterator, the underlying cursor remains open.

Client Side Development

After saving the source code, you need to compile it:

```
sqlj -passes -user=scott/tiger -ser2class
     sqlj\declarationsServer\ProductQuery.sqlj
```

Notice the -ser2class option here. You can leave the Profile classes with the .ser extension and the example work just the same.

Now provide the connect.properties file in the declarationsServer directory. For server-side SQLJ, you will need to use a special driver, the KPRB driver:

```
sqlj.url=jdbc:oracle:kprb:@
sqlj.user=scott
sqlj.password=tiger
```

Next, create a JAR file of the sqlj\declarationsServer package. The primary reason for using a JAR file is to make it easier to load the required classes into the server. You could load the classes into the server without using a JAR file by specifying the classes and other related files when you call the Oracle tool loadjava, which is provided with the installation.

```
jar -cvf0 productQuery.jar sqlj\declarationsServer
```

> It is advisable to create the JAR file with no compression (the –0 option) because the tolerance of the loadjava utility for compressed archives is unreliable.

551

Now you load the JAR file into the server:

```
loadjava -thin -user=scott/tiger@dbserver:1521:proead productQuery.jar
```

This command will use the thin driver to connect to the proead database on host dbserver, and load up the files. The syntax and capabilities of this tool are more fully explored in Chapter 11.

> The **loadjava** utility is located in **<ORACLE_HOME>\bin**. When Oracle is installed, that directory is automatically added to your **PATH** environment variable. If your **PATH** variable lacks this directory, you will need to add it yourself. Check the SQLJ documentation for other options for the **loadjava** utility.

After loading the classes into the server, you create an SQL wrapper so the procedure can be called. In SQL*Plus, execute the following:

```
set echo on
set serveroutput on
set termout on
set flush on

execute dbms_java.set_output(5000);

create or replace procedure GET_LOW_INVENTORY
as language java
name 'sqlj.declarationsServer.ProductQuery.doLowInventoryQuery()';
/
```

The name parameter must be a static fully qualified Java method name **including any package specification**. If the method takes parameters, you must use the fully qualified class name for any class parameters; for example, java.lang.String or java.util.Vector.

Finally, you call the stored procedure. From within SQL*Plus:

```
call GET_LOW_INVENTORY();
```

From a Java program:

```
#sql { call GET_LOW_INVENTORY() };
```

When calling a stored procedure from SQLJ, you need to use the dbms_output.get_line procedure if you need to read the output buffer. The get_line procedure takes two parameters: an int which is set to 1 for a successful call, and set to 0 for an unsuccessful call; and a string to hold the line from the buffer. Since the doLowInventoryQuery() sends its output to the buffer, here's a code snippet showing how to read the buffer:

```
String s;      //string to hold buffer contents
int x = 0;     //flag for status of get_line call

#sql { call dbms_output.enable(5000) }; //call enable before reading buffer
#sql { call dbms_output.get_line(:OUT x, :OUT s) };
while (x == 0) {
    System.out.println(s);
  #sql { call dbms_output.get_line(:OUT x, :OUT s) };
}
```

Any Java method that returns a value must be declared as a stored function. Here's a snippet demonstrating a Java method returning a primitive value:

```
package sqlj.serverside;

import java.sql.SQLException;

public class Product
{
  public static int getInventory(String productId)
  {
    Integer count;
    try {
      #sql { select count_in_stock into :count
               from product
               where product_id = :productId
            };
    } catch (SQLException e) {
      count = new Integer(-1);
    }
    return count.intValue();;
  }
}
```

The SQL statement to publish the method could be:

```
create or replace function GET_INVENTORY(productid varchar) return number
as language java
name 'sqlj.serverside.Product.getInventory(java.lang.String) return int';
/
```

It would be called from SQLJ like this:

```
String productId = "Rose-1";
int inventory;
#sql inventory = { call GET_INVENTORY(productId) };
```

Dropping Java Objects

If you have an error in your Java code, you may need to drop, reload, and republish the function or procedure. Most of the time, using the SQL syntax CREATE OR REPLACE will be sufficient. However, if you need to drop a function or procedure, you use the SQL call:

```
drop function GET_INVENTORY;
drop procedure GET_LOW_INVENTORY;
```

After dropping the function or procedure, you unload the Java class with the dropjava utility.

```
dropjava -oci8 -user=scott/tiger@proead sqlj\serverside\Product.class
```

This example uses the OCI driver and assumes a local TNS name proead is defined. Note that you should supply the same JAR file, or be in the same directory, as was specified when loadjava was originally called. This is because dropjava scans the file(s) specified in the command-line, and then drops the corresponding file(s) from the database.

Server Side Development

Developing and compiling the SQLJ code on the client and then loading it to the server provides great advantages; one of the best advantages is the ability to check the code semantics while the code is compiled. You can, however, write the code on the client, and let the server handle compilation when you load the source into the server.

Here's how you would do that for the method Product.getInventory() above. After writing the source code, but before compiling it, load it directly into the server:

```
loadjava -oci8 -user=scott/tiger@proead sqlj\serverside\Product.sqlj
```

If you have multiple .sqlj files, you can put them all in a single JAR file, and upload the JAR file. The advantage is that a single JAR file is easier to work with than multiple .sqlj source files.

Use the same CREATE OR REPLACE statement from above. The first time the function is called, the server will compile the source and execute the function. Subsequent calls will simply execute the compiled code. If you prefer to have the code compiled when it is loaded, call loadjava with the −resolve option:

```
loadjava -oci8 -resolve -user=scott/tiger@proead sqlj\serverside\Product.sqlj
```

Summary

This chapter was a brief introduction to SQLJ – SQL statements embedded in Java code. Here's what we have learned:

❑ SQLJ is used for static SQL code. The statement structure must be known at compile time, although the value of host expressions can be determined at run-time.

❑ With the limitation above, any SQL statement can be embedded in Java using the `#sql { SQL statement };` or `#sql result = { SQL statement };` syntax.

❑ An iterator declaration creates a new Java datatype that can be used to receive the result from a select expression that returns multiple rows.

❑ A connection context declaration creates a new Java datatype that can be used to create different connections to a database. Multithreaded code can be implemented using different connection contexts; when different threads are logically different transactions, then different connection contexts should be used.

❑ An execution context is a Java datatype that is used to refer to an instance of the `sqlj.runtime.ExecutionContext` class. Multithreaded code can be implemented using different execution contexts; when different threads are part of the same transaction, then different execution contexts should be used.

SQLJ code can be loaded into a server and run as stored procedures or stored functions. The chapter on Java Stored Procedures explains these processes further.

APPLICATIONPROGRAMMINGORACLE8i

Enterprise JavaBeans and Oracle

Applications can be considered to have three logical tiers: a presentation tier responsible for communicating to the end-user; an application-logic tier responsible for validating and transforming data and managing workflow; and a data tier responsible for maintaining a consistent representation of the application's state over time. Enterprise JavaBeans (EJBs) are aimed squarely at the application-logic tier, and specifically for applications that implement this application-logic tier on a server that is remote from the end-user. EJB technology is designed to help developers build distributed, scalable, secure, portable, transactional application-logic components. These should be able to interact with a wide variety of presentation-tier clients (JSPs; Java applets or applications; Visual Basic, PowerBuilder, or C++ applications; WAP clients or browsers; CORBA business-to-business components using XML; etc.) and a wide variety of enterprise resources (databases; messaging systems; mail systems; LDAP servers; ERP systems; security systems; etc.).

This chapter provides a very practical introduction to Enterprise JavaBeans. It explains:

- ❑ What an EJB component looks like
- ❑ How to construct and deploy an EJB 1.1 compliant component
- ❑ Where EJBs fit into Sun's plan for server-side Java
- ❑ Why you would use them in your application architecture, and when you might not
- ❑ How to construct and deploy an EJB 1.0 compliant application to the Oracle 8i JVM

We'll also build an application using Enterprise JavaBeans. This application, a restaurant finder, will demonstrate some of the design principles we'll talk about, and also provide concrete EJB examples that you can modify to build your own components. If there are any readers who are actually building restaurant portals, they will see that there are numerous simplifications and unrealistic assumptions in our application. This is done to avoid obscuring the use of EJBs and to conserve space for more general material.

Actually, we will build our restaurant finder twice: once using a type of component (entity beans) that represents data in the database; and once without this type of component. In the first part we will focus on EJB development with respect to the J2EE development and deployment standard. In the second part we will show how, with a few changes to the code and EJB architecture, we can deploy the example in the Oracle 8i JVM. We will discuss later the relative merits of the approaches.

To understand this chapter, you will need to know the Java programming language. You will probably get the most from this chapter if you also have some familiarity with basic terms such as transactions, connection pools, scalability, and persistence. To follow along with the examples, you need a Java compiler (available free from many sources) and a suitable EJB container. There are numerous EJB containers available, including open source containers that are free for any purpose and commercial containers that are free for development.

The Oracle 8i Java Virtual Machines in versions 8.1.5 and 8.1.6 provide an EJB container that supports the EJB specification 1.0. We will show how to deploy a version of our example to this container.

One of the first things that you should understand about EJB technology is that it is not a product sold by Sun or any other company. It is a **specification** for a technology. Part of this specification describes the requirements of the environment in which an EJB component runs. This environment, known as an **EJB container**, has been built by dozens of commercial and open-source vendors, who then sell (or give away) these competing containers. Another part of the specification describes how to build an **EJB component** that can run in any compliant container. This is the part of the specification that you, the reader, will implement – you will build EJB components that follow the rules in the specification, and you will then deploy them in a container that you purchase or download.

Like any actively-used technology specification, there are multiple versions of the EJB specification. Each version adds capabilities, corrects mistakes, and addresses various concerns not addressed in the previous version. There are three versions of the specification of which you should be aware. The current version as of this writing is 1.1. The examples in this book are written to work with a container that implements this version of the specification. There is also a draft of the next version of the specification – 2.0 – that has been released for comments by the community. An EJB 2.0-compliant container must be able to run an EJB 1.1-compliant component unchanged, so all the examples here will also apply to that version of the specification when containers that implement it are available. (Some of the proposed additions to the EJB 2.0 specification will be discussed in this chapter.) Finally, the previous version of the specification was 1.0. This version becomes more irrelevant with each passing day, but there are still books, articles, and EJB containers directed at this version of the specification. Unlike the version upgrade from EJB 1.1. to EJB 2.0, there were some incompatible changes made from version 1.0 to version 1.1. Components developed for EJB 1.0 may not run in an EJB 1.1 container.

Enterprise JavaBeans technology is a subject with a lot of content (the EJB 2.0 draft specification has more than 500 pages), and it may be that the material in this book does not fully address your needs. One additional source of information that I can recommend is Wrox Press's *Professional Java Server Programming J2EE Edition* (of which I am the author of much of the EJB material). There are also numerous resources available on the Internet, including tutorials, FAQs, forums, and sample applications. Sun has published a document that discusses various design strategies (the J2EE Blueprints) and a sample e-commerce application (the Java Pet Store). The EJB specifications themselves are freely available for download from Sun's web site, but their intended audience is not component writers, and the typical application developer will probably find that the cost of slogging through them outweighs the benefits of having read them.

I will clear up one potential source of confusion right at the start: an Enterprise JavaBean component is only tangentially related to a "garden-variety" JavaBean component. Many readers who are not familiar with EJBs will be familiar with JavaBean components (at least in their GUI incarnations, such as grids, lists, tree controls, and combo-boxes). This similarity in name is a marketing ploy more than anything else; EJB components have more in common with servlet or JSP components than they do with JavaBeans.

Varieties of EJB Components

A component is a packaged, reusable unit of software with a well-defined interface. Component reuse has been one of the most successful strategies to maximize an investment in software development. EJBs are server-side components that can be used concurrently by multiple clients – such as JSPs, servlets, applets, and other EJB components.

The Enterprise JavaBeans 1.1 specification provides two different models for EJB components: session beans and entity beans. Entity beans and session beans have different purposes, use different Java classes, provide different capabilities, and impose different requirements on the developer. (The EJB 2.0 draft specification adds a third model: message-driven beans, which will be briefly discussed later.)

A **session bean** is used by a single client. It provides that client with access to application logic calculations, workflow, and application state on a server. It is intended to be short-lived; in other words, it should exist for the duration that it is needed by a single client, and then should be discarded.

A session bean can be either stateful or stateless. A **stateful** bean can keep information across client method calls, whereas a stateless bean cannot. This is an extremely important distinction. Sometimes it is helpful or necessary for an application to keep temporary, private state (also known as conversational state) in memory on the server, so a stateful session bean must be used. However, if it is not necessary, **stateless** session beans provide significant advantages to scalability and application design. Stateless session beans – because they can be reused by multiple clients – can be pooled to provide huge differences in the demands on the server's memory, and should be your choice whenever possible.

> *Multiple stateful session beans should be used with care because of the difficulty of managing differing "time-out" values for the state's validity. Also for this reason one stateful session bean should never call another. Instead, if stateful session beans are used at all, a single bean should be given the responsibility to manage all state associated with a particular client application.*

An **entity bean** can be thought of as an object-oriented representation of data in a database. Like a database, multiple clients can safely access it simultaneously. It is intended to provide a persistent representation of data; as long as the corresponding data exists in the database, the entity is said to exist.

An entity bean's state needs to be synchronized with the database. The EJB container will manage the timing of this synchronization and will deal with concurrency issues, database connection pooling, caching, and so on. It can also provide the logic to actually move the entity's state to and from the database. This is known as **container-managed persistence** (CMP). Alternatively, the component developer can choose to provide this logic. This is known as **bean-managed persistence** (BMP). Allowing the EJB container to handle the persistence logic (thus freeing application programmers from having to write sometimes-difficult, always-tedious SQL code and logic) can be a tremendous productivity enhancer. Sometimes, however, it is not possible because the container cannot provide the object-relational mapping between the entity's state and the relational database; these are the circumstances in which it is necessary to use bean-managed persistence.

There are two models of container-managed persistence. The first, introduced in EJB 1.0 and modified only slightly in EJB 1.1, uses public variables in a Java class to represent the state of the entity. This approach had some drawbacks; for instance, it made it very difficult to represent dependent objects (for example line items for an order) in an efficient and portable manner. The second model of container-managed persistence was introduced with EJB 2.0. The state of an entity is represented by abstract accessor methods and abstract dependent objects for which EJB-container tools provide a concrete implementation.

In other words, you might have a customer entity with a `String` property called "name". Instead of defining a name variable in your entity bean, you would define two methods as follows: `abstract String getName();` and `abstract void setName(String name);`. When you deployed your entity bean, tools specific to your EJB container's **persistence manager** would generate a new version of the customer entity with implementations of `getName()` and `setName()`. New versions are also generated for the dependent objects in your model, such as the customer's orders and payments. Because all access to the customer's persistent state is through these generated classes and methods, it is possible for the persistence manager to provide sophisticated object-relational mapping in a portable manner. This new model of container-managed persistence solves many of the problems facing the earlier model, and will reduce the occasions for which bean-managed persistence is necessary.

The restaurant example in the first part of this chapter uses a restaurant entity with bean-managed persistence. Each restaurant entity has associated codes, which are modeled as dependent objects of the entity. Although some EJB 1.1-compliant containers can map these dependent objects to a normalized relational design using container-managed persistence, others cannot. This dependent object mapping is a good example of a situation that might require bean-managed persistence – depending on the capabilities of your target EJB containers. Note that an EJB 2.0-compliant container would almost certainly be able to map this entity state to a normalized relational database design. In my opinion, container-managed persistence will almost always be a better choice than bean-managed persistence with EJB 2.0.

The Enterprise JavaBeans 2.0 specification provides a final model for EJB components, known as a **message-driven bean**. This type of bean is similar in use to a stateless session bean, except that it is designed to process asynchronous notifications – Java Message Service (JMS) messages – rather than respond to a client's call. Message-driven beans do not maintain state on behalf of a particular client like stateful session beans, nor do they represent state in the database like entity beans. On the other hand, they may access the database either directly using JDBC or indirectly using entity beans.

Where EJBs Fit into Sun's Plans for Server-side Java

Sun and its partners have developed a series of specifications to provide coverage for all the services that a highly-available, secure, reliable and scalable server-based application might require. These specifications and the relationships between them are described in what is known as the Java 2 Platform Enterprise Edition (J2EE).

The J2EE platform provides for **components**, **containers** for those components, and **services** that the components may use. The three types of server-side components are JSPs, servlets, and EJBs. JSPs and servlets execute in a web container. EJBs execute in an EJB container. In addition, the J2EE platform describes client-side components, for instance applets and Java applications, and their containers.

There are several standard services available in the J2EE platform to clients or components such as EJBs. Remote communication is possible through HTTP, HTTPS (that is HTTP over SSL), and RMI-IIOP (RMI over the CORBA interoperable protocol), and often through other common protocols such as RMI-JRMP (Java Remote Method Protocol, or "standard" RMI). Access to relational databases is available through JDBC. Access to enterprise messaging systems is available through the Java Messaging Service (JMS). Access to enterprise e-mail systems is available through the JavaMail API. Access to enterprise directory services is available through the Java Naming Directory Interface (JNDI). The JNDI API is also used to acquire references to other enterprise resources in a standard, portable manner. This will be explained shortly.

The generic term for an operating environment designed to provide services to server-tier application components is an **application server**. Implementations of the J2EE platform APIs are often referred to by this term. The "EJB container" is a logical abstraction of the EJB-related services provided by an application server. For the most part, the provider of the application server will be the same as the provider of the EJB container, although it is possible for an API to be defined that would allow an application server to use different EJB containers, or an EJB container to be plugged into different application servers.

In addition to the standard services provided by well-defined Java APIs, there are implicit services provided by a component's container. The component developer need not do any programming to take advantage of these services, although he or she may need to declare how those services should behave by configuring them in a standard XML file (the deployment descriptor). For an EJB component, you may reasonably expect some or all of the following services:

❑ **Declarative Transactions**
A transaction is a set of changes to an application's state. These changes must be atomic (must succeed or fail as a group), consistent (must leave the database in a state that makes sense), isolated (must not be affected by other concurrent transactions), and durable (must be reflected in a permanent store). Transaction management can be complicated, particularly if multiple data-access components and/or multiple data sources are involved. Using EJBs, complex transactions can be managed without any coding.

❑ **Declarative Security**
In every real-world application, access to data and application logic functionality must be secure. Access to EJB components can be regulated without any coding.

❑ **Data Caching**
Under certain circumstances, EJB data caching can provide a significant improvement in both performance and scalability of an application without any coding on the part of the application developer.

❑ **Error Handling**
Few applications of any size will be successful without a clear and consistent error-handling framework. The EJB specification clearly defines how errors affect transactions, client results, server logging, and component recovery.

❑ **Scalability and Fail-Over**
Some J2EE applications must service a large number of users – throughout the enterprise or on the Web. The EJB specification does not make the component developer responsible for scaling his or her application. An appropriate EJB container will be able to efficiently manage finite enterprise resources across multiple threads, processes, or machines. An EJB container can also be designed to recover from the failure of any particular resource – including a server on which the J2EE platform is executing.

❑ **Manageability**
The administrator of an application must be able to monitor and control access to enterprise resources and application functionality. An appropriate implementation of the J2EE platform can provide a manageable environment.

❑ **Portability**

There are three types of portability available to EJB components. Since EJB components are written in Java, they can be used unchanged on many operating systems and on many computer architectures. Just as importantly, if an EJB component does not take advantage of any proprietary APIs offered by a particular EJB container vendor, it can be deployed in an EJB container from many container vendors. Finally, an EJB component can be deployed in different enterprise environments – against different databases, security systems, communication systems, etc. As a result, an application can be sold to companies that have existing infrastructures which they are unwilling to change. Furthermore, applications can be redeployed on EJB containers with different capabilities as the requirements of the application change.

Towards the end of this chapter, we will look closely at the deployment and resource acquisition issues for EJBs running in the Oracle 8i container.

Do You Need EJB Components in Your Architecture?

There is a definite development cost to using EJB components in your design. EJB component development requires a particular skill set that can be expensive or difficult for your project or organization to acquire. The question to be considered is: will you gain more than you pay? It's certainly true that server-tier application logic and web sites with dynamic content existed before EJB components, thus demonstrating that EJB technology is not, strictly speaking, necessary.

The answer, frankly, is sometimes yes, sometimes no. Like every other software decision, it depends on the requirements of your application and the available development resources of your project. To evaluate the appropriateness of the technology, it is useful to consider what it brings to the table.

The central idea behind the design of the Enterprise JavaBeans specification is to separate the concerns of system-level development from the concerns of application-level development. In other words, an application programmer should not need to know how to write a transaction manager, a security service, an error handling framework, and certainly not a load-balancing, fault-tolerant application framework. In the view of the EJB specification authors, these activities are the rightful domain of people who develop them full-time. The application programmer, who is presumably an expert on the domain of the application being developed, should be allowed to concentrate on application logic exclusively. By following a set of rules about how that application logic should be structured using EJB components, he or she can be freed from non-application-logic concerns.

I would say that it rarely, if ever, makes sense for an organization to write its own system-level services from scratch. If an application developer finds himself or herself developing the kinds of services that an EJB container can provide (such as transaction management, persistence, security, data caching, etc.) then yes, he or she should probably use EJBs instead. However, if the application is a simple one that does not require the services that an EJB container can provide, then it doesn't make sense to introduce the relative complexity of EJB component development.

Resource Acquisition in J2EE Components

EJB components are designed to be portable. As mentioned above, this portability extends to different enterprise environments that may use entirely different software infrastructures. An EJB component does not need to be written with the deployment environment in mind. Instead, it works with abstractions that are later mapped onto actual enterprise resources during the deployment process.

At some level, this process will be familiar to most programmers. Database access is the most obvious example. Unless you are using database-specific features, you can program using JDBC without regard to whether your target database is Oracle, Interbase, or SQL Server. The other Java APIs – such as JMS or JavaMail – work the same way.

Acquiring the resources for use within a component must also be done in a way that preserves the component's independence from its deployment environment. The JNDI API is used for this purpose. The component developer accesses a resource factory (such as `javax.sql.DataSource`) by name using this API, and then creates an instance of the resource (such as a JDBC connection) through this factory. (You'll see an example of this in just a few paragraphs.)

Accessing resources based on their name is done in an ad hoc manner throughout computing. For instance, files are referenced based on their file system name; web sites are referenced based on their URLs; and e-mail accounts are referenced based on their addresses. One role of the JNDI API is to provide a common programmatic interface for retrieving a resource based on its naming convention. The implementation of the API is provided through pluggable "service providers" provided by independent software vendors (including Sun), just like the implementation of the JDBC API is provided by pluggable database drivers. One service provider may allow you to access files in a file system; another may allow you to access an enterprise LDAP server. Your J2EE-compliant application server will include a service provider that allows your components to access resources by name.

In the JNDI API, names of objects are arranged in a hierarchy of contexts, just like names of files in your file system are arranged in a tree of directories. A context is represented by the Java class `javax.naming.Context`. The "root directory" is represented by the class `javax.naming.InitialContext`. Like a file system, the nested contexts can be navigated by retrieving them one at a time, or by specifying a compound name that indicates the path through the tree.

Although there are several operations possible on contexts, we are only interested right now in using them to look up resources. The process is quite simple, involving three steps.

1. Set up the properties for the initial context. For a component executing in a web or EJB container, this step is not necessary; the container will automatically provide the correctly configured initial context to the component. For a stand-alone Java application or applet, you can either configure a file called `jndi.properties` and make it available on the classpath, or set up a `java.util.Properties` object with the correct name-value pairs and pass it as a parameter to the constructor of the `IntialContext` object. (The exact contents of the file or values of the name-value pairs will depend on the server you are using.) Here is a class from the restaurant finder example that is used by the test clients to instantiate a properly configured `Properties` object for the Oracle 8i JVM. This is the file `restaurants.ClientPropertiesFactory` which we will use later:

```
package restaurants;

import javax.naming.Context;
import java.util.Properties;
import oracle.aurora.jndi.sess_iiop.ServiceCtx;

public class ClientPropertiesFactory {
  public static Properties getInitialContextProperties() {
     Properties   prop = new Properties();
    prop.setProperty( Context.SECURITY_PRINCIPAL, "scott" );
    prop.setProperty( Context.SECURITY_CREDENTIALS, "tiger" );
    prop.setProperty( Context.URL_PKG_PREFIXES, "oracle.aurora.jndi");
    prop.put(Context.SECURITY_AUTHENTICATION, ServiceCtx.NON_SSL_LOGIN);
    return prop;
  }
}
```

2. Instantiate a new InitialContext object – either by new InitialContext() or new InitialContext(properties).

3. Get the reference using the lookup method of the IntialContext class. The parameter of that method should be the name of the object you are trying to find. For instance, here is an excerpt from the ClientInterview class (which will be provided in full later in this chapter). This excerpt looks up a stateful session bean under the name PreferenceInterviewer (I'll describe later how it got that name):

```
String oracleservice = "sess_iiop://dbserver:2481:proead";
PreferenceInterviewerHome home = (PreferenceInterviewerHome)
    initial.lookup(oracleservice + "/test/PreferenceInterviewer");

interviewer = home.create("Schenectady");
```

As I mentioned, the EJB container is responsible for configuring a components JNDI name space (which is simply the complete set of available names and their bound objects), so the client will use the no-arguments constructor for the InitialContext class. The EJB component's environment (its available resources and its configured properties) is located in the "java:comp/env/" context. Take a look at this excerpt from our restaurant entity bean as it acquires a reference to a database connection (the entire class will be presented later). It retrieves the connection factory (DataSource) from the jdbc/restaurantDB location in the component's environment:

```
private Connection getConnection() {
  try {
    InitialContext initial = new InitialContext();
    DataSource ds = (DataSource)
      initial.lookup( "java:comp/env/jdbc/restaurantDB" );

    return ds.getConnection();
  }
  catch (Exception e) {
    e.printStackTrace();
    throw new EJBException(e);
  }
}
```

Access to database resources via a **DataSource** lookup is highly relevant when an EJB needs to be readily portable between enterprise containers, and needs to access arbitrary remote databases. In deploying EJBs to Oracle, then access to the local database is most appropriately obtained directly through the internal driver. Oracle provides support for the **DataSource** interface by way of the **oracle.jdbc.pool.OracleDataSource** object, (see Chapter 12 for an example of setting this up). In the working example later in this chapter, we will use the internal driver directly.

The JNDI name of a resource – whether it be an EJB reference, a JDBC connection, or something else – is arbitrary. When the application is deployed into a target environment, these references (such as jdbc/restaurantDB) will be linked to actual resources. This **indirection** in acquiring resources gives application developers great flexibility to mix and match components from different sources, and to build their own components without regard to the actual resources that will be in the target environments.

To ensure that the acquisition of EJB components is compatible with a CORBA-based server using RMI–IIOP as its communication protocol, the EJB specification recommends that down-casting to an EJB home or remote reference be done using the javax.rmi.PortableRemoteObject.narrow() method. From the point of view of the application developer, this is just a complicated way to cast an EJB interface class, and doesn't provide any other service except portability to environments that happen to require it. We could implement this as follows:

```
String oracleservice = "sess_iiop://dbserver:2481:proead";
Object home = initial.lookup(oracleservice + "/test/PreferenceInterviewer");
PreferenceInterviewerHome home = (PreferenceInterviewerHome)
    PortableRemoteObject.narrow(homeObject, PreferenceInterviewerHome.class);

//create a PreferenceInterviewer for the locale Schenectady
interviewer = home.create("Schenectady");
```

Transactional Resource Usage

One of the benefits of using EJB components is that the container will manage transactions for you. You declare to the container on a per-method basis the transactional behavior that you would like. The container will start, suspend, or join the appropriate transactions for you before your business method begins to execute, and will commit, maintain, or rollback the transaction as appropriate when the method completes. You don't need to write any code to support this behavior. Any time you use a resource (such as a database connection) within a business method or one of its helper methods, that resource is automatically enlisted into the appropriate transaction.

Because the container is responsible for transactions, the programmer must never use resource methods that would interfere with its transaction management. For a database connection, the EJB code must never call commit(), setAutoCommit(), and rollback(). (You can make the current transaction roll back by calling a method of the EJB's context class.)

The Enterprise JavaBeans specification supports only flat transactions. You cannot have child (nested) transactions. There are six options for how a method works with transactions:

❏ **NotSupported:** used primarily for non-transactional resources. Any existing transaction will be suspended while this method executes. Unless you have a non-transactional resource, you probably will not use this transaction attribute.

❏ **Required:** an existing transaction is joined. If there is no existing transaction, a new one is created. This is a good choice for methods that modify data.

❏ **Supports:** an existing transaction is joined. If there is no existing transaction, the method executes outside of a transaction context. You might want to use this attribute for a read-only method (for example one that retrieves a piece of data).

❏ **RequiresNew:** an existing transaction is suspended, and a new one is started. When the method completes, the existing transaction is resumed. You might use this attribute to get a sequential ID from a table that you didn't want to keep locked.

❏ **Mandatory:** this method can only be called with an existing transaction, or an exception is thrown.

❏ **Never:** this method must never be called with a transaction, or an exception is thrown.

The transactional attributes for a method can be specified in an XML, or other (vendor–specific) deployment descriptor. We will examine the Oracle format later in the chapter. An XML deployment descriptor uses `<container-transaction>` elements to indicate which transaction attributes apply to the various methods. Each `<container-transaction>` element has two child elements: a method, and the transactional attribute. The method has the name of the EJB and the name of the method (which can be a wild-card: "*", or can include method-param sub-elements to further distinguish the method's identity). Here is a simple example:

```
<container-transaction>
  <method>
    <ejb-name>Product</ejb-name>
    <method-name>*</method-name>
  </method>
  <trans-attribute>Required</trans-attribute>
</container-transaction>
```

For entity beans, transaction boundaries can be used by the container to determine:

❏ when EJB component callback methods related to persistence are triggered (these are named `ejbLoad()` and `ejbStore()`)

❏ when container-managed persistence functions are performed, if the entity uses container-managed persistence

In the latter case, just before the first business method of an entity is called within a transaction, the container may initialize the bean's state from the database (assuming that the data has not already been cached). Similarly, just before the transaction completes the container will actually move the state of the bean to the database.

To consider a typical example (and considering only the transaction and persistence aspects of the container's duty), assume that an entity bean has a business method with the signature `public void setName(String name);` and a transaction type of "Required." Here is the sequence of events for a remote invocation:

1. Before the container allows this method to execute, it will start a current transaction.

2. The container will load the data for that entity, if the entity has container-managed persistence and the data is not already cached.

3. The container will then indicate that the data has been loaded by using the callback method `ejbLoad()`, assuming that the data is not already cached.

4. The container will execute the code in our `setName()` method.

5. Before the remote business method returns, the container will invoke the `ejbStore()` callback method that indicates the component's state either should be (BMP beans) or will be (CMP beans) synchronized with the database.

6. For CMP beans, the container will actually synchronize the bean's state with the database.

7. Finally, the container will commit the transaction.

Don't worry too much about these entity bean callbacks right now. They will be discussed later in this chapter and (of course) sample code will be provided.

For session beans, there are no container callback methods indicating that the session bean should synchronize with the database. (There are optional callbacks that indicate the transaction is about to be committed. These can be used to similar effect.) However, resources are still enlisted into the transaction. Updates to transactional resources are always committed by the container for both session and entity beans according to the method attributes declared in the deployment descriptor.

Cooperation with Other Enterprise Technologies

Some project teams may have the luxury of writing their entire application from scratch. Others – and this may be the more common circumstance – will need to integrate with existing applications that are currently serving the demands of the enterprise. For instance, a manufacturing company may use an ERP (Enterprise Resource Planning) software package to manage their scheduling, inventory, labor allocation, and so on. Similarly, specialized software exists for managing the sales process, customer relationships, student enrollments, medical care, and almost any other major organizational activity that you can imagine. Enterprise JavaBeans technology has been designed to work with these existing technologies.

From the point of view of an EJB component, external software will be either a **client** or a **resource** (or both). External software acting as a client can access EJB components synchronously using a remote method call (for example RMI-IIOP) or through any request-response protocol (for instance by using a servlet front-end). As of EJB 2.0, external software can use messaging (JMS) and the new message-driven bean to access EJB components asynchronously as well.

An EJB component can be a "client" of enterprise software by accessing it as a resource. The access can take place with various levels of integration. The simplest and least integrated would be to **update shared tables** in a database. Of course, this bypasses all the application logic that exists in the other application. The next level of integration would be to **communicate directly with the enterprise application**, perhaps using sockets or RMI. Using this method allows the application logic in the resource to execute; however, there are three problems. First, the application logic would not execute in a transaction. If the EJB component rolled back its transaction, there would be no easy way to undo the effects of calling that application logic. Second, there is no easy way to extend EJB's security model to the resource. It would be necessary to manually authenticate and/or provide access control to that resource. Finally, there is no common mechanism that the EJB container can use to provide services for scalability – such as resource pooling.

The new **J2EE Connector Architecture**, part of the proposed J2EE 1.3 platform, provides a solution for these three problems. A resource that provides a compliant driver allows an EJB component to access that resource securely, within a transaction, and at large-scale transaction rates. It is the responsibility of the outside software solution provider – the ERP vendor – to provide a driver for the resource. As far as the component developer is concerned, the pattern for resource acquisition remains the same (as described in the previous section).

Constructing EJB Components

Both entity bean and session bean components are made up of at least four basic files. The **remote interface** exposes the business methods of the component to its user. The **home interface** provides to the user a factory for the management of the component's life-cycle. In other words, it has methods for creating new component instances and finding existing instances. The **implementation class** is where the component developer provides the application logic. The **deployment descriptor** is an XML file (however Oracle still requires a proprietary format, of which we will see an example later) in which is specified information about EJB components, such as its behavior with regard to transactions and security.

These files that make up an EJB are packaged into a Java archive (JAR) file. (There is only one deployment descriptor for a JAR file, regardless of the number of EJB components that it contains). This JAR file can be further packaged, along with other EJB JARs, WAR (web archive) files and support classes, into a single J2EE-standard file known as an enterprise archive (EAR file).

We'll talk more in this section about how these various components should look, and examine the sample code from our restaurant finder example. Before we do this, I'll describe what the restaurant finder application does.

Introducing the Restaurant Finder Application

We're developing a portal application that will interview its user about their preferences and make some recommendations about a restaurant that they might like to visit. There are two types of users (UML "actors") that interact with our system. The first is a "reviewer," who creates or updates the information about a particular restaurant. The second is someone who would like to find an appropriate restaurant in which to dine.

There are two example clients, corresponding to the two different types of user. Both clients are Java command-line applications, designed only to test the EJB components that we will develop. One sets up some sample data, using the class `PropertyUpdater`, which is the EJB stateless session bean façade designed for "reviewers."

The other **interviews a potential diner** about his or her dining preferences using
`PreferenceInterviewer`, which is the EJB stateful session bean façade designed for potential
restaurant patrons. Here is a sample interview session:

```
ClientInterview                                                        _ □ X
Are you looking for dinner, or do you want to book an event?
#0 Dinner
#1 An event
0
What price range (per meal) is appropriate?
#0 <10
#1 10-20
#2 20-40
#3 >40
0
What type of food are you interested in?
#0 French
#1 Italian
#2 Mexican
#3 Thai
#4 Fusion
#5 Diner
5
Do you require a vegetarian menu?
#0 Yes
#1 No
1
Do you need a restaurant that is open late?
#0 Yes
#1 No
0
The following restaurants meet your criteria:
Restaurant: Ground Round with chef: Day Cook
Restaurant: Gregs with chef: Ellen Daviero

Press Ctrl+C to terminate the application...
```

You can feel free to add restaurants and properties beyond what has been provided in the first
command-line application; failing this, you should keep an eye on the existing data when answering the
questions in the interview application (to make sure you get interesting results).

The design of the database is quite simple. There are two tables. One stores some basic information
about the restaurant: name, location, and chef. You can create it using the following statement:

```
CREATE TABLE RESTAURANT (
        NAME VARCHAR2(28) NOT NULL,
        LOCATION VARCHAR2(30) NOT NULL,
        CHEF VARCHAR2(25),
PRIMARY KEY (NAME));
```

The other table stores properties related to a particular restaurant, which consist of a code, a value, a
reviewer (essentially a "modified-by" field), and a review date (essentially a "modification-date" field). A
property might be a type of restaurant (for example French or Thai), the price range of the restaurant,
whether or not it's open late, etc. Of course, there can be many properties related to each restaurant.
The two tables are joined on `restaurant.name = restaurantproperty.restaurant`. You can
create the property table using the following statement:

```
CREATE TABLE RESTAURANTPROPERTY (
        RESTAURANT VARCHAR2(28) NOT NULL,
        CODE VARCHAR2(25) NOT NULL,
        VAL VARCHAR2(25) NOT NULL,
        REVIEWER VARCHAR2(25) NOT NULL,
        REVIEWDATE DATE,
PRIMARY KEY (RESTAURANT, CODE));
```

There are three components in this application: a stateful session bean, a stateless session bean, and an entity bean (one of each). The stateful session bean – **PreferenceInterviewer** – manages the interviewing process. Its state is the location of the user and the answers that he or she has given. This stateful session bean delegates much of its processing to a helper class called `QuestionStateMachine`. The stateless session bean – **PropertyUpdater** – provides an interface to the client for creating or updating a restaurant and its properties. Of course, the entity bean is **Restaurant**. It uses bean-managed persistence, so it should be portable to any EJB container, regardless of its object-relational mapping capabilities. (Remember, we'll shortly develop another version of this application that does not use an entity bean.) Here is a diagram that summarizes the relationships between the most important parts of this application:

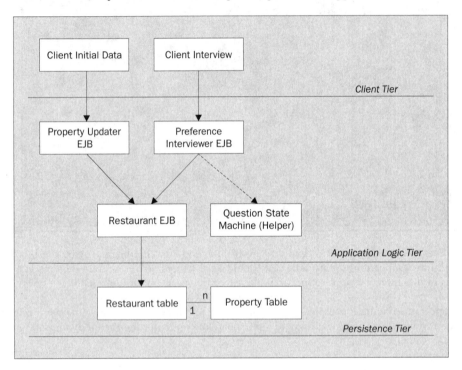

It almost goes without saying that the real purpose of this application is to help you to understand how to use EJB components, and not to actually help you select restaurants in which to eat. With this end in mind, several large compromises have been made regarding the application's design. One of the most significant ones (but certainly not the only one) is that the interview questions are hard-coded in the `restaurants.QuestionStateMachine` class. Those questions are things like appropriate price range, type of food, and vegetarian requirements. As I said earlier, if you're actually designing a restaurant portal you have a lot of work remaining. But you can take this example (and aspects of its design) and apply the concepts to any project requiring EJB components.

The following tables summarize the classes and their roles for this example. You may want to refer to it as you read the text:

EJB Components

The entity bean classes are as follows:

Bean	Restaurant
Type	Entity
Bean class files	RestaurantEJB RestaurantHome Restaurant ejb-jar.xml
Support class files	PropertyList RestaurantNotFoundException RestaurantProperty
Bean refs	–
Resource refs	jdbc/restaurantDB

The following table describes the session beans in a similar manner:

Bean	PreferenceInterviewer	PropertyUpdater
Type	Stateful Session	Stateless Session
Bean class files	PreferenceInterviewerEJB PreferenceInterviewerHome PreferenceInterviewer ejb-jar.xml	PropertyUpdaterEJB PropertyUpdaterHome PropertyUpdater ejb-jar.xml
Support class files	PropertyView InvalidChoiceException QuestionStateMachine	PropertyView PropertyNotFoundException RestaurantNotFoundException
Bean refs	Restaurant	Restaurant
Resource refs	–	–

Clients

Client	ClientInitialData	ClientInterviewer
Class files	ClientInitialData ClientPropertiesFactory	ClientInterviewer ClientPropertiesFactory RecommendationView QuestionStateMachine
Bean refs	PropertyUpdater	PreferenceInterviewer

In the following sections, you'll see all the classes and files that make up these three EJB components.

> We will put all the files for the entity bean version into a package **restaurant**. Later, when we modify the application for deployment to Oracle 8.1.6, we will copy most of the files to a new package **restaurant2**, and make a few further modifications. The class files that will not be deployed to Oracle are clearly indicated in the text.

Remote Interfaces

A remote interface provides access to the application logic of a component instance. Every remote interface of an EJB component – regardless of whether it is an entity or a session bean – must extend `javax.ejb.EJBObject`, which extends `java.rmi.Remote`. (An EJB 2.0 message-driven bean does not have a remote interface, because it is never called directly by clients.) `EJBObject` declares some common methods:

```
package javax.ejb;

public interface javax.ejb.EJBObject
   extends java.rmi.Remote {

   EJBHome getEJBHome()
           throws java.rmi.RemoteException;

   Handle getHandle()
           throws java.rmi.RemoteException;

   Object getPrimaryKey
           throws java.rmi.RemoteException;

   boolean isIdentical(EJBObject obj)
           throws java.rmi.RemoteException;

   void remove()
           throws java.rmi.RemoteException, javax.ejb.RemoveException;
}
```

PreferenceInterviewer Remote Interface and View Objects

As we look at the `PreferenceInterviewer`'s remote interface, we will also briefly discuss the use of view objects to move data between the client and the component. Here is the remote interface for the preference interviewer component:

```
package restaurants;

import java.util.Vector;
import java.rmi.RemoteException;
import javax.ejb.EJBObject;
import javax.ejb.EJBException;

public interface PreferenceInterviewer extends EJBObject {
```

```
    public void answerQuestion(Choice choice) throws RemoteException,
        InvalidChoiceException;

    public Choice[] getChoices() throws RemoteException;

    public String getQuestion() throws RemoteException;

    public Vector getRecommendations() throws RemoteException, EJBException;
}
```

Because EJBs can be accessed remotely, every method in the remote interface must be declared to throw `java.rmi.RemoteException`. Because `RemoteException` is a checked exception, this ensures that the client will be aware of issues such as the potential for network failure.

Experienced Java programmers will see the keyword `interface` and immediately wonder who implements that interface. The interesting answer is that the component developer does *not*; the EJB container is responsible for providing a suitable implementation itself. We briefly covered this earlier in the discussion on transaction and persistence management by the container. The container implementation of an EJB method in the remote interface will wrap various service specific method calls around the call to the actual EJB method in your implementation.

The `PreferenceInterviewer` component remembers the current question, and can compare the answer to the valid choices. The `InvalidChoiceException` would occur when the client input does not match the current state of the component. Here is that very simple class, located in `InvalidChoiceException.java`:

```
    package restaurants;

    public class InvalidChoiceException extends Exception {
        // marker class: no content necessary
    }
```

The `Choice` class and the `RecommendationView` class (instances of which are returned in the `Vector`) are examples of what are known as **view** classes. A view is just a thin state holder; its purpose is to efficiently return the information required by a remote client of a component. The alternative – accessing each element of the required state piece by piece – is untenable because of the overhead of repeated round trips across the network. There are actually three classes whose sole purpose is to provide clients with a view of application state:

❑   `Choice.java` provides the client with a code, value, and description

❑   `RecommendationView.java` provides the client with a restaurant name and chef name

❑   `PropertyView.java` provides the client with a code and value

Parameters and return types for remote methods in an EJB component must obey the rules of RMI over IIOP. In practical terms, this basically means that you must use native types (for example `int`, `long`, `double`) or serializable classes. To conform to this rule, I have made all three classes serializable. Here is the code for these simple classes:

Here is `Choice.java`:

```
package restaurants;

import java.io.Serializable;

public class Choice implements Serializable {
  private String code;
  private String value;
  private String description;

  public Choice( String code, String value, String description ) {
     this.code = code;
     this.value = value;
     this.description = description;
  }

  public String getCode() {
    return code;
  }

  public String getValue() {
    return value;
  }

  public String getDescription() {
    return description;
  }
}
```

Here is `RecommendationView.java`:

```
package restaurants;

import java.io.Serializable;

public class RecommendationView implements Serializable {
  private String restaurant;
  private String chef;

  public RecommendationView(String restaurant, String chef) {
     this.restaurant = restaurant;
     this.chef = chef;
  }

  public String getRestaurant() {
    return restaurant;
  }

  public String getChef() {
    return chef;
  }
}
```

Finally, here is `PropertyView.java`:

```java
package restaurants;

import java.io.Serializable;

public class PropertyView implements Serializable {
  private String code;
  private String value;

  public PropertyView(String code, String value) {
    this.code = code;
    this.value = value;
  }

  public String getCode() {
    return code;
  }

  public String getValue() {
    return value;
  }
}
```

PropertyUpdater Remote Interface and Session Bean façades

An interesting thing about the property updater component is that it has no significant application logic of its own, beyond the workflow implicit in calling other components. Instead, it provides an interface to the restaurant entity bean for a client to provide new data and updates to existing data.

One of the earliest and most useful design patterns used by EJB developers was a session bean **façade**, which you can use for all your clients. A façade is simply a higher-level interface that hides the details of your object model. The diagram below illustrates an example setup:

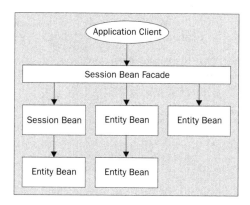

There are several advantages to using this higher level interface. Some of the major ones are:

❑ **Reduced complexity of the client code.** The façade component can aggregate application logic operations on behalf of the client. For instance, an e-commerce application that took an order for a product might then need to check inventory levels, order parts from suppliers, and schedule a job for manufacturing. As far as the client is concerned, this is all hidden behind a simple "place order" business method.

❏ **Reduced dependencies between sub-systems.** This is closely related to the previous point about reducing the complexity of the client code. Because a façade component can hide the details of the object model, a change in the application logic would not cascade through the other components in your application.

❏ **Decreased network traffic.** This is the particular advantage to a façade component that motivates its use in the case of the property updater component. Object oriented programming typically involves numerous calls to methods that implement discrete and limited functionality. The classic examples are 'get' and 'set' methods. If these method calls are occurring remotely, all the parameters and return values must be sent across the network. If the changes to application state are bundled into a single business method call to a façade component, that façade can often handle those calls on the application server where it resides without any further remote invocations.

❏ **Fewer calls on the container's services.** When a client makes a call to an EJB component, the container must ensure that the client is authorized to access that application logic. It must ensure that the application logic takes place in an appropriate transaction. It must ensure that the state of the component is properly synchronized with the state of the database. All of these container operations have a cost. Although the cost, in general, is outweighed by the benefits that the container can provide, the application should not make the container perform unnecessary work. A façade can make it possible to replace a larger number of transactions, authentications, and database synchronizations with a single one of each.

Here is the `PropertyUpdater` component's remote interface:

```
package restaurants;

import java.util.Vector;
import java.util.Date;
import java.rmi.RemoteException;
import javax.ejb.CreateException;
import javax.ejb.EJBException;
import javax.ejb.EJBObject;

public interface PropertyUpdater extends EJBObject {

    public void addProperties(String restaurantName, Vector properties) throws
        PropertyAlreadyExistsException,RestaurantNotFoundException,
        EJBException, RemoteException;

    public void changeChef(String restaurantName, String newChef) throws
        EJBException, RestaurantNotFoundException, RemoteException;

    public void changeProperties(String restaurantName, Vector properties)
        throws EJBException, PropertyNotFoundException,
            RestaurantNotFoundException, RemoteException;

    public void createRestaurant(String restaurantName,
            String location, String chef) throws CreateException,
        EJBException, RemoteException;

    public void moveRestaurant(String restaurantName, String newLocation)
        throws RestaurantNotFoundException, RemoteException, EJBException;

    public void removeProperties(String restaurantName, Vector propertyCodes)
        throws PropertyNotFoundException, RestaurantNotFoundException,
            EJBException, RemoteException;
}
```

There are three custom exception classes that these methods can throw. The `RestaurantNotFoundException` class is used to indicate that the restaurant argument passed to the business method does not correspond to an existing restaurant:

```
package restaurants;

public class RestaurantNotFoundException extends Exception {
}
```

The `PropertyNotFoundException` is used to indicate that a restaurant property that the user intended to change or remove does not exist:

```
package restaurants;

public class PropertyNotFoundException extends Exception {
}
```

The `PropertyAlreadyExistsException` is used to indicate that a restaurant property that the user intended to add already has a value:

```
package restaurants;

public class PropertyAlreadyExistsException extends Exception {
}
```

The `javax.ejb.CreateException` is used to indicate that a restaurant already exists and so cannot be created. This is a standard exception that can be thrown whenever an EJB component is created.

Restaurant Remote Interface

The restaurant remote interface provides simple "get/set" access to the restaurant's properties. Notice that the level of granularity is significantly lower than it was for the property updater component's remote interface. For instance, the restaurant component's remote interface adds, changes, or removes properties one at a time; the property updater component receives a collection of properties to be added, changed, or removed. This is a common and useful idiom. (Of course, in this simple case, there is nothing to prevent us from simply giving the restaurant component some accessor methods that take collections of properties. We could then let the client use these directly. In general, this is a bad practice for the reasons given earlier in discussing the façade pattern. I am trying to use this example to provide a pattern for a good design in more demanding situations.)

```
package restaurants;

import java.rmi.RemoteException;
import java.util.Date;
import javax.ejb.EJBObject;

public interface Restaurant extends EJBObject {
  public void moveRestaurant(String newLocation)
    throws RemoteException;

  public void changeChef(String newChef) throws RemoteException;
```

```
    public String getName() throws RemoteException;

    public String getLocation() throws RemoteException;

    public String getChef() throws RemoteException;

    public void addProperty(String code, String value, String reviewer,
       Date reviewDate) throws RemoteException, PropertyAlreadyExistsException;

    public void changeProperty(String code, String value, String reviewer,
       Date reviewDate) throws RemoteException, PropertyNotFoundException;

    public void removeProperty( String code )
       throws RemoteException, PropertyNotFoundException;
}
```

Home Interfaces

Throughout the J2EE platform, resource acquisition follows a common pattern. First, a factory object is obtained from the JNDI namespace. Second, an instance is acquired from this factory object. EJB components are resources that are acquired in exactly this way. The **home interface** represents to the client the factory object that is acquired from the JNDI namespace. The remote interface represents to the client the EJB component instance.

Every home interface, whether for a session bean or an entity bean, must extend javax.ejb.EJBHome. (An EJB 2.0 message-driven bean does not have a home interface, because it is never called directly by a client.) The EJBHome interface looks like this:

```
package javax.ejb;

public interface EJBHome extends java.rmi.Remote {

   EJBMetaData getEJBMetaData() throws java.rmi.RemoteException;

   HomeHandle getHomeHandle() throws java.rmi.RemoteException;

   void remove(Handle handle) throws java.rmi.RemoteException,
      javax.ejb.RemoveException;

   void remove(Object primaryKey) throws java.rmi.RemoteException,
      javax.ejb.RemoveException;
}
```

The component developer's home interface, derived from this interface, will add one or more methods depending on the type of bean.

PreferenceInterviewer Home Interface

A stateful session bean will add one or more create() methods. The parameters to the create() method are used by the component's implementation to initialize its state prior to use. Here is the home interface to the PreferenceInterviewer stateful session bean component from our example. The parameter to the create(String) method indicates the area in which restaurants should be located:

```
package restaurants;

import java.rmi.RemoteException;
import javax.ejb.CreateException;
import javax.ejb.EJBHome;

public interface PreferenceInterviewerHome extends EJBHome {

   PreferenceInterviewer create() throws RemoteException, CreateException;
   PreferenceInterviewer create(String s) throws RemoteException,
       CreateException;
}
```

Note that the Oracle deployment verification process **insists** that the home interface must have the no argument form of the create() method, even if it is not used in the implementation (we don't use it here). A general aim is to provide code in this section portable to the Oracle section later in the chapter while keeping to a maximum of generality with respect to the J2EE standard. That is to say, where we can make our classes compatible with both Oracle and J2EE, without affecting the implementation, we will do so.

PropertyUpdater Home Interface

A stateless session bean must define exactly one create() method with no parameters. A parameter to a create() method of a stateless session bean wouldn't make any sense – the component doesn't maintain state, so by the time the next business call came it would have forgotten all about the parameter. This makes home interfaces for stateless session beans the most boring part of EJB development; except for the class and package names, they all look exactly like our PropertyUpdater component's home interface. *(This class will not be used in the Oracle deployment)*:

```
package restaurants;

import java.rmi.RemoteException;
import javax.ejb.CreateException;
import javax.ejb.EJBHome;

public interface PropertyUpdaterHome extends EJBHome {
   PropertyUpdater create()
     throws RemoteException, CreateException;
}
```

Restaurant Home Interface, and Entity Create and Finder Methods

An entity component's home interface will have zero or more create() methods, and one or more finder() methods. As the method names imply, these correspond to creating a new instance of an entity, or finding an existing instance. If a client successfully calls create() on the home interface of an entity bean component, data will be inserted into the database. If a client destroys the component, data will be deleted from the database.

The life-span of an entity bean corresponds to the existence of its state in the underlying database. In other words, if there is an entry for a particular customer in your customer table, the customer entity bean is said to exist. If someone uses a command-line database administration tool to insert a new record into the customer table, a customer entity bean can be considered to have been created, *even if the EJB container isn't running.*

Obviously, if the enterprise has multiple paths for creating and destroying records in the database, different business logic will be called. For instance, if the record is inserted through a command-line tool or a C++ application, the application logic in the "create" methods in your EJB component will never be called.

There is a distinction between the life-cycles of session beans and entity beans that is of fundamental importance. As far as the client is concerned – ignoring any EJB container optimizations – a session bean comes into existence when the client first indicates a need for it and disappears forever when the client is finished. The client has complete and total control over its existence, and no one else is affected by these activities. No data is inserted into a database, or is accessible in any way except by that one client.

An entity bean component might have zero `create()` methods in its home interface. What would this mean? Simply that the application designer knew that there was another path for information to get into the database – perhaps an ERP system, or even a different entity component. Our restaurant component has a single method for creation that takes the restaurant name, the location, and the chef.

There are one or more finder methods in an entity's home interface that must start with the word "find." At a minimum, there will be one named `findByPrimaryKey` that takes the primary key of the entity component as a parameter, and either returns the corresponding entity or throws a `javax.ejb.ObjectNotFoundException` (which is a subclass of `javax.ejb.FinderException`).

Finder methods can return a `java.util.Collection` of matching entities, as well as a single instance of that entity type. If the finder method returns a collection, it does not throw an exception if no matching entities are found. In our restaurant application, a finder method `findByProperties` plays an important role in our application logic. It takes a location parameter and the relevant answers to the interview questions and returns a list of appropriate restaurant entities from which the session bean extracts the name and the chef and returns that information to the client. *(This class will not be used in the Oracle deployment.)*

```
package restaurants;

import java.rmi.RemoteException;
import java.util.Collection;
import javax.ejb.EJBHome;
import javax.ejb.CreateException;
import javax.ejb.FinderException;

public interface RestaurantHome extends EJBHome {
  public Restaurant create(String restaurant, String location, String chef)
    throws RemoteException, CreateException;

  public Restaurant findByPrimaryKey(String restaurant)
    throws RemoteException, FinderException;

  public Collection findByProperties(String location, Collection properties)
    throws RemoteException, FinderException;
}
```

The EJB 2.0 specification adds the ability for the component developer to add business methods to the home interface that will apply to that type of entity in general, rather than to a particular instance. For example, a business method in the home interface might provide a count of restaurants in a particular location.

Entity Primary Keys

In the previous section on home interfaces, I mentioned that the findByPrimaryKey() method takes the entity's primary key as its parameter. Every entity must have a primary key that uniquely identifies it. This key will be a Java class that follows certain rules.

If the entity's key can be represented by a simple Java type like java.lang.String or java.lang.Integer, the component developer can use that for an entity with either bean-managed or container-managed persistence. The restaurant entity falls into this category; it uses java.lang.String.

If the entity's key cannot be represented by a simple Java type (that is if the corresponding database state is identified by multiple columns), then the component developer must provide a custom key class. This custom key class must be a legal RMI-IIOP value type (basically, it must be serializable), and it must provide suitable implementations of the hashCode() and equals() methods.

For an entity component with bean-managed persistence, these are the only requirements. If the entity uses container-managed persistence, there are a few extra rules. First, because the container will need to create instances of the key, there must be a no-arguments public constructor available for its use. Second, because it must initialize the key to have appropriate values, the key class must have public state variables whose names and types correspond to the names and types of the fields in the entity that define its identity. For instance, if a restaurant entity were defined by name and location, rather than just name, it might have a primary key that looked like this *(this class is not actually used in the restaurant finder example)*:

```
package restaurants;

public class SampleRestaurantKey {
  public String name;
  public String location;

  public boolean equals(Object obj) {
    if (! (obj instanceof SampleRestaurantKey))
      return false;
    SampleRestaurantKey other = (SampleRestaurantKey) obj;
    return (name.equals( other.name ) && location.equals( other.location ));
  }

  public int hashCode() {
    return (name + location).hashCode();
  }
}
```

Implementation Classes

Most of the work in developing an EJB component will be in writing the implementation class. This class is the repository of the actual application logic of the application. Of course, like any Java class, the implementation class can call other "helper" classes.

The specific structure of the implementation class is dependent on the type of EJB component. An entity bean must implement the interface javax.ejb.EntityBean; a session bean must implement the interface javax.ejb.SessionBean; and an EJB 2.0 message driven bean must implement the interface javax.ejb.MessageDrivenBean. (This section does not cover message-driven beans further.) The bean class must implement the callbacks defined in the corresponding interface – although those callback methods will often be left blank.

The bean class must have a public method named `ejbCreate()` with matching arguments, corresponding to every `create()` method declared in the home interface. For a session bean, the return type will be `void`. For an entity bean, the return type will be the class of the primary key, and the returned value will either be `NULL` (for container-managed persistence) or an instance of the primary key (for bean-managed persistence). An entity bean must also implement a corresponding `ejbPostCreate()` method. For an entity bean with bean-managed persistence, methods must be implemented that correspond to the finder methods declared in the bean's home interface. For an entity bean with container-managed persistence, the container will implement the finder methods. For an entity using the EJB 1.1 container-managed persistence model, the deployer of the entity component will provide a description of what the finder should do in a container-specific format. For an entity using the EJB 2.0 container-managed persistence model, the component developer will provide a description of what the finder should do in a standard format.

Finally, the bean class must have business methods corresponding to those that were declared in the bean's remote interface. The signatures of those methods must match the ones in the remote interface. These methods are the *raison d'etre* for the whole of Enterprise JavaBeans technology.

You'll notice that a lot of the code that I'm going to present in this section is related to the persistence of the restaurant entity. If I had chosen to use container-managed persistence, I would not have needed to write this code. It might be useful to compare the restaurant entity to one from the e-store case study that uses container-managed persistence. You will see that no code related to persistence is necessary, and that a container-managed entity would be less costly to develop and easier to maintain. However, for those situations that require bean-managed persistence, you should find the persistence code in the restaurant entity a useful starting point. I think that the approach to managing the persistence of dependent objects (the restaurant properties) may be especially helpful if you are not already working within an object-relational mapping framework. (My recommendation is to buy, rather than build, this functionality if at all possible.)

You will also notice that the callback methods required by the EJB specification are often empty. This is not an unusual situation, even for a project of larger scope and complexity. Many of these callback methods are notifications that a certain event in the component's life-cycle has occurred. They present opportunities for resource acquisition or release, or similar management activities. Often these notifications are not relevant to a particular component and can be ignored.

There are several examples of resource acquisition in the implementation classes. These follow the familiar pattern of obtaining a factory from the JNDI namespace and getting an instance of the resource from the factory. The example of obtaining a JDBC connection in the restaurant entity bean is illustrative of another important principle of server-side programming. Once you are finished with a resource, *you should release it.* The database connection that we are using is a valuable and expensive resource. If we kept a reference to it after we were through using it for a particular purpose, the server would have to maintain that resource on our behalf. If, instead, we indicate we are finished with it (by closing the connection), the server can return it to a pool of connections for reuse on behalf of another client request. Sharing resources is the most important principle of scalable server applications, and the pattern that enables this is as follows: **acquire the resource right before you use it, and release it immediately after**. (If, for some reason, you want to keep a resource associated to a component between remote method calls, there are callbacks that allow you to manage the resource in conjunction with component life-cycle events. In general, this is not a recommended practice, but the callbacks are discussed in this chapter.)

There are several programming techniques that you won't see in the following implementation classes. In order to allow the EJB container to manage its EJB components and provide them with services, there are certain restrictions on what the EJB component developer can do. The most important ones are as follows:

❑ **You can't use threads or the threading API.** This means you can't use the `synchronized` keyword in any of your bean class methods. Synchronizing the accesses of multiple beans could lead to deadlock. (You can still use utility classes with synchronized methods, such as `Vector`.) You can't start, stop, suspend, or resume a thread.

❑ **You can't use the AWT (Abstract Windowing Toolkit).** EJBs cannot use the AWT to display information or to input information from a keyboard.

❑ **You can't act as a network server.** This means you can't listen, accept, or multi-cast on a socket. It doesn't mean you can't use sockets at all, a common misconception: you can use a socket as a client. If an EJB component were to act as a network server, it would interfere with the host application server's ability to manage its environment (resources, component life-cycle, etc.).

❑ **You can't use read/write static fields.** Static fields are only visible in one Java Virtual Machine. But many EJB containers will utilize multiple virtual machines (across multiple computers) for reasons of performance or reliability, and there is no way to propagate the update of a static field. This doesn't mean you can't use static fields at all: they just need to be read-only. You should probably declare any static field as `final` to enforce this requirement. Instead of writable static fields, you should use an appropriate shared resource, like a database. This will maintain maximum portability.

❑ **You can't use the `java.io` package.** If you want to load or store data, use a transactional resource (that is a database). The file system is not appropriate for use in a transactional environment.

❑ **You can't load a native library.** Any time you load a native library, you have security and portability concerns.

❑ **You can't use "this" as an argument to or return value from a business method.** Instead of passing the `this` reference, pass the result of `SessionContext.getEJBObject()` or `EntityContext.getEJBObject()`, which will be explained shortly.

PropertyUpdater Implementation Class

The implementation class for the property updater component is called `PropertyUpdaterEJB`. It is a stateless session bean, so it must implement the interface `javax.ejb.SessionBean`. The business methods all make use of one of the utility methods defined at the end of the class: `getRestaurantHome()` or `getRestaurant(String restaurantName)`. The `createRestaurant()` method gets the restaurant component's home interface and uses it to create a new restaurant instance. The other methods get an existing restaurant instance's remote interface and use it to update its data. *(This class will not be used in the Oracle deployment.)*

```
package restaurants;

import java.util.Collection;
import java.util.Iterator;
import java.rmi.RemoteException;
import javax.ejb.SessionBean;
import javax.ejb.SessionContext;
import javax.ejb.CreateException;
import javax.naming.InitialContext;
import javax.ejb.ObjectNotFoundException;
import javax.ejb.EJBException;

public class PropertyUpdaterEJB implements SessionBean  {
  public void createRestaurant(String restaurantName,
     String location, String chef) throws CreateException {
```

```
    try {
      RestaurantHome home = getRestaurantHome();
      home.create( restaurantName, location, chef );
    }
    catch (RemoteException re) {
      re.printStackTrace();
      throw new EJBException(re.toString());
    }
  }

  public void moveRestaurant(String restaurantName, String newLocation)
    throws RestaurantNotFoundException {
    try {
      Restaurant restaurant = getRestaurant( restaurantName );
      restaurant.moveRestaurant( newLocation );
    }
    catch ( RemoteException re ) {
      re.printStackTrace();
      throw new EJBException(re.toString());
    }
  }

  public void changeChef(String restaurantName, String newChef)
    throws RestaurantNotFoundException {
    try {
      Restaurant restaurant = getRestaurant( restaurantName );
      restaurant.changeChef( newChef );
    }
    catch (RemoteException re) {
      re.printStackTrace();
      throw new EJBException(re.toString());
    }
  }

  public void addProperties(String restaurantName, Collection properties)
    throws PropertyAlreadyExistsException, RestaurantNotFoundException {
    try {
      Restaurant restaurant = getRestaurant( restaurantName );
      Iterator iter = properties.iterator();
      while (iter.hasNext()) {
        RestaurantProperty property = (RestaurantProperty) iter.next();
        restaurant.addProperty( property.getCode(), property.getValue(),
          property.getReviewer(), property.getReviewDate() );
      }
    }
    catch ( RemoteException re ) {
      re.printStackTrace();
      throw new EJBException(re.toString());
    }
  }

  public void changeProperties(String restaurantName, Collection properties)
    throws PropertyNotFoundException, RestaurantNotFoundException {
    try {
      Restaurant restaurant = getRestaurant( restaurantName );
      Iterator iter = properties.iterator();
```

```
      while (iter.hasNext()) {
        RestaurantProperty property = (RestaurantProperty) iter.next();
        restaurant.changeProperty( property.getCode(), property.getValue(),
          property.getReviewer(), property.getReviewDate() );
      }
    }
    catch (RemoteException re) {
      re.printStackTrace();
      throw new EJBException(re.toString());
    }
  }

  public void removeProperties(String restaurantName, Collection
    propertyCodes) throws PropertyNotFoundException,
                          RestaurantNotFoundException {
    try {
      Restaurant restaurant = getRestaurant( restaurantName );
      Iterator iter = propertyCodes.iterator();
      while (iter.hasNext()) {
        restaurant.removeProperty( (String) iter.next() );
      }
    }
    catch ( RemoteException re ) {
      re.printStackTrace();
      throw new EJBException(re.toString());
    }
  }
```

The next two methods are the utility methods defined to encapsulate the acquisition of the home interface or a particular instance's remote interface for the restaurant component. We've discussed all these techniques (append this code to the previous code in the file `PropertyUpdaterEJB.java`):

```
// utility methods

private Restaurant getRestaurant( String restaurantName )
  throws RestaurantNotFoundException {
  RestaurantHome home = getRestaurantHome();
  try {
    return home.findByPrimaryKey( restaurantName );
  }
  catch (ObjectNotFoundException onfe) {
    throw new RestaurantNotFoundException();
  }
  catch (Exception e) {
    e.printStackTrace();
    throw new EJBException(e.toString());
  }
}

private RestaurantHome getRestaurantHome() {
  try {
    InitialContext initial = new InitialContext();
    RestaurantHome home = (RestaurantHome)
      initial.lookup( "java:comp/env/ejb/Restaurant" );
    return home;
  }
  catch (Exception e) {
    e.printStackTrace();
    throw new EJBException(e.toString());
  }
}
```

Finally, here are the life-cycle methods (again, append this code to the previous code in the file `PropertyUpdaterEJB.java`). The `ejbCreate()` method will often be empty for a stateless session bean. You should know that stateless session beans are almost always pooled by the EJB container and are used by more than one client (although not simultaneously; they do not need to be thread-safe). So the `ejbCreate()` method might be used to acquire resources for the component, but those resources must apply to any client:

```
// life-cycle methods

public void ejbCreate() {
}
```

Passivation and activation are described in the next section on stateful session beans. Right now, all you need to know is that the container never passivates (and therefore never activates) a stateless session bean. Therefore, these two callback methods will never be called. They need to be implemented because they are used for stateful session beans, and so are declared in the `SessionBean` interface.

```
public void ejbActivate() {
}

public void ejbPassivate() {
}
```

Any resources that were allocated in `ejbCreate()` should be deallocated in `ejbRemove()`:

```
public void ejbRemove() {
}
```

If the programmer wants to use the `SessionContext` in any business method, they must save a reference to it when the container calls `setSessionContext()`. The container will call this method right before `ejbCreate()`, so the programmer can access it in the `ejbCreate()` method if desired:

```
public void setSessionContext(SessionContext ctx) {
}
}
```

> **We will reimplement this class for the Oracle version later in this chapter. To ensure compatibility with older versions of JRE used by Oracle 8i JVM, we will not use the `Collection`, `LinkedList`, or `Iterator` API in the working example. The release notes for Oracle 8.1.7 state that a bug remains that prevents a `Collection` being returned to a client by an EJB , even though the JVM is JDK 1.2.2 compliant.**

The session context provides the following to the bean programmer:

- ❑ The `getEJBObject()` method returns the session bean's remote interface.

- ❑ The `getEJBHome()` method returns the session bean's home interface.

- ❑ The `getCallerPrincipal()` method returns the `java.security.Principal` that identifies the invoker of the bean instance's EJB object.

❏ The isCallerInRole() method tests if the session bean instance's caller has a particular role.

❏ The setRollbackOnly() method allows the instance to mark the current transaction such that the outcome of the transaction must be a rollback. Only instances of a session bean with container-managed transaction demarcation can use this method. (This is the normal case.)

❏ The getRollbackOnly() method allows the instance to test if the current transaction has been marked for rollback. Only instances of a session bean with container-managed transaction demarcation can use this method. (This is the normal case.)

❏ The getUserTransaction() method returns the javax.transaction.UserTransaction interface. The instance can use this interface to demarcate transactions and to obtain transaction status. Only instances of a session bean with bean-managed transaction demarcation can use this method. In general, you should let the container manage your transactions.

PreferenceInterviewer Implementation Class

The implementation class for the preference interviewer component is called PreferenceInterviewerEJB. It is a stateful session bean, so it must implement the interface javax.ejb.SessionBean. It has three state variables: an area in which restaurants should be found, a list of responses that the interviewee has made, and a class (called QuestionStateMachine) that keeps track of which question should be asked next:

```
package restaurants;

import java.util.Vector;
import java.util.Enumeration;
import java.rmi.RemoteException;
import javax.ejb.SessionBean;
import javax.ejb.SessionContext;
import javax.ejb.EJBException;
import javax.ejb.CreateException;
import javax.naming.InitialContext;

public class PreferenceInterviewerEJB implements SessionBean {

  private String area;
  private Vector listResponses = new Vector();
  private QuestionStateMachine questions = new QuestionStateMachine();
```

The implementation of the business methods are, for the most part, simply deferrals of processing to the restaurant entity bean and the question state machine. You should have no trouble understanding them, although I hardly recommend this hard-coded approach in your own restaurant portal application:

```
// if a question is boolean, only add it to the requirements
// when the answer was "yes"
private boolean isBooleanChoice(String code) {
    if (code.equals("vege") ||
      code.equals("late") ||
      code.equals("access") )
      return true;
    return false;
  }
```

```
private void addResponse( Choice choice ) {
  String code = choice.getCode();
  String value = choice.getValue();
  if (isBooleanChoice(code) && !value.equals( "true" ))
    return;
  listResponses.addElement( new PropertyView( code, value ) );
}

public String getQuestion() throws RemoteException {
  return questions.getNextQuestion();
}

public Choice[] getChoices() throws RemoteException {
  return questions.getChoices();
}

public void answerQuestion( Choice choice ) throws RemoteException,
  InvalidChoiceException {
  if (questions.indicateResponse( choice.getCode(), choice.getValue() ))
    addResponse( choice );
}
```

Notice how we use the restaurant's finder method to get the results, and then put those results in a collection of view objects:

```
public Vector getRecommendations() throws EJBException {
    try {
      InitialContext initial = new InitialContext();
      RestaurantHome home = (RestaurantHome)
          initial.lookup("java:comp/env/ejb/Restaurant");
      Vector recommendations = new Vector();
      Vector restaurants = (Vector) home.findByProperties(
          area, listResponses);
      Enumeration e = restaurants.elements();
      while (e.hasMoreElements()) {
        Restaurant restaurant = (Restaurant) e.nextElement();
        recommendations.addElement(new RecommendationView(
              restaurant.getName(), restaurant.getChef()));
      }
      return recommendations;
    }
    catch (Exception e) {
      e.printStackTrace();
      throw new EJBException(e.toString());
    }
  }
```

The life-cycle methods are mostly empty, except for the creation method, which takes a single parameter:

```
public void ejbCreate() throws RemoteException, CreateException {
}

public void ejbCreate(String area) throws RemoteException,
      CreateException {
  this.area = area;
}

public void ejbRemove() {
}
```

> A peculiarity of the Oracle 8.1.5/6 EJB deployment verification process is that implementation methods must throw the same exceptions as those specified in the home and remote interfaces, even if there is no code in the body of the method that could throw these exceptions. This is not incorrect code. However, since empty methods will compile fine without these exception declarations, it is a point worth bearing in mind when troubleshooting EJB deployment to Oracle. This deployment peculiarity has been fixed in 8.1.7.

Unlike stateless session beans, the EJB container cannot pool stateful session beans because they have state that is specific to a particular client. This means that if you have 10,000 people using your application, you might have 10,000 instances of that EJB component. To manage a large number of components, the EJB container can swap them in and out of temporary storage. Saving a stateful session bean to temporary storage is called **passivation**, and reactivating it is called **activation**.

The `ejbActivate()` and `ejbPassivate()` callbacks notify the stateful session bean about movement to and from temporary storage. If it has any state that cannot be serialized, it should release that state during `ejbActivate()` and reacquire it during `ejbPassivate()`:

```
    public void setSessionConnext(SessionContext ctx) {
    }

    public void ejbActivate() {
    }

    public void ejbPassivate() {
    }
}
```

The `QuestionStateMachine` class is just a simple Java support class. Two points are worth making. First, I have used static variables. While this is hardly a great design for a real restaurant portal, these variables are read-only and do not violate the programming restrictions on EJB components. Second, I have made this class serializable. This is so that passivation and activation can occur in `PreferenceInterviewerEJB` (which has an instance of `QuestionStateMachine`) without any work on my part in `ejbActivate()` and `ejbPassivate()`:

```
    package restaurants;

    import java.io.Serializable;

    public class QuestionStateMachine implements Serializable {
      private int index = 0;
      private String[] questionArray = basicQuestions;
      private Choice[][] choiceArray = basicQuestionChoices;
      boolean event = false;

      public boolean indicateResponse(String code,String value ) {
        if (code.equals("purpose")) {
          if ( value.equals("eve") )
            event = true;
          return false;
        }
        return true;
      }
```

```
public String getNextQuestion() {
  if (index == questionArray.length) {
    if (questionArray == basicQuestions) {
      questionArray = event ? eventQuestions : individualQuestions;
      choiceArray = event ? eventQuestionChoices : individualQuestionChoices;
      index = 0;
    }
    else
      return null;
  }
  return questionArray[index];
}

public Choice[] getChoices() {
  if (index == choiceArray.length)
    return null;
  return choiceArray[index++];
}

private static final String[] basicQuestions = new String[] {
  "Are you looking for dinner, or do you want to book an event?",
  "What price range (per meal) is appropriate?"
};

private static final String[] individualQuestions = new String[] {
  "What type of food are you interested in?",
  "Do you require a vegetarian menu?",
  "Do you need a restaurant that is open late?"
};

private static final String[] eventQuestions = new String[] {
  "How many people will be attending your event?",
  "Do you need a wheelchair-accessible facility?"
};

private static final Choice[][] basicQuestionChoices = new Choice[][] {
  {
    new Choice( "purpose", "din", "Dinner" ),
    new Choice( "purpose", "eve", "An event" )
  },
  {
    new Choice( "price", "a", "<10" ),
    new Choice( "price", "b", "10-20" ),
    new Choice( "price", "c", "20-40" ),
    new Choice( "price", "d", ">40" )
  }
};

private static final Choice[][] individualQuestionChoices = new Choice[][] {
  {
    new Choice( "type", "fr", "French" ),
    new Choice( "type", "it", "Italian" ),
    new Choice( "type", "mx", "Mexican" ),
    new Choice( "type", "ta", "Thai" ),
    new Choice( "type", "fs", "Fusion" ),
    new Choice( "type", "dn", "Diner" )
  }
```

```
 '
   {
     new Choice( "vege", "true", "Yes" ),
     new Choice( "vege", "false", "No" )
   },
   {
     new Choice( "late", "true", "Yes" ),
     new Choice( "late", "false", "No" )
   }
 };

 private static final Choice[][] eventQuestionChoices = new Choice[][] {
   {
     new Choice( "nmbr", "a", "fewer than 15" ),
     new Choice( "nmbr", "b", "15-30" ),
     new Choice( "nmbr", "c", "30-100" ),
     new Choice( "nmbr", "d", "100-250" ),
   },
   {
     new Choice( "access", "true", "Yes" ),
     new Choice( "access", "false", "No" )
   }
 };
}
```

Restaurant Implementation Class

The implementation class for the restaurant component is called `RestaurantEJB`. It is an entity bean, so it must implement the interface `javax.ejb.EntityBean`. It has four state variables: a name (which is also its key), a location, a chef, and a list of properties. Many of `EntityBean`'s callback methods relate to persistence. If this class used container-managed persistence, they could quite likely be left empty. Because the restaurant component uses bean-managed persistence, they will have implementations. We also provide implementations of the two finder methods that were declared in the home interface. As an implementation detail, the restaurant property collection class (`PropertyList`) cooperates in its intelligent persistence. *(This class will not be used in the Oracle deployment.)*

```java
package restaurants;

import java.sql.Connection;
import java.sql.ResultSet;
import java.sql.PreparedStatement;
import java.sql.SQLException;
import java.util.Collection;
import java.util.Iterator;
import java.util.LinkedList;
import java.util.Date;

import javax.sql.DataSource;
import javax.ejb.EntityBean;
import javax.ejb.EntityContext;
import javax.ejb.EJBException;
import javax.ejb.CreateException;
import javax.ejb.FinderException;
import javax.ejb.ObjectNotFoundException;
import javax.ejb.RemoveException;
import javax.naming.InitialContext;
```

```
public class RestaurantEJB implements EntityBean {
  private String name;
  private String location;
  private String chef;
  private PropertyList propertyList;

  EntityContext ctx;

  // business methods

  public void moveRestaurant(String newLocation) {
    location = newLocation;
  }

  public void changeChef(String newChef) {
    chef = newChef;
  }

  public String getName() {
    return name;
  }

  public String getLocation() {
    return location;
  }

  public String getChef() {
    return chef;
  }
```

For the business methods that operate on a property, I've defined a utility method that finds the property based on its code.

```
public void addProperty(String code, String value, String reviewer,
    Date date) throws PropertyAlreadyExistsException {
  if (findObject(code) != null)
    throw new PropertyAlreadyExistsException();
  propertyList.add( new RestaurantProperty(code, value, reviewer, date));
}

public void changeProperty(String code, String value, String reviewer,
  Date reviewDate) throws PropertyNotFoundException {
  RestaurantProperty property = findObject(code);
  if (property == null)
    throw new PropertyNotFoundException();
  property.setValue(value);
  property.setReviewer(reviewer);
  property.setReviewDate(reviewDate);
}

public void removeProperty(String code)
  throws PropertyNotFoundException {
  RestaurantProperty property = findObject(code);
  if (property == null)
    throw new PropertyNotFoundException();
  propertyList.remove(property);
}
```

The finder methods defined in the home interface must have corresponding `ejbFind()` methods in the implementation class of an entity with bean-managed persistence. The `ejbFindByPrimaryKey()` method will just do an "existence check":

```java
// finder methods

public String ejbFindByPrimaryKey(String restaurant)
  throws FinderException {
  Connection con = null;
  try {
    con = getConnection();

    PreparedStatement statement =
      con.prepareStatement(
      "select count(*) from restaurant where name=?" );
    statement.setString( 1, restaurant );
    ResultSet results =
      statement.executeQuery();
    if (!results.next())
      throw new EJBException(
        "Problem with SQL" );
    int count = results.getInt( 1 );
    results.close();
    statement.close();
    if (count == 1)
      return restaurant;
  }
  catch (Exception e) {
    e.printStackTrace();
    throw new EJBException(e.toString());
  }
  finally {
    try {
      if (con != null)
        con.close();
    }
    catch( Exception e) {
    }
  }
  throw new ObjectNotFoundException();
}
```

The `ejbFindByProperties()` method implements some significant application logic; it determines the list of appropriate restaurants based on the location and properties. The database access code is generated via the utility method `generatePreparedStatement()`:

```java
public Collection ejbFindByProperties( String location, Collection properties )
  throws FinderException {
  Connection con = null;
  try {
    con = getConnection();

    // This method calls a helper method to generate a prepared statement
    // that will select restaurants with the required criteria. It then
    // sets the parameters in the prepared statement--property codes
    // and values.
```

```
          String preparedStatement =
             generatePreparedStatement(properties.size());

          PreparedStatement statement =
            con.prepareStatement( preparedStatement );
          statement.setString( 1, location );

          Iterator iter = properties.iterator();
          int iterParam = 2;
          while (iter.hasNext()) {
            PropertyView property = (PropertyView) iter.next();
            statement.setString( iterParam++, property.getCode() );
            statement.setString( iterParam++, property.getValue() );
          }

          ResultSet results =
            statement.executeQuery();

          LinkedList keys = new LinkedList();
          while (results.next()) {
            keys.add( results.getString(1) );
          }
          results.close();
          statement.close();

          return keys;
        }
      catch (Exception e) {
        e.printStackTrace();
        throw new EJBException(e.toString());
      }
      finally {
        try {
          if (con != null)
            con.close();
        }
        catch( Exception e) {
        }
      }
    }
```

There must be corresponding `ejbCreate()` and `ejbPostCreate()` methods for every `create()` method defined in the home interface. (The `ejbPostCreate()` method is only used in specialized circumstances that require a reference to the component's remote interface during creation.) These methods in an entity with bean-managed persistence are responsible for initializing the state of the component and inserting that state into the underlying database and returning an instance of the primary key. For an entity that uses container-managed persistence, the `ejbCreate()` method just initializes the state of the component; the container will insert the state into the database.

If there were significant validation logic for this application, a question might exist as to the tier in which it should be placed: client, application logic, or persistence. The truth is, often it probably should exist on all three tiers. It should be placed in the EJB component for maximum portability of the component between environments, for clearer and more consistent error handling from the client's point of view, and possibly to save unnecessary processing in a transaction that should be rolled back because of an error. However, if the database will be modified outside of the EJB component, validation logic will need to exist there as well. And of course, it's helpful to performance and responsiveness to be able to validate data on the client without making a remote call to the server.

```java
// life-cycle methods

public String ejbCreate( String restaurant, String location, String chef )
  throws CreateException {
  this.name = restaurant;
  this.location = location;
  this.chef = chef;
  propertyList = new PropertyList( name );

  Connection con = null;
  PreparedStatement statement = null;
  try {
    con = getConnection();
    statement = con.prepareStatement(
      "insert into restaurant (name, location, chef ) " +
      "values (?, ?, ?)" );
    statement.setString(1, restaurant );
    statement.setString(2, location );
    statement.setString(3, chef );
    statement.executeUpdate();

    return restaurant;
  }
  catch (SQLException sqle) {
    sqle.printStackTrace();
    throw new CreateException(sqle.getMessage());
  }
  finally {
    try {
      if (con != null)
        con.close();
    }
    catch (Exception e) {
    }
  }
}

public void ejbPostCreate(String restaurant,
    String location, String chef) {
}
```

When the container calls `ejbLoad()`, a bean with bean-managed persistence must synchronize its state with that of the database. The property list's data is "lazy-loaded" in other words, the database access is deferred until the list is actually used. In some transactions, it may not need to be loaded at all. (A bean with container-managed persistence will often leave this method empty. It may, however, post-process its state after the EJB container loads it from the database.)

```java
public void ejbLoad() {
  Connection con = null;
  PreparedStatement statement = null;
  ResultSet results = null;
  try {
    con = getConnection();
```

```
        String primKey =
          (String) ctx.getPrimaryKey();
        statement = con.prepareStatement(
          "select location, chef from restaurant where name =?");
        statement.setString(1, primKey );
        results = statement.executeQuery();
        boolean hadData = results.next();
        if (hadData){
          this.name = primKey;
          this.location = results.getString(1);
          this.chef = results.getString(2);
          propertyList = new PropertyList( name );
        }
        results.close();
        statement.close();
        if (!hadData)
          throw new EJBException("Record not found");
      }
    catch (Exception e) {
      e.printStackTrace();
      throw new EJBException(e.toString());
    }
    finally {
      try {
        if (con != null)
          con.close();
      }
      catch( Exception e) {
      }
    }
  }
```

When a container calls `ejbRemove()` on a bean with bean-managed persistence, it must remove its state from the database. A bean with container-managed persistence will often leave this method empty, as the EJB container is responsible for its persistence operations.

```
public void ejbRemove() throws RemoveException {
    Connection con = null;
    PreparedStatement statement = null;
    try {
      propertyList.clear();
      propertyList.store();
      con = getConnection();
      statement = con.prepareStatement(
        "delete from restaurant where name = ?" );
      statement.executeUpdate();
    }
    catch (SQLException sqle) {
      sqle.printStackTrace();
      throw new EJBException(sqle.toString());
    }
    finally {
      try {
        con.close();
      }
      catch (SQLException sqle) {
      }
    }
  }
```

When the container calls `ejbStore()`, a bean with bean-managed persistence must save its state to the database. (A bean with container-managed persistence will often leave this method empty. It may, however, pre-process its state before the EJB container saves it to the database.)

```
public void ejbStore() {
  Connection con = null;
  try {
    con = getConnection();

    PreparedStatement statement =
      con.prepareStatement(
        "update restaurant set location=?, chef=? where name=?");
    statement.setString(1, location );
    statement.setString(2, chef );
    statement.setString(3, name );
    int updated = statement.executeUpdate();
     statement.close();
    if (updated != 1)
      throw new EJBException(
        "Record not updated" );
    propertyList.store();
  }
  catch (Exception e) {
    e.printStackTrace();
    throw new EJBException(e.toString());
  }
  finally {
    try {
      if (con != null)
        con.close();
    }
      catch( Exception e) {
    }
  }
}
```

The `ejbActivate()` and `ejbPassivate()` methods do not have the same purpose in an entity bean that they do in a stateful session bean; instead, they are called when the entity instance is associated or disassociated with an identity. The timing of these calls is related to the EJB container's caching strategy. The EJB component developer will usually leave them blank:

```
public void ejbActivate() {
}

public void ejbPassivate() {
}
```

To find the restaurant entity's data in the database, you will need the primary key. By the time that `ejbLoad()` is called, the primary key has been associated with the entity and is available from its context. This entity context is associated with the bean by a callback method, just like the session context is associated with a session bean. Because we'll be needing it in `ejbLoad()`, we save it in an instance variable. The `setEntityContext()` and `unsetEntityContext()` methods can also be used to associate and disassociate resources that can be used by the instance regardless of its identity. In general, you shouldn't maintain per-component resources (for example resources that you associate with a component between remote method calls, as discussed earlier in the section on resource acquisition).

```
  public void setEntityContext(EntityContext ctx) {
    this.ctx = ctx;
  }

  public void unsetEntityContext() {
    ctx = null;
  }
```

The private implementation methods don't present anything new as far as EJB components are concerned. The getConnection() method follows the normal resource-acquisition pattern of J2EE components.

```
  // implementation helpers

  private Connection getConnection() {
    try {
      InitialContext initial = new InitialContext();
      DataSource ds = (DataSource)
        initial.lookup( "java:comp/env/jdbc/restaurantDB" );
      return ds.getConnection();
    }
    catch (Exception e) {
      e.printStackTrace();
      throw new EJBException(e.toString());
    }
  }

  private String generatePreparedStatement(int count) {
    if (count == 0)
      return "select name from restaurant where location = ?";

    StringBuffer buffer = new StringBuffer(
      "select name from restaurant t1 where t1.location = ? and " );
    buffer.append( count );
    buffer.append( " = (select count(*) from restaurantproperty t2 where " );
    buffer.append( "t2.restaurant = t1.name and (" );

    for (int iter=0; iter<count; iter++) {
      if (iter!=0)
        buffer.append( " or " );
      buffer.append( " (code=? and val=?) " );
    }

    buffer.append( "))" );
    return buffer.toString();
  }

  private RestaurantProperty findObject( String code ) {
    // we could make an index of this w/ a map
    Iterator iter = propertyList.iterator();
    while (iter.hasNext()) {
      RestaurantProperty property = (RestaurantProperty) iter.next();
      if (property.getCode().equals( code ))
        return property;
    }
    return null;
  }
}
```

There are two features of the generatePreparedStatement() method which are worth mentioning in the context of this book. First, you will notice that it creates an SQL query string "dynamically", that is, it pieces together the query using some conditional logic and external parameters. This is at the same time powerful and dangerous: it is powerful because it is not an easy feature to code directly in this way in PL/SQL; it requires care because the dynamic creation of query strings can lead to efficiency and integrity problems within the database tier. Some issues of this nature are discussed in Chapter 16.

The RestaurantProperty class represents the dependent object of the restaurant component. For the most part, it is just a data-holder (and we even use it as a view object). It does have one interesting feature: a modified flag that allows us to tune our database updates (only modified properties are synchronized with the database).

```
package restaurants;

import java.util.Date;
import java.io.Serializable;

public class RestaurantProperty implements Serializable {
    private String code;
    private String value;
    private String reviewer;
    private Date reviewDate;

    private boolean modified;

    public RestaurantProperty() {
    }

    public RestaurantProperty( String code, String value,
        String reviewer, Date reviewDate ) {
        this.code = code;
        this.value = value;
        this.reviewer = reviewer;
        this.reviewDate = reviewDate;
        modified = true;
    }

    public String getCode() {
        return code;
    }

    public void setCode(String code ) {
        this.code = code;
        modified = true;
    }

    public String getValue() {
        return value;
    }

    public void setValue(String value ) {
        this.value = value;
        modified = true;
    }
```

```
    public String getReviewer() {
      return reviewer;
    }

    public void setReviewer(String reviewer) {
      this.reviewer = reviewer;
      modified = true;
    }

    public Date getReviewDate() {
      return reviewDate;
    }

    public void setReviewDate(Date date) {
      this.reviewDate = date;
      modified = true;
    }

    public boolean isModified() {
      return modified;
    }

    public void clearModifiedFlag() {
      modified = false;
    }
}
```

The interesting thing about the `PropertyList` class is how it cooperates in its own persistence. A collection class is often a convenient place to track additions, deletions, and modifications to an object's properties. These will correspond to SQL inserts, deletes, and updates. Also, the list is the most convenient place to implement lazy-loading; when it is used, it first checks to ensure it has been loaded. *(This class will not be used in the Oracle deployment.)*

```
package restaurants;

import java.util.Collections;
import java.util.Collection;
import java.util.LinkedList;
import java.util.HashSet;
import java.util.List;
import java.util.Set;
import java.util.Iterator;
import java.sql.Connection;
import java.sql.PreparedStatement;
import java.sql.ResultSet;
import java.sql.SQLException;
import javax.naming.InitialContext;
import javax.sql.DataSource;
import javax.ejb.EJBException;

public class PropertyList implements Collection {
    private LinkedList deletedItems = new LinkedList();
    private HashSet originalSet = new HashSet();
    private LinkedList backingList = new LinkedList();
    private boolean loaded = false;

    private String restaurant;

    public PropertyList(String restaurant) {
      this.restaurant = restaurant;
    }
```

We can't alter the interface of the `java.util.Collection` class to throw `SQLException`, which is a checked exception. Instead, we catch it here and throw an `EJBException` (which is an unchecked exception) instead. The EJB container behaves differently when an unchecked exception is thrown from a business method: it rolls back any current transaction and discards the instance from the container. This is to simplify error-handling for the component developer, who does not have to write recovery code.

```java
private void checkLoaded() {
  try {
    if (!loaded)
      load();
  }
  catch (SQLException sqle) {
    sqle.printStackTrace();
    throw new EJBException( sqle );
  }
}

void load() throws SQLException {
  Connection con = null;
  PreparedStatement statement = null;
  ResultSet results = null;
  try {
    con = getConnection();
    statement = con.prepareStatement(
      "select code, val, reviewer, reviewdate from restaurantproperty " +
        "where restaurant = ?" );
    statement.setString( 1, restaurant );
    results = statement.executeQuery();
    while (results.next()) {
      String code = results.getString(1);
      String value = results.getString(2);
      String reviewer = results.getString(3);
      java.sql.Date reviewDateSQL = results.getDate(4);
      java.util.Date reviewDate = new java.util.Date(
          reviewDateSQL.getTime() );
      RestaurantProperty property = new RestaurantProperty(
        code, value, reviewer, reviewDate );
      addFromStore( property );
    }
    loaded = true;
  }
  finally {
    try {
      if (con != null)
        con.close();
      if (results != null)
        results.close();
      if (statement != null)
        statement.close();
    }
    catch (Exception e) {
    }
  }
}
```

If the list hasn't even been loaded, then it certainly hasn't been modified.

```
void store() throws SQLException {
  if (!loaded) // don't bother if no changes made
    return;
  Connection con = null;
  PreparedStatement statement = null;
  try {
    con = getConnection();
```

We iterate through our list of deleted properties and delete them from the database.

```
// deleted objects
statement = con.prepareStatement(
  "delete from restaurantproperty where " +
  "restaurant=? and code=?" );
Iterator iterDeletedObjects =
  deletedItems.iterator();
while (iterDeletedObjects.hasNext()) {
  RestaurantProperty property =
    (RestaurantProperty) iterDeletedObjects.next();
  statement.setString( 1, restaurant );
  statement.setString( 2, property.getCode() );
  statement.executeUpdate();
}
statement.close();

// new objects
```

Any object that isn't in our set of original objects is a new object, and is inserted into the database.

```
statement = con.prepareStatement(
  "insert into restaurantproperty (restaurant, " +
    "code, val, reviewer, reviewdate) " +
    "values (?, ?, ?, ?, ?)" );
Iterator iterCurrentObjects =
  backingList.iterator();
while ( iterCurrentObjects.hasNext() )
{
  RestaurantProperty property =
    (RestaurantProperty) iterCurrentObjects.next();
  if (!originalSet.contains( property )) {
    statement.setString( 1, restaurant );
    statement.setString( 2, property.getCode() );
    statement.setString( 3, property.getValue() );
    statement.setString( 4, property.getReviewer() );
    statement.setDate( 5, new java.sql.Date(
      property.getReviewDate().getTime()) );
    statement.executeUpdate();
  }
}
statement.close();
```

For the remaining objects, we check to see if they have been modified. If yes, we update their records in the database.

```
      // updated objects
      statement = con.prepareStatement(
        "update restaurantproperty set val=?, " +
          "reviewer=?, reviewdate=? where restaurant=? " +
          "and code=?" );
      iterCurrentObjects =
        backingList.iterator();
      while (iterCurrentObjects.hasNext()) {
        RestaurantProperty property =
          (RestaurantProperty) iterCurrentObjects.next();
        if (originalSet.contains( property ) &&
          property.isModified()) {
          statement.setString(1, property.getValue() );
          statement.setString(2, property.getReviewer() );
          statement.setDate(3, new java.sql.Date(
            property.getReviewDate().getTime()));
          statement.setString(4, restaurant );
          statement.setString(5, property.getCode() );
          statement.executeUpdate();
        }
      }
      statement.close();

      // account for synchronization with database
      Iterator iterAll = backingList.iterator();
      while (iterAll.hasNext()) {
        RestaurantProperty prop = (RestaurantProperty) iterAll.next();
        prop.clearModifiedFlag();
      }
      originalSet.addAll( backingList );
      deletedItems.clear();
    }
    finally {
      try {
        if (con != null)
          con.close();
        if (statement != null)
          statement.close();
      }
      catch (Exception e) {
      }
    }
  }
```

This method is used when the properties are retrieved from the database.

```
  void addFromStore(RestaurantProperty property) {
    property.clearModifiedFlag();
    originalSet.add( property );
    backingList.add( property );
  }
```

We must implement the basic collection interface methods.

```
public int size() {
   checkLoaded();
   return backingList.size();
}

public boolean isEmpty() {
   checkLoaded();
   return backingList.isEmpty();
}

public boolean contains(Object o) {
   checkLoaded();
   return backingList.contains(o);
}
```

We make the iterator refer to an unmodifiable list so that it can't be used to change the contents without the property list's knowledge. A more sophisticated implementation would simply return a subclassed iterator, which would notify the property list about any changes.

```
public Iterator iterator() {
   checkLoaded();
   return Collections.unmodifiableCollection( backingList ).iterator();
}

public Object[] toArray(){
   checkLoaded();
   return backingList.toArray();
}

public Object[] toArray(Object[] a) {
   checkLoaded();
   return backingList.toArray( a );
}

public boolean add(Object o) {
   checkLoaded();
   return backingList.add( o );
}

public boolean remove(Object o) {
   checkLoaded();
   deletedItems.add( o );
   return backingList.remove( o );
}

public boolean containsAll(Collection c) {
   checkLoaded();
   return backingList.containsAll( c );
}
```

```
public boolean addAll(Collection c) {
  checkLoaded();
  return backingList.addAll( c );
}

public boolean removeAll(Collection c) {
  checkLoaded();
  deletedItems.addAll( c );
  return backingList.removeAll( c );
}

public boolean retainAll(Collection c) {
  checkLoaded();
  LinkedList tempList = new LinkedList();
  tempList.addAll( backingList );
  tempList.removeAll( c );
  deletedItems.addAll( tempList );
  return backingList.retainAll( c );
}

public void clear() {
  checkLoaded();
  deletedItems.addAll( backingList );
  backingList.clear();
}
```

Once again, we retrieve a resource using the standard pattern. Our helper class has exactly the same namespace as the EJB component (of which it is a part).

```
// implementation helpers
private Connection getConnection() {
  try {
    InitialContext initial = new InitialContext();
    DataSource ds = (DataSource)
      initial.lookup( "java:comp/env/jdbc/restaurantDB" );

    return ds.getConnection();
  }
  catch (Exception e) {
    e.printStackTrace();
    throw new EJBException(e);
  }
}
}
```

Deployment Descriptor

The deployment descriptor contains the structural information about the EJB components in a JAR, declares the bean's external dependencies, and specifies certain information about how services such as transactions and security should work. It must be named `ejb-jar.xml`, and must go into the META-INF directory within the JAR. You will most likely produce this file using a tool, probably one that comes with your chosen application server or IDE. I won't explain each entry – many of them are fairly self-explanatory – but I will comment on a few:

605

```xml
<?xml version="1.0"?>

<!DOCTYPE ejb-jar PUBLIC
   "-//Sun Microsystems, Inc.//DTD Enterprise JavaBeans 1.1//EN"
   "http://java.sun.com/j2ee/dtds/ejb-jar_1_1.dtd">

<ejb-jar>
 <enterprise-beans>

   <session>
      <ejb-name>RestaurantDataUpdater</ejb-name>
      <home>restaurants.PropertyUpdaterHome</home>
      <remote>restaurants.PropertyUpdater</remote>
      <ejb-class>restaurants.PropertyUpdaterEJB</ejb-class>
      <session-type>Stateless</session-type>
```

You should rarely have the need to manage transactions yourself. (If you did, the transaction type would be "Bean".)

```xml
      <transaction-type>Container</transaction-type>
```

Resource references, such as database connections or EJB references, must be declared in the deployment descriptor. These will be resolved to refer to actual resources when the JAR is deployed in an EJB container. The `<ejb-link>` element is a way to resolve an EJB reference to a particular EJB. You should organize your EJB references in a subcontext called `ejb`:

```xml
      <ejb-ref>
         <ejb-ref-name>ejb/Restaurant</ejb-ref-name>
         <ejb-ref-type>Entity</ejb-ref-type>
         <home>restaurants.RestaurantHome</home>
         <remote>restaurants.Restaurant</remote>
         <ejb-link>Restaurant</ejb-link>
      </ejb-ref>
   </session>

   <session>
      <ejb-name>PreferenceInterviewer</ejb-name>
      <home>restaurants.PreferenceInterviewerHome</home>
      <remote>restaurants.PreferenceInterviewer</remote>
      <ejb-class>restaurants.PreferenceInterviewerEJB</ejb-class>
      <session-type>Stateful</session-type>
      <transaction-type>Container</transaction-type>
      <ejb-ref>
         <ejb-ref-name>ejb/Restaurant</ejb-ref-name>
         <ejb-ref-type>Entity</ejb-ref-type>
         <home>restaurants.RestaurantHome</home>
         <remote>restaurants.Restaurant</remote>
         <ejb-link>Restaurant</ejb-link>
      </ejb-ref>
   </session>

   <entity>
      <ejb-name>Restaurant</ejb-name>
      <home>restaurants.RestaurantHome</home>
      <remote>restaurants.Restaurant</remote>
      <ejb-class>restaurants.RestaurantEJB</ejb-class>
         <persistence-type>Bean</persistence-type>
         <prim-key-class>java.lang.String</prim-key-class>
         <reentrant>False</reentrant>
```

Here is an example of declaring a reference to a database. You should organize your database references in a subcontext called `jdbc`:

```
    <resource-ref>
        <res-ref-name>jdbc/restaurantDB</res-ref-name>
        <res-type>javax.sql.DataSource</res-type>
        <res-auth>Container</res-auth>
    </resource-ref>
  </entity>


</enterprise-beans>
```

The `<assembly-descriptor>` element contains the information about how the EJBs are composed into a larger application deployment unit. The transaction and security attributes of the methods are defined here. (This example does not define any security.)

```
<assembly-descriptor>

  <container-transaction>
    <method>
        <ejb-name>RestaurantDataUpdater</ejb-name>
        <method-name>*</method-name>
    </method>
    <trans-attribute>Required</trans-attribute>
  </container-transaction>
  <container-transaction>
    <method>
        <ejb-name>PreferenceInterviewer</ejb-name>
        <method-name>*</method-name>
    </method>
    <trans-attribute>Required</trans-attribute>
  </container-transaction>
  <container-transaction>
    <method>
        <ejb-name>Restaurant</ejb-name>
        <method-name>*</method-name>
    </method>
    <trans-attribute>Required</trans-attribute>
  </container-transaction>

</assembly-descriptor>
</ejb-jar>
```

Deployment

You should package the class files and deployment descriptor in a JAR file using your development environment tools (or the command line tool in the JDK). The JAR should look like this:

```
restaurants/Choice.class
restaurants/InvalidChoiceException.class
restaurants/PreferenceInterviewer.class
restaurants/PreferenceInterviewerEJB.class
restaurants/PreferenceInterviewerHome.class
```

```
restaurants/PropertyAlreadyExistsException.class
restaurants/PropertyList.class
restaurants/PropertyNotFoundException.class
restaurants/PropertyUpdater.class
restaurants/PropertyUpdaterEJB.class
restaurants/PropertyUpdaterHome.class
restaurants/PropertyView.class
restaurants/QuestionStateMachine.class
restaurants/RecommendationView.class
restaurants/Restaurant.class
restaurants/RestaurantEJB.class
restaurants/RestaurantHome.class
restaurants/RestaurantNotFoundException.class
restaurants/RestaurantProperty.class
META-INF/ejb-jar.xml
```

You can now deploy this application and try it out. The deployment process is specific to the EJB container that you use and its proprietary tools. One thing you will need to do is to resolve any resource references to actual resources. For the restaurant finder example, this means that the reference to a database connection `jdbc/restaurantDB` will need to be tied to an actual database.

In the J2EE reference application server, you may add resource details to the `default.properties` file with, for example, the following two lines:

```
jdbc.drivers=oracle.jdbc.driver.OracleDriver
jdbc.datasources=jdbc/restaurantDB|jdbc:oracle:thin:@dbserver:1521:proead
```

This will instruct the server (on start up) to publish, in the JNDI namespace at `java:comp/env/jdbc /restaurantDB`, an object implementing `DataSource` from which the EJBs can acquire `java.sql.Connection` objects via the Oracle driver classes. In this configuration, the Oracle driver package `classes111.zip` or `classes12.zip` needs to be in the `lib/system` directory of the J2EE installation. Authentication for the connection should be configured using the program `deploytool` that comes with the installation, not in the driver URL.

Deploying the EJBs of this chapter to a server such as Sun's reference J2EE server (http://java.sun.com/j2ee) or the Orion server (http://www.orionserver.com) is an excellent exercise preliminary to dealing with the subleties of deployment on Oracle platforms.

Sample Clients

There are two sample clients. The first one sets up some initial restaurant data.

```
package restaurants;

import javax.naming.InitialContext;
import java.util.Properties;
import java.util.Date;
import java.util.Vector;

public class ClientInitialData {
  static String reviewer = "Christina Coughlin";
  static Date reviewDate = new Date();
  static Vector toVector(Object[] obs) {
    Vector v = new Vector();
    for (int i = 0;i < obs.length; ++i) {
```

```
            v.addElement(obs[i]);
        }
        return v;
    }

    static RestaurantProperty[] samplePropertyList1 = new RestaurantProperty[]
    {
        new RestaurantProperty("type","dn",reviewer,reviewDate),
        new RestaurantProperty("vege","false",reviewer,reviewDate),
        new RestaurantProperty("late","false",reviewer,reviewDate),
        new RestaurantProperty("price","a",reviewer,reviewDate)
    };

    static RestaurantProperty[] samplePropertyList2 = new RestaurantProperty[]
    {
        new RestaurantProperty("type","dn",reviewer, reviewDate),
        new RestaurantProperty("vege","true",reviewer,reviewDate),
        new RestaurantProperty("late","true",reviewer,reviewDate),
        new RestaurantProperty("price", "a",reviewer,reviewDate)
    };

    static RestaurantProperty[] samplePropertyList3 = new RestaurantProperty[]
    {
        new RestaurantProperty("type","fs",reviewer,reviewDate),
        new RestaurantProperty("vege","true",reviewer,reviewDate),
        new RestaurantProperty("late","true",reviewer,reviewDate),
        new RestaurantProperty("price","d",reviewer,reviewDate)
    };

    public static void main(String[] args) {
        try {
            Properties prop =
                ClientPropertiesFactory.getInitialContextProperties();
            InitialContext initial = new InitialContext( prop );

            String oracleservice = "sess_iiop://dbserver:2481:proead";

            PropertyUpdaterHome home = (PropertyUpdaterHome)
                initial.lookup(oracleservice + "/test/PropertyUpdater");
            // create some sample restaurants
            PropertyUpdater propertyUpdater = home.create();
            propertyUpdater.createRestaurant("McLanes","Schenectady","Ruth");
            propertyUpdater.addProperties("McLanes",
                toVector(samplePropertyList1));
            propertyUpdater.createRestaurant("Ground Round",
                "Schenectady","Day Cook");
            propertyUpdater.addProperties("Ground Round",
                toVector(samplePropertyList2));
            propertyUpdater.createRestaurant("Eds","Schenectady","Ed");
            propertyUpdater.addProperties("Eds", toVector(samplePropertyList1));
            propertyUpdater.createRestaurant("Gregs","Schenectady",
                "Ellen Daviero");
            propertyUpdater.addProperties("Gregs",toVector(samplePropertyList2));
            propertyUpdater.createRestaurant("Trio","Evanston","Shawn McClain" );
            propertyUpdater.addProperties("Trio",toVector(samplePropertyList3));
        }
        catch (Exception e)  {
            e.printStackTrace();
        }
    }
}
```

This second client performs an interview to determine an appropriate restaurant. It gives the logic a test, but it's light on the error handling. Obviously, a real restaurant portal would have a web client with more sophistication.

```java
package restaurants;

import javax.naming.Context;
import javax.naming.InitialContext;
import java.util.Properties;
import java.util.Date;
import java.util.Hashtable;
import java.util.Vector;
import java.util.Enumeration;

import oracle.aurora.jndi.sess_iiop.ServiceCtx;

public class ClientInterview {

    private PreferenceInterviewer interviewer = null;
    private Choice[] choices;
    private String question;

    public Choice[] getChoices() {
        return choices;
    }

    public String getQuestion() {
        return question;
    }


    public void init() throws Exception {
        Properties prop =
            ClientPropertiesFactory.getInitialContextProperties();
        Context initial = new InitialContext(prop);

        String oracleservice = "sess_iiop://dbserver:2481:proead";
        PreferenceInterviewerHome home = (PreferenceInterviewerHome)
            initial.lookup(oracleservice + "/test/PreferenceInterviewer");

        interviewer = home.create("Schenectady");
    }


    public void nextQuestion() {
        try {
            if ((question = interviewer.getQuestion()) == null) {
                choices = null;
            }
            else choices = interviewer.getChoices();
        }
        catch (Exception e) {
            e.printStackTrace();
        }
    }
}
```

```
    public void answerQuestion(int number) {
       try {
          interviewer.answerQuestion(choices[number]);
       }
       catch (Exception e) {
          e.printStackTrace();
       }
    }

    public Vector getRecommendations() {
      Vector recommendations = null;
      try {
        recommendations = interviewer.getRecommendations();
      }
      catch (Exception e) {
        e.printStackTrace();
      }
      return recommendations;
    }

    public void close() {
       try {
          if (interviewer != null) interviewer.remove();
       }
       catch (Exception ignore) {
       }
    }

    public static void main(String[] args) {
      ClientInterview ci = new ClientInterview();
      try {
        ci = new ClientInterview();
        ci.init();
        byte[] b = new byte[5];
        Choice choice = null;
        ci.nextQuestion();
        Choice[] chs = ci.getChoices();
        while ( chs != null ) {
          System.out.println( ci.getQuestion() );
          for (int iter=0; iter< chs.length; iter++) {
            choice = chs[iter];
            System.out.println( "#" + iter + " " +
                choice.getDescription() );
          }
          System.in.read(b);
          int chc = b[0]-48;
          ci.answerQuestion(chc) ;
          ci.nextQuestion();
          chs = ci.getChoices();
        }
        Vector recommendations = ci.getRecommendations();
        Enumeration e = recommendations.elements();
        System.out.println( "The following restaurants meet your criteria:");
        while (e.hasMoreElements()) {
          RecommendationView view = (RecommendationView) e.nextElement();
          System.out.println( "Restaurant: " + view.getRestaurant()
```

```
             + " with chef: " + view.getChef() );
      }
    }
    catch (Exception ie) {
      ie.printStackTrace();
    }
    finally {
      ci.close();
    }
  }
}
```

You will need to consult the documentation of your application server to work out how to configure the InitialContext object for your clients. That is, you should adapt accordingly the Context configuration properties in the ClientPropertiesFactory class. The above clients are configured for access to EJBs running in an Oracle 8i database with TNS name proead on host dbserver listening on port 1521. We now proceed to show how to deploy a session-bean-only approach to the Oracle JVM, such that these clients can connect to them and run.

A Solution without Entities

It is possible to modify this solution to avoid the use of entity beans. As mentioned earlier, this may be necessary or desirable for any one of several reasons: because your application server does not support entity beans; because your object-relational mapping tool does not integrate with entity beans in your container, but can be used from session beans; because you are using an object database back end and you perceive entity beans as adding little value; or for reasons of your own. I design my applications to use entity beans, but taking a session beans-only approach is a legitimate architectural decision.

It was not too difficult to port our restaurant finder application to a session bean-only approach and deploy it to the Oracle 8.1.6 JVM. We simply replace the code that used the restaurant entity bean with code that used data access components. In a real-world situation, these data-access components would often be generated by a tool. In chapter 17, we look at one technology for automatic generation of 'entity objects' directly from database schemas.

The changes to the above package are as follows:

❑   Two new classes: PropertyDataObject.java and RestaurantDataObject.java

❑   Two classes were changed: PreferenceInterviewerEJB.java, PropertyUpdaterEJB.java

❑   Four files became unnecessary: Restaurant.java, RestaurantHome.java, RestaurantEJB.java, and PropertyList.java

❑   In place of the ejb-jar.xml deployment descriptor we introduce the .ejb descriptor format currently supported by Oracle, one for each session bean

To keep things simple, we should copy all the files over to a new package (restaurants2 rather than restaurants). Here is a table summarizing the files used:

Bean	PreferenceInterviewer	PropertyUpdater
Type	Stateful Session	Stateless Session

Bean class files	`PreferenceInterviewerEJB`
	`PreferenceInterviewerHome`
	`PreferenceInterviewer`
		`PropertyUpdaterEJB`
		`PropertyUpdaterHome`
		`PropertyUpdater`

	`PreferenceInterviewer.ejb`	`PropertyUpdater.ejb`
Descriptor:		

Support class files	`PropertyView`
	`InvalidChoiceException`
	`QuestionStateMachine`
	`RestaurantDataObject`
		`PropertyView`
		`PropertyNotFoundException`
		`RestaurantNotFoundException`
		`PropertyDataObject`

Bean refs	–	–
Resource refs	Oracle 8i database via the internal `OracleDriver` `defaultConnection()` in `RestaurantDataObject`	Oracle 8i database via the internal `OracleDriver` `defaultConnection()` in `PropertyDataObject` and `RestaurantDataObject`

The clients are the same for this part.

The `RestaurantDataObject` object is mostly just SQL code (and could just as easily be calls to, for example, a stored procedure):

```
package restaurants2;

import java.sql.Connection;
import java.sql.PreparedStatement;
import javax.naming.InitialContext;
import java.util.Vector;
import java.util.Enumeration;
import java.sql.ResultSet;
import javax.ejb.EJBException;

public class RestaurantDataObject {
  void createRestaurant(String name, String chef, String location)
        throws EJBException {
    Connection con = null;
    PreparedStatement statement = null;
    try {
      con = getConnection();
      statement = con.prepareStatement(
        "insert into restaurant (name, location, chef ) " +
        "values (?, ?, ?)" );
      statement.setString(1, name );
      statement.setString(2, location );
      statement.setString(3, chef );
      statement.executeUpdate();
    }
    catch (Exception e) {
      e.printStackTrace();
      throw new EJBException(e.toString());
    }
```

You'll notice it's a little light on error-handling, failing to distinguish what caused a problem when an exception is thrown:

```
finally {
    try {
        if (con != null)
            con.close();
    }
    catch (Exception e ) {
    }
    }
}

void setChef(String name, String chef) throws EJBException {
    Connection con = null;
    try {
        con = getConnection();

        PreparedStatement statement =
            con.prepareStatement(
                "update restaurant set chef=? where name=?");
        statement.setString(1, chef );
        statement.setString(2, name );
        int updated = statement.executeUpdate();
        statement.close();
        if (updated != 1)
            throw new EJBException(
                "Record not updated");
    }
    catch (Exception e) {
        e.printStackTrace();
        throw new EJBException(e.toString());
    }
```

Always close a connection when you are done using it, so it can be returned to the pool:

```
finally {
    try {
        if (con != null)
            con.close();
    }
    catch (Exception e ) {
    }
    }
}

void setLocation(String name, String location) throws EJBException {
    Connection con = null;
    try {
        con = getConnection();

        PreparedStatement statement =
            con.prepareStatement(
                "update restaurant set location=? where name=?");
        statement.setString(1, location );
```

```
      statement.setString(2, name );
      int updated = statement.executeUpdate();
       statement.close();
      if (updated != 1)
        throw new RuntimeException("Record not updated" );
    }
  catch (Exception e) {
    e.printStackTrace();
    throw new EJBException( e.toString() );
  }
  finally {
    try {
      if (con != null)
        con.close();
    }
    catch( Exception e) {
    }
  }
}
```

The getRecommendations() and generatePreparedStatement() are taken directly from our first implementation:

```
Vector getRecommendations(String location, Vector properties)
  throws EJBException {
  Connection con = null;
  try {
    con = getConnection();

    String preparedStatement = generatePreparedStatement(properties.size());

    PreparedStatement statement =
      con.prepareStatement( preparedStatement );
    statement.setString( 1, location );

    Enumeration e = properties.elements();
    int iterParam = 2;
    while (e.hasMoreElements()) {
      PropertyView property = (PropertyView) e.nextElement();
      statement.setString( iterParam++, property.getCode() );
      statement.setString( iterParam++, property.getValue() );
    }

    ResultSet results =
      statement.executeQuery();

    Vector recommendationViews = new Vector();
    while (results.next()) {
      RecommendationView view =
        new RecommendationView( results.getString(1),
        results.getString(2) );
      recommendationViews.addElement( view );
    }
    results.close();
    statement.close();
```

```
            return recommendationViews;
        }
    catch (Exception e) {
        e.printStackTrace();
        return null;
    }
    finally {
        try {
            if (con != null)
                con.close();
        }
        catch( Exception e) {
        }
    }
}
}


private String generatePreparedStatement(int count) {
    if (count == 0)
        return "select name, chef from restaurant where location = ?";

    StringBuffer buffer = new StringBuffer(
        "select name, chef from restaurant t1 where t1.location = ? and ");
    buffer.append(count);
    buffer.append(" = (select count(*) from restaurantproperty t2 where ");
    buffer.append("t2.restaurant = t1.name and (" );

    for (int iter=0; iter<count; iter++) {
        if (iter!=0)
            buffer.append( " or " );
        buffer.append( " (code=? and val=?) " );
    }

    buffer.append( "))" );
    return buffer.toString();
}
```

To acquire its connection, we use the internal Oracle driver:

```
private Connection getConnection() throws EJBException {
    try {
        return new oracle.jdbc.driver.OracleDriver().defaultConnection();
    }
    catch (Exception e) {
        e.printStackTrace();
        throw new EJBException(e.toString() );
    }
}
```

The `PropertyDataObject` introduces nothing new. It simply implements the SQL code and the resource acquisition pattern that we saw earlier in the EJB:

```
package restaurants2;

import java.sql.Connection;
import java.sql.PreparedStatement;
import javax.naming.InitialContext;
import javax.ejb.EJBException;

public class PropertyDataObject {
  void createProperty( String restaurant, RestaurantProperty property )
    throws EJBException {
    Connection con = null;
    PreparedStatement statement = null;
    try {
      con = getConnection();

      // new objects
      statement = con.prepareStatement(
        "insert into restaurantproperty (restaurant, " +
          "code, val, reviewer, reviewdate) " +
          "values (?, ?, ?, ?, ?)" );
      statement.setString( 1, restaurant );
      statement.setString( 2, property.getCode() );
      statement.setString( 3, property.getValue() );
      statement.setString( 4, property.getReviewer() );
      statement.setDate( 5, new java.sql.Date(
        property.getReviewDate().getTime()) );
      statement.executeUpdate();

      statement.close();
    }
    catch (Exception e) {
      e.printStackTrace();
    }
    finally {
      try {
        if (con != null)
          con.close();
      }
      catch (Exception e) {
      }
    }
  }

  void updateProperty( String restaurant, RestaurantProperty property )
    throws EJBException {
    Connection con = null;
    PreparedStatement statement = null;
    try {
      con = getConnection();

      statement = con.prepareStatement(
        "update restaurantproperty set val=?, " +
```

```
         "reviewer=?, reviewdate=? where restaurant=? " +
         "and code=?" );
    statement.setString(1, property.getValue() );
    statement.setString(2, property.getReviewer() );
    statement.setDate(3, new java.sql.Date(
      property.getReviewDate().getTime()) );
    statement.setString(4, restaurant );
    statement.setString(5, property.getCode() );
    statement.executeUpdate();

    statement.close();
  }
  catch (Exception e) {
    e.printStackTrace();
  }
  finally {
    try {
      if (con != null)
        con.close();
    }
    catch (Exception e) {
    }
  }
}

void deleteProperty( String restaurant, String code )
  throws EJBException {
  Connection con = null;
  PreparedStatement statement = null;
  try {
    con = getConnection();

    statement = con.prepareStatement(
      "delete from restaurantproperty where " +
      "restaurant=? and code=?" );
    statement.setString( 1, restaurant );
    statement.setString( 2, code );
    statement.executeUpdate();
    statement.close();
  }
  catch (Exception e) {
    e.printStackTrace();
  }
  finally {
    try {
      if (con != null)
        con.close();
    }
    catch (Exception e) {
    }
  }
}

private Connection getConnection() throws EJBException {
  try {
```

```
        return new oracle.jdbc.driver.OracleDriver().defaultConnection();
      }
    catch (Exception e) {
      e.printStackTrace();
      throw new EJBException(e.toString());
    }
  }
}
```

The `PropertyUpdaterEJB` component was largely a façade to the restaurant entity. It is now largely a façade to the `RestaurantDataObject` and `PropertyDataObject` database code:

```
package restaurants2;

import java.util.Vector;
import java.util.Enumeration;
import java.rmi.RemoteException;
import javax.ejb.SessionBean;
import javax.ejb.SessionContext;
import javax.ejb.CreateException;
import javax.naming.InitialContext;
import javax.ejb.ObjectNotFoundException;
import javax.ejb.EJBException;

public class PropertyUpdaterEJB implements SessionBean {
  public void createRestaurant(String restaurantName, String location,
    String chef ) throws CreateException, RemoteException, EJBException {
    RestaurantDataObject rdo = new RestaurantDataObject();
    rdo.createRestaurant( restaurantName, chef, location );
  }

  public void moveRestaurant( String restaurantName, String newLocation )
   throws RestaurantNotFoundException, RemoteException, EJBException {
    RestaurantDataObject rdo = new RestaurantDataObject();
    rdo.setLocation(restaurantName, newLocation);
  }

  public void changeChef( String restaurantName, String newChef )
    throws RestaurantNotFoundException, RemoteException, EJBException {
    RestaurantDataObject rdo = new RestaurantDataObject();
    rdo.setChef( restaurantName, newChef );
  }

  public void addProperties( String restaurantName, Vector properties )
    throws PropertyAlreadyExistsException, RestaurantNotFoundException,
          RemoteException, EJBException {
    PropertyDataObject pdo = new PropertyDataObject();
    Enumeration e = properties.elements();
    while (e.hasMoreElements()) {
      RestaurantProperty property = (RestaurantProperty) e.nextElement();
      pdo.createProperty( restaurantName, property );
    }
  }
}
```

```
public void changeProperties( String restaurantName, Vector properties )
  throws PropertyNotFoundException, RestaurantNotFoundException,
     RemoteException, EJBException {
  PropertyDataObject pdo = new PropertyDataObject();
  Enumeration e = properties.elements();
  while (e.hasMoreElements()){
    RestaurantProperty property = (RestaurantProperty) e.nextElement();
    pdo.updateProperty( restaurantName, property );
  }
}

public void removeProperties( String restaurantName,
  Vector propertyCodes ) throws PropertyNotFoundException,
    RestaurantNotFoundException, RemoteException, EJBException {
  PropertyDataObject pdo = new PropertyDataObject();
  Enumeration e = propertyCodes.elements();
  while (e.hasMoreElements()) {
    String code = (String) e.nextElement();
    pdo.deleteProperty( restaurantName, code );
  }
}
```

The utility methods were used to acquire the restaurant entity's factory and remote interfaces, and are no longer necessary. The life-cycle methods are unchanged.

```
// life-cycle methods

public void ejbCreate() throws CreateException, RemoteException {
}

public void ejbActivate() {
}

public void ejbPassivate() {
}

public void ejbRemove() {
}

public void setSessionContext(SessionContext ctx) {
}
}
```

Only the getRecommendations() method of PreferenceInterviewerEJB class changes:

```
public Vector getRecommendations()
    throws EJBException, RemoteException {
  try {
    RestaurantDataObject rdo = new RestaurantDataObject();
    return rdo.getRecommendations(area, listResponses);
  }
  catch (Exception e) {
    e.printStackTrace();
    throw new EJBException(e.toString());
  }
}
```

Deployment Descriptors

Oracle 8.1.5 and 8.1.6 require the EJB developer to use Oracle's proprietary descriptor format for specifying transaction and container management attributes. This format has features in common with both Java code and the familiar J2EE compliant XML formats. Although Oracle 8.1.7 JVM now has support for XML descriptors, it is still a requirement that a different descriptor be produced for each bean, rather than being able to specify all the beans in a single file. Oracle provides a command-line tool `ejbdescriptor` which is capable of translating between the input format (Oracle or XML) and the serialized version which is actually uploaded to the JVM. However, the `deployejb` tool will also perform this translation for you. Full descriptions of these tools can be found in the *Oracle EJB and Corba Developer's Guide* at http://technet.oracle.com, or on your documentation CD.

A minimal Oracle deployment descriptor for the `PropertyUpdaterEJB` session bean is shown below. We briefly summarise the possible attributes and their meanings in the table below.

```
SessionBean restaurants2.PropertyUpdaterEJB {
    BeanHomeName = "test/PropertyUpdater";
    HomeInterfaceClassName = restaurants2.PropertyUpdaterHome;
    RemoteInterfaceClassName = restaurants2.PropertyUpdater;
    StateManagementType = STATELESS_SESSION;

    TransactionAttribute = TX_REQUIRED;
    RunAsMode = CLIENT_IDENTITY;
    AllowedIdentities = { scott };
}
```

Attribute	Possible Values	Mandatory
BeanHomeName	String that the bean will be named as in the JNDI context. Client's look up this string, to get a reference to the bean.	Yes
HomeInterface ClassName	The fully qualified class name of the home interface.	Yes
RemoteInterface ClassName	The fully qualified class name of the remote interface.	Yes
Reentrant	Boolean `true` or `false`. For entity beans. This value is not relevant for Oracle8i implementation because entity beans are not supported. Session beans are always non-reentrant.	No
State ManagementType	STATEFUL_SESSION or STATELESS_SESSION Determines whether a session beans is stateful or stateless. This value is not relevant for current Oracle8i implementation because all beans are treated as stateful session beans.	No
Transaction Attribute	TX_BEAN_MANAGED TX_MANDATORY TX_NOT_SUPPORTED TX_REQUIRED TX_REQUIRES_NEW TX_SUPPORTS Default value is TX_SUPPORTS.	No

Table continued on following page

Attribute	Possible Values	Mandatory
RunAsMode	CLIENT_IDENTITY SPECIFIED_IDENTITY SYSTEM_IDENTITY These are the same as the values defined in the javax.ejb.deployment.ControlDescriptor class.	No
RunAsIdentity	A username in the database. This is not a role. *Unless RunAsMode attribute is set.	No*
Allowed Identities	A list of permitted usernames or roles for the method, enclosed in braces. For example {SCOTT,ADMIN,SYS}.	No

The following is a fuller deployment descriptor for the PreferenceInterviewer session bean,
illustrating method-specific transaction and identity attributes.

```
SessionBean restaurants2.PreferenceInterviewerEJB {
  BeanHomeName = "test/PreferenceInterviewer";
  HomeInterfaceClassName = restaurants2.PreferenceInterviewerHome;
  RemoteInterfaceClassName = restaurants2.PreferenceInterviewer;

  SessionTimeout = 0;
  StateManagementType = STATEFUL_SESSION;

  TransactionAttribute = TX_SUPPORTS;
  RunAsMode = CLIENT_IDENTITY;
  AllowedIdentities = { scott };

  java.util.Vector getRecommendations() {
    TransactionAttribute = TX_SUPPORTS;
    RunAsMode = CLIENT_IDENTITY;
    AllowedIdentities = { public, scott };
  }

  restaurants2.Choice[] getChoices () {
    TransactionAttribute = TX_SUPPORTS;
    RunAsMode = CLIENT_IDENTITY;
    AllowedIdentities = { scott, keith };
  }
}
```

Deployment

We will deploy the EJBs using Oracle's deployejb tool and check that they are visible to the world using
the sess_sh tool. Both of these operations can be achieved remotely from the Oracle 8i instance. You
will, however, need the Oracle 8i command-line tools mentioned above on your machine. These are
available with most Oracle 8i client installations. You will need the following libraries in your classpath to
compile the EJB and client code and to run the clients. They are usually found in the following places:

- ❑ `<ORACLE_HOME>\lib\vbjapp.jar`

- ❑ `<ORACLE_HOME>\lib\vbjtools.jar`

- ❑ `<ORACLE_HOME>\lib\vbjorb.jar`

- ❑ `<ORACLE_HOME>\lib\aurora_client.jar`

- ❑ `<ORACLE_HOME>\jdbc\lib\classes111.zip, classes12.zip`

These libraries contain the necessary classes, in addition to the core JDK 1.1.x runtime library, that you need for JNDI (`InitialContext` etc.), EJBs, the IIOP protocol, and the Oracle database drivers. Compile with:

```
javac restaurants2\*.java
```

You will then need to put the package into an uncompressed (the 0 option) JAR file:

```
jar -cf0 PreferenceInterviewerSource.jar restaurants2\*.class
```

Deploy the EJBs, one at a time, specifying the deployment descriptor and the source library in the command line as follows:

```
deployejb -republish -u scott -p tiger \
    -s sess_iiop://dbserver:2481:proead -descriptor \
        PreferenceInterviewer.ejb PreferenceInterviewerSource.jar
```

The tool will then upload all the relevant Java files to the database, grant the necessary permissions on the published object, perform a "deployment verification" analysis on the EJB code, and generate the client-side "stub" files in the library `PreferenceInterviewerSource_generated.jar`. This library will need to be added to your classpath when running the clients. The idea behind the stub files is that they are client-side versions of the EJB classes. The client calls the methods in the stub class (once it has obtained a handle to the remote object) as if it were simply calling the methods of the original class. The automatically generated stub classes, however, implement the "marshaling" of the method calls into a form that can be sent over the network using the RMI-IIOP protocol. Similarly, the stub classes deal with unmarshaling the return values from the remote objects and passing them back to the client. All this is hopefully transparent to the client code. However, the extra burden on the client is that it has to deal with the possibility of a `RemoteException` being thrown by the remote method call.

> *Visit http://java.sun.com/rmi for further information and tutorials on the subject of the RMI-IIOP specification and implementation.*

sess_sh

This command lets you communicate with the CORBA 2.0 object request broker (ORB) in the Oracle 8i database. This is where the EJBs will have been published when you used the `deployejb` tool. The following line will start a session for user `SCOTT` on a database with hostname `dbserver`. The server must have a TNS listener configured to listen on port 2481 (the default Internet Inter-ORB Protocol (IIOP) port) and must be running an Oracle database instance with service name `proead`:

```
sess_sh -u scott -p tiger -s sess_iiop://dbserver:2481:proead
```

You can then interrogate the published objects by navigating through the directory:

```
Command Prompt - sess_sh -u scott -p tiger -s sess_iiop://dbserver:2481:proead    _ □ X
Microsoft(R) Windows NT(TM)
(C) Copyright 1985-1996 Microsoft Corp.

C:\>sess_sh -u scott -p tiger -s sess_iiop://dbserver:2481:proead
--Aurora/ORB Session Shell--
--type "help" at the command line for help message
$ ls
bin/      etc/      test/
$ cd test
$ ls
PreferenceInterviewer      PropertyUpdater
$
```

If you have a problem logging on or deploying EJBs, you may need to ensure that your database has the dedicated IIOP listener configured correctly. See the troubleshooting section below.

Running the Clients

Once your EJBs are deployed you can run the client programs:

```
java restaurants2.ClientIntialData
java restaurants2.ClientInterview
```

You will need to add the generated JAR libraries containing the stub files to your classpath, in addition to the client libraries listed above. Don't forget to delete the records from the RESTAURANT and RESTAURANTPROPERTY tables of your database before running the ClientInitialData application more than once. If you try and re-insert the data you will violate the unique constraint property of the NAME primary key. This will throw an SQLException which will be caught, wrapped in an EJBException, and thrown to the client.

Troubleshooting

Configuring Multi-threaded Server in the Database

You will need to ensure that your Oracle database instance is configured to run in multi-threaded server mode rather than in dedicated mode. See Appendix A.

Configuring IIOP Listener on the Server

You will need to make sure there is an IIOP listener active for your database instance. Go to Start | Oracle Home | Network Administration | Net8 Assisstant and select the Local | Listeners directory in the configuration tree. There should be a listener address dedicated to IIOP, usually on the standard port of 2481.

Exception Handling

In Sun's EJB specification 1.0 the exception `javax.ejb.EJBException` is not a subclass of `RuntimeException`, as it is in specification 1.1 (extract the exception class from `aurora_client.jar` and use `javap` to inspect its inheritance properties, if you want to confirm this). It is a direct subclass of `java.lang.Exception`. This means that it is a checked exception and methods that throw this exception will need to declare it in their `throws` clause. If you encounter problems with compiling your EJB code using the `aurora_client.jar` EJB 1.0 library, when you have already successfully compiled and run it on other platforms, then you will need to address this issue. The library classes that your EJBs will actually use while in the Oracle 8.1.5 or 8.1.6 JVM are in the `aurora_client.jar` library, so you will need to make sure your code **compiles using these library classes before you deploy it**.

It is unwise to consider throwing `RuntimeException` instead of `EJBException` in code that is implemented for an EJB 1.0 platform (in order to avoid the necessity of declaring it in the `throws` clause). This is because it would remove from the code the semantic transactional implications of the `EJBException`. When the container intercepts an `EJBException` thrown back to the client by a transaction-managed EJB, it will rollback any uncommitted database updates that the EJB is attempting. An `EJBException`, like a `RuntimeException`, is considered fatal to the intended execution of the code, and should therefore be a container-managed event, as well as a client-managed event. There is an excellent article on exception handling in EJB containers in *Java Developers Journal*, September 2000, issue 5:9.

Another issue in exception handling is that the Oracle `deployejb` verification tool mentioned above includes a check that the methods in the EJBs throw exactly the same exceptions as declared in the remote and home interfaces. We mentioned this earlier in the chapter at the first point this occurred. This appears to be related to EJB development with Oracle's Java IDE JDeveloper. An IDE will of course try to generate template methods for EJBs that declare all possible exceptions as specified in the interfaces. However, it seems that when it comes to deployment, these exceptions are made mandatory, rather than optional where the implemented code cannot throw the exception(s).

JDeveloper

The code in this chapter was not originally written to be run from, or ported to an IDE. However, it is possible to obtain from the Wrox web site, a JDeveloper project for the application, which should enable you to deploy the EJBs and run the clients using JDeveloper features.

Summary

This chapter introduced Enterprise JavaBeans, or EJBs for short. EJBs are designed to encapsulate application logic, and to protect the application developer from having to worry about system level issues. They are portable, reusable server-side components that execute in a container and are accessible from many different types of clients. The EJB container can provide many services, such as transactions, security, automatic persistence, scalability, and fail-over.

There are three basic types of EJB components: session beans, entity beans, and message-driven beans. Session beans can be stateful or stateless. Stateless session beans have scalability advantages over stateful session beans, and should be used whenever possible. Entity beans can use bean-managed persistence (BMP) or container-managed persistence (CMP). Entity beans with container-managed persistence are easier to develop, but the EJB container does not always provide sufficient capabilities to use CMP.

There are four major parts to entity and session beans: the home interface, the remote interface, the implementation class, and the XML deployment descriptor. (EJB 2.0 message-driven beans do not require home and remote interfaces.) These files and any necessary support classes are bundled into a JAR file for deployment.

An EJB component uses the JNDI API to acquire a resource factory, and that resource factory to retrieve a resource. These resources are declared in the deployment descriptor, and tied to an actual enterprise resource at deployment time.

One of the most important design patterns for EJB development is to use a session bean as a façade for a client to the other components in an application. The façade improves performance and reduces dependencies.

ORACLE8iAPPLICATIONPROGRAMMING

16
Inside the Database

This book uses some very powerful Java programming techniques and complex code-generating tools in conjunction with the Oracle database. Since we've just completed an application that used one of the more complex architectures in the J2EE programming model, namely EJB, and before we move on to use one of these code-generating tools (BC4J) let's take this chapter to get back inside this database.

Once you had your EJBs up-and-running, in the previous chapter, did you stop for a second and think, "exactly what code am I generating in the database and how well is it doing its job?" If you did not, then this chapter will try to illustrate why perhaps you should have, and furthermore, why you might want to further investigate the core, basic features of the Oracle database you have purchased.

Programming a database without understanding what is available to you and how it works is a lot like using just the blade of a Swiss Army knife – it has dozens of features beyond that blade. The database is a lot like that Swiss Army knife: it has everything. Understanding how it works and what it can (and sometimes cannot) do is crucial to the success of your application in the multi-user environment to which it will be exposed. The features I am talking about here go deeper than the high level, flashy features – here we're going to look at the "meat and potatoes" of the database. We will discuss why you need to understand:

- ❑ **How standards fit into the picture** – and how they can confuse it

- ❑ **How the database locks data** – to avoid programs that sit and wait for long periods of time

- ❑ **What happens in a heavy multi-user environment** – to avoid programs that work great in isolation but which fail in a multi-user environment

- ❑ **Which features are available to you** – features you do not have to code yourself. Oracle has put a lot into the database. There are over 60 supplied database packages to do everything from sending e-mails, to writing OS files, to scheduling jobs. There is no need for a development team to re-invent the wheel (but we see it all of the time – mostly due to "I didn't know it did that")

❑ **How to tune the application** – realizing that database tuning, tuning at the instance level, is not going to pay off in high double digit percentages – the majority of tuning is done at the application level. It is generally not possible to throw some switches in the database to fix a poorly performing application. We will examine the code generated in the database by the `ClientInterview` bean and look at how we can tune it

Notice that I said, "Why you need to understand them" not "How they work". We will not be going into lots of detail on each and every topic (many of which are topics of entire books) but rather will hope to expose you to some of the reasons you want to learn more about the database. So, if you read something that you don't understand – the point has been made. It is time to dig out the Oracle documentation (I particularly recommend that you read the Server Concepts Manual) and buy a companion book to learn these fundamentals.

Why You Really Need to Deal with the Database

Many people approach the database as if it were a "black box", something that they don't have to understand. The attitude is "it is just the thing that holds the bits and bytes, we don't need to learn about it". How does this attitude arise? Let's look at just two of the possible reasons:

❑ "We program in Java, and Java abstracts this database thing for me"

❑ "We have a tool that generates all our code and we don't have to understand what it generates"

Let's take the first point. Is there any such thing as a "database independent" application? – one that you can develop for one database and then port to another database and, with minor adjustments, get it up and running in the same way? I would say that the answer is most likely to be "no".

It is important to understand that one database is different from another in the same way that one operating system is from any other. Externally, they appear the same – they perform similar functions – but how they have each implemented that functionality is important. If you laid out the core functionality of Unix and NT in a bulleted list, they would not look very different. However, when you actually sit down and start using one or the other – you quickly discover there are fundamental differences between the two. What works fine on one OS will not work at all on the other. Understanding that all databases are not created equal, and experience in one does not imply knowledge of another, is important. There are significant differences between each. Many times people will "upsize" an application from a small database running MS Access and discover that it behaves extremely differently.

Different implementations and different techniques will work with different outcomes on the various databases. With the exception of some simple read-only reporting tools, having a truly "database independent" application is not something you should really hope to obtain. It is possible but, ironically, **only if you fully understand and appreciate how each database does what it does** and are willing to forgo some features in one database to accommodate another.

Let me give you one example of this. Oracle does not employ shared read locks for consistent results – **EVER**. MS SQLServer does. What this means is that an application coded using Oracle for development will not execute very well in SQLServer given that your developers made the assumption that a READ will never block a WRITE. In Oracle that is true (it is also true that a WRITE will never block a READ), in SQLServer it is not true. What will happen is that the application that runs fine in Oracle will not scale at all in SQLServer. The converse is true as well – if you started development in SQLServer and decided to deploy in Oracle, the techniques you used to code the application to avoid locking issues are simply not relevant in Oracle. Those techniques will hinder the Oracle implementation.

Understanding the database and how it works is crucial – even if the goal is not database independence. Time and time again we encounter development teams who do not have this understanding – the team, the "coders", consist of some great Java programmers or C/C++ programmers with absolutely no database experience whatsoever. This team, should they set about building a database application, is doomed to failure. I've seen cases where the "prototype" worked great – in single user mode or with a handful of users – but when multiple users accessed the application concurrently, the application would fail with an error or serialize access to the data. This is due to the developers not understanding the impact of using an isolation mode of serializable – or what repeatable reads really implies. Every choice you make during the development of a database application will have implications later.

Let's consider the second trap that people fall often fall into: "the tool generates the code and I don't have to understand what it generates". They will use a code generator that hides the "complexity" of SQL from them. They will write very small simple layers of abstraction (APIs) and rely on them to hide the "complexity". Such an approach will fail when building large scale, enterprise ready applications. Again, their applications may work fine in the laboratory and with a handful of users (sometimes) but when put under load they fail to perform, they run slow, and frequently do the wrong thing when concurrent actions are taking place.

An application built around the database – dependent on the database – will succeed or fail based on how it uses the database. A development team needs at least a core set of "database savvy" coders who are responsible for ensuring the database logic is sound and the system is tuned. They can do this by providing a set of PLSQL packages (stored procedures) that implements the database logic correctly. This involves much more than just understanding SQL and how to write a query, as we shall now see.

SQL/92 – A Whole Bunch of Standards

Did you know that many commercially available databases are SQL/92 compliant? Did you know that means very little as far as query portability goes?

The SQL/92 standard has four levels:

- ❑ **Entry level** – This is the level to which most vendors have complied. This level is a minor enhancement of the predecessor standard SQL/89. No database vendors have been certified higher

- ❑ **Transitional** – this is approximately halfway between Entry level and Intermediate

- ❑ **Intermediate** – Intermediate SQL adds many features including (not by any means an inclusive list):

Dynamic SQL

Cascade delete for referential integrity

DATE and TIME data types

Domains

Variable length character strings

A CASE expression

CAST functions between data types

- **Full** – Full SQL adds provisions for (again, not inclusive)

  Connection management

  A `BIT` string data type

  Deferrable integrity constraints

  Derived tables in the `FROM` clause

  Subqueries in `CHECK` clauses

  Temporary tables

The entry-level standard does not include features such as outer joins, the new inner join syntax, and so on. Transitional does specify outer join syntax and inner join syntax. Intermediate adds more and Full is all of SQL/92. Most books on SQL/92 do not differentiate between the various levels leading to confusion on the subject; they demonstrate what a theoretical database implementing SQL/92 FULL would look like. It makes it impossible to pick up a SQL/92 book and apply what you see in the book to just any SQL/92 database. For example, in SQLServer the inner join syntax is supported in SQL statements, whereas in Oracle it is not. But, they are both SQL/92 compliant databases. You can do inner joins and outer joins in Oracle – you will just do it differently than in SQLServer. The bottom line is that SQL/92 will not go very far at the entry level and, if you use any of the features of intermediate or higher, you risk not being able to port your application anyway.

You should not be afraid to make use of vendor specific features. You are paying a lot of money for those features. Every database has its own bag of tricks and we can always find a way to perform the operation in each database. Use what is best for your current database and reimplement components as you go to other databases. Use good programming techniques to isolate yourself from these changes – the same techniques employed by people writing OS portable applications. The goal is to fully utilize the facilities available to you but ensure you can change the implementation on a case-by-case basis.

For example, a common function of many database applications is the generation of a unique key for each row – when you insert the row, the system should automatically generate a key for you. Oracle has implemented the database object called a `SEQUENCE` for this. Informix has a `SERIAL` datatype. Sybase and SQLServer have an `IDENTITY` type. Each database has a way to do this, however the methods are different, both in how you do it and the possible outcomes. So, to the knowledgeable developer there are two paths that can be pursued:

- Develop a totally database independent method of generating a unique key

- Accommodate the different implementations and use different techniques when implementing in each database

The theoretical advantage of the first approach is that to move from database to database – you need not change anything. I call it a theoretical advantage because the con-side of this implementation is so huge that it makes this solution totally infeasible. What you would have to do to develop a totally database independent process is to create a table such as:

```
create table id_table ( id_name varchar(30), id_value number );
insert into id_table values ( 'MY_KEY', 0 );
```

Then, in order to get a new key, you would have to execute the following code:

```
update id_table set id_value = id_value + 1 where id_name = 'MY_KEY';
select id_value from id_table where id_name = 'MY_KEY';
```

Looks simple enough but the outcome is that only one user at a time may process a transaction. We need to update that row to increment a counter and that will cause our program to serialize on that operation. At best, one person at a time will generate a new value for this key. This issue is compounded by the fact that our transaction is much larger than we have outlined above – the UPDATE and SELECT we have in the example are only two statements of potentially many other statements that make up our transaction. We have to insert the row into the table with this key we just generated and do whatever other work it takes to complete this transaction. This serialization will be a huge limiting factor in scaling. Think of the ramifications if this technique was used on web sites that processed orders – and this was how we generated order numbers. There would be no multi-user concurrency; we would be forced to do everything sequentially.

The correct approach to this problem would be to use the best code for each database. In Oracle this would be (assuming the table that needs the generated primary key is T):

```
Create table t ( pk number primary key, ... );
Create sequence t_seq;
Create trigger t_trigger before insert on t for each row
Begin
    Select t_seq.nextval into :new.pk from dual;
End;
/
```

That will have the effect of automatically and transparently assigning a unique key to each row inserted. The same effect can be achieved in the other databases using their types – the create tables will be different; the net results will be the same. Here we have gone out of our way to use each database's feature to generate a NON-BLOCKING, highly concurrent unique key and have introduced no real changes to the application code – all of the logic is contained in this case in the DDL.

Another example of defensive programming to allow for portability, once you understand that each database **will implement features in different way,** is to layer your access to the database when necessary. Let's say you are programming using JDBC. If all you use is straight SQL SELECT, INSERT, UPDATE and DELETE statements – you probably do not need a layer of abstraction. You may very well be able to code the SQL directly in your application, as long as you limit the constructs you use to those supported by each of the databases you intend to support. Another approach, which is both more portable and offers better performance, would be to use stored procedures to return result sets. You will discover that every vendor can return result sets from stored procedures but that how they are returned is different – the actual source code you must write is different for different databases.

Your two choices here would be to either not use stored procedures to return result sets or to implement different code for different databases. I would definitely follow the different code for different vendors and use stored procedures heavily. This apparently seems to increase the amount of time it would take to implement on a different database however – you will find it is actually easier to implement on multiple databases with this approach. Instead of having to find the perfect SQL that works on *all* databases in the same way (perhaps better on some than on others), you will implement the SQL that works best on that database. You can do this outside of the application itself – permitting you more flexibility in tuning the application. We can fix a poorly performing query in the database itself and deploy that fix immediately – without having to patch the application. Additionally, you can take advantage of vendor extensions to SQL using this method freely. For example, Oracle supports hierarchical queries via the CONNECT BY operation in its SQL. This unique feature is great for resolving recursive queries. In Oracle you are free to utilize this extension to SQL since it is "outside" of the application (hidden in the database). In other databases, you would use a temporary table and procedural code in a stored procedure to achieve the same results perhaps. You paid for these features so you might as well use them.

These are the same techniques that developers who implement multi-platform code utilize. For example Oracle Corporation uses this technique in the development of its own database. There is a large amount of code (a small percentage of the database code overall) called OSD (Operating System Dependent) code that is implemented specifically for each platform. Using this layer of abstraction, Oracle is able to make use of many native OS features for performance and integration without having to rewrite the large majority of the database itself. The fact that Oracle can run as a multi-threaded application on Windows and a multi-process application on Unix attests to this feature. The mechanisms for inter-process communication are abstracted to such a level that they can be reimplemented on an OS by OS basis, allowing for radically different implementations that perform as well as an application written directly and specifically for that platform.

As we look into other considerations with respect to the database – such as understanding locking, concurrency models, how the different optimizers work, how to tune and so on – the need for specific SQL implementations for each database will become even clearer.

Locking Models

This is where people really get into trouble. They do not understand how the various databases implement locking. You have page level, and row level; some implementations escalate locks from row level to page level, some do not; some use read locks others do not; some implement serializable transactions via locking and others via read consistent views of data (no locks). These small differences can balloon into huge performance issues or downright bugs in your application if you do not understand how they work. Locks are the elements that both allow for and prohibit concurrency in the database. Without some locking model – to prevent concurrent updates to the same row for example – multi-user access would not be possible in a database. The database uses locks to ensure that, at most, one transaction is modifying a given piece of data. So, they allow for concurrency. Overused, or used improperly, they inhibit concurrency. If you or the database itself locks data unnecessarily, fewer people will be able to concurrently perform operations. Understanding what locking is and how it works in your database is vital in order to develop a scalable, correct application. Lack of understanding of database locking will not only inhibit concurrency but can actually lead to data integrity issues (as we will demonstrate in a moment).

This is not an attempt to promote one locking model over the other. There are lots of discussions on that subject – just go to the database news groups "comp.databases.*" and ask about them or search the newsgroup archives. Rather, this section will show that there are radically different ways to implement various features and if you do not understand the tool you are using you will fail. It is as simple as that. We will not cover what page level locking is versus row level or how lock escalation works or what serializable transactions are in this section. Rather, we will look at an example of how not understanding how these features work will lead to erroneous, buggy and error prone applications.

For example, let's look at a case where you need consistent results from the database and you need to get these results from a table that is actively being modified. As an example, we will use a table of bank accounts – a table in which we store checking and saving account balances. Assume the table looks like this:

```
Create table Accounts( account_name varchar2(30),
                       account_type varchar2(30),
                       account_bal  int );
```

You want to run a query such as:

```
Select sum(account_bal) from Accounts;
```

That is a pretty simple query; it seems totally unambiguous – very straightforward. Your requirements are to print on a report the total amount of money in the bank at that particular point in time. This number needs to be accurate and correlate with other values on that same report.

In actuality – depending on the database – you may get radically different results for the above query – given an identical set of circumstances. This is simply due to the different approaches taken by the databases in locking data. Unless you understand how this works, you will never be able to test your applications for correctness, as you will not know under what sorts of conditions you must test. You will also not be able to explain how certain results show up on reports and as such you do not fully understand how the data is retrieved in the first place. The fact that such a simple, straightforward query could result in a different answer from different databases – or cause a runtime error may come as a surprise to many people. We will explore what answers Oracle might return and then another database given the same set of circumstances.

For this example, we will assume that we will store one row per database block/page – this will eliminate discussions of row level versus page level locking (other things you need to consider) and make the example easier to understand. We will use a table with four blocks or pages of data as follows:

	Account-Name	Account-Type	Account-Bal
Block1	123	Savings	$100
Block2	456	Savings	$200
Block3	456	Checking	$300
Block4	123	Checking	$100

So, at this exact point in time, there is $700 in the bank. If we were the only user in the database and ran the select sum() query, we would be returned the value of $700. What we would like to consider is the impact of a user performing an ATM transaction to transfer $50 from the Savings account of Account 123 to the Checking account of Account 123. Further, we would like to consider what will happen if this account update takes place concurrently with our query. First, we will see how Oracle processes this and then how another database such as SQLServer would process it.

So, the scenario is we have two users – one summing the account balance and the other performing a transfer of accounts. The mix of work is as follows:

Time	Query	Update
T1	Reads block 1, sum = 100 so far	
T2	Reads block 2, sum = 300 so far	
T3		Updates block 1, puts an exclusive lock on block 1 preventing other updates. Block 1 now has $50
T4	Reads block 3, sum = 600 so far	
T5		Updates block 4, puts an exclusive lock on block 4 preventing other updates (but not reads). Block 4 now has $150

Table continued on following page

Time	Query	Update
T6	Reads block 4, discovers that block 4 has been modified. It will actually rollback the block to make it appear as it did at time = T1. The query will read the value $100 from this block – it cannot see the changes made by the Update. Sum = 700 so far.	
T7		Commits transaction;
T8	Presents $700 as the answer	

We see that Oracle gets the correct answer $700 – the amount of money in the bank as of the time T1. Oracle's philosophy toward locking is that it naturally inhibits concurrency and should be avoided when it can be. That does not mean that Oracle doesn't lock data when it should but rather that Oracle locks as infrequently as it can. The above shows how Oracle does this – by using multiple versions of the data. At time T6, Oracle discovered some of the data it was reading had been modified since the query began. That would make that data inconsistent with (out of sync with) the data that had already been read. Oracle will not read and process this altered data – rather it will reconstruct the modified information to appear as it did at time T1. It does this by reading the rollback segments (where Oracle stores UNDO information for a transaction). So, at time T6, Oracle reconstructs the data and continues on. There is no blocking, no contention between the Query and the Update transaction. It is as if the query ran from start to finish and then the update ran from start to finish – even though they ran concurrently. It is interesting to note that even if the commit performed at time T7 was performed right after T5 and before T6 (so that the update committed the changes to block 4 before our query read it) – the outcome would have been the same. At time T6, the query would have seen that the block it read had been modified and it would have reconstructed it even though the changes to it were committed. That is because, even though the changes were committed, they are out of sync with all of the other data already processed.

In Oracle, this feature is called multi-versioning. Multi-versioning is always done at the statement level (the above scenario happens for each and every query) and may be done at the transaction level as well via read-only or serializable transactions. Oracle accomplishes this without using locks – the only locks employed above were to ensure that two people did not update the same exact piece of data simultaneously.

Most other databases do not support multi-versioning for read consistency as Oracle does. In these other databases you must choose to either limit concurrency with shared read locks or live with potentially inconsistent results. A shared read lock differs from the Exclusive lock we used in that a shared read lock prevents any other transaction from updating that row – it makes sure the row does not change – but does not prevent others from reading that row. Let us look at the same example from above run in SQLServer in its default "read committed" mode of operation:

Time	Query	Update
T1	Reads block 1, sum = 100 so far	
T2	Reads block 2, sum = 300 so far	
T3		Updates block 1, puts an exclusive lock on block 1 preventing other updates. Block 1 now has $50

Time	Query	Update
T4	Reads block 3, sum = 600 so far	
T5		Updates block 4, puts an exclusive lock on block 4 preventing other updates and reads. Block 4 now has $150
T6	Reads block 4, discovers that block 4 has been modified. This session will block and wait for this block to become available. All processing on this query HALTS	
T7		Commits transaction;
T8	Reads block 4, sees 150 on this block as it sees the committed data. Sum = 750 so far	
T9	Presents $750 as the answer	

As you can see here – using this other database will result in a different answer – given the same exact set of circumstances. It will present the answer of $750, which interestingly is a value that never existed at any point in time in the database! There was never a time when the sum(account_bal) was $750. This is a side effect of committed read in many databases (not Oracle due to its read consistent model). So, if you understand that this is the case and you know you must get a consistent answer, you will run your query in a mode that gives a consistent result. In SQLServer it accomplishes this by leaving a shared read lock on data that was read. This guarantees that data you have read will not change during the course of your transaction (no updates will be permitted to data you have read) but that others can read this data. If we use this mode and do the above, we will find that:

Time	Query	Update
T1	Reads block 1, sum = 100 so far. Block 1 has a shared read lock on it.	
T2	Reads block 2, sum = 300 so far. Block 2 has a shared read lock on it.	
T3		Attempts to update block 1 but is blocked. This transaction is suspended as it cannot obtain an exclusive lock on the block.
T4	Reads block 3, sum = 600 so far. Block 3 has a shared read lock on it.	
T5	Reads block 4, sum = 700 so far. Block 4 has a shared read lock on it.	
T6	Presents $700 as the answer	
T7	Commits transaction	

Table continued on following page

Time	Query	Update
T8		Updates block 1, puts an exclusive lock on block 1. Block 1 has 50 on it now
T9		Updates block 4, puts an exclusive lock on block 4. Block 4 has 150 on it now
T10		Commits transaction

Here, we achieve the correct result of $700, however the price we paid was to physically serialize the two transactions. In order to ensure we get a consistent answer, we will block many other concurrent transactions from occurring. If this table was not simply a four block table but a four million block table, that update transaction may have been waiting for a very long time. This shared read lock method has another serious drawback, not only will reads block writes and writes block reads, but they can actually cause each other to fail. If we change the example a little – making the table look like:

	Account-Name	Account-Type	Account-Bal
Block1	123	Checking	$100
Block2	456	Savings	$200
Block3	456	Checking	$300
Block4	123	Savings	$100

Here we have simply moved the physical location of Account 123's checking and savings accounts – something you do not have control over. The checking account is at the top of the table and the savings at the bottom. Now, using the same sequence of operations:

Time	Query	Update
T1	Reads block 1, sum = 100 so far. Block 1 has a shared read lock on it.	
T2	Reads block 2, sum = 300 so far. Block 2 has a shared read lock on it.	
T3		Updates block 4, puts an exclusive lock on block 4 preventing other updates and shared read locks. Block 1 now has $50
T4	Reads block 3, sum = 600 so far. Block 3 has a shared read lock on it.	

Time	Query	Update
T5		Attempts to update block 1 but cannot due to the shared read lock. This transaction is suspended pending the availability of block 1.
T6	Attempts to read block 4 but cannot since block 4 has an exclusive lock on it.	

At this point in time we have just deadlocked ourselves. Our read-only query is deadlocked with our update transaction. The system will choose one of these transactions and raise an error in it. Either the user at the ATM will get an error message or the user running the report will. That is the only way to proceed further – to remove some of the locks.

So, as you can see – since the different databases have very different locking models, what works well in one will not work in the other (for example: a deadlock on a query). Not only that, but the results may be different – even when the circumstances are identical. Not understanding how your database locks data, how it provides for concurrent access, how it will function in a multi-user environment is a sure way to develop a database application that fails at runtime. It may fail silently by returning the wrong answer, it may fail more vocally with an error message, or it may not fail sometimes, only to fail again later with a different set of circumstances. The bottom line here is without understanding how your database locks data, your results may be completely unpredictable, as you can not determine the outcome of your application. If a simple, seemingly unambiguous query "select sum(balance) from accounts" can give us so many different outcomes in different databases, consider what could happen with more complex questions.

Concurrency

This is something people fail to test time and time again. What works in isolation falls apart in the real world. Techniques that work well if everything happens one after the other do not work so well when everyone does them simultaneously. These sorts of issues are the hardest to track down – the problem is similar to debugging a multi-threaded program. It works fine in the debugger but crashes horribly when running normally.

I remember a case I saw once where a developer was demonstrating a program they had developed. This application was to schedule resources such as conference rooms, projectors, and such. Since two people cannot schedule a resource for the same period of time (a business rule implemented by the application), the application had specific code embedded in it to check that no other user had allocated the time slot yet. It did this by querying the schedule table and then, if no rows existed that overlapped that time slot, it would insert those rows. So, the developer basically had two tables he was concerned with:

```
Create table resources ( resource_name varchar2(25) primary key, …. );
Create table schedules( resource_name varchar2(25) references resources,
                    Start_time    date,
                    End_time      date );
```

And before making a reservation they would query:

```
Select count(*)
  from schedules
 Where resource_name = :room_name
   And ( start_time between :new_start_time and :new_end_time
         Or
         end_time between :new_start_time and :new_end_time
       )
```

It looked bullet proof (to the developer anyway) – if the count came back zero, the room was yours. If it came back non-zero, you could not reserve it for those times. Once I knew what his logic was, I set up a very simple test to show him the error.

All I did was ask for him to get someone else to use the terminal next to him. They both went to the same screen on the different terminals and both tried to reserve the room for the same exact times. I told them that on the count of three both of them should hit the go button to save the reservation. When they did, both people got the reservation. The logic (which worked perfectly in isolation) failed in a multi-user environment. The fact was that both people had the reservation slipped into the system in spite of the business rule that was in place – since it had been implemented incorrectly.

What the developer in this case needed to do was to impose a little serialization himself. In order to correctly enforce this business rule, he must ensure that exactly one person at a time makes a reservation on a given resource. In addition to performing the count(*) above, the developer must first:

```
Select * from resources where resource_name = :room_name FOR UPDATE;
```

That FOR UPDATE clause is what makes this business rule work (or not). The developer must understand that in the multi user environment – they must employ techniques at times similar to techniques used in multi-threaded programming. The FOR UPDATE here is working like a semaphore or a mutex. It serializes access to the resources tables for that ROOM (Oracle does row level locking only, in a page level locking system your results may vary). If we do not serialize updates at the ROOM level, our business rule will not be enforceable. This is still highly concurrent as there are thousands of resources – what we have done is ensure that only one person modifies a resource at any time.

Locking is totally transparent 99% of the time and you need not concern yourself with it. It is that 1% you must be trained to recognize. There is no simple checklist of "if you do this, you need to do this" for this issue. This is a matter of understanding how your application will behave in a multi-user environment and how it will behave in your database. If you migrate your application from database to database – you will have to verify that it still works correctly in these different environments. What you need to implement in one database might very well be different than what you need to implement in another to achieve the same result.

For example, let's use the same example as above but let's assume we had initially deployed it in a database that employed page level locking and there was an index on the schedules table:

```
Create index schedules_idx on schedules( resource_name, start_time );
```

We also assume that the business rule was done via a database trigger (after the insert took place we would verify that only our row existed in the table for that time slot). In a page locking system, due to the update of the index page by `resource_name` and `start_time`, it is very likely that we would have serialized these transactions. The system would have processed these inserts sequentially due to the index page being locked (all of the `resource_names` with `start_times` near each other would be on the same page). In that page level locking database our application would be well behaved. When we moved it to a row level locking database however, it become ill behaved. The resulting data indicated that our implementation no longer works as we first specified. This is a direct consequence of not understanding how the database we have works in a multi-user environment.

I have seen many times when moving an application from database A to database B issues such as the one above come up. Applications that worked flawlessly in database A now do not work or work in an apparently bizarre fashion on database B. The first thought is database B is a bad database. In actuality the answer is database B does it differently – neither is necessarily wrong, they are just different. Knowing and understanding how they work will help you immensely in dealing with these issues.

Transactions

This is also an often overlooked area. The JDBC (and ODBC) API has `AutoCommit` set on by default so that each and every single statement is automatically committed after it executes. This is terrible – the first line of code in all JDBC programs after the connect should be: `conn.setAutoCommit(false);` to disable this default behavior. Transactions should always span:

- ❑ As few statements as possible
- ❑ As many statements as necessary

While this sounds like conflicting goals – what it really says is "your transaction should be as big as it should be, no more – no less". For example, consider an ATM transaction to move money from savings to checking. Suppose you used JDBC in its default mode to issue:

```
Update accounts set balance = balance - 100 where account = 55 and type =
'Savings';

Update accounts set balance = balance + 100 where account = 55 and type =
'Checking';
```

If the system crashed after the first statement but before the second, you would be out by $100, which is not acceptable. Only by using properly coded transactions can you solve this issue. The only way to have properly coded transactions is to ensure that the API you are using does not auto commit and to explicitly commit work yourself. Stored procedures are an excellent facility for this, as are EJBs and other technologies.

Stored procedures are perhaps the easiest and most accessible method to ensure correct transactions. If you follow a programming paradigm that says "a stored procedure call is a transaction", you'll have an easier time controlling your transactions and building new ones. You would code stored procedures that received all of the necessary inputs to perform its work. It would take the database from one consistent state to the next. When you invoke this procedure, you would do so in a block such as:

```
Begin
    Procedure( inputs … );
    Commit;
End;
```

Now, if PROCEDURE completes successfully, we will commit all of the work it did. If it fails and throws an exception, all of the work it has done will be rolled back for us. The reason I would not put the commit directly into PROCEDURE itself is because at some later date I might need to combine two or three transactions into one transaction. For example, let's go back to ATM transfer above. Assume we implemented a stored procedure to modify an account. This procedure takes as input the Account Number, the Account Type, and the amount to adjust the account by. I need to process two calls to this procedure as one call. If this routine did its own commit, I could not do both calls as one transaction. By leaving it up to the client to commit (which is where the choice belongs) I can assemble larger transactions as a collection of smaller ones. I can code:

```
Begin
    Update_Account( 55, 'Savings', -100 );
    Update_Account( 55, 'Checking', +100 );
    Commit;
End;
```

And be assured that they either both happen or neither happens.

Enterprise Java Beans (EJBs) are another viable method for doing this sort of operation without using stored procedures. Stored procedures are nice in that they are callable from many dozens of environments (SQLPlus, ODBC, JDBC, EJBs themselves, and so on) but some people want to avoid using them for whatever reason. The implementation of EJBs (effectively a remote procedure call – just like a stored procedure) makes them candidates for encapsulating your transactions as well. Given that EJBs have transaction semantics and features that are compatible with the database, they are also a nice way to encapsulate the transaction.

Once you have right-sized your transaction, we need to discuss why getting your DBA to correctly size rollback segments to do your job is paramount. Rollback segments are the place where Oracle stores its UNDO information – data needed to undo your database modifications in the event you rollback or the system fails for any reason. Frequently, I see commits in the middle of transactions. The reasoning is that if we do not commit, we will run out of rollback segment space and our transaction will fail. This is always the wrong answer to that specific problem. The only correct solution is to size the rollback segments correctly. They must be large enough to accommodate as many concurrently executing transactions as you believe you will have. It is not proper for you to artificially reduce the size of your transactions with commits to make your rollback needs smaller – it is your job to do as little as you have to, as much as you need to, in one transaction. Placing a commit in the middle of a large transaction is a sure way to logically corrupt your database. At some time, your transaction will fail after it has committed once but before it has committed all of the work. At that point in time you have a half done transaction. Unless you've carefully programmed it so you can restart your transaction exactly where it left off (and this is a manual process, you must restart it), you have a mess to clean up.

If there is one thing that sets the database apart from a file system, it is this ability, the ability to support transactions. A thorough understanding of what they are, what yours are, is needed.

Tuning Queries

Optimizers are not created equal. This is in some regards similar to the SQL/92 discussion above. I've seen cases where a query on one database performs excellently, whereas on another it doesn't ever finish. It goes both ways – for the database that performs this query poorly, there will be a query it does well that the other database does not.

Unless you use simple single table keyed reads of single rows using primary keys, you will encounter the case where you must tune the query for the database. Knowing how to find the queries to tune and then how to tune them is very important, almost as important as realizing you will ultimately need to do this in the end. In Oracle – you will use SQL_TRACE, TIMED_STATISTICS and TKPROF (see the section below). These tools will show you exactly what the application is doing in the database and help you find the "lowest hanging fruit".

I've used these tools with great success in every case where I've been called in to tune an application. I can, from outside the program, turn on trace, run the poorly performing application, and upon review of the TKPROF report describe how to make the program go faster. Typically this is a case of finding the poorly performing query or queries and rewriting them more optimally. These are the easy cases. In the harder cases, where there is no obvious query to tune, we can still use the TKPROF report to see what it is the application is doing. If you see the same query being executed tens of thousands of times – that will at least point you to a place to start looking.

The bottom line here, if you are developing an application to run on many databases, is that you will have to code some queries differently for the different databases. If you realize that in the beginning, you can use techniques to ensure this is possible without recoding the application itself. For example, using stored procedures to return results is a good defensive technique. You can freely recode these stored procedures without even stopping the application from executing. This flexibility is very powerful.

Openness

You put all of your data into the database. The database is a very open tool – it supports data access via SQL, EJBs, HTTP, FTP, SMB, and many other protocols and access mechanisms. Sounds great so far, the most open thing in the world.

Then, you put all of your application logic, and more importantly your security, outside of the database, perhaps in your beans that access the data. Perhaps in the JSP pages that access the data. Perhaps in your Visual Basic code running under Microsoft's Transaction Server (MTS). The end result is that you have just closed off your database – you have made it non-open. No longer can people hook in existing technologies to make use of this data – they *must* use your access methods (or bypass security all together). This sounds all well and fine today but what you must remember is the "whizz bang" technology of today, EJBs for example, are yesterday's concepts and tomorrow's tired, old technology. What has persevered for over twenty years in the relational world (and probably most of the object implementations as well) is the database itself. The front ends to the data change almost yearly, and as they do, the applications that have all of the security built inside themselves, not in the database, become obstacles, roadblocks to future progress.

By locating some things such as access control right next to the data (for example Fine Grained Access Control, a method of tightly integrating security with data) you are providing higher openness for your data. It no longer matters if the user comes at the data from a Bean, a JSP, a VB application using ODBC or SQLPlus – the same security protocols will be enforced – you are well situated for the next technology that comes along.

We will consider Fine Grained Access Control a little more here now. Fine grained access control is a feature whereby you can teach the database kernel to protect the data from unauthorized access, regardless of the technology used to get to the data. Whether you come in via an EJB, use a connection over ODBC, or utilize a JDBC based ad-hoc query tool, the data is protected just the same. With this feature, the database gives you the ability to attach, at runtime, a predicate to any and all objects accessed in the system. This predicate, developed by you to filter the data, can take into consideration many variables.

❏ Who is currently logged in

❏ Who owns the procedure accessing the data

❏ What time of day it is

❏ Which IP address is used by the client

❏ Whether the request is a web request or a client server application

The possibilities are limitless, and easy to implement. For example, you could set up a rule that limits the data based on the client's IP address. If the client of the database is in the domain of your company you get to see one set of data. If the IP address comes from outside of your company you get a restricted set of data. You would for example limit the data seen by time of day. You can query up the information from 9-5 but if you attempt to do it at 9pm, you'll get no data found. You can take any and all of these factors (and more) into consideration and develop a predicate to allow the user to see/modify only the rows they are allowed to. You do not need to use a specific program to access the data; you just need the database.

Ultimately the choice is yours. By utilizing the features inherent in your database you will maximize the return on your investment in the software. You can replicate many features contained within the database in your own software at the expense of custom development and ongoing maintenance, or you can choose to use the off the shelf functionality. You will find it more productive in the long run (and more open as well) to utilize to the fullest the software you have purchased.

Use the Tools the Database Provides

There really isn't such a thing as the most important tool, but the one I'll talk about here as an example definitely ranks up there in order of importance. This section isn't just about this one tool, it is really about getting to know the database product you are using. I've seen many cases where people develop tools and techniques to solve problems that already have solutions (some very old solutions in fact). The reason was simply due to ignorance of the tool set that was available to them. For example, I've seen people write DDL extraction tools over and over again – not realizing that a simple "EXP … rows=NO" and "IMP … indexfile=ddl.sql" could do it for them. Or they write complex functions in Java or PLSQL to perform date arithmetic, never realizing that it is as easy as adding 1/24 to a date to add an hour. The Oracle database can do anything – it is well worth the time to learn as much as possible about it.

Here we will discuss the usefulness of the SQL_TRACE setting, the results of a TKPROF report, how to use this to figure out what your program is doing and how to tune it (briefly, just to show what is possible). We will not go into an exhaustive review of SQL_TRACE, we will use it briefly to give you an idea of the power of it, and hopefully to make you curious about what other goodies the database has to offer.

I use this particular feature as my predominant method of tuning. I am typically called in to "make things go faster". I have no background information on the application – what it does or how it does it. This is the tool I use to find out what and how it is doing things, many times telling the people who actually wrote the application how their program behaves. You see this frequently when using a development environment that generates the SQL for you. For example, in Chapter 15, we find the statement:

*... It can also provide the logic to actually move the entity's state to and from the database. This is known as **container-managed persistence** (CMP). ... Allowing the EJB container to handle the persistence logic (thus freeing application programmers from having to write sometimes-difficult, always-tedious SQL code and logic) can be a tremendous productivity enhancer...*

This section shows there are two sides to this story. If the EJB container handles all of the SQL for you, you effectively have no idea what the application is doing in the database or how it is doing it. This can be a serious performance impediment. I will repeat – not understanding what your application does in the database or how it does it will lead to performance issues. I've worked with people using EJBs and CMP for the above reasons (the perception that it is too difficult to learn SQL, so they don't want to bother with it). What they quickly discovered was that what worked fine in their test database, with a small amount of data, in single user mode, fell apart when run against the live data, with many users. Issues surrounding serialization soon appeared, issues with non-performing queries appeared. The application did not run very well at all. Unfortunately, since the developers had been so carefully shielded from the database itself, they had no idea how to fix it, how to make it go faster, what tools they had at their disposal or *even what the program actually did in the database*. This made tuning this application a challenge to say the least. Using SQL_TRACE, I was able to inform the developers exactly what SQL was being executed and in what isolation level. We were able to see the exact "SELECT for UPDATE" statements causing the serialization and the queries that were performing poorly. Just by running their application through its screens in single user mode, we identified all of their serious performance issues and fixed them in a matter of minutes.

SQL_Trace

SQL_TRACE is a facility in the database whereby you can have the server record all of the SQL activity in a session. The information recorded includes:

- ❑   The actual SQL for the entire time tracing is on – executed by the server (ODBC users are often surprised to see that the SQL they thought they were sending to the database is not the same as the SQL the database actually received – some ODBC adapters try to rewrite the SQL)

- ❑   The amount and number of times we spent parsing that SQL

- ❑   The amount and number of times we spent executing the SQL

- ❑   How many rows were affected in the database

- ❑   How many physical disk reads we did

- ❑   How many logical IOs we performed

- ❑   What the query plans were

- ❑   How many rows passed through each phase of the query plan and so on

In order to demonstrate this feature, I am using the restaurant example from Chapter 15. I started with no understanding of what this application was, what it did, or how it did it. By enabling SQL_TRACE I was able to see the exact SQL submitted by this bean to the database and how it performed. I could then make some suggestions as to how this application would perform if it were scaled up (it works great on the small data set it uses but would not scale up over time as more restaurants were added).

In this particular example, I used a supplied package DBMS_SYSTEM and the procedure SET_SQL_TRACE_IN_SESSION to turn on trace in our bean while it was executing. I would start the sample Java client and before answering any of its prompts I went into the database, queried V$SESSION to find my EJB session and, using the SID and SERIAL# columns from V$SESSION, enabled trace. I ran the bean to completion at that point and that closed my session (hence ending the trace). I then used the command line tool TKPROF to format the raw trace file into a readable report. We'll investigate the contents of this report in a moment in the TKPROF section below. Right now, I'll just demonstrate the steps I went through to get the trace generated in this case in the first place:

1. I started the Java bean client program.

```
C:\> java restaurants2.ClientInterview
Are you looking for dinner, or do you want to book an event?
#0 Dinner
#1 An event
```

2. In another window, using SQLPlus, I identified my session in the database:

```
system@TKYTE816> select sid, serial#, username from v$session where username =
'SCOTT';

       SID    SERIAL# USERNAME
---------- ---------- ------------------------------
         8         44 SCOTT
```

3. I made sure TIMED_STATISTICS was on and turned on SQL_TRACE in that session. Note that you need DBA type privileges to change this system setting and to set SQL_TRACE in another session. I used the SYSTEM account in this example:

```
system@TKYTE816> alter system set timed_statistics=true;
System altered.
system@TKYTE816> exec sys.dbms_system.set_sql_trace_in_session( 8, 44, TRUE );
PL/SQL procedure successfully completed.
```

4. I completed the "interview" with the bean application and allowed it to exit.

That was it. I now have the raw trace file I need to generate the report and analyze exactly what the application did. We can find where trace files are generated to on the server via:

```
system@TKYTE816> show parameter user_dump_dest

NAME                                 TYPE    VALUE
------------------------------------ ------- ------------------------------
user_dump_dest                       string  C:\oracle\admin\tkyte816\udump
```

You need access to the dynamic performance view v$parameter to see this information. Before we look at our trace file, we will explore other ways to get trace output from our applications:

Using SQL_TRACE=TRUE in the init.ora

This has the advantage of being very easy. You do not have to identify your session; you don't have to run a procedure to get trace started. It has a distinct disadvantage in that you cannot control what sessions will be traced (they all are) and tracing will generate copious amounts of data. This can rapidly fill up your file system. The use of the init.ora parameter is only feasible on single user systems where you control all of the sessions. It is good for a developer working on their machine. I would recommend against this approach unless you have no other method of enabling trace.

Using an "ON LOGON" Trigger in the Database

This is one of my favorite methods. We can create a trigger much like this:

```
create or replace trigger login_trigger
after logon on schema
begin
        execute immediate
        'ALTER SESSION SET TIMED_STATISTICS=TRUE';
        execute immediate
        'ALTER SESSION SET SQL_TRACE=TRUE;
end;
/
```

and have SQL_TRACE and TIMED_STATISTICS set on for us when we logon.

Adding the SQL Commands Directly into Our Applications

This is an excellent thing to have – the ability to tell your application via switches or properties that it should or should not trace. For all new code you develop, this would be strongly encouraged. Your application would have some method of enabling SQL_TRACE via a command line switch or a property file or any other method you want. In this fashion, you can easily enable SQL_TRACE at any time.

Now we are ready to review the output of our trace file we generated via the restaurant example.

TKPROF

TKPROF is the command line tool that will take a raw trace file generated by SQL_TRACE and format it into a readable report containing the relevant data. TKPROF works only on these types of trace files (don't try to use it on a trace file generated by some server error – those are for support to deal with. TKPROF will not format these into anything you can use).

TKPROF has many command line options – we'll not be going into them here, those are for you to explore. Here we will simply use TKPROF to reformat the trace file and review its contents. We begin by finding our USER_DUMP_DESTINATION, where the server will place our trace files and going there. To find our trace file – it is typically easiest to do a sorted directory search (for example: ls -ltr on Unix or dir /o:d on Windows) and find the newest file. That should be your trace file. Once we have identified it, we simply execute:

```
C:\oracle\ADMIN\tkyte816\udump>tkprof <tracefilename>.trc tkprof.txt
TKPROF: Release 8.1.6.0.0 - Production on Wed Nov 15 16:14:56 2000
(c) Copyright 1999 Oracle Corporation.  All rights reserved.
```

Now we can edit this file. In this case, there are only two queries in this report. One of the queries is:

```
select longname
from
 javasnm$ where short = :1


call     count       cpu    elapsed       disk      query    current        rows
-------  ------  --------  ---------  ---------  ---------  ---------  ----------
Parse       40      0.04       0.05          0          0          0           0
Execute     40      0.01       0.01          0          0          0           0
Fetch       40      0.00       0.00          0        160          0          40
-------  ------  --------  ---------  ---------  ---------  ---------  ----------
total      120      0.05       0.06          0        160          0          40

Misses in library cache during parse: 0
Optimizer goal: CHOOSE
Parsing user id: SYS    (recursive depth: 1)


Rows     Row Source Operation
-------  --------------------------------------------------
      1  TABLE ACCESS BY INDEX ROWID JAVASNM$
      1   INDEX UNIQUE SCAN (object id 317)
```

This SQL query won't be found anywhere in our sample application, this SQL is actually what is known as recursive SQL – SQL performed in order to perform our SQL. There are many types of recursive SQL performed at various times – for space management, security checks and so on. In fact, if you run this example on a cold database, a database that was just started, you'll see dozens of SQL queries in your TKPROF report, not just two. These queries were executed to read the Java byte code, parse SQL queries for the first time and so on. Once executed, most of these queries need not be executed again as their output is stored in the shared pool for us. (The shared pool is a database caching area for shared query plans, stored procedure code, dictionary information and so on).

So, we will ignore this query for right now since we cannot do anything about it. We can avoid some, but not all, recursive SQL – for example, if we find our application is doing lots of space management, requesting new extents and the like, we can use locally managed tablespaces to completely avoid that recursive SQL. If we use dictionary-managed tablespaces we can still avoid much of this recursive SQL by changing our storage parameters so we request space less frequently. This small digression on recursive SQL points out that you might very well need to have more than a cursory understanding of the database in order to build a high-performance application. If you do not know what a dictionary-managed tablespace is and how it is different from a locally managed one is... Or if recursive SQL is news to you, you might now start realizing you have a need to know about these things as they materially affect the performance of your application.

Onto the query we can do something about in the TKPROF report. It is:

```
select name, chef
from
 restaurant t1 where t1.location = :1 and 4 = (select count(*) from
  restaurantproperty t2 where t2.restaurant = t1.name and ( (code=:2 and val=
  :3)  or  (code=:4 and val=:5)  or  (code=:6 and val=:7)  or  (code=:8 and
  val=:9) ))
```

call	count	cpu	elapsed	disk	query	current	rows
Parse	1	0.00	0.00	0	0	0	0
Execute	1	0.00	0.00	0	0	0	0
Fetch	1	0.01	0.01	0	33	4	2
total	3	0.01	0.01	0	33	4	2

```
Misses in library cache during parse: 0
Optimizer goal: CHOOSE
Parsing user id: 32       (recursive depth: 1)

Rows     Row Source Operation
-------  ---------------------------------------------------------
      2  FILTER
      5   TABLE ACCESS FULL RESTAURANT
      8   SORT AGGREGATE
     12    CONCATENATION
      2     TABLE ACCESS BY INDEX ROWID RESTAURANTPROPERTY
      8      INDEX UNIQUE SCAN (object id 21398)
      2     TABLE ACCESS BY INDEX ROWID RESTAURANTPROPERTY
      8      INDEX UNIQUE SCAN (object id 21398)
      4     TABLE ACCESS BY INDEX ROWID RESTAURANTPROPERTY
      8      INDEX UNIQUE SCAN (object id 21398)
      4     TABLE ACCESS BY INDEX ROWID RESTAURANTPROPERTY
      8      INDEX UNIQUE SCAN (object id 21398)
```

This report quickly shows us

❑   We processed 33 blocks of data in "query" mode (our consistent read mode).

❑   We processed four blocks of data in "current" mode. This mode is more expensive than current mode and may get blocked temporarily by other sessions. This mode means we need to get the block as it exists right now – we might have to wait for other transactions to commit. In this case, these blocks were needed to get the extent map of the restaurant table so we could full scan it (data dictionary blocks are commonly read in current mode).

❑   It took 1/100 of a CPU second and 1/100 of a wall clock second to execute.

The query that was executed:

```
select name, chef
from
  restaurant t1 where t1.location = :1 and 4 = (select count(*) from
    restaurantproperty t2 where t2.restaurant = t1.name and ( (code=:2 and val=
    :3)  or  (code=:4 and val=:5)  or  (code=:6 and val=:7)  or  (code=:8 and
    val=:9) ))
```

is known as a correlated query. The subquery "and 4 = (select count(*) … " is a correlated subquery since it refers to values from the outer query. A correlated subquery is executed once for each row in the outer query. The above query could procedurally be written as:

```
        for x in ( select name, chef from restaurant where location = :1 ) loop
    select count(*) into :cnt
        from restaurantproperty
      where restaurant = :x.name
        and ( (code=:2 and val= :3)
          or  (code=:4 and val=:5)
          or  (code=:6 and val=:7)
          or  (code=:8 and val=:9) ));

      if ( :cnt = 4 ) then
          OUTPUT record
      else
          IGNORE record, does not meet all of our criteria
      End if
    End loop
```

We can see that in our query plan below. It full scanned the restaurant table and then executed the subquery each time. The row counts bear that out. We can see it probing the restaurant property table many times – once for each row that met our location criteria. After all was said and done, two rows made it out of this query and were returned to the client. Look at how many rows were processed to find those two rows however – lots of work was done:

```
Rows      Row Source Operation
-------   -------------------------------------------------------
      2   FILTER
      5    TABLE ACCESS FULL RESTAURANT
      8    SORT AGGREGATE
     12     CONCATENATION
      2      TABLE ACCESS BY INDEX ROWID RESTAURANTPROPERTY
      8        INDEX UNIQUE SCAN (object id 21398)
      2      TABLE ACCESS BY INDEX ROWID RESTAURANTPROPERTY
      8        INDEX UNIQUE SCAN (object id 21398)
      4      TABLE ACCESS BY INDEX ROWID RESTAURANTPROPERTY
      8        INDEX UNIQUE SCAN (object id 21398)
      4      TABLE ACCESS BY INDEX ROWID RESTAURANTPROPERTY
      8        INDEX UNIQUE SCAN (object id 21398)
```

It is a good thing our sample had only five restaurants – four of which met our location criteria – and that a suitable index existed on our restaurant property table. If it had thousands of restaurants, our initial FULL SCAN of restaurant would have taken quite a while. Additionally – if many of them were in the correct location, we would have run that subquery many times in a loop. So, I see two problems with scaling this query up:

❑ The full scan on restaurant

❑ The inefficient subquery

Lets look at how we can possibly make this query more efficient for thousands of restaurants, if it had to read 33 blocks to get the answer with a set of data that should fit on a single block, what will happen when we have thousands of blocks to consider. What we might start by doing is consider indexing LOCATION in the restaurant table. We would do this if LOCATION were considered selective. We would want the query "select * from restaurant where location = 'some value'" to return a small percentage of the table (say 20% or less). If we can add that index, the query plan will change from a FULL SCAN to an index range scan + table access by ROWID. We can rapidly find the rows we want and perform the subquery on them. We might consider indexing (code, val) in the RESTAURANTPROPERTY table – we use them heavily in the predicate as well. The bottom line is there are perhaps dozens of ways to write this query, given that you have some knowledge of the underlying data, you can make a query that has a chance to perform better then some other query. For example, in the above example, a simple optimization is to use WHERE EXISTS in place of " 4 = (subquery)". By using the "4 = (subquery)" technique, we force the database to find *all* matching rows, then count them. Using a WHERE EXISTS many times, we can allow the database to stop processing a given row in our query as soon as it discovers one of the (code, val) pairs we are interested in no longer exist. For example, I rewrote the query as follows:

```
select name, chef
  from restaurant t1
 where t1.location = :x1
   and exists (select null
                 from restaurantproperty t2
                where t2.restaurant = t1.name
                  and code = :x6 and val = :x7 )
   and exists (select null
                 from restaurantproperty t2
                where t2.restaurant = t1.name
                  and code = :x4 and val = :x5 )
   and exists (select null
                 from restaurantproperty t2
                where t2.restaurant = t1.name
                  and code = :x8 and val = :x9 )
   and exists (select null
                 from restaurantproperty t2
                where t2.restaurant = t1.name
                  and code = :x2 and val = :x3 )
```

call	count	cpu	elapsed	disk	query	current	rows
Parse	1	0.00	0.00	0	0	0	0
Execute	1	0.00	0.00	0	0	0	0
Fetch	2	0.00	0.00	0	22	4	2
total	4	0.00	0.00	0	22	4	2

```
Misses in library cache during parse: 1
Optimizer goal: CHOOSE
Parsing user id: 32

Rows     Row Source Operation
-------  ---------------------------------------------------------
      2  FILTER
      5   TABLE ACCESS FULL RESTAURANT
      2   TABLE ACCESS BY INDEX ROWID RESTAURANTPROPERTY
      2    INDEX UNIQUE SCAN (object id 21398)
      2   TABLE ACCESS BY INDEX ROWID RESTAURANTPROPERTY
      2    INDEX UNIQUE SCAN (object id 21398)
      2   TABLE ACCESS BY INDEX ROWID RESTAURANTPROPERTY
      2    INDEX UNIQUE SCAN (object id 21398)
      4   TABLE ACCESS BY INDEX ROWID RESTAURANTPROPERTY
      6    INDEX UNIQUE SCAN (object id 21398)
```

As you can see, this query (which is 100% equivalent to the original) processed about two thirds of the number of blocks – it did less work. This is because as soon as ONE of the WHERE EXISTS failed – the database stopped processing the remaining subqueries.

Going a step further, I added an index on restaurantproperty(code,val) and substituted in this query:

```
select name, chef
  from restaurant
 where name in ( select name
                   from restaurantproperty
                  where ( (code=:x2 and val=:x3)
                       or (code=:x4 and val=:x5)
                       or (code=:x6 and val=:x7)
                       or (code=:x8 and val=:x9) )
                  group by name
                  having count(*) = 4)
   and location = :x1
```

call	count	cpu	elapsed	disk	query	current	rows
Parse	1	0.01	0.01	0	0	0	0
Execute	1	0.00	0.00	0	0	0	0
Fetch	1	0.00	0.00	0	17	4	0
total	3	0.01	0.01	0	17	4	0

```
Misses in library cache during parse: 0
Optimizer goal: CHOOSE
Parsing user id: 32
```

Rows	Row Source Operation
0	FILTER
5	TABLE ACCESS FULL RESTAURANT
4	FILTER
8	SORT GROUP BY
56	CONCATENATION
12	INDEX RANGE SCAN (object id 21484)
12	INDEX RANGE SCAN (object id 21484)
16	INDEX RANGE SCAN (object id 21484)
16	INDEX RANGE SCAN (object id 21484)

Now we have it down to 17 blocks processed – a 50% reduction.

Which one of these is best? Without knowing more about how the actual data is distributed, it is hard to say. Perhaps an index on location plus the WHERE EXISTS optimization would be best, if location is very selective. Maybe a bitmap index on (code, val) would be the most efficient method. Maybe some other query (I came with at least four other queries that are semantically the same as the original but syntactically different. These queries have very different plans from each other). If I was able to sit down with the people who knew the data, we would be able to figure out the best approach. I can only say this because I have the above information – without it, we would be able to draw no conclusions.

Hopefully, this shows that knowledge of the workings of the optimizer, a full grasp of SQL and all of its features, the ability to use the tools provided and understand their output are critical to a successful application. A single slow query can make or break your application. Take a look at this application. What if it were a web application that had restaurants worldwide and let people make these searches from anywhere. The performance of this single query – the amount of work it does – would make or break this application. This is not something you want to have in a "black box" that you feel you do not need to understand. This is something you want to have a firm grasp on – complete control over.

Summary

What we are trying to point out in this chapter is that a solid understanding of the core technologies you are using is extremely relevant. We have touched on a couple of points here – SQL/92 and "standard SQL", different locking models, concurrency controls, transactions, optimizers, "openness", and tools. These are some of the things you still need to be concerned about – even when using tools that are supposed to hide this from you. They can only hide it for so long, eventually you must address these issues and you can only do that by having a good understanding of what the database you are using actually does and how it does it.

If this chapter has started you thinking seriously about these issues then it has done its job. The basic point I've tried to make is this: no matter what tool or programming model you use with the Oracle database, you are never absolved or abstracted from needing to understand what the database can do and how it works.

17

Business Components for Java

Business Components for Java, or BC4J, is a framework from Oracle Corporation for writing the business logic tier of an application. As detailed in Chapters 15 and 22, enterprise applications are architected across at least three tiers: the client tier, the business logic tier and the database. Often the physical locations of these tiers will be different in each case.

BC4J is aimed at interacting with the same variety of clients as EJBs and, given that the EJB technology is already in place and so popular, one might wonder if indeed there is any need for another middle tier framework. The EJB model has been widely adopted, and provides services such as concurrency management, transaction management, security and so on, which free developers from system level plumbing, and help them to focus on the business logic. However, the model is still complex, and provides many development challenges.

This is where BC4J provides an alternative approach. The BC4J framework provides system level services similar to those provided by the EJB container. In conjunction with JDeveloper, BC4J provides wizard-driven facilities for object-relational mappings, and a host of generic functionalities for database interaction and transaction management. Customizations can be applied at all stages. Business logic developed with BC4J can be deployed as an EJB or a CORBA server object in the Oracle 8i JServer, to the visibroker CORBA ORB, or to any application server (although the present release of JDeveloper helps in deploying only to Oracle Application Server). Changing deployment platform does not necessitate any code changes. Developing applications with BC4J therefore becomes simpler than developing with EJBs.

This chapter will cover:

- ❑ The BC4J architecture, with a detailed discussion of the components that go into a typical BC4J application

- ❑ Rapid development of application logic using Oracle JDeveloper (we will use version 3.1.1.2)

- ❑ Deployment of the business logic as an EJB in the Oracle 8i JVM

- ❑ Developing client applications for the BC4J Application Logic

- ❑ Integration with Oracle's Web Beans using JavaServer Pages

- ❑ Deployment of the Web application to Oracle's Internet Application Server (iAS 1.0)

A simple application will be built to demonstrate the features of the architecture. Chapter 15 built a restaurant finder application. In this chapter we will build one to reserve tables in a restaurant and to place take-out orders.

Components of Oracle BC4J

The BC4J framework consists of the following components:

- ❑ **Application modules**
  These encapsulate the View Objects and business services required for a complete application and serve as a logical container for coordinated objects related to a particular task.

- ❑ **View objects**
  These are based on a SQL statement and are useful for joining, filtering, projecting, and sorting the business data for the specific needs of a given application scenario or task.

- ❑ **View links**
  View Links specify relationship between two view objects. The relationship can be one-to-one or one-to-many. Multiple view links can be used to create a many-to-many relationship.These are used to coordinate master-detail types of data in a declarative way.

- ❑ **Entity objects**
  These encapsulate the business logic and database storage details of the business entities.

- ❑ **Domains**
  These map the data types of the Entity Attributes.

- ❑ **Associations**
  These capture all the relationships between the business entities.

The relationships between these components are depicted in the schematic overleaf, which presents the architecture of a typical application built using BC4J.

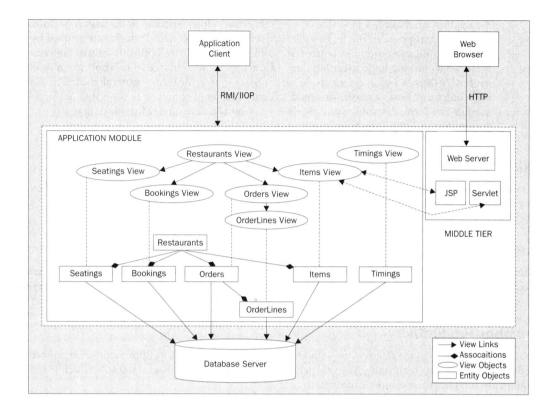

Features of BC4J

Encapsulated Business Logic

Business logic, including validation, that resides and executes in the middle tier, promotes thin clients, ease of customization, and reuse. This code can be placed at different levels within the BC4J framework for effective component reuse:

❏   An entity object contains business logic pertaining to a single business entity. All view objects based on the entity object share the logic. At the entity level, calculations are performed in Java code.

❏   A view object contains logic pertaining to a view, which is defined by a SQL SELECT statement. This can include SQL-calculated expressions, joins, unions, nested subselects, and so on. We can also add code to the Java source, for example, we can propagate events to the UI, or create a method that calls an entity method that we want to expose for this view.

❑ An application module's Java source files can contain logic specific to the task it performs – logic not appropriate to put in an entity object or view object, and which can be used by multiple application modules performing different tasks. If two applications use the same view, we would put logic specific to one of the applications in one of its application module source files instead of in the entity or view object source files. As a general guideline, if we have one form view per task, we could structure our application so there is one application module per form. An application module represents a data model for a task that is accomplished within one transaction.

Flexible Views Of Data

Views of data are SQL-based and completely separate from the underlying entities, enabling flexible presentation schemes, that is, different view objects might encapsulate different queries but be based on the same entity objects and thus present data in different forms.

Transaction Management

Business Components for Java caches data in entity objects, manages changes to the data and handles posting of changes to the database. It provides default transaction support without the developer having to write any code unless he wishes to customize the default behavior for transactions.

Developer Productivity

With the integration of the framework with Oracle JDeveloper, the BC4J approach can significantly reduce the product roll-out times. JDeveloper provides a powerful toolset of wizards which leads to significant increase in developer productivity.

Developing with BC4J

Development with BC4J involves tight integration with Oracle JDeveloper. BC4J allows us to define the characteristics of business objects: their attributes, relationships, and business rules. We then let JDeveloper generate the necessary Java and XML code which we customize with minimal effort.

JDeveloper enforces no particular methodology, but the development process typically involves answering questions like these:

❑ What are the entities and business objects?

❑ How are the entities related?

❑ What are the validation rules?

❑ What data will be presented and manipulated?

Enough of theory, let's get to the nitty-gritty of learning how to develop an application using the BC4J framework.

The Restaurant Example

In Chapter 15, we built a restaurant finder application, where the user enters his preferences for his choice of restaurants. Let's continue from where we left off by building a restaurant portal for online reservation of tables and for placing orders for home delivery. This application consists of four screens in the client tier. The first screen will present the user with a list of restaurants and their descriptions (we will assume the list is based on his preferences entered in the previous application!). If in the first screen the user chooses the **Book Seats** link, he is led to the second screen where he then enters his choice of seating-type in the restaurant, number of people visiting, credit card number, etc. and books a table. The third screen provides for cancellation of a table reservation. A fourth screen provides the user with an option of placing home-delivery orders for his food. The user can navigate to his choice of restaurant using the arrows on the navigator bar:

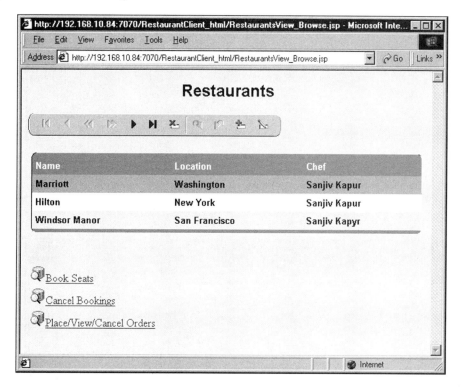

The functionality of this page also allows, by default, the customer to edit and to add or delete restaurants. This would be disabled according to the eventual business plan for the project. Next, click on the **Book Seats** link to get to the next page:

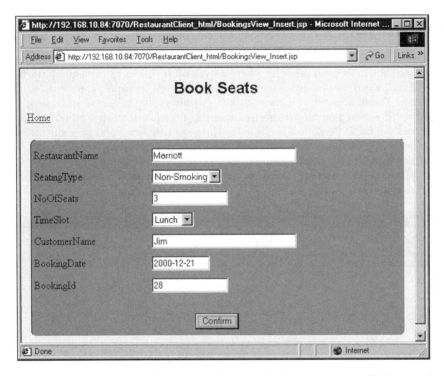

The booking identifier is automatically generated using a database sequence. If the user chooses the Cancel Bookings link they arrive at the screen below, where the bookings for each restaurant can be scrolled through and deleted as desired.

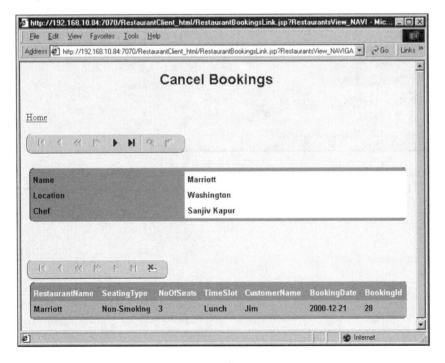

Orders for take-outs can be placed through the screen below, which is reached from the third hyperlink in the home page. A new order is created by clicking on the plus symbol in the navigator bar. The current sequence of orders is shown in the second table:

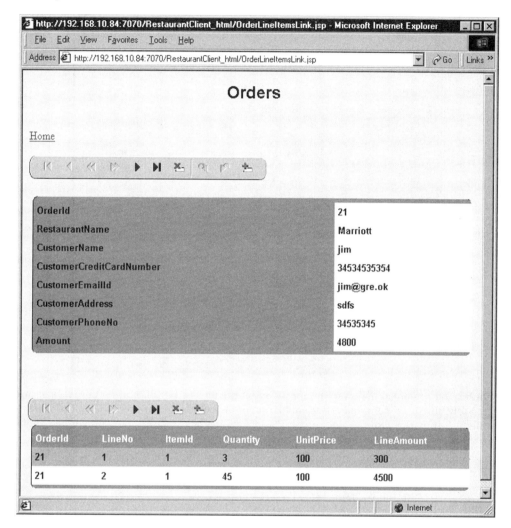

The customer edits the order in the next screen:

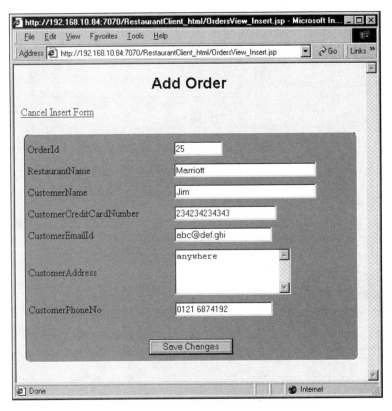

The application presented here is by no means a comprehensive portal. For the purposes of this chapter, only functional components essential to demonstrate the feature set of the BC4J framework are implemented. In particular, the generated JSP application would require some finetuning, and possibly additional pages, to complete a viable implementation.

The development process can be broken down into the following steps:

- Creating a Business Components Project
- Creating Entity Objects and Associations based on the database design
- Creating View Objects and View Links based on the Entity Objects and Associations
- Adding Validation logic using Domains and Built-In Validation Rules
- Writing Business Logic in the Entity Objects, or in remotely accessible methods in the Application Module and the View Objects
- Making the Application Module remotable
- Deploying the Application Module (we will be deploying it as a Session EJB in Oracle 8i)
- Building the client tier and deploying it on iAS

Creating a Database

The Restaurant example consists of seven database tables, which will hold information for our portal. It also has two sequences for generating primary keys. Create a new user called RESTAURANT and run the following SQL script which will create the database tables for us:

```
CREATE TABLE restaurants (
        name VARCHAR2(25) NOT NULL,
        location VARCHAR2(25) NOT NULL,
        chef VARCHAR2(25),
        PRIMARY KEY (name)
);

CREATE TABLE seatings (
        restaurant_name VARCHAR2(25), CONSTRAINT restaurant_seatings
          FOREIGN KEY (restaurant_name) REFERENCES restaurants(name),
        seating_type VARCHAR2(25),
        no_of_seats NUMBER(25) NOT NULL,
        PRIMARY KEY (restaurant_name, seating_type)
);

CREATE TABLE timings (
    time_slot VARCHAR2(50) PRIMARY KEY
);

CREATE TABLE bookings (
        restaurant_name VARCHAR2(25), CONSTRAINT restaurant_bookings
          foreign key (restaurant_name) REFERENCES restaurants(name),
        seating_type VARCHAR2(25),
        no_of_seats NUMBER(10) NOT NULL,
        time_slot VARCHAR2(50) NOT NULL,
          CONSTRAINT time_slot_bookings FOREIGN KEY (time_slot)
          REFERENCES timings(time_slot),
        customer_name VARCHAR2(25) NOT NULL,
        booking_date DATE NOT NULL,
        booking_id NUMBER(10),
        PRIMARY KEY (booking_id)
);

CREATE TABLE ITEMS (
        restaurant_name VARCHAR2(25), CONSTRAINT restaurant_items
          foreign KEY (restaurant_name) REFERENCES restaurants(name) ,
        item_id NUMBER(4),
        item_name VARCHAR2(25),
        description VARCHAR2(255),
        price NUMBER(5,2),
        PRIMARY KEY (restaurant_name, item_id)
);

CREATE TABLE orders (
        order_id NUMBER(4),
        restaurant_name VARCHAR2(25), CONSTRAINT restaurant_orders
          FOREIGN KEY (restaurant_name) REFERENCES restaurants(name) ,
        customer_name VARCHAR2(25) NOT NULL,
        customer_credit_card_number VARCHAR2(16),
        customer_email_id VARCHAR2(255),
        customer_address VARCHAR2(255),
        customer_phone_no VARCHAR2(255),
        amount NUMBER(10,2),
```

```
        PRIMARY KEY (order_id)
   );

CREATE TABLE order_lines (
        order_id NUMBER(4), CONSTRAINT order_line_items
        FOREIGN KEY (order_id)
        REFERENCES orders (order_id) on DELETE CASCADE ,
        line_no NUMBER(4),
        item_id NUMBER(4),
        quantity NUMBER(4) NOT NULL,
        unit_price NUMBER(10,2),
        line_amount NUMBER(10,2),
        PRIMARY KEY (ORDER_ID , LINE_NO)
   );

CREATE SEQUENCE booking_seq START WITH 1 INCREMENT BY 1;
CREATE SEQUENCE order_seq START WITH 1 INCREMENT BY 1;
```

Creating the Database Connections in JDeveloper

❏   Choose Tools | Connections from the menu bar.

❏   Choose New... in the Connections dialog box.

❏   Give an appropriate Connection Name and choose JDBC from the Connection Type radio group.

❏   Enter your authentication details, test the connection and press OK.

❏   Repeat the process but now choose Connection Type as IIOP. An IIOP connection is required to communicate with EJBs deployed in Oracle 8i. IIOP or "Internet Inter-ORB Protocol" is the protocol for such communication. You need to ensure that an IIOP listener is configured on the target database and make a note of the listener port (the default is 2481).

So we should now have a JDBC connection:

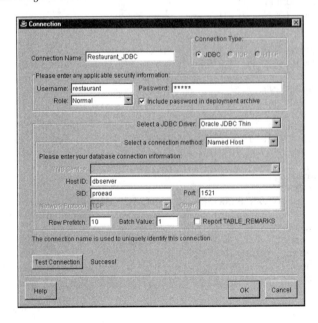

And an IIOP connection:

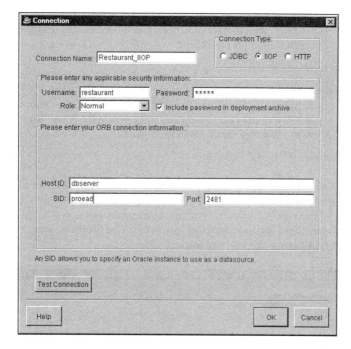

Creating a Business Components Project using JDeveloper

The following steps describe how to use JDeveloper to create Business Components for a Java Project:

- ❑ Start a new project by selecting File | New Project.

- ❑ On the Welcome panel, review the steps of this wizard and click Next.

- ❑ On the Project Type panel, type `<JDEV_HOME>\myprojects\RestaurantBooking.jpr` in the project filename field. (Use the full pathname of your JDeveloper root directory.) Choose to create "A Project Containing Business Components" and click Next.

- ❑ On the Project Options panel, enter the name of the default package as `restaurant`, and accept the default source path, and output directory. Click Next.

- ❑ Enter relevant information about our project in the Project Information panel. We can also choose to generate an HTML file for our project. Click Next when we are finished with this panel.

- ❑ The Finish panel shows a tree representing the options we have chosen. If we want to modify these values click Back. Otherwise, click Finish.

- ❑ The Business Component Project Wizard is chained into the Project Wizard and appears immediately. On the Welcome panel click Next to continue.

- ❑ On the Connections panel, choose the `Restaurant_JDBC` connection from the dropdown list. Click Next.

- ❑ On the **Package Name** panel we enter `restaurant`. Click **Next** to continue.

- ❑ In the **Create Entity Objects Tab** select `BOOKINGS`, `ITEMS`, `RESTAURANTS`, `SEATINGS`, `ORDERS`, `ORDER_LINES` and `TIMINGS`. Check the **View Objects** and **View Links** checkbox as well as the **Application Module** checkbox.

- ❑ Click **Finish** to close the wizard.

- ❑ Generate **View Row** classes for **each** of the views by launching the View Object Wizard. Right-click on the view object and choose **Edit** from the pop-up menu. On the View Object Wizard, the **Java** tab will provide the option to generate the View Row Class. In the **Java** tab check the **Generate view row class** checkbox.

- ❑ From the **File** menu, choose **Save All**.

A view row class is a very handy and elegant way to manipulate view rows as will be evident in the later sections of the chapter. A view row is an object that consists of data for a row. A view row helps manipulate the data of the view's query. A view row class generates accessor methods for each attribute, or column. Furthermore, these accessor methods provide the appropriate return types, so we also don't have to worry about typecasting or checking for null values.

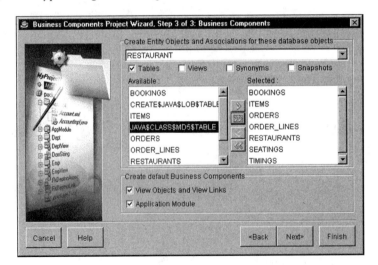

Implementing the Support Classes

We now have a **business components project** which has provided us with mappings for the database objects. We will eventually create an **application module** whose methods can be accessed by a remote client. For exchange of data between the client and the application module, we will also create some helper classes to allow us to transfer information over the wire. The following are the required helper objects: `Restaurant`, `Reservation`, `Order`, `OrderLine` and `Item`. These classes have fields corresponding to the columns in the database, and like all objects that are to be transferred across the network, they implement `java.io.Serializable`.

Create the following classes in the same project in the Jdeveloper navigation view.

Class Item

This class is defined for holding of the items available on the menu of a resataurant and transferring the information across the network:

```java
package restaurant;

import java.io.Serializable;

public class Item implements Serializable{

    public String restaurantName;
    public int itemId;
    public String itemName;
    public String description;
    public float price;

    public Item(      String aRestaurantName,
                      int aItemId,
                      String aItemName,
                      String aDescription,
                      float aPrice
                ) {
        restaurantName = aRestaurantName;
        itemId = aItemId;
        itemName = aItemName;
        description = aDescription;
        price = aPrice;
    }
}
```

Class Order

This class is defined for holding details of the take-out orders placed at a restaurant, and transferring information across the network:

```java
package restaurant;

import java.io.Serializable;

//This class holds information about an Order
public class Order implements Serializable {

    public int orderId;
    public String restaurantName;
    public String customerName;
    public String customerCreditCardNumber;
    public String customerEmailId;
    public String customerAddress;
    public String customerPhoneNo;
    public float amount;

    public OrderLine[] orderLines;
```

```
/**
 * Constructor
 */
public Order( int aOrderId,
              String aRestaurantName,
              String aCustomerName,
              String aCustomerCreditCardNumber,
              String aCustomerEmailId,
              String aCustomerAddress,
              String aCustomerPhoneNo,
              float aAmount,
          OrderLine[] aOrderLines

                ) {
        orderId = aOrderId;
        restaurantName = aRestaurantName;
        customerName = aCustomerName;
        customerCreditCardNumber = aCustomerCreditCardNumber;
        customerEmailId = aCustomerEmailId;
        customerAddress = aCustomerAddress;
        customerPhoneNo = aCustomerPhoneNo;
        amount = aAmount;

        orderLines = aOrderLines;
    }
}
```

Class OrderLine

An array of objects of this class is declared in the class `Order` and represents Line Items for a particular order:

```
package restaurant;

import java.io.Serializable;

//This class holds information about an order line
public class OrderLine implements Serializable {

    public int orderId;
    public int lineNo;
    public int itemId;
    public int quantity;
    public float unitPrice;
    public float lineAmount;

    /**
     * Constructor
     */
    public OrderLine( int aOrderId,
                      int aLineNo,
                      int aItemId,
                      int aQuantity,
                      float aUnitPrice,
                      float aLineAmount
                        ) {
```

```
        orderId = aOrderId;
        lineNo = aLineNo;
        itemId = aItemId;
        quantity = aQuantity;
        unitPrice = aUnitPrice;
        lineAmount = aLineAmount;
    }
}
```

Class Reservation

This class is defined for holding and transferring across the network information about a Reservation made at a restaurant:

```
package restaurant;

import java.io.Serializable;

//This class holds information about a booking made by the user
public class Reservation implements Serializable {
    public int bookingID = 0;
    public String seatingType = null;
    public String restaurantName = null;
    public int noOfSeats = 0;
    public String timeSlot = null;
    public String customerName = null;
    public String bookingDate = null;
    public Reservation(   String aSeatingType,
            String aRestaurantName,
            int aNoOfSeats,
            String aTimeSlot,
            String aCustomerName,
            String aBookingDate )
    {
        seatingType = aSeatingType;
        restaurantName = aRestaurantName;
        noOfSeats = aNoOfSeats;
        timeSlot = aTimeSlot;
        customerName = aCustomerName;
        bookingDate = aBookingDate;
    }

    public Reservation(   int aBookingID,
            String aSeatingType,
            String aRestaurantName,
            int aNoOfSeats,
            String aTimeSlot,
            String aCustomerName,
            String aBookingDate ) {
        bookingID = aBookingID;
        seatingType = aSeatingType;
        restaurantName = aRestaurantName;
        noOfSeats = aNoOfSeats;
        timeSlot = aTimeSlot;
        customerName = aCustomerName;
        bookingDate = aBookingDate;
    }
}
```

Class Restaurant

This class is defined for holding and transferring across the network information about a restaurant:

```java
package restaurant;

import java.io.Serializable;

//This class holds information about a Restaurant
public class Restaurant implements Serializable {

    public String name = null;
    public String location = null;
    public String chef = null;

    public Restaurant(String aName, String aLocation, String aChef) {
        name = aName;
        location = aLocation;
        chef = aChef;
    }
}
```

Entity Objects

Entity objects provide mappings to database objects. These encapsulate the logic of performing DML operations and queries on the database.

When we create an entity object using the Entity Object Wizard, JDeveloper creates an XML file which stores the metadata of the entity object. It stores information about its attributes, associated data types and precision and validation rules for the attributes.

Just as a database table can carry certain constraints, we can modify an entity object's attributes to specify validation rules (also called business rules) and methods. Validation rules can ensure that:

❑   The values returned by a query are valid

❑   Users do not enter invalid data into a table

We can define validation rules through the Entity Object Wizard. Along with an XML file, an entity object also creates a Java file. This class implements an object that extends from `oracle.jbo.server.EntityImpl`. Objects of this class map to one row of the underlying table. By default, this class contains accessor methods to access and manipulate the attributes of the entity object, that is the columns of the underlying table. We generally do not need to call these accessor methods, since all interaction with the entity object is taken care of by the view object. However, if we need to override the default behavior, we may change the code in the accessor methods.

Similar to the accessor methods, we can also have JDeveloper generate the `create()` method, which can help us override the default behavior of the entity object for performing inserts. For example, if we want a particular attribute to be based on a sequence number, we can write the logic in the `create()` method as described below:

We now write logic for generating primary keys using sequences. We will also edit some the methods of `OrderLinesImpl`, that is the `OrderLines` entity object, in order to: generate the order line number; to automatically calculate line amount; to populate item price based on item identifier; and to automatically update the order amount for the `Orders` entity.

To tell JDeveloper to generate the `create()` method, apply the following procedure:

❑ Launch the Entity Object Wizard by right-clicking on the `Bookings` entity object and choosing **Edit Bookings** from the pop up menu

❑ Click on the **Java** tab page and check the `create()` method checkbox.

❑ Click **Finish**.

❑ Repeat the same procedure for the `Orders` entity object

❑ In the `BookingsImpl.java` file, change the code in the `create()` method to make it look like this:

```
public void create(AttributeList attributeList) {
```

The call to `super.create()` creates an entity object, that is an empty row which will be inserted in the database:

```
super.create(attributeList);
```

Now obtain the next number from the sequence:

```
SequenceImpl s = new SequenceImpl("BOOKING_SEQ", getDBTransaction());
Integer next = (Integer)s.getData();
```

Set the primary key value with the sequence number obtained:

```
setBookingId(new Number(next.intValue()));
}
```

Now similarly edit the `create()` method of `OrdersImpl.java` with the sequence now being `ORDER_SEQ` instead, and call `setOrderId()` instead of `setBookingId()`.

The `OrderLines` entity object is a detail of the `Orders` entity object. So when a new order line is created, BC4J ensures that it already has the appropriate order id. We will now write code to automatically populate the **line number** attribute. Using the same procedure as above, generate the `create()` method for the `OrderLinesImpl` class by editing the `OrderLines` entity object. Edit its `create()` method as follows:

```
//generate the order line no
public void create(AttributeList attributeList) {
    super.create(attributeList);
```

`getOrders()` obtains us a reference to the `Orders` entity object for this `OrderLine`. Calling its `getOrderLines()` method obtains us an `oracle.jbo.RowIterator` object whose `getRowCount()` method provides us with the number of `OrderLines` already existing in the `Order`:

```
    int i = getOrders().getOrderLines().getRowCount();
    //increment the row count by 1 and obtain the
    //Order Line number.
    setLineNo(new Number(i + 1));
}
```

We have so far incorporated logic for automatic population of primary keys in the Bookings, Orders and OrderLines entity objects. In the OrderLines table we also need to automatically populate the unit price based on the items being ordered.

Based on the item type and the quantity, we need to populate the LineAmount for the OrderLine. For this we will edit the setItemId() and the setQuantity() methods of the OrderLinesImpl.java.

The setItemId() method calls a method dumpQueryResult() method of the Transaction interface. More discussion on this and other methods of Transaction is included in a later section.

```
//Populate the item price based on the item id
public void setItemId(Number value) {
    //The JDeveloper generated code is:
    setAttributeInternal(ITEMID, value);

    //Query the price from the database.
    //The dumpQueryResult() of the Transaction
    //interface feteches a String of the form:
    //<column>\n<value>\n
    String queryResult = getDBTransaction().dumpQueryResult(
        "select price from items where item_id = " + value.intValue(),
        "oracle.jbo.server.QueryDumpTab",
         null);
    try {
        //Obtain the value of price from the
        //String
        int n = queryResult.indexOf("\n")+1;
        String price = queryResult.substring(n).trim();
        //Call the setUnitPrice() method
        setUnitPrice(new Number(price));
    } catch(Exception ex) {
        throw new oracle.jbo.JboException (ex);
    }
}
```

Let us now write code to populate the Line Amount attribute:

```
//Populate the Line Amount based on the
//Item Id and the quantity
public void setQuantity(Number value) {
    //The JDeveloper generated code is:
    setAttributeInternal(QUANTITY, value);
    //compute the line amount from quantity
    //and unit price
    try {
        if (this.getItemId() != null) {
            Number n = new Number(getUnitPrice().doubleValue() * value.intValue());
            //set the Line Amount
            setLineAmount(n);
```

```
        }
        //the constructor of class
        //oracle.jbo.domain.Number is declared to
        //throw the SQLException, so catch it and
        //throw a JboException
    } catch(java.sql.SQLException sqe) {
        throw new oracle.jbo.JboException(sqe);
    } catch(Exception e) {
        throw new oracle.jbo.JboException(e);
    }
}
```

Note that we will be building the client JSP application using Oracle's web beans. The wizard-generated form will overwrite the automatically populated fields with NULL values (since we won't supply these values from the JSP form). In order to ensure that a unit price entry does not get overwritten by a NULL value, we will also have to edit the setUnitPrice() and setLineAmount() method as well. Change the method as follows:

```
public void setUnitPrice(Number value) {
    if (value != null) {
        setAttributeInternal(UNITPRICE, value);
    }
}

public void setLineAmount(Number value) {
    if (value != null) {
        setAttributeInternal(LINEAMOUNT, value);
    }
}
```

Defining Validation and Business Logic

When we use BC4J framework for building our applications, we can define validation rules and declaratively associate them with the Entity Object attributes. Having done this, we can rely on the framework to execute it consistently and ensure the enforcement of our business rules.

We can define validation rules using the methods described below.

Domain Objects

A domain represents the type of values an attribute can have. A Domain Object is a developer-defined data type, an immutable Java class encapsulating a scalar value with a simple validation check. Although the data type is defined by the developer, it still has to be an atomic data type, for example String, Date, and so on. If the database has aggregate data types defined as Oracle objects, then domains can consist of aggregate data types. The validation check occurs when an object of that domain type is created. Domains are a very elegant way of ensuring validity of our data. In particular, domains provide us with the following advantages:

❑ Simple validations are performed once, against the domain definition, when the data is created. Then, the data object can be passed between the tiers without the need for reconstruction or revalidation.

❑ We can define properties and then share them with all attributes which are based on a given domain.

Domains are mandatory in a certain situation. For example, if we are working with a relational table that contains an Oracle object, we must define a Domain for the object before we can create an Entity Object to represent the table.

The BC4J framework provides methods such as `validateEntity()` which can be overridden to contain custom validation code. This method is automatically called by the framework whenever appropriate. BC4J also provides for invoking entity validation explicitly by calling methods such as `Entity.validate()`, `Transaction.validate()`, `ApplicationModule.validate()`, or `Transaction.commit()`. When overriding the protected validate method, it is advisable to also call `super.validateEntity()` so that the default validation that BC4J performs is also invoked.

An entity requires validation when any of its attribute values changes. If there are container entities accessible through ownership associations, then each container will also require validation. For example, if the `OrderLines` entity requires validation, the `Orders` entity would also require validation.

Using Domain Objects

Step 1: Creating Domain Objects

❑ In the Navigator pane, right-click on the restaurant package and choose `Create Domain`.

❑ In the Domain wizard, in screen 1 of 2 Name panel, type `EmailId` in the Name field.

❑ In screen 2 of 2 Settings panel, keep the value for the Attribute Type (String) and choose `VARCHAR2` for the Database Column Type. Click Finish.

Step 2: Adding Validation Logic

❑ In the `EmailId.java` file, add the following code for validation, rebuild the project and save all files. The validation is simplified here for brevity. If a String has an @ and a '.' after @, it is a valid email identifier:

```
protected void validate() {
    // ### Implement custom domain validation logic here. ###
    if (mData.length() > 0) {
        if ( mData.lastIndexOf("@") > -1 ) {
            if ( mData.indexOf(".") > mData.indexOf("@") ) {
            } else {
                throw new oracle.jbo.domain.DomainValidationException(
                    "Not a valid email id : " + mData);
            }
        } else {
            throw new oracle.jbo.domain.DomainValidationException(
                "Not a valid email id : " + mData);
        }
    }
}
```

Step 3: Binding an Attribute with a Domain

❑ Right-click on the `Orders` entity and choose **Edit**

❑ Click the **Attribute Settings** tab

❑ Select `CustomerEmailId` from the list box

❑ From the **Attribute Type** list, choose `restaurant.EmailId`

❑ Click **Finish**. Save all files (*Alt-F + V*).

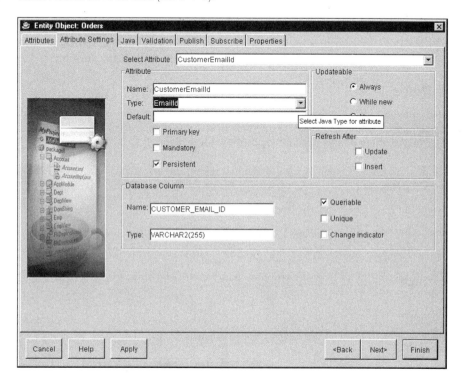

Important: Having done this, we must ensure that the `View Row` Class for `OrdersView` updates its accessor methods for `CustomerEmailId`. For this, launch the View Object Wizard by right-clicking and choosing **Edit** on the `OrdersView`, and click **Finish**.

Using Built-in Validation Rules

As an alternative to custom validation of entity attributes, we do this declaratively using built-in rules called **server validation rules**. The rule categories are: **compare**, **range**, and **list**.

Compare Validator

The compare validator performs a logical comparison between an attribute value and another value. This value can be either a literal value, the results of a SQL query, or the results of a View Object query.

Range Validator

The range validator tests for attribute values within specified minimum and maximum values. (inclusive). A range validator is used to validate numeric values. The range values are set in the constructor or by using set methods. The `validateValue()` method performs the actual comparisons and returns true on success.

List Validator

The list validator determines whether an attribute value is in a given list of values. The list can be either a list of literal values, the results of a SQL query, or the results of a View Object query.

Method Validator

To tell BC4J to validate an attribute using a method, we will have to define a method with the following signature: public void `validateXXX(Type)` where `Type` is the type of the attribute.

Validation Rules

In our restaurant example, we would want to ensure that a booking date is not in the past. This is a good place for a CompareValidator to validate the date against the database `sysdate`. To attach the Validator to the Attribute of an Entity Object, follow these steps:

❑ Launch the Entity Object Wizard by right-clicking the `Bookings` entity object, and click on the **Validation** tab

❑ Select the `BookingDate` attribute and click on **Add**.

❑ Select the rules of **Validator** as `CompareValidator`.

❑ Select `GreaterOrEqualTo` in the operator listbox.

❑ Choose `query result` in the compare with listbox and enter the query `select trunc(sysdate) from dual`.

❑ Click **OK**

❑ Click on **Finish** to close the Entity Object Wizard.

Working with Events

The BC4J framework also provides publishing and subscribing to events. An entity object can publish events which can be subscribed to by other entity objects. This model of event-driven programming can help our business components to be de-coupled from each other. For example whenever the user places an order through our portal, if we want to notify the nearest branch of the restaurant to make the delivery, we can create an `OrderPlaced` event which will be published by the `Orders` entity object. This could then be subscribed by other entity objects and containing the logic to fire the notification.

View Objects

View objects are like database views, in that they encapsulate a SQL statement. While the entity objects map the business entities, the view objects provide access to them. In a BC4J scenario, the entity object is never exposed to the client tier or even to the application module. View objects act as windows to the entity objects. They can sort, filter, hide data by way of their `WHERE`-clause, `ORDER-BY`-clause and thus allow for flexible interaction with data.

At run time, we can instantiate a view object from a design-time definition, a complete SQL statement, or SQL query clauses. We can also find and reuse view object instances. The key methods are:

❑ `createViewObject()` creates a view object at runtime based on an entity object.

❑ `findViewObject()` returns a reference to an existing view object.

❑ `createViewObjectFromQueryStmt()` creates a view object at runtime based on a query statement. Since such view objects are not based on entity objects, these are not updateable.

❑ `createViewObjectFromQueryClauses()` creates a view object based on query clauses. These can have their clauses changed any number of times by calls to `set<name-of-clause>()` methods.

We call the above methods on an application module. Whether created dynamically with SQL or from a design-time definition, a view object persists until it, or the application module from which it was created, is explicitly deleted (by calling the `remove()` method). We can use a given view object definition more than once within an application module; the Business Components for Java framework uses view instance names to distinguish between them.

Dynamically Created View Object

In our example, when a user wants to reserve a table in a restaurant, we want to first check for availability of seats in the restaurant. We dynamically create a view object based on this query. Once the view object is created, we can reuse it across multiple method invocations. Since our view object is based on a parameterized query, we can make it work much like a JDBC prepared statement, but the advantage is that we do not have to create it every time we want to execute the query or access the query results.

Add the following method to `RestaurantModuleImpl.java`. First add the imports:

```
import oracle.jbo.Row;
import oracle.jbo.domain.Date;
import oracle.jbo.Key;
```

The SEATINGS table holds the number of seats for each restaurant and the BOOKINGS table holds the number of bookings that have been commited. So we obtain the information for the total seats available and seats booked on the selected date and the selected time slot:

```
public boolean checkAvailability (restaurant.Reservation reservation) {
  String sqlStr =
    "select nvl(sum(Bookings.no_Of_seats), 0) bookingsSoFar," +
    " seatings.no_of_seats from Bookings, seatings " +
    " where seatings.restaurant_name = " +
    " Bookings.restaurant_name " +
    " and Bookings.restaurant_name = ? " +
    " and seatings.seating_type = Bookings.seating_type " +
    " and Bookings.seating_type = ? and " +
    " Bookings.booking_date = ? and " +
    " Bookings.time_slot = ? " +
    " group by seatings.no_of_seats" ;

  int noOfSeatsToBeReserved = reservation.noOfSeats;
```

If a view object is created at runtime, it still persists across multiple method invocations. So before creating a view object at runtime we have to check whether it has already been created in a previous call to this method:

```
  ViewObject v_NoOfBookingsDoneSoFar =
    findViewObject("v_NoOfBookingsDoneSoFar");
  if ( v_NoOfBookingsDoneSoFar == null ) {
    v_NoOfBookingsDoneSoFar =
      createViewObjectFromQueryStmt("v_NoOfBookingsDoneSoFar", sqlStr);
  }
```

Now set the where-clause of the view:

```
  v_NoOfBookingsDoneSoFar.setWhereClauseParam(0,
    reservation.restaurantName );
  v_NoOfBookingsDoneSoFar.setWhereClauseParam(1,
    reservation.seatingType);
  v_NoOfBookingsDoneSoFar.setWhereClauseParam(2,
    new Date(reservation.bookingDate));
  v_NoOfBookingsDoneSoFar.setWhereClauseParam(3,reservation.timeSlot);

  v_NoOfBookingsDoneSoFar.executeQuery();
```

If there is any booking done for this date and this time slot he following hasNext() will return true:

```
  if (v_NoOfBookingsDoneSoFar.hasNext()) {
    v_NoOfBookingsDoneSoFar.next();
    Row currRow = v_NoOfBookingsDoneSoFar.getCurrentRow();
    int seatsBookedSoFar =
      Integer.parseInt(currRow.getAttribute(0).toString());
    int totalNoOfSeats =
      Integer.parseInt(currRow.getAttribute(1).toString());
```

If the seats available exceed the seats demanded, return false:

```
    if ((seatsBookedSoFar + noOfSeatsToBeReserved) > totalNoOfSeats){
      return false;
    }
  } else {
```

Since the Seatings View is a detail view of the Restaurants View, it has a default WHERE clause for the restaurant name in the current row of that view. Hence we should make the appropriate row the current row in the Restaurants View and then execute the query in Seatings View:

```
      ViewObject restaurantsView = getRestaurantsView();
      restaurantsView.setWhereClause("name = '" +
        reservation.restaurantName + "'");
      restaurantsView.executeQuery();
      if (restaurantsView.hasNext() ) {
        restaurantsView.next();
        SeatingsView = getSeatingsView();
        SeatingsView.setWhereClause(" seating_type =
          '"+reservation.seatingType + "'");
        SeatingsView.executeQuery();
        if (SeatingsView.hasNext()) {
          SeatingsViewRowImpl row =
            (SeatingsViewRowImpl)SeatingsView.next();
          int noOfSeats = row.getNoOfSeats().intValue();
          //if the seats available exceed the seats demanded,
          //return false
          if (noOfSeats >= reservation.noOfSeats) {
            return true;
          } else {
            return false;
          }
        }
      }
    }
    return false;
  }
```

In the above code, we have set the WHERE clause of the views v_NoOfBookingsDoneSoFar and SeatingsView in two different ways to illustrate the different ways of setting a WHERE clause. While the first method is preferable since we do not have to remember to enclose strings in single quotes, the second way of doing it can come in handy when a view object is based on a design-time definition and we do not want to always provide parameters to execute its query. The key application module methods are findViewObject(), createViewObjectFromQueryStmt(), and the key view object methods are setWhereClauseParam() and setWhereClause().

More on Executing a View Object's Query

If the existing state of the view object includes pending changes (inserts, updates, deletes), they are cached in the underlying entity object caches and are not affected by refreshing the query. The changes are still pending and the inserted and updated rows will appear in their current pending state in the view object. This will be illustrated in our client application, where the JSPs will allow us to explicitly commit or rollback any DML operations arising from the session.

The executeQuery() method does not post, commit, or validate changes.

If other database users add new rows to the database in the meantime, and they meet the WHERE criteria of our view object, they will appear in the view object after calling executeQuery(). Methods such as setWhereClause() that change the query clauses do not execute the query. We can change the query clauses as many times as we want. However, the new query does not take effect until we call executeQuery().

We now implement some more methods of our application which return the results of a View Object's query:

getRestaurantList()	Returns an array of type restaurant.Restaurant. This array can be used to provide the user with information about the restaurants.
getBookings()	Provides a list of bookings already done, so that we can cancel them.
getSeatingTypes	Provides information about various sections in the restaurant (smoking, non-smoking, etc.)
getItems()	Provides the user with the menu of the desired restaurant.

When the client of the application is a BC4J JSP application generated using JDeveloper wizards, some of these methods may not be required. But we will make our business logic tier capable of catering to the needs of all types of clients.

Retrieving a View Object's Query Results

In RestaurantModuleImpl.java, add the following code, first add the imports:

```
import oracle.jbo.domain.Number;
```

Now we start with the methods in the above table:

```
public Restaurant[] getRestaurantList () {
    Restaurant[] restaurants = null;
    //Since we want to retrieve all the rows,
    //we should unset any previous
    //where-clause that might have been set
    //in other methods.
    ViewObject vo = getRestaurantsView();
    vo.setWhereClause(null);
```

Now execute the query on the Restaurants View:

```
    vo.executeQuery();
    int numRows = vo.getRowCount();
    restaurants = new Restaurant[numRows];
    //Store the View's data in the array
    //of Restaurant objects and return it.
    for ( int current = 0; current < numRows; current++ ) {
```

```
        //Each row obtained by the call to the next()
        //method is typecasted into the view row
        //class. The accessor methods of the view row
        //class make the code more readable and
        //less error-prone

        RestaurantsViewRowImpl row = (RestaurantsViewRowImpl)vo.next();
        restaurants[current] = new Restaurant(row.getName(),
        row.getLocation(),
        row.getChef());
    }
    return restaurants;
}

public Reservation[] getBookings(String restaurantName) {
    //The BookingsView has a View Link to RestaurantsView.
    // This makes it a detail view of the RestaurantsView
    //So it has a default WHERE clause corresponding to the
    //current Row in the RestaurantsView. Hence we should make the
    //appropriate row the current row in RestaurantsView

    ViewObject restaurantsView = getRestaurantsView();
    restaurantsView.setWhereClause("name = '" + restaurantName + "'");
    restaurantsView.executeQuery();
    Reservation [] bookings = null;
    if (restaurantsView.hasNext() ) {
        restaurantsView.next();
        ViewObject bookingsView = getBookingsView();
        //Execute the query of BookingsView
        bookingsView.executeQuery();
        int noOfBookings = bookingsView.getRowCount();
        BookingsViewRowImpl row = null;
        if (bookingsView.hasNext()) {
            bookings = new Reservation [noOfBookings];
            for (int i = 0; i < noOfBookings; i++) {
```

We store the view's data in the array of Reservation objects and return it. Each row obtained by call to the next() method is cast into the ViewRow class. The accessor methods of the view row class make the code more readable and less error-prone:

```
            row = (BookingsViewRowImpl)bookingsView.next();
            bookings[i] = new Reservation(
              row.getBookingId().intValue(),
              row.getSeatingType(),
              row.getRestaurantName(),
              row.getNoOfSeats().intValue(),
              row.getTimeSlot(),
              row.getCustomerName(),
              row.getBookingDate().toString()
            );
        }
      }
    }
    return bookings;
}
```

The `Seatings` view has a view link to `RestaurantsView`. This makes it a detail view of the `RestaurantsView`. So it has a default WHERE clause corresponding to the current row in the `RestaurantsView`. Hence we should make the appropriate row the current row in `RestaurantsView`:

```
public String[] getSeatingTypes(String aRestaurantName) {
  ViewObject restaurantsView = getRestaurantsView();
  restaurantsView.setWhereClause("name = '" + aRestaurantName + "'");
  restaurantsView.executeQuery();
  if (restaurantsView.hasNext() ) {
    restaurantsView.next();
    ViewObject vo = getSeatingsView();
    //For checkAvailability we had modified the
    //WHERE clause of this view object. Since the WHERE clause still
    //persists, we have to nullify it to obtain all the rows
    vo.setWhereClause(null);
    //Execute the query of SeatingsView
    vo.executeQuery();
    if (vo.hasNext()) {
      int numRows = vo.getRowCount();
      //Store the data in a String array and return it
      String[] seatingTypes = new String[numRows];
      for (int i = 0; i < numRows; i++) {
        Row row = vo.next();
        seatingTypes[i] = row.getAttribute("SeatingType").toString();
      }
      return seatingTypes;
    } else {
      return null;
    }
  }
  return null;
}

public Item[] getItems (String aRestaurantName) {
  Reservation [] bookings = null;
  Item[] items = null;
```

The Items View has a View Link to Restaurants View. This makes it a detail view of the RestaurantsView as with the Seatings View above:

```
getRestaurantsView().setWhereClause("name = '"+aRestaurantName+"'");
getRestaurantsView().executeQuery();
if (getRestaurantsView().hasNext() ) {
  getRestaurantsView().next();
  ItemsViewImpl itemsView = getItemsView();
  itemsView.executeQuery();
  ItemsViewRowImpl itemsViewRow = null;
  if (itemsView.hasNext()) {
    int numberOfItems = itemsView.getRowCount();
    items = new Item[numberOfItems];
    for (int i = 0; i < numberOfItems; i++) {
```

Typecast each row into the view row class:

```
        itemsViewRow = (ItemsViewRowImpl)itemsView.next();
        items[i] = new Item(
          itemsViewRow.getRestaurantName(),
          itemsViewRow.getItemId().intValue(),
          itemsViewRow.getItemName(),
          itemsViewRow.getDescription(),
          itemsViewRow.getPrice().floatValue()
        );
      }
    }
  }
  return items;
}
```

Notice that in the above code, the view row data is accessed using the View Row's accessor methods. This makes the code more readable, freeing us therefore from worrying about attribute names. These accessor methods also have the appropriate return types and eliminate all the typecasting and checking for null values.

Using a View Object to Insert and Delete Rows

A view object can be used for DML in two ways. In the application module we could write code as follows. Create a row and fill in the columns; assume vo is a view object declared and initialized:

```
Row newRow = vo.createRow();
newRow.setAttribute("<AttributeName>", value);
---
---
vo.insertRow(newRow);
// Call a helper method.
getTransaction().commit();
```

As in the previous code snippet, the view row accessor methods provide a better approach to doing the same work as will be demonstrated in the next code snippet.

We will now write a method in the OrdersView object that inserts rows into the orders as well as order lines tables. This method will then be called from the application module. We can also call this method directly from the client tier.

Creating View Object Methods That Can Be Used By the Client

The following method will create a home-delivery order for us.

In OrdersViewImpl.java, write the following code. We will then export the insertOrder() method, as will be described below. First add the import statement:

```
import oracle.jbo.domain.Number;
```

Typecast each row into the view row class:

```
public void insertOrder (Order order) {

    OrdersViewRowImpl newRow = (OrdersViewRowImpl)createRow();
    newRow.setRestaurantName(order.restaurantName );
    newRow.setCustomerName(order.customerName);
    //The attribute EmailId is of type EmailId
    newRow.setCustomerEmailId(new EmailId(order.customerEmailId));
    newRow.setCustomerPhoneNo(order.customerPhoneNo);
    newRow.setCustomerAddress(order.customerAddress);
    newRow.setAmount(new Number(order.amount));
    insertRow(newRow);

    Number orderId = newRow.getOrderId();

    OrderLine[] orderLines = order.orderLines;

    OrderLinesViewRowImpl orderLine = null;
    for (int i = 0; i < orderLines.length; i++) {
        orderLine = (OrderLinesViewRowImpl)
          newRow.getOrderLinesView().createRow();
        orderLine.setItemId(new Number(orderLines[i].itemId));
        orderLine.setQuantity(new Number(orderLines[i].quantity));
        orderLine.setUnitPrice(new Number(orderLines[i].unitPrice));
        getOrderLinesView().insertRow(orderLine);
    }
}

private OrderLinesViewImpl getOrderLinesView() {
    return (OrderLinesViewImpl)
      getApplicationModule().findViewObject("OrderLinesView");
}
```

In `RestaurantModuleImpl.java` call this method as follows:

```
public void createOrder(Order order) {
    getOrdersView().insertOrder(order);
    getTransaction().commit();
}
```

Having written this method, we should export the method to the client. In the JDeveloper Navigation pane, right-click the `OrdersView` object, and select **Edit**. In the **Client Methods** tab, select the methods we want to expose. Only exportable methods are displayed in the methods list. Click **Apply**, then **Finish**.

JDeveloper generates:

❑   A Java interface named for the view object row

❑   A view object row **proxy**

The generated interface contains the signature of the exported accessor method. The proxy object implements the generated `ViewObjectRow` interface.

Note that it is the row proxy that is deployed to the client; the object and its methods reside on the application tier. The client program can use the proxy to invoke the row accessor methods on the application tier. This requires that we make the application module remotable and deploy it. Making the application module remotable is discussed in a later section.

Accessing the View Object Methods from the Application Module

We now implement another method, bookSeats() for booking a table in the restaurant. The bookSeats() method relies on two other methods defined in the same application module, a private insertBooking() method and a checkAvailability() method.

One of the simplifications made for the sake of brevity is in the booking process. We assume that each section of the restaurant accommodates a fixed number of people. Based on the size of groups of people visiting, the table arrangements will be made. Hence, before confirming a booking, we check for availability of the seats and then proceed with actually confirming the booking.

In RestaurantModuleImpl.java write the following code:

```
private void insertBooking (Reservation reservation) {
    BookingsViewRowImpl newRow =
        (BookingsViewRowImpl)getBookingsView().createRow();
    newRow.setNoOfSeats(new Number(reservation.noOfSeats) );

    //The String reservation.bookingDate is of format yyyy-mm-dd
    newRow.setBookingDate(new Date(reservation.bookingDate) );
    newRow.setRestaurantName(reservation.restaurantName );
    newRow.setNoOfSeats(new Number(reservation.noOfSeats) );
    newRow.setSeatingType(reservation.seatingType);
    newRow.setCustomerName(reservation.customerName);
    newRow.setTimeSlot(reservation.timeSlot);
    getBookingsView().insertRow(newRow);
}
```

Having written the checkAvailability() and the insertBooking() methods, we are all set to implement our second remote method of the RestaurantModuleImpl.java:

```
public boolean bookSeats(Reservation reservation) {
    if (checkAvailability(reservation)) {
        //The insertBooking() was successful.
        insertBooking(reservation);
        //Time to commit!
        getTransaction().commit();
        return true;
    }
    return false;
}
```

Deleting Rows Using View Objects

When we have multiple rows to delete we can use the following approach: Get the row(s) to delete:

```
vo.setWhereClause(" <WHERE clause> ");
// Delete row(s).
vo.executeQuery();
while (vo.hasNext()) {
    vo.next();
    vo.removeCurrentRow();
}
getTransaction().commit();
```

We could also locate a row by calling the findByKey() method of the view object as in the following section.

Deleting Rows Using View Objects

In `RestaurantModuleImpl.java` write the following code:

```
public boolean cancelSeats(String bookingID, String restaurantName) {
  try {
    //Since BookingsView is a detail view of the Restaurants view,
    //We have to first make the appropriate row the current row
    //in the RestaurantsView
    getRestaurantsView().setWhereClause( " name = '" + restaurantName + "'" );
    getRestaurantsView().executeQuery();
    if (getRestaurantsView().hasNext()) {
      getRestaurantsView().next();
      Key key = BookingsImpl.createPrimaryKey(new Number(bookingID));
      //findByKey takes two arguments: the Key, and an int for maximum
      //expected rows
      Row[] row = getBookingsView().findByKey(key, 1);
      row[0].remove();
      getTransaction().commit();
      return true;
    }
    return false;
  } catch( Exception ex) {
    ex.printStackTrace();
    return false;
  }
}
```

View Links

A view link specifies a relationship between two view objects. As such, it is an expression of an association defined either by underlying entity objects or by literal SQL statements. A view link specifies source and destination view objects, and links them using attributes selected by those view objects. A view link can be traversed from master to detail, but not from detail to master. This means that a view row of the master view will have an accessor for all its details, but a detail view row will not have an accessor for its master row.

A view link is a very handy way of ensuring master-detail coordination among view objects. For example, when we traverse the view link between `OrdersView` and `OrderLinesView`, the `OrderLinesView` will always contain data for the current row in the `OrdersView`. Moreover, if a new row is created in the `OrderLinesView` view, the `OrderLinesView` will automatically contain the appropriate order identifier. This removes many possibilities for errors and facilitates cleaner code.

A view link can be created from a **view link definition** or from an **entity association**. We can also create view links at runtime using methods defined on the application module interface.

Using the Accessor of the Master View Row Class to Access the Rowset of a Detail View

In the following method we notice that the master view row class of the master view has an attribute of the type of the RowIterator which consists of the detail rows. This row iterator contains rows of the detail view row class which can be used to conveniently access the detail data. Thus the view link between Orders view and OrderLines view effectively filters the rows of the OrderLines view.

In RestaurantModuleImpl.java, write the following method which returns the details of a particular order based on an order identifier and a restaurant name passed to it:

```java
public Order getOrderDetails(String orderId, String aRestaurantName) {
   //Since OrdersView is a detail view of the Restaurants view,
   //We have to first make the appropriate row the current row
   //in the RestaurantsView
   getRestaurantsView().setWhereClause(" name = '" +
     aRestaurantName + "'");
   getRestaurantsView().executeQuery();
   if (getRestaurantsView().hasNext()) {
     getRestaurantsView().next();
     OrdersViewImpl ordersView = getOrdersView();
     ordersView.setWhereClause("order_id = " + orderId);
     ordersView.executeQuery();
     if (ordersView.hasNext()) {
       OrdersViewRowImpl row = (OrdersViewRowImpl)ordersView.next();
       OrderLinesViewImpl ordersLinesViewImpl =
          (OrderLinesViewImpl)getOrderLinesView();
       Order order = new Order(
         row.getOrderId().intValue(),
         row.getRestaurantName(),
         row.getCustomerName(),
         row.getCustomerCreditCardNumber(),
         //Check for null value before calling toString()
         row.getCustomerEmailId() != null ?
          row.getCustomerEmailId().toString() : null,
         row.getCustomerAddress(),
         row.getCustomerPhoneNo(),
         row.getAmount().floatValue(),
         null
       );
```

Due to the view link, the row class for orders will contain an accessor for the order lines rowset. This will be accessed by row.getOrderLinesView():

```java
       order.orderLines = getOrderLines(row.getOrderLinesView());
       return order;
     }
   }
   return null;
 }
```

This method extracts the details of all order lines for an order. The Orders view has an accessor for its order lines, which is passed as an argument to this method:

```java
private OrderLine[] getOrderLines (oracle.jbo.RowIterator rowIterator) {
```

```
OrderLinesViewRowImpl orderLinesViewRow = null;
OrderLine[] orderLines = new OrderLine[rowIterator.getRowCount()];
//Loop through the iterator and obtain the
//order line details
for (int i = 0; i < orderLines.length; i++) {
  //Type cast the iterator's row into the
  //View Row class of order lines view object.
  orderLinesViewRow = (OrderLinesViewRowImpl)rowIterator.next();
  orderLines[i] = new OrderLine(
    orderLinesViewRow.getOrderId().intValue(),
    orderLinesViewRow.getLineNo().intValue(),
    orderLinesViewRow.getItemId().intValue(),
    orderLinesViewRow.getQuantity().intValue(),
    orderLinesViewRow.getUnitPrice().floatValue(),
    orderLinesViewRow.getLineAmount().floatValue()
  );
}
return orderLines;
}
```

We have now added the main application methods to respond to view object queries.

Associations

While view links are relationships between view objects, **associations** are relationships between entity objects. Associations allow entity objects to access data of other associated entities.

To show exactly how associations are useful, we will add some more functionality to the application. We will now write code to automatically calculate the amount column in the order table. Whenever the line amount of the OrderLines entity object is set, it passes a message to its Orders entity object to refresh its amount. The Orders entity object in turn accesses all its OrderLines entity objects and recalculates its amount.

In OrdersImpl.java, write the following code. First add the imports:

```
import oracle.jbo.RowIterator;
import oracle.jbo.Row;
import oracle.jbo.domain.Number;
```

```
public void refreshAmount() {

  //Access the child entities using the accessor generated for
  //the association
  RowIterator iterator = getOrderLines();
```

```
      double amount = 0;
      try {
      //Traverse through the iterator and calculate the total
      //amount.
      while(iterator.hasNext()) {
        oracle.jbo.Row row = iterator.next();
        Number n = (Number)row.getAttribute("LineAmount");
        amount += n.doubleValue();
      }
      //Set the Amount
      setAmount(new Number(amount));
      } catch (Exception ex) {
        ex.printStackTrace();
        throw new oracle.jbo.JboException (ex);
      }
  }
```

In `OrderLinesImpl.java`, edit the `setLineAmount()` method to call the `refreshAmount()` method above as follows:

```
public void setLineAmount(Number value) {
  if (value != null) {
    setAttributeInternal(LINEAMOUNT, value);
    //Access the parent Orders Entity using the accessor
    //generated for the Association and call its
    //refreshAmount() method
    getOrders().refreshAmount();
  }
}
```

Also edit the `setAmount()` of `OrdersImpl`, that is the `Orders` entity object method to prevent `null` values from overwriting the calculated value:

```
public void setAmount(Number value) {
  if (value != null) {
    setAttributeInternal(AMOUNT, value);
  }
}
```

Application Module

The application module forms the business logic tier and is the interface between the client tier and the database. An application module is a business module which performs application specific tasks. Like an Enterprise JavaBean (EJB), the client invokes methods of the interface of an application module. However, unlike an EJB's remote interface, the application module's interface not only contains the developer-defined methods but also a host of additional methods for performing generic tasks such as committing a transaction.

The application module has a transaction context and a database connection. Application modules can be nested, and when they are, the top level application module provides the transaction context and the database connection to its constituent application modules.

In the `RestaurantModuleImpl` class, we have implemented the following methods to be invoked from the client tier:

- ❑ Check whether seats are available
  `boolean checkAvailability(restaurant.Reservation reservation);`

- ❑ Get details of restaurants
  `restaurant.Restaurant[] getRestaurantList();`

- ❑ Get booking details
  `restaurant.Reservation[] getBookings(String restaurantName);`

- ❑ Get the list of sections in the restaurant
  `java.lang.String[] getSeatingTypes(String aRestaurantName);`

- ❑ Provide the list of items on the menu
  `restaurant.Item[] getItems(String res_name);`

- ❑ Book a table in the restaurant
  `boolean bookSeats(restaurant.Reservation reservation);`

- ❑ Cancel the booking
  `boolean cancelSeats(java.lang.String bookingID, String restaurantName);`

- ❑ Provide the details of an order
  `Order getOrderDetails(String orderId, String aRestaurantName);`

- ❑ Create an order
  `void createOrder(Order order);`

Exception Handling Approaches with BC4J

In the EJB framework, all the remote methods are declared to throw `java.rmi.RemoteException`. The `RemoteException` can wrap a nested non-remote exception and throw it to the client tier. Similarly BC4J framework provides a remotable exception class `oracle.jbo.JboException` that can be thrown to the client tier. This exception is an unchecked exception, since it extends from `java.lang.RuntimeException`.

The BC4J framework also provides many exception classes (for example, `ValidationException` and `NameClashException`). These classes extend `oracle.jbo.JboException`. Therefore, a Business Component method can throw a BC4J exception without a throws clause in the signature. BC4J exceptions have an attribute that stores an error message, and they support National Language Support translation and message formatting. `JboException` uses `java.util.ListResourceBundle` to format its messages. A resource bundle class defines constants and strings to use as error messages.

We can extend from the `JboException`, or directly throw the `JboException` from our code.

However, since a `JboException` is a `RuntimeException` it usually indicates an unrecoverable situation

Another approach that could be followed for error handling is using result codes. A result code can be a single boolean value or a numeric value that is returned to the client side to indicate the outcome of a method invocation.

Exporting Application Module Methods to Clients

The application module houses the business logic of the application. The business logic is in the form of methods defined in the application module. To make these methods available to the client tier, we should export these methods using the Application Module Wizard. This will then generate an interface for application module (<ApplicationModuleName>.java in the common package) which contains the signature for all the exported methods.

Exporting application module methods lets a client invoke business logic within the context of an application module containing multiple view objects in the application tier. Right click on the RestaurantModule and select Edit. Then select all the methods in the Client Methods tab. Click Finish.

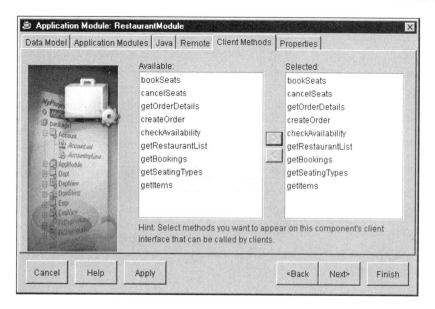

Deploying Business Components

JDeveloper lets us deploy business components without code changes to several different platforms. JDeveloper 3.1 supports four platforms for deploying business components:

❑ **Local**. In this configuration, the application runs on the client and uses JDBC to connect to an Oracle database. This mode is useful for two-tier client/server applications or servlets, prototyping, or for tasks like server-side batch processing of a day's transactions.

❑ **Oracle8i CORBA Server/EJB Session Bean**. In this configuration, the client uses IIOP to connect to the application tier which runs in the Oracle database; the application tier uses the internal driver (KPRB) to connect to the database.

❑ **Visibroker CORBA Server**. In this configuration, the client uses IIOP to connect to a VisiBroker ORB on the application tier; the application tier uses JDBC to connect to an Oracle database.

❑ **EJB Session Bean on the Oracle Application Server**. In this configuration, the client uses HTTP to connect to the Oracle Application Server; the Application Server uses JDBC to connect to an Oracle database. (JDeveloper does not support direct deployment to iAS yet.)

Deploying the BC4J components through JDeveloper involves three steps:

❑ Create a remotable application module

❑ Create a deployment profile

❑ Deploy the application module using the deployment profile

Creating a Remotable Application Module

A remotable application module is one that is configured to be deployed to a particular platform. When we make an application module remotable, JDeveloper generates the required helper classes to deploy to that particular platform. Also it creates client-side classes for the application module. When an application module is looked up, the result of the lookup is typecast to the client-side helper class.

❑ In JDeveloper, in the Navigator pane, right-click on the `RestaurantModule` application module and choose Edit, thus launching the Application Module Wizard

❑ Click on the Remote tab

❑ Check the Remotable Application Module checkbox

❑ Select the Oracle 8i Session Bean from the pick-list and click Finish

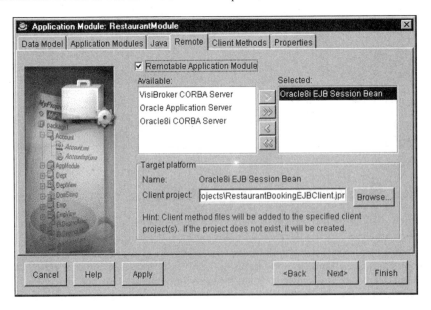

Notice that there is a textfield Client project in the wizard. When we click finish, a project by that name gets created in JDeveloper. It consists of classes which serve as clients to the remotable classes. For instance, if we have a remotable application module that consists of view objects with exported methods, we get a client class for the application module and the view object so that we can invoke remote methods on both. If our BC4J project has more than one application module, we get a client class for each one. At the end of this chapter we will provide a class for looking up an application module deployed as an EJB in Oracle 8i. We will also provide a JSP client and a command line client.

Creating the Deployment Profile

JDeveloper lets us create a deployment profile, a configuration file for executing a sequence of deployment processes, and deploy the application module in the same step.

Deployment profiles store our preferences for deploying a Java program. The Business Components for Java framework creates one profile for the entire project; then for each deployment platform and for each application module, it creates a target-specific common profile and a target-specific server profile.

To create a deployment profile, right-click on the RestaurantBooking project in the navigator pane and choose Create Deployment Profiles.

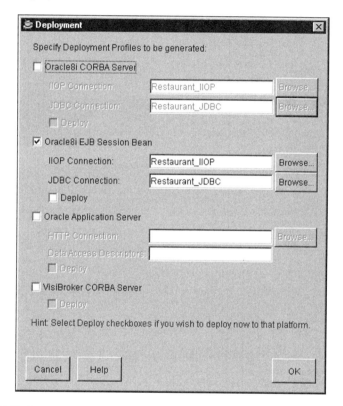

Chose Oracle 8i EJB Session Bean. Then for both IIOP connection and JDBC connection, click Browse and choose the appropriate connection and press OK. If we are deploying our first ever application module as an Oracle 8i Session Bean do not choose to deploy immediately. Instead, after creating the deployment profile, right-click on the project again and this time choose Deploy Business Components with the Deploy Business Components for Java Runtime checkbox checked.

When we deploy business components for the first time, all the classes that make up the BC4J runtime environment have to also be loaded in the database. Hence, we also check the Deploy Business Components for Java Runtime checkbox and press OK and sit back while JDeveloper takes over and deploys everything for us. This will take a long time. When deploying BC4J for the second time in the same schema, we do not need to deploy the BC4J runtime. So deploying BC4J components after the first timebe much quicker.

Connecting To the Deployed Application

Before running the BC4J application, we need to grant certain permissions to the user. Open SQL*Plus, connect as SYSTEM and execute the following SQL script. This script assumes our previous user, RESTAURANT. Therefore it needs to be edited for granting the permissions to the appropriate user, if the schema the tables were created on is not RESTAURANT.

```
SET VERIFY OFF
EXEC DBMS_JAVA.GRANT_PERMISSION('RESTAURANT', 'SYS:java.util.PropertyPermission',
  '*', 'write');
EXEC DBMS_JAVA.GRANT_PERMISSION('RESTAURANT', 'SYS:java.util.PropertyPermission',
  '*', 'read');
EXEC DBMS_JAVA.GRANT_PERMISSION('RESTAURANT', 'SYS:java.lang.RuntimePermission',
  'createClassLoader', null);
EXEC DBMS_JAVA.GRANT_PERMISSION('RESTAURANT', 'SYS:java.lang.RuntimePermission',
  'setContextClassLoader', null);
COMMIT;
SET VERIFY ON
```

Where Are We Now?

We have completed developing the business logic for the Restaurant Application using BC4J. In particular, we:

❏ Created a Business Components Project

❏ Created entity objects and associations based on the database design

❏ Created view objects and view links based on the entity objects and associations

❏ Added validation logic using domains and built-in validation rules

❏ Provided implementation for automatic generation of primary keys

❏ Provided implementation for automatic calculation of attributes

❏ Provided remotely accessible methods in the application module and a view object

❏ Created a remotable application module

❏ Deployed the application module as a session EJB in Oracle 8i

We can view the deployed application module from JDeveloper. For this, right-click on the Restaurant_IIOP connection in the Connections folder. JDeveloper will open a session window into the ORB that manages the namespace for IIOP clients:

You can also spot here the two EJBs, PreferenceInterviewer, and PropertyUpdater, that we deployed in Chapter 15.

Inserting Data

The following script will provide the data to get us started with the application:

```
INSERT INTO restaurants VALUES('Marriott', 'Washington', 'Sanjiv Kapur');
INSERT INTO restaurants VALUES('Hilton', 'New York', 'Sanjiv Kapur');
INSERT INTO restaurants VALUES('Windsor','San Francisco','Sanjiv Kapur');
INSERT INTO seatings VALUES('Marriott','Smoking',50);
INSERT INTO seatings VALUES('Marriott','Non-Smoking',100);
INSERT INTO seatings VALUES('Hilton','Smoking',50);
INSERT INTO seatings VALUES('Hilton','Non-Smoking',100);
INSERT INTO seatings VALUES('Windsor,'Smoking',50);
INSERT INTO seatings VALUES('Windsor','Non-Smoking',100);
INSERT INTO items VALUES('Marriott',1,'Russian Salad', 'nice thing', 100);
INSERT INTO items VALUES('Marriott',2,'Lobster Special','very spicy', 200);
INSERT INTO items VALUES('Windsor', 3, 'Chicken Stroganoff','hot',100);
INSERT INTO items VALUES('Windsor',4,'Golden Fried rawns','spicy',200);
INSERT INTO items VALUES('Hilton',5,'Russian Salad', 'nice thing', 100);
INSERT INTO items VALUES('Hilton',6,'Chicken Biryani','very spicy', 200);
INSERT INTO timings VALUES('Lunch');
INSERT INTO timings VALUES('Dinner');
COMMIT;
```

Building the JSP Client Application

Having built the middle tier, we now proceed to build the user interface for our client application. The client is a set of JSPs that connect to the application module and invoke its methods containing the business logic. We will build the JSPs through the Business Components JSP Application wizard. In JDeveloper, select **File | New Project** and choose a project containing a new Business Components JSP as the project type. Also provide an appropriate project name and a package name. This will launch the Business Components JSP Application wizard.

❑   On the Welcome screen, click **Next**

❑   Click **Next** on step 1 of the Business Components JSP Application Wizard

❑   Select the project `RestaurantBooking.jpr` from the combo box

❑   Click on **Next**

❑   Select the application template then click **Next**

❑   Specify the `Restaurant_JDBC` connection then click **Next**

❑   In step 5, from the **View Objects** column select `SeatingsView`, uncheck the generate-page checkbox from **Form Options** column

❑   Repeat for `TimingsView` also

❑   In step 6, select the theme of your choice and then click **Next**

❑   Click **Finish**

The wizard generates JSP files for the client tier. These JSP files provide default insert, update and delete functionality for all the updateable view objects in the application module. These also provide master-detail screens for each view link that the application module contains. However these default screens are seldom what we require in real applications. We will have to customize the default screens in order to provide the appropriate user interface for the application. We now show how to customize the JSPs generated by the wizard. However, please note that the modifications to the wizard generated code that we do here are by no means comprehensive and are merely pointers to the possible customization. In particular, we show how to call the remote methods of the application module, change and configure some of the GUI widgets, add and remove some of the default functionalities and perform minimal client-side validations.

We will now modify some of the wizard generated JSPs for our restaurant application.

RestaurantsView_Browse.jsp

Here we will customize the title, remove some unwanted buttons on the navigation bar, and make the name of the selected restaurant available to the next JSP. We will also add some links to the next screens.

Change the heading within the <h2> tag from "RestaurantsView" to "Restaurants". In the first jsp:useBean tag, delete (or comment out) the following individual lines:

```
tb.addSeparator();
tb.addButton(tb.NAVIGATE_FINDFORM ,RestaurantsView_Query.jsp");
tb.addButton(tb.NAVIGATE_BROWSE ,"RestaurantsView_Browse.jsp");
tb.addButton(tb.NAVIGATE_VIEW , "RestaurantsView.jsp");
```

Towards the very end of the file, just before the closing </body> tag, add the following lines of code to make the selected restaurant name accessible from the next JSP:

```
<%

    String name="";
    if (RowSetBrowser.getRowSet().getRowCount() > 0) {
      Object o =
      RowSetBrowser.getRowSet().getCurrentRow().getAttribute("Name");
      if (o != null){
        name=o.toString();
      }
    }
    session.putValue("name",name);

%>
```

Then add the following HTML code to add links to bookings, cancellation and orders screens:

```
<BR><BR>
<TABLE>
<TR><TD>
   <A HREF="BookingsView_Insert.jsp" ><IMG BORDER=0 SRC=ViewObject.gif>Book
   Seats</a>
</TD></TR>
<TR><TD>
   <A HREF="RestaurantBookingsLink.jsp" ><IMG BORDER=0 SRC=ViewObject.gif>Cancel
   Bookings</a>
</TD></TR>
<TR><TD>
   <A HREF="OrderLineItemsLink.jsp" ><IMG BORDER=0
   SRC=ViewObject.gif>Place/View/Cancel Orders</a></td></TR>
</TABLE>
```

Save the changes made to the file.

BookingsView_Insert.jsp

This is the screen for booking a table. We will customize this screen to populate and display comboboxes to select the section and the time slot for a booking. We will also change the text of the **Save Changes** button to **Confirm**.

Change the heading (the `<h2>` tag)to "**Book Seats**". Then add the following code after the heading:

```
<a href="javascript:history.go(-1)" >Home</a>
```

The default editors for fields in the wizard generated JSPs are text fields. But our application requires the Seating Type (the smoking areas in the restaurant) and the Time Slot fields to be combo-boxes. We will change them from text fields to combo-boxes. The former is populated by calling the `getSeatingsType(String restaurantName)` method of the application module, whereas for the latter, we will use the `useComboBox(String viewName, String selectStatement)` method of the `EditCurrentRecord` class. This method creates a view object at runtime based on the name and the query provided, and populates the combo-box with the results of the query. Such queries can not be parameterized queries, so whenever we want the combo-box data to be based on parameterized queries, we should write a method in the application module for this.

Replace the `jsp:usebean` tag by the code below:

```
<jsp:useBean id="RowEditor" class="oracle.jbo.html.databeans.EditCurrentRecord"
scope="request">
<%
  RowEditor.initialize(application, session , request, response, out,
    "restaurant_RestaurantModule.BookingsView");
  RowEditor.setTargetUrl("BookingsView_SubmitInsertForm.jsp");
  RowEditor.createNewRow();
  //obtain a reference to the Application Module
  restaurant.common.RestaurantModule appModule =
    (restaurant.common.RestaurantModule)
      oracle.jbo.html.jsp.JSPApplicationRegistry.getApplication
        ("restaurant_RestaurantModule");
  //Get the name of the chosen restaurant passed
  //from the previous jsp.
  String ResName =(String) session.getValue("name");
  if ( (ResName != null) && (ResName.length() > 0)) {
```

If we have navigated here from the `RestaurantsView_Browse.jsp`, ResName will have some valid value. We pass it to the application module's `getSeatingTypes()` method:

```
      String seatings[]=appModule.getSeatingTypes(ResName);
      //use the data to populate a combo box
      RowEditor.useStaticComboBox("SeatingType",seatings,seatings);
   }

   //Since this query is static, we can populate a combo box in this manner
   RowEditor.useComboBox("TimeSlot", "select TIME_SLOT from Timings",
       "TIME_SLOT","TIME_SLOT");
   //Changing the text of the submit button from Submit to Confirm
   RowEditor.setSubmitText("Confirm");
   RowEditor.setReleaseApplicationResources(true);
   RowEditor.render();
%>
</jsp:useBean>
```

Save the changes made to the file.

BookingsView_SubmitInsertForm.jsp

This screen is for submitting the insert data for the `Bookings` view. Recall that in the application module we have written a method called `checkAvailability()`. We will call this method in this screen to provide feedback to the user if the requested reservation is not available. If the requested reservation cannot be made, the use is redirected to a different screen and an error message is shown to the user. If, however, the reservation is available, the user can go ahead and confirm it.

Change the heading (the `<h2>` tag) to "Bookings". After the heading, add the following lines:

```
   <br><br>
   <A HREF="RestaurantsView_Browse.jsp" >
     <IMG BORDER=0 SRC=ViewObject.gif>Home</a>
   <br><br>
```

To allow the user to return to the home page, replace the first `jsp:usebean` tag (the one before the heading) by the code below:

```
   <jsp:useBean id="RowEditor" class="oracle.jbo.html.databeans.EditCurrentRecord"
   scope="request">
   <%
     RowEditor.initialize(application, session , request, response, out,
       "restaurant_RestaurantModule.BookingsView");
     //Obtain a reference to the Application Module
     restaurant.common.RestaurantModule appModule =
     (restaurant. common.RestaurantModule)
       oracle.jbo.html.jsp.JSPApplicationRegistry.getApplication
         ("restaurant_RestaurantModule");
     int SeatsNum=0;
     boolean seatsAvailable = false;
     try{
```

```
        SeatsNum=Integer.parseInt(request.getParameter("NoOfSeats"));
        //collect the details of the sought reservation
        restaurant.Reservation reservation=new restaurant.Reservation (
          request.getParameter("SeatingType"),
          request.getParameter("RestaurantName"),
          SeatsNum,request.getParameter("TimeSlot"),
          request.getParameter("CustomerName"),
          request.getParameter("BookingDate"));
        //check with the application module for availability of reservation
        seatsAvailable = appModule.checkAvailability(reservation);
      }
    catch(Exception e){
      }
    if (seatsAvailable){
      %>
      <script>var isAvailable=true;</script>
      <%
      //seats are available,so make the changes(i.e
      //insert the data into the table)
        RowEditor.execute();
    } else {
      %>
      <script>var isAvailable=false;
      </script>
      <%
      //if the reservation is not available, rollback
      ((RowEditor.getRowSet()).getCurrentRow()).setAttribute("NoOfSeats","0");
      RowEditor.execute();
      (appModule.getTransaction()).rollback();
      }
  %>
  </jsp:useBean>
```

Delete the next jsp:usebean tag. This tag is to display the Navigator Bar which is not required here.

Before the closing </body> tag, add the following lines:

```
<script>
  //provide a message to the user that seats required are not available
  if (!isAvailable){
    var txt= "<font color=#ff0000><center>";
    txt += "<h2>Number of seats required is not available.</h2>";
    txt += "</center></font>";
    document.write (txt);
    txt = "<center><h2>";
    txt += "<a href=javascript:history.go(-1) >Back</a>";
   txt += "</h2></center>";
    document.write(txt);
  }
</script>
```

Save the changes made to the file.

RestaurantBookingsLink.jsp

The default functionality of this screen is to display records from BookingsView. Since we have a link from RestaurantsView to the BookingsView, the records in this view will be corresponding to the restaurant chosen from the RestaurantsView. By default, the navigation bar has buttons to insert, update and to execute a custom query on the BookingsView. We change this functionality and only provide facility to delete records from Bookings, that is, to cancel his bookings. We will customize this screen to hide unwanted buttons on the navigation bar. We also hide the delete button in the navigation bar for Restaurants since we will only allow deletion of Bookings.

In the second jsp:usebean tag (just before the <h2> heading), delete (or comment) the following individual lines:

```
dtb.addSeparator();
dtb.addButton(dtb.NAVIGATE_FINDFORM, "BookingsView_Query.jsp");
dtb.addButton(dtb.NAVIGATE_INSERT , "BookingsView_Insert.jsp");
dtb.addButton(dtb.NAVIGATE_EDIT , "BookingsView_Edit.jsp");
```

Also, the following line has to be added:

```
(dtb.getButton(dtb.NAVIGATE_DELETE)).setButtonVisible(false);
```

This is to hide the delete button, which is also not required here. The jsp:useBean tag should now appear as:

```
<jsp:useBean class="oracle.jbo.html.databeans.NavigatorBar"
    id="dtb"  scope="page" >
<%
  dtb.setTargetUrl("RestaurantBookingsLink.jsp");
  dtb.setDetailMode(true);
  dtb.initialize(application,session,
      request,response,out,"restaurant_RestaurantModule.BookingsView");
  String sImageBase = (String)session.getValue("ImageBase");
  dtb.setDetailMode(true);
  dtb.setImageDir(sImageBase);
  dtb.setDetailMode(true);
  (dtb.getButton(dtb.NAVIGATE_DELETE)).setButtonVisible(false);
%>
</jsp:useBean>
```

Change the heading (the <h2> tag) to "Cancel Bookings". After the heading, add the following lines:

```
<br>
<a href="RestaurantsView_Browse.jsp" >Home</a>
<br>
<br>
```

In the next jsp:useBean tag, delete (or comment out) the following individual lines:

```
tb.addSeparator();
tb.addButton(tb.NAVIGATE_FINDFORM, "RestaurantsView_Query.jsp");
tb.addButton(tb.NAVIGATE_BROWSE , "RestaurantsView_Browse.jsp");
tb.addButton(tb.NAVIGATE_INSERT , "RestaurantsView_Insert.jsp");
tb.addButton(tb.NAVIGATE_EDIT , "RestaurantsView_Edit.jsp");
```

and add the following line as before:

```
(tb.getButton(dtb.NAVIGATE_DELETE)).setButtonVisible(false);
```

The jsp:useBean tag should now be:

```
<jsp:useBean class="oracle.jbo.html.databeans.NavigatorBar"  id="tb"
  scope="page" >
<%
  tb.setTargetUrl("RestaurantBookingsLink.jsp");
  tb.initialize(application,session, request,response ,
     out,"restaurant_RestaurantModule.RestaurantsView");
  String sImageBase = (String)session.getValue("ImageBase");

  (tb.getButton(dtb.NAVIGATE_DELETE)).setButtonVisible(false);
  tb.render();
%>
</jsp:useBean>
```

In the last jsp:useBean tag, add the following line:

```
(dtb.getButton(dtb.NAVIGATE_DELETE)).setButtonVisible(true);
```

This is to make the delete button visible. The full tag should read:

```
<jsp:useBean id="RowSetBrowser" class="oracle.jbo.html.databeans.RowSetBrowser"
scope="request">
<%
  (dtb.getButton(dtb.NAVIGATE_DELETE)).setButtonVisible(true);
   dtb.render();

   RowSetBrowser.initialize(application, session , request, response, out,
"restaurant_RestaurantModule.BookingsView");

   RowSetBrowser.setReleaseApplicationResources(true);
   RowSetBrowser.render();
%>
</jsp:useBean>
```

Save the changes made to the file.

OrderLineItemsLink.jsp

Like the screen in the above section, this is a master-detail screen with the master view being the OrdersView while the detail view is the OrderLinesView. Here we will retain most of the default functionality. However we will disable update of orders. When the user wishes to place a new order, he clicks on the insert button of the master view. When he wishes to add an item to the order, he will click on the insert button of the detail view. We will customize this page to remove unwanted buttons on the navigation bar.

Change heading (the <h2> tag) to "Orders".

In the `jsp:useBean` tag just before the heading, remove (or comment out) the following individual lines to remove the **Edit** and the **Find** buttons for the master view, that is, the `OrdersView`:

```
dtb.addSeparator();
dtb.addButton(dtb.NAVIGATE_FINDFORM, "OrderLinesView_Query.jsp");
dtb.addButton(dtb.NAVIGATE_EDIT , "OrderLinesView_Edit.jsp");
```

The tag should finally look like this:

```
<jsp:useBean   class="oracle.jbo.html.databeans.NavigatorBar"
   id="dtb"  scope="page" >
<%
   dtb.setTargetUrl("OrderLineItemsLink.jsp");

dtb.setDetailMode(true);
dtb.initialize(application,session,
request,response,out,"restaurant_RestaurantModule.OrderLinesView");
String sImageBase = (String)session.getValue("ImageBase");

   dtb.setDetailMode(true);

   dtb.setImageDir(sImageBase);
   dtb.setDetailMode(true);

   dtb.addButton(dtb.NAVIGATE_INSERT , "OrderLinesView_Insert.jsp");
%>
</jsp:useBean>
```

After the heading, add the following code:

```
<br>
<a href="RestaurantsView_Browse.jsp" >Home</a>
<br>
<br>
```

In the `jsp:usebean` tag after the heading, delete (or comment out) the following lines to remove the **Edit** and the **Find** buttons for the detail view, that is, the `OrderLinesView`:

```
tb.addSeparator();
tb.addButton(tb.NAVIGATE_FINDFORM, "OrdersView_Query.jsp");
tb.addButton(tb.NAVIGATE_BROWSE , "OrdersView_Browse.jsp");
tb.addButton(tb.NAVIGATE_EDIT , "OrdersView_Edit.jsp");
```

The `jsp:useBean` tag should finally look like:

```
<jsp:useBean   class="oracle.jbo.html.databeans.NavigatorBar"
   id="tb"  scope="page" >
<%
   tb.setTargetUrl("OrderLineItemsLink.jsp");
   tb.initialize(application,session,
     request,response,out,"restaurant_RestaurantModule.OrdersView");
   String sImageBase = (String)session.getValue("ImageBase");
   tb.addButton(tb.NAVIGATE_INSERT , "OrdersView_Insert.jsp");
   tb.render();
%>
</jsp:useBean>
```

Save the changes made to the file.

OrdersView_Insert.jsp

In this screen the customer provides his details before placing the order. Since we are programmatically generating the order amount, we will hide the **Amount** field. Since the width of the customer e-mail and phone number fields in the database is 255 characters, by default, these fields are rendered in a text area. We will specify that textfields should be used.

Change the heading to "Add Order". In the `jsp:usebean` tag after the heading, add lines following `RowEditor.createNewRow()` as follows:

```
RowEditor.useEditField("CustomerEmailId");
RowEditor.useEditField("CustomerPhoneNo");
RowEditor.useHiddenField("Amount");
((HTMLFieldRenderer)
   RowEditor.getFieldRenderer("CustomerEmailId")).setDisplayWidth(20);
((HTMLFieldRenderer)
   RowEditor.getFieldRenderer("CustomerAddress")).setDisplayWidth(20);
((HTMLFieldRenderer)
   RowEditor.getFieldRenderer("CustomerPhoneNo")).setDisplayWidth(20);
((HTMLFieldRenderer)
   RowEditor.getFieldRenderer("CustomerAddress")).setDisplayHeight(4);
```

The `jsp:useBean` tag should finally read:

```
<jsp:useBean id="RowEditor" class="oracle.jbo.html.databeans.EditCurrentRecord"
scope="request">
<%
   RowEditor.initialize(application, session , request, response, out,
"restaurant_RestaurantModule.OrdersView");
   RowEditor.setTargetUrl("OrdersView_SubmitInsertForm.jsp");
   RowEditor.createNewRow();
  RowEditor.useEditField("CustomerEmailId");
  RowEditor.useEditField("CustomerPhoneNo");
  //set the display width of the email id,phone
  //and address fields to 20
  ((HTMLFieldRenderer)
     RowEditor.getFieldRenderer("CustomerEmailId")).setDisplayWidth(20);
  ((HTMLFieldRenderer)
RowEditor.getFieldRenderer("CustomerAddress")).setDisplayWidth(20);
  ((HTMLFieldRenderer)
RowEditor.getFieldRenderer("CustomerPhoneNo")).setDisplayWidth(20);

  //set the display height of the address field
  //to 4
  ((HTMLFieldRenderer)
  RowEditor.getFieldRenderer("CustomerAddress")).setDisplayHeight(4);
  RowEditor.setReleaseApplicationResources(true);
  RowEditor.render();
%>
</jsp:useBean>
```

Save the changes made to the file.

OrdersView_SubmitInsertForm.jsp

Recall that we had created a domain object to validate the e-mail address of the user. We will use the same domain class to validate the e-mail in this screen.

Change the heading to "Order", and after the heading, add the following code:

```
<BR><BR>
<A href="OrderLineItemsLink.jsp" >Back</A>
<BR><BR>
```

In the first `jsp:useBean` tag, replace the code after the following line:

```
RowEditor.initialize(application, session , request, response, out,
    "restaurant_RestaurantModule.OrdersView");
```

by the following lines. This will create an object of the type of the `EmailId` domain. If the value is invalid, the constructor of the class will throw a `oracle.jbo.domain.DomainValidationException` which will be trapped to display the error message to the user:

```
    try {
       restaurant.EmailId emailId= new
       restaurant.EmailId(request.getParameter("CustomerEmailId"));
       //The email id passed is valid, so submit the form data.
       RowEditor.execute();
%>
    <script>var emailValid=true;</script>
<%
    }catch(Exception e) {
%>
    <script>
      var emailValid=false;
    </script>
<%
    }
%>
```

Next we replace the code in the second `jsp:usebean` tag after the following line:

```
RowViewer.setReleaseApplicationResources(true);
```

by the following lines:

```
    try{
       restaurant.EmailId emailId = new
       restaurant.EmailId(request.getParameter("CustomerEmailId"));
%>
       <a href="OrderLineItemsLink.jsp" >Back</a>
       <br><br><br>
<%
       RowViewer.render();
       } catch (Exception e)
       }
%>
```

Towards the very end of the file, just before the closing </body> tag, add the following lines:

```
<script>
  if (!emailValid){
    var txt= "<font color=#ff0000><center>";
    txt += "<h2>Email id entered is not valid.</h2>";
    txt += "<h2>Please enter a valid email id.</h2>";
    txt += "</center></font>";
    document.write (txt);
    txt = "<center><h2>";
    txt += "<a href=javascript:history.go(-1) >Back</a>";
    txt += "</h2></center>";
    document.write(txt);
  }
</script>
```

When a user tries to make an order with an invalid e-mail address the user will be redirected to another page where the error message is displayed and the user is prompted to enter a valid e-mail address before continuing.

Save the changes made to the file.

OrderLinesView_Insert.jsp

In this screen the user will specify the items he wants to order. We customize this screen to display a combo box for available items for the desired restaurant. Also, the user shall be able to see the price of the items below the form, for which we will display the records from the ItemsView. We will also hide fields that are automatically populated.

Change the heading to "Place An Order". After the heading, change the <a> tag from:

```
<a href="javascript:history.go(-1)" >Cancel Insert Form</a>
```

to:

```
<a href="javascript:history.go(-1)" >Cancel Order</a>
```

Replace the jsp:usebean tag after the heading by the entire code fragment below:

```
<jsp:useBean id="RowEditor" class="oracle.jbo.html.databeans.EditCurrentRecord"
  scope="request">
<%
  //get a reference to the application module
  restaurant.common.RestaurantModule appModule=
    (restaurant.common.RestaurantModule)
      oracle.jbo.html.jsp.JSPApplicationRegistry.getApplication
        ("restaurant_RestaurantModule");
  RowEditor.initialize(application, session , request,
    response, out, "restaurant_RestaurantModule.OrderLinesView");
  RowEditor.setTargetUrl("OrderLinesView_SubmitInsertForm.jsp");
  RowEditor.createNewRow();
  try {
```

```
//get the restaurant name which has been stored in the session
String ResName =(String) session.getValue("name");
//get the menu for the chosen restaurant
restaurant.Item[] items=appModule.getItems(ResName);

String ids[]=new String[items.length];
String names[]=new String[items.length];
for (int i=0;i<items.length;i++){
  ids[i]=(new Integer(items[i].itemId)).toString();
  names[i]=items[i].itemName;
}
//Populate the items combo box with the items data
RowEditor.useStaticComboBox("ItemId",names,ids);
RowEditor.getFieldRenderer("ItemId").setPromptText("Item");
}catch(NullPointerException npe) {
}
//Since unit price and line amount will be populated automatically,
//hide them
RowEditor.useHiddenField("UnitPrice");
RowEditor.useHiddenField("LineAmount");
//change the text of the submit button from Submit to Order Now
RowEditor.setSubmitText("Order Now");
RowEditor.setReleaseApplicationResources(true);
RowEditor.render();
%>
</jsp:useBean>
```

Just before the closing <body> tag, add the following code. This is to display the menu of the selected restaurant:

```
<center><h2>Menu</h2></center>
<br><br>

<br>
<jsp:useBean id="RowSetBrowser" class="oracle.jbo.html.databeans.RowSetBrowser"
scope="request">
<%
    RowSetBrowser.initialize(application, session , request, response, out,
"restaurant_RestaurantModule.ItemsView");
    RowSetBrowser.setReleaseApplicationResources(true);
    RowSetBrowser.render();
%>
</jsp:useBean>
```

Save the changes made to the file.

OrdersLinesView_SubmitInsertForm.jsp

Change the heading to "Your Order" and after the heading, add the following code:

```
<br><br>
<a href="OrderLineItemsLink.jsp" >Back</a>
<br><br>
```

Delete the jsp:usebean tag after the heading. This tag is to display the Navigator Bar which is not required here.

Run the Application

Recall that the BC4J EJB deployment process generates client side proxy classes. To run the application, we must first ensure that the client proxy classes to communicate with the application module are in the classpath of the client code:

- ❑ Select Project | Properties and click on the Libraries tab
- ❑ Click on Add, then New
- ❑ Enter the name as restaurant
- ❑ Click on the button beside Classpath
- ❑ Click on Add Zip/JAR and navigate to the myclasses folder
- ❑ Select the file RestaurantModuleEJBClient.jar
- ❑ Press OK
- ❑ Also ensure that from the available libraries, "JBO Runtime" is included in the project properties

From JDeveloper run RestaurantsView_Browse.jsp. This will launch the built-in Web-to-Go JSP container to test run the application.

> To view detailed logging of what is going on when running BC4J components, we can set a special debug option in the JDeveloper runtime parameters. Select Debug/Run from the project properties box. In the Java VM drop box, type a new value:
> **-Djbo.debugoutput=console**

Deploying the JSPs to iAS

- ❑ From the Project menu, choose Deploy | New Deployment Profile
- ❑ From the Deployment Profile Wizard, choose Web Application to Web Server as the deployment option
- ❑ Accept defaults for steps 2, 3, 4, 5 of the wizard.
- ❑ Select all libraries in the step 6
- ❑ Click Finish

The JSPs then get put together into a JAR file and all the archive files in the project classpath get copied into the <JDEV_HOME>\myclasses folder of JDeveloper. We are now ready to deploy the application to the Apache JServ JSP container built in to Oracle HTTP Server. Now follow these steps:

- ❑ In the document root <DOC_ROOT> of iAS, (normally <iAS_HOME>\apache\apache\htdocs), create a folder called restaurant.
- ❑ The myclasses folder in <JDEV_HOME> will contain a JAR file containing the JSP files. This JAR file has the same name as that of the JSP project: RestaurantClient.jar. Extract its contents into the restaurant folder. This creates a folder with a name RestaurantClient_html under restaurant. (You can use jar -xf <JARfile> from the command prompt.)
- ❑ In the restaurant folder, create a folder called jars.

- ❏ Copy the `RestaurantBooking.jar` and `RestaurantBookingCommonEJB.jar` files present in `<JDEV_HOME>\myclasses` to the `jars` folder. These files represent the classpath of the JSP application.

- ❏ Copy the files `restaurant_RestaurantModule.properties` and `connections.properties` present in `<JDEV_HOME>\myclasses` to the folder `jars` created in step 3.

- ❏ Add the following classpath statements in the `jserv.properties` file found in `<iAS_HOME>\apache\jserv\conf` (replace `<DOC_ROOT>` with the real document root of the server – usually `<APACHE_HOME>\apache\htdocs`):

```
wrapper.classpath=<DOC_ROOT>\restaurant\jars\RestaurantBooking.jar
wrapper.classpath=<DOC_ROOT>\restaurant\jars\RestaurantBookingCommonEJB.jar
wrapper.classpath=<DOC_ROOT>\restaurant\jars\RestaurantModuleEJBClient.jar
wrapper.classpath=<DOC_ROOT>\restaurant\jars
wrapper.classpath=<DOC_ROOT>\restaurant\jars\jboremoteejb.zip
wrapper.classpath=<DOC_ROOT>\restaurant\jars\jboremote.zip
wrapper.classpath=<DOC_ROOT>\restaurant\jars\jboo8i.zip
wrapper.classpath=<DOC_ROOT>\restaurant\jars\jbohtml.zip
wrapper.classpath=<DOC_ROOT>\restaurant\jars\connectionmanager.zip
wrapper.classpath=<DOC_ROOT>\restaurant\jars\aurora_client.jar
wrapper.classpath=<DOC_ROOT>\restaurant\jars\vbjorb.jar
wrapper.classpath=<DOC_ROOT>\restaurant\jars\vbjapp.jar
wrapper.classpath=<DOC_ROOT>\restaurant\jars\jdev-rt.zip
```

Note that not all these files may be necessary, since you may already have some BC4J set up on your installation. (The current version of iAS ships with a BC4J example and some of the above archives may already be present in your `jserv.properties` file. Note that all above files have been found to be necessary)

To configure the application to use the application module locally, check that the file `restaurant_RestaurantModule.properties` contains the following lines:

```
# can be 8i , EJB or local
ConnectMode=Local

#in 8i mode this is an IIOP connection name
ConnectionName=Restaurant_JDBC

# used only if password not provided by connection definition
Password=tiger
```

To configure the application for IIOP access to the application module we deployed to the database, check the following lines:

```
# can be 8i , EJB or local
ConnectMode=EJB

#in 8i mode this is an IIOP connection name
ConnectionName=Restaurant_IIOP

# used only if password not provided by connection definition
Password=tiger

#only used in 8i mode
JndiPath=test/restaurant/ejb
```

Now start the iAS HTTP server. Type the following URL to access the JSP application: http://<host name>/restaurant/RestaurantClient_html/RestaurantsView_Browse.jsp

Connecting To an Application Module

The JSP application above is built using Oracle's web beans which use generated code to handle all the logic of connecting to the application module. However, there may be times when we want our custom code to connect to the application module, for instance if we wanted to create DML clients from custom Swing components. We now introduce a class that will connect to our application module and make its methods accessible to a command line client:

```
import oracle.jbo.ApplicationModule;
import oracle.jbo.*;//JboContext;
import java.util.Hashtable;
import javax.naming.*;//Context;
import java.util.Hashtable;
import java.util.StringTokenizer;

public class ApplicationModuleClient {

    /**
       This class obtains the remote interface of an Application Module
       deployed as an EJB in the Oracle 8i JServer
    */
    public static ApplicationModule getApplicationModuleInstance(
        String userName,
        String password,
        String connectString,
        String amName,
        String applicationPath
    ) throws Exception   {
```

The argument `connectString` should be of the form `<host name>:<port no>:<SID>`; the default connect-string for an application module deployed as an EJB or CORBA server object to connect to the database is:

```
String connStr = "jdbc:oracle:kprb:";
```

The following obtains the hostname, port and SID of the deployed process from the command line argument:

```
StringTokenizer str = new StringTokenizer(connectString, ":");
ApplicationModule appMod = null;
if ( str.countTokens() == 3 ) {
    String machineNo = str.nextToken();
    String portNo = str.nextToken();
    String sid = str.nextToken();

    Hashtable env = new Hashtable(10);
    env.put(Context.INITIAL_CONTEXT_FACTORY,
        JboContext.JBO_CONTEXT_FACTORY);
    env.put(JboContext.CONNECTION_MODE,
            new Integer(ConnectionModeConstants.REMOTE));
    env.put(JboContext.DEPLOY_PLATFORM, JboContext.PLATFORM_EJB);
```

The default application path is test/<username>/ejb, (recall we deployed the application at test/restaurant/ejb):

```
        env.put(JboContext.APPLICATION_PATH, applicationPath);
        env.put(Context.SECURITY_PRINCIPAL, userName);
        env.put(Context.SECURITY_CREDENTIALS, password);
        env.put(JboContext.HOST_NAME, machineNo);
        env.put(JboContext.CONNECTION_PORT, portNo);
        env.put(JboContext.ORACLE_SID, sid);

        try {
          System.out.println("Setting up Initial Context...");
          Context ic = new InitialContext(env);
          System.out.println("Doing LookUp..." + amName);
          //Obtain the home interface
          ApplicationModuleHome home1 =
            (ApplicationModuleHome)ic.lookup(amName);
          System.out.println("Calling create...");
          //Obtain the remote interface
          appMod = (ApplicationModule) home1.create();

          //establish the database connection
          //This will also start a new transaction
          System.out.println("establishing Connection...");
          appMod.getTransaction().connect(connStr);
        } catch(Exception ex) {
          throw ex;
        }
    } else {
      throw new Exception ("Invalid connect string");
    }
        return appMod;
    }
  }
```

The following are the options for Context properties for this type of lookup code, and the possible values to be set for creating the InitialContext:

Context Property	Description	Required on Platforms
DEPLOY_PLATFORM	Platform to which an Application Module is deployed. One of PLATFORM_VB, PLATFORM_LOCAL, or PLATFORM_ORACLE8I.	ALL
INITIAL_ CONTEXT_FACTORY	Must be JBO_CONTEXT_FACTORY.	ALL
HOST_NAME	Host on which the Application Module server is started. Required on Visibroker for USE_BIND mode only.	Oracle8i CORBA Server, Visibroker
CONNECTION_PORT	Port number where the ORB listens for IIOP requests	Oracle8i

Context Property	Description	Required on Platforms
CONNECTION_MODE	Specifies how to connect to Application Module server. Clients can connect to an Application Module server started on a remote host (USE_BIND mode), find the server using the Visibroker naming service (REMOTE mode), or load the server in the client's VM (COLOCATED mode).	Visibroker
ORACLE_SID	Oracle8i CORBA Server service ID to identify the ORB service.	Oracle8i
APPLICATION_PATH	JNDI path under which an Application Module is registered. Full path under which an Application Module is published.	Oracle8i
USE_APPLET	Must be used whenever the client is an applet.	Visibroker, Oracle8i CORBA Server
SECURITY_ PRINCIPAL	User name. Required for connecting to an Oracle8i CORBA Server.	Oracle8i CORBA Server
SECURITY_ CREDENTIALS	Password. Required for connecting to an Oracle8i CORBA Server.	Oracle8i CORBA Server

Running the Command Line Client

To run the command line client, we will create a new class TestRestaurantApp.

First we need to set the appropriate classpath for the program. Launch the Project | Properties wizard and add the following libraries to the project:

- ❏ JBO Runtime
- ❏ JBO EJB Client
- ❏ JBO EJB Runtime

Also create a new library and include the following JAR files (found in the myclasses) in its classpath:

- ❏ RestaurantBooking.jar
- ❏ RestaurantBookingCommonEJB.jar
- ❏ RestaurantModuleEJBClient.jar

Add this library to the project libraries. In the code below, we illustrate how to access the Application Module from a remote client and how to access the functionality of the module once a handle to it has been obtained:

```
import restaurant.*;
import restaurant.common.*;
import restaurant.client.ejb.*;

public class TestRestaurantApp {

  public static void main(String[] args) {
    try {
      RestaurantModule restaurantModule =
        (RestaurantModuleEJBClient)
          //You will need to insert platform specific details here
          ApplicationModuleClient.getApplicationModuleInstance(
            "restaurant",
            "tiger",
            "dbserver:2481:proead",
            "restaurant.RestaurantModule",
            "test/restaurant/ejb"
          );

      Restaurant[] restaurants = restaurantModule.getRestaurantList();
      System.out.println("The restaurants currently available " +
        "for booking are:");
      for (int i = 0; i < restaurants.length; i++) {
        System.out.println("\t" + restaurants[i].name + "\t" +
          restaurants[i].location + "\t" + restaurants[i].chef);
      }

      Reservation reservation = new Reservation("Smoking","Hilton", 10,
       "Lunch", "James", "2000-12-10");
      boolean available = restaurantModule.checkAvailability(reservation);


      System.out.println("Availability of seats = " + available);

      System.out.println("The sections available in Hilton are:");
      String[] seatings = restaurantModule.getSeatingTypes("Hilton");
      for (int i = 0; i < seatings.length; i++) {
        System.out.println("\t" + seatings[i]);
      }
      restaurantModule.bookSeats(reservation);

      Reservation[] reservations = restaurantModule.getBookings("Hilton");
      System.out.println("The bookings made in Hilton so far are:");
      for (int i = 0; i < reservations.length; i++) {
        System.out.println("\t" + reservations[i].bookingID + "\t" +
          reservations[i].restaurantName + "\t" +
          reservations[i].seatingType + "\t" +
          reservations[i].noOfSeats + "\t" +
          reservations[i].bookingDate + "\t" +
          reservations[i].timeSlot);
      }
      System.out.println("Cancelling booking with id " +
        reservations[0].bookingID);
      restaurantModule.cancelSeats(""+reservations[0].bookingID,
      reservations[0].restaurantName);
```

```
          Item[] items = restaurantModule.getItems("Windsor");
          System.out.println("The items available for " +
            "ordering in Windsor are:");
          for (int i = 0; i < items.length; i++) {
            System.out.println("\t" + items[i].itemName +
            "\t" + items[i].price );
          }

          restaurant.OrderLine[] ols = new restaurant.OrderLine[2];

          //When creating an order, argument -1 indicates a calculated column.
          ols[0] = new restaurant.OrderLine( -1,-1,1,2,-1,-1);
          ols[1] = new restaurant.OrderLine( -1,-1,2,2,-1,-1);
```

Create a new order:

```
          restaurant.Order o = new restaurant.Order(
            -1,
            "Marriott",
            "Makarand",
            "1212",
            "m@a.com",
            "customerAddress",
            "customerPhoneNo",
            (float)10.2,
             ols
          );
          restaurantModule.createOrder(o);
```

The following assumes there is an order with sequence identifier 1, (which might not be the case if you have previously added and removed elements):

```
          Order ord = restaurantModule.getOrderDetails("1", "Marriott");
          System.out.println("The details of the order no 1 are ");
          System.out.println("Customer Name = "+ord.customerName+",\t" +
            "Restaurant Name = " +ord.restaurantName + ",\t" +
            "Order Amount = "+ord.amount);
          for (int i = 0; i < ord.orderLines.length; i++) {
            System.out.println("Item Id = " + ord.orderLines[i].itemId +
            ",\t" + "quantity = "+ord.orderLines[i].quantity +
            ",\t" + "unit price = "+ord.orderLines[i].unitPrice +
            ",\t" + "line amount = "+ord.orderLines[i].lineAmount);
          }

      } catch (Exception ex) {
         ex.printStackTrace();
      }
    }
  }
```

Troubleshooting

If you experience problems connecting to the EJB application module after redeploying it, this problem may be solved by restarting the database instance, which reinitializes the ORB server. In particular, it is possible that a `CreateException` may be thrown when trying to create an instance of a redeployed application module. If so, the only known fix is to stop and start the database (for example from the NT Services applet).

Transactions

A key service that is required for robust server-side development is the management of **transactions**. Transactions, when controlled properly, can make mission-critical operations run predictably and safely in an enterprise environment.

A transaction is a series of operations that execute as one large, atomic operation. All operations to modify data in a transaction must succeed before the server will accept the changes. These operations can include not just standard SQL DML statements but methods that set attribute values, and possibly calls to Java Stored Procedures or PL/SQL packages as well. When a transaction is committed, all operations persist; if rolled back, all the operations within that transaction are rolled back.

The Need for Transactions:

These are some of the issues that transactions address:

❏ **Atomic operations**. Multiple discrete operations can be treated as one contiguous atomic operation. Thus either the entire set of operations succeeds or the entire set fails. This ensures that no failure at any point would result in an inconsistent state of your data.

❏ **Hardware failures**. Transactions provide a reliable manner to handle network or hardware failures, which are a significant issue in distributed environments.

❏ **Multiple users**. When multiple users access different application servers that share the same database, there is a lot of potential for operations to become interleaved. Here again, we need to have a means to ensure that multiple users concurrently modifying data do not corrupt the data.

Transaction Support in BC4J

Transaction and concurrency support is provided by default by Business Component Application Modules. The transaction management from middle tier to database is the same as is from client to database. BC4J uses a batch-oriented approach to synchronize changes between the cache and the database. It does not support nested transactions, but it does support distributed transactions. Coding is required only if we want to customize the default behaviour.

Client applications connect to databases and manage transactions by using the `oracle.jbo.Transaction` interface. Some of its useful methods are:

`connect()`	Attempts to establish a connection to the given database URL.
`commit()`	Commits the transaction.
`rollback()`	Rolls back the transaction.
`disconnect()`	Disconnects the server from the database.
`getLockingMode()`	Gets the preferred locking mode for this transaction.
`setLockingMode()`	Sets the preferred locking mode for the current transaction.
`dumpQueryResult()`	Returns a string that contains a result of a query.
`executeCommand()`	Executes any SQL comman including DML

Transactions and Locks

Transactions use locks to control concurrent access to data, achieving two important database goals, Consistency and Integrity. The BC4J framework locking model provides the following features and benefits:

A lock is placed even if inconsistency is detected. It can determine that inconsistency is due to DELETE or UPDATE of data. It supports middle-tier server comparison of original data columns. Data is retrieved to correct inconsistencies when they occur, with no further roundtrips required.

We can customize the locking behavior by setting the **locking mode** of the Transaction. The locking mode can be set to:

❑   ApplicationModule.LOCK_PESSIMISTIC
    A lock is placed as soon as a row in a view object is changed by a client for the first time.

❑   ApplicationModule.LOCK_OPTIMISTIC
    A lock is placed on a changed row only at the time of posting the changes to the database.

❑   ApplicationModule.LOCK_NONE
    A lock is placed manually by the programmer at the appropriate point in the application by call to the lock() method of the view row object or the entity object.

After the initial lock call for a given row object, subsequent calls are ignored unless the corresponding database transaction has had the commit or rollback operation performed, because locks are automatically released at these times. Irrespective of the locking mode, we can check whether an entity row is locked or not by calling its isLocked() method.

When an attempt is made to lock a row, if the row is already locked, we get the oracle.jbo.AlreadyLockedException. If, on the other hand, the row has been changed by another client and the change has been committed, we get the oracle.jbo.RowInconsistentException.

Summary

The BC4J Framework enables a RAD approach at development of N-tier scalable, Java applications. It comes with a comprehensive set of out-of-the box components that are easy to learn and customize and enhance developer productivity and result in robust and scalable applications.

The framework provides API and components for database interaction, transaction and concurrency management, exception handling, validations and events. The framework also handles a data cache in the middle tier and enables thin clients. Along with the middle-tier components, JDeveloper provides client-side Swing as well as HTML components which are data aware and facilitate wizard-driven development with minimal custom code.

What we've seen in this chapter is a code-intensive introduction to the Business Components For Java framework. BC4J provides a simple means to abstract away the most susceptible-to-change part of your code, that is, the business logic.

The main components of a BC4J application are:

- Application modules
- View objects
- View links
- Entity objects
- Domains
- Associations

Validation support is provided by way of domain objects and built-in validation rules, for example the compare validator, the range validator, the list validator and the method validator.

BC4J provides a range of proprietary Java exceptions, each a subclass of `JboException` that could be thrown to the client tier. However, having error codes as return values is an efficient alternative way of handling exceptions.

BC4J supports transactions and controls them using locks. We can change the default locking behavior and set it to use optimistic, pessimistic or manual locking. BC4J manages concurrency by monitoring the locks.

BC4J gives you the flexibility to deploy your business logic classes as EJBs, as CORBA objects or even as local classes, by simply choosing from the various automated deployment options.

18

A Discussion Forum using PL/SQL and Java

With Oracle 8*i*, developers have a choice of two programming languages for building applications for the database engine: PL/SQL and Java. The two languages operate seamlessly within the database; Java application logic can extend existing PL/SQL programs, and Java stored programs can call PL/SQL within the server software.

This Chapter together with Chapter 20 will show a case study of how a fictitious Internet company uses Java, PL/SQL and interMedia Text to implement an online discussion forum for their web site. Many of the concepts we use for the study, such as JDBC, SQLJ, interMedia Text, and connection pooling have been introduced in previous chapters. Intermedia is introduced in the next Chapter.

In this chapter we will implement the actual discussion forum functionality (posting messages, watching topics, creating user profiles, etc.), set up the database, and program the user interface. In Chapter 20 we will further extend the project by embedding advanced search capabilities, using interMedia Text.

More specifically, for this chapter, we will:

- ❑ Setup a discussion forum database
- ❑ Use PL/SQL to program database functionality
- ❑ Call Java stored procedures from PL/SQL for message transport
- ❑ Use JDBC to call PL/SQL stored procedures from Java
- ❑ Use Java Server Pages to generate the user interface of the discussion forum

Case Study Overview

The aim of our project is to create an online discussion forum, where one can post a question and get replies and comments from a community of registered users. Our forum will be aimed at technical topics, such as Oracle and Java development. The idea is to keep the site fast and reliable, minimizing graphics and complex ornaments, such as applets, movies, and such.

A user wishing to join the forum will be required to subscribe (provide name, password, e-mail address, etc.). The user information will be captured and stored in the database. When the login procedure has been successfully completed, the member will be able to view a list of available forums, which they can enter. Once the user has entered a specific forum, they can browse the message threads of the forum, create a new thread, or reply to previous messages. Additionally, they can specify which messages they would like the server to keep a watch on and send e-mail messages when they are updated.

In addition to the demand for a tight design, we have a tight schedule. Therefore, to ensure efficiency, we had to combine the quality of two teams on this project: the database team, using PL/SQL, and the web team, using Java. The application could have been built exclusively using either PL/SQL or Java; but the two languages were designed with different focuses, and as a result, are suited for different tasks. Because PL/SQL is designed around the database, SQL datatypes are easier to use and SQL operations are generally faster in PL/SQL (http://technet.us.oracle.com/products/ oracle8i/htdocs/jserver_faq/#_35), whereas Java, with its more general type system, is better suited to creating a user interface. Because both languages are supported equally by the Oracle Database Server and interoperate easily, we can combine both in our project, using the best of both worlds.

Given the above, our project included all possible versions of combined PL/SQL and Java programming:

- ❑ PL/SQL functions: used to generate the database functionality, see *PL/SQL Stored Procedures*.

- ❑ PL/SQL calling Java: optional, used to send e-mail using the JavaMail API, see *Calling Java from PL/SQL*.

- ❑ Java calling PL/SQL: used to access the database PL/SQL functions, see *Calling PL/SQL from Java*.

- ❑ Java functions: used to store the forum user's identity during the session, create the user interface, and more. See *User Interface*.

Thus, in this case study, all database functionality is implemented using PL/SQL stored procedures, either to directly manipulate the database objects or to use Java objects that were loaded into the database. We use a Java class to access the PL/SQL functions, using JDBC to call the stored procedures. This class could be instantiated and used by JavaServer Pages to access the database and generate the user interface.

In this chapter, we will discuss every aspect of the forum implementation in detail, roughly splitting the content according to the previous programming combinations.

Application Architecture

We will implement the discussion forum as a four-tier application, where the four tiers of each request are: a client, a web server, an application server, and a database. In the actual implementation, we use the Apache web server in conjunction with the Tomcat application server, but both these can be obtained freely from the Apache and Tomcat web sites, at http://www.apache.org and http://jakarta.apache.org, respectively. The database used was Oracle, version 8.1.5. Of course, any type of compliant web and application servers can be used, as can any other version of Oracle 8*i*:

The following figure shows the basic architecture of the project.

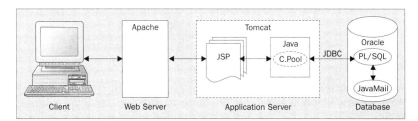

The diagram shows the relationship between the client's web browser, the web and application servers, and the database. In our implementation, all service requests are sent to the web server where they are handed over to Tomcat. To display the requested content, we will use Java Server Pages (JSP) to build HTML output. For database access, the JSP calls Java classes that use JDBC and pooled connection objects to access stored procedures (Java or PL/SQL) in the database.

To summarize:

❑ The client requests a page in the forum.

❑ The web server serves the HTTP request.

❑ The application tier contains JSP and Java classes. The JSP is used to generate the user interface (HTML) of the forum. The Java classes use pooled database connection objects to access stored procedures in the database.

❑ The database contains stored PL/SQL and Java procedures. The PL/SQL procedures provide the database functionality, enroll users, post messages, etc. The Java stored procedures are used to send e-mail notifications to forum users using JavaMail. (Optionally, for Oracle 8.1.6 users, the Java stored procedures can be replaced by the supplied utl_smtp PL/SQL package, as we will explain in more detail later.)

The Data Tier

Before we can start to implement any part of the discussion forum, we must prepare the database, create the necessary tables and sequences, and add a few initial categories.

Creating Tables

There are a few tables we will need for storing the transactions taking place on the discussion forum. The table schema is shown in the following diagram, while each table is further discussed below. The actual table scripts can be obtained from the Wrox web site.

721

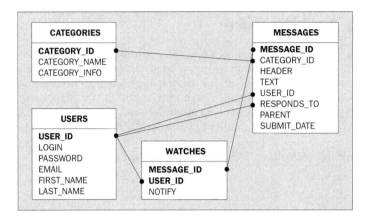

Storing Users

As you will see in the actual user interface implementation, we require that users log on before they can post or reply to messages. Before they can log on, however, they will have to create a user profile, which is stored in the users table.

We require each user to supply us with information on their login name and password, their e-mail address and full name. In an actual implementation, this table would probably contain more detailed information on the user, such as their address, company, zip code, etc. To keep things simple in this context, we have omitted all but the most relevant fields of the table.

Message Categories

Each message posted on the discussion forum belongs to a category. The categories correspond to a certain field of interest, and the messages in each category are somehow related to this field. Example categories include *Oracle JDBC*, *PL/SQL Stored Procedures*, etc. The community managers predefine the categories, although users could possibly come up with suggestions for new categories as new issues come to the focus. All categories are stored in the categories table. They are identified by their category_id and category_name. Optionally, the community managers may include a description of each category to better describe to the user which topics each category should cover.

Storing Messages

Once logged in, the users can post either new messages or reply to previously posted messages. We store information on the messages in the messages table. Each message consists of a header (header) and message body (text), so the member can browse the message headers and view full messages as desired. For those messages that reply to previously posted messages, we store the message_id of the parent message they belong to and to which user they replied. The user can reply either directly to the parent message or to another reply. We define parent messages as those messages that are posted at root level, directly below the category. Parent messages are identified by the fact that they have no parent (parent IS NULL). A *message thread* is defined as a parent message along with all its replies. Finally, we store: which category the message belongs to, which user posted it, and the date it was posted.

Keeping a Watch on Messages

Often, users want to be informed when certain topics are updated, regardless of whether they themselves posted the original topic or not. For example, when a user posts a question and needs a fast answer, they may have limited time for browsing the forum regularly to check for updates. Instead, they could have the forum keep a watch on the topic, and send them e-mail notifications when it is updated. All registered message watches are stored in the watches table. This table stores the user_id of the user, the message_id of the root message of the thread the user wants to watch, and whether they wish to receive e-mail notifications when the thread is updated.

Creating Sequences and Triggers

In addition to the tables, a few sequences have to be created. We maintain separate sequence, for the messages, users, and categories tables, the msg_seq, usr_seq, and cat_seq sequences, respectively.

```
CREATE SEQUENCE USR_SEQ;
CREATE SEQUENCE MSG_SEQ;
CREATE SEQUENCE CAT_SEQ;
```

To automatically insert correct sequence values for the primary keys of the users, messages, and categories tables (user_id, message_id, and category_id, respectively) we create triggers that take care of selecting and inserting the next value of the corresponding sequence. The trigger for the messages table is created with the following script; triggers for the users and categories are analogous:

```
CREATE OR REPLACE TRIGGER msgGetKey
BEFORE INSERT ON MESSAGES FOR EACH ROW
DECLARE
    new_id NUMBER;
BEGIN
    SELECT MSG_SEQ.NEXTVAL INTO new_id FROM DUAL;
    :new.MESSAGE_ID := new_id;
END msgGetKey;
```

In addition to the triggers we use to insert values for the primary keys of the messages, users, and categories tables, we create a trigger to validate the email field of the users table. The e-mail address supplied by each forum user must have a valid syntax, otherwise we will encounter problems when we try to send messages, as we will discuss in more detail in *Calling Java from PL/SQL*.

```
CREATE OR REPLACE TRIGGER usrEmail
BEFORE INSERT OR UPDATE ON USERS FOR EACH ROW
CALL UserProfile.validateEmail(:new.EMAIL)
```

The usrEmail trigger calls the validateEmail() procedure of the UserProfile package we define later in this chapter. This procedure will check if the address supplied is valid and throw an exception if it is not.

> **Please note that the usrEmail trigger cannot be created before you create the UserProfile package.**

Creating Initial Categories

Once we have created all tables, sequences and triggers, we can insert some initial categories. The following statements create the three categories, Oracle JDBC, PL/SQL Stored Procedures, and Oracle interMedia, which we will be mostly working with in our examples. The category keys are generated with the `cat_seq` sequence.

```
INSERT INTO CATEGORIES (CATEGORY_NAME,CATEGORY_INFO)
VALUES ('Oracle JDBC','The JDBC API provides universal database access from the
Java programming language');

INSERT INTO CATEGORIES (CATEGORY_NAME,CATEGORY_INFO)
VALUES ('PL/SQL Stored Procedures','Use this forum to discuss standard PL/SQL
programming, calling external procedures, and more.');

INSERT INTO CATEGORIES (CATEGORY_NAME,CATEGORY_INFO)
VALUES ('Oracle interMedia','Discuss interMedia topics, such as indexing and
searching, document loading, and more.');

COMMIT;
```

Once all the database objects have been created, we proceed to create the stored procedures that add the database functionality to the project.

PL/SQL Stored Procedures

The PL/SQL language implements Oracle's procedural extensions to SQL. In addition to the standard features of modern computer languages, such as looping, exception handling, and modularity, PL/SQL also supports object-oriented programming features, such as encapsulation, to some extent. PL/SQL programs can be stored in the database, executed as stand-alone blocks, or associated with object methods.

A PL/SQL package is a schema object that groups logically related types and subprograms. Usually, packages have two parts, a specification (spec), and a body. The spec is the interface to other applications, as it declares the types, constants, variables, exceptions, cursors, and subprograms available for use. The body fully defines cursors and subprograms, thereby implementing the specification.

In this section, we will describe the PL/SQL stored procedures we implement for our discussion forum project. For the implementation, we create two packages that each contain procedures with similar purpose:

❑ The `UserProfile` package contains procedures for storing and updating user profiles, for logging users on to the network, and for retrieving existing profiles.

❑ The `Forum` package contains methods for posting and watching messages, retrieving message threads, and more.

All the functions and procedures of these packages will use standard, built-in methods and packages of Oracle 8i (except for the optional `utl_smtp` package, as we will discuss later).

A complete overview of the packages can be seen in the following diagram. In addition to the package specs, it also depicts the `Mailer` Java class, which will be loaded into the database and called with the `sendMail()` wrapper function of the `Forum` package, to send mail messages. Optionally, we can use the `utl_smtp` package of Oracle 8.1.6 instead of JavaMail for the messaging functionality, as we will discuss later, in the *Calling Java from PL/SQL* section.

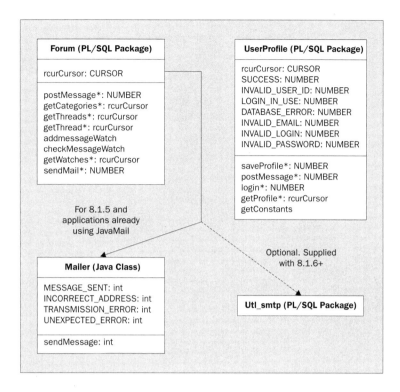

The UserProfile Package

The UserProfile package contains methods for storing new user profiles, for updating existing profiles, logging users onto the network, retrieving user profiles and validating e-mail addresses:

❑   saveProfile(): updates or creates a new user profile.

❑   getProfile(): retrieves an existing user profile.

❑   login(): logs the user on to the forum network.

❑   validateEmail(): validates an e-mail address, and raises an exception if it is invalid.

❑   getConstants: a simple procedure, with all OUT parameters, which serves the purpose of migrating the values of the package constants to the Java classes we implement later.

Package Spec

The UserProfile package specification is shown below. In addition to functions, types, and procedures, the specification contains a number of global constants that correspond to the return values of some of the functions of the package.

```
CREATE OR REPLACE PACKAGE UserProfile
IS

    TYPE rcurCursor IS REF CURSOR;
```

```
      -- Constants
      SUCCESS                CONSTANT      NUMBER    :=  1;
      INVALID_USER_ID        CONSTANT      NUMBER    := -1;
      LOGIN_IN_USE           CONSTANT      NUMBER    := -2;
      DATABASE_ERROR         CONSTANT      NUMBER    := -3;
      INVALID_EMAIL          CONSTANT      NUMBER    := -4;
      INVALID_LOGIN          CONSTANT      NUMBER    := -5;
      INVALID_PASSWORD       CONSTANT      NUMBER    := -6;

/*    ----------------------------------------
      Validates the given e-mail address. If it
      is invalid, an exception is raised.
      ---------------------------------------- */
      PROCEDURE validateEmail (
          v2Email            IN       VARCHAR2
      );

/*    ----------------------------------------
      Updates or creates a new user profile
      ---------------------------------------- */
      FUNCTION saveProfile (
          nUsr               IN OUT   NUMBER,
          v2Login            IN       VARCHAR2,
          v2Password         IN       VARCHAR2,
          v2FirstName        IN       VARCHAR2,
          v2LastName         IN       VARCHAR2,
          v2Email            IN       VARCHAR2
      ) RETURN NUMBER;

/*    ----------------------------------------
      Returns information on the user profile.
      ---------------------------------------- */
      FUNCTION getProfile (
          nUsr               IN       NUMBER
      ) RETURN rcurCursor;

/*    ----------------------------------------
      Logs the user on to the forum network
      ---------------------------------------- */
      FUNCTION login (
          v2Login            IN       VARCHAR2,
          v2Password         IN       VARCHAR2,
          nUsr               OUT      NUMBER
      ) RETURN NUMBER;

/*    ----------------------------------------
      Returns the package constants.
      ---------------------------------------- */
      PROCEDURE getConstants (
          nSuccess           OUT      NUMBER,
          nDatabaseError     OUT      NUMBER,
          nInvalidUserId     OUT      NUMBER,
          nLoginInUse        OUT      NUMBER,
          nInvalidEmail      OUT      NUMBER,
          nInvalidLogin      OUT      NUMBER,
          nInvalidPasswd     OUT      NUMBER
      );

END;
```

Package Body

For clarity, we will split up the package body and discuss each method separately.

```
CREATE OR REPLACE PACKAGE BODY UserProfile
IS
```

Validating e-mail Addresses

As we have already mentioned when we created the usrEmail trigger for the users table, we use the validateEmail() procedure to validate a given e-mail address. If the address is valid (that is, with a valid syntax; it might still be an invalid address, for example, either misspelled or invented), nothing is done. If, however, the address is invalid, we raise an error. This procedure is called every time the users table is modified and also from within the saveProfile() function we will implement later.

```
/*   ----------------------------------------
     Validates the given e-mail address. If it
     is invalid, an exception is raised.
     ---------------------------------------- */
     PROCEDURE validateEmail (
         v2Email          IN        VARCHAR2
     ) IS

     nTemp            NUMBER;
     v2Temp           VARCHAR2(100);

     BEGIN
         nTemp := INSTR(v2Email,'@');
         IF nTemp > 0 THEN
             v2Temp := SUBSTR(v2Email,nTemp+1,LENGTH(v2Email));

             -- Search for a dot:
             nTemp := INSTR(v2Temp,'.');
             IF (nTemp < 1 OR nTemp = LENGTH(v2Temp)) THEN
                 RAISE_APPLICATION_ERROR(-20101,'Invalid email address');
             END IF;
         ELSE
             RAISE_APPLICATION_ERROR(-20101,'Invalid email address');
         END IF;

     END validateEmail;
```

Creating and Updating User Profiles

Before users can participate in the forum discussion, they must log onto the network. In order to do so, however, they must have a valid user profile, which is created with the saveProfile() function. This function takes for parameters information on the user, which is used to insert into or update the users table.

The saveProfile() function is used both for the purpose of updating existing and creating new users. It does this by optionally taking the user_id as an attribute (nUsr), in which case we update the user corresponding to the presumably valid key. On the other hand, if nUsr is omitted, we create a new user.

Before updating the users table, saveProfile() verifies the supplied data. For example, all login names must be unique, and the e-mail address must also be valid. The function returns appropriate error codes if any of these conditions are not met. For a successful transaction, however, it returns a value of SUCCESS, and the user_id of the new or updated user is sent out with the nUsr parameter (which was defined to be IN/OUT).

727

```
        Updates or creates a new user profile

        Returns:

            1   On success
            0   Undefined database error
           -1   Invalid user ID supplied.
           -2   Login name already in use by another user
           -4   Invalid e-mail address supplied.
        ---------------------------------------- */
        FUNCTION saveProfile (
            nUsr            IN OUT  NUMBER,
            v2Login         IN      VARCHAR2,
            v2Password      IN      VARCHAR2,
            v2FirstName     IN      VARCHAR2,
            v2LastName      IN      VARCHAR2,
            v2Email         IN      VARCHAR2
        ) RETURN NUMBER IS

        -- Variables
        nTemp               NUMBER;
        nTempUsr            NUMBER;
        v2Temp              VARCHAR2(100);
        cur                 rcurCursor;
        loginInUse          EXCEPTION;
        invalidEmail        EXCEPTION;
        invalidUserID       EXCEPTION;

        BEGIN

            -- Validate the login
            IF nUsr IS NULL THEN
                BEGIN

                    OPEN cur FOR
                    SELECT login FROM users
                    WHERE login = v2Login;
                    FETCH cur INTO v2Temp;
                    CLOSE cur;

                    IF v2Temp IS NOT NULL THEN
                        RAISE loginInUse;
                    END IF;

                END;
            END IF;

            -- Validate the e-mail address
            BEGIN
                validateEmail(v2Email);
            EXCEPTION WHEN OTHERS THEN
                RAISE invalidEmail;
            END;

            -- Update the user profile
            IF nUsr IS NOT NULL THEN
```

```
            UPDATE users SET
                login = v2login,
                password = v2login,
                email = v2email,
                first_name = v2firstname,
                last_name = v2lastname
            WHERE user_id = nUsr;

            -- If this user did not exist, we raise an error.
            IF SQL%ROWCOUNT = 0 THEN
                RAISE invalidUserID;
            END IF;

        ELSE
            -- CREATE THE NEW USER
            INSERT INTO users (login,password,email,
                first_name,last_name)
            VALUES (v2Login,v2Password,v2Email,
                v2FirstName,v2LastName);

            -- Get the new user_id
                OPEN cur FOR
                SELECT usr_seq.currval FROM dual;
                FETCH cur INTO nUsr;
                CLOSE cur;
        END IF;
        RETURN SUCCESS;

    -- Handle exceptions and return corresponding
    -- numeric values.
    EXCEPTION
        WHEN loginInUse THEN
            RETURN LOGIN_IN_USE;
        WHEN invalidEmail THEN
            RETURN INVALID_EMAIL;
        WHEN invalidUserID THEN
            RETURN INVALID_USER_ID;
        WHEN OTHERS THEN
            RETURN DATABASE_ERROR;
    END saveProfile;
```

Retrieving User Profiles

At some point, we may want to obtain information on a specified user. For example, the user may wish to edit some part of their profile, such as the login name or password, in which case we must fetch the existing data for update. The getProfile() function takes a user ID and selects the matching profile information. The fields available from the cursor returned are:

❑   login: the user login and display name

❑   password: the user password

❑   first_name: first name of the user

❑   last_name: the user's surname

❑   email: the user's e-mail address

```
/*    ---------------------------------------
      Returns information on the user profile.

      Columns: login,password,first_name,last_name,email
      --------------------------------------- */
FUNCTION getProfile (
      nUsr             NUMBER
) RETURN rcurCursor IS

-- Variables
cur                    rcurCursor;

BEGIN
      OPEN cur FOR
      SELECT login,first_name,last_name,email
      FROM users WHERE user_id = nUsr;
      RETURN cur;
END getProfile;
```

Logging on to the Forum

We have already discussed the saveProfile() function, which updates existing or creates new user profiles. When a user has created a profile, they can use the login name and password supplied with their profile to log on to the network, in order to participate in the discussion. This login process is handled by the login() function.

The login() function takes the login name and password of the user and queries the database for matches. The function has three possible return values. If the login name supplied is not found in the users table, the function returns INVALID_LOGON. However, if the login name is valid but the password doesn't match, the function returns INVALID_PASSWORD. Finally, if the login name and password are both valid, we get SUCCESS returned. In that case, we can obtain the user_id of the user from the nUsr OUT parameter. The user_id can then be used to call getProfile() and thus obtain the full profile of the user (this is done in the User Java class we implement in the *User Interface* section later in this chapter).

> *If this procedure weren't to be called from JDBC methods, we would perhaps consider using the PL/SQL Boolean datatype to indicate whether the login was successful or not. However, due to a restriction in the OCI layer, the JDBC drivers do not support the passing of Boolean parameters to PL/SQL stored procedures and therefore we must use Number when migrating to Java (see http://oradoc.photo.net/ora81/DOC/java.815/a64685/tips3.htm#1005343).*

```
/*    ---------------------------------------
      Logs the user on to the forum network

      Returns:

           1  On success
          -5  Invalid login
          -6  Login and password do not match

      --------------------------------------- */
FUNCTION login (
      v2Login           IN       VARCHAR2,
```

```
        v2Password        IN        VARCHAR2,
        nUsr              OUT       NUMBER
) RETURN NUMBER IS

-- Variables
v2Temp                    VARCHAR2(100);
cur                       rcurCursor;
invalidLogin              EXCEPTION;
invalidPassword           EXCEPTION;

BEGIN

    -- Validate the login name
    OPEN cur FOR
    SELECT user_id,password
    FROM users WHERE login = v2Login;
    FETCH cur INTO nUsr,v2Temp;
    CLOSE cur;
    IF nUsr IS NULL THEN
        RAISE invalidLogin;
    END IF;

    -- Validate the password
    IF v2Password != v2Temp THEN
        RAISE invalidPassword;
    END IF;

    RETURN SUCCESS;

EXCEPTION
    WHEN invalidLogin THEN
        RETURN INVALID_LOGIN;
    WHEN invalidPassword THEN
        RETURN INVALID_PASSWORD;
END login;
```

Retrieving Package Constants

In the Java class we will later implement to access the stored procedures in the database, we must be able to get the proper values of the constant return types of the `UserProfile` package functions. The `getConstants()` procedure has as many OUT parameters as there are package constants. These parameters are given the values of their corresponding constants.

```
/* ---------------------------------------
   Returns the package constants.
   --------------------------------------- */
PROCEDURE getConstants (
    nSuccess          OUT       NUMBER,
    nDatabaseError    OUT       NUMBER,
    nInvalidUserId    OUT       NUMBER,
    nLoginInUse       OUT       NUMBER,
    nInvalidEmail     OUT       NUMBER,
    nInvalidLogin     OUT       NUMBER,
    nInvalidPasswd    OUT       NUMBER
) IS
```

```
       BEGIN
           nSuccess := SUCCESS;
           nDatabaseError := DATABASE_ERROR;
           nInvalidUserId := INVALID_USER_ID;
           nLoginInUse := LOGIN_IN_USE;
           nInvalidEmail := INVALID_EMAIL;
           nInvalidLogin := INVALID_LOGIN;
           nInvalidPasswd := INVALID_PASSWORD;

       END getConstants;
```

Finally, as we have implemented all the methods of the package, we close the package body:

```
   END;
```

The Forum Package

The Forum package contains methods for posting and gathering messages, watching registered message threads, and so on. More precisely, it contains the following methods:

- ❑ postMessage(): posts a new message.

- ❑ getCategories(): returns the available categories.

- ❑ getThreads(): returns the message threads of a specified category.

- ❑ getMessages(): returns a specified message thread.

- ❑ addMessageWatch(): sets a watch for a specific thread.

- ❑ checkMessageWatch(): checks for users awaiting updates on a specified topic and calls sendMail() to notify those who do.

- ❑ getWatches(): returns the messages being watched for a specified user.

- ❑ sendMail(): wrapper function for a Java class implementing the JavaMail API for message transport. Optionally, for 8.1.6 users, this can be replaced by using the utl_smtp package, as we will explain later.

Package Spec

The Forum package specification can be seen below. In addition to functions and procedures, the specification defines the date format used throughout the package and some of the return values of the Forum functions. Note that as we define the SUCCESS and DATABASE_ERROR constants with constants from the UserProfile package, we must create the UserProfile before we create the Forum package.

```
   CREATE OR REPLACE PACKAGE Forum
   IS

       SUCCESS            CONSTANT   NUMBER   :=   UserProfile.SUCCESS;
       DATABASE_ERROR     CONSTANT   NUMBER   :=   UserProfile.DATABASE_ERROR;
       DATE_FORMAT        CONSTANT   VARCHAR2(50):= 'dd.mm.yyyy HH24:MI';
       TYPE rcurCursor IS REF CURSOR;
```

```
/*  ----------------------------------------
    Posts a new message
    --------------------------------------- */
    FUNCTION postMessage (
        nCategory        IN        NUMBER,
        nUsr             IN        NUMBER,
        v2Header         IN        VARCHAR2,
        v2Text           IN        VARCHAR2,
        nRespondsTo      IN        NUMBER        DEFAULT NULL,
        nParent          IN        NUMBER        DEFAULT NULL,
        nMessage         OUT       NUMBER
    ) RETURN NUMBER;

/*  ----------------------------------------
    Returns the categories available
    --------------------------------------- */
    FUNCTION getCategories RETURN rcurCursor;

/*  ----------------------------------------
    Returns the message threads of the specified category.
    --------------------------------------- */
    FUNCTION getThreads (
        nCategory        IN        NUMBER,
        dLogon           IN        DATE
    ) RETURN rcurCursor;

/*  ----------------------------------------
    Returns the specified message along with
    all its replies.
    --------------------------------------- */
    FUNCTION getMessages (
        nMessage         IN        NUMBER
    ) RETURN rcurCursor;

/*  ----------------------------------------
    Registers the specfied user on a watch for
    the indicated message.
    --------------------------------------- */
    PROCEDURE addMessageWatch (
        nUsr             IN        NUMBER,
        nMessage         IN        NUMBER,
        nNotify          IN        NUMBER DEFAULT 0
    );

/*  ----------------------------------------
    Checks whether there are any users waiting
    for updates on the specified message.
    Calls the sendMail procedure if there are
    any messages to send.
    --------------------------------------- */
    PROCEDURE checkMessageWatch (
        nMessage         NUMBER
    );
```

```
/*    -------------------------------------------
      Returns the message watched for this user.
      ------------------------------------- */
FUNCTION getWatches (
     nUsr             NUMBER
) RETURN rcurCursor;


/*    -------------------------------------------
      Send blind carbon copy mail to the addresses
      specified.
      ------------------------------------- */
FUNCTION sendMail (
     v2To             IN      VARCHAR2,
     v2From           IN      VARCHAR2,
     v2Cc             IN      VARCHAR2,
     v2Bcc            IN      VARCHAR2,
     v2Subject        IN      VARCHAR2,
     v2Body           IN      VARCHAR2
) RETURN NUMBER;

END;
```

Package Body

As we did with the `UserProfile` package, we will split up the `Forum` package body and discuss each method separately.

```
CREATE OR REPLACE PACKAGE BODY Forum
IS
```

Posting Messages

When the user has created a profile and logged into the forum network, they can participate in the discussion. To do so, they can either create a new message thread, which will be listed directly under a specific category, or reply to previously posted messages. In either case, all message posts are handled by the `postMessage()` function.

The `postMessage()` function the following parameters:

❑   nCategory: the `category_id` of the category the message belongs to

❑   nUsr: the `user_id` of the user posting the message

❑   v2Header: the message header

❑   v2Text: the message content

❑   nParent: the `message_id` of the parent message, omitted for new threads

❑   nRespondsTo: the `user_id` of the user responded to, omitted for new threads

In the `postMessage()` function, there is no actual validation of the supplied data (no censorship either), however, if the foreign key values supplied (nCategory and nUsr) have no match in their referenced tables (`categories` and `users`, respectively), an exception will be thrown and the function returns an error value. If everything goes well, however, the function retuens a value of `success` and the `message_id` of the new message can be obtained from the nMessage OUT variable.

At the end of postMessage(), we call the checkMessageWatch() procedure, which checks if there are any users watching the thread our posted message belongs to. By including this call, we ensure a secure watch of all message threads, as each and every message reply must be posted with the postMessage() function. We will discuss the checkMessageWatch() procedure in detail later.

Note that as we only store specified root messages in the watches table, we only call the checkMessageWatch() procedure when we have a message with a parent. Otherwise, we would be creating a new message thread, which no one could be watching.

```
/* -------------------------------------------
   Posts a new message

   Returns:
        1  On success
        0  Unknown error
   ------------------------------------------- */
FUNCTION postMessage (
      nCategory        IN     NUMBER,
      nUsr             IN     NUMBER,
      v2Header         IN     VARCHAR2,
      v2Text           IN     VARCHAR2,
      nRespondsTo      IN     NUMBER      DEFAULT NULL,
      nParent          IN     NUMBER      DEFAULT NULL,
      nMessage         OUT    NUMBER
) RETURN NUMBER IS

   -- Variables
   cur                 rcurCursor;

BEGIN

      -- Add the message to the messages table
      INSERT INTO Messages (category_id,header,
          text,user_id,responds_to,parent)
      VALUES (nCategory,v2Header,v2Text,nUsr,
          nRespondsTo,nParent);
      COMMIT;

      -- Get the new message_id
      OPEN cur FOR
      SELECT msg_seq.currval FROM dual;
      FETCH cur INTO nMessage;
      CLOSE cur;

      -- Checks on the status of possible
      -- message watches if this is not a
      -- new root message.
      -- IF nParent IS NOT NULL THEN
      --     checkMessageWatch(nMessage);
      -- END IF;

      RETURN SUCCESS;

-- This is an unknown database error
EXCEPTION WHEN OTHERS THEN
      RETURN DATABASE_ERROR;
END postMessage;
```

Getting Categories

The getCategories() function queries the database for the currently defined categories. The method returns a cursor, with available fields:

- ❏ category_id: the category ID
- ❏ category_name: the name of the category
- ❏ category_info: information on the category

```
/* -----------------------------------------
   Returns the categories available

   Columns: category_id,category_name,category_info
   --------------------------------------- */
FUNCTION getCategories RETURN rcurCursor IS

   -- Variables
   cur                    rcurCursor;

BEGIN
    OPEN cur FOR
    SELECT category_id,category_name,category_info
    FROM categories ORDER BY category_name;
    RETURN cur;
END getCategories;
```

Getting Root Messages

Once the user has selected a category to browse, we display its message threads (root messages) in chronological order. The getThreads() function takes a category_id and specified logon date for parameters. The function selects the message threads of the specified category, along with the number of replies and the post dates of the latest replies. In addition, it examines whether the threads have been modified after the specified dLogon date (which indicates when the user last logged on to the network). This query is selected into a cursor, which the function returns. The fields that can be obtained from the cursor are:

- ❏ message_id: the message ID.
- ❏ header: the message header.
- ❏ post_date: the date the message was posted, as a string in the format *29.11.2000 23:11*.
- ❏ replies: the number of replies the message has had.
- ❏ last_reply_date: the date the latest message in the thread was posted or null if the message has not had any replies, as a string in the same format as post_date.
- ❏ modified: indicates whether any of the messages in the thread have been posted after the specified dLogon date. Returns an integer, where negative values mean that the thread has not been modified.

```
/*  ------------------------------------------
    Returns the root messages of the
    specified category.

    Columns:    message_id,header,post_date,
                replies,last_reply_date
    ------------------------------------------ */
FUNCTION getThreads (
    nCategory           IN      NUMBER,
    dLogon              IN      DATE
) RETURN rcurCursor IS

    -- Variables
    cur                 rcurCursor;

BEGIN
    OPEN cur FOR
    SELECT TO_CHAR(p.submit_date,DATE_FORMAT) AS post_date,
    (SIGN(p.submit_date-dLogon)
    + NVL(SIGN(MAX(r.submit_date)-dLogon),-1)) AS modified,
    p.header AS header,p.message_id AS message_id,
    COUNT(r.message_id) AS replies,
    TO_CHAR(MAX(r.submit_date),DATE_FORMAT)
    AS last_reply_date
    FROM messages p,messages r
    WHERE p.category_id = nCategory
    AND p.parent IS NULL
    AND p.message_id = r.parent (+)
    GROUP BY p.submit_date,p.header,p.message_id
    ORDER BY p.submit_date DESC,p.header;

    RETURN cur;
END getThreads;
```

It is probably necessary to explain this function a little bit further. In the SELECT statement, we query for the root messages of the specified category, which are recognized by the fact that they have no parent (i.e., parent IS NULL). We then join the messages table with itself, linking together the root messages and their replies. Since the root messages need not have any replies, we keep this an **outer join**, preserving the root messages:

```
FROM messages p, messages r
WHERE p.category_id = nCategory
AND p.parent IS NULL
AND p.message_id = r.parent (+)
```

We format the date fields with the TO_CHAR() function. In your own implementation, you can of course specify another date format, by changing the value of the DATE_FORMAT constant.

```
SELECT TO_CHAR(p.submit_date,'dd.mm.yyyy HH24:MI') AS post_date,
...
TO_CHAR(MAX(r.submit_date),'dd.mm.yyyy HH24:MI') AS last_reply_date,
```

To get the number of replies to each of the root messages, we select the COUNT() of rows that resulted from the outer join. If there are no replies, the COUNT() simply returns zero.

```
COUNT(r.message_id) AS replies
```

We also want to know whether the specified message thread (that is, the message or any of its replies) has been modified after the user last logged on to the discussion forum. (We store the logon date in the User object the user obtains when they log on, as we will describe in the *User Interface* section later.) To get this information, we add together the **key signatures** (+1 or -1) of the difference of the logon date and the post date of the root message, and the difference of the logon date and the post date of the newest reply. Note that we must take the NVL() of the latter term – that way, if there are no replies we get a difference of -1, which is the same as saying that there have not been any **new** replies.

```
(SIGN(p.submit_date-dLogon) + NVL(SIGN(MAX(r.submit_date)-dLogon),-1))
```

As the SIGN() function returns -1 if its attribute is below zero, zero if the attribute is exactly zero, and +1 if it is more than zero, a total sum equal to or more than zero indicates that the thread has been modified, but a sum of below zero indicates the opposite. Note that, with this assumption, messages that are posted at exactly the same time as the user logged on are actually defined as non-modified. Therefore, we define modified messages as those messages that were posted **after** the user logged on.

Getting a Message Thread

The getMessages() function takes the message_id of a specified root message as a parameter and returns a cursor pointing at the root message and all its replies, if any. The messages are returned in chronological order, so that the root message will be the first row fetched from the cursor (optionally, you may return the parent value of the messages for a more robust check).

The fields available from the cursor are:

❑ message_id: the message ID

❑ header: the message header

❑ text: the message body

❑ author: the name of the user who posted the message

❑ user_id: the user ID of the user who posted the message

❑ post_date: the date the message was posted

❑ reply_to: the name of the user this message replies to

```
/*  ---------------------------------------------
    Returns the specified message along with
    all its replies.

    Columns:    message_id,header,text,author,user_id,
                post_date,reply_to
    --------------------------------------------- */
FUNCTION getMessages (
    nMessage        IN      NUMBER
) RETURN rcurCursor IS
```

```
    -- Variables
    cur                rcurCursor;

    BEGIN

        OPEN cur FOR
        SELECT m.message_id AS message_id, m.header AS header,
        m.text AS text,u.login AS author,u.user_id AS user_id,
        TO_CHAR(m.submit_date,DATE_FORMAT) AS post_date,
        r.login AS reply_to
        FROM messages m,users r,users u
        WHERE (m.message_id = nMessage
            OR m.parent = nMessage)
        AND u.user_id = m.user_id
        AND m.responds_to = r.user_id (+)
        ORDER BY m.submit_date;

        RETURN cur;
    END getMessages;
```

Watching a Topic

We have already mentioned the `watches` table, which stores which users are watching which messages. By default, users will watch threads in which they post. Optionally, users can explicitly specify that they want to watch a certain topic. In either case, setting watches is handled by the `addMessageWatch()` procedure. This procedure takes as parameters the `message_id` of the root message of the thread and the `user_id` of the user wishing to keep a watch. In addition, users can specify being notified about updates with e-mail, by giving the `nNotify` parameter a value of 1 (the default is 0).

> *Logically, we should be using the PL/SQL Boolean datatype for indicating the type of notification. However, the same restriction as with the previously mentioned `login()` function applies here.*

Note that we only watch specific **topics**, that is, we only store the `message_id` of the root message of a certain message thread.

```
/*  -----------------------------------------
    Registers the specfied user on a watch for
    the indicated message.
    ----------------------------------------- */
PROCEDURE addMessageWatch (
    nUsr            IN      NUMBER,
    nMessage        IN      NUMBER,
    nNotify         IN      NUMBER DEFAULT 0
) IS

    -- Variables
    nNotiTemp          NUMBER;

    BEGIN

        -- Set the proper value.
        nNotiTemp := nNotify;
        IF nNotiTemp >= 1 THEN
```

```
            nNotiTemp := 1;
    ELSE
            nNotiTemp := 0;
    END IF;

        -- Add this user and message to the watches table.
        INSERT INTO watches (user_id,message_id,notify)
        VALUES (nUsr,nMessage,nNotiTemp);

    EXCEPTION WHEN OTHERS THEN NULL;
    END addMessageWatch;
```

Checking the Watch Status

We have already seen that the postMessage() function makes a call to the checkMessageWatch() procedure each time a new message reply is posted. The checkMessageWatch() procedure takes the message_id of a certain root message and queries for users who have specified receiving e-mail notifications when the message receives a reply. If the query has results, we construct a message and a list of recipients, and invoke the sendMail() procedure, which we will discuss later.

```
/*  ------------------------------------
    Checks whether there are any users waiting
    for updates on the specified message.
    Calls the sendMail procedure if there are
    any messages to send.
    ------------------------------------- */
PROCEDURE checkMessageWatch (
    nMessage        IN      NUMBER
) IS

    -- Variables
    v2Body              VARCHAR2(100)    := '';
    v2Subject           VARCHAR2(100)    := '';
    v2Header            VARCHAR2(100);
    v2TempEmail         VARCHAR2(100);
    v2EmailList         VARCHAR2(32767)  := '';
    nCount              NUMBER;
    nTemp               NUMBER;
    cur                 rcurCursor;

BEGIN

        -- Select the recipients
        OPEN cur FOR
        SELECT  u.email
        FROM users u,watches w
        WHERE w.message_id = nMessage
        AND u.user_id = w.user_id
        AND w.notify = 1;

        -- Create a list of all email addresses
        LOOP

            FETCH cur INTO v2TempEmail;
            EXIT WHEN cur%NOTFOUND;
            v2EmailList := v2EmailList || ',' || v2TempEmail;
```

```
          END LOOP;
          CLOSE cur;

          -- If there are any recipients, we continue.
          IF LENGTH(v2EmailList) > 0 THEN

               -- Skip the last comma
               v2EmailList := SUBSTR(v2EmailList,0,LENGTH(v2EmailList)-2);

               -- Construct the message subject
               v2Subject := 'Message Update from the Forum';

               -- Construct the message body
               OPEN cur FOR
               SELECT p.header AS header,COUNT(r.message_id) AS ncount
               FROM messages p,messages r
               WHERE p.message_id = nMessage
               AND p.message_id = r.parent (+)
               GROUP BY p.header;

               FETCH cur INTO v2Header,nCount;

               v2Body :=  'We wanted to let you know that the message '
                      || v2Header || ' has been updated and has now '
                      || nCount || ' replies. For more information, '
                      || 'visit the following page: '
                      || 'http://www.theforum.com/message.jsp?message='
                      || nMessage ;

               -- Call the sendMail procedure, with
               -- the recipient list, sender, subject
               -- and message body as parameters.
               -- that we do not actually do anything
               -- if we get an error status, although
               -- some logging could be done.
               nTemp := sendMail('','',v2EmailList,
               'info@theforum.com',v2Subject,v2Body);

          END IF;

     EXCEPTION WHEN OTHERS THEN NULL;
     END checkMessageWatch;
```

Getting Watched Messages

The getWatches() function takes the user_id of a specified user as a parameter and returns a cursor pointing at the messages this user is watching, if any. The fields available from the cursor are:

❑   header: the message header

❑   message_id: the message ID

```
/* ---------------------------------------
   Returns the messages watched for this user.
   --------------------------------------- */
   FUNCTION getWatches (
       nUsr           IN      NUMBER
   ) RETURN rcurCursor IS
```

```
        -- Variables
        cur                 rcurCursor;

    BEGIN
        OPEN cur FOR
        SELECT m.header AS header, m.message_id AS message_id
        FROM messages m, watches w
        WHERE m.message_id = w.message_id
        AND w.user_id = nUsr
        ORDER BY m.header;
        RETURN cur;
    END getWatches;
```

Now there is only one procedure in the Forum package left to discuss, the sendMail() procedure, which handles the network messaging and which we will cover in the next section.

Calling Java from PL/SQL

In our discussion forum, we need to be able to address some kind of mail sending application from within our PL/SQL procedures. Since Oracle8*i* supports loading Java classes directly into the database, where they can be manipulated by PL/SQL, using Java for the messaging process becomes a feasible choice.

We have already mentioned that we originally used Oracle 8.1.5 for this project. At that time, we used Java stored procedures to call JavaMail messaging classes that were stored in the database. In the first part of this section we will discuss this approach to messaging with PL/SQL.

However, with version 8.1.6 of Oracle came the supplied package UTL_SMTP that can be used to send messages from PL/SQL. This package uses stored Java for the message functionality. Using the UTL_SMTP package spares us the whole process of implementing a JavaMail class, as we have to do with 8.1.5.

Unlike our JavaMail implementation, the UTL_SMTP package can only send a message to a single recipient at a time. Because of this limitation, using JavaMail will probably be a better choice in this application.

In this section we will discuss the implementation of the Forum.sendMail() procedure using both methods of messaging. However, for your own application, you must select one of these methods. A short summary of the properties of both approaches follows:

❑ JavaMail: used with 8.1.5 and those 8.1.6 applications that already have implemented complex JavaMail programs. This method better suits our application, since it allows sending messages to **multiple recipients** simultaneously.

❑ UTL_SMTP: Used with 8.1.6, spares us the process of implementing JavaMail applications. This method can only send messages to a **single recipient** at a time.

Oracle 8.1.5: Messaging with JavaMail

In this section, we will discuss how to use JavaMail to construct a message transport service, which can be loaded into the database for further manipulation. To be more precise, we will:

❑   Discuss the JavaMail API

❑   Implement a `Mailer` class

❑   Use `loadjava` to load the classes to the database

❑   Create a wrapper procedure for the desired methods

> Note that in order to be able to use `loadjava`, you must have installed the SQLJ packages and set your **CLASSPATH** accordingly. For further information on this process, consult the *SQLJ Installation* appendix.

The JavaMail specification provides a collection of abstract classes that model a mail system. The API provides a platform and protocol-independent framework to build Java technology-based mail and messaging applications.

While the JavaMail abstract classes and interfaces are not directly usable (due to their abstract nature), it is up to the mail providers implementing the API to provide the functionality needed to communicate with specific protocols. Actually, implementations for the most commonly used mail protocols, including SMTP (Simple Mail Transport Protocol), POP3 (Post Office Protocol 3), IMAP (Internet Message Access Protocol) and MIME (Multipurpose Internet Mail Extensions), are available for download from Sun, in addition to various other third-party implementations.

Mail services are divided into two categories: transporting and storing. Transport services have the capability of delivering messages to a specified destination, such as mailboxes, where it is the role of the storing services to keep track of all incoming and outgoing deliveries. The most commonly used transport protocol is the SMTP protocol, while the POP3 and IMAP protocols are probably the most widely used mail protocols for storing. Using supplemented or custom implementations of the JavaMail interfaces allows applications to access these various message protocols in virtually the same manner.

Installation

Currently, JavaMail is not included in any standard distribution of the Java Runtime or Development Kits. The implementation distribution has to be downloaded separately from Sun's JavaMail page, at http://java.sun.com/products/javamail. The distribution archive contains lots of documentation and examples, in addition to the `mail.jar` archive, which contains the actual source code. This archive must be extracted to a location specified in the `classpath`, as we explain below.

The JavaMail distribution archive includes implementations of the core JavaMail API packages as well as implementations of the IMAP and SMTP transport service providers, as we have already mentioned. An implementation of the POP3 storing service must be obtained separately. Sun actually offers a sample implementation of this service, available for download at http://java.sun.com/products/javamail/pop3.html. Please note that the POP3 implementation is not required for our case study, as we will only be using SMTP transport services to send messages.

In addition to the core `mail.jar` archive, you will also need the JavaBeans Activation Framework (JAF) extension, in order to use JavaMail. This extension consists of the `activation.jar` file, which includes the `javax.activation` package. The archive is available for download at http://java.sun.com/beans/glasgow/jaf.html.

Compiling Outside Oracle

Using `loadjava` to load the Java classes into the database, you can either directly load the actual source code (`.java` file) and have it compiled in the database, or compile the class outside the database and load the resulting class file (`.class` file). Usually, the latter method is recommended, as it provides better error handling. To do so, however, you must properly set your CLASSPATH before compiling.

Once both the `mail.jar` and `activation.jar` packages have been downloaded and extracted to the right place, you must add them to your `classpath`. For example, if you extracted both files to the JAVA_HOME/lib folder, you should alter your CLASSPATH shell variable on a UNIX system:

```
CLASSPATH=$CLASSPATH:$JAVA_HOME/lib/mail.jar
CLASSPATH=$CLASSPATH:$JAVA_HOME/lib/activation.jar
export CLASSPATH
```

If you are deploying on Windows, you alter your CLASSPATH environment variable with:

```
SET CLASSPATH=%CLASSPATH%;%JAVA_HOME%\lib\mail.jar
SET CLASSPATH=%CLASSPATH%;%JAVA_HOME%\lib\activation.jar
```

Implementing a Mail Transport Class

With the `activation.jar` and `mail.jar` files in our CLASSPATH, we can now implement a simple mail transport Java class. This class, which we call `Mailer`, is the same one as depicted in the package diagram at the beginning of the last section. As we will later explain, we will load the `Mailer` class into the database where it will be accessible by the methods of the `Forum` package.

The `Mailer` class contains a few static constants, which are used to determine the proper return value of the `sendMessage()` method, which is used for the message transport. The SMTP host name used by the class is also kept constant; in our case this is the imaginary mail server `mail.theforum.com`.

Note that our implementation of the `Mailer` class is by no means designed to show the full capabilities of the JavaMail API. It contains the single static method `sendMessage()`, which takes for parameters comma separated lists of message recipients, along with the subject and body of the message itself.

```java
import java.io.*;
import java.net.*;
import java.util.*;
import javax.activation.*;
import javax.mail.*;
import javax.mail.internet.*;

public class Mail {

        final static int MESSAGE_SENT       =  1;
        final static int INCORRECT_ADDRESS  = -1;
        final static int TRANSMISSION_ERROR = -2;
        final static int UNEXPECTED_ERROR   = -3;
```

```
        final static String HOST = "mail.theforum.com";

        public static int sendMessage( String to,String from,String cc,
            String bcc,String subject,String text ) {
```

The method then proceeds to create a JavaMail `Session` instance, which is used to manage the mail configuration settings and to handle transports during the session. The `Session` object is obtained with the static `getInstance()` method of the `Session` class, which takes a `Properties` object, containing mail configuration settings, and an instance of the `Authenticator` class, which is actually `null` in our implementation, for parameters.

```
        try {
            // Create the JavaMail session
            Properties properties = System.getProperties();
            properties.put("mail.smtp.host",HOST);
            Session session = Session.getInstance(properties,null);
```

Next, a `MimeMessage` object is constructed from the `Session` instance. We then set necessary attributes for the `MimeMessage`, such as recipient addresses, message subject, and message text. Note that we construct a single `Address` instance for the address of the sender, as opposed to arrays of `Address` instances for the recipient addresses. The `Address` arrays are constructed with the static `parse()` method of the `InternetAddress` class, which splits a comma separated list of e-mail addresses to an array of valid `Address` objects.

```
            // Construct the message
            MimeMessage message = new MimeMessage(session);

            // Set the from address
            Address fromAddress = new InternetAddress(from);
            message.setFrom(fromAddress);

            // Parse and set the recipient addresses
            Address[] toAddresses = InternetAddress.parse(to);
            message.setRecipients(Message.RecipientType.TO,toAddresses);

            Address[] ccAddresses = InternetAddress.parse(cc);
            message.setRecipients(Message.RecipientType.CC,ccAddresses);

            Address[] bccAddresses = InternetAddress.parse(bcc);
            message.setRecipients(Message.RecipientType.BCC,bccAddresses);

            // Set the subject and text
            message.setSubject(subject);
            message.setText(text);
```

Finally, we call the `send()` method of the `Transport` class to send the message. At the end of the `sendMessage()` method, we handle all possible sorts of runtime exceptions and return an appropriate status code.

```
              // Send the message.
              Transport.send(message);
              return MESSAGE_SENT;

       } catch (AddressException e) {
           return INCORRECT_ADDRESS;
       } catch (SendFailedException e) {
           return TRANSMISSION_ERROR;
       } catch (MessagingException e) {
           return UNEXPECTED_ERROR;
       }
   }
}
```

Loading Java into the Database

Before we can call the `Mailer` methods from the PL/SQL procedures, we must load them into the Oracle RDBMS and publish them to SQL. Loading and publishing are separate tasks. Many Java classes, referenced only by other Java classes, are never published to SQL. This is actually the case with the `mail.jar` and `activation.jar` archives, which we have to load (but not publish!) to the database, before we can load the `Mailer` class, as it will depend on those archives.

To load Java stored procedures automatically, we use the command-line utility `loadjava`. It uploads Java source, class, and resource files into a system-generated database table, and then uses the SQL `CREATE JAVA` statement to load the Java files into the RDBMS. Detailed information on `loadjava` is found in the Java Stored Procedures chapter. We use `loadjava` to load the JAR archives before the `Mailer` class:

```
loadjava -user dbuser/dbpasswd -resolve -verbose activation.jar
loadjava -user dbuser/dbpasswd -resolve -verbose mail.jar
```

> **Note that when using `loadjava` to upload Java to a remote machine, you use the full TNS connect string together with the `-oci8` or `-thin` command-line arguments. See the Java Stored Procedures chapter for further details.**

Loading these archives will take some time on most platforms, as they are quite large and the JVM has to resolve all the class files that the archives contain. For example, loading the `activation.jar` will take around 6 minutes and for `mail.jar` some 15 minutes.

If you are using Oracle 8.1.5, you will not be able to load the archives into the user's schema, even with the `JAVASYSPRIV` privilege granted (consult the SQLJ chapter for more information on the `JAVASYSPRIV` privilege). Instead, you must load them into the `SYS` schema:

```
loadjava -user internal/passwd -synonym -resolve -verbose activation.jar
loadjava -user internal/passwd -synonym -resolve -verbose mail.jar
```

In addition, the `activation.jar` and `mail.jar` files come with some of the files compressed. You must unpack and repack the files without compression. This is how you can do it on the UNIX platform:

```
jar xvf activation.jar
rm activation.jar
rm META-INF/MANIFEST.MF
jar cf0 activation.jar META-INF javax com
rm -rf META-INF javax com

jar xvf mail.jar
rm mail.jar
rm META-INF/MANIFEST.MF
jar cf0 mail.jar META-INF javax com
rm -rf META-INF javax com
```

This is how you do it using Windows:

```
jar xvf activation.jar
del activation.jar
del META-INF\MANIFEST.MF
jar cf0 activation.jar META-INF javax com
del META-INF javax com

jar xvf mail.jar
del mail.jar
del META-INF\MANIFEST.MF
jar cf0 mail.jar META-INF javax com
del META-INF javax com
```

Once we have loaded the archives into the database, we can now load the `Mailer` class as well. For example, the following command will load the `Mailer` class to the user identified by `dbuser`/`dbpassword`:

```
loadjava -user dbuser/dbpasswd -resolve -verbose Mailer.class
```

Note that we loaded the compiled `Mailer` class, although we could have loaded the source file as well. A good rule of thumb, though, is to compile and test all Java source before loading it into the database. (We have already mentioned this, when we set the `CLASSPATH`, above.)

Implementing the sendMail() Procedure

In order to use the loaded `Mailer` class by PL/SQL procedures, we must create a call specification (or *call spec*) that looks like a PL/SQL function on the outside but is really nothing more than a pass-through to the underlying Java code. A call spec procedure is defined as `LANGUAGE JAVA`, and as such, it calls a stored Java method by mapping the attributes list of the spec to the attributes list of the Java method.

The `sendMail()` procedure we now implement, is a call specification for the `Mailer.sendMessage()` method. The parameter list of the procedure is mapped to the parameter list of the Java method, that is, the first parameter of `sendMail()` will be the first parameter of `sendMessage()`, the return value of `sendMail()` will be the return value of `sendMessage()`, and so on:

```
/*  ----------------------------------------
    Send blind a mail message to the addresses specified.
    ---------------------------------------- */
FUNCTION sendMail (
    v2To            IN      VARCHAR2,
    v2From          IN      VARCHAR2,
    v2Cc            IN      VARCHAR2,
    v2Bcc           IN      VARCHAR2,
    v2Subject       IN      VARCHAR2,
    v2Body          IN      VARCHAR2
) RETURN NUMBER
AS LANGUAGE JAVA
NAME 'Mail.sendMessage( java.lang.String,java.lang.String,
      java.lang.String,java.lang.String,java.lang.String,
      java.lang.String) return int';
```

Oracle 8.1.6: Messaging with UTL_SMTP

Messaging with PL/SQL is very simple and straight forward with the UTL_SMTP package supplied in Oracle 8.1.6. In order to send e-mail using the UTL_SMTP package, you first need to install the required Java classes, which are supplied with the Oracle installation.

Installing the Java Classes

By default, Oracle installs the Java classes required for UTL_SMTP. However, in the case of a custom installation, you might need to manually install these classes.

To install (load) the required Java classes, you need to connect as SYS and run a couple of installation scripts. Using UNIX, you would have to perform the following commands:

```
@<ORACLE_HOME>/javavm/plsql/jlib/initjvm.sql
@<ORACLE_HOME>/rdbms/java/install/initplsj.sql
```

To do the same, on Windows, this would be:

```
@<ORACLE_HOME>\javavm\plsql\jlib\initjvm.sql
@<ORACLE_HOME>\rdbms\java\install\initplsj.sql
```

> Note that you will have to supply the full path of <ORACLE_HOME>, not just the environment variable as shown above.

Implementing the sendMail() Procedure

Using the UTL_SMTP package, we implement the sendMail() procedure described in the Forum specification, as described in this section. As we have already mentioned, the UTL_SMTP package can only handle sending messages to a single recipient at a time. Therefore, we must split the input string we get from the checkMessageWatch() procedure (a comma-separated list of e-mail addresses) and send the message to a single recipient at a time.

The sendMail() procedure must ensure that the contents of the message conform to the RFC822 specification used by UTL_SMTP. Therefore, we must terminate each line of the message with a <CR><LF> sequence, as required by RFC821. This is done by using the v2Crlf variable.

We hard-code the name of our mail host in this procedure (it was hard-coded in the Mailer class in the JavaMail method). The port number on which SMTP server is listening is usually 25; modify this value in accordance with the correct mail server port if it is different from the standard.

To send a message with the UTL_SMTP package, we must invoke the following procedures, in this order:

- ❑ Open_connection(): Allows open connection to an SMTP server.
- ❑ Helo(): Performs initial handshaking with SMTP server after connecting.
- ❑ Mail(): Initiates a mail transaction with the server.
- ❑ Rcpt(): Specifies the recipient of the e-mail message.
- ❑ Data(): Specifies the content of the e-mail message (including subject).
- ❑ Quit(): Terminates an SMTP session and disconnects from the server.

The sendMail() procedure is implemented using UTL_SMTP as follows. (Note that we skip the processing of the v2Cc and v2Bcc e-mail lists; this would be analogous to the processing of the v2To list.)

```
/*  -------------------------------------------
    Send a mail message to the addresses
    specified.
    ------------------------------------- */
FUNCTION sendMail (
        v2To            IN        VARCHAR2,
        v2From          IN        VARCHAR2,
        v2Cc            IN        VARCHAR2,
        v2Bcc           IN        VARCHAR2,
        v2Subject       IN        VARCHAR2,
        v2Body          IN        VARCHAR2
) RETURN NUMBER
IS

-- Hard-coded mail host.
v2Mailhost          VARCHAR2(30)      := 'mail.theforum.com';
mail_conn           utl_smtp.connection;
v2Crlf              VARCHAR2(2)       := CHR(13) || CHR(10);
v2Message           VARCHAR2(1000);
v2Email             VARCHAR2(100);
v2List              VARCHAR2(100);

BEGIN
    mail_conn := utl_smtp.open_connection(mailhost, 25);

    -- Take the list of TO addresses.
    v2List := v2To;
    WHILE INSTR(v2List,',') > 0 LOOP
        v2Email := SUBSTR(v2List,1,INSTR(v2List,',')-1);
```

```
                -- Construct the message data.
                v2Message :='From:  <'  || v2From   || '>'      || v2Crlf ||
                            'Subject: ' || v2Subject|| v2Crlf   ||
                            'To: '      || v2Email  || v2Crlf   ||
                            ' '         || v2Crlf   || v2Body;

                -- Send the message.
                utl_smtp.helo(mail_conn, v2Mailhost);
                utl_smtp.mail(mail_conn, v2From);
                utl_smtp.rcpt(mail_conn, v2Email);
                utl_smtp.data(mail_conn, v2Message);
                utl_smtp.quit(mail_conn);

                -- Cut of the list.
                v2List := SUBSTR(v2List,INSTR(v2List,',')+1,LENGTH(v2List));
        END LOOP;

        -- The last address.
        IF LENGTH(v2List) > 0 THEN

                -- Construct the message data.
                v2Message :='From:  <'  || v2From   || '>'      || v2Crlf ||
                            'Subject: ' || v2Subject|| v2Crlf   ||
                            'To: '      || v2Email  || v2Crlf   ||
                            ' '         || v2Crlf   || v2Body;

                -- Send the message.
                utl_smtp.helo(mail_conn, v2Mailhost);
                utl_smtp.mail(mail_conn, v2From);
                utl_smtp.rcpt(mail_conn, v2Email);
                utl_smtp.data(mail_conn, v2Message);
                utl_smtp.quit(mail_conn);

        END IF;

        -- Repeat the previous procedure for the
        -- v2Cc and v2Bcc parameters.

    END sendMail;
```

With this last procedure, we have finished our implementation of the Forum package. In the next section, we discuss how we can call the package function from Java methods, using JDBC.

Calling PL/SQL from Java

Using JDBC, stored procedures can easily be called from any Java application with database access. In our implementation, we will create a single Java class that will give us access to the stored functions and procedures of the Forum package, using JDBC. This class will encapsulate all the JDBC objects necessary for database access, such as the Connection, ResultSet, and CallableStatement. Therefore, it will be our sole interface to the database, used for both updating tables and for obtaining scrollable result sets.

The key in calling PL/SQL stored procedures from Java is the CallableStatement class. Although we have already mentioned this class in Chapter 12, we will now briefly recap its most notable features.

CallableStatement Overview

A `CallableStatement` object provides a way to call PL/SQL stored procedures. The stored procedure call is written in an escape syntax that may take one of two forms, one with a result parameter, and the other without. A result parameter is the return value for the stored function. Both forms may have any number of parameters used for input (`IN` parameters), output (`OUT` parameters), or both (`IN`/`OUT` parameters). Using the `CallableStatement`, a question mark serves as a placeholder for a parameter. An example of both forms is given below:

```
// Calling a procedure
query = "BEGIN Forum.addMessageWatch (?,?,?); END;";

// Calling a function.
query = "BEGIN ? := UserProfile.login (?,?,?); END;";
```

Normally, anyone creating a `CallableStatement` object would already know that the DBMS being used supports stored procedures and what those procedures are. If one needed to check, however, various `DatabaseMetaData` methods will supply such information. For instance, the method `supportsStoredProcedures()` will return `true` if the DBMS supports stored procedure calls, and the method `getProcedures()` will return a description of the stored procedures available. For example, the following code lists the names of all available stored procedures for the specified database user:

```
// Gets a connection to the database from a specific dbUrl.
Connection conn = DriverManager.getConnection(dbUrl);
DatabaseMetaData dmd = conn.getMetaData();

// Creates a ResultSet of the stored procedures available.
ResultSet rs = dmd.getProcedures(conn.getCatalog(),null,null);
while ( rs.next() ) {
    System.out.println( proc.getString("procedure_name") );
}
rs.close();
conn.close();
```

The `CallableStatement` inherits both `Statement` methods, which deal with SQL statements in general, as well as `PreparedStatement` methods, which deal with `IN` parameters. All of the methods explicitly defined for `CallableStatement` therefore deal with `OUT` parameters, such as registering their JDBC types, retrieving their values, and checking for nulls. Whereas the `get()` methods defined in `ResultSet` retrieve values from a result set, the `get()` methods of the `CallableStatement` retrieve values from the `OUT` parameters and/or return values of stored procedures.

Further information on the `CallableStatement` can be obtained from Chapter 12, earlier in the book.

DatabaseAccess

For our discussion forum, we will implement a single Java class for calling the PL/SQL stored procedures in the database. This class, which we call `DatabaseAccess`, has methods corresponding to each procedure in the `Forum` package, in addition to general access methods that are relayed to the corresponding methods of the `ResultSet`, as we will see in more detail later. The following figure shows the `DatabaseAccess` class and its methods.

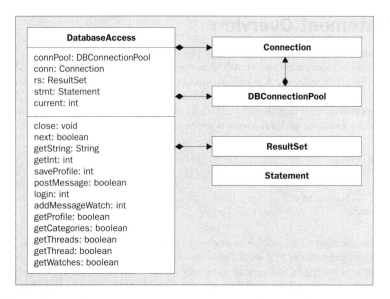

In our implementation of the DatabaseAccess class we will use JDBC 2.0 and Oracle extension packages. If you don't have the Oracle JDBC driver files, which contain these packages, you can download the appropriate archive from Oracle at http://technet.oracle.com/software. At the time this is written, the JDBC 2.0 driver archive is downloaded as classes12_01.zip. Once you have downloaded this archive, you must make sure it is in your classpath. For example, on a UNIX system, if you have downloaded the classes12_01.zip archive in JAVA_HOME/lib, you set:

```
CLASSPATH=$CLASSPATH:$JAVA_HOME/lib/classes12_01.zip
export CLASSPATH
```

On Windows, this would be:

```
SET CLASSPATH=%CLASSPATH%;%JAVA_HOME%\lib\classes12_01.zip
```

If you try to compile the DatabaseAccess class and get error messages like

```
D:\My Documents\code\DatabaseAccess.java:3: package oracle.jdbc.driver does not exist
import oracle.jdbc.driver.*;
^
```

you should check your CLASSPATH variable.

Connection Pooling

Since we are developing a web site application, which will possibly experience high traffic levels, we must consider the scheme we will use for database connectivity. Creating a new Connection instance each time we instantiate our DatabaseAccess class will cause a lot of overhead eventually, since creating and destroying physical database Connection objects is an expensive task. However, using connection pooling, which we discussed in Chapter 13, this overhead can be largely avoided. (Further information on the advantages of connection pooling can be obtained from Chapter 13.)

If you are familiar with the implementation discussed in Chapter 13, you will see that we can get pooled `Connection` objects from an instance of the `DBConnectionPool` class. In the `DatabaseAccess` class, we have to use a `Connection` instance directly, instead of using the `DBConnection` wrapper, since we have to be able to freely manipulate the `Connection Statement`. If we just make sure to return the `Connection` back to the pool once we close the `DatabaseAccess` class, we will have the full benefits of the `DBConnection` wrapper, but with more flexibility. Note that as we are using JDBC 2.0 with Oracle JDBC extensions in the `DatabaseAccess` implementation, we will use the modified version of the `DBConnectionPool`, which we implemented at the end of Chapter 13.

Class Construction

The `DatabaseAccess` class has a few instance variables, used for the database access. The class contains an instance of each of the JDBC classes `Connection`, `ResultSet`, and `Statement`, as well as the `DBConnectionPool`, which is used to get the initial `Connection`. In addition, the class keeps track of the current row being fetched from the `ResultSet` object, kept as the `current` variable. Actually, explicit `ResultSet` scrolling is purely optional, as we will see later.

In addition to the class variables, the `DatabaseAccess` class maintains a few `public` integer constants the clients can use to validate various return values. These values are instantiated with the values of their corresponding constants in the `UserProfile` package, in the `getConstants()` method, which is called by the constructor.

```
package forum;

import java.util.*;
import java.io.IOException;
import oracle.jdbc.driver.*;
import java.sql.*;
import pooling2.*;

public class DatabaseAccess {

    public int SUCCESS;
    public int DATABASE_ERROR;
    public int INVALID_USER_ID;
    public int LOGIN_IN_USE;
    public int INVALID_EMAIL;
    public int INVALID_LOGIN;
    public int INVALID_PASSWORD;

    private DBConnectionPool connPool;
    private Connection conn;
    private ResultSet rs;
    private Statement stmt;
    private int current;

    public DatabaseAccess( String poolname ) throws SQLException {
        DBPoolManager manager = DBPoolManager.getInstance();
        connPool = manager.getConnectionPool(poolname);
        current = 0;

        // Load the public "constants" with
        // values from the UserProfile package.
        getConstants();
    }
```

Opening a Connection

Before any of the access methods can execute a call to a stored procedure, they must call the open()
method to get a pooled Connection from the connection pool and to initialize the Statement instance:

```
private synchronized void open() throws SQLException {
    current = 0;
    if ( isOpen() ) {
        rsClose();
        stmtClose();
    } else {
        conn = connPool.getConnection();
    }
    stmt = conn.createStatement();
}
```

If the connection is currently open, as could happen when using the same DatabaseAccess instance
more than once in the same context, we close existing Statement and ResultSet instances by calling
the stmtClose() and rsClose() methods, respectively. This way, we already have a valid
Connection instance and simply create a new Statement.

The rsClose() and stmtClose() methods simply close the ResultSet and Statement instances
and set them to null, if they aren't already:

```
private synchronized void stmtClose() throws SQLException {
    if ( stmt != null) {
        stmt.close();
        stmt = null;
    }
}

private synchronized void rsClose() throws SQLException {
    if ( rs != null) {
        rs.close();
        rs = null;
    }
}
```

When checking whether the Connection was closed or not, we called the isOpen() method, which
returns true if the class Connection object is not null, and false otherwise. Possibly, this method
could include a more robust check for validity, such as by creating a test Statement, as we did in
Chapter 13. In this context, however, that is probably unnecessary.

```
private boolean isOpen() {
    return conn != null;
}
```

Accessing the Data

For our implementation, we must be able to access the table fields pointed at by returned database
cursors. In order to do so, we implement get() methods that relay a call to their corresponding
ResultSet counterparts. To be able to scroll the ResultSet on the client side, we implement the
next() method, that moves the row index of the ResultSet instance forward by one. In addition, the
client can also explicitly specify which row of the ResultSet to access, using overloaded get()
methods, which take an additional row index parameter. The latter methods will only be used when the
forum user can actually scroll a specific results list, such as the list of message threads.

The code for the next() method is shown below. This method calls the next() method of the ResultSet to move the row index forward by one.

```
public synchronized boolean next() throws SQLException {
    try {
        return rs.next();
    } catch (NullPointerException e) {
        throw new SQLException( "Please call get() only after "
                            +   "calling query() and next().");
    } catch (SQLException s) {
        return false;
    }
}
```

For our project, we need only implement get() methods for String and int, as these are the only datatypes we will get from the database cursors returned from the Forum package functions. The single-parameter getString() method takes a field name as an attribute and calls the getString() method that takes the row index parameter. Note that as the first getString() method gives the row index of zero, which is the value we initialize the current variable in the open() method, the latter getString() method will not move the ResultSet cursor, as current == index all the time. In general, we use the single-parameter get() methods combined with next(). The two getInt() methods more or less follow the same design pattern.

> Note that the cursors that we return from the various PL/SQL methods of the **Forum** and **UserProfile** packages are scrollable *forward only*. Therefore, we cannot use the **absolute()** method of the **ResultSet** to access a specified result row, which would be ideal for our **get()** methods (calling **absolute()** on a **ResultSet** object for a forward-only cursor will throw a **SQLException**). Instead, we implement the result scrolling by calling **next()** until we reach the desired row number.

```
public String getString( String field ) throws SQLException {
    return getString(field,0);
}

public String getString( String field,int index ) throws SQLException {
    if ( current != index ) {
        while( current++ < index ) next();
    }
    try {
        String s = rs.getString(field);
        return (s != null) ? s : "";
    } catch (NullPointerException e) {
        throw new SQLException( "Please call get() only after "
                            +   "calling query() and next().");
    }
}

public int getInt( String field ) throws SQLException {
    return getInt(field,0);
}
```

```
public int getInt( String field, int index ) throws SQLException {
    if ( current != index ) {
        while( current++ < index ) next();
    }

    try {
        return rs.getInt(field);
    } catch (NullPointerException e) {
        throw new SQLException( "Please call get() only after "
                        +    "calling query() and next()." );
    }
}
```

Loading Variables

Now that we have discussed all the general access and opening methods of the DatabaseAccess class, we can start to implement the actual PL/SQL migration methods.

First of all, we will implement the getConstants() method that was called by the DatabaseAccess constructor. This method calls the getConstants() procedure of the UserProfile package and obtains the values of constants defined for this package from OUT parameters. These values are then assigned to corresponding (not constant, though) public variables of the DatabaseAccess class.

```
private void getConstants() throws SQLException {

    CallableStatement cs;
    String query;
    query = "BEGIN UserProfile.getConstants(?,?,?,?,?,?,?); END;";

    open();
    cs = conn.prepareCall(query);
    cs.registerOutParameter(1, Types.INTEGER);
    cs.registerOutParameter(2, Types.INTEGER);
    cs.registerOutParameter(3, Types.INTEGER);
    cs.registerOutParameter(4, Types.INTEGER);
    cs.registerOutParameter(5, Types.INTEGER);
    cs.registerOutParameter(6, Types.INTEGER);
    cs.registerOutParameter(7, Types.INTEGER);
    cs.execute();

    // Get the constant values.
    SUCCESS             = cs.getInt(1);
    DATABASE_ERROR      = cs.getInt(2);
    INVALID_USER_ID     = cs.getInt(3);
    LOGIN_IN_USE        = cs.getInt(4);
    INVALID_EMAIL       = cs.getInt(5);
    INVALID_LOGIN       = cs.getInt(6);
    INVALID_PASSWORD    = cs.getInt(7);

    cs.close();
}
```

Saving the User Profile

The saveProfile() method is used to call the saveProfile function of the UserProfile package. The method has two forms: one with no usr specified (used when creating a new user) and another one that accepts a usr and calls the stored procedure. The first method simply calls the latter one, giving the usr ID of zero. In the actual procedure call, we set the first IN/OUT parameter as an OUT parameter when we have a usr ID of zero, indicating that the function should create a new user, which is just what we want in this case. On the other hand, if we have a valid usr ID, we set the first IN/OUT parameter as an IN parameter, and update the user corresponding to the supplied ID.

If the procedure call is successful, we return the user_id of the newly created or updated user.

```java
public int saveProfile( int usr, String login, String password,
    String firstName, String lastName, String email )
    throws SQLException {

    CallableStatement cs;
    int result;
    String query;

    query = "BEGIN ? := UserProfile.saveProfile (?,?,?,?,?,?); END;";

    open();
    cs = conn.prepareCall(query);
    cs.registerOutParameter(1, Types.INTEGER);
    if ( usr != 0 ) {
        cs.setInt(2,usr);
    } else {
        cs.registerOutParameter(2, Types.INTEGER);
    }
    cs.setString(3,login);
    cs.setString(4,password);
    cs.setString(5,firstName);
    cs.setString(6,lastName);
    cs.setString(7,email);
    cs.execute();

    result = cs.getInt(1);
    if ( result == SUCCESS && usr == 0 ) {
        usr = cs.getInt(2);
        cs.close();
        return usr;
    } else {
        cs.close();
        return result;
    }
}
```

Posting Messages

To either post new message threads or reply to previous messages, we call the postMessage() method of the DatabaseAccess class. This method, as the previous saveProfile() method, has two forms. The first form is used to omit the parent and respondsTo parameters of the latter form. New root messages are posted using the first method, while the second method posts message replies with a defined parent. If we get a value of zero for the parent or respondsTo parameters (the first method calls the latter one with these values), we call the PL/SQL function with these values set to NULL. This will create root messages, as we implemented the Forum package. If the transaction was successful, we obtain the new message_id from the nMessage OUT parameter of the postMessage() function.

```
public int postMessage( int category,int usr,String header,String text )
    throws SQLException {
    return postMessage(category,usr,header,text,0,0);
}

public int postMessage( int category,int usr,String header,
    String text,int respondsTo,int parent )
    throws SQLException {

    CallableStatement cs;
    int result;
    String query;

    query = "BEGIN ? := Forum.postMessage (?,?,?,?,?,?,?); END;";

    open();
    cs = conn.prepareCall(query);
    cs.registerOutParameter(1, Types.INTEGER);
    cs.setInt(2,category);
    cs.setInt(3,usr);
    cs.setString(4,header);
    cs.setString(5,text);
    if ( respondsTo != 0 && parent != 0 ) {
        cs.setInt(6,respondsTo);
        cs.setInt(7,parent);
    } else {
        cs.setString(6,"");
        cs.setString(7,"");
    }
    cs.registerOutParameter(8, Types.INTEGER);
    cs.execute();

    result = cs.getInt(1);
    if ( result == SUCCESS ) {
        result = cs.getInt(8);
    }
    cs.close();
    return result;
}
```

Login

To log on to the forum network, we call the `login()` method of `DatabaseAccess`, giving the user name and password of the specified user as parameters. The function returns the `user_id` of the matching user from an `OUT` parameter if the logon was successful, but appropriate error codes otherwise. The invoking client application can access public variables of the `DatabaseAccess` class to validate the return code (the variables we previously loaded with the `getConstants()` method).

```java
public int login( String login, String password ) throws SQLException {

    CallableStatement cs;
    int result;
    String query;

    query = "BEGIN ? := UserProfile.login (?,?,?); END;";

    open();
    cs = conn.prepareCall(query);
    cs.registerOutParameter(1, Types.INTEGER);
    cs.setString(2,login);
    cs.setString(3,password);
    cs.registerOutParameter(4, Types.INTEGER);
    cs.execute();

    result = cs.getInt(1);
    if ( result == SUCCESS ) {
        result = cs.getInt(4);
    }
    cs.close();
    return result;
}
```

Watching a Topic

If a user wants to keep a watch on specified topic, we call the `addMessageWatch()` method, giving the `user_id`, `message_id`, and a `boolean` indicating whether the user wants to receive e-mail notifications when the message gets updated, as parameters. This method calls the `addMessageWatch()` stored procedure, after transforming the `boolean` to an `int`.

```java
public void addMessageWatch( int usr, int message, boolean notify )
        throws SQLException {

    CallableStatement cs;
    int result;
    int index;
    String query;

    query = "BEGIN Forum.addMessageWatch (?,?,?); END;";

    open();
    cs = conn.prepareCall(query);
    cs.setInt(1,usr);
    cs.setInt(2,message);
    cs.setInt(3,notify ? 1 : 0);
    cs.execute();
    cs.close();
}
```

Getting the User Profile

When we successfully log a user on to the forum network, we also call the getProfile() method to access the data from the existing user profile, which we store in a session-bound user object. The getProfile() method calls the getProfile() stored procedure and creates a ResultSet from the cursor returned. The method returns true if the call was successful.

```
public synchronized boolean getProfile( int usr ) throws SQLException {

    CallableStatement cs;
    int result;
    int index;
    String query;

    query = "BEGIN ? := UserProfile.getProfile (?); END;";

    open();
    stmt = conn.prepareCall( query );
    ( (CallableStatement)stmt ).registerOutParameter(1,OracleTypes.CURSOR);
    ( (CallableStatement)stmt ).setInt (2,usr);
    ( (CallableStatement)stmt ).execute();
    rs = ( (OracleCallableStatement)stmt ).getCursor(1);

    return (rs != null);
}
```

Getting the Categories

The initial forum categories are accessed with the getCategories() method. This method creates a ResultSet instance from the cursor type returned from the getCategories() stored procedure called.

```
public synchronized boolean getCategories() throws SQLException {

    CallableStatement cs;
    int result;
    int index;
    String query;

    query = "BEGIN ? := Forum.getCategories; END;";

    open();
    stmt = conn.prepareCall( query );
    ( (CallableStatement)stmt ).registerOutParameter(1,OracleTypes.CURSOR);
    ( (CallableStatement)stmt ).execute();
    rs = ( (OracleCallableStatement)stmt ).getCursor(1);

    return (rs != null);
}
```

Getting Root Messages

Once the user has selected a specified category, we call the `getThreads()` method to access the message threads of the selected category. As the threads can become numerous, we define the corresponding `ResultSet` to be fully scrollable back and forth, so that the users may browse the message list from page to page (as we will only display 10 threads per page of the overview, as we will show later). In addition to the specified category, the method takes a `java.util.Date` object for a parameter – which stands for the date the user logged on to the network. If the user has not logged on, this `date` parameter is set to `null`, and we send some future date to the stored procedure.

```
public synchronized boolean getThreads( int category, java.util.Date date )
  throws SQLException {
    CallableStatement cs;
    int result;
    int index;
    String query;
    if ( date == null ) {
        date = new java.util.Date( ( new java.util.Date() ).getTime()*10);
    }

    query = "BEGIN ? := Forum.getThreads (?,?); END;";

    open();
    stmt = conn.prepareCall(query);
    ( (CallableStatement)stmt ).registerOutParameter(1,OracleTypes.CURSOR);
    ( (CallableStatement)stmt ).setInt (2,category);
    ( (CallableStatement)stmt ).setDate(3, new
        java.sql.Date(date.getTime()));
    ( (CallableStatement)stmt ).execute();
    rs = ( (OracleCallableStatement)stmt ).getCursor(1);
    return (rs != null);
}
```

Getting a Single Message Thread

Once the user has selected a specific root message, we can access all of the messages belonging to the parent's message thread with the `getThread()` method. This method calls the PL/SQL `getMessages()` stored procedure, which returns a cursor. Detailed information on the available database fields from the cursor can be seen in the PL/SQL implementation section.

```
public synchronized boolean getThread( int message ) throws SQLException {

    CallableStatement cs;
    int result;
    int index;
    String query;

    query = "BEGIN ? := Forum.getMessages (?); END;";

    open();
    stmt = conn.prepareCall( query );
    ( (CallableStatement)stmt ).registerOutParameter(1,OracleTypes.CURSOR);
    ( (CallableStatement)stmt ).setInt (2,message);
    ( (CallableStatement)stmt ).execute();
    rs = ( (OracleCallableStatement)stmt ).getCursor(1);

    return (rs != null);
}
```

Getting Watched Messages

On the forum site, the user may wish to see what messages they are currently watching. The
getWatches() method calls the PL/SQL getWatches() stored procedure, which returns a cursor,
containing message headers and keys.

```
public synchronized boolean getWatches( int usr ) throws SQLException {

    CallableStatement cs;
    int result;
    int index;
    String query;

    query = "BEGIN ? := Forum.getWatches (?); END;";

    open();
    stmt = conn.prepareCall( query );
    ( (CallableStatement)stmt ).registerOutParameter(1,OracleTypes.CURSOR);
    ( (CallableStatement)stmt ).setInt (2,usr);
    ( (CallableStatement)stmt ).execute();
    rs = ( (OracleCallableStatement)stmt ).getCursor(1);

    return (rs != null);
}
```

Cleaning Up Resources

Once the client application has finished using the DatabaseAccess class, it should call close() to clean
up all resources and return connections back to their pool. In addition to the close() method, we define
the finalize() method, which simply calls close(), which will be used by the garbage collector.

```
public synchronized void close() throws SQLException {
    if ( isOpen() ) {
    conn.setAutoCommit(true);
    conn.close();
    //connPool.freeConnection(conn);
    conn = null;
    }
}

protected void finalize() throws Throwable {
    close();
}
}
```

User Interface

Once all the actual programming is behind us, it is time to develop the forum user interface. As we have
already mentioned, we will use Java Server Pages (JSP) to generate the HTML output and call the
database access methods.

There are many pages comprising the full discussion forum site. We will discuss only the most relevant
pages in this context, although you may obtain the full source code for the site at the Wrox web site.
The pages we will discuss in this section are:

- ❏ categories.jsp: displays the forum categories
- ❏ threads.jsp: displays the message threads of a single category
- ❏ messages.jsp: displays all the messages of a single message thread
- ❏ reply_edit.jsp: edits/posts messages

Before we start describing the JSP, however, we implement a simple Java class that we use to represent users on the site.

User Class

The User class we will now implement is used to represent a single user on the forum site. When a user logs on to the network, we generate an instance of the class and store it in the HttpSession instance of the user as long as the user stays on the site. The User class has a number of public instance variables, which can be accessed by applications requesting the user data. The class is constructed with the user_id of a specified user and the name of a connection pool; these are used to instantiate the DatabaseAccess class and call its getProfile() method, in order to obtain the full user profile.

> Note that in order to test the forum and create sample threads, you must create a **User** object with a valid **user_id** and add it to the **HttpSession**.

```java
package forum;

import java.sql.SQLException;
import java.util.Date;

public class User {

    public int usr;
    public String login;
    public String password;
    public String firstName;
    public String lastName;
    public String email;
    public Date logondate;

    public User( int usr,String poolname ){

        DatabaseAccess dba = null;
        login = "";
        password = "";
        firstName = "";
        lastName = "";
        email = "";
        logondate = new Date();
        this.usr = usr;

        try {
            dba = new DatabaseAccess(poolname);
            dba.getProfile(usr);
```

```
            if( dba.next() ){
                login      = dba.getString("login");
                password   = dba.getString("password");
                firstName  = dba.getString("first_name");
                lastName   = dba.getString("last_name");
                email      = dba.getString("email");
            }

            // Close the database connection.
            if( dba != null ){
                dba.close();
            }
        } catch ( SQLException e ){}

    }
}
```

Page Footer

Each of the JSP pages we will implement uses the same footer script, which we will add to an includable file, which we call `footer.jsc`. This include file contains a single table that displays options based on whether the user has logged in or not.

```
<table width="550" border="0" cellpadding="2" cellspacing="0">
    <tr>
<% if( session.getAttribute("usr") == null ){ %>
    <td>
        <font face="Verdana,Arial" size="1">
        Hi! You have to <a href="login.jsp">log in</a>
        to participate in the forum.
        </font>
    </td>
    <td>
        <font face="Verdana,Arial" size="1">
        Click <a href="profile_edit.jsp">here</a> to create a new profile.
        </font>
    </td>
<% } else { %>
    <td>
        <font face="Verdana,Arial" size="1">
        Press <a href="logout.jsp">here</a> to log out.
        </font>
    </td>
    <td>
        <font face="Verdana,Arial" size="1">
        Click <a href="watches.jsp">here to view message watches.
        </font>
    </td>
<% } %>
    </tr>
</table>
```

Displaying the Categories

When the user first enters the discussion forum, they are sent to the categories page, which displays the available forum categories. Each of these categories is listed along with a short description, which indicates the type of discussion taking place in the category. The categories are displayed with the `categories.jsp` page, which instantiates the `DatabaseAccess` class and calls the `getCategories()` method for generating the output.

> Note that we assume that the name of the connection pool has been read during site initialization and added to the user **HttpSession** object. This is left up to you to actually implement.

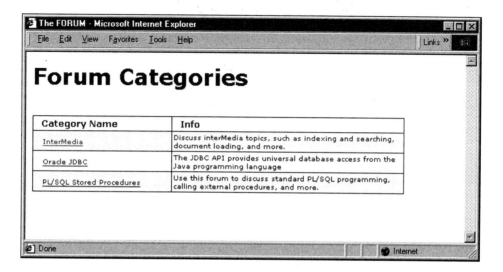

```
<%@ page import="forum.*" %>
<%@ page import="java.io.*" %>
<% response.setHeader("Expires", "-1"); %>
<% try { %>
<%
    // ************ DECLARATIONS *******************
    session.putValue("poolname","forum");
    String poolname = (String) session.getValue("poolname");

    //***You would not need to apply these if using the extra JSP
    //***functionality available from the Wrox download site.
    //***You need to have a user with ID 1, or change the 1 below.
    User u = new User(1,"forum");
    session.putValue("usr",u);
    //***

    String[] colors = {"#F4F4F4","#F9F9F9"};
    DatabaseAccess dba = new DatabaseAccess(poolname);
    int c = 0;
    // *********************************************
%>
```

```html
<html>
<head>
    <title>The FORUM</title>
</head>

<body bgcolor="#FFFFFF">

<h1><font face="Verdana,Arial">Forum Categories</font></h1><br>

<table width="550" border="0" cellpadding="2" cellspacing="1"
bgcolor="#000000">

    <tr bgcolor="#F9F9F9">
        <td width="200">
            <font face="Verdana,Arial" size="2">
              <b>Category Name</b>
            </font>
        </td>

        <td>
            <font face="Verdana,Arial" size="2">
              <b>Info</b>
            </font>
        </td>
    </tr>

<%
    // Display the forum categories.
    dba.getCategories();
    while( dba.next() ){
%>
    <tr bgcolor="<%=colors[c++%2]%>">
        <td>
              
            <a href="threads.jsp?category =<%= dba.getInt("category_id")%>
                &name= <%=dba.getString("category_name")%>">
            <font face="Verdana,Arial" size="1">
            <%=dba.getString("category_name")%>
            </font>
            </a>
        </td>
        <td>
            <font face="Verdana,Arial" size="1">
            <%=dba.getString("category_info")%>
            </font>
        </td>
    </tr>
<% } %>
</table>

<br>

<!-- This is the footer script -->
<%@ include file="footer.jsc" %>
```

```
        </body>
        </html>

<%
      } catch ( Exception e ) {
          ByteArrayOutputStream bytes = new ByteArrayOutputStream();
          PrintWriter writer = new PrintWriter(bytes, true);
          e.printStackTrace(writer);
          String stack = bytes.toString();
          out.println(stack);
      }
%>
```

Displaying the Message Threads

Once the user selects a specific category to browse, they are sent to the threads.jsp page. There, we list, in chronological order, the top messages of the message threads that belong to the specified category, with the getThreads() method of the DatabaseAccess class. As the number of message threads will inevitably grow larger as time will pass, we display only a fixed number of threads at a time, allowing the user to scroll back and forth for older messages.

Note that if the user is logged in and any of the messages in a message thread have been modified since the user logged on, we display an icon (mod.gif) in front of the thread header. In addition, if the user is logged in, we display a link to the reply_edit.jsp page, where the user can post a new message thread.

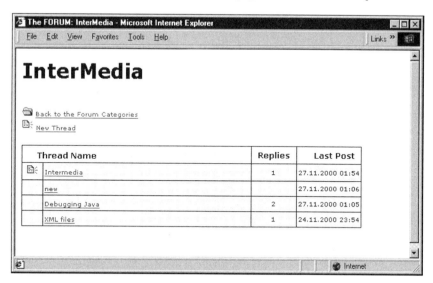

```
<% response.setHeader("Expires", "-1"); %>
<% try { %>
<%
    // ************* DECLARATIONS ********************
    String name = request.getParameter("name");
    String poolname = (String) session.getValue("poolname");
    String[] colors = {"#F4F4F4","#F9F9F9"};
    DatabaseAccess dba = new DatabaseAccess(poolname);
```

```
      final int RESULTS_PER_PAGE = 10;
      int category = Integer.parseInt( request.getParameter("category") );
      int c = 0;
      int i;
      int start;

      java.util.Date date = null;
      // ************************************************
%>
    <html>
    <head>
        <title>The FORUM: <%=name%></title>
    </head>

    <body bgcolor="#FFFFFF">

    <h1><font face="Verdana,Arial"><%=name%></font></h1><br>


    <img src="folder.gif" border="0">
    <a href="categories.jsp">
    <font face="Verdana,Arial" size="1">Back to the Forum Categories</font>
    </a>
    <br>

    <% if( session.getValue("usr") != null ){ %>
        <img src="mod.gif" border="0">
        <a href="categories.jsp">
        <a href="reply_edit.jsp?category=<%=category%>&name=<%=name%>">
        <font face="Verdana,Arial" size="1">New Thread</font>
        </a>
    <% } %>

    <br><br>


    <table width="550" border="0" cellpadding="2"
    cellspacing="1" bgcolor="#000000">
        <tr bgcolor="#F9F9F9">
            <td colspan="2" width="100%">
                <img src="space.gif" width="18" border="0">
                <font face="Verdana,Arial" size="2">
                <b>Thread Name</b>
                </font>
            </td>
            <td align="center">
                <font face="Verdana,Arial" size="2">
                <b><nobr>  Replies  </nobr></b>
                </font>
            </td>
            <td align="right">
                <font face="Verdana,Arial" size="2">
                <b><nobr>  Last Post  </nobr></b>
                </font>
            </td>
        </tr>
    <%
        // Get the starting thread row.
        try {
            start = Integer.parseInt(request.getParameter("start"));
        } catch ( NumberFormatException e ) {
            start = 0;
        }
```

```
        // Get the logon date from the User object in session, if any.
        if( session.getValue("usr") != null ){
            date = ( (User) session.getValue("usr") ).logondate;
        }

        // Select all the forum threads.
        if ( dba.getThreads(category,date) ){

            // Scroll through a portion of the ResultSet
            for( i=start-1; i < start+RESULTS_PER_PAGE-1; i++ ){
                if( !dba.next() ) break;
%>
            <tr bgcolor="<%=colors[c%2]%>">
                <td width="18">
                <% if( dba.getInt("modified",i) >= 0 ){ %>
                    <img src="mod.gif" border="0" vspace="0" hspace="5">
                <% } else { %>
                    <img src="space.gif" border="0" vspace="0" hspace="5">
                <% } %>
                </td>
                <td width="100%">
                    <a href="message.jsp?message=<%=dba.getInt("message_id",i)%>
                    &category=<%=category%>&name=<%=name%>">
                    <font face="Verdana,Arial" size="1">
                    <%=dba.getString("header",i)%>
                    </font>
                    </a>
                </td>
                <td align="center">
                    <font face="Verdana,Arial" size="1">
                <% if( dba.getInt("replies",i) != 0 ){
                        out.print(dba.getInt("replies",i));
                    } %>
                    </font>
                </td>
                <td align="right">
                    <font face="Verdana,Arial" size="1"><nobr>
                <% if( dba.getInt("replies",i) == 0 ){ %>
                    <%=dba.getString("post_date",i)%>
                <% } else { %>
                    <%=dba.getString("last_reply_date",i)%>
                <% } %>
                    </nobr></font>
                </td>
            </tr>
        <% } %>
    </table>
    <br>
    <!-- Display the 'next' and 'previous' links -->
    <table width="550" border="0" cellpadding="2" cellspacing="1">
        <tr>
            <td width="50%" align="left">
            <% if( start > RESULTS_PER_PAGE ){ %>
                <font face="Verdana,Arial" size="1">
                <a href="threads.jsp?category=<%=category%>
                &start=<%=(start-RESULTS_PER_PAGE)%>&name=<%=name%>">
                << Previous
                </a></font>
        <% } %>
            </td>
            <td width="50%" align="right">
```

```
        <% if( dba.next() ){ %>
            <font face="Verdana,Arial" size="1">
            <a href="threads.jsp?category=<%=category%>
            &start=<%=(i+1)%>&name=<%=name%>">
            Next >>
            </a></font>
        <% } %>
        </td>
    </tr>
</table>
<% } %>

<br>

<!-- This is the footer script -->
<%@ include file="footer.jsc" %>

</body>
</html>
<%
    } catch ( Exception e ) {
        out.println(e.getMessage());
    }
%>
```

Displaying Messages

When the user selects a specific message thread from the threads list, we send them to the
messages.jsp page. This page displays the root message of the thread along with all replies, with a
call to the getThread() method of the DatabaseAccess class:

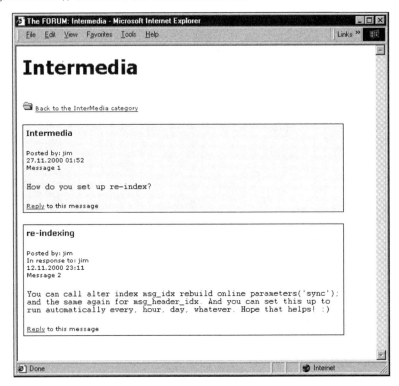

```jsp
<%@ page import="forum.*" %>
<%@ page import="java.io.*" %>
<% response.setHeader("Expires", "-1"); %>
<% try { %>
<%
    // ************* DECLARATIONS *******************
    String name = request.getParameter("name");
    String category = request.getParameter("category");
    String poolname = (String) session.getValue("poolname");
    String header;

    int message = Integer.parseInt(request.getParameter("message"));
    int count = 1;

    DatabaseAccess dba = new DatabaseAccess(poolname);
    // **********************************************

    // Get this thread
    dba.getThread(message);

    // This is the root message.
    if( dba.next() ){
        header = dba.getString("header");
%>
        <html>
        <head>
            <title>The FORUM: <%=header%></title>
        </head>

        <body bgcolor="#FFFFFF">

        <h1><font face="Verdana,Arial"><%=header%></font></h1><br>

        <img src="folder.gif" border="0">
        <a href="threads.jsp?category=<%=category%>&name=<%=name%>">
        <font face="Verdana,Arial" size="1">Back to the <%=name%> category</font>
        </a>

        <br><br>

        <table width="550" border="0" cellpadding="5"
            cellspacing="1" bgcolor="#000000">
            <tr bgcolor="#F4F4F4">
                <td colspan="2">
                    <font face="Verdana,Arial" size="2">
                    <b><%=header%></b>
                    </font><br><br>
                    <font face="Verdana,Arial" size="1">
                    Posted by: <%=dba.getString("author")%><br>
                    <%=dba.getString("post_date")%><br>
                    Message <%=count++%>
                    </font><br><br>
                    <font face="Courier" size="2">
                    <%=dba.getString("text")%>
                    </font><br><br>
```

```jsp
                    <% if( session.getValue("usr") != null ){ %>
                        <font face="Verdana,Arial" size="1">
                        <a href="reply_edit.jsp?parent=<%=message%> &replyTo=
                          <%=dba.getInt("user_id")%>
                          &header=<%=header%>&category=
                          <%=category%>&name=<%=name%>">
                        Reply</a> to this message
                        </font>
                    <% } %>
                    </td>
                </tr>
        </table>
        <br>
    <%
        // Continue with the thread, now list all replies.
        while( dba.next() ){
    %>
        <table width="550" border="0"
          cellpadding="5" cellspacing="1" bgcolor="#000000">
            <tr bgcolor="#FFFFFF">
                <td colspan="2">
                    <font face="Verdana,Arial" size="2">
                    <b><%=dba.getString("header")%></b>
                    </font><br><br>
                    <font face="Verdana,Arial" size="1">
                    Posted by: <%=dba.getString("author")%><br>
                    In response to: <%=dba.getString("reply_to")%><br>
                    12.11.2000 23:11<br>
                    Message <%=count++%>
                    </font><br><br>
                    <font face="Courier" size="2">
                    <%=dba.getString("text")%>
                    </font><br><br>
                <% if( session.getValue("usr") != null ){ %>
                    <font face="Verdana,Arial" size="1">
                    <a href="reply_edit.jsp?parent=<%=message%>&replyTo=<%=
                      dba.getInt("user_id")
                        %>&header=<%=header%>&category=<%=
                          category%>&name=<%=name%>">
                    Reply</a> to this message
                    </font>
                <% } %>
                </td>
            </tr>
        </table>
        <br>

    <%
        }
    }
    %>

        <!-- This is the footer script -->
        <%@ include file="footer.jsc" %>
```

```
            </body>
            </html>
<%
    } catch ( Exception e ) {
        ByteArrayOutputStream bytes = new ByteArrayOutputStream();
        PrintWriter writer = new PrintWriter(bytes, true);
        e.printStackTrace(writer);
        String stack = bytes.toString();
        out.println(stack);
    }
%>
```

Posting Messages

When the user has logged on to the forum, they may post new message threads or reply to previous messages. Both tasks are handled by the reply_edit.jsp page, which determines what action to perform based on received parameters. The page can perform four different tasks:

- ❑ Edit new message threads

- ❑ Save new message threads

- ❑ Edit a message reply

- ❑ Save a message reply

The page automatically knows whether to display the edit fields or to save the content based on certain parameters passed with the form post. If there are at any stage parameters missing, or if the message post was unsuccessful, we redirect the user to the start page of the forum, categories.jsp. If, however, we have a successful post, we redirect the user to the messages.jsp page, where the new message should appear.

```
<%@ page import="forum.*" %>
<%@ page import="java.io.*" %>
<% response.setHeader("Expires", "-1"); %>
<% try { %>
<%
        // ************* DECLARATIONS ********************
        String parent = request.getParameter("parent");
        String replyTo = request.getParameter("replyTo");
        String category = request.getParameter("category");
        String name = request.getParameter("name");
        String header = request.getParameter("header");
        String text = request.getParameter("text");
        String poolname = (String) session.getValue("poolname");

        DatabaseAccess dba;
        User user;
        int usr = 0;
        int message;
        int msg;

        boolean saving = (request.getParameter("save") != null);
        boolean newThread = (parent == null || parent.equals("null") );
        boolean notify = (request.getParameter("notify") != null &&
            request.getParameter("notify").equals("on"));
        // **********************************************
```

```
        // Get the User object
        if( session.getValue("usr") == null ){
           response.sendRedirect("categories.jsp");
        } else {
           user = (User) session.getValue("usr");
           usr = user.usr;
        }


        // Display the edit form if not saving.
        if( !saving ){
%>

<html>
<head>
    <title>The FORUM</title>
</head>

<body bgcolor="#FFFFFF">

<h1><font face="Verdana,Arial">Post a Message</font></h1><br>

<form name="postform" action="reply_edit.jsp" method="post">
<table width="550" border="0" cellpadding="2" cellspacing="0">
    <tr>
    <td>
        <font face="Verdana,Arial" size="2">
        Subject<br><input type="text" size="45" value="" name="header">
        </font><br><br>
    </td>
    </tr>

    <tr>
    <td>
        <font face="Verdana,Arial" size="2">
        Content<br><textarea name="text" cols="40" rows="10"></textarea>
        </font><br><br>
    </td>
    </tr>

    <tr>
    <td>
        <font face="Verdana,Arial" size="1">
        <input type="checkbox" checked name="notify"> 
            Send me mail when this thread is updated<br><br>
        </font>
    </td>
    </tr>

    <tr>
    <td>
        <font face="Verdana,Arial" size="1">
        <input type="submit" value="Submit">
        </font>
    </td>
    </tr>
</table>
```

```
                <input type="hidden" value="1" name="save">
                <input type="hidden" value="<%=category%>" name="category">
                <input type="hidden" value="<%=name%>" name="name">
                <input type="hidden" value="<%=parent%>" name="parent">
                <input type="hidden" value="<%=replyTo%>" name="replyTo">
                </form>

                </body>
                </html>
<%
                // This means we should save the content.
                } else {
                    dba = new DatabaseAccess(poolname);

                    // Save the new message thread.
                    if( newThread ){
                        message = dba.postMessage( Integer.parseInt(category),
                            usr,header,text );
                        out.println(message);
                    } else {
                        message = dba.postMessage( Integer.parseInt(category),
                            usr,header,text, Integer.parseInt(replyTo),
                            Integer.parseInt(parent) );
                    }

                    // Redirect the user
                    if( message > 0 ){
                        msg = newThread ? message : Integer.parseInt(parent);

                        // Users automatically watch their threads.
                        dba.addMessageWatch(usr,message,notify);

                        response.sendRedirect("message.jsp?message=" + msg
                            +   "&category=" + category + "&name=" + name);

                    // Some error has occurred.
                    } else {
                        out.println(saving);
                        System.out.println("" + message);
                        response.sendRedirect("categories.jsp");
                    }
                }

        } catch ( Exception e ) {
            ByteArrayOutputStream bytes = new ByteArrayOutputStream();
            PrintWriter writer = new PrintWriter(bytes, true);
            e.printStackTrace(writer);
            String stack = bytes.toString();
            out.println(stack);
        }
%>
```

More Pages

By now, we have implemented the JSP pages necessary to browse the categories, view messages and post replies. However, there are still a few pages left to implement for the site. In this section, we will list the remaining pages, and give a short description of their general functionality. Note that the full source code for these pages is available at the Wrox web site.

The remaining pages are:

- ❑ `profile.jsp`: This page will edit and save the user profile. If the user is logged on, the input forms will be filled with the data from the `User` object in session, and the profile will be updated, rather than creating a new one.

- ❑ `login.jsp`: This page logs the user on to the forum network. The user enters their login and password, which are submitted to the `login()` method of the `DatabaseAccess` class. If the login is successful, we take the user ID the `login()` method returns, and construct a new `User` instance. This `User` instance is then added to the `session`, with the `setAttribute()` method of the `HttpSession` interface.

- ❑ `logout.jsp`: This page logs the user out of the forum site. It simply removes the `User` instance from the `session`, by calling the `removeAttribute()` method of `HttpSession`.

- ❑ `watches.jsp`: This page displays the messages the user is currently watching, by calling the `getWatches()` method of the `DatabaseAccess` class.

Summary

In this chapter, we have implemented a discussion forum by using a combination of the PL/SQL and Java languages. More specifically, we have:

- ❑ Created database objects for the discussion forum
- ❑ Implemented a PL/SQL package for database access
- ❑ Implemented a Java class that uses JavaMail for message transport
- ❑ Loaded the messaging class into the database and called it from PL/SQL
- ❑ Implemented a Java class that accesses the PL/SQL stored procedures with JDBC
- ❑ Designed the user interface of the forum site, using JSP

19

Overview of Oracle interMedia Text

Introduction

In your travels around the internet, you have probably used many powerful search engines. Many of today's top search engines use the features such as those in interMedia text to provide the reliability of results that is expected from them. A case study that builds a search engine will be shown in a case study later in the book.

If you were a computer book addict, and were looking for info, you could search for the phrase `books`. The problem is you will receive results on everything from cooking books to books on trains in no useful order. By utilizing interMedia text, we can focus that search into a more useful result set. If you want to narrow down the search, you would specify a search like `books + potter - programming`. This tells the search engine that you are searching about `books`, and want `Potter` books ranked highest, also you want to eliminate or lower the rank of results with `programming` books in the search.

Modifiers, such as **+** and **–**, appear to be very useful in a search, but we must keep in mind that most people will not know that these special modifiers exist, and the average person will not want to spend time on reading through documentation or help. Users will not usually spend the time to learn the 'ins and outs' of proper usage. The average user will want to use natural language searches for 'themes' and 'gists'. A natural language search is a search in the form of a question: 'Where do I find out about books?' The theme of the previous question is 'books'. Oracle interMedia has integrated the ability to add to indexes 'themes' of documents or concepts within a document, though it is up to you to plan the design around your intended user.

interMedia text queries

InterMedia has been integrated very tightly into Oracle, so most queries on indexed text access components of interMedia text. This does not mean that you or your users will automatically see changes on search results the instant you install Oracle 8i and interMedia.

CONTAINS – the Heart of interMedia Text Searches.

The CONTAINS query operator is the main component of interMedia text searches. Using this within WHERE clause in a SELECT statement will tell the Oracle database to use the interMedia extensible architecture.

```
SQL> SELECT indexcolumn, content_column FROM content_table WHERE
     CONTAINS ( content_column, 'text' ) > 0;
```

The CONTAINS operator within the SELECT statement must be terminated with '> 0'; this requires that a result is returned from the rows that contain the text that is being searched for. The '0' corresponds to where there is no match for the search criteria in a particular row. Thus the CONTAINS query has to be greater than 0 for a result to be returned. Otherwise, all the rows will be returned, those with and those without the text! InterMedia text is tightly integrated with Oracle itself, and is a part of the core query engine that Oracle uses. interMedia is used in the CTX schema; this originates from when this used to be called the Context cartridge.

> **Anyone can use interMedia text to create indexes and tables, and to form queries. To create preferences, however, (which will be mentioned later) and to use the interMedia PL/SQL packages, you need to have the `ctxapp` role granted by the ctxsys user or the DBA.**

CONTAINS queries base their results on a score achieved, which is out of a hundred. In Oracle's words:

> *"To calculate a relevance score for a returned document in a word query, Oracle uses an inverse frequency algorithm based on Salton's formula."*

In English, this means that if the text 'Book' occurs in a small set of documents many times, then it would achieve a high score. If there are many hundreds or thousands of documents then only a few occurrences of 'Book' will give a similarly high score.

The use of the score is optional, and the syntax of the query is unusual in that each SCORE operator in a query must reference a label specified as the third parameter of the corresponding CONTAINS clause:

```
SQL> SELECT score(1), indexcolumn, content_column FROM content_table WHERE
CONTAINS ( content_column, 'text',1 ) > 0;
```

The main query operators are listed opposite. They are all used in conjunction with the CONTAINS operator and can be used instead of the 'text' in the above expression.

Term	Usage	How used
AND	`'Potter AND programming '`	Searches for both `Potter` and `programming` as in a normal Boolean search.
ACCUM (`'`)	`'Potter , programming'`	This searches for the combined score of both words, `Potter` and `programming`.
MINUS (`-`)	`'Potter - programming'`	This searches for documents with `Potter` but gives a low priority to a document that also includes `programming`.
NEAR (`;`)	`'near((potter, programming), X, FALSE)', 1 )'`	Using this the words being searched must be within X words of each other. `FALSE` is used to indicate that the words can appear in any order in the document. Using `TRUE` will ensure that `Potter` has to appear before `programming` in the document.
NOT (`~`)	`'potter NOT programming'`	This does not return any documents with `programming` in them.
OR (`|`)	`'Potter or programming'`	The `OR` operator searches for independent occurrences of each word, and scores results from the highest total of either of the words that exist.
FUZZY (`?`)	`'?pitter'`	Fuzzy searches work with binary similarities in words, and are used to return words based on searches that can include spelling mistakes.
SOUNDEX (`!`)	`'!hotter'`	SOUNDEX searches the database and compares data phonically or words that sound similar.
WITHIN	`'Potter WITHIN programming'`	WITHIN is an advanced operator used against documents stored into the database with parameter filters applied to index for searching document sections. There is more about this later in the chapter.
STEM (`$`)	`'$book'`	STEM finds the term that is entered with different endings in the database. Here we may get book, books, etc.
Wildcards (`%` `_`)	`'book%'`	`%` is used as a wildcard and would find book1 and booking, etc.
	`'bo_k'`	`_` is a single character wildcard used to find words with wildcards for a specific letter or character, here we could get book or bonk.
stored query	Will be shown later in the chapter	There is more on this at the end of the chapter.

One important thing to note is that, by default, interMedia text does case insensitive searches. However it can be forced to do case sensitive searches.

You may be wondering why not use DML statements to find information from the database? The reason is that interMedia text is used to search for text within whole documents, LOBs, CLOBs, etc in a column. Also, the search results are much faster than for a DML query. To check this, you can set the `timing` variable on in SQLPlus. This is under Options|Environment, scroll down the list until you find timing and change the value to custom and then to on. This is useful to find out how long it takes to query the database.

We shall come back to how query language is used later in the chapter but firstly you must understand how the indexes formed.

InterMedia Indexes

InterMedia Text's indexing methods are the backbone of interMedia Text; they also provide the means to increase the performance of your searches.

An interMedia text index creates four index tables against each table indexed. Below we see the tables and the contents. The interMedia index is an example of an inverted index, the industry standard for text indexing. This structure in its default use provides enough information to recreate the original documents in a narrowed form, without punctuation, type formatting, correct case, and stopwords. Theme/index words are added and linked to their corresponding rows off of 'token' or pointer references. If there are multiple occurrences of a word, there will be multiple token entries.

```
DR$Test_IDX$I (
   TOKEN_TEXT    VARCHAR2 (64)   NOT NULL,  TOKEN_TYPE   NUMBER (3)    NOT NULL,
   TOKEN_FIRST   NUMBER (10)     NOT NULL,  TOKEN_LAST   NUMBER (10)   NOT NULL,
   TOKEN_COUNT   NUMBER (10)     NOT NULL,  TOKEN_INFO   BLOB)

DR$Test_IDX$K (DOCID      NUMBER (38),  TEXTKEY   ROWID          NOT NULL)

DR$Test_IDX$N (NLT_DOCID  NUMBER (38)   NOT NULL, NLT_MARK    CHAR (1)        NOT
NULL)

DR$Test_IDX$R (ROW_NO   NUMBER (3),  DATA     BLOB)
```

On inserts and deletes, the token entries are changed, not usually the word itself. Each distinct token in the document set has a record. Also each record, there is a `DOCID` for each occurrence, and for each `DOCID` there are 'within-document' occurrences called token offsets. Later in the chapter, you can see the tokens in indexes we create by the following command, replacing `Test_IDX` with the name of the index:

```
SQL>select TOKEN_TEXT,
TOKEN_TYPE, TOKEN_FIRST,
TOKEN_LAST,
TOKEN_COUNT from
DR$Test_IDX$I;
```

The method that the database uses to create and insert these indexes is called the index pipeline. It can be seen in this diagram:

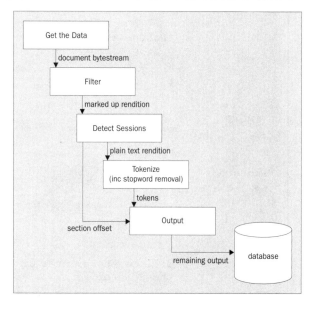

The indexes are built from different preference options that tell the database what it is indexing, and how to access and store the data.

This is an example of extended preferences in an index, the preferences in this index are highlighted and are discussed in more detail later in the chapter.

Once a table is loaded into the database, an interMedia index is created, which requires a primary key constraint to be present (which may be a composite). This is the command to create an interMedia index; it is similar to creating a normal index:

```
CREATE INDEX name_of_index ON content_table (content_column)
INDEXTYPE IS CTXSYS.CONTEXT
PARAMETERS (' …' );
```

In the above, CTXSYS.CONTEXT refers to the index type used to index the column. In oracle 8.1.6 and earlier there was only one type of index, which is the context index. This index was optimized for searching text in large documents within columns. In release 8.1.7 of the database there will be a new index type that will be called a catalog index, ctxcat; this will be used to index small amounts of text in columns and will offer increased performance. There also will be a new datatype called xmltype.

The PARAMETERS clause is optional, and if it is not present, defaults will be assumed. More of indexes, later in the chapter.

Indexing is controlled by preferences, objects which are inserted in sequence into a 'pipeline' of indexing functions (beginning with the column value) passing them along the pipeline and fulfilling all pipeline stages before an entry is made for that row in the index. The types of preference objects are Datastore, Filter, Section Group, Lexer, Stop List, Word List, and Storage (see the table below). Although a primary key may be composite during data load, indexes cannot currently be created on composite keys, only single columns, and the column must be of a supported datatype.

It is important to note that within interMedia text, the absence of a text index will not merely slow down queries, an index must be present to enable anything beyond the most basic DML. Although interMedia text index creation is designed to be as similar to conventional binary tree index creation as possible, creation of an index requires detailed understanding of the mechanism.

Preference	Description	Available Options
Datastore	Obtains the data from the table	DIRECT_DATASTORE – where data is stored in the column
		DETAIL_DATASTORE – where data is split into multiple lines
		USER_DATASTORE – where data is stored in OS files, column is file name
		URL_DATASTORE – where data is stored as web pages in the column
		FILE_DATASTORE – where data is stored in the column
		NESTED_DATASTORE – where data is stored in a column in a nested table

Table continued on following page

Preference	Description	Available Options
Filter	Converts the data into text such as XML or plain text	INSO_FILTER
		USER_FILTER
		CUSTOMNAME
Section Group	Is querying within sections enabled and how are the document sections defined?	AUTO_SECTIONGROUP
		HTML_ SECTIONGROUP
	This converts the document to plain text	XML_ SECTIONGROUP
		NULL_ SECTIONGROUP
Lexer	What language is being indexed?	DEFAULT_LEXER
		BASIC_LEXER
		CUSTOMNAME
Wordlist	How should stem and fuzzy queries be expanded?	DEFAULT_WORDLIST
		CUSTOMNAME
Storage	How should the index tables be stored?	DEFAULT_STORAGE
Stop List	What words or themes are not to be indexed?	DEFAULT_STOPLIST
		EMPTY_STOPLIST

DataStore

The DataStore object extracts the document from the columns in the database, prior to processing by a filter. Datastores read from tables, whether or not these contain the actual documents or references to external documents, using (URL_DATASTORE), such as operating system files and URLs. By default, the Datastore object is set to DIRECT_DATASTORE, which simply assumes that the documents to be indexed are stored in a column, and it can be used for any index. This can also be used for the BFILE data type, which is treated as being present within the column. If external files are used, then the FILE_DATASTORE class operates in a very similar way to using DIRECT_DATASTORE with BFILEs, using the column data as the file name for indexing. This class allows the path to the directory to be specified if it is not within the column data, nor in the default working directory. Specifying the path in the attribute will cause it to be prefixed to the column data, meaning that mixing full file specifications with a path attribute will cause the indexing to fail. Therefore, if a FILE_DATASTORE is created without an attribute:

```
Execute CTX_DDL.CREATE_PREFERENCE('file_pref', 'FILE_DATASTORE');
```

The first parameter, file_pref, is simply a name assigned to that object for future reference, and is defined by the developer. The second is the name of the class, a list of which may be found in the CTX_CLASSES view, created during installation. Then the columns of the database could contain information of the form:

```
C:\documents\intermedia\file1.doc
C:\documents\intermedia\file2.doc
C:\documents\intermedia\file3.doc
```

However, if an attribute is set for the Data Store object:

```
Execute CTX_DDL.SET_ATTRIBUTE('file_pref', 'PATH',
    'C:\documents\intermedia\');
```

...then the database columns would have to contain only:

```
file1.doc
file2.doc
file3.doc
```

The FILE_DATASTORE class attribute PATH can contain multiple paths, using semicolons to separate them. However, all file names must be unique within all the directories specified. For example:

```
Execute CTX_DDL.SET_ATTRIBUTE('file_pref', 'PATH', 'C:\documents\;
C:\documents\intermedia');
```

If the disk contains two files, only the first of that name will be indexed:

```
C:\documents\file1.doc            - indexed
C:\documents\intermedia\file1.doc - not indexed
```

The SET_ATTRIBUTE procedure is called after the class is instantiated as an object, and the name is required as a parameter, followed by the name of the attribute to be set, and the value of that attribute. This procedure is optional for FILE_DATASTORE, but offers far greater flexibility with the URL_DATASTORE class. This class is similar to the FILE_DATASTORE, in that it reads a reference to a document rather than the document itself from the database. It can read from the file system, an FTP server, or a web server, using the standard URL format for describing the document and its location. However, both FILE_DATASTORE and URL_DATASTORE suffer from the limitation that the index will not be updated if the document itself, which is located externally to the database, is modified, and manual intervention is necessary. The index needs to be rebuilt, or simply the value in the column needs to be updated to the same value, so that interMedia is able to register the update. Both these approaches may be triggered from external scripts monitoring resource modification times, and then issuing DML to the database. Reads using URL_DATASTORE are multi-threaded to maximise performance, although it is a current limitation of interMedia that index creation cannot be parallelized. To create an object of this class:

```
Execute CTX_DDL.CREATE_PREFERENCE('url_pref', 'URL_DATASTORE');
Execute CTX_DDL.SET_ATTRIBUTE('url_pref', 'TIMEOUT', '30');
```

The available preferences for URL_DATASTORE are related to the configuration of the local network topology and the server resources that should be devoted to the external communication activity. The networking parameters will have to be configured for each site on which interMedia is deployed, unless the defaults (no proxy-ing at all) are acceptable. These parameters are mostly self-explanatory (HTTP_PROXY and FTP_PROXY), with NO_PROXY specifying a domain with which the server will attempt to communicate directly, rather than going via a proxy. For example, no proxying would be required for machines on a local area network. These are visible by executing the following query:

```
SELECT prv_attribute, prv_value FROM ctx_preference_values WHERE
prv_preference='URL_DATASTORE';
```

The next class, in ascending order of complexity, is the DETAIL_DATASTORE. This class is designed for master/detail tables, in which large bodies of text are stored in a table column, with one line of text per table row. Cases where a document is spread across multiple columns are less common, but are addressed by the USER_DATASTORE. The DETAIL_DATASTORE simply joins the rows into a single document before indexing occurs, using the foreign key to identify the rows, and a sequential column to order them. The foreign key relationship must exist logically, but not necessarily as a database constraint. The document text column values are not directly used by interMedia, and again, if they are changed without changing the master table, the index will not be updated. The workaround to this is to update the value of the master column to itself, triggering the rebuilding of the index, or manually dropping and rebuilding the index. There should be an otherwise unused column to maintain the integrity of SQL syntax, for building indexes and running queries, in this case it is the text column in the intermedia_recipes table. This is best illustrated by an example; we will use the data from the recipe.xml document encountered in Chapter 21 but we will make new tables to illustrate the use of interMedia text. The first table holds all the recipes and methods and is the master table:

```
CREATE TABLE intermedia_recipes (
    id NUMBER PRIMARY KEY,
    name VARCHAR2(80),
    method VARCHAR2(80),
    text CHAR(1) );
```

This table is for the ingredients needed for each recipe and is the detail table:

```
CREATE TABLE intermedia_ingredients (
    id NUMBER,
    line NUMBER NOT NULL,
    text VARCHAR2(80) );
```

We will now insert some data into the two tables; as you notice we are inserting the data not the whole XML document here:

```
INSERT INTO intermedia_recipes (id, name, method) VALUES
    (1, 'Cookies', 'Baking');
INSERT INTO intermedia_ingredients (id, line, text) VALUES
    (1, 1, '130g of chocolate');
INSERT INTO intermedia_ingredients (id, line, text) VALUES
    (1, 2, '4 boxes of eggs');
```

Now we create the parameters for our index:

```
EXECUTE CTX_DDL.CREATE_PREFERENCE ('detail_pref', 'DETAIL_DATASTORE');
EXECUTE CTX_DDL.SET_ATTRIBUTE('detail_pref', 'DETAIL_TABLE',
    ' intermedia_ingredients ');
EXECUTE CTX_DDL.SET_ATTRIBUTE('detail_pref', 'DETAIL_KEY',
    'id');
EXECUTE CTX_DDL.SET_ATTRIBUTE('detail_pref', 'DETAIL_LINENO',
    'line');
EXECUTE CTX_DDL.SET_ATTRIBUTE('detail_pref', 'DETAIL_TEXT',
    'text');
```

The following will build the interMedia index on the `intermedia_recipes` table:

```
CREATE INDEX intermedia_recipe_index ON intermedia_recipes (text) INDEXTYPE IS
ctxsys.context PARAMETERS('datastore detail_pref');
```

To check that the index has been built, we have to get data from it:

```
SELECT name FROM intermedia_recipes WHERE CONTAINS(text, 'chocolate') > 0;
```

The result of this query is:

```
NAME
-------
Cookies
```

The most sophisticated of all the Datastores is the USER_DATASTORE. This class offers a great deal of flexibility with existing document storage conventions, and new designs, as it allows the developer to specify exactly how the documents are stored, and assemble them programmatically. This is accomplished by calling a stored procedure to assemble the document whenever indexing occurs. In fact, two stored procedures must be created, one owned by the schema in which the actual data is stored, or with SELECT granted on the tables, and one owned by the CTXSYS user, which is actually called by interMedia. The CTXSYS stored procedure simply calls the schema owner stored procedure, which assembles the document prior to indexing. This stored procedure returns the document as a CLOB, BLOB, or VARCHAR2. CLOB is most suitable for large documents, but for documents smaller than 32k, VARCHAR2 will give better performance. Non-textual documents can only use the BLOB type.

```
CREATE TABLE instructions (
    id NUMBER,
    line NUMBER,
    text VARCHAR2(80) );
```

We need to put some data into this table:

```
INSERT INTO instructions (id, line, text) VALUES (1, 1, 'Pre-heat the oven to
180C');
INSERT INTO instructions (id, line, text) VALUES (1, 2, 'Line the baking tin with
greaseproof paper');
```

This stored procedure simply concatenates the contents of the two detail tables into a single document, given a key from the master table:

```
CREATE OR REPLACE PROCEDURE intermedia_recipe_doc (p_id IN NUMBER, p_doc IN OUT
VARCHAR2) AS
    v_buf VARCHAR2(32767);
BEGIN
  FOR c_recipe IN (SELECT text FROM intermedia_ingredients WHERE id=p_id)
  LOOP
    v_buf := v_buf || ' ' || c_recipe.text;
  END LOOP;
  FOR c_recipe IN (SELECT text FROM instructions WHERE id=p_id)
  LOOP
    v_buf := v_buf || ' ' || c_recipe.text;
  END LOOP;
  p_doc := v_buf;
END;
```

The CTXSYS owned procedure is very simple, passing the parameters straight to the stored procedure belonging to the actual user:

```
CREATE OR REPLACE PROCEDURE ctxsys. intermedia_recipe_doc (p_id IN NUMBER, p_doc
IN OUT VARCHAR2) AS
BEGIN
    user.intermedia_recipe_doc (p_id, p_doc);
END;

GRANT execute ON ctxsys. intermedia_recipe_doc TO user;

EXECUTE CTX_DDL.CREATE_PREFERENCE('user_pref', 'USER_DATASTORE');
EXECUTE CTX_DDL.SET_ATTRIBUTE('user_pref', 'PROCEDURE', 'intermedia_recipe_doc');
```

Now, the index is created as before. If the stored procedure, or the detail rows are changed, the index will have to be re-created, as before:

```
DROP INDEX intermedia_recipe_index;
CREATE INDEX intermedia_recipe_index ON intermedia_recipes (text) INDEXTYPE IS
ctxsys.context PARAMETERS  ('datastore detail_pref');
```

The available preference classes, their attributes, and the valid values are described in data dictionary views; these are:

```
CTX_CLASSES
CTX_OBJECTS
CTX_OBJECT_ATTRIBUTES
CTX_OBJECT_ATTRIBUTE_LOV
CTX_PREFERENCES
CTX_PREFERENCE_VALUES
CTX_USER_INDEX_OBJECTS
CTX_USER_INDEX_VALUES
```

The first three in the above list each contain a description field explaining their contents. The CTX_DDL package also contains procedures for deleting objects. These are DROP_PREFERENCE, DROP_SECTION_GROUP, deleting from the interMedia Text data dictionary, and UNSET_ATTRIBUTE, which removes an attribute from a preference object. Since some attributes have default values, and some are by default blank, it would be clearer in your code to explicitly re-set attributes on objects that will continue in use.

Filters

Once the document is assembled, it is passed along the pipeline. This next stage is the Filter, which processes the document, if it is in a foreign format, to readable text for indexing. The default is the NULL_FILTER that, as the name suggests, simply passes the document straight through without modification. The CHARSET_FILTER is used to convert documents from a foreign character set to the database-wide character set, and has one attribute, CHARSET for the NLS name of the source character set, which must be supported by Oracle. It is created and set using the CTX_DDL.CREATE_PREFERENCE and SET_ATTRIBUTE procedures, in the same way that datastores' classes are.

The USER_FILTER differs from the USER_DATASTORE in that it is not a stored procedure within the database, but an executable in the <ORACLE_HOME>\ctx\bin directory on the file system, run once for every document submitted to the pipeline. This executable reads the document on standard input (STDIN) and sends the result to STDOUT, in the same way as most command line utilities. The name of the script or program to run is set in the EXECUTABLE attribute of the instantiated USER_FILTER object. For readers unfamiliar with shell scripting, a short example is provided, but an introduction to script programming is beyond the scope of this chapter. The following uses Unix syntax:

```perl
#!/usr/bin/perl

# translate UK English into American English

%translation=('cake',      'muffin',
              'biscuit',    'cookie' );

while (<STDIN>)
{
        foreach $english (keys %translation)
        {
                $american = $translation{$english};
                s/$english/$american/ig;
        }
        print;
}
```

If this script was saved in <ORACLE_HOME>\ctx\bin\translate.pl, the value of the EXECUTABLE attribute would be translate.pl. The appropriate ACLs (access control lists) must be set by the system administrator, allowing a designated user account for Oracle to execute the filter and the developer to write to the directory.

The final filter is provided by a third party, Inso Corporation, and is included with interMedia Text. This filter processes many proprietary formats into text, detecting the file type automatically. There are no attributes that can be set. It uses the USER_FILTER mechanism, with the EXECUTABLE attribute 'ctxhx', and can be run from the command line with two parameters, the input file, and the output file.

The output is in HTML format, which will be processed in the next stage of the pipeline, the SECTION_GROUP.

Section Groups

The Section Groups are key to using XML with interMedia. These process XML (or HTML) documents, and output two streams of data, the section boundaries, and the text content. The default is the NULL_SECTION_GROUP, which simply passes the document straight through without performing any processing or modification, but the most relevant are the BASIC_SECTION_GROUP, the XML_SECTION_GROUP and the AUTO_SECTION_GROUP. Unlike previous preference objects, they are created using the procedure:

```
Execute CTX_DDL.CREATE_SECTION_GROUP('sg_pref', 'BASIC_SECTION_GROUP');
```

The first argument, like the previous preferences, is the name the developer wishes to assign to the object. The second is the class to be instantiated to create the object. Different classes implement different parsing styles to the document, using definitions provided by the developer to set the conditions. The attributes of a section are TAG, which is the the name of the XML element in which the text occurs, NAME, the alias by which this item will be known within queries, and TYPE, of which there are different kinds. The section group type defines the behavior of the indexing engine upon encountering delimiters such as tags, and hence the capability of subsequent queries. The FIELD section group type indexes content separately from section beginnings and ends, leading to faster query performance, but at the cost of decreased flexibility, and a limit of 64 sections. The ZONE section type ignores the contents of its sections, but unlike FIELD, it treats repeating sections as distinct, not continuations. Field sections cannot be nested within one another, in these cases Zone sections must be used. The SENTENCE and PARAGRAPH section group types operate in conjunction with Lexer classes to decompose documents according to their punctuation, but as they are not directly applicable to XML, they will not be covered.

To demonstrate querying within a section group, we will put a couple of fragments of the Recipes.xml that was first encountered in Chapter 21 into a new tablefile into a new table:

```
CREATE TABLE xml_intermedia (
    id NUMBER PRIMARY KEY,
    text clob);
```

Firstly we put in the recipe for Chocolate Brownies:

```
INSERT INTO xml_intermedia VALUES (1, ' <recipe><name>Chocolate Brownies</name>
<ingredients><item><quantity>170g</quantity>
<description>Flour</description><supplier>Sainsburys</supplier></item><item><quant
ity>1 box of</quantity>
<description>Eggs</description><supplier>Tesco</supplier></item></ingredients>
<method><step> <number>1</number><task>Preheat the Oven for</task><time>40
mins</time><preheat>at 200C</preheat></step></method></recipe> ');
```

Next we put in the recipe for Blueberry Muffins:

```
INSERT INTO xml_intermedia VALUES (2, ' <recipe><name>Blueberry
Muffins</name><ingredients><item><quantity>1cup</quantity><description>Blueberries
</description><supplier>Sainsburys</supplier></item><item><quantity>2cups</quantit
y><description>sugar</description><supplier>Safeway</supplier></item></ingredients
><method><step><number>1</number><task>PreheattheOvenfor</task><time>30mins</time>
<preheat>at180C</preheat></step></method></recipe> ');
```

Now we create the section groups:

```
EXECUTE CTX_DDL.CREATE_SECTION_GROUP('recipe', 'BASIC_SECTION_GROUP');
EXECUTE CTX_DDL.ADD_ZONE_SECTION('recipe', 'name', 'name');
EXECUTE CTX_DDL.ADD_ZONE_SECTION('recipe', 'item', 'item');
EXECUTE CTX_DDL.ADD_ZONE_SECTION('recipe', 'quantity', 'quantity');
EXECUTE CTX_DDL.ADD_ZONE_SECTION('recipe', 'description', 'description');
EXECUTE CTX_DDL.ADD_ZONE_SECTION('recipe', 'supplier', 'supplier');
EXECUTE CTX_DDL.ADD_ZONE_SECTION('recipe', 'method', 'method');
EXECUTE CTX_DDL.ADD_ZONE_SECTION('recipe', 'step', 'step');
EXECUTE CTX_DDL.ADD_ZONE_SECTION('recipe', 'number', 'number');
```

And to create the indexes:

```
CREATE INDEX recipe_index ON xml_intermedia (text) INDEXTYPE IS ctxsys.context
PARAMETERS( 'SECTION GROUP recipe' );
```

Queries can now be executed on the indexed documents, here we find `Safeway` within the `supplier` tag, If there was a mention of Safeway within a tag other than supplier the id for that row would not be returned:

```
SELECT id FROM xml_intermedia WHERE CONTAINS (text, 'Safeway within supplier') >
0;
```

The `HTML_SECTION_GROUP` is a special case for HTML, and includes special cases for dealing with HTML documents in the form that they are currently transferred and stored on the world-wide web, for example, the use of escape sequences for particular character entities. For example, in an HTML document, the £ symbol is represented as `&#0163;` and the " symbol as `&quot;`. The HTML section group also indexes meta-information within the heading of an HTML document, which differs from normal attributes in that the names of the attributes actually are attributes themselves. For example, in XML, attributes are of the general form:

```
<TAG ATTRIBUTE_NAME="ATTRIBUTE_VALUE">
```

In HTML the `META` tag which describes the document properties is:

```
<META NAME="ATTRIBUTE_NAME" CONTENT="ATTRIBUTE_VALUE">
```

In this example, substitute a name-value pair for the text in italics. While an XML tag can have many attributes, an HTML tag has only the two illustrated above, with the pattern repeating for every name-value pair. Therefore, the HTML section group includes a special case for indexing existing documents:

```
EXECUTE CTX_DDL.CREATE_SECTION_GROUP('htmlsg', 'HTML_SECTION_GROUP');
EXECUTE CTX_DDL.ADD_FIELD_SECTION('htmlsg', 'ATTRIBUTE_NAME',
'META@ATTRIBUTE_NAME');
...
SELECT text FROM html_table WHERE CONTAINS(text, 'ATTRIBUTE_VALUE within
ATTRIBUTE_NAME') > 0;
```

There is an optional parameter to `ADD_FIELD_SECTION`, a Boolean value known as the visible flag. This defaults to `FALSE`, which means that the contents of the section are indexed separately from the main body of the document. Therefore, queries on the document, which do not explicitly state the section in which to search WITHIN the document, *will not match the document*. To disable this behavior, pass `TRUE` as the fourth parameter to `ADD_FIELD_SECTION`.

All name-value pairs within `META` tags that are to be indexed must be explicitly defined in the section group object attributes before the index is created, otherwise the indexing engine will not parse them. `META` tags not of the form illustrated above will also be ignored, as will HTML comments (delimited by `'<!--'` and `'-->'`), JavaScript or anything between `<SCRIPT>` tags, and cascading style sheets and their entire content. The class will index documents that are not well formed to XML standards, for example it is common in HTML to leave `<LI>` (list item) and `<TD>` (table cell data) tags unclosed, although it is bad programming practice to do so! XML documents are not considered syntactically valid unless elements are correctly terminated, and many XML parsers will fail and return an error message.

If you use field or zone sections, there are some other points to be aware of. Firstly, a tag must be unique within a section group. This is because interMedia Text becomes confused with identically named tags within a section, as it cannot resolve overlaps and determine where each tag is closed. The examples above show that only the content of the tag is passed to the section group: the surrounding text (<> or </>) is added transparently. However, tags can be assigned to more than one section, simplifying WITHIN queries. Zone and field section names share the same space, therefore each name must be unique, unless they are segregated into different groups. Only zone sections can be nested, and zone sections treat repeating tags as separate, whereas field sections treat them as continuations of the same tag, with the element delimited by the first of the opening tags and the last of the closing, with tags between ignored. Zone sections can even be used when the same tag is nested within one of an identical name, with structure maintained. Think of the analogy of placing a small box within a large box. A field section would remove the contents of the small box, place them into the larger box, and throw the small box away. A zone section would place the small box into the larger box, without disturbing the contents.

The XML section group includes the capability of mixing DTDs within the same data table, without becoming confused between identically named tags with different semantic meaning in each document. These DTDs are informally defined within the documents themselves, rather than validation being performed against an external specification. Each document must, however, include the <!DOCTYPE> declaration, defining the qualifier to a repeated tag name. Returning to the recipe example, imagine the following two documents are stored within the same table:

```
<!DOCTYPE recipe>
<recipe>
    <name>blueberry muffins</name>
        <ingredients>
            <name>flour</name>
            <quantity>170g</quantity>
        <ingredients>
    </name>
</recipe>
```

and:

```
<!DOCTYPE supermarket>
<supermarket>
    <name>tesco</name>
    <address>1004 Oracle Boulevard</address>
</suermarket>
```

Then, before an index can be built, the procedures to add the field sections must be executed, otherwise identically named tags of the same case are considered semantically equivalent. The query is run on the section name, not the tag:

```
EXECUTE CTX_DDL.CREATE_SECTION_GROUP('xmlsg', 'XML_SECTION_GROUP');
EXECUTE CTX_DDL.ADD_FIELD_SECTION('xmlsg', 'name', '(recipe)name');
EXECUTE CTX_DDL.ADD_FIELD_SECTION('xmlsg', 'sname', '(supermarket)name');
    ...
SELECT id FROM xml_intermedia WHERE CONTAINS
    (text, 'berry within name') > 0;
```

XML section group tag attributes are indexed using similar, but not identical, methods to the HTML section group. If the XML is of the form:

```
<!DOCTYPE recipe>
<recipe name = "Chocolate Brownies">
    <ingredients>
        <item>
            <name>flour</name>
            <quantity>170g</quantity>
        </item>
    </ingredients>
</recipe>
```

The "attribute section" is used to generate the index:

```
EXECUTE CTX_DDL.ADD_ATTR_SECTION('xmlsg', 'name', 'recipe@name');
SELECT id FROM xml_intermedia WHERE CONTAINS (text, 'brownie within name') > 0;
```

And reused attribute names are differentiated using the query syntax:

```
SELECT id FROM xml_intermedia WHERE CONTAINS
    (text, 'brownie within recipe@name') > 0;
```

However, the following query would return no matches, as attribute values are invisible for queries unless specifically declared:

```
SELECT id FROM xml_intermedia WHERE CONTAINS (text, 'blueberry') > 0;
```

Searching for a tag-delimited element within a section defined by a particular attribute is not possible; there is no way to query the records to find all the muffin recipes containing flour as an ingredient. If queries like this are necessary to support the application, a different XML DTD would need to be designed before the data was loaded, or the transformation would need to be performed external to the database using a USER_FILTER or equivalent.

AUTO_SECTION_GROUP is both powerful and easy to use, and if the requirement is to index and query on almost all tagged elements, rather than only on a minority subset, then it is the most suitable. Unlike the XML_SECTION_GROUP, it indexes all values within tags, ignoring ones that are specified prior to the creation of the index. A section is automatically added for every different and non-empty tag encountered in the indexed table, and attribute sections are automatically indexed for query using the tag@attribute syntax.

There is a bug in the version of interMedia Text shipping with Oracle 8.1.6, making this section group case-insensitive for queries but case-sensitive when specifying tags to ignore.

The Auto Section Group index supports nested tag queries, tag-delimited values, from the following code in the data base:

```
<!DOCTYPE recipe>
<recipe name = "Chocolate Brownies">
    <ingredients>
        <item>
            <name>flour</name>
            <quantity>170g</quantity>
        </item>
    </ingredients>
</recipe>
```

The following query is performed:

```
SELECT id FROM xml_intermedia WHERE CONTAINS(text, '(170g within quantity) within
recipe') > 0;
```

The result returned would be the 170g from quantity tags. However, suppose that in the table, all the recipes used flour and in the same quantity, 170g, then a query for that quantity of flour would return almost all the recipes, if a search was run within the <quantity> tag. But we want to exclude the values within the <quantity> tag from the index, otherwise there would be a great deal of unnecessary results returned. To do so, both the DOCTYPE and the name of the tag are specified. If this procedure is executed after an index is created, it will apply to documents added but not to previously indexed documents unless the index is dropped and rebuilt.

```
EXECUTE CTX_DDL.ADD_STOP_SECTION ('autosg', '(recipe)quantity');
```

Storage

The Storage group of classes contains only BASIC_STORAGE. The creation of interMedia Text indexes requires storage to be allocated for tables, and the Storage class gives the developer control in the same way as for the creation of normal tables and indexes. In fact, the value of the attributes is simply appended to the CREATE TABLE and CREATE INDEX DDL statements generated and executed by the indexing engine. By default, the attributes of the BASIC_STORAGE object are empty, and therefore the database objects are simply created in the default schema of the user who executes the package procedure, not the CTXSYS schema. Of course, if a suitable GRANT is in place, the index creation schema can be specified in the DDL, and this schema may default to another tablespace. Clauses to table and index creation DDL are covered elsewhere within the book, but the exception in this case is that index organised tables are not permitted. The Storage class uses identical syntax to the other preferences, and despite the fact that it is appended, there is no need for a preceding space in the clause:

```
EXECUTE CTX_DDL.CREATE_PREFERENCE('storpref', 'BASIC_STORAGE');
EXECUTE CTX_DDL.SET_ATTRIBUTE('storpref', 'I_INDEX_CLAUSE', 'TABLESPACE idx');
```

The command above, when the PARAMETERS ('storage storpref') qualifier is added to the CREATE INDEX DDL will instruct interMedia to build this index in the tablespace named 'idx'. This is the only clause that affects actual indexes; however, here the definition of an Oracle index and an interMedia Text index differ. A logical interMedia index is physically an Oracle B-tree index, and five Oracle tables. The tables are used to store index data, key mappings, row identifiers, patterns for wildcard expansion, and the negative list, and follow the convention of the first initial of the table usage, with the extension _TABLE_CLAUSE. For example, the clauses controlling the creation of the key mapping data table would be set in the attribute K_TABLE_CLAUSE.

Lexer and Lists

The last classes necessary before documents can be fully indexed to support an application are the Lexer, the Word List, and the Stop List. The Lexer encapsulates the logic for extracting individual words from documents, determining word boundaries and classifying non-alphanumeric characters. The Lexer only gets to see content after section group decomposition, and has no direct impact on the processing of XML-specific properties of a document. Of the six Lexer classes, four are required only for Oriental languages. Chinese and Japanese words are not clearly delimited by white space, as words are in Western languages, and Korean verb forms are dependant on context, and can have many different forms. These lexers operate either with local character sets, or Unicode. The other two classes are the BASIC_LEXER and the MULTI_LEXER.

Basic Lexer

The BASIC_LEXER by default divides entire documents into individual words for indexing, defining a word as a group of characters surrounded by white space (for example, spaces, tabs, new lines) or non-alphanumeric characters (for example, punctuation marks). Setting attributes within an object of this class, however, can modify the exact meaning of any individual character or set of characters. By this method, non-alphanumeric characters can be treated as parts of words to cope, for example with an e-mail address, a technical document or product identity code, or a trademark. The limitation exists that once set, a preference attribute applies to the entire indexing job, therefore a non-alphanumeric character that has multiple meanings within a document can confuse the indexing engine.

For example, a document that uses the '.' character to indicate the termination of an English sentence would not be able to index Internet domain names as single words. However, this problem may be evaded for characters such as '/' by adopting a convention of surrounding them by white space outside of URLs, and adding them to a Stop List. There is no interface, similar to a USER_FILTER for intelligently handling non-alphanumeric characters depending on the surrounding text, and if this became necessary, it would have to be done before interMedia indexed the documents, or even before they were loaded into Oracle itself. Two possible techniques are using a scripting language such as Perl, or the PL/SQL Web Toolkit.

There are four attributes used to decide what constitutes a word, and one to decide how to index a single number. The STARTJOINS and ENDJOINS attributes determine, respectively, what characters may be included at the start and end of a word. If a character set as STARTJOINS appears in the middle of an unbroken (by white space) string of characters, that string will be split on the STARTJOINS character. This character then forms the first letter of a word comprising it, and the rest of the string terminated by the next occurrence of a non-word character. The first part of the string, from the beginning to the character immediately prior to the STARTJOINS character is taken as a single, whole word.

The value of a STARTJOINS attribute may be a group of characters, and if more than one of these characters occur together within the unbroken character string, they will all be prefixed to the word. If for example, you mistakenly typed L as a STARTJOINS character when you meant >, then any words with a capital L would be split. An ENDJOINS character (or group of characters) behaves in the same way, but is appended to the first part of the string after the split.

A character defined within the PRINTJOINS attribute forms is a valid character within a word, and is treated as a part of that word by the indexer, and by subsequent queries. One of these characters may appear in the middle, or at either end of a word. Characters declared as SKIPJOINS do not split a word, but are not a part of the word either. They are ignored, and the character strings on either side of them are merged into a single word. If a SKIPJOINS character appears at the beginning or end of a word, it is ignored completely. A character appearing in the STARTJOINS attribute cannot also be used in the ENDJOINS, PRINTJOINS, or SKIPJOINS attributes. For example, consider the character '@' and the e-mail address 'blueberry@muffin'. (This may or may not be a valid e-mail address, either way it is used purely as an illustration). The effect of this within the different attributes is as follows:

Attribute	Indexed word(s)
STARTJOINS	'blueberry' '@muffin'
ENDJOINS	'blueberry@' 'muffin'
PRINTJOINS	'blueberry@muffin'
SKIPJOINS	'blueberrymuffin'

This class is also responsible for the case sensitivity of the index, via setting the attribute MIXED_CASE to 'YES' if you require case-sensitive queries. Accented characters are converted to their nearest equivalent 7-bit ASCII forms by setting BASE_LETTER to 'YES'. There are several characters relating to white space itself, rather than the words it surrounds. Spaces and tabs are hard-coded white space characters and cannot be re-defined, but additional white space characters can be added by setting the WHITESPACE attribute. CONTINUATION defines which characters indicate that a line continues as a single logical structure despite being wrapped to the width of the document. Typically, within English text, the hyphen is used to split words across lines, and the backslash is included by default, as this is used as the continuation symbol by convention in plain text editors such as GNU emacs on Unix. Unix systems typically use a single character to separate lines of text, whereas Windows uses a pair of characters together, signifying both 'new line' and 'carriage return'. This attribute (NEWLINE), once set to 'NEWLINE' or 'CARRIAGE_RETURN' (which actually means 'new line and carriage return'), affects the entire index. Punctuation marks within numbers (for example, '1,234.56') are treated differently, and have their own attributes, NUMGROUP for the "thousands" character, and NUMJOIN for the decimal point. These will automatically be derived from the global national language settings of the Oracle server.

Multi-Lexer

If there is a requirement to use a different Lexer for each row in the table, then the Multi Lexer is the master (or global) lexer for the index. It reads, for each row, a specific column that instructs it which secondary (or sub) lexer will actually perform the decomposition into individual words, sentences, and paragraphs. This is designed to support the storage of documents in multiple languages within a table, and the query engine is capable of detecting the NLS_LANG setting of the user running the query and chooses the appropriate row. Only English and French are supported languages at the time of writing, so if another language is required, you will need to set the relevant lexer parameters manually. From the perspective of indexing XML documents, it has no direct relation, as tag elements, are by definition independent of anything beyond their own DTDs. At present, version 8.1.6, interMedia cannot recognize namespaces in XML documents once the content is queried; however, national language becomes more important.

Lists

A Stop List is simply a list of words to be ignored by the index. These are usually words that are common, and that would not normally be queried upon anyway, therefore indexing them would be a waste of tablespace and processor cycles. In other, application-specific, cases, there may be words that occur too frequently in the particular corpus to be useful discriminants or words you wish to exclude, as having multiple meanings in different contexts, particularly product or brand names that are also common English words. A stop list may contain up to 4095 words of up to 64 characters each, and default lists are provided for English (containing common prepositions and conjunctions) and several other languages (Danish, Dutch, Finnish, French, German, Italian, Portuguese, Spanish, and Swedish). These may be examined by querying the views CTX_STOPLISTS and CTX_STOPWORDS, which are related by CTX_STOPWORDS.SPW_STOPLIST referencing CTX_STOPLISTS.SPL_NAME. The default list is CTXSYS.DEFAULT_STOPLIST. If the Lexer is set to case-sensitive mode, stop lists are also case sensitive. Stop lists are created and used as follows:

```
EXECUTE CTX_DDL.CREATE_STOPLIST('stoppref');
EXECUTE CTX_DDL.ADD_STOPWORD('stoppref', 'flour');

DROP INDEX intermedia_recipe_index;

CREATE INDEX intermedia_recipe_index INDEXTYPE IS ctxsys.context
PREFERENCES('stoplist stoppref');

ALTER INDEX intermedia_recipe_index REBUILD PARAMETERS('add stopword flour');
```

The final class that will be considered is the single Word List class, BASIC_WORDLIST. This class is not used when indexes are built, and is only used in certain advanced forms of query. The stem query uses technology licensed from Xerox Corporation to match words with a common linguistic root. For example, performing a stem query on the word 'bake' would match documents containing the words 'baker' and 'baked', even if the document did not contain 'bake' as a distinct word, and only exact word matches would normally be returned. This is because the query term is expanded prior to execution, and an OR search is performed. The fuzzy query locates words with similar spellings, for example it could be used to match 'flour' when searching for 'flower'.

Queries that match by pattern are referred to as 'wildcard queries', and are physically an Oracle LIKE query on the main index, followed by an interMedia search for all the matches of the initial query. Vague terms have the potential to consume large processing resources and interMedia takes two approaches to address this. The first is the wildcard pattern index, which attempts to avoid the need to perform a full table scan of the main index. The price for this increased performance is paid in storage space and processor cycles when the index is built, and will vary according to the uniqueness ratio of the words within the documents. Secondly, the maximum number of unique words a wildcard can refer to can be restricted, and interMedia will refuse to process queries which attempt to exceed it. Use these two restrictions:

```
EXECUTE CTX_DDL.CREATE_WORDLIST('wordpref', 'BASIC_WORDLIST');
EXECUTE CTX_DDL.SET_ATTRIBUTE('wordpref', 'SUBSTRING_INDEX', 'TRUE');
EXECUTE CTX_DDL.SET_ATTRIBUTE('wordpref', 'WILDCARD_MAXTERMS', '100');
```

Other Preferences

The other preferences are also related to the conservation and rationing of server resources. The MEMORY parameter, appended in the usual way to the PARAMETERS in CREATE INDEX, sets the amount of memory used to build or alter the index. This cannot exceed MAX_INDEX_MEMORY, which is set using CTX_ADM.SET_PARAMETER, as are the default memory and the logging directory. The indexing mechanism used by interMedia is more complex than the usual Oracle B-Tree, and documents are actually built within memory, rather than added to the B-Tree one row at a time. When the memory parameter is reached, the index is updated on disk, then the buffer reused for the next set of documents. The number of documents within the buffer at any one time varies (with size and uniqueness) and no sorting is done prior to index processing. Therefore, indexing a large set of documents in a small amount of memory will lead to a fragmented index.

Other available performance improvements, such as in-memory document services, parallel index creation, and index optimization are beyond the scope of this chapter.

Special Operators

Now that we know how the indexes are formed let's recap on the querying and how to use queries. We will concentrate on two main queries – within and stored query expression (SQE).

Within

This is an expression restricting a query to a section, either a zone, a field section, or a grammatical section (sentence or paragraph). These divisions are made by the Section Group and Lexer classes when the index is created. This operator does not influence the score per se: scores are assigned to the set that match. This operator is very sensitive to precedence, and care must be taken when designing queries that use it. For example, consider the queries:

```
SELECT id FROM intermedia_recipes WHERE CONTAINS (text, 'eggs and flour within
ingredients') > 0;

SELECT id FROM intermedia_recipes WHERE CONTAINS (text, '(eggs and flour) within
ingredients') > 0;

SELECT id FROM intermedia_recipes WHERE CONTAINS (text, 'eggs within flour and
flour within ingredients') > 0;

SELECT id FROM intermedia_recipes WHERE CONTAINS (text, ' eggs within ingredients
within recipe') > 0;
```

The first of the queries will match any document that contain the word `flour` within the `ingredients` section, and that contain the word `eggs` anywhere within the document, regardless of section. The second query will match documents containing the words `eggs` and `flour` within the same `ingredients` section. If the document contained two of these sections, with one of the query terms in each, the Text query engine would not recognize that as a match. This behavior differs from that of the field section group. Also, see the discussion of section groups and visibility above. The third query will return any document that contains the query terms within the named section, irrespective of whether or not the same section contains them both, so long as the section name matches the one in the query. The fourth query will fail – the `within` operator can only be nested as in the case below:

```
SELECT id FROM intermedia_recipes WHERE CONTAINS (text, ' (eggs within
ingredients) within recipe') > 0;
```

The way of nesting `within` operators is to for it to be enclosed in brackets around the inner expression like above. Also the left side of the nested `within` has to be a text query.

`within` can be combined with operators other than AND. The simplest of these are OR, ACCUM, and NOT. Whereas NOT is Boolean and does not affect score, OR and ACCUM introduce the ability to score documents, since they provide optional criteria. When AND is used, the score assigned is the lowest of the individual scores of each of the query terms, since a document may contain single or multiple instances of each of the terms, and multiple documents may match the query in different ways. A document returned by AND will contain at least one occurrence of each of the terms. The ACCUM and OR operators both give positive scores if one or more of their search terms are found within a document. OR simply returns a score based on the frequency of the most common term, but ACCUM scores are calculated by the number of the terms that are found in each document. For example, if we searched for `eggs` and `flour`, OR would award the highest score to a document that contained the word `eggs` many times, even if `flour` did not appear. However, ACCUM would give a better score to a document containing both `flour` and `eggs`, even if they only occurred a few times. The ACCUM operator may be abbreviated to ','.

```
SELECT id FROM intermedia_recipes WHERE CONTAINS (text, 'eggs accum flour') > 0;
SELECT id FROM intermedia_recipes WHERE CONTAINS(text, 'blueberry,muffin within
name') > 0;
```

The EQUIV operator is not a match for equality, as in conventional SQL, despite the fact that it is abbreviated to ' = '. Instead, it specifies alternatives for a search term. It can be used in place of the OR operator when assembling searches for complete phrases. As they are equivalent, score is assigned as if the query was executed for the single search term. So, to search for "blueberry muffin" or "cherry muffin" without matching "cherry pie", assuming we had cherry pie and cherry muffins in our database, of course:

```
SELECT id FROM intermedia_recipes WHERE CONTAINS (text, 'blueberry=cherry muffin
within name') > 0;
```

However, suppose that we wished to locate recipes containing cherries, but had baked muffins the previous week. While muffins are still an acceptable snack, perhaps another recipe would be better. In this case, the MINUS operator, abbreviated to ' – ' is used. This operator matches documents containing both search terms, but reduces the score of documents that contain both to lower than the score of those that only contain the first. This operator has no effect if the second term is not found.

```
SELECT id FROM intermedia_recipes WHERE CONTAINS (text, 'cherry minus muffin
within name') > 0;
```

More explicit control over a query like this is given by the WEIGHT operator, abbreviated to '*'. When a query has more than one term, the relative importance of each term can be specified. The query engine will first calculate the score for each term, then multiply each score by the weight of that term, then total all the scores to give the overall document score. If the result exceeds 100, a value of 100 will be returned (this indicates a perfect match anyway). Unlike the MINUS operator, by default WEIGHT increases the score of a term, rather than reducing the score of other terms, but using a negative weight (even -1) will cause the score to be lowered proportionally. Therefore, care must be taken when assigning weights, as overuse could cause all (or a high proportion of) documents to be considered perfect. This is purely a query operator, and does not bias the underlying index. Therefore, an alternative approach to searching for cherry recipes and reducing the relative ranking of muffins is:

```
SELECT id FROM intermedia_recipes WHERE CONTAINS (text, 'muffin,cherry*5 within
name') > 0;
```

or:

```
SELECT id FROM intermedia_recipes WHERE CONTAINS (text, 'muffin*-1,cherry within
name') > 0;
```

Neither of which is the same as:

```
SELECT id FROM intermedia_recipes WHERE CONTAINS (text, '(cherry not muffin)
within name') > 0;
```

Stored Queries

There is one more query expression. This is a stored query expression (SQE) which is conceptually similar to a stored procedure, and allows an interMedia Text query to be named and reused. Stored queries return scores in the same way as pre-defined operators, and can be combined with those operators, and multiple clauses within SELECT statements. To create a stored query, the parameters are the name to assign, and the interMedia Text operators and terms that comprise the query:

```
EXECUTE CTX_QUERY.STORE_SQE ('recipes', 'muffin or cookie');
```

The stored query is then embedded with a normal query expression, using the SQE operator. There is not an interface for passing a parameter to a stored query, unlike for example the prepared statements in JDBC, or conventional stored procedures. Note the use of brackets rather than quotes within the expression.

```
SELECT id FROM intermedia_recipes WHERE CONTAINS (text, 'sqe(recipes)') > 0;
```

Summary

In this chapter, the world of interMedia Text has been introduced. The various ways queries are formed should now be familiar to you. You should know the indexing pipeline and how interMedia indexes are formed. We have also examined techniques for indexing and searching XML documents. This is a large area and we have only explored the building blocks of the software. In the next chapter, we'll put together a web-based search engine, which uses the materials and tools of this chapter.

ORACLE8i APPLICATION PROGRAMMING

Building a Search Engine using Java and interMedia

Search engines are an important part of all network applications. Over the years, these engines have evolved to be user friendly and simple, yet powerful. Their actual implementation, however, is often complex, due to the diversity of valid search phrases.

With the emergence of interMedia Text for indexing and searching the Oracle database, application developers have been presented with a simple alternative to the task of designing a search engine. This powerful component can be used in conjunction with nearly any type of programming language, to deliver high-speed search results with ease.

In this chapter we will put into motion many of the concepts we have discussed in previous chapters. We will cover the design and implementation of a search engine, using features of interMedia Text, to search the discussion forum from a previous chapter. We assume that the reader has already installed the interMedia Text component and read the interMedia Text chapter of this book, which covers the installation, usage, and syntax of interMedia Text in detail.

To be exact, we will:

❑   Discuss the design of a search syntax

❑   Create a Java class to translate search phrases to valid interMedia queries

❑   Implement a search engine Java class

❑   Use servlets to execute searches and display search results

Introduction

In a previous chapter we presented an implementation of an online discussion forum, using PL/SQL and Java to create the functionality. In this chapter, we will use interMedia Text in conjunction with JDBC and Java to create a search engine to search the forum database for specified topics. Although we will frequently reference terms and use database structures we presented in the previous chapter, the search engine implementation should be general enough to be used as a part of any other application.

We will begin this chapter by discussing database preparation, then cover the actual search engine implementation, and finally create the user interface by using servlets to generate HTML output.

Index Creation

We have already covered the table creation for the discussion forum in a previous chapter. In this section, we will discuss the steps necessary in creating valid interMedia indexes for the forum tables we wish to search with our search engine. As interMedia index creation has already been covered in detail in the interMedia Text chapter, we assume that you are familiar with the procedure, and present it as such.

Database Tables

To recap, we store all messages of the discussion forum in the messages table. This is the table that will be searched, and thus indexed. The messages table is created as follows:

```
CREATE TABLE MESSAGES (
    MESSAGE_ID          NUMBER                      NOT NULL,
    CATEGORY_ID         NUMBER                      NOT NULL,
    HEADER              VARCHAR2(500)               NOT NULL,
    TEXT                VARCHAR2(2000)              NOT NULL,
    USER_ID             NUMBER                      NOT NULL,
    RESPONDS_TO         NUMBER                          NULL,
    PARENT              NUMBER                          NULL,
    SUBMIT_DATE         DATE DEFAULT SYSDATE NOT NULL,
    CONSTRAINT MSG_PKEY PRIMARY KEY (MESSAGE_ID),
    CONSTRAINT MSG_FKEY_CAT FOREIGN KEY (CATEGORY_ID)
        REFERENCES CATEGORIES,
    CONSTRAINT MSG_FKEY_USR FOREIGN KEY (USER_ID)
        REFERENCES USERS,
    CONSTRAINT MSG_FKEY_RT  FOREIGN KEY (RESPONDS_TO)
        REFERENCES USERS
);
```

We will create two indexes for the messages table, one to index the message body (text column) and another one to index the message headlines (header column).

Creating Section Groups

As we wish to keep our index general enough in this context, we have omitted all special PARAMETERS, such as LEXER and FILTER. However, all indexes should use stop lists for ignoring common words, and therefore we assign the interMedia-supplied DEFAULT_STOPLIST for both the indexes (this is a stop list of English words – feel free to use another one that suits your application better). In addition, since our forum users are likely to include HTML tags in their messages (this is a technical forum, remember), we wish to create a HTML section group that would enable searching within certain tags/fields, as we will describe in our discussion of the QueryBuilder class later. InterMedia comes with the predefined section group type HTML_SECTION_GROUP, which can be used for defining sections in HTML documents. What we want to do is to create a section group of the mentioned HTML_SECTION_GROUP type and add most commonly encountered HTML tags to the section. This can be done as shown in the following code. Please note that the list of fields and zones we present in this example is by no means exhaustive; we encourage you to expand it in you own implementation.

```
BEGIN
CTX_DDL.CREATE_SECTION_GROUP('HTM_GROUP', 'HTML_SECTION_GROUP');
CTX_DDL.ADD_ZONE_SECTION('HTM_GROUP', 'HEADLINE1', 'H1');
CTX_DDL.ADD_ZONE_SECTION('HTM_GROUP', 'HEADLINE2', 'H2');
CTX_DDL.ADD_ZONE_SECTION('HTM_GROUP', 'BOLD', 'B');
CTX_DDL.ADD_ZONE_SECTION('HTM_GROUP', 'UNDERLINED','U');
END;
/
```

The CREATE_SECTION_GROUP procedure creates our HTML section group, which we call HTM_GROUP. We then use the ADD_ZONE_SECTION procedure to create zone sections and add them to the group. Zone sections are section-delimited by start and end tags. The <B> and </B> tags, for instance, mark a certain zone. Zone sections can be nested one within another, can overlap, and can occur more than once in a document. The ADD_ZONE_SECTION procedure takes the group name it should belong to, the name of the zone, and the zone tag, as its parameters.

In addition to adding zones to the section group, we could have added individual fields with the ADD_FIELD_SECTION procedure. However, unlike zone sections, field sections cannot nest or overlap. As such, field sections are best suited for non-repeating, non-overlapping sections, such as <TITLE>...</TITLE>. Since we are indexing individual messages that are already enclosed by HTML tags on the forum web site, it is unlikely that forum users will be using this sort of HTML tags in their messages.

Creating Indexes

When the section group has been created, we proceed to create the indexes (connect as CTXSYS):

```
CREATE INDEX MSG_IDX ON MESSAGES(TEXT)
    INDEXTYPE IS CTXSYS.CONTEXT
    PARAMETERS (' STOPLIST CTXSYS.EMPTY_STOPLIST
    SECTION GROUP CTXSYS.HTM_GROUP ');

CREATE INDEX MSG_HEADER_IDX ON MESSAGES(HEADER)
    INDEXTYPE IS CTXSYS.CONTEXT
    PARAMETERS (' STOPLIST CTXSYS.EMPTY_STOPLIST
    SECTION GROUP CTXSYS.HTM_GROUP ');
Index created.
```

It is worthwhile to point out that this is just a basic setup for interMedia indexes. In fact, we encourage you to adjust the index PARAMETERS to better suit your application, for example by setting language settings, further section groups, stop lists, and so on.

Implementing the Search Engine

In this section, we will delve into the details of the actual search engine we wish to implement. Using interMedia Text for the searching actually eliminates most of the work of creating reasonable database queries from the user input. Therefore, our task of searching is basically about translating the search phrase entered by the user to an interMedia format, executing a search with the translated query, and keeping track of the search results.

Our implementation consists of the `SearchEngine` class, which executes the actual search and maintains search results, and the `QueryBuilder` class, which we use to translate search phrases to properly formatted queries as illustrated in the following diagram:

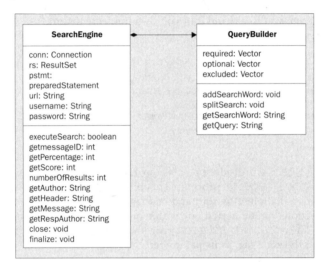

The client instantiates a `SearchEngine` instance and calls the `executeSearch()` method with a given search string to run the search. Then, through the various `get()` methods, the user may scroll through the search results, and display the data they find appropriate. The `SearchEngine` instance keeps an instance of the `QueryBuilder`, which is used to translate the search phrase given to the `executeSearch()` method to a valid query. These methods will be discussed in detail later.

Search Syntax

A critical part of designing the search engine is to define its search syntax. Most professional search engines use a very similar syntax for the search queries, with only slight alterations between individual models. In this section we will define and describe the syntax we will use in our implementation of the search engine. This syntax is mostly modeled after the common syntax of such commercial search engines as Google and AltaVista, although it is by no means as thorough. It should suffice however, in this context.

In the interMedia chapter of this book is a detailed coverage of the various query operators used by interMedia Text; you may wish to use some of those not covered here in your own implementation.

Common Phrases

Probably the most common form of a search phrase is a space separated list of words. If the words are enclosed with quotes, this means that it should search for the whole quoted sentence, in the order it was entered. For example, searching for "Oracle interMedia" will return only those messages that contain the words Oracle **and** interMedia next to each other. However, when entering a list of search words, omitting quotes, we search for as many of the words as possible. In terms of an interMedia query, this translates to **accumulating** the search words.

Generally, messages score higher when more of the search words are hit. For example, searching for the phrase Oracle interMedia Text will score any message with all three words higher than any document with two of the three, which will score higher than any document with only one of the three.

Required Words

Often, a search is meaningless if certain search words are not found. In our search syntax, we allow for specifying any of the words in the search phrase as required. Setting a word required means that messages will not score unless they contain that word, no matter what the rest of the search phrase looks like. To mark a word as required, one must set the plus operator (+) directly in front of the search word. A space separating a search word and a plus does not specify a required word.

For example, searching for Oracle +interMedia will return all documents containing interMedia, where messages that also contain Oracle are scored higher than those that do not.

Excluded Words

Sometimes, excluding certain irrelevant words from the search phrase can make a big difference in the search results. This is particularly true when searching for a word that has synonyms that should be omitted. For example, searching for information on the island of Java with the search phrase Java will probably not return any useful results! However, by excluding such words as programming, package, software, etc., the search will probably have more meaning. To exclude a word from a search phrase, one sets the minus operator (–) directly in front of the word to exclude. Thus, the latter search query would be something like Java -programming -software -package.

Section Fields

As we discussed in the *Index Creation* section, we can define certain section fields that the user may specify when searching. Searching for a word within a specified field will return only those messages where the indicated word actually appears within the tags that correspond to the given field name.

For example, searching for BOLD:solution will only return those messages where the word solution appears in boldface. This type of search might be useful when searching for specifically highlighted topics, that are more likely to lead to the right result (or solution, in this example).

As the field names specified must be valid in order to give results, it is a good rule to include a list of available field names on the web page that contains the search engine.

Wildcards

Given a search word, interMedia Text will search for a match among whole words only, omitting similar words or sentences. In other words, searching for horse will not return documents containing horsepower (unless they also contain horse, of course), because only whole words are matched. However, by setting appropriate wildcard characters (*) this can be avoided. With a wildcard character, searching for horse* will return messages containing horseshoe, horsepower, horse, and horsewhip, to name but a few.

Summary

The table below gives a quick summary of the simple search syntax we support for our search engine:

Search phrase	Description
Oracle interMedia	Finds messages containing either interMEdia or Oracle, or both.
+Oracle +interMedia	Finds only messages containing both words. The plus character marks a required word.
+Oracle interMedia	All messages must contain Oracle, but messages also including interMedia will be ranked higher than those not.
"Oracle interMedia"	Finds the exact phrase enclosed by the quotes.
Oracle -interMedia	Finds messages containing Oracle, but not the word interMedia.
inter*	Searches for words that begin with inter.
UNDERLINED:interMedia	Finds all messages where the word interMedia appears underlined.

QueryBuilder Class

Before we can execute a search with interMedia Text, we need to translate the search phrase entered by the user to a valid query. For this purpose, we define the QueryBuilder class, which serves the purpose of taking a search string and constructing a corresponding interMedia query.

SearchWord

When we parse the search phrase from the user and split it up into individual search words, we may want to keep various information on each search word. To encapsulate a single search word along with all the information that applies, we define the SearchWord class. In our implementation, the SearchWord contains only the actual search word and a possible field name. However, there is nothing to stop you from adding more instance variables to the class. Note that the SearchWord class is an *inner* class of the QueryBuilder class.

```
package forum.search;

import java.util.*;

class SearchWord {
    String text;
    String fieldName;
}
```

Note that class SearchWord is visible only to QueryBuilder since it is a private class defined in the same file as the public class QueryBuilder.

Instance Variables and Construction

The QueryBuilder is constructed with the default constructor. It keeps a few Vector objects as instance variables, which are used to store different types of search words during the parsing:

```
public class QueryBuilder {

    private Vector required;
    private Vector optional;
    private Vector excluded;
```

In order to simplify the code, the QueryBuilder defines three integer constants, corresponding to the three Vector instances from above:

```
public final int REQUIRED   = 0;
public final int OPTIONAL   = 1;
public final int NOT_WANTED = 2;
```

Splitting the Search String

To be able to work with each of the search words in the input from the user, we will need a method for taking the input string and splitting it up into individual words. For this purpose, we define the splitSearch() method. For the parsing, we define a *search word* as being either a single word, delimited by blank spaces, or a partial sentence, delimited by quotes.

The splitSearch() method starts by defining and initializing its variables. First of all, it defines the Vector instances required, optional, and excluded, that are to hold the search words, and the tokenizer StringTokenizer instance that will be used to split up the search phrase. The integer variable y is used to keep track of possible search fields included within any of the search words, the searchWord variable is used for storing individual search words of the input string, and fieldName is used for storing possible field names:

```
private void splitSearch ( String input ) {

    int y;
    int flag;

    String searchWord;
    String temp;
    String fieldName;
    StringTokenizer tokenizer;

    required = new Vector();
    optional = new Vector();
    excluded = new Vector();
    tokenizer = new StringTokenizer(input," ");
```

When all necessary variables have been defined, the method begins parsing the search string by looping through all the tokens of the StringTokenizer. Special notice must be taken of words containing quotes. When such a word is found, we skip the input tokens until we either find another quote character (a closing quote, by then) or come to the end of the input. In either case, we extract the quoted sentence and proceed:

```
while ( tokenizer.hasMoreTokens() ) {

    searchWord = tokenizer.nextToken();

    // Check for quoted phrase. If a quote is
    // found, we search for the closing quote.
    if ( searchWord.startsWith("\"") ) {
        searchWord = searchWord.substring(1);
        while ( tokenizer.hasMoreTokens() ) {
            temp = tokenizer.nextToken();
            if ( temp.endsWith("\"") ) {
                searchWord += " " + temp.substring(0,temp.length()-1);
                break;
            } else {
                searchWord += " " + temp;
            }
        }
    }
}
```

By now, we have identified a single search word. We then check whether the search word is preceded by either one of the plus or minus operators, and if so, set the appropriate value for the `flag` variable, which is used to identify the class of the search word. The flag gets the value of:

❑   REQUIRED when the search word is preceded by a plus (+)

❑   NOT_WANTED when the search word is preceded by a minus (–)

❑   OPTIONAL otherwise

Next, we replace the search syntax wildcard character (*) with the SQL wildcard operator (%) and search for field names possibly included in the search word. If a field name is found, it is extracted and stored. Finally, the search word we have parsed is added to the appropriate vector by a call to the `addSearchWord()` method, which we will discuss later. If there are any more unhandled search words available at this stage, we repeat the whole process until we reach the end of the input:

```
// We have now identified a single word in the
// search string. This word is either a traditional
// word, or a part of a sentence, identified by quotes.
// We now proceed to searching for the required/not
// wanted flags, +/-.

flag = OPTIONAL;
fieldName = "";

// Preceeded by a REQUIRED flag.
if ( searchWord.charAt(0) == '+' ) {
    flag = REQUIRED;
    searchWord = searchWord.substring(1);

// Preceeded by the NOT WANTED flag.
} else if (searchWord.charAt(0) == '-') {
    flag = NOT_WANTED;
    searchWord = searchWord.substring(1);
}
// Replace * wild cards with %
searchWord = searchWord.replace('*', '%');
```

```
        // Find field indicator ":"
        y = searchWord.indexOf(":");
        if ( y > 0 ) {
            fieldName = searchWord.substring(0, y);
            searchWord = searchWord.substring(y+1, searchWord.length());
        }
        addSearchWord(searchWord, flag, fieldName);
    }
}
```

The addSearchWord() method takes the search word, a field name, and the type of word as its input parameters. It wraps the search word and field name in an instance of the SearchWord class and adds the instance to one of the vectors required, optional, and excluded, based on the word type.

```
private void addSearchWord( String word, int type, String field ) {

    SearchWord w = new SearchWord();

    w.text = word;
    w.fieldName = field;

    // Add the search word to the
    // appropriate Vector instance.
    switch (type) {
        case REQUIRED:
            required.addElement(w);
            break;
        case OPTIONAL:
            optional.addElement(w);
            break;
        case NOT_WANTED:
            excluded.addElement(w);
            break;
    }
}
```

Formatting Search Words

As we have discussed, we use the addSearchWord() method to add the search words to their appropriate search words vectors. The opposite method, getSearchWord(), takes a Vector instance and integer as its parameters. It extracts a SearchWord object from the specified array index of the vector. It then reads the search word from the SearchWord instance and surrounds it with braces to avoid any reserved words and words containing characters that are query operators. If the SearchWord also contains a field name, we extract its value and attach a WITHIN clause:

```
private String getSearchWord (Vector words, int pos) {
    String str = "{" + ((SearchWord) words.elementAt(pos)).text + "}";
    if (((SearchWord)words.elementAt(pos)).fieldName.length() > 0) {
        str += " WITHIN " + ((SearchWord)words.elementAt(pos)).fieldName;
    }
    return str;
}
```

For example, if the search word BOLD:Oracle has been entered, meaning that the word Oracle should be searched for within a BOLD section, getSearchWord() would translate this to the phrase {Oracle} WITHIN BOLD.

Building the Query

When the `splitSearch()` method has categorized the words composing the search phrase, it is time to build the actual query. For that purpose, we will call the `getQuery()` method, which formats and returns the interMedia query form of the original input:

```
private String getQuery () {
    String tmp = "";

    String bool = "";      //   AND, OR, NOT operator
    int reqCount;          //   Count of required words
    int optCount;          //   Count of optional words
    int notCount;          //   Count of not wanted words
    int i;                 //   Loop control

    bool = "";
    reqCount = required.size();
    optCount = optional.size();
    notCount = excluded.size();
```

In building the query, `getQuery()` must evaluate the search words based on whether they were marked as required, optional, or not wanted.

First, it adds up all the required words (if any), separated by the AND Boolean operator (&):

```
if ( reqCount > 0 ) {

    tmp = "((";

    // Required words, first time.
    for ( i = 0; i < reqCount; i++ ) {
        tmp += bool + getSearchWord(required,i);
        bool = " & ";
    }
}
```

It then combines the required search words with the optional words, if there are any. The required words are first listed separately, separated by the & operator, and are given an additional weight over the other optional words. Next, the required words are accumulated in a comma-separated list, and we move to listing the optional words. Instead of resetting the `bool` variable at this stage, it simply proceeds with its prior value. This means, that if there were both required words and optional words, the optional words now listed will be added at the end of the required words accumulation. Otherwise, this will be a new list with the optional words only.

```
if ( reqCount > 0 && optCount > 0 ) {
    tmp += ") | ((";

    bool = "";

    // Required words, second time.
    for ( i = 0; i < reqCount; i++ ) {
        tmp += bool + getSearchWord(required,i);
        bool = " & ";
    }
    tmp += ")*10*10";
    tmp += " & ((";
```

```
            // Required words, third time
            // Accumulates with optional words.
            bool = "";
            for ( i = 0; i < reqCount; i++ ) {
                tmp += bool + getSearchWord(required,i);
                bool = " , ";
            }
        }
    } else {
        tmp = "(";
    }

    // Optional words, accumulated.
    for ( i = 0; i < optCount; i++ ) {
        tmp += bool + getSearchWord(optional,i);
        bool = " , ";   // Accumulate
    }

    if ( reqCount > 0 ) {
        if ( optCount > 0 ) {
            tmp += ")) )";
        } else {
            tmp += ")) ";
        }
    } else {
        tmp += ")";
    }
```

Finally it processes the excluded words, but only if there are also some optional or required words. If not, that means that our search query is comprised of excluded words only, which is meaningless and will return an empty query. Empty search queries are specifically handled in the SearchEngine class, as we will discuss later.

```
    if ( tmp.length() > 0 ) {
        bool = " NOT ";
    } else {
        bool = "";
    }

    for ( i = 0; i < notCount; i++ ) {
        tmp += bool + getSearchWord(excluded,i);
        bool = " NOT ";
    }
    return tmp;
}
```

Putting It All Together

The final method of the QueryBuilder is also the only public one. The build() method, which is called by the client to translate an input string, simply invokes the splitSearch() method and returns the value of getQuery():

```
public String build( String input ) {
    splitSearch(input);
    return getQuery();
}
}
```

SearchEngine Class

By now, we have studied the QueryBuilder class, which translates a given search phrase to a formatted interMedia query. The SearchEngine class, which we will discuss next, uses the QueryBuilder to build a query, which it then executes. It also keeps track of the search results and provides methods for retrieving necessary information for the overview of the results.

Instance Variables

The SearchEngine defines a few instance variables.

```
package forum.search;

import pooling2.*;
import java.util.*;
import java.sql.*;

public class SearchEngine {

    Connection conn;
    DBConnectionPool connPool;
    long time;
    PreparedStatement pstmt;
    QueryBuilder qbuilder;
    ResultSet rs;

    int current;
    int maxscore;
```

The two integer variables current and maxscore are used to keep track of the current row of the ResultSet and the maximum score from a query, respectively. The Connection, ResultSet, and PreparedStatement objects are used for database access while the QueryBuilder instance is used to translate the search query. The DBConnectionPool instance is used for obtaining pooled connections, as we discussed in the Discussion Forum chapter. Finally, we store in milliseconds the time that it took to execute the actual search (including the translation of the input) in the variable time.

Constructor

The SearchEngine constructor takes for a parameter the name of the connection pool to use for this instance. The pool name is used to obtain a DBConnectionPool instance from the DBPoolManager class; we discussed these classes in detail in the Connection Pooling and Discussion Forum chapters.

```
public SearchEngine( String poolname ) throws SQLException {
    connPool = DBPoolManager.getInstance().getConnectionPool(poolname);
    current = 0;
    maxscore = 0;
}
```

Executing the Search

The executeSearch() method executes the actual search. It takes a search phrase as its input and proceeds to translate the phrase to a proper interMedia query, with a call to the build() method of the QueryBuilder class. If the search phrase is just an empty string, we immediately return false, indicating a failed search. In case of a valid input, we obtain a Connection instance and construct the actual SQL query that is used to search the database. You may have noted that the CONTAINS keyword is used on both the message and header columns of the messages table – we search both the headlines and body content of the forum messages at the same time.

Note that we do not select all of the available columns from the messages table, since we are selecting only the most relevant fields for the results overview:

```
public boolean executeSearch( String search ) throws SQLException {

    // Return immediately if there is no search phrase.
    if ( search.trim().equals("") ) {
        return false;
    }
    long start;
    String sqlSelect;
    String query;

    // Take the time.
    start = System.currentTimeMillis();

    // Translate the search string to a ConText query.
    qbuilder = new QueryBuilder();
    query = qbuilder.build(search);
    System.out.println(query);

    // Obtain a Connection from the connection pool.
    conn = connPool.getConnection();

    // Build the SQL query.
    sqlSelect = "SELECT m.message_id AS message, m.header AS header,"
        +    "    m.text AS text,u.login AS author,"
        +    "    NVL(m.parent,-1) AS parent, "
        +    "    SUM(SCORE(1) + SCORE(2)) AS scr, "
        +    "    TO_CHAR(m.submit_date,'dd.mm.yyyy HH24') AS sdate, "
        +    "    c.category_id AS category,c.category_name AS catname "
        +    "FROM messages m,users u,categories c "
        +    "WHERE ( CONTAINS(m.header,?,1) > 0 "
        +    "    OR CONTAINS(m.text,?,2) > 0) "
        +    "    AND u.user_id = m.user_id "
        +    "    AND c.category_id = m.category_id "
        +    "GROUP BY m.message_id,m.header,m.text, "
        +    "    u.login, NVL(m.parent,-1), "
        +    "    TO_CHAR(m.submit_date,'dd.mm.yyyy HH24'), "
        +    "    c.category_id,c.category_name "
        +    "ORDER BY scr DESC";
    System.out.println(sqlSelect);
```

When we have constructed the query, we create a PreparedStatement instance by a call to the prepareStatement() method of the Connection. We explicitly specify that the ResultSet of the statement being executed should be scroll insensitive – we want to be able to scroll back and forth in the search results. If everything goes well, and no exception is thrown, we return true, indicating a successful search:

```
          pstmt = conn.prepareStatement(  sqlSelect,
                                 ResultSet.TYPE_SCROLL_INSENSITIVE,
                                 ResultSet.CONCUR_READ_ONLY);

      pstmt.setString(1, query);
      pstmt.setString(2, query);
      try {
          rs = pstmt.executeQuery();
      } catch (SQLException e) {
          e.printStackTrace();
          return false;
      }
      time = System.currentTimeMillis() - start;
      return true;
  }
```

Replacing Tags

When we display an overview of the search results, we may want to remove all HTML tags from the headline and message excerpt, since they might interfere with our own tags. For example, if we want to have all the headers link to the full version of the message, we would have to remove all possible links in the header before we can insert our own links. In addition, since we display only an extract of long messages, we must remove all tags from the message body. Otherwise we might accidentally cut an excerpt that ends in the middle of some HTML tag, which could produce strange results for the rest of the page (for example, not including an </a> tag in the excerpt, would cause the rest of the page to be active as a link to the same page that the previous <a> tag pointed to).

Therefore, we implement a couple of methods for extracting tags and replacing substrings in the message content. First, the replace() method returns a String that is the String base, with all occurrences of strOut replaced with strIn:

```
    private String replace ( String base,String strOut,String strIn ) {
        if (base.equals("") || strOut.equals("") ) {
            return base;
        }

        StringBuffer strBufBase = new StringBuffer(base);
        String check = new String();
        int j = 0;
        while(j < (strBufBase.length() - strOut.length() + 1) ) {

            check = strBufBase.substring(j, j+ strOut.length());

            if( check.equalsIgnoreCase(strOut) ) {
                strBufBase.replace(j, j+ strOut.length(),strIn);
                j += (strIn.length() - 1);
            }
            j++;
        }

        return strBufBase.toString();
    }
```

Secondly, we define the `removeTags()` method, which takes a `String` input and returns the same `String`, with all HTML tags removed. This method makes use of the previous `replace()` method in tag replacing:

```
private String removeTags (String str ) {
    String temp = str;
    int start, end;
    while( ((start=temp.indexOf('<')) != -1) &&
            ((end=temp.indexOf('>',start)) != -1) ) {
        temp = replace(temp,temp.substring(start,end+1),"");
    }
    return temp;
}
```

Fetching the Search Results

When we have executed the search, we may fetch any of the search results with an appropriate call to the `get()` methods of the `ResultSet`. For that purpose we define a number of methods that each return a certain part of the `ResultSet`. Each of these methods takes an integer index as input and jumps to the corresponding row of the `ResultSet` (if it isn't there already – note the use of the `current` variable) before calling an appropriate `get()` method. With this implementation, and because we defined the `ResultSet` scrollable, the search engine user can now scroll back and forth in the search results.

```
public String getMessage( int index ) throws SQLException {
    if ( current != index ) {
        rs.absolute(index);
        current = index;
    }
    String msg = rs.getString("text");

    // Cut an excerpt of the message body.
    // Take the first 50 characters plus the
    // number of characters to the next space.
    if ( msg.length() >= 50 ) {
        msg = msg.substring(0, msg.indexOf(" ",49)) + " ...";
    }
    return msg;
}

public String getHeader( int index ) throws SQLException {
    if ( current != index ) {
        rs.absolute(index);
        current = index;
    }
    return rs.getString("header");
}

public String getDate( int index ) throws SQLException {
    if ( current != index ) {
        rs.absolute(index);
        current = index;
    }
    return rs.getString("sdate");
}
```

```
        public String getAuthor( int index ) throws SQLException {
            if ( current != index ) {
                rs.absolute(index);
                current = index;
            }
            return rs.getString("author");
        }

        public int getMessageID( int index ) throws SQLException {
            if ( current != index ) {
                rs.absolute(index);
                current = index;
            }
            return rs.getInt("message");
        }

        public int getParent( int index ) throws SQLException {
            if ( current != index ) {
                rs.absolute(index);
                current = index;
            }
            return rs.getInt("parent");
        }

        public int getCategory( int index ) throws SQLException {
            if ( current != index ) {
                rs.absolute(index);
                current = index;
            }
            return rs.getInt("category");
        }
        public String getCategoryName( int index ) throws SQLException {
            if ( current != index ) {
                rs.absolute(index);
                current = index;
            }
            return rs.getString("catname");
        }
```

In addition to the methods above, which simply return the data from the messages, categories, and users tables, we define methods that return information on the search itself. For example, the getNumberOfResults() method returns the number of search results (it jumps to the last row and returns the index), getTime() returns the time (in seconds) that it took to search, and the getScore() method returns the score of the result in row number index of the ResultSet. However, since the interMedia score is probably of little value to the user, we define the getPercentage() method, which returns the percentage value of the score of the current row, compared with the score of the highest scoring message(s). That way, the highest scoring document gets a percentage rating of 100%, with lower scoring messages having percentage ratings below that.

```
        public int numberOfResults() throws SQLException {
            rs.last();
            return rs.getRow();
        }
```

```java
    public int getScore( int index ) throws SQLException {
        if ( current != index ) {
            rs.absolute(index);
            current = index;
        }
        return rs.getInt("scr");
    }

    public int getPercentage( int index ) throws SQLException {

        // Determine the max score.
        if ( maxscore == 0 ) {
            rs.first();
            maxscore = rs.getInt("scr");
            rs.absolute(index);
        }
        return (100*getScore(index))/maxscore;
    }

    public float getSearchTime() {
        return (float) time/1000;
    }
```

Closing the Search Engine

When we have executed a search with the SearchEngine and are done with displaying the results, we must call close() in order to return the Connection instance back to the connection pool:

```java
    public void close() throws SQLException {

        if ( rs != null ) {
            rs.close();
            rs = null;
        }
        if ( pstmt != null ) {
            pstmt.close();
            pstmt = null;
        }
        if ( conn != null ) {
            conn.close();
            conn = null;
        }
    }

    protected void finalize() throws Throwable {
        close();
    }
}
```

In addition, we define the finalize() method for garbage collection, which does nothing but call close().

Example Client

We will end this chapter with an example of how to use our search engine implementation. This example will consist of a servlet, which serves the purpose of displaying the search form, executing search queries, and listing results. With a given input, the servlet might produce the following display:

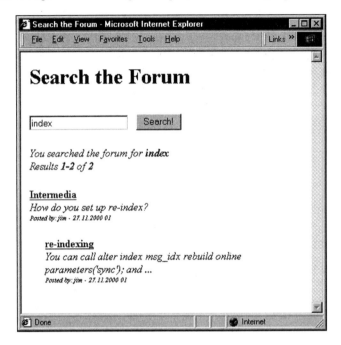

All the actual work of our servlet, which we simply call SearchServlet, is done through its doGet() method:

```
package forum.search;

import java.io.*;
import javax.servlet.*;
import javax.servlet.http.*;
import java.sql.*;

public class SearchServlet extends HttpServlet {

    protected void doGet( HttpServletRequest request,
                          HttpServletResponse response)
                    throws ServletException, IOException {
```

The doGet() method starts by defining the variables necessary for the search engine. The method gets an instance of the HttpSession object associated with the HttpServletRequest and reads from it the name of the connection pool being used for this application (we assume that the pool name has previously been added to the session). At this stage, we determine whether we have received a search phrase and a specified index of search results. If not, that means the user either entered a blank query or this is the first visit to the search page. In either case, this means no searching will be done for now.

```
SearchEngine engine = null;
ServletOutputStream out = null;
HttpSession session = request.getSession();

//***This is not necessary in the complete implementation.
//***The value would be set in the initial environment.
session.putValue("poolname","forum");

int start;
int end;
int results;
int index;
int lastMessage;
final int RESULTS_PER_PAGE = 10;

String search;
String poolname;

out = response.getOutputStream();
search = request.getParameter("search");
search = (search == null) ? "" : search;
try {
  start = Integer.parseInt(request.getParameter("start"));
} catch ( NumberFormatException e ) {
  start = 1;
}
index = start - 1;
lastMessage = -1;

poolname = (String) session.getValue("poolname");
```

Next, we print the opening HTML tags for the page and display the actual search form:

```
// Create the HTML page.
out.println("<html>");
out.println("<head>");
out.println("    <title>Search the Forum</title>");
out.println("</head>");
out.println("<body bgcolor=\"#FFFFFF\">");
out.println("<table width=\"400\" border=\"0\">");
out.println("<tr><td colspan=\"2\">");
out.println("<h1>Search the Forum</h1><br>");
out.print  ("<form name=\"searchform\" ");
//don't need action=URL to return to same servlet
out.println("method=\"GET\">");
out.print  ("<input type=\"text\" name=\"search\" length=\"20\" ");
out.println("value=\"" + search + "\">");
out.print  ("  <input type=\"button\" value=\"Search!\" ");
out.println("onClick=\"javascript:document.searchform.submit()\">");
out.println("<br><br>");
out.println("</tr>");
```

By now, we determine whether we should execute a search or not. As we have explained, we execute a search if we request a valid search phrase from the search form. If so, we instantiate the `SearchEngine` instance and call the `executeSearch()` method with the requested search phrase as the input. If the search is successful and the number of results above zero, we proceed.

Next, we determine the index of the last result we display for the current page. Special concern must be taken for the last results page, where we display a total of RESULTS_PER_PAGE + `results mod` RESULTS_PER_PAGE records (this is done because it looks weird to have just a couple of results on the last page).

If everything is well so far, we display the next RESULTS_PER_PAGE results (unless we are on the last page, as we have already mentioned), starting from the requested starting index. For each message, we display the message header, an excerpt from the message body, the name of the author and the date posted. We use the message header as a link to the full version of the message (in this example, we link to the `message.jsp` JSP page, which we implemented in an earlier chapter).

There is one thing to mention here: if we encounter a message that has for a parent the last message displayed, we choose to indent the child message, to further emphasize this parent-child relationship. For this purpose, we store the ID of the current message at the end of the output loop, to use in comparison with the parent message of the next result:

```
// Determine whether we had a search query.
if ( !search.trim().equals("") ) {
  try {

    // The database variables are added to the
    // session when the user first enters the forum.

    //engine = new SearchEngine(url,user,password); *********
    engine = new SearchEngine(poolname);
    if ( engine.executeSearch(search) && engine.numberOfResults()>0 ) {

      results = engine.numberOfResults();

      // This is the last page.
      if ( (results - results%RESULTS_PER_PAGE)-start
         < RESULTS_PER_PAGE ) {
        end = results;
      } else {
        end = start + RESULTS_PER_PAGE - 1;
      }

      out.println("<tr><td colspan=\"2\">");
      out.print  ("<i>You searched the forum for <b>");
      out.println( search + "</b></i><br>");
      out.print  ("<i>Results <b>" + start + "-" + end );
      out.println("</b> of <b>" + results + "</b></i><br><br>");
      out.println("</tr>");

      // Display the results for this page.
      while ( index++ < end ) {
        System.out.println("****************" + index);
```

```
                    // If the last message displayed is the parent
                    // of this message, we will indent it.
                    if ( lastMessage != -1 &&
                    engine.getParent(index) == lastMessage) {
                    out.println("<tr><td width=\"20\"> </td><td>");
                    } else {
                       out.println("<tr><td colspan=\"2\">");
                    }
                    out.print   ("<a href=\"message.jsp?message=" );
                    out.print   ( engine.getMessageID(index) );
                    out.print   ( "&category=" + engine.getCategory(index) );
                    out.println( "&name=" + engine.getCategoryName(index) );
                    out.print   ("\"><b>" + engine.getHeader(index) );
                    out.println("</b></a><br>");
                    out.println("<i>" + engine.getMessage(index) + "</i><br>");
                    out.print   ("<font size=\"1\"><i>Posted by: " );
                    out.println( engine.getAuthor(index) );
                    out.print   (" - " + engine.getDate(index) );
                    out.println("</i></font><br><br>");
                    out.println("</td></tr>");

                    // Store the ID of the last message.
                    lastMessage = engine.getMessageID(index);
                 }//while
```

When we have listed all the results for this particular page, we print a list of links to all the available result pages, as well as to the pages immediately before and after the current page. Note that we do this only if there is more than one page, as it would be rather pointless otherwise.

```
                    // Display the overview of result pages.
                    if ( results > RESULTS_PER_PAGE ) {
                    out.println("<tr><td colspan=\"2\">");
                    if ( start > RESULTS_PER_PAGE ) {
                       out.print   ("<a href=\"/servlet/SearchServlet?search=" );
                       out.print   ( search +"&start=" + (start-RESULTS_PER_PAGE) );
                       out.println( "\">Previous</a> ");
                    }

                    // Only display the page number if there are more than one page.
                    if ( results > 2*RESULTS_PER_PAGE-1 ) {
                       for ( int i=0; i < (int)results/RESULTS_PER_PAGE; i++ ) {

                          // Boldface the current page.
                          if ( (i*RESULTS_PER_PAGE + 1) == start ) {
                            out.print("<b>" + (i+1) + "</b>  ");
                          } else {
                             out.print("<a href=\"/servlet/SearchServlet?search=" );
                             out.print( search +"&start=" );
                             out.print( (1 + i*RESULTS_PER_PAGE) + "\">" );
                             out.println((i+1) + "</a>  ");
                          }
                       }//for
                    if ( results > end ) {
                       //You need to ensure this is pointing at this servlet.
```

```
                    out.print("<a href=\"/servlet/SearchServlet?search=" );
                    out.print( search +"&start=" + (start+RESULTS_PER_PAGE) );
                    out.println( "\">Next</a> ");
                }
            }//if
            out.println("</td></tr>");
        }//if
    } else {
        out.println("<tr><td colspan=\"2\">");
        out.println("<i>No messages were found to match your query</i><br>");
        out.println("</tr>");
    }//if
```

Finally, when we have displayed all the search results, we call the `close()` method of the
`SearchEngine` instance. We then end this method by closing the necessary HTML tags:

```
        // Close the search engine.
        //engine.close();      ***************
    } catch ( SQLException e ) {
        e.printStackTrace();
        out.println(e.getMessage());
        return;
    }
    finally {
        try {
            engine.close();
        }
        catch (Exception ignore) {
            ignore.printStackTrace();
            out.println(ignore.getMessage());
        }
    }


    // Close the page.
    out.println("</table>");
    out.println("</form>");
    out.println("</body>");
    out.println("</html>");
    }//if
    }//doGet
}
```

Summary

In this chapter, we have studied the implementation of a search engine using interMedia Text to index and query the database. To be more precise, we have:

- ❏ Defined a search syntax for the search engine, covering the requirements of the search capability including common phrases, required words, excluded words, section fields, and wildcards

- ❏ Implemented a query builder class and learned the benefits of splitting the search string to maximize the different forms of search words

- ❏ Implemented a search engine class, for executing and tracking the results of the search

- ❏ Created the search engine user interface using servlets, giving us a front-end to display the search form, execute queries, and list the search results

ORACLE8i APPLICATION PROGRAMMING

21

Oracle and XML

The use of XML to mark up data is becoming increasingly widespread. It is being used across all development tiers; from data storage to data transport and display and – crucially – it can be used in conjunction with many other programming languages (basically any language that you can write a parser for), including Java and PL/SQL.

The chapters in this section will cover some practical demonstrations of the use of XML in Oracle enterprise applications, including its role in application data exchange in and its use in conjunction with XSLT to publish data in an enterprise integration scenario (Chapter 22).

In this chapter, however, we will concentrate on what constitutes Oracle's core support for XML: the Oracle XML Developer's Kit (XDK). This is a set of tools and libraries for parsing XML documents, and generating XML programmatically from database queries, or from other XML documents. Most of the functionality provided is based on Java, but there is also support for PL/SQL and C++. In our examples we will concentrate on Java and PL/SQL, as these XML components are available on all Oracle platforms. The XDK is available as a collection of free downloads from the Oracle Technology Network at http://technet.oracle.com: each component is distinguished by base language, version, and specific function and forms a separate, self-contained archive, which is downloaded individually. A free registration is required before any of the libraries can be downloaded. At the time of writing, the XML components are found at http://technet.oracle.com/tech/xml. Also included in the kit are the Oracle XML SQL utility and the XSQL Servlet.

We will start this chapter with a discussion of the different ways of parsing an XML document using the Oracle XDK: we'll look at the two main programming interfaces, the Document Object Model (DOM), and the Simple API for XML (SAX), and we'll see where DTDs and Schemas fit into the picture.

We will then look at the higher-level interfaces for querying and manipulating XML documents: in particular, the XPath query language and the XSLT transformation language that uses it.

As one might expect, a particular feature of the Oracle XDK is the mechanisms it uses to integrate XML processing with the relational world of SQL. We will look in particular at the XSQL tool for bridging between these two worlds.

This will then equip us to look at the role of XML in designing distributed applications. In particular, we'll discuss the pros and cons of using XML as the mechanism for communication between applications versus Java mechanisms such as remote invocation and serialization, and the conventional SQL-based JDBC mechanisms. We will also look at the role of JavaServer Pages and see how they can be combined with other tools. In particular, we will see the various ways in which XSLT-based transformations can be integrated into a multi-tier application.

Finally, we will review the Transviewer JavaBeans provided with the Oracle XDK that enable all this functionality to be built into a component-based application.

XML Parsers

Oracle provide several XML parsers, which are available for C, C++, Java and PL/SQL languages:

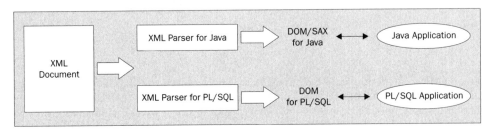

We will only be concentrating on the PL/SQL, and Java parsers. These parsers are provided as components suitable for incorporation within your own application, where they provide "black box" XML parsing functionality. There are two PL/SQL parsers that are suitable for use from stored procedures. The first requires the Java capability of Oracle 8*i*, as it is a "wrapper" around the Java functionality making it available from stored procedures. The second is a pure PL/SQL DOM parser, which is compatible with Oracle version 7.3.4 and above, but this is much more limited in functionality. The Java and C++ parsers support both DOM (Document Object Model) and SAX (Simple API for XML) interfaces. The parsers being used in this book are version 2, but beta releases of version 2.1 have been made available recently. The version 2 parsers support DOM 1.0 and SAX 1.0, but the new parsers will support DOM 2.0 and SAX 2.0.

DOM parsers load the entire XML document into the memory, building and maintaining a hierarchical data structure. This tree structure is made up of objects representing the elements identified in the source XML by XML tags, with the text content forming the leaves on the branches. A SAX parser, by contrast, reads the document from top to bottom and reports every tag as it is encountered to the application. It does this by means of events that the application traps by registering a call-back function for each type of event, such as start of element and end of element.

The Java parsers run on any platform on which a Java Runtime Environment version 1.1.6 or higher is available, including within Oracle 8*i*'s JVM (JServer) environment. The C/C++ parsers are only available for Windows (95, 98, NT, or 2000), Solaris, or GNU/Linux. The C++ parser is supplied in the form of a pre-compiled library, and because of incompatibility between method signature conventions to support function overloading, can only be used with the C++ compiler with which it was created (on Solaris this is Sun Pro C++, so the class library cannot be used with GNU G++).

Parsing XML

An XML parser is a self-contained library, providing functionality to an application, for analyzing an XML document, and storing it as a tree structure in memory (DOM) or generating a stream of events (SAX). DOM APIs allow the entire document to be accessed and manipulated by the application, whereas SAX presents a serial view, and is therefore is more useful for applications loading the data into some other structure, for example processing a third party news feed and integrating it into an Oracle database for use within a web site.

Oracle's XML parsers support version 1.0 of the DOM and SAX specifications, plus the XML Namespace standard, allowing XML elements to be distinguished in a similar way to Java classes. This means that even if different developers choose the same name for a tag, there will be no collision, and other developers can mix libraries from different vendors when reusing code, without overloading definitions. This feature has been seen in the use of XML tags prefixed `<xsl:...>`. The parsers can operate in either validating or non-validating mode, but in both cases will only operate with well-formed documents. The difference is that in **validating mode**, the document will be checked to ensure that it conforms with its associated Document Type Definition (DTD), for example to verify that all the elements that are used have been declared, and that all required attributes of an element are present.

This chapter relies on the XML Parser for Java version 2, downloaded from OTN as `xmlparserv2.jar`. This file must be added to the classpath whenever it is used in an application (for information on classpath, see Appendix B). The URL is http://technet.oracle.com/tech/xml.

Running the Oracle XML Parser

You can run the Oracle XML parser from the command line to verify the validity of an XML document. To validate an XML document enter:

```
C:\xml>java oracle.xml.parser.v2.oraxml -v -w recipe.xml
```

The output of this validation should be:

```
The input file parsed without errors
```

Parsing with SAX

A SAX parser does not transform the textual XML document into a data structure in memory, instead it calls a function registered by the user every time an event occurs. A typical event is the start or end of an element, and events occur sequentially as the document is read from the beginning to the end. These events are handled in Java by a class that implements the SAX `DocumentHandler` interface (or `ContentHandler` in the case of SAX2). A convenient way to write a `DocumentHandler` is to extend the `HandlerBase` class, provided with the parser, which defines methods to be called for each type of event, and within each implemented method the developer must decide which event of that type was received, and process it accordingly.

While the `DocumentHandler` interface notifies the events that most applications need to know about, such as elements, attributes, and text, there are other interfaces to provide lower-level information such as comments, CDATA sections, and entity boundaries. `HandlerBase` implements all four interfaces, providing a default "do nothing" method for each event. This means that when you write a subclass of `HandlerBase`, you only need to implement the methods for the events in which your application is interested. However, if you prefer, you can implement the interfaces directly rather than extending this class.

Interface	Description
EntityResolver	Provides an interface for handling external entities. By default, HandlerBase returns null for this interface's methods, so the parser uses the system handler. It allows entity resolution to be intercepted prior to parsing and directed to an alternative source under program control.
DTDHandler	Provides an interface for handling events related to entities within the DTD, that cannot be parsed. The application can then provide logic for processing the entity. The default behavior is to ignore them. Unusually, the parser reports these in an undefined order, rather than in the order in which they were declared, but always between events for the start of a document, and the first element event.
DocumentHandler	This is the main interface for parsing and handling a stream of SAX events. For each type of event, the corresponding method is implemented to provide the application-specific functionality. Examples of these are events for opening and closing element tags, character data within elements, "ignorable white space" (the white space between tags which the DTD says is insignificant), and XML processing instructions. Once a method has been called and has returned, parsing will continue until the end of the document, at which point the application will be notified.
ErrorHandler	Provides an interface for handling exceptions if the application wishes to do so. If it is used, the parser will generate events to be handled by methods implemented from this interface, instead of throwing exceptions for warnings and errors. If this interface is implemented, errors and warnings will be ignored by default. However, encountering a fatal error will still cause an exception to be thrown (a fatal error is anything that causes the document not to be "well formed"). This provides the opportunity for throwing application-specific exceptions in response to particular errors and warnings, allowing sophisticated handling or recovery, for example for a violation of a range of values constraint.

Let's look at an example application that will use SAX to process the recipe.xml document below:

```
<?xml version='1.0' ?>
<snack>
    <recipe>
        <name>Chocolate Brownies</name>
        <ingredients>
            <item>
                <quantity>170g</quantity>
                <description>Flour</description>
                <supplier>Sainsburys</supplier>
            </item>
            <item>
                <quantity>1 box of</quantity>
                <description>Eggs</description>
                <supplier>Tesco</supplier>
            </item>
        </ingredients>
        <method>
```

```
        <step>
            <number>1</number>
            <task>Preheat the Oven for</task>
            <time>40 mins</time>
            <preheat>at 200C</preheat>
        </step>
    </method>
</recipe>
<recipe>
    <name>Blueberry Muffins</name>
    <ingredients>
        <item><quantity>1 cup</quantity>
            <description>Blueberries</description>
            <supplier>Sainsburys</supplier>
        </item>
        <item>
            <quantity>2 cups</quantity>
            <description>sugar</description>
            <supplier>Safeway</supplier>
        </item>
    </ingredients>
    <method>
        <step>
            <number>1</number>
            <task>Preheat the Oven for</task>
            <time>40 mins</time>
            <preheat>at 200C</preheat>
        </step>
    </method>
</recipe>
</snack>
```

Here is the `SAXRecipe.java` class that extends the `HandlerBase` class. In this example this class serves two functions: it fires off the parser and it receives notification of the parsing events. It's common to combine these functions, though they can be done in separate classes if you prefer.

```java
import java.io.*;
import java.net.*;
import oracle.xml.parser.v2.*;
import org.xml.sax.*;

public class SAXRecipe extends HandlerBase {
    private boolean outputchars = false;

    /** Constructor method, performs the majority of the logic
     * of this class. Registers itself with the SAX parser to
     * handle events, then tells the parser to begin. From then
     * on, the parser takes control and the registered callback
     * events are simply invoked as and when events occur.
     */

    public SAXRecipe (String filename) throws SAXException, IOException {
        File xmlfile = new File(filename);
        FileReader xmlreader = new FileReader(xmlfile);
```

```
        SAXParser saxp = new SAXParser();
        saxp.setEntityResolver(this);
        saxp.setDTDHandler(this);
        saxp.setDocumentHandler(this);
        saxp.setErrorHandler(this);

        saxp.parse(xmlreader);
    }

    /** This method will be invoked every time a new
     * document is handed to the parser for processing.
     * note that the start of a document is not the same
     * thing as the event triggered when the document element is
     * parsed.
     */

    public void startDocument() {
        System.out.print("I'm hungry! ");
    }

    /** The method called when an element (which may be the document
     * element) starts. Within this method, decide what to do with
     * it
     */

    public void startElement(String element, AttributeList al)
                        throws SAXException {
        outputchars = false;

        if (element.equals("recipe"))
            System.out.print("Let's bake some ");
        else if (element.equals("name"))
            outputchars = true;
        else if (element.equals("ingredients"))
            System.out.println("We'll need:");
        else if (element.equals("item"))
            System.out.print("* ");
        else if (element.equals("quantity"))
            outputchars = true;
        else if (element.equals("description")) {
            System.out.print(" of ");
            outputchars = true;
        } else if (element.equals("supplier")) {
            System.out.print(" from ");
            outputchars = true;
        } else if (element.equals("method"))
            System.out.println("And here's the method:");
        else if (element.equals("number"))
            outputchars = true;
        else if (element.equals("task"))
            outputchars = true;
    }
```

The following method is called every time the end of an element is encountered. This will typically be an end tag such as </item>; but when an empty element tag such as <br/> is encountered, the parser notifies two events, a start element event and an end element event. In theory you could work out what the element name is, because tags will always occur in pairs, but the name is supplied as a parameter to save you the trouble:

```
    public void endElement(String element) throws SAXException {
        if (element.equals("name"))
            System.out.println(".");
        else if (element.equals("ingredients"))
            System.out.println();
        else if (element.equals("method"))
            System.out.println();
        else if (element.equals("number"))
            System.out.print(". ");
    }
```

Now we provide a method to handle the character data that occurs between the tags:

```
    /** This method is called for the contents of every element.
     * (pcdata means parsed character data, like in the DTD).
     * note that it doesn't natively deal with String
     */

    public void characters(char[] pcdata, int start, int length) {
        if (outputchars)
            System.out.print(new String(pcdata, start, length));
    }
```

and finally a method to be called when the end of the document is reached:

```
    /** called when the document is fully parsed and there are
     * no more events
     */

    public void endDocument() throws SAXException {
        System.out.println("Now it's time to eat!");
    }
```

Because this is just an example, we'll provide a main() method so the program can be called from the command line:

```
    public static void main (String[] args) {
        try {
            if (args.length != 1)
                System.err.println("Usage: java SAXRecipe <filename>");
            else
                new SAXRecipe(args[0]);
        } catch (IOException ioe) {
            System.err.println("Could not read " + args[0]);
        } catch (SAXException saxe) {
            System.err.println("Could not parse " + args[0]);
        }
    }
}
```

The example is invoked in the usual manner:

```
C:\Documents\xmldev>javac SAXRecipe.java
C:\Documents\xmldev>java SAXRecipe recipe.xml
```

The output is as shown below:

```
I'm hungry! Let's bake some Chocolate Brownies.
We'll need:
* 170g of Flour from Sainsburys* 1 box of of Eggs from Tesco
And here's the method:
1. Preheat the Oven for
Let's bake some Blueberry Muffins.
We'll need:
* 1 cup of Blueberries from Sainsburys* 2 cups of sugar from Safeway
And here's the method:
1. Preheat the Oven for
Now it's time to eat!
```

Parsing with the DOM

The DOM interface can be used to load, manipulate, then save an XML document, or to extract data from it into a new XML document. Manipulation includes adding and removing elements and changing the content of elements. The DOM parser is used to actually build the data structure, but is not involved in manipulating the structure after that, as the document is an object in its own right (of type `XMLDocument`) with its own methods and properties. This means that once a document has been parsed, the DOM objects created are used to query the document relative to the root node, without relying on the parser itself. The document consists of instances of the `Node` class, and its subclasses. A node may have child nodes, but these need not necessarily be subclasses of it, although they are often of type `Element`, which inherits from `Node`. These may have children, apart from `Text` nodes, which may not, and an exception will be raised if an attempt is made to add a child to a text node. `Text` extends `CharacterData` and `Node`, and represents the content of an element or attribute.

The `Node` class provides most of the methods for inserting and removing child nodes (or elements). `Element` objects may have attributes (that is, XML attributes, rather than attributes in the object-oriented sense, which are usually referred to as properties when speaking of Java) and these are retrieved by name as instances of `String`. However, attributes may also be manipulated by the `Attr` class, which gives greater flexibility in cases that contain entity references. A `NodeList` is an ordered collection of `Node` objects, indexed by an integer key, and a `NamedNodeMap` is a collection of nodes keyed to node name, similar to the `Hashtable` in the core Java classes.

In our example, we will load an XML document and then add a node to it, before performing other functions. The XML fragment `fragment.xml` (which will be merged into the main `recipe.xml` document) is as follows:

```xml
<?xml version = "1.0"?>
<item>
    <quantity>200g</quantity>
    <description>Self Raising Flour</description>
    <supplier>Safeway</supplier>
</item>
```

And here is the code `DOMAPIExample.java` that will merge `fragment.xml` as a child element into our parent document:

```java
import java.io.*;
import org.xml.sax.*;
import org.w3c.dom.*;
import oracle.xml.parser.v2.*;

/** This example will load two files from the disk, one containing an
  * XML document, and one containing a fragment of XML forming an element
  * of the first file. A new document will be formed from these two parts,
  * and this document saved to disk.
  */

public class DOMAPIExample {
    private File          file;
    private FileReader    fr;
    private XMLDocument   maindoc;
    private XMLDocument   fragmentdoc;
    private XMLDocument   newdoc;
    private DOMParser     parser;

    /** create a parser, and load both the documents from the disk. then
      * extract a node from the fragment document, and add it to the
      * main document, before writing out the result.
      */

    public DOMAPIExample(String main, String fragment)
                throws SAXException, IOException, FileNotFoundException,
                       XMLParseException, XSLException {

        /** create a new parser, which will be reused */
        parser = new DOMParser();
        parser.setValidationMode(false);
        parser.setPreserveWhitespace(false);

        /** load in the two files, and create XMLDocument objects for DOM */
        file = new File(main);
        fr = new FileReader(file);
        parser.parse(fr);
        maindoc = parser.getDocument();

        file = new File(fragment);
        fr = new FileReader(file);
        parser.parse(fr);
        fragmentdoc = parser.getDocument();

        /** Find the parent element of the item structure within the
          * main document, and the root node (also item) in the fragment.
          */
        XMLNode mainxn = (XMLNode)maindoc.selectSingleNode(
                                            "/snack/recipe/ingredients");
        XMLNode fragxn = (XMLNode)fragmentdoc.getDocumentElement();
```

Attempting now to use an API call such as `mainxn.appendChild(fragxn)` will fail, because you cannot add a node created from one document to a node that is a member of another document. It will result in an `XMLDOMException` being thrown. Therefore, we loop through the contents of each node (we know that they are semantically and syntactically the same) and copy the values of the fragment node into a clone of the node extracted from the main document. This cloned node can then be inserted back into the parent document. The parameter to `cloneNode` ensures that child elements will also be copied:

```java
XMLNode clone = (XMLNode)mainxn.cloneNode(true);
NodeList nl = fragxn.getChildNodes();

for (int i = 0; i <nl.getLength(); i++) {
    Node node = nl.item(i);

    /** The first child is a node of type Text */
    String value = node.getFirstChild().getNodeValue();

    /** Now find the matching node in the clone and reset its value */
    NodeList clonenode = clone.selectNodes("//"+node.getNodeName());

    /** We are assuming that the fragment and the main document share
     * a common structure - if not this will fail with an exception.
     */
    clonenode.item(0).getFirstChild().setNodeValue(value);
}

/** Now we can safely insert the new node into the parent structure */
mainxn.appendChild(clone);
maindoc.print(System.out);
}

public static void main(String[] args) {
    try {
        if (args.length != 2)
            System.err.println(
                        "Usage: java DOMAPIExample<input file> <fragment>");
        else
            new DOMAPIExample(args[0], args[1]);
    } catch (Exception e) {
        e.printStackTrace();
    }
}
}
```

The example may be executed as follows:

```
C:\xml>javac DOMAPIExample.java
C:\xml>java DOMAPIExample recipe.xml fragment.xml
```

The output to the console will be the XML file with the fragment inserted.

Parsing with a DTD

From the structure of the document used in these examples, we can see that a <snack> can contain a <recipe>, which has one <name>, one <ingredients> element, and one <method>. The <ingredients> element consists of one or more <item> elements, each of which contains one <quantity>, one <description>, and one <supplier>. A <method> contains one or more <step> elements, each of which contains one <number> defining the order in which the step is to be performed, and one <task> stating what needs to be done at that time.

This structure can be defined formally in a Document Type Definition, or DTD. For this structure, a snack.DTD can be defined as follows:

```
<!ELEMENT snack (recipe+)>
<!ELEMENT recipe (name,ingredients,method)>
   <!ELEMENT name (#PCDATA)>
   <!ELEMENT ingredients (item+)>
      <!ELEMENT item (quantity,description,supplier)>
      <!ELEMENT quantity (#PCDATA)>
      <!ELEMENT description (#PCDATA)>
      <!ELEMENT supplier (#PCDATA)>
   <!ELEMENT method (step+)>
      <!ELEMENT step (number,task,time,preheat)>
         <!ELEMENT number (#PCDATA)>
         <!ELEMENT task (#PCDATA)>
         <!ELEMENT time (#PCDATA)>
         <!ELEMENT preheat (#PCDATA)>
```

The DTD is conventionally referenced in the DOCTYPE tag of the document itself, as in <!DOCTYPE snack SYSTEM "snack.DTD">. The DOCTYPE directive resides between the XML declaration and the beginning of the document proper. The Oracle XML parser can be used to validate that the document conforms to all the rules defined in its DTD. This can be done either using the oraxml command line utility, or by invoking a Java class that is available if the xmlparserv2.jar file is within the classpath. This will parse the document, and output warnings when undeclared or inconsistent syntax is used:

```
C:\xml>java oracle.xml.parser.v2.oraxml -v -w recipe.xml
```

Parsing with an XML Schema

An XML schema is an alternative to DTDs, and it is widely expected that it will supersede the DTD as the formal definition of a well-formed and semantically intact document for advanced data exchange applications in which the validity of data types and their ranges must be ensured. There are several reasons for this. Firstly, the schema represents the structure of the document as an XML document in its own right, rather than using a separate construct, namely the DTD. Another reason is that it provides much richer definition of the data types occurring in the XML document: for example, a schema can define the range of values in a numeric field, or it can constrain a particular element to contain a valid date.

This approach means that the definition of the document can itself be manipulated using the same tools (for example, DOM parsers and XSLT) that are used to manipulate the XML document that it defines. However, the most important advantage schemas have over DTDs is that now the developer can impose constraints on the XML document before they even get to Oracle for insertion, reducing the probability of failure at this stage. Using a schema means less error-checking code is required within applications, since the #PCDATA in a DTD can contain almost any data. Schema validation can be made very strict or very flexible and is a valuable addition to relying on triggers or a combination of constraints and SQL*Loader scripts when importing from a foreign source.

In addition, if XML is being stored directly in an interMedia database, the schema is the best way to validate it, since using either database constraints or programmatic rules would necessitate decomposing the document first.

XML Schema is a relatively new addition to the XML range of standards, and this is reflected in the Oracle product set. The Oracle XML schema processor can validate XML schemas, but at this time cannot generate them from DTDs, nor from well-formed documents. In addition, it does not generate Oracle schemas from XML schemas. An Oracle schema is constructed from tables of rows and columns related by foreign keys, whereas an XML schema is a formal and detailed definition of a hierarchical data structure and it's valid contents, expressed in an XML document. This functionality is currently not expected to be incorporated in a future release.

This component of the XDK is downloadable from http://technet.oracle.com/tech/xml/schema_java. The file xschema.jar must then be added to the classpath. The download also contains a copy of the XML Parser version 2, which is also required to be in the classpath.

A document that conforms to a particular schema is referred to as an **instance document** of that schema, borrowing the jargon from the object-oriented world. An instance document is generally composed either of complex elements, which have hierarchically structured child elements, or of simple elements, which simply contain an item of data. Further detail on difference between the simple and complex types may be found in the XML primer in Appendix C.

Complex types may be nested. The parser does not require that a complex type be defined before being used, although the definition must occur later in the document. This allows for the earlier parts of the document to describe the entire document in a high-level, abstract fashion, with the details added later, a style often used in programming languages.

The schema language defines data types, which are represented textually (as a sequence of ASCII or Unicode characters) but which must conform to rules for that data type, for example a date, or a floating point number. Simple types are built into the schema specification, and others are derived from them. These types are used to ensure the correct parsing of times and dates (unique instants, durations of time, regularly recurring times) and numeric values. In the same way that Oracle stored procedures allow developers to derive more restricted data types from the basic number, XML Schema can parse decimals, integers, double precision floating point numbers, and other combinations. The following data types are defined natively to XML Schema:

Family	Types
XML 1.0 Entities	ID, IDREF, IDREFS, ENTITY, ENTITIES, NOTATION, LANGUAGE, NMTOKEN, NMTOKENS, name, Qname, NCname.
	All of these types are defined in the XML 1.0 specification, and provide XML schema with a means of ensuring validity of elements within XML that refer to other XML documents, original or target languages, addresses, etc. These should only be used within attributes, otherwise the document will not conform to XML 1.0.
Numeric	float, double, decimal, integer, non-positive-integer, negative-integer, positive-integer, long, int, short, byte, unsigned-long, unsigned-int, unsigned-short, unsigned-byte.
	Non-positive and negative integers differ in that a negative integer cannot be zero, but a non-positive can. Similarly, a positive-integer must be greater than zero. The other numeric types are very similar to the types found in C or Java.

Family	Types
Time and Date	`date` – of the form YYYY-MM-DD, where month ranges from 1 to 12. XML Schema will not validate dates beyond their syntax.
	`time` – of the form HH:MM:SS.mmm-ZZ:00 to millisecond precision, where ZZ represents the difference in hours between GMT and the local time zone.
	`timeInstant` – a full date and a time, separated by the character 'T'.
	`timeDuration` – this format specifies the length of the time span, in terms of years(Y) , months(M), days(D), hours(H), minutes(M) and seconds(S), prefixed by a 'P', then a number, then Y (specifying years), a number then M, etc. Between the years, months and days, there is a 'T' before the hours minutes and seconds. Therefore, a fully formed `timeDuration` would be `P0Y0M0DT0H40M0S`, signifying 40 minutes (for example, a baking time).
Others	`String` – a string of alphanumeric and punctuation characters.
	`Boolean` – true or false.
	`Binary` – a string of "1" and "0" – not Base64 encoded binary data.
Patterns	A pattern is a regular expression describing the formation of a string of characters in terms of specifying the order in which types of characters (for example, numbers, or capital letters) should appear, and the location and type of delineation and separation. They are derived from the `string` type. For example, in the `<quantity>` section of the recipe XML document, a new type can be defined of "one or more numbers followed by a space, then one or more letters", allowing values such as '100 grams' or '2 tablespoons'.
Enumerations	An enumeration, like a List of Values (LOV) in Oracle Developer/2000, lists all the values that a string is permitted to have. In the example, it will be used to constrain the `<supplier>` to one of the major supermarkets.
Facets	Patterns and Enumerations are both "facets" – attributes used to constrain the simple data types. The other facets include length, minlength, maxlength, precision and scale.

The XML schema class is unusual in the XDK in that the developer does not instantiate or make method calls to it directly. Rather, it is used by the regular XML parser when an XSD directive is encountered while processing a document. XSD is an XML schema definition, and namespaces are covered in the XML appendix. Therefore, even though an application, which requires XSD validation, will compile without being imported or mentioned, the file `xschema.jar` must be in the classpath at run time.

```
import  java.io.*;
import  oracle.xml.parser.v2.*;
import  org.xml.sax.*;

public class CheckSchema {

    /** Note the call to the setSchemaValidationMode() method which
     * is inherited from XMLParser, the parent class of DOMParser.
     * other then that, simply create a stream and parse it, as in
     * previous examples. this constructor is used when a reference
```

```
 * to the XSD is made within the XML document. There is no interface,
 * unlike the XSL processors, for specifying the XML and XSD (XML
 * Schema Definition) files separately - although there is a
 * setXMLSchema() method in XMLParser, there aren't the constructors
 * or methods in the oracle.xml.parser.schema.XMLSchema class to
 * allow the developer use of it.
 */

public CheckSchema(String xmlfilename) throws SAXException, IOException {

    File xmlfile = new File(xmlfilename);
    FileReader xmlreader = new FileReader(xmlfile);
    DOMParser parser = new DOMParser();
    parser.setValidationMode(false);
    parser.setSchemaValidationMode(true);
    parser.parse(xmlreader);
}

/** check the command line arguments, then instantiate the class
 * friendlier exception handling, describing to the user the problem
 */

public static void main (String[] args) {
    try {
        if (args.length != 1)
            System.err.println("Usage: java CheckSchema <xml>");
        else
            new CheckSchema(args[0]);
    } catch (FileNotFoundException fnfe) {
        System.err.println("Could not find file '" + args[0] + "'");
    } catch (SAXException sae) {
        System.err.println("Invalid XML in " + args[0]);
    } catch (Exception e) {
        e.printStackTrace();
    }
}
}
```

The recipe.xml file – in order to reference an XML schema – requires the following modification to the first snack tag:

```
<snack xmlns:xsd = "http://www.w3.org/1999/XMLSchema/instance"
    xsd:schemaLocation = "recipe.xsd">
```

Compare the XML Schema of a recipe with the DTD used for the class generator example earlier in the chapter. Although it is still decomposed hierarchically in the same way, each element can now be validated. The following is available as recipe.xsd for download from the Wrox web site (www.wrox.com):

```
<?xml version = "1.0"?>
<schema xmlns = "http://www.w3.org/1999/XMLSchema">

<complexType name = "snack">
    <sequence>
        <element name = "name" type = "string"/>
        <element name = "ingredients" type = "ingredientsType"/>
        <element name = "method" type = "methodType"/>
    </sequence>
</complexType>
```

```
<complexType name = "ingredientsType">
   <element name = "item" type = "itemType"/>
</complexType>

<complexType name = "itemType">
   <sequence>
      <element name = "quantity" type = "quantityType"/>
      <element name = "description" type = "string"/>
      <element name = "supplier" type = "supplierType"/>
   </sequence>
</complexType>

<simpleType name = "quantityType" base = "string">
   <pattern value = "/d+ [A-Za-z]+"/>
</simpleType>

<simpleType name = "supplierType" base = "string">
   <enumeration value = "Tesco"/>
   <enumeration value = "Sainsburys"/>
   <enumeration value = "Safeway"/>
</simpleType>

<complexType name = "methodType">
   <element name = "step" type = "stepType"/>
</complexType>

<complexType name = "stepType">
   <sequence>
      <element name = "number" type = "positive-integer">
      <element name = "task" type = "string">
      </sequence>
   </complexType>
</schema>
```

To verify the `recipes.xml` document against the `recipe.xsd` schema, for example, before processing into a database application, run the application from the command line:

```
C:\xml>java CheckSchema recipes.xml
```

Output will only be displayed in the event of an error occurring, either in one of the input files (if they are not found, or are not valid XML) in the form of an exception, or as a description in textual form if the schema is violated.

XML Query and Transformation

It isn't possible to use SQL to query an XML document directly, because the hierarchical Data model of XML is so different from the relational (tabular) model assumed by SQL.

A number of query languages for XML have been proposed, but the one that has gained the widest acceptance to date is XPath, a syntax that relies heavily on addressing nodes in the hierarchic structure using path expressions that are rather similar to the hierarchic filenames used in most operating systems. XPath is a standard defined by the World Wide Web Consortium(W3C) for addressing parts of a document. It is used in XSLT, the XML transformation language, which we will examine in the next section, and in XPointer, the standard for hyperlinking between documents.

XPath, Xpointer, and XLink (XML Link Language) are designed to avoid the inherent fragility of referring to subsections of HTML (or XML) documents using HREF anchors. There is always a possibility when you refer to a place in a document that when the document is updated, the reference will be wrong or meaningless. XPath syntax, which is used within XPointer, gives you a choice of referring to places by content (The section whose title is "Introduction") by position (The third bullet in section 2.4), by structure (The <glossary> element), or any combination of these. The syntax doesn't rely on any special anchors, like the HTML <A> tag, being present in the document to which you are referring.

XSLT is the W3C's transformation language for XML. Its primary purpose is to define transformations of one XML tree structure into another, but it also allows the result tree to be written out in other formats, such as HTML (which is probably the most common usage), comma-separated values, or other text-based formats such as EDI messages or PDF files. As more and more documents on the Web begin to be stored in XML as their native format, XSLT will likely be the method used to transform these documents from data-centric XML representations into presentation-friendly XHTML or WML representations, and into other XML vocabularies required by other applications. Within XSLT, the node selection language used is XPath – this language allows specific nodes or values to be selected from the source XML document for manipulation and presentation. We'll now describe the XPath and XSLT languages and give some examples of their use.

XPath

Once a well-formed and deeply nested XML document has been created, we would of course like to exploit this structure to navigate to or pinpoint a certain element of interest. For example, we might want to start drilling down from `Statement Request`, to `BankAccount`, to `AccountID` in order to get at the data associated with an `AccountID`. Xpath is designed to enable such **hierarchical traversal** or **navigation** to target specific elements, attributes, text fragments, etc.

XPath is syntax for expressing traversal paths. Its syntax is quite similar to the hierarchical directory traversal syntax familiar to command-line users of UNIX or DOS, though with one rather fundamental difference: UNIX and DOS filenames identify individual files, whereas many XML elements can have the same name. For example, to identify the `AccountID` in the Bank Statement example from the XML appendix, we would use the following XPath expression:

```
StatementRequest/BankAccount/AccountID
```

This expression might identify a single element in the document, but in general, it will identify all the `AccountID`s that are within a `BankAccount` that is within a `StatementRequest`. In XPath terminology, a **path** is a series of steps to a target location, and in general, it leads to a set of nodes. Like SQL, XPath deals with sets of nodes rather than individual ones. Paths may be **absolute** or **relative**. The starting point of an absolute path is the root node (the parent of the document element). An absolute path begins with the symbol /, indicating the root:

```
/StatementRequest/BankAccount/AccountID
```

A relative path, on the other hand, starts from an existing location in a document, referred to as the context node. For example:

```
account/address/postcode
```

identifies a `<postcode>` element within an `<address>` element within an `<account>` element that itself is within the context node.

The examples above all traverse down the hierarchy, but in fact, you can navigate in any direction. For example, given a context node, you can use the `..` construct to go to its parent. Given a `BankAccount`, the following XPath expression identifies the starting date of the recurring statement requested for this account:

```
../Recurrence/StartDate
```

When the names of all elements between the context element and the target are not known, the `*` symbol may be used to stand in for any element. Again, this notion is borrowed from traversal of directories in filing systems. So, if you know that there is an `AccountID` somewhere under `StatementRequest`, you can specify:

```
StatementRequest/*/AccountID
```

The `*` here represents a single element: the `AccountID` must be a grandchild of the `StatementRequest`. If you don't know how many levels you want to skip, you can use the '`//`' notation:

```
StatementRequest//AccountID
```

Whenever you say `AccountID` without qualification, that is:

```
AccountID
```

A relative path is assumed – in other words, it always refers to an `AccountID` element that is the child of the current element in context. You can also make this more explicit, using the `child::` notation:

```
child::AccountID
```

Similarly, the verbose `descendant-or-self::` notation can be used in place of `//` to find elements at any depth below the current element:

```
child::StatementRequest/descendant-or-self::node()/child::AccountID
```

The '`..`' notation, which is used to traverse up the hierarchy, is an abbreviation for '`parent::node()`'. Given the context of an `AccountID`, you can specify:

```
parent::node()/parent::node()/child::Recurrence/child::StartDate
```

Other navigational constructs such as `preceding-sibling::`, `following-sibling::`, etc. are also available, as is `ancestor::`.

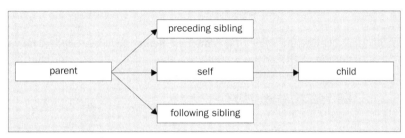

Predicates in XPath

All the XPath expressions we have seen so far select sets of nodes. What if you want to select individual nodes, or a subset of the nodes with a given name? You might have dozens of BankAccount elements in a StatementRequest. How do you find just the one we're looking for? The answer is the XPath equivalent of SQL's WHERE clause, which is known as a predicate.

XPath uses predicates to say which items you want to keep from a node-set. Predicates can select elements either by position, or by value. For a given StatementRequest context, the first BankAccount can be chosen by:

```
BankAccount[1]
```

The number in this case does not refer to the position among all the children of StatementRequest, but to the position among all the BankAccount children only. To select a BankAccount only when its position is the first among all the children of a given Statement Request, a more complex predicate must be used:

```
*[position() = 1 and self::BankAccount]
```

The * selects all the sibling elements one level below relative to the context, and then the filters in the predicate are applied. Here self::BankAccount is technically a navigation step, which goes from the current node to itself, if it is a BankAccount, and selects nothing otherwise. By using it in a predicate, the effect is to test whether the context node is a BankAccount.

Similarly, the following XPath expression can be used to find the last BankAccount:

```
BankAccount[last()]
```

Another useful function is count(), which can be used to determine how many occurrences of a particular element are in a document. From the context of a document that has multiple StatementRequest elements, the following XPath expression can be used to select only those StatementRequest elements that contain exactly one BankAccount:

```
child::StatementRequest[count(child::BankAccount) = 1]
```

We can also test contained elements. From the context of a StatementRequest, the following will select only those BankAccounts that directly contain a BankID:

```
child::BankAccount[BankID]
```

In addition to existence checks, the value of a contained element can be tested. (The value of an element is the concatenation of all the text it contains, ignoring attributes, and ignoring any other tags within the element content.)

```
child::BankAccount[BankID="310824233"]
```

Attributes can be tested using the attribute keyword, which can be abbreviated using the @ symbol. The following selects the numberingSystem attribute of the BankID element (or more precisely, it selects a set of attributes, containing the numberingSystem attribute of every child BankID element of the context node):

```
BankID/attribute::numberingSystem
BankID/@numberingSystem
```

Similarly, the following will select every `BankID` element that has a `numberingSystem` attribute with value 'American Routing and Transit'. Note the difference between selecting an attribute, and selecting an element that has a particular attribute:

```
BankID[@numberingSystem="American Routing and Transit"]
```

We can look for more than simply exact matches to strings. To check if the value of the `BankID` element contains a sub-string 'American', we can ask:

```
BankID[contains(., "American")]
```

A number of other string operators, such as `starts-with()`, `concat()`, `substring()`, etc. are provided. You can also convert strings to numbers where possible, using the `number()` function. Real numbers can be converted to integers using the `round()` function; the customary `floor()` and `ceiling()` functions are also provided.

XPointer

XPointer is the mechanism defined by the W3C to point to subsets of XML documents. It is not yet widely available in products, but will assume increasing importance over the next couple of years. Once you have found the document you want, typically by following a URL, you need to home in to the part of the document that interests you. XPointer, which is based on XPath expressions, allows specific nodes or sets of nodes to be selected. The closely-related XLink specification in turn uses XPointer as the way of specifying where within a document the end of a hyperlink resides.

HTML frequently uses **fragment identifiers** on the end of URLs to take you to a specific part of a HTML document. Any characters following a # character in a URL constitute a fragment identifier. For example, you could specify the following HTML to refer to an **anchor** named `xptr` in a document:

```
<p> See: <a href="xmlprimer.html#xptr">XPointer</a> </p>
```

XPointer adds to the fragment identifier capability in several ways:

❑   XPointers can point to specific places inside documents and unlike HTML anchors, you can point to a location that isn't specifically set up with an anchor for the purpose.

❑   XPointers provide finer-grained addressing into elements, string selections, and ranges inside documents.

❑   XPointers can navigate hierarchies (that is, the structure of XML documents), so that locations are human-readable and writeable.

XPointer expressions are simply appended to a URL. XPointer makes heavy use of XPath – XPath expressions are used inside Xpointers for navigation. For example, in order to navigate within a XML document containing StatementRequests, we can specify:

```
http://acmecorp.com/statements/StatementRequest.xml#xpointer(/BankAccount/AccountI
D)
```

The range functionality of XPointer goes beyond XPath, allowing you to select a range of account elements:

```
xpointer(AccountID("000000000")/range-to(AccountID("999999999")))
```

There are a number of other useful XPointer functions that go beyond XPath. The `unique()` function of XPointer can be used to determine whether an expression actually locates a single object in the document:

```
http://acmecorp.com/statements/StatementRequest.xml#xpointer(/BankAccount[unique()
]
```

Similarly, XPointer adds functions such as `here()` and `origin()`, which provide for addressing relative to the location of an XPointer expression itself; functions `start-point()` and `end-point()`, to identify beginning and ending locations, and so on. Together, these make XPointer ideal for pointing into the sub-parts of a document.

Using XPath

The best way to gain understanding of XPath is by example and experimentation. Conveniently, the Oracle XDK allows XPath expressions to be used directly from a Java application. The following Java application takes advantage of this: it will load an XML document, prompt the user for XPath queries, and display the resulting node sets. The application is saved as `XPathToy.class`.

Note that you will need a Java Development Kit and the XDK for Java installed (this can be obtained from http://technet.oracle.com/tech/xml).

```java
import java.io.*;
import oracle.xml.parser.v2.*;
import org.xml.sax.*;
import org.w3c.dom.*;

public class XPathToy {
    private XMLDocument document;
    private String query;

    public XPathToy(String filename) {
        try {
            document = loadXMLDocument(filename);
            BufferedReader in = new BufferedReader(
                                new InputStreamReader(System.in));
            do {
                System.out.print("XPath> ");
                query = in.readLine();
                try {
                    NodeList nodes = ((XMLNode)document).selectNodes(query,
                                     (NSResolver)document.getDocumentElement());
                    for (int i = 0; i < nodes.getLength(); i++)
                        System.out.println("Value: " + nodes.item(i).getNodeValue());
                } catch (XSLException e) {
                    System.out.println("Invalid XPath query: " + query);
                }
            } while (!(query.equals("quit")));
        } catch (IOException e) {
```

```
              System.err.println("Could not load '" + filename + "': " +
                                  e.toString());
       } catch (SAXException e) {
          System.err.println("Could not parse XML: " + e.toString());
       }
   }

   private XMLDocument loadXMLDocument(String filename)
                               throws IOException, SAXException {
       File file = new File(filename);
       FileReader reader = new FileReader(file);

       DOMParser parser = new DOMParser();
       parser.parse(reader);

       return parser.getDocument();
   }

   public static void main(String[] args) {
       if (args.length == 1)
          new XPathToy(args[0]);
       else
          System.err.println("Usage: java XPathToy <filename>");
   }
}
```

The XML document, `recipe.xml`, seen earlier, will be used for the examples:

To use the application, compile and run it in a Java compiler, with the name of an XML file as the sole argument; in this case it is called `recipe.xml`:

```
C:\xml>javac XPathToy.java
C:\xml>java XPathToy recipe.xml
```

Enter XPath statements at the prompt, and the matching nodes will be displayed, until the command `quit` is entered. The XPath queries select elements from the document. The document is loaded once, and multiple queries are performed on it.

```
XPath> /snack/recipe/name/text()
```

The output should be:

```
Value: Chocolate Brownies
Value: Blueberry Muffins
```

Stylesheets: XSLT

Included with Oracle's XML parser, as part of the XDK, is a command line utility, XSLT Processor; this is for processing XML documents using XSLT stylesheets. eXtensible Stylesheet Language Transformations(XSLT) describe how a source document should be transformed into a target document by specifying rules that govern the mapping of source elements to result elements (and other nodes), including simple logic such as iteration, string functions, Boolean branches, and numeric operations. XSLT uses XPath expressions to reference document elements. An XSLT stylesheet in its most basic form can be written as a template for the output document, into which the values of elements extracted from the source XML document are substituted as the transformation is processed.

As we have seen, both XPointer and XSLT use XPath as their foundation. The XSLT system is a method for transforming one XML document into another. The source and target documents may conform to the same Document Type Definition(DTD); for example, you can use XSLT to copy the parts of a document you are interested in. Alternatively, XSLT can be used to transform documents conforming to one DTD into documents conforming to another. The most common use is to take a dataset in the form of an XML document, and transform it into an HTML document for presentation to a client device. This approach is most powerful when multiple devices with differing capabilities are to access the same application; the developer needs only to build the business logic once to output XML, then for each device a unique transform is applied.

However, XSLT is not only for presentation: you can use it to implement parts of the business logic of your application. It enables an application (which may reside on the middle tier of a distributed application) to load data from any source in the form of an XML document, and then perform local queries on it without needing to access the network, nor the original data source. This technique can reduce network traffic and server query latency, and it allows complex data structures to be passed between applications without requiring a potentially difficult-to-use object framework (such as CORBA). It also means you can offload some of the computational work previously confined to the server. Of course, there are potential costs, such as an increased amount of data passed between the tiers of your multi-tier application, and as always you will have to make design trade-offs. XML documents are easily generated and cached, but less easily parsed than native SQL recordsets loaded into a Fourth Generation Language (4GL) such as Oracle Forms, where caching a set of records from a query is almost transparent to the developer.

However, let's get back to the most common use of XSLT, for defining how XML is to be presented to users on the screen.

Although this book is about Oracle, it's worth reminding ourselves at this stage that Oracle isn't the only vendor in town. In particular, when we discuss screen presentation it's hard to avoid mentioning one of their competitors, Microsoft. One of the great advantages of XSLT is that it's one of the few standards that has been implemented equally well for use "client-side" or "server-side". An XSLT stylesheet written to run in the Oracle back-end should work equally well as part of the Internet Explorer browser. (But note, Microsoft's MSXML3 product, which implements XSLT, is not currently a standard part of the browser: instead, Internet Explorer still ships by default with an older language, Microsoft XSL, which is quite incompatible).

While XML documents are marked up to be easily read by both people and software, people are typically more interested in seeing the content rather than the markup. Further, they are interested in seeing the content on different devices or media – PCs, TVs, PDAs, and more: including, of course, paper. Clearly, the display of XML on each of these would need different kinds of formatting. To display the content of XML documents on these devices, it necessary to replace the tags with appropriate text styles, and on occasion to transform between styles. The Extensible Stylesheet Language (XSL), of which the XSL Transformation (XSLT) standard forms part, is designed to address these requirements.

The content of an XML element such as <Address> has no explicit style. A single style would not be acceptable to all forms of publications – the weight of font, number of lines of display, purpose of presentation – all have to be taken into consideration when determining a style. A **stylesheet** lists the rules according to which the elements associated with a DTD or schema are to be formatted for display. Such stylesheets may be shared by a number of documents, reducing the effort needed to deal with large number of documents that need to be formatted in the same way.

Today, the most common way of rendering XML is by converting it to HTML using XSLT. However, W3C's ambitions extend beyond this, with the development of the other half of the XSL standard, XSL formatting objects. At the time of writing XSL Formatting Objects are a Candidate Recommendation, and no complete implementations are available. Because the standard is significant for the future, we'll describe it briefly here.

The most popular formatting objects are table cells, blocks, and so on. Each formatting object has a number of properties that can be used to lay out the document according to the tastes of the designer – for example, the block object has a property that determines the spacing between this block and the next. XSL makes the XML elements 'flow' into the formatting objects.

We could assign the individual elements of Address to different table cells. We could reduce the font if the display was on a device with a small screen, such as a cellphone. Some of the other tasks performed by stylesheets could be:

❑ Leave a gap of two lines between paragraphs.

❑ Increase the volume on a cellphone if emphasized text is to be spoken.

❑ Display hypertext links in black.

❑ Make a stock quote blink on a screen.

XSL has many more features; such as being able to process the same element twice, suppress elements in one location, and display them in another, add generated text before displaying, and even change the order of elements. Together, these capabilities are very useful for creating different presentations for the same data.

XSLT is a standard for transformations. When used with XSL formatting, it can:

❑ Transform data from one XML format to another XML format.

❑ Specify which XSL formatting objects need to be applied to an element.

❑ Reorder and sort source elements.

❑ Add prefixes or suffixes to elements in the source content.

XSLT transformation is useful whether the target is XSL formatting instructions, or any other vocabulary: for example SVG graphics, VoxML for sound, or plain old HTML for conventional PC browsers. XSLT instructions are distinguished from the target vocabulary by the use of the namespace http://www.w3.org/1999/XSL/Transform.

Let us see how this works in practice using HTML as the target.

Suppose we have a simple XML document name.xml containing a directory entry – a person and their phone number:

```
<?xml version="1.0"?>
<DirectoryEntry>
    <name>Oracle Tech Support</name>
    <number>(123)456-789</number>
</DirectoryEntry>
```

A simple stylesheet, name.xsl, would display the name, followed by number. In order to do so in a HTML browser, we have to create HTML out of the XML:

```
<xsl:stylesheet version="1.0" xmlns:xsl='http://www.w3.org/1999/XSL/Transform'>
<xsl:template match="/">
    <H1><xsl:value-of select="//name"/></H1>
    <H2><xsl:value-of select="//number"/></H2>
</xsl:template>
</xsl:stylesheet>
```

The above XSLT directives transform the XML document into a HTML document. If you have the Oracle XML Parser and JDK installed the command would be:

```
C:\xml>java oracle.xml.parser.v2.oraxsl name.xml name.xsl name.html
```

The result would be the following file, name.html, with HTML tags:

```
<H1>Oracle Tech Support</H1>
<H2>(123)456-789</H2>
```

As you can see, the XSLT above uses the xsl:value-of instruction to put the value of the element <name> between HTML tags <H1> and </H1>, and then the same instruction to put the value of the element <number> between <H2> and </H2> tags. This results in a display where the name is displayed bolder by a browser than the number.

If you wanted to create a different display, one in which the number precedes the name and both have the same font size, you could create another stylesheet, name2.xsl:

```
<xsl:stylesheet version="1.0" xmlns:xsl='http://www.w3.org/1999/XSL/Transform'>
<xsl:template match="/">
   <H1><xsl:value-of select="//number"/></H1>
   <H1><xsl:value-of select="//name"/></H1>
</xsl:template>
</xsl:stylesheet>
```

This would generate a different arrangement of HTML tags:

```
<H1>(123)456-789</H1>
<H1>Oracle Tech Support</H1>
```

We've explained these transformations in terms of the stylesheet outputting HTML tags. Actually, this is a simplification. An XSLT transformation is actually a three-stage process: first the XML parser processes the source document to construct a tree representation, rather like the DOM; then the XSLT instructions are applied to transform this to a different tree, and finally the resulting tree is **serialized** into an output file in XML, HTML, or some other text-based format.

The distinction is important when you come to write more complex transformations, because it means that you can never write tags that aren't properly paired up. It looks as if the <H1> in the stylesheet above causes an <H1> start tag to be written, and the </H1> causes an </H1> end tag. In actual fact, the <H1> and </H1> are combined into a single instruction element in the stylesheet tree, this is processed to create an <H1> element in the result tree, and when the result tree is serialized, this <H1> element produces an <H1> start tag and an </H1> end tag. Remember this if you ever want to write a start tag without an end tag, or vice versa: you can't write half an element node to the result tree.

The XSLT Processing Model

Let's discuss the XSLT processing model. An XSLT processor begins with a stylesheet and a **source tree**, which is akin to a DOM representation of the XML document. In the simplest case, the XSLT processor starts at the root node of the source tree and processes it by finding the template rule in the stylesheet that describes how that node should be displayed. This template rule describes what to do next; very often, the rule will use the `<xsl:apply-templates/>` instruction, which causes the children of the root node to be processed, each using the template rule in the stylesheet defined for that kind of node. Processing may invoke various XSLT transformation instructions.

In more complex cases, each template can specify which nodes to process, so some nodes may be processed more than once and some may not be processed at all.

All this processing creates a **result tree**. XSLT allows the result tree to be composed of any kind of elements, such as XSL formatting objects, HTML element names etc. The result tree always follows the XML structural rules, but the final stage of processing, called **serialization**, may create an output file in either XML, or another format such as HTML or plain text. When HTML elements are used in the result tree, the default is to serialize it as an HTML document. This process can be depicted as follows:

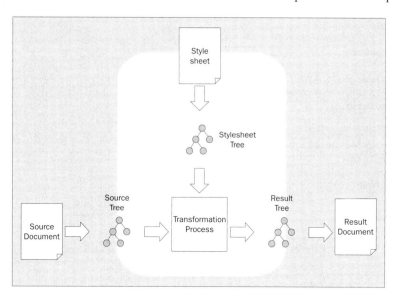

Suppose we had a `Lineitem` element, from the `Invoice` example in the XML appendix, in its own separate document, `purchaseitem.xml`, with an extra element, `comment`:

```
<?xml version = "1.0" ?>
<LineItem
itemCode ="ABC-123">
    <itemDescription>Kayak</itemDescription>
    <quantity>1</quantity>
    <price>567.80</price>
    <comment>Prefer green with yellow trim</comment>
</LineItem>
```

We might decide that when displaying the item fragment in a HTML browser, we want to choose different fonts, indentation, etc. for the different elements. Specifically, we want to display the productName and partNum in bold font, the quantity and price in italics, and the comment in blue to make it stand out. In XSLT, we can use **template rules** to define such formatting. The XSLT processor takes the current node in the tree and tries to find a matching template rule. If one is found, the instructions inside the matching template are evaluated.

The XSLT stylesheet, displayitem.xsl, for generating the HTML fragment to display the above item in a browser could look like this:

```
<xsl:stylesheet xmlns:xsl='http://www.w3.org/1999/XSL/Transform' version="1.0">

<xsl:template match="itemDescription">
   <P><B><xsl:value-of select="."/></B></P>
</xsl:template>

<xsl:template match="@itemcode">
   <P><B><xsl:value-of select="."/></B></P>
</xsl:template>

<xsl:template match="quantity">
   <P><i><xsl:value-of select="."/></i></P>
</xsl:template>

<xsl:template match="price">
   <P><i><xsl:value-of select="."/></i></P>
</xsl:template>

<xsl:template match="comment">
   <P style="color:blue"><xsl:value-of select="."/></P>
</xsl:template>

</xsl:stylesheet>
```

The result would be:

```
> java oracle.xml.parser.v2.oraxsl purchaseitem.xml displayitem.xsl

<?xml version= '1.0' encoding = 'UTF-8' ?>
<P><B>Kayak</B></P>
<P><B>ABC-123</B> </P>
<P><i>1</i></P>
<P><i>567.80</i></P>
<P style="color:blue">Prefer green with yellow trim. </P>
```

The string inside the select attribute of xsl:value-of is an XPath expression. In the example we've only used the simplest XPath expression possible, ".", which refers to the context node. However, it's possible to use any of the XPath expressions introduced earlier in the chapter. For example, by using a preceding @ symbol, attributes can be selected in the same way as elements.

You can create very complex result trees from very complex (or simple) sources, and the above should give you a flavor of how this is all done.

Notice that XPath can select nodes relative to the current node, which is initially the root, and that the value of the current node is referenced by the "." expression. The current context changes according to the last XPath statement in a surrounding block, which is why the `<xsl:value-of select="."/>` instructions in different template rules in the example above produce different results.

The stylesheet above is written as a collection of simple template rules. Contrast this with the section below that displays baking instructions. Here the XSLT instructions and the HTML formatting mark-up are freely mixed. The stylesheet uses a loop-like construct to repeat a block of instructions `for-each` node selected by the XPath expression. Also, note that the `for-each` instruction is an XML element that has content, while the `xsl:value-of` instruction is an empty XML element. The entire stylesheet must be a well-formed XML document, which means that when you use HTML tags, they too must follow the XML rules: for example an opening `<li>` tag must be matched by a closing `</li>`. Here is `recipe.xsl`:

```
<html xsl:version="1.0" xmlns:xsl="http://www.w3.org/1999/XSL/Transform">
<head>
   <title>Recipe</title>
</head>
<body>
<xsl:for-each select="snack/recipe">
<p>
   <h2><xsl:value-of select="name"/></h2>

   <h3>Ingredients</h3>
<ul>
   <xsl:for-each select="ingredients/item">
<li>
     <xsl:value-of select="concat(' You need ',quantity, ' of ', description,',
',' available from ',supplier)"/>
<!--- This selects the values of quantity, description and supplier using the
concat() function, which produces a string from our arguments and we have added
some text-->
</li>
</xsl:for-each>
</ul>

<h3>Method</h3>
<ul>

   <xsl:for-each select="method/step">
   <li><xsl:value-of select="concat(number, '. ',task,' ',time,' ',preheat)"/>
</li>
   </xsl:for-each>
</ul>
   </p>
   </xsl:for-each>
</body>
</html>
```

To use the XSLT Processor, save the above block of code as `'recipes.xsl'` and, from the command prompt, run the `oraxsl` command, as shown below. The three parameters are the source XML file, the source XSL file, and the destination HTML file, which will be overwritten if it already exists.

```
C:\xml>java oracle.xml.parser.v2.oraxsl recipe.xml recipe.xsl recipes.html
```

This destination file can be viewed in your browser:

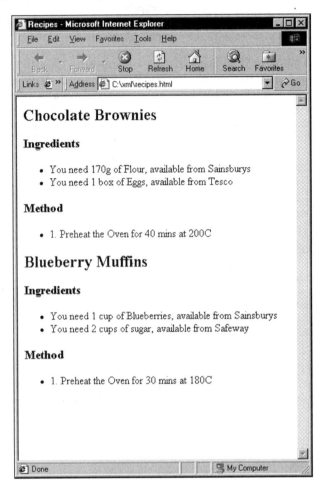

The `oraxsl` command can be run on large batches of XML documents using the same stylesheet, in which case it will write either to a directory, or to file names of a different extension from the source file. A possible use for this option, which is multi-threaded for efficiency, would be to process documents prior to loading into interMedia Text. For a full list of the available options of this command, execute the command with no arguments.

The command shown below processes a batch of XML documents located in the `source` directory into HTML documents in the `target` directory by using `stylesheet.xsl`. Also any errors that occur are logged into `error.log` and up to four documents at a time are processed:

```
C:\xml>java oracle.xml.parser.v2.oraxsl -e error.log -d source -o target \
    -r html -t 4 -s stylesheet.xsl
```

For production use, you will probably want to invoke the Oracle XSLT Processor in an application, rather than calling it from the command line. It is written as a set of Java classes, which are documented in the product specification, so this is straightforward to do.

JavaServer Pages and XML

JavaServer Pages (JSPs) are in many ways similar to XSLT stylesheets, mixing logical and structural elements with layout information and data items to produce a document containing embedded data. They are often used as a template system for delivering web content in HTML, but JSPs are also a convenient technique for generating XML documents for consumption by other applications, or for client-side rendering using XSLT in the browser. Java, unlike XSLT, is a fully featured programming language, and can be used to express algorithms of arbitrary complexity and perform arbitrary computation. Java is integrated with distributed object models (EJB and CORBA), and an XML document generated by a JSP is a convenient bridge between these and the 'lingua franca' of the Internet, HTML. Java accesses data in many ways including via an object broker or via DML over JDBC. Both Internet Application Server and the Oracle 8i Server itself are fully featured Java runtime environments.

A JavaServer Page is produced using a text editor, and stored in the file system until execution upon request by a client application. This differs from a servlet, discussed below, which is compiled and loaded into the process space of the server. After invocation, the JSP is compiled, and this class file is cached and reused by the web server for performance reasons. The compilation transforms the JSP file into a Java application within a framework, which makes the necessary objects for it to function available at run time. These objects fulfill functions such as exposing the parameters passed by the client, maintaining a user session, providing an interface for output, allowing instantiation of other Java classes, etc.

For the JSP example, we will use a relational data structure as the base, to generate an XML fragment similar to the previous example:

```
CREATE TABLE recipe (
    id number PRIMARY KEY,
    name VARCHAR2(80) );

CREATE TABLE ingredients (
    id number,
    line number,
    supplier_id number,
    quantity VARCHAR2(80),
    description VARCHAR2(80) );

CREATE TABLE supplier (
    supplier_id number,
    name VARCHAR2(80) );
```

We need to insert some values:

```
INSERT INTO recipe (id, name) VALUES (1, 'Treacle Sponge');
INSERT INTO ingredients (id, line, supplier_id, quantity, description)
    VALUES (1, 1, 1, '175g', 'self raising flour');
INSERT INTO ingredients (id, line, supplier_id, quantity, description)
    VALUES (1, 2, 2, '6 tablespoons', 'golden syrup');
INSERT INTO ingredients (id, line, supplier_id, quantity, description)
    VALUES (1, 3, 3, '3', 'eggs');
INSERT INTO supplier (supplier_id, name) VALUES (1, 'Tesco');
INSERT INTO supplier (supplier_id, name) VALUES (2, 'Safeway');
INSERT INTO supplier (supplier_id, name) VALUES (3, 'Sainsburys');
COMMIT;
```

The JSP `insertrecipe.jsp` code is a straightforward mix of XML, Java, and SQL. The content type and the `<?xml?>` declaration are both included, to specify that this is an XML document. The JavaBean included takes care of actually accessing the Oracle database. The bean must be within the classpath of the server when compiled, and the JSP in the document root will be compiled when requested.

```
<%@ page language="java"
            contentType="text/xml"
            import = "QueryBean"
            isThreadSafe = "false"
%>
<jsp:useBean id="query"
                class="QueryBean"
                scope="session"/>

<% //<?xml version = "1.0"?> %>
<%
    query.setQuery("SELECT name FROM recipe WHERE id = 1");
    query.runQuery();
    query.nextRow();
%>
<snack>
    <recipe>
        <name><%= query.getValue("name") %></name>
        <ingredients>
<%

    query.setQuery("select description, name from ingredients, supplier where
ingredients.supplier_id = supplier.supplier_id and ingredients.id = 1");
    /*
    query.setQuery("SELECT ingredients.description, name FROM ingredients,
                    supplier " + "WHERE ingredients.supplier_id =
                    supplier.supplier_id " + "AND ingredients.id = 1");*/
    query.runQuery();

    while (query.nextRow()) {
%>
        <item><%= query.getValue("description") %>
        <supplier><%= query.getValue("name") %></supplier>
        </item>

<%
    }
%>
        </ingredients>
    </recipe>
<snack>
```

The database access is contained within a JavaBean; the code of `QueryBean.java` is shown below, which can be used to encapsulate business logic for reuse, allowing the JSP to concentrate on XML generation. Exceptions are thrown, and could be intercepted by using the `<%@page errorPage= %>` directive in the main JSP. The value of this attribute is an absolute or relative URL to the page that reports errors to the client. The JavaBean could easily be written to use the Oracle SQL XML utility classes to generate XML itself, passed back to the client via String objects for inclusion within a template.

```
import java.beans.*;
import javax.servlet.http.*;
import javax.servlet.*;
import java.util.*;
import java.sql.*;

public class QueryBean {
    private Connection  connection;
    private Statement   statement;
    private ResultSet   results;
    private String      query;

    public QueryBean() throws SQLException {
        DriverManager.registerDriver(new oracle.jdbc.driver.OracleDriver());
        Connection connection = DriverManager.getConnection
                    ("jdbc:oracle:thin:@dbserver:1521:proead", "scott", "tiger");
        statement = connection.createStatement();
    }

    public void setQuery(String query) {
        this.query = query;
    }

    public String getQuery() {
        return query;
    }

    public void runQuery() throws SQLException {
        results = statement.executeQuery(query);
    }

    public boolean nextRow() throws SQLException {
        return results.next();
    }

    public String getValue(String column) throws SQLException {
        return results.getString(column);
    }
}
```

The output is shown below:

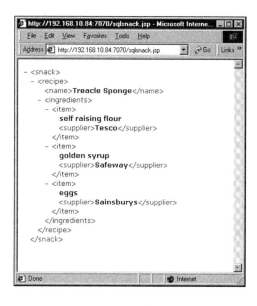

XSQL Pages

In the previous section we discussed Oracle's SAX and DOM parsers; we've looked at XSLT and XPath support, and we've looked at the use of XML with JavaServer Pages. Frankly, these components are not all that different from half a dozen other Java-based XML toolkits available from suppliers such as Apache and Sun. Where the Oracle XDK starts to differ from these commodity products is, as you might expect, in the area of SQL support.

Although a conventional relational table can always be transformed to an XML document, the reverse is not so straightforward. This is because XML documents are hierarchically structured, with parent and child nodes. It's easy to represent a table as a rather flat hierarchy, but representing a hierarchy as a table is not so easy.

The fact that XML and SQL use different data models means that there is a need for tools that bridge the gap between the two models.

The Oracle XSQL servlet is the simplest way to generate XML views of relational data, using XSLT stylesheets and reusing conventional SQL statements for transmission of data across open standards-based networks. It can also be used to provide functionality to off-line applications, using exposed methods or a command line stub, but the intended use is as a plug-in to an existing web server. This will enable it to execute pre-written SQL statements, which may accept parameters at run time using the standard HTTP form method, and format the output in XML, optionally transforming it before viewing. The XSQL servlet also functions as a general purpose XML/XSL processor, and can be used without a database connection. It is compatible with any web server that includes a servlet runtime virtual machine and uses a JDBC driver for connectivity to Oracle, although the developer is not exposed to the JDBC API (but it can be used with any data source for which a JDBC driver is available).

> The XSQL servlet and associated utilities are available for download from Oracle Technology Network. The release notes cover configuring XSQL for use with common web servers. For the purpose of this text, it is assumed that you are using the bundled Web-to-Go server included with the XSQL distribution on Windows NT/2000. In JDeveloper 3.1 you may simply add the included XSQL Runtime to your project libraries. An XSQL file can then be run, and this will launch it in the servlet runner. Note the configuration detail below.

The first example shows the simplest form of an XSQL page, using the schema from the first JSP example:

```
<?xml version="1.0"?>
<xsql:query xmlns:xsql="urn:oracle-xsql" connection="recipe">
    SELECT name FROM recipe WHERE id=1
</xsql:query>
```

There are several points to note about the structure of this page.

❑ The xmlns attribute is the XML namespace. In this case, it is set to the uniform resource name of 'oracle-xsql'. This provides resolution of the mark-up for the XSQL specific layout and logic tags. This is different from the name space for XSL page transformation documents. An XSQL page is a valid XML document in its own right.

❑ The connection attribute refers to a database connection specified within a configuration file, which must be present, well-formed, and correctly customized for your Oracle instance. This file is located in <XSQL_HOME>, the directory in which you installed the XSQL servlet, and is named XSQLConfig.xml. (Yes, it too is an XML document.) You should just need to modify the existing defaults to create a database connection descriptor. The tags to look for are a <connectiondefs> pair, within which you should write:

```
<connection name="recipe">
    <username>scott</username>
    <password>tiger</password>
    <dburl>jdbc:oracle:thin:@dbserver:1521:proead</dburl>
    <driver>oracle.jdbc.driver.OracleDriver</driver>
</connection>
```

❑ In JDeveloper 3.1, the default XSQLConfig.xml file is in the lib directory of <JDEV_HOME>.

❑ There is no semicolon terminating the SQL statement, which is embedded within the <xsql:query> tags. There are no layout tags at all, although they are not precluded. Care must be taken in using them, in the same way that mixing layout with XSL risks producing a badly formed document.

Viewing the XSQL page through a web browser (at present Internet Explorer is the only compatible browser), it will look like this:

```
<?xml version = '1.0'?>
<ROWSET>
    <ROW num="1">
        <name>Treacle Sponge</name>
    </ROW>
</ROWSET>
```

❑ The tags around a value are the name of the column it came from in the underlying table. You can set the tag to be something different by using the query syntax: SELECT name AS dessert FROM recipe WHERE id = 1.

❑ The <ROW> attribute "num" is simply the order in which the rows were returned by Oracle. It bears no relation to the id column in the table. Nor is it related to the Oracle rowid associated with each record. A single row is still a rowset, for consistency's sake.

❑ <ROWSET> and <ROW> are the defaults, and the name of the tag around each value is the same as the column heading given by Oracle. These, however, can be transformed into any other named tag by applying an XSLT transformation to the XML, or by adding attributes to the <xsql:query> tag. These are of the form name="value". See the table below for an explanation of the available attributes and their effects.

XSQL pages also accept parameters, passed in using the URL from a standard HTML form, or specified on the command line for batch generation of XML documents from template queries. (See the XSLT Processing Model section earlier for a technique for batch processing XML using XSL, and later we will see a more flexible approach for generating XML from the command line.) Modifying the previous XSQL page to accept a parameter, we can put recipe.xsql as:

```
<?xml version="1.0"?>
<xsql:query xmlns:xsql="urn:oracle-xsql" connection="recipe">
    SELECT name FROM recipe WHERE id={@id}
</xsql:query>
```

To invoke this page, the value for `id` must be a part of the request string sent by the web client, this assumes that 7070 is the port on which your web server is listening and that you are using IE as your browser:

```
C:\xml>ie.exe http://localhost:7070/xsql/recipe.xsql?id=1
```

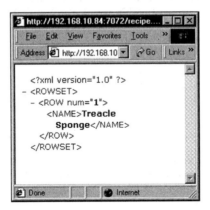

Or to generate the page from the command line:

```
C:\xml\java oracle.xml.xsql.XSQLCommandLine recipe.xsql id=1
```

XSQL queries are usually not mixed with direct PL/SQL calls to the HTP, HTF, or OWA_UTIL packages, which are part of the PL/SQL Web Toolkit. This is because these generate HTML natively not XML, and XSQL assumes the use of XSL to present the documents. An application and logical architecture mixing the two will still run, however the presentation will suffer, and maintainability will be reduced. However, using XSQL action handlers, stored procedures using the OWA packages can be used. The statements invoking the stored procedure are within `<xsql:include-owa>` tags, and the output will be substituted in the same way as it is when using `<xsql:query>`. `<xsql:include-xml>` will insert an arbitrary XML page, referenced by absolute or relative URL, and `<xsql:include-xsql>` will do the same thing for another XSQL page.

The `<xsql:ref-cursor-function>` tag builds canonical XML from a REF_CURSOR returned by an Oracle stored procedure, allowing straightforward reuse of existing queries. Together, these three handlers provide the functionality of the "server-side includes" used by early web servers. An SQL statement not returning rows, or an anonymous PL/SQL block can be executed for every page request by surrounding it with `<xsql:dml>` tags, and no substitution will be performed. All action elements will have parameter substitution performed on them before they are executed, either within the contents of a tag itself (a SELECT statement) or the attributes of the tags themselves. If an error occurs during the processing of an action element where that substitution would have occurred, the `<xsql-error>` tag will be placed instead, with nested `<message>` and `<statement>` elements containing further details. These may be accessed using XPath.

To apply an XSL to the output of an XSQL page, a single line must be added to the XSQL page, giving a reference to the stylesheet itself, and a MIME type. To cater for different client types XSQL contains logic for choosing a stylesheet for a particular client, for example Netscape Communicator or Spyglass. These directives are processed in the order in which they are encountered by the servlet; the first directive is found in the USER AGENT environment variable supplied in the HTTP header being used to transform the document. There may be as many of these as necessary, and because string matching is used, the system is capable of supporting multiple versions of a particular browser product.

If this feature is not used, the same stylesheet will be served to all clients, and if that stylesheet is last in a list of possible clients, it will be the default. To use this feature, add the following lines to the `.xsql` file, directly beneath the `<?XML?>` processing instruction. Note that they are not opened or closed in the same way as conventional XML processing instructions.

```
<?xml-stylesheet type="text/xsl" media = "Spyglass" href = "mosaic.xsl"?>
<?xml-stylesheet type="text/xsl" media = "Mozilla" href = "navigator.xsl"?>
<?xml-stylesheet type="text/xsl" href = "default.xsl"?>
```

They cannot be nested, and the set of directives is processed only once. It is impossible to apply multiple different stylesheets to different sub-sections of the document based on the client, so the way to work around this problem is to use a `<xsql:include>` tag and pass a parameter to it. Another alternative is to pass the name of the required stylesheet in the HTTP request string, generating this yourself and creating a link to it. URLs that use this feature refer to the stylesheet relatively or absolutely. Further, it is possible to specify whether the 'server' should process the stylesheet (which adds to the computational load of generating documents) or the 'client'. Requests are of the form:

```
C:\Xml\>ie.exe http://localhost:7070/xsql/page.xsql?xml \
    -stylesheet=iexplorer.xsl&transform=server
```

XML SELECT and INSERT

The XSQL servlet derives its functionality from classes contained within the Oracle XML SQL utility, a Java Archive containing a set of classes for many database functions. Two of these are `OracleXMLQuery`, which performs the function of generating an XML document from SQL and relational data, and `OracleXMLSave`, which generates relational data from XML documents. Both make use of a standard XML representation of relational tables, either generating it or parsing it. Therefore, just as XSLT can transform an XML document into HTML for presentation, it can also be used to transform an XML (or HTML) document into the standard relational form, for insertion into a relational structure. This is necessary as `OracleXMLSave` can only process documents conforming to this standard.

The question is then, what is this standard form and how do we derive the necessary transformation for a given set of XML documents that need to be loaded into a database? The answer is to do it in reverse: create an example of the required database structure, and generate a specimen XML document from it.

First, examine the document, and determine which elements and attributes are present. Using these and a standard modeling tool – whether that's an old blackboard or Oracle Designer running on a workstation – design a relational schema. Don't worry about integrity constraints at this stage; what we are interested in is the basic table definitions. Create the tables in your database, and then run a few INSERT statements to populate them with data. Make each value unique and easy to recognize. Next, construct SELECT statements that will return records in the same way as your application would see them (master-detail-detail). Copy and paste the SQL into an XSQL page and take a look at it in your web browser: You now have a perfect sample of the sort of XML you need to write an XSL which will transform your source!

The Oracle XML SQL utility includes both a command line interface and an API. We will use the command line to present an example of XML generation from a query, and for row insertion using XML. The basic form of the command is as follows:

```
C:\xml>java OracleXML getXML -user "scott/tiger" -conn \
    jdbc:oracle:thin@dbserver:1521:proead -rowSetTag "snacks" -rowTag "recipe" \
      -useLowerCase   "SELECT * FROM recipes"
```

Note this uses the Oracle JDBC thin driver to connect to your database. An alternative connect string would be `jdbc:oracle:oci8:@proead` if you have a local Oracle client installation. Alternatively, you may configure an appropriate environment variable (see below). The output is:

```
<?xml version="1.0"?>
<snacks>
    <recipe num="1">
        <id>1</id>
        <name>Treacle Sponge</name>
    </recipe>
</snacks>
```

The class is invoked using the Java runtime environment as shown above. The first argument is either `getXML` or `putXML`, and the parameters following this are used to define the operation. For example, when generating XML, the options `-useLowerCase` and `-useUpperCase` are available, specifying the case of the tag names (as opposed to the data itself). When inserting XML, however, the appropriate option is `-ignoreCase`, because although Oracle's SQL engine is not case sensitive, XML itself is case sensitive. The query is the last of the arguments, and is simply a normal SQL statement. The entire set of command line options are displayed when invoking the utility with no arguments, and most directly relate to API calls.

Command Line Options	Function
`-user`	The database connection for the query. The `-user` option is the most straightforward, simply of the form `"username/password"`, not `"username/password@service"` or SID - this will cause an error. The SID will be inherited from the environment variable.
`-conn`	If `-conn` is used, the parameter could be a full JDBC connection string, of the form `"jdbc:oracle:thin:@localhost:1521:ORCL"`, in which case the login credentials must be supplier by `-user`, or alternatively, the `-conn` could be `"jdbc:oracle:thin:scott/tiger@localhost:1521:ORCL"`.
`-filename`	`-filename` specifies, either absolutely or relatively to the current directory, the name of a plain text file containing a single SELECT statement. This statement may be spread over multiple lines, but must not be terminated by a semicolon.
`-rowsetTag` `-rowIdAttr`	These parameters control the tags around the column values of each row in the data set returned by the SQL statements. The `<ROWSET>` and `<ROW>` tags were replaced in the command line above.
`-rowIdColumn`	`-rowIdColumn` replaces the number of the row within the tag delimiting each row, even if it is renamed. The row ID attribute changes the name of the `<ROW>` attribute "num".
`-useNullAttrId`	`-useNullAttrID` configures whether or not null elements will have an attribute, otherwise it is omitted.
`-collectionIdAttr`	The `collectionIdAttr` attribute generates an attribute for each collection element.

Command Line Options	Function
-styleSheet -styleSheetType	The utility does not perform XSLT processing of the XML encapsulated query result set that it generates, but does allow the developer to specify the location of the stylesheet for another process to apply, and the MIME type of that stylesheet. These will be acted upon by an XSLT processor without being explicitly named at the invocation.
-errorTag	When errors occur in processing, for example a table not existing, the error report itself is in the form of an XML document. The -errorTag argument names the tag surrounding the text of the error message.
-raiseException	If the -raiseException option is used, however, instead of catching the exception and reporting it (still generating a valid document), the utility will throw a oracle.xml.sql. OracleXMLSQLException. This is useful when invoking the utility from a script, making it safe to assume that if a document was successfully generated, the database connection was established and the query executed, and if not, an error must have occurred.

-raiseNoRows Exception	Similarly, if the SQL is successfully executed but the query returned no matches, the default behavior is to generate an well-formed document that contains no rows, as follows:
	
	`<?xml version="1.0"?>`
	
	`<ROWSET />`
	
	This may cause problems if the output is expected by the next command in a batch script. The -raiseNoRowsException option will cause oracle.xml.sql.OracleXMLSQLNoRowsException instead.

-maxrows
 	
-skiprows
	When returning a large recordset in a consistent order, particularly over the Web, it is often necessary to break it into a series of smaller pages for quick downloading. -maxrows followed by an integer number instructs Oracle XML SQL to only return that number of rows in a document. -skiprows means to ignore the number of rows before assembling the document. On two subsequent command lines to produce two documents from a 100 row result set, these arguments would be:
	
	`-maxrows 50 "SELECT... ORDER BY id"`
	
	`-maxrows 50 -skiprows 50 "SELECT... ORDER by id"`
	
	This technique is highly suitable for automation via shell scripting.

A Java harness for calling exactly the same routines from within a program is straightforward, and provides yet another technique for generating XML from relational data. This is saved as XMLQuery.java:

```
import java.sql.*;
import oracle.jdbc.*;
import oracle.xml.sql.query.*;
import org.w3c.dom.*;

public class XMLQuery {

    public XMLQuery(String sql) {
        try {
            DriverManager.registerDriver(new oracle.jdbc.driver.OracleDriver());
            Connection connection = DriverManager.getConnection
                            ("jdbc:oracle:thin:scott/tiger@dbserver:1521:proead");
            OracleXMLQuery query = new OracleXMLQuery(connection, sql);
            // set query options here

            System.out.println(query.getXMLString());
        } catch (SQLException e) {
            System.err.println(e.toString());
        }
    }

    public static void main(String[] args) {
        if (args.length == 1)
            new XMLQuery(args[0]);
        else
            System.err.println("Usage: java XMLQuery 'SQL in double quotes'");
    }
}
```

Try the following:

```
C:\xml>java XMLQuery "select * from ingredients"
```

The output should be:

```
<ROWSET>
    <ROW num="1">
        <ID>1</ID>
        <LINE>1</LINE>
        <SUPPLIER_ID>1</SUPPLIER_ID>
        <QUANTITY>175g</QUANTITY>
        <DESCRIPTION>self raising flour</DESCRIPTION>
    </ROW>
    <ROW num="2">
        <ID>1</ID>
        <LINE>2</LINE>
        <SUPPLIER_ID>2</SUPPLIER_ID>
        <QUANTITY>6 tablespoons</QUANTITY>
        <DESCRIPTION>golden syrup</DESCRIPTION>
    </ROW>
    <ROW num="3">
        <ID>1</ID>
        <LINE>3</LINE>
        <SUPPLIER_ID>3</SUPPLIER_ID>
        <QUANTITY>3</QUANTITY>
        <DESCRIPTION>eggs</DESCRIPTION>
    </ROW>
</ROWSET>
```

Observe the following:

❑ The `org.w3c.dom` package is needed to use the `OracleXMLQuery` class, even though no DOM objects are used in the example above.

❑ The API is very simple to use, in fact there are only two lines in the code above that use it, and yet they do all of the useful work. The SQL statement on the command line must be passed within quotes, or Java will interpret it as several different arguments; this is the same as the supplied command line utility.

❑ Note the point in the source code directly after the OracleXMLQuery is created, using the database connection, and the SELECT statement. Here, you can call methods within the query object corresponding to the command line parameters. So, for example, valid code to control the output of the XML would be statements like `query.setErrorTag("ERR");` Here is also where you could perform XSL processing, using `query.setStyleSheet("recipe.xsl");` – the stylesheet will automatically be applied when `getXMLString()` is called.

Loading a Database Using XSLT

From the database schema, there are two tables (`recipes` and `ingredients`) in which data must be inserted; therefore, two XSLT transformations are required (or, equivalently, a transformation which produces multiple output files – most XSLT processors including Oracle's can now generate multiple output files from a single transformation). There is no need to perform these according to master-details relational integrity constraints, which means that the foreign key relationship logic and the matching of sequence numbers remain a concern. For the purpose of the example, we will assume that SQL triggers within Oracle itself will fulfill this.

The first transformation will extract values for the `recipes` table. As XSLT is a simple scripting language in its own right, there is no necessity for any configuration file, as the configuration information is the stylesheet itself. The `<ID>` element is computed from the `position()` function in XPath, with a dummy value added just to make sure it doesn't clash with existing data in the table. Save this file as `recipes_table.xsl`, and then run `oraxsl` to process the source XML file. Also, notice the strong similarity between this output and the format generated by OracleXML and similar tools – this is required if the parser is to understand it. The result should be saved as `recipe_table.xsl`:

```
<?xml version = "1.0"?>
<ROWSET xsl:version="1.0" xmlns:xsl="http://www.w3.org/1999/XSL/Transform">
<xsl:for-each select="snack/recipe">
<ROW>
    <ID><xsl:value-of select="position() + 2"/></ID>
    <name><xsl:value-of select="name"/></name>
</ROW>
</xsl:for-each>
</ROWSET>
```

The command for this is:

```
C:\xml>java oracle.xml.parser.v2.oraxsl newrecipe.xml recipe_table.xsl
```

The result is:

```
<?xml version = '1.0' encoding = 'UTF-8'?>
<ROWSET>
    <ROW>
        <ID>3</ID>
        <name>Rhubarb Crumble</name>
    </ROW>
</ROWSET>
```

Note that you can always use redirection (that is, *>filename*) in both Unix and Windows to output the result to a file. Next, we will do the same for the `ingredients` tag. Again, assumptions must be made for values we do not know. This code is again executed using the `oraxsl` utility. Save the result as `ingredients_table.xml`.

```
<?xml version = "1.0"?>
<ROWSET xsl:version="1.0" xmlns:xsl="http://www.w3.org/1999/XSL/Transform">
<xsl:for-each select="snack/recipe/ingredients/item">
<ROW>
    <ID>3</ID>
    <LINE><xsl:value-of select="position()"/></LINE>
    <supplier>2</supplier>
    <TEXT><xsl:value-of select="."/></TEXT>
</ROW>
</xsl:for-each>
</ROWSET>
```

The insertion is performed from the command line. The command line specifies both the name of the source XML file, and the table in which to insert it:

```
C:\xml>java OracleXML putXML -user "scott/tiger" -conn \
    "jdbc:oracle:thin:@dbserver:1521:proead" -ignoreCase -filename \
        recipes_table.xml recipe
successfully inserted 1 rows into recipes

C:\xml>java OracleXML putXML -user "scott/tiger" -conn \
    "jdbc:oracle:thin:@dbserver:1521:proead" -ignoreCase -filename \
        ingredients_table.xml ingredients
successfully inserted 3 rows into ingredients
```

This utility allows the row tag name to be set on the command line, but does not allow any other form of mapping, for example tag names to column names. The XSLT must therefore take care of this, in addition to extracting data into table format. This example shows that insertion of data from XML into Oracle can be very simple. The previous, all Java, example illustrates techniques for pre-processing XML beyond the ability of XSLT.

XML and Distributed Processing

An alternative to XML for inter-process communication in distributed, heterogeneous systems is the use of serialized Java objects. A Java class can be defined to include complex data structures and the logic that acts on these structures. This Java class can then be instantiated, populated, and converted to a byte stream for storage or transmission. Subsequently, these streams may be reconstituted into Java objects for processing, which may simply involve retrieving properties and loading them into a relational database table, or something more sophisticated. In this case, the functionality offered overlaps with that of XML. Theoretically, it is even possible to load an XML document into a Java DOM object and then use Java to serialize it, although in practice this will almost certainly be slower than reparsing the original document.

One scenario where sending serialized Java objects around the network might be more appropriate than sending XML is where the XML document is received from a third party application, but internal processing will be within a Java application, and you want to distribute the loading on the parser away from the main business logic for performance reasons. For example, a client application, or a process server located within a middle tier, would be likely to encounter an XML document for handling independently, retrieving a complex object or a multi-record result set before beginning a series of operations. Loading a document containing all the data required, rather than querying the database for each individual item, leverages a longer transmission time against reduced latency and causes protocol overheads on the network between the tiers.

A serialized Java class is able to transport its logic along with its data. This capability is not available to pure XML. Examples include both business logic and more generic object manipulation, for example Dictionary (Hash Table) extensions, sorting routines, or arithmetic functions. If this functionality is necessary, it indicates that the problem has become the design of a distributed process application, rather than database integration or content presentation. XML is purely designed for the transport and exchange of structured data, and while XML is an excellent standard on which to define the messages between distributed objects, it cannot be used in place of them.

A widely supported method for transferring relational data from a server to a client on demand is the JDBC API. There are advantages to using this mechanism for purely relational data, particularly when the query must be assembled at run time. Although there is an overhead in establishing a session with the database, the overhead of transporting result sets across the network is lower than with XML, especially in the case of large result sets. This is because XML embeds the meta-data of each column into each record, whereas a conventional relational query need only include this information at the start of each result set. While textual data with many repeating character sequences compresses very efficiently, this will not in general reduce network traffic unless additional processor resources are used to achieve the compression, for example transmission across Java Zip Streams. JDBC offers easy access to features such as prepared statements, explicit transaction control, and server stored procedures, which are taken for granted by many developers, and iterating across a returned recordset is straightforward.

However, in some circumstances, XML offers advantages over JDBC. Firstly, by adopting an XML based mechanism, the developer can use the same code to communicate bi-directionally between the client and the server, and can leverage push techniques. The same technique will also permit peer-to-peer communication between distributed components within each tier, in a way that JDBC cannot, as it would require each object to have a SQL parser embedded. XML does not require drivers or bridges to other binary protocols such as the common JDBC-ODBC, only a suitable parser at each end. XML can describe and deliver record structures including nested structures in a universally acceptable format, and ragged hierarchies (in which each branch has a different depth of children or number of leaf nodes).

Almost any data source can generate XML, and each source only needs to be XML-enabled once to become available to any other XML-aware application, rather then being reliant on third party protocols and drivers. As both documents and recordsets can be formatted as XML documents, template filling on the client application becomes unnecessary in many cases. If it is still necessary, modifying the client template does not require any modification to either the query submitted by the client, nor to the server logic. An example of this is in the generation and delivery of an HTML document to an HTTP client. If the browser supports it, an XML document will be sent by the server, with a cascading stylesheet applied within the browser itself, otherwise the server can use an XSLT template. In either case, the display logic and the application logic are entirely divorced. The key difference between XML and JDBC is tightness of coupling. Using XML is loosely coupled with regard to changing data structure, in terms of synchronous access (XML over asynchronous messaging), and in terms of server availability and security constraints.

In summary JDBC and XML have a significant overlap in terms of functionality, but each has its own particular strengths and weaknesses; both are fully supported by the Oracle platform, and can be combined in a single application.

This chapter has so far covered the integration of Oracle with XML from the perspectives of getting data into and out of the database, and manipulating XML both inside and outside of the database. We have examined techniques searching XML documents, and transforming them for presentation, as well as pre-processing XML for use in another application. We encountered how to index and search XML documents in Chapter 19, Oracle's XDK, available for download on http://technet.oracle.com, and interMedia Text are the core tools for working with XML in an Oracle environment, and allow the use of familiar programming languages such as Java and PL/SQL. In addition, the capability of command line execution means that the tools can be called from scripting languages.

The XML Class Generators

As we saw in the previous section, XML and Java both have a part to play in developing distributed applications. However, this invites the question of how the object model represented by the XML Document Type Definition, and the same object model as represented in the Java class and interface definitions, should be coordinated. Oracle's answer to this is to allow Java (or C++) class definitions to be generated automatically from the DTD.

Using a Document Type Definition (DTD) as the source, a class generator creates a series of classes that correspond to each element of the DTD, and can be instantiated and assembled within applications. One class is created for each named element within the DTD, and objects instantiated in these classes are nested within one another to represent the hierarchical structure of an XML document, where all nodes are descended from a root node. They provide a means for creating XML documents from within any application, through making the appropriate method calls, without explicitly writing raw XML, for example using the println() method. In straightforward applications, the use of a class generator is a significant overhead; however, in production their true value is that they greatly simplify constructing a well-formed document. The class generators make use of the XML parsers, but currently work from DTDs rather than XML Schemas. Schemas also include support for validation, but this functionality will not be provided by the present version of the generated classes.

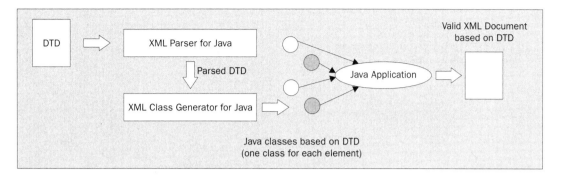

The class generators allow you to create classes that represent the specific structure of your documents: if your documents refer to bank accounts, customers, and transactions, then you can create classes that relate to these business objects. This provides an alternative to the approach of using the DOM, where the application instead has to deal in terms of completely generic classes such as Elements, Attributes, and Text nodes.

The Java Class Generator

The XML Class Generator is a Java utility for simplifying the creation of well-formed XML documents from individual data elements. These documents, for example, may subsequently be stored within an Oracle database for indexing, or later retrieval and manipulation.

> *To use the Class Generator, the library* `classgen.jar` *and the XML Parser* `xmlparserv2.jar` *must be installed, and their JAR files included within the classpath. These are available for download from http://technet.oracle.com as part of the XML/JAVA class generator download. There are versions of both of these libraries for Unix and NT, but the actual JAR files are identical, just the archive method is different. Documentation is included within the download.*

In this example, we will take a DTD and generate the corresponding Java classes for each element within that DTD. From the fields entered via an HTML form we will create an XML document, using the Java classes we have generated, and then load it into an Oracle database table. This HTML form will generate the input for a JavaServer Page, which will use a JavaBean to create an XML document from the submitted data, using the APIs generated previously.

Other uses for this tool are in the field of inter-process communication between applications, possibly running on different platforms and connected only via an interface carrying textual data. This is especially useful where applications are developed by different teams, perhaps in different companies. The development teams would only need to agree the DTD, and then generate an interface, before communication of structured data could commence. Defining the interface between applications in the form of a DTD gives the two teams much more flexibility to develop their code independently than if the interface was defined in terms of Java classes and methods.

The XML document used in the example is `recipe.xml`, which was shown at the beginning of the chapter, and the DTD `snack.DTD` corresponding to this, which we gave earlier.

However, `snack.DTD` is separated from the document for generating a Java wrapper around the document, in essence an API to the document structure for populating its elements using method calls that pass parameters into an object representing the document itself. In principle, this is the same as declaring a class containing nothing but properties and methods to set and retrieve values of those properties for encapsulating a particular data structure. Generating the source code for the API class requires a simple harness, again written in Java (before this code can be compiled, ensure that the classpath on your system includes `classgen.jar`):

```java
import java.awt.*;
import java.io.*;
import oracle.xml.classgen.*;
import oracle.xml.parser.v2.*;
import org.w3c.dom.*;
import org.xml.sax.*;

public class ClassGenExample extends Frame {

    private FileDialog fd;

    /** To generate a Java class API for an XML document defined
      * by a DTD, load the DTD from disk (could just as easily have
      * been from a URL), process the DTD from its root node,
      * and finally output the new Java source file. For more
      * industrial grade usage, this class could be modified to
      * parse all the XML documents in one directory and send the
      * results to another. In this case, exception handling would
      * have to be at the level of an individual file, so one
      * malformed document wouldn't stop the entire batch.
      */

    public ClassGenExample() {
        try {
            processDTD(getInputFileReader());
        } catch (Exception e) {
            System.err.println(e.toString());
            e.printStackTrace();
        }
        System.exit(0);
    }

    /** parse the parameter into the DOM, then generate a
      * java source file, and return it as a String.
      */

    private void processDTD(FileReader input)
                    throws SAXException, XMLParseException, IOException {
        /** Instantiate a parser, and process the document into
          * data structures needed by the next stage
          */

        DOMParser parser = new DOMParser();
        parser.setValidationMode(true);
        parser.parse(input);
        XMLDocument xmldoc = parser.getDocument();
        xmldoc.print(System.err);
        DTD xmldtd = (DTD)xmldoc.getDoctype();

        /** find out which tag is the root of the document
          */

        String root = xmldoc.getDocumentElement().getTagName();
```

```
        /** now use the ClassGenerator to convert the DTD into Java.
         * by default, javadoc comments will be included, and the
         * XML will be validated. The output of the class generator
         * can be either a text source code file, or a serialised
         * Java object.
         */

        ClassGenerator generator = new ClassGenerator();
        generator.generate(xmldtd, root);
    }

    /** We extended Frame in this class in order to be able to use
     * the AWT FileDialog. Note that this method returns a FileReader,
     * not the file itself, as the Parser prefers to do its own reading.
     */

    private FileReader getInputFileReader() throws FileNotFoundException {
        fd = new FileDialog(this, "Select XML File", FileDialog.LOAD);
        fd.show();
        File file = new File(fd.getDirectory(), fd.getFile());
        return new FileReader(file);
    }

    public static void main (String[] args) {
        if (args.length != 0)
            System.err.println("Usage: java ClassGenExample");
        else
            new ClassGenExample();
    }
}
```

If you execute this code on the file snack.DTD, it will generate a series of Java files in the same directory as the XML document. These are:

```
Description.java
Ingredients.java
Item.java
Method.java
Name.java
Number.java
Quantity.java
Recipe.java
Snack.java
Step.java
Supplier.java
Task.java
```

The process will also generate the file Snack_DTD.txt containing the generated code's own version of the DTD. On my system, there appears to be a bug with this part, and the file may be empty. In that case, copy the snack.DTD to Snack_DTD.txt.

We will now use these generated classes to generate the XML document from a submission of the following HTML form:

```html
<HTML>
    <HEAD><TITLE>Recipe input form</TITLE></HEAD>
    <BODY>
        <FORM method="POST" ACTION="insertrecipe.jsp">
            Recipe Name:<BR/>
            <INPUT TYPE="TEXT" name="name"/><P/>
            Ingredients:<BR/>
            <TABLE COLS=3>
            <TR>
                <TH>Quantity</TH>
                <TH>Description</TH>
                <TH>Supplier</TH>
            </TR>
            <TR>
                <TD><INPUT TYPE="TEXT" name="quantity"/></TD>
                <TD><INPUT TYPE="TEXT" name="description"/></TD>
                <TD><INPUT TYPE="TEXT" name="supplier"/></TD>
            </TR>
            <TR>
                <TD><INPUT TYPE="TEXT" name="quantity"/></TD>
                <TD><INPUT TYPE="TEXT" name="description"/></TD>
                <TD><INPUT TYPE="TEXT" name="supplier"/></TD>
            </TR>
            <TR>
                <TD><INPUT TYPE="TEXT" name="quantity"/></TD>
                <TD><INPUT TYPE="TEXT" name="description"/></TD>
                <TD><INPUT TYPE="TEXT" name="supplier"/></TD>
            </TR>
            </TABLE>
            <P/>
            Method:<BR/>
            <INPUT TYPE="TEXT" name="task"/><BR/>
            <INPUT TYPE="TEXT" name="task"/><BR/>
            <INPUT TYPE="TEXT" name="task"/><BR/>
            <P/>
            <INPUT TYPE="SUBMIT"/>
        </FORM>
    </BODY>
</HTML>
```

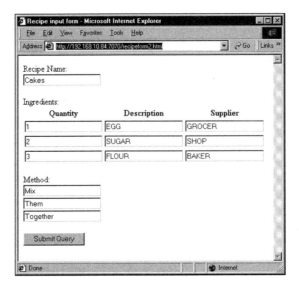

JavaServer Pages are executed within the Oracle Application Server in these examples. The default login (username `scott`, password `tiger`) is used, and we create a table in which to hold the data:

```
CREATE TABLE xml_recipes (id number PRIMARY KEY, text CLOB);
CREATE SEQUENCE seq_recipe START WITH 1 INCREMENT BY 1;
```

The JSP file, and all the compiled classes must be visible to the web server, as must the file `Snack_DTD.txt`, which is required by the tool-generated `Snack.java` class.

Here is the code for the JSP page, `insertrecipe.jsp`. Place this file on the JSP web server in the same directory as the HTML page above (which references it):

```
<%@ page language = "java"
         contentType = "text/html"
         import = "RecipeXMLBean"
         isThreadSafe = "false"
         errorPage = "xerrorpage.jsp"
%>
<jsp:useBean id = "rxb"
             class = "RecipeXMLBean"
             scope = "request"/>
<%
   // Set the name of the /snack/recipe this method
   // is defined in the bean code RecipeXMLBean.java

   rxb.setName(request.getParameter("name"));

   // The quantity, description and supplier parameters
   // are returned as arrays. We are assuming that if
   // quantity is filled in, the other fields will be to.
   // more rigorous error checking would be used in
   // production. In addition, an errorpage directive should be
   // used. These are added to /snack/recipe/ingredients

   String[] quantity = request.getParameterValues("quantity");
   String[] description = request.getParameterValues("description");
   String[] supplier= request.getParameterValues("supplier");

   for (int i = 0; i < quantity.length; i++)
      rxb.addItem(quantity[i], description[i], supplier[i]);

   // The same technique is used to add method information
   // to /snack/recipe/method

   String task[] = request.getParameterValues("task");
   for (int i = 0; i < task.length; i++)
      rxb.addStep(i + 1, task[i]);

   // Now finalise the newly created XML document in the
   // database

   rxb.persistXML();

%>
<HTML>
<HEAD><TITLE>Recipe saved</TITLE></HEAD>
<BODY>
Your recipe has been saved in the database. <A HREF = "recipeform.html">
Enter another?</A>
</BODY>
```

Finally, here is the JavaBean that assembles the XML document, and stores it in the database via a JDBC connection (this bean must be compiled and within the classpath of the JSP server):

```java
import java.io.*;
import java.sql.*;
import java.util.*;
import oracle.xml.classgen.*;
import oracle.xml.parser.v2.*;

public class RecipeXMLBean {
    private Connection    connection;
    private Statement     statement;
    private ResultSet     results;
    private String        query;

    private Snack         snack;
    private Recipe        recipe;
    private Ingredients   ingredients;
    private Method        method;

    /** Open a connection to Oracle when this bean is instantiated, and
      * create a new Snack document for populating with the form's data.
      * We are assuming that a Snack contains one Recipe.
      */

    public RecipeXMLBean() throws SQLException,
                                  InvalidContentException {
        DriverManager.registerDriver(new oracle.jdbc.driver.OracleDriver());
        Connection connection = DriverManager.getConnection
                    ("jdbc:oracle:thin:@dbserver:1521:proead","scott","tiger");
        statement = connection.createStatement();

        snack = new Snack();
        System.out.println("Snack created");
        System.out.println("Connection " + connection);
        recipe = new Recipe();
        ingredients = new Ingredients();
        method = new Method();
    }

    /** Sets the <NAME> tag of the document. alternative syntax is
      * NAME recipename = new NAME(); recipename.addData(name);
      */

    public void setName(String name) throws InvalidContentException {
        Name recipe_name = new Name(name);
        recipe.addNode(recipe_name);
    }

    /** Constructs the <ITEM> element, populates it, and adds it to
      * <Ingredients>. There are multiple elements, therefore no
      * conventions ITEM(quantity, description, supplier) constructor :0(
      * however, addNode() is overloaded in such a way that it can be
      * called with the class representing any of its child nodes, and
      * the correct node will be added (which cannot be done in the
      * equivalent PL/SQL toolkit). variable names indicate position
      * within the hierarchy.
      */
```

```java
public void addItem(String quantity, String description, String supplier)
            throws InvalidContentException {
    Item ingredients_item = new Item();
    Quantity item_quantity = new Quantity(quantity);
    Description item_description = new Description(description);
    Supplier item_supplier = new Supplier(supplier);

    ingredients_item.addNode(item_quantity);
    ingredients_item.addNode(item_description);
    ingredients_item.addNode(item_supplier);

    ingredients.addNode(ingredients_item);
}

/** Add a step to the method. note the abbreviated syntax */
public void addStep(int number, String task)
            throws InvalidContentException {
    Step method_step = new Step();
    method_step.addNode(new Number(Integer.toString(number)));
    method_step.addNode(new Task(task));

    method.addNode(method_step);
}

/** INSERTs the completed XML document into an Oracle table. get
  * the next value from seq_recipe, then insert into table xml_recipe.
  * there is no method for retrieving the generated XML document as
  * a string, therefore some manipulation is required.
  */

public void persistXML() throws InvalidContentException, SQLException {
    snack.addNode(recipe);
    recipe.addNode(ingredients);
    recipe.addNode(method);

    results = statement.executeQuery("SELECT seq_recipe.NEXTVAL FROM DUAL");
    results.next();
    String id = Integer.toString(results.getInt("NEXTVAL"));

    ByteArrayOutputStream stream = new ByteArrayOutputStream();
    snack.print(stream);
    String xml = stream.toString();

    statement.executeUpdate("INSERT INTO xml_recipes (id, text) VALUES ('"
                        + id + "', '" + xml + "')");
}
}
```

Using the Oracle XSL Transformation Engine

Earlier in this chapter we looked at the XSLT language and its use for defining transformations. Now we'll look at how this can be exploited within a distributed web application.

Transforming Before Display

Once the content is in the database, there must be a mechanism for viewing the data. Ideally, the web server will minimize the number of trips it needs to make to the database, and will be able to present the content appropriately to different web browsers. The implementation method will again be a JavaServer Page and a JavaBean, using Oracle class libraries. An XSLT transform operates on an XML document to produce a different XML document. This can be used to extract the contents of particular elements, substitute elements for differently named elements, or convert the document into a different XML vocabulary, for example taking XML data and producing HTML for display in a web browser.

The following example generates two possible forms of XML document, a list of all the recipes stored within the database, or the full document corresponding to a particular recipe, identified by the primary key of the table. These documents will be processed using a different XSLT stylesheet, depending on the HTTP client that is used to access them. In this case, the presentation logic is embedded within the stylesheet, and the JSP is required purely to interface between the HTTP protocol and the logic contained within the Java class. Note that no bean-specific functionality is required for these examples, and that they are ordinary Java classes.

```
<%@ page language = "java"
         contentType = "text/html"
         import = "XSLQueryBean"
         isThreadSafe = "false"
%>
<jsp:useBean id = "xqb" class = "XSLQueryBean" scope="session"/>
<jsp:setProperty name="xqb" property="*" />
<%
%>
<%= xqb.getDocument(request) %>
```

The JSP passes the entire request to the JavaBean and it will process the parameters, generate an XML document, process it with the appropriate XSLT stylesheet for the client platform, and output the resulting HTML here (see contentType, above). This bean persists for the life of the user session, so only needs to speak to the database when it is instantiated. The problem with this approach is that it will miss updates that occur to the underlying data set during the life of the session. In addition, we are performing the XSLT transformation for every request, which uses processor resources. Therefore, this technique should be used when you have fairly static datasets of which different portions of the same documents need to be used by widely varying client applications. An example of this type of profile is found in the multiple channel delivery scenario, where many different types of device, each with its own characteristics, need to look at the same information, for example, to check television listings (or to look at snack recipes). If so, there is little to gain by caching transformed documents here, as the data will not change over a session, and for performance, reverse proxy caches can be implemented between the bean server and the client device, if devices and delivery channels can be matched (for example, by subnet range).

All the XML and XSLT processing is contained within the bean. The XSLT transforms are essentially the same as in the examples earlier in the chapter, but with the addition of processing directives for the <LIST><LINK> elements, and the <ERROR> tag. If the XSLT does not specify template rules for these elements, the error "Expected EOF" will be reported by the transformation method. A full description of JSP error and exception handling is beyond the scope of this chapter.

To use this code, the Oracle XML Parser version 2 must be installed as outlined earlier in the chapter, and the Oracle JDBC library, which is installed along with the Oracle database. To use this bean, save the code as XSLQueryBean.java, compile it, and place the class file in the classpath of the servlet engine.

```java
import java.io.*;
import java.net.*;
import java.sql.*;
import java.util.*;
import javax.servlet.http.*;
import oracle.xml.parser.v2.*;
import org.w3c.dom.*;
import org.xml.sax.*;

public class XSLQueryBean {
    private Connection   connection;
    private Statement    statement;
    private ResultSet    results;

    private Hashtable    cache;           // the XML documents
    private DOMParser    parser;
    private static int CLOBSIZE = 4096;

    /** When instantiating the class, open a connection to Oracle
      * to grab the entire record set from the xml_recipe table.
      * Just in case, limit the length of the CLOB to 4k - increase
      * this depending on the size of your documents, and the capacity
      * of your server. The CLOB interface requires JDBC 2.0. The CLOB
      * API holds a pointer to the CLOB on the server rather than the
      * value itself, until a method like getSubString() is called.
      * Note that CLOB substrings start from 1, not 0. Also load the
      * XSL templates into a Hashtable, if you store them in Oracle[f190]
      */

    public XSLQueryBean() throws SQLException {
        DriverManager.registerDriver(new oracle.jdbc.driver.OracleDriver());
        Connection connection = DriverManager.getConnection
                    ("jdbc:oracle:thin:@dbserver:1521:proead","scott","tiger");
        statement = connection.createStatement();

        results = statement.executeQuery("SELECT id, text FROM xml_recipes");
        cache = new Hashtable();
        while (results.next()) {
            String id  = results.getString("id");
```

You will need the Oracle JDBC driver archive `classes12.zip` as opposed to `classes111.zip` in your classpath in order to read a `Clob`:

```java
            Clob c = results.getClob("text");
            cache.put(id, c.getSubString(1, CLOBSIZE));
        }

    statement.close();
    connection.close();

    parser = new DOMParser();
}

/** The only public method, acting as a dispatcher for the real
 * work of this bean. The request from the client device
 * is passed in, giving access to parameters in the same
 * way as JSP. First, create the XML document, then perform
 * the platform-specific transformation. All errors are passed
 * up the hierarchy for handling at the JSP server level (i.e.
 * one set of exception handling for the whole application).
 */

public String getDocument(HttpServletRequest request)
                   throws XMLParseException, SAXException,
                          IOException, XSLException {
    String xml;
    String id = request.getParameter("id");
    if (id == null)
        xml = listAllRecipes();
    else
        xml = displayRecipe(request.getParameter("id"));

    return transformXML(xml, request.getHeader("User-Agent"));
}

/** List all the recipes, defined by the contents of
 * /snack/recipe/name. Note that the entire XML documents
 * are returned. The documents are queried using XPath,
 * and a new, temporary XML document is built. This is
 * so that a single XSL handles presentation for each client
 *(using //name is easy, but a performance hit, because
 * all nodes must be traversed to find it! )
 */

private String listAllRecipes() throws XMLParseException, SAXException,
                                IOException, XSLException {
    StringBuffer xmlbuffer = new StringBuffer();
    StringBuffer resultbuffer = new StringBuffer();

    resultbuffer.append("<LIST>");

    Enumeration e = cache.keys();
    while (e.hasMoreElements()) {
        String key = e.nextElement().toString();
        String currentdoc = cache.get(key).toString();
        XMLDocument xmldoc = stringToDoc(currentdoc);
```

```
            NodeList nl = ((XMLNode)xmldoc).selectNodes("//name/text()",
                        (NSResolver)xmldoc.getDocumentElement());
        // should only be one node matched, but just in case...
        for (int i = 0; i < nl.getLength(); i++)
            resultbuffer.append("<LINK><LINKID>" + key + "</LINKID><LINKname>" +
                        nl.item(i).getNodeValue() + "</LINKname></LINK>");

            resultbuffer.append("</LIST>");
        }

    return resultbuffer.toString();
    }

    /** Return a String containing the XML of a recipe specified by id
      * in the method parameter. We are catching the NullPointerException
      * thrown by toString() if there isn't a match, and returning an XML
      * fragment anyway. If there were lots of errors to trap, we would
      * wrap generating the <ERROR> document in a method of its own.
      */

    private String displayRecipe(String id) {
        try {
            String xml = cache.get(id).toString();
            return xml;
        } catch (NullPointerException e) {
            return "<ERROR>No such Recipe!</ERROR>";
        }
    }
}
```

Depending on the value of the target client device or browser software, we may perform a different XSLT transformation. The suggested mapping is hard-coded here, but the styles could easily be loaded from an Oracle table, or even from another XML document on the server, using a URL. The stylesheet requires the URL in order to find any includes or external references in the XML (although we aren't using any). Note that this technique will not necessarily handle Unicode:

```
    private String transformXML(String xml, String target)
                    throws SAXException, MalformedURLException,
                        XSLException, IOException {
        /** A possible implementation of conditional stylesheet application:
        String transform = "mozilla.xsl";
        if ((target.indexOf("MSIE")) > 0) transform = "msie.xsl";

        URL base = new URL("http://localhost:7070");
        URL url = new URL(base,transform);
        parser.parse(url);
        XMLDocument xsl = parser.getDocument();

        XSLStylesheet xsls = new XSLStylesheet(xsl, url);
        XSLProcessor xp = new XSLProcessor();

        ByteArrayOutputStream stream = new ByteArrayOutputStream();
        xp.processXSL(xsls, stringToDoc(xml), stream);
```

```
          return stream.toString();
          */
      return xml;
      }

      /** Utility method to create an XMLDocument from a string. To do
       * this, we need to create a stream source from a string. Using
       * an InputSource saves having to set the base URL for the parser.
       */

      private XMLDocument stringToDoc(String xml)
                            throws IOException, SAXException, XMLParseException {
          StringReader sr = new StringReader(xml);
          InputSource is = new InputSource(sr);
          parser.parse(is);
          return parser.getDocument();
      }
  }
```

The Oracle XML Development Kit classes are generally designed to deal with streams and URLs rather than Strings or character arrays. For example, in the `stringToDoc()` method of the `XSLQueryBean` class above, the `StringReader` and `InputSource` objects are used to convert the `String` object into an acceptable form. Similar type conversions are also needed for the `transformXML()` method. This is one of the reasons that it is easier to load the XSLT from the web server rather than storing it in Oracle itself, although writing a JSP to run a JDBC query and output the relevant database column would be trivial. It might seem more elegant to transfer XML around within and between applications within `XMLDocument` objects. By doing so you lose sight of one of the key justifications for XML in the first place: that it encapsulates complicated structured data within one of the simplest data formats: plain text. Passing complex data can easily be accomplished by wrapping the structures (using, say, Java `Vector` and `Dictionary` classes) within a JavaBean, but doing so sacrifices the true openness of XML. There are Oracle components, such as interMedia Text, that rely on plain text to perform their functions, and will parse XML for themselves.

The address `http://localhost:7070/` refers to an HTTP server, running on the local workstation, on port 7070, which is a convention for development web servers (in this case, Oracle Web-to-Go Server). This URL will need to be modified to refer to your own development server, which can be any of those capable of providing a runtime environment for JavaServer Pages and servlets, configured according to your own development system. There is no way to instantiate the `XSLStylesheet` without providing a URL for resolving external entities (this URL is needed as the base for relative references), but reusing the URL used previously is sufficient. It is often more convenient to work with `String` and `StringBuffer` classes as opposed to the native `XMLDocument` and related classes, even though APIs are provided for assembling XML documents, since many fragments are simple. However, even for simple or small documents, the XPath query system of returning matching nodes is easy to use and quite powerful. Hopefully, this code will be useful for utilizing the functionality provided by Oracle in more flexible ways. An improvement to the example would be to store the mapping rules of client device to XSLT within the database for easy reuse and modification, and to cache the XSLT, since the client device cannot (currently) change within a single session. To accomplish this, query the Oracle table containing the XSLT, and copy the CLOBs and the name of the transform into the built-in hash table class provided as part of the Java language. This would particularly be of value if there are many different client devices accessing the same application, for example, PDAs, mobile phones, games consoles, and set-top boxes for televisions.

Transforming before Insertion

An alternative use for XSLT is to transform documents before they are loaded into Oracle, rather than before they are delivered to a client device after having been retrieved via an Oracle query. The following example, making use of methods defined in previous Java classes, shows an application that will listen on a TCP/IP port for a stream of XML documents, each one delineated by its tags, before transforming them and writing them to Oracle over a JDBC connection. The format of each document within the incoming stream will be the same as `recipe.xml`, that is, conforming to the same DTD.

We wouldn't necessarily recommend this approach for a production application. TCP/IP is a rather low-level interface, and it leaves all the complexities of routing, error handling, and recovery to be handled at application level. In production, a service such as this would be need to be fully multi-threaded, capable of concurrently and asynchronously handling many connections, and would be more configurable, for example supporting multiple tables and transforms. In addition, logic would be required, depending on data volume, server capacity and other factors, to determine when commits should occur, by batching multiple rows together independent of the size of the documents. Therefore, in practice you would probably want to send XML documents using a higher-level protocol such as HTTP or CORBA if you needed synchronous transmission, or over a message-passing service if you wanted secure, recoverable asynchronous delivery. However, the APIs for TCP/IP are simple, so it provides a good example of a simple communication protocol for tutorial purposes.

A new table is required to support this application. For this example, assume that a caterer is receiving an XML stream of orders, and wishes to collate in an Oracle table everything that will be required:

```
CREATE TABLE shopping_list (
    quantity VARCHAR2(80),
    description VARCHAR2(80),
    supplier VARCHAR2(80));
```

The source code for the service is a standalone Java application:

```
import java.io.*;
import java.net.*;
import java.sql.*;
import oracle.xml.sql.dml.*;
import oracle.xml.parser.v2.*;
import org.w3c.dom.*;
import org.xml.sax.*;

public class XSLStreamListener {
    private Connection     connection;
    private OracleXMLSave  oxs;
    private XSLProcessor   xp;
    private XSLStylesheet  xsls;
    private StringBuffer   xmlbuffer;
    private DOMParser      parser;
    private String         currentline;
    private boolean        readflag;
    private boolean        exitflag;
    private boolean        startflag;
```

Below is the sole constructor method, which initializes all the objects and variables required to perform the service. These are to establish a connection to Oracle, instantiate the Oracle-supplied classes for transforming documents and inserting into Oracle tables, and finally the routines needed for networking. This class can only handle a single stream at a time (the complexity of the Java required for a fully-fledged server is beyond the scope of this chapter). This type of service would be used where information is constantly generated and needs to be made available for query, possibly prior to being re-packaged into another XML document, and delivered to a client device (after another XSLT transformation) for example, share prices. For brevity's sake, the constructor also contains the main thread:

```
public XSLStreamListener(String port, String xslfile, String tablename)
                   throws SQLException, IOException,
                          XMLParseException, SAXException, XSLException {
   DriverManager.registerDriver(new oracle.jdbc.driver.OracleDriver());
   Connection connection = DriverManager.getConnection
                      ("jdbc:oracle:thin:scott/tiger@dbserver:1521:proead");

   oxs = new OracleXMLSave(connection, tablename);
   oxs.setIgnoreCase(true);
   oxs.insertXML("<?xml version='1.0'?>" +
             "<ROWSET><ROW><quantity>1</quantity>" +
             "<description>2</description>" +
             "<supplier>4</supplier></ROW></ROWSET>");

   // Load the XSLT stylesheet, from the disk this time, using the
   // XSU utility method to convert a filename in a string to a URL.
   // then instantiate a processor.
   URL xslurl = oxs.createURL(xslfile);
   parser = new DOMParser();
   parser.setPreserveWhitespace(true);
   parser.parse(xslurl);
   XMLDocument xsldoc = parser.getDocument();
   xsls = new XSLStylesheet(xsldoc, xslurl);
   xp = new XSLProcessor();

   // Initialize the networking - easy in Java :0)
   // the port should be >1024 if you are working on UNIX
   // NT users can use any port that isn't already in use
   ServerSocket server = new ServerSocket(Integer.parseInt(port));

   // Repeat until the exit flag is set within the loop:
   // wait for a connection to the server socket, then process the
   // text that is sent.
   exitflag = false;
   Socket socket = server.accept();
   InputStreamReader isr = new InputStreamReader(socket.getInputStream());
   BufferedReader br = new BufferedReader(isr);

   do {
       currentline = br.readLine();
       readflag = (currentline != null);
       //listen for a special 'eof' comment
       exitflag = readflag && currentline.startsWith("<!--XLISTENEOF-->");
       //listen for the beginning of an xml document
       startflag = readflag && currentline.startsWith("<?xml");
   } while (!startflag && !exitflag);
   if (!exitflag) xmlbuffer = new StringBuffer(currentline);
```

```
        readflag = true;
        while (!exitflag && readflag) {
            currentline = br.readLine();
            System.out.println(currentline);
            readflag = (currentline != null);
            exitflag = readflag && currentline.startsWith("<!--XLISTEN");
            if (!exitflag) xmlbuffer.append(currentline);
        }

        System.out.println("Processing");
        processDocument(xmlbuffer.toString());

        // terminate the session cleanly, ready for the next one.
        br.close();
        isr.close();
        socket.close();

        connection.close();
    }
```

Apply the XSLT transform previously loaded to the document received from the TCP stream. If this renders it into an acceptable form, save it in relational form to an Oracle table. Note that we are decomposing the document and storing it in columns, unlike previous examples where we have stored XML documents intact within single CLOB or VARCHAR2 columns. OracleXMLSave (part of XSU), unlike the rest of the XDK, is happy working with strings:

```
    private void processDocument(String document)
                    throws XSLException, IOException,
                           XMLParseException, SAXException {
        ByteArrayOutputStream baos = new ByteArrayOutputStream();
        xp.processXSL(xsls, stringToDoc(document), baos);
        System.out.println(baos.toString());
        oxs.insertXML(baos.toString());
        System.out.println("Inserted to Database");
    }

    /** See XSLQueryBean.java */
    private XMLDocument stringToDoc(String xml)
                        throws IOException, SAXException, XMLParseException {
        StringReader sr = new StringReader(xml);
        InputSource is = new InputSource(sr);
        parser.parse(is);
        return parser.getDocument();
    }

    /** Verify that the correct number of command line arguments are
      * present, then instantiate the class. No attempt to verify the
      * syntactic or semantic validity of any of the arguments, but that
      * will be caught by the exception handler. A different catch clause
      * for each subclass of exception would make the program more user
      * friendly.
      */
```

```
public static void main (String[] args) {
    try {
        if (args.length == 0) {
            new XSLStreamListener("2222","streamexample.xsl","shopping_list");
        }
        else if (args.length == 3) {
            new XSLStreamListener(args[0], args[1], args[2]);
        }
        else {
            System.err.println("Usage: java XSLStreamListener
                                <port><xsl><table>");
        }
    } catch (Exception e) {
        e.printStackTrace();
    }
}
}
```

The XSL transform `streamexample.xsl` used by this example is straightforward:

```
<?xml version = "1.0"?>
<ROWSET xsl:version="1.0" xmlns:xsl="http://www.w3.org/1999/XSL/Transform">
<xsl:for-each select="snack/recipe/ingredients/item">
    <ROW>
        <quantity><xsl:value-of select="quantity"/></quantity>
        <description><xsl:value-of select="description"/></description>
        <supplier><xsl:value-of select="supplier"/></supplier>
    </ROW>
</xsl:for-each>
</ROWSET>
```

To start this service, use the command line, passing in the port number, the XSLT filename, and the name of the database table:

```
C:\Documents\xmldev\>java XSLStreamListener 2222 streamexample.xsl shopping_list
```

To test this, from the command line, call `telnet localhost 2222` and paste in the XML document `recipe.xml`, followed by a newline. To send an end-of-file signal to the listener, type in `<!--XLISTENEOF-->` followed by a newline. The code will insert the record into the `shopping_list` table.

XSLT Performance

The performance of the XSLT transformation engine is affected by the structure of the XML document it processes, in terms of both speed and memory usage. An XML DTD or schema will be designed to fulfill the requirements of an application, but design decisions are a result of considering many factors. In some cases, it is necessary to trade the elegance of a data structure for additional performance. In particular, processing XML documents using XSLT can be performed 'on the fly', that is, in response to every request, or it can be performed off-line as a batch process, with content published to the web server in bulk. In either case, the entire document must be loaded before a transformation occurs, an extremely memory-intensive operation, making XSLT unsuitable at present for handling very large documents.

Clearly, the technology is advancing rapidly and each new release will bring improved performance. Nevertheless, we thought it would be useful to present a snapshot of some performance measurements using the current version of the software. The Java Development Kit runtime provides simple profiling tools, which we used to measure the performance of XSLT transformation on a document containing identical data elements, formatted as follows, but with each `<item>` repeated 1000 times:

	XML Format	XSLT Transform
Attributes only	```<ingredients>
<item quantity=
"1 cup"
description=
"Blueberries"
supplier=
"Safeway"/>
</ingredients>```	```<?xml version = "1.0"?>
<HTML xsl:version="1.0"
xmlns:xsl="http://www.w3.org/1999/XSL/
Transform">
<BODY>
<UL>
<xsl:for-each select=
"ingredients/item">
<LI>
<xsl:value-of select=
"@quantity"/>
of <xsl:value-of select=
"@description"/> from
<xsl:value-of select=
"@supplier"/>
</LI>
</xsl:for-each>
</UL>
</BODY>
</HTML>```
Elements only	```<ingredients>
<item>
<quantity>
1 cup
</quantity>
<description>
Blueberries
</description>
<supplier>
Safeway
</supplier>
</item>
</ingredients>```	```<?xml version = "1.0"?>
<HTML xsl:version="1.0"
xmlns:xsl="http://www.w3.org/1999/XSL/
Transform">
<BODY>
<UL>
<xsl:for-each select =
"ingredients/item">
<LI>
<xsl:value-of select ="
quantity"/> of
<xsl:value-of select =
"description"/> from
<xsl:value-of select =
"supplier"/>
</LI>
</xsl:for-each>
</UL>
</BODY>
</HTML>```
Mixed	```<ingredients>
<item description =
"Blueberries">
<supplier>
Safeway
</supplier>
<quantity>
1 cup
</quantity>
</item>
</ingredients>```	```<?xml version = "1.0"?>
<HTML xsl:version="1.0"
xmlns:xsl =
"http://www.w3.org/1999/XSL/Transform">
<BODY>
<UL>
<xsl:for-each
select="ingredients/item">
<LI>
<xsl:value-of select =
"quantity"/> of
<xsl:value-of select =
"@description"/> from
<xsl:value-of select =
"supplier"/>
</LI>
</xsl:for-each>
</UL>
</BODY>
</HTML>```

The first and most obvious point is the difference in information density between the first two examples. The first has a much better ratio of content to meta-content, but the disadvantage of adopting purely this structure is the limitation to record structure, with no nesting of hierarchical elements. The second, using elements instead of attributes increases the space required to describe each data element by about 61%. This effect will be multiplied for more complex structures. The third example is a compromise between the two. The XML document types are saved on the disk as `format1.xml`, `format2.xml`, and `format3.xml`, with their corresponding transforms saved as `format1.xsl`, `format2.xsl`, and `format3.xsl`. The general form of the Java profiling command, using the Sun JDK version 1.2.2 is:

```
C:\Documents\xmldev>java -Xrunhprof:cpu=times oracle.xml.parser.v2.oraxsl
    format1.xml format1.xsl format1.html
```

Information on additional profiling features may be obtained using `java -Xrunhprof:help`. Each of the XML documents is transformed 10 times, and average statistics gathered, and the statistics are divided into time spent within the `oracle.xml.parser.v2.*` package, and other packages used from the standard Java distribution. Other time is spent in `sun.*` classes.

Format	Total CPU time (ms)	Oracle %	Java %	Peak Memory Usage (k)
Attributes Only	4180	48.62%	44.26%	14404k
Elements Only	5600	57.82%	37.77%	16684k
Mixed	5190	51.99%	42.20%	15520k

The Oracle XSL transformer performs better, in this case, using attributes only as a means of representing data, sacrificing some of the richness of XML in the process. The tests used exactly the same raw data, and generated identical target documents, but with a 34% variance in speed on this machine configuration (Pentium III 450Mhz, 320M memory). The use of attributes only reduces the memory required for the job (86% of that required for elements-only), however much of the memory will be occupied by the Java runtime itself, making the actual memory used by each technique vary more widely. Predictably, the results for the mixed document structure are between the two extremes, in terms of both memory and CPU time.

Performance statistics may also be gathered for an XML parse without transformation, using the same source documents. These figures show that much of the work is actually performed by the Java runtime environment, and that XSLT transformation performance bears a close relationship to XML parsing performance.

Format	Total CPU time (ms)	Oracle %	Java %	Peak Memory Usage (k)
Attributes Only	2070	35.37%	60.34%	9336k
Elements Only	2390	45.27%	51.18%	8844k
Mixed	2190	41.17%	53.03%	8804k

One point to note is that XSLT syntax of the form `//item` is slower than `/snack/recipe/ingredients/item`, because it forces the parser to traverse all nodes searching for a match, rather than choosing a known path through the DOM tree.

The actual performance figures will vary for other DTDs, operating systems, Java virtual machines, and many other factors, but this example illustrates a technique, and the necessity, for profiling and analyzing XML structure in the early stages of application development.

Transviewer JavaBeans

The Transviewer JavaBeans are reusable components, similar in principle to COM or OCX controls used by Windows developers. They are used within visual development environments such as Oracle JDeveloper (also available via OTN, currently version 3.1) to encapsulate XDK functionality. JDeveloper is free to download, but subject to license restrictions, a copy of XDK is included within this package. There are five beans:

- ❏ The DOM Builder provides a bean interface to the XML parser. This allows asynchronous operation.

- ❏ The XSL Transformer, which performs a similar role for XSLT. This also allows asynchronous operation.

- ❏ The Source Viewer bean, which displays an XML document as source.

- ❏ The TransformPanel, a visual bean for running XSL transformations.

- ❏ The Tree Viewer bean displays an XML document as a tree, allowing manipulation and editing.

The `transview_v1_03.zip` package can currently be downloaded from http://technet.oracle.com.

A JavaBean is a reusable software component designed to provide abstracted services when embedded within an application, and to be manipulated using visual development tools, even if it does not have a graphical component itself, unlike Microsoft's OCX controls. The application-building tool will use Java's reflection and introspection mechanisms to determine which properties, methods and events are made publicly accessible by the bean, and offer a graphical interface for configuring the instance of the bean to be used within the application itself. Methods for accessing the values of properties, and for subscribing to events generated by the bean are public, as are bean-specific methods for invoking internal, encapsulated business logic. Subscribers are either passively informed when a property changes, or in some cases, they are offered the opportunity to block the change occurring. Most Java objects can be treated as beans to a limited extent, if they provide `get()` and `set()` methods for their properties, as in the previous JSP based examples. Beans may provide an auxiliary class offering additional information on the Bean itself, its methods, properties, events, and parameters, for use by the application-building tool, and these are referred to as Bean Info classes. Beans often also provide `Customizer` classes, which may offer wizard interfaces for configuring the Bean, but these are generally used only with sophisticated Beans.

Oracle provides a tool for building Bean applications, named JDeveloper, currently at release 3.1, and available for download from Oracle Technology Network. JDeveloper users can choose which Java version to use when starting the tool, and JDK version 1.2 must be selected to use the Transviewer Beans. To add the Beans to JDeveloper, use the following procedure:

1. Select Configure Palette from the Tools menu. This will present a tabbed dialog box, showing the available groups of Beans, their packages, and icons (which are specific to each individual Bean).

2. Select Add on the Pages tab and enter the text Transviewer. This is the name that will appear on the tabbed panel in the palette. If the palette is invisible, use the Toolbar option of the View menu to select it.

3. Select the newly created Transviewer page in the left hand panel, then switch to the Add from Archive pane by clicking the tab at the top of the dialog. Browse to the directory where you have unzipped the Transviewer archive, and select `xmlcomp.jar`. This file is located in the `lib` subdirectory of the installation.

4. *Shift-click* on all the available options, and click Install, then OK when this is complete.

5. Create a new library for the Transviewer package. Select Project | Properties from the Tools menu. On the Libraries tab, select New and then, on the dialog that will appear, enter the name `Transview` and select the button to the right of the classpath textbox. Select Add Zip/JAR and browse to the `lib` directory of the Transviewer installation. Choose xmlcomp.jar and OK out of all boxes.

Oracle's XDK includes five JavaBeans:

Name	Description
DOMBuilder	This Bean acts as a wrapper for the XML parser included with the XDK, supporting both visual programming and asynchronous parsing. This technique provides functionality similar to a batch queue, in that documents are submitted to the parser with control returning immediately to the controlling program, with parsing continuing in the background. Applications are notified of completion by registering listeners, which implement methods that are invoked on occurrence of events, for example a document being fully parsed.
XSL Transformer	The XSL Transformer bean is similar to the DOM Builder, in that it returns control to the calling program immediately, and notifies progress via registered listener classes, in which it invokes methods when events occur. In addition, like the DOM Builder, it simply wraps functionality offered by the XSL transformer provided by the XML Parser for Java component of the XDK. The difference is the provision of the bean interface, and the asynchronous execution. The XSL Transformer Bean and the DOM Builder Bean are both within the `oracle.xml.async` package, and hence their own namespace. Objects within this package are managed by the `ResourceManager` class, which provides an interface for the calling application to check whether or not any outstanding tasks have yet to complete. The manager is created with a numerical parameter defining expected maximum concurrency.
XML SourceView	This Bean is a graphical component for displaying the contents of an XML file with syntax highlighting, either read-only or for editing. It uses the Swing classes for its interface, and allows different fonts and colors for XML attribute names and values, data element contents, comments, processing instructions, and tags. Inconsistently, it takes a `Document` as input, and returns a `String`, containing either the original data, or the data post-editing (it does not have any methods for actually manipulating XML documents via DOM).
XMLTransform Panel	This visual Bean applies XSL transformations and displays the results. A listener responds to callback events, rather than exposing an API for direct manipulation by the developer.
XMLTreeView	Another Swing-based graphical component, the Tree Viewer displays an explorer-style interface to an XML document, allowing hierarchically nested elements to be expanded and collapsed. The document can be browsed, but not edited within this panel. It can therefore take as input a `Document` object, although it can return a tree data structure for use within other Swing components. The input objects are instances of `org.w3c.dom.Document` rather than Oracle's own `XMLDocument`.

To use Oracle JDeveloper to create a simple application using a Transviewer Bean, use the following procedure:

1. Select File | New Project. A wizard will be launched to guide you through the process. After the welcome screen (on step 1 of 3), name your project and click A project containing a new... then choose Application.

2. Click Next, bringing you to a screen for setting package and paths. These can be left as the defaults. The next panel's items are only used to generate comments in the source code, and can safely be left as defaults, cleared, or fully completed.

3. When this wizard is complete, the Application Wizard will automatically be started. Set the class name to be `TransviewExample` and leave the package name as the default. Choose to use a New Empty Frame as the default frame. The next screen of the wizard asks for a class and package name for the frame. These may be left as defaults for the purpose of the example. Ensure that the Extends option is set to `javax.swing.JFrame`. Select OK.

4. In the Navigator pane on the left-hand side of the JDeveloper interface, there will now be an icon for `TransviewExample`. If this interface is not visible, select View | Navigator. The icon has a green traffic light next to it, indicating that it is executable. Right-click on the icon for the frame (the default name is "Frame1") for a contextual menu, then choose Open Viewer As, then Visual Designer from the submenu.

5. On the Bean palette, choose the `Transview` pane created earlier. This will display five icons, but they will be identical, as the Transviewer beans to not define unique, descriptive icons. You will need to select the `XMLSourceView` Bean by using the tooltips displayed by the IDE. With this highlighted, drag a box in the middle of the Frame displayed on the visual designer. Click on the background, so that the Property Palette (similar to Developer/2000) is editing `jPanel1`, then using the LOV change the layout property to PaneLayout.

6. At the bottom of the screen, there will be four tabbed panes, Source, Design, Class and Doc. Currently Design is selected, so switch to Source. Modify the text in this view as follows:

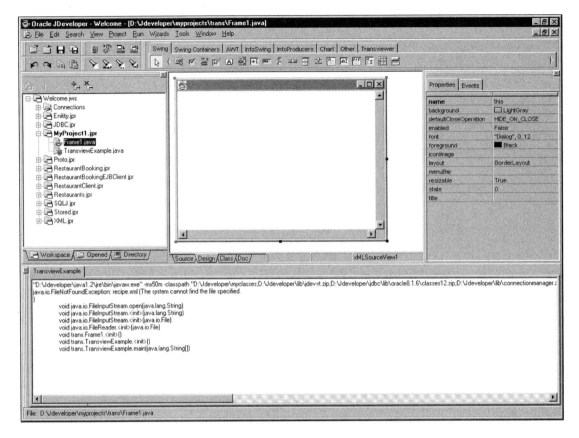

7. To the import statements at the beginning of the file, add `import java.io.*;` and `import oracle.xml.parser.v2.*;`

8. If the package import for the XML parser shows up in red, ensure that the Oracle XML Parser is within the project default properties' libraries.

9. Next, modify the constructor method. Although the file is hard-coded, it would be simple to use a dialog box to select a file: however programming Swing applications is beyond the scope of this chapter.

```
public Frame1() {
    super();
    try {
        bInit();
        File file = new File ("C:\\xml\\recipes.xml");
        FileReader reader = new FileReader (file);
        DOMParser parser = new DOMParser();
        parser.parse(reader);
        xMLSourceView1.setXMLDocument(parser.getDocument());
    } catch (Exception e) {
        e.printStackTrace();
    }
}
```

10. Finally, click the icon in the toolbar that resembles a green traffic light, or select Run from the Run menu. You will see a frame appear, containing a formatted and syntax-highlighted XML document.

Summary

The XDK provides a variety of tools for parsing and generating XML, as well as manipulating existing XML documents. These are used to provide functionality to applications, standalone or components, which are able to quickly add XML capability for storing and querying data structures, with or without connecting to the main Oracle server. This means that the XDK can be used in non-database applications also. The XDK in its present form does have its limitations, but in most cases, these can be worked around by understanding the breadth of the API.

In this chapter we have covered:

❑ What the Oracle XML Developer's Kit (XDK) comprises

❑ The different ways of parsing an XML document using the Oracle XDK:

  ❑ The Document Object Model (DOM)

  ❑ The Simple API for XML (SAX)

  ❑ DTDs and XML Schemas

❑ The higher-level interfaces for querying and manipulating XML documents:

  ❑ The XPath query language

  ❑ The XSLT transformation language that uses it

  ❑ The XSQL tool for integrating XML processing with the relational world of SQL

❑ The role of XML in designing distributed applications

❑ XML versus Java mechanisms for communication between applications

❑ The role of JavaServer Pages and how they can be combined with other tools

❑ The ways in which XSLT-based transformations can be integrated into a multi-tier application

❑ The Transviewer JavaBeans that enable the functionality to be built into a component-based application

22

A Case Study in Enterprise Application Development

Way back in Chapter 2 of this book we discussed in detail the nature of the challenges facing modern enterprise application developers. In particular we discussed the principles involved in building component-based n-tier applications, which can be briefly summarized as follows:

❑ Applications must be designed from a cross-functional (typically, in the real world, cross-departmental), perspective.

❑ Applications must be envisioned as a collection of loosely coupled distributed components delivering services to multiple applications throughout the organization.

❑ The services provided by the application must focus on reuse, consistency, and abstraction.

There are of course pros and cons to adopting these design principles – the pros being that such applications could, potentially, provide flexibility, scalability, and the ability to integrate smoothly with existing information systems; the cons being that these applications require a lot of time and expertise to get right (both of which are often in short supply). Many developers still find that their most successful projects in terms of productivity and stability are with 2-tier projects.

Ultimately, however, the costs and benefits of using Enterprise Application Design (EAD) principles in application development are often difficult to assess without a case study. In the preceding chapters you've had a thorough grounding in Java application development on an Oracle platform. Technologies such as Java stored procedures and EJBs have been discussed in detail and also, in the preceding chapter, the integration of XML into your Oracle applications. You will put all of this knowledge into practice in this chapter and, at the same time, consolidate your understanding of the intricacies of EAD.

We are going to discuss a case study – illustrating a common integration problem in which EAD principles can be applied. This case study has been selected because it is an enterprise integration problem. Within an enterprise environment very few applications are truly stand-alone. These applications need to integrate data and functionality that is present in other systems within the organization. However, many corporate Information Technologies (IT) systems are not "home-grown" systems built by an internal IT staff. Instead, they are often third-party packages purchased from a variety of vendors that offer varying degrees of integration capability and openness.

This is the case for Company ECall. ECall is a Fortune 100 company that maintains several call centers across the country. These call centers handle thousands of customer inquiries, complaints, and technical support questions every day. The call-center data is entered and stored in a dedicated Customer Relationship Management (CRM) system. It is then manually transferred (re-keyed) to a Knowledge Management System (KMS). The KMS, which is accessible to several groups of people outside the call center, is used as a knowledge base to locate previously solved solutions and as a marketing analysis tool to help identify customer needs and wants. The lack of integration between the various departments within Company ECall and their corresponding IT systems is a classic example of the "stovepiping" that can occur within an organization.

In this chapter you can imagine you work for a large Information Technologies (IT) shop for a Fortune 100 company. Your team is responsible for designing and implementing an integration application that will solve many of the inherent problems in the current system. It is not enough for this new application to simply "link" the two existing systems: it must allow the company to apply some highly specific business rules and it must make these rules reusable, to allow for the smooth integration of other systems in the future. The application architecture must ultimately be able to support customer self-service activity over the Internet. You must analyze the existing system, propose and evaluate several different application architectures, and implement the one that is most appropriate for the company's needs. Thus, we will:

- ❑ Discuss the Company ECall's current system and its inherent weaknesses

- ❑ Propose and evaluate three possible Oracle-based application architectures:

    - ❑ A quick and easy two-tier client/server architecture using Oracle PL/SQL and Java Stored procedures

    - ❑ A three-tier client/server architecture once again using Oracle PL/SQL and Java Stored Procedures

    - ❑ An N-Tier architecture using Java Servlets, XSL and XML, Enterprise JavaBeans; we will undertake a minimal working implementation of this solution

- ❑ Finish this discussion by examining some migration strategies for moving an application from a two-tier to N-tier model

The Current Setup

The term EAD leads many people to think of external web applications used by customers. Companies develop web applications to introduce a customer self-service element that will allow them to cut down on their overhead costs, while at the same time building and maintaining a loyal customer base. However few realize that the majority of development effort is not in developing the web-based front-end. The majority of development effort is EAD work involving "back-office" development that allows smooth integration of heterogeneous systems. Each of Company ECall's departments, and the customers they support, needs efficient access to the same data but for different reasons (they need different analysis options, they need to see different "views" of the data, and so on). Enterprise-level applications cross organizational boundaries and involve many end-users.

The specific demands of each department often lead companies to buy packaged applications that are designed to fulfill a specific need within a department. However, once the third-party package is installed, most companies run into the 80/20 rule. In the 80/20 rule, a packaged application will fit 80% of an organization's needs. The last 20% of the functionality needed (often the most critical functionality) can only be obtained through customized development and integration with other systems within an organization. Company ECall is no exception.

Let's start by taking a look at how ECall's current customer and technical support system works. The following diagram describes the current set-up:

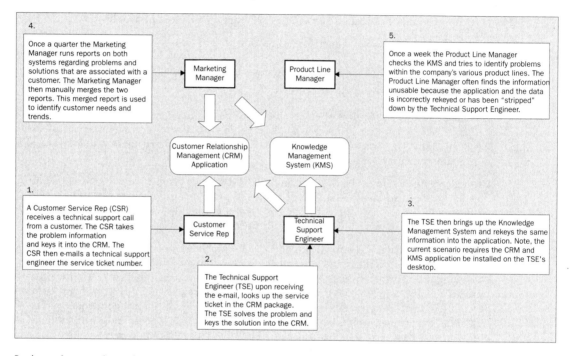

Let's analyze each application in this system in more detail.

CRM System

Call center data is entered into the CRM system. It is a vendor bought, two-tier, "fat-client" application. The client is a PowerBuilder application running on the CSR's desktop. The back-end operates on a Sun Server running Oracle 8i.

The CRM application is more than just a customer database. It is the central repository and integration point for all data and processes involving the customer. It provides a 360 degree view of the customer.

The data entered into the system allows the end-user within the company to identify such information as:

❑ Who is the customer? This includes such basic information as the customer name, the primary contact for the customer, their address, etc.

❑ What is the status of a customer's order?

The CRM application is more then just a data repository for customer information. It is fully integrated with the company's Financial and Order Entry system so that a CSR can tell such information as:

- ❏ Whether or not an order has been shipped?
- ❏ Who was used for shipping?
- ❏ Customer billing information
- ❏ The customer outstanding balance and credit history.
- ❏ What resources are available to assist a customer with a problem?
- ❏ Does the customer have an on-site support contract with Company ECall?
- ❏ What is the service level agreement for the customer?

In addition, the data in the CRM application provides a lot of additional "hidden" information on the following issues:

- ❏ **Customer Needs** – Customers often call the customer service department when they are having difficulty getting a product to work or get the product to do something it was never designed to do. The data keyed in from the customer service department provides a wealth of information on customer needs and wants.

- ❏ **Customer Satisfaction** – The data within the CRM application provides key insights into how happy the customers are with the product they are using. This data can be analyzed by the marketing and customer service department to identify where customer satisfaction can be improved.

- ❏ **Market Segmentation** – Companies spend a lot of time and money trying to figure out what is the optimal mix of products and services they can sell to customers. Much of the effort is spent classifying their customers and identifying who their biggest customers are. A rather common mistake of many companies is that because they cannot readily identify these "big" customers, they tend to treat every customer calling their customer service department equally. The marketing department would like to know the problems their biggest, most profitable customers are having so that they can make sure that these customers receive the best service.

From the points stated above, we can see that the CRM application contains a tremendous amount of data on customer problems and their corresponding solutions. The management team for the customer service department believes that the information locked in the CRM application could be used by the customer service representatives to analyze and solve customer queries without having to involve the technical support team. Unfortunately the CRM system does not possess the advanced search and knowledge management capabilities required to take full advantage of this data.

Therefore, in order to make the data available as a company-wide resource and to analyze and search it effectively, Company ECall has invested in a Knowledge Management System (KMS) that will allow users to search for problem solutions by using a web-based interface that walks them through a question and answer wizard. Unfortunately, there is no automated integration between the CRM and KMS application. As noted above, a technical support engineer has to manually transfer all of the problem and solution data from the CRM to the KMS system.

KMS System

The KMS is a vendor purchased, two-tiered client-server application. The front-end client is written in Microsoft's Visual Basic 6.0 and its back-end database is running on Windows NT 4.0 and SQL Server 7.0. The KMS system is more powerful than the CRM in that:

❏ The KMS application has advanced search capabilities. These search capabilities include the ability to perform keyword and contextual searches and allow the user to post questions in the form of a sentence. In addition, the KMS system will rate each result returned by a query based upon various business rules set up and defined by Company ECall.

❏ The KMS application has extensive Knowledge-Management features that allow information to be reviewed and published by individuals throughout the organization. The CRM is a tool for managing customer information. It does not possess the specialized editing and publishing tools that the KMS application possesses.

❏ The KMS application provides a web-browser based interface that allows internal end-users and customers to easily locate solutions to their problems. The browser interface is easy to use and does not require a "fat" client installed on each user's desktop, like the CRM application, to run. Benefits of using the KMS web application include:

❏ The customer service department being able to quickly locate solutions without having to go to the technical support staff.

❏ The product line manager using the KMS information to identify defects within ECall products.

The CRM application is a highly integrated tool that allows Company ECall to support its customers throughout all of the departments within its organization. It is a tool for managing customer data and processes. The KMS application is a highly specialized application that enables the company to build and maintain a knowledge base of problems and solutions it has encountered with its products.

CRM-KMS Integration System

It is decided that the Integration Application will be a web-based application that will "link" the CRM and KMS applications.

Initial Development

The first step in assessing the requirements of a new system is to learn the lessons of the old system. It is clear to the upper management of Company ECall, that their current business processes are not streamlined. Key customer data is constantly being re-keyed into the CRM and KMS applications. There is no data integration or single point of entry for this information. As a direct result of this:

❏ Redundant information is being keyed into multiple systems. Redundant data entry often leads to poor quality data in both applications. End-users who know they have to re-key information will often purposely cut down the amount of detailed information they are providing in order to save themselves time. This detailed information is critical in a Knowledge Management system. In addition, data quality goes down because of keying errors. Keying errors might not seem like a big deal until you consider the product your company is selling is a heart monitor or fire control system.

❏   There is no 360-degree view of the customer. Customer support involves a great deal of cross-department communication and interaction. Many times, when a technical support engineer is trying to resolve a problem, they must call the customer directly. Because there is very little system and data integration, the technical support engineer has to ask the customer for basic information the customer has already provided to the customer service representative. This wastes the customer's time and results in the customer feeling as if the organization does not really "know" them as a customer.

❏   The transaction costs for dealing with a customer are higher than they need to be. Customer service representatives and technical support engineers looking for information scattered throughout the organization translates into higher ovehead costs. Company ECall must hire more staff then it needs to process customer inquiries. These extra employees mean extra salaries, benefits, and managerial bureacracy. Integrated, enterprise-level applications streamline business processes and let employees do more with less.

In addition to these known problems, the company has, through experience, come to realize that there are several major business rules that need to be applied at the time the technical support engineer moves the data from the CRM application to the KMS application. These business rules cannot be found in either one of these systems.

One such business rule has to do with how the company would like to tie problems and solutions found in its products to a hierarchy of product lines, product families, parts, and components. It would like to capture these relationships and be able to pass that information to the KMS application. Once this data is in the KMS application Company ECall can perform keyword search on the above categories and also look for trends in each of these different categories. These categories and how they are structured are very industry-specific. It would be an extremely expensive effort to build this grouping functionality into the CRM and KMS applications. Company ECall would like to build this functionality into the web application being used as an integration tool and give the technical support engineers the ability to tie the problem and solution to these different categories. This grouping function must be performed by a human being because the Company ECall has literally hundreds of products spanning over ten to fifteen years of use out in the field.

> *This is a good illustration of the fact that the any packaged application will usually fit 75-80% of a company's need. The other 25%-30% of need is filled by custom solutions.*

Thus, the core objectives in the initial development phase could be summarized as follows:

❏   Solve the problems associated with redundant data entry by providing a single point of entry for information

❏   Incorporate the company business rules

Future Development

Ultimately, it is envisaged that the application will become a web portal to which customers and internal staff can come to find information and solutions to problems with the company's products. For example, in the future:

❏   The application will provide a customer self-service model where the customer can carry out many of the tasks traditionally performed by a customer service representative. These tasks include placing an order, checking order status, and answering product support questions. This means at some point in the future the application will have to serve many more users then originally anticipated.

The ability to scale must be one of the fundamental features built into this application's architecture.

❑ Every area of company activity will be able to input useful data into the system. For example, Front-Line Service Personnel (FLSP) visit the client site on a regular basis and perform basic account management duties and make sure that the products installed are working properly. Many times a customer will talk to the FLSP about a problem without calling the customer support line. At the moment the FLSPs have their own set of applications for logging and tracking their day-to-day movement but the knowledge captured in their applications would be an invaluable addition to the central KMS systems. Company ECall upper management is envisioning the day when FLSPs will be able to access corporate data and systems by using a database package like Oracle 8i Lite to run applications on such PDAs (Personal Digital Assistant).

The business rules developed for the integration application must be re-usable by other systems and be accessible from a variety of hardware and software platforms.

The Pilot Project

The director of customer services, acting on the above tenets, has identified a pilot project that he believes will significantly reduce transaction costs of technical support questions. After some thought, the IT team you are part of proposes a solution that they believe will help achieve the objectives set out for the initial development: eliminate redundant data entry and poor information quality within the KMS, and add key business rules within the CRM and the KMS. Furthermore, as an added bonus, this solution will let the company leverage the code written in the integration to develop a set of reports that the marketing manager and product line manager can use. The proposal looks like this:

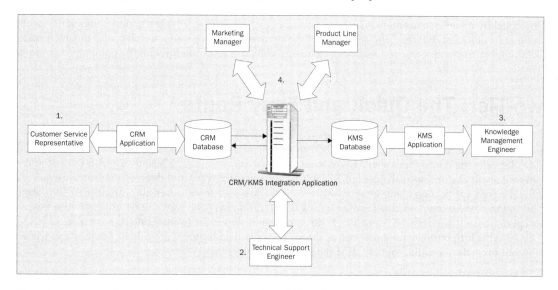

The above proposal uses an IT team developed, web-based application for retrieving and submitting customer data between these two systems. The system would basically work like this:

1. A Customer Service Representative (CSR) receives a technical support call from a customer. The CSR takes the problem information and keys it into the CRM system. Upon keying in all relevant information, the CSR assigns the case to a Technical Support Engineer. The CRM application then automatically sends an e-mail to the selected Technical Support Engineer.

2. The Technical Support Engineer (TSE) receives an e-mail from the CSR. The e-mail contains a URL that points to the C-K integration application. Upon clicking on the URL, a web page is brought up with all of the relevant customer and problem information presented. The TSE solves the problem and posts the solution via the C-K integration application. The TSE only has to key in the solution information once because the C-K intergation application will post the solution to both the CRM and KMS systems. After the data is posted to both of these systems, the C-K application will send an e-mail to a Knowledge Management Engineer (KME).

3. The role of the Knowledge Management Engineer is to ensure that the data going into the KMS application is clear and understandable. In a real-world example, the role of the KMS is to make sure that the information keyed in is clear and accurate. TSEs often need prodding to make sure that the solutions being keyed are accurate and understandable. The KMEs essentially act as editors. When they receive an e-mail indicating that a technical service engineer has just submitted a problem/solution set, they will use the KMS application to perform any additional editing. They will then use the KMS application to post the problem/solution set for general company-wide consumption.

4. The Marketing Manager and Product Line Manager now use web-based reports run from the C-K integration application to pull together data from both the KMS and CRM applications. These reports are written by the IT development team and reuse much of the code written for integrating the CRM and KMS applications together.

Your proposal to link the two systems together by providing a web-based application has been well received by upper-management. They not only see your solution as solving the data redundancy problems that currently exist, but they also see this application eventually becoming a web portal to which customers and internal staff can come to find information and solutions to problems with the company's products.

Two-Tier: The Quick and Easy Route

In many organizations, the knee-jerk response from the IT development team in charge of implementing this project would be to code this application as quickly as possible. After all, there are deadlines to meet and the last thing you want is some "know-nothing", businessperson ranting and raving about the unresponsiveness of IT. So the team gets together and decides that they are going to build a web-application using Oracle's PL/SQL and Java web tools. After all, web applications are cool, all of the development team is familiar with PL/SQL and everyone wants to be able to claim Java experience on their résumé. Since the KMS application they have to integrate to have a set of Java-based APIs for getting data in and out of the system, the development team believes they can use a Java Stored procedure residing in the CRM database to invoke these APIs.

For the sake of simplicity (and space limitations within this text) the team decides they will need four screens to capture all of the basic functionality:

❑ A retrieval screen – This screen will be used to display a text box in which the technical support engineers can key in the CRM service ticket number (the number assigned to the user's call) that they want to retrieve. This screen will validate the number the TSE entered and retrieve the service ticket data into a web page.

❑ A display screen. This screen will display the CRM service ticket information and provide the end-user the opportunity to add additional detailed information regarding the product line, product family, part, and component that the problem is related to. As stated earlier this information is not available in the CRM or KMS applications. This screen is where the user will be able to key in the solution to the customer's problem and have this data sent to both the CRM and KMS application.

❑ A query criteria screen that will let marketing and product line managers select from a set of pre-defined query criteria.

❑ A canned report that will show problem and solution data from the CRM and KMS applications. The data presented will be based on the query criteria on the query criteria screen.

Your development team has broken the above functionality out into two stored procedures. The first stored procedure is written in PL/SQL and has three methods for the retrieving of data from the CRM system and the drawing and posting of the web screens. The second stored procedure is written in Java and has one method. This method is used for inserting the data into the KMS application.

The overall flow and structure of this "quick and easy" solution looks like this:

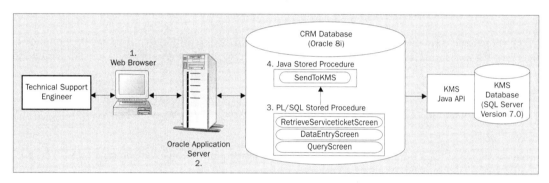

The basic flow of the application is as follows:

1. A technical support engineer wants to retrieve a service ticket and process the order through the CRM/KMS application. He makes his request to via web browser.

2. The request is sent from the web browser to Oracle Application Server. In this case, the application server is filling two roles. First, it is acting as web server to handle and process end-user requests. Secondly, it is acting a traffic cop, routing the various end-user's request to the appropriate PL/SQL stored procedure sitting within the CRM database.

3. When one of the methods is called on the PL/SQL stored procedure, the request is processed, business rules are applied, and HTML is generated. This HTML is returned to the Oracle Application Server and in turn returned to the end-user's browser.

4. If the request coming from the end-user is to submit a finished problem/solution set to the KMS application, the PL/SQL stored procedure will invoke the Java Stored Procedure.

5. The Java Stored Procedure will call classes and methods on the KMS Java API. Remember, this API is provided by the vendor as a means of moving data in and out of the application.

Your team has now put together an application that meets their immediate customer needs and probably did it in a very short amount of time. However, this "collapsing" of the presentation, business, and data logic has consequences. These consequences include:

❑ The loss of reuse. Since the logic for the application has been partitioned at a screen level it will be impossible to reuse any of the business or data retrieval rules in other places. These rules are locked within each display and post procedure.

❑ Increased maintenance costs. This application is extremely small. However, if the application consisted of more screens code maintenance costs could become extremely high. Every time an application change was needed, whether the change involved a code or database change, the entire application would have to be searched for any dependencies. If the application code were designed to be more partitioned and granular, a change in the code would have significantly less impact on the system as a whole.

❑ Difficulty scaling the application. The application is not logically partitioned. All of the code is written as stored procedures that do not break out presentation, business, or data into separate, distinct tiers. This lack of partitioning means that if there are performance problems, one or more of the tiers cannot be moved to a different machine. The only scaling option available is to buy bigger and often more expensive hardware.

The three issues raised above center around granularity. Any application that is or has the potential to be used at the enterprise level needs to be properly modeled so as to achieve the right level of granularity.

> **Achieving the right level of granularity within your application directly determines the amount of reuse, abstraction, and scalability you will get out of the application.**

Unfortunately, this is the extent of thinking that has taken place before the coding started. The problem with this mentality is three fold:

❑ The development team feel they are under time constraints and are going to spend a minimal amount of time in the design phase of the project. This means very little attention will be paid to partitioning the application for ease of reuse and long-term maintainability.

❑ The development team, to minimize the amount of development time, have not looked beyond the immediate problem at hand. Remember, upper-management is hoping this site will eventually become a portal site servicing far more users then they are currently anticipating.

❑ The development team have not been fully diligent in selecting their application architecture. They are using a traditional two-tier development model to build the CRM/KMS application. How can a web application be implemented as two-tier architecture? After all, a web application usually has three physically distinct layers: the thin-client web-browser acting as the presentation tier, the web-server serving as the business logic tier, and of course a backend database server serving as a data tier. The developers, by having all code reside in the database as PL/SQL and Java stored-procedures, are not logically partitioning the application. Thus, their solution will put presentation, business, and data-retrieval logic all within the same code.

Obviously, this application has been oversimplified. As a reader you may make the observation that this example is over-exaggerated and can be easily knocked down as unrealistic. However, more IT and IS shops then you can imagine pursue this type of development. This unstructured development occurs because many companies do not use EAD principles in their application development process. EAD principles focus on breaking an application into smaller granular and reusable parts. Directly related to EAD is the use of Object-Orientated Analysis and Design modeling techniques (OOAD). OOAD, an entire subject in itself, is a powerful tool for implementing EAD design principles. The lack of EAD and OOAD principles, as shown in the above example, often results in undisciplined development that focuses on application deployment schedules rather then delivering an application that will smoothly integrate into the existing IT infrastructure.

Three Tier: A Better Approach

The first version of the application, while solving the immediate business problem, did not lay the framework for a long-term solution. The application was not properly partitioned and Company ECall, had they deployed the version of the application above, would have faced several challenges in maintaining the application, adding new functionality to it, and scaling the application for more users.

Recognizing these challenges you and your IT team take a step back and begin to redesign the C-K application's core architecture. This time you are going to use a three-tier architecture, logically split into three distinct tiers: a presentation tier, a business tier, and data tier. Graphically, the application will look like this:

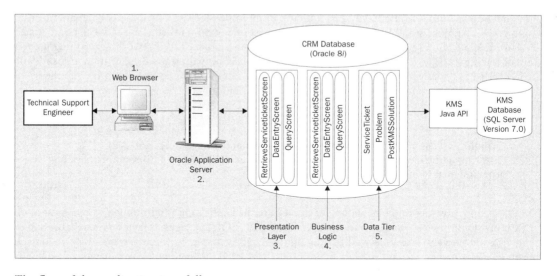

The flow of the application is as follows:

1. A technical support engineer who wants to retrieve a service ticket and process the order through the CRM-KMS integration application makes a request via a web browser.

2. The request is sent from the web browser to Oracle Application Server. The web server processes the user's request and calls the appropriate stored procedure residing in the database. However, in the previous example the OWS is calling a stored procedure with the presentation, business, and data logic all embedded within it. In this example, the OWS is calling a stored procedure that only contains presentation logic.

3. All of the presentation logic for the application will be written as PL/SQL stored procedures. Each screen will be broken out into a separate package. Only logic that deals with drawing the web page and doing client-side validation (JavaScript code in the web browser) will reside in this tier. Any business logic will be delegated to a separate set of stored procedures.

4. The business logic will be written as a set of Java stored procedures. The business logic tier will represent distinct business processes that are carried out by the application. These processes include any calculations, server-side data validation, or decision trees that the application must use. It is extremely critical that there is a minimal amount of direct database access from the business process code.

5. The data tier for this application will again be written as a set of Java stored procedures. Each stored procedure at this layer represents a discrete business entity existing with the CRM/KMS problem domain. An example of a business entity within this problem domain might be a service ticket from the CRM application or a problem/solution set for the KMS application. The stored procedure written for each of these business entities should contain all of the CRUD (Create, Replace, Update, and Delete) logic. The data layer stored procedures know nothing about the processes (the business layer components) that use them.

Why go through all of this additional work to split the application into multiple partitions? The primary reason is to reap the benefits of decoupling. The code in the first implementation, while achieving its immediate business goals, was very tightly coupled together. If performance bottlenecks were found in the first application, it would have been difficult, if not impossible, to break the code apart and run the split code on a more scalable technology (such as a set of components running in a clustered, load-balanced application server farm). This would have taken a great deal of reworking and might even entail rewriting the application. If the application was a big hit within the organization and suddenly you needed to be able to handle an additional 500 end-users would you be able to rewrite the application quickly enough? This is an extremely important point to consider when the ultimate goal of this work is to build more then just an integration point between two applications.

> **Applications need to have scalability designed from the beginning, not as an afterthought. Decoupling the application into several distinct and discernable tiers is the first step to building a scalable application.**

In the second three-tier implementation, each piece of the application is partitioned so you have a lot more flexibility. For instance, you can port the presentation PL/SQL packages to Java servlets that reside on multiple web servers. This relieves the strain on the database server by removing the presentation code from the Oracle database and spreading the resources needed to generate the web page over several (relatively inexpensive) machines. The business logic and data tier can still be invoked from one of these Java servlets. If one of the business tier Java stored procedures is the performance bottleneck, you can easily port that package to be an Enterprise JavaBean (EJB) running under OAS (Oracle Application Server) or iAS (Oracle Internet Application Server). Once the code has been written as a EJB, it can be deployed across multiple load-balanced application servers. The advantage of using Java servlets and EJBs over a PL/SQL or Java Stored Procedures is that with servlets and EJBs you can move the processing of the code outside the database and onto another server – or perhaps you might decide not to by deploying the components to OSE and CORBA within the Oracle database itself. In either case, you have more flexibility in how your logical tier structure maps to a physical deployment. Stored procedures lock your code into the database and ensure that the business logic running inside the database will be competing for the same CPU and IO resources that that the database is competing for.

Building a loosely coupled, three-tier implementation is an extremely powerful concept because it promotes flexibility. By using the three-tier approach, an organization can often develop their application using tools and concepts that are familiar to them. In addition they can incrementally change and move pieces of their application to an N-Tier implementation. The example given above highly leverages Oracle's Java stored procedures. Oracle's decision to move to Java as a development platform is an extremely enlightened decision. They have given Oracle developers a bridge to move much of their code away from PL/SQL and into the much more vendor-neutral Java language. The use of the Java language as a stored procedure language along with Oracle's commitment to Sun Microsystems Enterprise Java platform has provided Oracle developers with a smooth migration path from two-tiered application to N-Tier applications.

We have discussed two different examples of how to implement our C-K integration. The first example was a short term, quick and easy solution that while solving the immediate business needs of the organization does not provide a long-term enterprise integration strategy. The logic within the application was too tightly coupled together to reuse. In addition the code was written in a completely proprietary technology. The second example partitioned the code logically into three tiers. This application design broke the tight coupling that existed in the previous example. However it is still faces the same reuse and scalability issues the first example did. The real strength of the second example architecture is that the company is positioned for a smooth migration from a two-tier to an N-Tier implementation. Each piece of the application, while residing physically within an Oracle database, has been broken into the three tiers of presentation, business, and data logic. Any one of these tiers can, with a small amount of effort, be ported out of the Oracle database to a separate technology. The three-tier example is an appropriate way to implement an application if you suspect you are going to need to move to an N-Tier architecture within the near future.

Finally, remember that technology advances at a horrendously fast speed. Often times we start developing with a technology only to see it radically change before the project is even complete. Many developers, including myself, have written applications using Oracle's PL/SQL web development toolkit because it was the only web development environment available for Oracle at the time. It has only been since OAS 4.0.8.1 and Oracle 8i that there has been support for such technologies as Java servlets and Enterprise JavaBeans. Using the partitioned development approach described in this section a development team can react to sudden technological innovations without a "big-bang" rewrite of the code. Instead, they can leverage new technology by incrementally implementing it at the different logical partitions within the application.

N-Tier: The Long-Term Solution

The next architecture that is going to be covered is the N-Tier implementation. This section will be far more in-depth then previous sections. We will be covering the following:

❑   The basics pieces of an N-Tier architecture and the Oracle tools for developing each one of these tiers.

❑   What a Model-View-Controller (MVC) Framework is and how it can be used to build a robust and flexible N-Tier application.

❑   A simple example showing how to build one web-based screen using an MVC Framework.

When this section is completed you should have a basic understanding of the pieces of an N-Tier architecture and the Oracle development tools you can use to build it.

N-Tier Architectures: An Overview

An N-Tier architecture focuses on building a very loosely coupled application that is split across multiple machines and multiple tiers. This design, while much more time and skill intensive to implement, offers a higher degree of scalability, fault-tolerance, and reuse. The N-Tier application architecture for the C-K integration application looks like this:

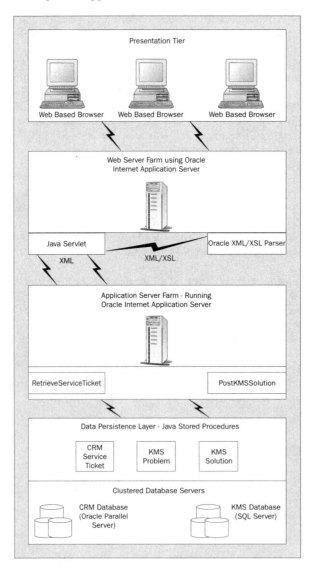

This application model above depicts code being partitioned on a physical and logical perspective. The model has the presentation, business, and data tiers split across multiple machines. If you compare this with the three-tier model from the previous section you see that that all of the tiers from the previous model can be moved to the N-Tier model. The graphic on p.909 shows how each of the tiers from the three-tier model described in the previous section can be mapped to the different tiers in the N-Tier model.

Lets look at this picture in a greater detail:

❑ The PL/SQL stored procedures that handle all of the presentation logic can now be rolled over to the web application server as Java servlets.

❑ The PL/SQL stored procedures that handle all of the business logic are now ported as Enterprise JavaBeans (EJB).

❑ All of PL/SQL and Java Stored Procedures in the original three-tier architecture's data tier can stay in the database. In the long-term we will probably want to port all of the PL/SQL stored procedures over to Java Stored Procedures. Porting the code to Java will make it that much easier if we decide to remove the data access code out of the database and use a technology like Oracle Business Components for Java or Enterprise Entity Beans.

From the figure above we can surmise three things:

❑ The application can be migrated incrementally from a three-tier architecture to an N-Tier architecture. We could first move the presentation PL/SQL packages to Java Servlets with a minimal amount of effort. The rest of the PL/SQL package would not be affected because they are unaware of how the package calling them is implemented.

❑ The model breaks our dependence on Oracle. If there is a decision within Company ECall that all of the company's web-servers must be Microsoft's Internet Information Server (IIS), we could move the PL/SQL stored procedures containing our presentation logic out of the database and to IIS as Java servlets. Oracle has great products, but there are few Chief Information Officers who are willing to lock themselves into one vendor's technology.

❑ Moving the code out of the Oracle database will allow the application to achieve better scalability and redundancy because the code can be split across multiple servers at the presentation, business logic, and data tier. The hardware can be clustered together to provide a great deal more scalability and fault-tolerance than can be found in an Oracle database server alone (even using the Oracle Parallel Server).

Clustering and Load Balancing

In the N-tier model depicted above, scalability and redundancy is achieved by taking advantage of the clustering technology found in Oracle Internet Application Server (iAS) and Oracle Parallel Server (OPS).

Oracle iAS provides load balancing of user requests at the web server and application server level. Both of Oracle's application servers, Oracle iAS and OAS, are implemented as share-nothing clusters. Each machine in a share-nothing cluster has its own CPU, memory, disk, and if necessary, copy of the application code. It is important to note that there are several different load-balancing algorithms available with iAS and OAS. The load-balancing algorithms range from simplistic round-robin load balancing to the more complicated algorithms of server weighting and utilization. These load-balancing methods will be available depending on the version of iAS or OAS you are using.

Oracle Parallel Server is used to load-balance user requests at the database level. However, OPS is not a share-nothing cluster. Each OPS instance resides on its own box, with its own CPU, memory, and local instance of the database binaries. The database files (the data files, redo logs, etc.) are stored on a central shared disk that all members of the OPS cluster have access to. So while OPS applications have a high degree of redundancy, they still have the single-point of failure with the shared disk. However, even this single point-of-failure can be mitigated by using a good RAID strategy to ensure your database will always have hard drives to run against. The clustering capabilities of Oracle iAS and database technologies have only been briefly described here.

At this point we need to shift gears and look at how the code is logically partitioned across the different tiers within our N-Tier architecture. We have chosen what is known as a Model-View-Controller Framework to provide structure and flexibility with out implementation.

Using a Model-View-Controller Framework with N-Tier

In the previous diagram we looked at how N-Tier architectures are physically partitioned. We also pointed out the different Oracle technologies that can be used in each of the different tiers in an N-Tier architecture. It is now time to shift gears and look at a basic N-Tier architecture.

This chapter will take one screen from the C-K integration application and show how to split that screen across the different tiers in the N-Tier architecture. The screen example itself is pretty simplistic. A TSE has just selected a service ticket from a drop down box and is now waiting for the C-K integration application to return the detailed service ticket information as a web page in his web browser.

This example was chosen because it has very little "business" logic in it and will provide the reader a simple N-Tier implementation that does not get cluttered in detail. The following topics will be covered:

❑ The Model-View-Controller (MVC) framework and how it can be used to build a flexible and extensible N-Tier architecture that completely separates an application's presentation, business, and data access logic.

❑ Code examples for each of the pieces of the MVC framework. The code examples will cover the following technologies:

  ❑ Java Servlets

  ❑ Enterprise JavaBeans (EJB)

  ❑ Java Stored Procedures

  ❑ The Oracle XML and XSL Parser

The Model-View-Controller

The N-Tier implementation of the C-K integration application has been designed using a Model-Viewer-Controller (MVC) framework. An MVC framework consists of three pieces:

❑ The **controller**. This is a single point of entry for handling all user requests. The controller acts like a supervisor. It identifies and interprets requests from the user and then routes them to the second piece of the MVC, the **model**.

❑ The **model** is a piece of business logic that manages the behavior and data of the application. The model responds to the user's request and acts on behalf of the user. When the model has finished processing the end user's request it will return back to the **controller**.

❑ After the **model** has finished processing the user's request, control will be returned to the **controller**. The **controller** will then take any data returned from the **model** and forward the data to the **view** component. The **view** component is solely responsible for the presenting data and information to the end-user

In the C-K application, the MVC model looks like this:

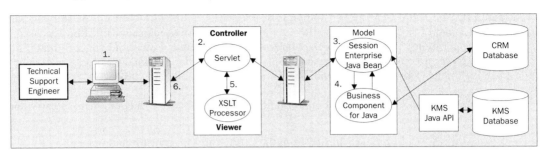

Using the diagram above, we are going to walk through what happens when a technical support engineer requests a service ticket via the C-K integration application. Do not get worried about all of the technologies being presented in these steps. These technologies will be covered in greater detail in later sections of this chapter and elsewhere in the book. Instead focus on the process and how the application works across all three tiers of the application:

1. The end-user makes a request for a service ticket to the C-K integration application. The web server takes the request and passes it to a Java servlet.

2. The Java servlet is acting as the **controller**. It is physically residing on each of the machines in the web server farm. As the servlet receives a request, it will check the HTTP request for two parameters: `Request` and `Action`. The `Request` will contain the name of the Enterprise JavaBean (EJB) that encapsulates the business process the end-user wants to carry out. The action parameter will be a specific method on the EJB that the end-user wants to invoke. The Java servlet will then instantiate the desired EJB and pass the HTTP request parameters into the method being invoked.

3. The session EJB is the **model** in our MVC framework. The session EJB is the place where the business logic for the application is applied. However, our example has very little business logic. In our example, we use the model to retrieve the service ticket data via a Java Stored Procedure. The service ticket data will be packaged as an XML document. The data is packaged as an XML document because the XSLT processor expects the data passed to it to be packaged in this format. After the session EJB has packaged the data, the data will be returned to the the servlet (the controller). The servlet will then pass the returned XML document to the XSLT processor (which is the **view** component in our MVC model).

4. The session EJB in the course of doing its work will need to access the CRM and KMS databases. Rather then going to the databases directly, the session EJB will use a Java Stored Procedure. The Java Stored Procedure abstracts away how the data is physically stored within the Oracle database. Any data that needs to be sent to the SQL server database will be done through the KMS Java API.

5. The XSLT processor, upon being invoked by the Java servlet, will take the XML and an XSL template and transform the two items into an HTML document.

6. This HTML document will be returned back to the calling servlet and then returned back to the end-user. The end-user will see the data entry screen pre-populated with service ticket information.

Controller

The controller for our N-Tier implementation is a Java servlet running on Oracle iAS. The Java servlet technology is part of Sun Microsystems's Java 2 Enterprise Edition specifications (J2EE). It is used to build web applications. The Java servlet can be considered a compiled piece of byte-code that resides on the web server. In our application we have only one Java servlet. It contains no presentation or business logic code. This servlet's sole purpose is to perform the following tasks:

❏ Identify the request of the user and instantiate the appropriate EJB component to carry out the user's request

❏ Pass the XML document returned from the EJB to the XSL transformation engine

❏ Take the resulting HTML produced from the XSL transformation and pass it back to the end-user making the request

```java
package eadcasestudy.servlet;

import java.util.*;
import java.io.*;

import javax.servlet.*;
import javax.servlet.http.*;
import javax.naming.*;
import eadcasestudy.javabean.*;


/*To get the latest Oracle XML Parser you have to go to Oracle's Web site
(www.oracle.com)*/
import oracle.xml.parser.v2.*;

public class CrmKmsIntegrationServlet extends HttpServlet{

  /*
    Contains all of the file names for the Request.Actions being posted
  */
    private Properties xslFileNames = new Properties();

  /*
    Constructor. This method will load all of the XSLStylesheet filenames
    into a property object.  The property object will be populated on startup
  */
    public void init(ServletConfig servletConfig) throws ServletException{
      super.init(servletConfig);

      try{
        xslFileNames.load(new FileInputStream("xslConfig.txt"));
      }
      catch(Exception e){
        System.out.println("Major problem has occurred. Nothing will work: " + e);
        System.exit(0);
      }
    }
}
```

```
/*
   Retrieve an XSL FileName from the property object
*/
private String getXslFileName(HttpServletRequest request){
   String key = request.getParameter("request") + "." +
      request.getParameter("action");

   return (String) xslFileNames.getProperty(key);
}


/*
   This is the controller piece of the MVC.
   When a request is submitted via a web FORM it can come in as a POST or a
   GET.  A GET will have paramet7ers coming in on the URL.  A POST will
   Have the parameters embedded within the HTTP header and not visible to
   the end-user.
*/
public void doPost (HttpServletRequest request, HttpServletResponse response)
   throws ServletException, IOException {

/*
   I am always calling the doGet method.  That way I will perform the action
   regardless of if the user does a POST via form or a get via data coming as
   parameters on the URL.
*/
   doGet(request, response);
}

public void doGet (HttpServletRequest request, HttpServletResponse response) {
   try{
      RequestProcessor reqProcessor = new RequestProcessor();
      XMLDocument       responseDOM = reqProcessor.process(request);
      String            xslFileName = getXslFileName(request);

      //check we've got the xml okay
      responseDOM.print(System.out);

      XSLTManager xsltMgr = new XSLTManager();
      xsltMgr.processOutput(response, responseDOM, xslFileName);
   }
   catch (Exception e){
      System.out.println(e);
      buildErrorPage(response, e);
   }
}


/*
   If any major exceptions occur.  Just send a bogus error screen
   to the end-user and print the exception to system console.
*/

private void buildErrorPage(HttpServletResponse response, Exception ex){
   try {
      response.sendRedirect("/invalidrequest.htm");
   }
   catch (Exception e){
      System.out.println ("Unable to read invalidrequest.htm: " + ex);
   }
}
}
```

Let's now look in more detail at how the servlet does its work. When the servlet is first loaded the `init` method is called:

```
public void init(ServletConfig servletConfig) throws ServletException{
  super.init(servletConfig);

  try{
    xslFileNames.load(new FileInputStream("xslConfig.txt"));
  }
  catch(Exception e){
    System.out.println("Major problem has occurred. Nothing will work: " + e);
    System.exit(0);
  }
}
```

In our particular `init` method we are loading all XSL filenames from a text file called `xslConfig.txt`. This file contains entries of all of the bean and methods that can be invoked by the application. These names are then mapped to XSL files that will be used to display the data returned by the called bean and method. The file could look like this:

```
CrmKmsIntegration.retrieveServiceTicket=file:serviceTicketDisplay.xsl
CrmKmsIntegration.problemSolutionPost=file:problemSolutionPost.xsl
```

These values are loaded into a Java property object called `xslFileNames`. When we wish to display the results of a user's request we call the `getXslFileName` method of this object in order to retrieve the file name of the appropriate XSL file. This method appends the request and action values passed in via the HTTP header and uses the appended value as a key to look up the appropriate file name in our `xslFileNames` object:

```
private String getXslFileName(HttpServletRequest request){
  String key = request.getParameter("request") + "." +
               request.getParameter("action");

  return (String) xslFileNames.getProperty(key);
}
```

The `xslFileName` will become important when it is time to take the results returned from the session EJB and transform them into HTML.

We are using two helper classes in the `CrmKmsIntegration` servlet: `RequestProcessor` and `XSLTManager`. The `RequestProcessor` class wrappers all the code needed to dynamically create the EJB needed to process the user's request. It also invokes the appropriate method on the EJB. The second helper class, `XSLTManager`, wrappers the Oracle XSLT engine used to transform XML and XSL into an HTML format. We are wrapping the Oracle XSLT parser so that we can easily switch to another parser if we so desire. Both of these helper classes help hide EJB and XSL implementation details from the Java servlet.

The `RequestProcessor` class is instantiated and used as follows:

```
RequestProcessor reqProcessor = new RequestProcessor();
Document   responseDOM        = reqProcessor.process(request);
```

These two lines instantiate a `RequestProcessor` class. After the `RequestProcessor` class has been instantiated, the `process` method on the class is invoked. In this method, the request (the EJB the user wants to access) and the action (the method the user wants to call) will be used to dynamically instantiate an Enterprise JavaBean. An XML document is returned from the call and is then forwarded to the `XSLTManager`.

```
XSLTManager xsltMgr = new XSLTManager();
xsltMgr.processOutput(response, responseDOM, xslFileName);
```

The `XSLTManager` (which we see later) is passed the `HttpServletResponse` object (called `response`), the XML document containing the data to be presented to the end user, and the filename of the stylesheet that instructs the `XSLTManager` to display the code. As you can tell, this is a very simplistic Java servlet. The servlet contains little functionality and minimal error handling. Java servlets are currently supported in Oracle iAS HTTP Server, which is essentially Apache JServ. From 8.1.7 you will be able to deploy servlets to the Oracle Servlet Engine (OSE) in the 8i JVM. You can then access them through a special Apache plug-in that diverts requests through HTTP back and forth to the database.

Now lets take a look in more detail at the `RequestProcessor` class:

```
package eadcasestudy.javabean;

import javax.servlet.http.*;
import oracle.xml.parser.v2.*;
import javax.naming.*;
import javax.ejb.*;
import java.rmi.RemoteException;
import java.util.*;
import org.w3c.dom.*;
import oracle.aurora.jndi.sess_iiop.ServiceCtx;
import eadcasestudy.ejb.*;

public class RequestProcessor{

    private final static String oracleservice =
        "sess_iiop://dbserver:2481:proead/test/";

    public XMLDocument process(HttpServletRequest request)
      throws NamingException, NoSuchMethodException, IllegalAccessException  {

    /*
     Pulling the name of the request out of the servlet HTTP
     Header
    */
    String serviceTicket = request.getParameter("soTicket");
    System.out.println("Got param " + serviceTicket);
```

We use a JNDI lookup to retrieve the home object from the application container. In this case we are accessing the EJB at `test/CrmKmsIntegration` published to the Oracle 8i CORBA server and with appropriate permissions for `scott`. The permissions are automatically granted if you have deployed the EJB through a connection to the `scott` schema. (These issues are covered further in Chapter 15).

```
        Hashtable env = new Hashtable();
        env.put(Context.URL_PKG_PREFIXES,"oracle.aurora.jndi");
        env.put(Context.SECURITY_PRINCIPAL,"scott");
        env.put(Context.SECURITY_CREDENTIALS,"tiger");
        env.put(Context.SECURITY_AUTHENTICATION,ServiceCtx.NON_SSL_LOGIN);
        Context ic = new InitialContext(env);

        CrmKmsIntegrationHome ckih = (CrmKmsIntegrationHome)
            ic.lookup(oracleservice + "CrmKmsIntegration");
        System.out.println("Got Home");
        CrmKmsIntegration cki = null;
        try {
            cki = ckih.create();
            System.out.println("Created EJB");
        } catch (Exception e) {
            e.printStackTrace();
        }
        XMLDocument xmld = null;
        try {
            xmld = (XMLDocument)cki.retrieveServiceTicket(serviceTicket);
            System.out.println("Retrieved document");
        } catch (Exception e) {
            e.printStackTrace();
        }
        return xmld;
    }
}
```

The following snippet shows how you can implement the above search for the home interface and
retrieval of a Document when given strings holding the EJB name requestName, the name of a
method to call requestAction, and some method argument locator. These strings might be
arguments generated at the presentation layer to direct the request to the appropriate business logic and
retrieve the appropriate document. The difficulty here is that we have to somehow convert syntactic
objects (strings) into real objects (EJB and a method instance). In the case of the EJB we have already
the JNDI mechanism for obtaining a handle to the object. All we have to do is pass in a new parameter
requestName to the lookup call. In the second case, we can use the java.lang.reflect package to
extract the method <requestAction>(java.lang.String) from the bean, where we supply
requestAction as a String argument. We then call our argument on some general locator
parameter (possibly just a String), which provides the EJB method with the information it needs to get
return requested Document:

```
        EJBHome home = (EJBHome) new InitialContext(env).lookup(oracleservice +
            requestName);

        Class homeClass = home.getClass();

        Method createMethod = homeClass.getMethod("create", null);

        /*Getting the bean class from the EJB*/
        bean = (EJBObject) createMethod.invoke(home, null);

        /*Getting the method we want to invoke off of the bean class*/
        Class beanClass= bean.getClass();
        Class[] classArray  = { String.class };
```

```
Method action= beanClass.getMethod( requestAction, classArray );

/*Setting up the parameter list and invoking the ction*/
Object[] objectArray = { locator };
Object doc =  action.invoke( bean, objectArray);

return (XMLDocument)doc;
```

One advantage of this approach is that it decouples our presentation logic from the necessity to import individual EJB packages into the lookup environment. A major disadvantage is how to deal with error handling. Since we are 'creating' new method objects and then calling them, we do not have a clear idea of what exceptions they might throw and what to do with them when caught.

Model

Enterprise JavaBeans (EJBs) are used to build the model portion of the MVC framework used in this application. An EJB is a Java-based software component used in middle-tier application development. The EJB specification originates from Sun Microsystems. Sun has developed a specification for developing server-side component software that is based completely on the Java programming language. Since Java is a platform-neutral tool, EJBs can be deployed on a wide variety of operating systems and hardware platforms. Some of the more common EJB deployment platforms include: Linux, Windows NT, Solaris, HP-UX, and AIX.

Just because the EJBs are written in Java does not mean you can put them on your server and just immediately start using them. EJBs are a standard for writing software components. Software component standards focus on letting you build reusable pieces of business logic. These software components rarely contain the infrastructure services that are needed to make an application using these components robust. EJBs are deployed via a piece of software called an application server. This application server provides many of the basic infrastructure services like: transaction management of data across multiple EJB components, clustering of EJB components to increase scalability and redundancy, and naming and directory services that enable applications to locate and remotely invoke EJBs residing on application servers residing through an organization. Oracle 8i database and Internet Application Server provide these services. However, it is important to note that the infrastructure services provided by an application server are in many cases proprietary to that application server.

There are two basic EJB types: Session EJBs and Entity EJBs. Session EJBs are the business process components used to develop the integration services frameworks described in Chapter 15. Session beans have been supported in since Oracle Application Server (OAS) V4.0.8. There are two types of session beans:

- **Stateless** – Stateless session beans hold the state of their internal variables for the length of one method call. As soon as a method has been called on a stateless session bean, all internal state on the component is lost.

- **Stateful** – Stateful session beans are the exact opposite of stateless beans. A stateful session bean will hold its internal state across multiple method invocations. A stateful session bean is often used to capture complex business processes that cannot be performed in a linear fashion inside one method call. Instead, the business process is carried out through a set of method calls on the bean.

For the purposes of our application the model piece of the MVC framework will be implemented using stateless session beans. Our application is a web-based application that needs, potentially, to service a large number of transactions. Web-based applications work to a request/response model where the application makes a request and the web/application server process the request and send a response back. Each response/request made is often stateless, meaning that the web and application server do not remember who the user is between calls. Each request/response made is an independent transaction.

Stateful session beans, because they store state between user calls, do not scale well. Stateful session beans require physical memory to maintain their state. Individually the memory used by a stateful session bean is quite small. However, in a high-volume environment, multiply that small amount of memory on the server by 10,000 end-users. You will quickly find that you run out of memory on the server.

Listed below is an example EJB with a method for retrieving data from the CRM database system. A stateless EJB is composed of three classes that implement the following: a home interface, a remote interface, and a bean class.

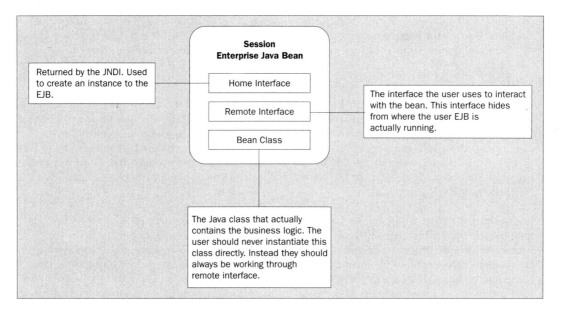

Do not get too hung up in the code details. We are not going to go into great depth explaining each part of the EJB. This would be out of scope for this chapter. Rather, we are going to look at the overall structure of the bean and see how it used by the controller (the servlet). We will start with the home interface:

```
package eadcasestudy.ejb;

/*Home Interface*/
import javax.ejb.*;
import java.rmi.*;

public interface CrmKmsIntegrationHome extends EJBHome {

    CrmKmsIntegration create() throws RemoteException, CreateException;

}
```

In the RequestProcessor class, discussed previously, the process method retrieved the home interface of the EJB it wanted to create. It did this through JNDI. Once the home interface was returned through JNDI, the process method invoked the create() method on the CrmKmsIntegrationHome interface:

```
package eadcasestudy.ejb;

/*Remote Interface*/
import javax.ejb.EJBException;
import javax.ejb.EJBObject;
import org.w3c.dom.*;
import java.rmi.RemoteException;

public interface CrmKmsIntegration extends EJBObject {

  public Document retrieveServiceTicket(String serviceTicket)
      throws RemoteException, EJBException;

  //test method to check architecture in case of transmission problems
  public int test()  throws RemoteException, EJBException;

}
```

The previous two code examples are interfaces. As such, they cannot be instantiated directly – instead they are "implemented" by a Java class and act as contract guaranteeing that the class will have all of the methods defined in the interface. As you can see, interfaces contain only method declarations and no actual code. So, if there is no code present and Java interfaces cannot be instantiated directly, how can these interfaces be used in the `RequestProcessor` class above? Remember, how I said the EJBs must be deployed within an application server. Before you can use the EJBs, you need to run them through a process that will generate stub classes for the remote and home interface. These stub classes are what the `RequestProcessor` deals with. The process of generating these stub classes is specific to the application server and highly detailed. For details on how to generate these stub classes and deploy an EJB from Oracle, please refer to the Oracle Technology Network (OTN) web site (http://otn.oracle.com/software/products/ias/software_index.htm). There are several white papers available on this topic. We will not be going to this level of detail at this point.

The bean class is the heart of the matter. It is the actual code that carries out our business logic:

```
package eadcasestudy.ejb;

/*Bean Class*/
import javax.ejb.*;
import oracle.xml.parser.v2.*;
import java.sql.*;
import org.w3c.dom.*;
import java.io.StringReader;
import java.rmi.RemoteException;

public class CrmKmsIntegrationBean implements SessionBean{
  private transient SessionContext sessionCtx;

  /*
     Used by the application server to retrieve a bean from
     temporary storage.  This method is called by the application
     server when there are too many beans running and resources need
     to be freed up.  THIS METHOD IS NOT USED IN A STATELESS BEAN,
     BUT THE METHOD DOES NEED TO BE IMPLEMENTED IN ORDER FOR THE
     COMPILE TO TAKE PLACE.
  */
```

```
public void ejbActivate(){
}

/*
   Used by the application server to send a bean to
   temporary storage.  This method is called by the application
   server when there are too many beans running and resources need
   to be freed up.  THIS METHOD IS NOT USED IN A STATELESS BEAN,
   BUT THE METHOD DOES NEED TO BE IMPLEMENTED IN ORDER FOR THE
   COMPILE TO TAKE PLACE.
*/
public void ejbPassivate() {
}

/*
   Used to clean up any resources the bean might use.  This method is
   called by the application server and gives the developer a change to end
   things gracefully (close network connections, files, etc...)
*/
public void ejbRemove() {
}

/*
  Used to set the context of the session bean.  This is a mechanism
  for interacting with the application server.  This context can
  contain transaction state, security information, etc....

  Required method by the SessionBean interface.  Not needed for our example.
*/
public void setSessionContext(SessionContext ctx){
  this.sessionCtx = ctx;
}

/*
   Used to initialize your bean. Corresponds to the create method on the
   CrmKmsIntegrationHome class.  We are not using it for anything.
*/
public void ejbCreate() throws RemoteException, CreateException{
}

/* Call this from a remote client to test your architecture if you are
   experiencing problems with marshalling, memory or timeout.  */
public int test()  throws RemoteException, EJBException {return 42;}

/*
   The business method used for retrieving your service ticket data.  This
   method must match the method you define in your CrmKmsIntegration
   interface.

   NOTE:  There can be more then one business method defined in your
   interface.  We have only one method to keep things simple.
*/
 public Document retrieveServiceTicket(String serviceTicket)
     throws RemoteException, EJBException {
```

```
        XMLDocument xmlDoc=null;

        /*
          We will use this buffer to track our process through the method. This can
          be useful for debugging a remotely deployed bean.
        */
        StringBuffer log = new StringBuffer();

        try{
          DOMParser parser = new DOMParser();

          Connection conn = new
            oracle.jdbc.driver.OracleDriver().defaultConnection();

          log.append("Openned connection okay;");

          String sql="{? = call retrieveserviceticket(?) }";

          /*Calling the stored procedure*/
          CallableStatement cs = conn.prepareCall(sql);
          cs.registerOutParameter(1, Types.VARCHAR);
          cs.setString(2,serviceTicket);

          //if (true) return  new (Document)XMLDocument();
          cs.executeUpdate();
          log.append("Executed query okay;");

          /*Getting the results and creating an XML DOM From them*/

          StringReader in = new StringReader(cs.getString(1));
          parser.parse(in);
          log.append("Parsed xml okay;");
          xmlDoc = parser.getDocument();
          log.append("Got document okay;");
          cs.close();
          //don't close database internal driver
        }
        catch(Exception e){
          throw new EJBException(e.toString() + log);
        }

        /*Returning the XML Document*/
        return (Document)xmlDoc;
    }
  }
```

Finally here is an Oracle 8i proprietary deployment descriptor to deploy the bean to the test directory of the ORB server:

```
SessionBean eadcasestudy.ejb.CrmKmsIntegrationBean
{
  BeanHomeName = "test/CrmKmsIntegration";
  HomeInterfaceClassName = eadcasestudy.ejb.CrmKmsIntegrationHome;
  RemoteInterfaceClassName = eadcasestudy.ejb.CrmKmsIntegration;
```

```
    SessionTimeout = 0;
    StateManagementType = STATEFUL_SESSION;

    TransactionAttribute = TX_REQUIRED;
    RunAsMode = CLIENT_IDENTITY;
    AllowedIdentities = { scott };

    org.w3c.dom.Document retrieveServiceTicket
        (javax.servlet.http.HttpServletRequest)
    {
      TransactionAttribute = TX_SUPPORTS;
      RunAsMode = CLIENT_IDENTITY;
      AllowedIdentities = { scott };
    }

    EnvironmentProperties
    {
    }
}
```

Please see Chapter 15 for more specific details on deployment to Oracle 8i. You will need to deal with various factors like listener configuration and multithreaded-servers.

Java Stored Procedures

In order to achieve a clean separation of business and data logic in the CRM-KMS integration application, we used a data persistence layer. Business process components are not allowed to talk directly to tables in either the CRM or KMS databases. Instead all the database work for these components is performed using Java Stored Procedures. In the example above, the `retrieveserviceticket` stored procedure is used to retrieve a string variable containing XML that holds the service ticket information retrieved from the CRM application. The stored procedure looks like this:

```
package eadcasestudy.jstoredproc;

import oracle.xml.parser.v2.*;
import oracle.jdbc.*;
import oracle.jdbc.driver.*;
import java.io.*;
import java.util.*;
import java.sql.*;
import org.w3c.dom.*;

public class CRMServices{

  /*
     Helper class to help build the text node (i.e. a node with an actual value
     <TEST>100</TEST>) I did not want to be doing the same step over and over
     again.
  */
  private static void buildTextNode(Element element, String textValue,
                              Element parent, XMLDocument xmlDoc){
    element.appendChild(xmlDoc.createTextNode(textValue));
    parent.appendChild(element);
  }
```

```
/*
    Building the Service order lines in the DOM. Looping through the
    resultset using a do while.
*/
private static Element buildServiceTicketLine(ResultSet rs,
                                              XMLDocument xmlDoc)
    throws Exception{

    Element lines       = xmlDoc.createElement("Lines");

    do{
      /*Building the Service Ticket Line information*/
      Element line = xmlDoc.createElement("Line");

      Element lineNumber    = xmlDoc.createElement("LineNumber");
      Element underWarranty = xmlDoc.createElement("UnderWarranty");
      Element problem       = xmlDoc.createElement("Problem");

      buildTextNode(lineNumber, rs.getString("so_line_number"),line, xmlDoc);
      buildTextNode(underWarranty, rs.getString("under_warranty"),
         line,xmlDoc);
      buildTextNode(problem, rs.getString("problem"), line, xmlDoc);

      /*Building the part information*/
      Element part       = xmlDoc.createElement("Part");
      Element partName    = xmlDoc.createElement("Name");
      Element partModel  = xmlDoc.createElement("Model");
      Element partSerial= xmlDoc.createElement("SerialNumber");

      buildTextNode(partName,  rs.getString("part_name"),  part, xmlDoc);
      buildTextNode(partModel, rs.getString("part_model"), part, xmlDoc);
      buildTextNode(partSerial, rs.getString("serial_number"), part, xmlDoc);

      line.appendChild(part);
      lines.appendChild(line);
    }while(rs.next());

    return lines;
}

/*
  Building the actual Service Ticket.
*/
private static XMLDocument buildServiceTicketDOM(ResultSet rs)
    throws Exception{
  XMLDocument xmlDoc = new XMLDocument();
  rs.next();

  Element root = xmlDoc.createElement("ServiceTicket");
  xmlDoc.appendChild(root);

  Element header = xmlDoc.createElement("Header");
  root.appendChild(header);
```

```
      /*Building my service order header information*/
      Element ticketNumber   = xmlDoc.createElement("TicketNumber");
      Element accountManager = xmlDoc.createElement("AccountManager");
      Element technician     = xmlDoc.createElement("Technician");
      Element urgency        = xmlDoc.createElement("Urgency");

      buildTextNode(ticketNumber, rs.getString("so_ticket_number"),header,
          xmlDoc);
      buildTextNode(accountManager, rs.getString("account_manager"), header,
          xmlDoc);

      buildTextNode(technician, rs.getString("technician"), header, xmlDoc);
      buildTextNode(urgency, rs.getString("urgency"), header, xmlDoc);

      /*Building my customer information*/
      Element customer = xmlDoc.createElement("Customer");
      header.appendChild(customer);

      Element name    = xmlDoc.createElement("Name");
      Element contact = xmlDoc.createElement("Contact");
      Element address = xmlDoc.createElement("Address");
      Element phone   = xmlDoc.createElement("Phone");

      buildTextNode(name, rs.getString("customer_name"), customer, xmlDoc);
      buildTextNode(contact, rs.getString("customer_contact"),
          customer, xmlDoc);
      buildTextNode(phone, rs.getString("phone"), customer, xmlDoc);

      /*Building the customer's address information*/
      Element street      = xmlDoc.createElement("Street");
      Element city        = xmlDoc.createElement("City");
      Element state       = xmlDoc.createElement("State");
      Element zip         = xmlDoc.createElement("Zip");

      buildTextNode(street, rs.getString("street_address"), address, xmlDoc);
      buildTextNode(city,  rs.getString("city"), address, xmlDoc);
      buildTextNode(state, rs.getString("state"), address, xmlDoc);
      buildTextNode(zip,   rs.getString("zip"),    address, xmlDoc);
      customer.appendChild(address);

      /*Building the service order line information*/
      root.appendChild(buildServiceTicketLine(rs, xmlDoc));

      return xmlDoc;
}

/*
    This method will retrieve a service ticket from the CRM application
    (running in Oracle) and build an XML DOM and return the DOM in a string
    format to the caller.  This stored procedure is written in Java.  The
    main point of entry is the static retrieveServiceTicketEntry.
*/
public static String retrieveServiceTicket(String serviceTicketNumber){
    try{
```

```java
Connection conn = new oracle.jdbc.driver.OracleDriver().defaultConnection();

StringBuffer sqlStr = new StringBuffer(2048);
sqlStr.append("SELECT                                                        ");
sqlStr.append("so_header.so_ticket_number ,   ");
sqlStr.append("so_header.account_manager   ,   ");
sqlStr.append("so_header.technician         ,   ");
sqlStr.append("so_header.urgency            ,   ");
sqlStr.append("customer.customer_name      ,   ");
sqlStr.append("customer.customer_contact   ,   ");
sqlStr.append("customer.street_address     ,   ");
sqlStr.append("customer.city                ,   ");
sqlStr.append("customer.state               ,   ");
sqlStr.append("customer.zip                 ,   ");
sqlStr.append("customer.phone               ,   ");
sqlStr.append("so_line.so_line_number       ,   ");
sqlStr.append("so_line.under_warranty       ,   ");
sqlStr.append("so_line.problem              ,   ");
sqlStr.append("part.part_name               ,   ");
sqlStr.append("part.part_model              ,   ");
sqlStr.append("part.serial_number           ");
sqlStr.append("FROM                                                         ");
sqlStr.append("   so_header                 ,                     ");
sqlStr.append("   so_line                   ,                     ");
sqlStr.append("   so_line_part              ,                     ");
sqlStr.append("   part                      ,                     ");
sqlStr.append("   customer                                        ");
sqlStr.append("WHERE                                              ");
sqlStr.append("   so_header.so_ticket_number=so_line.so_ticket_number ");
sqlStr.append("AND                                                ");
sqlStr.append("   so_line.so_line_number=so_line_part.so_line_number ");
sqlStr.append("AND                                                ");
sqlStr.append("so_line.so_ticket_number = so_line_part.so_ticket_number
                ");
sqlStr.append("AND                                                ");
sqlStr.append("   so_line_part.part_id = part.part_id           ");
sqlStr.append("AND                                                ");
sqlStr.append("   so_header.customer_id=customer.customer_id   ");
sqlStr.append("AND                                                ");
sqlStr.append("   so_header.so_ticket_number=?");

System.out.println(sqlStr);


/*Preparing my SQL Statement*/
PreparedStatement ps = conn.prepareStatement(sqlStr.toString());
ps.clearParameters();
ps.setString(1, serviceTicketNumber );

/*Executing the results*/
ResultSet rs = ps.executeQuery();

/*Building my DOM*/
XMLDocument serviceOrder = buildServiceTicketDOM(rs);
```

```
              /*Converting the DOM to a string*/
              ByteArrayOutputStream output = new ByteArrayOutputStream();
              PrintWriter            pw      = new PrintWriter(output);
              serviceOrder.print(pw);

              /*
              A stored procedure should not close the internal connection.
              But it should close statements and restultsets.
              */
              rs.close();
              ps.close();
              return output.toString();
          }
        catch(Exception e){
            System.out.println(e);
        }

          /*If I have not returned anything by now return a null*/
          return null;
      }
    }
```

Typically, you would load this into your Oracle database with:

```
loadjava -user scott/tiger@dbserver:1521:proead -thin -v \
    eadcasestudy.jstoredprocs.CRMServices.class
```

Please refer to Chapter 11 for more specific details. The command will use the JDBC thin driver to connect with the database and upload the class file. Then you should wrap the procedure by creating a PL/SQL function:

```
CREATE OR REPLACE FUNCTION RETRIEVESERVICETICKET(
    serviceTicketNumber IN VARCHAR2)
RETURN VARCHAR2
AS LANGUAGE JAVA
    NAME
  'eadcasestudy.jstoredproc.CRMServices.retrieveServiceTicket(java.lang.String)
return java.lang.String';
```

This is the PL/SQL method that is called by the CrmKmsIntegrationBean to retrieve the XML given the service ticket number (as a string). We now enter some tables and data into the Oracle database:

```
--
--    Creates the customer table for the EAD case study.
--
CREATE TABLE customer (
    customer_id         NUMBER PRIMARY KEY,
    customer_name       VARCHAR2(255)    ,
    customer_contact    VARCHAR2(255)    ,
    street_address      VARCHAR2(512)    ,
    city                VARCHAR2(255)    ,
    state               VARCHAR2(2)      ,
    zip                 VARCHAR2(100)    ,
    phone               VARCHAR2(12)
```

```
);


--
--    Creates the service order header table for the EAD case study.
--
CREATE TABLE so_header(
   so_ticket_number      VARCHAR2(255) PRIMARY KEY   ,
   account_manager       VARCHAR2(255)            ,
   technician            VARCHAR2(255)            ,
   urgency               VARCHAR2(255)            ,
   customer_id           NUMBER
);


--
--    Creates the service order line table for the EAD case study.
--
CREATE TABLE so_line(
   so_line_number           NUMBER            ,
   so_ticket_number         VARCHAR2(255)       ,
   under_warranty           VARCHAR2(10)        ,
   problem                  VARCHAR2(1024)      ,
   PRIMARY KEY    (so_line_number, so_ticket_number)
);


--
--   Creates a join table between the so_line and part table.
--
CREATE TABLE so_line_part(
   so_line_number        NUMBER            ,
   so_ticket_number      VARCHAR2(255)         ,
   part_id               NUMBER            ,
   PRIMARY KEY    (so_line_number, so_ticket_number, part_id)
);


--
--   Creates the part table for the EAD case study.
--
CREATE TABLE part(
   part_id            NUMBER PRIMARY KEY,
   part_name          VARCHAR2(255)         ,
   part_model         VARCHAR2(255)         ,
   serial_number      VARCHAR2(100)
);


--
--    Loading the example data
--
INSERT INTO customer VALUES(34356,'Leary Medical Supplies','Mary
      Valenti','1803 N. Woods Avenue','Milwaukee',
      'WI','53201','262-431-8945');
INSERT INTO so_header VALUES('343241','Jewell Ehlert', 'Robert Sell',
      'Medium Priority - 24 Hours',34356);
INSERT INTO so_line   VALUES(1,'343241','Y',
      'Monitor flickered and then died');
INSERT INTO part      VALUES(1,'15X3 Montior','X-TV1','343-45-22222-9');
INSERT INTO so_line_part VALUES(1,'343241',1);
```

```
--
--   Adding the foreign key constaints for the table definitions
--
ALTER TABLE so_header
   ADD   CONSTRAINT so_header_customer_id FOREIGN KEY (customer_id) REFERENCES
customer(customer_id);

ALTER TABLE so_line
   ADD   CONSTRAINT so_line_so_ticketNumber FOREIGN KEY (so_ticket_number)
REFERENCES so_header(so_ticket_number);

ALTER TABLE so_line_part
   ADD   CONSTRAINT so_line_part FOREIGN KEY (so_line_number, so_ticket_number)
REFERENCES so_line(so_line_number, so_ticket_number);

ALTER TABLE so_line_part
   ADD   CONSTRAINT so_line_part2 FOREIGN KEY (part_id) REFERENCES part(part_id);
```

You can now test the stored procedure using:

```
select RETRIEVESERVICETICKET(343241) from dual
```

This should yield the XML <ServiceTicket> document that is shown later in this chapter.

For more details on these techniques, see Chapter 11.

This code was written as a Java Stored Procedure for both application development and illustrative reasons. From an application development perspective writing a Java Stored Procedure as the data persistence layer makes a great deal of sense for two reasons:

❑ Java Stored Procedures are extremely flexible. Developers using Java Stored Procedures can work with any data store that has a JDBC driver available. This is extremely useful for our application because at some point we are going to need to connect to a Microsoft SQL Server database.

❑ Because the stored procedure is written in Java, you have more flexibility in deploying the code. If it turns out the code is too resource-intensive to run in the database, you could easily move the code out of the database and have the EJB call it directly. The EJB can be deployed on a different server and the processing load can be taken off of the database server.

From an illustrative perspective Java Stored Procedures were used because:

❑ The Java class written above gives a basic idea of how to use Java to connect to an Oracle database and retrieve data using JDBC.

❑ The stored procedure shows how to use the Oracle XML parser to build an XML Document Object Model (DOM). We could have used the Oracle XML SQL utility to build the XML Document DOM for us from the SQL statement, but the author is a firm believer in learning how to do a task yourself, before letting a tool do it for you.

❑ This chapter focuses on building an MVC framework with an N-Tier architecture. Using a technology like Oracle Business Components for Java or Sun Microsystem's Entity JavaBeans would bog us down in a great deal of detail without adding a great deal of value to our MVC example.

Oracle does provide several other tools for building the data persistence tier. These tools include PL/SQL, Entity EJBs, and Oracle Business Components for Java (BC4J). These tools were not used because:

❑ PL/SQL stored procedures are extremely proprietary. PL/SQL stored procedures, while providing a host of functionality for working with Oracle, provide no means to access other data stores like SQL Server. The KMS application is running on SQL Server. Rather then trying to support multiple data tier development tools (both PL/SQL and Java Stored Procedures) EJBs were chosen because of their cross-platform/cross-database capability.

❑ Entity EJBs, like Session EJBs, are part of the Sun Microsystems J2EE standard. This standard provides a mechanism by which developers can build an object persistence layer over a data store. A data store is typically a relational database, but it does not always have to be. Entity EJBs are not currently supported in Oracle Application Server. There are supported in iAS Release 3 and Oracle 8.1.7. However a number of restrictions on their use relative to Sun's standard EJB 1.1, are still in place. (See the EJB chapter, or the product Release Notes for more details.)

❑ Oracle BC4J is a technology for modeling and implementing an object-based data persistence layer to run on top of an Oracle database. BC4J are Java based software components that developers can use to implement database CRUD (Create, Replace, Update, and Delete Logic). This tool eliminates much of the coding that often takes place with writing data access components. BC4J are deployed as session EJBs. BC4J run on any of the Oracle platforms that support session EJBS. These platforms include:

  ❑ Oracle 8i (up to 8.1.6 supports EJB1.0; 8.1.7 supports EJB1.1 with some restrictions such as one bean per descriptor)

  ❑ Oracle Application Server 4.0.8

  ❑ Oracle Internet Application Server (EJB1.1 with some restrictions such as restricted JDBC access of entity beans to database)

  ❑ Any EJB compliant application server such as BEA's WebLogic or IBM's WebSphere

Java stored procedures still place a great deal of code within the Oracle database. A more ideal solution would be to build a set of data access components that reside outside the database and that all other business components could interact with. To do this we could use a technology like Oracle Business Components for Java (BC4J).

BC4J have an advantage over other data modeling development tools. BC4J are easier to develop for Oracle deployment than other data-access software components like Sun's Entity EJBs, for which Oracle support has been lagging. BC4J modeler, included with the latest version of JDeveloper, provides a variety of modeling and code-generation tools.

We have only briefly touched on some of the Oracle tools for developing a data persistence layer. The reader is referred to Chapters 15 and 17 for more details on these technologies.

View

The view piece of our MVC framework is going to use XML and eXtensible Stylesheet Language (XSL) to generate the output that the end user sees in their web browser. Our view piece consists of a Java class called the XSLTManager. This class takes an XML document, an XSL Stylesheet, and Oracle's XSL process to generate the HTML that appears in the end-user's browser.

On a very high level, the XSLTManager class performs the following actions:

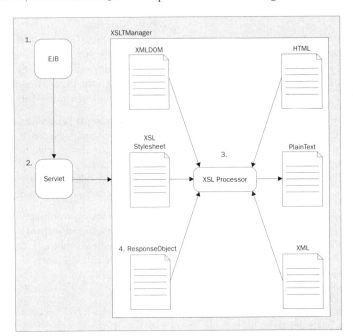

1. The EJB performs its business logic and returns any data that needs to be presented in the form of an XMLDocument object.

2. The servlet passes three things into the XLSTManager via the processOutput call: The XML Document containing the data, the file name of the XSL stylesheet that is used to present the data, and the HttpServletResponse object passed in from the servlet.

   The XSL Transformation Engine will merge the XMLDocument object and XSL stylesheet. The results of this merge will be HTML. We are using the Oracle XSL processor, which can return HTML, plain text, and XML. Other XSL transformation engines, such as infoTeria's iXSLT, can return other formats like Adobe's PDF and Wireless Access Protocol (WAP) for cellular phones.

3. After the XSL processor has merged the XMLDocument and the XSL Stylesheet objects, HTML will be generated and returned back to the end-user via the HttpServletResponse object.

XML and XSL are being used because this allows us to completely separate the business and presentation logic in our application. The model (the EJB) returns all of the data it wants to display back to the controller (the Java servlet). This data is then passed via the controller (the Java Servlet) to an XSL transformation engine. The XSL transformation uses an XSL Stylesheet and the XML document passed in to generate HTML. The XSL Stylesheet describes how the data should be presented to the end-user. By using XSL and XML we can completely change how the data is presented to the end-user without having to the change the business logic used to get the data. For this application XSL and XML were used because upper management could see aspects of the C-K integration application being run on some other device then a web browser (such as a PDA or even a cell phone).

The XSL transformation for our application is occuring in the `XSLTManager` class. Conceptually, the `XSLTManager` is pretty simple. However, before we start diving into `XSLTManager` code let's take a step back. We need to have a basic understanding of some of the key technologies being used.

Extensible Markup Language (XML)

XML was developed by the World Wide Web Consortium (W3C) as a self-describing notation for defining the layout of data. Traditionally when two organizations, or even two software systems within the same organization, wanted to exchange data electronically, the IT departments in both groups would get together and come up with file format for laying out the data. One group would then write a program to export that data in the agreed upon format and the other side would write an application to parse the data. This process was very time-consuming and error-prone. In addition, these import and export programs were often very specific to the integration at hand and offered little in the way of reuse.

XML breaks this model by defining a very precise, universal, and vendor-independent method for defining the structure of data. XML is quickly becoming the universal language for data exchange. As you can tell, this is a pretty formal explanation. In simpler terms, XML is a mechanism for formally defining a data format that is independent of how the data is being used or presented. Any application, regardless of the operating system or hardware platform it is running on, can parse and process XML documents if it has an XML parser available to it.

In our example we are retrieving a service ticket from the CRM database and presenting this data in a web screen. If we used XML, the data structure would look like this:

```
<?xml version = '1.0' ?>
<ServiceTicket>
    <Header>
        <TicketNumber>343241</TicketNumber>
        <AccountManager>Jewell Ehlert</AccountManager>
        <Technician>Robert Sell</Technician>
        <Urgency>Medium Priority - 24 Hours</Urgency>
        <Customer>
            <Name>Leary Medical Supplies</Name>
            <Contact>Mary Valenti</Contact>
            <Address>
                <Street>1803 N. Woods Avenue</Street>
                <City>Milwaukee</City>
                    <State>WI</State>
                    <Zip>53201</Zip>
            </Address>
            <Phone>262-431-8945</Phone>
        </Customer>
    </Header>
    <Lines>
        <Line>
            <LineNumber>1</LineNumber>
            <UnderWarranty>Y</UnderWarranty>
            <Part>
                <Name>15X3 Monitor</Name>
                <Model>X-TV1</Model>
                <SerialNumber>343-45-22222-9</SerialNumber>
            </Part>
            <Problem>Monitor flickered and then died</Problem>
        </Line>
    </Lines>
</ServiceTicket>
```

As you can see, XML is nothing more then a way of defining how data is packaged. The packaging of the data is hierarchical in nature and each piece of the data is "closed". When we say the data is closed, this means there is a very clear beginning and end tag for each one of the elements in the XML DOM (Document Object Model). Looking at the example above, we can clearly see where one piece of data ends and another piece begins. This XML standard is so powerful for data exchange because it allows applications and organizations to pass data back and forth in a consistent manner. The XML standards also encourage development of XML parsers that can interpret the data regardless of the platform where the parsing is taking place. XML is a simple concept that for once frees developers from having to write a unique file parser every time they want to move data back and forth between applications.

Currently there are two types of XML parsers: the DOM (Document Object Model) parser and the SAX (Simple API for XML) parser. The major difference between the DOM and the SAX parser is that the DOM parser loads all of the elements within an XML document as a tree in physical memory. Since the document is represented as a tree it very easy to reorder, add, and delete elements. However, loading the XML document into memory is not always advantageous. Large XML documents in a high transaction environment can quickly eat up memory on even the largest server. The more memory used to hold these XML documents, the less memory is available for processing user requests.

The SAX API does not load the entire XML document into memory and avoids the scalability problem that the DOM API can have. The SAX API is an event-based parser. It will parse pieces of the XML document as the user requests it. This means that as a consumer (that is, program using the SAX API) requests information from the XML document, the parser will start searching the document until it finds the data the user is looking for. As soon as the data is found a callback is made and the consumer requesting the information from the document is notified. The SAX API can be very fast when used to perform a simple, linear search for an element within the XML document. However, one significant disadvantage of using the SAX API is it cannot be used to modify the structure of an XML document.

The decision to use the DOM or SAX API is going to be based on need. If you have small XML documents that will be modified during the course of a transaction use the DOM API. If you need an API that can quickly parse large documents and not modify their underlying structure, use the SAX API. Fortunately, Oracle provides us both with a SAX and DOM version of their parser. In addition Oracle's parser is available for programmers using PL/SQL, Java, C, and C++. This is just the start of the XML tools Oracle offers. For more information on other Oracle XML tools please refer to Chapter 21.

Extensible Stylesheet Language (XSL)

While XML is a very powerful tool for data interchange, it is even more powerful when used in conjunction with XSL. If XML describes the structure of data, XSL is a description of how data should be visually presented and formatted. For the CRM/KMS integration application, the following XSL stylesheet could be used to present a form that would contain service ticket information and a place for the technical support engineer to key in and clean up a problem and solution:

```
<?xml version='1.0' ?>
<xsl:stylesheet xmlns:xsl="http://www.w3.org/1999/XSL/Transform" version="1.0">
  <xsl:template match="/">
  <HTML>
    <Title>CRM to KMS Integration</Title>
    <BODY>
    <TABLE align="left">
      <TR>
```

```
        <TD><IMG src="know-how.gif" width="74" height="72"></IMG></TD>
        <TD><H2>Know How - Your Link to Customer
                Problems and Solutions</H2></TD>
    </TR>
</TABLE>
<BR></BR>
    <FORM method="POST" action="default.html">
        <INPUT type="hidden" name= "Request" value = "CrmKmsIntegration">
        </INPUT>
        <INPUT type="hidden" name="Action"  value = "PostProblemSolution">
        </INPUT>
        <xsl:for-each select="ServiceTicket">
            <BR></BR><BR></BR><BR></BR><BR></BR>
            <TABLE border="0" align="left">
              <TR>
                <TD align="left"><B>Customer Order Number:</B></TD>
                <TD align="left">
                  <xsl:value-of select="Header/TicketNumber"/>
                </TD>
              </TR>
              <TR>
                <TD align="left"><B>Customer Name:</B></TD>
                <TD align="left">
                  <xsl:value-of select="Header/Customer/Name"/>
                </TD>
              </TR>
              <TR>
                  <TD align="left"><B>Customer Contact:</B></TD>
                  <TD align="left">
                    <xsl:value-of select="Header/Customer/Contact"/>
                  </TD>
              </TR>
              <TR>
                  <TD align="left"><B>Phone Number:</B></TD>
                  <TD align="left">
                    <xsl:value-of select="Header/Customer/Phone"/>
                  </TD>
              </TR>
              <TR>
                  <TD align="left"><B>Address:</B></TD>
                  <TD align="left">
                    <xsl:value-of select="Header/Customer/Address/Street"/>
                  </TD>
              </TR>
              <TR>
                  <TD align="left"></TD>
                  <TD align="left">
                    <xsl:value-of select="Header/Customer/Address/City"/>,
                    <xsl:value-of select=  "Header/Customer/Address/State"/>
                       
                    <xsl:value-of select="Header/Customer/Address/Zip"/>
                  </TD>
              </TR>
            </TABLE>
            <BR></BR><BR></BR><BR></BR><BR></BR>
```

```
<BR></BR><BR></BR><BR></BR><BR></BR>
<HR></HR>
<xsl:for-each select="/ServiceTicket/Lines/Line">
   <TABLE border="1">
    <TR>
     <TD align="center" bgcolor="#C0C0C0"><B>Line #</B></TD>
     <TD align="center" bgcolor="#C0C0C0"><B>Part Name</B></TD>
     <TD align="center" bgcolor="#C0C0C0"><B>Model</B></TD>
     <TD align="center" bgcolor="#C0C0C0"><B>Serial Number
       </B>
     </TD>
     <TD align="center" bgcolor="#C0C0C0"><B>Under Warranty </B>
     </TD>
    </TR>
    <TR>
     <TD align="center">
        <xsl:value-of select="LineNumber"/>
     </TD>
     <TD align="center">
        <xsl:value-of select="Part/Name"/>
     </TD>
     <TD align="center">
        <xsl:value-of select="Part/Model"/>
     </TD>
     <TD align="center">
        <xsl:value-of select="Part/SerialNumber"/>
     </TD>
     <TD align="center">
        <xsl:value-of select="UnderWarranty"/>
     </TD>
    </TR>
    <TR>
     <TD align="center"><B>Problem:</B></TD>
     <TD align="center">
        <TEXTAREA cols="50" rows="5" wrap="physcial">
           <xsl:attribute name="name">
               Problem<xsl:value-of select="LineNumber"/>
           </xsl:attribute>
           <xsl:value-of select="Problem"/>
        </TEXTAREA>
     </TD>
    </TR>
    <TR>
     <TD align="center"><B>Solution</B></TD>
     <TD align="center">
     <TEXTAREA cols="50" rows="5" wrap="physcial">
        <xsl:attribute name="name">
            Solution<xsl:value-of select="LineNumber"/>
        </xsl:attribute>
     </TEXTAREA>
     </TD>
    </TR>
   </TABLE>
<BR></BR>
<TABLE align="center">
```

```
        <TR>
            <TD align="center">
                <INPUT type="submit" value="Submit Solution"
                    name="submit1"></INPUT>
            </TD>
        </TR>
    </TABLE>
    </xsl:for-each>
    </xsl:for-each>
    </FORM>
    </BODY>
    </HTML>
    </xsl:template>
</xsl:stylesheet>
```

Using the XSLTManager below and the XML DOM and XSL stylesheet from the previous examples we get the following output:

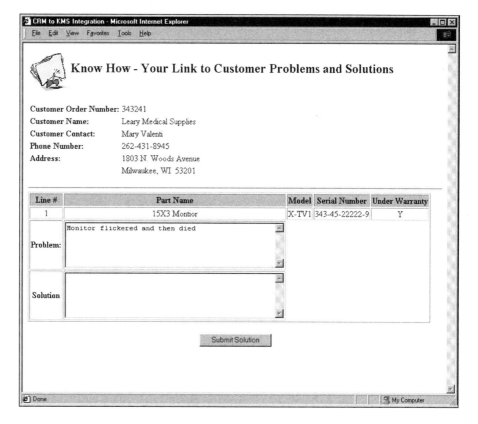

The XSLTManager

Now that we have covered some of the basic concepts of XML and XSL, lets take a look at the code used to develop the XSLTManager. The code might seem a little overwhelming but when broken down step-by-step, it is pretty straightforward.

```
package eadcasestudy.javabean;

import java.util.*;
import java.io.*;
import java.net.*;

import oracle.xml.parser.v2.*;
import javax.servlet.http.HttpServletResponse;
import javax.servlet.http.*;


public class XSLTManager{
    /*
        This method will take an XMLDocument and a XSL stylesheet and generate HTML
        that will be returned back to the end user.
    */
    public void processOutput(HttpServletResponse response,
        XMLDocument xmlDoc, String xslFileName){

        /*Creating my parser*/
        DOMParser parser = new DOMParser();

        try{
          /*************Step 1***************/
          /*Converting the file name to a URL object*/
          URL xslURL = new URL(xslFileName);
          parser.parse(xslURL);

          /*************Step 2***************/
          XMLDocument xslDoc = parser.getDocument();

          /*************Step 3***************/
          XSLStylesheet xslStyleSheet = new XSLStylesheet(xslDoc, xslURL);
          XSLProcessor processor = new XSLProcessor();
          processor.showWarnings(true);
          processor.setErrorStream(System.out);

          /*Telling the response object we are going to write out HTML*/
          response.setContentType("text/html");

          /*************Step 4***************/
          PrintWriter out = response.getWriter();

          /*************Step 5***************/
          processor.processXSL(xslStyleSheet, xmlDoc, out);
          //out.close();
        }
        catch (Exception e){
          e.printStackTrace();
        }
    }
}
```

The code above can be somewhat overwhelming. So let's walk through it step-by-step and make sure we understand it.

```
URL xslURL = new URL(xslFileName);
parser.parse(xslURL);
```

The method loads the XSL file based upon the filename that is passed in. This filename is used as a constructor for the Java URL object xslURL. This means that the file name passed in must be passed in as a URL. For example, if the file c:\wrox\serviceTicketDisplay were the XSL file we wanted to load then the filename would be denoted as `file:\\c:\\wrox\\serviceTicketDisplay.xsl:`

The XSL file is then parsed into an XMLDocument object called xslDoc. The Oracle XML V2 parser is used to parse the XSL file:

```
XMLDocument xslDoc = parser.getDocument();
XSLStylesheet xslStyleSheet = new XSLStylesheet(xslDoc, xslURL);
XSLProcessor processor = new XSLProcessor();
processor.showWarnings(true);
processor.setErrorStream(System.out);
PrintWriter out = response.getWriter();
```

The xslDoc and xslURL objects are then used in the constructor for the XSLStylesheet to instantiate an XSLStylesheet object called xslStyleSheet. The xslStyleSheet object is what is actually passed into the XSL processor for parsing.

A PrintWriter object called out is retrieved from the HttpServletResponse object. This object will be passed into the XSL processor when we are ready to merge the xslDoc and xslStylesheet.

```
processor.processXSL(xslStyleSheet, xmlDoc, out);
```

The xslDoc, xslStylesheet, and the out object are all passed into the XSL processor via the processXSL method call. The XSL processor will internally generate HTML and write the HTML to the out object passed into the method call.

When the XSLTManager is broken down, the concepts it embodies become quite simple. With the XSLTManager as the view piece of our MVC framework we are completing separating how the data is presented from how the data is structured or retrieved. However, we have made one basic assumption in the above code. We have assumed that the only desired output is HTML. If you wanted to present other output formats, like output for a cell phone or PDA, you would need to refactor the controller (the servlet) and the view (XSLTManager) to be able to accommodate these different formats.

The MVC framework is a very powerful concept in an N-Tier architecture design and implementation. Each piece of the MVC framework offers unique opportunities. The controller is a central point for managing all user requests. In the Controller, code can be placed to do such things as auditing or even performing security checks to make sure the user is authorized to perform an action. In the Model, a business rule can be modified without the fear that it will break any of your presentation logic. The model just needs to handle the business logic and returning data to be passed back to the controller. With the View, you can completely change the look-and-feel of an application by modifying the XSL stylesheets. Imagine being able to build a web-based interface that can be completely customized to meet the individual needs of each one of your customers. Now, imagine being able to do this in a day. There are companies out there right now using the MVC framework and N-Tier architectures to accomplish exactly these tasks.

Deployment

We can point out a few things to help you deploy the servlet to Oracle HTTP Server (Apache JServ), or to run it in JDeveloper, (a JDeveloper project for this chapter is available on the Wrox web site). There are also further resources in this book, namely in Chapters 11,15 and 19.

For JServ, you need to edit the `jserv.properties` and `zone.properties` files, normally found below <APACHE_HOME>\Jserv. Add the following declarations, which assume that the EJB stub class archive generated by `deployejb` is named `CrmKmsIntegrationGenerated.jar`. To `jserv.properties`, add (substituting suitable full pathnames):

```
wrapper.classpath=<DEPLOY_HOME>\CrmKmsIntegrationGenerated.jar
wrapper.classpath=<DEPLOY_HOME>
wrapper.classpath=<XML_LIB>\xmlparserv2.jar
wrapper.classpath=<ORACLE_HOME>\lib\aurora_client.jar
wrapper.classpath=<ORACLE_HOME>\lib\vbjorb.jar
wrapper.classpath=<ORACLE_HOME>\lib\vbjapp.jar
wrapper.classpath=<ORACLE_HOME>\lib\vbjtools.jar
```

Note that <DEPLOY_HOME> should be the directory containing the `eadcasestudy` directory. Also, add to the `zone.properties` file:

```
repositories=<DEPLOY_HOME>
servlets.startup=eadcasestudy.servlet.CrmKmsIntegrationServlet
servlet.ead.code=eadcasestudy.servlet.CrmKmsIntegrationServlet
```

This should enable you to access the servlet via a URL:
http://localhost/servlet/ead?request=CrmKmsIntegration&action=retrieveServiceTicket&soTicket=343241

In JDeveloper you can register the servlet in the built-in servlet runner (Web-to-Go). Select **Wizards | Web Object Manager**, go to the servlets folder, and register the servlet class with alias `ead`. Running it will launch the servlet in the built-in servlet runner.

Troubleshooting

A few tips that may be of use in this application:

❑ Ensure that the version of Oracle XML Parser you are using is identical in both database and development/deployment area. Otherwise you may encounter problems reading serialized objects from the EJB over the network. Serialization is the technology that allows a Java object like `Document` to be sent from one Java virtual machine to another. If the object reader and writer produce incompatibilities, then you may receive obscure errors. To upload the XML Parser JAR file to the database, you use the `loadjava` command, which is covered elsewhere in the book.

❑ Ensure that your applications are finding any XSL files and `xslConfig.txt`.

❑ See Chapter 15 for Oracle EJB troubleshooting tips.

❑ For Apache JServ make sure that all relevant class files are visible to the server (not just source).

Migrating from Legacy Applications

So, far most of our discussion has been focusing on building N-Tier applications from the ground up. However, very few of us have the luxury of developing stand-alone, new applications. As our C-K application illustrates, most EAD efforts involve either integrating applications or re-factoring existing applications to be more reusable, scalable, and fault-tolerant.

When you are faced with migrating a two-tier closed, architecture to the more extensible N-Tier model, there are four principles, that I like to call the GATE principles, that must be kept in mind:

- ❑ Generalize your key business processes.

- ❑ Abstract away technical implementation details.

- ❑ Technology choices should be a means to solving a problem, not an end in itself.

- ❑ Enough is enough.

Generalizing your key business processes is essential to developing enterprise-level applications. Businesses remain competitive by constantly and consistently embracing change. Generalization shields your application(s) from changes in a business process. Use these legacy migration projects as an opportunity to generalize your business processes. Generalization allows you to change the underlying rules and steps that take place in a business process. By generalizing your business processes you can avoid the ripple effects that often occur when you change a business rule in a tightly coupled two tiered application. Generalization also promotes reuse. Inevitably, applications have to be integrated. By designing coarse-grained services that wrapper a business process you can significantly cut down on other application development efforts. Other applications can use the business process without a significant amount of work. When looking to migrate an application to a N-Tier architecture look to the following:

1. Identify the key business processes that are being supported by the migration. Ask yourself two questions. Which of these business processes will change on a regular basis? Which of these business processes will most likely be used in other applications? What is the importance of the business process?

2. Wrapper these business processes so that other applications are completely unaware of how these components work. A wrappered business process can be thought of as a single transaction containing multiple steps. A consumer of the business process should not care about the steps involved within each business process.

3. As you are porting the application make sure that all pieces of the application interact with the business process through its wrapper. Many times there is a temptation to "skirt" the business process because the code needs to do something special. If you come across this temptation, you are probably not generalizing the business process properly. Stop, go back, and make sure the business process can handle these exceptions.

4. After you have written the business processes and migrated the application publish the fact that this service now exists. As other applications are being integrated with the newly ported application force them to use the services you have written. Never let them talk directly to the newly ported application's data stores.

The abstraction of technical implementation details will help in two ways. First, abstracting away technical detail will help you break the trap of vendor dependency. Third-party software tools and components can significantly cut down on development time. However, never let your applications directly use the vendor's tools. Wrapping your vendor tools will protect you from a significant amount of rework if the software vendor goes out of business or you choose to use a different tool. Secondly, by abstracting away technical details, you can prevent your applications from knowing how data is stored or manipulated. By using abstraction, your application will no longer care that the data it is using is stored in Oracle, Sybase, or even on a Mainframe. The Generalization and Abstraction principles of GATE can be summed up as:

> **Your applications are consumers of services. They do not care about the steps involved in carrying out the services or how the services are carried out. They only care that they can use the services to get a job done.**

The third principal of GATE, emphasizes that technology is merely a tool. The application developers of the first CRM/KMS integration application violated this principle. They built their entire application centered on development tools rather than a development platform. When doing your migration make sure to pick a development platform that is open and standards-based. Don't move from one short-term solution to another. In the N-Tier example of the CRM/KMS integration application, we used a development platform, Sun Microsystems's J2EE platform, to write our application. Oracle was just a particular implementation of that platform. If Oracle's Application Server was found to be lacking we could with relatively little work, port the application over to a different application server running on a completely different hardware platform. Luckily, for the CRM/KMS team in the second architecture model, Oracle chose to embrace the J2EE platform. They have a gradual migration path to move their application over to a standards-based, N-Tier architecture. Imagine what would have happened if they had written the entire application using a Sybase's PowerBuilder web development tools. If they found this platform unscalable, they would have faced a significant amount of rewrite of the application.

The last principle of GATE is enough is enough. Recognize when it is time to stop designing and start coding. It is easy when migrating a two-tier to an N-Tier model to focus too much on building the perfectly componentized, partitioned application and lose sight of what's important. N-Tier architectures provide long-term solutions. This means things will change and whatever design you come up with has to be extensible enough to accommodate change. Focus on the 80-20 rule. Any model you build should be 80% complete. The last 20% of the model will be the part that constantly evolves and is impossible to capture in a static model. Accept the uncertainty and build your application. This author has seen too many N-Tier applications die a quick death because the computer scientists in the development team wanted to build the perfect model.

Many of the GATE principles can be accomplished by using Object-Oriented Analysis and Design (OOAD) techniques. Unfortunately, OOAD is a large, complicated topic that cannot be adequately covered in one or two chapters of a book on Oracle Application Programming. OOAD is a critical piece of designing granular and flexible business and data tiers. This author highly recommends that before you design and implement a large-scale N-Tier application you familiarize yourself with these topics.

Summary

In this chapter we presented a case study that showed many of the challenges organizations face in building enterprise-level applications. These challenges include:

❑ Building an application to solve the common problem of data integration. This application had to integrate two systems built on different technologies and different levels of integration capability.

❑ Choosing an application architecture that is scalable enough to meet not only the demands of the current user, but also a large number of future users. This scalability needs to be implemented with a minimal amount of code rewrite.

❑ Building an integration framework that will allow other applications to integrate easily with the CRM and KMS applications.

We have looked at three application architecture models and explored how they meet the objectives stated above. These models are:

❑ The quick and easy two-tier application implementation. This implementation is typical of the mentality "Just get it done." The two-tier model will get the job done quickly, but will not solve the long-term problems of scalability and reuse.

❑ A more structured three-tier implementation that focuses on logically separating the application into different pieces. This application is easy to implement and offers a migration path to the more powerful and extensible N-Tier model.

❑ A N-Tier implementation. We used a Model-Viewer-Controller framework. This model separates the application into three distinct and physically separated tiers. The MVC framework acts as a software construct that further decouples the presentation, business, and data logic from one another. The N-Tier architecture and the MVC framework best meet the three objectives stated above.

Finally, we looked at migration strategies for moving legacy applications to an N-Tier model. This migration strategy uses the GATE principles to help guide us in our design and technology decisions. The four principles of GATE are:

❑ Generalize key business processes

❑ Abstract away technical implementation details.

❑ Technology choices should be a means not an end to solving a problem.

❑ Enough is enough.

In conclusion, when applying EAD to your application development processes always remember this: Enterprise Application Design (EAD) is for long-term solutions, not short-term problem solving. The short cuts you take now are the messes you have to deal with in the future.

23

Application Integration using SOAP

Approaching the design of a new Web application or the integration of different systems – from portals to CRM – or simply an interface to a company's ERP software is a daunting task. Today, businesses need a much higher level of integration between heterogeneous systems.

The "old" Internet applications imply an innovative way to work: a user connected with a server anywhere in the world. The server provides the user with HTML pages using the HTTP protocol, often statically taken from a file system.

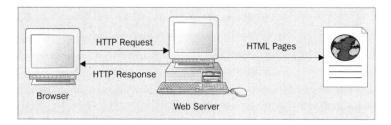

With this approach, you can provide catalogs, brochures, and any kind of information on-line, without the need for intermediaries, complex inter-connection infrastructures and proprietary software: just a browser. This caused a stir with the IT companies first and the entire world later. Within a few years, companies of all kinds embraced this technology.

The e-Commerce world, however, requires a new pattern in browser-server cooperation. The previous one was a 'pull-like' communication protocol: the browser asks for a page and the server provides it. In the new one, the browser acts as a terminal in our information system, similar to a client in the more traditional, client-server application. We need to authorize lesser-known users to perform some operations using our site as a server and we need dynamically generated pages, usually from multiple applications collaborating together, in order to try to satisfy the needs of the customer.

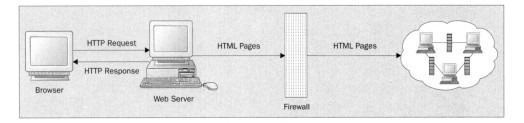

Companies such as Amazon.com have led the way in E-Commerce. The vast infrastructures that are now available – communications lines, routers, domain name servers etc. – have enabled a new information technology world, with costs that were unthinkable a few years ago.

Let's take a closer look at a simplified version of the process that is involved in selling a book at a site such as Amazon.com:

❏   Get a credit card charge authorization from a Bank

❏   Inform the carrier of a new shipping

❏   Charge the customer credit card

❏   Prepare a payment for the book provider

❏   Prepare a payment for our carrier

❏   Adjust the customer profile

❏   Update the selling statistics

For an e-Commerce site, these processes need be carried out quickly and efficiently and in a manner that minimizes cost.

> *Speed is a very important factor in an Internet business. Speed is a relevant aspect not only for the system architects who are working on the infrastructure but also for the marketing people and their important objective: to maximize sales. Recent studies proved that an Internet customer has an attention span of 8 seconds and in that length of time, your site has the opportunity to catch him. If the site isn't fast enough to satisfy his needs, you could lose a prospective client. The main portal site has to offer its service not only with careful graphic design, but backed up with a strong technical architecture.*

This is a significant challenge because even the simplified process presented above is unlikely to be supported by a single company operating a single monolithic server. In reality many companies have to cooperate in the book-selling process: not just the company running the main portal site but also business partners of this company including publishers, delivery companies, banks, and so on.

Each company will have their own technical infrastructures and business rules and for an effective, profitable B2B operation, we need the ability to combine heterogeneous systems and achieve a high level of application integration across these multiple organizations. The objective of this chapter is to show how you can achieve this goal using Oracle and Simple Object Access Protocol (SOAP).

What is SOAP?

Every once in a while an idea comes along that on the surface appears very simple, yet has the power to affect the way applications are designed. SOAP (Simple Object Access Protocol) is such an idea. XML-based SOAP messages have the potential to transform the way we write distributed applications. SOAP is a protocol for client-server communications across a network.

XML is a W3C standard and defines a platform-neutral way to represent data that can be shared among different devices. We can easily define our different types of business data – expedition orders, invoices, sales receipts, bank orders etc. – and send them using SOAP and HTTP.

SOAP is platform-neutral, language-neutral and is not dependent on any object model. Therefore, a SOAP-enabled distributed application could span multiple operating systems, consisting of objects from different vendors, written in different languages, and based on different objects.

This is a protocol that combines two existing and widely accepted technologies: HTTP and XML. It makes use of our investments in those technologies by building upon them.

HTTP is a generic, stateless and broadly adopted protocol and, thus, using it with SOAP we have the means to connect an Oracle 8i Database to different applications and systems, regardless of platform and avoiding the difficulties associated with firewalls that block non-HTTP requests. As a server, Oracle 8i can expose its services without the need for complex client configurations.

SOAP is another mechanism that permits remote procedure calls, or remote method invocation, just like DCOM (Distributed COM), IIOP (Internet Inter-ORB Protocol), and others. In fact, SOAP isn't as fully featured as some of these. It does not attempt to support:

- ❑ Distributed garbage collection

- ❑ Bi-directional HTTP communications

- ❑ Boxcarrying or pipelining of messages (batching multiple method calls into a single message as an optimization and to reduce network traffic)

- ❑ Objects by reference

- ❑ Activation (creating components and establishing connections to components)

> **It is perhaps because of its inherent simplicity that it stands a good chance of succeeding where the others have not made significant inroads. SOAP has the potential to standardize the way distributed applications communicate.**

SOAP strives to set out what the envelope for an XML message should look like, current SOAP protocol is focused on remote method invocation and message exchanges via HTTP.

The SOAP specification defines what a remote object method call should look like. The fact that the method calls and data travel as plain text on the widely accepted and deployed HTTP ports means that SOAP-enabled distributed applications will be easier to deploy than DCOM-based distributed applications.

SOAP is a real-time communications protocol. It usually uses HTTP as a transport, although it can use other types such as SMTP. There is no notion of persisting a message and sending it later. This raises a potential drawback: the system you are communicating with needs to be online when you send your message. The action to take if the recipient is not online is an implementation detail left to be resolved at an architectural level. You could keep retrying until you do get a response, or you could have some mechanism to provide a fail-over recipient, or perhaps you may want to serialize the message and queue it up to be sent once the recipient machine is reachable.

Conversation and Message Types

SOAP enables distributed applications through two types of web communication scenarios: request/response and fire-and-forget. In the fire-and-forget one-way communication scenario, the originator invokes a method call in a remote object, but doesn't require a return value. In the request/response scenario, objects can have a bi-directional communication, with the sender invoking a method call and receiving a return value. However, as stated above, there is no real-time bi-directional communication; method calls, and return values are passed back and forth through HTTP.

A SOAP message will always fall into one, and only one, of the following categories:

- ❑ A method invocation, a Request
- ❑ The result of a method invocation, a Response
- ❑ A Fault

The method invocation originates on the SOAP client, and the SOAP server returns the result and fault. If a SOAP message is a fault, then, by definition, it cannot also contain a return value.

SOAP Envelope

The SOAP protocol defines an envelope for a message, and a format for the XML payload container. The SOAP protocol includes custom HTTP headers, in addition to the XML of the message envelope and payload. The following is a graphical representation of a SOAP message:

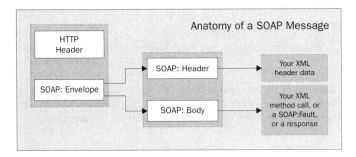

Here is a typical example of a method invocation:

This would go in the HTTP header:

```
POST /myserver HTTP/1.1
Host: www.mydomain.com
Content-Type: text/xml
Content-length:nnnn
SOAPMethodName: my-name-space#myMethod
```

This would go in the SOAP envelope:

```
<SOAP:Envelope xmlns:SOAP="urn:schemas-xmlsoap-org:soap:v1.1">
  <SOAP:Header>
    <t:transactionID xmlns:t="a-name-space" SOAP:mustUnderstand="1">
      19
    </t:transactionID>
  </SOAP:Header>
  <SOAP:Body>
    <m:myMethod xmlns:myMethod="my-name-space">
      <par1>foo</par1>
      <par2>bar</par2>
    </m:myMethod>
  </SOAP:Body>
</SOAP:Envelope>
```

A benefit of having the method name in the header is that it enables creation of routers that can grant or deny access to a SOAP call, and properly dispatch the SOAP calls just by reading the header, without requiring the ability to parse the XML in the message itself. A typical response could look something like this.

First the HTTP header:

```
HTTP/1.1 200 OK
Content-Type: text/xml
Content-length:nnnn
```

And now the contents of the SOAP envelope, or the payload:

```
<SOAP:Envelope xmlns:SOAP="urn:schemas-xmlsoap-org:soap:v1">
  <SOAP:Body>
    <m:myMethodResponse xmlns:m="my-name-space">
      <return>hello</return>
    </m:myMethodResponse >
  </SOAP:Body>
</SOAP:Envelope>
```

The payload is a standard well-formed XML file. You could send binary data as part of the invocation or response, using Base64 encoding – the XML standard for encoded binaries. This would allow you to do things such as sending images with your SOAP request. Alternatively, rather than making binaries or resources part of the SOAP message, you can include a URI that points back at them.

The SOAP Header

The `<SOAP:Header>` element is optional. The intention behind the header is to send extended information along with the method call. `<SOAP:Header>` elements are used to pass implicit information. For example, a purchase transaction may consist of several individual messages that are part of a transaction. A `<SOAP:Header>` could be used to tie the related messages together. To enforce compatibility, elements contained inside a header can have a `mustUnderstand` attribute. If this attribute has a value of "1", it indicates to the receiving application that it must be able to understand and correctly process it. If the attribute has a value of "0", then it is functionally equivalent to it not being present.

Proper usage of this attribute will help in the creation of more robust applications that are extensible, but also able to raise errors if they receive messages containing data that is not fully understood.

Faults

The SOAP protocol includes a way for the invoked method to return an error message to the requestor. This is achieved by having a `<SOAP:Fault>` tag as a child of the `<SOAP:Body>`. It is important to remember that there are only three types of SOAP messages: a request, a response, and an error condition. Any given SOAP message will fall into one and only one of those categories. As a result of this, the only items that will ever appear as children of the `<SOAP:Body>` tag are details of the error.

The SOAP protocol defines four different error codes:

Code	Name	Description
100	Version Mismatch	The request was made by an unsupported version of the SOAP protocol.
200	Must Understand	The request contained a `<SOAP:Header>` element that had a `mustUnderstand` attribute with a value of "1", and the application did not understand it.
300	Invalid Request	The request was not supported by the application.
400	Application Faulted	The application was able to understand the request, but an error occurred.
500	Internal Server Error	There was an error whilst processing the SOAP request on the server and a fault message is returned stating the error

The SOAP protocol dictates that a standard SOAP Fault message shall contain the following child elements:

Element	Contents
`<faultcode>`	One of the four numeric values presented above.
`<faultstring>`	One of the strings listed above.
`<runcode>`	An enumerated value that indicates whether or not the request was actually sent to the application. The three possible values are `Maybe`, `No` and `Yes`.
`<detail>`	If present, contains application-specific error information.

You may add additional sub-elements, provided they are namespace qualified. Any additional information you may wish to convey would, more than likely, be application-specific, and as such should be placed inside the `<detail>` element.

Serving It Up

The SOAP protocol defines what the message envelopes should consist of the implementation details are completely up to the developer.

Whichever form the implementation takes, there will need to be some form of SOAP server that either acts upon, or acts as a routing agent for the SOAP message. This is the URI end point of the `POST`ed HTTP request.

The above are only a few samples of SOAP end points. It is the fact that SOAP only defines a protocol, and that the entire implementation is left to the developer, that makes it so open and flexible.

Security

SOAP messages can be sent using the firewall-friendly and generally open port 80. The bad news is that any methods you expose will now be accessible to anyone that knows how to call them, so security is a concern.

However, this is not as serious a problem as many have envisioned. SOAP messages can be sent through normal secure mechanisms such as SSL or HTTPS, and use normal access control and authentication processes. Firewalls and other HTTP filters can be configured to block messages based on the content of the HTTP header, thereby determining which methods can be called, and even by whom. The fact that the method name is in the header (as well as in the body) means that messages can be blocked without needing to be able to understand the structure and content of the message itself. In order for someone outside your firewall to wreak havoc, you would first need to give them the capability by exposing the objects and methods to do so when invoked, give them access privileges, and even then, they would need to know what to call. In other words, if a little attention is paid to security during the architecture phase, security should not be a problem. There is no inherent security breach created when you write a distributed application that uses SOAP messages. Good design practices coupled with an eye to security considerations will result in applications that can safely be exposed.

Encoding Data

The SOAP protocol defines a formal method for encoding data, and supports all simple and compound data types required by a modern application. It supports the passing of strings, integers, arrays (including multi-dimensional and partially transmitted arrays) and more.

Exposing Services

We've talked about "exposing services" so let's consider in more detail exactly what we mean by this and how it comes about. What are these services? For example, an Administration department may offer to "register an invoice" service. Using this service, employees in other internal departments can electronically send the invoice entry request to the Admin department, thereby avoiding all of the paper-intensive work usually required

In a similar way, a carrier can offer a book delivery service. We can insert a book delivery request into a SOAP bubble and pass it to the carrier over the Internet. This sounds simple, but bear in mind that in order to achieve this we need to have full knowledge of the **interface** defined by the service provider. We can think about the interface of the service in a COM or Java analogous way: a contract between the implementer of interface and the client in terms of functionality provided and signature of the functions. If someone breaks the contract, nothing will work!

In the examples presented later in this book, we know these details, but clearly there would be advantages to being able to "discover" all the details of a service. This is achieved by all the interfaces being constructed according to standard specifications:

> The idea is to take a standard interface specification from http://www.w3.org/TR/SOAP/ where soap specification is at the time this book is being published at the stage of being a NOTE.

We can describe an interface using XML instead of a proprietary mechanism like a Java class file or Microsoft COM type library. Using an XML representation of the interface, every platform that supports XML and HTTP can "read" the interface specification and use it to call the service. In a simpler way: you can, programmatically create a local proxy and invoke the object's methods on the proxy, as you would call them on a local object; the proxy, knowing the object's interface, can build the SOAP call transparently.

This is a good idea but, unfortunately, there are many different approaches to this problem: Microsoft's Services Description Language (SDL) and IBM's Network Accessible Service Specification Language (NASSL) for example. Both of them were the first attempts to describe the service's interface using XML, today all the efforts are in the Universal Description, Discovery, and Integration (UDDI) specification. The first result was the WSDL specifications released less than a month after the initiative was launched.

The main goal of this initiative is to create a platform-independent, open framework for describing services, discovering businesses, and integrating business services using the Internet. The UDDI standard is supported by many members: IBM, Microsoft and SUN above all, although not Oracle yet. You can find up-to-date information on UDDI and WSDL specifications at:

❑ http://www.uddi.org.

❑ http://msdn.microsoft.com/xml/general/wsdl.asp

❑ http://www-4.ibm.com/software/developer/library/w-wsdl.html.

Implementing SOAP

From an architectural standpoint, we want to expose our services in a platform-neutral way and we want to use our Oracle Server like any other information or service provider in our network of heterogeneous systems.

To have a schematic view you can think of encapsulating our various "servers" in SOAP bubbles:

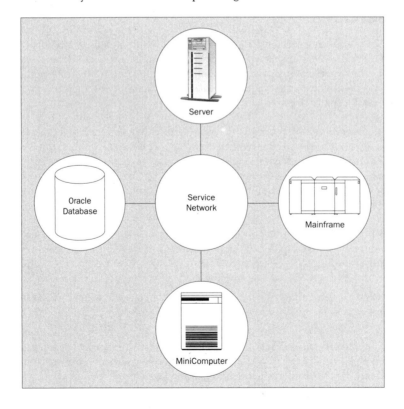

Every bubble can be a consumer (client) or a provider (server) of a service. We can think about our SOAP bubble network like a peer-to-peer "services" network. We can think of SOAP not only as glue between heterogeneous systems but also as a mediator between different architectures, or as an agent integrator.

In this scenario we can enable every service in a peer to peer way so every service can be, at the same time, a server and a client and they can interact with each other disregarding languages, transmission protocol, physical server site, and so on.

We can invoke a MTS/COM+ Visual Basic service from inside an Oracle stored procedure or, vice versa, you can invoke an Oracle stored function from a Perl module without any other middleware other than SOAP, even if they reside on a different server and even if servers are separated by firewalls.

In other words you can connect a client written in any language, based on whichever technology is used with an Oracle DB using SOAP and a small amount of infrastructure to implement it, without any need for proprietary protocols: no NET8 dependency, ODBC drivers, JDBC, nor any CORBA services.

All you need is HTTP/SMTP, XML, and the SOAP infrastructure to expose your Oracle services worldwide.

SOAP Architecture

To use SOAP we need a framework for each platform we want to use. Today we can find a lot of SOAP implementations for different platforms, for example:

- ❑ Apache SOAP implementation
- ❑ Microsoft SOAP toolkit

The first one is written in Java and is based on a previous IBM version; as this book is going into publication, this is undergoing a revision and a name change, it may be called Axis (which will be version 3) by the time you read this chapter, you can find more recent information at http://xml.apache.org/soap.

The second one is the Microsoft toolkit and you can find more details at http://msdn.microsoft.com/xml/general/toolkit_intro.asp and the whole .NET initiative. The forthcoming vs.net brings SOAP full-circle, making SOAP and web services development a seamless part of the development environment.

All the implementations share a common goal:

> *To simplify the use of SOAP services.*

As application developers we don't want to deal with a lot of implementations details like envelope, body or transport protocol issues: we want to make a call to a service and we'd like the infrastructure to take care of all the SOAP specification details.

Usually in a SOAP network, we've got an architecture like this.

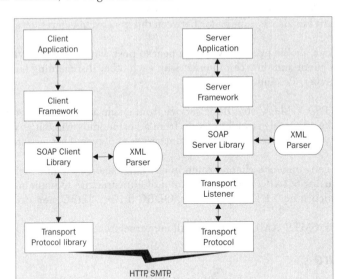

In this chapter, we want to show you how to create, set-up and use a network of SOAP services. Firstly we will examine the Apache and Microsoft SOAP libraries, then show the design and the development of a framework to make evident the PL/SQL use of SOAP "bubble" services and how to access Oracle services from heterogeneous clients. In a SOAP network, we can identify, for each server, two major players: the SOAP Client and the SOAP Server. We don't look for how a service is implemented, we only talk with a SOAP server; and our services do not have to know that they are inserted in a SOAP bubble; they only expose their service. The infrastructure takes care of all the details. We have prepared the infrastructure to use Oracle both as a client and as server with the objective of integrating it with other SOAP-enabled services.

In other words, we want to insert Oracle into a bubble.

We prepared the complete client side Oracle SOAP implementation and a simple Enterprise JavaBean to insert a row in an Oracle table. It is quite simple to extend our JavaBean to create a more general component able to call an object stored in the Oracle DB such as a stored procedure or execute PL/SQL code to return a resultset.

In the absence of an existing Oracle-SOAP implementation, we need to write our own framework and a PL/SQL interface for SOAP in order to transform our Oracle Database into a SOAP client. To make Oracle a SOAP server is easier than to transform it into a client, the intriguing thing is to transform it into a client so you can use Oracle in a peer-to-peer SOAP network. Using this framework you can easily call any SOAP service you need from inside the PL/SQL: trigger, stored procedure, stored function, or SQL query.

> **Later, we're going to show you the details of our implementation and from the Wrox website you'll be able to download the source code both of the framework and all of the samples. In this chapter only the full code for the Java calculator and the Oracle framework are shown. To incorporate all the code for the case study into this chapter would obscure the important details of how the SOAP is implemented.**

The Apache-SOAP

The Apache SOAP is a Java, open-source, and free implementation of the SOAP 1.1 specifications. It supports most of the 1.1 requirements except:

❑   `mustUnderstand` attribute

❑   `root` attribute

❑   `actor` attribute and SOAP intermediaries

❑   `ID/href` links and `multi-ref` accessors

In the Apache download you can find: two tools for managing services, a tool for debugging SOAP, a servlet listener for the HTTP protocol, the `soap.jar` archive containing all the classes and the complete documentation set. As you saw in the previous diagram, we have the API for both the client side and the server side.

The main class for the client side API is `org.apache.soap.rpc.Call`. Using this class you can invoke remote SOAP service, the required steps to invoke a remote service are:

❑   Instantiate a new Call Object

❑   Identify the remote object

❑   Set the name of the method

❑   Add the parameters required (if any)

❑   Invoke the method

The result is a Response object that contains the actual response or the generated fault.

SOAP is based on XML and if you want to implement SOAP, you will always need an XML parser. The Apache SOAP uses, as default, the Apache XML parser: Xerces. Thus, you need to add the `xerces.jar` file to your CLASSPATH in order to use this implementation.

The Apache-SOAP Listener

Even though SOAP 1.1 doesn't rely on a particular RPC protocol, it is usually used with HTTP. If you want to you can change the transport protocol and use SMTP or something else. In this case study, we present all the implementation samples based on HTTP. The Apache SOAP implementation uses HTTP as the main protocol and if you want to use SMTP as a transport a lot of the e-mail infrastructure must be made available: you will need a SMTP server, a POP3 server and an e-mail address that you need as the equivalent of the server-side HTTP router. When the SMTP server-side bridge receives mail sent to the SOAP router mail address via POP3, it extracts the envelope from the e-mail body and posts it to an existing HTTP SOAP infrastructure. When it receives the response it prepares a response mail and sends it back to the original sender. However we are unable to go into detail in this chapter on using SMTP, but this is just a brief view of how SOAP can be used.

In the current Apache SOAP implementation (version 2), the HTTP listener is a servlet (pre-version 2 it was a JavaServer Page). This servlet resides inside a servlet engine and its job is to respond to the SOAP service requests.

> The Apache SOAP implementation requires a servlet engine compliant with the JSDK 2.2 servlet specifications. We cannot use internet Application Server (iAS), at least in the current implementation (which is 8i, release 2), because it uses Jserv (JSDK 2.0) and SOAP requires JSDK2.2. However, in Oracle 8.1.7 there will be a servlet engine within the actual database, called Oracle Servlet Engine (OSE), which will be JSDK 2.2 compliant, a module, (mod_OSE) in iAS that will make use of this servlet engine.

The Apache SOAP listener can work on every web server supporting the above Servlet specifications. We will use Tomcat 3.1, which is the reference implementation for JavaServer Pages and Servlets.

The Servlet listener is contained in the package named `org.apache.soap.server.http` and it's called `RPCRouterServlet`. This class is quite simple and has only two methods:

- `doGet()`
- `doPost()`

The first one is provided only as a test. Simply direct your browser over your listener URI and if you can see the following message then it means that your environment is correctly functioning. This assumes that you have set up Tomcat as shown in the installation appendix, and you are going to the SOAP home URI:

Sorry, I don't speak via HTTP GET- you have to use HTTP POST to talk to me

The `doPost()` method is the correct way to talk with a listener, using HTTP protocol, as indicated by the SOAP specification. The main steps that the listener performs are as follows:

1. Extract the SOAP payload

2. Parse the payload

3. Validate the method name

4. Discover the service provider

5. Activate it

6. Invoke the method

7. Prepare the envelope with the response

8. Send the answer to the client as HTTP response

We can recap all the concepts with the following picture; we've got the following elements:

Client side

- A transport protocol provided by the SOAP library (HTTP and SMTP)
- The SOAP Client library (with the Call object)
- The Client application (the service consumer)

Server side:

- ❑ The servlet engine
- ❑ A transport listener (RPCRouterServlet)
- ❑ The SOAP server library
- ❑ The server application (the service provider)

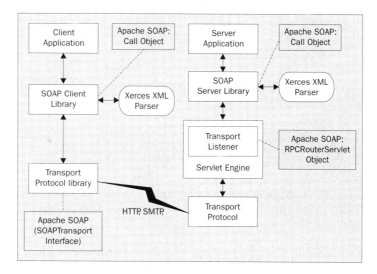

The Microsoft SOAP Toolkit

The July 2000 SOAP Toolkit is the version of the Microsoft SOAP implementation used at the time of writing, although as the book is being published, another version is being released. The .NET framework will be replacing these in the near future. In the package, we can find: an ASP-based and an ISAPI version of the SOAP listener and some COM objects implementing the SOAP client and server side code. You can find more details and download the toolkit at http://msdn.microsoft.com/xml/general/toolkit_intro.asp.

The COM objects are in the process server packaged in the ROPE.dll file, where ROPE stands for Remote Object Proxy Engine. The most important objects are:

- ❑ The Proxy Object
- ❑ The SOAPPackager
- ❑ The WireTransfer

The Proxy object provides an RPC programming model for client and server applications that is based on sending and receiving SOAP messages. This model allows your application to access remote services exposed by a SOAP protocol binding as if they were implemented as a local COM component; it only requires the SDL file to describe the remote service.

The SOAPPackager object provides functionality for accessing the contents of a SOAP envelope, and for sending and receiving SOAP messages, while the WireTransfer object permits to send or post HTTP requests.

In the July 2000 release, there isn't any support for other transport protocols except HTTP.

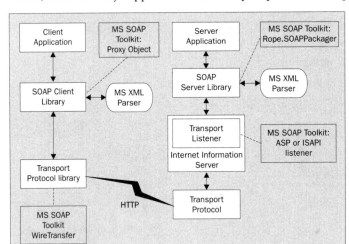

To create a SOAP service consumer, the easiest way is to use the `Proxy` object provided with the Toolkit. This component is useful and easy to use. It has a `LoadServiceDescription` method, which can load, from a String or an URI, a formal definition of services. After the definition is loaded, we can call every function exposed by the interface.

If you look in the ROPE distribution sample directory, you will find an example of a proxy object for a stock quotation sample:

```
Dim oProxy As ROPE.Proxy

    Screen.MousePointer = vbHourglass
    ' create objects
    Set oProxy = New ROPE.Proxy

    ' load ServicesDescription
    oProxy.LoadServicesDescription icSTRING, ServicesDescription

    ' get quote
    sBuffer = oProxy.GetStockQuote(txtSymbol.Text, "any company")

    Screen.MousePointer = vbNormal
    'display price
    MsgBox "Share price = " & sBuffer, vbOKOnly, txtSymbol.Text

    'clean up
    Set oProxy = Nothing
```

In this function the SDL specification of the services is already loaded in a `ServicesDescription` global String, so the proxy can parse it and get the information it needs. The proxy object then calls the `GetStockQuote` service and displays the value of a particular stock in a message box.

The first problem is that without the SDL description of that service, the Microsoft Proxy cannot work! The proxy loads and parses the SDL file looking through it to create the infrastructure needed to interact with the Web service. This could be an unwanted overhead caused by the round-trip over the net if you already know the correct specification of the service, moreover you must prepare the SDL file even if you're writing both the client side and server side part of your Web Service.

Another problem is that there are a lot of incompatibilities between the Microsoft's SOAP implementation and the Apache one due to the poor support of SOAP 1.1 specifications of the Microsoft toolkit; this may change with the latest edition (November 2000) of the toolkit .

A possible way to overcome this problem is to use the `WireTransferObject` directly and create the SOAP envelope by hand. This object is the lower level object designed to execute `HTTP POST` and `GET` actions for SOAP Web Services.

To simplify the use of `WireTransfer` object and with the help of the `SOAPPackager` object we will create two new Visual Basic objects, the code for these is shown below:

❑ `SOAPParam`

❑ `NewSOAPProxy`

Using these new objects, we can wrap all the SOAP details and decouple our application from the MS SOAP toolkit requirements (and bugs) with a more standard SOAP 1.1 implementation. This is not "production code". If you want to use services in a Microsoft environment you can wait for a further implementation of the SOAP toolkit or find a more conformant COM implementation on the World Wide Web. We prepared this implementation as a reference and as a sample for the reader.

We can now describe the relationship between the client application and transport protocol via the `WireTransfer` COM object as shown below:

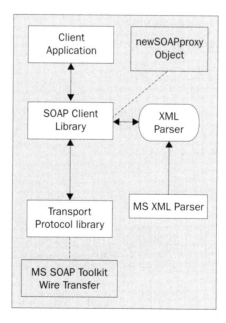

The purpose of the `SOAPParam` object is to represent the parameters in a SOAP call. This class is very simple. It has only two properties:

❑ `Name`

❑ `Value`

And the code for this SOAPParam class is:

```
Private m_Value As Variant
Private m_strName As String
Public Property Get Name() As String
    Name = m_strName
End Property
Public Property Let Name(strName As String)
    m_strName = strName
End Property
Public Property Get Value() As Variant
    Value = m_Value
End Property
Public Property Let Value(vValue As Variant)
    m_Value = vValue
End Property
```

The first property is a String and represents the name of the parameter as specified in its interface description while the property Value is a Variant containing the value of the param object.

The other object, newSOAPProxy, is a little more complicated and it tries to encapsulate the envelope construction details. It has a read-only property, a method, the constructor/destructor pair, and a private method:

❑   Value property: returns the value of the response

❑   Invoke function: builds the envelope, calls the service and gets the result

❑   Initialize: constructor

❑   Terminate: destructor

❑   getSOAPType private method: an helper "serializer" that creates the SOAP representation of all the parameters eventually used in the call. In this simple case, we use only integers and strings.

Here is the code for the newSOAPProxy object:

```
Private m_strStdEnv As String
Dim m_objWireT As WireTransfer
Dim m_oSoapP As SOAPPackager
Public Function invoke(ByVal serverUri As String, _
                       ByVal objectName As String, _
                       ByVal functionName As String, _
                       ParamArray parameters()) As String

' this function invoke a SOAP method
' without using SDL, SCL, or anything else

Dim strEnv As String
' ... building the Envelope

strEnv = m_strStdEnv + "<ns1:" + functionName
strEnv = strEnv + " xmlns:ns1 = " + Chr(34)
strEnv = strEnv + objectName + Chr(34)
```

```
    strEnv = strEnv + " SOAP-ENV:encodingStyle=" + Chr(34)
    strEnv = strEnv + "http://schemas.xmlsoap.org/soap/encoding/" + Chr(34)
    strEnv = strEnv + ">" + vbCrLf
    ' Now we start with parameters
    Dim soapp As SOAPParam
    Dim para As Variant
    For Each para In parameters
        If VarType(para) = vbObject Then
            Set soapp = para
            If Len(soapp.Name) > 0 Then
                strEnv = strEnv + "<" + soapp.Name + " xsi:type=" + Chr(34)
                strEnv = strEnv + getSOAPType(VarType(soapp.Value)) + Chr(34)
                strEnv = strEnv + ">" + CStr(soapp.Value) + "</" + soapp.Name + ">" +
    vbCrLf
            End If
        End If
    Next para

    strEnv = strEnv + "</ns1:" + functionName + ">" + vbCrLf
    strEnv = strEnv + "</SOAP-ENV:Body>" + vbCrLf
    strEnv = strEnv + "</SOAP-ENV:Envelope>" + vbCrLf

    Dim res, sTemp As String
    m_objWireT.SetHeader "Content-Type", "text/xml"
    m_objWireT.SetHeader "Content-Length", CStr(Len(strEnv))

    res = m_objWireT.PostDataToURI(serverUri, strEnv)

    'set SOAP payload
    m_oSoapP.SetPayload icRESPONSE, res

    strEnv = m_oSoapP.GetParameter(icRESPONSE, "return")

    End Function
    Private Function getSOAPType(vbType As Integer) As String
    Select Case vbType
        Case vbEmpty ' 0 Empty (uninitialized)
        Case vbNull  ' 1 Null (no valid data)
        Case vbInteger ' 2 Integer
            getSOAPType = "xsd:int"
        Case vbLong ' 3 Long integer
        Case vbSingle ' 4 Single-precision floating-point number
        Case vbDouble ' 5 Double-precision floating-point number
        Case vbCurrency '6 Currency value
        Case vbDate    ' 7 Date value
        Case vbString  ' 8 String
            getSOAPType = "xsd:string"
        Case vbObject  ' 9 Object
        Case vbBoolean ' 11 Boolean value
        Case vbVariant ' 12 Variant (used only with arrays of variants)
        Case vbDataObject ' 13 A data access object
        Case vbDecimal    ' 14 Decimal value
        Case vbByte       ' 17 Byte value
        Case vbArray      '

    End Select
    End Function
```

957

```
Public Property Get Value(Name As String) As String
    Value = m_oSoapP.GetParameter(icRESPONSE, Name)
End Property
Private Sub Class_Initialize()
' Standard Constructor
    Set m_oSoapP = New SOAPPackager
    Set m_objWireT = New WireTransfer

    m_strStdEnv = "<SOAP-ENV:Envelope xmlns:SOAP-ENV=" + Chr(34)
    m_strStdEnv = m_strStdEnv + "http://schemas.xmlsoap.org/soap/envelope/" +
Chr(34)
    m_strStdEnv = m_strStdEnv + " xmlns:xsi=" + Chr(34)
    m_strStdEnv = m_strStdEnv + "http://www.w3.org/1999/XMLSchema-instance" +
Chr(34)
    m_strStdEnv = m_strStdEnv + " xmlns:xsd=" + Chr(34)
    m_strStdEnv = m_strStdEnv + "http://www.w3.org/1999/XMLSchema" + Chr(34)
    m_strStdEnv = m_strStdEnv + ">" + vbCrLf

    m_strStdEnv = m_strStdEnv + "<SOAP-ENV:Body>" + vbCrLf
End Sub

Private Sub Class_Terminate()

    Set m_oSoapP = Nothing
    Set m_objWireT = Nothing

End Sub
```

For the server side implementation of SOAP, we have to choose between the ISAPI listener and the ASP version. In this chapter, we only use the ASP version, as it is simpler to install, to understand, and to patch.

Both the ASP and ISAPI listeners of the MS SOAP toolkit are not full implementations of the SOAP 1.1 specification and, usually, they cannot work with the Apache client implementation. If you navigate to http://www.soap-wrc.com/webservices/default.asp you can find a lot of useful information, as well as the modified listener.asp named apache_listener.asp. This patched file permits us to exchange SOAP messages between the Microsoft and Apache implementations.

The apache_listener.asp file is more SOAP 1.1 conformant and it can be used by an Apache client so we'll use that in the rest of the chapter.

To create a SOAP service starting from a COM component you can use an automatic procedure contained in the Microsoft SOAP toolkit. In the Wizard sub directory of your Microsoft SOAP toolkit installation you can find the SDLWizard.exe file. This program helps us to create all the files needed to expose your COM components like SOAP services. Start the program, choose the COM component you want to "SOAP-enable" and follow the wizard's instructions.:

❑ Start the SDLWizard program

❑ Choose a COM object (or a SDL URL)

❑ Choose all the methods of the interfaces implemented by the object

❑ Choose the listener type (ASP, ISAPI) and the Listener URI

❑ And finally the destination directory for all the files

At the end of its execution the wizard creates all the files needed to "bubbleize" your COM component. To give the Apache client the opportunity to use these services you must change the ASP listener generated by the wizard. The include line `<!--#include file="listener.asp"-->` must be the corrected in `<!--#include file="apache_listener.asp"-->`. If you want to use the ISAPI listener the steps are more complex and you need to modify directly the C++ source code or wait for a standard implementation.

Simply by changing the include file with the patched one in the generated ASP file your listener becomes fully SOAP 1.1 compliant and you will be able to call the COM component from any SOAP 1.1 compliant client, as you are able to from the Apache one.

The Oracle client SOAP Implementation

Now we describe the Oracle client SOAP implementation that we will be using for the rest of the chapter. The main goal of this implementation is to simplify the use of SOAP services from Oracle. In the following diagram we'll show all the building blocks of the framework.

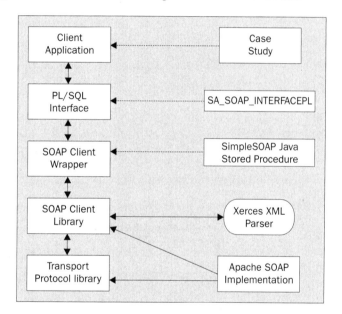

On the lower level, we have got the transport protocol library, in our case this is the Apache SOAP implementation, this package can be used as a transport client library and as a SOAP client library. It is a SOAP 1.1 conformant implementation, it is free and open source. The library can use both HTTP and SMTP as transport protocol. The Apache SOAP uses many XML parsers provided they are namespace aware but, for now, there is complete support only for the Apache Java parser: Xerces; so we are using this. In the installation appendix, A, you will see all the details on how to load both the parser and the SOAP library.

In order to use the SOAP client from a PL/SQL client we need a Java stored procedure. A Java stored-procedure has an important requirement: methods to be called from PL/SQL must be static.

So, we decided to create a simple class named `SimpleSOAP` with all static members that act as a bridge between the Apache SOAP implementation and the PL/SQL procedure that will be built later in the chapter.

We create a static vector of `Call` objects so all the static methods can use a `Call` object. This class is used to provide a static wrapper for the Apache SOAP client and it's the first block of our infrastructure.

When we instantiate a new call, calling the `newCall` function, we actually insert a new `Call` object into the static Java vector and we return the index of the vector to use in all the following calls. This index represents an entry in the vector and maps a SOAP `Call` object. Doing so you also need a method to clean up the memory, informing the garbage collector that the object is used no more: in our case this method is `freeCall`.

```java
package soapclient;

import java.io.*;
import java.net.MalformedURLException;
import java.net.URL;
import java.sql.SQLException;
import java.util.Vector;
import org.w3c.dom.*;
import org.apache.soap.util.xml.*;
import org.apache.soap.*;
import org.apache.soap.encoding.*;
import org.apache.soap.encoding.soapenc.*;
import org.apache.soap.rpc.*;

public class StaticCall {

    static Vector calls = new Vector(10);

    public StaticCall() {
    }

public static void freeCall(int i) {
        calls.setElementAt(null, i);
}
public static int newCall() {
    Call call = new Call();
    // Create new params Vector for future use
    Vector params = new Vector();
    call.setParams(params);
    // Set standard Mapping registry
    SOAPMappingRegistry smr = new SOAPMappingRegistry();
    BeanSerializer beanSer = new BeanSerializer();

    call.setSOAPMappingRegistry(smr);

    calls.addElement(call);
    return calls.size() - 1;
}

    private static Call getCall(int aCall) {
        return (Call)calls.elementAt(aCall);
    }

    public static void setIntParam(int aCall,String name,
                        int value,
                        String encodingStyleURI) {
      Call call = getCall(aCall);
      Vector p = call.getParams();
      p.addElement(new Parameter(name,Integer.class,new Integer(value),
                        encodingStyleURI));
      call.setParams(p);
    }
```

```
    public static void setStringParam(int aCall,String name,
                              String value,
                              String encodingStyleURI) {
    Call call = getCall(aCall);
    Vector p = call.getParams();
    p.addElement(new Parameter(name,String.class,value, encodingStyleURI));
    call.setParams(p);
  }
```

Set the method name for the target object:

```
    public static void setMethodName(int aCall, String methodName) {
        getCall(aCall).setMethodName(methodName);
    }
    /** Set the URI of the Target Object
    */
    public static void setTargetObjectURI(int aCall, String uri) {
        getCall(aCall).setTargetObjectURI(uri);
    }
    public static void setEncodingStyleURI(int aCall, java.lang.String
    encodingStyleURI) {
        getCall(aCall).setEncodingStyleURI(encodingStyleURI);
    }
    public static String invoke(int aCall, String strUrl,String SOAPActionURI) {
      try {
          URL url = new URL(strUrl);
          Response rp = getCall(aCall).invoke(url,SOAPActionURI);
          return rp.getReturnValue().getValue().toString();
      }
      catch(SOAPException se) {
          return "SOAP Fault=" + se.getFaultCode();
      }
      catch(Exception e) {
        StringWriter log = new StringWriter();
        PrintWriter pw = new PrintWriter(log);
        e.printStackTrace(pw);
        return log.toString();
      }
    }
```

this is the `Main()` method. In this method, we create two `Call` objects directly into the vector and we make two fixed calls.

```
    public static void main(String[] args) throws Exception{
      int iCall = newCall();
      setEncodingStyleURI(iCall,Constants.NS_URI_SOAP_ENC);

      setTargetObjectURI(iCall,"urn:Calc");
      setIntParam(iCall,"x",5,null);
      setIntParam(iCall,"y",8,null);
      setMethodName(iCall,"sum");

    System.out.println(invoke(iCall,"http://localhost:2020/soap/servlet/rpcrouter","")
    );
    }
  }
```

To use this class from inside PL/SQL code we need a PL/SQL wrapper for the class. We created a package named `SimpleSOAP`. This package contains only the PL/SQL definitions for the `StaticCall` class.

In the `SimpleSOAP` package, we defined all the methods of the `StaticCall` class so they can be called by Oracle stored procedures.

```
create or replace package SimpleSOAP is

FUNCTION newCall return number is language java
    name 'soapclient.StaticCall.newCall() return int';

PROCEDURE freeCall(aCall number) is language java
    name 'soapclient.StaticCall.freeCall(int)';

PROCEDURE setIntParam(aCall number,name varchar2, value number, encStyle varchar2)
is language java
    name
'soapclient.StaticCall.setIntParam(int,java.lang.String,int,java.lang.String)';

PROCEDURE setStringParam(aCall number,name varchar2, value varchar2, encStyle
varchar2) is language java
    name
'soapclient.StaticCall.setStringParam(int,java.lang.String,java.lang.String,java.l
ang.String)';

 PROCEDURE setMethodName(aCall number,methodName varchar2) is language java
    name 'soapclient.StaticCall.setMethodName(int,java.lang.String)';

PROCEDURE setTargetObjectURI(aCall number,targetObject varchar2) is language java
    name 'soapclient.StaticCall.setTargetObjectURI(int,java.lang.String)';

PROCEDURE setEncodingStyleURI(aCall number,encodingStyle varchar2) is language
java
    name 'soapclient.StaticCall.setEncodingStyleURI(int,java.lang.String)';

function invoke(aCall number, url varchar2, actionURI varchar2) return varchar2 is
language java
    name 'soapclient.StaticCall.invoke(int,java.lang.String,java.lang.String) return
java.lang.String';

end SimpleSOAP;
```

The most important methods of the package are:

- ❏ newCall
- ❏ freeCall
- ❏ setIntParam
- ❏ setStringParam
- ❏ setMethodName
- ❏ invoke

The `newCall` method creates the `Call` object, places it in the `Vector` and returns a "handle" to the `Call` object. The `freeCall` method frees the corresponding `Call` object. The two methods `setIntParam` and `setStringParam` insert a new parameter of type `String` or `Int` in the parameter array of the corresponding `Call` object; the `setMethodName` sets the method that will be called and, last but not least, the method invoked does the actual SOAP call.

As you can easily see in the code all the methods require a lot of parameters which are sometimes unclear, like encodingStyle, actionURI and so on. In order to simplify the use of the SimpleSOAP package we designed a façade package that encapsulates the SimpleSOAP details and also provides useful default values for some parameters. We have defined a new type named CALL_ITEM_TYPE:

```
CREATE OR REPLACE TYPE "CALL_ITEM_TYPE"
as object
  ( aCall           NUMBER,
  EncodingStyle VARCHAR2(600),
  TargetObj     VARCHAR2(600))
```

We prepared the PL/SQL package named SA_SOAP_INTERFACEPL that makes straightforward calls to SOAP services in an Oracle database environment.

This package contains some functions and procedures, like newCall, freeCall, setIntParam, Invoke. These functions hide the calls to the SimpleSOAP Oracle Java stored procedure. Create these packages in your database.

```
CREATE OR REPLACE PACKAGE SA_SOAP_INTERFACEPL IS
---
FUNCTION newCall
            RETURN call_item_type;
---
FUNCTION newCall (
            vTargetObj        VARCHAR2,
            vEncodingStyle    VARCHAR2    DEFAULT SA_SOAP_GLOBAL.NS_URI_SOAP_ENC)
            RETURN call_item_type;
---
  PROCEDURE freeCall (
            theCall      call_item_type);
---
PROCEDURE setEncodingStyleURI (
            theCall            IN OUT call_item_type,
            vEncodingStyle   VARCHAR2    DEFAULT SA_SOAP_GLOBAL.NS_URI_SOAP_ENC);
---
PROCEDURE setTargetObjectURI (
            theCall        IN OUT call_item_type,
            vTargetObj    VARCHAR2);
---
PROCEDURE setMethodName (
            theCall        call_item_type,
          vMethodName   VARCHAR2);
  ---
FUNCTION invoke (
            theCall        call_item_type,
            vHostName     VARCHAR2 DEFAULT 'localhost',
            nPortNum      INTEGER  DEFAULT 80,
            vSoapListener VARCHAR2 DEFAULT 'soap/servlet/rpcrouter',
            vAction       VARCHAR2 DEFAULT '')
            RETURN VARCHAR2;
---
PROCEDURE setIntParam (
            theCall        call_item_type,
            vParam        VARCHAR2,
            nValueParam   NUMBER,
```

```
                vEncodingStyle VARCHAR2 DEFAULT NULL);
---
PROCEDURE setStringParam (
            theCall         call_item_type,
            vParam          VARCHAR2,
            vValueParam     VARCHAR2,
            vEncodingStyle VARCHAR2 DEFAULT NULL);
END SA_SOAP_INTERFACEPL;
/
```

The above code has created the packages, and now the PL/SQL package bodies will be created for the SA_SOAP_INTERFACEPL interface:

```
CREATE OR REPLACE PACKAGE BODY SA_SOAP_INTERFACEPL IS
---
   FUNCTION newCall
            RETURN call_item_type
   IS
     aCall NUMBER;
     tCall call_item_type;
   BEGIN
     aCall := SimpleSoap.newCall();
     tCall := call_item_type(aCall,NULL,NULL);
     return tCall;
   END newCall;
---
FUNCTION newCall (
            vTargetObj      VARCHAR2,
            vEncodingStyle  VARCHAR2    DEFAULT SA_SOAP_GLOBAL.NS_URI_SOAP_ENC)
            RETURN call_item_type
IS
     aCall   NUMBER;
     tCall   call_item_type;
BEGIN
   aCall := SimpleSoap.newCall();
   SimpleSoap.setEncodingStyleURI(aCall,vEncodingStyle);
   SimpleSoap.setTargetObjectURI(aCall,vTargetObj);
   tCall := call_item_type(aCall,vEncodingStyle,vTargetObj);
   return tCall;
END newCall;
---
PROCEDURE freeCall (
            theCall     call_item_type)
   IS
BEGIN
    SimpleSoap.freeCall(theCall.aCall);
END freeCall;
---
PROCEDURE setEncodingStyleURI (
            theCall           IN OUT call_item_type,
            vEncodingStyle    VARCHAR2    DEFAULT SA_SOAP_GLOBAL.NS_URI_SOAP_ENC)
IS
BEGIN
    SimpleSoap.setEncodingStyleURI(theCall.aCall,vEncodingStyle);
    theCall.EncodingStyle := vEncodingStyle;
END setEncodingStyleURI;
```

```
---
PROCEDURE setTargetObjectURI (
        theCall       IN OUT call_item_type,
        vTargetObj    VARCHAR2)
IS
BEGIN
    SimpleSoap.setTargetObjectURI(theCall.aCall,vTargetObj);
    theCall.TargetObj := vTargetObj;
END setTargetObjectURI;
---
PROCEDURE setMethodName (
        theCall       call_item_type,
        vMethodName   VARCHAR2)
IS
BEGIN
    SimpleSoap.setMethodname(theCall.aCall,vMethodName);
  END setMethodName;
```

Now the function invokes the SOAP Listener, to listen at port 80:

```
FUNCTION invoke (
        theCall       call_item_type,
        vHostName     VARCHAR2 DEFAULT 'localhost',
        nPortNum      INTEGER  DEFAULT 80,
        vSoapListener VARCHAR2 DEFAULT 'soap/servlet/rpcrouter',
        vAction       VARCHAR2 DEFAULT '')
        RETURN VARCHAR2
  IS
    str    VARCHAR2(1000)  := NULL;
    ret    VARCHAR2(32767) := NULL;
    tCall  call_item_type;
  BEGIN
    str := 'http://' || vHostName || ':' || TO_CHAR(nPortNum) || '/' ||
vSoapListener;
    ret := SimpleSoap.invoke(theCall.aCall,str,vAction);
    return ret;
END invoke;
---
PROCEDURE setIntParam (
        theCall       call_item_type,
        vParam        VARCHAR2,
        nValueParam   NUMBER,
        vEncodingStyle VARCHAR2 DEFAULT NULL)
IS
BEGIN
    SimpleSoap.setIntParam(theCall.aCall,vParam,nValueParam,vEncodingStyle);
END setIntParam;
    ---
PROCEDURE setStringParam (
        theCall       call_item_type,
        vParam        VARCHAR2,
        vValueParam   VARCHAR2,
        vEncodingStyle VARCHAR2 DEFAULT NULL)
IS
BEGIN
```

```
        SimpleSoap.setStringParam(theCall.aCall,vParam,vValueParam,vEncodingStyle);
    END setStringParam;
    ---
    END SA_SOAP_INTERFACEPL;
    / show errors;
```

Finally, we wrote a package named SA_SOAP_GLOBAL containing useful constants concerning SOAP environment that can be used from other stored procedures.

```
create or replace package SA_SOAP_GLOBAL is
  -- Namespace prefixes.
  NS_PRE_XMLNS     CONSTANT VARCHAR2(5) := 'xmlns';
  NS_PRE_SOAP     CONSTANT VARCHAR2(4) := 'SOAP';
  NS_PRE_SOAP_ENV  CONSTANT VARCHAR2(4) := '-ENV';
  NS_PRE_SOAP_ENC  CONSTANT VARCHAR2(4) := '-ENC';
  NS_PRE_SCHEMA_XSI  CONSTANT VARCHAR2(3) := 'xsi';
  NS_PRE_SCHEMA_XSD  CONSTANT VARCHAR2(3) := 'xsd';

  -- Namespace URIs.
  NS_URI_XMLNS     CONSTANT VARCHAR2(300) := 'http://www.w3.org/2000/xmlns/';
  NS_URI_SOAP_ENV  CONSTANT VARCHAR2(300) :=
                          'http://schemas.xmlsoap.org/soap/envelope/';
  NS_URI_SOAP_ENC  CONSTANT VARCHAR2(300) :=
                          'http://schemas.xmlsoap.org/soap/encoding/';
  NS_URI_SCHEMA_XSI  CONSTANT VARCHAR2(300) :=
                          'http://www.w3.org/1999/XMLSchema-instance';
  NS_URI_SCHEMA_XSD  CONSTANT VARCHAR2(300) := 'http://www.w3.org/1999/XMLSchema';
  NS_URI_XML_SOAP  CONSTANT VARCHAR2(300) := 'http://xml.apache.org/xml-soap';
  NS_URI_XML_SOAP_DEPLOYMENT CONSTANT VARCHAR2(300) :=
                          'http://xml.apache.org/xml-soap/deployment';
  NS_URI_LITERAL_XML CONSTANT VARCHAR2(300) :=
                          'http://xml.apache.org/xml-soap/literalxml';
  NS_URI_XMI_ENC   CONSTANT VARCHAR2(300) := 'http://www.ibm.com/namespaces/xmi';

  -- HTTP header field names.
  HEADER_POST     CONSTANT VARCHAR2(4) := 'POST';
  HEADER_HOST     CONSTANT VARCHAR2(4) := 'Host';
  HEADER_CONTENT_TYPE   CONSTANT VARCHAR2(12) := 'Content-Type';
  HEADER_CONTENT_LENGTH CONSTANT VARCHAR2(14) := 'Content-Length';
  HEADER_SOAP_ACTION CONSTANT VARCHAR2(10) := 'SOAPAction';

  -- HTTP header field values.
  HEADERVAL_CONTENT_TYPE CONSTANT VARCHAR2(8) := 'text/xml';
  HEADERVAL_CONTENT_TYPE_UTF8 CONSTANT VARCHAR2(30) := 'text/xml; charset=UTF-';

  -- Element names.
  ELEM_ENVELOPE  CONSTANT VARCHAR2(8) := 'Envelope';
  ELEM_BODY    CONSTANT VARCHAR2(4) := 'Body';
  ELEM_HEADER  CONSTANT VARCHAR2(6) := 'Header';
  ELEM_FAULT   CONSTANT VARCHAR2(5) := 'Fault';
  ELEM_FAULT_CODE CONSTANT VARCHAR2(9) := 'faultcode';
  ELEM_FAULT_STRING CONSTANT VARCHAR2(11) := 'faultstring';
  ELEM_FAULT_ACTOR CONSTANT VARCHAR2(10) := 'faultactor';
  ELEM_DETAIL  CONSTANT VARCHAR2(6) := 'detail';
```

```
-- Attribute names.
ATTR_ENCODING_STYLE CONSTANT VARCHAR2(13) := 'encodingStyle';
ATTR_MUST_UNDERSTAND  CONSTANT VARCHAR2(14) := 'mustUnderstand';
ATTR_TYPE    CONSTANT VARCHAR2(4) := 'type';
ATTR_NULL    CONSTANT VARCHAR2(4) := 'null';
ATTR_ARRAY_TYPE CONSTANT VARCHAR2(9) := 'arrayType';

-- Attribute values.
ATTRVAL_TRUE  CONSTANT VARCHAR2(4) := 'true';
```

Next we have the SOAP defined fault codes.

```
FAULT_CODE_VERSION_MISMATCH CONSTANT VARCHAR2(20) := NS_PRE_SOAP_ENV ||
        ':VersionMismatch';
FAULT_CODE_MUST_UNDERSTAND CONSTANT VARCHAR2(20) := NS_PRE_SOAP_ENV ||
        ':MustUnderstand';
FAULT_CODE_CLIENT CONSTANT VARCHAR2(20) := NS_PRE_SOAP_ENV || ':Client';
FAULT_CODE_SERVER CONSTANT VARCHAR2(20) := NS_PRE_SOAP_ENV || ':Server';
FAULT_CODE_PROTOCOL CONSTANT VARCHAR2(20) := NS_PRE_SOAP_ENV || ':Protocol';

-- Error messages.
ERR_MSG_VERSION_MISMATCH CONSTANT VARCHAR2(600) := FAULT_CODE_VERSION_MISMATCH ||
        ': Envelope element must be associated with the ' || NS_URI_SOAP_ENV ||
        ' namespace.';
end SA_SOAP_GLOBAL;
/ show errors;
```

We can see a diagram showing all the building blocks for this framework:

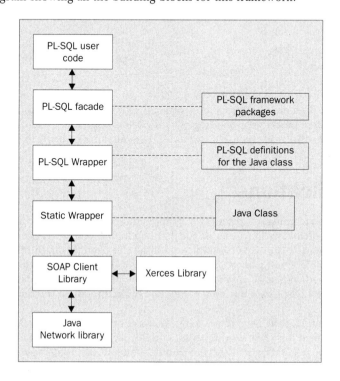

We use PL/SQL for SOAP calls; and, for example, a SOAP service can be called using a few lines of code like in the following sample. Don't worry if you can't understand all the details, we will investigate them later. For now, you can see how easy it is to make a SOAP call. To do so we prepared a stored function named `test` that will be used later to test our calculator example. The purpose of this function is to call the SOAP service named "`sum`" of the "`urn:Calc`" object, and passes it two integers, returning the result of the sum.

```
create or replace function test(x in number, y in number) return varchar2 is
/* Simple SOAP Client
*/
    aCall number;
    tCall call_item_type;
    result VARCHAR2(32767):= '';
BEGIN
  tCall := SA_SOAP_INTERFACEPL.newcall('urn:Calc');
  SA_SOAP_INTERFACEPL.setIntParam(tCall,'x',x,null);
  SA_SOAP_INTERFACEPL.setIntParam(tCall,'y',y,null);
  SA_SOAP_INTERFACEPL.setMethodname(tCall,'sum');
  result := SA_SOAP_INTERFACEPL.invoke(tCall);
  SA_SOAP_INTERFACEPL.freeCall(tCall);
    return result;
END test;
```

Now you can use the function to perform a sum:

```
select test(11,20) from dual;
```

or

```
declare x number;
    begin x:=test(11,20);
    DBMS_OUTPUT.put_line(x);
  end;
```

Using the framework presented in this chapter you can call any SOAP service from PL/SQL code, it does not matter which platform you are using. The service is also independent of the programming languages being used. Also, you can use a variety of transmission protocols like HTTP or SMTP.

Sample Applications

In this case study, we are going to present two sample applications. The first one is very simple, a fantastic distributed calculator. The other one is that of a motor-vehicle reseller. We will present two examples because the calculator is very simple and it doesn't need all the infrastructure code needed by the LUMA-cars example. So, if you are interested just in SOAP you can try the Calculator without the need for an Enterprise JavaBean Container and the entire infrastructure needed for the other example. You can then skip the LUMA-cars business model and jump directly to the implementation paragraph.

The LUMA-cars example is the abstraction and transposition of a real world B2B and B2C project. The infrastructure is designed for a real world project and it's quite complex. The idea is to provide the minimal infrastructure needed by a SOAP environment and all the implementation code is left as simple as possible in order to better understand the big picture.

The Calculator Example

The first sample is a simple Calculator. It is able to perform the four fundamental operations. In this sample we've got a calculator server implemented both in Java and in Visual Basic, and we want to publicize their services in a SOAP network so we can call them from any client provided that they are SOAP-enabled.

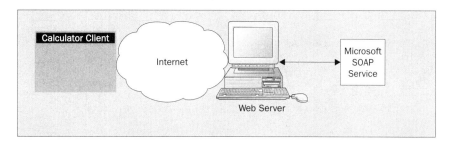

Server Components

We prepared two different Server implementations:

❑   Java

❑   Visual Basic

Java Calculator Server Component

This is the Java implementation of our component. It is a Java class with four methods representing the four fundamental operations:

```java
public class Calculator
{
    public int sum(int x, int y) {
    return x+y;
    }
    public int subtract(int x, int y) {
    return x-y;
    }
    public int multiply(int x, int y) {
    return x*y;
    }
    public int divide(int x, int y) throws Exception {
        if(y == 0) {
            Exception e = new Exception("cannot divide by zero :)");
            throw e;
        }
    return x/y;
    }
```

Visual Basic Calculator Server component

The following piece of code shows the Visual Basic implementation of our simple calculator:

```
Public Function sum(x As Integer, y As Integer) As Integer
    sum = x + y
End Function
Public Function subtract(x As Integer, y As Integer) As Integer
    subtract = x - y
End Function
Public Function multiply(x As Integer, y As Integer) As Integer
    multiply = x * y
End Function
Public Function divide(x As Integer, y As Integer) As Integer
    If y = 0 Then
        Err.Raise vbError + 1, "", "Cannot divide by zero :)"
    Else
        divide = x / y
    End If
End Function
```

As you can see the code is very similar to the Java counterpart.

Client Components

After the server code we can see the client code: the service consumer of our Calculator service. We prepared four clients for different platforms, they are:

❑ Java Swing Client

❑ Visual basic Client

❑ Oracle Client

❑ Pocket PC Client

Java Swing Client

The Java client uses a standard Swing interface and you can run it on any platform you like. This simple Swing program allows you to perform the mathematical operations. To make a SOAP call in Java make sure that the `soap.jar` and `xerces.jar` are in your system CLASSPATH.

The steps needed to use our simple Java calculator are:

1. Instantiate a `Call` Object

2. Create the destination URL

3. Set the standard mapping registry

4. Create a 'params' vector

5. Invoke the remote method

6. Check the response

We prepared a `DlgCalc` class, but let's see the code:

```java
package calcclient;

import java.awt.*;
import javax.swing.*;
import java.awt.event.*;

import java.io.*;
import java.util.*;
import java.net.*;
import org.w3c.dom.*;
import org.apache.soap.util.xml.*;
import org.apache.soap.*;
import org.apache.soap.encoding.*;
import org.apache.soap.encoding.soapenc.*;
import org.apache.soap.rpc.*;

public class DlgCalc extends JDialog {
  JLabel jLabel1 = new JLabel();
  JLabel jLabel2 = new JLabel();
  JTextField txtOp1 = new JTextField();
  JTextField txtOp2 = new JTextField();
  JButton btnSum = new JButton();
  JButton btnMul = new JButton();
  JButton btnSub = new JButton();
  JButton btnDiv = new JButton();
  JLabel lblRes = new JLabel();
  JLabel jLabel4 = new JLabel();
  JLabel jLabel3 = new JLabel();
  JComboBox cmbRouter = new JComboBox();
  JLabel jLabel5 = new JLabel();
  JLabel lblTiming = new JLabel();

  public DlgCalc(Frame frame, String title, boolean modal) {
    super(frame, title, modal);
    try {
      jbInit();
      pack();
    }
    catch(Exception ex) {
      ex.printStackTrace();
    }
  }

  public DlgCalc() {
    this(null, "", false);
  }
```

Now we create the graphical interface for the calculator:

```
void jbInit() throws Exception {
  jLabel1.setFont(new java.awt.Font("Dialog", 0, 18));
  jLabel1.setText("Operand 1");
  jLabel1.setBounds(new Rectangle(22, 85, 91, 16));
  this.getContentPane().setLayout(null);
  jLabel2.setFont(new java.awt.Font("Dialog", 0, 18));
  jLabel2.setText("Operand 2");
  jLabel2.setBounds(new Rectangle(21, 118, 116, 27));
  txtOp1.setFont(new java.awt.Font("Dialog", 0, 18));
  txtOp1.setText("12");
  txtOp1.setBounds(new Rectangle(150, 84, 221, 25));
  txtOp2.setFont(new java.awt.Font("Dialog", 0, 18));
  txtOp2.setText("14");
  txtOp2.setBounds(new Rectangle(152, 118, 222, 26));
  btnSum.setFont(new java.awt.Font("Dialog", 1, 18));
  btnSum.setText("Sum");
  btnSum.setBounds(new Rectangle(15, 239, 108, 23));
  btnMul.setBounds(new Rectangle(122, 239, 108, 23));
  btnMul.setText("Multiply");
  btnMul.setFont(new java.awt.Font("Dialog", 1, 18));
  btnSub.setBounds(new Rectangle(229, 239, 108, 23));
  btnSub.setText("Subtract");
  btnSub.setFont(new java.awt.Font("Dialog", 1, 18));
  btnDiv.setBounds(new Rectangle(336, 239, 108, 23));
  btnDiv.setText("Divide");
  btnDiv.setFont(new java.awt.Font("Dialog", 1, 18));
  lblRes.setFont(new java.awt.Font("Dialog", 1, 18));
  lblRes.setBounds(new Rectangle(152, 179, 307, 25));
  jLabel4.setFont(new java.awt.Font("Dialog", 1, 18));
  jLabel4.setText("Result");
  jLabel4.setBounds(new Rectangle(23, 177, 90, 31));
  jLabel3.setBounds(new Rectangle(25, 49, 118, 16));
  jLabel3.setText("SOAP Router");
  jLabel3.setFont(new java.awt.Font("Dialog", 0, 18));
  cmbRouter.addItem("http://localhost:3030/soap/servlet/rpcrouter");
  cmbRouter.addItem("http://localhost:2020/calc/calculator.asp");
  cmbRouter.setFont(new java.awt.Font("Dialog", 1, 18));
  cmbRouter.setEditable(true);
  cmbRouter.setBounds(new Rectangle(148, 43, 433, 26));
  this.setTitle("Calculator Java Client");
  jLabel5.setBounds(new Rectangle(18, 275, 70, 27));
  jLabel5.setText("Timing:");
  jLabel5.setFont(new java.awt.Font("Dialog", 0, 18));
  lblTiming.setBounds(new Rectangle(115, 276, 116, 27));
  lblTiming.setFont(new java.awt.Font("Dialog", 0, 18));
  this.getContentPane().add(jLabel1, null);
  this.getContentPane().add(txtOp1, null);
  this.getContentPane().add(txtOp2, null);
  this.getContentPane().add(jLabel2, null);
  this.getContentPane().add(btnDiv, null);
  this.getContentPane().add(btnSum, null);
  this.getContentPane().add(btnMul, null);
  this.getContentPane().add(btnSub, null);
```

```
this.getContentPane().add(jLabel4, null);
this.getContentPane().add(lblRes, null);
this.getContentPane().add(jLabel3, null);
this.getContentPane().add(cmbRouter, null);
this.getContentPane().add(jLabel5, null);
this.getContentPane().add(lblTiming, null);


btnSum.addActionListener(new java.awt.event.ActionListener() {
  public void actionPerformed(ActionEvent e) {
    exec(0);
  }
});

btnMul.addActionListener(new java.awt.event.ActionListener() {
  public void actionPerformed(ActionEvent e) {
    exec(1);
  }
});
btnSub.addActionListener(new java.awt.event.ActionListener() {
  public void actionPerformed(ActionEvent e) {
    exec(2);
  }
});

btnDiv.addActionListener(new java.awt.event.ActionListener() {
  public void actionPerformed(ActionEvent e) {
    exec(3);
  }
});

}
public static void main(String[] args) throws Exception {
  DlgCalc cc = new DlgCalc();
  // Add the listener
  cc.addWindowListener(new WindowAdapter() {
    public void windowClosing(WindowEvent e) {
      System.exit(0);
    }
  });
  // Show the frame
  cc.setSize(600,400);
  cc.setVisible(true);
}

void exec(int op) {
```

This function is called when we need to perform a SOAP Call:

```
long start = System.currentTimeMillis(); // A simple timer

  try {

    String encodingStyleURI  =  Constants.NS_URI_SOAP_ENC;
    URL url = new URL( cmbRouter.getSelectedItem().toString());
    SOAPMappingRegistry smr = new SOAPMappingRegistry();
```

```
// Build the call.

Call call = new Call();
call.setSOAPMappingRegistry(smr);
call.setTargetObjectURI("urn:Calc"); // Target Object URI

call.setEncodingStyleURI(encodingStyleURI);

switch (op) // Calling a different function:
{
  case 0:
    call.setMethodName("sum"); // a sum and so on ...
    break;
  case 1:
    call.setMethodName("multiply");
    break;
  case 2:
    call.setMethodName("subtract");
    break;
  case 3:
    call.setMethodName("divide");
    break;
}

Vector params = new Vector(); // we need a new Vector of params

Integer x = new Integer(txtOp1.getText());
Integer y = new Integer(txtOp2.getText());
```

We add the two `Integer` parameters: x and y

```
params.addElement(new Parameter("x",int.class,x, null));
params.addElement(new Parameter("y",int.class,y, null));
```

Here we set the `Params` for this call then we invoke the call and check the response

```
call.setParams(params);

Response resp;
resp = call.invoke(url, "");

if (!resp.generatedFault())
{
  Parameter ret = resp.getReturnValue();
  Object value = ret.getValue();
  lblRes.setText(value.toString());
  lblTiming.setText((System.currentTimeMillis() - start) + " msec");
}
else
{
  Fault fault = resp.getFault();
```

```
        System.err.println("Generated fault: ");
        System.out.println ("  Fault Code   = " + fault.getFaultCode());
        System.out.println ("  Fault String = " + fault.getFaultString());
      }
    } // End try block
    catch (SOAPException e) {
      System.err.println("Caught SOAPException (" +
                          e.getFaultCode() + "): " +
                          e.getMessage());
      return;
    }
    catch (Exception e) {
      System.err.println("Caught Exception (" +
                          e.getMessage());
      return;
    }
  } // End of exec method
} // End of the class
```

This Calculator is invoked by the command below, assuming you have setup Tomcat webserver, and the deployment descriptor, as described in the installation appendix:

```
java DlgCalc http://localhost:8080/soap/servlet/rpcrouter
```

The result is a Java client as follows:

Visual Basic Client

The Visual Basic client is analogous to the Java client. It is provided to demonstrate the intrinsic platform independence achieved by SOAP. Using this Visual Basic client you can simply do all the things you can do with the other clients, but in a Windows box.

The syntactical differences between this client and the previous Java one can be seen. There is a different approach followed by Microsoft and the Apache team in performing the SOAP client calls.

To make a SOAP call, using our framework as shown in a previous paragraph, you have to instantiate the newSOAPProxy object, and as many SOAPParams as you need and then call the invoke method.

Here is how we call the Visual Basic Client of our calculator:

```
Private Sub Command1_Click(Index As Integer)
Dim x As New newSOAPProxy
Dim p1 As New SOAPParam
Dim p2 As New SOAPParam
Dim strURI As String

If Combo1.ListIndex >= 0 Then
    strURI = Combo1.List(Combo1.ListIndex)
Else
    strURI = Combo1.Text
End If
p1.Name = "x"
p1.Value = CInt(Text1.Text)
p2.Name = "y"
p2.Value = CInt(Text2.Text)

Dim mycalc As New mycalc.Calculator

Dim counter As New CPerformance
counter.StartCounter

Select Case Index
    Case 0
        x.invoke strURI, "urn:Calc", "sum", p1, p2
        lblRes.Caption = x.Value("return")
    Case 1
        x.invoke strURI, "urn:Calc", "multiply", p1, p2
        lblRes.Caption = x.Value("return")
    Case 2
        x.invoke strURI, "urn:Calc", "subtract", p1, p2
        lblRes.Caption = x.Value("return")
    Case 3
        x.invoke strURI, "urn:Calc", "divide", p1, p2
        lblRes.Caption = x.Value("return")
    Case 4
        lblRes.Caption = CStr(mycalc.Sum(Text1.Text, Text2.Text))
    Case 5
        lblRes.Caption = CStr(mycalc.multiply(Text1.Text, Text2.Text))
    Case 6
        lblRes.Caption = CStr(mycalc.subtract(Text1.Text, Text2.Text))
    Case 7
        lblRes.Caption = CStr(mycalc.divide(Text1.Text, Text2.Text))
End Select
counter.StopCounter
Label2.Caption = CStr(CInt(counter.TimeElapsed))

End Sub
```

```
Private Sub Form_Load()
    Combo1.AddItem "http://localhost:3030/soap/servlet/rpcrouter"
    Combo1.AddItem "http://localhost:2020/calc/calculator.asp"
End Sub
```

We prepared all the samples with URLs like localhost:3030 *or* localhost:2020 *because we used the Apache Tunnel program, shown in the installation appendix in order to see all the packets sent and received by the client. We suggest this approach to better understand (and debug) the SOAP protocol and its implementations.*

Oracle Client

Using the SA_SOAP_INTERFACEPL package you have to create a new Call object, set the parameters and invoke the remote method. We created a stored function that performs a sum between two integers:

```
create or replace function SOAP_SUM(x in number, y in number) return varchar2 is

    aCall number;
    tCall call_item_type;
    result VARCHAR2(32767):= '';
BEGIN
SimpleSoap.setEncodingStyleURI(aCall,'http://schemas.xmlsoap.org/soap/encoding/');
  tCall := SA_SOAP_INTERFACEPL.newcall('urn:Calc');
  SA_SOAP_INTERFACEPL.setIntParam(tCall,'x',x,null);
  SA_SOAP_INTERFACEPL.setIntParam(tCall,'y',y,null);
  SA_SOAP_INTERFACEPL.setMethodname(tCall,'sum');
  result := SA_SOAP_INTERFACEPL.invoke(tCall);
  SA_SOAP_INTERFACEPL.freeCall(tCall);
    return result;
END SOAP_SUM;
```

You can now perform sums using a similar syntax using PL/SQL:

```
SELECT SOAP_SUM(34,14) from dual;
```

Or, if you prefer, you can create a trigger that updates a column in a table as a result of a sum from two others columns.

You can see in the following picture the Oracle server encapsulates the request in a SOAP message and sends it to the destination URI. The request is carried out using a standard HTTP post and so it can pass inside a firewall. In this case, the request can be accomplished by a Visual Basic COM+ component and the Microsoft SOAP toolkit can return the result back to the Oracle server.

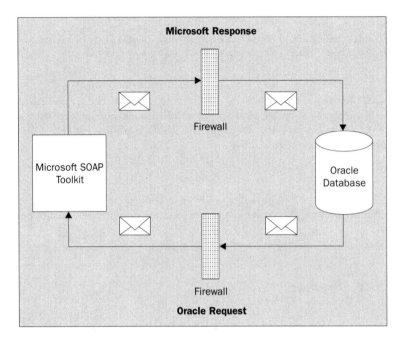

Pocket PC Client

As we saw at the beginning of the chapter, SOAP is platform neutral and language independent. To prove this we created an "unusual" SOAP-enabled client: a Windows CE client. The Windows CE 3.0 operating system has built-in support for XML and HTTP, so we can use that as a SOAP client. We prepared an example of how to use this client in a SOAP network.

We've got four buttons with the operation to be performed, and a combo box with a list of pre-set URL representing the Java and MS-VB service provider. We load the combo with the URLs, in the `form_load` event,

```
Combo1.AddItem "http://localhost:2020/calc/calculator.asp"
Combo1.AddItem "http://localhost:8080/soap/servlet/rpcrouter"
Combo1.AddItem "http://localhost:2025/soap/servlet/rpcrouter"
Combo1.ListIndex = 0
```

And when the user press a button we call a subroutine that builds the SOAP request and send it to the service provider. When the response arrives it parses the XML result and extracts the return value:

```
Public Function op(op1 As Integer) As String
    Dim strStdEnv As String
    Dim objWireT
    Dim docResp

    Dim XMLHTTP
    Dim objDOM
    Dim strXML      As String
    Dim strResponse As String
    Dim strOp As String
```

```
Set XMLHTTP = CreateObject("Microsoft.XMLHTTP")
XMLHTTP.Open "POST", Combo1.Text, False
XMLHTTP.setRequestHeader "Content-Type", "text/xml"
Select Case op1
    Case 0
    strOp = "sum"
    Case 1
    strOp = "multiply"
    Case 2
    strOp = "divide"
    Case 3
    strOp = "subtract"
End Select
```

This is where we build the SOAP envelope and the body

```
strXML = "<SOAP-ENV:Envelope xmlns:SOAP-
ENV=""http://schemas.xmlsoap.org/soap/envelope/""
xmlns:xsi=""http://www.w3.org/1999/XMLSchema-instance""
xmlns:xsd=""http://www.w3.org/1999/XMLSchema"">"
strXML = strXML + "<SOAP-ENV:Body><ns1:"
strXML = strXML + strOp + " xmlns:ns1 = ""urn:Calc"" SOAP-
ENV:encodingStyle=""http://schemas.xmlsoap.org/soap/encoding/"">"
strXML = strXML + "<x xsi:type=""xsd:int"">"
strXML = strXML + Text2.Text + "</x>"
strXML = strXML + "<y xsi:type=""xsd:int"">"
strXML = strXML + Text3.Text + "</y>"
strXML = strXML + "</ns1:"
strXML = strXML + strOp
strXML = strXML + "></SOAP-ENV:Body></SOAP-ENV:Envelope>"

XMLHTTP.send (strXML)

'MsgBox XMLHTTP.responsetext

Set objDOM = CreateObject("Microsoft.XMLDOM")


objDOM.LoadXml XMLHTTP.responsetext
op = objDOM.getelementsbytagname("return").Item(0).nodetypedvalue
End Function
```

LUMA Cars

Business Needs

For this case study we are pleased to bring you back to the LUMA cars example. The LUMA cars example was first presented in "*Professional ASP XML*", Wrox Press, ISBN 1-861004-02-8. For those who missed it, here is just a simple recap.

The company's name is LUMA and it is a car retailer. With the ongoing growth of the Internet, LUMA managers decided to put their business on the Net.

At the same time, they want to simplify and speed up bureaucracy by automating the various tasks involved in the processing of an order. Right now, all of these tasks are performed in a very paper-intensive way. They want to start saving some tropical trees...

The company thinks it all makes sense. So after some time, they finally decide to call a young and brilliant software-managing director to get the job done. But suddenly things get really complex.

Description of the Application Domain

Unfortunately, LUMA is not the center of the world. It can't force all its partners to modify their systems to process LUMA orders in a specified way. Each single company has its own way to process orders and LUMA has no power to make them change, not even in this LUMA-friendly test case. The problem is therefore the integration of different systems.

We must take into account security, scalability, graphical appeal and all the usual challenges of modern web-based applications. Moreover, integration adds a strange twist to the mix.

We have got four main departments: Administration, Assembly, Marketing, and Information technology.

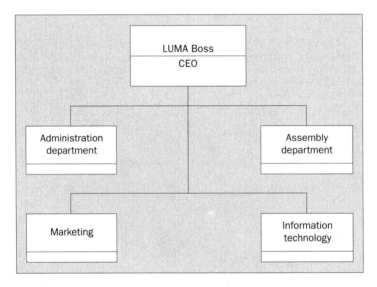

The Administration department is responsible for all administrative tasks: from invoicing to payments and bank relationships. The assembly department is responsible for motor-vehicle assembly and control of suppliers. Marketing has the overall main goal of the site's design and its promotion.

We represent the information technology department and we are responsible for the whole technical infrastructure. Our chairman also designates us to implement security surveillance.

When we arrived in LUMA cars, it was a startup company without an information technology manager and every department, as you can easily imagine, chose a different platform.

For a long time things have not changed and the administration department runs on an IBM machine, the assembly department with a Unix one, and the marketing people love their Windows 2000 workstations.

We also need to set up a B2B e-commerce system which will permit tight integration with our partners. In this case, we have to integrate not only our internal department but also our external partners.

With a limited budget, we can redesign the architecture, keeping in mind our primary goals:

- ❑ Integration among systems
- ❑ Speed in response
- ❑ Efficiency in the overall process

We also want to adopt an Oracle 8i server as our standard database machine.

Let's look at a new working scenario for the LUMA Company:

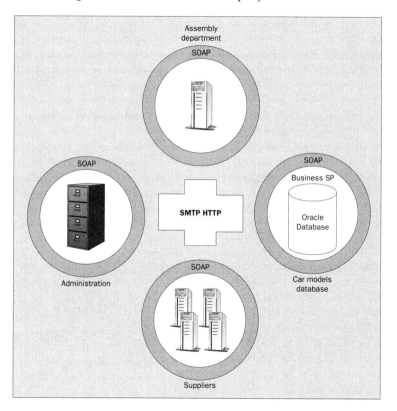

Our job is to integrate all the services, modifying them as little as possible. We decided to put every single "tile" of our big puzzle in a SOAP bubble. Another consideration to take into account is that the main portal web server, used by our customers to place their numerous orders, will be very loaded. Or, at least, we hope so.

We can devise a lot of "Use Cases Diagrams" involved in the project of putting the LUMA Company on the Web, too many to be described here. We will concentrate on the two main ones. These are on the core of the LUMA business, which is selling cars.

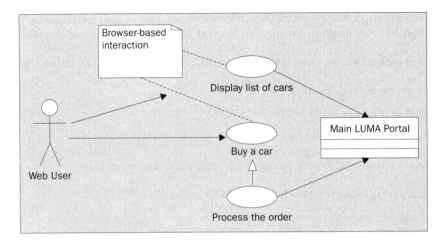

Every time a customer buys a car there are a number of operations that must be generated which involve all the departments. There are various transactions that involve communicating with our suppliers. These are:

1. Invoicing and customer credit card charge for the administration department

2. The marketing department will need to adjust its statistics

3. The assembly department must prepare the car

4. Our main database has to change the status of the car

5. The supplier has to place an order

As previously mentioned all our departments are protected by firewalls and their services are carried by heterogeneous systems. We will choose a simple architecture available for all our systems: SOAP.

Our job in designing, developing and installing the infrastructure is to permit a tight integration among the systems preserving them in the same form as much as possible.
In this section we enter deep into the code and we'll see the details of our simple solution with special care on the overall architectural design.

First of all a simple picture shows us all the components involved.

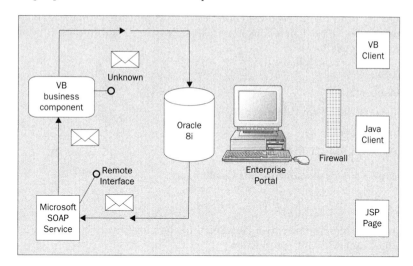

We prepared five different clients:

- Visual Basic
- Java
- JSP page
- Oracle PL/SQL client
- Pocket PC Client

Each client is able to perform two main jobs:

- Get a list of cars
- Order a car

On the server side, as previously seen, we have many technical platforms to manage:

- An Oracle 8i server
- An Enterprise Java Bean
- A Visual Basic business component

Our enterprise portal is a web server acting as an interface for the external user and as a glue between the service providers. As the interface it exposes the "Get a list of cars" and "Order a car" services to a Client whether it be a Visual Basic, Java, JSP, etc . As glue, it permits the tight integration between our systems that are needed in a B2B environment. In particular, it is the HTTP server used by the SOAP server to carry out the SOAP requests synchronously. We have got a lot of existing code in production and have to reuse as much software as we possibly can.

To do so we left our Microsoft Visual Basic components without modifying them. We have only set up our framework wrapping these components in a SOAP shell, or bubble, so we can call them from any SOAP enabled client, from every platform.

We have installed a Microsoft SOAP environment and have published our components; in a following paragraph we will provide all the details to start it up.

LUMA Cars Server Components

In this case study we preferred to keep the code as simple as possible without sacrificing the overall architectural design. So we used an architecture taken from a real world project. In this architecture we have to deal with these platforms:

- A web Server
- A servlet container
- An Enterprise JavaBean Container
- An Oracle 8i Server
- A COM+ Windows 2000 Server

We have prepared a simple example for each technology.

EJB Component

We prepared two very simple Enterprise Java Beans to complete the design of the infrastructure and easily migrate this framework into production.

We defined an Entity Bean and a Session Bean. The session bean performs the same job as its Visual Basic counterpart. It checks for whatever business rule you have and instantiates an Entity Bean representing our `Order` object.

The Entity Bean is Container managed and, in our case it inserts a row in our Oracle DB. All the issues of persistence will be taken care of by the server. As iAS is unable to deploy entity beans, for this example we have used JBoss with Tomcat. However, Oracle 9iAS will support entity beans.

Here we implement the Entity bean and need two interfaces, the Remote interface and the Home interface and two classes, the Primary and the Bean class.

The Home interface is used by any client to create and retrieve instances of the entity bean.

```
package soapimpl.EntOrders;

import javax.ejb.EJBHome;
import javax.ejb.CreateException;
import javax.ejb.FinderException;
import java.rmi.RemoteException;
import java.util.Enumeration;

public interface orderHome extends javax.ejb.EJBHome {

    public order create(int orderid, String userid,
        String cardid, double amount)
        throws RemoteException, CreateException;

    public order findByPrimaryKey(orderPK primaryKey)
        throws RemoteException, FinderException;

    public Enumeration findByCardID(String cardid)
        throws RemoteException, FinderException;

    public Enumeration findByUserID(String userid)
        throws RemoteException, FinderException;

    public Enumeration findAll()
        throws RemoteException, FinderException;
}
```

The Remote interface is the client's view of an instance of the entity bean. This is returned to the client by the Home interface after creating or finding an entity bean instance. The interface contains the business methods of the enterprise bean. For each method in this remote interface there must be a matching method in the bean implementation class.

```
package soapimpl.EntOrders;

import java.rmi.RemoteException;
import javax.ejb.EJBObject;

public interface order extends EJBObject {
    public int getOrderID ()
        throws RemoteException;
    public String getUserID ()
        throws RemoteException;
    public void setUserID (String userid)
        throws RemoteException;
    public String getCardID ()
        throws RemoteException;
    public void setCardID (String cardid)
        throws RemoteException;
    public double getAmount ()
        throws RemoteException;
    public void setAmount (double amount)
        throws RemoteException;
}
```

The Primary key class is necessary for entity beans only and it encapsulates the fields representing the primary key of an entity bean in a single object and then provides a pointer into the database.

```
package soapimpl.EntOrders;

import java.io.Serializable;

public class orderPK implements java.io.Serializable {
    public int orderid;
    public orderPK() {}
    public orderPK(int value) {
        this.orderid = value;
    }
    public int hashCode() {
        return orderid;
    }
    public boolean equals (Object obj) {
        if (obj == null || !(obj instanceof orderPK))
            return false;
        else if (((orderPK)obj).orderid == orderid)
            return true;
        else
            return false;
    }
    public String toString() {
        return String.valueOf(orderid);
    }
}
```

The Bean class actually implements the bean's business methods of the remote interface and the methods dedicated to the EJB environment, the interfaces of which are explicitly defined in the EJB specification.

```java
package soapimpl.EntOrders;

import javax.ejb.EntityBean;
import javax.ejb.EntityContext;

public class orderBean implements EntityBean {
    public int orderid;
    public String userid;
    public String cardid;
    public double amount;
    protected EntityContext context;
    public orderPK ejbCreate(int orderid, String userid,
            String cardid, double amount) {
        this.orderid = orderid;
        this.userid = userid;
        this.cardid = cardid;
        this.amount = amount;
        return null;
    }
    public void ejbPostCreate(int orderid, String userid,
        String cardid, double amount) {}
    public void setEntityContext(EntityContext ctx) {
        context = ctx;
    }
    public void unsetEntityContext() {
        context = null;
    }
    public void ejbActivate() {}
    public void ejbPassivate() {}
    public void ejbLoad() {}
    public void ejbStore() {}
    public void ejbRemove() {}

    public int getOrderID() {
        return orderid;
    }
    public String getUserID() {
        return userid;
    }
    public void setUserID(String user) {
        userid = user;
    }
    public String getCardID() {
        return cardid;
    }
    public void setCardID(String card) {
        cardid = card;
    }
    public double getAmount() {
        return amount;
    }
    public void setAmount(double n) {
        amount = n;
    }
}
```

Here we implement the Session bean and we need two interfaces, the Remote interface and the Home interface, and one class, the Bean class.

This bean acts as a simple interface between the client and the Entity bean and it is a Stateless session bean because it does not maintain its state across method calls.

Unlike entity beans, session beans are not persistent and do not represent data in a database.

The Home interface for a session bean defines the create methods that initialize a new session bean for client use: find methods are not used in session beans.

```
package soapimpl.SessOrders;

import javax.ejb.EJBHome;
import javax.ejb.CreateException;
import javax.ejb.FinderException;
import java.rmi.RemoteException;
import java.util.Enumeration;

public interface orderSessHome extends javax.ejb.EJBHome {

    public orderSess create()
        throws RemoteException, CreateException;
}
```

The Remote interface defines the business purpose of the enterprise bean.

```
package soapimpl.SessOrders;

import java.rmi.RemoteException;
import javax.ejb.EJBObject;
import java.util.Enumeration;
import java.util.Vector;

public interface orderSess extends EJBObject {
    /* Return 0->OK */
    public int newOrder (int orderid, String userid,
        String cardid, double amount)
        throws RemoteException;
    public Vector findByUserID(String userid)
        throws RemoteException;
    public Vector findByCardID(String Cardid)
        throws RemoteException;
    public Vector findAll()
        throws RemoteException;
}
```

The Bean class is created using the Remote interface as a guide; examining the implementation we note the use of JNDI to locate the orderHome Home interface and obtain a reference to the beans EJB home. So beans are other bean's clients, just like client applications.

```
package soapimpl.SessOrders;

import java.util.Enumeration;
import java.util.Properties;
import java.util.Vector;
```

```
import javax.ejb.SessionBean;
import javax.ejb.SessionContext;
import javax.naming.InitialContext;
import javax.naming.Context;
import javax.rmi.PortableRemoteObject;
import soapimpl.EntOrders.order;
import soapimpl.EntOrders.orderHome;

public class orderSessBean implements SessionBean {

    protected SessionContext context;

    //Private constant
    private static int OK = 0;
    private static int KO = 1;

    public void ejbCreate() {    }

    public void setSessionContext(SessionContext ctx) {
        this.context = ctx;
    }
    public void unsetSessionContext() {
        this.context = null;
    }
    public void ejbActivate() {}
    public void ejbPassivate() {}
    public void afterBegin() {}
    public void beforeCompletion() {}
    public void ejbRemove() {}

    public int newOrder(int orderid, String userid,
        String cardid, double amount) {
        try {
            Object obj = lookupObj();
            orderHome home = (orderHome)
PortableRemoteObject.narrow(obj,orderHome.class);
            order sd = home.create( orderid, userid, cardid, amount);
            //System.out.println(". Dopo create() sd.getUserID-" + sd.getUserID());
            return OK;
        } catch (Exception e) {
            e.printStackTrace();
            return KO;
        }
    }
    public Vector findByUserID(String userid) {
        try {
            Object obj = lookupObj();
            orderHome home = (orderHome)
PortableRemoteObject.narrow(obj,orderHome.class);
            Enumeration en = home.findByUserID(userid);
            Vector ret = new Vector();
            String s;
            while (en.hasMoreElements()) {
                obj = en.nextElement();
```

```
                    order aOrder = (order) PortableRemoteObject.narrow(obj,order.class);
                    s = String.valueOf(aOrder.getOrderID()) + "," + aOrder.getUserID()
                        + "," + aOrder.getCardID() + "," + aOrder.getAmount();
                    ret.addElement(s);
                }
                return ret;
            } catch (Exception e) {
                e.printStackTrace();
                return null;
            }
        }
    }
    public Vector findByCardID(String Cardid) {
        try {
            Object obj = lookupObj();
            orderHome home = (orderHome)
PortableRemoteObject.narrow(obj,orderHome.class);
            Enumeration en = home.findByCardID(Cardid);
            Vector ret = new Vector();
            String s;
            while (en.hasMoreElements()) {
                obj = en.nextElement();
                order aOrder = (order) PortableRemoteObject.narrow(obj,order.class);
                s = String.valueOf(aOrder.getOrderID()) + "," + aOrder.getUserID()
                    + "," + aOrder.getCardID() + "," + aOrder.getAmount();
                ret.addElement(s);
            }
            return ret;
        } catch (Exception e) {
            e.printStackTrace();
            return null;
        }
    }
    public Vector findAll() {
        try {
            Object obj = lookupObj();
            orderHome home = (orderHome)
PortableRemoteObject.narrow(obj,orderHome.class);
            Enumeration en = home.findAll();
            Vector ret = new Vector();
            String s;
            while (en.hasMoreElements()) {
                obj = en.nextElement();
                order aOrder = (order) PortableRemoteObject.narrow(obj,order.class);
                s = String.valueOf(aOrder.getOrderID())
                    + "," + aOrder.getUserID() + "," + aOrder.getCardID() + "," +
aOrder.getAmount();
                ret.addElement(s);
            }
            return ret;
        } catch (Exception e) {
            e.printStackTrace();
            return null;
        }
    }
```

```
        private Object lookupObj() throws javax.naming.NamingException {
            String contextFactory = "com.sun.jndi.rmi.registry.RegistryContextFactory";
            String pkgPrefix = "org.objectweb.jonas.naming";
            String anUrl = "rmi://localhost:1099";
             String EntOrdersJNDI = "ORDERSJNDI";
            Properties p = new Properties();
            p.put(Context.INITIAL_CONTEXT_FACTORY, contextFactory);
            p.put(Context.URL_PKG_PREFIXES, pkgPrefix);
            p.put(Context.PROVIDER_URL, anUrl);
            InitialContext ctx = new InitialContext(p);
            Object objRet = ctx.lookup(EntOrdersJNDI);
            return objRet;
        }
    }
```

The bean programmer has the responsibility to provide the Deployment Descriptor associated to the developed enterprise Java beans. This Deployment Descriptor must respect the XML DTD defined in the EJB 1.1 specification, as you can see at: http://java.sun.com/products/ejb/docs.html.

To deploy the Enterprise Java Beans on the EJB server we need information that is not defined in the standard XML deployment descriptor. Examples of this type of information are the mapping of the bean to the underlying database and the JNDI name of the beans.

In order to test the enterprise bean here is the code of a client Java program. The client program does not interact directly with the Entity Bean, but uses the Session Bean as a mediator.

```
public class orderSessClient {
    /**         */
    private static Object lookupObj(String sBeanJndi)
            throws javax.naming.NamingException {
        String contextFactory = "com.sun.jndi.rmi.registry.RegistryContextFactory";
        String pkgPrefix = "org.objectweb.jonas.naming";
        String anUrl = "rmi://localhost:1099";
        Properties p = new Properties();
        p.put(Context.INITIAL_CONTEXT_FACTORY, contextFactory);
        p.put(Context.URL_PKG_PREFIXES, pkgPrefix);
        p.put(Context.PROVIDER_URL, anUrl);
        InitialContext ctx = new InitialContext(p);
        Object objRet = ctx.lookup(sBeanJndi);          .
        return objRet;

    /**          */
    public static void main(String[] args) {
        String sBeanName = "ORDERSSessJNDI";
        int i = 0;
        String sUser = null;
        String sCard = null;
        String search = null;
        double d = 0;
        Vector en;
        if (args[0].equals("cr")) {
            i = Integer.parseInt(args[1]);
            sUser = args[2];
            sCard = args[3];
```

```
            if (args[4].equals(null)) {
                d = 0;
            } else {
                try {
                    d = Double.parseDouble(args[4]);
                } catch(Exception e) {
                    d = 0;
                }
            }
        }
        else if (args[0].equals("fa")) {
        }
        else if (args[0].equals("fu")) {
            if (args[1].equals(null))
                search = "";
            else
                search = args[1];
        }
        else if (args[0].equals("fc")) {
            if (args[1].equals(null))
                search = "";
            else
                search = args[1];
        }
        else {
            return;
        }
        System.out.println("sBeanName-" + sBeanName);
        //--
        try {
            Object obj = lookupObj(sBeanName);
            orderSessHome home = (orderSessHome)
                          PortableRemoteObject.narrow(obj,orderSessHome.class);
            orderSess sd = home.create();
            //---
            if (args[0].equals("cr")) {
                int tmp = sd.newOrder(i,sUser,sCard,d);
                System.out.println(". Dopo newOrder() sd.newOrder->" + tmp);
            }
            else if (args[0].equals("fa")) {
                en = sd.findAll();
                System.out.println(". findAll() en->" + en);
            }
            else if (args[0].equals("fu")) {
                en = sd.findByUserID(search);
                System.out.println(". findByUserID() search=" + search);
                System.out.println("   en->" + en.toString());
            }
            else if (args[0].equals("fc")) {
                en = sd.findByCardID(search);
                System.out.println(". findByCardID() search=" + search);
                System.out.println("   en->" + en.toString());
            }
        }
        catch(Exception e) {
            e.printStackTrace();
        }
    }
}
```

Visual Basic Server Component

The Visual Basic component is very simple. Its job is registering the client's order in an Oracle database for the marketing department.

They have a lot of software to analyze sales, customer profiles, statistical analysis and so on. So our new architecture doesn't change their habits and they can play with their drill-down, pivot whatever data. To do so we can rewrite our code using the same interfaces or, more simply, use their old components. Obviously, we used the last approach.

Technically this is a COM+ configured component started up from a SOAP call, it uses the OLE_DB provider for Oracle and the COM+ transaction services to perform its job. It implements the IObjectConstruct interface so you can define the ADO connection string administratively without the need for changing the code.

Here is the code:

```
Implements COMSVCSLib.IObjectConstruct
Private strConnection As String
Public Function ProcessOrder(ByVal CreditCardID As String, _
                    ByVal carID As String, _
                    ByVal orderDate As Date) As String
    Dim ctx As ObjectContext
    Set ctx = GetObjectContext()
    Dim cmd As New ADODB.Command
    Dim strSQL As String

    Dim count As New CPerformance
    count.StartCounter
    strSQL = "INSERT INTO Marketing (CarID,CustomerID) VALUES( "
    strSQL = strSQL & "'" & carID & "','" & CreditCardID & "')"

    On Error GoTo errPO
    cmd.ActiveConnection = strConnection
    cmd.CommandText = strSQL
    cmd.CommandType = adCmdText

    cmd.Execute
    If carID = "ERROR" Then
        ctx.SetAbort
        Err.Raise vbObjectError + 5, "LegalAgency.Prepare",
"LegalAgency.Prepare:Cannot prepare the documents"
    Else
        ctx.SetComplete
    End If
    count.StopCounter
    ProcessOrder = CStr(count.TimeElapsed)
    Exit Function
errPO:
    Set cmd = Nothing
    ctx.SetAbort
    Err.Raise Err.Number, "GetOrder", Err.Description
End Function

Private Sub IObjectConstruct_Construct(ByVal pCtorObj As Object)
    Dim strOC As IObjectConstructString
    Set strOC = pCtorObj
    strConnection = strOC.ConstructString
End Sub
```

Client Implementation

For the LUMA cars sample, we prepared five different clients. So we can see how different technologies can collaborate with each other using the SOAP technology. They are:

- ❑ JavaServer Page
- ❑ Java Swing Client
- ❑ Visual basic Client
- ❑ Oracle PL/SQL Client
- ❑ Pocket PC Windows CE Client

JSP Client

Here we have three JSP pages showing HTML forms in which a user can submit his orders on our database. It's very simple: the first page shows us the LUMAcars catalog taken from an Oracle DB, the second page ask the user for the credit card to be charged and the third page confirms the selling. When a user submits an order the submit page activates an EJB containing the business logic.

The first page is named `Default.jsp` and it connects to the database, thus it has the JDBC connection details:

```
<%@ page import="lumacars.*,java.lang.System,
java.io.*,java.util.*,java.beans.*,java.sql.*,
javax.naming.InitialContext, javax.naming.Context, javax.naming.NamingException,
javax.rmi.PortableRemoteObject"%>

<%
     String className = "oracle.jdbc.driver.OracleDriver";
     String url = "jdbc:oracle:thin:@localhost:1521:ORCL";
     String user = "scott";
     String passwd = "tiger";

     Class.forName(className);
     Connection conn = DriverManager.getConnection(url, user, passwd);
     Statement stmt = conn.createStatement();

     ResultSet res = stmt.executeQuery("select * from luma_catalog");
%>
```

Here, all the data is retrieved from the database:

```
<%   while (res.next())
   {
     String CarID = res.getString("CarID");
     String Description = res.getString("Description");
     String Price = res.getString("Price");
%>
     <tr>
```

The result is a page like this:

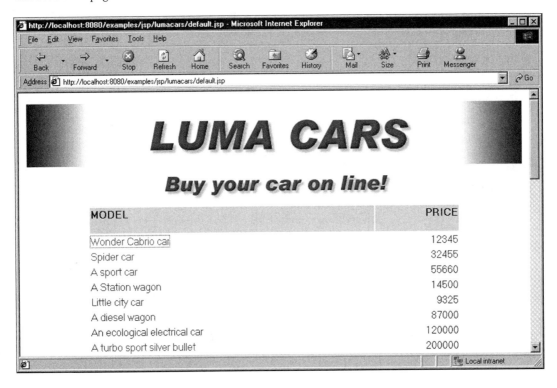

The second page, named `confirm.jsp` is:

```
<%@ page import="java.lang.System,java.io.*,java.util.*"%>

<%  String CarID=request.getParameter("CarID");
    String Price=request.getParameter("Price");
    String Model=request.getParameter("Model");
%>
<html>
```

The credit card details are taken:

```
<table>
  <tr>
    <td>Please enter your Credit Card Number</td>
    <td>
    <input type="text" name="CardID">
    <input type="submit" value="Submit" name="submit1">
    </td>
  </tr>
</table>
```

and the result is:

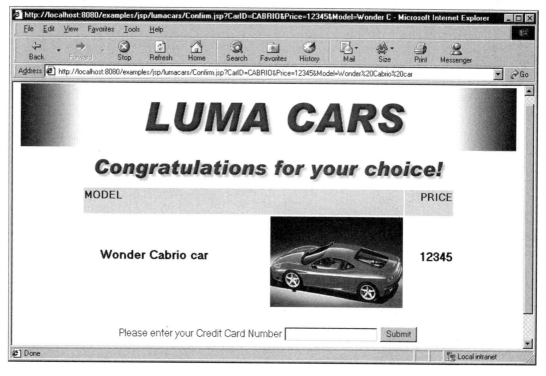

The last page named `submit.jsp` is used to instantiate our EJB and the code is:

```
<%@ page import="lumacars.*,java.lang.System,java.io.*,java.util.*,java.sql.Time,
javax.naming.InitialContext, javax.naming.Context, javax.naming.NamingException,
javax.rmi.PortableRemoteObject"%>

<%    String CardID = request.getParameter("CardID");
      String CarID = request.getParameter("CarID");

      String contextFactory = "org.jnp.interfaces.NamingContextFactory";
      String pkgPrefix = "org.jnp.interfaces";
      String anUrl = "localhost";

      Properties p = new Properties();
      p.put(Context.INITIAL_CONTEXT_FACTORY, contextFactory);
      p.put(Context.URL_PKG_PREFIXES, pkgPrefix);
      p.put(Context.PROVIDER_URL, anUrl);
      InitialContext ctx = new InitialContext(p);
      Object obj = ctx.lookup("ORDERSSessJNDI");

      orderSessHome home =
(orderSessHome)PortableRemoteObject.narrow(obj,orderSessHome.class);
      orderSess sd = (orderSess)home.create();
      int ret = sd.newOrder(CarID, CardID, 1);
      String res="";
      if (ret!=0)
```

```
            out.write ("Error");
        else
            res = "the Car " + CarId + " has been ordered !";
%>

<html>
<style>
TD{ FONT-FAMILY: 'MS Sans Serif';
     TEXT-ALIGN: center}
A{  FONT-FAMILY: 'MS Sans Serif';
    TEXT-DECORATION: none}
H6{ FONT-FAMILY: 'MS Sans Serif';
    FONT-SIZE: xx-small;
    FONT-WEIGHT: 100;
    COLOR: #0000ff;
    TEXT-DECORATION: none}
</style>

<body>
<table border="0" width="100%">
  <tr>
    <td>
      <img SRC="images/Bg1.gif">
    </td>
    <td width="100%" Align="middle">
      <img SRC="images/Luma.gif">
    </td>
     <td>
       <img SRC="images/bg2.gif">
     </td>
  </tr>
  <tr>
    <td colspan="3">
      Your transaction returned the following result:
    </td>
  </tr>
  <tr>
    <td colspan="3"><h3><%=res%></h3></td>
  </tr>
   <tr>
    <td colspan="3">
      <a HREF="Default.jsp">Order a new car</a>
    </td>
  </tr>
  <tr>
    <td valign="top">
      <img SRC="images/bg4.gif">
    </td>
    <td width="100%">
      <h6 align="right"><a href="mailto:c.ulivi@datasiel.net"> Cristina Ulivi
 </a></h6>
    </td>
     <td valign="top">
        <img SRC="images/bg3.gif">
     </td>
  </tr>
</table>

</body>
</html>
```

SOAP-enabled Service

Until now, there is nothing special, a JSP page that instantiates an EJB to perform some business logic, but now we want to "bubbleize" the EJB service and to prepare for a more realistic scenario. The first step is to create a Java class that exposes the `orderACar` service, this class hides all the EJB instantiation details:

```java
import lumacars.*;

import java.util.Date;
import java.sql.Time;
import java.util.Vector;
import java.util.Properties;
import java.util.Enumeration;
import java.util.Collection;
import java.util.Collections;
import javax.naming.InitialContext;
import javax.naming.Context;
import javax.naming.NamingException;
import javax.rmi.PortableRemoteObject;

public class soapOrder {
    /**        */
    public String orderACar(String carId,String customerId) {
        String contextFactory = "org.jnp.interfaces.NamingContextFactory";
        String pkgPrefix = "org.jnp.interfaces";
        String anUrl = "localhost";
        String sBeanName = "ORDERSJNDI";

        long start = System.currentTimeMillis();
        Properties p = new Properties();

        p.put(Context.INITIAL_CONTEXT_FACTORY, contextFactory);
        p.put(Context.URL_PKG_PREFIXES, pkgPrefix);
        p.put(Context.PROVIDER_URL, anUrl);
        try {
            //---
            InitialContext initial = new InitialContext(p);
            Object obj = initial.lookup(sBeanName);
            orderHome home =
(orderHome)PortableRemoteObject.narrow(obj,orderHome.class);
            //---
            order sd = home.create(carId,customerId,null,1);
        }
        catch(Exception e) {
            e.printStackTrace();
            return "Error!";
        }
        return " " + (System.currentTimeMillis() - start);
    // End of orderACar
    }
    public static void main(String[] args) {
        //int i;
        //double d;
        String carId = args[0];
        String customerId = args[1];

        soapOrder ord = new soapOrder();
        System.out.println("Result = " +
            ord.orderACar(carId,customerId));
    }
}
```

Then we need to expose the `orderAcar` method as a SOAP enabled service. To do so we used the SOAP admin toolkit from the Apache implementation and we created the `carOrder` service from the `soapOrder` class exposing only the `orderAcar` method. You can see all the details in Appendix A and from the code download.

Java Client

We prepared a simple Java SWING client performing car orders. Using this client you can order a car without the need of a browser. The code is:

```
package newcar;

   public DlgCar(Frame frame, String title, boolean modal) {
     super(frame, title, modal);
     try {
       jbInit();
       pack();
     }
     catch(Exception ex) {
       ex.printStackTrace();
     }
   }

   public DlgCar() {
     this(null, "", false);
   }

   void jbInit() throws Exception {
```

The code to build the visual interface has been left out::

```
   void exec() {
     long timeE = System.currentTimeMillis();
     try {
       String encodingStyleURI  =  Constants.NS_URI_SOAP_ENC;
       URL url = new URL(txtURI.getText());
       SOAPMappingRegistry smr = new SOAPMappingRegistry();
       // Build the call.
       Call call = new Call();
       call.setSOAPMappingRegistry(smr);
       call.setTargetObjectURI("carOrder");
       call.setEncodingStyleURI(encodingStyleURI);
       call.setMethodName("orderACar");
       Vector params = new Vector();
       String carID = txtOp1.getText();
       String customerID = txtOp2.getText();
       params.addElement(new Parameter("carId",String.class,carID, null));
       params.addElement(new Parameter("customerId",String.class,customerID,
  null));

       call.setParams(params);
```

We invoke the call and check the response:

```
        Response resp;
        resp = call.invoke(url, "");


        if (!resp.generatedFault())
        {
          Parameter ret = resp.getReturnValue();
          Object value = ret.getValue();
          lblRes.setText(value.toString());
        }
        else
        {
          Fault fault = resp.getFault();

          System.err.println("Generated fault: ");
          System.out.println ("  Fault Code   = " + fault.getFaultCode());
          System.out.println ("  Fault String = " + fault.getFaultString());
        }
      } // End try block
      catch (SOAPException e) {
        System.err.println("Caught SOAPException (" +
                          e.getFaultCode() + "): " +
                          e.getMessage());
        return;
      }
      catch (Exception e) {
        System.err.println("Caught Exception (" +
                          e.getMessage());
        lblRes1.setText(" " + (System.currentTimeMillis()-timeE));
        return;
      }
    } // End of exec method
}
```

Using the Swing Java Client you can access our SOAP Oracle service from any platform, the result is:

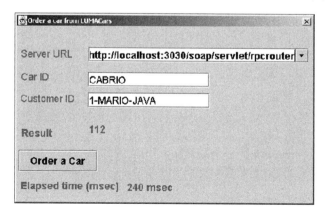

Visual Basic Client

The Visual Basic client permits to order a car not using the Web interface but instead you can use your usual Win32 program to access an Oracle service using SOAP and the World Wide Web network. The result is:

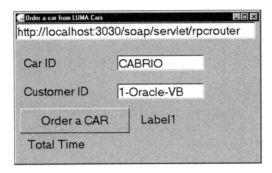

and the code is:

```
Private Sub submit_Click()
    Dim x As New newSOAPProxy
    Dim p1 As New SOAPParam
    Dim p2 As New SOAPParam
    Dim count As New CPerformance
    count.StartCounter
    On Error GoTo errOrd
        Me.MousePointer = vbHourglass
        p1.Name = "carId"
        p1.Value = Text1.Text
        p2.Name = "customerId"
        p2.Value = Text2.Text

        x.invoke txtURI.Text, "carOrder", "orderACar", p1, p2
        lblRes.Caption = x.Value("return")
        Me.MousePointer = vbNormal
        count.StopCounter
        Label3.Caption = CStr(CInt(count.TimeElapsed))
        Exit Sub
    errOrd:
        Me.MousePointer = vbNormal
        MsgBox "Error - " & Err.Description


    End Sub
```

Pocket PC Client

You can also call this service from a hand held device like a Pocket PC equipped by Windows CE. The idea is quite simple, we can exploit the HTTP and XML features of the Microsoft library. So we created a `Microsoft.XMLHTTP` object in order to set up a HTTP call and then we can instantiate the `Microsoft.XMLDOM` parser to parse the response and get the result.

The code is similar to that used in the calculator example:

```
Public Function op(op1 As Integer) As String
    Dim strStdEnv As String
    Dim objWireT
    Dim docResp

    Dim XMLHTTP
    Dim objDOM
    Dim strXML       As String
    Dim strResponse As String
    Dim strOp As String

    Set XMLHTTP = CreateObject("Microsoft.XMLHTTP")
    XMLHTTP.Open "POST", Combo1.Text, False
    XMLHTTP.SetRequestHeader "Content-Type", "text/xml"

    strOp = "orderACar"

    strXML = "<SOAP-ENV:Envelope xmlns:SOAP-
ENV=""http://schemas.xmlsoap.org/soap/envelope/""
xmlns:xsi=""http://www.w3.org/1999/XMLSchema-instance""
xmlns:xsd=""http://www.w3.org/1999/XMLSchema"">"
    strXML = strXML + "<SOAP-ENV:Body><ns1:"
    strXML = strXML + strOp + " xmlns:ns1 = ""carOrder"" SOAP-
ENV:encodingStyle=""http://schemas.xmlsoap.org/soap/encoding/"">"
    strXML = strXML + "<carId xsi:type=""xsd:string"">"
    strXML = strXML + Text2.Text + "</carId>"
    strXML = strXML + "<customerId xsi:type=""xsd:string"">"
    strXML = strXML + Text3.Text + "</customerId>"
    strXML = strXML + "</ns1:"
    strXML = strXML + strOp
    strXML = strXML + "></SOAP-ENV:Body></SOAP-ENV:Envelope>"

    XMLHTTP.send (strXML)

    'MsgBox XMLHTTP.responsetext

    Set objDOM = CreateObject("Microsoft.XMLDOM")

    'MsgBox
    objDOM.LoadXml XMLHTTP.responsetext

    op = objDOM.getElementsByTagName("return").Item(0).NodeTypedValue

End Function
```

Oracle Client

If you have to use the Visual basic component that inserts some statistical records in the marketing database the easier and faster solution could be to insert a trigger in the LUMA_orders table and call the VB component as a SOAP service exploiting the Oracle SOAP client features.

We have prepared a stored function named `marketing` that calls the VB component for the marketing people, the code is:

```
create or replace function i_marketing(CreditCardID in varchar2, CarID in
varchar2) return varchar2 is
/* Simple SOAP Client
*/
    aCall number;
    tCall call_item_type;
    result VARCHAR2(32767);
BEGIN
  tCall := SA_SOAP_INTERFACEPL.newcall();
  SA_SOAP_INTERFACEPL.setStringParam(tCall,'CreditCardID',CreditCardID,null);
  SA_SOAP_INTERFACEPL.setStringParam(tCall,'carID',CarID,null);
  SA_SOAP_INTERFACEPL.setMethodname(tCall,'ProcessOrder');
  result :=
SA_SOAP_INTERFACEPL.invoke(tCall,localhost:2020',8080,'/LegalAgency/Prepare.asp');
  SA_SOAP_INTERFACEPL.freeCall(tCall);
  return result;

END marketing;
```

To add this feature to transparently respect our client we have prepared a trigger. We use the trigger, which calls the marketing component for each order submitted using a SOAP call. We can call any service from inside the trigger without influencing the whole architecture. The code for this trigger is:

```
create or replace trigger marketing_INS
    before insert on LUMA_ORDERS
    for each row          .
    DECLARE
          res VARCHAR2(512);
    begin
        res := i_marketing(:new.CUSTOMERID,:new.CARID);
end Prova;
```

The LUMA cars server architecture is now represented in the following picture, we've got:

❑   A JSP engine
❑   The Apache SOAP implementation
❑   An EJB Container
❑   An Enterprise JavaBean with the LUMA Cars business logic
❑   An Oracle DB
❑   A trigger
❑   An IIS Web server
❑   A COM+ configured component with the marketing business logic

All kept together by the SOAP infrastructure.

Summary

In this chapter, we presented Oracle from a new perspective: as a SOAP provider and as a SOAP service consumer.

SOAP is a protocol you can use to exchange information between heterogeneous systems using different transport agent like HTTP or SMTP.

You can use HTTP, SMTP or any other protocol, as SOAP is not tied to a specific transport protocol. Using HTTP, for example, you can transport a SOAP envelope describing your request in a standard, synchronous way; or you can use SMTP to deliver your message asynchronously. This intrinsically flexible way of delivering messages gives designers a powerful weapon in designing a network of heterogeneous systems: you can simply think of your network in terms of a service producer and a service consumer without the influence of the media that you will use.

SOAP will play a very important role in a B2B environment for the following reasons:

- ❑ It's based on XML
- ❑ It's extensible
- ❑ It's easy to implement
- ❑ It's broadly adopted
- ❑ You can use whatever firewall friendly protocol you want

In this chapter we've seen how we can use whatever language like Java or Visual Basic or even embedded Visual basic for pocket PC in whatever operating system like Linux, Windows 2000 and Pocket PC. In our network of services we've got our Oracle 8i database too, and it plays an important role: it's not only our database machine but we can use it as a Client of different service providers in a transparent way thanks to SOAP.

In a modern e-Commerce world we'll use more and more "web services" even without realize it and from a technical point of view we can figure out SOAP not only a protocol but like an agent integrator.

We've got a long path to travel and have to improve the security mechanisms, we need a transaction protocol to manage transactions distributed over different sites but we're on the right way.

24

Wireless Applications with Oracle Portal-to-Go

With the wide-spread proliferation of mobile devices facilitating Internet access, and the exponential growth rate predicted in terms of the number of users projected to use such devices, it has never been more imperative to re-align content and business-logic for the wireless Internet. As is the case with most other Internet technologies, such an effort is largely influenced by the need to rapidly prototype and deploy the final solution. Oracle's Portal-to-Go attempts to solve development and deployment issues on this front by reusing existing content and logic, shortening development cycles and providing customizable and extensible components.

In this chapter we shall explore Portal-to-Go from the perspectives of a content-adaptation platform and a development and deployment platform for wireless services. Specifically we shall be focusing our attention on the following aspects of Portal-to-Go:

- ❑ Architecture and user abstractions of Portal-to-Go based wireless services
- ❑ Installing the Portal-to-Go setup
- ❑ Portal-to-Go Object and XML and style sheet framework
- ❑ Auxiliary tools
- ❑ Developing services using default adapters and writing custom adapters
- ❑ A sample Application – phone book application using a custom LDAP adapter

Portal-to-Go as a Wireless Solution

Traditionally web sites have been designed with a certain average bandwidth in mind and often this corresponds to that *enjoyed* by users accessing these sites from full-featured browsers and content delivered to general-purpose workstations. With the emergence of mobile Internet access, access issues have taken a more complex turn. The workstation is no longer the only device or machine to access content from; most wireless devices have smaller keypads with many fewer keys and screens with very small form factors. These hardware constraints apart from limited and expensive bandwidth greatly influence the access capabilities that these devices allow. To further compound the problem, there exist several standards for displaying and negotiating content on these devices, when compared to traditional browsers which are chiefly software for interpreting HTML.

Further, the nature of interaction is different; the wireless Internet devices of today are more suited for accessing small pieces of information rather than browsing graphic-rich content. The challenge lies in enabling existing web sites with vast amounts of content to be accessible from these devices; rewriting content for wireless devices is not always feasible owing to the sheer volume of information and the task of maintaining content for each of these different devices. In the real world, these devices are ideal for receiving stock alerts, short message e-mails, and weather information, delivered synchronously or asynchronously. However, with all these limitations, mobile Internet access brings unprecedented features to the mobile user. The most obvious of these being ubiquitous access to content and applications, and the latest being location-based services – such as a device which is aware of your current geographic position, and guides you to the nearest gas station when you realize that you that you are fast running out of fuel.

Deploying wireless-enabled content and applications is fraught with several obstacles, one of the most challenging being the afore-mentioned issue of the multitude of devices, browsers and interfaces to contend with. Re-writing content to support each of these devices is a highly time and resource consuming exercise, if not altogether impossible. Equally daunting is the task of migrating existing content and logic to the wireless world. Portal-to-Go addresses this pair of issues quite adequately for most development and deployment scenarios. It is important to understand how Portal-to-Go appears to the end user and what it means to the developer.

A User's View

Subscribers to wireless services enabled by Portal-to-Go use the micro-browser (or any other interface) on their mobile device to access the services hosted by Portal-to-Go. We shall call such an interface or micro-browser the Device Portal from now on. Using the device portal, subscribers can interact with services, create a list of favorite services, and organize services in folders. Apart from using a mobile device for such customization, the user can use a conventional browser to access a web interface to customize his or her device portal. Such a web interface is what we shall call the Personalization portal.

The Developer's Perspective

The Portal-to-Go developer uses the transformer mechanism provided by Portal-to-Go to ensure that the content is accessible by a variety of devices (in other words, the various flavors of the device portals). They will further modify the Personalization portal's look and feel, and sometimes the logic, to reflect the site and services that are being hosted by Portal-to-Go. A typical case would be to modify the look-and-feel of the Personalization portal to resemble the existing web user interface of the site. The developer can publish services that access data from various data sources (say from an existing web site, or a SQL database) using any of the bundled adapters, or they may choose to write a custom adapter that can be used to access data from a source that is not supported by any of the bundled adapters.

Portal-to-Go Architecture

The diagram below sets out the basic architecture that we will consider in this chapter:

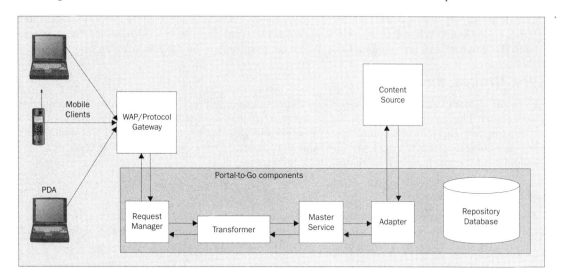

Let us look at what transpires when a user invokes a service hosted by Portal-to-Go from their mobile device. The request is often encapsulated in a protocol (such as WAP) that is specific to the telecommunication provider and the device. This request is converted into an HTTP request by an intermediary protocol gateway, say a WAP gateway. The WAP gateway (or any other protocol-specific gateway) by itself is not part of the Portal-to-Go, but exists as part of the deployment framework to facilitate conversion of client requests to HTTP. This is because the Portal-to-Go core runs as Servlets in an Apache/JServ environment.

The web server (Apache) directs the request to a JServ instance from where the Portal-to-Go Servlet takes over. The **Request Manager** module authenticates the user and does some other initial processing, such as determining the user's location (in some cases, where location-based services are provided).

The request manager now creates a request object and passes it on to the appropriate **Master Service**. Each service hosted by Portal-to-Go has a master service associated with it. The master service now invokes an **Adapter** specific to the service. An adapter is an object that has the logic necessary to connect to a specific content source and retrieve information. An example is a SQL adapter that retrieves content from a SQL database.

The data returned by the adapter is in XML that conforms to a DTD specified by Portal-to-Go. This data format is, however, a generic format and needs to be customized for the requesting device's rendering capabilities. This is where the **Transformer** comes in. Broadly speaking, each device has a transformer associated with it and the transformer has the know-how to convert the result data, returned by the adapter in a generic format, into the device-specific format.

We shall be revisiting most of these components in detail during the course of the chapter.

Objects and the Repository

Portal-to-Go's object-oriented design results in almost all of its modules, or more precisely entities, being objects. The users, services, folders, adapters, and almost everything else are all objects. These objects are stored in a repository – the repository being a database accessed by Portal-to-Go through JDBC connections. When Portal-to-Go is started for the first time, several of these objects are fetched from the database and instantiated. Let's take a look at some of the more interesting object types.

Users, Groups, and Folders

Each subscriber of any of the Portal-to-Go services is a unique Portal-to-Go user and is associated with a user object. The user belongs to a group which, of course, is represented by a group object. All users belonging to a group have a common set of access and visibility privileges, in other words, they can access a common set of services with the same permissions. Users can organize their services or references to services (known as aliases) into folders.

Master Services

The `master service` object corresponds to a unique service hosted by Portal-to-Go. An example of a master service is one that displays the temperature conditions of a city when the ZIP code is provided. The master service uses an adapter to connect to the actual data source.

Adapters and Transformers

An `adapter` object exists for each content source that is accessed by the services. We shall see more about content sources in the next section and, later in this chapter, we will also see how to implement a custom adapter. A transformer converts from the device-neutral data format output by the adapter into a device-specific format. Supported target formats include WML1.1, Tiny THML, VoxML, HDML, and Plain Text. A default transformer exists for each device type, although it is possible to develop a custom transformer, which works only with a specific device and master service pair.

Logical Device

The actual device, such as a Palm handheld or a wireless web-enabled phone is grouped under a logical device, which is basically an abstraction grouping together all devices that have the same rendering capabilities. Most often a new device fits into a logical device category and when it does, it eliminates the need to do anything special to deploy content on that device.

Content Sources

As we saw earlier, adapters insulate the master services from the idiosyncrasies of the data sources, both in terms of connecting to them and also in terms of the data format. Let us take a look at some of the interesting data sources that can be accessed using the default adapters provided with Portal-to-Go. To access a new data source with a different format and connection semantics, we would have to implement a custom adapter. This adapter should possess the logic to connect, retrieve and parse the data from the new content source and also represent it in the generic XML format. This generic XML format into which adapters convert data from disparate sources is called the **SimpleResult** format. It conforms to the `SimpleResult` DTD.

Web Integration Adapter

This is one of the most useful adapters as it allows the immediate deployment of content that is already accessible through a conventional web browser. For the web integration adapter to work, we need an operational web integration server (bundled with Portal-to-Go). The adapter connects to the web integration server and requests data based on a interface agreed upon between the adapter and the we integration server. The adapter then converts this into the generic `SimpleResult` XML and passes it on to the transformer for the requesting device.

SQL Adapter

This adapter connects to JDBC-capable data sources. It can issue queries, execute procedures, and invoke stored procedures in the remote database.

Servlet Adapter

This adapter allows applications that are developed as Java servlets to be readily deployed as Portal-to-Go services.

Stripper Adapter

This adapter fetches data from a URL source and performs actions as specified on encountering tags in the retrieved document. An external class can define the action for the tags.

URL Adapter

The URL adapter fetches a URL pointing to an XML document, which conforms to the `SimpleResult` DTD. This is especially useful when integrating applications that have been developed with a wireless interface in mind (apart from a web interface or some other traditional interface). The application needs to generate data in `SimpleResult` format and therefore integrates easily with Portal-to-Go. Note that the URL adapter is available from 1.0.2.2 release onwards.

Provisioning Adapter

This is not an adapter in the true sense, but nevertheless is used for user management on Portal-to-Go. It facilitates an interface that integrates seamlessly with any user management front-end that can talk to it.

Development Tools

Portal-to-Go comes with several supplementary tools that are used mainly for designing services, repository management, and user management. Let us take a closer look at some of the more useful ones.

Service Designer

The service designer, as the name implies, is the utility to design and publish services on to the Portal-to-Go server. It provides a browse able tree interface to the repository objects. Running a batch script, `run.bat`, which can be found in `\panama\ServiceDesigner`, will start the service designer.

Upon starting, the service designer needs to connect to the running instance of the Portal-to-Go server for which the services are to be designed or to the repository. The preferred mode is to connect to the Portal-to-Go server by specifying the machine information for the server, for example, `myptgserver.wrox.com`. You must also specify a port number if you are running Portal-to-Go at a port other than the default one, for example, `myptgserver.wrox.com:8765`. We shall look at the service designer in detail in the next section, where we design a weather lookup service.

Web Integration Developer

The Web Integration adapter talks to the Web Integration server, asking it to fetch a web page parsed on criteria specified in a mutually agreed interface (in the WIDL interface format). We develop this interface using the Web Integration Developer and then publish it to the Web Integration server under a particular interface name. We specify this interface name when we build a service that uses the Web Integration adapter. This discussion is illustrated in the weather lookup service.

LoadXml Utility

This utility is used to convert the repository data to and from XML format and download or upload it consequentially. This is useful especially in distributing data between two JDBC sources. Again, it is useful to selectively download a particular type of object only. LoadXml, with default options, can be invoked using upload.bat *inputxmlfile.xml*, to upload data represented in XML to a repository or using download.bat *outputxmlfile.xml* to download the data. LoadXml checks for object dependencies and uniqueness of the object, though it does not do any validation of the XML (since the repository XML has no DTD associated with it, due to external references in it). Neither does it do any error checking other than checking for well-formedness of the XML when uploading. If the object does not exist in the repository, it creates the object and performs a database commit.

CopyObjects Utility

The CopyObjects utility is used to copy services from one instance of a Portal-to-Go server to another. It is quite similar to the LoadXml utility in that it uses an XML representation when copying services. In fact the utility copies a folder from one server to another; hence it is necessary to place the service in a folder before copying it. The configuration of the origin and destination servers must be the same, since the utility sends only service and folder information and not configuration-related information. Consider the following code:

```
java oracle.panama.core.util.CopyObjects -f /master/finance \
    -s user1/pw1@//:2008/PanamaServer \
        user2/pw2@//targetsrv:2008/PanamaServer
```

It causes the folder /master/finance on the local machine, belonging to the user user1 with a password of pw1, to be copied to the server running on port 2008 of the machine targetsrv, under the user user2 with the password pw2.

Installing Portal-to-Go

The latest complete release of Portal-to-Go is version 1.0.2.1, although it has been followed by a major patch release, 1.0.2.2, which contains many performance improvements. Portal-to-Go releases can be downloaded from http://technet.oracle.com.

In this section we will go through the step-by-step installation of version 1.0.2.1 on Windows NT, followed by installation of the 1.0.2.2 patch. We will run Portal-to-Go using the Apache web server and JServ as the Servlet Container. Apache can be downloaded from http://www.apache.org, and JServ can be downloaded from http://java.apache.org. Note that if you are installing Portal-to-Go on an existing iAS platform, you will be able to use the Apache web server that is part of Oracle HTTP Server.

The installation of Portal-to-Go can be divided into the following main steps:

- ❏ Installing Portal-to-Go Binaries
- ❏ Creating and Populating Portal-to-Go Repository
- ❏ Configuring Apache and JServ
- ❏ Configuring Web Integration Developer and Web Integration Server
- ❏ Applying the 1.0.2.2 patch

We will cover each of these steps in detail in the following subsections. Before starting the installation of Portal-to-Go, install apache version 1.3.9 or later and JServ 1.1 (refer to the documentation that comes along with the Apache/JServ distribution or to a book such as *Professional Apache*, published by Wrox Press ISBN 1-861003-02-1.

Installing Portal-to-Go Binaries

In this section we will install the Portal-to-Go distribution using the Oracle Universal Installer.

1. Unzip the downloaded Portal-to-Go version 1.0.2.1 distribution file (`ptg10210_exp.zip`) in a temporary directory (`C:\temp\Portal-to-Go`).

2. Go to the temporary directory where the `Zip` file is extracted and run `setup.exe`. This will launch the Oracle Universal Installer.

3. Click the Next button in the Oracle Universal Installer's main Welcome window.

4. Enter the name and path of an Oracle home directory, or create a new Oracle home directory, and click on the Next button. Portal-to-Go binaries will be installed in the specified path. Do not change the entry of the Source Path field.

5. Select the Portal-to-Go server as the Product to Install and click on the Next button.

6. In the Installation Types window, select Typical Installation, and click on the Next button.

7. In the Portal-to-Go Repository Information window, enter the details of the database where the Portal-to-Go repository will be installed. In the Host Name field enter the name of the machine where the Oracle database is running; in the Port field enter the network port on which the listener listens for the SQLNet requests; in the SID field enter the System Identifier of the database. After entering the values for all the fields click on the Next button.

8. In the Portal-to-Go Schema Information window enter the name and password of the database user, used by the Portal-to-Go to connect to the repository. This user should not exist in the database.

9. In the Enter the System Password window, enter the password of the database user SYSTEM, and click on the Next button. This is used by the Oracle Universal Installer to create the database user and schema for the Portal-to-Go repository.

10. In the Repository Configuration window select No, and click on the Next button.

11. In the Repository Loading Information window click on the Next button.

12. In the Summary window click on the Next button. Now the installer will install Portal-to-Go binaries in the specified Oracle home directory.

13. Once the installation is complete, click on the Next Install button to install Portal-to-Go client. Select the Typical installation as the Installation Type for the Portal-to-Go client.

Creating and Populating Portal-to-Go Repository

The Oracle Universal Installer has an option of creating and populating the Repository automatically (Step 10 of *"Installing Portal-to-Go Binaries"*). This option requires the Oracle database client installation (SQL*Plus and other related tools) to be on the machine where Portal-to-Go is installed, which may not always be the case. Instead, we decided to create and load the repository manually.

The following steps are involved in creating and loading the Portal-to-Go repository:

1. Start SQL*Plus from any machine where an Oracle database client is installed.

2. Connect to the Portal-to-Go repository database as user SYSTEM.

3. Execute create_aq_user.sql script to create Portal-to-Go database user; this script in present in <ORACLE_HOME>panama\sql directory. The arguments to the script are the database user name and the password used by Portal-to-Go to connect to the Repository. Note that the user name and the password should be same as specified in Step 8 of *"Installing Portal-to-Go binaries"*:

```
sqlplus> @d:\Portal-to-Go\panama\sql\create_aq_user.sql PTG_USER welcome
```

4. Connect as the Portal-to-Go database user:

```
sqlplus> connect PTG_USER@ptgserver/welcome
```

5. Execute create_all.sql script. This script creates the schema for the Portal-to-Go repository:

```
sqlplus> @d:\Portal-to-Go\panama\sql\create_all.sql
```

6. Load the repository by running upload.bat script from the command line:

```
d:\Portal-to-Go\panama\sample> upload.bat bootstrap.xml
```

This will load the repository with all the adapters shipped with the current version, and will create a Portal-to-Go user Administrator with password manager. More users, adapters, and services can later be added to the repository using the Service Designer tool.

Configuring Apache and JServ

The next step of installation is to run Portal-to-Go on Apache and JServ. Here we will be changing the configuration files of Apache and JServ.

Changes to the Apache Configuration File (httpd.conf)

1. Create an alias for accessing the personalization portal, which is implemented as a set of JSP files. We create an alias so that these JSP files can be accessed from Apache. Add the following line at the end of the Alias section in the `httpd.conf` file:

```
Alias /papz D:\Portal-to-Go\panama\server\papz/
```

2. On Solaris, please make sure that the `papz` directory is readable by the user on whose context the Apache server runs. On Windows, note the trailing /.

3. Include JServ's main configuration file (`JServ.conf`) at the end of the `httpd.conf` file, so that JServ gets automatically started when Apache server is started:

```
Include d:\apache\JServ1.1\conf\JServ.conf
```

Changes to JServ's configuration file (JServ.conf)

1. Map `*.jsp` to `oracle.jsp.JspServlet`, in order to allow Oracle's JServ engine to handle all the JSP pages:

```
ApJServAction .jsp /servlets/oracle.jsp.JspServlet
ApJServAction .sqljsp /servlets/oracle.jsp.JspServlet
```

2. Create a servlet mount point called p2g. This will allow the Portal-to-Go Request Manager interface to be accessed as http://hostname/p2g/rm. You can also access servlets from the /servlet/rm mount point:

```
ApJServMount /p2g /root
```

Changes to JServ's properties file (JServ.properties)

Add all the JAR files required by the Portal-to-Go in the classpath of JServ. Apart from the libraries shipped with the Portal-to-Go distribution, Portal-to-Go requires Java Servlet Library (`jsdk.jar`), and the `tools.jar` library, which is shipped with JDK1.2.2. These libraries can be downloaded from http://java.sun.com:

```
wrapper.classpath=D:\jsdk2.0\lib\jsdk.jar
wrapper.classpath=D:\jdk1.2.2\lib\tools.jar
wrapper.classpath=D:\Portal-to-Go\panama\lib\panama\server\classes
wrapper.classpath=D:\Portal-to-Go\panama\lib\panama_core.zip
wrapper.classpath=D:\Portal-to-Go\panama\lib\panama_papz.zip
wrapper.classpath=D:\Portal-to-Go\panama\lib\classes111.zip
wrapper.classpath=D:\Portal-to-Go\panama\lib\ojsp.jar
wrapper.classpath=D:\Portal-to-Go\panama\lib\servlet.jar
wrapper.classpath=D:\Portal-to-Go\panama\lib\jndi.jar
wrapper.classpath=D:\Portal-to-Go\panama\lib\xmlparserv2.jar
wrapper.classpath=D:\Portal-to-Go\panama\lib\client.zip
wrapper.classpath D:\Portal-to-Go\panama\lib\server.zip
```

Changes to zone.properties

We carry out the following tasks on the `jserv.properties` file:

1. Include the Personalization Portal's JSP files in the list of repositories:

    ```
    repositories=D:\apache\JServ1.1\servlets,D:\Portal-to-Go\panama\server\papz
    ```

    Note the directory should correspond to the one in which you install Portal-to-Go.

2. Specify that the JServ should load the servlet `oracle.panama.ParmImpl` on startup:

    ```
    servlets.startup=oracle.panama.ParmImpl
    ```

3. Create a servlet alias for the Request Manager:

    ```
    servlet.rm.code=oracle.panama.ParmImpl
    ```

Configuring Web Integration Developer and Web Integration Server

If the machine on which the Portal-to-Go server is running is inside a firewall, then we will have to configure the proxy settings in the Web Integration Developer and the Web Integration Server, so that they can access web sites outside the firewall.

Configuring Web Integration Developer

1. Run the Web Integration Developer. On Windows this can be accessed from Start | Oracle for NT | Portal-to-Go menu.

2. In the main window of the Web Integration Developer, from the Edit menu, select Preferences and then Configuration.

3. Enter the Proxy (HTTP) and the Secure Proxy (HTTPS) settings for your computer (hint: check what's in your IE or Netscape connection/LAN settings).

4. Click on the OK button.

Configuring Web Integration Server

1. Run the Web Integration Server. This is done by running the `server.bat` script in the `WebIntegration\Server\bin` directory. (On installation it may be set up as an NT service.)

    ```
    D:\Portal-to-Go\panama\WebIntegration\Server\bin> server
    ```

2. From the browser go to http://hostname:5555.

3. Log in to the web integration server as user `Administrator`. The default password for the user `Administrator` is manage. (Yes, you need to remember to use manager and manage in different contexts!)

4. Click on the Settings link; this will show the default settings of the Web Integration Server

5. Click on the Edit button.

6. Enter the Proxy (HTTP) and the Secure Proxy (HTTPS) settings.

7. Click on the Submit button.

Testing the Installation

After carrying out the above steps, test whether all of the components are installed correctly. If any of these tests fail then do check if all the steps were done as described. Check Apache is starting correctly (look in `Apache\Apache\logs\error_log`), and check that your database connection to the repository is OK – these services use the installed repository for initialization.

Testing the Personalization Portal

From your browser navigate to http://hostname/papz/login.jsp. The login page should appear. You can log in under the user name of `Administrator` with the password manager.

Testing the Request Manager Interface (oracle.panama.ParmImpl)

From your browser, navigate to http://hostname/servlet/rm. The login page should appear. You can log on as user `Administrator`.

Testing the Service Designer

Run the Service Designer. In the login window enter the host name of the machine on which the Portal-to-Go server is running in the location field, `Administrator` in the username field, manager in the password field, and click on the OK button. The main window of the Service Designer should appear after logging in.

Applying 1.0.2.2 patch

This patch contains performance improvements such as connection pooling, XML transformer pooling, and bug fixes. In order to apply the patch, follow the following steps:

1. Download `ptg10210_exp.zip` from the Portal-to-Go area at Oracle Technology Network (http://technet.oracle.com) web site.

2. Extract the ZIP file in a temporary directory.

3. Go to the temporary directory.

4. Set the environment variable `ORACLE_HOME` to point to the `ORACLE_HOME` path used while installing the binaries.

5. Run the `client.bat` script for upgrading the client distribution.

6. Run `server.bat` script for upgrading the server distribution.

The distribution of Portal-to-Go comes with the following documentation (see `panama\doc` directory):

❑ **Installation Guide** – instructions for installing Portal-to-Go.

❑ **Implementation Guide** – describes Portal-to-Go Concepts.

❑ **API Specification** – Java Documentation for the public API's of Portal-to-Go. The Portal-to-Go system can be extended using these API's.

Changing the Default Configuration of Portal-to-Go

Portal-to-Go is installed with the default configuration, which might not be suitable for all deployment scenarios. The default configuration can be changed by modifying the `system.properties` file in the `panama\server\classes\oracle\panama\core\admin` directory. All valid parameters of the `system.properties` file are explained in the Implementation Guide. In this section we will cover few of the most important parameters.

Portal-to-Go Repository-related Parameters

db.connect.string

This is the database connect string, used by the JDBC driver to connect to the database:

```
db.connect.string=PTG_USER/welcome@hrawat-sun.us.oracle.com:1521:hrawat
```

db.driver

This specifies the JDBC driver used by the Portal-to-Go to connect to the repository. By default Oracle's thin driver is used; in the final deployment you should consider using OCI8 driver for performance reasons:

```
db.driver=THIN
```

db.session.min

This specifies the number of database sessions kept open by Portal-to-Go. In real deployment, where a large number of users are accessing Portal-to-Go, one should keep the value of this parameter high:

```
db.session.min=1
```

Session-related Parameters

session.expiration.time

This specifies the number of seconds, after which an inactive session is destroyed:

```
session.expiration.time=600
```

session.expiration.checkinterval

This specifies the interval (in seconds) at which the monitor thread checks for inactive sessions:

```
session.expiration.checkinterval=60
```

Logging-related Parameters

log.level

This specifies which levels of messages will be logged:

```
log.level=Warning, Error, Notify
```

log.directory

This specifies the directory where the log file is maintained:

```
log.directory=C:\temp
```

log.file.name

This specifies the name of the log file:

```
log.file.name=sys_panama.log
```

Designing a Web Integration Service

In this section we will design a service using the Portal-to-Go server and related tools. The service to be designed is based on the Web Integration adapter. For this reason, we need to do the following to get the service up and running:

❑   Use the Web Integration Developer to create the Web Integration Definition Language (WIDL) interface.

❑   Publish the interface to the Web Integration server.

❑   If necessary, create users and groups.

❑   Create the service using the Service Designer, specifying the same interface.

❑   Publish the service to the Portal-to-Go server.

The service that we will create takes an input of a Zip Code and returns some information about today's weather. We shall connect to Yahoo's weather web site at http://weather.yahoo.com to retrieve the actual information.

Creating the WIDL Interface

To create the WIDL interface, we launch the Web Integration Developer. Usually this will be accomplished by running the batch script `developer.bat` found in the `panamaWebIntegration\server\bin` directory. Alternatively, follow Start | Oracle for NT | Portal-to-Go. The script has the necessary classpath information set up, although if the standard class libraries are in a different directory, we might have to set the classpath by hand.

We will extract our web content from a weather information provider. One drawback of this approach is that we cannot guarantee the consistency of results from such a web site, even on consecutive visits. However, it will be fun, and will illustrate the techniques and tools that we describe in this chapter. From the File menu, select Open URL and enter the URL http://weather.yahoo.com.

Close the cookie dialog that follows. The cookie dialog box shows the cookies, which are set by the URL. This is of no concern to us, because the Web Integration Server takes care of storing and sending the cookies. Now the Web Integration Developer retrieves the content from the site and parses it and organizes into simple elements, from which we could choose the elements of interest to us and discard the rest. The form shown below appears:

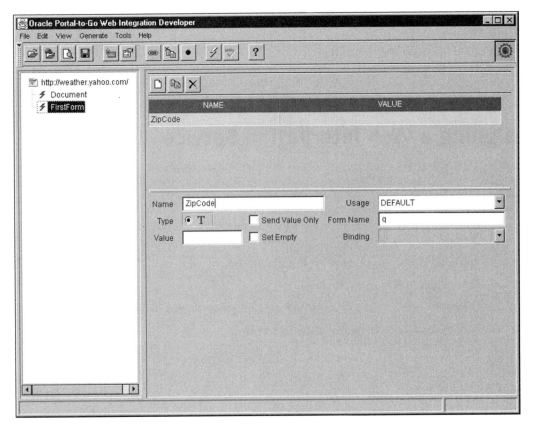

Highlight `FirstForm` in the left panel. Each HTML form element in the original HTML documentation has a representation in the Web Integration Server (WIS) parsed schema. Change the name of the variable by modifying the text area labeled Name in the bottom half of the screen. Change the name from q to `ZipCode` and hit *return*.

Next, choose **Generate** and select **WIDL**. Specify the name of the interface as `TodaysWeather` and the Query as `WeatherQuery`. Now enter a valid Zip Code in the consequent dialog box and submit. This causes the WIS developer to contact the actual web site to get a response for that particular Zip Code. It then parses the output and builds its structure of elements. From this we need to choose the output elements of interest to us and discard the rest.

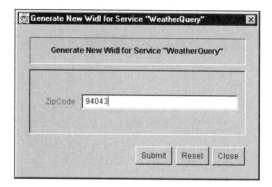

Open the **Bindings** node of the tree on the left panel and highlight **WeatherQueryInput**. This is the part of the interface that contains the elements corresponding to the HTML page that a conventional browser would have received on fetching the URL http://weather.yahoo.com. We need to make no modifications here, since we already have the variable with the right name: **ZipCode**. We can delete all other variables: if any other variables appear in the upper table, select them then hit the delete key.

Next, highlight **WeatherQueryOutput** on the left pane and scroll down the list of variables until you reach **table6** (this may vary as the original site changes). Highlight this and in the bottom half, click on the **Sample** tab and choose the element corresponding to row number 2 and column number 2 (again, this might vary if the site changes overnight). Right-click and select **Create new variable from session** and name it `Weather`.

We can now delete all other variables. Select all rows, other than the `Weather` row just created, and delete them.

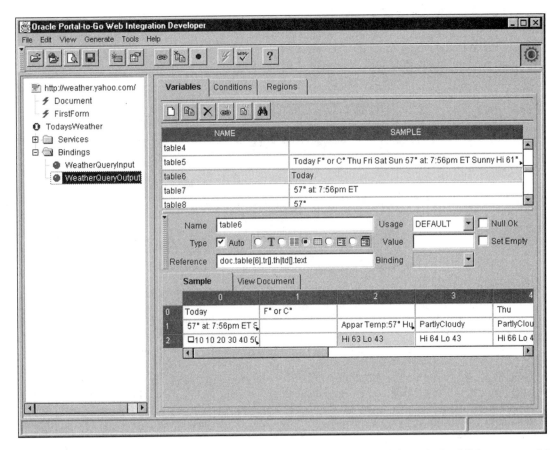

From the File menu, choose Publishing and then select Publish Interface. Specify the full hostname of the Web Integration server with the port name, for instance localhost:5555. Port 5555 is the default port for the Web Integration Server. Let the package choice on this dialog box remain as default. Again enter the name of the server in the next dialog box. You need to have a user name (usually Administrator) and a password (default manage) to publish interfaces on the Web Integration server.

Creating User Accounts

If you do not have a user account to test out the new service, now is a good time to create one. For this you need to start the Service Designer, which can be invoked by the batch script run.bat found in \panama\ServiceDesigner (on NT you should have it in the Start | Oracle for NT | Portal-to-Go folder). In order to create new accounts, the Service Designer needs to connect to the Portal-to-Go server as Administrator (default password manager).

Before you create the user's root folder, create a root folder that will hold all the root folders of all users. For this purpose, expand the Services tree in the left panel of the service designer, right-click, choose Create New Folder, and complete the form. In the Name field, enter Users Folders then select Valid and Visible to ensure that the object created is valid and is visible to other objects that might access it.

The next step is to create a group (if you don't have any at present). Click on the Group folder on the object tree on the left panel, right-click, and select Create New Group. In the form that follows, name it WeatherGroup and click Finish. We need not bother about the other fields on the right panel for now.

Finally, to create the user and user's root folder, highlight the user branch on the object tree and right-click to select **Create New User**. In the form that follows, enter appropriate values for **Name**, **Display Name**, **Password**, and **Password Hint**. Browse the **User Root Parent** field and choose **Users Folders**. Choose WeatherGroup for the **Group** section, select the **Enabled** and **Anonymous** (default options for standard users), and click **Finish**:

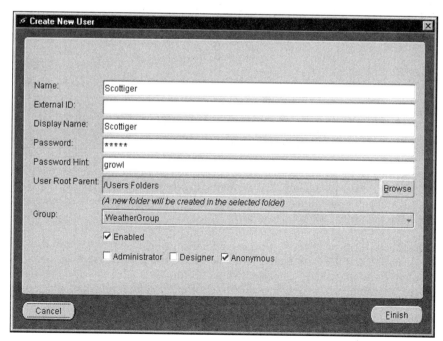

Creating the Service

Now, we need to create the actual service. First we create a master service, then we create a folder in the services tree and, in this folder, we create an alias to the actual service. Finally, so that the service is accessible to the user, this folder is made accessible to the group we just created and thereby to our user, who is a member of the group.

To create a master service, highlight the Master Services branch of the object tree in the left panel and choose Create New Master Service. In the following form, choose a name for the service (we've used WeatherInfo here). Choose WebIntegrationAdapter to be the adapter for this service. Let the owner remain as Administrator. As always, check the Valid and Visible boxes. If you desire, add additional information in the Description box and click Finish:

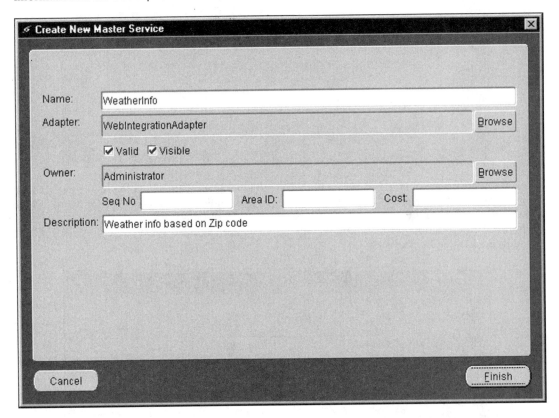

Now that the Service Designer knows that the service is a Web Integration server based service, it needs to be informed of the other parameters that are particular to this adapter type. For this, click the Init Parameters tab and enter the full machine name of the server running the Web Integration server, and specify the port in the format *machine_name:port*.

Enter the Interface as TodaysWeather (this is the interface name we published to the Web Integration server). Leave the WIDL_FILE field blank. When you click Apply, the Service Designer populates the Input and Output Parameters tabs. Choose the Input Parameters tab and select the ZipCode variable to be User Customizable. You may ignore the Output Parameters in this particular case.

Now we need to create a folder and an alias for it, pointing to the service we just created. So, right-click on the Services tree, choose Create New Folder and complete the form as before, using the name WeatherFolder (or perhaps something less drab!).

Now right-click the newly created folder and choose Create New Alias. Name the alias MyWeatherService. At the Services item choose WeatherInfo. The defaults work fine for the rest of the items on this form. Remember to select Visible and Valid, and then click Finish:

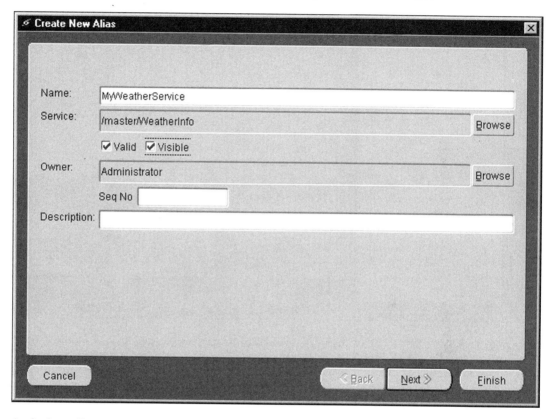

At the Input Parameters tab on the same screen, select the variable ZipCode to be User Customizable and then click Apply.

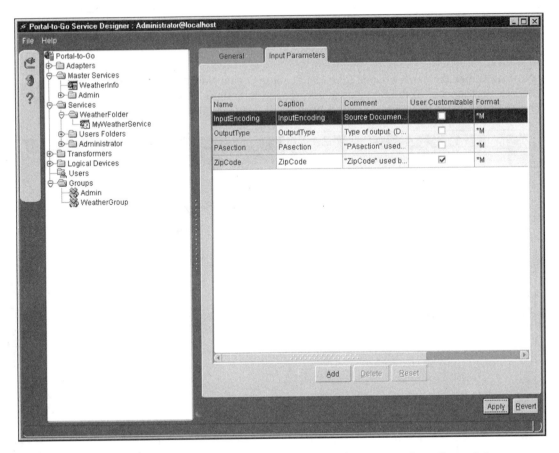

We now have a user belonging to a new group, a newly created service, and an alias to it in a new folder. The last thing to do is to make the service available to the new group, WeatherGroup, and thereby to its member Scottiger, who ultimately is the user. We start by expanding the Group part of the object tree and clicking WeatherGroup. Click the Service Folders tab on the right panel to display the Service Folders panel, which actually comprises two frames, Service Folders and Selected Service Folders. We expand the Services Folder under the Service Folders frame. We click on WeatherFolder, and then on the right arrow to move it into the Selected Service Folders frame. We click Apply for the changes to be effective, thus completing the service deployment.

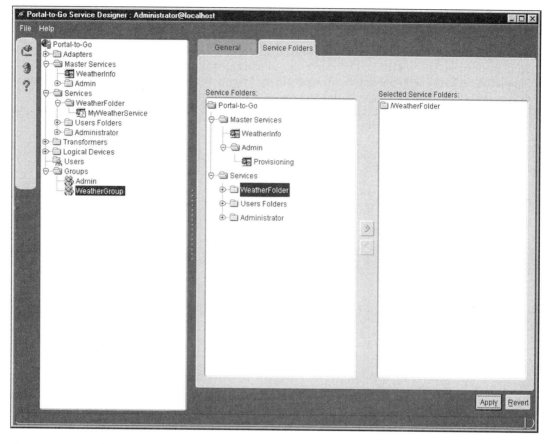

One way to test the new service is to use the URL http://hostname/servlet/rm. This page authenticates the user and simulates a device portal. However to see a simulation on a mobile phone emulator, you could download the UP SDK from Phone.com. See below for how this service appears on a mobile phone after the login phase:

If we connect successfully, we should see something like the following:

Please visit http://developer.phone.com for installation details of this emulator.

Portal-to-Go SimpleResult XML

One of the main features of Portal-to-Go is that it allows end users to access the same applications across multiple devices. This is achieved by converting all the content retrieved by the adapters into SimpleResult XML, and applying device-specific stylesheets to convert the SimpleResult XML to the device-specific markup language. In this section we will briefly look at the SimpleResult DTD. Understanding SimpleResult DTD will be important for people who wish to write their own adapters, modify existing transformers or write new transformers.

The following diagram will remind us of the transformation stages between the content source (say a weather report web page) and the device specific output language (say WML):

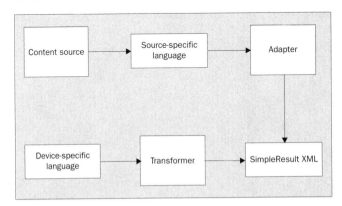

The way the adapter works is that it retrieves content from the outside source – database, web, or other network resource – and converts it into SimpleResult XML. Depending on the device type, the Portal-to-Go system applies the appropriate stylesheet to convert SimpleResult XML to the device-specific markup language. The return value of the invoke() method of the adapter is an XML ELEMENT, conforming to the SimpleResult DTD. All the Transformers (XSL stylesheets) are written against SimpleResult DTD. So adapter and transformer writers should understand SimpleResult XML.

> *Please refer to Appendix C and Chapter 21 for more information regarding on XML, DTD, and ELEMENT.*

The SimpleResult DTD defines the elements for displaying text, menus, forms, and tables. In the next section we will cover all the elements defined in SimpleResult XML. The full reference is the *Portal-to-Go Implementation guide*, Revision 1.0.2.

SimpleResult

SimpleResult is the root element of SimpleResult XML documents and contains one or more SimpleContainer elements.

Name	Optional	Description
name	yes	The name of the element
title	yes	The title of the element
link	yes	A link for this element

SimpleContainer

The SimpleContainer element is the logical container for one or more elements. It contains one or more SimpleText, SimpleForm, SimpleMenu, or SimpleTable elements.

Name	Optional	Description
name	yes	The name of the element
title	yes	The title of the element
link	yes	A link for this element

SimpleText

The SimpleText element contains one or more blocks of plain text. It contains one or more SimpleTextItem.

Name	Optional	Description
name	yes	The name of the element
title	yes	The title of the element
link	yes	A link for this element

SimpleTextItem

The SimpleText Item represents a block of plain text.

Name	Optional	Description
name	yes	The name of the element
title	yes	The title of the element
link	yes	A link for this element

The following SimpleResult XML document generates the text Sun Nov 19 08:22:28 GMT 2000:

```
<SimpleResult name="Time Service">
    <SimpleContainer name="Time Service">
        <SimpleText>
            <SimpleTextItem name="Time">
                Sun Nov 19 08:22:28 GMT 2000
            </SimpleTextItem>
        </SimpleText>
    </SimpleContainer>
</SimpleResult>
```

SimpleMenu

The `SimpleMenu` element represents a simple menu with selectable menu items. It contains one or more `SimpleMenuItem`.

Name	Optional	Description
name	Yes	The name of the element
title	Yes	The title of the element
link	Yes	A link for this element

SimpleMenuItem

The `SimpleMenuItem` element represents a single, selectable option in a menu.

Name	Optional	Description
name	Yes	The name of the element
title	Yes	The title of the element
link	Yes	A link for this element
target	No	The link target for this item.
section	Yes	Used by the Web Integration Adapter
separator	Yes	Whether a separator should precede or follow the menu item; possible values are "before", "after", "none"

SimpleForm

The `SimpleForm` element contains one or more form input fields.

Name	Optional	Description
name	Yes	The name of the element
title	Yes	The title of the element
link	Yes	A link for this element
target	No	The link target for this item
section	Yes	Used by the Web Integration Adapter

SimpleFormItem

The SimpleFormItem element is a single input item in a form. The content of this element, which is in parsable character format, specifies default values for the form item.

Name	Optional	Description
name	Yes	The name of the element
title	Yes	The title of the element
link	Yes	A link for this element
default	Yes	Provides a default value for the field
mandatory	Yes	Indicates whether the item is mandatory; possible values are "yes", "no"; the default value is "no"
maxlength	Yes	Specifies the maximum input length

SimpleFormSelect

The SimpleFormSelect element is a selectable option menu in a form. The content of this element, which is in parsable character format, specifies default values for the form item.

Name	Optional	Description
name	Yes	The name of the element
title	Yes	The title of the element
link	Yes	A link for this element

SimpleFormOption

The SimpleFormOption element is an item in a selectable option menu. The content of this element, which is in parsable character format, specifies default values for the form item.

Name	Optional	Description
name	Yes	The name of the element
title	Yes	The title of the element
link	Yes	A link for this element
value	No	The value assigned to the name variable when the option is selected

The following `SimpleResult` XML document, generates a form with one input item, TIME_ZONE:

```
<SimpleResult name="Time Service">
   <SimpleContainer name="Time Service">
      <SimpleForm name="inputs" target="rm?PAoid=243">
         <SimpleFormItem name="TIME_ZONE"
        title="Enter the TIME_ZONE">Enter the TIME_ZONE" />
      </SimpleForm>
   </SimpleContainer>
</SimpleResult>
```

SimpleTable

The `SimpleTable` represents tabular data. It contains an optional `SimpleTableHeader` and a `SimpleTableBody` element

Name	Optional	Description
name	Yes	The name of the element
title	Yes	The title of the element
link	Yes	A link for this element

SimpleTableHeader

The `SimpleTableHeader` element represents column headings. It contains one or more `SimpleCol` element.

Name	Optional	Description
name	Yes	The name of the element
title	Yes	The title of the element
link	Yes	A link for this element

SimpleTableBody

The `SimpleTableBody` element contains the actual tabular data. It contains one or more `SimpleRow` elements.

Name	Optional	Description
name	Yes	The name of the element
title	Yes	The title of the element
link	Yes	A link for this element

SimpleRow

The `SimpleRow` element represents a single row of data. It contains one or more `SimpleCol` elements.

Name	Optional	Description
name	Yes	The name of the element
title	Yes	The title of the element
link	Yes	A link for this element

SimpleCol

The `SimpleCol` element represents a single table cell. It stores a single value for a table cell.

Name	Optional	Description
name	Yes	The name of the element
title	Yes	The title of the element
link	Yes	A link for this element

Simple but Powerful

The combination of an adapter/transformer mechanism is the key to the fact that Portal-to-Go is able to aggregate content from various sources and cater to different client devices. Summarizing the process: the adapters and transformers are the converters, the data itself that is converted is first pulled in from a content source by the adapter, which represents it in SimpleResult XML. The SimpleResult XML serves as input for the transformers, which convert it into device-specific markup languages. As we have indicated, it is possible to write custom adapters to extend the functionality of the ready-made adapters shipped with Portal-to-Go. In the next section we will write two different adapters.

Writing Your Own Adapter

The current version of Portal-to-Go is shipped with pre-built adapters, which can be used to access content from a variety of content sources such as a web site or database. These are good enough for developing most of the wireless applications. However, you may want to develop applications that retrieve content from a custom data source, or data sources like LDAP, or e-mail (IMAP/ POP3) that are not supported in the current release.

To access these data sources, a custom adapter can be implemented and added to the Portal-to-Go repository, and services can be built using the newly added custom adapter. Portal-to-Go supports several API's (refer of the *API Specification* documentation) through which end users can implement their own adapters and add them to the Portal-to-Go System.

All the Portal-to-Go adapters implement the `oracle.panama.Adapter` interface. Like the `javax.servlet.Servlet` interface for servlets, the Portal-to-Go `Adapter` interface contains methods for initializing and invoking the adapter. It contains additional methods for describing the adapter – the `init` arguments required for initializing the adapter, the `input` arguments required for invoking the adapter, and the `output` arguments generated by the adapter. Tools such as the Service Designer use these methods.

Let's look at the methods of the `Adapter` interface:

- ❑ `AdapterDefinition getAdapterDefinition()` This method returns the definition of `init`, `input`, and `output` arguments as an `AdapterDefinition` object

- ❑ `AdapterDefinition getInitDefinition()` This method returns the definition of `init` arguments

- ❑ `void init(Arguments args)` Initializes the adapter with supplied arguments

This last method is called once, when the adapter is loaded by the Portal-to-Go run time system. The adapter implementation should allocate all the resources, which can be used by the adapter across invocations, in this method. The argument `args` contains the values for the `init` arguments.

- ❑ `org.w3c.dom.Element invoke(ServiceRequest serviceReq)` This method is called by the Portal-to-Go runtime system, whenever the Portal-to-Go run time system receives a request for any master service based on this adapter. The `serviceReq` method argument, contains the values for `input` arguments. The invoke method returns the content as an XML document (conforming to the SimpleResult DTD).

A typical sequence in which these methods are called in run time is as follows:

1. Construct the adapter.

2. Initialize the adapter: call `init()` method. The arguments passed to the `init()` method are picked from the master service, which points to this adapter. These arguments are stored in the repository when the master service is created in the Service Designer.

3. Call `invoke()`.

Let's implement a simple time adapter, which takes a local time zone string identifier, such as "PST", "America/Los_Angeles" or "GMT -8:00", as an argument and returns the local time of that zone.

Let's look at the implementation of the adapter:

```
package oracle.panama.adapter;

import java.util.Date;
import java.util.Calendar;
import java.util.TimeZone;

import org.w3c.dom.Element;
import org.w3c.dom.Document;

import oracle.panama.Argument;
import oracle.panama.InputArgument;
import oracle.panama.ArgumentType;
import oracle.panama.Arguments;
import oracle.panama.ServiceRequest;
import oracle.panama.PAPrimitive;
```

```
import oracle.panama.adapter.Adapter;
import oracle.panama.adapter.AdapterHelper;
import oracle.panama.adapter.AdapterDefinition;
import oracle.panama.adapter.AdapterException;
public class TimeAdapter implements Adapter {
   private final String TIME_ZONE = "TIME_ZONE";
   private AdapterDefinition initDef;
   private AdapterDefinition adpDef;
   private boolean initialized;

   public AdapterDefinition getAdapterDefinition() {
```

If the adapter definition is not created then create it using the `AdapterHelper` class. The adapter has only one input argument, `TIME_ZONE`:

```
   if (adpDef == null) {
     synchronized(this) {
       if (adpDef == null) {
         adpDef = getInitDefinition();
```

Add the definition of the argument to the adapter definition:

```
         InputArgument arg = adpDef.createInput(ArgumentType.SINGLE_LINE,
           TIME_ZONE, "Time Zone of the place", null);
       }
     }
   }
   return adpDef;
}

   public AdapterDefinition getInitDefinition() {
```

If the `init` definition of the adapter is not created, then create it now. There are no initialization arguments for this adapter:

```
   if (initDef == null) {
     synchronized(this) {
       if (initDef == null) {
         initDef = AdapterHelper.createAdapterDefinition();
       }
     }
   }
   return initDef;
}

   public void init(Arguments args) {
```

Set the initialized flag to `true`:

```
     initialized = true;
   }

   public Element invoke(ServiceRequest serviceReq) throws AdapterException{
```

If the adapter is not initialized then throw an `AdapterException`:

```
if (!initialized) {
   throw new AdapterException("Adapter is not initialized");
}
```

Get the `Document` object from the `ServiceRequest`:

```
Document doc = serviceReq.getOwnerDocument();
```

Create a `SimpleResult` element, and add a container to it. The helper class `PAPrimitive` contains methods for creating XML elements defined in the `SimpleResult` DTD:

```
Element simpleResult = PAPrimitive.createSimpleResult(doc, "Time Service");
Element simpleContainer = PAPrimitive.createSimpleContainer(doc,
   "TimeService");
simpleResult.appendChild(simpleContainer);
```

Get the value of the input argument `TIME_ZONE`:

```
String timeZoneStr = null;
Argument arg = serviceReq.getArguments().getArgument(TIME_ZONE);
if (arg != null) {
   timeZoneStr = arg.getValue();
}
```

If the value of the input argument `TIME_ZONE` is `null`, then generate a form with `TIME_ZONE` as an input field. And add the form to the `simpleContainer` element.

```
if (timeZoneStr == null) {
```

Note that the action of the form should again point to the same adapter. You can do this using `getURLPAoidParameter` of the `AdapterHelper` class. The `getURLPAoidParameter` method generates a URL pointing to the same Service:

```
Element simpleForm = PAPrimitive.createSimpleForm(doc, "inputs",
AdapterHelper.getURLPAoidParameter(serviceReq.getArguments()));
simpleContainer.appendChild(simpleForm);
String formInputs[] = {TIME_ZONE};
AdapterHelper.createInputFields(simpleForm, formInputs,
   serviceReq.getArguments());
} else {
```

Get the local time:

```
TimeZone localTimeZone = TimeZone.getDefault();
TimeZone timeZone = TimeZone.getTimeZone(timeZoneStr);
TimeZone.setDefault(timeZone);
Calendar calendar = Calendar.getInstance();
calendar.getInstance(timeZone);
Date date = calendar.getTime();
String dateValue = date.toString();
TimeZone.setDefault(localTimeZone);
```

Create a `simpleText` item element containing the local time, and add the simple text to the `simpleContainer`:

```
Element simpleText = PAPrimitive.createSimpleText(doc);
Element simpleTextItem = PAPrimitive.createSimpleTextItem(doc,
  "Time", dateValue);
simpleText.appendChild(simpleText);
simpleContainer.appendChild(simpleText);
    }
```

Return the `simpleResult`:

```
    return simpleResult;
    }
  }
```

The adapter class file should be placed such that it is in the classpath of the JServ process (`wrapper.classpath` parameter of the `jserv.properties` file). We will place the class file of the adapter in `<ORACLE_HOME>\panama\server\classes\oracle\panama\adapter`.

The implemented adapter can be added to the Portal-to-Go repository using Service Designer tool. Start the Service Designer and Log in as user `Administrator`/`manager`. In the main view of the Service Designer right-click on the **Adapter** link, and select **Create New Adapter**. In the **Create New Adapter** pop-up window enter the name and the class of the new adapter, check the **Valid** checkbox, and click on the **Finish** button. This will add the information about the adapter in the Portal-to-Go repository:

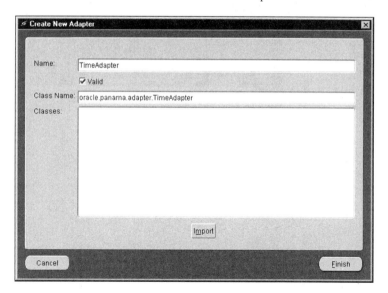

Now we can create services based on this adapter. First we need to create a Master Service. Again, Service Designer can be used to create Master Services. In the main view of the Service Designer right-click on the **Master Services** link, and select **Create New Master Service** option. In the **Create New Master Service** window, enter the name of the Master Service, select the newly created **TimeAdapter** as **Adapter**, check the **Valid** and **Visible** check boxes, and click on the Finish button.

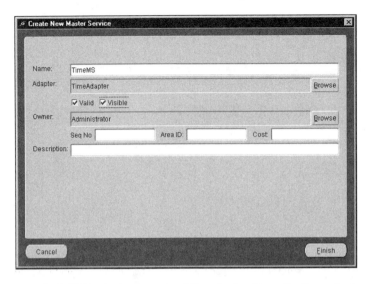

Now we need to enter the initialization arguments of the adapter. Since the time adapter doesn't have any initialization parameters, we don't have to enter the values for the arguments. Click on the Input Parameters tab. This will show all the input arguments for the adapter. Make the TIME_ZONE input argument User Customizable by checking the User Customizable check box, and clicking on the Apply button:

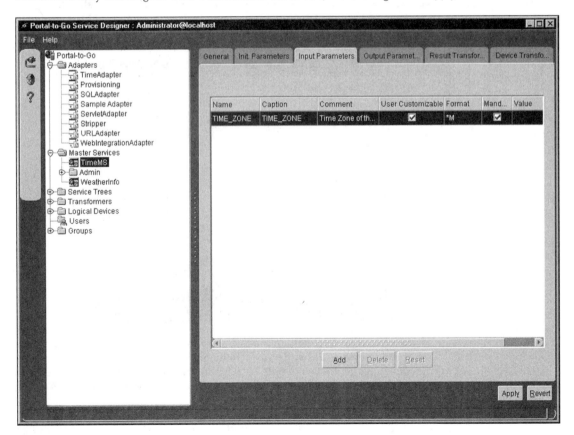

Now let's create the Aliases to the Master Service, so that it can be accessed by the Portal-to-Go user. Let's use the `Scottiger` user from the weather example, whose root folder is `/Users Folders/Scottiger`. Right-click on the Users folder, and select the Create New Alias link. In this window, enter the name of the Alias, select the newly created master service as Service, check the Valid and Visible check boxes, and click on Finish. Now the user `Scottiger` can access this Service from his root folder.

Create New Alias		
Name:	TimeService	
Service:	/master/TimeMS	Browse
	☑ Valid ☑ Visible	
Owner:	Administrator	Browse
	Seq No	
Description:		

Cancel   Back   Next »   Finish

The following screenshots show the Service Screens when accessed from the Phone.com Simulator. The first screenshot shows the main menu of the Service where the user enters the time zone:

This screenshot shows the local time at the specified time zone:

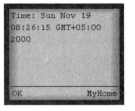

When invoking the `TimeService` from the phone, the user enters the `TIME_ZONE` string in the Input Form. Entering data into an actual phone is not a very pleasant experience. Portal-to-Go supports mechanisms by which the value of input arguments of a Service can be stored in the repository, and can be picked-up by the service whenever it gets invoked. Let's assume that Scottiger checks the local time in India (GMT +5.5) very frequently from his phone. To save him from typing the `TIME_ZONE` string every time he invokes the service, we can create an India Time service for him.

To create an India Time service, first create an alias, specifying **TimeMS** as the Master Service. In the **Input Parameters** tab of the **India Time** alias, enter the value of `TIME_ZONE` argument as GMT +5.5, and click on the **Apply** button. Now when the **India Time** service is invoked the Portal-to-Go runtime loads the input argument directly from the repository.

Input values for the services can also be configured using the Personalization portal.

Writing and Modifying Existing Stylesheets

The Portal-to-Go distribution comes with a default set of transformers, which are used to convert the SimpleResult XML document generated by the Adapter to device-specific markup languages (like WML). End users may want to modify existing transformers or add a new transformer for a logical device, or to change the look and feel of the content that is delivered through their wireless portal. For example, they may want to add their company Logo to the WML pages that are delivered from their portal. It is possible to modify existing transformers or to write a new transformer for a logical device, using the Service Designer tool.

Steps for modifying an existing transformer:

1. Start the Service Designer Tool.

2. Connect to the Portal-to-Go instance as user `Administrator`.

3. Expand the Transformers link.

4. Select the Transformer that you want to modify. Now the right portion of the screen shows the Stylesheet for the transformer.

5. Make changes to the Stylesheet in the editable text window; or you can import an XSL Stylesheet file, by clicking on the **Import** button

6. After making the modifications, click on the **Apply Button.**

Personalization Portal

Portal-to-Go is also shipped with a default implementation of the web-based personalization portal, which can be used by the portal users from their web browsers, to create services they want to access from their mobile devices. It can also be used to store frequently-used input parameters by creating Aliases.

The Personalization portal is implemented as a set of Java Server Pages (JSP) files, which interact with the Portal-to-Go Servlet. These JSP files can be modified to build a custom personalization portal.

To access the personalization portal, go to http://hostname/papz/login.jsp from your web browser. You can also drill into your `Scottiger` home directory here and access your services via a slightly flashier set of web pages than the request manager.

A Sample Phone Book Application with LDAP

Lets develop a real-life application using Portal-to-Go. Most organizations use some kind of directory services (mostly LDAP), to store information like e-mail ID, phone number etc., about employees. Employees within the organization access this information using some web-based application, which access the LDAP (Lightweight Directory Access Protocol) directory in the back end.

> *For more information on LDAP and programming for LDAP, please refer to* Implementing LDAP *by Mark Wilcox, Wrox Press ISBN 1-861002-21-1.*

It would be nice to have such an application available on mobile devices, so that employees can search phone numbers, e-mail addresses, and so on, while they are on the move. Portal-to-Go is an ideal choice for building such an application, because the same application can be made available to all the devices supported by Portal-to-Go. Support for new devices can be added very easily by defining new logical devices.

To deploy and test this sample application, you need to have a running LDAP server. There are several LDAP vendors offering several solutions and for our test purposes, we could use the OpenLDAP server available under open source at http://www.openldap.org. Of course, we need to have a working installation of Portal-to-Go, installed as described earlier. Next, we briefly describe the installation of the OpenLDAP Server

Installing OpenLDAP Server

A Unix/Linux distribution can be downloaded from http://www.openldap.org. Unpack the distribution and follow the install and make instructions. Then edit the following entries in the configuration file (usually /usr/local/etc/sldap.conf):

```
suffix "dc=wrox,dc=com"
rootdn "cn=Manager,dc=wrox,dc=com"
rootpw welcome
```

Start the Stand-alone LDAP Server (SLAPD). You will need to be logged in as root to start the server:

```
% /usr/local/libexec/slapd
```

Add the following entries, in the entries.ldif file, to the LDAP server:

```
ldapadd -x -D "cn=Manager,dc=wrox,dc=com" -W -f entries.ldif
```

It will ask for the password: enter welcome in the password prompt.

The LDIF File

Let's assume that the following employee information is stored in the LDAP server. The entries.ldif file describing the LDAP entries is given here:

```
dn: dc=wrox, dc=com
objectclass: dcObject
dc:wrox.com
```

```
dn: uid=cagarwal, dc=wrox, dc=com
uid: cagarwal
cn: Chacho
sn: Agarwal
mail: cagarwal@wrox.com
telephoneNumber: 101 650 8128
objectclass: inetOrgPerson
objectclass: dcObject
dc: wrox.com

dn: uid=cbeller, dc=wrox, dc=com
uid: cbeller
cn: Cathy
sn: Beller
mail: cbeller@wrox.com
telephoneNumber: 101 650 8129
objectclass: inetOrgPerson
objectclass: dcObject
dc: wrox.com
```

The application will require Portal-to-Go to retrieve information from the LDAP content source. Unfortunately, such support is not available in the current version (1.0.2.2) of Portal-to-Go LDAP based adapter. Therefore, we will have to write a custom adapter that retrieves information from a LDAP-based server. We will write the adapter in such a way that it can be deployed easily.

The application will allow users to search for employees, and also to see the details of the selected employees. Lets look at the screenshots to get a feel for the application.

This is the first screen of the application. Here the end user enters the search string, and clicks the OK button, which takes the user to the search results screen:

This screen displays the list of all the employees matching the search criteria. The user can select any entry from the list to get the details of that employee:

This screen shows the details of the selected employee:

Let's look at the code of `EmployeeSearchAdapter.java`:

```
package oracle.panama.adapter;

import java.util.Hashtable;

import javax.naming.*;
import javax.naming.directory.*;
import com.sun.jndi.ldap.LdapCtxFactory;

import org.w3c.dom.Element;
import org.w3c.dom.Document;

import oracle.panama.Argument;
import oracle.panama.InitArgument;
import oracle.panama.ArgumentType;
import oracle.panama.Arguments;
import oracle.panama.ServiceRequest;
import oracle.panama.PAPrimitive;

import oracle.panama.adapter.Adapter;
import oracle.panama.adapter.AdapterHelper;
import oracle.panama.adapter.AdapterDefinition;
import oracle.panama.adapter.AdapterException;
public class EmployeeSearchAdapter implements Adapter {
    private static final String LDAP_SERVER = "LDAP_SERVER";
    private static final String SEARCH_BASE = "SEARCH_BASE";
    private static final String COMMAND = "COMMAND";
    private static final String SEARCH_STRING = "SEARCH_STRING";
    private static final String CMD_SEARCH = "search";
    private static final String CMD_GET_DETAILS = "getDetails";

    private AdapterDefinition initDef=null;
    private AdapterDefinition adpDef=null;
    private DirContext ctx;
    SearchControls constraints;
    private String ldapServer;
    private String searchBase;
    private boolean initialized = false;

    public AdapterDefinition getAdapterDefinition() {
```

If the adapter definition is not yet created then create it with two input arguments, `COMMAND` and `SEARCH_STRING`. The input argument `COMMAND` is of type `ENUM` and can have `CMD_SEARCH` or `CMD_GET_DETAILS` as its value. The Input argument `SEARCH` contains the search string if the value of `COMMAND` argument is `CMD_SEARCH`, otherwise it contains the `uid` of an entry if the value of `COMMAND` argument is `CMD_GET_DETAILS`:

```
    if (adpDef == null) {
  synchronized(this) {
     if (adpDef == null) {
  adpDef = getInitDefinition();
  String options[] = {CMD_SEARCH, CMD_GET_DETAILS};
  initDef.createInput(ArgumentType.ENUM, COMMAND,
     "The comand to  execute", options);
```

```
         initDef.createInput(ArgumentType.SINGLE_LINE, SEARCH_STRING,
           "The search string", null);
     }
       }
     }
   return adpDef;
     }


   public AdapterDefinition getInitDefinition() {
```

If the `init` definition is not yet created, then create it with two `init` arguments: `LDAP_SERVER` and `SEARCH_BASE`. The `init` argument `LDAP_SERVER` specifies the LDAP server URL, and the `init` argument `SEARCH_BASE` specifies the root for the LDAP search operation.

```
       if (initDef == null) {
         synchronized(this) {
         if (initDef == null) {
         initDef = AdapterHelper.createAdapterDefinition();
         InitArgument arg = initDef.createInit(ArgumentType.SINGLE_LINE,
         LDAP_SERVER, "The ldap sever url", null);
         arg = initDef.createInit(ArgumentType.SINGLE_LINE, SEARCH_BASE,
           "The Search base in the ldap directory tree", null);
       }
       }
     }
     return initDef;
   }


   public void init(Arguments args) throws AdapterException {
```

If the adapter is not yet initialized then create an LDAP context, and the search constraints object. It is a good idea to create all the objects that can be used across adapter invocations in the `init` method. This will reduce the time taken to invoke the services:

```
       if (!initialized) {
         synchronized(this) {
           if (!initialized) {
           ldapServer = args.getInputValue(LDAP_SERVER);
           searchBase = args.getInputValue(SEARCH_BASE);
           Hashtable env = new Hashtable();
           env.put(Context.INITIAL_CONTEXT_FACTORY,
           "com.sun.jndi.ldap.LdapCtxFactory");
           env.put(Context.PROVIDER_URL, ldapServer);
           try {
             ctx = new InitialDirContext(env);
             constraints = new SearchControls();
             constraints.setSearchScope(SearchControls.SUBTREE_SCOPE);
           } catch (NamingException ex) {
             throw new AdapterException(ex);
           }
           initialized = true;
         }
       }
       }
     }


   public Element invoke(ServiceRequest serviceReq) throws AdapterException {
```

If the adapter is not yet initialized then throw an exception:

```
if (!initialized) {
  throw new AdapterException("Adapter not initialzied");
}
```

Get the value of the COMMAND argument, if it is null then throw an exception. When creating a master service based on this adapter, remember to pre-set the value of the COMMAND argument to CMD_SEARCH:

```
String command = serviceReq.getArguments().getInputValue(COMMAND);
if ((command == null) || (command.length() == 0)) {
  throw new AdapterException("Command missing");
}
```

Get the value of the SEARCH_STRING argument:

```
String searchString  = serviceReq.getArguments().getInputValue(
  SEARCH_STRING);
```

Create the simpleResult and add simpleContainer to it:

```
Document doc = serviceReq.getOwnerDocument();
Element simpleResult = PAPrimitive.createSimpleResult(doc,
  "Employee Search");
Element simpleContainer = PAPrimitive.createSimpleContainer(doc,
  "Employee Search");
simpleResult.appendChild(simpleContainer);
if ((searchString == null) || (searchString.length() == 0)) {
```

If the value of the SEARCH_STRING argument is null, then generate a form with one input entry item, SEARCH_STRING:

```
Element simpleForm = PAPrimitive.createSimpleForm(doc, "inputs",
  AdapterHelper.getURLPAoidParameter(serviceReq.getArguments()));
  simpleContainer.appendChild(simpleForm);
  String formInputs[] = {SEARCH_STRING};
  AdapterHelper.createInputFields(simpleForm, formInputs,
    serviceReq.getArguments());
} else if (command.equalsIgnoreCase(CMD_SEARCH)) {
```

If the value of COMMAND argument is CMD_SEARCH, then search the directory:

```
NamingEnumeration results;
try {
  results = ctx.search(searchBase,
    "(&(objectclass=inetOrgPerson)(cn=*"+searchString+"*))", constraints);
```

Create a simple menu:

```
Element simpleMenu = PAPrimitive.createSimpleMenu(doc, "Search Results");
while (results != null && results.hasMore()) {
  SearchResult result = (SearchResult) results.next();
```

Get the details of each search result entry:

```
String cn = (String)result.getAttributes().get("cn").get();
String sn = (String)result.getAttributes().get("sn").get();
String uid = (String)result.getAttributes().get("uid").get();
    String mail= (String)result.getAttributes().get("mail").get();
    String telephoneNumber = (String)
result.getAttributes().get("telephoneNumber").get();
```

Store the details of each search result entry in the panama session:

```
serviceReq.getPanamaSession().putValue(uid, new InetOrgPerson(cn,
    sn, uid, mail, telephoneNumber));
String name = cn + " "+sn;
 String target =
    AdapterHelper.getURLPAoidParameter( serviceReq.getArguments());
```

Create a simple menu item pointing to the same service with the value of the COMMAND argument as CMD_GET_DETAILS and the value of SEARCH_STRING as uid:

```
Element simpleMenuItem = PAPrimitive.createSimpleMenuItem(doc, name,
    target+"&"+COMMAND+"="+CMD_GET_DETAILS+"&" +SEARCH_STRING+"="+uid,
    false);
    simpleMenu.appendChild(simpleMenuItem);
 }
 simpleContainer.appendChild(simpleMenu);
} catch (NamingException ex) {
    throw new AdapterException(ex);
}
} else if (command.equalsIgnoreCase(CMD_GET_DETAILS)) {
try {
```

If the value of the COMMAND argument is CMD_GET_DETAILS:

```
Element simpleText = PAPrimitive.createSimpleText(doc);
```

Get the details of the user from the Session of the user:

```
        InetOrgPerson obj = (InetOrgPerson)
serviceReq.getPanamaSession().getValue(searchString);
if (obj == null) {
```

If the details of the selected user are not present in the panama session, then display an error message:

```
Element simpleTextItem = PAPrimitive.createSimpleTextItem( doc, "Failure",
    "Could not get details of the user");
simpleText.appendChild(simpleTextItem);
} else {
```

Display the details of the selected user:

```
    Element simpleTextItem = PAPrimitive.createSimpleTextItem( doc,
    "First Name", obj.getCn());
    simpleText.appendChild(simpleTextItem);
      simpleTextItem = PAPrimitive.createSimpleTextItem(doc, "Last Name",
        obj.getSn());
    simpleText.appendChild(simpleTextItem);
    simpleTextItem = PAPrimitive.createSimpleTextItem(doc,
      "E-mail Id", obj.getMail());
    simpleText.appendChild(simpleTextItem);

    simpleTextItem = PAPrimitive.createSimpleTextItem(doc, "Telephone Number",
    obj.getTelephoneNumber());
    simpleText.appendChild(simpleTextItem);
    }
  simpleContainer.appendChild(simpleText);
} catch (Exception ex) {
  throw new AdapterException(ex);
  }
}
return simpleResult;
}

}
```

Class `InetOrgPerson` stores the details of a person:

```
class InetOrgPerson {
  private String cn;
  private String sn;
  private String uid;
  private String mail;
  private String telephoneNumber;

  public InetOrgPerson(String cn, String sn, String uid, String mail,
                       String telephoneNumber) {
    this.cn = cn;
    this.sn = sn;
    this.uid = uid;
    this.mail = mail;
    this.telephoneNumber = telephoneNumber;
  }

  public String getCn() {
    return cn;
  }

  public String getSn() {
    return sn;
  }

  public String getMail() {
    return mail;
  }

  public String getTelephoneNumber() {
    return telephoneNumber;
  }
}
```

The adapter-based architecture allows the rest of the Portal-to-Go components to be insulated from the idiosyncrasies of the various content sources; they need be aware only of `SimpleResult` XML. Furthermore, the system itself is extensible when it comes to supporting new content sources. In fact it is possible to add a new adapter while the system is still running. On the other hand, the adapter approach has its limitations, the most obvious being that, while adapters mimic the Servlet approach, they do not specify a `destroy()` method. At the moment adapters can be written only in Java, and no other languages. In a way, this is not altogether bad, because the discipline of the language helps adapter developers to write applications conforming to the object framework of the system.

Summary

The world of wireless Internet access has never been more promising, and never more challenging. The main challenges at the moment are expensive and constrained bandwidth, small form-factor access devices supporting varying standards and pre-existing content that needs to be rapidly made available to such devices. Portal-to-Go greatly alleviates these issues by using logical device abstractions and content-adapters and transformers, allowing both existing content to be made available to mobile Internet devices and new content to be created transparently for these disparate devices. We started out by installing and configuring Portal-to-Go. We looked at the default `WebIntegration` adapter and also looked at how to write custom adapters. We also familiarized ourselves with the various auxiliary tools to assist development of content and maintaining the Portal-to-Go server. The sample LDAP application illustrates the use of custom adapters among other features of Portal-to-Go.

APPLICATIONPROGRAMMINGORACLE8i

25

ASP, XML and Oracle

Active Server Pages (ASP) is a server-side web technology that allows developers to use scripting languages to dynamically generate HTML code. First introduced with Microsoft Internet Information Server 3.0 (IIS3), ASP has become one of the leading server-side programming technologies, competing with rival technologies such as PHP, Cold Fusion, and Java Server Pages (JSP). It allows developers to use their existing experience of languages such as Visual Basic and JavaScript to rapidly develop web solutions that rival traditional client/server applications in the functionality they are able to offer.

While ASP started life on an NT platform, Chilisoft (http://www.chilisoft.com) has ported ASP functionality to other platforms such as Sun Solaris and Linux with Apache. There is also an open source project that aims to further spread the reach of ASP (http://www.activescripting.org/).

This chapter will look at how ASP can interface with Oracle databases in particular, and will examine such areas as:

- ❏ Connecting to an Oracle 8i database
- ❏ Techniques for retrieving data
- ❏ Executing stored procedures
- ❏ Implications of developing database applications in a stateless environment
- ❏ Replication of client Oracle forms functionality using ASP
- ❏ Using ASP to retrieve an XML document from a database

Why Use ASP with Oracle?

The first question we must answer in this chapter is why we should want or need to use ASP, after all this is a book about Oracle 8i programming and ASP has no obvious direct links with Oracle in any way. The answer to this question very much depends upon the scenario, but a few common reasons include:

❑ **Cost of development.** There are no separate licensing costs involved with using ASP technology because, unlike other technologies such as Cold Fusion, the interpreter is built into the IIS web server.

❑ **Ease of development.** This is always a contentious reason to state, as it naturally depends upon the particular circumstances. However, through its support for VBScript and JavaScript, ASP provides an opportunity for a wide base of client-side web developers and Visual Basic Windows developers to leverage their existing skills.

One common use of ASP, as with other server-side technologies, is the web enabling of existing or legacy corporate systems. ASP is suitable for this type of application through its extensible architecture, and the simple fact that resulting applications are accessible on any platform that can run a web browser. There is no need for ActiveX controls or Java Applets. This means there is no need to upgrade older machines to a specification that will support the latest version of any client software. For larger organisations this saving can pay for the development of the software many times over.

Of course, this move away from the traditional client-server model, towards web deployment of applications also affects traditional Oracle-based technologies such as Forms and Reports applications.

This may not involve the whole application, but only a subset, such as allowing remote offices to directly update a central system database, or providing access to a subset of reports on a corporate intranet.

Forms Server allows existing Forms applications to be deployed over the web with minimal modification. However, they are not really suitable for deployment over the Internet to large numbers of clients. The dependency upon the large JInitiator download, which allows forms to run within a client browser, makes it impractical in an Internet environment, and performance is also much slower than the pure HTML content delivered by an ASP solution. Oracle promises that future versions of Forms will be more HTML-centric, so this situation may change.

The first sentence of this chapter stated that ASP allows developers to dynamically generate HTML code. While this is true, it is a huge simplification of the potential of ASP. In actual fact, ASP can be used to generate any text based data format as required or supported by the client user agent. This means it is wholly suitable for generating XML in a data service environment or WML for WAP-enabled devices. The nature of the information generated by the ASP application is entirely at the developer's discretion.

One of the negative aspects of ASP development is that you often need to write more code than would normally be required in a typical 4GL language to carry out a particular task. This is partly due to the restrictions imposed by its dependency on scripting languages, and also because of the stateless HTTP environment in which it functions. Scripting languages typically aren't well structured – the "spaghetti-like" code doesn't promote reuse.

The next generation of ASP, called ASP.NET, aims to challenge this. ASP.NET is part of Microsoft's .NET initiative. As well as supporting a much wider range of languages, including C++ and other languages not developed by Microsoft, it will also adopt a more traditional event-based programming model. There are many other improvements promised for ASP.NET when it is released, so hopefully this will reduce the effort required to implement ASP solutions in future.

However, while these developments look promising, they don't affect ASP currently and therefore don't improve the current situation. In the meantime, there are several sets of tools available that will ease the burden of the developer:

❑ Microsoft has attempted to ease the development of data-driven applications with the design-time controls included in Visual InterDev 6. These are essentially a collection of server-side ActiveX components that wrap much of the database functionality, such as data connections, recordsets, paging, etc.

❑ Similarly, Macromedia's DreamWeaver UltraDev product provides a point and click environment that allows developers to connect to databases and build pages that display and maintain the information in the database. UltraDev generates pure ASP code to implement the functionality, and does not rely upon additional server-side components or files.

❑ Oracle also has a tool for generating ASP code, namely the Oracle AppWizard for Microsoft Visual InterDev. We will cover it briefly again towards the end of this chapter.

I normally do not advocate the use of point-and-click development tools, as they invariably fail to deliver on the promise of true WYSIWYG development – at some point it almost always becomes necessary to roll up your sleeves and start writing the code manually. As this requires a proper understanding of the underlying technology, a developer may as well skip the point-and-click approach and jump straight in at the deep end anyway.

ASP for the Uninitiated

This chapter is by no means intended to provide a comprehensive discussion on ASP development (if this is what you were hoping for I strongly recommend two other Wrox publications, *Beginning Active Server Pages 3.0* - ISBN 1-861003-38-2 and *Professional Active Server Pages 3.0* - ISBN 1-861002-61-0). However, a brief introduction to ASP is appropriate for those readers that haven't already encountered it.

As previously discussed, ASP is a server side technology that allows the development of dynamic web pages for Intranet, Extranet, and Internet applications. Typical applications may include e-commerce solutions over the Internet for either B2B or B2C, or as mentioned earlier, the provision of an interface for legacy corporate systems.

To use ASP you need MS Internet Information Server (IIS) for Windows NT Server or Windows 2000 Server. This is available as part of the NT Option pack, which is freely available for licensed copies of the operating system. Alternatively, for the Windows 9x operating system, you can also use Personal Web Server. This is available as part of the components distributed with the Windows 98 operating system or available from `http://www.microsoft.com/ntserver/nts/downloads /recommended/NT4OPTPk/default.asp` as part of the NT 4 Option Pack. The code can be written in any text editor, however for serious development I recommend Microsoft Visual InterDev, as this provides a much richer environment geared towards ASP and database development.

The glue that forms the heart of ASP applications is developed using a scripting language, similar to the scripting used in client-side browser development. The two scripting libraries typically used for ASP development are VBScript and JavaScript, however the open architecture supports any scripting language – PerlScript is another alternative that can be used.

ASP pages contain both HTML and scripting code, and are denoted by the `.asp` extension of the file name. When a request is received by the web server for a `.asp` file, the processing of the file is passed to a server side component, `asp.dll`. This processes the page, line by line, looking for particular tags that denote blocks of server-side script. These tags can appear in one of two ways, either as a `<script>` ... `</script>` tag pair with the special `runat="server"` attribute, or as `<% ... %>`. When it comes across one of these tags it passes the scripting code to the appropriate scripting engine. ASP can determine which scripting engine should be used as it is passed either as the `LANGUAGE` attribute of the `<script>` tag, or if using the `<%...%>` delimiters, then as a special `@`directive as the very first line of code on any ASP page:

```
<%@ LANGUAGE="VBSCRIPT"%>
```

The scripting engine then compiles the code "on the fly" and returns any output as HTML. As a server side technology, the client browser never sees the scripting code, only the resulting HTML. This process is summarised in the following diagram:

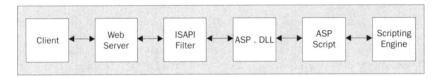

One non-functional service provided by ASP is the ability to build up a file from a series of other smaller files, a feature known as server-side includes. This allows for greater reusability of code, as common procedures or blocks of HTML code can be kept in a single place and reused again and again.

Probably one of the main reasons for the success of ASP is its support for the Microsoft Common Object Model (COM). This extensibility is extremely powerful as it allows ASP to integrate with most other software systems, using the intrinsic Microsoft objects, third party products, or custom bespoke components developed to address a particular need.

The ASP Objects

ASP is actually an extension to your web server that allows server-side scripting. At the same time it also provides a compendium of objects and components, which manage interaction between the web server and the browser. These objects form the **Active Server Pages Object Model**. These 'objects' can be manipulated by scripting languages.

ASP itself provides five main intrinsic COM objects that are available to the script code. These are described in the following table:

Object Names	Description
Request	The `Request` object is used when handling any information coming from the client browser. This may be data passed in a form either in the HTTP headers, or as parameters appended to the URL, or data held on the client computer in a cookie file.
Response	The `Response` object is used to control all content and functionality related to sending information back to the client. The most common use of the `Response` object is to stream HTML back to the client from within a server-side code block – indeed it is this that provides much of the dynamic capabilities of ASP.

Object Names	Description
Server	The Server object is a very powerful object, as it allows access to and control of a variety of information about the client, the application, and the operating environment. Perhaps most importantly though, it allows us to instantiate other COM components and interface to these through our ASP code.
Session	The Session object may be used to maintain state between individual page requests. Each user has their own session; hence the Session object is typically used to persist user-specific data between page requests.
Application	The Application object is similar to the session object in that it is also typically used to persist data, except the data is available to all users of, or sessions in, the application.

In addition, the ASP 2.0 and ASP 3.0 upgrades have added an ASP Error object to aid error handling and debugging, and an ObjectContext object which can help non-scripting programming languages interface with the objects contained within ASP. These last two objects are of little interest to us in this chapter, as we will not be covering the areas in which they are employed. However, we'll take a brief look at the five main objects now.

The Request Object

When your web page is requested, much information is passed along with the HTTP request, such as the URL of the web page request and format of the data being passed. It can also contain feedback from the user such as the input from a text box or drop down list box. The Request object allows you to get at information passed along as part of the HTTP request. The corresponding output from the server is returned as part of the Response. The Request object has several collections to store information that warrant discussion.

The Request Object's Collections

The Request object has five collections. Interestingly, they all act as the default property for the object. That is to say, you may retrieve information from any of the five collections by using the abbreviated syntax:

```
ClientIPAddress = Request("REMOTE_ADDR")
```

The REMOTE_ADDR value lies in the ServerVariables collection. However, through the use of the collection cascade, it can be retrieved with the above notation. Please note that for ASP to dig through each collection, especially if they have many values, to retrieve a value from the last collection is inefficient. It is always recommended to use the fully qualified collection name in your code. Not only is this faster, but it improves your code in that it is more specific, and less cryptic.

ASP searches through the collections in the following order:

- ❑ QueryString
- ❑ Form
- ❑ Cookies
- ❑ ClientCertificate
- ❑ ServerVariables

If there are variables with the same name, only the first is returned when you allow ASP to search. This is another good reason for you to fully qualify your collection. Only three of these collections are of any interest to us here, `QueryString`, `Form` and `ServerVariables`.

QueryString

The `QueryString` collection contains a collection of all the information attached to the end of an URL. When you make an URL request, the additional information is passed along with the URL to the web page appended with a question mark. This information takes the following form:
`URL?item=data[&item=data][...]`

The clue to the server is the question mark. When the server sees this, it knows that the URL has ended, and variables are starting. So an example of a URL with a query string might look like this:

http://www.buythisbook.com/book.asp?bookname=ASPProgrammersReference

A `QueryString` is just a name/value pair. In this example `bookname` is the name and `ASPProgrammersReference` is the value. When ASP gets hold of this URL request, it breaks apart all of the name/value pairs and places them into this collection for easy access. Query strings are built up using ampersands to delimit each name/value pair so if you wished to pass the user information along with the book information, you could pass the following:

http://www.buythisbook.com/book.asp?bookname=ASPProgrammersReference&buyer=JohnDoe

A `Querystring` can be generated in one of three ways. The first is, as discussed, by a user typed URL. The second is as part of a URL specified in an Anchor tag.

```
<A HREF="book.asp?bookname=ASPScriptProgrammersReference">Go to book buying
page</A>
```

So when you click on the link, the name/value pair is passed along with the URL. The third and final method is via a form sent to the server with the `GET` method.

```
<FORM ACTION="book.asp" METHOD="GET">
Type your name: <INPUT TYPE="TEXT" NAME="buyer"><BR>
Type your requested book:  <INPUT TYPE="TEXT" NAME="bookname" SIZE=40><BR>
<INPUT TYPE=SUBMIT VALUE=Submit>
</FORM>
```

You input the information onto the text boxes on the form and the text is submitted when you click on **Submit** and two `Querystrings` are generated.

Next you need to be able to retrieve information, and you use this technique to retrieve from each of the three methods used to generate a query string.

```
Request.QueryString("buyer")
Request.QueryString("bookname")
```

Please note that these lines won't display anything by themselves, you need to add either the shorthand notation (equality operator) to display functions in front of a single statement, or when a number of values need displaying then use Response.Write to separately display each value in the collection.

for example <%=Request.QueryString("buyer")%> or
Response.Write(Request.QueryString("bookname"))

The first of the two `Request` object calls should return the name of John Doe on the page and the second of the two should return ASP Programmers Reference. Of course you could always store this information in a variable for later access.

```
sBookName = Request.QueryString("bookname")
```

Form

The Form collection contains a collection of all the form variables posted to the HTTP request by an HTML form. Query strings aren't very private as they transmit information via a very visible method, the URL. They also provide a fairly small limit on the amount of information you wish to transmit (dependent on the allowable length of a URL). If you want to transmit information from the form more privately, or transmit larger amounts of information, then you can use the form collection to do so which sends its information as part of the HTTP Request body.

If we go back to our previous example, the only alteration we need to make to our HTML form code is to change the METHOD attribute. Forms using this collection must be sent with the POST method and not the GET method. It is actually this attribute that determines how the information is sent by the form. So if we change the method of the form as follows:

```
<FORM ACTION="book.asp" METHOD="POST">
Type your name: <INPUT TYPE="TEXT" NAME="buyer"><BR>
Type your requested book:  <INPUT TYPE="TEXT" NAME="bookname" SIZE=40><BR>
<INPUT TYPE=SUBMIT VALUE=Submit>
</FORM>
```

Once the form has been submitted in this style, then we can retrieve and display the information using the following:

```
=Request.Form("buyer")
```

ServerVariables

When the client sends a request and information is passed across to the server, it's not just the page that is passed across, but information such as who created the page, the server name, and the port that the request was sent to. The HTTP header that is sent across together with the HTTP request also contains information of this nature such as the type of browser, and type of connection. This information is combined into a list of variables that are predefined by the server as environment variables. Most of them are static and never really change unless you change the configuration of your web server. The rest are based on the client browser.

These server variables can be accessed in the normal method. For instance, the server variable HTTP_USER_AGENT, which returns information about the type of browser being used to view the page, can be displayed as follows:

```
<%=Request.ServerVariables("HTTP_USER_AGENT")%>
```

Alternatively you can print out the whole list of server variables and their values with the following code:

```
For Each key in Request.ServerVariables
   Response.Write "<B>" & (Key) &"</B> "
   Response.Write (Request.ServerVariables(key)) & "<BR>"
Next
```

This displays each of the `ServerVariables` collection in bold, and the contents of the key (if any) after it.

Server variables are merely informative, but they do give you the ability to customize page content for specific browsers, or to avoid script errors that might be generated.

The Response Object

After you've processed the request information from the client browser, you'll need to be able to send information back. The `Response` object is just the ticket. It provides you with the tools necessary to send anything you need back to the client.

The Response Object's Write Method

To understand how the `Response` Object works, we need to examine the workings of how ASP sends a response in more detail. When an ASP script is run, an **HTML output stream** is created. This stream is a receptacle for the web server to store details and create the dynamic/interactive web page in. As mentioned before, the page has to be created entirely in HTML for the browser to understand it (excluding client-side scripting, which is ignored by the server).

The stream is initially empty when created. New information is added to the end. If any custom HTML headers are required then they have to be added at the beginning. Then the HTML contained in the ASP page is added next to the script, so anything not encompassed by `<% %>` tags is added. The `Response` object provides two ways of writing directly to the output stream, either using the `Write` method or its shorthand technique.

`Write` allows you to send information back to the client browser. You can write text directly to a web page by encasing the text in quotation marks:

```
Response.Write "Hello World!"
```

Or to display the contents of a variant you just drop the quotation marks:

```
sText = "Hello World!"
Response.Write sText
```

For single portions of dynamic information that only require adding into large portions of HTML, you can use the equality sign as shorthand for this method, as specified earlier, for example:

```
My message is <% =sText %>
```

This technique reduces the amount of code needed, but at the expense of readability. There is nothing to choose between these techniques in terms of performance.

The Application and Session Objects

The `Application` and `Session` objects like `Request` and `Response` work very closely together. `Application` is used to tie all of the pages together into one consistent application, while the `Session` object is used to track and present a user's series of requests to the web site as a continuous action, rather than an arbitrary set of requests.

Normally, you will declare a variable for use within your web page. You'll use it, manipulate it, then perhaps print out its value, or whatever. But when your page is reloaded, or the viewer moves to another page, the variable, with its value, is gone forever. By placing your variable within the Contents collection of the Application or Session objects, you can extend the life span of your variable!

Any variable or object that you declare has two potential scopes: procedure and page. When you declare a variable within a procedure, its life span is limited to that procedure. Once the procedure has executed, your variable is gone. You may also declare a variable at the web page level but like the procedure-defined variable, once the page is reloaded, the value is reset.

Enter the Application and Session objects. The Contents collections of these two objects allow you to extend the scope of your variables to session-wide, and application-wide. If you place a value in the Session object, it will be available to all web pages in your site for the life span of the current session (more on sessions later). Good session scope variables are user ids, user names, login time, etc, things that pertain only to the session. Likewise, if you place your value into the Application object, it will exist until the web site is restarted. This allows you to place application-wide settings into a conveniently accessible place. Good application scope variables are font names and sizes, table colors, system constants, etc, things that pertain to the application as a whole.

The global.asa File

Every ASP application may utilize a special script file. This file is named global.asa and it must reside in the root directory of your web application. It can contain script code that pertains to the application as a whole, or each session. It is also used as a place to initialize variables that you want to exist across the whole application, or for the duration of a user's session. You may also create ActiveX objects for later use in this scripting file.

The Application Object

ASP works on the concept that an entire web site is a single web application. Therefore, there is only one instance of the Application object available for your use in your scripting at all times. Note that it is possible to divide up your web site into separate applications, but for the purposes of this discussion we'll assume there is only one application per web site.

Collections

The Application object contains two collections: Contents and StaticObjects. The Contents collection is discussed above. The StaticObjects collection is similar to Contents, but only contains the objects that were created with the <OBJECT> tag in the scope of your application. This collection can be iterated just like the Contents collection.

You cannot store references to ASP's built-in objects in Application's collections.

Methods

The Application object contains two methods as detailed below.

Lock	The Lock method is used to "lock-down" the Contents collection so that it cannot be modified by other clients. This is useful if you are updating a counter, or perhaps grabbing a transaction number stored in the Application's Contents collection.
Unlock	The Unlock method "unlocks" the Application object thus allowing others to modify the Contents collection.

Events

The `Application` object generates two events: `Application_OnStart` and `Application_OnEnd`. The `Application_OnStart` event is fired when the first view of your web page occurs. The `Application_OnEnd` event is fired when the web server is shut down. If you choose to write scripts for these events they must be placed in your `global.asa` file.

The most common use of these events is to initialize application-wide variables. Items such as font names, table colors, database connection strings, perhaps even writing information to a system log file. The following is an example `global.asa` file with script for these events:

```
<SCRIPT LANGUAGE=VBScript RUNAT=Server>
Sub Application_OnStart
    'Globals…
    Application("ErrorPage") = "handleError.asp"
    Application("SiteBanAttemptLimit") = 10
    Application("AccessErrorPage") = "handleError.asp"
    Application("RestrictAccess") = False


    'Keep track of visitors…
    Application("NumVisits") = Application("NumVisits") + 1
End Sub
</SCRIPT>
```

The Session Object

Each time a visitor comes to your web site, a `Session` object is created for the visitor if the visitor does not already have one. Therefore there is an instance of the `Session` object available to you in your scripting as well. The `Session` object is similar to the `Application` object in that it can contain values. However, the `Session` object's values are lost when your visitor leaves the site. The `Session` object is most useful for transferring information from web page to web page. Using the `Session` object, there is no need to pass information in the URL.

The most common use of the `Session` object is to store information in its `Contents` collection. This information would be session-specific in that it would pertain only to the current user.

Many web sites today offer a "user personalization" service. That is, to customize a web page to their preference. This is easily done with ASP and the `Session` object. The user variables are stored in the client browser for retrieval by the server later. Simply load the user's preferences at the start of the session and then, as the user browses your site, utilize the information regarding the user's preferences to display information.

Suppose your web site displays stock quotes for users. You could allow users to customize the start page to display their favorite stock quotes when they visit the site. By storing the stock symbols in your `Session` object, you can easily display the correct quotes when you render your web page.

This session management system relies on the use of browser cookies. The cookies allow the user information to be persisted even after a client leaves the site. Unfortunately, if a visitor to your web site does not allow cookies to be stored, you will be unable to pass information between web pages within the `Session` object.

Collections

The Session object contains two collections: Contents and StaticObjects. The Contents collection we discussed above. The StaticObjects collection is similar to Contents, but only contains the objects that were created with the <OBJECT> tag in your HTML page. This collection can be iterated just like the Contents collection.

Methods

The Session object contains a single method, Abandon. This instructs ASP to destroy the current Session object for this user. This method is what you would call when a user logs off your web site.

Events

The Session object generates two events: Session_OnStart and Session_OnEnd. The Session_OnStart event is fired when the first view of your web page occurs. The Session_OnEnd event is fired when the web server is shut down. If you choose to write scripts for these events they must be placed in your global.asa file.

The most common use of these events is to initialize session-wide variables. Items like usage counts, login names, real names, user preferences, etc. The following is an example global.asa file with script for these events:

```
<SCRIPT LANGUAGE=VBScript RUNAT=Server>
Sub Session_OnStart
    Session("LoginAttempts") = 0
    Session("LoggedOn") = False
End Sub

Sub Session_OnEnd
    Session("LoggedOn") = False
End Sub
</SCRIPT>
```

The Server Object

The last object we'll look at in the ASP object model is the Server object. The Server object enables you to create and work with ActiveX controls in your web pages. In addition, the Server object exposes methods that help in the encoding of URLs and HTML text. However, it's the CreateObject Method we're going to focus on, as we will need it when interfacing with the Oracle database.

The CreateObject Method

Using this method, we can instantiate a new instance of an object. The result can be placed into the Application or Session Contents collection to lengthen its life span.

Generally you'll create an object at the time the session is created and place it into the Session.Contents collection. For example, let's say you've created a killer ActiveX DLL with a really cool class that converts Fahrenheit to Celsius and vice versa. You could create an instance of this class with the CreateObject method and store it in the Session.Contents collection like this:

```
Set Session("MyConverter") = Server.CreateObject("KillerDLL.CDegreeConverter")
```

This object would be around as long as the session is and will be available for you to call.

ASP also comes with its own built in set of components that you can create instances of using the `CreateObject` method. These are:

- ❑ **Ad Rotator** – used to display a random graphic and link every time a user connects to the page.

- ❑ **Browser Capabilities** – manipulates a file `browscap.ini` contained on the server computer to determine the capabilities of a particular client's browser.

- ❑ **Content Linker** – provides a central repository file from where you manage a series of links and their URLs, and provide appropriate descriptions about them.

- ❑ **Content Rotator** – a cut down version of the Ad Rotator that provides the same function but without optional redirection.

- ❑ **Page Counter** – Counts the number of times a page has been hit.

- ❑ **Permission Checker** – checks to see if a user has permission before allowing them to access a given page.

- ❑ **Counters** – counts any value on an ASP page from anywhere within an ASP application.

- ❑ **MyInfo** – can be used to store personal information about a user within an XML file.

- ❑ **Status** – used to collect server profile information.

- ❑ **Tools** – a set of miscellaneous methods that are grouped under the generic heading of Tools.

- ❑ **IIS Log** - allows you to create an object that allows your applications to write to and otherwise access the IIS log.

There is another set of objects that come with ASP, and can be used as part of ASP, but are a separate set of objects in their own right, which help enable web database access. This set of components, which we will be referring to regularly in this chapter, is known as the Microsoft ActiveX Data Object (ADO) library. Let's have a look at them now.

ActiveX Data Objects (ADO)

ADO is a key component of Microsoft's drive for Universal Data Access (UDA): it can be used for accessing data wherever it may be stored, either in Oracle or SQL Server databases, flat formatted text-files, Microsoft Exchange, LDAP directories, or many other forms of repositories.

The foundation of UDA is OLE DB, a system-level programming interface (consisting of classes written in powerful O-O languages such as C++ or Java). Unfortunately, scripting languages are simply not powerful enough to manipulate OLE DB objects directly. ADO is the "friendly face" of OLE DB. It works at the application rather than system level and provides a set of COM-based objects that provide a thin wrapper around the complex OLE DB interfaces.

The following diagram shows the software layers that your ASP program must traverse in order to access the database. The **bold** squares pick out the route most commonly used in this section:

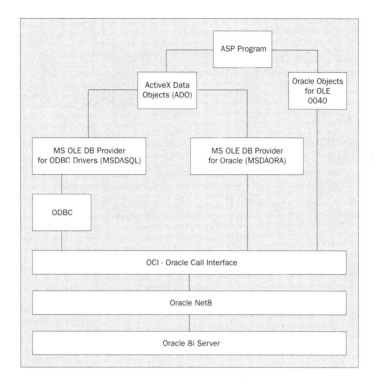

OLE DB for ODBC

MSADASQL effectively acts as a conversion layer, mapping OLE DB interfaces to ODBC APIs. It is the default provider for ADO and, since ODBC is still the only driver that provides access to all Oracle functionality, it is very useful in many circumstances. However, this route takes you through the most software layers and, hence, performance inevitably suffers.

OO4O

Oracle Objects for OLE is a Oracle's proprietary COM layer by which VB and C++ can converse with an Oracle database and provides similar functionality to ADO. Unlike OO4O, however, ADO is not bound to any particular type of database or data store. In fact with the introduction of version 2.5 of ADO in Windows 2000, applications can now access non-regular data stores where each record has a different set of attributes (or columns).

I personally prefer ADO rather than OO4O as it allows the development of generic code that can easily be adapted to many different data sources. As I work not only with Oracle, but also SQL Server it means I can reuse code with only minor changes needed to SQL, etc. If, however, you are familiar with OO4O and have no previous exposure to ADO then OO4O may also be used with ASP to provide an interface to an Oracle database. The following code, taken from the Oracle 8i documentation, explains how to instantiate OO4O with ASP.

```
<object runat="Server" scope="Application" id="OraSession"
        progid="OracleInProcServer.XOraSession"></object>
```

It should be added to the global.asa file in the ASP application.

The ADO Object Model

ADO is the result of much revision and consolidation in Microsoft's data access strategy. It is the successor to such technologies as Data Access Objects (DAO) and Remote Data Objects (RDO).

The relationship between ADO and OLE DB can be compared to that of RDO and ODBC: RDO was a thin wrapper over the ODBC API.

ADO, OLE DB and ODBC are now grouped together in a single installable component called Microsoft Data Access Components (MDAC). MDAC has gone through a number of iterations from version 1.0 through 1.5, 2.0, 2.1 and most recently 2.5, introduced with Windows 2000. The latest version of MDAC may be downloaded from the Microsoft web site at http://www.microsoft.com/data/. I strongly recommend that you use at least ADO 2.1, and preferably ADO 2.5. Most of the changes in each new version simply extend the functionality provided by previous versions and fix any bugs, and so are backward compatible.

As before, this section is not intended to be a comprehensive reference to ADO (please see the Wrox book "*ADO 2.6 Programmers Reference*" ISBN 1-861004-63-x for this), however as with the intrinsic ASP objects it is important that we cover the key ADO objects here for those readers not already familiar with them.

Object Name	Description
Connection	The Connection object is used to create a connection to the data source, effectively a pipe through which we can communicate with the database.
Recordset	The Recordset object is used whenever we need to work with records. A recordset may contain zero or more records.
Command	It shouldn't come as too much of a surprise that the Command object allows commands to be executed against the database. Typically these commands would be non-recordset returning SQL statements, for example DELETE, or stored procedures.
Parameter	The Parameter object is used in conjunction with the Command object when interacting with a stored procedure that requires or returns parameter values.

Creating a Connection

In order to connect to an Oracle 8i database it is necessary to have Net8 installed on the web server, just as we would normally require it for client/server development. The first action that must be performed before any interaction can be performed between ASP and the Oracle database is the creation of a connection to the database. This is indeed an important concept to understand – the client never actually connects to the database; only the server connects to the database.

There are a number of ways of instantiating a connection, however the following is a typical example:

```
Set mcon_Connection = Server.CreateObject("ADODB.Connection")

mcon_Connection.Open "DSN=ProfOra8;UID=scott;PWD=tiger"

If mcon_Connection.State = adStateOpen Then
    ' ...
    ' Do whatever database work we are going to do here
    ' ...
```

```
      mcon_Connection.Close
   End If

   Set mcon_Connection = Nothing
```

The first line `Server.CreateObject("ADODB.Connection")` instantiates the ADO `Connection` COM object. We then open the connection to the database, passing all the connection information in as a single string to the `Open` method of the `Connection` object:

`"DSN=ProfOra8;UID=scott;PWD=tiger"`.

The DSN part of this parameter refers to a system ODBC Data Source Name (DSN) that has been configured on the server to point to the Oracle database instance. The UID and PWD parts specify the username and password that will be used to connect to the database instance. When a specific provider is not specified, as in this case, ADO will automatically use the default OLE DB provider for ODBC (MSDASQL), which is more than adequate for most circumstances. However, in order to use the OLE DB provider for Oracle, we must change the connection string as follows:

```
   lcon_Connection.Open "Provider=MSDAORA;data source=profOra8;" & _
                        "User ID=scott;Password=tiger"
```

Notice that the username and password parameter names are changed, due to the different requirements of the OLE DB provider for Oracle. We can also provide the username and password as separate parameters to the `Open` method, as follows:

```
   lcon_Connection.Open "Provider=MSDAORA;data source=ProfOra8", "scott", "tiger"
```

Normally, a system DSN would be created on the server to point to the correct Oracle instance, and indeed the previous code assumes that a DSN is defined with the name ProfOra8. ADO does support the creation of DSN-less connections. For an Oracle database we can use the following syntax, where TNS_NAME is the name of the database in the `TNSNAMES.ORA` configuration file.

```
   lcon_Connection.Open "Provider=MSDAORA;Data Source=TNS_NAME; " & _
                        "User ID=scott;Password=tiger;"
```

The versions of the MDAC components installed with IIS, and all subsequent versions, have connection pooling enabled by default. This means that connections to the database remain open for a period of time, even when explicitly closed in the code. This improves performance, especially in ASP where connections are opened and closed all the time as different pages are requested. Further information on connection pooling can be found in *Knowledge Base* article Q169470 in MSDN.

Best coding practice in ASP development is always to request resources as late as possible, and release them as early as possible. This practice is true for the ADO objects, and storing open connections in either session or application context is discouraged. Typically the connection string may be stored at an application or session level, with individual connection objects instantiated on each page. Another alternative for sites where the majority of pages are interfacing to a database is to instantiate the connection object in an include file that is included at the top of every page. Another include file can then also be included at the end of every page to close the connection and release the object references. This practice is not advised for high traffic Internet sites, but may be suitable for intranet-based applications, where there are many different pages interfacing to the database and simplicity and reuse during development may be more important.

If you experience problems with connecting to an Oracle database from IIS Microsoft have published a good knowledge base article (Q255084) to assist with troubleshooting. At time of press this was available from:

`http://support.microsoft.com/support/kb/articles/Q255/0/84.asp`.

One final point to note with connecting to the database concerns the account used by the web server to connect to the database. In a typical client-server environment each user has an individual account and hence connection to the database. Using this approach with a web application that may have many hundreds or thousands of concurrent users is not normally practical. It also does not make best use of the connection pooling capabilities of MDAC.

Consequently a typical ASP data driven application will use a single account that has the highest level of access required by the application to connect to the database. Security is then handled at an application level by the ASP code. One possible way of implementing application-level security is described later on in this chapter.

Retrieving Records

Just as with creating connections, ADO is flexible in the techniques we may use to retrieve records from the database. Whatever technique we employ, we use the ADO `Recordset` object when working with one or more records.

The first and simplest way of returning a set of records from the database is to invoke the `Execute` method of the `Connection` object, passing in the appropriate SQL string as a parameter. Assuming the SQL executed is of the type that returns records, for example a SELECT statement, the `Execute` method automatically returns a `Recordset` object populated with the appropriate records. This is sometimes known as the fire-hose method, and returns a read-only, forward-only recordset. In the following example, `mcon_Connection` represents an ADO connection object, `mrec_Employees` represents an ADO Recordset object, whilst `mstr_Sql` is a string containing the SQL string to be executed.

```
<%
Set mcon_Connection = Server.CreateObject("ADODB.Connection")
mcon_Connection.Open "Provider=MSDAORA;DSN=ProfOra8", "scott", "tiger"
If mcon_Connection.State = adStateOpen Then
  Set mrec_Employees = mcon_Connection.Execute(mstr_Sql)

  ...

  mrec_Employees.Close
  Set mrec_Employees = Nothing
  mcon_Connection.Close
End If
Set mcon_Connection = Nothing
%>
```

The second method, and the one I prefer, as the code is more explicit in its actions, is to create a `Recordset` object and use the `Open` method to retrieve the records from the database. This method also allows us a greater degree of flexibility in the type of recordset we wish to open. In the following example, the `mcon_Connection`, `mrec_Employees`, and `mstr_Sql` variables behave as before, while the `adOpenForwardOnly`, `adLockReadOnly`, and `adCmdText` are all constants, which specify the cursor type, locking type and option value respectively. This passes information that specifies the type of recordset values we wish to open.

Before ADO can identify the constant values though, we have to add an include file to the head of the ASP page, known as `ADOVBS.ASP`. This is a standard file that comes with ADO and sets values for all of the constants mentioned:

```
<!--#include file="include/adovbs.asp"-->
```

Without this file the constants have no value, and you will generate unexpected errors in the page. Another way of adding the constant values is to include the `msado15.dll` which also contains this information, as follows:

```
<!—METADATA TYPE="typelib" FILE="C:\Program Files\Common
Files\System\ado\msado15.dll" -->
```

We'll consider the most common constant types that are supplied in ADO now.

Cursor Type

There are four cursor type constants in total, as follows:

❑ **Forward-only** (adOpenForwardOnly): this is the default type and gives you a non-scrollable recordset. It's also static, so changes to the underlying data are not represented.

❑ **Static** (adOpenStatic): this is similar to a forward-only recordset, except that it is scrollable, so you can move back to previous records as well as moving forwards.

❑ **Dynamic** (adOpenDynamic): the recordset is fully dynamic, and lets you see additions, amendments and deletions that are made by other users. It's fully scrollable so you can move around the recordset any way you like.

❑ **Keyset** (adOpenKeyset): this is similar to the dynamic recordset, but you can't see records that other users add, although you *can* see changes to existing records. Any records that other users delete become inaccessible.

Locking Type

There are four types of locking you can use:

❑ **Read-only** (adLockReadOnly): This gives you a non-updateable recordset. No locking is performed, since you can't change the data in a read-only recordset. This is the default.

❑ **Pessimistic** (adLockPessimistic): This gives you an updateable recordset, in which the lock type is very protective. In this case, the copy of the record that exists in the data store is locked as soon as you start editing it. This means that no one else can change the record until you release the lock, which is after you finished editing the record and have committed the update.

❑ **Optimistic** (adLockOptimistic): This also gives you an updateable recordset, but the lock type is a little more carefree. In this case, the copy of the records in the data store remains unlocked while you're editing your changes within the recordset. The data store records are *only* locked when you update your changes.

❑ **Optimistic Batch** (adLockBatchOptimistic): Batch update mode allows you to modify several records, and then have them updated all-at-once, so this only locks each record as it is being updated.

Option Values

The `Options` parameter tells the recordset what form the data source will take. The most common options you can set are as follows:

❑ **Text command** (`adCmdText`) is used to indicate that `Source` parameter holds command text, for example, a SQL command.

❑ **Table name** (`adCmdTable`) is used to indicate that `Source` parameter holds the name of a table.

❑ **Stored procedure** (`adCmdStoredProc`) is used to indicate that `Source` parameter holds the name of a stored procedure or query.

❑ **Table** (`adCmdTableDirect`) is used to indicate that `Source` parameter holds the name of a table.

❑ **Saved Recordset** (`adCmdFile`) is used to indicate that `Source` parameter holds the file name of a saved recordset.

❑ **URL** (`adCmdURLBind`) is used to indicate that `Source` parameter holds a URL.

So if we pass on this information as part of our query, our code will look like this:

```
<%
Set mcon_Connection = Server.CreateObject("ADODB.Connection")
mcon_Connection.Open "Provider=MSDAORA;DSN=ProfOra8", "scott", "tiger"
If mcon_Connection.State = adStateOpen Then
  Set mrec_Employees = Server.CreateObject("ADODB.Recordset")
  mrec_Employees. Open mstr_Sql, mcon_Connection, _
                        adOpenForwardOnly, adLockReadOnly, adCmdText

  . . .

  mrec_Employees.Close
  Set mrec_Employees = Nothing
  mcon_Connection.Close
End If
Set mcon_Connection = Nothing
%>
```

The BOF and EOF Properties

Once we have retrieved a recordset we typically iterate through the records contained with it. This is possible using two important Boolean properties of the ADO Recordset object, BOF (Beginning of File) and EOF (End of File). The BOF property is set to True when we are at the very beginning of the recordset, while EOF is set to True when we are at the very end. When BOF and EOF are both True the recordset does not contain any records. Consequently, two snippets of code often used are:

```
If mrec_DemoRecordset.BOF And mrec_DemoRecordset.EOF Then
  ' Recordset is empty
End If
```

and

```
Do While Not mrec_DemoRecordset.EOF
   ' Do something with the current record, for example read data
   mrec_DemoRecordset.MoveNext
Loop
```

It is very important to remember to include the `.MoveNext` method when looping through a recordset. This is a common omission when first developing a page, and causes the server to go into an endless loop. If your application is timing out when trying to retrieve records from a database, this is the first thing to check.

The RecordCount Property

One important point to remember when working with recordsets is that many properties are dependent upon the settings or values of other properties. A common problem experienced by developers concerns the use of the `RecordCount` property. The documentation states that this property contains the number of records in a recordset, however much confusion results when this returns -1, even when it is obvious that there are records in the database. The `RecordCount` property in fact returns -1 in most cases, including the fire-hose method of retrieving records we discussed earlier. In order to retrieve the number of records successfully we must use a client-side cursor, rather than the default server-side type. This can be achieved by including the following code before we open the recordset.

```
mrec_DemoRecordset.CursorLocation = adUseClient
```

Other Useful Properties

One final word of advice on working with recordsets is to restrict the amount of data returned to the client. Executing a query that returns hundreds of matching records is not a problem for Forms applications as the records are retrieved only when required, however it is something that must be considered when using ASP. If it is only necessary to retrieve a fixed amount of records, for example the top 10 matches, then the `MaxRecords` property of the `Recordset` object can be set before the recordset is opened, for example:

```
mrec_Employees.MaxRecords = 10
mrec_Employees. Open mstr_Sql, mcon_Connection, _
                     adOpenForwardOnly, adLockReadOnly, adCmdText
```

Another solution is to display pages of records that the user may navigate through. This approach is typically seen when using an Internet search engine. ADO provides three properties of the `Recordset` object that may be used to generate paging functionality, `.PageSize`, `.PageCount`, and `.AbsolutePage`. `PageSize` either sets or returns the number of records per page, `PageCount` returns the total number of pages, whilst `AbsolutePage` either sets or returns the current page in the recordset.

Executing Stored Procedures and Functions

There are several methods that are used to execute stored procedures and functions. I won't go into all of them here (I would again refer you to *Professional ADO 2.6*, ISBN 1-861004-63-x by Wrox Press), but before moving on I want to cover the method I use most of the time. I use this method, despite its verbosity, because it's proven to be the most reliable way of executing Oracle stored procedures without encountering problems such as truncation of parameter values and other errors.

Firstly we create an ADO `Command` object using the following code, assuming a `Connection` object called mcon_Connection has already been instantiated and opened.

```
Dim mcmd_DemoStoredProc

Set mcmd_DemoStoredProc = Server.CreateObject("ADODB.Command")
```

We then set the properties of the `Command` object, namely the reference to the open `Connection` object, and the `CommandText` property to the name of the stored procedure. We also set the `CommandType` of the `Command` object to be `adCmdStoredProc` to save ADO from having to work this out for itself.

```
mcmd_DemoStoredProc.ActiveConnection = mcon_Connection
mcmd_DemoStoredProc.CommandText = "VALIDATE_USER"
mcmd_DemoStoredProc.CommandType = adCmdStoredProc
```

We will assume that this stored procedure has two IN parameters, `PI_USERNAME` and `PI_PASSWORD`, and a single OUT parameter called `PO_LEVEL`. For each parameter we first instantiate an ADO `Parameter` object. We then set the name of the parameter to be the same as the name of the parameter expected by the stored procedure. We must also set the data type and size of parameter and for the input parameters the values we wish to supply. Finally each parameter is appended to the `Command` object.

```
Set mpar_Username = Server.CreateObject("ADODB.Parameter")
mpar_Username.Name = "PI_USERNAME"
mpar_Username.Type = adVarChar
mlpar_Username.Direction = adParamInput
mpar_Username.Size = 20
mpar_Username.Value = "TestUser"
mcmd_ConvertOrder.Parameters.Append mpar_Username

Set mpar_Password = Server.CreateObject("ADODB.Parameter")
mpar_Password.Name = "PI_PASSWORD"
mpar_Password.Type = adVarChar
mpar_Password.Direction = adParamInput
mpar_Password.Size = 10
mpar_Password.Value = "TestPass"
mcmd_ConvertOrder.Parameters.Append mpar_Password

Set mpar_Level = Server.CreateObject("ADODB.Parameter")
mpar_Level.Name = "PO_LEVEL"
mpar_Level.Type = adVarChar
mpar_Level.Direction = adParamOutput
mpar_Level.Size = 5
mpar_Level.Value = Null
mcmd_ConvertOrder.Parameters.Append mpar_Level
```

Record Locking in a Stateless HTTP Environment

It is easy to take record locking for granted when developing traditional client server applications, where a connection to the database is maintained between requests. In the stateless HTTP environment however, record locking becomes a serious issue that must be considered in the design of an application. The following illustration depicts the traditional mechanism for allowing a user to update a database record with ASP.

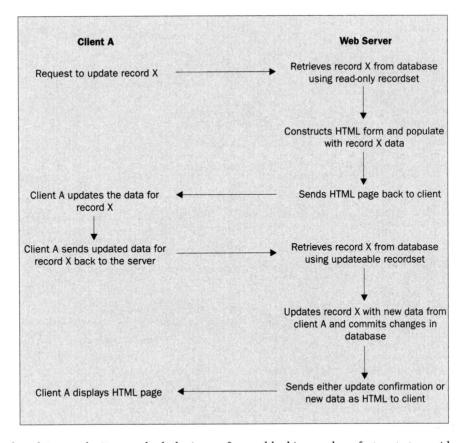

Many data driven web sites overlook the issue of record locking, and are fortunate to avoid problems because the likelihood of more than one user updating the same record at the same time is minimal. For web applications that solely exist for the purpose of interfacing to a database, for example the web enablement of a legacy Oracle Forms application, locking becomes critical in ensuring the integrity of the information in the database. Take the following scenario for example, where Client B overwrites changes made by Client A without either Client A or Client B realizing.

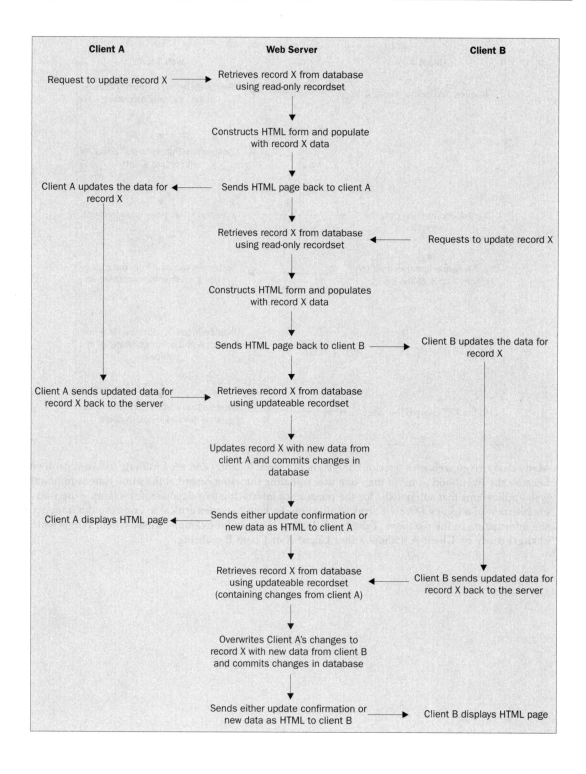

Following are three possible ways of implementing a pseudo record locking mechanism, using ASP:

The first method is to add a date/time stamp column to all tables in the database. Whenever a change is made to a record the timestamp column should be set with the current date and time. The current value of the date/time stamp is extracted along with the other fields in the record and stored in a hidden field in the HTML form containing all the editable field values. When the client resubmits the modified data the ASP page must first check that the value of the timestamp column in the database is the same as the stored value in the HTML form field. If the values are different the application can cancel the update and inform the user.

The primary benefit of this approach is that it's a relatively easy solution to implement in ASP, requiring only a minor modification to the SQL statement, together with some additional HTML to hold the timestamp value between requests. The flip side of the coin is that the addition of the timestamp column to all tables in the database is messy, and in many cases may not be a realistic option.

The second way of implementing record locking does not require any modifications to the database, however it does require much more ASP development effort. Essentially, all of the column values for the record are duplicated in hidden fields in the HTML form when the record data is first retrieved by the application. When the client returns the modified form data the ASP code is able to compare values in the updateable recordset with the values stored in the hidden form fields. Again if any of the values is different the application can cancel the update and inform the user that the record has been updated in the interim period.

The positive aspect of this approach is that it requires no modifications at all to the database structure, and allows greater feedback to be provided to the user about any changes that may have occurred. The arguably larger negative aspect is that all the extra hidden field data unnecessarily increases the volume of data transmitted between client and web server. Over lower bandwidth connections, or for forms containing many fields, this is clearly a situation to be avoided. Also, the additional processing required to compare each individual column can be a significant overhead, especially for tables with a large number of columns. A final negative aspect to this approach is from a maintenance point of view. The addition of a single column to the table means a lot of modification to the ASP code, even if this column isn't displayed in the HTML page.

The final pseudo record locking mechanism is a happy medium of the first two methods. This is to generate a checksum for the record and store this single checksum as a hidden form field. Checksums are commonly used to verify the successful and accurate movement of data between two sources, or to validate the accuracy of data such as a credit card number. The key benefit of a checksum is that a large volume of data can be represented by a much smaller amount of data, normally an integer value. Applying an algorithm to the source data, typically summing the bytes or words of information, generates the checksum value.

For our pseudo locking mechanism, the ASP page can derive a checksum for the data held in all columns in the recordset when first requested by the client. The checksum value is then placed into a hidden form field and sent with the rest of the data back to the client. When the client resubmits the data, the ASP application can retrieve the data from the database for updating and again generate a checksum using the same algorithm. If the new checksum value has changed from the checksum stored in the hidden form field then the update can be cancelled as before.

Rather than having to generate our own checksums in ASP, Oracle provide a package called OWA_OPT_LOCK that will generate a 32-bit integer checksum when supplied with the name of the table, the name of the table owner, and the rowid of the record. It should be noted that this package is only available if the Oracle PL/SQL web toolkit has been installed, as it is not a default package.

Replicating Oracle Forms Functionality

One of the biggest problems with porting legacy Forms application to the web is the lack of functionality such as triggers, blocks, and rich controls such as List Of Values (LOV). It is however possible to replicate these in ASP with a little bit of imagination and creative development!

Replicating Visual Attributes

Replicating Visual Attributes is not really a function of ASP, however the concept of defining the appearance of components within the application is possible through the use of Cascading Style Sheets (CSS). CSS is a technology that isn't used as often as it might be, partly because of varying degrees of support for and compatibility issues with the various flavors and versions of browsers. Another reason is that many of the WYSIWYG tools on the market for creating HTML pages simply use the older method of `<font>` tags and color attributes.

It's worth investing a little time learning about CSS, and tools like the CSS editor in Visual InterDev make it much easier by allowing style-sheets to be created in a graphical environment. Using CSS allows you to define a standard and consistent appearance for your entire application, setting default fonts, colors, and alignment, to name a few. If your application is to be deployed in an Internet Explorer only environment you can even apply the principles to the intrinsic HTML controls, so mandatory text fields may have a different background color from optional fields, etc.

Replicating Function Blocks

The concept of blocks does not exist in an HTML page, as there are no individual sections to a page. Consequently it can be difficult to replicate master-detail relationships; the replication of updateable multi-line blocks would typically require either excessive client-side scripting, or a complicated state machine in the ASP page to handle multiple round trips to the server.

Replicating updateable single record blocks is more straightforward, and may be achieved through the use of HTML frames. The simple example we will work through here is based upon the default scott/tiger schema, and uses the `target` attribute of a frame to load the department details of an employee into a different frame.

The first file we need to create is the frameset, `BlocksFrame.htm`, page that will provide the container for the master and detail pages. This is a simple file that specifies the two frames and assigns a name to each, **Master** for the master page containing the list of employees, and **Detail** for the detail page containing the department for the employee selected in the master page.

```
<html>
  <head>
    <title>Replicating Blocks</title>
  </head>
  <frameset rows="*,*">
    <frame name="Master" src="MasterBlock.asp">
    <frame name="Detail" src="DetailBlock.asp">
    <noframes>
      <body>
        <p>
          This page uses frames, but unfortunately
          your browser doesn't support them.
        </p>
      </body>
    </noframes>
  </frameset>
</html>
```

The next file we need to create is `MasterBlock.asp`. This ASP page will retrieve an ADO recordset containing the `Ename` and `DeptNo` columns from the `EMP` table and simply list the names of the employees in a `<SELECT>` dropdown list. We then iterate through the records in the recordset and dynamically write out the HTML `<OPTION>` tags that will display the details in the `<SELECT>` list. For the sake of simplicity, the `DeptNo` for each employee is assigned to the value of each item in the list, which, together with a submit button, is held within a standard HTML form. The `target` attribute of the form is set to be the name of the detail frame in the frameset. Note that the second line includes the ADO constants library, and should point to the location of this on the server, relative to the ASP file

```asp
<%@ Language=VBScript %>
<!--#include file="include/adovbs.asp"-->
<html>
  <head>
    <title>Master Block</title>
  </head>
  <body>
    <form action="DetailBlock.asp" method="get" target="Detail">
      Employee:
<%
Dim mcon_Connection
Dim mrec_Employees
Dim lstr_Sql

lstr_Sql = "SELECT EName, DeptNo FROM Emp ORDER BY EName"

Set mcon_Connection = Server.CreateObject("ADODB.Connection")

mcon_Connection.Open "Provider=MSDAORA;Data Source=proead;" & _
                     "User ID=scott;Password=Tiger;"

If mcon_Connection.State = adStateOpen Then
  Response.Write "<select id=""deptno"" name=""deptno"">"
  Set mrec_Employees = Server.CreateObject("ADODB.Recordset")
  mrec_Employees.Open lstr_Sql, mcon_Connection, adOpenForwardOnly, _
                      adLockReadOnly, adCmdText

  Do While Not mrec_Employees.EOF
  Response.Write "<option value=""" & mrec_Employees.Fields("DeptNo") & _
                 """>" & mrec_Employees.Fields("EName") & "</option>"
  mrec_Employees.MoveNext
  Loop
  mrec_Employees.Close
  Set mrec_Employees = Nothing
  mcon_Connection.Close
  Response.Write "</select>"
End If
Set mcon_Connection = Nothing
%>
      <input name="cmdSubmit" type="submit" value="Get Department Details">
    </form>
  </body>
</html>
```

The final page is `DetailBlock.asp`, which displays the departmental details for the selected employee. First, we have the standard HTML header block for the page:

```
<%@ Language=VBScript %>
<!--#include file="include/adovbs.asp"-->
<html>
<head>
<title>Detail Block</title>
</head>
<body>
```

We then read the `Deptno` value from the data submitted by the form in the master page. If the `Deptno` value is empty we can assume that this is the first time the page has been loaded.

```
<%
  Dim mstrDeptNo
  Dim mcon_Connection
  Dim mstr_Sql
  Dim mrec_Department

  mstrDeptNo = Request.QueryString("deptno")
  If mstrDeptNo = "" Then
    Response.Write "Please select an employee."
```

We then use the `deptno` value to dynamically build the appropriate SQL statement to execute against the database. We then write out the details of the department and location matching the supplied department number.

```
  Else
  lstr_Sql = "SELECT DName, Loc FROM Dept WHERE DeptNo = '" & mstrDeptNo & "'"

  Set mcon_Connection = Server.CreateObject("ADODB.Connection")

  mcon_Connection.Open "Provider=MSDAORA;Data Source=proead;" & _
                  "User ID=scott;Password=Tiger;"

  If mcon_Connection.State = adStateOpen Then
    Set mrec_Department = Server.CreateObject("ADODB.Recordset")

    mrec_Department.Open lstr_Sql, mcon_Connection, _
                    adOpenForwardOnly, adLockReadOnly, adCmdText

    If Not (mrec_Department.BOF And mrec_Department.EOF) Then
      Response.Write "Department: " & mrec_Department.Fields("DName") & "<br>"
      Response.Write "Location: " & mrec_Department.Fields("Loc")
    End If
    mrec_Department.Close
    Set mrec_Department = Nothing
    mcon_Connection.Close
  End If
  Set mcon_Connection = Nothing
  End If
%>
  </body>
</html>
```

Initially when the page loads it looks like this:

Clicking on Get Department Details retrieves the data for employee Adams.

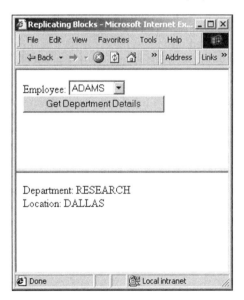

Selecting James from the list and then pressing the button again loads the details of James's department into the detail frame.

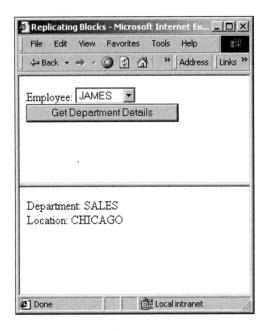

Replicating Controls

The Oracle Forms environment is a rich development environment, with a large array of controls and functionality available to the developer. To further supplement the intrinsic controls, Forms also allows custom functionality to be developed through support for Java Beans and ActiveX controls. Unfortunately, when developing applications to be deployed using HTML as the GUI, the variety of intrinsic controls available is greatly reduced.

At a first glance, it would appear that only a small number of controls are available, as there are only four HTML tags that are used to display controls in HTML. However the same tag is used in a number of instances to display different controls, configured using attribute values of the tag. Some of the controls available include: button, check box, radio button, text box and scrollable fields.

Again, it is possible to extend the controls available through the use of Java applets and ActiveX controls – however this is not always feasible due to variations in client browser capabilities and the development effort involved.

Replicating Item-Level Triggers

It is possible to replicate triggers using a combination of both client and server-side validation routines. On the client the validation logic is possible using the intrinsic browser event model. Here we may use either the onBlur() event for individual fields, or the onSubmit() event of a form to perform basic validation, such as data type validation, numeric domain validation, or simple masking validation (for example for e-mail addresses). The downside of client-side validation is that it is typically limited to basic numeric domain validation (does value x fall within defined boundaries) and type validation (is x a number, a string, a valid date, etc.). Since the client browser never has a physical connection to the database it isn't usually possible to validate against other existing data in the database. In order to perform this sort of remote validation we can use a technology called **Remote Scripting**.

Remote Scripting

Remote Scripting is one of those technologies that seems to sit quietly on the sidelines, just waiting to be noticed. Developed by Microsoft, it uses a client-side Java applet to communicate over HTTP with server-side ASP pages. The principles are the same as those employed by Oracle's JInitiator and Developer Server, to allow Forms applications to be deployed in a web browser.

Remote Scripting is not an Internet Explorer proprietary technology – all it requires is a Java compatible browser. In practice however, it can be difficult to develop solutions that work satisfactorily in other browsers such as Netscape.

> *For simplicity and ease of coding all of the examples in this chapter will assume the browser is Internet Explorer 4.01 or greater running on a Windows 9x/NT/2000 platform.*

If you are creating your ASP applications using Visual InterDev then the necessary Remote Scripting files will automatically be installed in the _Scripts directory of the web application. Otherwise, you can download the Remote Scripting kit for free from the Microsoft site at http://msdn.microsoft.com /scripting/. I can't stress enough how important it is to thoroughly test server-side functions from within a normal ASP page before porting to the Remote Scripting "environment". Debugging Remote Scripting procedure at runtime will only cause endless hours of frustration, as the true cause of any errors can be masked by a generic Remote Scripting error message.

> *A detailed discussion of Remote Scripting is out-of-scope for this chapter. There are, however, a number of good articles on the ASPToday site (http://www.asptoday.com).*

Uses for Remote Scripting

One area in particular where remote scripting is useful, is in providing more advanced field validation. It allows us to validate values entered by the user in a client-side HTML <INPUT> control using server-side code, without having to do a complete server round trip with the whole page. A useful feature of Remote Scripting is that it allows us to call the server-side functions either synchronously, or asynchronously. This gives us increased flexibility because it means that we can perform the validation either at the field or at the form level.

Let's build on our previous example uses the default scott/tiger schema again, but validating on the server, the department id entered by the user at the client, to ensure the department already exists in the database. The key point to note is that this is achieved without refreshing the entire HTML page, as would normally be necessary.

We will start by building the server side code that will validate the department ID. In order to use remote scripting we enable it both within the client-side source page **and** in the server-side ASP code. This is done in the ASP file, ValidateDept.asp, as follows:

```
<% RSDispatch %>
<!--#include virtual="/_ScriptLibrary/rs.asp"-->
<!--#include file="../include/adovbs.asp"-->
```

The second line must point to the location of the rs.asp file on the server. When Remote Scripting is installed this is located by default in the _ScriptLibrary folder off the web root. Unfortunately it isn't possible to build up this line dynamically, as the ASP engine processes server side includes before any script code is executed. This is therefore one of the first things to check when debugging Remote Scripting code. Similarly, I prefer to group Remote Scripting pages in a separate RemoteScripting folder off the root, which is where ValidateDept.asp is stored in these examples.

We then include a standard JavaScript function in the page, MyServerMethods() to handle the requests from the client as follows:

```
<script runat="server" language="JavaScript">
  var public_description = new MyServerMethods();
  function MyServerMethods()
  {
    this.ValidateDept = Function('DeptNo','return
ValidateDepartment(DeptNo)');
  }
</script>
```

The remote scripting ASP page may contain any number of functions or procedures, and it is the responsibility of this function to pass the request from the client to the appropriate function that performs the work. While the MyServerMethods() function must always be coded in JavaScript, the functions and procedures actually performing the work may be coded in either JavaScript or VBScript, depending upon the preferences of the developer.

The this.ValidateDept... line exposes the private ValidateDepartment() VBScript function as ValidateDept, and identifies it as expecting a single argument, DeptNo.

The remainder of the page is the VBScript ValidateDepartment () function that actually validates the supplied department ID against the database.

```
<script runat="server" language="VBScript">
  Function ValidateDepartment(ByVal vlng_DeptNo)

  Dim lcon_Connection
  Dim lrec_Department
  Dim lstr_Sql
```

```
    If IsNumeric(vlng_DeptNo) Then
        Set lcon_Connection = Server.CreateObject("ADODB.Connection")
        lcon_Connection.Open "Provider=MSDAORA;Data Source = proead;" & _
                            "User ID=scott;Password=tiger;"

        If lcon_Connection.State = adStateOpen Then
            Set lrec_Department = Server.CreateObject("ADODB.Recordset")
            lstr_Sql = "SELECT DName FROM Dept WHERE DeptNo = " & vlng_DeptNo
            lrec_Department.Open lstr_Sql, lcon_Connection, adOpenForwardOnly, _
                            adLockReadOnly, adCmdText

        If lrec_Department.BOF And lrec_Department.EOF Then
            ValidateDepartment = "Department does not exist."
        Else
            ValidateDepartment = ""
        End If
            lrec_Department.Close
            Set lrec_Department = Nothing
            lcon_Connection.Close
        End If

        Set lcon_Connection = Nothing
    Else
        ValidateDepartment = "Department ID must be numeric."
    End If

End Function
</script>
```

From the above code you can see that first of all a check is made that the data is numeric as expected.

```
If IsNumeric(vlng_DeptNo) Then

 ...<etc.>...

Else
  ValidateDepartment = "Department ID must be numeric."
End If
```

Assuming that a numeric value has been supplied, we create a connection to the database.

```
        Set lcon_Connection = Server.CreateObject("ADODB.Connection")
        lcon_Connection.Open "Provider=MSDAORA;Data Source = proead;" & _
                            "User ID=scott;Password=tiger;"
```

Having checked that a connection has been opened successfully we then attempt to retrieve the name of the department matching the supplied ID.

```
If lcon_Connection.State = adStateOpen Then
    Set lrec_Department = Server.CreateObject("ADODB.Recordset")
    lstr_Sql = "SELECT DName FROM Dept WHERE DeptNo = " & vlng_DeptNo
    lrec_Department.Open lstr_Sql, lcon_Connection, adOpenForwardOnly, _
                adLockReadOnly, adCmdText
```

If the recordset doesn't contain any records then we can deduce that the supplied ID is invalid. Having performed the check we properly close the recordset and the connection and release the object references.

```
If lrec_Department.BOF And lrec_Department.EOF Then
  ValidateDepartment = "Department does not exist."
Else
  ValidateDepartment = ""
End If
lrec_Department.Close
Set lrec_Department = Nothing
lcon_Connection.Close
End If
Set lcon_Connection = Nothing
```

Having completed the server-side validation process, we will now look at the client-side functionality in the file RSValidation.asp. As with the server-side code we must first enable the page for remote scripting.

```
<html>
  <head>
    <title>Validation using Remote Scripting</title>
    <script language="JavaScript"
            src="http://WEB_SERVER/_ScriptLibrary/rs.htm"></script>
    <script language="JavaScript">
      serverURL = "http://WEB_SERVER/_ScriptLibrary";
      RSEnableRemoteScripting(serverURL);
    </script>
```

The WEB_SERVER part should be replaced with the name of the web server. Should the client page also be generated using ASP we can achieve this automatically by taking advantage of one of the server variables as follows:

```
<script language="JavaScript"
src="http://<%=Request.ServerVariables("SERVER_NAME")%>/_ScriptLibrary/rs.htm"></s
cript>
serverURL = _
        "http://<%=Request.ServerVariables("SERVER_NAME")%>/_ScriptLibrary";
```

We then include the client side code that calls the server-side function.

```
    <script language="javascript">
      function ValidateDept()
      {
        var objRS = RSExecute("http://<%=Request.ServerVariables("SERVER_NAME")%>/
RemoteScripts/ValidateDept.asp","ValidateDept", txtDeptId.value);
        if (objRS.status != 0)
        {
          alert("An error occurred whilst validating the data.");
        }
        else
        {
            if (objRS.return_value)
            {
            alert(objRS.return_value);
        }
        }
      }
    </script>
  </head>
```

This simply calls the `ValidateDept()` function within the `ValidateDept.asp` page, passing in the value from the local text input field. Remote scripting calls always return an object with a `Status` property that can be used to detect whether a problem occurred during the execution of the remote script (in this case we simply display an error message). Another property of the object is the return value from the remote function. If the supplied department was invalid for whatever reason this would contain some error text that we can display in an error dialog, as shown below.

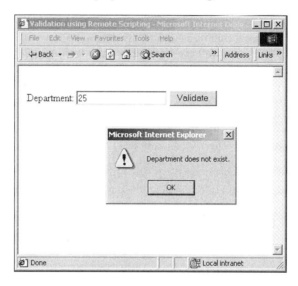

If a valid department code was supplied then no message is displayed.

The final part of the client HTML page simply displays the prompt, the text box, and the **Validate** button itself. The `onClick()` event of the **Validate** button calls the `ValidateDept()` function declared in the `<head>` section of the page.

```
<body>
  <table>
    <tr>
      <td>Department:</td>
      <td>
        <input id="txtDeptId" name="txtDeptId" type="text" value="" />
      </td>
      <td>
        <button id="cmdValidate"
                onclick="javascript:ValidateDept();">Validate</button>
      </td>
    </tr>
  </table>
</body>
</html>
```

In this example we have used a separate Validate button to validate the code. In reality the user cannot, and should not, be expected to click on a command button to validate the values he enters. One way to overcome this is to sink the call to the remote script in the onBlur() event for the control. This would cause the value entered by the user to be validated as soon as the control lost focus. In an Intranet environment this might be acceptable but in an Extranet or Internet scenario, where speed is more of a consideration, the time required to perform the validation could prove to be annoying for the user. A way to circumvent this is to use the asynchronous capabilities of Remote Scripting to validate the values in the background whilst the user continues to enter other data. The validation messages can then be displayed when the user presses a Submit button. If invalid values have been entered then a suitable message can be displayed to the user, otherwise the form data is submitted to the server.

Replicating LOVs

One of the great features provided by Oracle Forms is the List Of Values (LOV) functionality. LOVs provide an intuitive way of finding a specific value from within a large data set of possible records. There are no intrinsic controls that allow us to replicate this functionality in HTML, however using Remote Scripting, some ASP, and a little client-side DHTML we can provide LOV functionality in our web applications.

A sample of the LOV we shall build over the next few pages is shown in the following screenshot.

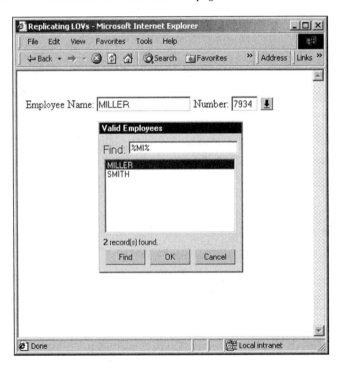

For this example we shall construct two ASP files, LOV.asp and SearchEmployee.asp, together with a Cascading Style Sheet (CSS) file, LOV.css that sets the appearance of the various parts of the LOV. The complete style sheet is described below.

```
<STYLE>
BODY
{
    BACKGROUND-COLOR: #ffffff
}
DIV.LOV
{
    BACKGROUND-ATTACHMENT: fixed;
    BACKGROUND-COLOR: #cccccc;
    BACKGROUND-IMAGE: url(images/lov.gif);
    BACKGROUND-REPEAT: no-repeat;
    BORDER-BOTTOM: #333333 1px solid;
    BORDER-LEFT: #cccccc 1px solid;
    BORDER-RIGHT: #333333 1px solid;
    BORDER-TOP: #cccccc 1px solid;
    CURSOR: hand;
    FONT-SIZE: 8pt;
    HEIGHT: 18px;
    MARGIN: 0px;
    PADDING-BOTTOM: 1px;
    PADDING-LEFT: 1px;
    PADDING-RIGHT: 1px;
    PADDING-TOP: 1px;
    WIDTH: 18px
}
DIV.LOV_Dialog
{
    BACKGROUND-COLOR: #000066;
    BORDER-BOTTOM: #666666 2px solid;
    BORDER-LEFT: #d0d0d0 2px solid;
    BORDER-RIGHT: #666666 2px solid;
    BORDER-TOP: #d0d0d0 2px solid;
    COLOR: #ffffff;
    CURSOR: move;
    FONT-FAMILY: 'MS Sans Serif', Arial;
    FONT-SIZE: 8pt;
    FONT-WEIGHT: bold;
    HEIGHT: 200px;
    MARGIN: 0px;
    PADDING-BOTTOM: 0px;
    PADDING-LEFT: 0px;
    PADDING-RIGHT: 0px;
    PADDING-TOP: 1px;
    POSITION: absolute;
    WIDTH: 200px
}
DIV.LOV_Dialog TABLE
{
    CURSOR: default;
    MARGIN: 2px 0px 0px;
    PADDING-BOTTOM: 0px;
    PADDING-LEFT: 0px;
    PADDING-RIGHT: 0px;
    PADDING-TOP: 0px;
    WIDTH: 100%
}
```

```
DIV.LOV_Dialog TD
{
    BACKGROUND-COLOR: #e0e0e0;
    FONT-FAMILY: 'MS Sans Serif', Arial;
    MARGIN: 0px;
    PADDING-BOTTOM: 0px;
    PADDING-LEFT: 0px;
    PADDING-RIGHT: 0px;
    PADDING-TOP: 0px
}
DIV.LOV_Dialog TABLE TD.Buttons
{
    PADDING-BOTTOM: 10px;
    PADDING-TOP: 5px;
    TEXT-ALIGN: center
}
DIV.LOV_Dialog TABLE TD.Title
{
    BACKGROUND-COLOR: darkblue;
    COLOR: #ffffff;
    FONT-WEIGHT: 700;
    TEXT-ALIGN: left
}
DIV.LOV_Dialog BUTTON
{
    BORDER-BOTTOM: #333333 1px solid;
    BORDER-LEFT: #cccccc 1px solid;
    BORDER-RIGHT: #333333 1px solid;
    BORDER-TOP: #cccccc 1px solid;
    CURSOR: hand;
    FONT-FAMILY: 'MS Sans Serif', Arial;
    FONT-SIZE: 8pt;
    HEIGHT: 22px;
    MARGIN-LEFT: 4px;
    MARGIN-RIGHT: 4px;
    WIDTH: 60px;
    FONT-FACE: Arial
}
DIV.LOV_Dialog TABLE TD.Prompt
{
    PADDING-LEFT: 5px;
    PADDING-RIGHT: 5px;
    PADDING-TOP: 10px;
    WIDTH: 30px
}
DIV.LOV_Dialog TABLE TD.Find
{
    FONT-SIZE: 8pt;
    PADDING-BOTTOM: 5px;
    PADDING-RIGHT: 5px;
    PADDING-TOP: 10px;
    WIDTH: 180px
}
DIV.LOV_Dialog TABLE TD.Results
{
```

```
        PADDING-LEFT: 5px;
        PADDING-RIGHT: 5px;
        TEXT-ALIGN: center
    }
    DIV.LOV_Dialog TABLE TD.Count
    {
        FONT-SIZE: 8pt;
        PADDING-LEFT: 5px;
        PADDING-TOP: 5px
    }
    DIV.LOV_Dialog TABLE TD.Find INPUT
    {
        FONT-FAMILY: 'MS Sans Serif', Arial;
        FONT-SIZE: 8pt
    }
    DIV.LOV_Dialog TABLE TD.Results SELECT
    {
        FONT-FAMILY: 'MS Sans Serif', Arial;
        FONT-SIZE: 8pt
    }
    </STYLE>
```

Placing the settings for the LOV in a separate style-sheet allows their reuse across a web application in different files, taking advantage of file caching as well as allowing the appearance to be defined from a single location.

The first of the ASP files is the server side file that queries the database, `SearchEmployee.asp` (again stored in the **RemoteScripting** folder)

As with the earlier example, we first include the necessary code to enable remote scripting and provide a mapping for our server-side function `getEmployees()`, that will query the database.

```
<% RSDispatch %>
<!--#include virtual="/_ScriptLibrary/rs.asp"-->
<!--#include file="../include/adovbs.asp"-->
<script runat="server" language="JavaScript">
    var public_description = new MyServerMethods();
    function MyServerMethods()
    {
        this.getEmployees = Function('filter','return GetEmployeeList(filter)' );
    }
</script>
```

We then include the code for the `getEmployees()` function. This accepts a single parameter, `vstr_Search` that is used as part of a LIKE statement to filter the number of employee records returned. We create a `Connection` and `Recordset` object as before, and execute the SQL against the database.

```
<script runat="server" language="VBScript">
    Function GetEmployeeList(ByVal vstr_Search)

    Dim lcon_Connection
    Dim lrec_Employees
    Dim lstr_Html
    Dim lstr_Sql
```

```
lstr_Sql = "SELECT EmpNo, EName FROM Emp WHERE EName LIKE '" & _
           CStr(vstr_Search) & "' ORDER BY EName"

Set lcon_Connection = Server.CreateObject("ADODB.Connection")
lcon_Connection.Open "Provider=MSDAORA;DSN=ProfOra8", "scott", "tiger"
If lcon_Connection.State = adStateOpen Then

  Set lrec_Employees = Server.CreateObject("ADODB.Recordset")
  lrec_Employees.Open lstr_Sql, lcon_Connection, adOpenForwardOnly, _
                      adLockReadOnly, adCmdText
```

Once the recordset containing the matching records is populated we can start to build the HTML that is returned to the client to allow the records to be displayed in a list box. We must supply the HTML code for the entire list, including the <select> tags.

```
lstr_Html = "<select id=""lstRecords"" name=""lstRecords"" " & _
            "size=""8"" onchange=""javascript:" & _
            "btnOkDisabled.style.display='none';" & _
            "btnOk.style.display='';"" " & _
            "ondblclick=""javascript:" & _
            "setEmployee(lstRecords.value, " & _
            "lstRecords.children(selectedIndex).innerText);"" " & _
            "style=""width:200px"">"

If Not (lrec_Employees.BOF And lrec_Employees.EOF) Then
  Do While Not lrec_Employees.EOF
    lstr_Html = lstr_Html & "<option value=""" & _
                CStr(lrec_Employees.Fields("EmpNo") & "") & """>" & _
                CStr(lrec_Employees.Fields("EName")) & "</option>"
  lrec_Employees.MoveNext
  Loop
End If
```

Finally we close the `Recordset` and `Connection` objects as normal and release the object references.

```
    lrec_Employees.Close
    Set lrec_Employees = Nothing
    lcon_Connection.Close
  End If

  Set lcon_Connection = Nothing
  lstr_Html = lstr_Html & "</select>"
  GetEmployeeList = lstr_Html

  End Function
</script>
```

Having completed the server-side code we must now develop the client page LOV.asp, which displays the input form and LOV. Again, we must first include the standard HTML header code and enable the page to support Remote Scripting.

```
<%@ Language=VBScript %>
<html>
  <head>
    <title>Replicating LOVs</title>
    <script language="JavaScript" src="_ScriptLibrary/rs.htm"></script>
    <script language="JavaScript">
      serverURL =
"http://<%=Request.ServerVariables("SERVER_NAME")%>/_ScriptLibrary";
      RSEnableRemoteScripting(serverURL);
    </script>
```

We also include the local scripting function, `DisplayLOV()` that interacts with the remote script and displays the results. This function first hides the normal OK button and displays the disabled OK button, as the resulting list returned from the remote script will not have an item selected initially. This code is not really necessary, just a nice esthetic touch. The procedure then calls the remote script, passing the contents of the search text box as a parameter.

```
<script language="javascript">
  function DisplayLOV()
  {
    btnOk.style.display='none';
    btnOkDisabled.style.display='';
    var objRS =
RSExecute("http://<%=Request.ServerVariables("SERVER_NAME")%>/PO8P/" +
"RemoteScripts/SearchEmployee.asp","getEmployees", Search_Employee_Surname.value);
```

The script then checks the status property of the Remote Scripting object returned to determine if any errors occurred. If an error did occur an error message is displayed to the user, otherwise the contents of the <div> tag surrounding the existing list is replaced with the HTML returned by the remote script. This should contain the entire HTML necessary to display the list, together with the client-side script that will sink the various events of the control. The final action performed by the script is to display the number of records returned by the search. This is achieved simply by counting the number of items in the list.

```
    if (objRS.status != 0)
    {
      alert("An error occurred whilst retrieving the records.");
    }
    else
    {
                divEmployees.innerHTML = objRS.return_value;
                divEmployeeCount.innerHTML =
'<b>'+lstRecords.children.length+'</b> record(s) found.";
    }
  }
```

The next client-side function we include passes the value selected by the use in the LOV list back to the appropriate controls on the main form.

```
  function setEmployee(empNo,empName)
  {
    Employee_Id.innerText = empNo;
    Employee_Name.innerText = empName;
    Search_Employee.style.display = "none";
  }
```

The final client-side script we include is simply used to position the `<div>` containing the entire pseudo LOV control in the centre of the window. The last part of the `<head>` tag contains a link to the CSS file containing all the styles for the LOV.

```
function positionLov()
{
   Search_Employee.style.left = ((document.body.clientWidth/2) - 100);
   Search_Employee.style.top = ((document.body.clientHeight/2) - 120);
}
</script>
<link rel="stylesheet" type="text/css" href="LOV.css">
</head>
```

We sink a couple of the body tags events. Both the `onresize()` and `onload()` events cause the LOV to be maintained in the centre of the window by calling the `positionLov()` function. We include a couple of `<input>` controls that will contain the name and id of the employee selected in the LOV.

```
<body onresize="javascript:positionLov();"
      onload="javascript:positionLov();">
  <table>
    <tr>
      <td>Employee Name:</td>
      <td>
        <input id="Employee_Name" name="Employee_Name"
               readonly="readonly" type="text" value="" />
      </td>
      <td>Number:</td>
      <td>
        <input id="Employee_Id" name="Employee_Id" style="width:40px"
               readonly="readonly" type="text" value="" />
      </td>
```

This has the following appearance in the HTML page.

We use a `<div>` tag that the user may click on to display the LOV. This CSS style for the class assigned to this tag automatically displays the appropriate image file.

```
      <td>
        <div class="LOV"
onclick="javascript:Search_Employee.style.display='';Search_Employee_Surname.focus
();"> </div>
      </td>
    </tr>
  </table>
```

The next block of code defines the master `<div>` tag that contains all of the HTML necessary to display the LOV. The first section of this HTML defines the `<input>` text box that allows the user to specify the search criteria. We sink the onkeypress event so that when the user presses the return key (keycode 13) the function to communicate with the server side script is called. The initial value of the text box is set to `%`.

```
<div id="Search_Employee" class="LOV_Dialog" style="display:none">
   Valid Employees
  <table cellspacing="0">
    <tr>
      <td class="Prompt">Find:</td>
      <td class="Find">
        <input id="Search_Employee_Surname"
               name="Search_Employee_Surname"
               onkeypress="javascript:if(event.keyCode==13)DisplayLOV();"
               style="width:165px" type="text" value="%" />
      </td>
    </tr>
```

The next section of HTML code defines the list that will display the results. This is essentially a placeholder at this stage, as it will be replaced by the HTML returned by the remote ASP function.

```
    <tr>
      <td class="Results" colspan="2">
        <div id="divEmployees">
          <select id="lstRecords" name="lstRecords" size="8"
                  style="width:200px"></select>
        </div>
      </td>
    </tr>
```

We also define another <div> tag that will be used to display the number of matching records returned by the remote script. Whilst this functionality is not displayed on a normal Oracle LOV, it's easy for us to implement with little overhead.

```
    <tr>
      <td class="Count" colspan="2">
        <div id="divEmployeeCount"> </div>
      </td>
    </tr>
```

The final block of HTML code defines the three buttons displayed in the LOV. In fact we actually include four buttons, as the easiest way to toggle the appearance of the OK button between a disabled or enabled appearance is actually to include a dummy button with a disabled appearance. The style of each button is then dynamically modified to hide or show the appropriate button.

```
    <tr>
      <td class="Buttons" colspan="2">
        <button id="btnFind" onclick="javascript:DisplayLOV();">
          Find
        </button>
        <button id="btnOkDisabled" disabled style="display:''">
          OK
        </button>
        <button id="btnOk"
            onclick="javascript:setEmployee(lstRecords.value,
                lstRecords.children(lstRecords.selectedIndex).innerText);"
            style="display:none">
          OK
```

```
        </button>
        <button id="btnCancel"
              onclick="javascript:Search_Employee.style.display='none';">
          Cancel
        </button>
      </td>
    </tr>
  </table>
 </div>
 </body>
</html>
```

The appearance of our LOV initially looks as follows, before any search is executed:

Unlike the Oracle LOV, we do not automatically load all records by default when the LOV is first displayed. This is for performance reasons, as retrieving all of the records may take some time. After all, if the user needs to use a LOV, the likelihood is that they need to filter the available records to locate the one they require.

Simply clicking on the OK button at this stage will search for all employee records and populate the list. The number of matching records is also displayed:

By selecting a specific employee, we enable the **OK** button:

Clicking **OK**, or double-clicking on a specific employee in the list, will close the LOV and copy the details of the selected employee into the text boxes on the main page:

Replicating Menu Security

Menu security in Oracle Forms applications is based upon the database roles configured for each user in the database. We may also use the same principles in our ASP applications, if the account used by the web server to access the database has select permissions for the DBA_ROLE_PRIVS system table. By performing a simple SQL statement we may determine the appropriate permissions for a particular user and apply them at an application level to restrict access to certain levels of functionality, assuming that the database username assigned to the user is held in the mstr_DbUsername variable.

```
mstr_Sql = "SELECT granted_role " & _
           "FROM dba_role_privs " & _
           "WHERE grantee = '" & mstr_DbUsername & "'"

Set lrec_Privileges = Server.CreateObject("ADODB.Recordset")
lrec_Privileges.Open lstr_Sql, mcon_Connection, adOpenForwardOnly, _
                adLockReadOnly, adCmdText

Do While Not lrec_Privileges.EOF
  Session(lrec_Privileges.Fields("granted_role")) = True
  lrec_Privileges.MoveNext
Loop
lrec_Privileges.Close
Set lrec_Privileges = Nothing
```

Assuming that one of the roles defined in the database is called APP_ADMIN then we can simply check at any time whether the current user has that privilege using the following code.

```
If Session("APP_ADMIN") = True
   ' User has the role assigned
End If
```

Oracle AppWizard for Microsoft Visual InterDev

A chapter on using ASP to interface with Oracle 8i would not be complete without briefly mentioning the Oracle AppWizard for Microsoft Visual InterDev. This product integrates into the Visual InterDev environment and allows developers to quickly develop an interface to the data, in a similar way to the intrinsic Visual InterDev design time controls. The AppWizard for Visual InterDev uses OO4O to provide the link between the ASP pages and the Oracle 8i database, and generates all the code necessary to view, insert, update and delete single records, as well as navigating through multiple records and master details blocks.

The AppWizard is a great product if you are completely new to ASP and ADO development, but already very familiar with OO4O. However, as with all "wizards" it will only hold your hand for so long before leaving you high and dry when things get tough, and you try to do something a little out of the ordinary.

Integration with Oracle Developer Server

An application need not be created using just ASP or just Developer Server. It is possible to integrate the two products, especially for the generation of reports. An ASP page can take the information submitted in an HTML form and use this to construct an appropriate URL query string to pass to Developer Reports Server using the Oracle Web CGI cartridge. This cartridge parses the information in the HTTP URL request and runs the specified report with any parameters also supplied. The resultant report is then automatically sent back to the client in either HTML or PDF format by using the DESTYPE=CACHE setting.

A word of caution when using this method of interfacing to Reports Server is that it is only suitable for reports that do not take longer than a few minutes to run. Any longer and the client browser will timeout, assuming that the server has died.

Using ASP and XML with Oracle

Lastly, as mentioned earlier in our introduction, the ASP code we use doesn't just have to generate HTML code, it can generate any code that has a text format, and that includes XML. XML support in Oracle is provided through the **XML SQL Utility**, a set of special components, which allow us to retrieve an XML document from the database by executing a SQL query, and to update a database by parsing an XML document. The ASP can be used to create a SQL query and we can use ADO to retrieve an XML document from the database, which returns the result of that query.

The XML SQL Utility

The XML SQL Utility (often abbreviated to XSU) can be downloaded from Oracle's TechNet site at:

http://technet.oracle.com/software/tech/xml/oracle_xsu/software_index.htm

The xmlgen Package

Now that we've got the XSU installed, it's time to see what we can do with it. As we said above, we'll restrict ourselves to the PL/SQL API, since that is the component that is most likely to be useful to an ASP developer.

The PL/SQL API is essentially a wrapper that sits on top of the Java API, and consists of a single Oracle package called xmlgen. This package contains too many functions to go through each one, so we will instead look at how we can accomplish the most important tasks using the XSU, and see how we can use these features from an ASP application.

Retrieving an XML Document from the Database

The most common Oracle/XML task will probably be to retrieve a recordset in XML format as a result of a database query. True, we can do this easily enough with ADO but the structure of ADO XML recordsets is hardly intuitive. Fortunately, Oracle allows us to retrieve far more intuitively structured XML documents from a database using the getXML function of the xmlgen package. The syntax for this function is:

```
XMLDoc := xmlgen.getXML(sql_statement, [meta_type])
```

Where:

Name	Data Type	Description
XMLDoc	CLOB	The generated XML document.
sql_statement	varchar	The query which will be used to generate the XML document.
meta_type	number	Optional. Specifies whether a DTD is to be generated with the XML document.

The following stored procedure illustrates the use of this function. In this procedure, we will simply pass a hard-coded SQL query into getXML and return the generated XML document as a varchar output parameter:

```
CREATE OR REPLACE PROCEDURE spGetEmpXml
(strXML OUT varchar)
AS
clobXML CLOB;
intLength integer;
BEGIN
    intLength := 4000;
    clobXML := xmlgen.getXML('SELECT * FROM EMP');
    DBMS_LOB.READ(clobXML, intLength, 1, strXML);
END;
```

The getXML function returns a CLOB (Character Large Object), rather than a varchar, so we need to convert this to a string before returning it from our procedure. To do this, PL/SQL provides the DBMS_LOB.READ method. This takes four parameters: the CLOB we wish to read from, the number of characters we want to read, the offset (the position in the CLOB where we want to start reading), and a varchar variable which will be used to hold the result. Note that the second of these parameters is in/out, so it cannot be passed in as a literal – we have to use a variable.

The `genXML` function returns an XML document in the following format:

```
<?xml version="1.0" ?>
<ROWSET>
    <ROW num="n">
        <column>value</column>
        <!-- an element for each column -->
    </ROW>
</ROWSET>
```

Each row in the resultset is represented by a <ROW> element in the XML document, and these are enclosed by a root <ROWSET> element. The individual <ROW> elements are identified by a num attribute. Each column is represented by an element with the same name as the column, and contains the column's value in a child text node.

Calling the Stored Procedure from ASP

Now that we've got our XML document as a stored procedure output parameter, it's a very simple job to access this via ADO from an ASP page or an ASP component. After connecting to the database, we simply create an ADO `Command` object, set its `CommandType` to `adCmdStoredProc`, and create a `Parameter` object. This should be an output parameter of type adVarChar, with a length of 4000 characters, since that's the number of characters we read from the CLOB in our stored procedure. Next, we call the `Command` object's `Execute` method to call the procedure, set `Response.ContentType` to `"text/xml"`, and display the XML document. This is returned as an output parameter from our procedure, so our `Parm1` `Parameter` object is populated when we call `cmd.Execute`:

```
<!-- METADATA TYPE="TypeLib"
            FILE="C:\Program Files\Common Files\System\ADO\msado15.dll" -->
<%
Set cn = Server.CreateObject("ADODB.Connection")

cn.Open "Provider=MSDAORA;Data Source=ProfOra8;" & _
        "User ID=scott;Password=tiger"

Set cmd = Server.CreateObject("ADODB.Command")
Set cmd.ActiveConnection = cn
cmd.CommandText = "spGetEmpXML"
cmd.CommandType = adCmdStoredProc

Set Parm1 = cmd.CreateParameter("strXML", adVarChar, adParamOutput, 4000)
cmd.Parameters.Append Parm1

cmd.Execute

Response.ContentType = "text/xml"
Response.Write Parm1.Value
%>
```

When viewed in IE5+, the output from this ASP page will be:

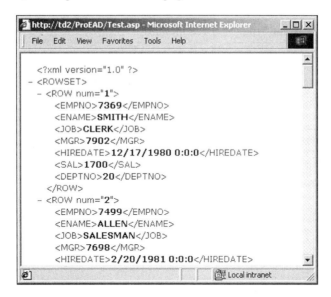

Retrieving the DTD

Before moving on, let's just make a couple of small changes to our stored procedure so that our generated XML document contains an inline DTD. As we saw above, the `getXML` function can take an optional parameter `meta_type`. If we set this to the value 1, the XSU will include a DTD with the document. This DTD is automatically generated according to the structure of the data returned by the SQL query.

```
CREATE OR REPLACE PROCEDURE spGetEmpXml
(strXML OUT varchar)
AS
DTD CONSTANT NUMBER := 1;
clobXML CLOB;
intLength integer;
BEGIN
    intLength := 4000;
    clobXML := xmlgen.getXML('SELECT * FROM EMP', DTD);
    DBMS_LOB.READ(clobXML, intLength, 1, strXML);
END;
```

Alternatively, the `xmlgen` package also has a `getDTD` function, which will generate and return a DTD on its own from a supplied SQL query. This has the syntax:

```
DTD := xmlgen.getDTD(sql_statement, [with_version])
```

Where:

Name	Data Type	Description
DTD	CLOB	The generated DTD.
sql_statement	varchar	The query which will be used to generate the DTD.
with_version	number	Optional. Specifies whether the DTD is to include the XML declaration with the version information, `<?xml version = '1.0'?>`.

The following stored procedure calls this function to retrieve a DTD. The code is very similar to that for retrieving an XML document:

```
CREATE OR REPLACE PROCEDURE spGetEmpDtd
(strDTD OUT varchar)
AS
intLength integer;
clobXML CLOB;
BEGIN
    intLength := 4000;
    clobXML := xmlgen.getDTD('SELECT * FROM EMP', TRUE);
    DBMS_LOB.READ(clobXML, intLength, 1, strDTD);
END;
```

The DTD returned by this stored procedure is:

```
<?xml version = '1.0'?>
<!DOCTYPE ROWSET [
<!ELEMENT ROWSET (ROW)*>
<!ELEMENT ROW (EMPNO, ENAME?, JOB?, MGR?, HIREDATE?, SAL?, COMM?, DEPTNO?)>
<!ATTLIST ROW num CDATA #REQUIRED>
<!ELEMENT EMPNO (#PCDATA)>
<!ELEMENT ENAME (#PCDATA)>
<!ELEMENT JOB (#PCDATA)>
<!ELEMENT MGR (#PCDATA)>
<!ELEMENT HIREDATE (#PCDATA)>
<!ELEMENT SAL (#PCDATA)>
<!ELEMENT COMM (#PCDATA)>
<!ELEMENT DEPTNO (#PCDATA)>
]>
```

Inserting Rows Into the Database

Now that we've seen how to retrieve XML data from an Oracle database, you're perhaps wondering how we can use an XML file to update the database and insert and delete rows. Again, the xmlgen package contains functions which allow us to do this.

To insert rows into a database table, we use the insertXML function. This takes an XML document and decomposes it into a row in a specified table. If the document contains elements which do not match a column name in the table, or if data integrity constraints are infringed, an error will be raised.

The syntax for `insertXML` is:

```
numRows := xmlgen.insertXML(strTableName, strXML)
```

Where:

Name	Data Type	Description
numRows	number	The number of rows successfully inserted into the database.
strTableName	varchar	The name of the table into which the rows should be inserted.
strXML	varchar	The XML document which contains the data to be inserted into the table.

So, let's have a look at a stored procedure which calls this function. We pass into the procedure two input parameters, `strTable` (the name of the table to update) and `strXML` (our XML document), which we pass directly into the function. We also have one output parameter – the number of rows inserted. This is passed directly from the return value of the function into an output parameter:

```
CREATE OR REPLACE PROCEDURE spInsertXML
(strTable IN varchar,
 strXML IN varchar,
 intRows OUT integer)
AS
BEGIN
   intRows := xmlgen.insertXML(strTable,strXML);
END;
```

An XML file for updating the EMP table using this procedure might look like this:

```
<ROWSET>
   <ROW num='1'>
      <EMPNO>7503</EMPNO>
      <ENAME>ROBINSON</ENAME>
      <JOB>CLERK</JOB>
      <MGR>7902</MGR>
      <HIREDATE>10/21/1980 0:0:0</HIREDATE>
      <SAL>1700</SAL>
      <DEPTNO>20</DEPTNO>
   </ROW>
</ROWSET>
```

As we stated above, there must be no elements within a <ROW> which do not correspond to a column in the table. Also, if we try to insert a row that infringes any constraints (for example if we attempt to insert a row with no value for a column which is not nullable, or if we try to insert a duplicate primary key or UNIQUE column), an error will be raised.

The following page shows how we might call this stored procedure from an ASP page. It is similar to the previous example, but we create three parameters (two input and one output) to match the parameters of our stored procedure. We read in the XML document from a file on the server using a `TextStream` object and the `FileSystemObject`:

```
<!-- METADATA TYPE="TypeLib"
             FILE="C:\Program Files\Common Files\System\ADO\msado15.dll" -->
<%
Set cn = Server.CreateObject("ADODB.Connection")

cn.Open "Provider=MSDAORA;Data Source=ProfOra8;" & _
        "User ID=scott;Password=tiger"

Set cmd = Server.CreateObject("ADODB.Command")
Set cmd.ActiveConnection = cn
cmd.CommandText="spInsertXML"
cmd.CommandType=adCmdStoredProc

Set objFSO = Server.CreateObject("Scripting.FileSystemObject")
Set objTStream = objFSO.OpenTextFile
                       ("C:\inetpub\wwwroot\xml\oracle\insert.xml")
strXML = objTStream.ReadAll
objTStream.Close

Set Parm1 = cmd.CreateParameter("strTable", adVarChar, adParamInput, 4000, _
                                "scott.emp")
Set Parm2 = cmd.CreateParameter("strXML", adVarChar, adParamInput, 4000, _
                                strXML)
Set Parm3 = cmd.CreateParameter("intRows", adInteger, adParamOutput)

cmd.Parameters.Append Parm1
cmd.Parameters.Append Parm2
cmd.Parameters.Append Parm3

cmd.Execute

Response.Write Parm3.Value & " rows inserted."
%>
```

Deleting Rows from the Database

If we can insert rows using an XML document, then we must be able to delete them as well, right? And, sure enough, `xmlgen` provides a `deleteXML` function which does just that. The syntax is very similar to that for `insertXML`:

```
numRows := xmlgen.insertXML(strTableName, strXML)
```

Where:

Name	Data Type	Description
numRows	number	The number of rows successfully deleted from the database.
strTableName	varchar	The name of the table from which the rows should be deleted.
strXML	varchar	The XML document which indicates which rows are to be deleted from the table.

The XML document we pass into this function acts very much like the WHERE clause in a SQL DELETE statement. We don't need to include elements for all rows, and any rows that match the criteria we do specify will be deleted. For example, if we call this function on the EMP table with the XML document:

```
<ROWSET>
    <ROW num='1'>
        <ENAME>SMITH</ENAME>
    </ROW>
</ROWSET>
```

This will be equivalent to the SQL command:

```
DELETE FROM EMP WHERE ENAME='SMITH'
```

The following stored procedure can be used to call the deleteXML function; it is virtually identical to the spInsertXML procedure above:

```
CREATE OR REPLACE PROCEDURE spDeleteXML
(strTable IN varchar,
 strXML IN varchar,
 intRows OUT integer)
AS
BEGIN
    intRows := xmlgen.deleteXML(strTable,strXML);
END;
```

We won't show the code for calling this procedure from an ASP page, since it's identical to the code for calling spInsertXML: all we need to do is change the name of the stored procedure that we are calling:

```
cmd.CommandText="spDeleteXML"
```

And possibly also the name of the XML file to load.

Updating the Database

So, we can use XML documents to retrieve, insert and delete rows in the database. But can we modify existing rows with the XSU? Again, the xmlgen package provides a function (called updateXML) to meet our needs. The syntax for this function will come as no surprise either:

```
numRows := xmlgen.updateXML(strTableName, strXML)
```

Where:

Name	Data Type	Description
numRows	number	The number of rows successfully updated in the database.
strTableName	varchar	The name of the table where the rows should be updated.
strXML	varchar	The XML document which specifies what updates are to occur.

But how does the XSU know which rows to update? This is where things get a bit more complicated than the last couple of examples. Before we call this function, we must tell the XSU which columns we want to use as key columns for identifying individual records. We can add a column to the list of key columns using the setKeyColumn procedure:

```
xmlgen.setKeyColumn(strColumnName)
```

Where:

Name	Data Type	Description
strColumnName	varchar	The name of the column to add to the list of key columns.

If we call the updateXML function without specifying the key column(s), or with a value for the key column which is not found in the database, no update will occur, although no error will be generated.

We can clear the list using the clearKeyColumnList method:

```
xmlgen.clearKeyColumnList
```

A similar list of columns is maintained to indicate which columns should be updated. Any columns not in this list will not be updated by the updateXML function, even if they are included in the XML document. We can add columns to the list using the setUpdateColumn procedure:

```
xmlgen.setUpdateColumn(strColumnName)
```

Where:

Name	Data Type	Description
strColumnName	varchar	The name of the column to add to the list of columns that can be updated.

If a value isn't specified in the XML document for one of the update columns, it will be set to NULL. This will generate an error if the column is not nullable.

We can clear this list of updateable columns using the clearUpdateColumnList method:

```
xmlgen.clearUpdateColumnList
```

So let's see an example of a stored procedure that updates the database based on an XML document. It is similar to the insert and delete procedures, but before calling the updateXML function, we first clear the key column list. We will identify rows based on the primary key of the EMP table, the EMPNO column, since this is guaranteed to be unique, so we add this to the key column list. Then we clear the update column list and add the ENAME column. This will ensure that users can only change this column when updating the table, and can't change, for example, the salary details.

```
CREATE OR REPLACE PROCEDURE spUpdateXML
(strTable IN varchar,
 strXML IN varchar,
 intRows OUT integer)
AS
BEGIN
    xmlgen.clearKeyColumnList;
    xmlgen.setKeyColumn('EMPNO');
    xmlgen.clearUpdateColumnList;
    xmlgen.setUpdateColumn('ENAME');
    intRows := xmlgen.updateXML(strTable,strXML);
END;
```

Oracle XML Example

We'll finish off this section on Oracle and XML by providing a simple example which makes use of the Oracle XML SQL Utility and IE5 data binding to allow client-side editing of our Oracle data over the Internet or over an intranet. Data binding is a feature of IE5+ (although an earlier version also existed in IE4) which allows us to bind HTML elements to a data source. This data source can be an **XML data island**. These are islands of XML data embedded into an HTML page, enclosed in <XML></XML> tags. Data binding allows us to bind an HTML table to the XML document contained in one of these data islands, and to bind the cells in the table to individual elements in the document.

The Stored Procedures

This application will use very slightly modified versions of the select and update stored procedures we looked at above. In the case of the update procedure, the only difference is that we only retrieve three columns from the EMP table – EMPNO, ENAME and JOB:

```
CREATE OR REPLACE PROCEDURE spGetEmpXml2
(strXML OUT varchar)
AS
clobXML CLOB;
intLength integer;
BEGIN
    intLength := 4000;
    clobXML := xmlgen.getXML('SELECT EMPNO, ENAME, JOB FROM EMP');
    DBMS_LOB.READ(clobXML, intLength, 1, strXML);
END;
```

For the update procedure, the only change is that we will allow both the ENAME and JOB columns to be updated:

```
CREATE OR REPLACE PROCEDURE spUpdateXML2
(strTable IN varchar,
 strXML IN varchar,
 intRows OUT integer)
AS
BEGIN
    xmlgen.clearKeyColumnList;
    xmlgen.setKeyColumn('EMPNO');
    xmlgen.clearUpdateColumnList;
    xmlgen.setUpdateColumn('ENAME');
    xmlgen.setUpdateColumn('JOB');
    intRows := xmlgen.updateXML(strTable,strXML);
END;
```

The ASP Page

The rest of the code is contained entirely within an ASP page. The page submits to itself; when the user opts to update the database, the entire XML document will be posted to the page in a hidden element, hdnXML. We therefore start by checking the Request.Form collection to see if an XML document has been submitted. If so, we call our update stored procedure, display a link to return to the edit page, and end the execution of the page:

```
<!-- METADATA TYPE="TypeLib"
            FILE="C:\Program Files\Common Files\System\ADO\msado15.dll" -->
<HTML>
<HEAD>
    <TITLE>Oracle XML Example</TITLE>
</HEAD>
<%
If Request.Form("hdnXML") <> "" Then
    strXML = Request.Form("hdnXML")

    Set cn = Server.CreateObject("ADODB.Connection")

    cn.Open "Provider=MSDAORA;Data Source=ProfOra8;" & _
            "User ID=scott;Password=tiger"

    Set cmd = Server.CreateObject("ADODB.Command")
    Set cmd.ActiveConnection = cn
    cmd.CommandText="spUpdateXML2"
    cmd.CommandType=adCmdStoredProc

    Set Parm1 = cmd.CreateParameter("strTable", adVarChar, adParamInput, _
                                    4000, "scott.emp")
    Set Parm2 = cmd.CreateParameter("strXML", adVarChar, adParamInput, _
                                    4000, strXML)
    Set Parm3 = cmd.CreateParameter("intRows", adInteger, adParamOutput)

    cmd.Parameters.Append Parm1
    cmd.Parameters.Append Parm2
    cmd.Parameters.Append Parm3
```

```
      cmd.Execute
      varRows = Parm3.Value
      Set Parm1 = Nothing
      Set Parm2 = Nothing
      Set Parm3 = Nothing
      Set cmd = Nothing
      cn.Close
      Set cn = Nothing
      Response.Write varRows & " rows were updated.<BR><BR>"
      Response.Write "<A HREF='update.asp'>Return to edit page</A>"
      Response.End
   End If
```

If no XML document has been submitted, we call our stored procedure to retrieve the XML document from the database:

```
   Set cn = Server.CreateObject("ADODB.Connection")

   cn.Open "Provider=MSDAORA;Data Source=ProfOra8;" & _
           "User ID=scott;Password=tiger"

   Set cmd = Server.CreateObject("ADODB.Command")
   Set cmd.ActiveConnection = cn
   cmd.CommandText="spGetEmpXML2"
   cmd.CommandType=adCmdStoredProc

   Set Parm1 = cmd.CreateParameter("strXML", adVarChar, adParamOutput, 4000)
   cmd.Parameters.Append Parm1

   cmd.Execute

   varXML = Parm1.Value
   Set Parm1 = Nothing
   Set cmd = Nothing
   cn.Close
   Set cn = Nothing
   %>
```

Once we have this, we can store it in an XML data island embedded in the HTML page, so we can access it on the client:

```
   <XML ID="dsoEmp"><%= varXML %></XML>
```

Now we display our data-bound table. The table itself will be bound to the XML document as a whole, while each cell contains a textbox which is bound to one of the columns we retrieved from the database. We use textboxes (rather than, say, <SPAN> elements) because this will allow the user to change the entries. Any changes made here will be reflected in the XML document stored on the client:

```
   <TABLE ID="tblData" DATASRC="#dsoEmp">
      <THEAD>
         <TH>Employee Number</TH>
         <TH>Name</TH>
         <TH>Job Description</TH>
```

```
   </THEAD>
   <TBODY>
      <TR>
         <TD><INPUT TYPE="TEXT" ID=txtHireDate DATAFLD="EMPNO"></TD>
         <TD><INPUT TYPE="TEXT" ID=txtName DATAFLD="ENAME"></TD>
         <TD><INPUT TYPE="TEXT" ID=txtSal DATAFLD="JOB"></TD>
      </TR>
   </TBODY>
</TABLE>
<HR>
```

Finally come the form we use to submit the updated XML document and a short piece of client-side JScript which will store the XML document in the hidden element before submitting the form:

```
<FORM ACTION="update.asp" NAME="frmUpdate" ID="frmUpdate" METHOD="POST">
<INPUT TYPE="HIDDEN" ID="hdnXML" NAME="hdnXML"></INPUT>
<BUTTON NAME="btnSubmit" ONCLICK="fnSubmit()">Update database</BUTTON>
</FORM>
<SCRIPT>
function fnSubmit() {
    hdnXML = document.all['hdnXML'];
    hdnXML.value = dsoEmp.xml;
    frmUpdate.submit();
}
</SCRIPT>
</HTML>
```

And this is how our page looks:

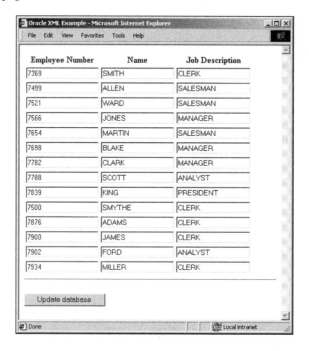

We've kept things as simple as possible, so there are no fancy graphics here, and we've kept functionality to a minimum, too. We haven't incorporated the ability to insert or delete records, although this would be easy to do with the `deleteXML` and `insertXML` functions we saw earlier in the chapter. Finally, remember that this code will only work in IE5+, so at present XML data binding is of limited use in an internet scenario. However, the data binding techniques shown here are very useful if you can rely on the IE5 browser, and the Oracle XML SQL Utility is a great way of extracting XML data, for example for business-to-business applications. We haven't covered all of the XSU's functionality here, but we have shown how you can accomplish the most important data manipulation tasks, and how you can use the XSU from within an ASP application.

Summary

In this chapter we started with a quick overview of ASP and its related data access technology ADO. We explained briefly the benefits of using ASP to integrate with an Oracle 8 database, as well as how to go about connecting to a database, retrieving records, and executing stored procedures. We have considered the implications on record locking associated with developing for the web, and looked at possible ways of overcoming these problems. For the second half of the chapter we have looked at how, with a bit of creativity, we may replicate a number of areas of functionality provided by Oracle Forms. This has included the replication of blocks, triggers, and LOVs, together with using database-defined roles to implement permission-based security. We rounded things off by looking at how we can use ASP applications to retrieve XML documents from a database, using the Oracle XML SQL utility.

Installation Issues

Installing Oracle 8i

Oracle 8i is the latest iteration of Oracle's world-class legacy of relational database systems. Although one of the advantages of working with a database such as Oracle is its platform independence, we're going to make the assumption here that you're installing on a Windows NT machine. However, be aware the exact same installation utility can be used on the Sun Solaris Operating systems with similar functionality.

There are many enhancements in 8i even if you are a previous Oracle user. I will cover briefly what they are, but the intent of this appendix is to help a Web Developer install and configure Oracle 8i, so this will not be an in-depth discussion of Oracle, SQL, or any of its utilities.

8i is an extensive new release with enhanced functionality across almost all aspects of the core product. This is the first Oracle database product that is designed for the Internet and will help you to harness its business potential. Among the most notable new features are tremendously enhanced security, the Java-based Oracle Universal Installer and Packager, the Java-based Oracle Enterprise Manager, a new Row ID format, enhanced Parallel Query optimizations, and better Memory Management. All of these changes make for substantial performance improvements and product refinement over previous releases.

Overview

In this appendix we will cover the following installation issues:

- ❑ Installing Oracle 8i database and client software
- ❑ Installing and configuring Net8 listeners
- ❑ Configuring the multi-threaded server for EJB deployment
- ❑ Installing Oracle SQLJ
- ❑ Installing Oracle XSU
- ❑ Installing the necessary components for the SOAP case study

Preparing for Oracle

Let's start by examining what you need to do in order to get ready to install Oracle 8i. Like any major system change or update, especially if you're in a production environment (as opposed to a test or development environment), you should take every precaution to make sure that you can recover no matter what happens. Some of my steps may seem a little extreme, but I've been able to recover from more than one system failure (including new – brand name – hard drives) without loosing my hair, my job, and the trust of my employer.

While most of what we cover for installation will be equally valid for Sun Solaris, some of the recovery recommendations are Windows NT specific. You will need to substitute appropriate steps (where applicable) if you are performing an Oracle 8i install on Solaris. All of the Oracle-specific installation will apply to you, however, since the Universal Installer is a Java product.

Always Prepare for Disaster

It's just that simple – and that tough. You and I know that before these products are released they go through extensive testing. They are installed and uninstalled, tested with extremely large data stores and processing-intensive queries and scripts, and in many cases several large businesses are beta sites for the vendor. They've done everything they could except install it on your machine. Chances are that you're not the one unlucky individual out of a million (figuratively speaking) who will have installation or operating system problems. But if you do have a failure, no amount of good testing by the vendor will save your data better than preparing for the worst ahead of time. Along the way to installation, I'm going to cover my best practice recommendations as to what you should do.

Be Prepared to Use Outside Resources

If you work for a large enough organization, you may have support agreements with any number of major vendors and local value added resellers (VARs). Make sure you have the technical support numbers available, know who the point(s) of contact are, and the terms of your organization's service agreement(s). Don't forget that you can also use resources on the web both to research an upgrade or product and for technical support and questions.

Two of the best that come to mind are the Microsoft Developer Network (MSDN) at http://msdn.microsoft.com/default.asp and the Oracle Technology Network (OTN) at http://technet.oracle.com/software/download.htm. The Web-based resources are always accessible (although you may have to register) and in general are made available for free.

Backup Essential/Mission-Critical Files

The best type of backup when you're performing a major system change or upgrade is a full-system (all files) backup. There are many products – software and hardware – to help facilitate this process if you don't already have a system in place. Two that come to mind that I have used with success are Contemporary Cybernetics 8mm tape drives and ARCserve backup software. Regardless of what backup system you use, the <u>absolute minimum</u> you should do is to backup user data files. If you do not backup the entire system, be prepared, in the event of an emergency, to reload and configure all the server software including the operating system and all applications. I don't need to warn you that this can be an extremely time consuming endeavor.

Obtain Critical Network Information

If you are installing Windows NT Server de novo, make sure you have the appropriate information from your networking staff. This should include the domain administrator's username and password, any relevant IP addresses (including the one assigned to the new server), domain names, DHCP, DNS, and WINS servers. You should decide ahead of time what password to use for the Oracle DBA. You will need at least five passwords. One is for the default user "sys" and one for the default user "system". I recommend that you add at least one additional DBA Account, a prototypical User Account, and a prototypical Developer Account too. Be careful about assigning away the admin privilege, because if you do, any user granted such could revoke the administrator's rights.

Backup the Registry

Backing up the registry should be something that you do with any Windows NT server at every opportunity (mainly when you're down for scheduled maintenance, and both before and after any major upgrade). Call me old-fashioned, but when I back up the registry, I use `regedit.exe`, which is located in your Windows NT home directory (`C:\WinNT\Regedit.exe` on my machine). If only authorized personnel have access to your server and the admin password, it's a good idea to add a shortcut to `regedit` on your desktop. In order to back up the registry, open `regedit`, click Registry on the menu, select "Export Registry File" and select a location. Once you have exported the file, you need to do one of two things, either save it to another machine on the network (like your workstation) or, save it to a sufficiently large removable media drive (Zip, Superdisk, Orb, etc.). This facilitates taking the registry data off-site and occasionally dropping it in a safe deposit box or a pre-arranged safe location in case of a catastrophic failure (like the building burning down).

Create an Emergency Repair Disk

Just as important as backing up the registry is preparing an emergency repair disk (ERD). It should be another thing that you do with a production server at every opportunity (again the best time to do this is when you're down for scheduled maintenance and before any major upgrade). To run the ERD program, use the Rdisk.exe program which is located in your windows NT home, System 32 directory (call `C:\WinNT\system32\rdisk.exe /s` on my machine). My personal best practices include making a shortcut for `rdisk` on the desktop of the server, if only authorized personnel have access to it. I use the /s as well to make sure that the security database is backed up (this also skips the confirmation dialog). You should not use the /s option if you have a large number of users or groups defined in the user manager! Either use `rdisk` itself or backup the Windows NT home, repair directory (`C:\WinNT\Repair` on my machine). For additional information about this problem refer to Microsoft Knowledge Base article Q122857. Once again, this is another area where it makes sense to store the completed ERD disk both at work (where it can always be used, if needed) and off site.

Have All Operating System Disks Available

This may seem obvious, but make sure that you have all the operating system disks readily available (check and make sure – more than once someone may have a patch or service pack sitting on their desk or worse at home). This includes the basic Windows NT Server CD, all updates and patches, the NT Option pack (if you use any of those products), the updates and patches that apply to option pack products, and the back office family of products and patches if you use those, too. One of my best practices is when a new update, patch, or service release comes out for a product that I use is to burn a CD for it (or order the media) soon after it becomes available.

Have All Patches/Service Packs Available

This is not a re-hash of what was previously mentioned. I believe in the operating system update "aging" process that I learned from a "Unix Head" (please note that this is not a derogatory term) earlier in my career. His philosophy was that an aged operating system or update was a good operating system or update, and he generally waited a few months before he installed any new software. Personally, I have heard horror stories about those who have rushed to install the latest, greatest patch or service release only to hear that the vendor has distributed an "all points bulletin" not to install the update until something is fixed.

So here is my personal best practice: I generally like to stay one patch or service pack behind (developer products excluded, I usually need the bug fixes). However, even if you want to stay more current than that, make sure you have the minimum patch or service pack level installed on your server and apply whatever update(s) you need at least a couple of weeks before you install any new major product. This "waiting period" gives you time to work out any kinks that may be evident and any software incompatibilities that arise. Even if you follow my best practice, always have the latest update physically available! You may find, after calling a support number, that you need the latest update for some reason that was not apparent before you started the installation.

Clean the Registry

This is another area that is often overlooked. Over time any machine that gets used frequently will develop a "polluted" registry. Get a copy of RegClean from Microsoft. The version that I have on my system is RegClean 4.1a (build 7364.1). I suspect from the date in the readme file, 3/13/98, that there is a newer version. One issue with the program's ZIP file when I decompressed it is that it does not have an install program that creates its own directory or shortcut. I suggest you create a directory named `RegClean` below the `Program Files` directory and place the expanded files there. Once you have set up the shortcut, click on it to run RegClean. Once it has completed running, you have the choice of making the changes or exiting. You can always roll back the registry changes since a Microsoft-compliant `.reg` file is created in the `RegClean` directory allowing you to access it from Windows Explorer and perform a registry merge provided you are logged in to that NT machine with administrative rights.

Verify that You Have Enough Disk Space and Memory

This probably seems obvious too, but remember, server resources get used all the time and you can't be sure that you don't need a new drive. Also remember that in addition to the product, you will need space for the company's database(s), so consider likely database sizes (estimated record size * number of records * .1 for database overhead) and adjust your estimates accordingly. Oracle says that you will need 586 Megabytes (Mb) of hard drive storage for a minimal Installation. Personally, I don't know why anyone would buy such an industrial-strength database like Oracle 8i and then only perform a minimal installation. The full install requires that you have 719 Mb of storage space. In addition to this, you will need at least 96 Mb of system RAM, preferably 250Mb or more, and should have a swap/paging file size equal to twice the system RAM (e.g. if system RAM = 96 Mb then the paging file should be 192 Mb). In my server environment the actual space used was much less that Oracle required, so I feel they may have included enough room for a "typical" database. For our purposes, try to start with enough space for a full install of Oracle, your pagefile, and 300 Mb to install developer support.

Shutdown All Potentially Conflicting Services and Applications

Perform a restart on the machine to purge any "leaky" applications that may have corrupted the operating environment and remove any errant modules from memory. Log onto the system under a user account that has administrative rights on the local machine, preferably the domain account with administrative rights created as explained above.

Any programs that might conflict with the installation process then should be shut down or stopped. Such applications can usually be shut down using the Services applet found in the Control Panel:

- ❑ All IIS services, including all of the following:
    - ❑ Certificate Authority
    - ❑ Content Index
    - ❑ FTP Publishing Service
    - ❑ IIS Admin. Service
    - ❑ World Wide Web (WWW) Publishing
- ❑ All Microsoft Exchange services, including all of the following:
    - ❑ Microsoft Exchange Server service
    - ❑ Microsoft Exchange Directory Service
    - ❑ Microsoft Exchange Information Store
    - ❑ Microsoft Exchange Message Transfer Agent
    - ❑ Microsoft Exchange System Attendant
    - ❑ Microsoft Exchange Internet Mail Connector (IMC)
- ❑ All Microsoft SQL Server products
- ❑ Microsoft SNA Server
- ❑ Remote Access AutoDial
- ❑ Microsoft DBWeb
- ❑ ARCserve, Backup Exec, or any other backup service
- ❑ Any antiviral software or services
- ❑ Microsoft NNTP Service
- ❑ Microsoft SMTP Service
- ❑ Disk Keeper, or disk management service
- ❑ SNMP Service(s) MSDTC
- ❑ Any other client-server or ODBC applications that are running
- ❑ Microsoft Windows NT® Event Viewer and `regedit32.exe`

> **Pay particular attention to closing down services before deinstalling any product. Processes still executing may not be fully deinstalled, and may later make it difficult to upgrade or reinstall.**

Installing Oracle 8i

The Oracle Universal Installer and Packager is an excellent tool to aid you in installing and setting up your Oracle database. When you insert the Oracle CD, the autorun.inf file will automatically start the Installer. You should see the autorun screen shown below. Note that from here you can access the extensive online documentation. In Oracle 8.1.5 you can also choose to optionally load the documentation on the server or a workstation, but it will take approximately 130 Mb of space to do so.

Click on the Install/Deinstall Products button. You should see the Welcome page shown below:

If you click on Installed Products, it should tell you what products are installed (there should be none). This is also where you have the option of de-installing previous installations. Note also that you can choose to view Help from this screen, but it's not very helpful other than telling you a little about silent, script-driven installations.

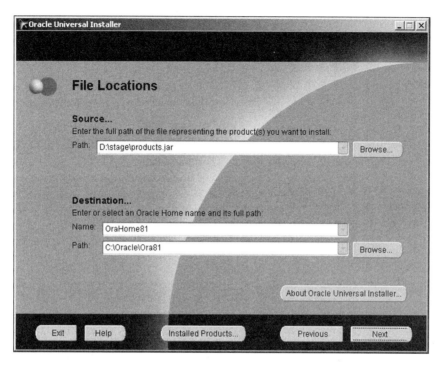

Continuing on, you will be prompted for the location from which you are installing and where you want to install the product(s). I generally find that the default locations are a good choice for these types of questions, although often you will need to alter the drive letter to allow for enough space (the UI automatically chooses the drive with the most space as its default install location). If you have a special network storage device or Redundant Array of Inexpensive Disks (RAID) drive, by all means install to that device, but if you are dealing with a more basic setup, try to deviate only as much as needed to accomplish you goal.

When installing multiple Oracle products on one machine, then the issue of which Oracle Home to install them in will become a significant question. The Oracle installer makes significant use of the registry to keep notes of where things are installed, and you will find it difficult to fool it. The reason why you install different Oracle products in different homes is so that similar processes and services don't overwrite each other. The installation process inserts the HomeName into NT services to avoid naming conflicts. For example, if you installed into `OraHome81`, then you might have a service called `OracleOraHome81ManagementServer`, which would not conflict with the different version software installed in another Home.

When installing these products, the installer will use the registry information of previous installs to suggest a list of possible Oracle Homes. If you try to install a product in an incompatible home, the installer will generally stop you. But this is a step to think about very carefully. You should find a README note about using different Homes on NT in the Oracle for NT menu item in your Start | Programs menu.

Clicking on the Next button will cause Oracle to scan the CD to determine what products are available for installation. You should see the dialog shown below. At this point, we want to install the core Oracle 8i core product, which is version 8.1.6 Enterprise Edition (as of the time of writing 8.1.7 is about to be released, but the installation procedure should not differ greatly from this), and should be the default as you can see in the figure below. We will cover the other Client option as we move on.

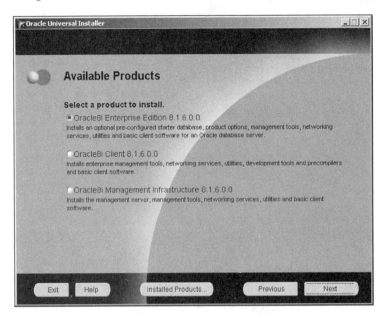

Next the Universal Installer will give three options: Typical, Custom or Minimal Installation.
I would choose Typical here. You can always do a custom install of odd bits later. The next two pieces of information that the Universal Installer asks for are absolutely critical. The Global Database Name and System ID are requested from the Database information dialog box.

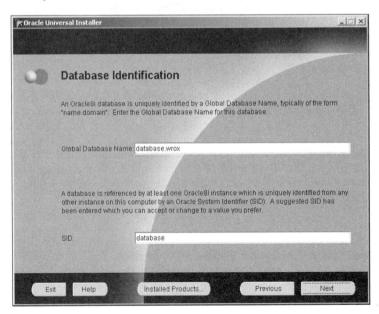

These two names have massive implications as we move forward. The main limitation is that no two Oracle databases in the same Oracle domain can have the same SID. I recommend that you assign your database a global database name such as `database.wrox` (or similar) and use `database` as the SID. Once you have entered the information, click next to continue with installation.

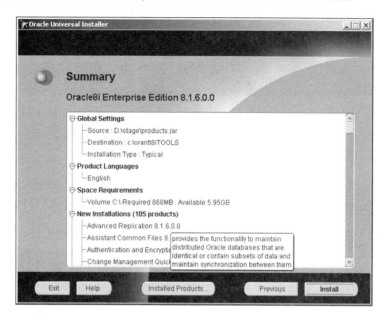

At this point, Oracle will display what products are included in the installation as shown in the figure above. One feature that I really liked was the ability to "hover" over any item and see a tool tip that indicated what the item does and why it was being loaded. Basically, you may want to review this list, but do not modify any options, just click on Install when you are finished reviewing the list.

At this point you will need to wait for Oracle to expand and copy all the files that it needs from the CD. This will take some time, but you will get a rough indication from the progress bar as to how much time is left. Another excellent touch is the install log that is kept and screen notification of where to find it should anything fail. The path is `<ORACLE_HOME>\inventory\logs\installActions.log`. Even though we have cleaned the system logs, it is nice to know that Oracle provides more specific information and an easy way to get at that important file.

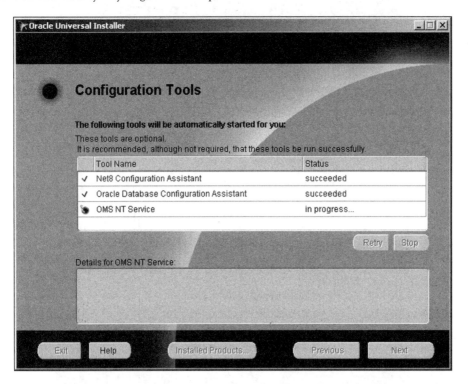

Next come the configuration tools. These items help you to get the most out of Oracle by simplifying some of the more complex issues such as setting up Net8 (which we will cover below under client installations – essentially identical) and configuring a database. The figure above shows what this screen looks like and that it is fully automated. This stage actually starts services for you. Just watch and make sure that these programs execute properly. Do not worry if something fails, the process can be re-run manually, or you can de-install and re-install Oracle. In testing this installer, I did both and had no problems. The next process is where Oracle installs its sample database and sets up a set of control files. For a small to medium database, you will probably not need to adjust these.

As your database grows in size and complexity, you will need to have a skilled DBA examine the database and determine what you need to get the most out of Oracle. For now, just be aware that you will have a sample database that you can play with and that, by installing the sample, we are allowing Oracle to create a set of basic control files.

In the next section, we look at an install of the networking software for a client. Following this will clarify some of the steps that occur when the automatic configurations are invoked as above.

Oracle Clients and Net8

If you're only going to use one computer, then you're all set. You should have an Oracle database and networking all set up. Otherwise, to connect to an Oracle database, you're going to need to set up Net8 networking on your computer. In fact, you don't *have* to use Net8, you can use JDBC thin drivers to access your database from a remote machine. But installing client networking will generally make your life a lot easier – and it's a good way to start work on Oracle fundamentals if you're new to it all.

In all Oracle products, you are required to run a special network product in order to communicate with other Oracle machines including the server. In past iterations prior to Oracle 8, that product was named SQL*Net. In Oracle 8 and 8i, the name of the networking product has been changed to Net8 corresponding with a large number of enhancements made in the client product.

The main point to keep in mind is that Net8 must be running on a client machine in order for it to communicate with any Oracle server that has Net8 installed. Also you should know that Net8 is backwards compatible (in case you already have SQL*Net installed). Even if you already have SQL*Net installed, you probably will want to switch to Net8 as time permits in order to take advantage of the enhancements. One advantage to Oracle's approach to integrating products is that as long as you have Net8 installed, the exact protocol that you are using at the network level is irrelevant. For example, while you probably will use TCP/IP, if you chose to run IPX/SPX (Novell's Protocol) to maintain compatibility with some older hardware or equipment, you can still use Net8 without any problems and have total connectivity between your workstations and clients.

Installing Client Networking Software

We will now examine a client install of Net8 and look at what is required in order for your client machines to communicate with your Oracle server. If all the steps above have been completed successfully, you have a working Oracle server on your network! The next section will cover troubleshooting if a step above failed (in my testing of this product, I made it fail twice and recovered both times). Place the Oracle CD in the drive on a client computer where you want to load the Net8 client. You must use a client for this, Oracle will do a "direct connect" if you try to use the server for this and Net8 will not be properly tested.

1. Insert the CD you used to install Oracle 8i. You will see the autorun screen shown earlier. Click on the Install/Deinstall button as you did earlier and you will once again see the welcome screen.

2. I always feel better verifying that other Oracle products are not already installed, so by clicking on the Installed Products button, you can check this as you did before.

3. Close the Installed Products screen once you have verified that there is no prior installation and click the Next button. At this point, you will be presented with the file location dialog which is similar to the one you saw during the Server install:

4. You may need to adjust your destination location. Note that it is possible to host the Oracle JAR files on a server for client installation through a script. While it is beyond the scope of this book to discuss this in detail, it is an important factor to keep in mind if you have hundreds of workstations or remote sites without technical support personnel.

5. Finally, you will see the available products screen shown below. At this point, you will select the Oracle 8i Client 8.1.6 as shown below and click the Next button.

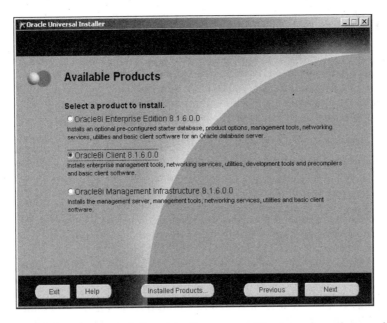

Oracle allows you to select the type of client install you want. You have four choices, **Administrator**, **Programmer**, **Application User**, and **Custom**, as show below. In my testing I did a custom install and tried to de-select some trivial looking options and quickly found that I had no Net8 connectivity. If you have an 8i experienced DBA on the staff or a very persistent networking individual, they may be able to cut this down some, but I believe based on my testing that the total reduction may not be significant. **Programmer** will probably be sufficient for your needs unless you want to use a lot of administration consoles. Choose **Application User** if you merely want to use SQL*Plus and other tools.

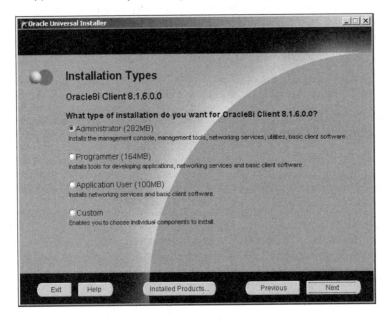

After clicking Next, you will see a summary screen. As we saw earlier it is useful to look through this to check that the installation is doing what you want. You can always go to Previous and change the configuration. I suggest that you browse through the list provided to see exactly what is being installed. It seems like some of the installed modules could be pruned, but take my word for it: it will take some trial and error to reduce the size of the client install if you're short of resources on your client machines. This is a case where if it is an issue of significance, you should consider an outside consultant or vendor who does a lot of Oracle work, as familiarity with the product is key to this process.

Once you have completed reviewing this information, click on the install button to move along. You will see the install progress screen, as shown below which will guide you through the loading of the software. On my machine this was a time consuming process, but the software worked flawlessly.

I liked several things about this screen and this part of the install process. First, the progress bar was consistent in its representation of how much time was left on the install. Secondly, as I mentioned before, it tells you up front where to find the log file (just logging the install in case of errors is a great idea). On top of these features, it gives you the option of canceling if the need arises. When the install has completed, click on the Next button.

This screen comes up to help guide you through the configuration and set up of Net8. You do not have to run these two tools, but I recommend that you do. If you choose not to, select the process that is running and you will see the Retry and Stop buttons below the grid active. Click on the Stop button and the process will end, but you will have to configure Net8 manually if you want to communicate with Oracle. Since this wizard is provided it seems like a wise choice to allow it to make sure you are configured correctly.

The first optional wizard, the Net8 Configuration assistant runs without the need for any information from you. Useful information concerning the placement of configuration files and status information is displayed in the shaded test box. When you progress to the Net8 Easy config, you will be prompted for several pieces of information that you will need to supply for the wizard to configure the rest of the software to connnect you with the Oracle database on the server. The screen above will still be present.

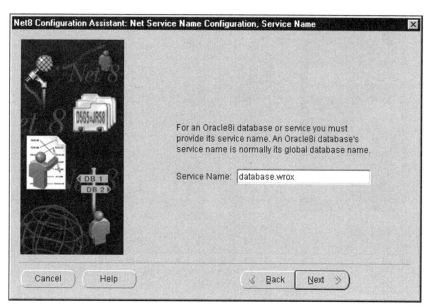

The screen above requires that you enter the origin database global name. I used `database.wrox` for this, which is also the global name I used to name the database. The only recommendation I have is that you use a meaningful name. Click Next when you are ready to continue. You will be presented with the Net8 Protocol Settings Screen shown below:

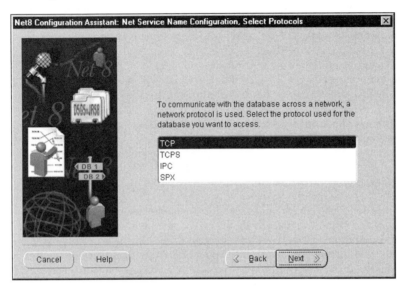

You will probably want to select TCP/IP as this is almost certain to be available on your setup. Note that you can configure multiple Net Service Names on your machine: you could configure different names to access the same database using different protocols.

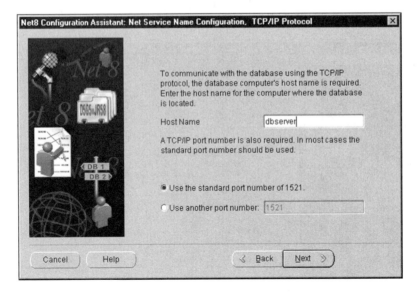

The TCP/IP screen asks that you enter the machine name and port for the Oracle server. If you have installed the database this sould be easy, but you may have to request the data from your DBA or open Network Neighborhood and see if you can find the net name of the database server. Here we are using an unqualified hostname of a computer on the LAN. You could use the full domain name, or even the IP address, of the computer if it has one. If you are configuring another service name on the same machine, use `localhost`. The default port for Oracle is re-loaded into the port number box. Unless you know the port has been changed, do not alter this value. When you are done, click the Next button and you will see the screen shown below.

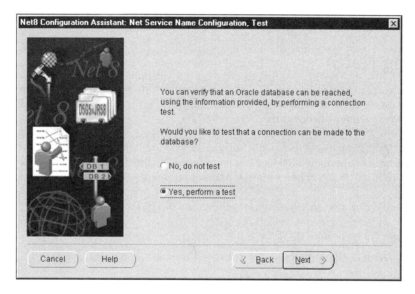

The test connection screen is a great addition to the install and an excellent way to make sure that everything is working. It assumes that you installed the sample database, since it uses the familiar scott/tiger name and password combinations. I highly recommend that you test your connection here and make sure that you have connectivity. If you do, you will see the screen shown below. It will indicate that you have a valid Oracle database that is available for communication.

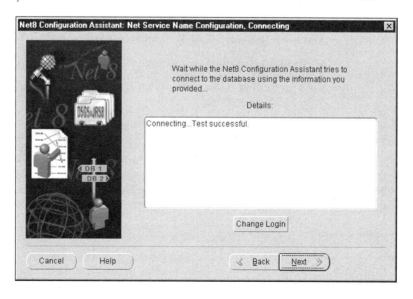

This screen shows the results of the connection test. If there is an error, look very closely at these results and make sure that nothing was entered incorrectly. If it was, close this dialog and use the Back button to go back and change the erroneous information and do a re-test. When you achieve success, click the Close button. If you have deleted user scott for some reason then you will need to use the Change Login option to log in as another user. (This improves over earlier versions of this test, which forced you to log in as a specfic user to test the service – if you were experiencing network problems, then this could be annoyingly frequent.)

This is the end of the installation for Oracle. At this point you should be able to communicate through Net8 without problems.

Configuring Net8

As mentioned earlier, we need to install a layer of network software on our web server that allows us to communicate with Oracle. By selecting the **Client** installation, the Oracle Installer will have installed Net8, which we now have to configure.

Net8 supports standard network protocols, such as TCP/IP, to connect to Oracle8 servers through the use of user-friendly aliases called **Service Names**. A service name is simply a name used to refer to an Oracle database instance much like we use URLs in preference to hard-to-remember IP addresses.

You have a number of ways in which to store these lists of service names:

- ❏ Domain Name System (DNS)
- ❏ Local client configuration files
- ❏ Oracle Names Server
- ❏ Non-Oracle name server

Net8 uses **Oracle Protocol Adaptors** to map the following industry-standard network protocols into a standard that it can recognize internally:

TCP/IP	Widely-used Internet network protocol
SPX	Another relatively commonly-used network protocol
Named Pipes	Microsoft's networking protocol specific to PC-based LANs
Bequeath	Used for local Windows 95 and 98 Personal Oracle8 installations and other local connections
Logical Unit Type	Part of IBM's peer-to-peer SNA network

Oracle8 comes with two utilities to configure Net8: **Net8 Easy Config**, to edit our list of service names, and **Net8 Assistant**, an advanced utility that allows us to configure service names, network listeners, Oracle Names Servers and local configuration files. Configuration using Net8 Assistant is primarily a DBA role so we won't cover it here. We will be using the Net8 Easy Config application to configure our client.

There are a number of ways to store the list of service names with the two most commonly used methods being:

❑ **Host Naming** – Uses existing DNS-based or a centrally maintained HOSTS file for name resolution. By simply using the host's network name, no client configuration is required.

❑ **Local Naming** – Uses a local configuration file – TNSNAMES.ORA – to resolve names.

Host Naming does not required any client configuration so we will take a look at **Local Naming** using the Net8 Easy Config program. Net8 Easy Config edits a file called TNSNAMES.ORA in the <installation_folder>\Net80\Admin folder, which can be edited manually using Notepad or by using the Net8 utility. In many Oracle installations it is common practice to simply copy the TNSNAMES.ORA file from the Oracle server machine onto the client.

> **TNS stands for** Transparent Network Substrate (TNS). **This is a non- proprietary low-level interface that manages the opening and closing of sessions and the sending or receiving of requests.**

Start the Oracle Net8 Easy Config and select **Add New Service**. Our DBA has called the Oracle8i server dbserver, so we'll type that name in – you'll have to use the name of your own Oracle8i server. You may find that this is the name of the actual server, provided that it is only running one instance of Oracle.

> **You may see a dialog box warning you that Net8 Easy Config has found a number of comments in the configuration file TNSNAMES.ORA. It is generally safe to ignore this warning message.**

Before you can enter the Oracle8i service name, choose the Local Net Service Name configuration option, click **Next** and then choose the **Add Item** to add a new service name before pressing Next again. Finally you must tell the Oracle8i Configuration Assistant that you want to access an Oracle8i database. Clicking Next will take you to the Service Name screen.

The next step is to choose the type of network protocol used to communicate with the server. Typically this will most likely be TCP/IP.

The host name is the resolved name used to refer to the server, which in our case is the same name given to this service name – for ease. It is possible to install the Oracle server software to listen on a different TCP/IP port number. By default, port number 1521 is used for Oracle installations, in much the same way that port number 80 is used for HTTP requests. Unless your DBA has used a different port number for additional security, select the default option.

There is one additional step to complete before testing an Oracle8 connection: you have to type in the name of the database System Identifier, or **SID** to connect to. It is possible to run more than one **instance** of Oracle on the same server by giving each instance a unique SID by which it can be identified.

> **If you do have a number of database instances per server then it might be a good idea to set up service names as the name for each service.**

To test the new service name, you must enter a valid user name and password. The Oracle8i version actually defaults to using scott/tiger for you.

If you've entered the correct host name and username/password then you should receive a message saying that the connection test was successful. If you receive the error message ORA-12545: connect failed because target host or object does not exist, you need to recheck the values of your host name, port number and SID. You should also confirm that Oracle is actually running on the host specified and has been configured to listen for that database.

The message ORA-01017: invalid username/password; logon denied is a lot more encouraging; it means that you successfully communicated with the Oracle server, but you entered the wrong username or password.

ORA-12545 and ORA-01017 are the common error messages that you are likely to come across, but you may receive any of the following messages as well:

Error	Possible Solution
ORA-12154: TNS:could not resolve service name	Net8 could not find the service name specified in your TNSNAMES.ORA file.
	Make sure that the TNSNAMES.ORA file actually exists and that you do not have multiple copies of the TNSNAMES.ORA file
	Make sure that you do not have duplicate copies of the SQLNET.ORA file.
	When using domain names ensure that your SQLNET.ORA file contains a NAMES.DEFAULT_DOMAIN value.
ORA-12198 TNS:could not find path to destination and ORA-12203: TNS:unable to connect to destination	The client could not find the required database
	Is the service name spelt correctly?
	Is TNSNAMES.ORA file in the correct folder?
	Check that the service name ADDRESS parameter in the connect descriptor of your TNSNAMES.ORA file is correct.
	Get your DBA to check that the Oracle Listener on the remote server has started and is running.
ORA-12224: TNS:no listener	Could not connect because the listener is not running.
	Does the destination address match one of the addresses used by the listener.
	Are you running the correct version of Net8 or SQL*Net?

Much like SQL Server's **user spaces**, Oracle groups database objects, such as tables, indexes and procedures, into what is called a **schema**. A schema maps to an actual login name. So, in the case of the scott login name you will find a whole host of database objects under the scott account. Scott is the sample database schema created by the Oracle Installer when you first install the Oracle server. Typically, a new default Oracle installation will have the following logins created:

Username	Password	Password
scott	tiger	Sample login.
sys	change_on_install	Can perform all operations such as stopping and starting the database.
system	manager	The user 'system' is the database administrator. The 'system' user is normally granted the SYSDBA privilege. DBA's then set up another user as an operations user which is granted the SYSOPER privilege

We've now gone through the process of installing Oracle's client networking software and Net8, and have then added and tested a new Net8 service name to connect to an Oracle8i server called database.

Multi-Threaded Server

If you intend to use EJB or CORBA features, the Multithreaded Server (MTS) option must be enabled for the database. If the only Java application components you expect to run are Java Stored Procedures, you can run in dedicated mode or MTS mode. In that case, the choice comes down to how many client connections the database must support and the type of application. Most OLTP (On-Line Transaction Processing) Internet applications will enable the MTS option for improved scalability.

> **Note that multi-threaded server support for IIOP (Internet Inter-ORB Protocol) clients is automatically enabled when you install Oracle Java option in a typical Enterprise Edition installation.**

The easiest way to check and enable the MTS option is using the Oracle Database Configuration Assistant. When the assistant dialog comes up, select the "Change database configuration" option, select the instance you want to modify, then select Shared Server Mode.

Next, the Assistant will prompt you to accept or override the default MTS settings with the dialog shown below. These settings are used to modify your init.ora configuration file.

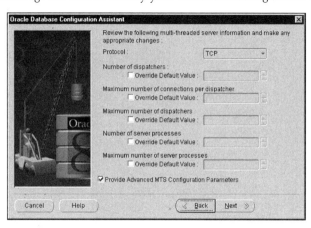

The first setting is for MTS_DISPATCHERS. In the MTS architecture, dispatcher processes are used to manage multiple client requests. Basically, as client requests come into the dispatcher, it sends them to a Request queue. As a shared server process become available on the database server, client requests are dequeued, processed, and the result sent to a Response queue. A dispatcher can realistically handle only a certain number of concurrent connections. The rough guide suggested in the Oracle 8i documentation (the Net8 Administrators Guide, available from http://technet.oracle.com) is to start with 1 dispatcher for every 1024 connections. 1 dispatcher is the default setting in the Assistant.

The second setting also affects MTS_DISPATCHERS. It is used to set a limit to the number of connections allowed to each dispatcher. For example, setting "Number of dispatchers" to 1 and "Maximum number of connections per dispatcher" to 501 results in the following entry in init.ora:

```
mts_dispatchers = "(protocol=TCP)(disp=1)(con=501)"
```

The third setting is for MTS_MAX_DISPATCHERS. Additional dispatchers can be started once a database is up and running using the ALTER SYSTEM statement. Usually this is in response to an unexpected increase in load. The MTS_MAX_DISPATCHERS setting places a limit on how many dispatchers can be running. Setting "Maximum number of dispatchers" to 2 results in this entry in init.ora:

```
mts_max_dispatchers = 2
```

The fourth and fifth settings are for MTS_SERVERS and MTS_MAX_SERVERS respectively. The MTS_SERVERS setting specifies the minimum number of shared server processes that should be running in the database. When the database instance is started, it will create this number of shared processes. MTS_MAX_SERVERS specifies the maximum number of shared server processes allowed. As load increases and decreases, the Oracle instance dynamically creates and destroys server processes up to a maximum of MTS_MAX_SERVERS and down to a minimum of MTS_SERVERS. The best setting for an application can be determined over time, but the Oracle 8i documentation recommends starting with one shared server process for every 10 anticipated connections. Setting these to 2 and 100 respectively results in these entries in init.ora:

```
mts_servers = 2
mts_max_servers = 100
```

Memory Initialization Parameters

To run the script initjvm.sql which initializes the database, you need at least 50Mb of shared pool memory and 20Mb of Java pool memory. These settings are changed in the init.ora configuration file for the instance:

```
shared_pool_size = 51200000
java_pool_size = 20480000
```

Note: these values are to support running initjvm.sql. After the Java options have been installed, you'll want to adjust these to support the normal operational environment.

System Tablespace and Rollback Segments

You also need about 30Mb of available system tablespace and about 20M of rollback segments. You can take care of the tablespace problem by making sure the system tablespace is set to auto-extend. If the query:

```
SELECT AUTOEXTENSIBLE FROM dba_data_files WHERE tablespace_name = 'SYSTEM';
```

returns YES the `system` tablespace will auto-extend. If not, execute the following statement to change the setting (logged on as user SYS):

```
ALTER DATABASE DATAFILE 'C:\Oracle\Ora81\ORADATA\orcl\System01.DBF' AUTOEXTEND ON;
```

Replace `C:\Oracle\Ora81\ORADATA\orcl\System01.DBF` with the path to your system data file. If you aren't sure what it is run:

```
SELECT file_name FROM dba_data_files WHERE tablespace_name = 'SYSTEM';
```

The easiest way to handle the rollback segments requirement is to use auto-extend as well. If the query:

```
SELECT AUTOEXTENSIBLE FROM dba_data_files WHERE tablespace_name = 'RBS';
```

returns YES the rollback segment data file will auto-extend. Otherwise, follow the same procedure described above for the rollback segment data file. An alternative solution is to create additional rollback segments.

> Some of the changes made require restarting the Oracle instance. Once that is complete, you can execute the **initjvm.sql** script.

The remainder of this chapter is consists of rather brief, but we hope useful, instructions for installing various Oracle client components and tools. We start by outlining an installation of Oracle SQLJ.

Installing Oracle SQLJ

To translate and compile SQLJ files, you need the following archives:

- `<ORACLE_HOME>\sqlj\lib\translator.zip`
- `<ORACLE_HOME>\jdbc\lib\classes111.zip`

If you need NLS support, a third file is needed:

- `<ORACLE_HOME>\jdbc\lib\nls_charset11.zip`

For Java 2 and JDBC 2, the JDBC files are

- `<ORACLE_HOME>\jdbc\lib\classes12.zip`
- `<ORACLE_HOME>\jdbc\lib\nls_charset12.zip`

If Oracle is Installed on Your Computer

Find the Oracle Home directory on your computer (we will refer to it as <ORACLE_HOME>)

The SQLJ archive files are normally located in <ORACLE_HOME>\sqlj\lib. On the machine where this appendix was written, <ORACLE_HOME> is defined as C:\Oracle\Ora81; so the SQLJ files are located in C:\Oracle\Ora81\sqlj\lib. Check that the translator.zip file is located in the sqlj\lib directory.

Next, check that the jdbc files classesnnn.zip and nls_charsetnn.zip are in the directory <ORACLE_HOME>\jdbc\lib.

> **If you are working in a UNIX environment, the locations will be the same, just change the path separator. For example, <ORACLE_HOME>\sqlj\lib\translator.zip becomes <ORACLE_HOME>/sqlj/lib/translator.zip**

If the files are not located as shown above, try searching in other directories. If the files cannot be located on your computer, you will need to install or download the files as explained below.

Oracle is Not Installed – You Have an Installation CD

If Oracle is not installed on your computer, simply install it. All the various types of Oracle installations (server, client, programmer, etc.) for any platform should install the class files for SQLJ and JDBC automatically. In the event Oracle is installed but the class files are not installed, you can perform a custom installation:

1. Follow the installation procedure to the point where the type of installation is selected. Select Custom Installation

2. When presented with the list of components to install, find the JDBC and SQLJ components in the list, and select them for installation

3. Complete the installation

Downloading the Files

If you don't have a distribution CD or installation files, you can download the needed drivers from Oracle's web site at http://technet.oracle.com. Click the link to Software, then select Oracle JDBC Drivers or SQLJ Translator from the Select a Utility or Driver drop down menu. Place the downloaded files into the directories shown above.

Installing Java

Install a Java Development Kit, if one is not already installed. When you install Oracle 8.1.5, it will install Java Runtime Environment 1.1.7. If you have an 8.1.6 installation, you will have JRE1.2.2. If you want JDK 1.1.8 or Java 2 (either JDK 1.2.2 or JDK 1.3), you will need to install it yourself. Consult the installation instructions that came with the JDK.

The installation procedure will change the path and classpath settings for your system. However, if the new settings in the path or classpath statement come after the Oracle settings, then the Oracle settings will take precedence. In general, when using any command line program, your system will use the first file it encounters as it searches the path for the executable.

If your path setting includes the JDK 1.1.7 bin directory before the JDK 1.1.8 bin directory, then it will use the compiler from JDK 1.1.7. This would not be a big problem, because the Java API for JDK 1.1.7 and JDK 1.1.8 are the same. However, if you used classes or methods from the Java 2 API, and the system used the JDK 1.1.7 compiler, then your code may not compile because the Java 2 API includes classes and methods that are not in the JDK 1.1.7 API.

If your classpath included `classes111.zip` prior to `classes12.zip`, the compiler and virtual machine will use the JDBC 1.0 classes over the JDBC 2.0 classes. Again, this could be a problem, because the JDBC 2.0 API has classes and methods that are not available in the JDBC 1.0 API.

To resolve this conflict, you'll need to set your classpath properly. This is explained in the section "Setting Environment Properties" later in this appendix.

> **If you are using Java 2, the SQLJ translator that is part of Oracle 8.1.5 will throw a Java exception when you attempt to translate your source file. The hard way to resolve this problem is to translate using a Java 1.1 virtual machine, and then compile the translated file with Java 2. The easy way is to download a patch from Oracle that fixes the problem. The patch is available at http://technet.oracle.com. Click the link to Software, then select "SQLJ Translator" from the "Select a Utility or Driver" drop down menu.**

Configuring the Environment

Win98

To configure the environment for Windows98, you will need to edit the `autoexec.bat` file. This file is normally located in the root directory `C:\`. In the file may be two lines, one that sets the variable `CLASSPATH` and the other sets the variable path:

```
set CLASSPATH=C:\Oracle\Ora81\sqlj\lib\translator.zip;c:\Oracle\Ora81\jdbc\lib\cla
sses111.zip;.
set PATH=C:\Oracle\Ora81\bin;"C:\PROGRAM FILES\ORACLE\JRE\1.1.7\BIN";C:\;C:\WINDOW
S;C:\WINDOWS\SYSTEM32
```

You will edit the line by adding or removing file paths to the two lines as described below. If either line is not in the Autoexec.bat file, you can add it to the file. You will need to reboot to use these environment settings.

> **When you reboot, the changes affect all programs. You can make these changes effective for a single DOS window without rebooting. Create a batch file with the desired changes, and run that batch file in a DOS window. The changes will affect that DOS window and programs run in that DOS window.**

WinNT/2000

System properties are set from a dialog. To access the dialog, right-click on the My Computer icon, and select the Properties option from the drop-down menu; in the tabbed dialog that follows, select the Environment tab. In Win 2000 you have to select the Advanced tab then the Environment button You can also change the environment settings from the Control Panel, System application. (Start Menu|Settings|Control Panel, double click icon labeled System, select the Environment tab, for Win 2000 this is the advanced tab and environment button).

The Environment tab has two windows with system properties. One window, accessible only to administrators, will allow the properties to be set for all users; the other window allows you to change settings for yourself. In NT click on a name in either of the windows; the name and its value appear in two text boxes at the bottom of the dialog. In Win 2000 you have click on the Edit button after highlighting the variable and a new window pops up with name and value of the variable like in NT. You can then change the name or its value. Click the "Set" button to set the value. (If you select a different name, or click the OK button before you click Set, then any changes you made will be lost.) After you click OK, the changes will be in effect.

Unix

Unix settings are set by a script file that is run when you log into the system. The name of the file varies, depending upon which shell you use when entering command line options. For example, if your default shell is the C shell (csh), the script file is named .cshrc. If you use the Bash shell bash then the settings may be in .bash_profile (set once per login) or .bashrc (set for every new terminal window). For example, here are the relevant lines from .cshrc:

```
setenv CLASSPATH ${CLASSPATH}:/usr1/oracle/sqlj/lib/translator.zip:/usr1/oracle/jd
bc/lib/classes111.zip:.
set PATH = ($PATH /usr/local/java/bin)
```

The exact syntax will vary based on the shell. You will add or remove file paths to the two lines as described below. If either line is not in the file, you can add it. The changes become effective when you source the resource file:

```
source .cshrc
```

or when you open a new terminal window.

Setting Environment Properties

Before running the translator, you need to ensure your environment is set correctly. You set the environment by changing the path and CLASSPATH environment variables for your operating system (as described above). Oracle recommends the following directories be added to your path and classpath settings. (The path separator for Windows is shown, change to a '/' for a UNIX environment).

Path

❑ <ORACLE_HOME>\bin

❑ <ORACLE_HOME>\sqlj\bin

Classpath

❑   `<ORACLE_HOME>\sqlj\lib\translator.zip`

❑   `<ORACLE_HOME>\jdbc\lib\classes111.zip`

❑   `<ORACLE_HOME>\jdbc\lib\nls_chaset11.zip`

As necessary, add or change the path and classpath for your system so that the directory and file paths shown above are part of the path or classpath. If you are adding a ZIP or JAR file to the classpath, the entire path including the file name must be added. If you are including `.class` files, you must include the path up to the start of the root of the package tree containing the files. (Refer to the Java appendix for information on packages). For example, if you had a Java class that was in the `com.wrox.database` package:

```
package com.wrox.database;
public class Example {
    //class members and methods
}
```

and the .class file was located at:

```
C:\Wrox\projects\oracle_programming\com\wrox\database\Example.class
```

then the `CLASSPATH` entry would include the directories up to `\com`:

```
set CLASSPATH=c:\Wrox\projects\oracle_programming
```

The Java compiler (or virtual machine) takes the package specification `com.wrox.database`, converts it to a directory structure `com\wrox\database\` and then appends that to each path in the classpath:

```
C:\Wrox\projects\oracle_programming\com\wrox\database
```

Then it attempts to find the class file in those directories.

If you are using Java 2, you might be able to eliminate most of the classpath statement. When using the Java 2 development environment, the compiler and virtual machine will automatically use any Java archives located in the JRE extension directory (for example `C:\java\jdk1.3\jre\lib\ext`). If you copy the SQLJ and JDBC zip files into this directory, you can remove them from the classpath statement. For deployment, you will need to copy the files to the runtime JRE directory. On my Windows 98 system, that directory is

```
C:\Program Files\JavaSoft\JRE\1.3\lib\ext
```

As mentioned previously, there may be a conflict between different executables or class files as listed in the path or classpath. The first way to resolve this conflict is to remove any Java archives from the classpath that are not used. Similarly, if there are directory paths to class files that you do not want linked to your program, remove those directory paths from the classpath. Finally, set the classpath so that the desired archives or directories appear in the classpath prior to the undesired archives or directories. Do the same for the path statement. For example, suppose your path statement looked like this:

```
SET Path=c:\Oracle\Ora81\bin;"C:\PROGRAM FILES\ORACLE\JRE\1.1.7\BIN";C:\;C:\WINDOW
S;C:\WINDOWS\SYSTEM32;C:\java\jdk1.2\jre\bin
```

1131

As shown, if you ran a Java program using the Java Runtime Environment (JRE) virtual machine, the Oracle JRE would be used rather than the JDK1.2 JRE (because the Oracle JRE directory appears before the JDK1.2 JRE). To use the JDK 1.2 JRE instead, fix the path by moving `C:\java\jdk1.2\jre\bin;` to the beginning of the classpath:

```
SET Path= C:\java\jdk1.2\jre\bin;c:\Oracle\Ora81\bin;"C:\PROGRAM FILES\ORACLE\JRE\
1.1.7\BIN";C:\;C:\WINDOWS;C:\WINDOWS\SYSTEM32;
```

Usage

Now that SQLJ is installed we will need to test it:

Testing the Installation

In a terminal or DOS window, type `sqlj` at a command prompt and press return. You should receive a usage message:

```
Usage:   sqlj [options] file1.sqlj [file2.java] ...
   or    sqlj [options] file1.ser  [file2.jar]  ...
where options include:
    -d=<directory>            root directory for generated binary files
    -encoding=<encoding>      Java encoding for source files
    -user=<user>/<password>   enable online checking
    -url=<url>                specify URL for online checking
    -status                   print status during translation
    -compile=false            do not compile generated Java files
    -linemap                  instrument compiled class files from sqlj source
    -profile=false            do not customize generated *.ser profile files
    -ser2class                convert generated *.ser files to *.class files
    -P-<option> -C-<option>   pass -<option> to profile customizer or compiler
    -P-help   -C-help         get help on profile customizer or compiler
    -J-<option>               pass -<option> to the JavaVM running SQLJ
    -version                  get SQLJ version
    -help-alias               get help on command-line aliases
    -help-long                get full help on all front-end options
```

If you do not get a usage message, or you get an error message or exception stack trace, check that

❑ The SQLJ and JDBC ZIP files exist on your computer as described at the beginning of this appendix

❑ The classpath points to the SQLJ and JDBC ZIP files, or that they exist in the JRE extension directory

❑ The path points to the directory where the JDK is installed

❑ The path points to the directory where the `sqlj.exe` file (Windows) or the `sqlj` script (Unix) exists (this is normally <ORACLE_HOME>\bin or <ORACLE_HOME>\sqlj\bin).

Basic Translator Operations

After writing a Java source file with SQLJ, you translate and compile the code using the SQLJ translator. At its simplest, here's the command to compile your SQLJ code from the command line:

```
sqlj file.sqlj
```

In a Windows environment, sqlj is actually sqlj.exe, an executable program; in a UNIX environment, sqlj is a script. The Oracle translator itself is actually a Java program. The executable or script launches the Java program. The Java program reads the .sqlj file and translates it.

If the translator and compiler encounter no problems, they will silently complete and the command prompt will return. If you see no messages, you can safely assume that the SQLJ file was compiled successfully.

A common problem when compiling a class for the first time is the following error message:

```
C:\sqlj\projects\ch1>sqlj Customer.sqlj
Customer.sqlj:6: Class oracle.jdbc.driver.OracleDriver not found in import.
import oracle.jdbc.driver.OracleDriver;
            ^
1 error
```

This error message (class not found in import) always means that the compiler was not able to find the class. Either the classpath does not contain the correct directory or archive, or the class does not exist on your system. See the "Setting Environment Properties" section above for the proper way to set the classpath.

If you get any unusual exceptions (not compiler errors or warnings, but actual exceptions with stack traces) such as the following:

```
unexpected error occurred...
java.lang.ExceptionInInitializerError: java.lang.NullPointerException
     at sqlj.framework.ClassFileReader.attribute_info(ClassFileReader.java,
     Compiled Code)
.....
     [LONG STACK TRACE CUT]
.....
     at sqlj.translator.Main.runTranslation(Main.java:85)
     at sqlj.tools.Sqlj.statusMain(Sqlj.java, Compiled Code)
     at sqlj.tools.Sqlj.main(Sqlj.java:125)
Customer.sqlj: Error: Exception caught:
Total 1 error.
```

You are using Java 2, and the SQLJ version you have is not compatible with Java 2. See the Note above in the "Installing Java" section for the patch that fixes this problem.

See the chapter on SQLJ for more information on translator usage.

Integrated Development Environment

SQLJ capability is pre-installed in Oracle JDeveloper. We give here the instructions for installing SQLJ into JBuilder.

JBuilder

First, configure the Project properties for the desired JDK:

❑   Select **Project** | **Properties** from the JBuilder menubar.

❑   In the tabbed dialog box, select the **Paths** tab. Check the **Target JDK**. Use the drop down box to select the desired JDK. If the desired JDK is not on the list, go to the next step.

❑   Select the Define button. The **Available JDK Versions** dialog box appears. Click the New button; click the button to the right of the **Path of JAVA.EXE** text box (the button labeled with three dots). Use the file browser to locate the `java.exe` file for the desired Java version. Close the dialog boxes. If you selected a Java 2 version, see the Note above in the "Installing Java" section.

❑   Click the **Add** button under the **Java Libraries** window. Click the **New** button in the dialog box. Create a library for SQLJ. Type a name in the **Name** text field. (SQLJ would be a good name). Use the **File Chooser** button (the button labeled with three dots) to find the `translator.zip` file. Click **OK**. Click on the library you just created and click **OK**.

❑   Click the **Add** button under the Java Libraries window. Click the **New** button in the dialog box. Create a library for JDBC. Type a name in the Name text field. (JDBC would be a good name). Click the **File Chooser** button (the button labeled with three dots) and find the `classes111.zip` file. Click **OK**. Click on the library you just created and click **OK**.

Second, configure JBuilder to use the SQLJ translator:

❑   Click **Tools** | **Tool** Options on the JBuilder menu.

❑   Click the **Add** button.

❑   Type a name for the tool in the **Title** box .

❑   Click the browse button and use the **File Chooser** dialog to find the `sqlj` executable (probably `<ORACLE_HOME>\bin\sqlj.exe` or `<ORACLE_HOME>\sqlj\bin\sqlj.exe`).

❑   In the Macros list, find and click on the `$NodeName` macro. Click the Insert button.

❑   Check the **Is Service** box.

❑   Click the OK button and then close the **Tool Options** dialog.

When you are ready to translate a SQLJ file, just select the tool you created from the **Tools** menu. JBuilder will run the translator. Then when the Java file(s) have been created from the SQLJ source file(s), build them in the normal way.

JDeveloper

If you have JDeveloper 2 or JDeveloper 3 from Oracle, SQLJ support is built into the development environment. Check the JDeveloper documentation for information on how to use the built-in support.

Installing XSU

The XML SQL Utility (XSU) can be downloaded from Oracle's TechNet site at:

http://technet.oracle.com/software/tech/xml/oracle_xsu/software_index.htm

The Windows version of the utility can be downloaded as a single Zip file, named
XSU12_ver1_2_1.zip (for XSU 12), or XSU12_ver1_1_1.zip (for version XSU 111). To install the
XSU, extract all the files from this Zip archive. This will create a directory named by default
C:\OracleXSU12 (for XSU 12), which contains the installation files, documentation files and samples.

The XSU consists of three separate components:

❑   A client-side front-end. This is a command-line utility that acts as a front-end to the XSU.

❑   A Java API, for access to the XSU from Java programs.

❑   A PL/SQL API, which allows us to use the XSU from within PL/SQL (in stored procedures).

We won't look at the first two of these components, because we have already seen the Java side from the
point of view of Java Stored Procedures (see the relevant chapter).

Setting up the XSU

To use the XSU, we need to have certain components already installed. The actual components we need
installed on the machine vary according to whether we are using that machine as a client or as the
database server. If the same machine is serving both as a client and server (e.g. if the web server and
database server are on the same machine, or if we are developing on a single test machine), then of
course all the components must be installed.

	XSU 12	XSU 111
Client-side	Java JDK 1.2.x or later.	JDK 1.1.x or later
	Oracle's JDBC 2.0-compliant drivers.	Oracle's JDBC 1.x-compliant drivers.
	Oracle XML parser v. 2+	Oracle XML parser v. 2+
Server-side	Oracle 8.1.6 or later.	Oracle 8.1.5
	Oracle XML parser v. 2+	Oracle XML parser v. 2+

The Oracle XML parser is included with the XSU itself, and the JDK (Java Developer's Kit) and Oracle
JDBC (Java DataBase Connectivity) drivers are installed with Oracle.

The installation itself is simply a matter of running a couple of scripts which are supplied with the XSU.
To enable the command-line front-end and Java API on the client, run the env.bat batch file in the
XSU's install directory (for example C:\OracleXSU12). If you didn't install the XSU or Oracle to the
default directory you may have to edit the file to ensure all the directories are correct.

To install the Java and PL/SQL APIs on the database server, we just need to run the `oraclexmlsqlload.bat` file (installed by default to the `lib` directory of the XSU directory. The only alteration we need to make to this file is the username/password pair, which is set at the start of the file:

```
set USER_PASSWORD="scott/tiger"
```

This batch file performs four tasks:

❑ It installs the Oracle XML parser. If this is already installed, we can comment out the line:

```
rem call loadjava -r -v -u %USER_PASSWORD% xmlparserv2.jar
```

❑ Loads the classes for the XSU's Java API into the database.

❑ Installs the PL/SQL API on top of the Java API.

❑ Tests that the PL/SQL API has correctly installed.

SOAP Installation

To install the whole SOAP environment is a little bit tricky, and there are many variables you have to choose values for.

> There is a download available from the Wrox website which contains all the code for the SOAP case study and also jar file to allow easy deployment of the code.

We need the following system software:

❑ A SOAP implementation

❑ A servlet engine

❑ An EJB server

❑ An Oracle 8i instance up and running

In all the samples we tested and developed the entire framework using the following configuration:

❑ Operating systems: Windows 2000, Linux and Sun Solaris

❑ EJB server: jBoss 2 (http://www.jboss.org)

❑ SOAP Apache distribution (http://xml.apache.org/soap)

❑ Microsoft SOAP toolkit (http://msdn.microsoft.com/xml/general/toolkit_intro.asp)

❑ Oracle 8i Release 2 (8.1.5)

❑ Servlet engine: Tomcat (http://jakarta.apache.org/tomcat) Release 4 milestone 4

We will now take you through the installation steps needed for the whole system.

Oracle SOAP Client installation

To permit Oracle access all the SOAP services we need to install the SOAP Client infrastructure inside Oracle. We used the Apache SOAP implementation derived from the IBM one. This implementation is based on Java it is a free and open source software in the terms of the Apache license, you can download it from http://xml.apache.org/soap.

The first step is to load the SOAP, and all related, jar files into Oracle.
We started by loading Xerces 1.2 (the latest update available at http://xml.apache.org/xerces-j_) into our Oracle 8i instance. The fastest way is to use the `loadjava` utility provided by Oracle:

```
loadjava -r -v -f -u username/password@database xerces.jar
```

After loading and resolving all the Xerces classes we have to load the SOAP ones. If you only want to use HTTP as transport protocol you can only load `soap.jar` (don't worry if you see loading errors, the reason for these is mentioned below) otherwise you have to load the POP3 beans if you want to use SMTP.

```
loadjava -r -v -f -u username/password@database soap.jar
```

Now after loading the SOAP Apache implementation into Oracle you have to load our Java stored procedure which is the bridge between the Apache SOAP implementation, you can find it at `<INSTALL>\examples\OracleFramework` directory:

```
loadjava -r -v -f -u username/password@database StaticCall.class
```

Finally you have to load the PL/SQL side of our framework; we prepared a simple script file to create and compile our packages:

```
sqlplus username/password@database @load.sql
```

> *Attention: using Oracle 8.1.6 when the method `addSymbolToCache` of the class `org.apache.xerces.util.SymbolCache` tries to double a 2 dimensional array size we got a `NullPointer` exception. This is possibly due to a bug in Oracle 8.1.6 JVM that should be fixed in Oracle 8.1.7. If you want to use 8.1.6 release you must load our "brutally" patched `SymbolCache` class.*

```
loadjava -r -v -f -u username/password@database SymbolCache.class
```

Or you can simply import the export **sample.dmp** we prepared in the `<INSTALL>/examples/sample.zip` file that is available for download.

Tomcat installation

Tomcat is the Jakarta Project implementation of Java Servlets 2.2 and JSP 1.1 specifications. It's the Sun reference implementation for servlet and JSP.

The Tomcat installation is pretty easy. Download the latest binary distribution from the Tomcat site: `http://jakarta.apache.org/site/binindex.html` (zip or tar format). Decompress it, go to the bin directory and start it using: `tomcat start` (or tomcat run if you want see the log messages).

To use our case study you need to change the classpath used by tomcat. To change the classpath you can change the Tomcat startup file, `tomcat.bat`. (For Tomcat 4 it is `Catalina.bat` if you're using Windows or `Catalina.sh` if you're using a Unix operating system.) Add the following lines. It is very important to add `Xerces.jar` in the classpath **before** the `xml.jar` that already exists in the batch file, otherwise you will have difficulties in starting up tomcat.

```
# Add SOAP to CLASSPATH
CP=$CP:/usr/local/soap-2_0:/usr/local/soap-2_0/lib/soap.jar
CP=$CP:/usr/local/xerces-1_2_0/xerces.jar
# Add the jBoss Client, see below to the CLASSPATH
JBOSS_HOME=/usr/local/jBoss-2.0_BETA_PROD_02
CP=$CP:$JBOSS_HOME/deploy/lumacars.jar
CP=$CP:$JBOSS_HOME/client/jndi.jar
CP=$CP:$JBOSS_HOME/client/connector.jar
CP=$CP:$JBOSS_HOME/client/jboss-client.jar
CP=$CP:$JBOSS_HOME/client/jnp-client.jar
CP=$CP:$JBOSS_HOME/client/ejb.jar
CP=$CP:$JBOSS_HOME/lib/ext/classes12.jar
```

The `classes12.jar` file is the jar containing the Oracle JDBC classes used by the examples. You can test your Tomcat installation using http://localhost:8080 to see if tomcat is working. Then you can copy the lumacars directory under the `<TOMCAT_HOME>/webapps/examples/jsp` directory, you can try the following URL to see if the sample is correctly installed:

```
http://localhost:8080/examples/jsp/lumacars/Default.jsp
```

If you want to configure Apache (iAS) to use Tomcat as a servlet engine then refer to the "Tomcat - A Minimalistic User's Guide" which is in `<TOMCAT_HOME>/doc`. But ` this means that you will be unable to use OJSP (Oracle JSPs) with this set up.

JBoss installation

You can download jBoss at http://www.jboss.org, on the site you can also find the instruction on how to install it on your platform. Jboss, if you're using the JDK 1.3, has an interesting feature: automated deployment. In order to deploy your Enterprise JavaBeans you can simply put your JAR file in the deploy directory and jBoss takes care of all the details.

So we provided only the `lumacars.jar` in the `<INSTALL>/examples/lumacars` directory. You only need to put this file in the jBoss deployment directory: that's all. The `lumacars.jar` file contains also the source file for the LUMACars implementation. After you installed the EJB side of LUMACARs example you can navigate over the JSP pages in order to verify that all is working.

Apache SOAP installation

After the Tomcat installation you can install the Apache SOAP implementation. You can download the latest binary distribution at http://xml.apache.org/soap and then extract all the files on to your disk. In the `docs\install` subdirectory there are two HTML files giving the instruction on how to install Apache SOAP. You can carefully read the documentation or directly modify your Tomcat startup files as previously stated. Then the easiest way to set up tomcat is to modify the `server.xml` configuration file in the `conf` folder adding a new context:

```
<Context path="/soap" docBase="path-to-apache-soap/webapps/soap"
        debug="1" reloadable="true">
</Context>
```

Now you can try the Apache SOAP implementation using the following URL:

```
http://localhost:8080/soap
```

Following the URL on the page you should be able to test the Admin JSP-based client and the SOAP RPC router. Keep in mind that the router is a servlet and the SOAP specifications require, if you use HTTP, a `POST` (or `M_POST`) method so you shouldn't see a response from a `GET` request. In the Apache RPC router implementation there is a very simple `doGET` method that shows a nice error message:

Sorry, I don't speak via HTTP GET- you have to use HTTP POST to talk to me.

This shows you that everything is working.

Now you can deploy the first sample: the Calculator in chapter 23.

Go to the SOAP service administration page following the previous URL and choose the Deploy link. Now you can deploy the calculator sample provided by our framework. The parameters required are:

Property	Details
ID	`urn:Calc`
Scope	`Request`
Provider Type	`java`
Provider Class	`samples.calculatorj.Calculator`
Use Static Class	`false`
Methods	`sum subtract multiply divide`

You also need to deploy the LUMACars `carOrder` class. This class is used as a bridge from a SOAP call and the EJB components. The parameters are:

Property	Details
ID	`carOrder`
Scope	`Request`
Provider Type	`java`
Provider Class	`soapOrder`
Use Static Class	`false`
Methods	`orderACar`

> **Remember: you have to include the Framework (provided in the code download) directory in the Tomcat classpath.**

If everything is working and your classpath is set properly you can use the Oracle SOAP client components of the framework. Start a SQL-PLUS session, and execute the following query, after the installation of Oracle's SOAP framework:

```
SELECT test(5,6) FROM DUAL;
```

And you should see the result of the sum. With the Apache SOAP distribution there is a very nice utility that permits you to see all the traffic on a TCP port. This utility acts as a proxy and you can start it with the following command:

```
java org.apache.soap.util.net.TcpTunnelGui 2020 localhost 8080
```

Now you have to redirect your SOAP request to `http://localhost:2020/soap/servlet` `/rpcrouter` doing so the Java proxy can show the request and the response string on the screen like this:

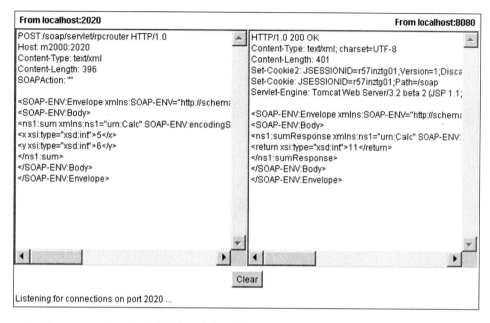

This tool will prove to be very helpful to debug SOAP especially when nothing else is working.

Microsoft SOAP toolkit for Visual Studio

To install the Microsoft toolkit for SOAP you have first to download it from the Microsoft site, you can search the last SOAP engine at http://msdn.microsoft.com. In this sample we used the July 2000 version, (although as this book was being published there was a new release, in November 2000, which we were unable to test). In this version we've got an installer `.msi` file that performs the actual installation using the standard Microsoft Installer services.

Microsoft Environment

In order to use all the server side implementations of our samples you have to install the Microsoft version too. To install the calculator the steps are very simple:

❑ Register the `MyCalc.dll` file in the `<INSTALL>\examples\Microsoft\Calculator\Server` directory

❑ Share the `examples\Microsoft\Calculator\Server` directory as the Web `/calc` URI

❑ Start the `ClientCalculator.exe` program found in the `<INSTALL>\examples\Microsoft \Calculator\Clients` directory and choose the right URL

To install the LUMA cars example you have to:

- ❑ Create a new COM+ application named `Marketing`
- ❑ Register the DLL `marketing.dll` found in
  `<INSTALL>\examples\Microsoft\LUMACars\Marketing`
- ❑ Configure the component `Marketing.GetOrder` enabling the object construction flag and setting the Constructor String with the value, for example, of

```
Provider=MSDAORA.1;User ID=user;Password=pwd;Data Source=orcl;Persist Security
Info=False
```

This is the connection string used by the component to connect with our Oracle DB
Use the `examples\Microsoft\LUMACars\Marketing` as the `Web/marketing` URI

Summary

This appendix has presented some of the more common issues that arising when installing and configuring Oracle 8i databases and clients as well as some of the tools and utilities Oracle provides for development such as Jdeveloper, the XSU and Oracle SQLJ.

ORACLE8iAPPLICATIONPROGRAMMING

Java Primer

This appendix is not supposed to be a replacement for or a condensed version of the many books that actually teach the Java language. The reader is encouraged to refer to a foundational programming manual such as *Beginning Java 2, JDK 1.3 Edition*, Ivor Horton, Wrox Press, March 2000, ISBN 1861002238. This appendix should rather be viewed as a quick reference companion to this book, which will allow readers new, or relatively new, to Java to brush up on some of the core features of the language and specification.

Java's History

The history of Java is quite unusual as computer languages go. For a start, it has one. Or at least, it has one which is celebrated and widely known, as opposed to most languages which are taken as they come and whose origins are buried deep within old and forgotten coding and business decisions.

In the early 1990s, Sun was busy trying to become to network technologies what Microsoft was to the PC market. A team codenamed 'Green', which included James Gosling, invented an object-oriented architecture independent language called Oak. It grew out of their work on networked devices such as cellular phones, personal digital assistants, and interactive TV. The work they did in these areas unfortunately did not break any boundaries, but when Oak was redeveloped for the increasing popular internet, and renamed 'Java', Sun had finally found an area in which they could expand.

Java was an instant hit on the Internet, largely because its self-contained and robust nature made it ideal for writing applets to run in web pages. Suddenly everyone could have scrolling text brightening up their fledgling websites, and that was just the sort of thing to capture the imagination and the purse strings of businesses worldwide.

The Java Virtual Machine

Today, of course, Java's importance and position in the industry is about much more than dancing icons on web pages. Perhaps the most important thing about it is its famous 'write once, run anywhere' credentials. With most languages, code written in them needs to be compiled for a particular platform. Java, on the other hand, is not compiled into native machine code, but into a bytecode format. Bytecode is executed by the Java Virtual Machine, or JVM, an abstract computing machine. Versions of the JVM are available for all the most popular platforms, and are embedded in all the most popular internet browsers.

What the virtual machine actually runs can be anything from simple applets to multi-tiered enterprise applications. At one end of the scale, a traditional application could use a JVM and Java applications just on the client, perhaps to carry out some user-interface processing in a friendly and pretty way. Or the application could push Java further, and use the application server's JVM as well, to provide the core processing required by the system in a way that is easily deployable and maintainable. With the Oracle 8i JVM, it is possible to take Java all the way back to the database server, and have Java code manipulating data from inside the database. These different levels, and how they are applicable in the context of Oracle, are discussed later in this appendix.

Developing with Java

The history and nature of Java are not just important because they make an interesting story. Gosling and his team made the earliest versions of Java available on the Internet, for free. They did this because they knew it would be the perfect way to ensure that the development community warmed to it, and indeed this was one of the reasons for the speed with which Java became the language of the Internet. Java was created because of the vision and tenacity of a small group of developers. Despite the fact that it is now one of the most desired programming skills in the industry and is used extensively by major corporations, the feeling of a small community with a common and inspiring goal still pervades throughout the Java development world.

The Java Developer Connection (http://developer.java.sun.com) is perhaps the best example of this. It is a rich resource for developers, with endless documentation about all the Java products, tutorials, code forums, and, possibly most importantly, the bug database. This lists everything which has been submitted by developers as a bug, and gives its evaluation by the Sun team, including any workarounds and the status of fixes. Developers can vote for bugs and so raise their priority in the fixing schedules.

The Java Platform and the SDK

If you have an Interactive Development Environment (IDE) such as Borland's JBuilder or Symantec's VisualCafé, you can follow the manuals which come with it and use it to write, compile and run your Java code.

There are some advantages to learning Java with a development tool. You will be able to quickly compile and run simple Java programs. Most of these tools have excellent compiler error reporting systems that should enable you to find and fix typos and other problems in your code. In contrast, the command-line compiler can be less accessible to the beginner.

There are many good reasons to start learning Java using Sun's reference Java platforms. Perhaps most importantly, you will be able to share your learning experience with others. If you hit an intractable problem doing something with an obscure IDE, it is much less likely that anyone will be able to tell you what is wrong with your setup or your code. If your problem can be replicated using a reference JDK, then you have vast resources of knowledge available to help clarify your problem.

Sun provide several Java platforms. The Java™ 2 Platform, Standard Edition, or J2SE™, is the main one. The platform provides abstract functionality, and the JDK is the software which implements the platform. It is worth taking a moment to look at Java platforms, development kits and versions, as they can be confusing.

With early versions of Java technology, such as 1.1.7 and 1.1.8, products were split into the Java Runtime Environment, or JRE, and the Java Development Kit, or JDK. These versions are still being used in Oracle 8i, so you may well come across these terms.

The 1.2 versions of these products included significant changes in functionality, and Sun decided to adopt the name **Java 2** to refer to all versions from 1.2 onwards. They also amalgamated the JDK and JRE into the one SDK. The most recent available version of the SDK for J2SE™ is 1.3, and this is labeled under the Java 2 name.

Other platforms available are for the Java™ 2 Platform, Enterprise Edition (J2EE™) and the Java™ 2 Platform, Micro Edition (J2ME™). The J2EE™ provides the functionality required to build enterprise server-side applications, while the J2ME™ provides functionality specialized for devices such as pagers and cellular phones. These platforms have their own versioning in place, but you do not need to worry about them until you have become familiar with the basics of Java, and they are not dealt with in this appendix.

The SDK for J2SE™ can be downloaded from http://java.sun.com/j2se/1.3. Follow the instructions given. Once you have successfully downloaded and installed it, you are ready to start running Java code.

Writing, Compiling and Running Code

To write, compile and run your first Java program, follow these steps:

Ensure that you have downloaded and installed the SDK as mentioned above. Then, open your text editor of choice, and type in the code below. This is a very simple program, which just prints out a line of text saying 'Goodbye'. Don't worry about what the code means at the moment.

```
public class Originality
{
public static void main(String[] args)
    {
        System.out.println("Goodbye!");
    }
}
```

Create a temporary directory somewhere for your first coding attempts, such as C:\Code. Save this code as a file, called Originality.java, in that directory.

Now you need to compile the code. You can do this using the javac tool, which comes with the SDK. It will be located in the \bin directory wherever you have installed the SDK. At the command line, invoke the program, passing it the name of the file you want to compile. For example, if you have installed the SDK in C:\jdk1.3, and you have saved the file in C:\Code, you will need to type in:

```
C:\jdk1.3\bin\javac C:\Code\Originality.java
```

There should now be an extra file in C:\Code (or wherever you saved the file) called Originality.class. This represents the compiled code.

Classpath

To run this class, you can use the `java.exe` tool located in the `\bin` directory of the SDK installation. First, however, you need to tell it where to find the compiled Java code. You do this by setting the `CLASSPATH` environment variable, which you can do either on the command file, or in the System Properties window. With the latter, it would look something like this:

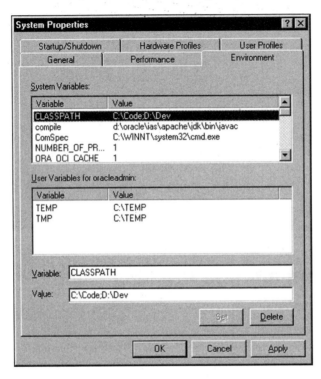

As you can see, you can specify more than one location for the classpath; the order in which they are specified will be the order in which they are searched to find the compiled code. As we are often running files from within the same directory it is necessary to tell the JVM to also look in the current directory, which it doesn't do by default. To achieve this we have to include a full stop at the beginning of the path, like this: `.;C:\Code;D:\Dev`

Now you can run the compiled code, `Originality.class`. However, you do not need to specify the `.class` extension. Neither do you need to specify its location, since the `CLASSPATH` variable does that for you. So all you need is something like:

```
C:\jdk1.3\bin\java Originality
```

And you should see Goodbye! printed out on the screen. The entire session would look something like this:

```
Command Prompt                                                    _ □ ×
Microsoft(R) Windows NT(TM)
(C) Copyright 1985-1996 Microsoft Corp.

C:\>cd Code

C:\Code>C:\jdk1.3\bin\javac Originality.java

C:\Code>cd ..

C:\>C:\jdk1.3\bin\java Originality
Goodbye!

C:\>_
```

You can also specify where your package can be found by using the -classpath option when you execute the java command. This has the advantage that it only applies for the current execution so you can easily set it to suit each run.

> Note that when you compile code using **javac** you have to include the whole filename (with **.java** extension) whereas when you run the code using the Java command you just type the filename without the **.class** extension.

Later we will be using slightly more sophisticated code examples, but the process is always the same: save the code as a file with a .java extension, compile this using the javac tool provided by the SDK, and then run it using the java tool.

The Java Language

Now it is time to start looking at the language itself. But before any actual code is introduced, it will be worth examining how programs written in Java are constructed.

Object Orientation

Key Concepts

Java is an **object-oriented** language, which means that writing a program in it consists of defining discrete objects providing specific functionality. These objects represent entities, along with their attributes, the operations which can be performed on them, and the methods they are capable of carrying out.

The entities represented by the objects may be something concrete which can be found in the real world, such as a movie. A movie's state might consist of, among other things, a title, director, and classification, and operations which could be performed on it might be awarding it an Oscar, or giving it a critical rating.

Objects can also be more conceptual, such as a string. A string's state consists of the number and type of characters it has, and a method it can carry out is giving you a specified subsection of itself.

Although it is not the place of this appendix to go deeply into the principles of object orientation (usually referred to as OO), it is important to understand a little bit about them. OO is a powerful tool when used properly, as it can be used to develop systems which are built on reusable components, and which are easy to extend as the business needs underpinning them change.

Encapsulation

An object in an OO system is an entity which encapsulates both data, and operations to control that data. The interaction between those objects in an object-oriented system will provide the system's behaviour and functionality. These operations are usually known as **methods** of the object, and if the system has been well written, they will be the only way to access and manipulate the object's data. For this reason objects are said to be **encapsulated**.

Objects forming part of an OO system act as building blocks, capable of being assembled together to provide the required behaviour and functionality. Assembling a different selection from the same body of objects could provide different behaviour, and the same object could provide different functionality by being put together with another group of objects.

Polymorphism

The collection of methods which an object provides for accessing it and its data are known as the object's **interface**. Because objects can only be accessed through their interfaces, clients which make calls on those objects do not need to be aware of what is going on in the object itself. And because different objects can share interfaces, this means that a client object can make calls asking for a certain operation to be performed, without having to know exactly what type of object is going to fulfill its request.

The ability to swap in different objects with the same interfaces is known as **polymorphism**, and it is crucial to object orientation. It can make it easier to write the code which is requesting that operations be carried out, since very little needs to be known about the object providing the operation. It also enables objects to be implemented in different ways, while code that uses the object is unaffected.

Inheritance

Another key feature of OO is **inheritance**, which is the ability for objects to inherit functionality from each other. Many systems, for example, might have objects representing Employees, with functionality to deal with their job title, manager, home address, and so on. If the system designer then decided that more specialised objects were needed, in order to maintain the difference between employees who were paid on commission and employees who were paid by the hour, they would not need to start from scratch with the new objects, redefining all the functionality from the Employee object. Instead they could just inherit from the Employee object, and include in their new objects just the functionality specific to them.

Design Patterns

You may be wondering how, armed only with this short introduction to OO, you will be able to design a system to take advantage of any of OO's strengths. Fortunately, it is not necessary to start from a blank page, because there are many **design patterns** of which you can take advantage. Design patterns are general solutions to the specific problems which confront designers of object oriented systems, and they not only provide a solution to the problem, but they describe the problem in such a way that the solution can be applied to it.

Design patterns are not unique to software engineering. Football players, for example, do not just run blindly on to the pitch at the starting whistle and scuttle around randomly for ninety minutes – at least, not when they are playing well. Instead, they use carefully planned formations which will enable them to overcome the strengths and take advantage of the weaknesses of the opposing side. Design patterns are comparable to footballing tactics, and enable you to solve problems such as not having your objects too tightly coupled. Coupling is the practice of writing code so that different objects are dependent on each other, and, while it is inevitable, it needs to be very carefully handled.

> **The seminal work on design patterns** *is Design Patterns: Elements of Reusable Object-Oriented Software*, **by Erich Gamma, Richard Helm, Ralph Johnson and John Vlissides (Addison-Wesley, 1995).**

Frameworks

You may also come across frameworks in the design of good OO systems. A framework is a library of classes which forms the basis for the common functionality shared by components in a system. Frameworks make the design of the components which use the framework easier, but the difficulty which is inherent to OO is simply shifted into the framework design. All the principles of OO design are magnified when it comes to frameworks. If the design is not truly reusable, then even a perfectly designed application may have its functionality curtailed by the restrictions the framework places upon it. If the framework is too tightly coupled to the classes which use it, then whenever it is changed (which it inevitably will be), all the application classes will have to be changed as well – which makes the whole point of a framework somewhat irrelevant. However, since frameworks can contribute more to an OO system's possibility for reuse than any other single concept, they can be very useful things.

Writing Java Code

An Introduction to Java Classes and Objects

Any application written in Java will consist of one or more objects interacting with each other, calling methods on each other and providing each other with information. An object is created by writing a program which defines a class to represent it, as well as its internal state and the operations it supports. The source code for the class will be a file with the extension `.java`. When compiled, the source code will generate a file with a `.class` extension (strictly speaking, more than one `.class` file might be generated, but this will be dealt with later). Class files can be loaded by the JVM. So, if your application needed to deal with movies, you might have a `Movie.java` file representing, through its code, all the information you needed to store about movies, as well as all the ways of manipulating that information. This would constitute your Movie class.

Unless you are lucky enough to be writing an extremely simple application however, you will probably be dealing with more than one movie. In order to do this, you have to be able to create *instances* of your Movie class. The instances you create are the *objects*, and they instantiate all the features represented in the Movie class. For example, the Movie class has the concept of a movie title, but you need an actual movie object to get access to a real title, such as "It's a Wonderful Life".

We will see exactly how to create objects later, but for the moment it is important to understand the difference between a class, which represents an entity, and an object, which *is* one of those entities, capable of doing everything the class says it can. A common analogy is that of a template such as a cookie cutter, where a class is like a cookie cutter and the objects are like the cookies that it can produce.

Java has only a few primitive data types, and so most of the Java code you write will deal with classes and objects. There are a great many classes available with the Java platform, which give you a lot of functionality for free. The String class is one example of these: strings are not primitive data types in Java, but objects of the class `String`.

Two Simple Classes

This is an example of a fairly simple class `SimpleMovie.java`:

```java
public class SimpleMovie
{

    protected String title;
    private float budget = 1000000;
    protected int rating;

    /**
     * Creates a movie with a default title
     */
    public SimpleMovie()
    {
        this("Unnamed");
    }

    /**
     * Creates a movie with a specific title
     */
    public SimpleMovie(String movieTitle)
    {
        title = movieTitle;
    }

    /**
     * Returns the movie's title
     */
    public String getTitle()
    {
        return title;
    }


    /**
     * Returns the movie's budget
     */
    protected float getBudget()
    {
        return budget;
    }

    /**
     * Gives the movie a critical rating, out of ten
     */
    public void rateMovie(int newRating)
    {
```

```
        // Check that the rating is between 1 and 10
        if (newRating > 0 && newRating < 11)
        {
            rating = newRating;
        }
        else
        // If not, give it a default rating
        {
            rateMovie();
        }

        switch ( getRating() )
        {
            // If the rating satisfies any of the following conditions (i.e. is
            // less than 5), then 'Lousy Movie' will be printed out
            case 1:
            case 2:
            case 3:
            case 4:
                System.out.println("Lousy movie");
                break;
            // If the rating satisfies any of the following conditions (i.e. is
            // less than 8 but greater than 4), then 'OK Movie' will be printed out
            case 5:
            case 6:
            case 7:
                System.out.println("OK movie");
                break;
            // If the rating satisfies any of the following conditions (i.e. is
            // greater than 7), then 'Great Movie' will be printed out
            case 8:
            case 9:
            case 10:
                System.out.println("Great movie");
                break;
            // If no conditions have been satisfied, then 'Invalid Rating' will
            // be printed out
            default:
                System.out.println("Invalid Rating");
                break;
        }

    }

    /**
     * Gives the movie a default critical rating, out of ten
     */
    public void rateMovie()
    {
        rating = 5;
    }

    /**
     * Returns the movie's rating
     */
```

```
    public int getRating()
    {
        return rating;
    }

    public String setSequel(String sequelNo)
    {
        title = title + " " + sequelNo;
        return title;
    }

}
```

And this is an example of another class which creates an instance of the first one (an object) and does something with it (filename: MovieTester.java):

```
public class MovieTester
{
    public static void main(String[] args)
    {
        SimpleMovie movie = new SimpleMovie("I Know You Had a Nightmare" +
            " in Woodsboro Last Halloween Part XXXVII");

        System.out.println("The movie's title is " + movie.getTitle());
        System.out.println("The movie's budget is £" + movie.getBudget());

        System.out.println("Critics rated it as a");
        movie.rateMovie(7);

        movie.setSequel("The Second");
        System.out.println(movie.getTitle());

    }
}
```

You should be able to compile these two classes as described before, and then run the second one. The output will look like this:

```
The movie's title is I Know You Had a Nightmare in Woodsboro Last Halloween Part
XXXVII
The movie's budget is £1000000.0
Critics rated it as a
OK movie
I Know You Had a Nightmare in Woodsboro Last Halloween Part XXXVII The Second
```

You will, however, probably not be satisfied with this state of affairs, and would rather write and run your own classes. So we are going to go through the steps needed to create a simple class.

Creating a class

Each class usually has its own separate *.java* file. The exception is classes containing inner classes, which will have more than one class within one *.java* file. We will see more about this when we discuss inner classes.

Within a .java file, the necessary code to create a class is as follows:

```
public class Movie extends Object
{
}
```

By convention, the names of classes always start with a capital letter, have no spaces, and are capitalized on word boundaries, such as StackOverflowError and ZipFile. So first you need to declare the class by name, which in this case is Movie.

You then need to specify what the class **extends**. The concept of inheritance has already been mentioned, and it is likely that most of your classes will extend, or be a subclass of, another class. This is how objects inherit from each other in Java.

If you do not specify which class a new class extends, then by default it will extend the Object class, which is part of the Java platform. In fact, if your class does extend Object you do not need to specify this explicitly, and can leave out the extends <class> declaration. It has simply been included here as an illustration. We will be looking at subclassing in more detail later.

The name of the class must match the name of the .java file you save it as. Class names are case-sensitive. Create a file called Movie.java in the directory you have created for your code, and copy the code above into it.

You will have noticed that there is also a public modifier before the class declaration. This is necessary to make the class accessible to others. We will look more at public modifiers in a moment.

Classes are usually organized into packages, which are logical groupings carrying out a similar purpose to directories on a file server. Package names, like class names, are case-sensitive, but conventionally they are lower-case.

In the same way that classes extend Object if nothing else is specified, classes will implicitly be in the java.lang package if no package is specified for them explicitly. Object is itself in the java.lang package, which is part of the Java platform. Objects are sometimes referred to by what is known as their fully-qualified class name. This is the package name followed by the class name, for example java.lang.Object.

Normally you would create your own packages for your classes, but for the time being we will not be worrying about them. We will be looking at packages in more detail later, for now you only need to know what they are, so you can recognize references to them when you see them.

Properties and Methods

Visibility

As you would expect of any program, a class can have constants, variables and methods. All of these can have **public**, **protected**, **private** and **package** visibility, and their visibility affects the ability of other classes to see and make references to them.

Public visibility is the least restrictive. If something is declared to be public, it can be seen and accessed by any class. The methods by which other objects manage and manipulate instances of a class should be declared public.

Protected visibility is more restrictive. Protected methods and properties can be only be accessed by other classes which are in the same package, or by classes which are not in the same package, but which extend the class in which the protected item is found (subclasses).

Package visibility is the default. It means that only classes in the same package can access whatever has the package visibility.

Private visibility is the most restrictive: private attributes and methods can only be seen within the class in which they are created.

Visibility Level	Meaning
Public	Any other class can access method/property
Protected	Subclasses and classes in same package can access method/property
Package	Classes in same package can access method/property
Private	Method/property can only be accessed from class it belongs to

Private methods should be used with care, and only if you are certain that the functionality they provide would never be implemented differently by a subclass. On the other hand, it is quite rare to have public variables. This is because variables represent something about the state of a class, and classes which form part of an object-oriented system should be capable of completely managing their own state, and should rarely allow other classes direct access to that state. This is known as **encapsulation**. If it is possible for another class to access an object's variables, that class can change the variable's value, and possibly make the class inconsistent. Instead the object should provide methods to get and set the variable. That way, when an attribute is being set, an object can check that it is being set to a valid value, and update anything about its state which depends on the attribute.

Primitive Data Types

The Java language has eight primitive data types, such as **boolean** and **integer (int)**. A boolean can have a value of true or false, while an `int` is a whole number between -2^{31} and $2^{31}-1$. The other six types are **char**, **byte**, **short**, **float**, **long** and **double**. Primitive data types are not Java objects (although, just to confuse things, wrapper classes, such as `Integer`, do exist to make coding with them simpler).

Add the following three lines to your class between the curly brackets:

```
public class Movie extends Object
{
    protected String title;
    private float budget = 1000000;
    protected int rating;
}
```

Properties

Properties can be constants or variables. The three lines you have just added are declaring variable properties of the class (we will come to constants later). The first one is a Java object of the class String, which was mentioned earlier. The second is a primitive float data type, while the third is a primitive int data type.

As you can see, the visibility is specified first (protected), then the data type of the object variable (String), then its name (in this case, title). The second property (the float) shows how properties can be declared and initialized in one go.

The equals ("=") sign is used to assign a value to a variable. Be careful when using this: it does not mean equality! Testing for equality will be discussed further later.

It is conventional to use lower case names for variables, to distinguish them from classes. However, they are usually capitalized on word boundaries if they are formed of more than one word:

```
protected String directorName;
protected String producerName;
```

Methods

The code below is an example of a method. You can add it to your class below the variables:

```
public class Movie extends Object
{
    protected String title;
    private float budget = 1000000;
    protected int rating;
    public String setSequel(String sequelNo)
    {
        title = title + " " + sequelNo;
        return title;
    }
}
```

The first word, public, specifies the visibility of the method. The second specifies the type of what is returned by the method. This may be a class, a Java primitive data type, or void if nothing is returned from the method (a method must "return" the type void if it has no explicit call to return). The third word is the method name, which, like a variable name, conventionally starts with a lower case letter and is capitalized on word boundaries. Then, in brackets, come the method parameters, declared by type and then a name. The body of the method is enclosed in curly braces.

This method is taking a string which represents the name of the sequel, and adding that to the variable which represents the movie's title (The + symbol is the Java operator which concatenates strings). It is returning the new title. If you go back to the earlier examples of two classes, you can in the second class see how this method might be called.

Add these other methods to your class:

```java
/**
 * Returns the movie's title
 */
public String getTitle()
{
    return title;
}


/**
 * Returns the movie's budget
 */
protected float getBudget()
{
    return budget;
}


/**
 * Gives the movie a default critical rating, out of ten
 */
public void rateMovie()
{
    rating = 5;
}

/**
 * Returns the movie's rating
 */
public int getRating()
{
    return rating;
}
```

Method Overloading

It is possible to have more than one method with the same name in a class, as long as the different methods have different parameters. The different methods can have different numbers of parameters, or the same number, but different types. They can have different return types, but it is not sufficient *just* to have different return types; the parameters must differ as well. The combination of a method's name and number and types of parameters is called its signature, and having the same methods with the same names but different signatures in a class is called *method overloading*. Overloading is useful when a class has methods which perform similar operations, or where a class might be called with different parameters depending on where it is called from. It should not be used in other circumstances.

Below is an example of method overloading, which you can add to your class. Suppose that the Movie class has a rateMovie() method allowing it to be given a mark out of 10. It might be desirable to have a way of doing this without having a specific value to assign to the movie, in which case it will be given an average rating. This could be expressed:

```java
public void rateMovie(int newRating)
{
    if (newRating > 0 && newRating < 11)
    {
        rating = newRating;
    }
    else
    {
        rateMovie();
    }
}
public void rateMovie()
{
    rating = 5;
}
```

The above example shows how one method can be called from another, as well as introducing conditions. It is checking that any rating passed to the method is between 1 and 10, and modifying the rating if it is in the range. Otherwise it is calling the no-parameter method, which simply assigns an average rating. We will look more at conditional statements later.

Structuring Code

The syntax of Java code is not difficult to pick up, especially for programmers who have any experience of C or C++. Since the point of this appendix is more to introduce Java than to teach it in-depth, we will not be exploring every nuance of the language, but it is still worth introducing the most important points.

You may have already noticed that statements end with a semicolon. You have probably also noticed the use of braces to group statements together, in a method body and after `if` statements, for example. Code grouped together by such braces is known as a block. Any variables declared within that block are only visible in the block, and will normally cease to exist once the path of execution has left the block. Whether or not to indent the code within a block is a matter of personal (and sometimes company) taste, but it does make the code more readable. Blocks do not need semicolons at the end of them.

Braces are required for method bodies, and for try and catch blocks, which we will come on to later. Additionally, they are often used in flow control, to group together sections of code which should be executed as a result of some condition being satisfied.

If Statements

The *if* statement is one you will probably use a lot in your code. It takes the form:

```java
if (expression which equates to a boolean)
{
    statement;
}
else if (another boolean expression)
{
    another statement;
}
else
{
    a third statement
}
```

An 'expression which equates to a boolean' is usually known as a *boolean expression*. Some examples are:

```
10 == 20;
3 < 5;
object1.equals(object2);
```

You can see that there is no end if statement in Java. The else statement is optional. The braces enclosing the blocks to be executed are also in fact optional if the block contains one statement only, but it is good coding practice always to use them, as it can lead to unexpected behavior if you do not. The following is an example:

```
int movieRating = 2;

    if (movieRating > 5)
        System.out.println("This movie is");
        System.out.println("worth seeing");

    if (movieRating < 5)
    {
        System.out.println("This movie is");
        System.out.println("not worth seeing");
    }
    System.out.println("Normal processing resumed");
```

If you do not use braces after an if statement, then the first line of code after it will be executed if the statement equates to true, and control will continue from there. On the other hand, if you use braces, then all the code in the block enclosed by the braces will be executed, and control will continue from outside the block. If you run the above code (which is in the FlowControl class), you will see that the output is:

```
worth seeing
This movie is
not worth seeing
Normal processing resumed
```

whereas you would actually want it to be:

```
This movie is
not worth seeing
Normal processing resumed
```

Switch Statements

Sometimes, rather than using a long if...else if statement, it is possible to use a switch statement instead, which looks like this:

```
switch ( getRating() )
    {
        case 1:
        case 2:
        case 3:
        case 4:
            // If the rating is equal to any of the four
            // values above, the next line of code will be
```

```
                          // executed
                          System.out.println("Lousy movie");
                          break;
                     case 5:
                     case 6:
                     case 7:
                          System.out.println("OK movie");
                          break;
                     case 8:
                     case 9:
                     case 10:
                          System.out.println("Great movie");
                          break;
                     default:
                          System.out.println("Invalid rating");
                          break;
             }
```

The expression following the `switch` keyword must be one of the following expressions: an `int`, `byte`, `short` or `char`, but it cannot be any other primitive data type like `long` or any type of object. The expressions following the `case` keywords (1, 10, etc.) must be constants: either literals, or static final properties. If the expression following the switch keyword matches any of the labels after the `case` keywords, the following statements are executed, right up until the end of the `switch` statement.

The break keyword can be used to force execution out of the `switch` statement and into the statement which follows it. Case labels will not force execution out of the switch statement, so it is important to use `break` – otherwise all your statements will be executed, regardless of which case was satisfied.

The statement after the `default` keyword, which is optional, will be executed if no match is found.

Add the code above to the end of your `public void rateMovie(int newRating)` method.

Loops

Another way of controlling the flow of execution in your programs is with loops. There are three types of loops in Java: `while` loops, `do` loops, and `for` loops.

`While` loops are the simplest kind of loop. They take the form:

```
int i = 1;
while (i < 10)
{
    System.out.println("Not reached 10 yet");
    i = i +1;
}
```

The statement in the block will be executed as long as the boolean expression evaluates to true. The statement can of course change something which affects the value of the condition; in this example, the `while` statement is checking whether a number is smaller than a certain value, and the statement inside the loop is incrementing this number each time. `Do` loops are similar to `while` loops, but they take the form:

```
do
{
    statement;
}
while (boolean expression);
```

Do loops are guaranteed to be executed once, because the condition is not evaluated until after the statement has been executed. For loops, on the other hand, might never be executed if the condition evaluates to false the first time it is checked. For loops are slightly more sophisticated. A typical for loop is:

```
for (int j = 1; j < 11; j++)
{
    System.out.println(j + "green bottles hanging on a wall");
}
```

(What is typical about this loop is its initialization, not its content; obviously in not many applications is it necessary to print out fragments of nursery rhymes).

The for expression has three parts: the first int j = 1; specifies the starting position, the second j < 11; specifies a condition which must be met for the iteration to continue, and the third j++ is a statement which must be executed at the end of every iteration.

As you can see from the initialization of this loop, it is possible to declare and initialize the initial expression in one go, although this is not actually necessary. You will probably also notice the j++ syntax, which may be familiar to you: this is just shorthand for j = j+1.

The outcome of these loops can be seen by running the FlowControl program.

Execution can be transferred out of a loop and to the statement following it by using the break statement, in the same way as in switch statements. Control can also be passed to the end of the loop body (but not out of the loop) by using the continue; statement. Execution will then start again with the next iteration of the loop.

Equality

In fact, a double equal == tests for equality, but again this should be used with care, since it actually compares instances in memory, and it is unlikely that two **objects** you are comparing will have the same memory address. You will usually need to use the equals() method from Object for most equality tests. The exception is primitive data types, which can be compared using ==.

The following code illustrates the different uses of equality:

```
public class Equality
{

    public static void main(String args[])
    {
        int i = 10;
        int j = 20;
        int k = j - i;

        String hello1 = "Hello World";
        String hello2 = "Hello";
        String hello3 = hello1.substring(0, 5);

        if (i == j) System.out.println("10 is the same as 20");

        if (k == i) System.out.println("20 is the same as 20");
```

```
        if (hello2 == hello3)
            System.out.println("These two strings have the same address in memory");

        if (hello2.equals(hello3))
            System.out.println("These two strings have the same characters");

    }

}
```

Three `ints` have been defined, equal to 10, 20 and 20-10. If you compile and execute this code, you will see that two `ints` with the same value will be considered equal if you use the `==` operator.

Three strings have also been defined, `"Hello"`, `"Hello World"`, and a substring of `"Hello World"` which is equal to `"Hello"`. If you run this code, you will see that the two strings with a value of `"Hello"` are not considered equal if you use the `==` operator, but they are if you use the `equals()` method.

Constructors

We have clarified the distinction between classes and objects, we have seen how to declare and use properties and methods, and we have seen how constants and methods can be accessed without having an object which instantiates the class which provides them. What we have not seen is how to create an instance of a class.

This is very straightforward. Objects are created in the following way:

```
Movie myMovie = new Movie();
```

The above code snippet is doing two things: declaring a variable and assigning a newly created `Movie` object to it. This can also be done in two stages:

```
Movie myMovie;
myMovie = new Movie();
```

The `new` keyword is the important one here. The Java compiler will treat this as a cue to create a new instance of the object whose class is named after the `new` keyword. To do this, it will call a special method in the class called a **constructor**. A constructor is a method which has the same name as the class, and no return type. If you look at the example below, you will see that the method declaration begins `public Movie(...`, whereas all the methods we have seen so far have something between the visibility modifier and the method name (such as `String` or `void`) to specify the type of what is returned by the method.

If you do not specify a constructor in a class, the compiler will generate a default one with no arguments, which you can then access, even though it has not been declared. It is also possible to have constructors with arguments, if you explicitly define them.

An example of a constructor with arguments might be:

```
public Movie(String movieTitle)
{
    title = movieTitle;
}
```

Add this constructor to your class.

To create a Movie object using this constructor, you would do something like:

```
Movie anotherMovie = new Movie("Nightmare on Elm Street 3829");
```

Subclassing

Because Java is an object-oriented language, classes can *extend* other classes. What this means is that if Class B extends Class A, B inherits all the functionality A has, and will either change the implementation of some of that functionality, or add some new functionality. B can be referred to as a **subclass** of A, while A is a **superclass** of B. This is the concept of inheritance, which we visited briefly earlier, and it is one of the most powerful features of Java. It should be used when you need to create a subclass which is a more specialized version of a class: for example, you might want to extend the class Movie with a subclass HorrorMovie. Horror movies have everything which has been defined in the Movie class, such as a title, director, and critical rating, and they also have other things as well, such as horror type (vampire or zombie) and so on.

It is often suggested that you can test whether a class should be a subclass of another simply by testing whether predication holds between them. If B **is an** A – like a horror movie is a movie, then B should usually be a subclass of A. However, this maxim should be used with care, although it will suffice for the time being. Proper use of subclassing is not as easy as it looks, and is beyond the scope of this appendix.

We have already seen that if you create a class and do not specify whether it extends any other class, it will implicitly extend java.lang.Object, the Object class in the java.lang package. Although classes do not need to be in any package at all, all the J2SE™ classes are in packages, and the java.lang package is the one in which many of the key J2SE™ classes are found.

The Object class provides some very basic functionality: it has an equals() method for example, which tests whether two objects are the same. It also has toString() method, which returns a string representation of the object. Normally this will just be the object's class name, but for certain classes it can contain more information about the object, such as some of the data it contains. We will be looking at inheritance in more detail later – because it is so powerful, it can also be quite destructive if used improperly, so it is important to understand it in detail. It is also important to note that, unlike some other languages, Java does not support multiple inheritance, where a class can inherit functionality from more than one superclass. The multiple inheritance in languages like C++ can make things very complicated, and so Java avoids it in its bid to be as simple a language as possible.

We are going to create a HorrorMovie class, which will be a subclass of the Movie class you have already created. First, add a variable and a method to the Movie class:

```
protected String genre;
public boolean canHaveSequel()
    {
        if (genre.equals("ACTION"))
        {
            return true;
        }
        else
        {
            return false;
        }
    }
```

Now create a `HorrorMovie` class:

```java
public class HorrorMovie extends Movie
{
    /**
     * Always returns true, as horror movies can always have sequels
     */
    public boolean canHaveSequel()
    {
        return true;
    }
}
```

Save this as a file called `HorrorMovie.java`.

If one class extends another (as the new `HorrorMovie` class extends the `Movie` class), then by doing so it will inherit all the superclass's methods and properties which are not private. The subclass is then free to **override** the methods of the superclass, which means implementing them with the same signature and return type, but giving them a different body, so that they perform their function differently.

What we have done is defined a method in the `Movie` class which specifies whether or not a film can have a sequel. In the `HorrorMovie` subclass, this method is overridden, because horror movies can always have sequels.

Final Methods and Properties

Setting a property to be a constant is pretty straightforward in Java; you just need to use the keyword `final`. If something is declared as `final`, its value cannot be reassigned.

Create a `BoardOfClassification` class using the following code:

```java
public class BoardOfClassification
{
    public static final String U = "U";
    public static final String PG = "PG";
    public static final String TWELVE = "12";
    public static final String FIFTEEN = "15";
    public static final String EIGHTEEN = "18";

    public BoardOfClassification()
    {
    }

    public void classifyMovie(Movie movie)
    {
        if (movie instanceof HorrorMovie)
        {
            movie.setClassification(EIGHTEEN);
        }
        else
        {
            movie.setClassification(TWELVE);
        }
    }
}
```

This has five constants representing the five types of film classification. We can assume, at least for the purposes of our little application, that these will never change. They are therefore suitable for being defined as constants.

The class also has a simplistic method to classify a movie. It is just rating all horror movies as 18s, and everything else as a 12. This is a nice example of inheritance in practice: the method just receives a `Movie` object to classify. Because a `HorrorMovie`, being a subclass of `Movie`, is also a `Movie` object, then it may well be receiving a `HorrorMovie` object. It is checking whether this is the case by using the `instanceof` keyword. Unfortunately further discussions of this OO feature are beyond the scope of this appendix, but this should give you an idea of how inheritance can be used in Java.

There is obviously less of an issue with making constants public than there is with public variables, since their value cannot be changed by any object anyway.

Final Methods

Methods can also be declared as `final`, and the effect this has is to prevent them from being overridden in subclasses. Although overriding is a great and useful thing, sometimes you might not want a subclass to provide a different implementation of a method, and in this case you would declare the method in the class as `final`, to prevent any overriding implementation. An example of this is having two methods with different signatures, where one simply calls the other.

Create an `Actor` class using the code below:

```java
public class Actor
{
    public static final String MALE = "male";
    public static final String FEMALE = "female";

    protected int box_office_successes;
    protected String gender;
    protected int last_movie_fee;
    protected String fullName;

    public Actor(String gender, int num_successes, float last_fee)
    {
        box_office_successes = num_successes;
        if (gender.equals(MALE))
        {
            gender = MALE;
        }
        else
        {
            gender = FEMALE;
        }
    }

    public int getNumberBoxOfficeSuccesses()
    {
        return box_office_successes;
    }

    public String getGender()
    {
        return gender;
```

```
    }

    public int getLastMovieFee()
    {
        return last_movie_fee;
    }

    public String getName()
    {
        return fullName;
    }

    // This method can be overridden if subclasses want to
    // include different functionality when the name is set
    public void setName(String newFullName)
    {
        fullName = newFullName;
    }

    // This method cannot be overridden.
    public final void setName(String forename, String title, String surname)
    {
        setName(title + " " + forename + " " + surname);
    }

}
```

Look at the last two methods, which are both called `setName()`. In this example, the first method is the one which is providing the functionality. It is setting the `fullName` attribute, and is therefore changing the class's state. The second method, on the other hand, is not changing the class's state. It is simply calling the first, passing in a `String`, which is composed of the three parameters passed in to it concatenated together.

Subclasses might want to do something different with `setName()`; for example, they might want to generate an `id` the first time the name is set. If this were the case, then you would only want them to change the functionality in the first method, and have the second one just call the first, in the same way as before. This is why the first method has been declared as final, to prevent subclasses from overriding it.

Sharing Methods and Properties Across Instances of a Class: the Static Modifier

So far all the examples we have looked at have been **instance** methods and properties: methods and properties which every instance of a class will have. Every director will have a date of birth, for example, and that will usually be different from any other director's date of birth.

Java also provides the possibility of having methods and properties which are shared by every instance of a class, and this can greatly improve a class implementation. To specify that a method or property is shared by every instance of a class you need to use the **static** modifier.

Static methods and properties belong to a class, rather than to an object which is an instance of that class. An example might be the board responsible for film classification. Such a board will be shared by all the movies in our system, so there will only ever be one of them.

For this reason, if there was a reference to a film classification in the Movie class, it would be declared as static. Any methods which operated on it would be declared as static, too. Add the following code to the Movie class.

```
protected static BoardOfClassification classifyingBoard;

public static void setClassifyingBoard(BoardOfClassification board)
{
    classifyingBoard = board;
}

static
{
    board = new BoardOfClassification();
}
```

The final bit of this code is what is called a static initializer. It is like a method, except that you cannot call it directly. Instead it will be called for you when the class is first used. It is therefore, as the name suggests, a good place to initialize your static properties.

So why might you want to have class methods and properties rather than instance ones? Well, for a start, it neatly overcomes the problem that object creation is one of the most expensive operations in Java. If you are going to be writing Java applications, you will probably find out just how memory-hungry Java code can be, and spend a great deal of time optimizing your code to make it more efficient. There are very few hard and fast rules for making Java code run more quickly, and no nice tools, such as the Oracle performance tools EXPLAIN_PLAN and TKPROF, for tracking down problem areas (although there are some third-party tools for analyzing performance which can be quite useful). One thing which is always true, however, is that the fewer objects you can get away with the better.

For this reason, if you have an entity which is going to be shared by all instances of a class, you do not want to create an object within each instance to represent it. Instead, you should declare it as static so that it only needs to be created once. Constants should also be declared static as well as final; if they are truly constant then there should only ever be one instance of them.

Static methods are useful because you do not need an instance of the class to be able to call them. Static methods cannot access instance methods and variables, obviously, because if there is more than one object in existence there will be more than one of the methods and properties, and so operating on them from a static method is senseless. The flipside of this is that you do not need to instantiate a class to be able to call its static methods. An example of this would be:

```
System.exit(0);
```

The System class provides static methods which represent and control the entire system, and exit() is one of these: it terminates the currently running Java Virtual Machine, and is called with a parameter which represents how the system is exiting (normally or abnormally). You do not need to instantiate a System object to be able to call its exit() method: in fact you cannot instantiate a System object.

The fact that System starts with a capital letter rather than a lower case letter points to the fact that the exit() method is being called on the class itself, rather than on an instance of the class: objects represented by variables conventionally start with a lower case letter in Java, whereas classes conventionally start with an upper case letter. Note that it is possible to use a class instance variable to access static methods as in (new SomeObject()).staticMethod(), however this should rarely if ever be used.

It is entirely possible and sometimes highly desirable to have classes in Java which can never be instantiated, and which only provide static utility methods. It is also possible for a normal, non-utility class to provide static methods for those functions of the class which do not need to access instance methods and properties:

```
Math.random();
```

which will return a randomly generated double precision floating point number between 0.0 and 1.0.

Constants, that is final variables of a class, can also be referenced through the class itself rather than an instance of it. This is done in the same way, by prefacing the property with the class name, for example:

```
Math.PI
```

Where `PI` is a constant in the `Math` class, representing the value of π to twenty decimal places.

When properly used, static properties and methods provide information and functionality which can be used across an application in an invaluable and efficient way.

The 'this' and 'super' Keywords

It is possible to call one constructor from another in the same class, by using the `this` keyword. The reference `this` is a reference to the object you are in, and acts like a variable. If, for example, you wanted all movies which were created without a title to be assigned a default title until a proper one had been assigned, you could do it like this:

```
public Movie()
{
    this("Unnamed");
}
```

Add this constructor to your movie class.

The `this` keyword can also be useful when you want to pass the object itself to a method of another object. For example, you could add the following line to your `Movie` class:

```
board.classifyMovie(this);
```

Look at the sample code which comes with this appendix if you are unsure where to do this.

Constructors of a superclass can also be accessed, by using the keyword `super`. For example, in the `HorrorMovie` class you might want to create a horror movie with a default title if none is supplied. Rather than redefining a method to do this, you can do it this way instead:

```
public HorrorMovie()
{
    super("Unspecified horror");
}
```

Add this constructor to the `HorrorMovie` class. Also add the following one:

```
public HorrorMovie(String title)
{
    super(title);
}
```

The `super` keyword can also be used to call other methods of a superclass. If you are overriding a `doSomething()` method which you have inherited from a superclass, and you want to first carry out the processing of the superclass before adding some extra processing of your own, you could do so as follows:

```
public void doSomething()
{
    super.doSomething();
    doSomethingElse();
}
```

Inner Classes

Classes do not have to be stand-alone entities: they can also be contained within other classes. Such classes are known as **inner classes**. They are defined within the body of a main (or enclosing) class in the same way that properties and methods are defined.

Inner classes can provide greatly enhanced functionality, and so can be quite a complex area. This section will not explore them in any detail, but will just give a brief introduction to what they are. They will be visited again however when we come to look at actions and events.

An inner class can be one of three types:

Member classes are, as their name suggests, members of the class in which they are located. Their instances can be created within their enclosing class, and these instances have access to all the methods and properties of the enclosing class. Member classes can be useful for packaging up functionality which is part of the enclosing class, but which can be thought of as acting on a separate entity. An example of a member class, `MemberClass`, inside another class `OuterClass`, would be:

```
public class OuterClass
{
    public void methodOne()
    {
    }

    public Class MemberClass
    {
        public void memberMethodOne()
        {
        }
    }
}
```

Local classes are defined within a block of code, and are only visible within that block. They can use the properties and methods of the enclosing class, and they can also use any final variables which are local to the block in which they are declared. An example of a local class is:

```
public int predictPersonnelCosts()
{
    class LeadAssessor
    {
        public int assess(Actor actor)
        {
            int basic = actor.getLastMovieFee() *
                actor.getNumberBoxOfficeSuccesses();
            if (actor.getGender().equals(Actor.MALE))
            {
                basic = basic * 2;
            }
            return basic;
        }
    }
    LeadAssessor assessor = new LeadAssessor();
    return ((assessor.assess(leadMale) + assessor.assess(leadFemale)) * 2);
}
```

The class is `LeadAssessor`, which has one method, to assess how much the lead of a movie will need to be paid. The method which is predicting the personnel costs is creating a `LeadAssessor` object to assess both the male and female leads. It is predicting that the overall personnel costs will be double what needs to be paid to the two leads. The `LeadAssessor` class can only be accessed from inside the `predictPersonnelCosts()` method. There are of course other ways of doing what this method does, but this way illustrates the use of local classes.

Add this method to your `Movie` class. You will also need to add some variables:

```
protected Actor leadMale;
protected Actor leadFemale;
```

Anonymous classes are similar to local classes, except that they allow the declaration and instantiation of the class to be combined into a single step, which can make the code neater and easier to understand. This means that only one instance of an anonymous class can ever be created. Like local classes, anonymous classes can use instance properties and methods of the enclosing class, as well as final local properties. An example of an anonymous class is:

```
button.addActionListener(new ActionListener()
    {
        public void actionPerformed(ActionEvent ae)
        {
            System.out.println("Button pressed");
        }
    });
```

When you compile a class which contains inner classes of any type, the compiler will construct separate `.class` files for each inner class.

Abstract Classes

Abstract classes are 'partially complete' classes, which cannot be instantiated. Classes must be declared as abstract if they do not provide implementations of all their methods. If a class is abstract, subclasses of it must instantiate the abstract methods, otherwise they will be treated as abstract too.

1171

Abstract classes are useful for encapsulating functionality which will be shared across subclasses, when those subclasses need to implement certain behavior in ways which are specific to them. You might decide for example to make the `Movie` class abstract, since it could be argued that decisions about a movie's score will be dependent on that movie's genre, and must be defined by the subclasses corresponding to each genre. In this case, you could provide a lot of common functionality in the `Movie` class, so that different genres did not have to redefine it. You could then also leave areas concerned with the score as abstract methods, so that it would be up to subclasses to decide how to implement them.

Create a new `AbstractMovie` class like this:

```
public abstract class AbstractMovie
{
    ...
}
```

Between the braces which contain the method body, copy in the method body from your `Movie` class. Change the `predictPersonnelCosts()` method so that it is abstract:

```
public abstract int predictPersonnelCosts();
```

Now change the `HorrorMovie` class so that it extends `AbstractMovie`:

```
public class HorrorMovie extends AbstractMovie
{
    ...
}
```

If you try to compile this, you will get an error, because you have not provided an implementation for the `predictPersonnelCosts()` method. Copy this method in from the original `Movie` class.

The `AbstractMovie` class still contains all the methods which do things common to all movies.. However, because it is abstract, can no longer be instantiated. Only concrete subclasses, such as `HorrorMovie`, can be instantiated, and they inherit all these methods for free. Subclasses also get the abstract methods, which are methods, and they have to provide their own implementation of these, unless they themselves are also declared abstract. In this way you can share common functionality across classes, while still enforcing different functionality in areas where those classes differ.

Interfaces

One aspect of Java which some developers might find restricting is that multiple inheritance is not possible. Classes can only ever extend one other class; they cannot inherit functionality from more than one class.

Java's solution to some of the problems this might pose is the concept of **interfaces**. Interfaces are somewhat like abstract classes, except that none of the methods defined within them can have an implementation. All variables declared within an interface must also be static and final; in other words, they must be constants.

Interfaces can extend other interfaces, but they cannot extend classes. Interfaces can however extend more than one interface. Whereas a class would *extend* another class, it *implements* an interface. A class must provide definitions for all the methods in an interface which it implements.

Interfaces are used to define shared *behavior*, as opposed to abstract classes, which are used to group together functionality which is shared by subclasses. The non-abstract methods in an abstract class perform actual functions, and subclasses will inherit those functions. Interfaces, on the other hand, provide no method bodies at all, and so there is no functionality for their implementing classes to inherit. They only stipulate which methods a class implementing the interface should contain, and provide no clue as to how that class might implement a method.

An example of an interface which fits in with Movie and its friends might be something like TVProgramme. A movie can be a TV programme, but so can a documentary, a sitcom, or a news broadcast. For this reason, TVProgramme would be defined as an interface rather than a class. Create an interface using the code below (the steps are the same for creating a class – save the code as a file called TVProgramme.java):

```
public interface TVProgramme
{
    public boolean beforeWatershed();
}
```

This interface is a simple one, just having the one method which specifies whether a programme can be shown before the watershed or not. Make the AbstractMovie implement the interface, by changing the class definition as follows:

```
public abstract class AbstractMovie implements TVProgramme
{
    ...
}
```

You will now need to provide an implementation of the beforeWatershed() method. Look at the example code for a suggestion as to how to do this.

Testing Your Code

You should now be able to compile the classes you have created so far. Create a class to test them, using the following code:

```
public class MovieTester
{

    public static void main(String[] args)
    {
        HorrorMovie movie = new HorrorMovie("I Know You Had a Nightmare"
            + " in Woodsboro Last Halloween Part XXXVII");

        System.out.println("The movie's title is " + movie.getTitle());
        System.out.println("The movie's budget is £" + movie.getBudget());

        System.out.println("Critics rated it as a");
        movie.rateMovie(7);

        // You can experiment here by calling different methods
        // on the movie, and printing out different things
        movie.setSequel("The Second");
        System.out.println(movie.getTitle());

    }

}
```

You can change the code of this class to test different aspects of your classes.

There are just a couple more things about the Java language which we need to examine, before moving on to look at some wider issues. These are packages and exceptions.

Packages

It has already been mentioned that classes are arranged into packages, which are analogous to directories on a file server. Packages are specified from the top level down, with dots to separate the different levels:

```
com.moviecompany.product
```

Packages conventionally are lowercase. The `com.moviecompany` top level package has, in the example above, had a subpackage `product` added to it.

In fact, when you compile your classes, as long as you use the -d option, the .class files will be generated and placed in a directory structure which exactly mirrors the package structure. For the example above, the structure would be `com/moviecompany/product`.

Packages provide a way of grouping classes with similar or related functionality, and also are useful for overcoming naming conflicts. Since classes have meaningful names, and even a fairly simple application could use hundreds of classes, it is not hard to see how quickly there will be thousands of classes with the same name on the market. Specifying a class with its full package name on the other hand resolves all conflicts, since there should never be two classes in the same package with the same name.

To put a class into a package, you do so before the class declaration:

```
package com.moviecompany.product;

public class HorrorMovie extends AbstractMovie
{...
```

If you want to refer to other classes in this one without specifying the full package name each time you do so, you can import the classes. Importing a class just means that you can reference it by name, rather than having to use its fully qualified class name. For example, the class `Applet` is located in the package `java.applet`. If you wanted to reference it in your code, you would need to refer to it as `java.applet.Applet`, unless you had imported it. If you have imported it, you can just refer to it as `Applet` instead.

You import classes after you have specified the package, and before you declare the class:

```
package com.moviecompany.product;

import java.applet.Applet;

public class HorrorMovie extends Movie
{...
```

Alternatively, you can import all the classes in a package, by using the * symbol instead of the class name:

```
package com.moviecompany.product;

import java.applet.*;

public class HorrorMovie extends Movie
{...
```

Note that to run a class which is in a package using the `java` tool, you need to refer to it by its fully qualified name:

```
C:\jdk1.3\bin\java com.moviecompany.product.MovieTester
```

JAR Files

You will probably come across many references to Java Archive (JAR) files in your dealings with Java. These are simply a type of ZIP compressed archive. They mostly contain either `.class` or `.java` files, but they can also contain images, HTML, or text files to be used by the Java programs, or indeed any other type of file you wish to include. The JVM can run classes directly from within JAR files, so they are useful for packaging up all of an application's code in one place. They are the format in which most commercially available code is packaged, so it is worth knowing what they are, even though a more detailed discussion of them is beyond the scope of this appendix.

Exceptions

Exceptions in Java are objects used to signal that some of the processing has not been performed as expected. Java provides quite sophisticated ways of handling exceptions, but as with anything powerful, care has to be taken to use them properly.

Exceptions are Java objects; they all extend the class `java.lang.Throwable`. The base class for all exceptions is `java.lang.Exception`, and subclasses are things like `SQLException`, `IOException`, and so on, used when a particular type of exception has occurred.

The class structure is as follows:

```
java.lang.Throwable
extended by
    java.lang.Exception
extended by
        java.lang.RuntimeException
        java.sql.SQLException
        java.io.IOException
```

In Java, **throwing** an exception means signaling that a situation represented by an exception has occurred. When an exception is thrown, it will be passed up the call stack until it encounters code to catch it. **Catching** is what you do to such exceptions so that you can handle and recover from them.

An important subclass of `Exception` is `java.lang.RuntimeException`; runtime exceptions are those which should only happen as a result of programmer error and which should not therefore occur in a properly coded production application. A classic example is the `NullPointerException`, which will probably become a great acquaintance; this exception occurs when you attempt to call a method on a variable which has not been assigned to an existing object or which represents a null object. A null object is one which has no value. `NullPointerException` can often be avoided through being more careful with code, and can always be eliminated by checking whether an object is `null` before calling a method on it.

```
Director director = movie.getDirector();
If (director != null)
{
    director.setFee(movie.getBudget() / 20);
}
```

1175

The above example ensures that the setFee() call will not throw a NullPointerException, although really it should be checking that getBudget() does not return null either.

The usual code for handling exceptions is:

```
try
{
    body of statement(s);
}
catch (Exception ex)
{
    handle ex;
}
catch (AnotherException aex)
{
    handle aex;
}
finally
{
    clean up;
}
```

The try block simply establishes that any exceptions thrown by the code within it may be handled by the catch blocks below. As soon as any exceptions are encountered, control passes to the catch block.

The catch blocks must stipulate the type of exceptions they are trying to catch. This may simply be the superclass Exception, but it may be one of the subclasses of this, such as java.sql.SQLException, or it may be an Exception subclass you have defined yourself. If you are going to catch more than one exception, you must be careful to try to handle the most specific ones first. In the above example, if the second exception had been an SQLException, it would never have been caught: because SQLException is also an Exception, it would have been caught by the first catch block. Luckily the compiler will flag such errors, so that they will not make it into your code.

The exception should be handled in the body of the catch block. If, for example, an exception has been thrown because the user is trying to move off a screen which is showing updated and unsaved data, you may wish to ask them to save or roll back their changes.

The finally block is always executed, no matter how control leaves the try and catch blocks. In fact it can be used without a catch block, just with a try block. The finally block can be useful for code which should always be executed, such as clearing up file resources or setting busy cursors back to normal. What it should not be used for is returning values from a method (except in very unusual circumstances). Because the finally block is always executed, the value will be returned from the finally block, even if the try block exited normally!

If your code may cause non-runtime exceptions to be thrown, whether they are Java exceptions or your own, then the method which may cause them to be thrown must either catch them, or declare that they themselves throw the exception:

```
public void changeDirector throws PropertyVetoException
{
    ...
}
```

Methods which call this one will then themselves have to catch it or declare that they throw it. The Java compiler will let you know if this is not the case! `RuntimeException`, on the other hand, does not have to be (and usually should not be) declared.

It has been mentioned that Java is a straightforward language to learn, and this appendix will hopefully have shown you that it is. There is naturally a great deal more to the language than has been covered here. The concepts introduced in this appendix should however at least be sufficient to help you understand the code samples in the book, and to get you started in writing your own.

Summary

Although it is one of the youngest players in the programming world, Java is showing a great deal of potential. Its aims of being a distributed, interpreted, secure, architecture neutral, portable, dynamic language are not only realised, but are only going to become more important as large-scale deployment of Internet applications create computing needs of technologies which incorporate these features. This appendix, while not attempting to teach the language in any depth, has nevertheless introduced some of the most important concepts which anyone who is going to be developing in Java needs to understand. Some of the concepts are developed further in this book, while some are explored elsewhere, but this appendix should at least have made it clear why anyone would want or need to investigate them in more detail.

ICATIONPROGRAMMINGORACLE8iAPPLICATIONPROGRAMMINGORA

C
XML Primer

In this Appendix, we're going to take a quick look at the basics of XML. If you use XML on a daily basis already, you can skip this. For those of you who are coming from a pure relational database background, or if you can't remember the difference between an element and an attribute, read on.

We will be looking at:

❑ Basics of XML Markup

❑ Well-formed and valid documents

❑ Related technologies and how they fit in

Of course, there are whole books devoted to teaching XML, such as *Beginning XML*, from Wrox Press *ISBN 1861003412*, and this is just intended to get you up to speed with what you need to know for this book.

The first thing to make clear is that, assuming you are familiar with HTML, XML offers a new way of tagging (or marking up) your data that is so straight forward you will wonder why it is making such big waves. Yet, while HTML and XML may look very similar, they are in fact quite different.

Before we dive into using XML and showing you how it can be used, it would be helpful to have a quick look at markup languages in general and what markup is.

What is a Markup Language?

While you may not realize it, we come across markup every day. Quite simply, markup refers to anything put on a document that adds special meaning or provides extra information. For example, highlighted or bolded text is a form of markup.

But unless others understand our markup it is of little use, so we need a set of rules encompassing the following points for it to be understood:

❑ To declare what constitutes markup

❑ To declare exactly what our markup means

A markup language is such a set of rules. A familiar example is HTML – which is a markup language that enables you to write a document for display on the Web.

Tags and Elements

Even those of us who are familiar with HTML still often get the meaning of tags and elements mixed up. Just to clarify, tags are the angled brackets (known as delimiters), and the text between them. Here are some examples of tags used in HTML:

<P> is a tag that marks the beginning of a new paragraph
<I> is a tag indicating that the following text should be rendered in italic type
</I> is a tag that indicates the end of a section of text to be rendered in italic type

Elements, however, refer to the tags *plus* their content. So the following is an example of an element:

<B>Here is some bold text</B>

In general terms, tags are a label that tells a user-agent (such as a browser or parser) to do something to whatever is encased in the tags.

A user-agent is anything that acts on your behalf. You are a user agent working for your boss, your computer is a user agent working for you, your browser is a user agent working for you and your computer, and so it goes on.

Empty elements which don't have closing tags, such as the <IMG> element in HTML, have to be treated differently in XML to make up for them not having a closing tag, but don't worry about that for now, we will come back to them later.

The following diagram illustrates the parts of an element:

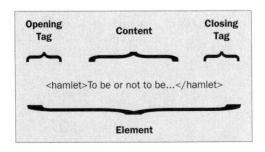

Attributes

Any tag can have an attribute as long as it is defined. They take the form of name/value pairs (also referred to as attribute/value pairs), in that the element can be given an attribute (with a name), and the attribute must carry a text value surrounded in quotation marks. They take the form:

```
<tagname attribute="value">
```

For example, in HTML 4.0 the <BODY> tag can take the following attributes:

```
CLASS ID    DIR       LANG    STYLE   TITLE
BACKGROUND  BGCOLOR   ALINK   LINK    VLINK   TEXT
```

So, for example, in HTML <BODY> could take the following attributes:

```
<BODY BGCOLOR="#000000" ALINK="#999999" LINK="#990099" VLINK="#888888"
TEXT="#999999">
```

As we shall see shortly there are other types of markup, but these are the two most used parts.

What is XML?

XML, or Extensible Markup Language to give its full name, is an example of a markup language, and just like HTML it makes extensive use of tags and attributes.

With HTML you have a fixed set of markup you can use – there is a prescribed set of tags and attributes with which you can write web pages.

XML, however, is a lot more flexible. You can make up your own tags and attributes, and its uses go beyond displaying information in a web browser. Because you can create your own tags and attributes in XML you can use markup that actually describes the content of the element, rather than just using tags that tell you how to present the data on a web page.

Because you can use tags that describe the content of an element, XML has become a general format for marking up all kinds of data – not just data that will be presented on the web. Let's dive straight in and look at an example so that we get a feel for it.

At its simplest level XML is just a way of marking up data so that it is **self-describing**. What do we mean by this? Well, imagine that you were running an e-commerce system, and that part of this system generates invoices. If a customer wanted to check their invoice over the web, it may be displayed to them marked up in HTML, and the HTML could look something like this:

```
<DOCTYPE HTML PUBLIC "-//W3C//DTD HTML 4.0 //EN">
<HTML>
    <HEAD><TITLE>Invoice</TITLE></HEAD>

<BODY>
    <H3>Invoice: Kevin Williams</H3>
```

```
<TABLE>
    <TR>
        <TD valign="top">
            <H4>Billing Address</H4>
                <UL>
                    <LI>Kevin Williams</LI>
                    <LI>742 Evergreen Terrace</LI>
                    <LI>Springfield</LI>
                    <LI>KY</LI>
                    <LI>12345</LI>
                </UL>
            </TD>

        <TD valign="top">
            <H4>Shipping Address</H4>
                <UL>
                    <LI>742 Evergreen Terrace</LI>
                    <LI>Springfield</LI>
                    <LI>KY</LI>
                    <LI>12345</LI>
                    <LI><B>Shipping Company</B> Fed Ex</LI>
                </UL>
            </TD>
    </TR>
</TABLE>

Item
    <UL>
        <LI><B>Item Description </B>Widget (3 inch)</LI>
        <LI><B>Item Code </B>1A2A3AB</LI>
        <LI><B>Quantity </B>17</LI>
        <LI><B>Price </B> 0.10</LI>
    </UL>

Item
    <UL>
        <LI><B>Item Description </B>Grommet (0.5 inch)</LI>
        <LI><B>ItemCode </B>1A2A3AB</LI>
        <LI><B>Quantity </B>22</LI>
        <LI><B>Price </B>0.05</LI>
    </UL>

</BODY>
</HTML>
```

While this may be fine for display on a web page, and we will see the result in the next screenshot, tags like <LI> don't tell you that here they are containing information about a product you just ordered. There is nothing in the HTML markup to tell you that this is an invoice.

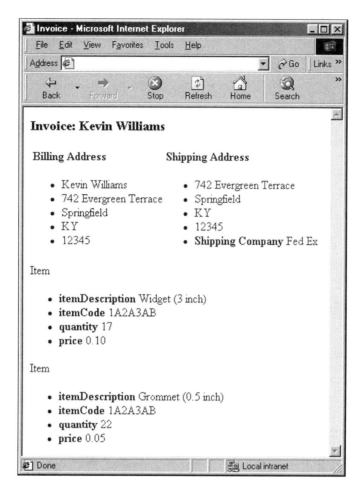

This is all very good for display on the web, but remember that we are running an e-commerce system here. Now, imagine that this e-commerce system is written in PHP, and that once it has generated the invoice information other parts of the company may need the same data:

❑ the packing department might need a copy to send the items out – but they run a UNIX-based system written in C

❑ the customer support team who can track the package may need it if there is a problem with delivery – but their system is written in Visual Basic

❑ the service department may need to check it if the product is returned because it is faulty – and they run an application written in Java

The potential number of uses for the data goes on, accounts, marketing, etc.; all of these users may need a copy of it. This means that there are a lot of uses for the same data, but the different departments that need the data use software written in different programming languages, and run on different operating systems. Wouldn't it be great if we could have a platform independent way of passing this data between programs, and of telling the programs what each piece of data that was marked up did?

Well, let's change the markup language and use XML instead of HTML. As I said, we can create our own tags with XML, so how about we use tags that describe what we are trying to say about the document – that it represents an invoice, and what the invoice contains... Let's make up some of our own tags and we can recreate this information with tags that describe the data we are marking up:

```
<?xml version="1.0" ?>

<Invoice
    customerName="Kevin Williams"
    billingAddress="742 Evergreen Terrace"
    billingCity="Springfield"
    billingState="KY"
    billingPostalCode="12345"
    shippingAddress="742 Evergreen Terrace"
    shippingCity="Springfield"
    shippingState="KY"
    shippingPostalCode="12345"
    shippingCompany="FedEx">
    <LineItem
        itemCode="1A2A3AB"
        itemDescription="Widget (3 inch)"
        quantity="17"
        price="0.10" />
    <LineItem
        itemCode="2BC3DCB"
        itemDescription="Grommet (0.5 inch)"
        quantity="22"
        price="0.05" />
</Invoice>
```

OK, if you opened this up in a browser, it would not look like a web page, it would look like this:

But, we do know that in the Invoice element we will find an invoice, and that in the customerName attribute, we will find out the customer whose invoice it is.

Furthermore, this XML file is just plain text, so the data in an XML file would be available for any programming language, and it would be available on any platform, and it can easily be passed over HTTP... So, we could actually use this data we had marked up in XML in a lot more ways that we could the HTML version. Because it is just text, and because we know that every time there is a invoice element there will be details about an invoice inside, the data becomes a lot more flexible.

Now you have to move your thoughts away from just displaying data in a web browser... think about anywhere that you need to exchange information, or you need to store information, and there *may* be a use for XML...

Let's just look at one last example so that you can really see why this is important. Pick a programming language, any programming language in which you may write an object. If you had to represent the invoice we have just seen in an object as part of the e-commerce system, we could pass the state into and out of the object as XML. Take a look at this:

```
<? xml version="1.0" ?>
<ObjectData id="customer125" classname="Invoice.Customer">
        <string name="sCustomerName">Kevin Williams</string>
        <string name="sAddress">742 Evergreen Terrace</string>
        <string name="sCity">Springfield</string>
        <string name="sState">KY</string>
        <string name="sPostalCode">12345</string>
    </Object>

    <Object id="order9876" classname="Invoice.Order">
        ...
    </Object>
</ObjectData>
```

Again, we are using markup that describes its content, it is simple text, it will be available to any programming language and any platform, and we can pass it easily in this form across a network. (In fact, we could even translate this into the invoice we saw earlier using a language called extensible stylesheet language.)

This set of tags and attributes that we have written to markup the invoice data are what we call an XML **vocabulary**. Vocabularies have already been created for a number of purposes, and it is always worth checking whether one has already been created for the task that you need to perform. But if one does not exist, you can always create your own and share it with others.

As you are able to create your own tags and attributes in XML, we obviously need some way to define a vocabulary in order for us to be able to share it with others, and get them using the same syntax. The XML 1.0 specification uses **Document Type Definitions** (**DTD**s) to do this. The DTD defines what markup can be used in a document that is supposed to conform to that vocabulary. For example, it can set out which elements a document can contain, how many instances of an element can occur, and in which order they should appear. It can set out which attributes an element can take, whether they must appear on a given element, if there is a default value should none be specified, and so on. So, in our invoice example we might have defined our markup in a way that says that every invoice element must contain a customerName attribute, a billingAddress attribute, and so on.

There is an interesting distinction to note here. When an XML document, using any vocabulary, conforms to the rules laid down in the XML 1.0 specification, it is said to be a **well-formed** document. When a well-formed document correctly corresponds to the rules laid out in a DTD describing that vocabulary, it is also said to be **valid**.

How XML Documents are Processed

XML documents are processed by a piece of software called a **parser**, which reads the XML document as plain text. Furthermore, they implement one or more **application programming interface**(s) (or **APIs**), such as the **Document Object Model** (**DOM**) or the **Simple API for XML** (**SAX**) either of which you may have heard of – if not, do not worry, we will introduce them later. The API offers programmers a set of functionality that they can call from a program to request information from the parser as it processes the document. For example, a program can ask the parser for the first child of the root element, and the text in it. Of course, there is a lot more you can do with an API implemented by a parser, but this gives you the idea of how the XML documents are actually made use of by processing applications.

Some parsers are able to check an instance of an XML document against the DTD that is used to describe the vocabulary, to check whether the markup used conforms to the intended markup. Parsers that have this functionality are known as **validating** parsers (although most validation parsers allow you to specify that they validate as an option, because validation takes up extra processing time and resources).

We now know that you can use XML to create your own markup language, and you can tell others how to use it. So, let's take a closer look at how we really structure an XML file, and then at how we declare the language we create.

The Basic Building Blocks of XML

We have seen that we can create tags and attributes that describe their content – and these usually constitute the majority of our markup – but there are also some other forms of markup available in our XML toolbox. In all we have:

- ❏ The XML Declaration
- ❏ Elements
- ❏ Attributes
- ❏ Character Data (CDATA)
- ❏ Processing Instructions
- ❏ Comments
- ❏ Entity References

Let's look at each of these in turn.

The XML Declaration

You might have noticed this at the start of the earlier examples. The **XML declaration** is actually optional, although you are strongly advised to use it so that the receiving application knows that it is an XML document and also the version used (although there is only one version of XML at the moment, it does future-proof your documents as well as indicate their format).

```
<?xml version="1.0"?>
```

If you use the XML declaration, also known as the **XML prolog**, it must be right at the start of the document (there should be nothing before it, not even white space), and the xml should be in lowercase.

In this declaration, you can also define the language in which you have written your XML data. This is particularly important if your data contains characters that aren't part of the English ASCII character set. You can specify the language encoding using the optional encoding attribute:

```
<?xml version="1.0" encoding="iso-8859-1"?>
```

The most common ones are shown in the following table:

Language	Character set
Unicode (8 bit)	UTF-8
Latin 1 (Western Europe, Latin America)	ISO-8859-1
Latin 2 (Central/Eastern Europe)	ISO-8859-2
Latin 3 (SE Europe)	ISO-8859-3
Latin 4 (Scandinavia/Baltic)	ISO-8859-4
Latin/Cyrillic	ISO-8859-5
Latin/Arabic	ISO-8859-6
Latin/Greek	ISO-8859-7
Latin/Hebrew	ISO-8859-8
Latin/Turkish	ISO-8859-9
Latin/Lappish/Nordic/Eskimo	ISO-8859-10
Japanese	EUC-JP or Shift_JIS

Elements

The most important components of XML documents are elements. Every XML document must have at least one in which all other markup is nested. In the following document there is just one element, SampleDoc:

```
<?xml version="1.0"?>
<SampleDoc>
    This is a simple, sample XML document.
</SampleDoc>
```

The highest-level element is termed the document element (although you may also see it referred to as the root element).

Elements may be used in one of two ways:

❑   as shown in this example with an opening tag and a closing tag where the element has three parts:

❑   A start-tag (<SampleDoc>)

❑   Followed by some content (the string This is a simple XML document.)

❑   Followed by an end-tag (</SampleDoc>). End-tags always start with a forward slash, followed by the name of the start-tag to which they correspond or

❑   as an **empty element**. These are used where there is no content between a start and end tag, instead a single tag is used with a forward slash before the closing bracket, for example:

```
<?xml version="1.0"?>
<SampleDoc />
```

At first, this seems pretty silly – what's the point of having an element without any content? However, it could be that in your document the presence of the element is all that's significant – think about how the <BR> element is used in HTML. Also, additional information can be attached to the empty element by using attributes, which we'll talk about next.

> Note that XML is case-sensitive, so apart from the forward slash, the elements must be exactly the same; `<SampleDoc>` and `<sampledoc>` are different tags.

Tag names can start with a letter, an underscore (_), or a colon character (:), followed by any combination of letters, digits, hyphens, underscores, colons, or periods. The only exception is that you cannot start a tag with the letters XML in any combination of upper or lowercase letters. You are also advised not to start a tag with a colon, in case it gets treated as a namespace (something we shall meet later on).

All tags must nest properly; this means that there must be no **overlapping elements**. For example, this is correct:

```
<SampleDoc>
   <SomeData>Some character data</SomeData>
</SampleDoc>
```

while this would be incorrect:

```
<SampleDoc>
      <SomeData>
            Some character data
</SampleDoc>
      </SomeData>
```

This is because the closing </SomeData> tag is after the closing </SampleDoc> tag.

Attributes

You've probably used attributes before in HTML – for example, when using the HREF attribute on the <A> element to define a hyperlink:

```
<A HREF="http://www.wrox.com">Go to Wrox's web site</A>
```

They work exactly the same way in XML. Attributes are included in an element's start-tag, and are expressed as **name-value pairs**. The value must always be wrapped in single or double quotes (it doesn't matter which ones, as long as you use the same quote before and after the value). For example:

```
<?xml version="1.0"?>
<SampleDoc Author="Ron Obvious">
    This is a simple XML document.
</SampleDoc>
```

In this sample document, the SampleDoc element has one attribute associated with it. The attribute **name** is Author, and the **value** is Ron Obvious.

Also, each attribute name may only appear once for a particular start-tag. So, the following is not allowed in XML:

```
<?xml version="1.0"?>
<SampleDoc Author="Ron Obvious" Author="Ken Shabby">
    This is a simple XML document.
</SampleDoc>
```

However, the following is perfectly acceptable:

```
<?xml version="1.0"?>
<SampleDoc>
    <Sentence Author="Ron Obvious">
        This is a simple XML document.
    </Sentence>
    <Sentence Author="Ken Shabby">
        This is the second sentence of the document.
    </Sentence>
</SampleDoc>
```

It should go without saying that attributes are always associated with elements (since they appear only in start-tags or empty-element-tags, which are always part of elements). Also, attributes may not contain the characters <, &, ' or ".

Finally, it does not matter in which order you put your attributes in an element – so the following two documents are semantically identical:

```
<?xml version="1.0"?>
<SampleDoc Author="Ron Obvious" CreateDate="7/23/2000">
    This is a simple XML document.
</SampleDoc>
```

and

```
<?xml version="1.0"?>
<SampleDoc CreateDate="7/23/2000" Author="Ron Obvious">
    This is a simple XML document.
</SampleDoc>
```

Character Data

In the examples we have been looking at so far, the element `SampleDoc` contains the text `This is a simple XML document`. It is the **element content**, although it has a special name in XML and is called **character data**. If you remember back to the section on how XML documents are processed, we said that they are processed by an application called a parser, the parser can read the content of the elements and pass it to applications that request it. We make this distinction now, because, as you will soon see, it is also possible to have data that is not parsed by the parser in this way.

As you'll see when looking further into XML technologies, contiguous blocks of text within an element are treated as one unit when being parsed or manipulated. Let's take a look at a slightly more complex example.

```
<?xml version="1.0"?>
<AlarmProcedure>
    This is a <alarmtype>test</alarmtype> of the Emergency Broadcast System.
</AlarmProcedure>
```

In this example, the element `AlarmProcedure` contains three pieces of data:

- ❏ the text block "This is a"
- ❏ the alarmtype element
- ❏ the text block "of the Emergency Broadcast System."

In turn, the alarmtype element contains one piece of data:

- ❏ the text block test

This character data can appear anywhere inside elements, or as values of attributes. However, there are some special characters that are not allowed in text blocks: the ampersand symbol (&) and the less-than symbol (<). This is because these symbols are interpreted by XML parsers as the start of markup; specifically, as the start of an entity instance and as the start of element start-, end-, or empty-element-tags. If you need to include these characters in your XML document (either in attribute values or in text blocks), you need to either use a CDATA section or entities (which we will deal with next).

CDATA Section

If you want to embed markup in your XML document, one way to do so is by wrapping the markup in a **CDATA section**. XML parsers ignore any characters wrapped in a CDATA section declaration when they are attempting to determine whether markup is present. For example, the following document will not produce the desired result:

```
<?xml version="1.0"?>
<MarkupSample>
    To start an element, use a start-element tag: <myTag>
</MarkupSample>
```

When a parser attempts to process this document, it will identify the string <myTag> as the beginning of a new element, and then complain when it doesn't find the matching end-tag </myTag>. One solution would be to embed the relevant text in a CDATA section:

```
<?xml version="1.0"?>
<MarkupSample>
    <![CDATA[To declare an element, use a start-element tag: <Foo>]]>
</MarkupSample>
```

As you can see, CDATA sections start with the CDATA start marker:

```
<![CDATA[
```

and end with the CDATA end marker

```
]]>
```

When the parser encounters the CDATA start marker, it turns off all scanning for markup except for the detection of the CDATA end marker. In the above document, the MarkupSample element contains one CDATA section item with the value "To declare an element, use a start-element tag: <myTag>."

It's important to remember that CDATA section items and text items are treated as two separate beasts by XML parsers. For example, the following two documents would seem to contain the same information:

```
<?xml version="1.0"?>
<MarkupSample>
    <![CDATA[To declare an element, use a start-element tag: <myTag>]]>
</MarkupSample>
```

```
<?xml version="1.0"?>
<MarkupSample>
    To declare an element, use a start-element tag: <![CDATA[<myTag>]]>
</MarkupSample>
```

In the second document, the parser will report the MarkupSample element as containing two items: the text string "To declare an element, use a start-element tag:" and the CDATA section item <myTag>. This can throw off a parser that is specifically looking for one item contained in the MarkupSample element.

This approach is good if you want to escape a number of characters that a parser might treat as markup, however, if you only want to escape occasional characters, you may be better off using an entity reference.

Entity References

As we mentioned before, CDATA sections are only one way to include characters like < and & in your XML documents. The other way is by using an **entity reference**. Before we dive into how entities work, let's take a look at an example.

```
<?xml version="1.0"?>
<MarkupSample>
    To declare an element, use a start-element tag: &lt;Foo>
</MarkupSample>
```

In this example, the string < is an entity reference; specifically, it's an instance of the entity called lt. Entity references in XML documents (as opposed to in document type definitions) always begin with an ampersand and end with a semicolon. When a parser encounters an entity reference, it goes to the symbol table created when the document type declaration was parsed (we'll take a look at document type declarations later).and extracts the relevant string, if it's present (it might not be, as we'll see a little later). It then substitutes that string in place of the entity instance. Entities that are treated this way are known as parsed entities. It is also possible to declare unparsed entities in an XML document – we'll see how this is done a little later.

There are two types of parsed entities that may be instanced in an XML document:

❑   internal entities, which actually have their replacement content embedded in the document type declaration for the document

❑   external entities, which point to some external resource (via a URI) that contains the replacement text

A non-validating processor is not necessarily obligated to resolve external parsed entity references to their replacement content (although most do), and this can lead to the non-substituted value for an entity reference alluded to above.

There are some standard entities that are defined for XML documents:

Entity	Character
<	<
>	>
&	&
'	'
"	"

Any conforming XML parser will automatically recognize these entities and expand them to their proper values.

Additionally, you may include character references in your documents – they look almost like entities, but they are treated differently by the processor (that is, they are immediately resolved without resorting to an entity lookup). Any decimal code, preceded by &# and followed by ;, is treated as a character reference; the Unicode character with the stated decimal character code is substituted for the reference. Similarly, any hex code preceded by &#x and followed by ; is treated as a character reference stated in hex. So the following two character references:

```
&#38;
&#x26;
```

both correspond to the ampersand character.

Another frequently needed character in XML documents is the non-breaking space – in HTML, this is represented by the entity reference . You can specify this in your XML document by using the numeric equivalent:

```
 
```

You could also declare an entity called nbsp to have the value   and then reference that entity in your document using the name rather than the number. We'll see how this is done a little later in this appendix.

Processing Instructions

If you want a processing application to take some action when it reaches a certain point in a document, you can embed a processing instruction to indicate that some action needs to take place where it was reported. The parser indicates this – either by showing a processing instruction node at the appropriate place in the node tree (in the case of DOM parsers), or by firing a processing instruction event (in the case of SAX parsers). The code that is driving the processor may then take some action on the document based on the type and value of the processing instruction. Processing instructions start with the processing instruction markup start string <?, and end with the string ?>.

```
<?xml version="1.0"?>
<Book>
    <Author>
        <?archive 17?>
        <Name>Kevin Williams</Name>
        <Address>742 Evergreen Terrace</Address>
        <City>Springfield</City>
        <State>KY</State>
        <PostalCode>12345</PostalCode>
    </Author>
</Book>
```

In this example, the string <?archive 17?> is a processing instruction declaration. For example, this processing instruction might indicate that the author information presented is the authoritative copy of that information, and older versions of the data should be stored to an archive for the author whose primary key is 17. Processing instruction declarations always come in two parts: the processing instruction target (in this case, the string archive) and the string to be operated upon (in this case, 17). Everything in the processing instruction declaration before the first whitespace is considered to be the processing instruction target, and everything after that whitespace is the string used to govern the processor's behavior. So, in the following example:

```
<?xml-stylesheet type="text/xml" href="#style1"?>
```

the target would be xml:stylesheet, and the additional information string would be the rest of the text up to, but not including, the question mark at the end of the tag declaration – in other words, the entire string type="text/xml" href="#style1". Note that if you want to access the contents of this string, you'll need to parse it manually – it's not returned as name-value pairs.

The processing instruction target may not begin with the string XML, in upper, lower, or mixed cases – these targets are reserved by the W3C for future extensions to the XML specification.

Comments

Comments may be added to an XML document, using exactly the same syntax as comments in HTML. They always begin with the comment markup start string <!-- and end with the comment markup end string -->:

```
<?xml version="1.0"?>
<!-- Created on 8/8/2000 -->
<DocumentElement/>
```

Note that you can't embed the string "--" in a comment – the parser will think you are indicating the end of the comment and become confused. It's important to note that comments may or may not be retained by an XML parser. When developing processing strategies, make sure to avoid processing based on statements like "the text I want is always the first item in the Foo element" – because it might not always be, unless you exclusively control the source of the XML documents. For example, say you had the following document fragment:

```
<Book>
  <!-- This is an updated book element -->
  <Author>Kevin Williams</Author>
</Book>
```

Some processors will return two child nodes of the Book node – one for the comment, and one for the Author element. Other processors will only return one node – the Author element. Thus, if you were relying on the Author element to be the second child node of the Book element, you might or might not see it where you were expecting it. It's a good practice to always use names when navigating your XML structures.

Namespaces

In a distributed web environment, we must assume that the same type or element name may mean different things to different people. One XML document may use Address elements to specify where people live, and another may use Address elements to describe locations of computer memory. An XML application has no way of knowing how to process an Address element unless it has some additional information about whose definition we are dealing with.

In XML 1.0, element type names and attribute names are considered **local names.** The W3C (World Wide Web Consortium) XML Namespaces Recommendation tries to improve this situation by extending the data model to allow element type names and attribute names to be qualified with a **URI** (Universal Resource Identifier) that identifies the namespace. This URI should be unique and persistent over time. Note that the URI doesn't actually have to point to anything – although sometimes navigating to the URI using a web browser will bring you to a specification describing that namespace, nothing is obligated to be found at the URI for the namespace. In our example, then, the wrox: namespace prefix is declared to map to the namespace http://www.wrox.com/oracle. The combination of a local name and a qualifying URI creates **universal names**. The role of the URI in a universal name is purely to allow applications to recognize the name.

Except in very unusual circumstances, you should declare all of the namespaces for your document as attributes of the root element to ensure that they are in scope for the entire document. It is also worth noting that an XML document can contain many namespaces. In XSLT (you will encounter XSLT in Chapter 21) the namespaces are very important – XSLT matches both the local name and the namespace, so you need to declare the namespaces properly in your XSLT stylesheet to have it recognize the corresponding elements in your documents.

Here is an example of Namespaces:

```
<document  xmlns:wrox:"http://www.wrox.com/oracle"
<wrox:address wrox:addressingSystem="US">
        <wrox:name> Kevin Williams </wrox:name>
        <wrox:street>744 Evergreen Terrace </wrox:street>
        <wrox:city> Springfield </wrox:city>
        <wrox:state> KY </wrox:state>
        <wrox:postcode>12345</wrox:postcode>
</wrox:address>
</document>
```

Here, we declare a **namespace** wrox, which is the local name for this namespace to be associated with the URI http://www.wrox.com/oracle. This immediately distinguishes these addresses from those developed by others. Having defined the namespace, we qualify all elements and attributes with wrox:, thus distinguishing them from identically named elements and attributes in other namespaces.

Document Type Definitions

In the XML 1.0 specification, a mechanism is provided for (loosely) constraining the content that may appear in an XML document. This is done by means of a document type definition, or DTD, which is basically a set of rules that any XML document it is applied to should follow. Some XML parsers are able to validate an XML document against its respective DTD, and if it doesn't follow the rules imposed on it by the DTD, it will throw up an error. These kinds of parsers are referred to as validating parsers. If the XML is found to conform to the rules of a DTD, then it can be referred to as **valid** XML, rather than merely well formed.

The Document Type Definition can either be an external file or it can be included in the XML document. If the DTD is in an external file it is referred to in the XML document using a **Document Type Declaration** which is written using the syntax <!DOCTYPE... >:

```
<!DOCTYPE MyXMLDoc SYSTEM "http://www.yoursite.com/xml/MyXMLDoc.dtd">
```

Here we are pointing to a DTD called MyXMLDoc, note that the name of your DTD must correspond to the root element of the XML document, so the root element of XML documents written according to this DTD must be <MyXMLDoc>. The use of the SYSTEM keyword indicates that the DTD is in an external file, whose location is referenced in the quotation marks. This type of DTD is known as an **external** DTD, because it is in an external file. It is also possible to declare a DTD with the PUBLIC keyword – this allows you to specify the location of the DTD in some way that is understood by many different processors, eliminating the need for an always-on connection to the Internet to validate the documents. However, there isn't one well-defined way to resolve DTDs declared as PUBLIC, so you're better off using the system identifiers to point to your DTDs.

The name of the DTD does not have to be the same as the name of the root element. The DTD itself can be called anything you want, as long as it is declared in the !DOCTYPE declaration to match the root element name.

The DTD can also be written inside the document type declaration, in which case it is known as an **internal** document type definition, like so:

```
<!DOCTYPE MyXMLDoc [
    <!ELEMENT MyXMLDoc (#PCDATA)>
]>
```

Here, all the constraints on the content of the document are provided as declarations inside the square brackets [...]. (Don't worry too much about the element declaration just yet – we'll be getting to that soon enough.

When a validating parser encounters an external document type definition, it accesses the resource indicated in the URI and pulls the document constraints from it; it then behaves as if these constraints were declared in-line.

If you have a situation where you can benefit from it, you can also mix the two declaration modes:

```
<!DOCTYPE MyXMLDoc SYSTEM "MyXMLDoc.dtd" [
    <!ELEMENT MyXMLDoc (#PCDATA)>
]>
```

For example, this technique would allow you to customize the allowable content of the Bar element. Note that in the above example, only the file name is included, rather than the whole path as well. This would only be suitable if the external file is in the same location as this one.

It's usually more helpful to have the document type definition be external to the document itself – this allows multiple documents to use the same rules without having to include the set of constraints in each document.

> Note, it is easy to get confused between the terms document type declaration and document type definition. To clarify, the document type definition constrains the markup and this is either contained in, or referenced to using, a document type declaration.

The Standalone Declaration

There is an attribute on the XML declaration that indicates whether a document type definition is standalone or not; that is, whether all of the declarations for the XML document are stated in the !DOCTYPE declaration, or whether some external URI needs to be accessed to obtain all the declarations (either through an external parameter entity, which we'll talk about later, or an external DTD). This attribute should also be used when your document declares namespaces. You don't have to explicitly declare this, but it might be useful to help streamline workflow and the transmission of XML documents.

To declare that a document stands alone, use this XML declaration:

```
<?xml version="1.0" standalone="yes"?>
```

If the declaration is omitted, the assumed default is that the document is not stand-alone.

Next, let's take a look at the various declarations you can use within a DTD to constrain the types of content an XML document conforming to that DTD may contain.

Element Declarations

The most important type of declaration in a DTD is the element declaration. Each DTD will have at least one of these (the declaration of the root element).

We saw how to simply declare an element in the previous example, but we did not explain what it was doing there:

```
<!ELEMENT MyXMLDoc (#PCDATA)>
```

We declare an element using the syntax:

```
<!ELEMENT elementName (contentModel)>
```

where `elementName` is the name of the element, and the contentModel is what that element can contain. This is the basic declaration that we need to start, so in our example we were declaring an element called `MyXMLDoc`. This element contains text only content – defined using the syntax `#PCDATA`.

There are five different types of element content that may be declared with an element declaration:

- ❑ Element content
- ❑ Mixed content
- ❑ Text-only content
- ❑ The EMPTY content model
- ❑ The ANY content model

Let's take a look at each, in turn.

Element Content

In the first type of element declaration, the element is defined as only containing other elements. The declaration specifies the order and cardinality with which each contained element may appear. For example, the declaration:

```
<!ELEMENT Foo (A, B, C)>
```

States that, within the Foo element, the elements A, B, and C must each appear exactly once, in that order. So for the following DTD:

```
<!ELEMENT Foo (A, B, C)>
<!ELEMENT A (#PCDATA)>
<!ELEMENT B (#PCDATA)>
<!ELEMENT C (#PCDATA)>
```

This example XML document conforms to the DTD:

```
<?xml version="1.0" standalone="no"?>
<!DOCTYPE Foo SYSTEM "Foo.DTD">
<Foo>
    <A> Some content <A />
    <B> Some more content <B />
    <C> Even more content <C />
</Foo>
```

But the following three examples do not. The first is missing a C element:

```
<?xml version="1.0" standalone="no"?>
<!DOCTYPE Foo SYSTEM "Foo.DTD">
<Foo>
    <A> Some content <A />
    <B> some more content <B />
</Foo> <!-- the C element is missing -->
```

The next one does not contain the elements in the correct order:

```
<?xml version="1.0" standalone="no"?>
<!DOCTYPE Foo SYSTEM "Foo.DTD">
<Foo>
    <B> Some more content <B />
    <A> Some content<A />
    <C> Even more content <C />
</Foo> <!-- the elements are not in the right order -->
```

And the final one uses too many A elements:

```
<?xml version="1.0" standalone="no"?>
<!DOCTYPE Foo SYSTEM "Foo.DTD">
<Foo>
    <A> Some content <A />
    <A> Some content <A />
    <B> Some more content <B />
    <C> Even more content <C />
</Foo> <!-- too many A elements -->
```

It is also possible to define a set of elements, only one of which may be present. This is indicated by separating the possibilities with the pipe character |. So the declaration

```
<!ELEMENT Foo (A | B | C)>
```

States that the Foo element should contain either an A element, a B element, or a C element - but only one of the above.

Child elements declared in the element declaration may also take cardinality suffixes. These suffixes indicate how many of each element (or element group, which we'll talk about later) may occur at that location in the element content. The following four cardinality operators exist:

Operator	Meaning
?	Optional (may occur 0 or 1 times)
*	Optional multiple (may occur 0 or more times)
(no suffix)	Required (must occur exactly once)
+	Required multiple (must occur 1 or more times)

Additionally, child elements may be grouped together in the element declaration. They may be grouped in either a sequence or a choice list. These groupings may also have the cardinality operators specified in the previous table applied to them. At this point, some examples are probably in order.

Example 1:

This states that zero or more A elements may appear as child elements of the Foo element, followed by one or more B elements; the B element or elements may then be followed by no more than one C element.

```
<!ELEMENT Foo (A*, B+, C?)>
```

The following XML fragments for the Foo element are all valid:

```
<Foo>
    <A> Some content <A />
    <B> Some more content <B />
</Foo>

<Foo>
    <B> Some more content <B />
    <B> Some more content<B />
    <B> Some more content<B />
</Foo>

<Foo>
    <A> Some content <A />
    <A> Some content <A />
    <B> Some more content <B />
    <C> even more content <C />
</Foo>
```

Example 2:

This states that either an A element or a B element comes first in the Foo element; that element must then be followed by a C element.

```
<!ELEMENT Foo ((A | B), C)>
```

So the following two examples are the only possible examples of valid content for Foo:

```
<Foo>
    <A> Some content <A />
    <C> Even more content <C />
</Foo>
```

```
<Foo>
    <B> Some more content <B />
    <C> Even more content <C />
</Foo>
```

Example 3:

In this example, Foo must contain either one or more A elements followed optionally by a B element, or this group can all be replaced by zero or more C elements.

```
<!ELEMENT Foo ((A+, B?) | C*)>
```

Again, the following are all valid:

```
<Foo>
    <A> Some content <A />
    <A> Some content <A />
    <A> Some content <A />
</Foo>
```

```
<Foo>
    <A> Some content <A />
    <B> Some more content <B />
</Foo>
```

```
<Foo>
    <C> Even more content <C />
    <C> Even more content <C />
    <C> Even more content <C />
</Foo>
```

For the purposes of the XML structures we'll be creating, elements that have all element content, we'll avoid the choice operator and stick to sequences with cardinality:

```
<!ELEMENT Foo (A?, B*, C?, D, E+)>
```

Mixed Content

Elements may also be declared as having mixed content. Elements declared this way may contain any of the elements included in the content list, in any order, with text interspersed anywhere in between. A mixed-content element declaration looks like this:

```
<!ELEMENT Foo (#PCDATA | A | B | C)*>
<!ELEMENT A (#PCDATA)>
<!ELEMENT B (#PCDATA)>
```

The #PCDATA is required to be the first thing in the pipe-delimited list – it indicates that text may be present in the element. The other listed elements may or may not appear. Note that no constraint is imposed on the order in which the elements may appear, or how many times. This is the only allowable declaration for mixed content – you are not allowed to constrain the location or number of the various subelements in a mixed-content element. Thus, the following fragments are all valid:

```
<Foo>
   Here is some <A>text</A> with interspersed <B>elements</B>.
</Foo>


<Foo>
   <C /><C /><C />Why so many C elements?
</Foo>


<Foo>
   There are no child elements in this element at all.
</Foo>


<Foo />
```

If you're familiar with relational databases, you're probably wincing right now, and you have a right to be – representing mixed content in a relational database is a real headache. Suffice it to say that you should always avoid the mixed content model for elements whenever possible when designing XML structures for data.

Text-only Content

A special case of the mixed content model, however, may prove quite useful – that case where an element may contain only text. Elements that are defined to contain only text look like this:

```
<!ELEMENT Foo (#PCDATA)>
```

This is one of the two major ways that a data point (a value) should be represented in XML for data:

```
<!ELEMENT Author (Name, Address, City, State, PostalCode)>
<!ELEMENT Name (#PCDATA)>
<!ELEMENT Address (#PCDATA)>
<!ELEMENT City (#PCDATA)>
<!ELEMENT State (#PCDATA)>
<!ELEMENT PostalCode (#PCDATA)>


<Author>
   <Name>Kevin Williams</Name>
   <Address>742 Evergreen Terrace</Address>
   <City>Springfield</City>
   <State>KY</State>
   <PostalCode>12345</PostalCode>
</Author>
```

The EMPTY Content Model

The EMPTY content model for elements states that an element may not contain anything. Empty elements are declared as follows:

```
<!ELEMENT Foo EMPTY>
```

Elements declared this way must take one of the two following forms:

```
<Foo />
```

```
<Foo></Foo>
```

However, it is strongly advised that you stick to the first form, as the second can easily get confused with an empty PCDATA element.

We talked about the reasons you might want to define an element that has no allowable content earlier in the chapter. For our purposes, however, we will only be defining elements this way if they have attributes associated with them. We'll see how attributes are declared for elements a little later on.

The ANY Content Model

If an element is declared to have a content model of ANY, that's just what it may contain – any well-formed XML whatsoever as long as any child elements validate against their own content models as defined elsewhere, in the DTD. Elements of this type are declared like so:

```
<!ELEMENT Foo ANY>
```

The following examples are valid for this declaration:

```
<Foo>
    Here's some random thing.
</Foo>
```

```
<Foo>
    <A><B><C><D><E></E></D></C></B></A>
</Foo>
```

```
<Foo>
    <A>This</A><B>is</B><C>marked</C><D>up</D>
</Foo>
```

Note that the subelements do not inherit the "free content properties" of the Foo element – they must still conform to their own declarations. So in our second example above, a single B element must be acceptable content for the A element, a single C element acceptable for B, and so on.

For the representation of data, this syntax is perilous. Allowing users to simply include whatever elements or text they feel like in an element is another relational database nightmare, worse than that caused by mixed element content declarations because you can't even narrow down the list of elements that might occur. You should avoid using the ANY content model for elements when designing XML structures for data.

Attribute Declarations

The next most common type of declaration in DTDs is the attribute declaration. This allows you to define what attributes may or must appear for a given element. The general syntax for an attribute declaration looks like this:

```
<!ATTLIST element-name attribute-definition*>
```

where an attribute definition looks like this:

```
attribute-name attribute-type default-declaration
```

So, let's say we have this pair of definitions in our DTD:

```
<!ELEMENT Foo EMPTY>
<!ATTLIST Foo
    Texture CDATA #REQUIRED>
```

This says that the Foo element, which must be empty, has one required attribute called Texture that may take any string value. So the following document fragment is valid:

```
<Foo Texture="bumpy" />
```

Next, let's take a look at the various attribute types that may be defined in a DTD.

The CDATA Attribute Type

The most commonly encountered attribute type in a DTD is CDATA. Attributes that take this type may take any string value. Remember that in all attribute values, the markup characters <, &, >, ", and ' should always be escaped to prevent parser confusion. So for this example:

```
<!ELEMENT Foo EMPTY>
<!ATTLIST Foo
    Texture CDATA #REQUIRED
    Color CDATA #REQUIRED
    Shape CDATA #REQUIRED>
```

the following document fragment follows the rules of the above DTD:

```
<Foo Texture="bumpy" Color="red&amp;blue" Shape="sphere" />
```

The ID Attribute Type

DTDs provide a way to assign unique identifiers to elements. This can be very useful when expressing more complex relationships in XML documents than can be shown by simple nesting, as we'll see later. In order for a document to be valid, every element that has an ID attribute associated with it in a single document must have a unique ID value. Also, the values for ID attributes must be valid XML names – in other words, they must begin with a letter (as defined by the Unicode standard) or an underscore (colons are also allowed, but their use is discouraged because of namespaces) – so simply using an identity or autoincrement value from a relational database is not sufficient. One strategy that works is to prefix that relational value with a string (unique across all elements in your document) that corresponds to the entity.

Let's see some examples. For this document declaration fragment:

```
<!ELEMENT Foo EMPTY>
<!ATTLIST Foo
    FooID ID #REQUIRED>
```

```
<!ELEMENT Bar EMPTY>
<!ATTLIST Bar
    BarID ID #REQUIRED>
```

the following would be valid:

```
<Foo FooID="foo1" />
<Bar BarID="bar1" />
```

but the following examples would not:

```
<Foo FooID="17" /> <!-- ID value is not a proper XML name -->
```

```
<Foo FooID="foo1" />
<Foo FooID="foo1" /> <!-- no two elements may have the same ID value -->
```

```
<Foo FooID="foo1" />
<Bar BarID="foo1" /> <!-- no two elements may have the same ID value -->
```

It is illegal to define more than one ID attribute on the same element.

The IDREF Attribute Type

The IDREF attribute type provides a way to "point" one element to another – in effect, expressing a one-to-one relationship between the two attributes. Values for attributes that are defined as IDREF attributes must match an ID attribute found somewhere in the XML document. So for the following DTD fragment:

```
<!ELEMENT Author EMPTY>
<!ATTLIST Author
    AuthorID ID #REQUIRED>
<!ELEMENT Book EMPTY>
<!ATTLIST Book
    BookID ID #REQUIRED
    AuthorIDREF IDREF #REQUIRED>
```

the following would be valid:

```
<Author AuthorID="author1" />
<Book BookID="book1" AuthorIDREF="author1" />
```

```
<Author AuthorID="author1" />
<Book BookID="book1" AuthorIDREF="book1" />
```

The second example makes an important point. IDREF attributes do not define the type of element their value points to, so it's equally valid to have an attribute called AuthorIDREF match an ID value for a Book element. If you want to strictly enforce the types of elements that may be matched by an IDREF attribute, you'll need to do so in your processing code.

The following example, of course, is not valid, and a validating processor will throw an error:

```
<Author AuthorID="author1" />
<Book BookID="book1" AuthorIDREF="author2" /> <!-- ID does not exist -->
```

The IDREFS Attribute Type

You can think of the IDREFS attribute as a way to include multiple IDREF values in one attribute. The value for an IDREFS attribute must be a whitespace-separated list of XML names that correspond to one or more ID attribute values defined in the document. Just as IDREF can be used to express a one-to-one relationship, so can IDREFS be used to express a one-to-many relationship. Here's an example:

```
<!ELEMENT Foo EMPTY>
<!ATTLIST Foo
    FooID ID #REQUIRED>
<!ELEMENT Bar EMPTY>
<!ATTLIST Bar
    BarID ID #REQUIRED
    FooIDREF IDREFS #REQUIRED>
```

For this DTD fragment, the following document fragments are valid:

```
<Foo FooID="foo1" />
<Foo FooID="foo2" />
<Bar BarID="bar1" FooIDREF="foo1" />

<Foo FooID="foo1" />
<Foo FooID="foo2" />
<Bar BarID="bar1" FooIDREF="foo1 foo2" />

<Foo FooID="foo1" />
<Foo FooID="foo2" />
<Bar BarID="bar1" FooIDREF="foo1 foo1" />
<!-- uniqueness is not enforced -->
```

but the following examples are not valid:

```
<Foo FooID="foo1" />
<Foo FooID="foo2" />
<Bar BarID="bar1" FooIDREF="" />
<!-- there must be at least one ID value -->

<Foo FooID="foo1" />
<Foo FooID="foo2" />
<Bar BarID="bar1" FooIDREF="foo1+foo2" />
<!-- not a space-separated list -->
```

The ENTITY Attribute Type

Attributes defined with the ENTITY attribute type must match the name of an unparsed entity declared elsewhere in the DTD. Typically, you'd use this to insert non-text content into your XML document, like an image or a sound file. Here's an example (don't worry too much about the entity and notation declarations – we'll take a look at those later in this appendix):

```
<!NOTATION gif PUBLIC "GIF">
<!ENTITY BlueLine SYSTEM "blueline.gif" NDATA gif>
<!ELEMENT Separator EMPTY>
<!ATTLIST Separator
    img ENTITY #REQUIRED>
```

A valid document would then be:

```
<Separator img="BlueLine" />
```

We won't spend much time talking about this type of attribute in this book, but you might find it useful if you want to build XML documents with embedded non-XML entities.

The ENTITIES Attribute Type

Briefly, ENTITIES is to ENTITY as IDREFS is to IDREF – it's a way to include multiple unparsed entity references in the same attribute by using a space-separated list of entity names. So, for example:

```
<!NOTATION gif PUBLIC "GIF">
<!ENTITY BlueLine SYSTEM "blueline.gif" NDATA gif>
<!ENTITY RedLine SYSTEM "redline.gif" NDATA gif>
<!ELEMENT Separator EMPTY>
<!ATTLIST Separator
    img ENTITIES #REQUIRED>
```

A valid document would then be:

```
<Separator img="BlueLine RedLine" />
```

The NMTOKEN Attribute Type

Attributes with a type of NMTOKEN must have a value that contains only letters, digits, underscores, hyphens, colons, periods, and other Unicode characters that are acceptable in XML names. So for the following declaration:

```
<!ELEMENT Foo EMPTY>
<!ATTLIST Foo
    FooToken NMTOKEN #REQUIRED>
```

the following document fragments are valid:

```
<Foo
    FooToken="17" /> <!-- no leading letter or underscore is required -->
```

```
<Foo
    FooToken="_____" /> <!-- underscores are fine -->
```

but the following are not:

```
<Foo
    FooToken="red&amp;blue" /> <!-- ampersands are not allowed -->
```

```
<Foo
    FooToken="bad token" /> <!-- whitespace is not allowed -->
```

Attributes with the type NMTOKEN (or NMTOKENS) give you a little more control over the allowable data in an attribute, by making the value (or each value, in the case of NMTOKENS) abide by the rules for proper XML names.

The NMTOKENS Attribute Type

Like IDREFS and ENTITIES, the NMTOKENS attribute type allows one attribute to contain a list of whitespace separated NMTOKEN values. For this example:

```
<!ELEMENT Foo EMPTY>
<!ATTLIST Foo
    FooToken NMTOKENS #REQUIRED>
```

the following fragments are valid:

```
<Foo
    FooToken="17 19 23" />
```

```
<Foo
    FooToken="_ _ - - ." />
```

Enumerated Value Sets

Another great feature of attribute declarations in DTDs is the ability to constrain the possible values that may appear for an attribute. This is very helpful if you have data points that correspond to a well-defined set of values. Let's see how this is done.

```
<!ELEMENT Foo EMPTY>
<!ATTLIST Foo
    Color (Red | Green | Blue) #REQUIRED>
```

As you can see, in an enumerated value set declaration the possible values for an attribute are listed, separated by pipe characters. As with anything else in XML, these values are case-sensitive. For this DTD fragment, the following document fragment is valid:

```
<Foo Color="Red" />
```

but this one is not:

```
<Foo Color="Orange" />
```

This is one of the few ways to strongly constrain the allowable values for a data point in a DTD.

Notation Attribute Declaration

Using this declaration, you can associate a particular notation (or one of a set of notations) with an element. This is useful if the element content, which for all other intents and purposes looks like text, actually needs to be processed another way – say, if it happens to be PostScript or a base-64 encoded block.

```
<!NOTATION ps PUBLIC "PostScript level 3">
<!NOTATION base64 PUBLIC "Base-64 encoded">
<!ELEMENT Foo (#PCDATA)>
<!ATTLIST Foo
    Datatype NOTATION (ps | base64) #REQUIRED>
```

Note that each possible value for the notation attribute must match the name of a notation defined elsewhere in the DTD.

A valid example of a document:

```
<Foo Datatype="ps">gsave 112 75 moveto 112 300 lineto showpage grestore</Foo>
```

Next, we need to look at the various ways in which cardinality and default values may be specified for attributes.

#REQUIRED

You've probably noticed that we've been using the #REQUIRED default declaration for all of our examples. This means what you'd expect – that the attribute value must be supplied in the XML document in order for it to be valid. So for this declaration:

```
<!ELEMENT Foo EMPTY>
<!ATTLIST Foo
   Color (Red | Green | Blue) #REQUIRED>
```

this is a valid XML fragment:

```
<Foo Color="Red" />
```

but this is not:

```
<Foo /> <!-- the Color attribute is required! -->
```

#IMPLIED

The #IMPLIED default declaration for an attribute means that the attribute may or may not be supplied. If the attribute is not supplied, then no value is available to the XML parser for that attribute when parsing that document. So in this case, with the declaration:

```
<!ELEMENT Foo EMPTY>
<!ATTLIST Foo
   Color (Red | Green | Blue) #IMPLIED>
```

both of the following are valid document fragments:

```
<Foo Color="Red" />
```

```
<Foo /> <!-- the Color attribute does not have to be supplied -->
```

Default Value Declarations

There is a third default declaration that is available when declaring an attribute. In this declaration, a value is provided for the attribute; if the attribute value is not supplied in the XML document, the default value is substituted and available to the XML parser as if it were explicitly stated in the XML document. An example is in order. For the declaration:

```
<!ELEMENT Foo EMPTY>
<!ATTLIST Foo
   Color (Red | Green | Blue) "Red">
```

When the document fragment

```
<Foo Color="Green" />
```

is parsed by the XML processor, the value Green will be returned for the Color attribute of this Foo element. Now, suppose that we have this document fragment:

```
<Foo />
```

In this case, since the Color attribute is missing from the XML fragment, the processor will automatically substitute and return the value Red for the attribute.

#FIXED Value Declarations

Finally, you may use the #FIXED declaration to indicate that the value of the attribute is always taken from the value specified in the attribute declaration. For example, you could have these declarations:

```
<!ELEMENT Foo EMPTY>
<!ATTLIST Foo
   Color CDATA "Red" #FIXED>
```

When an XML parser reads a document created using this set of declarations, the value Red will **always** be provided for the attribute Color on **all** Foo elements – even though the Color attribute is never mentioned in the XML document itself. In fact, it's an error to provide any other value – a document that looks like this will not validate against the declarations above:

```
<Foo Color="Orange" />
```

Instead, you must omit the attribute altogether, or provide the exact value in the attribute declaration:

```
<Foo />
<Foo Color="Red" />
```

One very good use for this technique is to pass version information about the DTD to the XML parser so that it can make intelligent guesses as to the available content in the XML document. You might declare a Version attribute that has a #FIXED value of 1.0, for example, and this would be available as if the XML document itself contained this value.

Notation Declarations

If you are going to use notations in your XML document (for unparsed entities, to specify a URI for the target of a processing instruction, or to annotate an element, for example), you need to declare them in the DTD. A notation declaration looks like this:

```
<!NOTATION gif PUBLIC "GIF">
```

It includes the name of the notation, as well as a system and/or public identifier that a processor can use to determine the application or information type to which the notation pertains. For the purposes of this book, we won't be spending much time on notations, but if you come across a notation declaration in an existing DTD you'll be able to figure out what it means. Several of the subsequent sections of this appendix detail various uses of these declarations.

Entity Declarations

There are two types of entities that may be declared: internal entities and external entities.

Internal Entities

Internal entities contain their replacement value in their declaration; when a parser encounters a reference to the specified internal entity, it substitutes the replacement value found in that entity's declaration.

For example:

```
<!ENTITY DocumentStatus "Draft">
<!ELEMENT About (#PCDATA)>
```

```
<About>
    This document is currently in &DocumentStatus; status.
</About>
```

When the parser reads this document, it substitutes the string provided in the entity declaration for the entity reference string "&DocumentStatus;". To a processor, the document looks like this:

```
<About>
    This document is currently in Draft status.
</About>
```

External Entities

By contrast, external entities refer to resources outside the context of the XML document. A system identification containing a URI where the external entity content may be found is provided; additionally, some sort of public identifier may be provided so that a processor can attempt to generate an alternate URI. Here are two examples of external entity declarations:

```
<!ENTITY SalesData SYSTEM "sales/summary.xml">
```

```
<!ENTITY SiteMap SYSTEM "http://www.yoursite.com/sitemap.xml"
               PUBLIC "//yoursite//sitemap.xml">
```

When entities are declared this way, their content is retrieved and substituted in the place where they are referenced. They are known as parsed entities because they must conform to the rules of XML. It's also possible to declare external unparsed entities, as we mentioned earlier in this appendix – we'll see how that's done a little later.

Say we have the following DTD, called invoice.dtd:

```
<!ENTITY InvoiceLineItems SYSTEM "lineitems.xml">
<!ELEMENT Invoice (CustomerName, LineItem+)>
<!ELEMENT CustomerName (#PCDATA)>
<!ELEMENT LineItem (Item, Quantity, Price)>
<!ELEMENT Item (#PCDATA)>
<!ELEMENT Quantity (#PCDATA)>
<!ELEMENT Price (#PCDATA)>
```

and the following document, called invoice.xml:

```
<?xml version="1.0"?>
<!DOCTYPE Invoice SYSTEM "invoice.dtd">
<Invoice>
   <CustomerName>Kevin Williams</CustomerName>
   &InvoiceLineItems;
</Invoice>
```

If the document lineitems.xml contains the following:

```
<LineItem>
   <Item>Widget</Item>
   <Quantity>50</Quantity>
   <Price>75.00</Price>
</LineItem>
<LineItem>
   <Item>Sprocket</Item>
   <Quantity>25</Quantity>
   <Price>100.00</Price>
</LineItem>
```

Then the document, after substitution, will be:

```
<?xml version="1.0"?>
<!DOCTYPE Invoice SYSTEM "invoice.dtd">
<Invoice>
   <CustomerName>Kevin Williams</CustomerName>
   <LineItem>
      <Item>Widget</Item>
      <Quantity>50</Quantity>
      <Price>75.00</Price>
   </LineItem>
   <LineItem>
      <Item>Sprocket</Item>
      <Quantity>25</Quantity>
      <Price>100.00</Price>
   </LineItem>
</Invoice>
```

Note that we still had to declare the substructure of the external parsed entity in our DTD. Parsed entities (whether internal or external) must conform to any document type definition provided for the document that references them. So if your lineitems.xml was instead formed like this:

```
<LineItem>
   <Item>Widget</Item>
   <Quantity>50</Quantity>
</LineItem>
```

a validating parser would complain because the Price subelement is missing from the LineItem element.

Parameter Entities

It's also possible to declare entities that are substituted into the DTD itself, rather than into the XML document. These are called parameter entities, and here's an example declaration:

```
<!ENTITY % ThirdColorChoice "Blue">
<!ELEMENT Foo EMPTY>
<!ATTLIST Foo (Red | Green | %ThirdColorChoice;)>
```

As you might imagine, substitution works just like it does for other entity references. To the validating parser, the DTD looks like this:

```
<!ELEMENT Foo EMPTY>
<!ATTLIST Foo (Red | Green | Blue)>
```

External parameter entities may also be declared:

```
<!ENTITY % ColorChoiceList SYSTEM "colorchoices.txt">
<!ELEMENT Foo EMPTY>
<!ATTLIST Foo (%ColorChoiceList;)>
```

And in colorchoices.txt, we might have:

```
Red | Green | Blue
```

Leading to the substituted DTD looking like this:

```
<!ELEMENT Foo EMPTY>
<!ATTLIST Foo (Red | Green | Blue)>
```

Unparsed Entities

Unparsed entities (entities that do not have their values extracted) may also be declared. These are the entity types we discussed when talking about attribute declarations. They may only appear as the values of attributes that are declared as having the ENTITY or ENTITIES type. To declare an unparsed entity, you use the same declaration as for an external parse entity but add a notation declaration to the end of it:

```
<!NOTATION gif PUBLIC "GIF">
<!ENTITY PropertyImage SYSTEM "image.gif" NDATA gif>
```

```
<!NOTATION midi PUBLIC "MIDI 1.0">
<!ENTITY BackgroundMusic SYSTEM "http://www.yoursite.com/music.mid"
                 NDATA midi>
```

The notation name at the end of the unparsed entity declaration must also be declared, in a notation declaration elsewhere in the document type definition, as seen in the above examples.

Conditional Sections

In a DTD, you can choose to include or ignore sections of the DTD by enclosing them in **conditional sections**. External entities may be used to control the inclusion or exclusion of document type declarations in much the same way that #define and #ifdef/#ifndef macros may be used to control the compilation of C++ source code. Let's see how this works.

If you want to include a section of declarations, you wrap them in the conditional section include markers - <![INCLUDE[at the beginning and]]> at the end. Similarly, to exclude a section of declarations, start with <![IGNORE[and end with]]>. For example, the first set of declarations in the following DTD will be included (used for validating XML), and the second set will be ignored:

```
<![INCLUDE[
<!ELEMENT Foo (#PCDATA)>
]]>

<![IGNORE[
<!ELEMENT Foo EMPTY>
]]>
```

To the validating parser, this will look like

```
<!ELEMENT Foo (#PCDATA)>
```

If we add parameter entities to the mix, we can turn on or off sections at will by changing the values of the parameter entities:

```
<!ENTITY % TextContent "INCLUDE">
<!ENTITY % AttributesOnly "IGNORE">

<![&TextContent;[
<!ELEMENT Foo (#PCDATA)>
]]>

<![&AttributesOnly;[
<!ELEMENT Foo EMPTY>
]]>
```

Using parameter entities this way allows us to easily control the structure of our DTD.

Thinking in Trees

Now that we've taken a look at the building blocks that go together to make up XML documents, we need to talk about how these building blocks fit together. To do this, we're going to need to stop thinking about XML documents as serial files and start thinking about them as node trees.

Take this sample XML document:

```
<Invoice>
  <CustomerName>Kevin Williams</CustomerName>
  <ShipTo>
    <Address>742 Evergreen Terrace</Address>
```

```
      <City>Springfield</City>
      <State>KY</State>
      <PostalCode>12345</PostalCode>
   </ShipTo>
   <LineItem>
      <Item>Widget</Item>
      <Quantity>15</Quantity>
      <Price>25.00</Price>
   </LineItem>
   <LineItem>
      <Item>Sprocket</Item>
      <Quantity>22</Quantity>
      <Price>44.00</Price>
   </LineItem>
</Invoice>
```

If you're used to working with flat files, such as comma-delimited files, you are probably thinking about this file serially: there's the invoice start tag, then the customer name start tag, then the customer name, and so on. However, most of the XML technologies we'll be using in this book don't model the information this way. Instead, the information is modelled as a tree:

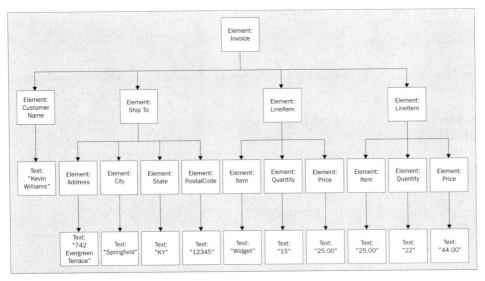

When you're working with XML documents through the DOM, see later in the chapter, or using XPath, this is explained in Chapter 21 to specify a particular location in an XML document, everything is expressed in terms of child lists and branch traversals. For example, if you had to apply the following XPath expression:

```
/Invoice/LineItem[position()=2]/Quantity
```

to the serialized document, it's not immediately apparent what's being referenced. However, once you understand that this expression describes a navigation through the node tree in our diagram - "go to the Invoice element, then to the second LineItem child of that element, then to the Quantity child of that element" (which gives us 22), it's obvious what's being requested.

Learning to think of XML documents in terms of node trees, rather than in terms of serialized text, will help you to more easily query and manipulate those documents from code.

Technology Overview

Let's take a quick look at the XML technologies covered in this book. We will see how each of these technologies may be used to facilitate our access to, and manipulation of, data stored in XML documents.

XML Schemas

XML Schemas are a new mechanism that the W3C is working on to define XML Vocabularies, as a replacement for DTDs. As of this time, XML Schemas are in working draft last call status. This means that they are fairly stable, but may still change somewhat before they reach recommendation status.

The Document Object Model (DOM)

You could treat the XML document as just a text file, and write a text file reader that interprets the information in the XML document in a way that your application code can use. This would, however, be quite tedious, and require you to understand all the constructs of XML. Also, such code would have to be written repeatedly by whoever wants to access information in XML documents. W3C realized that this would be a problem, and they created a standard way to create these XML document processors or XML parsers. Typically, XML processors parse an XML document, build a tree model of the elements in the document, and then allow the application to access this tree by means of a standard API called the Document Object Model or DOM.

A DOM XML parser is, quite simply, a program that converts your XML documents into a Java object model. You point a DOM XML parser to an XML document; it parses the document, and gives you a bunch of objects in the memory of your Java Virtual Machine. When you need to manipulate any information stored in the XML document, you can do so through these objects in memory. So, a DOM XML parser creates a Java document object **representation** of your XML document file. There are lots of free DOM XML parsers out there, including one from Oracle as part of the XDK.

The parser also performs some simple text processing as it creates the object model. It expands all entities, compares the structure of the information in the XML document to a DTD or schema (if one is used), and if this processing is successful, the XML document is converted into a tree of nodes in memory. The tree of nodes contains all the data and structure of the information contained in the XML document. This node tree can be accessed and modified using the DOM API.

The DOM API consists of a set of **interfaces**. The XML parser implements these interfaces. If you want to access XML documents from within Java, you need to import the `org.w3c.dom` package in Java, and then simply use these classes to get at the tree of nodes.

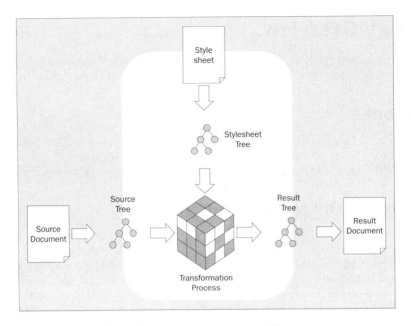

The W3C decided DOM would apply to common constructs like elements, comments, processing instructions, text content etc. that are present in both HTML and XML, and would, in addition, have some HTML-specific extensions.

In the document object tree, everything is a **node**. A node may have other nodes nested inside it. The node can hold information, like its tag-name, its value, and its child nodes (if any). This hierarchical organization reminds one of a file-system view of data, with the big difference that in a file system, the names name instances, whereas in XML they name types. Items are organized hierarchically, a folder may have files in it or other folders, and everything is descended from one root folder.

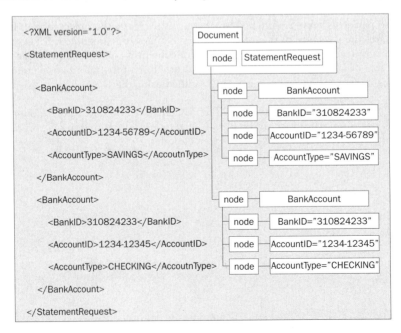

A document object itself is a node, it is descended from one node, and it may have other nodes inside it. The Node interface is central to DOM – most of the time, you can get by using just this interface. There are also other interfaces like `DocumentType`. Most of the interfaces are, however, subclasses of Node, and extend it to provide specific functionality.

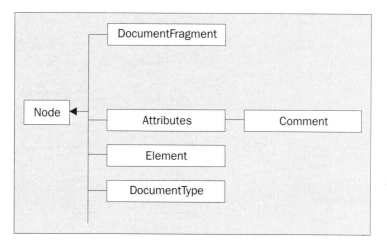

What kinds of behavior or methods do these interfaces have? For the most part, programmers want to get a node's value, its child Nodes and so on, and of course such methods are provided. In other situations, programmers want to know what the type of a node is (for example whether it is an Element or a piece of Notation), so these methods are provided as well.

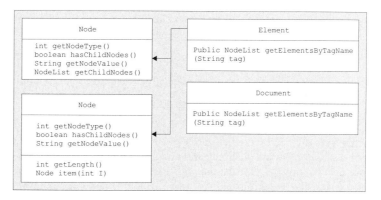

What answers would we get if we called these methods on the Nodes in our XML fragment?

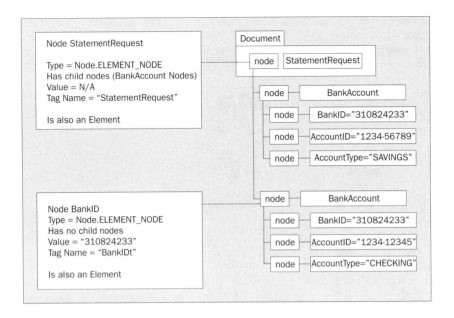

Simple API for XML (SAX)

The Simple API for XML, or SAX, is the development community's response to the DOM. It also parses XML documents, but is **event driven** rather than **document-model driven** like DOM. That is, it streams the document through the parse window and issues events to the caller when parts of the document are found (an element starts, an element ends, a processing instruction is read, and so on). Compared to the DOM, SAX has a very small memory footprint. The event model of SAX works like this:

❏   The SAX XML parser processes elements serially

❏   The XML application registers for those events that it is interested in and provides callback functions to handle the element

❏   When the events of interest are encountered, the callback functions are invoked.

The callback functions are defined by the interfaces `DocumentHandler`, `ErrorHandler`, `DTDHandler` and `EntityResolver`. For example, an application might be interested in the `DocumentHandler` interface and hence provide callbacks for the methods in this interface – viz. `StartDocument`, `EndDocument` , `StartElement`, and `EndElement`. The application might also want to implement the methods defined by the `ErrorHandler` interface for example `Warning` or `FatalError`. The SAX parser then informs the application when it encounters these events, and the application in turn invokes methods to process the events.

The SAX API is a fast API. It has a lighter computational footprint than DOM – that is it consumes less memory and CPU resources. The DOM API must construct a tree out of the whole document before any processing can be done. DOM is ideal for interactive applications that require an object representation in memory. SAX is more suited for server side applications that do not need to create a tree structure. SAX may be a good choice for network-oriented programs that send and receive XML documents. SAX is particularly useful for filtering very large XML documents, because DOM uses a lot of memory on these. SAX, in general requires a lot more coding than the DOM interface. Unfortunately, if the XML document is complexly connected (perhaps through the use of ID to IDREF relationships), using SAX can necessitate either multiple parses of a document or sophisticated buffering to retrieve needed information that has already passed through the parse window.

Summary

In this appendix, we've spent some time bringing you up to speed (or back up to speed) on the building blocks of XML and how they fit together. We've also taken a quick look at some of the technologies we'll be using to access and manipulate XML documents throughout the remainder of the book. If you found this chapter a little overwhelming, you might find a book like *Beginning XML* from Wrox Press *ISBN 1861003412* helpful to flesh out some of the details of the subjects we've discussed.

Support, Errata, and p2p.wrox.com

One of the most irritating things about any programming book is when you find that bit of code you've just spent an hour typing simply doesn't work. You check it a hundred times to see if you've set it up correctly and then you notice the spelling mistake in the variable name on the book page. Of course, you can blame the authors for not taking enough care and testing the code, the editors for not doing their job properly, or the proofreaders for not being eagle-eyed enough, but this doesn't get around the fact that mistakes do happen.

We try hard to ensure no mistakes sneak out into the real world, but we can't promise that this book is 100% error free. What we can do is offer the next best thing by providing you with immediate support and feedback from experts who have worked on the book and try to ensure that future editions eliminate these gremlins. We also now commit to supporting you not just while you read the book, but once you start developing applications as well through our online forums where you can put your questions to the authors, reviewers, and fellow industry professionals.

In this appendix we'll look at how to:

- ❑ Enroll in the **Programmer To Programmer**™ forums at http://p2p.wrox.com
- ❑ Post and check for errata on our main site, http://www.wrox.com
- ❑ E-mail technical support a query or feedback on our books in general

Between all three of these support procedures, you should get an answer to your problem in no time at all.

The Online Forums at p2p.wrox.com

Join the Professional Oracle 8*i* Enterprise Applications Development mailing list for author and peer support. Our system provides **Programmer To Programmer**™ support on mailing lists, forums, and newsgroups all in addition to our one-to-one e-mail system, which we'll look at in a minute. Be confident that your query is not just being examined by a support professional, but by the many Wrox authors and other industry experts present on our mailing lists.

How to Enroll for Support

Just follow these simple instructions:

1. Go to http://p2p.wrox.com in your favorite browser. Here you'll find any current announcements concerning P2P – new lists created, any removed and so on:

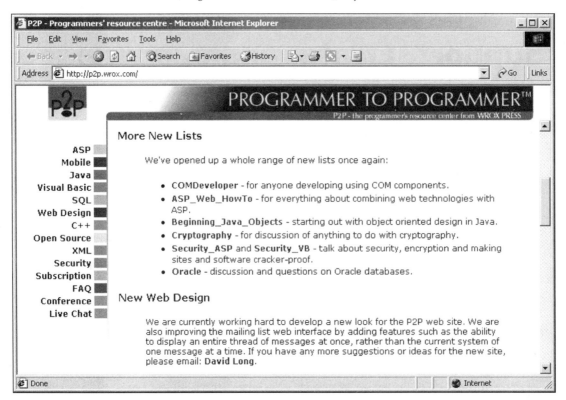

2. Choose to access the Oracle list.

3. If you are not a member of the list, you can choose to either view the list without joining it or create an account in the list, by hitting the respective buttons.

4. If you wish to join, you'll be presented with a form in which you'll need to fill in your e-mail address, name, and a password (of at least 4 alphanumeric characters). Choose how you would like to receive the messages from the list and then hit Save.

5. Congratulations. You're now a member of the Oracle mailing list.

Why This System Offers the Best Support

You can choose to join the mailing lists to receive mails as they are contributed, or a daily digest, or you can receive them as a weekly digest. If you don't have the time or facility to receive the mailing list, then you can search our online archives. You'll find the ability to search on specific subject areas or keywords. As these lists are moderated, you can be confident of finding good, accurate information quickly. Mails can be edited or moved by the moderator into the correct place, making this a most efficient resource. Junk and spam mail are deleted, and your own e-mail address is protected by the unique Lyris system from web-bots that can automatically hoover up newsgroup mailing list addresses. Any queries about joining, or leaving lists, or any query about a list should be sent to: support@wrox.com.

Checking the Errata Online at www.wrox.com

The following section will take you step-by-step through the process of posting errata to our web site to get that help. The sections that follow, therefore, are:

❑ Finding a list of existing errata on the web site

❑ Adding your own erratum to the existing list

There is also a section covering how to e-mail a question for technical support. This comprises:

❑ What your e-mail should include

❑ What happens to your e-mail once it has been received by us

Finding an Erratum on the Web Site

Before you send in a query, you might be able to save time by finding the answer to your problem on our web site – http://www.wrox.com.

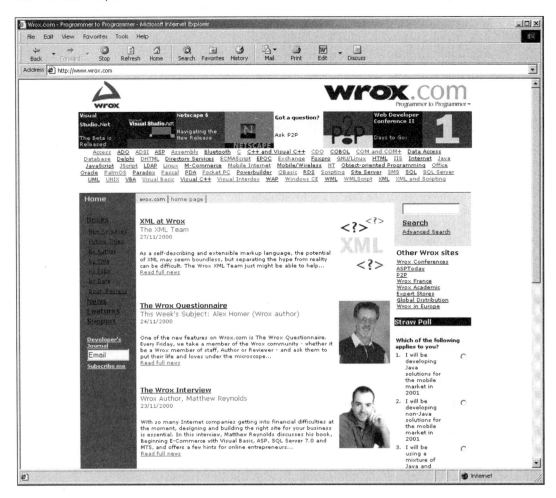

Each book we publish has its own page and its own errata sheet. You can get to any book's page by clicking on Books on the left hand navigation bar. To view the errata for that book, click on the Book errata link on the right-hand side of the book information pane, underneath the book information.

We update these pages regularly to ensure that you have the latest information on bugs and errors.

Add an Erratum

If you wish to point out an erratum to be put up on the web site or directly query a problem in the book page with an expert who knows the book in detail then e-mail support@wrox.com, with the title of the book and the last four numbers of the ISBN in the subject field of the e-mail. Clicking on the submit errata link on the web site's errata page will send an e-mail using your e-mail client. A typical e-mail should include the following things:

❏ The **name**, **last four digits of the ISBN**, and **page number** of the problem in the Subject field.

❏ Your **name**, **contact info**, and the **problem** in the body of the message.

We won't send you junk mail. We need the details to save both your time and ours. If we need to replace a disk or CD we'll be able to get it to you straight away. When you send an e-mail it will go through the following chain of support:

Customer Support

Your message is delivered to one of our customer support staff who will be the first people to read it. They have files on most frequently asked questions and will answer anything general immediately. They answer general questions about the book and the web site.

Editorial

Deeper queries are forwarded to the technical editor responsible for that book. They have experience with the programming language or particular product and are able to answer detailed technical questions on the subject. Once an issue has been resolved, the editor can post the erratum to the web site.

The Authors

Finally, in the unlikely event that the editor can't answer your problem, they will forward the request to the author. We try to protect the author from any distractions from writing. However, we are quite happy to forward specific requests to them. All Wrox authors help with the support on their books. They'll mail the customer and the editor with their response, and again all readers should benefit.

What We Can't Answer

Obviously with an ever-growing range of books and an ever-changing technology base, there is an increasing volume of data requiring support. While we endeavor to answer all questions about the book, we can't answer bugs in your own programs that you've adapted from our code. So, while you might have loved the chapters on file handling, don't expect too much sympathy if you cripple your company with a routine that deletes the contents of your hard drive. But do tell us if you're especially pleased with the routine you developed with our help.

How to Tell Us Exactly What You Think

We understand that errors can destroy the enjoyment of a book and can cause many wasted and frustrated hours, so we seek to minimize the distress that they can cause.

You might just wish to tell us how much you liked or loathed the book in question. Or you might have ideas about how this whole process could be improved. If this is the case, you should e-mail feedback@wrox.com. You'll always find a sympathetic ear, no matter what the problem is. Above all you should remember that we do care about what you have to say and we will do our utmost to act upon it.

Index

A Guide to the Index

The index is arranged hierarchically, in alphabetical order, with symbols preceding the letter A. Most second-level entries and many third-level entries also occur as first-level entries. This is to ensure that users will find the information they require however they choose to search for it.

C

1237

R

U

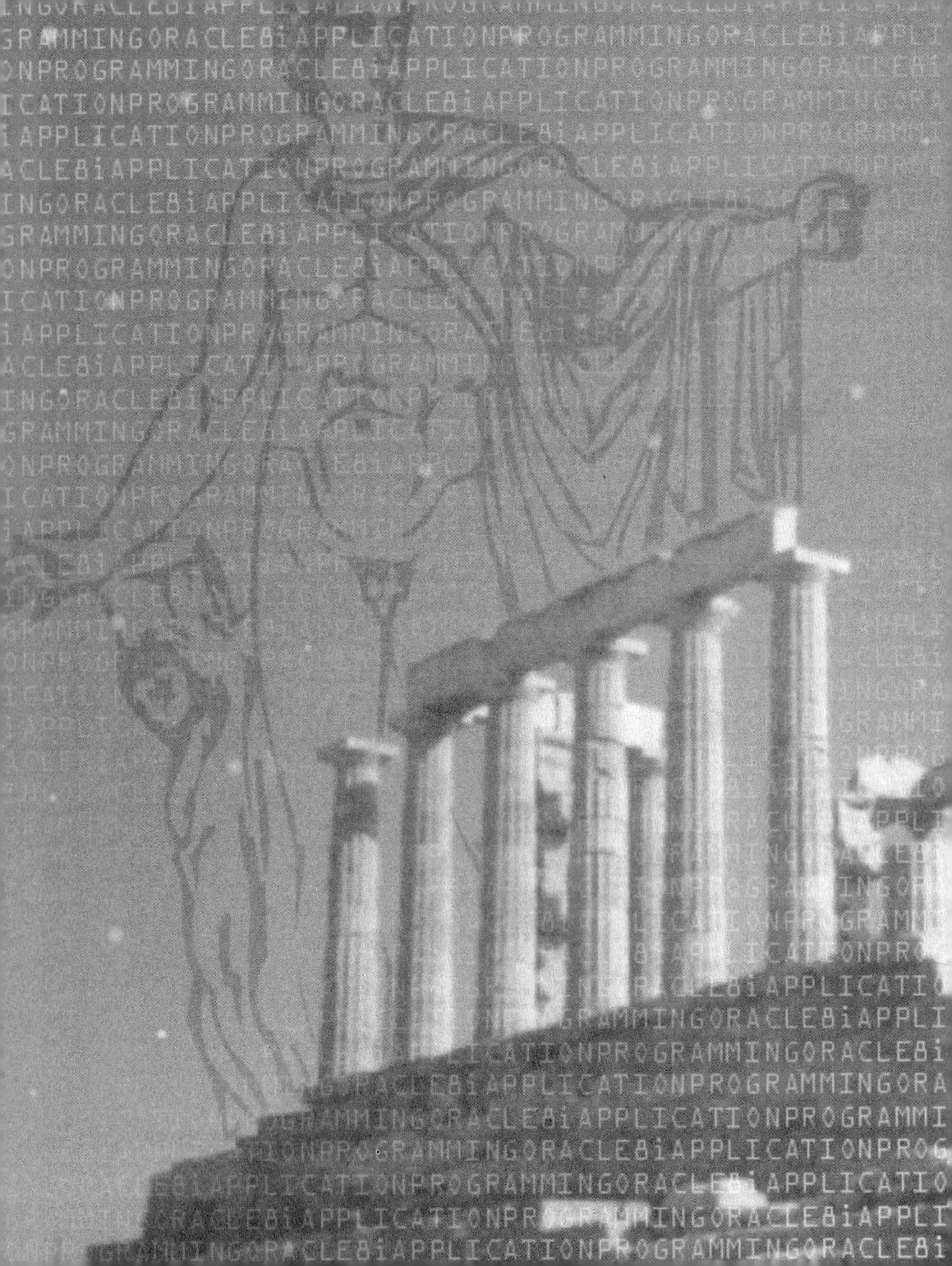
ORACLE8i APPLICATION PROGRAMMING